Lecture Notes in Computer Science 16488

Founding Editors

Gerhard Goos
Juris Hartmanis

Editorial Board Members

Elisa Bertino, *Purdue University, West Lafayette, IN, USA*
Wen Gao, *Peking University, Beijing, China*
Bernhard Steffen, *TU Dortmund University, Dortmund, Germany*
Moti Yung, *Columbia University, New York, NY, USA*

The series Lecture Notes in Computer Science (LNCS), including its subseries Lecture Notes in Artificial Intelligence (LNAI) and Lecture Notes in Bioinformatics (LNBI), has established itself as a medium for the publication of new developments in computer science and information technology research, teaching, and education.

LNCS enjoys close cooperation with the computer science R & D community, the series counts many renowned academics among its volume editors and paper authors, and collaborates with prestigious societies. Its mission is to serve this international community by providing an invaluable service, mainly focused on the publication of conference and workshop proceedings and postproceedings. LNCS commenced publication in 1973.

Chryssis Georgiou

Editor

Structural Information and Communication Complexity

33rd International Colloquium, SIROCCO 2026
Durham, UK, June 9–11, 2026
Proceedings

 Springer

Editor
Chryssis Georgiou
University of Cyprus
Nicosia, Cyprus

ISSN 0302-9743 ISSN 1611-3349 (electronic)
Lecture Notes in Computer Science
ISBN 978-3-032-26464-0 ISBN 978-3-032-26465-7 (eBook)
https://doi.org/10.1007/978-3-032-26465-7

This Springer imprint is published by the registered company Springer Nature Switzerland AG
The registered company address is: Gewerbestrasse 11, 6330 Cham, Switzerland

If disposing of this product, please recycle the paper.

Preface

SIROCCO, *the International Colloquium On Structural Information and Communication Complexity*, is devoted to the study of the interplay between structural knowledge, communication, and computing in decentralized systems of multiple communicating entities. Special emphasis is given to innovative methodological and solution approaches leading to a better understanding of the relationship between computing and communication. SIROCCO has a tradition of interesting and productive scientific meetings in a relaxed and pleasant atmosphere, attracting leading researchers in a variety of fields in which communication and knowledge play a significant role.

This volume contains the papers presented at the 33rd instance of SIROCCO, which was held on June 9–11, 2026 in the UNESCO world heritage city of Durham, UK, at the premises of Durham University (England's third-oldest University). It also includes the citation for the 2026 Prize for Innovation in Distributed Computing, which was awarded to *Dariusz R. Kowalski* (Augusta University, USA) for his pioneering advancements in distributed computing over shared channels. Dariusz, as the recipient of the prize, delivered a keynote lecture on "Distributed Protocols on Shared Channels". SIROCCO 2026 featured another two keynote lectures, presented by *Maria Potop-Butucaru* (Sorbonne University, France) on "Smart Contracts and Distributed Cross-Chain Protocols" and *Jukka Suomela* (Aalto University, Finland) on "Distributed Quantum Advantage". An abstract of each keynote lecture is included in these proceedings.

SIROCCO 2026 received 65 submissions. Each submission was reviewed by at least three members of the Program Committee, assisted by 32 external reviewers, using a single-blind reviewing process. Once all reviews for a given paper were completed, an intra-paper discussion among the reviewers took place in an attempt to harmonize the paper's evaluation. This phase was followed by an inter-paper discussion involving all PC members, yielding the final selection of 28 regular papers (a 43% acceptance ratio).

The Best Paper Award of SIROCCO 2026 went to *Caterina Feletti, Paola Flocchini, Debasish Pattanayak, Giuseppe Prencipe*, and *Nicola Santoro*, for their paper "Universal Dancing by Luminous Robots Under Sequential Schedulers". The Best Student Paper Award of SIROCCO 2026 was given to *Laurent Feuilloley, Soumyadeep Paul*, and *Ami Paz*, for their paper "Polynomial Time Local Decision Revisited" (contributing student: Soumyadeep Paul). Revised and expanded versions of several additional selected regular papers will be considered for publication in a special issue of the journal *Theoretical Computer Science*.

I would like to thank the authors who submitted their work to SIROCCO 2026, as well as the Program Committee members and subreviewers for their valuable reviews and discussions. The SIROCCO Steering Committee, chaired by Keren Censor-Hillel, provided essential guidance throughout the process. Special thanks go to Ulrich Smith for sharing his experience as last year's PC chair, and Roman Kuznets for his assistance with the proceedings. The EasyChair system was used to manage the submission of papers, the review process, and the generation of this proceedings volume. The support of the

Springer Nature editorial team was invaluable. I am grateful to the conference General Chair, Amitabh Trehan, who made the conference possible alongside his local organizing team at Durham University, including Peter Davies-Peck (Webmaster), William K. Moses Jr. (Publicity), and Karl Southern (Treasurer). Last but not least, I would like to thank the supporters of SIROCCO 2026, Durham University, the University of Cyprus, and Springer LNCS; the last provided a monetary award for the Best Student Paper.

March 2026   Chryssis Georgiou

SIROCCO 2026 Supporting Organizations

2026 Prize for Innovation in Distributed Computing

We are pleased to announce that the 2026 Prize for Innovation in Distributed Computing is awarded to **Dariusz (Darek) Kowalski** from Augusta University, USA. Darek has been a major contributor to the field of distributed protocols on shared channels. His contributions appear in numerous research papers published in leading conferences, including 9 papers in SIROCCO throughout the years.

Darek, with collaborators, started the subfield of adversarial shared channels (e.g., [1–4]). In a simplified setting, a multiple of autonomous processes, also called stations, are connected to a shared communication channel, in which a packet can be successfully transmitted if exactly one station attempts to transmit it at a time. Packets occur in stations according to some adversarial (worst-case) pattern, unknown to the distributed algorithm run by the stations, and are stored in local queues until successfully transmitted on the channel. The goal is to design algorithms that keep the queues bounded and achieve high throughput (of successfully transmitted packets) and low packet latency in arbitrarily long computations.

Darek produced a very large body of work that addresses and resolves several fundamental issues for the adversarial distribution of the input in time (even in an unbounded time period). The input could be packets, but also other resources or faults (e.g., jamming, crashes). In his papers (e.g., [1, 2]), a first model for analyzing arbitrarily long executions of communication on a shared channel was introduced, and later developed, together with latency analysis, and later with fairness, queue sizes, etc. Darek also introduced a classification of protocols and proved separation bounds between them. The results included, for example, an adversarial version of the renowned Little's Law from stochastic queuing theory, and the development of a new theory that combines queue sizes with latency and throughput.

Darek's contributions include further aspects of shared channels, such as asynchronous communication on the channel [5], consensus and mutual exclusion [6], adversarial models for analyzing stability and latency of transactional memory and sharding [7], classic scheduling with adversarial jamming [8, 9], and many others. Several novel and technically involved results and techniques have been developed (e.g., [10–12]) while pursuing his research on dynamic channels: a connection of adversarial dynamicity with online and stochastic models of shared channels, a construction of ultra-resilient superimposed codes which exploit close links with information theory and improve not only communication on dynamic shared channels but also in multi-hop beeping networks, contributions to the theory of selective families for radio networks, and more (e.g., [13–15]).

For his pioneering advancements on distributed computing over shared channels, we are proud to present the 2026 Prize for Innovation in Distributed Computing to Dariusz Kowalski. The prize will be awarded at SIROCCO 2026, to be held on June 9–11, 2026, in Durham, UK.

The 2026 Award Committee

Keren Censor-Hillel, Chair (Technion, Israel)
Yuval Emek (Technion, Israel)
Magnus Halldorsson (Reykjavik University, Iceland)
Sergio Rajsbaum (Universidad Nacional Autónoma de México, Mexico)
Ulrich Schmid (TU Wien, Austria)

References

1. Dariusz R. Kowalski: On the Selection Problem in Radio Networks. PODC 2005: 158–166.
2. Bogdan S. Chlebus, Dariusz R. Kowalski, Mariusz A. Rokicki: Adversarial Queuing on the Multiple Access Channel. ACM Trans. Algorithms 8(1): 5:1–5:31 (2012).
3. Lakshmi Anantharamu, Bogdan S. Chlebus, Dariusz R. Kowalski, Mariusz A. Rokicki: Medium Access Control for Adversarial Channels with Jamming. SIROCCO 2011: 89–100.
4. Vicent Cholvi, Pawel Garncarek, Tomasz Jurdzinski, Dariusz R. Kowalski: Optimal Packet-Oblivious Stable Routing in Multi-hop Wireless Networks. SIROCCO 2020: 165–182.
5. Paweł Garncarek, Dariusz R. Kowalski, Shay Kutten, Lauren Murach: The Impact of Asynchrony on Stability of MAC. ICDCS 2024: 151–16.
6. Jurek Czyzowicz, Leszek Gasieniec, Dariusz R. Kowalski, Andrzej Pelc: Consensus and Mutual Exclusion in a Multiple Access Channel. IEEE Trans. Parallel Distributed Syst. 22(7): 1092–1104 (2011).
7. Ramesh Adhikari, Costas Busch, Dariusz R. Kowalski: Stable Blockchain Sharding under Adversarial Transaction Generation. SPAA 2024: 451–461.
8. Gianluca De Marco, Dariusz R. Kowalski: Ultra-Resilient Superimposed Codes: Near-Optimal Construction and Applications. ICALP 2025: 65:1–65:20.
9. Antonio Fernández Anta, Chryssis Georgiou, Dariusz R. Kowalski, Elli Zavou: Adaptive Packet Scheduling over a Wireless Channel under Constrained Jamming. Theor. Comput. Sci. 692: 72–89 (2017).
10. Marcin Bienkowski, Tomasz Jurdzinski, Miroslaw Korzeniowski, Dariusz R. Kowalski: Distributed Online and Stochastic Queueing on a Multiple Access Channel. ACM Trans. Algorithms 14(2): 21:1–21:22 (2018).
11. Gianluca De Marco, Dariusz R. Kowalski: Fast Nonadaptive Deterministic Algorithm for Conflict Resolution in a Dynamic Multiple-Access Channel. SIAM J. Comput. 44(3): 868–888 (2015).
12. Marek Chrobak, Leszek Gasieniec, Dariusz R. Kowalski: The Wake-Up Problem in MultiHop Radio Networks. SIAM J. Comput. 36(5): 1453–1471 (2007).
13. Pawel Garncarek, Dariusz R. Kowalski, Shay Kutten, Miguel A. Mosteiro: Beeping Deterministic CONGEST Algorithms in Graphs. ESA 2025: 20:1–20:17.
14. Bogdan S. Chlebus, Dariusz R. Kowalski: Almost Optimal Explicit Selectors. FCT 2005: 270–280.
15. Tomasz Jurdzinski, Dariusz R. Kowalski: Searching for and Avoiding Hidden Sets Using Queries with Local Feedback. AAAI 2025.

Organization

Program Committee Chair

Chryssis Georgiou — University of Cyprus, Cyprus

Program Committee

Ittai Abraham	a16z, Israel
Vitaly Aksenov	Logical Intelligence, USA
Timothé Albouy	IMDEA Software Institute, Spain
Emmanuelle Anceaume	CNRS/IRISA, France
Hagit Attiya	Technion, Israel
Costas Busch	Augusta University, USA
Armando Castañeda	National Autonomous University of Mexico, Mexico
Joshua Daymude	Arizona State University, USA
Gianluca De Marco	University of Salerno, Italy
Giuseppe Antonio Di Luna	University of Rome - Sapienza, Italy
Antonio Fernández Anta	IMDEA Software & Networks Institutes, Spain
Ran Gelles	Bar-Ilan University, Israel
George Giakkoupis	Inria, France
Alexey Gotsman	IMDEA Software, Spain
Magnús M. Halldórsson	Reykjavik University, Iceland
Taisuke Izumi	Osaka University, Japan
Tomasz Jurdzinski	University of Wrocław, Poland
Mikel Larrea	University of the Basque Country UPV/EHU, Spain
Othon Michail	University of Liverpool, UK
Avery Miller	University of Manitoba, Canada
Miguel A. Mosteiro	Pace University, USA
Rotem Oshman	Tel Aviv University, Israel
Andrzej Pelc	Université du Québec en Outaouais, Canada
Sathya Peri	Indian Institute of Technology Hyderabad, India
Maria Potop-Butucaru	Sorbonne University, France
Christian Scheideler	University of Paderborn, Germany
Elad Michael Schiller	Chalmers University of Technology, Sweden
Gokarna Sharma	Kent State University, USA

Jukka Suomela	Aalto University, Finland
Sara Tucci Piergiovanni	Université Paris-Saclay, CEA LIST, France
Jennifer Welch	Texas A&M University, USA
Prudence Wong	University of Liverpool, UK

Organizing Committee

Amitabh Trehan (General Chair)	Durham University, UK
Karl Southern (Treasurer)	Durham University, UK
Peter Davies-Peck (Webmaster)	Durham University, UK
William K. Moses Jr. (Publicity)	Durham University, UK

Steering Committee

Keren Censor-Hillel (Chair)	Technion, Israel
Yuval Emek	Technion, Israel
Andrzej Pelc	Université du Québec en Outaouais, Canada
Sergio Rajsbaum	Universidad Nacional Autónoma de Mexico, Mexico
Ulrich Schmid	TU Wien, Austria

Additional Reviewers

Artmann, Matthias	Liedtke, David
Baligacs, Julia	Manaswini, Piduguralla
Bampas, Evangelos	Miyamoto, Masayuki
Bhardwaj, Gaurav	Montealegre, Pedro
Blondin, Michael	Morawietz, Nils
Bourreau, Yann	Parzych, Garrett
D'Amore, Francesco	Polevoy, Gleb
Feletti, Caterina	Poudel, Pavan
Ghinea, Diana	Pramanick, Subhajit
Gil, Yuval	Rao, M.V. Panduranga
Gujar, Sujit	Sangnier, Arnaud
Hillebrandt, Henning	Shibata, Masahiro
Karmegam, Arivarasan	Tseng, Lewis
Kitamura, Naoki	Werthmann, Julian
Kokkou, Maria	Yamauchi, Yukiko
Kshemkalyani, Ajay	Ziccardi, Isabella

Abstracts of Keynote Lectures

Distributed Protocols on Shared Channels

Dariusz R. Kowalski

Department of Computer & Cyber Sciences, Augusta University, USA

Abstract. A shared channel is an abstract model framework to study autonomous processes that interact and receive feedback as a function of the states of interacting processes. It first emerged more than 50 years ago in attempts to model wireless and local networks, in renowned works of Abramson on ALOHANET and of Metcalfe and Boggs on Ethernet. Both these communication settings assume that a message transmitted by a process (also called a station in this scenario) is received only if there is no other overlapping transmission. The primary performance measure is time complexity.

This talk reviews selected research directions following those prominent works. One of them is the impact of channel feedback on performance of the system; in other words, how the information stored at processes (e.g., messages to be transmitted or other types of local inputs) can be efficiently "recovered" from feedback received during an execution of a distributed protocol. Examples of such study include radio networks with/without collision detection, beeping models, SINR networks, and optical networks.

Another reviewed aspect of shared channels is dependent channels, typically modeled as spacial, graphical, or hypergraph (e.g., modeling multi-frequency) multi-hop networks, in which every neighborhood follows the rules of a shared channel. Here, however, a station initiating some action, e.g., packet transmission, automatically interacts in channels associated with the surrounding neighborhoods. This creates an additional challenge of coordinating simultaneous activities in overlapping neighborhoods.

While a vast majority of theoretical work focuses on slotted synchronized settings, in reality clock shifts or even (bounded) asynchrony may occur. We give examples of different impacts that these features may have on system performance or, in some cases, tasks' feasibility.

The last discussed aspect of shared channels targets continuity and stability of shared-channel communication. In particular, when the states/inputs of the processes may change dynamically by intervention of external stochastic/adversarial forces. Example includes packets injected dynamically into the processes, which then have to be successfully transmitted on the channel. The goal is to assure bounded packets' latencies (and thus, bounded queue sizes at stations) for as high a packet injection rate as possible, no matter how long the execution continues.

For each of the abovementioned aspects, major results and open directions will be presented. Due to time limitation, this talk will not be able to cover many

---

2026 Prize for Innovation in Distributed Computing Keynote Lecture

other features related to shared channels, such as fault-tolerance, security, equilibria, labeling schemes, quantum communication, energy efficiency, applications in shared memory, transactional memory, blockchains, etc., as well as relationships of shared channels with information theory and codes, communication complexity, (group) testing, machine learning, databases and other areas of computer science. For some of them, though, examples and references will be provided.

Keywords: Shared channels · Distributed algorithms · Collision models · Stability

Smart Contracts and Distributed Cross-Chain Protocols

Maria Potop-Butucaru

LIP6, Sorbonne University, France

Abstract. Many challenges in blockchains and decentralized finance can be understood as modern variations of classical distributed computing problems. This talk introduces a smart contract model that highlights both the parallels and the key distinctions between traditional distributed systems and blockchain-based environments.

The discussion centers on cross-chain protocols, where multiple parties—some honest, others potentially adversarial—interact through trusted smart contracts deployed across independent ledgers. While these protocols are capable of supporting general computation, their primary application lies in managing ownership of assets such as cryptocurrencies and other valuable data.

This asset-centric focus leads to important differences from classical models of distributed and concurrent computing. In particular, because participants may behave in a Byzantine manner, problems are framed using fundamental game-theoretic concepts that account for each party's incentives and possible outcomes.

As in traditional settings, parties provide inputs and agree on a sequence of intended asset transfers. However, unlike classical systems, it is the smart contracts—not the participants—that ultimately determine the outcomes by executing these transfers, as they alone control asset ownership.

Keywords: Blockchains · Smart contracts · Distributed models

Distributed Quantum Advantage

Jukka Suomela

Department of Computer Science, Aalto University, Finland

Abstract. How much room is there for quantum advantage in the distributed setting? If we have a large computer network, and we replace classical computers with quantum computers and classical communication links with quantum communication links, can we solve some distributed tasks asymptotically faster? In particular, can we reduce the number of communication rounds? Formally, is the quantum-LOCAL model asymptotically stronger than the classical LOCAL model?

In recent years, we have made substantial progress in understanding this question, and an intriguing picture has emerged. On the one hand, we can now show that there are distributed graph problems that admit a quantum advantage. On the other hand, all known examples of such tasks are artificial problems, designed only to demonstrate a provable quantum advantage, and serving no practical purpose beyond that.

In this talk, I will give an overview of the state of the art in this area. I will survey techniques that we can use to place limits on quantum advantage; in particular, I will discuss non-signaling arguments that conveniently allow us to establish such limits without directly dealing with quantum computation. I will give examples of artificial problems that admit quantum advantage, and I will also discuss key barriers that prevent us from understanding, for example, quantum advantage for symmetry-breaking tasks.

Keywords: Distributed computing · Distributed graph algorithms · Quantum computing · LOCAL model · Quantum-LOCAL model

Contents

A Simple Distributed Deterministic Planar Separator

Yaseen Abd-Elhaleem$^{(\boxtimes)}$, Michal Dory , and Oren Weimann

Department of Computer Science, University of Haifa, Haifa, Israel
`yaseenuniacc@gmail.com`, `mdory@ds.haifa.ac.il`, `oren@cs.haifa.ac.il`

Abstract. A balanced separator of a graph G is a set of vertices whose removal disconnects the graph into connected components that are a constant factor smaller than G. Lipton and Tarjan [FOCS'77] famously proved that every planar graph admits a balanced separator of size $O(\sqrt{n})$, as well as a balanced separator of size $O(D)$ that is a simple path (where D is the graph's diameter). In the centralized setting, these separators can both be found in linear $O(n)$ time. In the distributed setting, since the diameter D is a trivial universal lower bound for the number of rounds required to solve many optimization problems, separators of size $O(D)$ are preferable over those of size $O(\sqrt{n})$.

It was not until [Ghaffari, Parter DISC'17] that an algorithm was devised to compute such an $O(D)$-size separator distributively in $\tilde{O}(D)$(The $\tilde{O}(\cdot)$ notation is used to omit $\operatorname{poly}\log n$ factors.) rounds, by adapting the Lipton-Tarjan algorithm to the distributed model. Since then, this algorithm was used in several distributed algorithms for planar graphs, e.g., [Ghaffari, Parter DISC'17], [Li, Parter STOC'19], [Abd-Elhaleem, Dory, Parter and Weimann PODC'25]. However, the algorithm is randomized, deeming the algorithms that use it to be randomized as well. Obtaining a deterministic algorithm remained an interesting open question until very recently, when a (complex) deterministic separator algorithm was given by [Jauregui, Montealegre and Rapaport PODC'25]. In this paper, we present a much simpler deterministic separator algorithm with the same (near-optimal) $\tilde{O}(D)$-round complexity. While previous works devise either complicated or random ways of transferring weights from vertices of G to faces of G, we show that a straightforward way also works: Each vertex simply transfers its weight to one arbitrary face it belongs to. That's it!

We note that a deterministic separator algorithm directly derandomizes the state-of-the-art distributed algorithms for classical problems on planar graphs such as single-source shortest-paths, maximum-flow, directed global min-cut, and reachability.

Keywords: Distributed Computing · Planar Graphs · Balanced Separator

C. Georgiou (Ed.): SIROCCO 2026, LNCS 16488, pp. 1–20, 2026.
https://doi.org/10.1007/978-3-032-26465-7_1

1   Introduction

A c-balanced separator of a vertex-weighted graph G is a set of vertices whose removal disconnects the graph into connected components, each weighing at most a c fraction of G's total weight. In their classical paper from the 70's [16], Lipton and Tarjan showed that every planar graph admits a balanced separator of size $O(\sqrt{n})$. This has been used in numerous divide-and-conquer centralized algorithms. Their proof first shows that given any spanning tree T of G, there is a balanced separator of G consisting of a path in T. If G is *triangulated*, then this separator is a *fundamental cycle* (a cycle consisting of the path in T plus an edge e of G connecting the path's endpoints). Taking T to be a BFS tree produces a separator of size $O(D)$, where D is the graph's hop-diameter. In the distributed setting, since D is a trivial lower bound for the number of rounds required to solve many optimization problems, separators of size $O(D)$ are preferable over those of size $O(\sqrt{n})$.

Lipton and Tarjan reduce the problem of computing a balanced separator in T to computing a *balanced cut* in the *dual tree* T^*. It relies on the cut-cycle duality in planar graphs (see Sect. 2 for definitions of duality), and on the fact that one can transfer the weights from vertices of G to faces of G (i.e., to nodes of the dual graph G^*). In order for T^* to have a balanced cut, it is crucial that T^* has a constant degree. In the centralized setting, this can easily be achieved by triangulating G, i.e., adding artificial edges to G to make every face of size 3 (thus making every node in T^* to be of degree at most 3). In the distributed setting however, one cannot afford to triangulate G (as artificial edges cannot be communicated on). Instead, Ghaffari and Parter [10] gave a distributed implementation of Lipton-Tarjan that circumvents this using a randomized procedure that approximates the face-weights assigned by Lipton-Tarjan. Since then, their separator algorithm was used in several state-of-the-art distributed algorithms for planar graphs, including depth-first search, single-source shortest-paths, maximum flow, routing, and diameter [1,6,10,15]. However, since the distributed separator algorithm was randomized, all algorithms that used it were randomized as well. In fact, in most of them, finding the separator is the only randomized component. Very recently in PODC 2025, using a different approach, Jauregui, Montealegre, and Rapaport [13] provided a *deterministic* distributed separator algorithm. Their algorithm avoids computations on the dual graph by instead considering a collection of triangulation edges. This however leads to a complex analysis, as we discuss in Sect. 3.

Our Result. The standard way to compute a balanced separator in the primal graph (with respect to vertex-weights) is to translate it to the problem of computing a balanced cut (a cut whose sides are roughly of the same weight) in the dual graph. To do so, one needs to give weights to the dual nodes (faces of the primal graph) such that a balanced cut in the dual graph translates to a balanced separator in the primal graph. A natural way to transfer weights from vertices to faces is to set a face weight to be the sum of weights of its vertices. This however does not work, since a vertex can belong to an arbitrary number of faces which leads to overcounting. This issue was the source of [10] resorting to randomization and of [13] being complex. We give a very simple and natural alternative: Each vertex transfers its weight to one arbitrary face it belongs to. That's it! Since each vertex transfers its weight to one face it is counted exactly once which overcomes the problem of overcounting, and we show that a balanced cut with respect to this weight assignment translates to a balanced separator. Our result is summarized by the following theorem.

Theorem 1. *Let G be an embedded planar graph of hop-diameter D, T be a spanning tree of G, and $w(\cdot)$ be a weight assignment to G's vertices s.t. no vertex weighs more than $\frac{1}{12}$ fraction of the total weight of G. There is a deterministic $\tilde{O}(D)$-round distributed algorithm that finds a u-to-v path P in T that is a $\frac{3}{4}$-balanced separator of G. Adding the edge $e = (u, v)$ to G (if it does not already exist), closes a fundamental cycle $P \cup \{e\}$ in T. Setting T to be a BFS tree produces a separator of size $O(D)$.*

We note that a deterministic separator algorithm directly derandomizes the state-of-the-art distributed algorithms for classical problems on planar graphs such as depth-first search (DFS), single-source shortest-paths, maximum-flow, directed global min-cut, and reachability. This already follows from [13]. However, in [13] they only mention the application of DFS. We elaborate on the above other applications in Sect. 6.

Our algorithm works with vertex-weighted graphs, where previous works [10, 13] focused on the unweighted case (i.e., the unit-weight case. In particular, note that no vertex weighs more than $1/n$ fraction of the total weight). Finally, it is often useful for applications to compute a separator in multiple vertex-disjoint subgraphs of G simultaneously. Our algorithm can be easily extended to support this as we show in Sect. 5.

Roadmap. In Sect. 2 we give the necessary preliminaries. In Sect. 3 we overview related work and our technical contribution. Our deterministic separator algorithm is presented in Sect. 4, and its distributed implementation in Sect. 5. The applications are discussed in Sect. 6. Finally, the full version [2] includes some deferred details from Sects. 4 and 5.

2   Preliminaries

The CONGEST Model. We work in the standard distributed CONGEST model [18]. Initially, each vertex knows only its unique $O(\log n)$-bit ID and the IDs of its neighbors. Communication occurs in synchronous rounds. In each round, each vertex can send each neighbor a distinct $O(\log n)$-bit message. When the edges of G are weighted we assume that the weights are polynomially bounded integers. Thus, the weight of an edge can be transmitted in $O(1)$ rounds. This is a standard assumption in the CONGEST model. Input and output are local, e.g. when rooting a spanning tree, we assume that all vertices know (as an input) the ID of the root r, and their incident edges in the tree. When the algorithm halts, each vertex knows the ID of its parent in the tree.

Basic Notation and Graph Theory. We denote by $G = (V, E)$ the vertex-weighted or face-weighted simple (connected) planar graph of communication. We denote by D the hop-diameter of G and by F the set of faces of G in a given planar embedding (defined next). When the weights are assigned to vertices (resp. faces), we denote the weight function by $w_V(\cdot)$ (resp. $w_F(\cdot)$). We denote by $w_A(G)$ the total weight of G w.r.t. $w_A(\cdot)$ where $A \in \{V, F\}$. When A is clear from context we may omit it from the subscript and write $w(\cdot)$.

Planar Embedding. The *geometric* planar embedding of a planar graph G is a drawing of G on a plane so that edges intersect only in vertices. In such embedding, there is a distinguished face f_∞ (called the infinite face) surrounding the graph. When we consider a cycle C in G, we refer to C's *exterior* (resp. *interior*) as the side of C that contains (resp. does not contain) f_∞. We denote by C_{in} (resp. C_{out}) the interior (resp. exterior) of C, including C itself. We denote the *strict* interior (resp. exterior) of C (i.e., excluding C) by C_{in}^- (resp. C_{out}^-).

A *combinatorial* planar embedding of G provides for each vertex $v \in G$, the local clockwise ordering of its incident edges, such that the ordering is consistent with some geometric planar embedding of G. See Chap. 3.4 of [14] for more information. Throughout, we assume that a combinatorial embedding of G is known locally for each vertex. This is achieved in $\tilde{O}(D)$ rounds using the *deterministic* distributed planar embedding algorithm of Ghaffari and Haeupler [7].

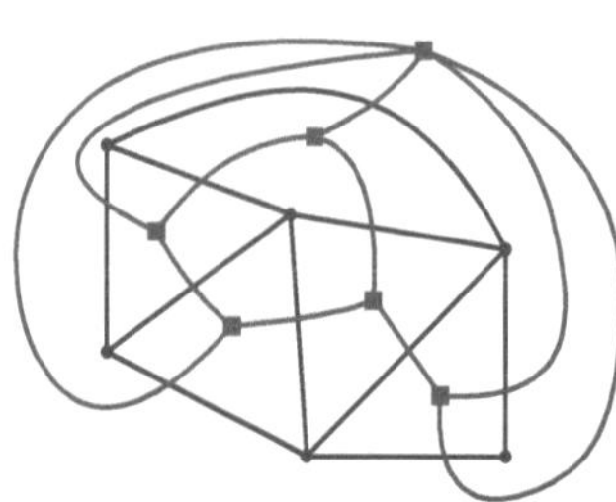

Planar Duality. The *dual* of a *primal* embedded planar graph G is a planar graph G^* whose nodes[1] correspond to the faces of G. For each edge $e \in G$ that belongs to two faces in G, there is an edge e^* in G^* between the faces' corresponding nodes (and a self-loop when the same face appears on both sides of an edge). We sometimes abuse notations and denote both e and e^* as e. See the figure for an illustration (the primal graph G in blue and its dual graph G^* in red).

Lemma 1. (Tree and cotree, Chap. 4.5 of [14]). *T is a spanning tree of G iff the* cotree *$T^* = E \setminus T$ is a spanning tree of G^*.*

Fundamental Cuts and Cycles. We use the duality between cycles defined by T and cuts defined by T^*:

Definition 1 (Fundamental cuts). *Removing an edge $e \in T$ from T, breaks T into two connected components. The set $\delta_G(T, e)$ of edges of G that have one endpoint in each component is called the fundamental cut of T with respect to e in G.*

---

[1] For clarity, we will refer to faces of the primal graph G as *nodes* (rather than vertices) of the dual graph G^*.

Definition 2 (Fundamental cycles). *Adding an edge $e \in G \setminus T$ to T, closes one simple cycle $C_G(T, e)$ with T. The cycle $C_G(T, e)$ is called the fundamental cycle of T with respect to e in G.*

When G is clear from the context, we use $\delta(T, e)$ and $C(T, e)$ to denote $\delta_G(T, e)$ and $C_G(T, e)$ respectively.

Lemma 2 (Fundamental cut-cycle duality [14]). *Let T^* be a spanning tree of G^* and $T = E \setminus T^*$ be its cotree. T^* defines a fundamental cut in G^* w.r.t. an edge e^* iff T defines a fundamental cycle in G w.r.t. e. That is, $\delta_{G^*}(T^*, e^*) = C_G(T, e)$.*

Separators. Let $w_A(\cdot)$ be a weight function on $A \in \{V, F\}$.

Definition 3 (α-proper weights). *$w_A(\cdot)$ is α-proper for $\alpha \in (0, 1)$ if $w_A(a) \leq \alpha \cdot w_A(G)$ for each $a \in A$.*

Definition 4 (Balanced separators). *Let $c < 1$ be a constant. A c-balanced separator S is a set of vertices s.t. the connected components of $G \setminus S$ are of size at most $c \cdot w_A(G)$.*

Definition 5 (Fundamental cycle separators). *Let $c < 1$ be a constant, and let T be a spanning tree of G. A fundamental cycle separator of G is a c-balanced separator S which constitutes a fundamental cycle of T. I.e., there exists an edge $e \notin T$ s.t. $S = C(T, e)$, and $w_A(S_{in}^-), w_A(S_{out}^-) \leq c \cdot w_A(G)$.*

Balanced and Critical Nodes. We use the following definitions of [10] that discusses rooted trees. For a node $f \in T^*$, let T_f^* denote the subtree of T^* rooted at f. We denote by $w(T^*)$ the total weight of all nodes of T^*.

Definition 6 (Balanced node). *$f \in T^*$ is (α, β)-balanced for constants $\alpha < \beta \leq 1$ if $\alpha \cdot w(T^*) \leq w(T_f^*) \leq \beta \cdot w(T^*)$.*

Definition 7 (Critical node). *$f \in T^*$ is (α, β)-critical for constants $\alpha < \beta \leq 1$ if $w(T_f^*) > \beta \cdot w(T^*)$, and $w(T_h^*) < \alpha \cdot w(T^*)$ for every child h of f in T^*.*

3 Technical Overview and Related Work

Computing a balanced separator is a fundamental building block in many algorithms for planar graphs. In distributed algorithms, it is desired that the separator is a path P in some given spanning tree T s.t. adding to P an edge $e \notin T$ (perhaps even $e \notin G$) that connects P's endpoints closes a fundamental cycle $C(T, e)$ in G (or in $G \cup \{e\}$ if $e \notin G$). Setting T to be a BFS tree, we get a separator of size $O(D)$. The goal is therefore to find such an edge e where $C(T, e)$ encloses a constant $0 < c < 1$ fraction of G's total weight of vertices. Finding such an edge e is not an easy task.

However, if the weights were assigned to faces (rather than vertices), then the problem becomes easy, as it amounts to finding a balanced node f in the dual tree T^*. Indeed, such a node f naturally defines a fundamental cut $\delta_{G^*}(T^*, e^*)$ in G^* (i.e., $e^* = (f, \mathsf{parent}(f))$) and hence a fundamental cycle $C(T, e)$ in G (Lemma 2). See Fig. 1. Since f is balanced, the weight of f's subtree T^*_f in G^* (the weight of all faces enclosed by $C(T, e)$ in G) is a constant fraction of G's total weight of faces. Formally:

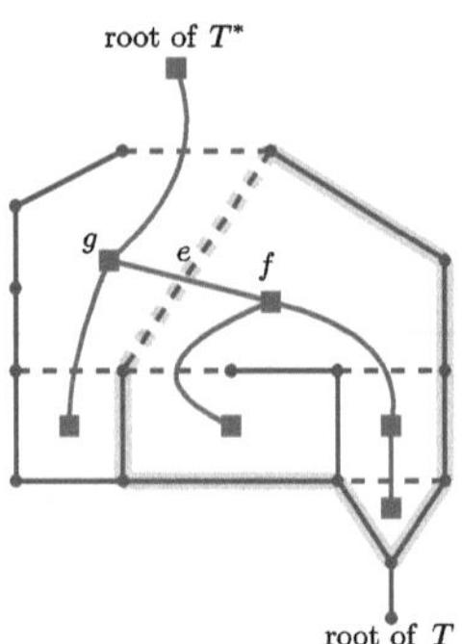

Fig. 1. The primal graph G is in blue. Solid blue edges are in T and dashed blue edges are not in T. I.e., their duals (in red) are in T^*. Removing the dual edge $e^* = (g, f)$ from T^* breaks T^* into T^*_f (f's subtree in T^*) and $T^* \setminus T^*_f$. The fundamental cycle $C(T, e)$ (highlighted in yellow) encloses all faces that correspond to nodes of T^*_f, and does not enclose any face that corresponds to nodes of $T^* \setminus T^*_f$.

Lemma 3 (See e.g., [14]). *Let T be a spanning tree of G and $e^* = (g, f)$ an edge of the cotree T^* of T. If we root T^* s.t. g is closer to the root than f, then each node of T^*_f maps to a face enclosed by $S = C(T, e)$. Analogously, each node of $T^* \setminus T^*_f$ maps to a face not enclosed by S. I.e., $w(T^*_f) = w_F(S_{in})$, and $w(T^* \setminus T^*_f) = w_F(S_{out})$.*

Alas, the weights in the input graph G are assigned to vertices and not to faces. Therefore, the idea is to transfer the vertex-weights to face-weights s.t. a balanced separator w.r.t. these face-weights is also a balanced separator w.r.t. the original vertex-weights (perhaps with a different balance constant). There are two challenges with this approach:

Challenge I - Assigning Weights to Faces. The natural naive assignment that assigns each face a weight equal to the total weight of its vertices, does not work. This is because a vertex may belong to many faces. Thus, a (primal) subgraph might have a small total vertex-weight but a large total face-weight. In T^*, this means that a subtree T^*_f of some node f might have a large weight, where in fact it corresponds to a cycle that encloses a small-weight subgraph, while the external subgraph has a large weight. Such a subtree might be mistakenly chosen to define the separator. I.e., f can be a balanced node in the dual tree, but it does not necessarily translate to a balanced separator in the primal graph with respect to vertex-weights.

Challenge II - Existence of a Balanced Node. Even if we overcome the first challenge, since faces can be arbitrarily large, it is not guaranteed that a balanced node f exists in T^*. It may be the case that all subtrees of T^* either weigh too much, or weigh too little. For example, when T^* is a star.

We next describe how prior work dealt with the above challenges, and how we deal with them.

Lipton-Tarjan [16]. In the 70's, Lipton and Tarjan introduced the above approach in the centralized setting. To overcome Challenge I, each vertex of G transfers its weight to an arbitrary face that it participates in. Thus, for any cycle of G, the weight of its (non-strict) interior w.r.t. faces and w.r.t. vertices is similar (each vertex assigns its weight to exactly one face that it lies on). In the centralized setting, Challenge II is easily dealt with by *triangulating* G. I.e., augmenting G with artificial edges to make each of its faces consist of exactly three edges. In the augmented graph, it is not hard to show that T^* always admits a balanced node f. This is because now the dual graph G^* is 3-regular, thus T^* is a binary tree, and the weight assignment to faces is 3α-proper if the weight to vertices was originally α-proper. In the distributed setting however, triangulation is not an option, since it may require adding a linear number of artificial edges which we cannot communicate on (and simulating them is too costly). This has motivated the following alternative direction of [10].

Ghaffari-Parter [10]. In 2017, Ghaffari and Parter [10] provided the first (near-optimal, $\tilde{O}(D)$-rounds) distributed procedure that computes a path separator. Their procedure is *randomized* and overcomes the above challenges as follows.

To overcome Challenge I, they compute for each node f of T^* a weight $w'(T_f^*)$ that approximates the total vertex-weight of the primal subgraph corresponding to T_f^*. Intuitively, instead of assigning each face the weight of all its vertices (which as mentioned above leads to overcounting), they sample each vertex with a certain probability. The weight of a face is 1 if at least one of the vertices of the face is sampled and it is 0 otherwise.[2] Eventually, for each node f in T^* they compute the subtree OR of it (to check if at least one of the values in the subtree is 1). They repeat the process a poly-logarithmic number of times with different sampling rates, and show that this allows them to estimate the total vertex-weight of the corresponding primal subgraph. This allows them to overcome Challenge I. However, the approach is heavily based on randomization.

To overcome Challenge II, they prove that if no balanced node exists in T^*, then a critical node f must exist. After finding such critical node f, a single artificial edge $e = (u, v)$ is added to the interior of the corresponding primal face f in G, splitting f into two faces (replacing the node f in T^* with two nodes connected by the new dual edge e^*). Finally, they prove that one of the two

---

[2] This assumes *unit* vertex-weights, however it can be extended to arbitrary weights by adjusting the sampling probability.

new nodes is a balanced node, hence defining a cycle separator consisting of the u-to-v path P in T, and the single artificial edge $e \notin G$.

Apart from being randomized, the only drawback of the Ghaffari-Parter algorithm is that it requires the input graph to be bi-connected (i.e., the removal of any single vertex does not disconnect the graph). Nonetheless, they show that the bi-connectivity assumption is not a restriction for the specific application of computing a Depth-First Search (DFS) tree in near-optimal $\tilde{O}(D)$ rounds (following an approach given in the parallel algorithm of [3]).

Li-Parter [15]. In 2019, Li and Parter [15] showed how to entirely remove the bi-connectivity assumption of [10], by augmenting G with certain (non-triangulation) artificial edges that do not violate planarity and can be simulated efficiently in the distributed setting. Another important contribution of [15], is showing how to apply the separator algorithm recursively, obtaining a *Bounded Diameter Decomposition (BDD)* in $\tilde{O}(D)$ rounds. The BDD is a recursive decomposition of planar graphs using separators. It is the distributed analog of the centralized recursive separator decomposition. It is highly non-trivial since, in contrast to the centralized decomposition, the distributed decomposition is required to preserve a low $\tilde{O}(D)$ diameter for all subgraphs in the decomposition.

Since the BDD works with [10]'s separator, it is also randomized. Nevertheless, it extends the applications of the separator to include (randomized) distributed algorithms for classical problems such as shortest-paths [15], maximum st-flow [1], diameter [15], and reachability [17]. See also Sect. 6.

Jauregui-Montealegre-Rapaport [13]. Very recently, in PODC '25, Jauregui, Montealegre and Rapaport showed how to obtain a near-optimal $\tilde{O}(D)$-rounds distributed *deterministic* separator algorithm, following a completely different approach than [10], which does not use planar duality at all. Instead, they address Challenge I directly on the primal graph, and show how to approximate what they call *fundamental face weights*, which are the total vertex-weight of the primal subgraphs enclosed by $C(T, e)$ for all $e \in G$. In our terminology, they approximate the total vertex-weight of the primal graph corresponding to a dual subtree T_f^* for all $f \in T^*$.

After computing the fundamental face weights, they check for one that can be used as a separator. If one does not exist, then there is no edge $e \in G$ that closes a cycle in T that can be used as the separator. To handle this (Challenge II), they approximate the total vertex-weight of subgraphs enclosed by fundamental cycles $C(T, e)$ defined by a certain set of what they call *augmentation edges* $e \notin G$. They prove that one such edge e exists that closes a cycle $C(T, e) = P \cup \{e\}$ in $G \cup \{e\}$, where P is the desired separator path, and compute it. The computational tasks they do on T for both cases are not very complicated, however, the proofs of correctness are. Namely, they involve examining multiple cases of augmentation edges and G edges, related to properties of augmentation edges, to DFS tours on T, and to the embedding of G.

As an application of their algorithm, they show that a deterministic DFS algorithm follows from using their separator in the DFS algorithm of Ghaffari-Parter.

Our Approach. We show that a simple approach where each vertex transfers its weight to a single face works also in the distributed setting and without triangulation. Since each vertex transfers its weight to exactly one face this overcomes the issue of overcounting (Challenge I). It extremely simplifies upon the approach of [13] for computing face-weights. Both [10] and [13] design other solutions that lead to either complicated or random algorithms to deal with the two challenges above.

We achieve the best of both worlds. Our algorithm is a combination of Lipton-Tarjan [16] and Ghaffari-Parter [10], that allows us to exploit the power of planar duality, which significantly simplifies the algorithm and its correctness compared to [13]. Concretely, we deal with Challenge I exactly like Lipton-Tarjan (i.e. every vertex transfers its weight to an arbitrary face it lies on), and we deal with Challenge II exactly like Ghaffari-Parter (i.e. using the fact that if there is no balanced node then there must be a critical node). Our contribution is in showing that this simple approach works, and can be implemented distributively.

Our correctness proof is inspired by the proofs of Lipton-Tarjan and Ghaffari-Parter. However, as we cannot triangulate the graph, we need to carefully handle the case of a critical node. In addition, we handle vertex-weighted graphs and adapt the proof to our weight assignment to faces. Finally, the distributed implementation is similar to both [10,13] and uses very standard tools in distributed computing such as low-congestion shortcuts and part-wise aggregation.

4   A Deterministic Separator Algorithm

Our algorithm begins by transferring weights from vertices to faces using a simple procedure: Each vertex transfers its weight to one arbitrary face it belongs to. The weight of the face is then the total weight of vertices that transferred their weight to this face. Then, we find a node f in the dual tree T^* that is either a balanced node or a critical node (where the weights are now on nodes of T^*). We prove that the fundamental cycle separator defined by f is also a separator w.r.t. the original vertex-weights. A pseudocode of the algorithm is given in Algorithm 1. The algorithm mostly follows the (distributed) algorithm of [10]. The highlighted steps are the steps where we differ from [10]. For each such step we provide a proof of correctness. We assume that the input graph is *bi-connected*. This assumption can be removed as in [15]. We discuss this in more detail in the next section.

Proposition 1. *Let G be a planar graph with vertex-weights $w_V(\cdot)$, and S a cycle in G. Then, the weight assignment where each vertex transfers its weight to an arbitrary face it belongs to satisfies $w_V(S_{in}^-) \leq w_F(S_{in}) \leq w_V(S_{in})$. Moreover, $w_F(G) = w_V(G)$.*

Proof. As each vertex transfers its weight to exactly one face, we clearly have $w_F(G) = w_V(G)$. In addition, if S is a cycle, we have $w_V(S_{in}^-) \leq w_F(S_{in}) \leq w_V(S_{in})$. The reason is that all vertices that are in the strict interior of S transfer

---

Algorithm 1: Separator

Input: A bi-connected D-diameter graph G, a spanning tree tree T of G, and a $\frac{1}{12}$-proper weight assignment $w_V(\cdot)$ to the vertices of G.

Output: A 3/4-balanced path separator P of G and an edge $e \notin T$ s.t.
$P \cup \{e\} = C(T, e)$.   (If $e \notin G$ then adding e to G
preserves planarity).

1. Compute the cotree T^*;
2. Transfer vertex-weights to face-weights. I.e., to nodes of T^* (Proposition 1);
3. Detect a $(\frac{1}{4}, \frac{3}{4})$-balanced dual node or a $(\frac{1}{4}, \frac{3}{4})$-critical dual node (Lemma 4);
4. Mark the separator path P in T, and learn vertices $u, v \in G$ s.t. $S = P \cup \{e\}$, where $e = (u, v)$ is possibly not in G (Lemma 5) :
   (a) If a balanced dual node f was found, mark P and $e = (u, v)$ where P is the u-to-v path in T and $e^* = (f, \mathsf{parent}(f))$ in T^* ;
   (b) If a critical dual node f was found, find vertices u, v on the face f s.t. if $e = (u, v)$ is added to f it creates a balanced node in T^*. Mark the u-to-v path P in T as before.

---

their weight to a face in S_{in} as all the faces that contain them are in S_{in}, hence $w_V(S_{in}^-) \le w_F(S_{in})$. Vertices that are part of the cycle S, can belong both to faces that are in S_{in} and to faces that are in S_{out}, so they may transfer their weight to a face in S_{in} or not. Vertices that are in the strict exterior of S are only contained in faces outside S and do not transfer their weight to a face in S_{in}. So overall we have $w_V(S_{in}^-) \le w_F(S_{in}) \le w_V(S_{in})$.

This simple proposition is the core of our algorithm, and the place where we differ from the previous distributed solutions that deal with Challenge I (see Sect. 3) in an either randomized or complicated way. Next, we prove that we can indeed find a fundamental cycle separator w.r.t. vertex-weights using this observation.

Our separator would easily follow if one finds an (α, β)-balanced dual node, as in Lipton-Tarjan, perhaps with different constants α, β. However, since we do not triangulate the graph, an (α, β)-balanced node does not necessarily exist. If that is the case, then there must exist an (α, β)-critical node as shown by [10]. We provide a proof in the full version of the paper [2] for completeness as we use different constants in our algorithm.

Lemma 4 ([10]). *Let G be a planar graph with face-weights $w_F(\cdot)$, T^* a spanning tree of G^* rooted at an arbitrary node, and constants $\alpha < \beta < 1$. Then, T^* either contains an (α, β)-balanced node, or an (α, β)-critical node.*

Now, we show that a 3/4-balanced separator exists w.r.t. our weight assignment, by detecting either a balanced or a critical node. If a balanced node f exists, then the edge $e^* = (f, \mathsf{parent}(f))$ in T^* is the edge (dual to the edge e) that closes a cycle with T forming the desired fundamental cycle separator. Otherwise, a critical node f exists. Intuitively, this node has a large subtree but its children have small subtrees, so none of them can define a balanced separator, but a consecutive subset of them can. In other words, we add artificial edges that are not in T to the interior of f, creating multiple new nodes in T^* resulting from partitioning f to smaller faces. Those nodes are connected to the children of f such that one of them is balanced. The edge e connecting this balanced node to its parent, determines which children of f are in which side of the separator. By proving that, we prove that there always exist two vertices u, v s.t. the u-to-v path P in T is a balanced path separator of G. Then, adding e (whether it exists in G or not), we have that $S = P \cup \{e\}$ is a fundamental cycle separator of $G \cup \{e\}$.

A similar statement was proven by [10], but for their way of dealing with the face weight challenge (Challenge I in Sect. 3). We show a proof that works with our weight assignment to faces. In addition, [10] focused on unit vertex-weights and we allow arbitrary vertex-weights.

Lemma 5. *Let G be a bi-connected planar graph, T a spanning tree of G, and a $\frac{1}{12}$-proper weight assignment $w_V(\cdot)$ to the vertices of G. After transferring vertex-weights $w_V(\cdot)$ to face-weights $w_F(\cdot)$ as in Proposition 1, then:*

1. *If a $(\frac{1}{4}, \frac{3}{4})$-balanced node f in T^* exists w.r.t. $w_F(\cdot)$, let u, v be the endpoints of the edge e that is dual to the edge $(f, \mathsf{parent}(f))$ in T^*. Then, the u-to-v path P in T is a $\frac{3}{4}$-balanced separator of G w.r.t. $w_V(\cdot)$. I.e., $P \cup \{e\} = C(T, e)$.*
2. *Otherwise, there exists a $(\frac{1}{4}, \frac{3}{4})$-critical node f in T^* w.r.t. $w_F(\cdot)$. Then, there are two vertices u, v on f s.t. the u-to-v path P in T is a $\frac{3}{4}$-balanced separator of G w.r.t. $w_V(\cdot)$. Moreover, if we add the edge $e = (u, v)$ to G, it does not violate planarity, and $P \cup \{e\} = C(T, e)$.*

Proof. By Lemma 4, either a $(\frac{1}{4}, \frac{3}{4})$-balanced node or a $(\frac{1}{4}, \frac{3}{4})$-critical node exists w.r.t. $w_F(\cdot)$.

Case 1: If a $(\frac{1}{4}, \frac{3}{4})$-balanced node f in T^* exists w.r.t. $w_F(\cdot)$, then consider the fundamental cut $\delta(T^*, e^*)$, where $e^* = (f, \mathsf{parent}(f))$. The cut is dual to a fundamental cycle $S = C(T, e)$ in G, such that its interior corresponds to T_f^* (Lemma 3). See Fig. 1 for an illustration. We next prove that the total vertex weight of the strict interior and strict exterior of S are both bounded by $\frac{3}{4} \cdot w_V(G)$. Then, setting P to be $S \setminus \{e\}$ gives the balanced path separator. By Lemma 3, $w(T_f^*) = w_F(S_{in})$. Also, as f is $(\frac{1}{4}, \frac{3}{4})$-balanced we have: $\frac{1}{4} \cdot w_F(G) \leq w(T_f^*) = w_F(S_{in}) \leq \frac{3}{4} \cdot w_F(G)$, and since $w_V(S_{in}^-) \leq w_F(S_{in}) \leq w_V(S_{in})$ (Proposition 1), we get that $w_V(S_{in}^-) \leq w_F(S_{in}) \leq \frac{3}{4} \cdot w_F(G)$ and $\frac{1}{4} \cdot w_F(G) \leq w_V(S_{in})$. Finally, because $w_F(G) = w_V(G)$ (Proposition 1) we get that both the strict interior is bounded by $w_V(S_{in}^-) \leq \frac{3}{4} \cdot w_V(G)$ and the strict exterior is bounded as we have $\frac{1}{4} \cdot w_V(G) \leq w_V(S_{in})$, which implies that $w_V(S_{out}^-) = w_V(G) - w_V(S_{in}) \leq w_V(G) - \frac{1}{4} \cdot w_V(G) = \frac{3}{4} \cdot w_V(G)$. Hence, we get a $\frac{3}{4}$-balanced separator with respect to vertex-weights.

Case 2: If a $(\frac{1}{4}, \frac{3}{4})$-critical node f exists in T^* w.r.t. $w_F(\cdot)$, then by the bi-connectivity assumption, f is a simple cycle in G^3. If f has no children in T^*, then this cycle has only one of its edges $e = (f, \mathsf{parent}(f))$ in T^*. The rest of its edges form a path P in T (by Lemma 1). In this case, P is the balanced separator, because the strict interior of the face (cycle) f is empty (so weighs zero), and the strict exterior is of weight at most $\frac{3}{4} \cdot w_V(G)$. This is because as f is a critical node with no children in T^*, we have that $w(T_f^*) = w_F(f) > \frac{3}{4} \cdot w_F(G) = \frac{3}{4} \cdot w_V(G)$, where the last equality follows from Proposition 1. Now, if the weight of f is larger than $\frac{3}{4} \cdot w_V(G)$ it means that the total weight of vertices in f is at least $\frac{3}{4} \cdot w_V(G)$, because the weight of f is the total weight of vertices in f that transferred their weight to f. This means that the strict exterior of f weighs
$$w_V(G \setminus f) = w_V(G) - w_V(f) \le w_V(G) - \frac{3}{4} \cdot w_V(G) < \frac{3}{4} \cdot w_V(G).$$

Otherwise, f has at least one child, and each child's subtree weighs less than $\frac{1}{4} \cdot w_F(G)$. We show that there are two vertices u, v on f s.t. the u-to-v path P in T is a balanced separator for G w.r.t. $w_V(\cdot)$. We do that by reducing this case to Case 1. In other words, we show that if one would triangulate f with artificial edges (see Fig. 2b), then one of the resulting faces is $(\frac{1}{4}, \frac{3}{4})$-balanced. By Case 1, this implies that such two nodes u, v exist. In this case, only the edge (u, v) will be artificial.

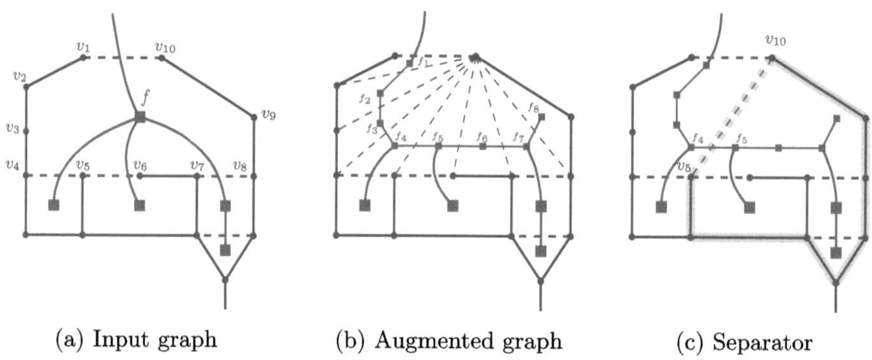

(a) Input graph (b) Augmented graph (c) Separator

Fig. 2. The primal graph is blue. The dual tree T^* is red. The solid blue edges are edges of the primal tree T. Dashed edges are not in T (i.e., their duals are in T^*). (a) f is the face with vertices $v_1, v_2, \ldots, v_{10}$. The edge $e = (v_1, v_{10})$ corresponds to the dual edge $e^* = (f, \mathsf{parent}(f))$ in T^*. (b) Adding the artificial triangulation edges (thin dashed) to the interior of f partitions f into faces $f_1, f_2, \ldots, f_8$. In the new dual tree T^*, node f_{i+1} is the child of f_i. The path $P(f)$ is the path from f_1 to f_8. (c) In this example, $f_j = f_4$. The dual edge $e^* = (f_4, f_5)$ in T^* corresponds to the artificial primal edge $e = (v_5, v_{10})$ and defines the separator (highlighted in yellow). (Color figure online)

---

³ I.e, if not, then f consists of a simple cycle and trees hanging from it. Then, removing a single vertex from the tree disconnects the graph, contradicting the assumption that it is bi-connected.

Formally, consider the primal edge e whose dual is the edge $(f, \mathsf{parent}(f))$ in T^*. Let $v_1, \ldots, v_k$ be the vertices of f such that $e = (v_1, v_k)$, and f's vertices are enumerated counter-clockwise from v_1 to v_k. See Fig. 2a. For the sake of the proof, we triangulate f by adding artificial edges between v_k and vertices $v_2, \ldots, v_{k-2}$ of f. This creates $k - 2$ new faces $f_1, f_2, \ldots, f_{k-2}$, where f_i is the face that contains the edge (v_i, v_{i+1}) of f (see Fig. 2b). Adding the triangulation edges changes T^* as follows: (1) The node f is replaced by a f_1-to-f_{k-2} path $P(f)$ of artificial edges, (2) The parent of f is now the parent of f_1, (3) Every f_i (where $i < k - 2$) has one (artificial) child f_{i+1} and perhaps one more (real) child g, if g was a child of f in T^* (i.e., when (f, g) is the dual edge of (v_i, v_{i+1})), (4) f_{k-2} is the last vertex of $P(f)$ so it does not have an artificial child, but it may have (at most) two real children (connected to f_{k-2} via the edges dual to (v_{k-2}, v_{k-1}) and (v_{k-1}, v_k)).

Consider T^*, where each node is assigned a weight as in Proposition 1. Recall that each vertex v transfers its weight to one face. If this face is not f, then v transfers its weight to the same face as before. If v originally transferred its weight to f, then v is contained in at least one face f_i. We then have v transfer its weight to one such (arbitrary) face f_i. By this weight assignment the total weight of the new faces f_i is exactly equal to the original weight of the face f. Since the original vertex weights were $\frac{1}{12}$-proper and each f_i has size 3 (i.e., gets the weight of at most 3 vertices), we have the following.

Lemma 6. *The weight of every f_i is $\frac{1}{4}$-proper.*

We next prove that one of the dual nodes f_i is balanced.

Lemma 7. *Let f_j be the lowest node on $P(f)$ whose subtree weighs more than $\frac{3}{4} \cdot w_F(T^*)$ but its children in T^* have subtrees weighing at most $\frac{3}{4} \cdot w_F(T^*)$. The child f_{j+1} of f_j is $(\frac{1}{4}, \frac{3}{4})$-balanced.*

Proof (of Lemma 7.). First we prove that such f_j exists. Recall that f was chosen such that it is a $(\frac{1}{4}, \frac{3}{4})$-critical node. This means that $w(T_f^*) > \frac{3}{4} \cdot w(T^*)$, but all its children in T have subtrees of weight smaller than $\frac{1}{4} \cdot w(T^*)$. After we replace the face f with the path $P(f)$, the total weight of all nodes f_i in $P(f)$ is the same as the original weight of f, and the weight of all other nodes is the same. Therefore, we have that $w(T_{f_1}^*) > \frac{3}{4} \cdot w(T^*)$. On the other hand, consider the last node f_{k-2} on $P(f)$. We show that $w(T_{f_{k-2}}^*) < \frac{3}{4} w(T^*)$. For this, first note that each face f_i has three vertices, which means that in the dual graph the node f_i has at most three neighbors. One of the neighbors of f_{k-2} is the node f_{k-3} of $P(f)$ (the parent of f_{k-2} in T^*) and it has at most two children not in $P(f)$. Since f is a critical node, each one of these neighbors g not in $P(f)$ has $w(T_g^*) < \frac{1}{4} \cdot w(T^*)$, as explained above. Also, as the weights of the nodes f_i are $\frac{1}{4}$-proper (Lemma 6), we get that $w(T_{f_{k-2}}^*) < \frac{1}{4} \cdot w(T^*) + 2 \cdot \frac{1}{4} \cdot w(T^*) = \frac{3}{4} \cdot w(T^*)$.

Hence, there exists a node f_j in $P(f)$ whose subtree weighs more than $\frac{3}{4} \cdot w_F(T^*)$ but its children in T^* have subtrees weighing at most $\frac{3}{4} \cdot w_F(T^*)$ (note that the children not on $P(f)$ weigh less than $\frac{1}{4} \cdot w(T^*)$ as explained above, and we are looking for the first f_j in $P(f)$ where this condition holds). Note that

$f_j \neq f_{k-2}$ as we showed that $w(T^*_{f_{k-2}}) < \frac{3}{4} \cdot w(T^*)$. Hence, f_j has a child f_{j+1}. By definition, we have that $w(T^*_{f_{j+1}}) \leq \frac{3}{4} \cdot w(T^*)$. To show that f_{j+1} is balanced we will show that $w(T^*_{f_{j+1}}) > \frac{1}{4} \cdot w(T^*)$. Recall that $w(T^*_{f_j}) > \frac{3}{4} \cdot w(T^*)$. Recall, f_j has at most one child g not on $P(f)$, in addition to the child f_{j+1} on $P(f)$. The child g not on $P(f)$ has $w(T^*_g) < \frac{1}{4} \cdot w(T^*)$ as explained above. And since the weights are $\frac{1}{4}$-proper we have that $w_F(f_j) \leq \frac{1}{4} \cdot w(T^*)$. On the other hand $w(T^*_{f_{j+1}}) = w(T^*_{f_j}) - w_F(f_j) - w(T^*_g) > \frac{3}{4} \cdot w(T^*) - \frac{1}{4} \cdot w(T^*) - \frac{1}{4} \cdot w(T^*) = \frac{1}{4} \cdot w(T^*)$. Hence, f_{j+1} is indeed a $(\frac{1}{4}, \frac{3}{4})$-balanced node as needed.

By the above lemma, Case 2 indeed reduces to Case 1. That is, the edge $e = (f_j, f_{j+1})$ in the new dual tree defines two nodes $u, v \in G$ s.t. the u-to-v path P in T is a 3/4-balanced path separator (in the augmented graph). See Fig. 2c. It is not difficult to see that this is also the case after removing the artificial edges. A simple proof appears in the full version of the paper [2].

Lemma 8. *The u-to-v path P in T is a 3/4-balanced path separator for the input graph (without artificial edges).*

Finally, P and e (if added to G) constitute a fundamental cycle $C(T, e)$ in $G \cup \{e\}$, and obviously e does not violate planarity as it was embedded inside a face. This concludes the proof of Lemma 5.

The above concludes the correctness of Algorithm 1 which we summarize in the following Theorem 2. In Sect. 5 we show how to implement it distributively thus proving Theorem 1.

Theorem 2. *Let G be a bi-connected embedded planar graph, T a spanning tree of G, and $w(\cdot)$ a 1/12-proper weight assignment to G's vertices. Then, Algorithm 1 deterministically finds a 3/4-balanced path separator P of G, where P is a path in T. Moreover, there exists an edge $e \notin T$ (maybe even $e \notin G$), such that, $S = P \cup \{e\}$ is a 3/4-balanced fundamental cycle separator of G (after adding e in case $e \notin G$, in which case, e does not violate planarity).*

5   A Distributed Implementation

In this section we present the distributed implementation of Algorithm 1. We first define some notions and briefly overview a set of existing tools in distributed algorithms. More details appear in the full version [2].

5.1   Distributed Tools

The main computational task our algorithm performs is computing *aggregations*. This is by now a simple and standard building block in CONGEST algorithms. The advantage of an algorithm that works only with aggregations is that, it can be easily extended to be applied on multiple subgraphs of G simultaneously, which is useful for applications. We elaborate on this more in Sect. 5.2 and in the full version of the paper [2].

Low-Congestion Shortcuts and Aggregations. *Low-congestion shortcuts* is a well known tool, first introduced in [8], that allows us to solve the classic *part-wise aggregation (PA)* problem efficiently. The PA problem considers the setting where a partition $\{G_i\}_{i=1}^{k}$ of G is given s.t. each part G_i is a connected subgraph of G, in addition each vertex $v \in V$ initially has some input x_v. The objective is then, for each subgraph G_i to compute an *aggregate operator* over all inputs x_v of vertices $v \in G_i$. An aggregate operator is a function that allows to replace $\tilde{O}(1)$-bit strings by one $\tilde{O}(1)$-bit string. This is usually a simple commutative function such as taking a minimum or a sum. Since G_is are given as an input, they might be of arbitrarily large diameter. This is the challenge that low-congestion shortcuts resolve. As these primitives are now classic in distributed computing, we omit their their formal for lack of space and refer the reader to the full version of the paper [2] for more information.

Lemma 9 (PA in planar graphs [9,12]). *The PA problem can be solved in the given partition deterministically in $\tilde{O}(D)$ rounds on a planar graph G.*

The PA problem is a very powerful building block that is used in many state-of-the-art algorithms. In our case, we will use the following procedure repeatedly.

Lemma 10 (Lemma 16 of [11]). *Let T be a tree, and r be a vertex of T. There is a deterministic algorithm that roots T at r, and for each node $u \in T$ computes the subtree sum using $\tilde{O}(1)$ part-wise aggregations.*

Dual Computations. We will also perform computations related to faces of G and to the dual tree T^*. To do that, we use procedures of [10] that rely on low-congestion shortcuts and PA on a related graph $\hat{G}$, which can be fully simulated in CONGEST via G with a constant overhead in the round complexity. See also Sects. 3, 4 and appendix A of [1]. For formal statements, see the full version of the paper [2].

Lemma 11. (Lemma 4, Corollary 5, and Sect. 4.2.2 of *[10]*- informal). *The following tasks can be done in $\tilde{O}(D)$ deterministic rounds: (1) Vertices $v \in G$ learn the IDs of faces that contain them, and their incident edges correspondence to edges of G^*. (2) Assuming each vertex $v \in G$ has an input for each face f that contains it. Then, for each face f, any aggregate operator can be computed over the input of its vertices, s.t. each vertex $v \in f$ learns f's output. Finally, (3) Let g be a face that is known to all $v \in G$ and let T^* be a spanning tree of G^*, s.t. each vertex v knows its incident edges correspondence to edges of T^*. Assume that for each face f, there is an input value that is known to its vertices. Then, T^* can be rooted in g and subtree sums can be computed on T^* w.r.t. g as the root, s.t. each vertex v on a face f knows f's output.*

Derandomized Components. Procedures that use [10] (like Lemma 11) were originally randomized. However, they can be easily derandomized. In particular, those procedures use a classic randomized connectivity algorithm [8]. But, by [1] (footnote 20 in Appendix A), this can be derandomized using a derandomization of [11] for the same connectivity algorithm. In more detail, the connectivity algorithm is Boruvka-like [4]. Initially, each vertex is its own component. Then, distinct components merge over incident edges in phases. In order to have only a small (polylogarithmic) number of phases, it is beneficial if the merges have a simple structure, like star-shape. One common way to achieve it is to use a fair coin flip. It is however well-known, as shown for example in [11], that this can be achieved deterministically using the classical Cole-Vishkin [5] coloring algorithm. In addition, traditional methods of aggregating information on the low-congestion shortcuts were originally randomized [8], but since then were derandomized [9,12]. Those components are standard, and used in [13]'s deterministic separator algorithm as well.

5.2 The Algorithm

We now give a distributed deterministic implementation of Algorithm 1. Recall that Algorithm 1 mostly follows Ghaffari-Parter [10], the lines highlighted in blue in Algorithm 1 specify which components differ from Ghaffari-Parter. For each such component, we describe the intuition behind its implementation and sketch a proof, highlighting the main ideas, especially those that differ from [10], where formal statements, full proofs, and discussions are provided in the full version of the paper [2] (also for steps that we borrow from [10]). The computational tasks we use are mainly the standard part-wise aggregation primitive.

It is highly beneficial to describe the algorithm in terms of part-wise aggregations. Then, the algorithm can be applied simultaneously in multiple subgraphs via low-congestion shortcuts. This is often used in the applications, where also the spanning tree T of G might be arbitrary, which (from our perspective) is given as input. Thus, we assume a given partition of G into vertex-disjoint biconnected subgraphs $\{G_i\}_{i=1}^{k}$, and for each G_i an arbitrary spanning tree T_i, and describe the algorithm for a specific subgraph G_i assuming we have low-congestion shortcuts constructed. This guarantees the algorithm can run on all G_i simultaneously at the same round complexity. If one only wants to compute a separator of $O(D)$ vertices in G, then we compute a BFS tree T of depth $O(D)$ of G in $O(D)$ rounds [18], and apply the algorithm on G with T as an input. To simplify notation, in the remainder of this section we use G and T instead of G_i and T_i.

Learning the cotree T^* (Step 1). This step is the same as that of [10]. Intuitively, the given spanning tree T of G defines a dual cotree T^* s.t. an edge is in T^* iff it is not in T (Lemma 1). Since vertices of G know their incident T edges, they also know their incident T^* edges. The correspondence between primal edges and dual edges (IDs of faces that contain them) is known in $\tilde{O}(D)$ rounds by Lemma 11.

Reducing Vertex-Weights to Face-Weights (Step 2). This step simplifies upon the approaches of [10,13] for computing face-weights and is the core of our algorithm. To compute the face weights, we compute a summation operator over the faces of G, and the result is then the faces' weights as in Proposition 1. The input of a vertex v for a face f that contains it is simply v's weight if v chose to transfer its weight to f and zero otherwise (e.g., v transfers its weight to the minimal ID face that contains it). Note that IDs of faces are known to vertices they contain from the previous step. Hence, using Lemma 11 the weights for all faces are computed in $\tilde{O}(D)$ rounds.

Balanced or Critical Node Detection (Step 3). Given the cotree T^* (computed in Step 1), either a $(\frac{1}{4}, \frac{3}{4})$-balanced node or a $(\frac{1}{4}, \frac{3}{4})$-critical node exists in T^* (by Lemma 4). In order to implement this step, we mainly use Lemma 11 to compute subtree sums on T^*, where the input for each node of T^* is its assigned weight from the previous step. Vertices of G then detect locally a balanced (or critical) node that they participate in. Then, vertices elect some balanced or critical node by aggregating the IDs of these nodes on a BFS tree (or low-congestion shortcuts) of G in deterministic $\tilde{O}(D)$ rounds by [18] (resp. by Lemma 9).

Marking the Separator (Step 4). In this step, we mark the u-to-v path separator P of T and inform the vertices u, v that they are the endpoints of the (possibly artificial) edge e that closes a cycle with P. We first detect the vertices u, v. Then, we mark the path P by a simple subtree sum computation on T: u, v have an input of 1, and other vertices 0. Thus, the edges that have some endpoint that has a sum of 1 are the edges of P. This terminates in $\tilde{O}(D)$ rounds (Lemmas 9 and 10).

The detection of u, v is done by using a procedure of [10] (Appendices B.2 and B.3) with different constants. In a high level, they investigate two cases (similar to what we do in Theorem 2). Namely, the case where a balanced node exists, and the case where a critical node exists, and for each they show how to deduce the vertices u, v. Note, in Lemma 5 we proved that given a balanced or a critical node, such a separator exists using our way of assigning weights. The procedure uses simple primitives: subtree sums and previously computed weights (so, it can easily be made deterministic).

Removing the Bi-connectivity Assumption. Finally, to conclude Theorem 1, we remove the bi-connectivity assumption as in [15]. We mention that [15]'s procedure was originally randomized for using the connectivity algorithms of [8, 10]. Hence, it is easily derandomized as in Sect. 5.1.

Theorem 1. *Let G be an embedded planar graph of hop-diameter D, T be a spanning tree of G, and $w(\cdot)$ be a weight assignment to G's vertices s.t. no vertex weighs more than $\frac{1}{12}$ fraction of the total weight of G. There is a deterministic $\tilde{O}(D)$-round distributed algorithm that finds a u-to-v path P in T that is a $\frac{3}{4}$-balanced separator of G. Adding the edge $e = (u, v)$ to G (if it does not already exist), closes a fundamental cycle $P \cup \{e\}$ in T. Setting T to be a BFS tree produces a separator of size $O(D)$.*

Generalization to Multiple Subgraphs. Note, given a partition $\{G_i\}_{i=1}^k$ of G into vertex-disjoint connected subgraphs, with spanning trees $\{T_i\}_{i=1}^k$, where

T_i is an arbitrary spanning tree of G_i, we have described the algorithm for computing a separator of a single subgraph G_i in deterministic $\tilde{O}(D)$ rounds. It easily extends to run on all subgraphs G_i simultaneously in the same round complexity. This follows from standard use of low-congestion shortcuts [10,11, 19].

6   Applications

Computing a balanced separator lies at the core of state-of-the-art distributed algorithms for many classical optimization problems in planar graphs. In most cases, the separator algorithm is their *only* randomized component. In particular, it was shown in [13] that the (near-optimal) randomized algorithm of [10] for computing a DFS tree can be derandomized by replacing the randomized separator algorithm with the deterministic one of [13]. However, it was not mentioned in [13], that a deterministic separator algorithm implies a derandomization to a collection of other state-of-the-art algorithms that use the *Bounded Diameter Decomposition* (BDD) as their only randomized component.[4] Recall from Sect. 3 that the BDD is a recursive decomposition of planar graphs using separators, s.t. all subgraphs in the decomposition have a low $\tilde{O}(D)$ diameter. The implementation of the BDD [15] assumes a black-box fundamental cycle separator algorithm that runs in $\tilde{O}(D)$ rounds and applies it recursively. In case there is no such separator, it is sufficient that the algorithm provides a path separator and (the endpoints and embedding) of a virtual edge, that if added, closes a cycle with the path separator. Replacing the black-box randomized separator algorithm in the BDD construction with ours (or with that of [13]) immediately derandomizes the BDD and hence the following state-of-the-art algorithms for classical problems in *directed* planar graphs:

- Computing $\tilde{O}(D)$-bit distance labels to every vertex (in a planar graph with positive and negative weights) in $\tilde{O}(D^2)$ rounds [15] (s.t. the distance between any two vertices can be deduced by their labels alone), hence also single-source shortest-paths in $\tilde{O}(D^2)$ rounds.
- Computing $\tilde{O}(D)$-bit reachability labels to every vertex in $\tilde{O}(D)$ rounds [17] (s.t. the reachability between any two vertices can be deduced by their labels alone), hence also single-source reachability in $\tilde{O}(D)$ rounds.
- Detecting strongly connected components in $\tilde{O}(D)$ rounds [17].
- Maximum st-flow in $\tilde{O}(D^2)$ rounds [1].
- Global directed minimum cut in $\tilde{O}(D^2)$ rounds [1].
- Minimum weight cycle in $\tilde{O}(D^2)$ rounds [17].

Acknowledgments. Y. Abd-Elhaleem was supported in part by the Israel Science Foundation grant No. 810/21 and No. 2829/25. M. Dory was supported in part by the Israel Science Foundation grant No. 2829/25. O. Weimann was supported in part by the Israel Science Foundation grant No. 810/21.

---

[4] Many of those algorithms use low-congestion shortcuts, that were originally randomized, but as mentioned in Sect. 5 were since then derandomized.

Disclosure of Interests. The authors have no competing interests to declare that are relevant to the content of this article.

References

1. Abd-Elhaleem, Y., Dory, M., Parter, M., Weimann, O.: Distributed maximum flow in planar graphs. In: 44th PODC, pp. 278–286 (2025). https://doi.org/10.1145/3732772.3733521
2. Abd-Elhaleem, Y., Dory, M., Weimann, O.: A simple distributed deterministic planar separator (2026). https://doi.org/10.48550/arXiv.2602.22916, full version of this paper
3. Aggarwal, A., Anderson, R.J.: A random NC algorithm for depth first search. Comb pp. 1–12 (1988). https://doi.org/10.1145/28395.28430
4. Bor?vka, O.: Über ein Minimalproblem. Práce moravské přirodovědecké společnosti pp. 37–58 (1926)
5. Cole, R., Vishkin, U.: Deterministic coin tossing with applications to optimal parallel list ranking. Inf. Control **70**(1), 32–53 (1986). https://doi.org/10.1016/S0019-9958(86)80023-7
6. Dou, J., Götte, T., Hillebrandt, H., Scheideler, C., Werthmann, J.: Brief announcement: Distributed construction of near-optimal compact routing schemes for planar graphs. In: 42nd PODC, pp. 67–70 (2023). https://doi.org/10.1145/3583668.3594561
7. Ghaffari, M., Haeupler, B.: Distributed algorithms for planar networks I: planar embedding. In: 35th PODC, pp. 29–38 (2016). https://doi.org/10.1145/2933057.2933109
8. Ghaffari, M., Haeupler, B.: Distributed algorithms for planar networks II: low-congestion shortcuts, mst, and min-cut. In: 27th SODA, pp. 202–219 (2016). https://doi.org/10.1137/1.9781611974331.ch16
9. Ghaffari, M., Haeupler, B.: Low-congestion shortcuts for graphs excluding dense minors. In: 40th PODC, pp. 213–221 (2021). https://doi.org/10.1145/3465084.3467935
10. Ghaffari, M., Parter, M.: Near-optimal distributed DFS in planar graphs. In: 31st DISC, Vienna, Austria. Schloss Dagstuhl - Leibniz-Zentrum für Informatik (2017). https://doi.org/10.4230/LIPIcs.DISC.2017.21
11. Ghaffari, M., Zuzic, G.: Universally-optimal distributed exact min-cut. In: 41st PODC, pp. 281–291 (2022). https://doi.org/10.1145/3519270.3538429
12. Haeupler, B., Izumi, T., Zuzic, G.: Low-Congestion shortcuts without embedding. Distrib. Comput. **34**(1), 79–90 (2020). https://doi.org/10.1007/s00446-020-00383-2
13. Jauregui, B., Montealegre, P., Rapaport, I.: Deterministic distributed DFS via cycle separators in planar graphs. In: 44th PODC, pp. 268–277 (2025). https://doi.org/10.1145/3732772.3733558, full version in https://arxiv.org/pdf/2504.21620
14. Klein, P., Mozes, S.: Optimization Algorithms for Planar Graphs. https://planarity.org, book draft
15. Li, J., Parter, M.: Planar diameter via metric compression. In: 51st STOC, pp. 152–163 (2019). https://doi.org/10.1145/3313276.3316358
16. Lipton, R.J., Tarjan, R.E.: Applications of a planar separator theorem. SIAM J. Comput. **9**(3), 615–627 (1980). https://doi.org/10.1137/0209046

17. Parter, M.: Distributed planar reachability in nearly optimal time. In: 34th DISC, pp. 38:1–38:17 (2020). https://doi.org/10.4230/LIPIcs.DISC.2020.38
18. Peleg, D.: Distributed computing: a locality-sensitive approach. Soc. Ind. Appl. Math. (2000). https://doi.org/10.1137/1.9780898719772
19. Rozhon, V., Grunau, C., Haeupler, B., Zuzic, G., Li, J.: Undirected $(1+\epsilon)$-shortest paths via minor-aggregates: near-optimal deterministic parallel and distributed algorithms. In: 54th STOC, pp. 478–487 (2022). https://doi.org/10.1145/3519935.3520074

Maintaining Bipartite Colourings on Temporal Graphs on a Budget

Duncan Adamson[1]([✉]) [iD], George B. Mertzios[2] [iD], and Paul G. Spirakis[3] [iD]

[1] School of Computer Science, University of St Andrews, St Andrews, UK
duncan.adamson@st-andrews.ac.uk
[2] Department of Computer Science, University of Durham, Durham, UK
george.mertzios@durham.ac.uk
[3] School of Computer Science and Informatics, University of Liverpool,
Liverpool, UK
p.spirakis@liverpool.ac.uk

Abstract. Graph colouring is a fundamental problem for networks, serving as a tool for avoiding conflicts via symmetry breaking, for example, avoiding multiple computer processes simultaneously updating the same resource. This paper considers a generalisation of this problem to *temporal graphs*, i.e., to graphs whose structure changes according to an ordered sequence of edge sets. In the simultaneous resource updating problem on temporal graphs, the resources which can be accessed will change, however, the necessity of symmetry breaking to avoid conflicts remains.

In this paper, we focus on the problem of *maintaining proper colourings* on temporal graphs in general, with a particular focus on bipartite colourings. Our aim is to minimise the total number of times that the vertices change colour, or, in the form of a decision problem, whether we can maintain a proper colouring by allowing not more colour changes than some given *budget*. On the negative side, we show that, despite bipartite colouring being easy on static graphs, the problem of maintaining such a colouring on graphs that are bipartite in each snapshot is NP-Hard to even approximate within *any* constant factor unless the Unique Games Conjecture fails. On the positive side, we provide an exact algorithm for a temporal graph with n vertices, a lifetime T and at most k components in any given snapshot in $O(T|E|2^k + nT2^{2k})$ time, and an $O\left(\sqrt{\log(nT)}\right)$-factor approximation algorithm running in $\tilde{O}((nT)^3)$ time.

Our results contribute to the structural complexity of networks that change with time with respect to a fundamental computational problem.

Keywords: Temporal Graph · Graph Colouring · Bipartite Graphs

---

G.B. Mertzios—Supported by the EPSRC grant EP/P020372/1.
P.G. Spirakis—Supported by the EPSRC grant EP/P02002X/1.

C. Georgiou (Ed.): SIROCCO 2026, LNCS 16488, pp. 21–33, 2026.
https://doi.org/10.1007/978-3-032-26465-7_2

1   Introduction

Graph colouring is one of the most fundamental questions in graph theory. Informally, this problem asks for an assignment of colours from a palette, normally represented by a set of integers $1, 2, \ldots, C$, such that no two adjacent vertices share a colour. This has many applications, particularly in networks where coordination is needed between various agents to avoid conflicts, for example, avoiding system resources being updated simultaneously. Given the broad applicability of this problem, there is a large body of work for both centralised [6,14] and distributed [7–9] computing. See [12] for an overview of several applications.

In this paper, we introduce and study a new generalisation of this problem to *temporal graphs*, graphs formed by a sequence of *snapshots*, with changing edgesets over a constant set of vertices. In our variant, the goal to construct a sequence of colourings such that each snapshot is properly coloured, while minimising the number of changes between snapshots. This allows us to capture the problems of avoiding conflicts between neighbouring vertices, while also incorporating the changing nature of temporal graphs. To date, there has been a reasonable body of work on colouring temporal graphs [1,5,10,13,15,16], with the primary, but by no means exclusive, focus being on *sliding window colourings*, colourings where each edge is properly coloured at least once within each window.

In this paper, we focus primarily on *bipartite graphs*, graphs which can be coloured with a palette of size two, traditionally $\{0, 1\}$. Our primary reason for this focus is that the problem of maintaining a colouring for any palette of size three or greater is trivially NP-hard, from the general problem of 3-colouring graphs. On the other hand, finding a bipartite colouring can be done in time linear relative to the number of edges, making this setting far more interesting from a technical standpoint.

We mention some of the other results on generalisations of the colouring problem to temporal graphs. First is the work by Yu et al. [16], who study a similar definition to ours, with the objective of minimising the sum $C+\alpha A$ where C is the palette size, A is total number of changes, and α is some parameter chosen by the user. The authors study six colouring algorithms, providing both an experimental comparison and explicit classes in which the algorithms perform best. We note that, unlike this work, they do not provide constraints on the size of the palette, and while their formulation remains NP-hard, the reduction follows explicitly from the hardness of the colouring problem in general, without any reference to bipartite graphs. More recent is the work by Mertzios et al. [15] on sliding window colourings, who showed that the problem of finding such a colouring is NP-hard even in several restricted classes, while also providing strong FPT results for finding such colourings in general. This work was built upon by Marino and Silva [13], who study parameters under which such a colouring can be found in polynomial time, specifically relating to how frequent, and for how long, each edge is active.

Our Contribution. We show that the problem of maintaining a colouring when restricted to bipartite graphs occupies an interesting position in terms of complexity. Determining whether there exists a colouring that does not require any vertex to be recoloured in any snapshot can be done in linear time, however, determining the minimum number of changes needed for any non-trivial instance is NP-hard. On the positive side, for a temporal graph with n vertices and a lifetime (number of discrete snapshots) T, we present an algorithm that is a fixed-parameter tractable in the maximum number k of connected components in each snapshot, running in $O(T|E|2^k + nT2^{2k})$ time, and an approximation algorithm with a factor of $O\left(\sqrt{\log(nT)}\right)$ running in $\tilde{O}((nT)^3)$ time, where $\tilde{O}(f(n))$ denotes complexity ignoring polylogarithmic factors. To complete the picture, we prove that, for every $C \geq 3$, it is NP-hard even to determine whether there exists a C-colouring with recolouring cost zero, i.e., a C-colouring that does not require any vertex to be recoloured in any snapshot.

2   Preliminaries

We denote by $[i]$ the ordered sequence of integers $1, 2, \ldots, i$, and by $[i, j]$ the sequence $i, i + 1, \ldots, j$, for any $i, j \in \mathbb{Z}$, $i \leq j$. We define a *temporal graph* by an ordered sequence of *snapshots*, each of which is a graph over a common set of vertices. Formally, let $\mathcal{G}$ be a temporal graph, then $\mathcal{G} = G_1, G_2, \ldots, G_T$ where $G_t = (V, E_t)$. We call the number of snapshots, by convention denoted T, the *lifetime* of the temporal graph, and G_t the tth *snapshot* of the temporal graph. Where confusion may arise, we refer to non-temporal graphs as *static graphs*. The *underlying graph* of a temporal graph, $\mathcal{G}$, denoted $U(\mathcal{G})$, is the static graph formed by the union of all edge sets in the temporal graph, i.e., $U(\mathcal{G}) = \left(V, \bigcup_{t \in [T]} E_t\right)$.

Given a vertex $v \in V$ in a temporal graph $\mathcal{G}$, we denote by $N_t(v)$ the set of *neighbours* of v in the snapshot $G_t = (V, E_t)$, formally $N_t(v) = \{u \in V \mid (v, u) \in E_t\}$. The *degree* of a vertex v in the snapshot G_t, denoted $\deg_t(v)$, is the number of neighbours of v in G_t, formally $\deg_t(v) = |N_t(v)|$. We ommit the subscript denoting snapshot for both the set of neighbours and degree of a vertex in a static graph, thus $N(v)$ denotes the set of neighbours, and $\deg(v) = |N(v)|$ the degree. Given multiple static graphs, we denote by $N_G(v)$ (resp., $\deg_G(v)$) the set of neighbours (resp. degree) of v in the graph G. A *component* in a static graph $G = (V, E)$ is a subgraph $K = (V_K, E_K)$ such that $\forall v \in V_K$, $N(v) \subseteq V_K$ and $E_K = E \cap (V_K \times V_K)$.

We define a colouring of a graph as a function $\psi : V \mapsto [0, C - 1]$ for some palette size C. We call a colouring over a palette of size C a *C-colouring*. A 2-colouring, as studied in this paper, is called *bipartite*, assigning to each vertex a colour in the set $\{0, 1\}$. A colouring of the (static) graph $G = (V, E)$ is *proper* if, given any edge $(v, u) \in E$, we have $\psi(v) \neq \psi(u)$. An edge (v, u) is called *monochrome* if $\psi(v) = \psi(u)$. For the remainder of this paper, we assume by default that any given colouring is proper unless explicitly stated to be otherwise. We denote by $\phi_C(G)$ the set of all proper C-colourings of a given static graph G.

We define a *temporal sequence C-colouring* of a temporal graph of lifetime T as a sequence of T proper C-colourings, $\Psi = \psi_1, \psi_2, \ldots, \psi_T$. We denote by $\Phi_C(\mathcal{G})$ the set of all temporal sequence C-colourings of the temporal graph $\mathcal{G}$. The *cost* of a temporal sequence colouring, denoted $\mathrm{Cost}(\Psi)$, is the total number of colour changes of each vertex over the lifetime of the graph. Formally,

$$\mathrm{Cost}(\Psi) = \sum_{v \in V} \sum_{t \in [T-1]} \begin{cases} 0 & \psi_t(v) = \psi_{t+1}(v) \\ 1 & \psi_t(v) \neq \psi_{t+1}(v) \end{cases}.$$

A *minimum cost temporal sequence C-colouring* of a temporal graph $\mathcal{G}$ is a temporal sequence C-colouring $\Psi \in \Phi_C(\mathcal{G})$ such that $\mathrm{Cost}(\Psi) \leq \mathrm{Cost}(\Psi')$, $\forall \Psi' \in \Phi_C(\mathcal{G})$. The primary problem we study in this paper is TEMPORAL RECOLOURING. As a decision problem, we ask whether there exists a temporal sequence C-colouring of a given temporal graph $\mathcal{G}$ with a cost of at most some given budget $B \in \mathbb{N}$. In the optimisation version of the problem, we are not given B along with the input, but we rather aim at computing the cost of a minimum cost temporal sequence colouring.

TEMPORAL RECOLOURING (TREC)

Input: A temporal graph $\mathcal{G}$, a palette of size $C \in \mathbb{N}$, and budget $B \in \mathbb{N}$.
Question: Does there exist a temporal sequence C-colouring $\Psi : V \times [T] \mapsto [C]$ such that $\mathrm{Cost}(\Psi) \leq B$?

Furthermore, whenever the size C of the palette in the problem TREC is a constant (and not part of the input), we refer to the problem as C-TREC.

2.1   Non-bipartite Temporal Sequence Colourings

Before presenting our main results, we make a small number of observations on some general properties of temporal sequence colourings for non-bipartite graphs. First, we justify our focus on bipartite colourings with the following:

Observation 1. TREC *is NP-Hard for any $C \geq 3$.*

Note that this follows from the hardness of finding a 3-colouring in static graphs. We extend to the more complex setting of $\Delta + 1$ colourings, where Δ represents the maximum degree of any vertex in any snapshot, i.e. $\Delta = \max_{v \in V} \max_{t \in [T]} \deg_t(v)$. Unlike a 3-colouring a $(\Delta+1)$-colouring can be found in $O(|E|)$ time for any given static graph $G = (V, E)$, and thus admits a less trivial proof of hardness.

Proposition 1. *For every $C \geq 3$, it is NP-hard to determine whether the minimum cost of a temporal sequence C-colouring of a temporal graph $\mathcal{G}$ is zero, even when every vertex has degree at most 1 in every snapshot.*

Proof. Let $G = (V, E)$ be a static graph, and let $m = |E|$ be the number of its edges and $C \geq 3$ be arbitrary. We construct a temporal graph

$\mathcal{G} = G_1, G_2, \ldots, G_m$, where every snapshot has exactly one of the edges of G. Now, observe that no vertex can have a degree greater than 1 in any given snapshot. Furthermore, note that there exists a temporal sequence C-colouring in this graph with a cost of 0 if and only if there exists a C-colouring of G. Therefore, since $C \geq 3$, this problem is NP-hard. $\qquad\qquad\square$

We note that Proposition 1 does not directly apply to bipartite graphs, as we can determine if a zero-cost temporal 2-colouring exists in linear time by determining if the underlying graph is bipartite. Thus, our results in the following sections are directly motivated in closing this bound.

3 Hardness Results for Bipartite Colourings

Our first major result is in showing that the TREC is NP-hard and hard to approximate (subject to specific plausible computational complexity assumptions), even when every snapshot only consists of a disjoint union of paths (see Theorem 1). For the proof of Theorem 1 we present a reduction from the problem MINUNCUT, which is the dual problem of MAXCUT:

MINUNCUT
Input: A (static) graph $G = (V, E)$.
Task: Partition the vertex set V of H into two colour-classes such that the number of monochromatic edges in E is as small as possible.

It is known that MINUNCUT is NP-hard and that it is known that there does not exist any polynomial-time constant approximation algorithm unless the Unique Games Conjecture fails [11]. Note that MINUNCUT can be reformulated as the problem of maximising the number of satisfied clauses in a 2SAT instance, where we have a variable b_v for every vertex $v \in V$, and a clause $(b_v \wedge \overline{b_u})$ for every edge $(v, u) \in E$, with the goal of finding an assignment of variables minimising the number of unsatisfied clauses.

Theorem 1. TREC *is NP-hard, even when $C = 2$, $\mathcal{G}$ consists of a disjoint union of paths at every time step, and the lifetime of $\mathcal{G}$ is 2. Further, there is no polynomial-time constant approximation algorithm unless the Unique Games Conjecture fails.*

Construction. From an input instance H of MINUNCUTwith n vertices $v_1, \ldots, v_n$ and m edges, we build the temporal graph $\mathcal{G} = G_1, G_2$, as follows. For every $i = 1, \ldots, n$ denote by d_i the number of neighbours $\deg_H(v_i)$ of v_i in the graph H. At a high level, we represent each vertex by a set of $2d_i - 1$ vertices, connected in G_1 to form a *vertex gadget*. In G_2, we replace the vertex gadgets with *edge gadgets*. We represent the colours of the vertices of H by the initial colouring of the vertex gadgets. We now provide the explicit construction.

The vertex gadget of each vertex v_i is a path with $2d_i - 1$ vertices. The vertex set of $\mathcal{G}$ consists of these $\sum_{i=1}^{n}(2d_i - 1) = 4m - n$ vertices. The vertices of the vertex gadget of v_i are denoted $a_i^1, b_i^1, \ldots, a_i^{d_i-1}, b_i^{d_i-1}, a_i^{d_i}$, as shown in Fig. 1, where the edges of this path are $\{(a_i^j, b_i^j), (a_i^j, b_i^{j+1}) \mid j = 1, \ldots, d_i - 1\}$. Note that for every 2-colouring of this (static) vertex gadget, all vertices $a_i^1, \ldots, a_i^{d_i}$ are coloured with one colour and all vertices $b_i^1, \ldots, b_i^{d_i-1}$ are coloured with the other colour. Our first snapshot, G_1, corresponds exactly to the set of variable gadgets.

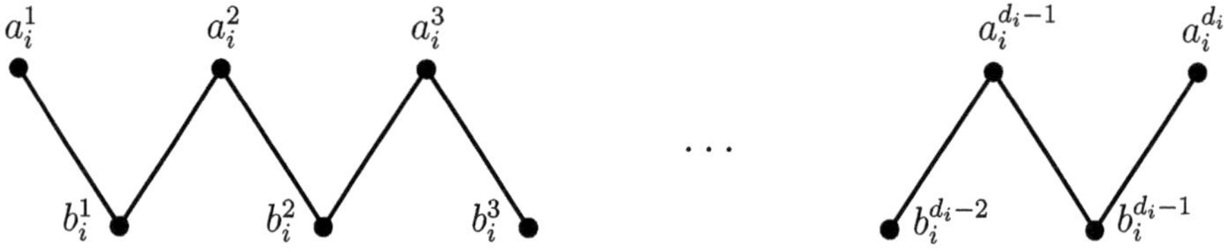

Fig. 1. The variable gadget for vertex v_i.

In the second snapshot G_2, we remove all edges from all variable gadgets and, for each edge of the input graph H, we add one edge to G_2, as follows. For every vertex v_i in the input graph H, we arbitrarily enumerate its edges. Let now $(v_i, v_j) \in E$ be an edge of H, which is the pth edge of vertex v_i and the qth edge of vertex v_j, where $1 \leq p \leq d_i$ and $1 \leq q \leq d_j$. Then, we add to G_2 the edge (a_i^p, a_j^q). That is, the second snapshot G_2 is a matching of m edges. This completes the construction of the temporal graph $\mathcal{G} = (G_1, G_2)$.

Lemma 1. *Given an instance $H = (V, E)$ of* MinUnCut *with m edges, the temporal graph $\mathcal{G}$ admits a 2-colouring with a cost at most k if and only if there exists a partition of V into two colour classes such that there are at most k monochromatic edges in E.*

Proof. ($\Leftarrow$) Let (A, B) be a partition of V into two colour classes such that there are at most k monochromatic edges in the colouring induced by (A, B) on H, i.e., $|E \cap (A \times A)| + |E \cap (B \times B)| \leq k$. In the first snapshot G_1, for every $i = 1, \ldots, n$, we assign colours to the vertices of the vertex gadget as follows: if $v_i \in A$, we assign colour 1 to vertices $a_i^1, \ldots, a_i^{d_i}$ and colour 0 to vertices $b_i^1, \ldots, b_i^{d_i-1}$. If $v_i \in B$, we assign colour 0 to vertices $a_i^1, \ldots, a_i^{d_i}$ and colour 1 to vertices $b_i^1, \ldots, b_i^{d_i-1}$.

Consider now an arbitrary edge (v_i, v_j) of H, which is the pth edge of v_i and the qth edge of v_j. If v_i and v_j belong to different colour classes in H (i.e., if either $v_i \in A$ and $v_j \in B$, or $v_i \in B$ and $v_j \in A$), then the edge (v_i, v_j) is not monochromatic in H, and the edge (a_i^p, a_j^q) is also properly coloured in G_2. Otherwise, if both v_i and v_j belong to the same colour class of H (i.e., if either $v_i, v_j \in A$ or $v_i, v_j \in B$) then the edge (v_i, v_j) is monochromatic in H; in this case, we flip the colour of vertex a_i^p in G_2, such that the edge (a_i^p, a_j^q) becomes properly coloured in G_2.

Therefore, if with the vertex partition (A, B) we have $t \leq k$ monochromatic edges in H, then in the transition from G_1 to G_2 we recolour exactly t vertices. Therefore, we constructed a proper temporal sequence colouring of $\mathcal{G}$ with a palette $C = \{0, 1\}$ and cost at most k.

($\Rightarrow$) Let Ψ be a minimum cost temporal sequence colouring of $\mathcal{G}$ with a palette $C = \{0, 1\}$ and cost at most k. By the construction of $\mathcal{G}$, for every $i = 1, \ldots, n$, all vertices $a_i^1, \ldots, a_i^{d_i}$ are coloured with the same colour in G_1. We define from the temporal sequence colouring Ψ a vertex partition (A, B) of the input graph H as follows. For every $i = 1, \ldots, n$, we add v_i to A (resp. to B) if the vertices $a_{i,1}^1, \ldots, a_{i,1}^{d_i}$ are coloured 1 (resp. 0) in G_1.

Consider an arbitrary edge $a_i^p a_j^q$ of the second snapshot G_2. By the construction of $\mathcal{G}$, this edge corresponds to the edge (v_i, v_j) of H which is the pth edge of v_i and the qth edge of v_j. First, suppose that, in the transition from G_1 to G_2 in $\mathcal{G}$, the colouring Ψ recolours neither a_i^p nor a_j^q. Then, by the construction of the vertex partition (A, B) of H, the edge (v_i, v_j) is not monochromatic in the partition (A, B). That is, either $v_i \in A$ and $v_j \in B$, or $v_i \in B$ and $v_j \in A$. Now suppose that, in the transition from G_1 to G_2 in $\mathcal{G}$, the colouring Ψ recolours one of the vertices a_i^p or a_j^q. Then, by the construction of the vertex partition (A, B) of H, the edge (v_i, v_j) is monochromatic in the partition (A, B). That is, either $v_i, v_j \in A$ or $v_i, v_j \in B$.

Therefore, if the minimum cost temporal sequence colouring Ψ of $\mathcal{G}$ has cost $t \leq k$, then in the vertex partition (A, B) of H we have exactly $t \leq k$ monochromatic edges. This completes the proof. $\qquad\square$

4 $O\left(\sqrt{\log(nT)}\right)$-Approximation

We now present our first positive algorithmic contribution in the form of an algorithm to find an $O\left(\sqrt{\log(nT)}\right)$ approximation of the minimum budget needed to maintain a bipartite colouring. Recall that we can determine if there exists a zero-cost colouring in $O\left(\sum_{t \in [T]} |E_t|\right)$ time by checking if the underlying graph is bipartite. Thus, our algorithm is a "true" approximation in that it returns a non-optimal budget if and only if there is no solution where the budget is zero.

Our approximation itself stems from the $O\left(\sqrt{\log(n)}\right)$-approximation of the MinUnCut problem due to Agarwal et al. [2], computable in $\tilde{O}(n^3)$ time due to Arora et al. [4], where $\tilde{O}(n^3) = O(n^3 \log^c n)$ for some constant c.

Our approach is to formulate the problem of finding a minimum budget temporal sequence 2-colouring of a temporal graph $\mathcal{G}$ as a MinUnCut instance, allowing this approximation algorithm to be applied directly.

Formulation. The high-level idea behind our formulation is to construct an auxiliary static graph $\alpha(G) = (V_\alpha, E_\alpha)$ such that the number of monochromatic edges in a partition of V_α corresponds to at most twice the cost of some temporal sequence colouring. The vertex set V_α contains a new vertex for each vertex in $V = \{v_1, v_2, \ldots, v_n\}$ and snapshot $G_1, G_2, \ldots, G_T$, formally $V_\alpha = \{v_{i,t} \mid i \in [n], t \in [T]\}$, where $v_{i,t}$ represents the vertex v_i in snapshot G_t. We define our edge set E_α by two subsets, C and S. The set C connects vertices between snapshots, which we use to represent the cost of changing the colour of a given vertex. Formally, $C = \{(v_{i,t}, v_{i,t+1}) \mid \forall v_i \in V, t \in [T-1]\}$.

The set S represents the components in the temporal graph within the new static graph. Given a component K containing the set of vertices $V_K = \{v_1, v_2, \ldots, v_m\}$ in G_t and 2-colouring ψ of K, we add the edge $(v_{i,t}, v_{j,t})$ to S for every pair $v_i, v_j \in V_K$ where $\psi(v_i) \neq \psi(v_j)$. This way, if $(v_{i,t}, v_{j,t}) \in S$, then ψ_t is a proper colouring of G_t only if $\psi_t(v_i) \neq \psi_t(v_j)$.

Lemma 2. *Let Ψ be a temporal sequence 2-colouring of the temporal graph $\mathcal{G} = (G_1, G_2, \ldots, G_T)$. Then, there exists a 2-colouring of $\alpha(\mathcal{G})$ with $\mathrm{Cost}(\Psi)$ monochromatic edges.*

Proof. We define our 2-colouring on $\alpha(\mathcal{G})$ by a pair of sets A and B, constructed as follows. Given a vertex v_i and snapshot G_t, we assign $v_{i,t}$ to the set A if $(\psi_t(v_i) + t) \bmod 2 \equiv 0$, and to set B otherwise. We use this construction so that if $\psi_t(v_i) = \psi_{t+1}(v_i)$, then either $v_{i,t} \in A$ and $v_{i,t+1} \in B$, or $v_{i,t} \in B$ and $v_{i,t+1} \in A$. Otherwise, if the colour of v_i changes between snapshots, we have $v_{i,t}, v_{i,t+1} \in A$ or $v_{i,t}, v_{i,t+1} \in B$.

Observe that, as ψ_t is a proper colouring of G_t, we have that, for any edge $(v_i, v_j) \in E_t$, $\psi_t(v_i) \neq \psi_t(v_j)$, thus either $v_{i,t} \in A$ and $v_{j,t} \in B$, or $v_{i,t} \in B$ and $v_{j,t} \in A$. Similarly, if $(v_{i,t}, v_{j,t}) \in E_\alpha$ and $(v_i, v_j) \notin E_t$, then v_i and v_j are in the same component in G_t, with the condition that they must belong to different colour classes of any bipartite colouring of the component. Hence, (v_i, v_j) can not form a monochromatic edge in V_α without contradicting the assumption that ψ_t is a proper colouring of G_t.

Therefore, any monochromatic edge in the colouring on $\alpha(\mathcal{G})$ induced by the partition A and B must be of the form $(v_{i,t}, v_{i,t+1})$, for some $t \in [T-1]$. Further, by construction, $(v_{i,t}, v_{i,t+1})$ will be a monochromatic edge in $\alpha(\mathcal{G})$ if and only if $\psi_t(v_i) \neq \psi_{t+1}(v_i)$. Thus, the total number of monochromatic edges in this partition is exactly equal to the cost of Ψ.

$\square$

Lemma 3. *Let $\mathcal{G} = (G_1, G_2, \ldots, G_T)$ be a temporal graph and let A, B be a partition of V_α inducing at most C monochromatic edges in $\alpha(\mathcal{G})$. Then, there exists a temporal sequence colouring Ψ of $\mathcal{G}$ with a cost of at most $2C$.*

Proof. We initially set $\psi_t(v_i)$ to 0 if either $v_{i,t} \in A$ and $t \bmod 2 \equiv 0$, or $v_{i,t} \in B$ and $t \bmod 2 \equiv 1$. Otherwise, we set $\psi_t(v_i)$ to 1. Note this matches the construction used in Lemma 2 to create a partition from the colouring, with the same property that a vertex changes colours between snapshots if and only if there is a corresponding monochromatic edge in the partition of the auxiliary graph. Therefore, given a monochromatic edge in the partition of V_α between some pair of vertices of the form $(v_{i,t}, v_{i,t+1})$, v_i changes colour in the corresponding colouring, and thus the colouring has an associated cost of 1 for each such edge.

Now, consider some component K with the vertex set $V_K = \{v_1, v_2, \ldots, v_m\}$ in snapshot G_t such that K is not properly coloured by our initial assignment. Further, let k be the number of monochromatic edges between the vertices $\{v_{1,t}, v_{2,t}, \ldots, v_{m,t}\}$. We partition K into the sets K_A and K_B where $K_A = \{v_i \mid \psi(v_1) = \psi(v_i) \text{ and } (v_{1,t}, v_{i,t} \notin E_\alpha)\} \cup \{v_i \mid \psi(v_1) \neq \psi(v_i) \text{ and } (v_{1,t}, v_{i,t} \in E_\alpha)\}$, and $K_B = K \setminus K_A$. Observe that the set of vertices K_A are properly coloured with respect to $v_{1,t}$, and thus each other, while the set of vertices are improperly coloured relative to $v_{1,t}$, and thus properly coloured with respect to each other. Therefore, to convert this into a proper colouring, we can "flip" the colours of the vertices in either K_A or K_B, setting $\psi_t(v_i)$ to 0 if it was originally 1, or 1 if it was originally 0, for each v_i in the flipped set.

To determine the corresponding cost of this new colouring, we now show that $\min(|K_A|, |K_B|) \leq k$. First, assume that there exists a pair of vertices $v_{1,t}, v_{2,t} \in K_A$ such that $(v_{1,t}, v_{2,t}) \in E_\alpha$. Then, for every vertex $v_i \in K_B$, there must be at least one monochromatic edge to either $v_{1,t}$ or $v_{2,t}$ in the original partition of V_α. Thus, in this case $|K_B| \leq k$. Otherwise, if no such pair exists, then $\{v_{j,t} \in K \mid (v_{1,t}, v_{j,t}) \in E_\alpha\} \subseteq K_B$ and, by extension, there exists some vertex $v_{i,t} \in K_B$ such that, $\forall v_{j,t} \in K_A$, $(v_{i,t}, v_{j,t})$ is monochromatic, and thus $|K_A| \leq k$, completing the claim.

Note that for each vertex v_i where the colour is changed when flipping the colours in either K_A or K_B we add at most two changes to v_i in Ψ, corresponding to potentially changing v_i between snapshots $t-1$ and t, and t and $t+1$. Thus, recolouring this component adds a cost of at most $2k$ and therefore the final colouring has a cost of at most $2C$.

$\square$

Theorem 2. *Given an always-bipartite temporal graph $\mathcal{G}$ with a lifetime T and n vertices we can find a temporal sequence 2-colouring $\Psi = \psi_1, \psi_2, \ldots, \psi_T$ such that $\mathrm{Cost}(\Psi)$ that is at most a factor of $O\left(\sqrt{\log(nT)}\right)$ greater than the minimum budget of any such colouring in $\tilde{O}((nT)^3)$ time.*

Proof. Let Ψ' be some minimum cost temporal 2-colouring of $\mathcal{G}$ and observe that, per Lemmas 2 and 3, $2M \geq \mathrm{Cost}(\Psi') \geq M$, where M minimum number of monochromatic edges in $\alpha(\mathcal{G})$. By the results of Agarwal et al. [2], and Arora et al. [4], we can find a partition of $\alpha(\mathcal{G})$ with M' monochromatic edges, where M' is a factor of at most $O\left(\sqrt{\log(nT)}\right)$ more than M. From Lemma 3, we can convert this assignment to a temporal 2-colouring Ψ of $\mathcal{G}$ that requires a budget of at most $2M'$. Thus, $2M' \geq \mathrm{Cost}(\Psi) \geq \mathrm{Cost}(\Psi') \geq M$, hence $\mathrm{Cost}(\Psi)$ is a factor of at most $O\left(\sqrt{\log(nT)}\right)$ greater than $\mathrm{Cost}(\Psi')$, giving the bound on the approximation factor. To get the time complexity, observe that we can find, by Arora et al. [3], a soloution to any MinUnCut instance in $\tilde{O}(m^3)$, where m

is the number of vertices in the input instance, in our case nT, giving a time complexity of $\tilde{O}((nT)^3)$.

$\square$

5   Parameterised Algorithm for Bipartite Colourings

Finally, we provide an algorithm for finding the optimal 2-temporal sequence colouring parameterised by the maximum number k of connected components in any given snapshot. Our algorithm works in a dynamic manner, computing the $2^k \times T$ sized table, B, indexed by the set of potential 2-colourings of $\mathcal{G}$ and the set of timestamps, $[T]$. Formally, let $\mathcal{G} = G_1, G_2, \ldots, G_T$ be a temporal graph such that each snapshot contains at most k connected components. Observe that, for a bipartite graph with at most k components, $\phi_C(G) \leq 2^k$, corresponding to the two unique ways of colouring each component. We use the following observation to aid in the construction of the table B and for determining the time complexity.

Observation 2. *The set of all bipartite colourings of a graph $G = (V, E)$, $\phi_C(G)$ with at most k components can be output in $O(|E|2^k)$ time.*

Algorithm. Let B be a table of size $2^k \times T$ such that $B[\psi, t]$ is the minimum budget needed to have a graph with the colouring ψ in snapshot G_t, for any $\psi \in \phi_C(G_t)$ and $t \in [T]$. As a base case, we set $B[\psi, 1]$ to 0, for every $\psi \in \phi(G_1)$. For $t \in [2, T]$, the value of $B[\psi, t]$ is determined from the set of colourings of G_{t-1} by looking for the colouring ψ' of $\mathcal{G}$ minimising $B[\psi', t-1] + \text{Cost}((\psi', \psi))$, formally:

$$B[\psi, t] = \min_{\psi' \in \phi_C(G_{t-1})} B[\psi', t-1] + \text{Cost}(\psi', \psi).$$

We provide pseudocode for computing the table B in Algorithm 1, and for converting the table B into a temporal sequence colouring in Algorithm 2.

Lemma 4. *The value of $B[\psi, t]$ can be computed in $O(n2^k)$ time, assuming the value of $B[\psi', t-1], \forall \psi' \in \phi_C(G_{t-1})$ has been precomputed.*

Proof. Observe that the minimum cost of any temporal sequence colouring $\Psi = \psi_1, \psi_2, \ldots, \psi_t$ such that $\psi_t = \psi$ for the given colouring ψ_t can be determined by finding the colouring ψ' of G_{t-1} such that there exists a temporal colour $\Psi' = \psi'_1, \psi'_2, \ldots, \psi'_{t-1}$ such that $\psi'_{t-1} = \psi'$ and $B[\psi', t-1] + \text{Cost}(\psi', \psi)$ is minimal amongst all colourings of G_{t-1}. As there are at most 2^k colourings of G_{t-1}, and we can compute $\text{Cost}(\psi', \psi)$ in $O(n)$ time, we can find $\min_{\psi' \in \phi_C(G_{t-1})} B[\psi', t-1] + \text{Cost}(\psi', \psi)$ from B in $O(n2^k)$, we get the claim. $\square$

Theorem 3. *The minimum cost of any temporal sequence 2-colouring on the temporal graph $\mathcal{G} = G_1, G_2, \ldots, G_T$ where no snapshot contains more than k components can be computed in $O(T|E|2^k + nT2^{2k})$ time.*

Algorithm 1. Bipartite Colouring Cost Table Algorithm

---

procedure $\textsc{ColourCostTable}(\mathcal{G} = (G_1, G_2, \ldots, G_T))$
    $k \leftarrow \max_{t \in T} |\mathrm{Components}(G_t)|$
    $B \leftarrow$ Empty $2^k \times T$ Table
    $\Psi \leftarrow$ Empty Temporal Sequence Colouring
    $B[1, \psi] \leftarrow 0, \forall \psi \in \phi_C(G_1)$
    for $t \in [2, T]$ **do**
        for $\psi \in \phi_C(G_t)$ **do**   ▷ Iterate over the set of all colourings of the graph G_t.
           $B[\psi, t] \leftarrow \infty$ ▷ Add a place holder value for $B[\psi, t]$.
           for $\psi' \in \boldsymbol{\Psi}(G_{t-1})$ **do**   ▷ Iterate over the set of all colourings of G_{t-1}.
              if $B[\psi', t-1] + \mathrm{Cost}(\psi, \psi') < B[\psi, t]$ **then**
                 $B[\psi, t] \leftarrow B[\psi', t-1] + \mathrm{Cost}(\psi, \psi')$
              end if
           end for
        end for
    end for
    return B
end procedure

Proof. From Lemma 4 we can compute each entry in B in $O(n2^k)$ time, provided we only compute $B[\psi, t]$ once $B[\psi', t-1]$ has been computed for all $\psi' \in \phi_C(G_{t-1})$. As there are $O(T2^k)$ entries in B, and we can output the set of all entries in $O(T|E|2^k)$, we get a total complexity of $O(T|E|2^k + nT2^{2k})$ for computing the full table B. Once the table B has been computed, we can determine the minimum cost colouring of $\mathcal{G}$ in $O(2^k)$ by finding $\min_{\psi \in \phi_C(G_T)} B[\psi, T]$, concluding the proof. $\qquad\square$

Note that Theorem 3 thus gives an $O(T|E|)$ time algorithm when the number of components is constant in each round, most notably when the graph is always connected. Finally, we make a brief observation on the complexity of determining a minimum-cost temporal 2-colouring from the table B.

Proposition 2. *We can determine a temporal 2-colouring of the temporal graph $\mathcal{G} = G_1, G_2, \ldots, G_T$ in $O(T|E|2^k + nT2^{2k})$*

Proof. Let $\Psi = \psi_1, \psi_2, \ldots, \psi_T$ be the temporal sequence colouring, and let B be the table as computed in Theorem 3. We work from the colouring ψ_T such that $B[\psi_T, T] = \min_{\psi' \in \phi_C} B[\psi', T]$. We determine the value of ψ_t, for every $t \in [T - 1]$, from the value of ψ_{t+1} by finding a colouring ψ such that $B[\psi, t] + \mathrm{Cost}(\psi, \psi_{t+1}) = B[\psi_{t+1}, t + 1]$, which can be done in $O(n2^k)$ time in a brute force manner, giving the bound.

$\qquad\square$

Algorithm 2. Bipartite Colouring Algorithm

---

   procedure COLOURING($\mathcal{G} = (G_1, G_2, \ldots, G_T)$)
      $B \leftarrow$ COLOURCOSTTABLE($\mathcal{G}$)
      $\Psi = (\psi_1, \psi_2, \ldots, \psi_T) \leftarrow (\emptyset, \emptyset, \ldots, \emptyset)$
      for $\psi \in \ominus(G_T)$ **do**
         if $\psi_T = \emptyset$ or $B[\psi, T] < B[\psi_T, T]$ **then**
            $\psi_T \leftarrow \psi$
         end if
      end for
      for $t \in T - 1, T - 2, \ldots, 1$ **do**
         for $\psi \in \ominus(G_t)$ **do**
            if $C[\psi, t] + \mathrm{Cost}(\psi, \psi_{t+1}) = B[\psi_{t+1}, t + 1]$ **then**
               $\psi_t \leftarrow \psi$
               break
            end if
         end for
      end for
      return Ψ
   end procedure

---

6 Conclusion

In this paper, we have introduced and studied the problem of maintaining a temporal sequence colouring, with a focus on two colourings of bipartite graphs. In doing so, we have provided a strong analysis of the complexity landscape of this problem, including hardness results, a fixed parameter tractability result for the number of components, an $O\left(\sqrt{\log(nT)}\right)$-factor approximation algorithm, and a hardness of constant factor approximation.

There are two natural directions in which to continue this work. The first is to extend the algorithmic results, most naturally the approximation result, to colourings with a larger palette size. It seems likely that a polynomial-time algorithm can be found with a similar approximation factor for maintaining degree $+$ 1 colourings in general, where degree here refers to the maximum degree of any vertex in any snapshot. On one hand, as with bipartite graphs, these can be determined in linear time relative to the number of edges, avoiding the natural problems due to the hardness of the colouring problem in general. On the other hand, unlike with bipartite graphs, the same freedom may preclude the same techniques used here for our approximation results.

The second direction is to improve the approximation bound. While a constant factor approximation bound has been ruled out unless the unique games conjecture fails, it is still possible that an improvement can be found in general, or for some particular classes of graphs. In particular, as our construction requires the use of long paths, the question of approximation remains open for temporal graphs in which each timestep is a matching.

References

1. Adamson, D.: Harmonious colourings of temporal matchings. Theoret. Comput. Sci., 115437 (2025)
2. Agarwal, A., Charikar, M., Makarychev, K., Makarychev, Y.: $O(\sqrt{\log(n)})$ approximation algorithms for min uncut, min 2cnf deletion, and directed cut problems. In: Proceedings of the Thirty-Seventh Annual ACM Symposium on Theory of Computing, pp. 573–581 (2005)
3. Arora, S., Hazan, E., Kale, S.: Fast algorithms for approximate semidefinite programming using the multiplicative weights update method. In: 46th Annual IEEE Symposium on Foundations of Computer Science (FOCS'05), pp. 339–348. IEEE (2005)
4. Arora, S., Kale, S.: A combinatorial, primal-dual approach to semidefinite programs. In: Proceedings of the Thirty-Ninth Annual ACM Symposium on Theory of Computing, pp. 227–236 (2007)
5. Barba, L., et al.: Dynamic graph coloring. In: Workshop on Algorithms and Data Structures, pp. 97–108. Springer (2017)
6. Formanowicz, P., Tanaś, K.: A survey of graph coloring - its types, methods and applications. Found. Comput. Decis. Sci. **37**(3), 223 (2012)
7. Fuchs, M., Kuhn, F.: Distributed $(\delta + 1)$-coloring in graphs of bounded neighborhood independence. arXiv preprint arXiv:2510.21549 (2025)
8. Ghaffari, M., Kuhn, F.: Deterministic distributed vertex coloring: Simpler, faster, and without network decomposition. In: 2021 IEEE 62nd Annual Symposium on Foundations of Computer Science (FOCS), pp. 1009–1020. IEEE (2022)
9. Halldórsson, M.M., Kuhn, F., Nolin, A., Tonoyan, T.: Near-optimal distributed degree+1 coloring. In: Leonardi, S., Gupta, A. (eds.) STOC '22: 54th Annual ACM SIGACT Symposium on Theory of Computing, Rome, Italy, 20—24 June 2022, pp. 450–463. ACM (2022)
10. Ibiapina, A., Nguyen, M.H., Rabie, M., Robin, C.: How to color temporal graphs to ensure proper transitions. arXiv preprint arXiv:2505.10207 (2025)
11. Khot, S.: On the power of unique 2-prover 1-round games. In: Proceedings on 34th Annual ACM Symposium on Theory of Computing (STOC), pp. 767–775 (2002)
12. Lewis, R.: Guide to Graph Colouring. Springer (2021)
13. Marino, A., Silva, A.: Coloring temporal graphs. J. Comput. Syst. Sci. **123**, 171–185 (2022)
14. Matula, D.W., Marble, G., Isaacson, J.D.: Graph coloring algorithms. In: Graph Theory and Computing, pp. 109–122. Elsevier (1972)
15. Mertzios, G.B., Molter, H., Zamaraev, V.: Sliding window temporal graph coloring. J. Comput. Syst. Sci. **120**, 97–115 (2021)
16. Yu, F., Bar-Noy, A., Basu, P., Ramanathan, R.: Algorithms for channel assignment in mobile wireless networks using temporal coloring. In: Proceedings of the 16th ACM International Conference on Modeling, Analysis & Simulation of Wireless and Mobile Systems, pp. 49–58 (2013)

Formal Certification of ASYNC Protocols: The Case of Gathering in $\mathbb{R}^2$ Using Weber Points

Maria-Virginia Aponte[1], Mathis Bouverot-Dupuis[1], Quentin Bramas[2], Pierre Courtieu[1], Lionel Rieg[3], and Xavier Urbain[4,5]

[1] CNAM, CEDRIC, Paris, France
[2] Université de Strasbourg, ICUBE, Strasbourg, France
[3] Grenoble INP - UGA, Verimag, Saint-Martin-d'Hères, France
[4] CNRS, Sorbonne UniversitÃl', LIP6, UMR 7606, Paris, France
[5] Université Lyon 1, Villeurbanne, France
Xavier.Urbain@univ-lyon1.fr

Abstract. Asynchronous executions of robotic swarm algorithms are challenging to reason about because they allow robots to compute their next destination based on observations that may be outdated. To add formal guarantees in such a context where subtle mistakes lead to dramatic errors, we propose a formalization for the ROCQ prover of asynchronous executions in the Look-Compute-Move model, as an extension to the PACTOLE formal library, and we illustrate how algorithms can be proved correct in this setting. Intuition makes it easy to overlook crucial details that formal methods would request when used, leading to published algorithms which can be, at best, seriously underspecified. This is particularly the case when problems seem easy, as with solving Gathering using Weber points. Attempts at formalization show that going blindly (or for that matter cautiously) towards the Weber point, a strategy often claimed to solve Gathering, is indeed incorrect under certain assumptions. We propose in this work an original and formally certified algorithm for Gathering in ASYNC. As this algorithm uses Weber points, we also provide a comprehensive formalization for Weber points and their properties. Interestingly, the use of our formalization for asynchronous executions does not come with an explosion of the proof size, which stays at a very reasonable level.

Keywords: Mobile robots · Proof assistant · Self-stabilization · Gathering

1 Introduction

The numerous applications of swarms of autonomous mobile robots have brought them into the limelight of the distributed computing community. Under a distributed algorithm, these autonomous entities aim at fulfilling tasks of various

C. Georgiou (Ed.): SIROCCO 2026, LNCS 16488, pp. 34–52, 2026.
https://doi.org/10.1007/978-3-032-26465-7_3

intricacy, ranging from fundamental challenges (akin to Leader election or Gathering) to practical and critical missions found in Search and Rescue scenarios.

In order to study this kind of robotic swarms, Suzuki & Yamashita [29] introduced in 1999 what is now considered to be the classical mathematical model, in which robots operations follow Look-Compute-Move cycles (LCM). Basically: for a robot, each cycle consists of the capture of a snapshot of the positions of other robots, then the computation of a destination based on this snapshot, and finally a movement to the calculated location.

To explore what is achievable, robots' capabilities are limited as much as possible. They are anonymous and indistinguishable, run the same algorithm (*uniformity*). No assumption is made about their orientation (*disoriented*) and in particular the frames of reference in which they compute their destination may not coincide. When they cannot remember their previous states, robots are said to be *oblivious.*

One may categorize executions in this context depending on the synchronization level of robots. Fully-synchronous (FSYNC) executions have *all* robots perform their cycles atomically and simultaneously. For semi-synchronous executions (SSYNC), only a subset of the robots are activated to run their cycles atomically and simultaneously while the others stay idle. Finally, asynchronous executions (ASYNC) drop the atomicity requirement of robots' actions, thus defining the most challenging mode of synchrony where robots may compute their next destination based on a snapshot that is possibly outdated.

No assumption is made about whether the computed destination is reached or not before the next activation, with the noticeable exception of an unknown minimal travel distance δ that is guaranteed before reactivation (thus eliminating Zeno-like counterexamples). Such movements are said to be *non-rigid.*

This work focuses on ASYNC executions of oblivious, disoriented, anonymous robots, with non-rigid movements in $\mathbb{R}^2$ along straight lines.

As with all distributed algorithms, establishing functional correctness of robotic swarm algorithms is a tremendous task. The use of formal methods is thus invaluable in trying to overcome errors of human origin, whether in algorithm designs or in the proofs of theoretical results. Main approaches for robotic swarms include model-checking and formal proof [27].

On the one hand, *model-checking* and its powerful automation have proved most useful for finding bugs in the existing literature [5,18,19], and to formally assess algorithms [5,15,17]. However, these results are limited to instances with few robots, and generalizing them to an arbitrary number remains doubtful as safety and reachability problems are undecidable in some cases [28].

On the other hand, *formal proof*, that is, mathematical proof development mechanically certified by a proof assistant like ROCQ [30], Isabelle [26] or Lean [25], is not limited to *particular instances* of algorithms. Yet, this approach usually requires some expertise as developments are mostly interactive. The standard ROCQ library dedicated to mobile robots is PACTOLE[1] [11], successfully used to formally prove both the correctness of algorithms [2,7,13] and

---

[1] https://pactole.liris.cnrs.fr.

the soundness of theoretical impossibility results [3,12]. A comprehensive introduction to PACTOLE for ROCQ, underlining the differences between formal proof and model-checking may be found in the first three sections of Courtieu *et al.* [11].

Most notably, to our knowledge, no formal proof approach has been used so far to formally establish the properties of a mobile robot algorithm in ASYNC. *Contributions.* Our contributions are threefold. Firstly, to allow formal proof in the context of ASYNC execution, we enrich PACTOLE with *the first full formal mechanized definition of the ASYNC execution model* for mobile robots.

The computability-centric approach of the Suzuki and Yamashita model directed efforts towards few benchmark problems that are theoretically interesting (such as impossibility results or correctness certification). Among them, *Gathering* consists of moving all robots to a location unknown beforehand, and keeping them there. It is known (and formally proved) to be impossible to solve with a deterministic algorithm when the initial configuration is *bivalent*, that is, consists of only two locations hosting the same number of robots [12,29].

We consider this problem, and illustrate the usability of our development by providing and certifying as correct *an original algorithm, GatherW, that solves Gathering*, in ASYNC, with non-rigid movements, in the Euclidean plane, provided that the initial configuration is not bivalent. This is our second contribution. Interestingly, our formalization of ASYNC *does not come with an explosion of the proof size.*

This new algorithm makes use of Weber points, that is, points minimizing the sum of distances to elements of a set of points. Finally, we provide, as an addition to the PACTOLE library, *a formal mechanized definition of the Weber point, generalized to multisets of points, and of its properties.* This is our third contribution.

Setting and Hypotheses. The setting considered in this work is the following. Robots move in the Euclidean plane under the non-rigid ASYNC model and no faults, crashes or Byzantine behaviour are allowed. Robots are oblivious and disoriented, they have strong global multiplicity detection, that is, they have unlimited vision and know the number of robots occupying the same location. They can compute exactly on real numbers (can decide equality of reals). They can compute the Weber points of a multiset of locations without any restriction. In initial configurations, all robots must be *idle*, that is, waiting for their first LCM cycle. This corresponds to the weak self-stabilization gathering property in the usual taxonomy.[2] The source code[3] of our formal development for ROCQ 9 is available at the following URL: https://pactole.liris.cnrs.fr.

Roadmap. Section 2 briefly compares this work with other solutions to the Gathering problem. Sect. 3 provides the needed formal definitions for the Weber point

---

[2] To our knowledge, this is (implicitly) assumed in almost all proofs of ASYNC algorithms.

[3] The code used in this article is archived by Software Heritage with the permanent link https://archive.softwareheritage.org/swh:1:rev: 989ae2a2521a2a8cd54fdb4c5375891c1a39e2e0.

and its properties. Sect. 4 introduces our algorithm and the informal key ideas suggesting that it solves Gathering in all non-impossible cases. As we require formal guarantees, Sect. 5 describes how PACTOLE encodes the ASYNC mode. Sect. 6 presents the main aspects of the formal proof (for the ROCQ proof assistant) that our algorithm actually solves Gathering. We conclude in Sect. 7 with remarks about the proof effort.

2   Related Work

On Formal Methods. The Look-Compute-Move model is distinct from message passing and shared memory models, in particular because of its use of unrelated local frames of reference and ASYNC movements. Hence formal approaches akin to TLA/TLA+ [14,24] do not apply.

Model-checking proved successful in discovering errors and inaccuracies in existing literature [5,18,19]. It allows also for formal verification of algorithms [5, 15,17], though hitting two limitations: these case studies can only be special instances with few robots, and they consider discrete topologies. Défago *et al.* [15] succeed in model-checking rendez-vous algorithms in a continuous space, using an abstract model that is however highly specific to rendez-vous.

Formal proof uses proof management systems, *proof assistants*, to check that a proof (interactively developed) is sound. Based on very expressive mathematical languages, it is not limited to particular instances of algorithms and problems but, being mostly interactive, requires a reasonable amount of expertise from the user. During the past twenty years, the use of tool-assisted verification has extended to the validation of distributed processes, in contexts such as process algebras [6,20], symmetric interconnection networks [22], message passing settings [23], self-stabilization [1,16]. Regarding robotic swarms, the standard ROCQ library is PACTOLE [11]. Offering more than 300 theorems, and while including various topologies, case studies and execution models, it does not propose a full proof framework for ASYNC executions. This work is based on PACTOLE and provides, as its first contribution, the needed formal developments for ASYNC.

On the Gathering Problem. Gathering is impossible to solve with deterministic algorithms in SSYNC, therefore also in ASYNC [12,29]. The configuration whence oblivious robots cannot deterministically gather consists in exactly two distinct positions occupied by the same number of robots, and is said to be *bivalent*. In particular, any non-gathered configuration with two robots is bivalent. Consequently, deterministic solutions exclude bivalent initial configurations, and an invariant of deterministic algorithms is that they must not lead to a bivalent configuration from a non-bivalent one.

A Weber point displays the interesting property of staying invariant when one moves towards it, making it a potentially useful tool for Gathering. Cicerone *et al.* [9] study the properties of Weber points in the context of Gathering to a predefined finite set of meeting points. Cieliebak *et al.* [10] solve Gathering under the ASYNC non-rigid model, assuming all initial positions are distinct (no multiplicity > 1), with more than two robots, and using the Weber point only in situations where it is known to be unique and computable with radicals.

In contrast, we provide, as a second contribution, a solution handling arbitrary (non-bivalent) configurations, and using Weber points without restrictions.

3   Weber Points in Rocq

We provide here the necessary concepts about Weber points required to define and prove our protocol in Sect. 4.2.

Definition 1 (Sum of distances). *Given a finite collection X of points in $\mathbb{R}^2$, we define the* sum of distances *of X to p as follows:* $D_X(p) = \sum_{x \in X} \|p - x\|_2$.

Definition 2 (Weber point). *Given a finite collection X of points, a point p is a Weber point of X if and only if it minimizes D_X.*

Figures 1 and 4 show examples of Weber points. Rocq definitions for the D_X function (`dist_sum`) and the Weber point are as follows. Note that, relying on lists of points, they allow for multiple occurrences of points.

```
Definition dist_sum (pts: list R2) (x: R2) :=
 list_sum (List.map (dist x) pts).
(* argmin f x means that x is a minimum for f *)
Definition argmin {A: Type} (f: A → R): A → Prop :=
 fun a ⇒ ∀ b, (f a ≤ f b) ℝ.
Definition Weber (pts: list R2): R2 → Prop := argmin (dist_sum pts).
```

3.1   (Non-)uniqueness of Weber Points

As illustrated in cases (c), (d) and (e) of Fig. 4, the Weber point is not always unique. Algorithms relying on the Weber point will be forced to use different strategies depending on its uniqueness. However, for most configurations the Weber point is unique: in particular whenever the points of X are not all aligned (*i.e.*, X contains three non-colinear points).

When all points of X are aligned, there can be several distinct Weber points, which are simple to characterize. The *Weber segment*, containing all Weber points, is the set of points that split the occupied segment into two parts containing the same number of robots. Let us define this formally. To take multiplicities into account, we consider X as a multiset of points. Let p be a point, and $\text{left}(p)$ (resp. $\text{on}(p)$ and $\text{right}(p)$) the sub-multiset of points of X that are strictly to the *left* of p (resp. *on* p and strictly to the *right* of p), given any orientation of the occupied segment. We denote by $\#E$ the cardinal of a multiset E.

Lemma 1 (Characterization of the Weber segment[8]). *Let X be a multiset of aligned points. A point p is a Weber point of X if and only if $|\#left(p) - \#right(p)| \leq \#on(p)$. Moreover p is the unique Weber point of X if and only if $|\#left(p) - \#right(p)| < \#on(p)$.*

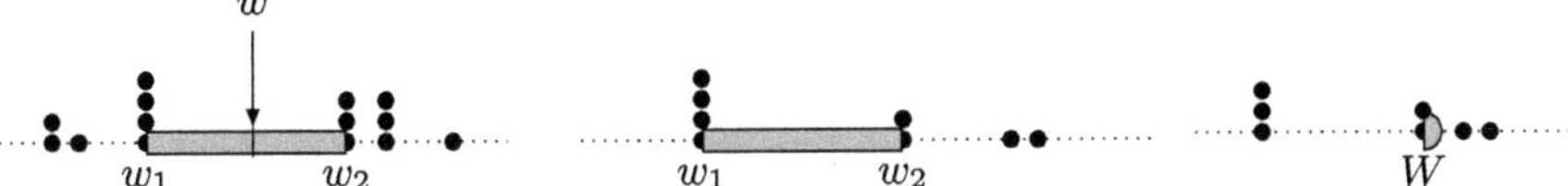

(a) Any point w in $[w_1, w_2]$ is such that $\#\mathrm{on}(w) = |\#\mathrm{left}(w) - \#\mathrm{right}(w)|$. The segment $[w_1, w_2]$ is thus the Weber segment.

(b) $[w_1, w_2]$ is the Weber segment for the same reason. Because w_1 holds $n/2$ robots, it has to be a border of the occupied segment.

(c) Only W fulfils the characterization property: it is the unique Weber point.

Fig. 1. Illustration of the characterization of Weber points in the aligned case.

This characterization (Fig. 1) allows us to state several useful corollaries:

Corollary 1. *The set of Weber points is a segment with endpoints in X and no other point of the segment belongs to X.*

Corollary 2. *Whenever $\#X$ is odd, every Weber point is included in X and thus there is a unique Weber point (Fig. 1c).*

Corollary 3. *If a point has a multiplicity of at least $\lceil \frac{\#X}{2} \rceil = \lfloor \frac{\#X+1}{2} \rfloor$, then it is a Weber point, and it is also an endpoint of the segment delimited by X (Fig. 1b).*

3.2   Preservation Under Contraction

What makes Weber points convenient for solving Gathering is that they are *preserved under contraction*. Informally (Fig. 2), if robots move along a straight line towards (*i.e.*, contract around) one or more Weber points, then all the Weber points around which they contract (and only them) are still Weber points after contraction.

Definition 3. *Let $X = (x_i)_{i \in I}$ and $Y = (y_i)_{i \in I}$ be two multisets of points. We say that X contracts to Y around p if and only if $\forall i \in I, y_i$ belongs to segment $[x_i, p]$. Points in Y are said to be* contraction points.

Lemma 2 (Preservation under contraction). *If there is a Weber point p_0 of X such that X contracts to Y around p_0, then for all points p the two following propositions are equivalent:*

- *p is a Weber point of Y,*
- *p is a Weber point of X and X contracts to Y around p.*

In particular (Fig. 2a) if p_0 is the unique Weber point of X then it is also the unique Weber point of Y.

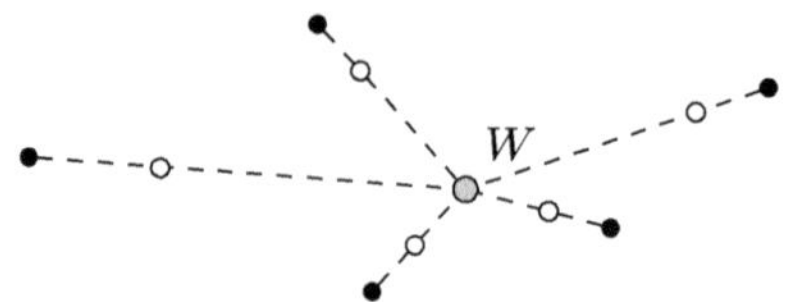

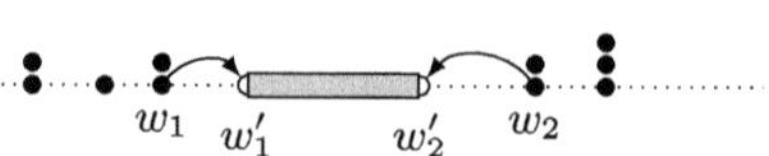

(a) A set X of points (in black) contracts to a set Y (in white) around the unique Weber point W of X. By preservation under contraction, W is also the unique Weber point of Y.

(b) $[w_1, w_2]$ is the initial Weber segment and two robots move from w_1 and w_2 to w_1' and w_2'. All points in $[w_1', w_2']$ are contraction points. The new Weber segment is thus $[w_1', w_2']$.

Fig. 2. Illustration of the preservation under contraction.

4   Gathering Asynchronously in $\mathbb{R}^2$, Overview

The Weber point (also known as the Fermat or Torricelli point), which minimizes the sum of distances to all robot positions, appears to be a convenient solution to solve Gathering in ASYNC as it *stays invariant* when robots move toward it along straight lines (*preservation under contraction*). Hence, robots moving asynchronously to it do not interfere with others' decisions. This strategy is frequently mentioned in the literature and often considered algorithmically obvious [21]. It is, in fact, incorrect without additional assumptions, and fails when the Weber point is not unique (see Sect. 3.1) as, in this case, robots may select different Weber points. We present hereafter a novel algorithm which relies solely on the use of Weber points, and which achieves Gathering in ASYNC with non-rigid moves in more general cases than previous solutions.

4.1   Preliminary Definitions

We consider $n > 2$ robots in the Euclidean plane, viewed as points in $\mathbb{R}^2$, and which can occupy the same locations. Let $\mathcal{P}$ denote the multiset of robot locations. The multiplicity of a location in $\mathcal{P}$ accounts for the number of robots occupying that location. Upon *activation*, a robot starts a cycle by receiving an observation (*Look* phase), namely, the multiset $\mathcal{P}$ in a local, self-centered coordinate system, and executes the algorithm (*Compute* phase) deciding on a destination in $\mathbb{R}^2$ solely based on this observation. Then it moves toward this destination (*Move* phase) in a straight line over a finite but unpredictable amount of time, during which other robots may be activated. A robot may be reactivated before reaching its destination, but only after it has travelled a distance greater than a predefined yet unknown threshold $\delta > 0$. When all robots are aligned, they form an *occupied segment* $[s_1, s_2]$. A *configuration* describes the system state at a given time, including robots' positions and motion statuses. We consider only *non-bivalent initial configurations without any activated robot*.

Algorithm `GatherW`:

```
1   let [w₁, w₂] be the Weber segment
2   if w₁ = w₂ then w₁                          { Phase 1 (unique Weber point) }
3   else                                        { From now P is aligned and n is even }
4     let M be the middle of P
5     if ∃p ∈ P of multiplicity n/2
6       then if ∃m′ ∈ P such that m′ ∈ [(0,0),p[ then (0,0) else p      { Phase 2 }
7     else
8       if M ∈ [w₁, w₂] then if (0,0) ∈ {w₁, w₂} then M else (0,0)          { Phase 3 }
9       elsif w₁ ∈ ]M; w₂[ then if (0,0) = w₂ then w₁ else (0,0)   { Phase 4 left }
10      elsif w₂ ∈ ]M; w₁[ then if (0,0) = w₁ then w₂ else (0,0)  { Phase 4 right }
```

Fig. 3. Informal description of our algorithm, `GatherW`. (0,0) is the current robot's location.

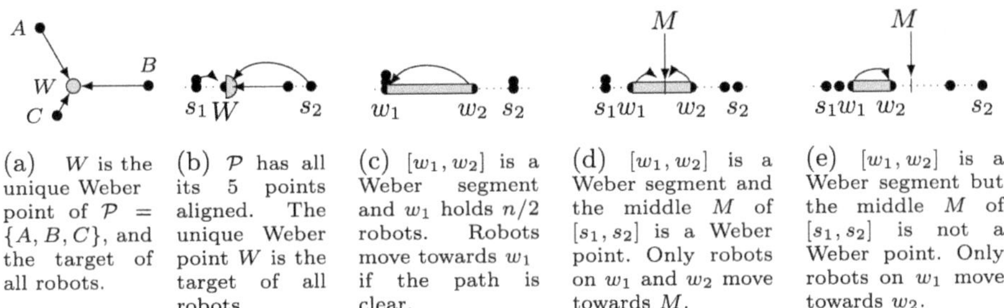

(a) W is the unique Weber point of $P = \{A, B, C\}$, and the target of all robots.

(b) P has all its 5 points aligned. The unique Weber point W is the target of all robots.

(c) $[w_1, w_2]$ is a Weber segment and w_1 holds $n/2$ robots. Robots move towards w_1 if the path is clear.

(d) $[w_1, w_2]$ is a Weber segment and the middle M of $[s_1, s_2]$ is a Weber point. Only robots on w_1 and w_2 move towards M.

(e) $[w_1, w_2]$ is a Weber segment but the middle M of $[s_1, s_2]$ is not a Weber point. Only robots on w_1 move towards w_2.

Fig. 4. Illustration of the algorithm's phases for a multiset P of points (in black, multiplicity shown vertically). Weber points of P appear in grey: when multiple, they form a *Weber segment* $[w_1, w_2]$; when unique, it is noted W. When robots are all aligned, they form an *occupied segment* $[s_1, s_2]$. Arrows (some bended to ease visualization) show destinations of robots. 4a and 4b correspond to Phase 1, 4c to Phase 2, 4d to Phase 3, and 4e to Phase 4.

4.2   The Algorithm `GatherW`.

From the self-centered[4] observation by the robot, the algorithm (Fig. 3) classifies the current configuration into one of four *phases*, and computes a destination accordingly (Fig. 4). When the Weber point is unique, only Phase 1 is executed (Fig. 4a and 4b). When multiple (Figs. 4c to 4e), all robots are necessarily aligned and n is even. Phases 2, 3, and 4 avoid creating a bivalent configuration which would amount to an ungatherable situation. Recall that the initial configuration is supposed non-bivalent.

Phase 1 (Fig. 4a and 4b). The Weber point is unique and robots move towards it. Thanks to the preservation property, the robots in any subsequent configuration continue to execute Phase 1, and eventually gather at the unique Weber point.

Phase 2 (Fig. 4c). There exists a point p of multiplicity $n/2$. By non-bivalent hypothesis this point is necessarily unique. All robots having a segment devoid

---

[4] The position of a robot when considered by itself is always $(0, 0)$.

of robots connecting their own location to p move towards p (*cautious move*). By doing so, the multiplicity of p does not decrease, and no bigger or equal multiplicity is created. Hence, Phase 2 continues in subsequent configurations until p becomes the unique Weber point, that is Phase 1 is reached.

Preliminaries on phases 3 and 4: In both remaining phases, robots are aligned. Let $[s_1, s_2]$ be the occupied segment and let M be its middle. In that case, Weber points form a segment $[w_1, w_2]$ ($w_1 \neq w_2$) (Sect. 3.1). Moreover, w_i cannot be equal neither to s_1 nor to s_2 since this would imply w_i having multiplicity $n/2$, already covered by Phase 2.

Phase 3 (Fig. 4d). M belongs to the Weber segment $[w_1, w_2]$, and all robots on this segment (which are either on w_1 or w_2, see Corollary 1 in Sect. 3.1) are ordered to move towards M. Notice that M does not change when robots on the Weber segment move, because $w_i \neq s_i$ (see remark above). Hence, M eventually becomes the unique Weber point, and Phase 1 is reached.

Phase 4 (Fig. 4e). M *does not* belong to the Weber segment $[w_1, w_2]$. Without loss of generality, we assume w_1 to be the endpoint of this segment that is farthest from M. Then, robots at w_1 move towards w_2. While they move, M does not change, and robots in w_1 will eventually reach w_2, which eventually becomes the unique Weber point, and Phase 1 is reached.

5   Customizing PACTOLE for ASYNC

PACTOLE [11] is a ROCQ library dedicated to the formal definition and proof of algorithms in the LCM model.

This section summarises the notions needed to understand the proofs at hand, in particular how ASYNC scheduling is defined.

An *execution* is an infinite sequence of configurations, determined by the interaction between a *robogram* (the algorithm executed by each robot) and a *demon* (a sequence of adversarial decisions). Robots perceive their environment through an observation, derived from the configuration and their own frame of reference. A transition from one configuration to the next, called a *round*, is solely determined by: (1) the configuration at the start of the current round, (2) the robogram running on all robots and (3) the influence of the environment represented by decisions of an adversary demon. The demon decides when a robot is *activated*, if so the robot does the Look and Compute phases in that same round. In subsequent rounds the robot may be moving but it is said to be *inactive*.

To adapt to the numerous variants of the LCM model, PACTOLE is defined as a set of fixed *ROCQ definitions* and a set of *parameters* left abstract. The fixed part corresponds to the structure common to all variants of the LCM model, whereas the abstract parameters are to be instantiated to account for a given variant. The central (fixed) function in PACTOLE is round which computes the configuration at the end of the current round (or the start of the next one) as follows:

- Each activated robot observes a configuration (Look) from its local point of view, determines an action to perform (Compute), and the demon decides which part of this action is actually performed at this round.
- Any other (non activated) robot may continue its current action if any.

The round function can be seen as a *template* as it uses *parameters* whose instantiation allows to specialize the execution model into many variants. The description of round in its full generality is presented in other works [11], here we only describe its instantiation to ASYNC for our purpose.

Instantiation to ASYNC

In the ASYNC non-rigid model, a robot may travel towards its target location over *several subsequent rounds*, while remaining non-activated. The demon determines the move ratio of an inactive robot (by a call to the inactive function below). If (re)activated before reaching its current target (and provided it has travelled the minimal distance δ), the robot computes a new target. The parameters and instances we use are described below:

- datatype State is the state of a robot, instantiated by a triple (s, d, ρ) where s is the location of the robot's last activation, d is its last computed target location, and ρ is the ratio already travelled on the segment $[s, d]$.
- function obs_from_config computes an observation from a configuration; it is instantiated by a function computing the multiset of occupied locations.
- function update computes the new state of the robot by applying the demon's decision to the robogram's result. From the current state (s, d, ρ), the instance computes the new state $(s', d', 0)$ where s' is the current position of the robot and d' is the target computed by the robogram.
- function inactive determines what non-activated robots do, depending on the demon's decision. From the current state (s, d, ρ) the instance computes the new state $(s, d, min(1, \rho + \rho_d))$ where ρ_d is a ratio chosen by the demon.

This instantiation leads to the following inlined version of round:

```
(* round function within Async + non-rigid moves + no byzantine
   + strong multiplicity detection *)
Definition round (r:robogram)(da:demonic_action)(cfg:configuration)  :=
  fun id ⇒
   if activate da id then
    (* demon choses a frame of reference *)
    let local_cfg := map_config (localize da cfg id) cfg in
    (* the observation is the multiset of occupied positions *)
    let obs := mk_multiset local_cfg in
    (* computed new target *)
    let target := r obs in
    (* new state of the robot *)
    let new_st := (get_location (local_cfg id), target, 0) in
    globalize da cfg id new_st
   else (* robot is inactive: demon may extend its pending move *)
     let '(s, d, ratio) := cfg id in
     (s, d, add_ratio ratio (choose_inactive da cfg id)).
```

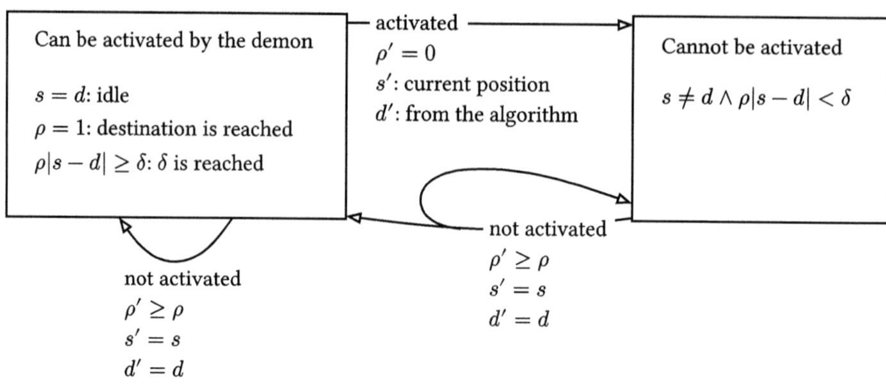

Fig. 5. ASYNC round for each robot. ρ', s' and d' are respectively the new ratio, source position, and target position of the robot after the round.

In a round, the state of a robot is updated when it is activated or when it is inactive. When it is activated, s and d are updated, and the ratio ρ is set to 0 (the robot does not move in this round, so it has to be inactive at least once to start moving). When it is not activated, only the ratio ρ can be updated (the robot may only move towards the previously computed destination). Since we are dealing with non-rigid movements, a robot can be activated even if it has not reached its destination, provided that it has traveled at least a distance δ. Figure 5 summarizes how the state of a robot is updated during a round. The fact that a demon cannot activate a robot that has not reached its destination and has not traveled at least δ is expressed by the following property:

```
Definition flex_da_prop (da:demonic_action) :=
  ∀ (id:identifier) (config : configuration),
    activate da id = true →
    get_location (config id) ≡ get_destination (config id)
    ∨ δ ≤ dist (get_start (config id)) (get_location (config id)).
```

Now we can define the main theorem of correctness of GatherW (defined formally in Sect. 5.1). It states that, given a fair demon, with non-rigid movements, if the initial configuration is valid (*i.e.*, not bivalent) and all robots are idle (their current destination d coincides with their current position s), then the robots will eventually gather at the same point and stay gathered forever:

```
Theorem gather_correct : ∀ config demon,
  (* The demon is fair. *)
  Fair demon →
  (* The frame changes (chosen by the demon)
   * are similarities centered on the observing robot. *)
  (Stream.forever (Stream.instant similarity_da_prop)) demon →
  (* We are in a non-rigid setting *)
  (Stream.forever (Stream.instant flex_da_prop)) demon →
  (* Initially, the configuration is not bivalent. *)
  ¬ bivalent config →
  (* Initially, all robots are idle. *)
```

```
config_stay config →
(* Following GatherW, the robots will eventually gather
 * and stay gathered at the same point forever. *)
WillGather (execute GatherW demon config).
```

Note that fairness (`Fair`) and non-rigidity (`flex_da_prop`) are not encoded in the model (which aims to be more general), but are rather explicit hypothesis of lemmas and theorems. Further note that in the ASYNC model fairness in conjunction with non-rigidity implies that each robot eventually computes a destination and each destination computation is eventually followed by a move toward this destination (unless the robot is already at its destination).

5.1   A Universal Robogram in ROCQ

A general solution based on Weber points must account for both cases: either the Weber point of a multiset X is unique or several exist. When not unique, the Weber points form a segment whose endpoints only belong to X. Let `weber_seg` be a function returning the endpoints of this segment, and let `segment w1 w2 w` denote the property $w \in [w1, w2]$. The `weber_seg` function cannot be defined in ROCQ without additional axioms as it is not computable. Therefore, we introduce it as an axiom, together with its specification. This is no different than the case of (classical) real numbers, which are axiomatized in the standard library.

```
Axiom weber_seg : list R2 → R2 * R2.
Axiom weber_seg_correct : ∀ (points:list R2) (w:R2),
 let (w1,w2) := weber_seg points in Weber points w ↔ segment w1 w2 w.
```

As explained in Sect. 4 the algorithm runs different *phases*. Let w_1 and w_2 be the endpoints of the Weber segment. When robots are aligned, let s_1 and s_2 be the endpoints of their occupied segment, and let m be its middle.

1. Phase 1: $w_1 = w_2$. In this case all robots move towards w_1.
2. Phase 2: $w_1 \neq w_2$, and there is a location t of multiplicity exactly $\frac{n}{2}$. In this case all robots move towards t.
3. Phase 3: $w_1 \neq w_2$, all locations have a multiplicity less than $\frac{n}{2}$, and m is in the segment $[w_1, w_2]$. In this case robots on w_1 or w_2 move towards m.
4. Phase 4: $w_1 \neq w_2$, all locations have multiplicity less than $\frac{n}{2}$, and m is *not* in the segment $[w_1, w_2]$. Assume without loss of generality that $w_1 \in [m, w_2]$. In this case all robots on w_2 move towards w_1.

Note that in Phases 2, 3 and 4, robots are aligned and there is not a unique Weber point. Therefore, by the properties of Sect. 3.1, the number n of robots is even, robots are aligned, and every point has a multiplicity of at most $\frac{n}{2}$.

Let us denote `segment_decb a b x` and `strict_segment_decb a b x` the tests whether x is respectively in the closed and open segment with endpoints a and b. We write = for the (axiomatized) boolean equality on $\mathbb{R}$, and `existsb pred mset` for the boolean predicate deciding the existence in a multiset `mset` of an element satisfying a predicate `pred`. Additionally `Nat.div2 x` stands for $\lfloor x/2 \rfloor$. The formal ROCQ definition of our algorithm is thus:

```
Definition gatherW (obs:observation) : location :=
 let (w1, w2) := weber_seg obs in
 if w1 = w2 then w1 else          (* phase 1: go to the unique weber pt *)
 match robot_with_mult (Nat.div2 (cardinal obs + 1)) obs with
 | Some t ⇒                              (* ph 2: move to t cautiously *)
   if existsb (strict_segment_decb 0 t) obs then 0 else t
 | None ⇒
 let m := middle_obs obs in
 if segment_decb w1 w2 m then     (* ph 3: if on w1 or w2 go to middle *)
   if (w1 = 0) || (w2 = 0) then m else 0
 else if segment_decb m w1 w2 then        (* ph 4: if on w1 go to w2 *)
   if w1 = 0 then w2 else 0
 else if w2 = 0 then w1 else 0            (* ph 4: if on w2 go to w1 *)
 end.
```

6   Proof of Correctness

We can now formalize completely the proof of gather_correct in the formal framework. As explained in [4], the proof is correct by construction: a theorem can only be compiled in ROCQ if it comes with a mechanically verified proof. Therefore, a reader who is convinced by the descriptions provided in the previous sections should consider the proof complete. The only thing left to check is the match between this work and the ROCQ statements: do we prove what we claim to prove?

This section is thus dedicated only to the explanation of the keys steps of the implementation of the proof for educational purposes, and to help future developers to prove correctness of their own robograms. The key steps of the proof are as follows.

Firstly, we show that, for any execution starting from a non-bivalent configuration, every configuration falls into one of the phases. Then we exhibit a measure in $\mathbb{R}$ over configurations such that (1) in each phase, unless the robots are already gathered, eventually the measure decreases by a constant amount, (2) the measure stays non-negative, (3) the configuration never becomes bivalent. From this, we conclude that any execution from a non-bivalent configuration eventually leads to a gathered configuration. A fundamental property of our algorithm is that when the phase changes, robots already in motion do not change their destination, even if they are reactivated before reaching it. This follows from the preservation under contraction property defined above.

6.1   Characterizing the Phases of GatherW

We attach an invariant to each phase of the robogram, stating the desired outcome of the phase. The following example shows the ROCQ code for the simple invariant of Phase 1, inv1, and the more complex one of Phase 2, inv2:

```
Definition inv1 config w : Prop :=
 (* All moving robots are moving towards [w]. *)
 config_stg config w ∧
```

```
(* [w] is the unique weber point. *)
OnlyWeber (pos_list config) w.

Definition inv2 c L : Prop :=
  let ps := pos_list c in
  aligned_on L ps ∧  (* The robots are aligned on L. *)
  (* The weber point isn't unique. *)
  (let (w1, w2) := weber_seg ps in w1 =/= w2) ∧
  (* There is a point with multiplicity (n+1)/2. It is necessarily
     an endpoint (if it isn't, then w1 = w2 (phase 1)).
     With the right choice of [L], it is the minimum point. *)
  (!! c)[left_endpoint L ps] = Nat.div2 (n+1) ∧
  (* The maximum has multiplicity less than [(n+1)/2],
     i.e. the configuration is valid. *)
  (!! c)[right_endpoint L ps] < Nat.div2 (n+1) ∧
  (* All robots are moving towards the minimum. *)
  config_stg c (left_endpoint L ps) ∧
  (* Both extrema aren't moving. left one because it is the target,
     the other because we perform cautious moves. *)
  endpoints_stay c L.
```

In this code, `ps` is the list of occupied locations in configuration c, the predicate `config_stg c w` expresses that all robots either stay where they are or move towards w; `endpoints_stay c L` means that (c being aligned) all robots standing on the end points of the occupied segment have reached their current destination and will not move if activated; `!!c` stands for the *observation* of configuration c in the global frame of reference, and `(!!c)[x]` stands for the multiplicity of point x in this observation; `left_endpoint L ps` (resp. `right_endpoint L ps`) is the minimum (respectively maximum) point of ps on the (oriented) line L.

We have to prove the crucial property that our set of invariants covers all possible initial configurations that are valid (*i.e.*, non bivalent and where all robots are idle).

```
Lemma inv_initial c :
  ¬bivalent c → config_stay c →  (* c valid initial configuration *)
  (∃ w, inv1 c w) ∨ (∃ L, inv2 c L) ∨
  (∃ L w1 w2, inv3 c L w1 w2) ∨ (∃ L w1 w2, inv4 c L w1 w2).
```

Using these invariants, we prove that executions of the robogram follow a transition diagram of the different phases (Fig. 6).

The diagram is described as ROCQ lemmas. For example, the following lemmas describe which phases can be reached from Phase 1 and Phase 2, and how:

```
Lemma phase1_transitions (c:configuration)(da:demonic_action)(L:line):
  similarity_da_prop da →  (* if the new frame is self-centered *)
  inv1 c w →                (* from P1... *)
  inv1 (round gatherW da c) w. (* to P1        *)

Lemma phase2_transitions (c:configuration)(da:demonic_action)(L:line):
  similarity_da_prop da →  (* if the new frame is self-centered *)
  inv2 c L →                (* from P2...*)
  inv1 (round gatherW da c) (left_endpoint L (pos_list c))) (* to P1 *)
  ∨ inv2 (round gatherW da c) L.                    (* or to P2 *)
```

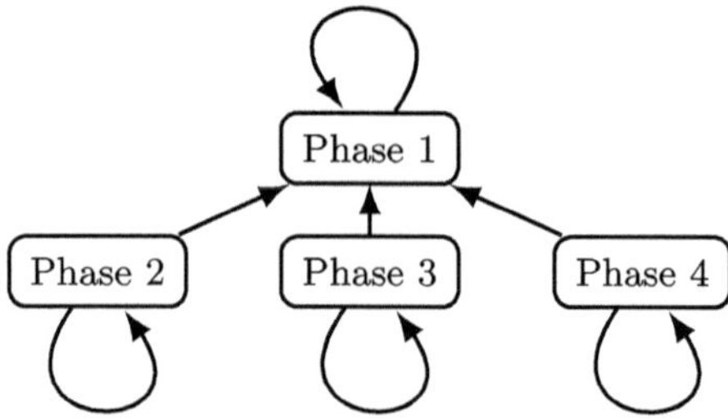

Fig. 6. Phase transition diagram.

We proceed similarly with all phases. From these lemmas and invariants we conclude on the *invariance of destination*: the destination is, and stays the same for all robots, even when a phase transition occurs. For example, `phase2_transitions` states that when transitioning from Phase 2 to Phase 1 the destination of robots is the left endpoint which was already the destination during Phase 2. Lemma `phase1_transitions` states that in Phase 1 the target of robots stays the same forever.

We also establish that each invariant implies that the configuration is not bivalent. For instance:

Lemma `inv1_valid config w : inv1 config w → ¬bivalent config.`

6.2   Decreasing Measure

Idle/Progressing/In Motion Robots. A robot is said to be *idle* on a point p if its starting point S and destination D are both equal to p. Otherwise, it is *in motion*. Note that these definitions are independent of the current location of the robot and that a robot in motion intends to move but may not be moving depending on the choice of the demon which may stop a robot movement before its destination. A robot is finally said to be *progressing* if it is both activated and in motion. Further note that when non-activated robots are moving they are not progressing.

Measure. Let D be the common destination point of all robots in motion. We define our measure on configuration as the sum of:

1. The number of robots that are *not* idle on D, and
2. The sum of all distances between D and the starting point of every robot.

It is in $\mathbb{R}$ and non-negative. Thanks to the invariance of destination (Sect. 6.1) it is always non-increasing between rounds. Moreover, this measure strictly decreases at every round that involves a *progressing* robot. Whenever there is a progressing robot r in a round, there are indeed two possible cases:

1. Either r is not on D (Figure 7), and since movements are non-rigid and r is activated: the starting point of r is now closer by at least δ to D; the sum

(a) Round i (b) Round $i+1$

Fig. 7. Robot r travels from its starting location S to its destination D. In round i, r is activated (thus is *progressing*). Since r is *not* on D, its new start (at current location of r) at round $i+1$ is at least δ closer to its (unchanged) destination D.

(a) Round i (b) Round $i+1$

Fig. 8. Robot r has reached its destination location D. In round i, r is activated (thus it is *progressing* since it is not yet idle). Its new start (at current location of r) becomes equal to its destination, thus it is idle at next round.

of distances, component 2 of the measure, decreases by at least δ while the other component does not increase.

2. Or r is on D (Fig. 8), and in the next round, r will be idle on D; the number of non-idle robots, component 1 of the measure, decreases by 1 while the other component does not increase.

The measure thus decreases by at least $\min(\delta, 1)$ at each round where a robot is progressing. For example for a round from Phase 1 to Phase 1 the corresponding `phase1_decrease` lemma will be:

```
Lemma phase1_decrease c da w :
  similarity_da_prop da → flex_da_prop da → (* model assumptions *)
  inv1 c w →
  inv1 (round gatherW da c) w →
  progress c da →
  (measure w (round gatherW da c) ≤ measure w c - Rmin 1ℝ δ)ℝ.
```

The last step is to prove that there will always eventually be a progressing robot unless the robots are already gathered: this is a consequence of the *fairness* assumption, that states that a robot is always eventually activated.

7   Concluding Remarks, Proof Effort

We described a formal model for ASYNC extending the PACTOLE library, and illustrated its use with the proof of correctness of an original algorithm solving Gathering for oblivious robots with non-rigid moves and strong global multiplicity. Our algorithm is based on Weber points which, contrary to popular belief, does not make it trivial, thus emphasizing the usefulness of formal methods.

The proof effort is shared between the enrichment of PACTOLE with Weber points definitions and properties, and the case study that is the definition and proof of correctness of our algorithm.

The library defining the Weber points and their properties is completely generic (it is defined for any Euclidean space). It consists of 1150 lines of reusable specifications and theorems, and of 4500 lines of proofs.

The case study itself includes the specifications, intermediate lemmas, and the proof for the main theorem (page 11). The total effort amounts to about 500 lines of specifications and 2900 lines of proofs only.

Keeping in mind that this is on a specific example, the reasonable and manageable size of proof suggests firstly that the model is well-suited for ASYNC, and secondly that it is possible to develop a formal proof in an ASYNC context without facing combinatorial explosion. This hints at PACTOLE as an interesting framework for proving formally the correctness of possibly more involved algorithms, akin to the ones of Cieliebak *et al.*. [10].

Acknowledgments. The authors would like to thank the referees whose remarks helped improving this article.

Disclosure of interest. The authors have no competing interest.

References

1. Altisen, K., Corbineau, P., Devismes, S.: A framework for certified self-stabilization. In: Albert, F., Lanese, I. (eds.) Formal Techniques for Distributed Objects, Components, and Systems - 36th IFIP WG 6.1 International Conference, FORTE 2016, Held as Part of the 11th International Federated Conference on Distributed Computing Techniques, DisCoTec 2016, Heraklion, Crete, Greece, June 6-9, 2016, Proceedings. LNCSvol. 9688, pp. 36–51. Springer-Verlag (2016). https://doi.org/10.1007/978-3-319-39570-8_3
2. Balabonski, T., Delga, A., Rieg, L., Tixeuil, S., Urbain, X.: Synchronous gathering without multiplicity detection: a certified algorithm. Theory Comput. Syst., 200–218 (2019). https://doi.org/10.1007/s00224-017-9828-z
3. Balabonski, T., Pelle, R., Rieg, L., Tixeuil, S.: A foundational framework for certified impossibility results with mobile robots on graphs. In: Bellavista, P., Garg, V.K. (eds.) Proceedings of the 19th International Conference on Distributed Computing and Networking, ICDCN 2018, Varanasi, India, January 4-7, 2018, pp. 5:1–5:10. ACM (2018). https://doi.org/10.1145/3154273.3154321
4. Bauer, A.: How to review formalized mathematics. Blog post (2013). http://math.andrej.com/2013/08/19/how-to-review-formalized-mathematics/
5. Bérard, B., Lafourcade, P., Millet, L., Potop-Butucaru, M., Thierry-Mieg, Y., Tixeuil, S.: Formal verification of mobile robot protocols. Distrib. Comput. **29**(6), 459–487 (2016). https://doi.org/10.1007/s00446-016-0271-1
6. Bezem, M., Bol, R., Groote, J.F.: Formalizing process algebraic verifications in the calculus of constructions. Formal Aspects Comput. **9**, 1–48 (1997)
7. Bonnet, F., et al.: Deterministic color-optimal self-stabilizing semi-synchronous gathering: a certified algorithm. In: Schmid, U., Kuznets, R. (eds.) Structural Information and Communication Complexity - 32nd International Colloquium (SIROCCO 2025). LNCS, vol. 15671, pp. 127–143. Springer Nature Switzerland, Delphi, Greece (2025). https://doi.org/10.1007/978-3-031-91736-3_8, https://hal.science/hal-04988128

8. Bouzid, Z.: Modèles et algorithmes pour les systèmes émergents. Ph.D. thesis, Université Pierre et Marie Curie, Paris, France (2013)
9. Cicerone, S., Stefano, G.D., Navarra, A.: Gathering of robots on meeting-points: feasibility and optimal resolution algorithms. Distrib. Comput. **31**, 1–50 (2018). https://api.semanticscholar.org/CorpusID:861053
10. Cieliebak, M., Flocchini, P., Prencipe, G., Santoro, N.: Distributed computing by mobile robots: gathering. SIAM J. Comput. **41**(4), 829–879 (2012). https://doi.org/10.1137/100796534
11. Courtieu, P., Rieg, L., Tixeuil, S., Urbain, X.: Swarms of mobile robots: towards versatility with safety. Leibniz Trans. Embed. Syst. **8**(2), 02:1–02:36 (2022). https://doi.org/10.4230/LITES.8.2.2, https://drops.dagstuhl.de/entities/document/10.4230/LITES.8.2.2
12. Courtieu, P., Rieg, L., Tixeuil, S., Urbain, X.: Impossibility of gathering, a certification. Inf. Process. Lett. **115**, 447–452 (2015). https://doi.org/10.1016/j.ipl.2014.11.001
13. Courtieu, P., Rieg, L., Tixeuil, S., Urbain, X.: Certified universal gathering algorithm in $\mathbb{R}^2$ for oblivious mobile robots. In: Gavoille, C., Ilcinkas, D. (eds.) Distributed Computing - 30th International Symposium, (DISC 2016). LeNCS, vol. 9888, pp. 187–200. Springer-Verlag, Paris, France (2016). https://doi.org/10.1007/978-3-662-53426-7_14
14. Cousineau, D., Doligez, D., Lamport, L., Merz, S., Ricketts, D., Vanzetto, H.: TLA + proofs. In: Giannakopoulou, D., Méry, D. (eds.) FM. Lecture Notes in Computer Science, vol. 7436, pp. 147–154. Springer-Verlag, Paris, France (Aug (2012)
15. Défago, X., Heriban, A., Tixeuil, S., Wada, K.: Using model checking to formally verify rendezvous algorithms for robots with lights in euclidean space. In: International Symposium on Reliable Distributed Systems, SRDS 2020, Shanghai, China, September 21-24, 2020, pp. 113–122. IEEE (2020). https://doi.org/10.1109/SRDS51746.2020.00019
16. Deng, Y., Monin, J.F.: Verifying self-stabilizing population protocols with COQ. In: Chin, W.N., Qin, S. (eds.) Third IEEE International Symposium on Theoretical Aspects of Software Engineering (TASE 2009), pp. 201–208. IEEE Computer Society, Tianjin, China (Jul (2009)
17. Devismes, S., Lamani, A., Petit, F., Raymond, P., Tixeuil, S.: Optimal grid exploration by asynchronous oblivious robots. In: Richa, A.W., Scheideler, C. (eds.) SSS 2012. LNCS, vol. 7596, pp. 64–76. Springer, Heidelberg (2012). https://doi.org/10.1007/978-3-642-33536-5_7
18. Doan, H.T.T., Bonnet, F., Ogata, K.: Model checking of a mobile robots perpetual exploration algorithm. In: Liu, S., Duan, Z., Tian, C., Nagoya, F. (eds.) Structured Object-Oriented Formal Language and Method - 6th International Workshop, SOFL+MSVL 2016, Tokyo, Japan, November 15, 2016, Revised Selected Papers. LNCS, vol. 10189, pp. 201–219 (2016). https://doi.org/10.1007/978-3-319-57708-1_12

19. Doan, H.T.T., Bonnet, F., Ogata, K.: Model checking of robot gathering. In: Aspnes, J., Felber, P. (eds.) Principles of Distributed Systems - 21st International Conference (OPODIS 2017). Leibniz International Proceedings in Informatics (LIPIcs), Schloss Dagstuhl–Leibniz-Zentrum fuer Informatik, Lisbon, Portugal (2017)
20. Fokkink, W.: Modelling Distributed Systems. EATCS Texts in Theoretical Computer Science, Springer-Verlag (2007). https://doi.org/10.1007/978-3-540-73938-8
21. Frei, F., Wada, K.: Invited paper: gathering oblivious robots in the plane. In: Stabilization, Safety, and Security of Distributed Systems: 26th International Symposium, SSS 2024, Nagoya, Japan, October 20–22, 2024, Proceedings, pp. 39–54. Springer-Verlag, Berlin, Heidelberg (2024). https://doi.org/10.1007/978-3-031-74498-3_3
22. Gaspar, N., Henrio, L., Madelaine, E.: Bringing COQ into the world of GCM distributed applications. Int. J. Parallel Programm. **42**(4), 643–662 (2014)
23. Küfner, P., Nestmann, U., Rickmann, C.: Formal verification of distributed algorithms. In: Baeten, J.C.M., Ball, T., de Boer, F.S. (eds.) TCS 2012. LNCS, vol. 7604, pp. 209–224. Springer, Heidelberg (2012). https://doi.org/10.1007/978-3-642-33475-7_15
24. Lamport, L., Merz, S.: Specifying and verifying fault-tolerant systems. In: Langmaack, H., de Roever, W.-P., Vytopil, J. (eds.) FTRTFT 1994. LNCS, vol. 863, pp. 41–76. Springer, Heidelberg (1994). https://doi.org/10.1007/3-540-58468-4_159
25. de Moura, L.M., Kong, S., Avigad, J., van Doorn, F., von Raumer, J.: The lean theorem prover (system description). In: Felty, A.P., Middeldorp, A. (eds.) CADE. LNCS, vol. 9195, pp. 378–388. Springer (2015). https://doi.org/10.1007/978 3 319 21401-6, http://dblp.uni-trier.de/db/conf/cade/cade2015.html#MouraKADR15
26. Nipkow, T., Paulson, L.C., Wenzel, M.: Isabelle/HOL — a proof assistant for higher-order logic, LNCS, vol. 2283. Springer-Verlag (2002). https://doi.org/10.1007/3-540-45949-9
27. Potop-Butucaru, M., Sznajder, N., Tixeuil, S., Urbain, X.: Formal methods for mobile robots. In: Flocchini, P., Prencipe, G., Santoro, N. (eds.) Distributed Computing by Mobile Entities, Current Research in Moving and Computing, LNCS, vol. 11340, pp. 278–313. Springer (2019). https://doi.org/10.1007/978-3-030-11072-7_12
28. Sangnier, A., Sznajder, N., Potop-Butucaru, M., Tixeuil, S.: Parameterized verification of algorithms for oblivious robots on a ring. Formal Methods Syst. Des. **56**(1), 55–89 (2020). https://doi.org/10.1007/s10703-019-00335-y
29. Suzuki, I., Yamashita, M.: Distributed anonymous mobile robots: formation of geometric patterns. SIAM J. Comput. **28**(4), 1347–1363 (1999)
30. Team, T.C.D.: The COQ proof assistant. Tech. rep. (2024). https://doi.org/10.5281/zenodo.11551307

Equivalence and Separation Between Heard-Of and Asynchronous Message-Passing Models

Hagit Attiya[1] , Armando Castañeda[2] , Dhrubajyoti Ghosh[3](✉) ,
and Thomas Nowak[3,4]

[1] Technion – Israel Institute of Technology, Haifa, Israel
`hagit@cs.technion.ac.il`
[2] Instituto de Matemáticas, Universidad Nacional Autónoma de México,
Mexico City, Mexico
`armando.castaneda@im.unam.mx`
[3] Université Paris-Saclay, CNRS, ENS Paris-Saclay, Laboratoire Méthodes Formelles,
Gif-sur-Yvette, France
`dghosh@lmf.cnrs.fr, thomas@thomasnowak.net`
[4] Institut Universitaire de France, Paris, France

Abstract. We revisit the relationship between two fundamental models of distributed computation: the asynchronous message-passing model with up to f crash failures (AMP_f) and the Heard-Of model with up to f message omissions (HO_f). We show that for $n > 2f$, the two models are equivalent with respect to the solvability of colorless tasks, and that for colored tasks the equivalence holds only when $f = 1$ (and $n > 2$). The separation for larger f arises from the presence of *silenced processes* in HO_f, which may lead to incompatible decisions. The results are proved through bidirectional simulations between AMP_f and HO_f, using an intermediate model that captures this notion of silencing. The results extend to randomized protocols against a non-adaptive adversary, indicating that the expressive limits of canonical rounds are structural rather than probabilistic. Together, these results help to delineate where round-based abstractions capture asynchronous computation, and where they do not.

Keywords: Equivalence of models · Asynchronous message-passing model · Heard-Of model · Message adversaries · Task solvability

1 Introduction

Distributed computing has been studied through a variety of models that differ in communication primitives, synchrony assumptions, and failure types. A natural question is how these models compare in their computational power. Specifically, we compare the sets of *tasks* solvable in different models. This is particularly valuable when two models are equivalent, but one offers a simpler setting for

C. Georgiou (Ed.): SIROCCO 2026, LNCS 16488, pp. 53–72, 2026.
https://doi.org/10.1007/978-3-032-26465-7_4

analysis or verification. Simulations are often used to provide these relationships, relating models that differ in synchrony or fault tolerance.

The standard *Asynchronous Message-Passing model with f The Heard-Of modelfailures* (AMP_f) assumes unbounded message delivery times and allows up to f process crashes. Many protocols in this model proceed in *rounds*: each process broadcasts a message tagged with its current round number and waits for $n - f$ messages from that round before advancing to the next. This round-based behavior is formalized in the *Heard-Of model* [11], which describes communication through *Heard-Of sets*, the sets of processes from which each process receives a message in a given round. The variant with f message omissions, denoted HO_f, corresponds to executions in which every process hears from at least $n - f$ processes per round.

The HO_f model is well suited to algorithm design and verification, partly because its executions form a compact set in a topology based on common prefixes (proved in Appendix A.1). Compactness implies that every infinite execution has finite, well-defined prefixes that can be reasoned about independently. As a result, correctness can be expressed through safety predicates and locally finite execution trees, avoiding the need to handle liveness properties explicitly as in AMP_f. This makes the HO_f model particularly amenable to both manual proofs and automated verification.

The precise relationship between HO_f and AMP_f has remained unclear. In particular, it is not known whether canonical rounds are fully general, or whether all tasks solvable in AMP_f can be solved also in HO_f. Indeed, not every protocol in AMP_f conforms to the canonical-round pattern. For example, the renaming task [4], is solved in AMP_f by a protocol in which each process maintains and shares the set of initial names it knows and decides once it has received $n - f - 1$ additional copies of this set. Here, decisions depend on the number of identical messages, rather than on the number of messages associated with a particular round. This example highlights that not all asynchronous protocols are expressed in terms of canonical rounds, motivating a closer examination of the precise boundary between AMP_f and HO_f.

The most relevant prior work is due to Gafni and Losa [17], who showed that HO_1 and AMP_1 solve the same set of *colorless* tasks for $n > 2$. (Roughly speaking, in a colorless task, like consensus, processes can adopt each other's decisions.) However, to the best of our knowledge, the case of colored tasks and larger fault thresholds ($f > 1$) has not been explored.

In this work, we complete the characterization of the relative computational power of HO_f and AMP_f *for arbitrary f*, considering both colorless and colored tasks.

To relate HO_f and AMP_f, we introduce an intermediate model based on the notion of silenced processes. A process in HO_f is considered *silenced* when its influence eventually stops propagating: only a proper subset of processes continue to hear from it, directly or indirectly. The *Silenced-Faulty* model, SFHO_f, treats such processes as faulty, while in HO_f they are still required to decide. Thus, establishing the equivalence between HO_f and AMP_f reduces to proving

Table 1. Conditions under which tasks solvable in HO_f are also solvable in AMP_f and vice versa.

	$0 \leq f \leq 1$ colorless	$0 \leq f \leq 1$ colored	$f > 1$ and $n > 2f$ colorless	$1 < f < n/2$ colored	$f \geq n/2$
HO_f in AMP_f	✓Lemma 1	✓Lemma 1	✓Lemma 1	✓Lemma 1	✓Lemma 1
AMP_f in HO_f	✓[17]	✓Theorem 2	✓Theorem 1	✗Theorem 3	unknown

the equivalence between HO_f and $SFHO_f$. Whether this holds depends on the number of failures and on whether the task is colorless or colored.

We use bidirectional simulations to prove the following results (see Table 1):

- For $n > 2f$, AMP_f and HO_f solve the same set of colorless tasks (Theorem 1).
- For $n > 2$ and $f \leq 1$, AMP_f and HO_f solve the same set of colored tasks (Theorem 2).
- For $f > 1$ and $n > 2f$, the renaming task, which is colored, is solvable in AMP_f but *not* in HO_f (Theorem 3).

We also show that the results carry over to randomized protocols with private local coins and a non-adaptive adversary, i.e., one whose behavior is fixed independently of the protocol's random choices; see Theorems 4, 5, and 6. With an adaptive adversary, the separation result still holds because they are stronger than non-adaptive adversaries; however, the equivalence results remain open.

Details of some of the proofs can be found in the Appendix and the full version of this article [5].

Additional Related Work: A long line of work has sought to bridge asynchronous and round-based message-passing models by placing them within a common framework for reasoning about protocols and impossibility results. The Heard-Of model of Charron-Bost and Schiper [11], Gafni's round-by-round fault detectors [16], and the unification framework of Herlihy, Rajsbaum, and Tuttle [18] are central to this direction. The problem of finding a round-based message-passing model equivalent to the read-write wait-free model was addressed by Afek and Gafni [1]. More recently, it was shown that canonical rounds are not fully general, when failures are Byzantine [6]. Our work contributes to this line by refining the comparison between asynchronous and round-based computation and pinpointing conditions under which equivalence holds.

Another body of research studies how asynchronous message-passing models can be characterized directly in round-based terms. Shimi, Hurault, and Quéinnec [19] introduce *delivered predicates* and show how they generate Heard-Of predicates for asynchronous models, providing a formal mechanism for deriving round-based behavior from asynchronous assumptions. Our approach differs in that we focus on *task solvability* and use the notion of *silenced processes* to identify where the Heard-Of abstraction HO_f diverges from AMP_f.

The Heard-Of abstraction has also proved valuable for the verification of distributed algorithms. Several works, including [8,12–14,19], have used it to reason about correctness within purely safety-based frameworks. Balasubramanian and Walukiewicz [8] formalized this connection, showing that verification in the Heard-Of model can be reduced to reasoning over locally finite trees. Because HO_f is defined by safety predicates and its executions form locally finite trees, automated verification is often more tractable than in AMP_f, which also requires liveness properties. The compactness result we establish for HO_f provides a theoretical explanation for this practical advantage.

Beyond verification, other comparisons between message-passing models have focused on the relationship between failure assumptions. Analyses such as Gafni's round-by-round fault detectors [16] investigate reductions between crash and omission failures, highlighting algorithmic reductions between models. Our perspective differs: we study *computational equivalence*, namely, whether two models can solve exactly the same set of tasks, rather than the existence of specific simulation-based transformations. This shift in focus clarifies the boundaries between asynchronous and round-based computation. In particular, our results refine the Heard-Of framework by identifying when the abstraction of canonical rounds captures the behavior of asynchronous message passing, and when it does not.

2   Models and Preliminaries

We consider message-passing models where processes modeled as deterministic automata with infinite state spaces communicate by broadcasting and receiving messages. A *protocol* is a set of n processes $\mathcal{P} = \{p_1, \ldots, p_n\}$. We assume our protocols to be *full-information*, where each process always broadcasts its current *view*, which is initially its initial state and afterwards its complete local history. A configuration of the system consists of the local states of all the processes and also the state of the environment, e.g., messages in transit, etc. A *schedule* describes the order in which processes broadcast and receive messages, and which processes' messages are obtained during each receive. An initial configuration I and a schedule S determine a *run* $\alpha(I, S)$ of the system which is an alternating sequence of configurations and broadcast or receive events. Each model describes a set of possible schedules and for each schedule, a set of processes that are *faulty*.

The AMP_f Model: In the *Asynchronous Message-Passing Model with $f \geq 0$ process failures* (AMP_f), there is no fixed upper bound on the time it takes for a message to be delivered nor on the relative speeds of the processors. Processes proceed in atomic steps, where they execute a receive, then a local computation and finally a broadcast. In a broadcast event, denoted as amp-bc$_i(m)$, process p_i broadcasts message m to all processes including itself. In a receive event, denoted amp-recv$_i(m)$, process p_i receives message $m \in M \cup \{\bot\}$ where M is the message domain and $\bot$ denotes "no message".

There are multiple definitions for AMP; we present one that is equivalent to the classical definition by Fischer, Lynch, and Patterson [15] (see [5, Appendix C]). A process that has infinitely many steps in a run is said to be *non-faulty*, and *faulty* otherwise. There can be at most $f \geq 0$ faulty processes. Messages broadcast by a non-faulty process are received by all non-faulty processes (Non-faulty Liveness). All messages *but* the last broadcast by a faulty process are received by all non-faulty processes (Faulty Quasi-Liveness). Every message received by a process was previously sent to the process (Integrity). No message is received more than once at any process (No Duplicates).

The HO_f Model: The Heard-Of model [11] is a round-based model. Here we consider one of its instances, the *Heard-Of model with $f \geq 0$ message omissions*. In each round, every process does a broadcast, then a receive, and finally a local computation. In a broadcast event, denoted ho-bc$_i(m)$, process p_i broadcasts m to all processes including itself. In a receive event, denoted ho-recv$_i(M')$, it gets a subset M' of the messages sent to it during the round. Messages missed in a round are lost forever.

Conceptually, processes proceed in lockstep; to represent the computation in the form of a sequence, we impose a total order on the events that is consistent with the order of events at each process, e.g., the round-robin pattern [7, Section 11.1]. In each round, a process may lose at most f messages from other processes; it always hears from itself (Weak Liveness). Every message received by a process in round k must have been broadcast in round k by some process (Integrity). A receive event can contain at most one message from each neighbor (No Duplicates). We remark that no process is defined to be faulty.

Tasks: In a run of a protocol, every process p_i has a non-$\perp$ *input* value in its initial state and *decides* on an *output* value *at most once*. If a process does not decide, its output is denoted by $\perp$.

A *task* is a tuple $T = (\mathcal{I}, \mathcal{O}, \Delta)$ where $\mathcal{I}$ is a set of input vectors (one input value for each process), $\mathcal{O}$ is a set of output vectors (one output value for each process), and Δ is a total relation that associates each input vector in $\mathcal{I}$ with a set of possible output vectors in $\mathcal{O}$. An output value of $\perp$ denotes an *undecided* process. We require that if $(I, O) \in \Delta$, then for each O' resulting after replacing some items in O with $\perp$, $(I, O') \in \Delta$.

In a *colorless* task, processes are free to copy the inputs and outputs of other processes. Formally, let $val(U)$ denote the *set* of non-$\perp$ values in a vector U. In a colorless task, for all input vectors I, I' and all output vectors O, O' such that $(I, O) \in \Delta$, $val(I) \subseteq val(I')$, and $val(O') \subseteq val(O)$, we have $(I', O) \in \Delta$ and $(I, O') \in \Delta$.

A task is *colored* if is not colorless.

A protocol $\mathcal{P}$ *solves* T in model $\mathcal{M}$, if in every run R of $\mathcal{P}$ with input vector I and output vector O, we have (1) $(I, O) \in \Delta$ and (2) $O[i] = \perp$ only if p_i is faulty in $\mathcal{M}$ in R. Finally, task T is *solvable* in model $\mathcal{M}$ if there exists a protocol $\mathcal{P}$ that solves T in $\mathcal{M}$.

Simulations: The definition of simulations follows [7, Chapter 7]. A simulation of model $\mathcal{M}_2$ in model $\mathcal{M}_1$ consists of three layers: (1) n *simulated processes*

$p_1, \ldots, p_n$, (2) n *simulating machines* $P_1, \ldots, P_n$, with machine P_i assigned to simulated process p_i, and (3) the communication system of $\mathcal{M}_1$ (see Fig. 1). Each simulated process p_i interacts with its simulating machine P_i via $\mathcal{M}_2$-communication primitives, as if the communication system is that of $\mathcal{M}_2$. The simulating machines interact with each other through $\mathcal{M}_1$ using $\mathcal{M}_1$-communication primitives. Transitions between states in simulated processes and simulating machines are triggered by the occurrence of events in $\mathcal{M}_1$ and $\mathcal{M}_2$. The occurrence of an event between p_i and P_i entails a transition in both p_i and P_i. A simulation is described by specifying the automaton for the simulating machines.

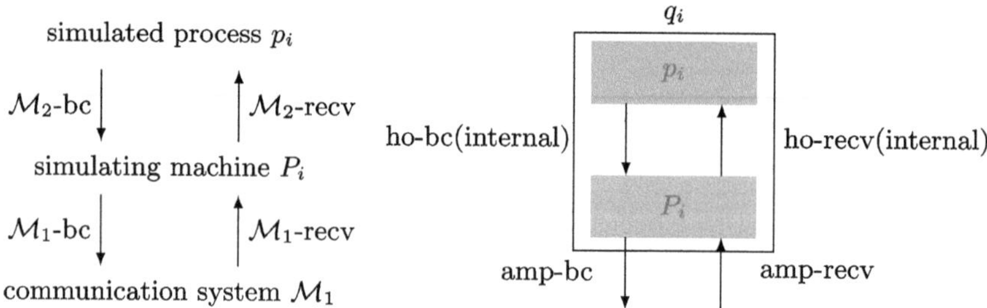

Fig. 1. Simulating $\mathcal{M}_2$ in $\mathcal{M}_1$.   **Fig. 2.** Constructing q_i from p_i and P_i.

A *configuration* of the system consists of the states of all the simulated processes and simulating machines and the state of the network. A schedule of a simulation is defined similarly to the schedule of a protocol, except it now involves the primitives of both $\mathcal{M}_1$ and $\mathcal{M}_2$. A *run* of a simulation consists of an initial configuration I and a schedule α such that the events in α are enabled in turn starting from I.

Given run α, we define the *simulated run top(α)* by restricting the initial configuration of α to the simulated processes and the schedule of α to the events of the upper interface.

3   Simulating HO$_f$ in AMP$_f$

In this section, we show that tasks solvable in HO$_f$ are solvable in AMP$_f$, with a simple simulation showing that an HO$_f$ protocol can be executed in AMP$_f$, as a consequence of the canonical-round construction technique in AMP. This helps to prove one direction of Theorems 1 and 2.

Lemma 1. *Any task that is solvable in* HO$_f$ *is also solvable in* AMP$_f$ *for* $0 \leq f \leq n$.

Proof. We first simulate a variant of the HO$_f$ model, called CFHO$_f$ (for *Crashed-Faulty* HO$_f$), in AMP$_f$ and then show the inclusion of HO$_f$ in CFHO$_f$. The

---

Algorithm 1. Pseudocode for machine P_i

1: Initialize counter $round \leftarrow 0$
2: Initialize empty sets $received[r]$ for all $r \geq 0$

3: When ho-bc$_i(m)$ occurs:
4:      $round \leftarrow round + 1$
5:      Add m to $received[round]$ ▷ Ensure that p_i hears from itself in HO$_f$
6:      Enable amp-bc$_i(\langle m, round \rangle)$

7: When amp-recv$_i(\langle m, r \rangle)$ occurs:
8:      Add m to $received[r]$

9: Enable ho-recv$_i(received[round])$ when:
10:      $|received[round]| \geq n - f$

CFHO$_f$ model is identical to HO$_f$ except that we allow a subset of processes to crash, i.e., have a finite number of events. Crashed processes do not need to decide as they are considered faulty processes. The number of messages that a non-crashed process does not receive in a round due to process crashes and message omissions is at most f.

Suppose a protocol $\mathcal{P}$ solves a task T in CFHO$_f$. Each round of CFHO$_f$ can be emulated in AMP$_f$ by waiting for $n-f$ messages before proceeding, preserving the causal structure of message delivery. We can construct a simulation system that simulates CFHO$_f$ in AMP$_f$ so that for $1 \leq i \leq n$, (1) the i-th simulated process is p_i and (2) the i-th simulation machine P_i is specified by Algorithm 1.

A protocol $\mathcal{Q}$ solving task $T = (\mathcal{I}, \mathcal{O}, \Delta)$ in AMP$_f$ can be constructed as in Fig. 2 by converting the simulation system into a network of automata $\mathcal{Q} = \{q_1, \ldots, q_n\}$ such that q_i runs both p_i and the i-th simulation machine P_i internally, and interacts with the communication system of AMP$_f$ using amp-bc and amp-recv events. The ho-bc and ho-recv events between p_i and P_i become part of q_i's internal computation.

The simulator q_i works as follows. The input of q_i is also used as the input for p_i. When p_i does an internal ho-bc(m) for round r to P_i, q_i does an amp-bc$(\langle m, r \rangle)$ and waits to receive at least $n - f$ messages of the form $\langle \cdot, r \rangle$, and collects their first components in a set M'. Then q_i performs an internal ho-recv(M') from P_i to p_i and changes p_i's state accordingly. If p_i internally decides an output o, then q_i decides o as well.

Since machine P_i waits to receive $n - f$ messages tagged with its current round counter before incrementing it, p_i receives $n - f$ messages in every round of a simulated run before broadcasting in the next round. The Integrity and No Duplicates properties are straightforward to verify and thus the simulated run is locally valid at every process, though it need not be globally valid. Indeed, due to the asynchronous nature of AMP$_f$, machine P_i could receive $n - f$ round-r tagged messages much earlier than machine P_j does, meaning p_i could then move on to do a round-$(r+1)$ ho-bc before p_j has a ho-recv for round r. However once the local history of events at the processes are correctly interleaved to follow the round-robin pattern, the rearranged simulated run is valid in CFHO_f. Thus the vector of outputs (which only depends on the local histories) of all the internal p_i and thus all q_i is valid for the input vector.

We now claim that if q_i is non-faulty in a run of AMP_f then p_i does not crash in the corresponding simulated run. To see this, let $\mathcal{Q}_{\mathrm{NF}}$ be the set of processes in $\mathcal{Q}$ that are non-faulty in the run of AMP_f. Let $q_i \in \mathcal{Q}_{\mathrm{NF}}$. In round 0, q_i does an internal ho-bc from p_i and does a corresponding round-0 tagged amp-bc. As $|\mathcal{Q}_{\mathrm{NF}}| \geq n - f$, there are $n - f$ such amp-bc events. Thus q_i receives $n - f$ round-0 tagged messages in AMP_f and enables a ho-recv from P_i to p_i; in turn, p_i enables a ho-bc for the next round. Thus for every $q_i \in \mathcal{Q}_{\mathrm{NF}}$, process p_i does a ho-bc for round 1. We can now continue our argument in an inductive fashion to conclude that p_i does not crash in the simulated run, which proves the claim.

By the above claim, every non-faulty q_i receives a non-$\perp$ output from p_i and hence decides. Thus protocol $\mathcal{Q}$ solves task T in AMP_f, showing that any task that is solvable in CFHO_f is also solvable in AMP_f for $0 \leq f \leq n$.

Finally, suppose that a protocol $\mathcal{P}$ solves a task T in HO_f. We show that $\mathcal{P}$ can also solve T in CFHO_f. Consider a run γ of $\mathcal{P}$ in CFHO_f. We can consider a run γ' of $\mathcal{P}$ in HO_f where every process that crashes in γ, say at the beginning of some round r, does not crash in γ' but instead from round r, (1) its messages are still lost to all other processes and (2) it hears from all non-crashed processes in γ (by Weak Liveness, there are at least $n - f$ such processes). By definition of HO_f, all processes decide in γ'. We show that (i) all processes that decide in γ output the same value they decide in γ', meaning that the output vector of γ is valid and (ii) all non-faulty processes in γ decide. For (i), if process p crashes in round r in γ, as γ and γ' are indistinguishable till round r to p, it will decide a value in γ if and only if it decides the same value before round r in γ'. If p does not crash in γ, as γ and γ' are indistinguishable, it decides in γ the same values that it necessarily decides in γ'. This also implies (ii). $\qquad\square$

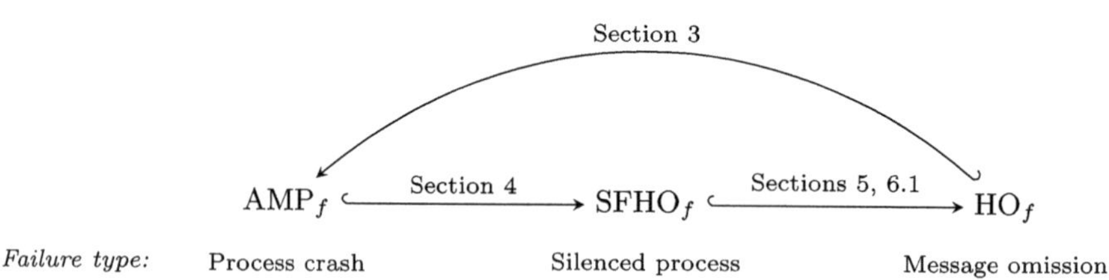

Fig. 3. Strategy for equivalence results; $\mathcal{M}_1 \hookrightarrow \mathcal{M}_2$ denotes a simulation of $\mathcal{M}_1$ in $\mathcal{M}_2$.

4   From AMP_f to HO_f

We now examine the conditions under which tasks solvable in AMP_f are solvable in HO_f. Instead of directly simulating AMP_f in HO_f, we introduce the *Silenced-Faulty Heard-Of* (SFHO_f) model, a variant of HO_f, which simplifies our proofs. The proof strategy for the equivalence results is outlined in Fig. 3.

4.1   The Silenced-Faulty Heard-Of Model

The schedules in SFHO_f must satisfy exactly the same conditions as they do in HO_f (Round-robin property, Integrity, No Duplicates, Weak Liveness). The difference between the models is that we can also declare a process to be faulty in SFHO_f. We first define the notion of a *silenced* process.

The *reach* of a process p_i from round r can be defined as the union of the set of processes that hear from p_i in round r, the set of processes that hear from one of these processes in round $r+1$, the set of processes that hear from one of the previous processes (of rounds r and $r+1$) in round $r+2$ and so on. Intuitively, the reach captures the transitive closure of message deliveries originating from p_i until a particular round. Formally,

Definition 1. *Let* $\mathrm{RCV}_i(r)$ *be the set of processes that receive a message from process* p_i *in round* r. *The* reach *of process* p_i *between rounds* r *and* $s \geq r$, *denoted* $\mathrm{REACH}_i(r, s)$, *is defined as*

$$\mathrm{REACH}_i(r, s) \stackrel{def}{=} \begin{cases} \{p_i\}, & \text{if } s = r \\ \bigcup_{p_j \in \mathrm{REACH}_i(r, s-1)} \mathrm{RCV}_j(s - 1), & \text{if } s > r. \end{cases}$$

The reach $\mathrm{REACH}_i(r, \infty)$ *of* p_i *starting from round* r *is* $\bigcup_{s \geq r} \mathrm{REACH}_i(r, s)$.

Definition 2. *A process* p_i *is* silenced from round r *if* $|\mathrm{REACH}_i(r, \infty)| \leq f$. *We say that* p_i *is* silenced *if there exists* r *such that* p_i *is silenced from round* r.

Definition 3. *A process is* faulty *in a run* σ *in* SFHO_f *if it is silenced in* σ.

We make the following simple but crucial observation about non-silenced processes for $n > f$, which also explains the term "silenced". If a process p_i is not silenced, then for any round r, there is a round $s \geq r$ such that $|\mathrm{REACH}_i(r, s)| = |\mathrm{REACH}_i(r, \infty)| \geq f + 1$. This implies that in round $s + 1$ every process hears from some process in $\mathrm{REACH}_i(r, s)$, which implies:

Lemma 2. *If* $n > f$ *then* p_i *is not silenced if and only if for any round* r, $|\mathrm{REACH}_i(r, \infty)| = n$.

When $n > 2f$, another important observation is that at most f processes are silenced.

Lemma 3. *If* $n > 2f$, *there are at most* f *silenced processes.*

Proof. Let *Sil* be the set of silenced processes. Suppose that $p_i \in Sil$ is silenced from round r_i. Then all the processes in $\mathrm{REACH}_i(r_i, \infty)$ must be silenced. Indeed, if some process $p_j \in \mathrm{REACH}_i(r_i, \infty)$ is not, then by Lemma 2, $|\mathrm{REACH}_j(r', \infty)| = n$ for some $r' > r_i$ and so $|\mathrm{REACH}_i(r_i, \infty)| = n$, contradicting our assumption that p_i is silenced.

By the definition of reach, there is a round after which no message broadcast by a process in $\text{REACH}_i(r_i, \infty)$ is received by a process outside the set. As we have shown for any $p_i \in Sil$ that $\text{REACH}_i(r_i, \infty) \subseteq Sil$, there is a round after which no message broadcast by a process in Sil is received by a process outside Sil.

We next argue that when $n > 2f$, at least one process is not silenced. Otherwise, all processes are silenced by some round R. In any round $r > R$, a message broadcast by any process is received by at most f processes in round r. So the total number of successfully received messages in round r is at most nf. However, by Weak Liveness, this number is at least $n(n - f)$, which is a contradiction as $n - f > f$.

Let p_k be a non-silenced process, that is, $p_k \notin Sil$. Since p_k misses at most f messages from other processes in any round and eventually does not hear from processes in Sil, it follows that $|Sil| \leq f$; that is, there are at most f silenced processes.

4.2   From AMP_f to SFHO_f

Lemma 4. *If $n > 2f$, then any task that is solvable in AMP_f is also solvable in SFHO_f.*

Proof. Let $T = (\mathcal{I}, \mathcal{O}, \Delta)$ be a task that is solvable in AMP_f by a protocol $\mathcal{P} = \{p_1, \ldots, p_n\}$. We use a hard-coded unique identifier id_i for each process p_i.

We construct a simulation system that simulates AMP_f in SFHO_f so that for $1 \leq i \leq n$, (1) the i-th simulated process is p_i and (2) the i-th simulation machine P_i has the specification given by Algorithm 2. Roughly, to simulate broadcasting a message in AMP_f, it is echoed in every round of SFHO_f by the processes that have already received it, in the hope that all processes eventually receive it. This fails when the message's original process is silenced in SFHO_f, and the simulated run risks violating the Non-faulty Liveness condition of AMP_f. So processes rely on acknowledgements to determine if their messages have reached everyone, until which they temporarily block themselves from proceeding in AMP_f. Thus if they are silenced in SFHO_f, they are faulty in AMP_f, and the Faulty Quasi-Liveness condition allows their last message to be not received by everyone in the simulated run.

To solve a task T in SFHO_f, a protocol $\mathcal{Q} = \{q_1, \ldots, q_n\}$ can again be constructed in the same manner as in Sect. 3, except that now the main events of q_i are ho-bc and ho-recv, while its internal events are amp-bc and amp-recv.

The simulator q_i works as follows. The input of q_i is also used as the input for p_i. When p_i does an internal $\text{amp-bc}_i(m)$, q_i broadcasts $latest = \langle id_i, m, T \rangle$ for some time value T in every subsequent round of SFHO_f. Also in every round, it broadcasts all previously received messages and acknowledgements for messages of the form $\langle \cdot, \cdot, \cdot \rangle$. It waits to receive at least f acknowledgements for $\langle id_i, m, T \rangle$ before unblocking p_i by enabling an internal $\text{amp-recv}_i(m')$ for every pending received message of the form $\langle \cdot, m', \cdot \rangle$. If p_i internally decides an output o, then q_i decides o as well.

Algorithm 2. Pseudocode for machine P_i

1: Initialize set *seen* $:= \emptyset$ ▷ History of messages received since the beginning
2: Initialize set *old* $:= \emptyset$ ▷ History of messages received before p_i's last amp-bc
3: Initialize variable *latest* $:=$ **null**
4: Initialize variable $T := 0$ ▷ For timestamping
5: Enable ho-bc$_i$(*seen*)   ▷ Enable broadcast for the first round of SFHO$_f$

6: When amp-bc$_i(m)$ occurs:
7:      *latest* $\leftarrow \langle id_i, m, T \rangle$
8:      Add *latest* to *seen*
9:      $T \leftarrow T + 1$

10: When ho-recv$_i(M')$ occurs:
11:      Add previously unseen messages in M' to *seen* and acknowledge those of type $\langle s, m', t \rangle$ by adding $ack(id_i, \langle s, m', t \rangle)$ to *seen*
12:      If *latest* $\neq$ **null** and $ack(j, latest)$ occurs in M' for at least f distinct values of $j \neq id_i$:
13:          Initialize set *pending* $:= \emptyset$
14:          Add messages of type $\langle s, m', t \rangle$ in *seen*$\setminus$*old* to *pending*
15:          If *pending* is empty:
16:              Enable amp-recv$_i(\bot)$
17:          Else:
18:              For each $\langle s, m', t \rangle \in$ *pending*:   ▷ Release all newly received messages
19:                  Enable amp-recv$_i(m')$
20:          *old* $\leftarrow$ *seen*
21:          *latest* $\leftarrow$ **null**   ▷ Update *old* and reset *latest* for next AMP step

22:      Enable ho-bc$_i$(*seen*)   ▷ Enable broadcast for the next round of SFHO$_f$

Every P_i tags every message m from p_i with the identifier id_i and a timestamp T, to distinguish an AMP$_f$ message that is broadcast multiple times by a process or by different processes.

The first observation is that if q_i is non-faulty (in SFHO$_f$) then p_i is also non-faulty (in AMP$_f$). By Lemma 2 and since q_i is non-silenced, every non-null *latest* value that occurs at q_i eventually reaches all processes in $\mathcal{Q}$. After a *latest* value by q_i is acknowledged by all the processes, q_i receives at least $n - f > f$ acknowledgements and thus allows p_i to continue in the simulated run.

Lemma 3 implies that there are at most f faulty processes in $\mathcal{P}$ in the simulated run.

In the simulated run, if a process p_i has an amp-bc(m) event eventually followed by an amp-recv event, it means that q_i received at least f acknowledgements to $\langle id_i, m, T \rangle$ (for some T) from others before allowing further amp-recvs at p_i. Thus eventually all processes q_j receive $\langle id_i, m, T \rangle$ and as all non-faulty processes p_j have infinitely many amp-recvs, amp-recv(m) must be one of them. Non-faulty Liveness and Faulty Quasi-Liveness hold as a consequence. Finally, it is straightforward to show that the simulated run satisfies the Integrity and No Duplicates properties.

We conclude that the simulated run is valid in AMP_f, meaning the vector of outputs of the simulated processes p_i and thus that of the q_i is valid. Moreover, a non-faulty q_i gets a non-$\bot$ output from its internal p_i. Thus task T is also solvable in SFHO_f, proving the lemma.

The next sections study the conditions under which a task solvable in SFHO_f is also solvable in HO_f, and then apply Lemma 1 and Lemma 4.

5   Equivalence for Colorless Tasks

We now show that when $n > 2f$, HO_f and AMP_f solve the same set of colorless tasks. Let $T = (\mathcal{I}, \mathcal{O}, \Delta)$ be a colorless task that is solvable in SFHO_f by a protocol $\mathcal{P} = \{p_1, \ldots, p_n\}$. One can easily construct a protocol $\mathcal{Q} = \{q_1, \ldots, q_n\}$ that solves T in HO_f. In every round, every process q_i runs p_i, and if a yet undecided process q_i hears from process q_j such that q_j has already decided o, then q_i decides o.

Let α be a run of $\mathcal{Q}$ with input vector I and output vector $O_{\mathcal{Q}}$ in HO_f. We first prove that all processes of $\mathcal{Q}$ decide on a value.

Lemma 5. *All processes q_i have non-$\bot$ output values in $O_{\mathcal{Q}}$.*

Proof. Since $n > 2f$, at least $n - f$ processes in $\mathcal{Q}$ are not silenced by Lemma 3 and decide by some round. In the next round, any q_i that has not yet decided hears from a decided process due to Weak Liveness and copies its output.

It remains to show that $\mathcal{Q}$ gives a valid output vector for the input vector of α. Let $O_{\mathcal{P}}$ be the output vector of $\mathcal{P}$ on α. Then $(I, O_{\mathcal{P}}) \in \Delta$ as α can be viewed as a run of $\mathcal{P}$ in SFHO_f.

Lemma 6. $val(O_{\mathcal{Q}}) \subseteq val(O_{\mathcal{P}})$ *and thus* $(I, O_{\mathcal{Q}}) \in \Delta$.

Proof. Suppose q_i decides output o in some round. This must be because either p_i decides o in that round in which case $o \in val(O_{\mathcal{P}})$, or q_i heard from some q_j that had already decided o in which case we can argue by induction that $o \in val(O_{\mathcal{P}})$. Thus $val(O_{\mathcal{Q}}) \subseteq val(O_{\mathcal{P}})$ and as T is colorless, $(I, O_{\mathcal{Q}}) \in \Delta$. $\square$

Thus protocol $\mathcal{Q}$ solves colorless task $T = (\mathcal{I}, \mathcal{O}, \Delta)$ in HO_f, proving that for $n > 2f$, colorless tasks solvable in SFHO_f are solvable in HO_f. Together with Lemma 1 and Lemma 4, this implies:

Theorem 1. *For $n > 2f$, models HO_f and AMP_f solve the same set of colorless tasks.*

6   Equivalence and Separation for Colored Tasks

6.1   Equivalence with One Fault

We now show for $f \leq 1$ and $n > 2f$ that HO_f and AMP_f solve the same set of colored tasks. When $f = 0$, there are no silenced processes in SFHO_0, and it is

---

Algorithm 3. Pseudocode for process q_i

1: Round r: Broadcast and receive messages and change the state of p_i accordingly
2: If q_i does not have an output yet, then
3:     If p_i decides o in round r, then q_i decides o
4:     Else if q_i determines from its round-r view that every other process has decided
5:         Then q_i chooses an output that together with the others' outputs and the input vector, satisfies the task

---

the same model as HO_0 and thus AMP_0 (by Lemma 1 and Lemma 4). Thus, it suffices to consider the case $f = 1$ and $n > 2f = 2$.

Let $T = (\mathcal{I}, \mathcal{O}, \Delta)$ be a colored task that is solvable in SFHO_1 by a protocol $\mathcal{P} = \{p_1, \ldots, p_n\}$. We show that the following protocol $\mathcal{Q} = \{q_1, \ldots, q_n\}$ solves task T in HO_1.

Recall that unlike colorless tasks, colored tasks require each process to produce its own output; thus decisions cannot be freely adopted from other processes. Thus, while process q_i runs p_i in each round, the decision rule is modified as in Algorithm 3.

Let α be a run of $\mathcal{Q}$ in HO_1 with input vector I and output vector $O_\mathcal{Q}$.

Lemma 7. *If q_i executes line 4 in round r, then there is a value for q_i to choose in line 5.*

Proof. Process q_i starts constructing a run α' by using the view of each q_j for the round where q_i last hears from q_j. It can then fill in the missing events in α' till round r by going over all possibilities (there is at least one that is valid, namely run α till round r). From round $r + 1$ onwards, it assumes that no messages are lost, so no process is silenced in α'. Thus p_i decides an output in α', which q_i uses in α. To see that q_i's choice leads to $O_\mathcal{Q}$ being a valid output vector, note that it is equal to the output vector yielded by $\mathcal{P}$ on α'. $\qquad\square$

We complement Lemma 7 with the observation that if a process is silenced, then it has nearly up-to-date information about the entire system.

Lemma 8. *If process q_i is silenced from round R in α, then for every round $r \geq R + 1$, its round-r view contains the round-$(r - 2)$ views of all processes.*

Proof. The round-r view of q_i contains the round-$(r - 1)$ views (and hence the round-$(r - 2)$ views) of at least $n - 1$ processes including itself. Let q_j be an exception. All processes in $\mathcal{Q} \setminus \{q_i, q_j\}$ must hear from q_j in round $r - 1$ as q_i is already silenced and no one hears from it. Thus q_i receives the round-$(r - 2)$ view of q_j from $\mathcal{Q} \setminus \{q_i, q_j\}$ in round r. $\qquad\square$

It remains to show that all processes decide and the run yields a valid output vector.

Lemma 9. *All processes q_i have non-$\perp$ output values in $O_\mathcal{Q}$.*

Proof. If q_i is not silenced then it is guaranteed to decide using p_i. Now suppose that q_i is silenced from round R and it does not get to decide using line 3. By Lemma 3, since no other process in $\mathcal{Q}$ is silenced, all processes in $\mathcal{Q} \setminus \{q_i\}$ decide by some round R'. Thus by Lemma 8, q_i satisfies the condition in line 4 by round $\max(R, R') + 2$ and also decides, by Lemma 7. $\qquad\square$

Lemma 10. $(I, O_{\mathcal{Q}}) \in \Delta$.

Proof. There can be at most one process q_i that decides using line 5. Indeed, if there were two such processes, both must have satisfied line 4, meaning each decided their outputs before the other; this is absurd. If *all* processes in $\mathcal{Q}$ decide their outputs in line 3, then $\mathcal{P}$ must yield output vector $O_{\mathcal{Q}}$ on run α in SFHO_1 and thus $(I, O_{\mathcal{Q}}) \in \Delta$. Otherwise, some process q_i decides in line 5, and thus, all other processes q_j decide in line 3. By Lemma 7, q_i's output combined with the others' outputs and the input vector I satisfy the task and thus $(I, O_{\mathcal{Q}}) \in \Delta$. $\square$

Hence protocol $\mathcal{Q}$ solves task $T = (\mathcal{I}, \mathcal{O}, \Delta)$ in HO_1, which implies:

Lemma 11. *For $f \leq 1$ and $n > 2f$, colored tasks solvable in SFHO_f are solvable in HO_f.*

Combining this with Lemma 1 and Lemma 4 implies:

Theorem 2. *For $f \leq 1$ and $n > 2f$, HO_f and AMP_f solve the same set of colored tasks.*

6.2 Separation with More Than One Fault

Algorithm 3 cannot be generalized to the case where $f > 1$, since it is possible to have a run with two silenced processes such that they are the only ones hearing from themselves. Since the two silenced processes will never have information about each other, getting them to decide compatible outputs is a challenge due to symmetry. Indeed, this prevents HO_f and AMP_f from coinciding for colored tasks and $f > 1$. We demonstrate this with the renaming task [4].

The *renaming task* with initial name space of potentially unbounded size M and new name space of size N and $M > N$ is defined as follows. Every process initially has as input a distinct identifier from the initial name space. Every process with a non-$\bot$ output must return a distinct output name from the new name space. To avoid trivial protocols for this task (e.g., for $N = n$, the protocol where process p_i always chooses i as output), we use the *anonymity assumption* on renaming protocols used in [4]. In particular, we can assume that the initial state of a process is a function of only its initial name and that all processes have the same decision function δ that maps the sequence of views at a process to an output name.

The anonymity assumption states that for any pair of processes and any input name i, both the processes have the same initial state when given i as input. Furthermore, let π be a permutation of $\{1, \ldots, n\}$ and let J and J' be two initial configurations such that for any $1 \leq i \leq n$, processes p_i in J and $p_{\pi(i)}$ in J' have the same state. Let R be a run of the renaming protocol starting from J. Consider $\pi(R)$, also a run of the protocol, starting from J' such that the sequence of events executed by p_i in R is instead executed by $p_{\pi(i)}$ in $\pi(R)$ for all i. Then p_i in R and $p_{\pi(i)}$ in $\pi(R)$ must have the same sequence of states.

Theorem 3. *For $1 < f < n/2$, the renaming task with an initial name space of size $N + n - 1$ and new name space of size $N = n + f$ is solvable in AMP_f but is not solvable in HO_f.*

Proof. For $n > 2f$, the renaming task with an unbounded initial name space and a new name space of size $N = n + f$ is solvable in AMP_f [4, Theorem 7.9]. Trimming the size of the initial name space to $N + n - 1$ clearly preserves the result. It is worth noting that the specifications of the AMP_f model in [4] differ in that all messages sent to non-faulty processes are required to be received. However it can be checked that the protocol works even if we weaken this by assuming Faulty Quasi-Liveness.

To show the separation, assume by way of contradiction that there is a protocol $\mathcal{P}$ solving the task in HO_f. We show how to obtain an input vector on which $\mathcal{P}$ fails. Fix arbitrary distinct initial names $x_1, \ldots, x_{n-2}$ for processes $p_1, \ldots, p_{n-2}$. Let processes p_{n-1} and p_n have initial names a and b that will be chosen later. Consider a run of $\mathcal{P}$ in HO_f with input vector $(x_1, \ldots, x_{n-2}, a, b)$ such that: (1) $p_1, \ldots, p_{n-2}$ hear from each other in every round, (2) p_{n-1} and p_n are not heard of by any other process in any round, and (3) p_{n-1} and p_n get to hear from $p_1, \ldots, p_{n-2}$ in every round.

With $x_1, \ldots, x_{n-2}$ fixed, the sequence of views of p_{n-1} is the value of some function $f(a)$ that does not depend on b, and its new name is some value $\delta(f(a))$. The sequence of views of p_{n-1} and p_n are symmetric, so the sequence of views of p_n is $f(b)$ and its new name is $\delta(f(b))$. As there are $N + 1$ initial names apart from $x_1, \ldots, x_{n-2}$ and only N possible new names, there exist values for a, b such that such that $x_1, \ldots, x_{n-2}, a, b$ are distinct and $\delta(f(a)) = \delta(f(b))$. Thus $\mathcal{P}$ fails on the input vector $(x_1, \ldots, x_{n-2}, a, b)$; a contradiction. $\qquad\square$

7 Randomized Protocols with a Non-Adaptive Adversary

In this section, we extend our study to randomized protocols under a *non-adaptive adversary*, which fixes process crashes and message omissions independently of the protocol's random choices. Randomization can break symmetry among processes, but it cannot repair lost communication: once two processes are silenced with respect to each other, their random choices evolve independently and their outputs may diverge. We prove that the equivalence between AMP_f and HO_f for colorless tasks persists in this setting, while the separation for colored tasks remains. Thus, the expressive boundary between the two models is *structural*, determined by the flow of information rather than by deterministic constraints.

More specifically, we assume processes are equipped with their own local coins, which they may flip an arbitrary number of times during the local computation of each step. Together with an initial configuration and schedule, the sequences of local coin flips determine a run. An overview of randomized protocols can be found in [3].

We assume that the scheduling of processes and messages is handled by a *non-adaptive adversary*, which must fix the schedule of the run in advance. Once fixed, the results of the coin flips are the only remaining unknowns that determine the run of the protocol. We also alter the definition of task solvability in Sect. 2 by replacing the second condition that says that all non-faulty processes must decide. Instead, we require that once the adversary fixes the scheduling, all non-faulty processes must decide with probability 1. The first condition remains unchanged, i.e., the output vector of a run always has to satisfy the task specification.

The following randomized versions of Theorems 1 and 2 are proved by identical simulation constructions, detailed in [5, Appendix A]. The only difference is in showing almost-sure termination.

Theorem 4. *For $n > 2f$, AMP_f and HO_f solve the same set of randomized colorless tasks.*

Theorem 5. *For $f \leq 1$ and $n > 2f$, AMP_f and HO_f solve the same set of randomized colored tasks.*

In order to show the randomized counterpart of the separation result (Theorem 3), we will use a probabilistic version of the pigeonhole principle that shows a positive probability of name collisions of randomized renaming protocols in HO_f (proved in [5, Appendix A]).

Lemma 12. *Let $N \geq 1$ be a positive integer and let $0 < c < 1/N$. There exists an integer $L = L(N, c)$ with the following property: for every collection $X_1, \ldots, X_L$ of L pairwise independent random variables in the set $\{a_1, \ldots, a_N\}$, there exist distinct indices $a, b \in \{1, \ldots, L\}$ such that $\mathbb{P}(X_a = X_b) \geq c$.*

To demonstrate separation, we will use the renaming task as in the deterministic version, only with a potentially larger initial name space because of Lemma 12.

Theorem 6. *For $1 < f < n/2$, there exists $L \geq 2$ such that the renaming task with initial name space of size $n - 2 + L$ and new name space of size $N = n + f$ is solvable in AMP_f but not in HO_f.*

Proof. The task is solvable for any $L \geq 2$ in AMP_f even by a deterministic protocol. Assume for all $L \geq 2$ that there is a randomized protocol solving it in HO_f against a non-adaptive adversary.

We choose the same message schedule and input vector $(x_1, \ldots, x_{n-2}, a, b)$ as in the proof of Theorem 3, with a and b to be chosen later. Let R be the set of runs having the chosen input vector and schedule. In run $r \in R$, let $c'(r)$

be the sequence of random choices of the processes $p_1, \ldots, p_{n-2}$ and let $c_{n-1}(r)$ and $c_n(r)$ be those of p_{n-1} and p_n. Write $\mathcal{C}'$ for the set of sequences of random choices $c'(r)$. Once $x_1, \ldots, x_{n-2}$ are fixed, the new names of p_{n-1} and p_n depend on their own initial names, their own sequences of random choices and those of $p_1, \ldots, p_{n-2}$, and thus can be written as $\delta(a, c_{n-1}(r), c'(r))$ and $\delta(b, c_n(r), c'(r))$. We use the fact that all processes almost-surely decide distinct non-$\perp$ values and the law of total probability [9, Theorem 34.4] to obtain

$$
\begin{aligned}
1 &= \mathbb{P}\big(\delta(a, c_{n-1}(r), c'(r)) \neq \delta(b, c_n(r), c'(r))\big) \\
&= \int_{\mathcal{C}'} \mathbb{P}(\delta(a, c_{n-1}(r), c'(r)) \neq \delta(b, c_n(r), c'(r)) \mid c'(r) = c')\, d\mathbb{P}(c').
\end{aligned}
\tag{1}
$$

Once $c'(r)$ is fixed to c' and values for a and b are chosen, the new names $\delta(a, c_{n-1}(r), c')$ and $\delta(b, c_n(r), c')$ are independent random variables because of $c_{n-1}(r)$ and $c_n(r)$being independent. Moreover they must be chosen from a set of $k = N - (n - 2)$ names. By setting $c = 1/2k$ in Lemma 12, there exists a choice of initial names a and b from a set of $L = L(N, c)$ names such that

$$
\mathbb{P}(\delta(a, c_{n-1}(r), c'(r)) \neq \delta(b, c_n(r), c'(r)) \mid c'(r) = c') \leq 1 - \frac{1}{2k}.
\tag{2}
$$

Combining (1) and (2) gives

$$
1 \leq \left(1 - \frac{1}{2k}\right) \int_{\mathcal{C}'} d\mathbb{P}(c') = 1 - \frac{1}{2k} < 1 \;,
\tag{3}
$$

a contradiction. $\qquad\square$

8   Summary and Discussion

This work establishes a precise correspondence between AMP_f, the asynchronous message-passing model with crash failures, and HO_f, the round-based Heard-Of model with message omissions. The two coincide for colorless tasks when $n > 2f$, and for colored tasks only when $f = 1$ (and $n > 2$). The distinction stems from *silenced processes* in HO_f: when several processes become permanently unheard, their views diverge and they may reach incompatible decisions. With a single such process, compatibility can still be preserved; with more, it cannot. The results extend to randomized algorithms with non-adaptive adversaries, indicating that the limitations arise from communication structure rather than determinism.

The notion of silencing offers a new perspective on the limits of coordination in asynchronous systems, showing that failures of propagation, rather than timing, define what is computable. One open question involves understanding the case $n \leq 2f$. While it initially appears that the landscape of solvable problems in both AMP_f and HO_f might only contain trivial tasks, it turns out that $(n-1)$-set agreement is solvable in both for $f = n - 2$: this is done by doing one round of exchanging input values and deciding on the minimal value received. Other open directions include identifying broader task classes for which the models coincide, and clarifying the role of the intermediate model SFHO_f for colored tasks with $f > 1$ and $n > 2f$. More broadly, reasoning in terms of information propagation may help reveal similar boundaries in models of partial synchrony and Byzantine behavior.

Acknowledgments.. Dhrubajyoti Ghosh and Thomas Nowak are supported by the ANR projects DREAMY (ANR-21-CE48-0003) and COSTXPRESS (ANR-23-CE45-0013). Hagit Attiya is supported by the Israel Science Foundation (grant number 25/1849). Armando Castañeda is supported by research projects DGAPA-PAPIIT IN108723 and IN103126, and SECIHTI CBF-2025-I-393.

Disclosure of Interests.. The authors have no competing interests to declare that are relevant to the content of this article.

A   Appendix

A.1   Compactness of HO_f

In this section, we prove that the set of runs of a protocol in HO_f with a *finite* number of possible initial configurations is compact with respect to the *longest-common-prefix* metric. Given two sequences $\alpha = (\alpha_k)_{k \in \mathbb{N}_0}$ and $\beta = (\beta_k)_{k \in \mathbb{N}_0}$, their *longest-common-prefix distance* [2] is:

$$d(\alpha, \beta) = 2^{-\inf\{k \in \mathbb{N}_0 \mid \alpha_k \neq \beta_k\}}. \tag{4}$$

If α and β are identical, then the infimum is $+\infty$ and their distance is zero. If not, then their distance is equal to 2^{-K} where K is the smallest index at which the sequences differ.

We first define schedules using *communication graphs* and show that the set of schedules is compact when equipping it with the longest-common-prefix metric. We then show that the mapping from schedules to protocol runs in HO_f is continuous. This then proves that the set of runs is compact, as the continuous image of a compact set.

We define $\mathcal{G}_{n,f}$ as the set of directed graphs $G = (V, E)$ such that:

1. the set of vertices of G is equal to $V = [n]$,
2. every vertex has a self-loop in G, i.e., $(i, i) \in E$ for all $i \in [n]$,
3. the set of incoming neighbors of every vertex has size at least $n - f$, i.e., $|\{j \in [n] \mid (j, i) \in E\}| \geq n - f$ for every $i \in [n]$.

A *communication graph* is a graph $G \in \mathcal{G}_{n,f}$. A *schedule* is an infinite sequence $G_1, G_2, \ldots$ of communication graphs.

To prove compactness of the set of schedules, we use Tychonoff's theorem (see, *e.g.* [10, Chapter I, §9, no. 5, Theorem 3]).

Theorem 7 (Tychonoff). *The product of a family of compact topological spaces is compact with respect to the product topology.*

Lemma 13. *The set of schedules is compact with respect to the longest-common-prefix metric.*

Proof. The set of schedules is equal to $\mathcal{G}_{n,f}^{\mathbb{N}}$. It is straightforward to show that the product topology is induced by the longest-common-prefix metric if every copy of $\mathcal{G}_{n,f}$ is equipped with the discrete metric. Each $\mathcal{G}_{n,f}$ is compact since it is finite. Thus, applying Theorem 7 shows that the set of schedules is compact as well. $\qquad\square$

Given a protocol in HO_f, denoting by Σ the set of schedules, by $\mathcal{S}$ the set of runs of HO_f, and by $\mathcal{C}_0$ the set of initial configurations of the protocol, we define the mapping $f : \mathcal{C}_0 \times \Sigma \to \mathcal{S}$ inductively on every element $(C_0, \alpha) \in \mathcal{C}_0 \times \Sigma$ by simulating the protocol starting from the given initial configuration C_0 and delivering messages in round r according to the round-r communication graph G_r of schedule α.

Lemma 14. *The function $f \colon \Sigma \times \mathcal{C}_0 \to \mathcal{S}$ is continuous when equipping Σ and $\mathcal{S}$ with the longest-common-prefix metric and $\mathcal{C}_0$ with the discrete metric.*

Proof. Since the round-r prefix of $f(\alpha, C_0)$ is entirely determined by C_0 and the round-r prefix of α, we have $d(f(\alpha, C_0), f(\beta, C_0)) \leq d(\alpha, \beta)$ for all $\alpha, \beta \in \Sigma$ and all $C_0 \in \mathcal{C}_0$. $\qquad\square$

Lemma 15. *For a protocol $\mathcal{P}$ whose set $\mathcal{C}_0$ of initial configurations is finite, the set of runs of $\mathcal{P}$ in HO_f is compact with respect to the longest-common-prefix metric.*

Proof. It is straightforward to check that the set of runs of $\mathcal{P}$ is the image of the function f. We thus have $\mathcal{S} = \bigcup_{C_0 \in \mathcal{C}_0} f(\Sigma, C_0)$. Each set $f(\Sigma, C_0)$ is compact as the continuous image of a compact set. Then, if $\mathcal{C}_0$ is finite, the set $\mathcal{S}$ is compact as the finite union of compact sets. $\qquad\square$

References

1. Afek, Y., Gafni, E.: Asynchrony from synchrony. In: Frey, D., Raynal, M., Sarkar, S., Shyamasundar, R.K., Sinha, P. (eds.) ICDCN 2013. LNCS, vol. 7730, pp. 225–239. Springer, Heidelberg (2013). https://doi.org/10.1007/978-3-642-35668-1_16
2. Alpern, B., Schneider, F.B.: Defining liveness. Inf. Process. Lett. **21**(4), 181–185 (1985). https://doi.org/10.1016/0020-0190(85)90056-0
3. Aspnes, J.: Randomized protocols for asynchronous consensus. Distrib. Comput. **16**(2–3), 165–175 (2003). https://doi.org/10.1007/s00446-002-0081-5
4. Attiya, H., Bar-Noy, A., Dolev, D., Peleg, D., Reischuk, R.: Renaming in an asynchronous environment. J. ACM **37**(3), 524–548 (1990). https://doi.org/10.1145/79147.79158
5. Attiya, H., Castañeda, A., Ghosh, D., Nowak, T.: Equivalence and separation between Heard-Of and asynchronous message-passing models (2025). https://doi.org/10.48550/arXiv.2511.21859. arXiv:2511.21859 [cs.DC]

6. Attiya, H., Flam, I., Welch, J.L.: Brief announcement: communication patterns for optimal resilience. In: Kowalski, D.R. (ed.) Proceedings of the 39th International Symposium on Distributed Computing (DISC 2025). LIPIcs, vol. 356, pp. 46:1–46:7. Schloss Dagstuhl – Leibniz-Zentrum fü, address = Dagstuhlr Informatik (2025). https://doi.org/10.4230/LIPIcs.DISC.2025.46

7. Attiya, H., Welch, J.: Distributed Computing: Fundamentals, Simulations and Advanced Topics. Wiley, Hoboken (2004). https://doi.org/10.1002/0471478210

8. Balasubramanian, A.R., Walukiewicz, I.: Characterizing consensus in the Heard-Of model. In: Konnov, I., Kovács, L. (eds.) Proceedings of the 31st International Conference on Concurrency Theory (CONCUR 2020). LIPIcs, vol. 171, pp. 9:1–9:18. Schloss Dagstuhl – Leibniz-Zentrum fü, address = Dagstuhlr Informatik (2020). https://doi.org/10.4230/LIPIcs.CONCUR.2020.9

9. Billingsley, P.: Probability and Measure. Wiley Series in Probability and Mathematical Statistics, 3rd edn. Wiley, New York (1995)

10. Bourbaki, N.: General Topology, Chapters 1–4. Elements of Mathematics, Springer, Heidelberg (1989)

11. Charron-Bost, B., Schiper, A.: The Heard-Of model: computing in distributed systems with benign failures. Distrib. Comput. **22**(1), 49–71 (2009). https://doi.org/10.1007/s00446-009-0084-6

12. Damian, A., Drăgoi, C., Militaru, A., Widder, J.: Communication-closed asynchronous protocols. In: Dillig, I., Tasiran, S. (eds.) CAV 2019. LNCS, vol. 11562, pp. 344–363. Springer, Cham (2019). https://doi.org/10.1007/978-3-030-25543-5_20

13. Debrat, H., Merz, S.: Verifying fault-tolerant distributed algorithms in the Heard-Of model. Arch. Formal Proofs **2012** (2012)

14. Drăgoi, C., Henzinger, T.A., Veith, H., Widder, J., Zufferey, D.: A logic-based framework for verifying consensus algorithms. In: McMillan, K.L., Rival, X. (eds.) VMCAI 2014. LNCS, vol. 8318, pp. 161–181. Springer, Heidelberg (2014). https://doi.org/10.1007/978-3-642-54013-4_10

15. Fischer, M.J., Lynch, N.A., Paterson, M.S.: Impossibility of distributed consensus with one faulty process. J. ACM **32**(2), 374–382 (1985). https://doi.org/10.1145/3149.214121

16. Gafni, E.: Round-by-round fault detectors (extended abstract): unifying synchrony and asynchrony. In: Coan, B.A., Afek, Y. (eds.) Proceedings of the 17th ACM Symposium on Principles of Distributed Computing (PODC 1998), pp. 143–152. ACM, New York (1998). https://doi.org/10.1145/277697.277724

17. Gafni, E., Losa, G.: Invited paper: time is not a healer, but it sure makes hindsight 20:20. In: Dolev, S., Schieber, B. (eds.) Proceedings of the 25th International Symposium on Stabilization, Safety, and Security of Distributed Systems, SSS 2023. LNCS, vol. 14310, pp. 62–74. Springer, Cham (2023). https://doi.org/10.1007/978-3-031-44274-2_6

18. Herlihy, M., Rajsbaum, S., Tuttle, M.R.: Unifying synchronous and asynchronous message-passing models. In: Coan, B.A., Afek, Y. (eds.) Proceedings of the 17th ACM Symposium on Principles of Distributed Computing, PODC 1998, pp. 133–142. ACM, New York (1998). https://doi.org/10.1145/277697.277722

19. Shimi, A., Hurault, A., Quéinnec, P.: Characterization and derivation of Heard-Of predicates for asynchronous message-passing models. Log. Meth. Comput. Sci. **17** (2021). https://doi.org/10.46298/lmcs-17(3:26)2021

Minimum Deviation Distance Realization

Amotz Bar-Noy[1], David Peleg[2], Mor Perry[3(✉)], Yingli Ran[4], and Dror Rawitz[5]

[1] City University of New York (CUNY), New York, USA
`amotz@sci.brooklyn.cuny.edu`
[2] Weizmann Institute of Science, Rehovot, Israel
`david.peleg@weizmann.ac.il`
[3] The Academic College of Tel-Aviv-Yaffo, Tel Aviv, Israel
`morpy@mta.ac.il`
[4] Zhejiang Normal University, Jinhua, China
`ranyingli@zjnu.edu.cn`
[5] Bar Ilan University, Ramat-Gan, Israel
`dror.rawitz@biu.ac.il`

Abstract. A DISTANCE REALIZATION problem asks, given an $n \times n$ matrix D of nonnegative integers, to find an n-vertex graph G and an integral weight function on the edges realizing D, i.e., such that $dist_G(i, j)$, the weighted distance from i to j, equals $D_{i,j}$ for every i and j, or decide that no such realizing graph exists. This paper introduces and studies the MINIMUM DEVIATION DISTANCE REALIZATION optimization problem, where given a matrix D, the goal is to find a weighted graph (G, w) that realizes D as closely as possible, i.e., such that the *deviation* $\phi(D, G)$ between D and the matrix of pairwise distances in G is minimized. We focus on four different types of deviation functions ϕ: the maximum difference over all matrix entries, ϕ_{MAX}, the sum of differences of all matrix entries, ϕ_{SUM}, the number of matrix entries exhibiting a mismatch, ϕ_{NUM}, and the multiplicative difference over all matrix entries, ϕ_{MULT}. For each deviation function ϕ, we consider the following variants of minimum deviation distance realization problems: (i) The deviation of the realizing graph (G, w) from the matrix D is allowed to be only upwards, only downwards, or in both directions; and (ii) The entries of D may specify exact values or *ranges* of permissible values. For each problem in this wide spectrum of variants, we either present a polynomial-time algorithm or show hardness and give a polynomial-time approximation algorithm.

Keywords: Distance realization · Approximate realization · Approximation algorithms · LP-rounding · Range realization

1 Introduction

1.1 Background and Motivation

The DISTANCE REALIZATION problem is a natural network design problem, where given a matrix specifying the desired requirements on distances between

This work was supported by US-Israel BSF grant 2022205.

C. Georgiou (Ed.): SIROCCO 2026, LNCS 16488, pp. 73–92, 2026.
https://doi.org/10.1007/978-3-032-26465-7_5

nodes, it is required to find a graph compatible with the specification. The output graph is said to be a *realization* of the given matrix. Network realization algorithms (and in particular, DISTANCE REALIZATION algorithms) can be used in different contexts, including engineering applications, where the input represents a specification given by the client, and science applications, where the network exists but is unknown to us, and we try to learn its structure based on a set of given experimental measurements.

In the *precise* DISTANCE REALIZATION problem, the given input is an $n \times n$ symmetric matrix D, such that each entry $D_{i,j} \in \mathbb{N}^+ \cup \{\infty\}$, for $1 \le i < j \le n$, and $D_{i,i} = 0$, for every $1 \le i \le n$. We view $D_{i,j}$ as specifying the required (minimum) distance between the vertices i and j in the network. A pair consisting of an undirected graph $G = (V, E)$ and a weight function $w : E \to \mathbb{N}^+$ on the edges is a *realization* of D, if $dist_G(i,j) = D_{i,j}$, for every $i < j$, where $dist_G(i,j)$ denotes the distance between i and j in G. In the *range* DISTANCE REALIZATION problem, each entry in the matrix D, for $i < j$, specifies a *range* $[D_{i,j}^-, D_{i,j}^+]$, and a realizing pair (G, w) must satisfy $D_{i,j}^- \le dist_G(i,j) \le D_{i,j}^+$, for every $i < j$.

Note that an alternative definition for the problem, studied for instance in [7], may use *fractional* (rather than integral) weights. Depending on the context, both variants may be of interest. Specifically, in many engineering contexts, it may be appropriate to design networks with non-integral weights. In some scientific contexts, however, one may be required to cope with the need to reconstruct an (existing) network involving integer distances. This can happen in a variety of situations. For example, one of the applications of distance realization is Phylogenetic trees, where the distance between two nodes (representing different species) is measured by the number of mutations. In other cases, the distance between nodes may be measured in wire segments, hops (e.g., in VPNs) or any other integral units. In this work we address this kind of situations, hence we study the problem variant where the edge lengths of the realizing graph are required to be integral. We remark that in many cases, the fractional variant of a problem is computationally easy whereas integrality constraints make it harder.

The above realization problems are *exact*, in the sense that a pair (G, w) is considered a feasible realization for the input matrix D only if all the constraints are met. In certain settings, this might be too rigid. In particular, the distance specification matrix might be infeasible, and yet it may be desirable to find a graph that "roughly" realizes it. Consequently, in this paper we are interested in *relaxed* variants of distance realization problems, where the realization is allowed to violate some of the constraints, and the goal is to minimize those deviations.

Let ϕ be a *deviation function*, which for every distance matrix D and a pair (G, w) gives a nonnegative value indicating the deviation of the pairwise distances in G from the distance matrix D. We consider four deviation functions (which are described using range terminology):

1. $\phi_{\mathrm{MAX}}(D, G) = \max_{i,j} \max\{0, D_{i,j}^- - dist_G(i,j),\ dist_G(i,j) - D_{i,j}^+\}$ is the maximum difference of a matrix entry (i.e., the ℓ_∞-norm in the precise case).

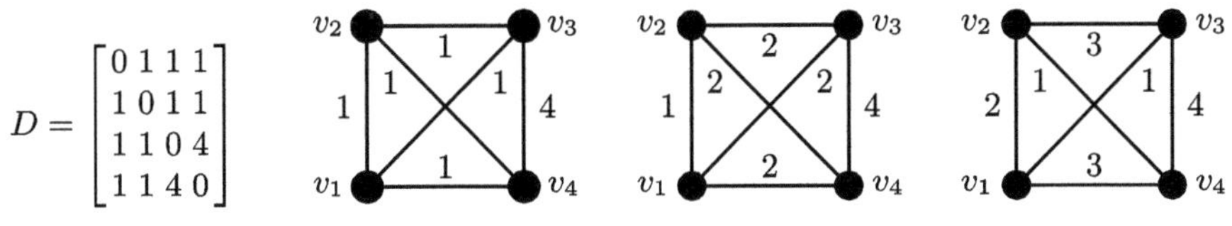

(a) Input matrix.   (b) Realization #1.   (c) Realization #2.   (d) Realization #3.

Fig. 1. Depiction of realizations related to Example 1.

2. $\phi_{\text{SUM}}(D,G) = \sum_{i<j} \max\{0, D_{i,j}^- - dist_G(i,j), \; dist_G(i,j) - D_{i,j}^+\}$ is the sum of differences of all matrix entries (i.e., the ℓ_1-norm in the precise case).

3. $\phi_{\text{NUM}}(D,G) = |\{(i,j) \mid i < j, \; dist_G(i,j) \notin [D_{i,j}^-, D_{i,j}^+]\}|$ is the number of matrix entries exhibiting a mismatch, i.e., for which the range $[D_{i,j}^-, D_{i,j}^+]$ and $dist_G(i,j)$ disagree (sometimes called the ℓ_0-norm).

4. $\phi_{\text{MULT}} = \max_{i,j}\{D_{i,j}^-/dist_G(i,j), \; dist_G(i,j)/D_{i,j}^+, \; 1\}$ is the maximum ratio, or multiplicative difference, of a matrix entry.

The MINIMUM DEVIATION DISTANCE REALIZATION (MD^{2}R) problem is defined as follows. Given a deviation function ϕ and a matrix D, find a graph G and a weight function w such that $\phi(D,G)$ is minimized.

We consider different variants of MD^{2}R denoted MD^{2}R$(\phi, D_{type}, O_{type})$, which are categorized by three parameters:

- $\phi \in \{\phi_{\text{MAX}}, \phi_{\text{SUM}}, \phi_{\text{NUM}}, \phi_{\text{MULT}}\}$, the deviation function.
- $D_{type} \in \{\mathsf{P}, [\,]\}$ indicates whether the matrix D specifies precise values or ranges.
- $O_{type} \in \{\uparrow, \downarrow, \updownarrow\}$ indicates whether the realization (G, w) is allowed to deviate from the matrix D only *upwards* (i.e., (G, w) is feasible only if $dist_G(i,j) \geq D_{i,j}$ for every $i < j$), only *downwards*, or in both directions. (A realization deviating from the constraints in a "forbidden" direction is deemed infeasible.)

Example 1. Consider the distance matrix D in Fig. 1a. Figure 1b describes an optimal realization for MD^{2}R$(\phi, \mathsf{P}, \downarrow)$, for $\phi \in \{\phi_{\text{MAX}}, \phi_{\text{SUM}}, \phi_{\text{NUM}}, \phi_{\text{MULT}}\}$. All distances are equal to 1, except the distance from v_3 to v_4 which is 2. Hence, the deviations of ϕ_{MAX}, ϕ_{SUM}, ϕ_{NUM}, and ϕ_{MULT} are 2, 2, 1, and 2, respectively. Figure 1c shows an optimal realization for MD^{2}R$(\phi, \mathsf{P}, \uparrow)$, where $\phi \in \{\phi_{\text{MAX}}, \phi_{\text{SUM}}, \phi_{\text{MULT}}\}$. In this case, $dist(v_1, v_2) = 1$, $dist(v_3, v_4) = 4$, and all other distances are 2. The deviations of ϕ_{MAX}, ϕ_{SUM}, and ϕ_{MULT} are 1, 4, and 2, respectively. Finally, Fig. 1d describes an optimal realization for MD^{2}R$(\phi_{\text{NUM}}, \mathsf{P}, \uparrow)$. In this case, $dist(v_1, v_3) = dist(v_2, v_4) = 1$, $dist(v_1, v_2) = 2$, $dist(v_1, v_4) = dist(v_2, v_3) = 3$, and $dist(v_3, v_4) = 4$. The deviation with respect to ϕ_{NUM} is 3.

1.2 Related Work

Precise Distance realization problems, where the realizing graph G must satisfy $dist_G(i,j) = D_{i,j}$ for every $i < j$, were first considered and solved by Hakimi and Yau [19]. Patrinos and Hakimi [25] considered the case where weights can be negative. Distance realization by weighted trees was considered by Baldisserri [2], who presented a characterization for realizability. For unweighted trees, there is a straightforward realization algorithm, based on the algorithm of [19] and on the fact that the realization, if it exists, is unique. Distance realization by bipartite graphs was studied in [5], where it was observed that it is sufficient to check the unique realization or the (inclusion-wise) minimal realization, in both the unweighted and weighted cases. Criteria for realization by graphs from several additional graph families were given in [3].

The distance realization problem was studied also for *distance ranges*. Tamura et al. [31] obtained necessary and sufficient conditions for the realizability of a range distance matrix. A polynomial-time realizability algorithm was given in [26]. A more general distance realization problem, where $D_{i,j}$, for each pair i and j, is a *set* of possible distances, rather than a contiguous range, was considered in [6].

The *optimal distance realization* problem was also introduced and studied in [19]. In this problem, a distance matrix D is given over a set S of n terminal vertices, and the goal is to find a *minimum-weight* graph G containing S, with possibly additional *auxiliary* vertices, that realizes the given D for S. In contrast, our minimum deviation distance realization problem requires the realizing graph to have exactly n vertices, and does not allow adding auxiliary ones. The optimal distance realization problem and some related problems were studied further in $[1,4,8\text{--}11,13,16,20,24,27\text{--}30,32,35]$.

Variants of $\mathrm{MD^2R}(\phi, \mathsf{P}, O_{type})$, for $\phi \in \{\phi_{\mathrm{MAX}}, \phi_{\mathrm{SUM}}\}$ were studied in [7]. They considered the Metric Nearness problem in which the input is a weighted complete graph, and the goal is to modify the weights resulting in a metric graph. Metric Nearness and $\mathrm{MD^2R}$ are closely related, but there are two main differences. The first difference is that in $\mathrm{MD^2R}$ the weights of the realizing graph G are *not* required to satisfy the triangle inequality, i.e., its distance matrix and its weight matrix may be different. However, given a realization (G, w), one can easily compute a weight function w', such that (G, w') is a realization and w' is a metric (see Observation 2). The second difference is that in the Metric Nearness problem the input and output need not be integral. As demonstrated by our results, the addition of integrality constraints may render a problem computationally harder. The ϕ_{SUM} and ϕ_{MAX} versions of Metric Nearness were studied in [7] and were given linear programs that solve both problems.

The variant of Metric Nearness where the deviation is measured under ϕ_{NUM} was studied in [15,17]. It is called the Metric Violation Distance (MVD) problem. That is, they considered variants of $\mathrm{MD^2R}(\phi_{\mathrm{NUM}}, \mathsf{P}, O_{type})$, for $O_{type} \in \{\uparrow, \downarrow, \updownarrow\}$. Both [15,17] proved that the downwards version of MVD is polynomial time solvable. While Gilbert and Jain [17] focused on heuristics for the upwards and bidirectional deviation versions, Fan et al. [15] showed that both are APX-hard using an approximation preserving reduction from VERTEX COVER. Note that VERTEX COVER cannot be approximated within a ratio less than $\sqrt{2}$, unless P = NP [12,21,22], and within a ratio less than 2, if the Unique Games Conjecture holds [23]. Fan et al. [15] also presented an $O(\sqrt[3]{\text{OPT}})$-approximation algorithm for both versions. Note that these algorithms do not apply to the corresponding MD^2R variants, since their computed output may be fractional. An extended version of this problem, where the input graph need not be complete, was studied in [14].

1.3 Our Results

We formalize the MINIMUM DEVIATION DISTANCE REALIZATION (MD^2R) problem and study a number of its variants. For each variant we either present a polynomial time algorithm for computing an optimal solution or prove that finding an optimal solution is APX-hard and give a polynomial-time approximation algorithm.

We give a polynomial time algorithm that solves each of the considered deviation functions (ϕ_{MAX}, ϕ_{SUM}, ϕ_{NUM}, and ϕ_{MULT}), when only downwards deviation $O_{type} = \ \downarrow$ is allowed. Our algorithm is similar to the algorithm for downwards MVD [15,17]. We show how to extend the algorithm to the range variants. We use a different approach to obtain a polynomial time algorithm that finds an optimal solution for the ϕ_{MAX} and the ϕ_{MULT} deviation functions, for every possible deviation direction, $O_{type} \in \{\updownarrow, \updownarrow\}$ for both the precise and range cases.

For all other variants, i.e., $\phi \in \{\phi_{\text{SUM}}, \phi_{\text{NUM}}\}$ with deviation allowed only upwards or in both directions (i.e., $O_{type} \in \{\uparrow, \updownarrow\}$), we show that the problem is computationally hard using an approximation preserving reduction from VERTEX COVER. Our reduction is an integral version of the reduction to MVD from   [15]. On the other hand, we give polynomial time approximation algorithms. In the precise case, the approximation ratio is a (linear or quadratic) function of $D_{\max} = \max_{i,j}\{D_{i,j}\}$, while in the range case, the ratio is a function of $D^-_{\max} = \max_{i,j}\{D^-_{i,j}\}$. Our approximation algorithms are based on LP-rounding. We note that the approximation ratio of all of our algorithms is at most n. Moreover, the fact that the distances are integral, and in particular the minimum distance is 1, implies that the approximation factor does not depend on the scale.

Table 1 summarizes the results for the MD^2R problems.

2 Preliminaries

Definitions and Notation. Let $G = (V, E)$ be a simple graph and let $w : E \to \mathbb{N}^+$ be a positive weight function on the edges. A path P in G is a sequence of edges $((v_1, u_1), \ldots, (v_k, u_k))$ such that $v_{i+1} = u_i$ for every $i \in \{1, \ldots, k - 1\}$. A path P is *simple* if all its vertices are distinct. The weight or length of a path P in G is $w(P) = \sum_{i=1}^{k} w(v_i, u_i)$.

Table 1. The symbol ✓ means solvable in polynomial time; ρ-apr means that there is a polynomial time ρ-approximation algorithm. Throughout, $K = \min\left\{D^-_{\max}, n\right\}$.

ϕ, D_{type} \ O_{type}	$\downarrow$	$\uparrow$	$\updownarrow$
$\phi_{\text{MAX}}, \{\mathsf{P},[\,]\}$		✓ (Thm. 2)	
$\phi_{\text{MULT}}, \{\mathsf{P},[\,]\}$		✓ (Thm. 3)	
$\phi_{\text{SUM}}, \{\mathsf{P},[\,]\}$	✓ (Thm. 1)	APX-hard (Thm. 4) $(K-1)$-apr (Thms. 6 & 7)	APX-hard (Thm. 5) $2K$-apr (Thms. 8 & 9)
$\phi_{\text{NUM}}, \mathsf{P}$		APX-hard (Thm. 4) $(K-1)$-apr (Thm. 10)	APX-hard (Thm. 5)
$\phi_{\text{NUM}}, [\,]$		APX-hard (Thm. 4) $(K-1)(D^-_{\max}-1)$-apr (Thm. 11)	$2K(D^-_{\max}-1)$-apr (Thm. 12 & 13)

Given an undirected graph G and a weight function $w : E \to \mathbb{N}^+$ on the edges, one may assume that $w(i,j) = \infty$, if $(i,j) \notin E$. Hence, w can be treated as a matrix. Let δ^w be the distance matrix induced by w, where $\delta^w_{i,j} = dist_w(i,j)$, for every $1 \le i, j \le n$. We omit the superscript w when it is clear from the context.

Note that the existence of an infinite weight in D may make it impossible to obtain a realization within the deviations ϕ_{MAX} and ϕ_{SUM} (e.g., an instance where $D_{1,2} = D_{2,3} = 1$, but $D_{2,3} = \infty$.). Nevertheless, a matrix representing a graph composed of several disconnected components can still be handled. More specifically, suppose that there exist pairwise disjoint subsets $I_1, \ldots, I_t$ such that $D_{i,j} = \infty$ if and only if $i \in I_p$ and $j \in I_q$ for $p \ne q$. Such a case can be identified using DFS, and then each subset can be solved separately.

Solution Properties. We show that one may consider only a certain kind of solutions, without loss of generality. This section is written in range terms, but it applies to the precise case as well. One only needs to recall that $D^-_{\max} = D^+_{\max} = D_{\max}$ in the precise case.

Definition 1. *For deviation types ϕ_{MAX}, ϕ_{NUM} and ϕ_{SUM}, define:*

1. In the downwards deviation case, every weighted graph (G, w) satisfying the constraints $\delta^w_{i,j} \le D^+_{i,j}$ for every $1 \le i < j \le n$ is feasible.
2. In the upwards deviation case, every weighted graph (G, w) satisfying the constraints $\delta^w_{i,j} \ge D^-_{i,j}$ for every $1 \le i < j \le n$ is feasible.
3. In the bi-directional deviation case, every weighted graph (G, w) is feasible.

The purpose of the next observation is to allow us to assume from now on that G is a complete graph, and to focus only on the weight function w.

Observation 1. *Given a feasible solution (G, w) with respect to D and a non-negative integer deviation Δ (under ϕ_{MAX}, ϕ_{NUM} or ϕ_{SUM}), there is a weight function w' that satisfies that $w'(i,j) \le D^-_{\max}$, for every i, j, and (K_n, w') is a feasible solution with deviation at most Δ.*

Proof. Given (G, w), define $w'(i, j) = \min\{w(i, j), D_{\max}^-\}$, for every i and j. Let P be a path from i to j. Clearly, $w'(P) \leq w(P)$. More specifically, if $w(e) \leq D_{\max}^-$ for all edges in P, then $w'(P) = w(P)$. Otherwise, there is at least one edge e in P such that $w(e) \geq D_{\max}^- + 1$. Hence, $w'(P) \geq D_{\max}^- \geq D_{i,j}^-$. It follows that

(a) If $w(P) \leq D_{i,j}^-$, then $w'(P) = w(P) \leq D_{i,j}^-$. That is, a path whose length is shorter than $D_{i,j}^-$ with respect to w has the same length with respect to w'.

(b) If $w(P) > D_{i,j}^-$, then $w'(P) \in [D_{i,j}^-, w(P)]$. That is, a path whose length is not shorter than $D_{i,j}^-$ with respect to w remains not shorter than $D_{i,j}^-$ with respect to w'.

Hence, $\delta_{i,j}^{w'} \leq \delta_{i,j}^{w}$, and moreover,

(i) If $\delta_{i,j}^{w} < D_{i,j}^-$, then $\delta_{i,j}^{w'} = \delta_{i,j}^{w}$ by (a) and (b).
(ii) If $\delta_{i,j}^{w} \in [D_{i,j}^-, D_{i,j}^+]$, then $\delta_{i,j}^{w'} \in [D_{i,j}^-, D_{i,j}^+]$ as well by (b).
(iii) If $\delta_{i,j}^{w} > D_{i,j}^+$, then $\delta_{i,j}^{w'} \in [D_{i,j}^-, \delta_{i,j}^{w}]$ by (b).

It follows that, for every i and j, $\delta_{i,j}^{w'}$ may only get closer than $\delta_{i,j}^{w}$ to the range of i and j. Hence, (K_n, w') is feasible and its deviation is at most Δ. $\square$

Corollary 1. *Without loss of generality, given a feasible weighted graph (G, w) with respect to D and deviation Δ (under ϕ_{MAX}, ϕ_{NUM} or ϕ_{SUM}), one may assume that G is a clique and that $w(i, j) \leq D_{\max}^-$ for every i, j.*

The above observation implies that one may shrink the ranges as follows.

Corollary 2. *One may assume w.l.o.g. that $D_{i,j}^+ \leq D_{\max}^-$, for every $i < j$.*

3 Polynomially Solvable Problems

We first show that $\mathrm{MD}^2\mathrm{R}(\phi, [\,], \downarrow)$ is solvable in polynomial time, for any deviation type. This implies the same for $\mathrm{MD}^2\mathrm{R}(\phi, \mathsf{P}, \downarrow)$. A similar algorithm was used for the downwards deviation version of METRIC VIOLATION DISTANCE in [15,17]. (Recall that this is a variant of $\mathrm{MD}^2\mathrm{R}(\phi_{\mathrm{NUM}}, \mathsf{P}, \downarrow)$ where the weights can be non-integral.) The crux is to construct a complete graph $\mathcal{G}$ and a weight function w such that $w(i, j) = D_{i,j}^+$, for every i and j. We prove that this downwards realization is optimal.

Theorem 1. $\mathrm{MD}^2\mathrm{R}(\phi, [\,], \downarrow)$ *is solvable in polynomial time for every deviation function* $\phi \in \{\phi_{\mathrm{MAX}}, \phi_{\mathrm{SUM}}, \phi_{\mathrm{NUM}}, \phi_{\mathrm{MULT}}\}$.

Proof. Given a distance matrix D with range specification, construct the clique graph $\mathcal{G}$ as follows. For every edge (i, j) assign the weight $w(i, j) = D_{i,j}^+$, for every i and j. By construction, $dist_{\mathcal{G}}(i, j) \leq D_{i,j}^+$ for every i and j, i.e., there are no upwards deviations in G. Hence, $\mathcal{G}$ is a feasible solution to $\mathrm{MD}^2\mathrm{R}(\phi, [\,], \downarrow)$.

We prove that every graph whose distance matrix deviates only downwards from D satisfies that for every i and j, the deviation of (i, j) is at least

$\max\{0, D_{i,j}^- - dist_{\mathcal{G}}(i,j)\}$, i.e., $\mathcal{G}$ is a minimum deviation graph. Let $\mathcal{G}'$ be a downwards realization of D. Consider a path $(i = v_0, \ldots, v_\ell = j)$ in $\mathcal{G}$ for which the total weight is $dist_{\mathcal{G}}(i,j)$. This path implies a set of requirements $D_{v_k, v_{k+1}}$, for $k \in \{0, \ldots, \ell-1\}$, such that the distance between v_k and v_{k+1} is at most $D_{v_k, v_{k+1}}^+ = w(v_k, v_{k+1})$. Since the realizing graph $\mathcal{G}'$ is not allowed to deviate upwards, the distance between i and j in $\mathcal{G}'$ is at most $dist_{\mathcal{G}}(i,j)$, i.e.,

$$\max\left\{0, D_{i,j}^- - dist_{\mathcal{G}'}(i,j)\right\} \geq \max\left\{0, D_{i,j}^- - dist_{\mathcal{G}}(i,j)\right\} .$$

$\square$

Next we show that $\mathrm{MD}^2\mathrm{R}(\phi, [\,], O_{type})$, for $\phi \in \{\phi_{\mathrm{MAX}}, \phi_{\mathrm{MULT}}\}$ and $O_{type} \in \{\uparrow, \updownarrow\}$, are solvable in polynomial time. Intuitively, since DISTANCE REALIZATION with ranges is solvable in polynomial time, and the goal is to minimize the maximum deviation, we can gradually expand the ranges (uniformly for all entries) and check realizability.

Theorem 2. $\mathrm{MD}^2\mathrm{R}(\phi_{\mathrm{MAX}}, [\,], \uparrow)$ *and* $\mathrm{MD}^2\mathrm{R}(\phi_{\mathrm{MAX}}, [\,], \updownarrow)$ *are solvable in polynomial time.*

Proof. Let D be a distance matrix with range specifications. Let $\Delta > 0$ be an (integer) additive deviation parameter. Define a distance matrix $D'(\Delta)$ in which the entry for i and j is the range $[D_{i,j}^-, D_{i,j}^+ + \Delta]$ (or $[\min\{1, D_{i,j}^- - \Delta\}, D_{i,j}^+ + \Delta]$, in the bidirectional case). Our goal is to find the minimum value of Δ for which $D'(\Delta)$ is realizable, and a realization G of $D'(\Delta)$.

Observe that a clique of n vertices where all edges have weight D_{max}^- is an upwards realization of $D'(\Delta)$. Hence the optimal additive upwards (bidirectional) deviation is between 0 and D_{max}^-. Over this range of values we perform a binary search. The number of inspected values in the binary search is $O(\log D_{\mathrm{max}}^-)$. Since D_{max}^- is part of the input, the number of iterations is polynomial in the input size. For each inspected value Δ, one can check the realizability of $D'(\Delta)$ (and find a realization if one exists) using the algorithm from [26, Thm. 10].

$\square$

Theorem 3. $\mathrm{MD}^2\mathrm{R}(\phi_{\mathrm{MULT}}, [\,], \uparrow)$ *and* $\mathrm{MD}^2\mathrm{R}(\phi_{\mathrm{MULT}}, [\,], \updownarrow)$ *are solvable in polynomial time.*

Proof. Given a distance matrix D with range specification, obviously, its minimum deviation $\phi_{\mathrm{MULT}}(D) \geq 1$, since for a realizable D it holds that $\phi_{\mathrm{MULT}}(D) = 1$, and otherwise $\phi_{\mathrm{MULT}}(D) > 1$, by definition. Let β be a multiplicative stretch parameter, such that every original entry $[D_{i,j}^-, D_{i,j}^+]$ of D is replaced with the range $[D_{i,j}^-/\beta, \beta D_{i,j}^+]$ (or $[D_{i,j}^-, \beta D_{i,j}^+]$ for only upwards deviation) in the transformed matrix D''. Our goal is to find the minimum value of β for which D'' is realizable, and a realization G of D''.

Unlike the additive deviation parameter, β is not necessarily an integer, since other values may induce integer entries in D''. For example, for $D_{i,j}^+ = 2$, if $\beta = 3/2$ then $\beta D_{i,j}^+ = 3$. Let $D^{\mathrm{all}} = \prod_{i \neq j} D_{i,j}^+$, let $\epsilon = 1/D^{\mathrm{all}}$, and observe that

$\beta D_{i,j}^{+}$ may be an integer only for $\beta = x \cdot \epsilon$, where x is an integer. For every $D_{i,j}^{-}$, $D_{i,j}^{-}/\beta$ may be an integer only for $\beta = D_{i,j}^{-}/x$, where x is an integer.

Recall that $D^{\max} = \max_{i,j}\{D_{i,j}^{-}\}$ is the highest lower bound of an entry in D. For $\beta = D^{\max}$, all entries of D'' include the value $D^{\max}$, and therefore D'' is realizable by a clique with edges of weight $D^{\max}$. It follows that $\phi_{\mathrm{MULT}}(D) \leq D^{\max}$. Since all entries of the input matrix are assumed to be integers, and we consider realizations with integral weights, the minimum deviation ϕ_{MULT} must be of the form $x \cdot \epsilon$, or of the form $D_{i,j}^{-}/x$ for some integer x.

For the first form, $x \cdot \epsilon$, there are at most $D^{\max} \cdot D^{\mathrm{all}}$ possible values for ϕ_{MULT}: $\epsilon, 2\epsilon, \ldots, (D^{\max} \cdot D^{\mathrm{all}})\epsilon$. Over this range of values we perform a binary search. The number of inspected values in the binary search is logarithmic in the number of possible values, i.e., $O(\log D^{\mathrm{all}})$. Since $D^{\mathrm{all}} \leq (D^{\max})^{n}$, the number of iterations is $O(n \log D^{\max})$, which is polynomial in the input. For each inspected value, we can check realizability of D'' (and find a realization if one exists) using the polynomial-time algorithm from [26, Thm. 10].

For the second form, $D_{i,j}^{-}/x$, there are at most $n^{2} \cdot D^{\max}$ possible values for ϕ_{MULT}: at most $D^{\max}$ for every entry. We perform a binary search over the range of possible values for every entry in $O(\log D^{\max})$ time.

Finally, $\phi_{\mathrm{MULT}}(D)$ is the minimum value we found over all binary searches. This concludes our polynomial-time algorithm for $\mathrm{MD}^{2}\mathrm{R}(\phi_{\mathrm{MULT}}, [\,], W, \updownarrow)$ (or $\mathrm{MD}^{2}\mathrm{R}(\phi_{\mathrm{MULT}}, [\,], W, \uparrow)$). $\qquad\square$

4 Hard Problems

In this section we prove that $\mathrm{MD}^{2}\mathrm{R}(\phi, \mathsf{P}, D_{type})$, for $\phi \in \{\phi_{\mathrm{SUM}}, \phi_{\mathrm{NUM}}\}$ and $D_{type} \in \{\uparrow, \updownarrow\}$, are APX-hard. These results extend to the range variants $\mathrm{MD}^{2}\mathrm{R}(\phi, [\,], D_{type})$, for $\phi \in \{\phi_{\mathrm{SUM}}, \phi_{\mathrm{NUM}}\}$ and $D_{type} \in \{\uparrow, \updownarrow\}$, in a straightforward manner.

The hardness result is obtained using approximation-preserving reductions from the VERTEX COVER problem, where the input is a graph $G = (V, E)$, and the goal is to find a minimum-size subset of vertices $C \subseteq V$ that covers all the edges, i.e., such that $C \cap e \neq \emptyset$, for every $e \in E$. VERTEX COVER cannot be approximated within a ratio less than $\sqrt{2}$, unless $\mathrm{P} = \mathrm{NP}$ [12, 21, 22], and within a ratio less than 2, if the Unique Games Conjecture holds [23]. Our reductions are integral versions of the reduction that was used for METRIC VIOLATION DISTANCE in [15].

We start with $\mathrm{MD}^{2}\mathrm{R}(\phi_{\mathrm{NUM}}, \mathsf{P}, \uparrow)$ and $\mathrm{MD}^{2}\mathrm{R}(\phi_{\mathrm{SUM}}, \mathsf{P}, \uparrow)$.

Theorem 4. $\mathrm{MD}^{2}\mathrm{R}(\phi_{\mathrm{NUM}}, \mathsf{P}, \uparrow)$ *and* $\mathrm{MD}^{2}\mathrm{R}(\phi_{\mathrm{SUM}}, \mathsf{P}, \uparrow)$ *are APX-hard.*

Proof. Given a graph $G = (V, E)$, where $n = |V|$, construct an $(n+1) \times (n+1)$ matrix D for i, j such that $i < j$ as follows:

$$D_{i,j} = \begin{cases} 3 & (i,j) \in E, \\ 2 & (i,j) \notin E \text{ and } i, j \leq n, \\ 1 & j = n + 1. \end{cases}$$

We show that a vertex cover C of G induces a realization $(\mathcal{G}, w)$ of D with deviation at most $|C|$, and that $(\mathcal{G}, w)$ realizing D induces a vertex cover C whose size is at most the deviation of $(\mathcal{G}, w)$, both with respect to ϕ_{NUM} and with respect to ϕ_{SUM}. Note that this reduction is approximation-preserving and it preserves the value of the optimum as well.

Let C be a vertex cover of G. Define the following realization $(\mathcal{G}, w)$ of D. Let $\mathcal{G} = (V', E')$ be a complete graph, where $V' = V \cup \{v_{n+1}\}$. In addition,

$$w(i,j) = \begin{cases} 3 & (i,j) \in E, \\ 2 & (i,j) \notin E \text{ and } i,j \leq n, \\ 2 & i \in C, j = n+1, \\ 1 & i \in V \setminus C, j = n+1. \end{cases}$$

Consider i and j.

- If $(i,j) \notin E$, then $\delta^w_{i,j} = w(i,j) = 2 = D_{i,j}$ as required.
- If $(i,j) \in E$, then either $i \in C$ or $j \in C$. Since $w(i,j) = 3$ and any other path contains at least two edges, it must be that $\delta^w_{i,j} \geq 2$. We claim that $\delta^w_{i,j} = w(i,j) = 3$. Suppose that $\delta^w_{i,j} < 3$. Then, there must be a 2-edge path from i to j through vertex $n+1$. However, either $w(i, n+1) = 2$ or $(j, n+1) = 2$, since either $i \in C$ or $j \in C$. A contradiction.
- If $j = n+1$, then $\delta^w_{i,j} = w(i,j) \geq 1 = D_{i,j}$, as required.

Hence, $(\mathcal{G}, w)$ is feasible upwards realization. Moreover, a deviation occurs only when $w(i, n+1) = 2$ for $i \in C$. Hence, the total deviation is at most $|C|$ both with respect to ϕ_{NUM} and with respect to ϕ_{SUM}.

For the other direction, let $(\mathcal{G}, w)$ be an upwards realization of D. Let $C = \{i : w(i, n+1) \geq 2\}$. We claim that C is a vertex cover in G. Consider an edge $(i,j) \in E$. It must be that $\delta^w_{i,j} \geq D_{i,j} = 3$. Hence, either $w(i, n+1) \geq 2$ or $w(j, n+1) \geq 2$, which means that either $i \in C$ or $j \in C$, as required. Also, notice that $|C|$ is not larger than the deviation of $(\mathcal{G}, w)$, both with respect to ϕ_{NUM} and with respect to ϕ_{SUM}. $\qquad\square$

A similar approach works for $\mathrm{MD}^2\mathrm{R}(\phi_{\mathrm{NUM}}, P, \updownarrow)$ and $\mathrm{MD}^2\mathrm{R}(\phi_{\mathrm{SUM}}, P, \updownarrow)$.

Theorem 5. $\mathrm{MD}^2\mathrm{R}(\phi_{\mathrm{NUM}}, P, \updownarrow)$ *and* $\mathrm{MD}^2\mathrm{R}(\phi_{\mathrm{SUM}}, P, \updownarrow)$ *are APX-hard.*

Proof. We use the same reduction as in the proof of Theorem 4. Showing that a vertex cover C induces a realization of deviation at most $|C|$ can be done as in the proof of Theorem 4. It remains to show that a bidirectional realization $(\mathcal{G}, w)$ of D with deviation Δ implies a vertex cover whose size is at most Δ.

Let $C = \{i : w(i, n+1) \geq 2\}$ and let $C' = \{i : (i,j) \in E, i < j, \delta^w_{i,j} \leq 2\}$. We claim that $C \cup C'$ is a vertex cover in G. Consider an edge $(i,j) \in E$, such that $i < j$. There are two options. If $\delta^w_{i,j} \geq D_{i,j} = 3$, then $w(i, n+1) + w(j, n+1) \geq 3$, which means that either $w(i, n+1) \geq 2$ or $w(j, n+1) \geq 2$, thus either $i \in C$ or $j \in C$. Otherwise, if $\delta^w_{i,j} \leq 2$, then $w(i, n+1) = 1$, $w(j, n+1) = 1$, and $w(i,j) \leq 2$. Hence, $i,j \notin C$ and $i \in C'$. As for the deviation, notice that each deviation is represented by a vertex in $C \cup C'$. It follows that $|C| + |C'|$ is bounded by the deviation of $(\mathcal{G}, w)$. $\qquad\square$

5 Approximation Algorithms

We turn to *approximate* realizations for MD^2R problems. We give approximation algorithms for the *precise* and *range* versions of the problem for both ϕ_{NUM} and ϕ_{SUM}. Throughout, the approximation ratios of our algorithms are expressed in terms of the parameter $K = \min\{D_{\max}^-, n\}$, where $D_{\max}^- = \max_{i,j}\{D_{i,j}^-\}$. (Recall that $D_{\max}^- = D_{\max}$ in the precise case.) We assume that $K \geq 2$, since otherwise the problem becomes trivial. Note that some of the proofs of this section were omitted for lack of space.

Observation 2. *Without loss of generality, given a weight function w that realizes D, one may assume that $w(i,j) = \delta_{i,j}^w$ for every i and j.*

Proof. Let w be a realization of D. By definition $w_{i,j} \geq \delta_{i,j}^w$ for every i and j. It is not hard to verify that $w' = \delta^w$ realizes D with the same deviation. Finally, notice that $w' = \delta^{w'}$. $\qquad\square$

Let $\mathcal{P}_{s,t}$ be the set of paths from s to t in the complete graph K_n, and let

$$\mathcal{P}_{s,t}^{<\ell} = \{P \in \mathcal{P}_{s,t} \mid P \text{ contains fewer than } \ell \text{ edges}\} .$$

The next observation implies that when computing $\delta_{s,t}^w = \min_{P \in \mathcal{P}_{s,t}} w(P)$, it suffices to consider "short" paths, for a suitable ℓ.

Observation 3. *For a feasible realization w of D, $\delta_{s,t}^w = \min_{P \in \mathcal{P}_{s,t}^{<K}} w(P)$ for any $s \neq t$, where $K = \min\{D_{\max}^-, n\} \geq 2$. If w is feasible with respect to $\mathcal{P}_{s,t}^{<K}$, then it is feasible.*

Proof. First, assume that $K = n$. Since edge weights are positive, a shortest path must be simple, with at most $n - 1$ edges. Therefore, $\delta_{s,t}^w = \min_{P \in \mathcal{P}_{s,t}^{<K}} w(P)$ in this case. Otherwise, $K = D_{\max}^-$. Notice that $\delta_{s,t}^w \leq w(s,t) \leq D_{\max}^-$, where the second inequality follows by Observation 1. If $\delta_{s,t}^w = D_{\max}^-$, then $\delta_{s,t}^w = w(s,t) = D_{\max}^-$, which means that there exists a shortest path containing a single edge. Otherwise, $\delta_{s,t}^w \leq D_{s,t}^- \leq D_{\max}^- - 1$, therefore $\delta_{s,t}^w = \min_{P \in \mathcal{P}_{s,t}^{<K}} w(P)$. Combining the two cases, the observation follows. $\qquad\square$

5.1 Sum of Upwards Differences

We start with the problem $MD^2R(\phi_{\mathrm{SUM}}, \mathsf{P}, \uparrow)$, whose goal is to minimize the objective function $\varphi(w) = \sum_{i<j}(\delta_{i,j}^w - D_{i,j})$. Recall that in this case, a weighted graph (G, w) is *feasible* if it satisfies the constraints $\delta_{i,j}^w \geq D_{i,j}$, for every $i < j$.

We show that $MD^2R(\phi_{\mathrm{SUM}}, \mathsf{P}, \uparrow)$ can be described using the following integer linear program (ILP) which has an integer variable $x_{i,j}$ for every $i < j$, which represents the difference between $w(i,j)$ and $D_{i,j}$. For any path P, let $x(P) =$

$\sum_{(i,j)\in P} x_{i,j}$ and $D(P) = \sum_{(i,j)\in P} D_{i,j}$. Recall that by Observation 3 we only need to look at paths with fewer than $K = \min\{D_{\max}, n\}$ edges.

$$\min \sum_{i<j} x_{i,j} \quad \text{s.t.} \begin{cases} x(P) \geq D_{s,t} - D(P), & \forall\, P \in \mathcal{P}_{s,t}^{<K}, \forall\, s < t, \\ 0 \leq x_{i,j} \leq D_{\max} - D_{i,j}, & \forall\, i < j, \\ x_{i,j} \in \mathbb{N}, & \forall\, i < j. \end{cases} \tag{1}$$

We first show that $\mathrm{MD}^2\mathrm{R}(\phi_{\mathrm{SUM}}, \mathsf{P}, \uparrow)$ and the ILP (1) are equivalent.

Lemma 4. *(i) If x is feasible for (1), then $w = x + D$ is a feasible realization for $\mathrm{MD}^2\mathrm{R}(\phi_{\mathrm{SUM}}, \mathsf{P}, \uparrow)$ and $\varphi(w) \leq \sum_{i<j} x_{i,j}$. (ii) If w is a feasible realization for $\mathrm{MD}^2\mathrm{R}(\phi_{\mathrm{SUM}}, \mathsf{P}, \uparrow)$, then $x = w - D$ is feasible for (1) and $\sum_{i<j} x_{i,j} = \varphi(w)$.*

Proof. Assume x is a feasible solution for (1) and $w = x + D$. Then the first constraint of (1) guarantees that $w(P) \geq D_{s,t}$, for any $P \in \mathcal{P}_{s,t}^{<K}$ and $s < t$. Observation 3 implies that (1) guarantees that $\delta_{s,t}^w \geq D_{s,t}$, for every $s < t$. Thus, w is a feasible solution for $\mathrm{MD}^2\mathrm{R}(\phi_{\mathrm{SUM}}, \mathsf{P}, \uparrow)$. Also, $\varphi(w) = \sum_{i<j}(\delta_{i,j}^w - D_{i,j}) \leq \sum_{i<j}(w(i,j) - D_{i,j}) = \sum_{i<j} x_{i,j}$.

Conversely, assume w is a feasible solution for $\mathrm{MD}^2\mathrm{R}(\phi_{\mathrm{SUM}}, \mathsf{P}, \uparrow)$. Then without loss of generality $w(i,j) \leq D_{\max}$, for every i and j, by Observation 1, and $w = \delta^w$ by Observation 2. As w is feasible, it allows only upwards deviations, which ensures that $x = w - D$ satisfies the constraints of the first type in (1). It also satisfies the constraints of the second type since $w(i,j) \leq D_{\max}$ for every i and j. Hence $x = w - D$ is a feasible solution for (1). Finally, $\sum_{i<j} x_{i,j} = \sum_{i<j}(\delta_{i,j}^w - D_{i,j}) = \varphi(w)$. $\qquad\square$

The LP-relaxation of (1) can be solved in polynomial time, even when K is nonconstant, using the ellipsoid method and a polynomial time separation oracle. Such a separation oracle, considers a solution to the LP, and either decides that it is feasible or find a constraint which is violated. (cf. [33, Section 12.3.1] and [34, Section 4.3]). In our case, observe that checking whether a solution satisfies the first set of constraints amounts to finding a shortest path that contains fewer than K edges, for every s and t, and this can be done using the Bellman-Ford algorithm.

We use LP-rounding on (1) to design an approximation algorithm for $\mathrm{MD}^2\mathrm{R}(\phi_{\mathrm{SUM}}, \mathsf{P}, \uparrow)$. Let (x^*, y^*) be an optimal fractional solution of (1). The idea is to round down $x_{i,j}^*$ if its non-integral part is smaller than $\frac{1}{K-1}$. Otherwise $x_{i,j}^*$ is rounded up. Let $\bar{x}_{i,j}$ be the rounded value of $x_{i,j}^*$, and for any path P, let $\bar{x}(P) = \sum_{(i,j)\in P} \bar{x}_{i,j}$. Also, $\bar{w}(i,j)$ is set to $D_{i,j} + \bar{x}_{i,j}$. (See Algorithm 1.)

Algorithm 1: Round ϕ_{SUM} Precise Up

---

1   Compute an optimal fractional solution (x^*, y^*) of (1)

2   **forall** $1 \leq i < j \leq n$ **do**

3     $\bar{x}_{i,j} \leftarrow \left\lfloor x_{i,j}^* + \frac{K-2}{K-1} \right\rfloor$

4     $\bar{w}(i,j) \leftarrow D_{i,j} + \bar{x}_{i,j}$

Theorem 6. $\mathrm{MD}^2\mathrm{R}(\phi_{\mathrm{SUM}}, P, \uparrow)$ *has a* $(K-1)$-*approximation algorithm.*

Proof. We first show that $\bar{x}$ is a feasible solution of (1). Let $\ell_{i,j} = x^*_{i,j} - \bar{x}_{i,j}$ and for any path P, let $\ell(P) = \sum_{(i,j)\in P} \ell_{i,j}$. Consider the vertices s, t, and path $P \in \mathcal{P}^{<K}_{s,t}$. Since (x^*, y^*) is feasible, we have $D(P) + \bar{x}(P) + \ell(P) = D(P) + x^*(P) \geq D_{s,t}$. Now $|P| \leq K-1$ implies that $\ell(P) < 1$, and therefore $D(P) + \bar{x}(P) \geq D_{s,t} - \ell(P) > D_{s,t} - 1$. Hence, $w(P) = \bar{x}(P) + D(P) \geq D_{s,t}$. By Lemma 4, $\bar{w}$ is a feasible realization of D. Also, $\varphi(\bar{w}) = \sum_{i,j} \bar{x}_{i,j} \leq (K-1)\sum_{i,j} x^*_{i,j} \leq (K-1)\sum_{i,j} x^I_{i,j}$, where x^I is an optimal integral solution of (1). By Lemma 4, $\bar{x}$ is $(K-1)$-approximate. $\qquad\square$

Next, consider approximating $\mathrm{MD}^2\mathrm{R}(\phi_{\mathrm{SUM}}, [\,], \uparrow)$. In this case, a feasible realization is a weight function w, such that $\delta^w_{i,j} \geq D^-_{i,j}$, for every i and j. The goal is to find a weight function w minimizing the objective function $\varphi(w) = \sum_{i,j} \max\{0, \delta_{i,j} - D^+_{i,j}\}$

Denote the *range width* by $r_{i,j} = D^+_{i,j} - D^-_{i,j}$ for any $i < j$. The following ILP extends (1). Similarly to (1), $x_{i,j}$ represents the difference between $w(i,j)$ and $D^-_{i,j}$. The variable $y_{i,j}$ captures the deviation of $\delta^w_{i,j}$.

$$\min \ \sum_{i,j} y_{i,j} \quad \text{s.t.} \quad \begin{cases} x(P) \geq D^-_{s,t} - D^-(P), & \forall\, P \in \mathcal{P}^{<K}_{s,t}, \forall\, s < t, \\ y_{i,j} \geq x_{i,j} - r_{i,j}, & \forall\, i < j, \\ 0 \leq x_{i,j} \leq D^-_{\max} - D^-_{i,j}, & \forall\, i < j, \\ y_{i,j} \geq 0, & \forall\, i < j. \end{cases} \tag{2}$$

We show that $\mathrm{MD}^2\mathrm{R}(\phi_{\mathrm{SUM}}, [\,], \uparrow)$ and the program (2) are equivalent.

Lemma 5. *(i) If* (x, y) *is a feasible solution for* (2)*, then* $w = x + D^-$ *is a feasible realization for* $\mathrm{MD}^2\mathrm{R}(\phi_{\mathrm{SUM}}, [\,], \uparrow)$*, and* $\varphi(w) \leq \sum_{i,j} y_{i,j}$*. (ii) If* w *is a feasible realization for* $\mathrm{MD}^2\mathrm{R}(\phi_{\mathrm{SUM}}, [\,], \uparrow)$*, then* $x = w - D^-$*,* $y = \max\{0, w - D^+\}$ *is a feasible solution for* (2) *and* $\sum_{i,j} y_{i,j} = \varphi(w)$*.*

Proof. If (x, y) is a feasible solution of (2), then $w(P) \geq D^-_{s,t}$, for any $P \in \mathcal{P}^{<K}_{s,t}$ and $s < t$. Moreover, $\delta^w_{s,t} \geq D^-_{s,t}$, for any $s < t$, by Observation 3. Hence, w is a feasible solution for $\mathrm{MD}^2\mathrm{R}(\phi_{\mathrm{SUM}}, [\,], W, \uparrow)$. In addition,

$$\varphi(w) = \sum_{i<j} \max\{0, \delta^w_{i,j} - D^+_{i,j}\} \leq \sum_{i<j} \max\{0, w(i,j) - D^+_{i,j}\} = \sum_{i<j} y_{i,j}\ .$$

On the other hand, we may assume without loss of generality that $w(i,j) \leq D^-_{\max}$, for every i and j, by Observation 1, and that w is the distance matrix by Observation 2. Since w is feasible, it allows only upwards deviations, which ensures that $x = w - D^-$ satisfies the constraints of the first type in (2). The second type of constraints are satisfied by definition of y. It also satisfies the constraints of the third type since $w(i,j) \leq D^-_{\max}$ for every i and j. Hence (x, y) is a feasible solution for (2). Also,

$$\sum_{i<j} y_{i,j} = \sum_{i<j} \max\{0, w(i,j) - D^+_{i,j}\} = \sum_{i<j} \max\{0, \delta^w_{i,j} - D^+_{i,j}\} = \varphi(w)\ .$$

$\qquad\square$

We use LP-rounding on (2) to design an algorithm for $\mathrm{MD^2R}(\phi_{\mathrm{SUM}}, [\,], \uparrow)$. Similarly to (1), this LP is solvable in polynomial time using a separation oracle that computes a shortest path containing less than K edges, for every s and t. Let (x^*, y^*) be an optimal fractional solution of (2). As in the precise case, the idea is to round down $x^*_{i,j}$ if its non-integral part is smaller than $\frac{1}{K-1}$. Otherwise $x^*_{i,j}$ is rounded up. Let $\bar{x}_{i,j}$ be the rounded value to $x^*_{i,j}$. Variable $\bar{y}_{i,j}$ is set to $\max\{\bar{x}_{i,j} - r_{i,j}, 0\}$ and $\bar{w}(i,j)$ is set to $D^-_{i,j} + \bar{x}_{i,j}$. (See Algorithm 2.) Since $x^*_{i,j}$ is rounded down only if its non-integral part is strictly smaller than $\frac{1}{K-1}$, the total decrease of the left-hand side of an inequality that corresponds to a path containing at most $K-1$ edges is below 1. Thus, $(\bar{x}, \bar{y})$ is feasible.

Algorithm 2: Round ϕ_{SUM} Range Up

---

1 Compute an optimal fractional solution (x^*, y^*) of (2)
2 **forall** $1 \le i < j \le n$ **do**
3 $\quad$ $\bar{x}_{i,j} \leftarrow \left\lfloor x^*_{i,j} + \frac{K-2}{K-1} \right\rfloor$ and $\bar{y}_{i,j} \leftarrow \max\{\bar{x}_{i,j} - r_{i,j}, 0\}$
4 $\quad$ $\bar{w}(i,j) \leftarrow D^-_{i,j} + \bar{x}_{i,j}$

Theorem 7. $\mathrm{MD^2R}(\phi_{\mathrm{SUM}}, [\,], \uparrow)$ *has a* $(K-1)$*-approximation algorithm.*

Proof. We first show that $(\bar{x}, \bar{y})$ is a feasible solution of (2). Let $\ell_{i,j} = x^*_{i,j} - \bar{x}_{i,j}$. Consider the vertices s and t, and a path $P \in \mathcal{P}^{<K}_{s,t}$. Since (x^*, y^*) is feasible, we have that

$$D^-(P) + \bar{x}(P) + \ell(P) = D^-(P) + x^*(P) \ge D^-_{s,t} \ .$$

Since $|P| \le K - 1$ and $\ell_{i,j} < \frac{1}{K-1}$ by the rounding process, it follows that $\ell(P) < 1$, and we have that $D^-(P) + \bar{x}(P) \ge D^-_{s,t} - \ell(P) > D^-_{s,t} - 1$. Hence, $w(P) = \bar{x}(P) + D^-(P) \ge D^-_{s,t}$. By Lemma 5, $\bar{w}$ is a feasible realization of D.

Let $A = \{(i,j) : \bar{x}_{i,j} > r_{i,j}\}$. Observe that $y^*_{i,j} = x^*_{i,j} - r_{i,j}$, for every $(i,j) \in A$. Hence, $\bar{y}_{i,j} = \left\lfloor y^*_{i,j} + \frac{K-2}{K-1} \right\rfloor$, for every $(i,j) \in A$. It follows that

$$\varphi(\bar{w}) \le \sum_{i<j} \bar{y}_{i,j} \le (K-1) \sum_{i<j} y^*_{i,j} \le (K-1) \sum_{i<j} y^I_{i,j} \ ,$$

where (x^I, y^I) is an optimal integral solution of (2). Lemma 5 implies that $(\bar{x}, \bar{y})$ is $(K-1)$-approximate. $\qquad\square$

5.2   Sum of Bidirectional Differences

We now turn to problems allowing both upwards and downwards deviations ($\updownarrow$). We first present an approximation algorithm for the precise problem $\mathrm{MD^2R}(\phi_{\mathrm{SUM}}, \mathrm{P}, \updownarrow)$, where the goal is to find a weight function w minimizing the objective function $\varphi(w) = \sum_{i<j} |\delta_{i,j} - D_{i,j}|$.

We write an ILP for $\mathrm{MD}^2\mathrm{R}(\phi_{\mathrm{SUM}}, \mathsf{P}, \updownarrow)$, with variable matrices x and y, where $x_{i,j}$ represents the deviation from $D_{i,j}$ and $y_{i,j}$ is the absolute value of $x_{i,j}$.

$$
\min \sum_{i<j} y_{i,j} \quad \text{s.t.} \quad
\begin{cases}
D(P) + x(P) \geq D_{s,t} + x_{s,t}, & \forall\, P \in \mathcal{P}_{s,t}^{<K}, \forall\, s < t \\
y_{i,j} \geq x_{i,j}, & \forall\, i < j \\
y_{i,j} \geq -x_{i,j}, & \forall\, i < j \\
1 \leq x_{i,j} + D_{i,j} \leq D_{\max}, & \forall\, i < j \\
x_{i,j}, y_{i,j} \in \mathbb{Z}, & \forall\, i < j
\end{cases}
\tag{3}
$$

We show that $\mathrm{MD}^2\mathrm{R}(\phi_{\mathrm{SUM}}, \mathsf{P}, \updownarrow)$ and the ILP (3) are equivalent.

Lemma 6. *(i) If (x, y) is a feasible solution of (3), then $w = D + x$ is a feasible realization of $\mathrm{MD}^2\mathrm{R}(\phi_{\mathrm{SUM}}, \mathsf{P}, \updownarrow)$ and $\varphi(w) \leq \sum_{i<j} y_{i,j}$. (ii) If w is a feasible realization of $\mathrm{MD}^2\mathrm{R}(\phi_{\mathrm{SUM}}, \mathsf{P}, \updownarrow)$, then (x, y), where $x = w - D$ and $y_{i,j} = |x_{i,j}|$, for every i and j, is a feasible solution of (3) and $\sum_{i<j} y_{i,j} = \varphi(w)$.*

Consider the following LP-rounding algorithm. Let (x^*, y^*) be an optimal fractional solution of (3). As before, this LP is solvable in polynomial time using a separation oracle that computes a shortest path that contains fewer than K edges, for every s and t. Here we round down $x_{i,j}^*$ if its non-integral part is smaller than $1/K$. Otherwise $x_{i,j}^*$ is rounded up. Moreover, $\bar{w}(i,j)$ is set to $D_{i,j} + \bar{x}_{i,j}$. (See Algorithm 3.)

Algorithm 3: Round ϕ_{SUM} Precise Up&Down

---

1 Compute an optimal fractional solution (x^*, y^*) of (3)
2 **forall** $1 \leq i < j \leq n$ **do**
3     $\bar{x}_{i,j} \leftarrow \lfloor x_{i,j}^* + \frac{K-1}{K} \rfloor$
4     $\bar{w}(i,j) \leftarrow D_{i,j} + \bar{x}_{i,j}$

Theorem 8. $\mathrm{MD}^2\mathrm{R}(\phi_{\mathrm{SUM}}, \mathsf{P}, \updownarrow)$ *has a $2K$-approximation algorithm.*

Finally, we consider the range problem $\mathrm{MD}^2\mathrm{R}(\phi_{\mathrm{SUM}}, [\,], \updownarrow)$, seeking a weight function w that minimizes $\varphi(w) = \sum_{i,j} \max\{0, \delta_{i,j}^w - D_{i,j}^+, D_{i,j}^- - \delta_{i,j}^w\}$.

ILP (4) extends (3) to the range case. Recall that $r_{i,j} = D_{i,j}^+ - D_{i,j}^-$, for every $i < j$. As in (3), $x_{i,j}$ represents the difference between $w(i,j)$ and $D_{i,j}^-$, while $y_{i,j}$ stands for the deviation associated with the pair (i,j).

$$
\min \sum_{i,j} y_{i,j} \quad \text{s.t.} \quad
\begin{cases}
D^-(P) + x(P) \geq D_{s,t}^- + x_{s,t}, & \forall\, P \in \mathcal{P}_{s,t}^{<K}, \forall\, s < t \\
y_{i,j} \geq x_{i,j} - r_{i,j}, & \forall\, i < j \\
y_{i,j} \geq -x_{i,j}, & \forall\, i < j \\
1 \leq x_{i,j} + D_{i,j}^- \leq D_{\max}^-, & \forall\, i < j \\
x_{i,j} \in \mathbb{Z}, y_{i,j} \in \mathbb{N}, & \forall\, i < j
\end{cases}
\tag{4}
$$

We show that $\mathrm{MD}^2\mathrm{R}(\phi_{\mathrm{SUM}}, [\,], \updownarrow)$ and the ILP (4) are equivalent.

Lemma 7. *(i) If (x, y) is a feasible solution of (4), then $w = D^- + x$ is feasible for $\mathrm{MD}^2\mathrm{R}(\phi_{\mathrm{SUM}}, [\,], \updownarrow)$ and $\varphi(w) \leq \sum_{i<j} y_{i,j}$. (ii) If w is a feasible realization of $\mathrm{MD}^2\mathrm{R}(\phi_{\mathrm{SUM}}, [\,], \updownarrow)$, then (x, y), where $x = w - D^-$ and $y_{i,j} = \max\{0, \delta^w_{i,j} - D^+_{i,j}, D^-_{i,j} - \delta^w_{i,j}\}$, for every i and j, is a feasible solution of (4) and $\sum_{i<j} y_{i,j} = \varphi(w)$.*

Consider the following LP-rounding algorithm. As before, this LP is solvable in polynomial time using a separation oracle that computes a shortest path containing less than K edges, for every s and t. Given a fractional optimal solution (x^*, y^*) of (4), it uses a rounding approach similar to the case of $\mathrm{MD}^2\mathrm{R}(\phi_{\mathrm{SUM}}, \mathsf{P}, \updownarrow)$ to create $\bar{x}$, but it does not actually compute an integral solution for (4). Weight $\bar{w}(i, j)$ is set to $D^-_{i,j} + \bar{x}_{i,j}$. (See Algorithm 4.)

Algorithm 4: Round ϕ_{SUM} Range Up&Down

---

1 Compute an optimal fractional solution (x^*, y^*) of (4)
2 **forall** $1 \leq i < j \leq n$ **do**
3 $\quad$ $\bar{x}_{i,j} \leftarrow \left\lfloor x^*_{i,j} + \frac{K-1}{K} \right\rfloor$
4 $\quad$ $\bar{w}(i, j) \leftarrow D^-_{i,j} + \bar{x}_{i,j}$

Theorem 9. $\mathrm{MD}^2\mathrm{R}(\phi_{\mathrm{SUM}}, [\,], \updownarrow)$ *has a $2K$-approximation algorithm.*

5.3   Number of Upwards Mismatches

Consider the number of upwards mismatches, namely $\mathrm{MD}^2\mathrm{R}(\phi_{\mathrm{NUM}}, \mathsf{P}, \uparrow)$. In this problem the goal is to minimize $\psi(w) = |\{(i, j) : \delta_{i,j} > D_{i,j}, \ i < j\}|$.

$\mathrm{MD}^2\mathrm{R}(\phi_{\mathrm{NUM}}, \mathsf{P}, \uparrow)$ can be described using the following ILP with the binary variables $z_{i,j}$, for every $i < j$, where $z_{i,j} = 1$ represents a deviation related to the pair (i, j).

$$\min \ \sum_{i<j} z_{i,j} \quad \text{s.t.} \begin{cases} z(P) \geq 1, & \forall\, P \in \mathcal{P}^{<K}_{s,t} \ \text{s.t.}\ D_{s,t} > D(P), \forall\, s < t, \\ z_{i,j} \in \{0, 1\}, & \forall i < j. \end{cases} \tag{5}$$

The key observation here is that, while (5) does not generate a solution to $\mathrm{MD}^2\mathrm{R}(\phi_{\mathrm{NUM}}, \mathsf{P}, \uparrow)$, it does provide the necessary indications on which weights $w_{i,j}$ need to be corrected. In this sense, $\mathrm{MD}^2\mathrm{R}(\phi_{\mathrm{NUM}}, \mathsf{P}, \uparrow)$ and (5) are equivalent. This is shown formally in the next lemma.

Lemma 8. *(i) If z is a feasible solution of (5), then $w = D + (K - 1)z$ is a feasible solution of $\mathrm{MD}^2\mathrm{R}(\phi_{\mathrm{NUM}}, \mathsf{P}, \uparrow)$ and $\psi(w) \leq \sum_{i<j} z_{i,j}$. (ii) If w is a feasible solution of $\mathrm{MD}^2\mathrm{R}(\phi_{\mathrm{NUM}}, \mathsf{P}, \uparrow)$, then the Boolean matrix z, such that $z_{i,j} = 1$ if and only if $w(i, j) > D_{i,j}$, is a feasible solution of (5) and $\sum_{i<j} z_{i,j} = \psi(w)$.*

Observe that (5) is a SET COVER instance. Therefore, its relaxation is solvable in polynomial time using a separation oracle that computes a shortest path containing less than K edges, for every s and t [18].

Theorem 10. $\mathrm{MD}^2\mathrm{R}(\phi_{\mathrm{NUM}}, \mathsf{P}, \uparrow)$ *has a* $(K-1)$-*approximation algorithm.*

Next we consider the range variant, $\mathrm{MD}^2\mathrm{R}(\phi_{\mathrm{NUM}}, [\,], \uparrow)$, in which a weight function w is feasible if $\delta_{i,j}^w \geq D_{i,j}^-$, for every $i < j$, and the goal is to minimize $\psi(w) = |\{(i,j) : \delta_{i,j}^w > D_{i,j}^+,\ i < j\}|$.

We write an integer linear program for $\mathrm{MD}^2\mathrm{R}(\phi_{\mathrm{NUM}}, [\,], \uparrow)$:

$$\min \ \sum_{i,j} z_{i,j} \quad \text{s.t.} \quad \begin{cases} D^-(P) + x(P) \ \geq\ D_{s,t}^-, & \forall\, P \in \mathcal{P}_{s,t}^{<K}, \forall\, s < t, \\ (D_{\max}^- - 1)z_{i,j} \geq x_{i,j} - r_{i,j}, & \forall\, i < j, \\ 0 \leq x_{i,j} \leq D_{\max}^- - D_{i,j}^-, & \forall\, i < j, \\ x_{i,j} \in \mathbb{N}, z_{i,j} \in \{0,1\} & \forall\, i < j. \end{cases} \tag{6}$$

Notice that in the precise case (i.e., $D^- = D^+$), $x_{i,j} > 0$ implies $z_{i,j} = 1$. Hence, this program extends (5). We show that $\mathrm{MD}^2\mathrm{R}(\phi_{\mathrm{NUM}}, [\,], \uparrow)$ and the ILP (6) are equivalent.

Lemma 9. *(i) If (x, z) is a feasible solution of (6), then $w = D^- + x$ is feasible for $\mathrm{MD}^2\mathrm{R}(\phi_{\mathrm{NUM}}, [\,], \uparrow)$ and $\psi(w) \leq \sum_{i<j} z_{i,j}$. If w is feasible for $\mathrm{MD}^2\mathrm{R}(\phi_{\mathrm{NUM}}, [\,], \uparrow)$, then (x, z), where $x_{i,j} = w(i,j) - D_{i,j}^-$, and $z_{i,j} = 1$ if and only if $w(i,j) > D_{i,j}^+$, for every $i < j$, is a feasible solution of (6) and $\sum_{i<j} z_{i,j} = \psi(w)$.*

We provide an LP-rounding algorithm for $\mathrm{MD}^2\mathrm{R}(\phi_{\mathrm{NUM}}, [\,], \uparrow)$. As before, (6) can be solved efficiently using a separation oracle. Let (x^*, y^*) be an optimal fractional solution of (6). As in the ϕ_{SUM} case, the idea is to round down $x_{i,j}^*$ if its non-integral part is smaller than $1/(K-1)$. Otherwise $x_{i,j}^*$ is rounded up. Let $\bar{x}_{i,j}$ be the rounded value to $x_{i,j}^*$. Variable $\bar{z}_{i,j}$ is set to 1 if and only is $\bar{x}_{i,j} > r_{i,j}$ and $\bar{w}(i,j)$ is set to $D_{i,j}^- + \bar{x}_{i,j}$. (See Algorithm 5.)

Algorithm 5: Round ϕ_{NUM} Range Up

---

1 Compute an optimal fractional solution (x^*, y^*) of (6)

2 **forall** $1 \leq i < j \leq n$ **do**

3    $\displaystyle \bar{x}_{i,j} \leftarrow \left\lfloor x_{i,j}^* + \frac{K-2}{K-1} \right\rfloor$ and $\bar{z}_{i,j} \leftarrow \begin{cases} 1 & \bar{x}_{i,j} > r_{i,j}, \\ 0 & \text{otherwise.} \end{cases}$

4    $\bar{w}(i,j) \leftarrow D_{i,j}^- + \bar{x}_{i,j}$

Theorem 11. $\mathrm{MD}^2\mathrm{R}(\phi_{\mathrm{NUM}}, [\,], \uparrow)$ *has a* $(K-1)(D_{\max}^- - 1)$-*approximation algorithm.*

5.4 Number of Bidirectional Mismatches

We move to consider two-way deviation. In $\mathrm{MD}^2\mathrm{R}(\phi_{\mathrm{NUM}}, \mathsf{P}, \updownarrow)$, the goal is to find a weight function w minimizing $\psi(w) = |\{(i,j) : |\delta_{i,j} - D_{i,j}| > 0, i < j\}|$.

We present an integer linear program for $\mathrm{MD}^2\mathrm{R}(\phi_{\mathrm{NUM}}, \mathsf{P}, \updownarrow)$:

$$\min \sum_{i,j} y_{i,j} \quad \text{s.t.} \quad \begin{cases} D(P) + x(P) \geq D_{s,t} + x_{s,t}, & \forall\, P \in \mathcal{P}^{<K}_{s,t}, \forall\, s < t \\ (D^-_{\max} - 1) \cdot z_{i,j} \geq x_{i,j}, & \forall\, i < j \\ (D^-_{\max} - 1) \cdot z_{i,j} \geq -x_{i,j}, & \forall\, i < j \\ 1 \leq x_{i,j} + D_{i,j} \leq D_{\max}, & \forall\, i < j \\ x_{i,j} \in \mathbb{Z}, z_{i,j} \in \{0,1\}, & \forall\, i < j \end{cases} \tag{7}$$

Lemma 10. *(i) If (x,z) is a feasible solution of (7), then $w = D + x$ is feasible for $\mathrm{MD}^2\mathrm{R}(\phi_{\mathrm{NUM}}, \mathsf{P}, \updownarrow)$ and $\psi(w) \leq \sum_{i<j} z_{i,j}$. (ii) If w is a feasible solution of $\mathrm{MD}^2\mathrm{R}(\phi_{\mathrm{NUM}}, \mathsf{P}, \updownarrow)$, then (x,z), where $x_{i,j} = w(i,j) - D_{i,j}$, and $z_{i,j} = 1$ if and only if $w(i,j) \neq D_{i,j}$, for every $i < j$, is a feasible solution of (7) and $\sum_{i<j} z_{i,j} = \psi(w)$.*

Consider the following LP-rounding algorithm for $\mathrm{MD}^2\mathrm{R}(\phi_{\mathrm{NUM}}, \mathsf{P}, \updownarrow)$. As before (7) can be solved efficiently using a separation oracle. The rounding is done as in the case of $\mathrm{MD}^2\mathrm{R}(\phi_{\mathrm{SUM}}, \mathsf{P}, \updownarrow)$. (See Algorithm 6.)

Algorithm 6: Round ϕ_{NUM} Precise Up&Down

---

1 Compute an optimal fractional solution (x^*, z^*) of (7)
2 **forall** $1 \leq i < j \leq n$ **do**
3 $\quad \bar{x}_{i,j} \leftarrow \lfloor x^*_{i,j} + \frac{K-1}{K} \rfloor$
4 $\quad \bar{w}(i,j) \leftarrow D_{i,j} + \bar{x}_{i,j}$

Theorem 12. $\mathrm{MD}^2\mathrm{R}(\phi_{\mathrm{NUM}}, \mathsf{P}, \updownarrow)$ *has a $2K(D^-_{\max} - 1)$-approximation algorithm.*

Finally, we consider $\mathrm{MD}^2\mathrm{R}(\phi_{\mathrm{NUM}}, [\,], \updownarrow)$, where the goal is to compute a weight function w minimizing $\psi(W) = |\{(i,j) : \delta_{i,j} > D^+_{i,j} \text{ or } D^-_{i,j} > \delta_{i,j}\}|$.

We provide the following ILP for $\mathrm{MD}^2\mathrm{R}(\phi_{\mathrm{NUM}}, [\,], \updownarrow)$,

$$\min \sum_{i,j} z_{i,j} \quad \text{s.t.} \quad \begin{cases} D^-(P) + x(P) \geq D^-_{s,t} + x_{s,t}, & \forall\, P \in \mathcal{P}^{<K}_{s,t}, \forall\, s < t \\ (D^-_{\max} - 1) z_{i,j} \geq x_{i,j} - r_{i,j}, & \forall\, i < j \\ (D^-_{\max} - 1) z_{i,j} \geq -x_{i,j}, & \forall\, i < j \\ 1 \leq x_{i,j} + D^-_{i,j} \leq D^-_{\max}, & \forall\, i < j \\ x_{i,j} \in \mathbb{Z}, z_{i,j} \in \{0,1\}, & \forall\, i < j. \end{cases} \tag{8}$$

Lemma 11. *(i) If (x,z) is a feasible solution of (8), then $w = D^- + x$ is feasible for $\mathrm{MD}^2\mathrm{R}(\phi_{\mathrm{NUM}}, [\,], \updownarrow)$ and $\psi(w) \leq \sum_{i<j} z_{i,j}$. (ii) If w is feasible for $\mathrm{MD}^2\mathrm{R}(\phi_{\mathrm{NUM}}, [\,], \updownarrow)$, then (x,z), where $x_{i,j} = w(i,j) - D^-_{i,j}$, and $z_{i,j} = 1$ if and only if $w(i,j) \notin [D^-_{i,j}, D^+_{i,j}]$, for every $i < j$, is a feasible solution of (8) and $\sum_{i<j} z_{i,j} = \psi(w)$.*

Consider the following LP-rounding algorithm for $\mathrm{MD}^2\mathrm{R}(\phi_{\mathrm{NUM}}, [\,], \updownarrow)$. As before (8) can be solved efficiently using a separation oracle. The rounding is done as in the case of $\mathrm{MD}^2\mathrm{R}(\phi_{\mathrm{SUM}}, [\,], \updownarrow)$ (see Algorithm 7).

Algorithm 7: Round ϕ_{NUM} Range Up&Down

---

1   Compute an optimal fractional solution (x^*, z^*) of (8)
2   **for** $1 \leq i < j \leq n$ **do**
3     $\bar{x}_{i,j} \leftarrow \left\lfloor x^*_{i,j} + \frac{K-1}{K} \right\rfloor$
4     $\bar{w}(i,j) \leftarrow D^-_{i,j} + \bar{x}_{i,j}$

Theorem 13. $\mathrm{MD^2R}(\phi_{\mathrm{NUM}}, [\,], \updownarrow)$ *has a* $2K(D^-_{\max} - 1)$-*approximation algorithm.*

Disclosure of Interests. The authors have no competing interests to declare that are relevant to the content of this article.

References

1. Althöfer, I.: On optimal realizations of finite metric spaces by graphs. Discr. Comput. Geometry **3**(2), 103–122 (1988). https://doi.org/10.1007/BF02187901
2. Baldisserri, A.: Buneman's theorem for trees with exatcly n vertices. Tech. Rep. 1407.0048, arXiv (2014)
3. Baldisserri, A., Rubei, E.: Distance matrices of some positive-weighted graphs. Australian J. Combinat. **70**(2), 185–201 (2018)
4. Bandelt, H.: Recognition of tree metrics. SIAM J. Discret. Math. **3**(1), 1–6 (1990)
5. Bar-Noy, A., Peleg, D., Perry, M., Rawitz, D.: Composed degree-distance realizations of graphs. Algorithmica **85**(3), 665–687 (2023)
6. Bar-Noy, A., Peleg, D., Perry, M., Rawitz, D.: Graph realization of distance sets. Theor. Comput. Sci. **1019**, 114810 (2024)
7. Brickell, J., Dhillon, I.S., Sra, S., Tropp, J.A.: The metric nearness problem. SIAM J. Matrix Anal. Appl. **30**(1), 375–396 (2008)
8. Buneman, P.: A note on the metric properties of trees. J. Combinat. Theory B **17**, 48–50 (1974)
9. Chung, F.R.K., Garrett, M.W., Graham, R.L., Shallcross, D.: Distance realization problems with applications to internet tomography. J. Comput. Syst. Sci. **63**(3), 432–448 (2001)
10. Culberson, J.C., Rudnicki, P.: A fast algorithm for constructing trees from distance matrices. Inf. Process. Lett. **30**(4), 215–220 (1989)
11. Dahlhaus, E.: Fast parallel recognition of ultrametrics and tree metrics. SIAM J. Discret. Math. **6**(4), 523–532 (1993)
12. Dinur, I., Khot, S., Kindler, G., Minzer, D., Safra, M.: Towards a proof of the 2-to-1 games conjecture? In: 50th ACM STOC, pp. 376–389 (2018)
13. Dress, A.W.M.: Trees, tight extensions of metric spaces, and the cohomological dimension of certain groups: a note on combinatorial properties of metric spaces. Adv. in Math. **53**, 321–402 (1984)
14. Fan, C., Gilbert, A.C., Raichel, B., Sonthalia, R., Buskirk, G.V.: Generalized metric repair on graphs. In: 17th SWAT. LIPIcs, vol. 162, pp. 25:1–25:22 (2020)
15. Fan, C., Raichel, B., Buskirk, G.V.: Metric violation distance: Hardness and approximation. In: 28th ACM-SIAM SODA, pp. 196–209 (2018)

16. Feder, T., Meyerson, A., Motwani, R., O'Callaghan, L., Panigrahy, R.: Representing graph metrics with fewest edges. In: Alt, H., Habib, M. (eds.) STACS 2003. LNCS, vol. 2607, pp. 355–366. Springer, Heidelberg (2003). https://doi.org/10.1007/3-540-36494-3_32
17. Gilbert, A.C., Jain, L.: If it ain't broke, don't fix it: Sparse metric repair. In: 55th IEEE Allerton Conference on Communication, Control, and Compution, pp. 612–619 (2017)
18. Grötschel, M., Lovász, L., Schrijver, A.: The ellipsoid method and its consequences in combinatorial optimization. Comb. **1**, 169–197 (1981)
19. Hakimi, S.L., Yau, S.S.: Distance matrix of a graph and its realizability. Quart. Appl. Math. **22**, 305–317 (1965)
20. Imrich, W., Simões-Pereira, J.M.S., Zamfirescu, C.: On optimal embeddings of metrics in graphs. J. Comb. Theory, Ser. B **36**(1), 1–15 (1984)
21. Khot, S., Minzer, D., Safra, M.: On independent sets, 2-to-2 games, and grassmann graphs. In: 49th ACM STOC, pp. 576–589 (2017)
22. Khot, S., Minzer, D., Safra, M.: Pseudorandom sets in grassmann graph have near-perfect expansion. In: 59th IEEE FOCS, pp. 592–601 (2018)
23. Khot, S., Regev, O.: Vertex cover might be hard to approximate to within 2-epsilon. J. Comput. Syst. Sci. **74**(3), 335–349 (2008)
24. Nieminen, J.: Realizing the distance matrix of a graph. J. Inf. Process. Cybern. **12**(1/2), 29–31 (1976)
25. Patrinos, A.N., Hakimi, S.L.: The distance matrix of a graph n and its tree realizability. Quart. Appl. Math. **255** (1972)
26. Rubei, E.: Weighted graphs with distances in given ranges. J. Classif. **33**, 282–297 (2016)
27. Simões-Pereira, J.M.S.: A note on the tree realizability of a distance matrix. J. Combinat. Theory B **6**, 303–310 (1969)
28. Simões-Pereira, J.M.S.: A note on distance matrices with unicyclic graph realizations. Discret. Math. **65**, 277–287 (1987)
29. Simões-Pereira, J.M.S.: An optimality criterion for graph embeddings of metrics. SIAM J. Discret. Math. **1**(2), 223–229 (1988)
30. Simões-Pereira, J.M.S.: An algorithm and its role in the study of optimal graph realizations of distance matrices. Discret. Math. **79**(3), 299–312 (1990)
31. Tamura, H., Sengoku, M., Shinoda, S., Abe, T.: Realization of a network from the upper and lower bounds of the distances (or capacities) between vertices. In: IEEE ISCAS, pp. 2545–2548 (1993)
32. Varone, S.C.: A constructive algorithm for realizing a distance matrix. Eur. J. Oper. Res. **174**(1), 102–111 (2006)
33. Vazirani, V.V.: Approximation algorithms. Springer (2001)
34. Williamson, D.P., Shmoys, D.B.: The Design of Approximation Algorithms. Cambridge University Press (2011)
35. Zaretskii, K.A.: Constructing a tree on the basis of a set of distances between the hanging vertices. Uspekhi Mat. Nauk **20**, 90–92 (1965)

Online Bisection with Ring Demands

Mateusz Basiak[1] , Marcin Bienkowski[1] , Guy Even[2,3] ,
and Agnieszka Tatarczuk[1(✉)]

[1] University of Wrocław, Wrocław, Poland
{mateusz.basiak,marcin.bienkowski,agnieszka.tatarczuk}@cs.uni.wroc.pl
[2] Max Planck Institute for Informatics, Saarbrücken, Germany
guyeven@mpi-inf.mpg.de
[3] School of Electrical Engineering, Tel-Aviv University, Tel Aviv, Israel

Abstract. The online bisection problem requires maintaining a dynamic partition of n nodes into two equal-sized clusters. Requests arrive sequentially as node pairs. If the nodes lie in different clusters, the algorithm pays unit cost. After each request, the algorithm may migrate nodes between clusters at unit cost per node. This problem models datacenter resource allocation where virtual machines must be assigned to servers, balancing communication costs against migration overhead.

We study the variant where requests are restricted to edges of a ring network, an abstraction of ring-allreduce patterns in distributed machine learning. Despite this restriction, the problem remains challenging with an $\Omega(n)$ deterministic lower bound. We present a randomized algorithm achieving $O(\varepsilon^{-3} \cdot \log^2 n)$ competitive ratio using resource augmentation that allows clusters of size at most $(3/4 + \varepsilon) \cdot n$.

Our approach formulates the problem as a metrical task system with a restricted state space. By limiting the number of cut-edges (i.e., ring edges between clusters) to at most $2k$, where $k = \Theta(1/\varepsilon)$, we reduce the state space from exponential to polynomial (i.e., $n^{O(k)}$). The key technical contribution is proving that this restriction increases cost by only a factor of $O(k)$. Our algorithm follows by applying the randomized MTS solution of Bubeck et al. [SODA 2019].

The best result to date for bisection with ring demands is the $O(n \cdot \log n)$-competitive deterministic online algorithm of Rajaraman and Wasim [ESA 2024] for the general setting. While prior work for ring-demands by Räcke et al. [SPAA 2023] achieved $O(\log^3 n)$ for multiple clusters, their approach employs a resource augmentation factor of $2 + \varepsilon$, making it inapplicable to bisection.

Keywords: Online bisection · Competitive analysis · Resource augmentation · Ring Network

Supported by Polish National Science Centre grant 2022/45/B/ST6/00559.

C. Georgiou (Ed.): SIROCCO 2026, LNCS 16488, pp. 93–111, 2026.
https://doi.org/10.1007/978-3-032-26465-7_6

1 Introduction

This work is motivated by the increasing interest in online graph partitioning problems. Among these, one of the most elegant and succinctly defined problems is the *online bisection problem* [5]. The goal is to maintain a time-varying partition of n nodes into two clusters, each of capacity $n/2$. The input is a sequence of requests, each corresponding to a pair of nodes. Serving a pair whose nodes are in different clusters incurs a unit cost, while serving requests between nodes in the same cluster is free. After serving a request, the algorithm may update the partition, paying a unit cost for each node that changes clusters.

The objective is to minimize the total incurred cost. This is an *online problem*: requests arrive sequentially, and the algorithm has to serve each before observing the next. The performance of an algorithm is measured by its competitive ratio [11], defined as the worst-case ratio between its total cost and that of an optimal offline algorithm OPT that knows the entire sequence in advance.

Motivation. Node pairs are ephemeral: once a request is served, it no longer incurs any cost. The online bisection problem models trade-offs that naturally arise in datacenters, where virtual machines (nodes) exchanging data have to be assigned to racks or physical servers (clusters). When two virtual machines are colocated (in the same cluster), their communication is cost-free; otherwise, it incurs latency and consumes bandwidth. Modern virtualization enables migration of virtual machines between servers (i.e., changes of node clusters), but such migrations incur network cost of their own.

1.1 Previous Results

This seemingly simple problem has proved surprisingly challenging, and despite substantial effort over the past decade, our understanding remains limited.

Exact Online Bisection. The first algorithm, proposed by Avin et al. [3,5], was a simple deterministic $O(n^2)$-competitive algorithm that maintained connected components of nodes that had communicated so far, mapping each component to a single cluster. This idea was later refined by Bienkowski and Schmid [9], who proved that a slightly randomized version of this approach achieves a sub-quadratic competitive ratio of $\widetilde{O}(n^{2-1/12})$.

A polynomial dependence on n is unavoidable for deterministic algorithms: via a reduction from online paging [34], one obtains a lower bound of $\Omega(n)$ [3]. For randomized algorithms, however, the known lower bound is merely $\Omega(\log n)$ [17], leaving an exponential gap between the best upper and lower bounds.[1]

---

[1] The lower bound of [17] was established for the so-called learning-model, but repeating their construction multiple times yields a lower bound for the general variant of the problem.

Resource Augmentation. The limited progress on exact bisection prompted the exploration of *resource-augmented* variants, where the online algorithm is permitted to relax the requirement of equal-sized clusters. More precisely, a $(1 + \varepsilon)$-*augmented* algorithm allows at most $(1 + \varepsilon) \cdot (n/2)$ nodes in each cluster, while being compared against a non-augmented O_{PT} with clusters of equal size $n/2$. We refer to $1 + \varepsilon$ as the *augmentation factor* or *balance parameter* of the algorithm. This relaxation is well motivated in practice because servers often have spare capacity that can be exploited to improve performance.

Surprisingly, the lower bound for deterministic algorithms in this setting remains $\Omega(n)$, and it holds for any nontrivial amount of augmentation, as long as it is not possible to place all nodes in a single cluster [3]. On the positive side, Rajaraman and Wasim [29] presented an $O(n \log n)$-competitive deterministic algorithm for any fixed $\varepsilon > 0$.[2] No randomized algorithm achieving a better bound than $O(n \log n)$ is known.

Multiple Clusters. The online bisection problem has also been studied in a generalized form, known as *online balanced graph partitioning*, where there are $\ell \geq 2$ clusters, each of size n/ℓ [3,5,7,16,23,26,29]. This generalization has also been investigated in models with a large augmentation factor of $1 + \varepsilon \geq 2$ [3,5,16,26], which would trivialize the online bisection problem, as all nodes could then be placed in a single cluster.

Ring Demands. Another natural restriction is to assume that requests must belong to a predefined subset $Q \subseteq V \times V$ that is known *a priori* to the online algorithm.

The case when Q is a cycle connecting all nodes is of particular theoretical and practical interest. In fact, the ring-allreduce communication pattern [32] used in distributed machine learning follows this structure. For the theoretical perspective, the deterministic lower bound of $\Omega(n)$ holds even under ring demands [3,5]. Ring demands were also studied by Räcke et al. in the multi-cluster case, for which they presented an $O(\log^3 n)$-competitive randomized algorithm [27]. However, their algorithm crucially requires an augmentation factor $2 + \varepsilon$, which makes it inapplicable to the online bisection problem.

1.2 Our Contribution

In this work, we present a randomized online algorithm for the online bisection problem with ring demands. The augmentation factor is $3/2+\varepsilon$, for $\varepsilon \in (0, 1/2]$,[3]

---

[2] Their algorithm also applies to the multi-cluster variant and uses an approach of Henzinger et al. [17] as a subroutine, thereby inheriting an exponential dependence on $1/\varepsilon$ hidden in the O-notation. However, for the online bisection, a straightforward extension of the component-based algorithm of [3] to the resource-augmented setting would trivially yield an $O(\varepsilon^{-1} \cdot n \log n)$-competitive algorithm.

[3] In other words, each cluster may contain at most $(3/4 + \varepsilon/2) \cdot n$ nodes.

and the competitive ratio is $O(\varepsilon^{-3} \cdot \log^2 n)$. For this setting, the best known solution to date is the $(1 + \varepsilon)$-augmented, $O(n \log n)$-competitive deterministic algorithm by Rajaraman and Wasim [29], which remains the state of the art even when randomization and arbitrarily high augmentation are permitted.

Overview. The bisection problem can be viewed as a *metrical task system* (MTS) [10] in which every state is a partition, and distances between states are the "edit distances" between these partitions. Let $\mathcal{S}$ denote the set of states. The randomized online MTS algorithm of Bubeck et al. [12] yields a competitive ratio $O(\log^2 |\mathcal{S}|)$, which is $O(n^2)$ since $|S| = \binom{n}{n/2}$.

To reduce the competitive ratio, we restrict the number of states to $n^{O(k)}$, for $k = \Theta(1/\varepsilon)$, as follows. Any partition of the cycle into two clusters can be represented by an even set of *cut-edges*, meaning ring edges between nodes assigned to different clusters. A natural choice for restricting the state space is to consider sets of at most $2k$ cut-edges.

More formally, let $\mathrm{MTS}(2k, \alpha)$ denote the MTS in which every state is an α-balanced partition induced by at most $2k$ cut-edges. As the number of states of this MTS is $O(n^{O(k)})$, the randomized online MTS algorithm of Bubeck et al. [12] has cost at most $O(k^2 \cdot \log^2 n)$ times that of an *optimal offline* α-balanced algorithm using at most $2k$ cut-edges.

This approach shifts the challenge to bounding the increase in cost caused by this sparsification of the set of states, i.e., bounding the ratio between the costs of the optimal solutions for $\mathrm{MTS}(n, 1)$ and $\mathrm{MTS}(2k, \alpha)$. We succeed in bounding this ratio by $O(k)$ if $\alpha = 3/2 + 1/k$ (see Theorem 1).

Our analysis works in phases in which an offline solution OFF for $\mathrm{MTS}(2k, \alpha)$ (for $\alpha = 3/2 + 1/k$) "chases" an optimal solution OPT for $\mathrm{MTS}(n, 1)$ until the α-balance parameter is violated. At all times, we maintain the invariant that the cut-edges in OFF form a subset of the cut-edges of OPT. This invariant guarantees that a request incurs a cost on OFF only if it incurs cost on OPT.

At the beginning of each phase, we start by sparsifying the cut-edges of OPT to a subset of cardinality at most $2k$. Lemma 1 proves that this is possible with balance parameter of $1 + 1/k$. The phase proceeds with OFF iteratively responding to changes in OPT and ends when this response leads to a partition that is no longer α-balanced.

We show that changes in OFF (in response to the single-node changes of OPT) incur amortized cost that is bounded by the cost of OPT within the phase (see Corollary 2). Moreover, the $O(n)$ rebalancing cost per phase can be charged to the cost of OPT within the phase, which we lower-bound by $\Omega(n/k)$ (see Lemma 7).

Comparison to Prior Work. Superficially, our algorithm shares certain similarities (the notion of cut-edges and the use of MTS routines) with the algorithm of Räcke et al. [27], but the underlying mechanisms differ. In particular, in their approach, the number of cut-edges corresponds to the number of clusters, whereas in our case it serves as a parameter that affects both the cost and the augmentation factor. Moreover, the partition of the cycle in their approach is more rigid, since cut-edges are confined to specific segments of the cycle that remain fixed throughout the execution, whereas in our approach the partition is more flexible, allowing cut-edges to appear anywhere on the cycle.

1.3   Other Related Work

The online bisection problem and its generalization to the online balanced partitioning problem were also studied in several relaxed variants, such as the learning model [17,18,22,23,27,28] (where the input admits a partition incurring no service cost) and stochastic inputs [4].

The offline counterparts of these problems (bisection and k-balanced partitioning) are NP-hard, and their approximation ratios have been improved in a long line of works; see [2,14,15,19,25,31] for bisection and [1,13,20,33] for k-balanced partitioning. Recently, balanced partitioning was also studied in a setting where the input and output are as in the online model, but the algorithm operates offline and has access to the entire input [26].

Closely related online problems include online disengagement (a "dual" of online bisection, where the algorithm pays for requests whose endpoints lie in the same cluster) [6,24,30] and the minimum linear arrangement problem, where the goal is to maintain a dynamically changing linear ordering of nodes [8,21].

1.4   Problem Definition

In the online bisection problem, we are given n nodes $v_1, v_2, \ldots, v_n$, where n is even. Instead of defining the problem in terms of partitions, we use an equivalent but more convenient coloring formulation: the algorithm maintains a coloring of all nodes with two colors, red and blue. There is a fixed initial coloring, where half of the nodes are colored red and the other half blue.

Requests arrive online. Each request is a pair of nodes, referred to as its endpoints. For every request in an input sequence:

- if its endpoints have the same color, the algorithm pays a *hit cost* of 0;
- if its endpoints have different colors, the algorithm pays a *hit cost* of 1;
- after paying the hit cost, the algorithm may *recolor* any number of nodes, paying a *recoloring cost* equal to the number of recolored nodes.

For an algorithm A_{LG} and input σ, we write $A_{LG}(\sigma)$ for the total cost on σ. We denote by A_{LG}_{HIT} and A_{LG}_{REC} the *hit cost* and *recoloring cost*, respectively.

Resource Augmentation. A coloring is α-*balanced* (for $\alpha \geq 1$) if at most $\alpha \cdot (n/2)$ nodes are assigned each color. An algorithm is α-*augmented* if, once it performs the recoloring in response to a request, the resulting coloring is α-balanced.

An (α-augmented) algorithm A_{LG} is R-*competitive* if there exists β such that, for every input σ, it holds that $A_{LG}(\sigma) \leq R \cdot O_{PT}(\sigma) + \beta$, where O_{PT}

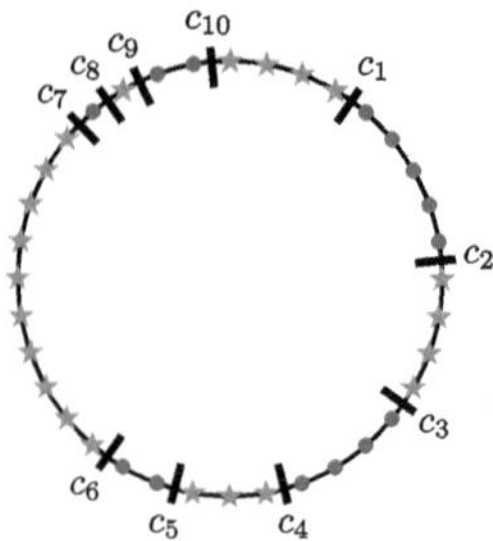

Fig. 1. An example coloring of a cycle with the set of cut-edges $\mathcal{C} = c_1, c_2, \ldots, c_{10}$. The cycle contains 22 blue (stars) and 14 red (circles) nodes; hence the less frequent color is red, and $\text{LESS}(\mathcal{C}) = 14$. (Color figure online)

denotes the optimal offline algorithm that maintains a 1-balanced coloring. The parameter β cannot depend on σ, but may be a function of n. For randomized algorithms, we replace $\text{ALG}(\sigma)$ above by its expected value and assume standard, oblivious adversary [11] that does not see random bits used by the algorithm.

Ring Demands. In the variant studied in this paper, all requests correspond to edges of a cycle. Thus, there are n possible request types: $(v_1, v_2), (v_2, v_3), \ldots,$ (v_n, v_1).

2 Outline of Our Solution

We show that for every $\varepsilon \in (0, 1/2]$, there exists an online $(3/2 + \varepsilon)$-augmented randomized algorithm that is $O(\varepsilon^{-3} \cdot \log^2 n)$-competitive. Below we outline our approach, starting with several necessary definitions.

Cut-Edges. At any time, the coloring maintained by algorithm ALG induces a set of *cut-edges*, denoted $\text{CUT}(\text{ALG})$, consisting of edges of the cycle whose endpoints have different colors. Note that $|\text{CUT}(\text{ALG})|$ is even. Conversely, each even-cardinality set $\mathcal{C}$ of cut-edges corresponds to two equivalent colorings of the nodes, obtained from each other by swapping color names. A set of cut-edges is *valid* if its cardinality is even. Hence, a valid set $\mathcal{C}$ of cut-edges uniquely represents a coloring, up to a swap of color names.

Fix any valid set $\mathcal{C}$ of cut-edges. The set $\mathcal{C}$ partitions the cycle into monochromatic arcs of alternating colors. Each such arc consists entirely of red or blue nodes, and we refer to it as a red or blue arc, respectively. We also define other arcs: for edges e_i and e_j, let $A(e_i, e_j)$ denote the set of nodes on the shorter path between e_i and e_j along the cycle. Let $d(e_i, e_j) \triangleq |A(e_i, e_j)|$.

Color Frequency. For a given coloring, a color is called *more frequent* if the number of nodes of that color exceeds $n/2$, and *less frequent* otherwise. When both colors contain exactly $n/2$ nodes, either color may be treated as more frequent. For a valid set $\mathcal{C}$ of cut-edges, let $\textsc{less}(\mathcal{C})$ denote the number of nodes assigned the less frequent color in the coloring induced by $\mathcal{C}$; cf. Fig. 1.

Global Rebalancing. As stated in the introduction, we consider algorithms that use at most $2k$ cut-edges, for an integer constant k. However, although the initial coloring is 1-balanced, it may involve more than $2k$ cut-edges. To address this, we introduce a *global rebalancing* procedure; its properties are stated in the lemma below and proved in Sect. 3.1. The procedure is executed at the beginning and may also be invoked later during the execution of the algorithm.

Lemma 1 (Global rebalancing procedure). *For any valid 1-balanced set $\mathcal{C}$ of cut-edges, there exists a deterministic procedure that computes a subset $\mathcal{C}_{2k} \subseteq \mathcal{C}$ of size $\min\{2k, |\mathcal{C}|\}$ such that $\mathcal{C}_{2k}$ is $(1 + 1/k)$-balanced.*

For every integer $k \geq 1$ and $\alpha \geq 1+1/k$, define the class $\mathcal{A}_\alpha^k$ of algorithms that (i) are α-augmented, (ii) perform global rebalancing, as specified in Lemma 1, before processing the input sequence, and (iii) during execution, maintain at most $2k$ cut-edges. Algorithms in $\mathcal{A}_\alpha^k$ may be either offline or online.

Main Bounds and Paper Organization. The main technical contribution of this paper is the following theorem on *offline* algorithms.

Theorem 1. *Fix an integer $k \geq 1$ and let $\alpha \triangleq 3/2+1/k$. There exists an offline algorithm $\textsc{Off} \in \mathcal{A}_\alpha^k$ such that, for every input σ, it holds that $\textsc{Off}(\sigma) \leq O(k) \cdot \textsc{Opt}(\sigma) + O(n)$.*

The theorem guarantees the *existence* of an algorithm $\textsc{Off}$; the algorithm need not be efficient. Section 3 presents its construction and analysis.

Next, we show that within the class $\mathcal{A}_\alpha^k$, one can construct an online randomized algorithm that is $O(k^2 \cdot \log^2 n)$-competitive against *any offline algorithm in the same class*. The proof proceeds by formulating the problem as a metrical task system [10] and applying the algorithm of Bubeck et al. [12]. It is given in Sect. 4.

Theorem 2. *Fix an integer $k \geq 1$ and $\alpha \geq 1 + 1/k$. It is possible to construct an online randomized algorithm $\textsc{Onl} \in \mathcal{A}_\alpha^k$ such that, for a fixed β, it holds that $\mathbf{E}[\textsc{Onl}(\sigma)] \leq O(k^2 \cdot \log^2 n) \cdot \textsc{Off}(\sigma) + \beta$, for every offline algorithm $\textsc{Off} \in \mathcal{A}_\alpha^k$ and every input σ.*

Corollary 1. *For any $\varepsilon \in (0, 1/2]$, there exists a $(3/2 + \varepsilon)$-augmented and $O(\varepsilon^{-3} \cdot \log^2 n)$-competitive online randomized algorithm for the online bisection problem on n nodes, where all requests correspond to edges of a cycle connecting all nodes.*

Proof. Let $k \triangleq \lceil 1/\varepsilon \rceil$ and $\alpha \triangleq 3/2 + 1/k \leq 3/2 + \varepsilon$. Consider the online randomized algorithm $ONL \in \mathcal{A}_\alpha^k$ guaranteed by Theorem 2.

Since $ONL \in \mathcal{A}_\alpha^k$, it is α-augmented, and thus also $(3/2 + \varepsilon)$-augmented. Fix an input σ and the offline algorithm $OFF \in \mathcal{A}_\alpha^k$ provided by Theorem 1. Let β be the parameter from the statement of Theorem 2. Then, for every input σ,

$$
\begin{aligned}
\mathbf{E}[ONL(\sigma)] &\leq O(k^2 \cdot \log^2 n) \cdot OFF(\sigma) + \beta && \text{(Theorem 2)} \\
&\leq O(k^3 \cdot \log^2 n) \cdot OPT(\sigma) + O(n \cdot k^2 \cdot \log^2 n) + \beta && \text{(Theorem 1)} \\
&\leq O(\varepsilon^{-3} \cdot \log^2 n) \cdot OPT(\sigma) + O(\varepsilon^{-2} \cdot n \cdot \log^2 n + \beta).
\end{aligned}
$$

This completes the proof of the claimed competitive ratio.

3   Offline Algorithm

In this section, we fix an integer $k \geq 1$, set $\alpha \triangleq 3/2 + 1/k$, and we construct an offline algorithm $OFF \in \mathcal{A}_\alpha^k$ that generates a solution on the basis of actions of OPT.[4] Before processing the input, OFF applies Lemma 1 to compute a coloring that uses at most $2k$ edges derived from the initial coloring of OPT.

Definition 1. *An offline algorithm OFF maintains* cut-edge invariants *if*

- $CUT(OFF) \subseteq CUT(OPT)$ and
- $|CUT(OFF)| = \min\{2k, |CUT(OPT)|\}$.

Note that the cut-invariants imply that if $CUT(OPT) \leq 2k$, then $CUT(OFF) = CUT(OPT)$. By Lemma 1, the cut-edge invariants hold after the global rebalancing procedure is applied at the beginning. We will also show that OFF maintains these invariants throughout execution.

As $CUT(OFF) \subseteq CUT(OPT)$, OFF never incurs hit cost unless OPT does. Hence, $OFF_{\text{HIT}}(\sigma) \leq OPT_{\text{HIT}}(\sigma)$ for every input σ. Therefore, our goal is to construct OFF such that $OFF_{\text{REC}}(\sigma) \leq O(k) \cdot OPT_{\text{REC}}(\sigma) + O(n)$ for every input σ.

Steps. Recall that in response to a single request, OPT may recolor multiple nodes, and after these changes are executed, the coloring of OPT has to be 1-balanced. In Sect. 3.3, we define the changes that OFF performs to mimic a single-node recoloring by OPT. Each such change maintains the cut-edge invariants (cf. Definition 1), but does not necessarily preserve color balance. Thus, when OFF processes all node recolorings of OPT in response to a single request, it verifies whether its coloring is α-balanced. If this is not the case, OFF executes the global rebalancing procedure described in Lemma 1. This procedure produces an α-balanced coloring and preserves the cut-edge invariants.

---

[4] Although the algorithm is well defined for any integer $k \geq 1$, only values $k \geq 3$ yield non-trivial augmentation factors.

For succinctness, we number the node recolorings performed by OPT and assume that each such recoloring corresponds to a single *step*, while a single request may correspond to multiple recoloring steps. We use superscript t to indicate that the state (or cost) refers to step t, and omit it when the considered step is clear from the context.

3.1   Global Rebalancing

In this section, we prove Lemma 1 by presenting a procedure that selects a subset of cut-edges from $CUT(OPT)$ guaranteeing the cut-edge invariants (cf. Definition 1). Note that this procedure disregards the current set of cut-edges of OFF. The construction begins with the cut-edges of OPT and removes them iteratively until the desired number of cut-edges is reached, controlling the color imbalance introduced at each step.

Proof (of Lemma 1). If $|\mathcal{C}| \leq 2k$, we simply set $\mathcal{C}_{2k} = \mathcal{C}$ and the claim follows since $LESS(\mathcal{C}_{2k}) = n/2$. Therefore, in what follows, we assume that $|\mathcal{C}| = 2m > 2k$.

We now describe how to iteratively construct the sets $\mathcal{C}_{2m}, \mathcal{C}_{2m-2}, \ldots, \mathcal{C}_{2k+2},$ $\mathcal{C}_{2k}$. For every $j \in \{k, \ldots, m\}$, we maintain the invariant $LESS(\mathcal{C}_{2j}) \geq n/2 - n/(2j)$. The final set $\mathcal{C}_{2k}$ is then $(1 + 1/k)$-balanced as required.

We start with $\mathcal{C}_{2m} \triangleq \mathcal{C}$. Clearly, the invariant holds since $LESS(\mathcal{C}_{2m}) = n/2$.

It now suffices to describe how to choose $\mathcal{C}_{2j-2}$ based on $\mathcal{C}_{2j}$ (for $m \geq j > k$), so that if the invariant holds for $\mathcal{C}_{2j}$, it also holds for $\mathcal{C}_{2j-2}$. Let $c_0, c_1, \ldots, c_{2j-1}$ denote the cut-edges of $\mathcal{C}_{2j}$ in clockwise order, starting from an arbitrary one. These cut-edges are numbered modulo $2j$, that is, c_{i+2j} is identified with c_i.

Fix one of the two colorings induced by $\mathcal{C}_{2j}$; without loss of generality, red is more frequent in $\mathcal{C}_{2j}$. Let $A(c_i, c_{i+1})$ be the smallest red arc. Define $\mathcal{C}_{2j-2} \triangleq \mathcal{C}_{2j} \setminus \{c_i, c_{i+1}\}$. In other words, $\mathcal{C}_{2j-2}$ is obtained from $\mathcal{C}_{2j}$ by changing the color of arc $A(c_i, c_{i+1})$ from red to blue. The resulting number of blue nodes in $\mathcal{C}_{2j-2}$ equals $LESS(\mathcal{C}_{2j}) + d(c_i, c_{i+1})$.

We first upper-bound $d(c_i, c_{i+1})$. Since the invariant holds for $\mathcal{C}_{2j}$, we have $LESS(\mathcal{C}_{2j}) \geq n/2 - n/(2j)$, and therefore the number of red nodes in $\mathcal{C}_{2j}$ is at most $n/2 + n/(2j)$. Because $\mathcal{C}_{2j}$ contains j red arcs and $A(c_i, c_{i+1})$ is the smallest among them, we obtain $d(c_i, c_{i+1}) \leq n/(2j) + n/(2j^2)$.

If blue remains the less frequent color also in $\mathcal{C}_{2j-2}$, the invariant follows immediately, since $LESS(\mathcal{C}_{2j-2}) = LESS(\mathcal{C}_{2j}) + d(c_i, c_{i+1}) \geq LESS(\mathcal{C}_{2j}) \geq n/2 - n/(2j) > n/2 - n/(2j - 2)$.

Otherwise, red becomes the less frequent color in $\mathcal{C}_{2j-2}$. Then

$$\begin{aligned}
LESS(\mathcal{C}_{2j-2}) &= n - LESS(\mathcal{C}_{2j}) - d(c_i, c_{i+1}) \\
&\geq n - n/2 - n/(2j) - n/(2j^2) \quad (\text{as } LESS(\mathcal{C}_{2j}) \leq n/2) \\
&> n/2 - n/(2j - 2).
\end{aligned}$$

In either case, the invariant holds for $\mathcal{C}_{2j-2}$, and the construction is therefore complete.

3.2 Distance Between OPT and OFF (Green Sectors)

We define Φ as the "edit distance" between OPT and OFF, representing the smallest set of nodes that must switch clusters to transform the partition of OFF into that of OPT.

To this end, we adapt the notion of an arc: a *clockwise arc* $A^\circ(c_i, c_j)$ includes all nodes between c_i and c_j in the clockwise order (not necessarily along the shorter path connecting them). The symbol $\uplus$ denotes the disjoint union of sets.

Definition 2. *If* $CUT(OPT)=CUT(OFF)$*, then* $\Phi = \emptyset$*. Otherwise, let* $c_1, c_2, \ldots,$ c_m *denote the cut-edges from* $CUT(OPT) \setminus CUT(OFF)$ *listed in clockwise order. Define*

- $\Phi_0 \triangleq A^\circ(c_1, c_2) \uplus A^\circ(c_3, c_4) \uplus \ldots \uplus A^\circ(c_{m-1}, c_m)$*, and*
- $\Phi_1 \triangleq A^\circ(c_m, c_1) \uplus A^\circ(c_2, c_3) \uplus \ldots \uplus A^\circ(c_{m-2}, c_{m-1})$*.*

Then, Φ is the smaller of the two sets, with ties broken arbitrarily; cf. Fig. 2.

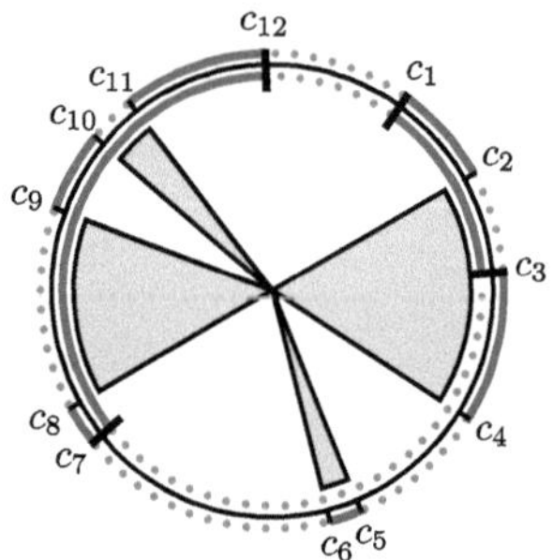

Fig. 2. An example configuration of OPT and OFF with $CUT(OPT) = c_1, c_2, \ldots, c_{12}$ and $CUT(OFF)= c_1, c_3, c_7, c_{12}$. Cut-edges of OFF are shown with thicker lines. The coloring outside the circle corresponds to OPT, while the coloring inside corresponds to OFF. The set Φ consists of nodes indicated by green (filled) sectors. The endpoints of these sectors coincide with $CUT(OPT) \setminus CUT(OFF)$. (Color figure online)

Lemma 2. *Φ is the minimum-cardinality set of nodes that OFF has to recolor to make its coloring either identical to or completely opposite to the coloring of OPT.*

Proof. First, observe that Φ_0 and Φ_1 are disjoint, and their union is the set of all nodes. Second, either Φ_0 or Φ_1 consists of the nodes on which the colorings of OPT and OFF differ. Consequently, the other set contains nodes on which the colorings of OPT and OFF coincide.

As an extreme illustration, consider the case in which the coloring of OFF is the "inverse" of the coloring of OPT (nodes that are blue in the OPT solution are red in OFF, and vice versa). In this case, the colorings correspond to the same partitions, and $\Phi = \emptyset$.

3.3   A Single Color Change of OPT: Definition of OFF

We say that the state of an edge is *flipped* if, due to some action of an algorithm, the edge becomes a cut-edge when it was not one, or ceases to be a cut-edge when it was one.

Observation 1. *Fix two edges e_1 and e_2. Flipping their states is equivalent to recoloring all nodes on arc $A(e_1, e_2)$ (and only them).*

Recall that to serve a single request, OPT may recolor several nodes. We refine its recolorings per request to subsequences of recolorings of single nodes. Using the definition of set Φ, we now specify how OFF responds to a single color change performed by OPT in step t. Let w denote this node.

By Observation 1, this color change flips the states of the two edges adjacent to w. Consequently, OPT either introduces two new adjacent cut-edges, deletes two adjacent cut-edges, or shifts an existing cut-edge by one position. We consider these three cases and specify how OFF responds to each, both in terms of recoloring and the resulting cut-edge modifications.

In the description below, $CUT(OFF^{t-1})$, $CUT(OPT^{t-1})$, and Φ^{t-1} denote the sets of cut-edges of OFF and OPT, and the value of Φ, respectively, immediately before step t. Recall that $CUT(OFF^{t-1}) \subseteq CUT(OPT^{t-1})$ by the cut-edge invariants.

- **OPT shifts a cut-edge** c_i. If $c_i \in CUT(OFF^{t-1})$, then OFF also recolors w, thereby shifting c_i as well; otherwise, it does nothing.
- **OPT introduces two new adjacent cut-edges** c_i, c_j. If $|CUT(OFF^{t-1})|$ is smaller or equal than $2(k-1)$, then OFF also recolors w, thereby adding c_i and c_j to $CUT(OFF)$; otherwise, it does nothing.
- **OPT removes two adjacent cut-edges** c_i, c_j. We consider four sub-cases:
    - If $c_i, c_j \notin CUT(OFF^{t-1})$, then OFF takes no action.
    - If $c_i, c_j \in CUT(OFF^{t-1})$ and $CUT(OFF^{t-1}) = CUT(OPT^{t-1})$, then OFF also recolors w, thereby removing c_i and c_j from $CUT(OFF)$.
    - If $c_i, c_j \in CUT(OFF^{t-1})$ and $CUT(OPT^{t-1}) \setminus CUT(OFF^{t-1}) \neq \emptyset$, then OFF first recolors w, thereby removing c_i and c_j. Next, OFF selects an arbitrary arc $A(c_x, c_y) \in \Phi^{t-1}$ (guaranteed by Definition 2) and recolors all nodes on $A(c_x, c_y)$. By Observation 1, this operation adds c_x and c_y to $CUT(OFF)$.
    - In the final sub-case, exactly one of $\{c_i, c_j\}$, say c_i, does not belong to $CUT(OFF^{t-1})$. Since $c_i \in CUT(OPT^{t-1}) \setminus CUT(OFF^{t-1})$, Definition 2 implies the existence of an arc $A(c_i, c_y) \in \Phi^{t-1}$. In this situation, OFF recolors all nodes on $A(c_j, c_y)$. By Observation 1, this operation removes c_j from $CUT(OFF)$ and adds c_y to it.

It is straightforward to verify that in each of the above cases, OFF preserves the cut-edge invariants. In particular, every cut-edge added by OFF is present in $CUT(OPT^t)$. Hence, it suffices to analyze the recoloring cost of OFF, which will be done in the next section.

3.4   A Single Color Change of OPT: Cost Analysis

We analyze a single step t in which O_{PT} recolors a node w.

Let Φ^{t-1} and Φ^t denote the values of Φ immediately before and after step t. Let Φ^t_* be equal to Φ^t_0 if $\Phi^{t-1} = \Phi^{t-1}_0$, and to Φ^t_1 otherwise. That is, Φ^t_* represents the "continuation" of Φ^{t-1}, disregarding a possible switch between Φ_0 and Φ_1. Clearly $|\Phi^t| \leq |\Phi^t_*|$.

We define the potential function as $\phi \triangleq |\Phi|$. Let $\Delta^t \phi = \phi^t - \phi^{t-1}$, and let $\Delta^t_* \phi = \phi^t_* - \phi^{t-1}$.

In the following three lemmas, we analyze the possible changes performed by O_{PT}. In each lemma, we show that $O_{FF}^t{}_{REC} + \Delta^t_* \phi \leq 1$. Since $\phi^t \leq \phi^t_*$, it follows that $O_{FF}^t{}_{REC} + \Delta^t \phi \leq O_{FF}^t{}_{REC} + \Delta^t_* \phi \leq 1 = O_{PT}^t{}_{REC}$. The symbol $\oplus$ denotes the symmetric difference of sets.

Lemma 3. *If O_{PT} shifts a cut-edge, then $O_{FF}^t{}_{REC} + \Delta^t_* \phi \leq 1$.*

Proof. Let c_i denote the shifted cut-edge.

- If $c_i \in C_{UT}(O_{FF}^{t-1})$, then O_{FF} recolors w, paying a cost of 1. As a result, O_{FF} reproduces the shift of a cut-edge (cf. Figure 3a and 3b). This leaves Φ unchanged, and thus $\Delta^t_* \phi = 0$.
- Otherwise, $c_i \notin C_{UT}(O_{FF}^{t-1})$, and then O_{FF} does nothing, thus its cost is 0, cf. Figure 3c. In this case, $\Phi^t_* = \Phi^{t-1} \oplus \{w\}$, and therefore $\Delta^t_* \phi = \pm 1$.

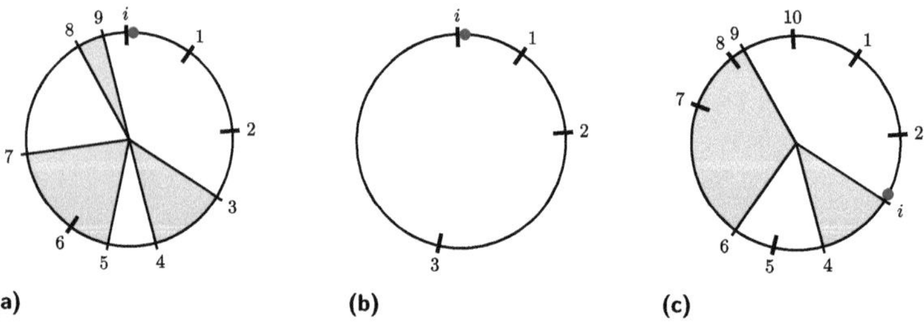

Fig. 3. Φ right before O_{PT} shifts a cut-edge. For simplicity, we label cut-edges by i instead of c_i. The purple dot represents the node w recolored by O_{PT}, thick cut-edges belong to $C_{UT}(O_{FF}^{t-1})$, and nodes in Φ^{t-1} are marked with green (filled) sectors. (Color figure online)

Lemma 4. *If O_{PT} adds two new adjacent cut-edges, then $O_{FF}^t{}_{REC} + \Delta^t_* \phi \leq 1$.*

Proof. We distinguish two cases based on the cardinality of $C_{UT}(O_{FF}^{t-1})$.

- If $|C_{UT}(O_{FF}^{t-1})| = 2k$, O_{FF} takes no action, and hence incurs no cost, cf. Figure 4a and 4b. In this case, $\Phi^t_* = \Phi^{t-1} \oplus \{w\}$, and thus $\Delta^t_* \phi = \pm 1$.

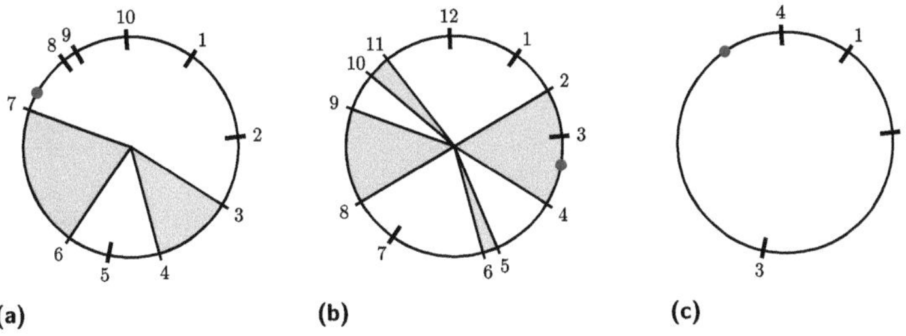

Fig. 4. Φ right before OPT introduces two new cut-edges. Notation as in Fig. 3.

- Otherwise $|CUT(OFF^{t-1})| \leq 2(k-1)$. Then, OFF recolors w paying a cost of 1, cf. Figure 4c. In this case, Φ remains unchanged, and thus $\Delta^t_* \phi = 0$.

Lemma 5. *If OPT removes two adjacent cut-edges, then $OFF^t_{REC} + \Delta^t_* \phi \leq 1$.*

Proof. Let c_i, c_j denote the cut-edges removed by OPT.

- If $c_i, c_j \notin CUT(OFF^{t-1})$, OFF takes no action and therefore incurs no cost, cf. Figure 5a. In this case, $\Phi^t_* = \Phi^{t-1} \oplus \{w\}$, implying $\Delta^t_* \phi = \pm 1$.
- If $c_i, c_j \in CUT(OFF^{t-1})$ and $CUT(OFF^{t-1}) = CUT(OPT^{t-1})$, then OFF recolors w paying a cost of 1. In this case, Φ remains unchanged, and hence $\Delta^t_* \phi = 0$.
- In the next case, $c_i, c_j \in CUT(OFF^{t-1})$ and $CUT(OPT^{t-1}) \setminus CUT(OFF^{t-1}) \neq \emptyset$. Let $A(c_x, c_y) \in \Phi^{t-1}$ be the arc selected by OFF; see Fig. 5b, where this arc is marked with a star. We first examine the effect of both OPT and OFF recoloring w, and then subsequent recoloring of $A(c_x, c_y)$ by OFF. When both recolor w, OFF pays a cost of 1, and Φ remains unchanged. Next, when OFF recolors $A(c_x, c_y)$, it pays and additional cost of $d(c_x, c_y)$, and $\Phi^t_* = \Phi^{t-1} \oplus A(c_x, c_y)$. Since $A(c_x, c_y) \subseteq \Phi^{t-1}$, we have $\Phi^t_* = \Phi^{t-1} \setminus A(c_x, c_y)$. Overall, $OFF^t_{REC} = 1 + d(c_x, c_y)$ and $\Delta\phi = -d(c_x, c_y)$.
- In the final case, $c_i \notin CUT(OFF^{t-1})$ and $c_j \in CUT(OFF^{t-1})$. By Definition 2, there exists an arc $A(c_i, c_y) \subseteq \Phi^{t-1}$, marked with a star in Fig. 5c and 5d. OFF recolors all nodes in $A(c_j, c_y)$ (note that $A(c_j, c_y) = A(c_i, c_y) \oplus \{w\}$), incurring cost of at most $d(c_i, c_y) + 1$. In this case, $\Phi^t_* = \Phi^{t-1} \oplus A(c_j, c_y) \oplus \{w\} = \Phi^{t-1} \oplus A(c_i, c_y)$. Since $A(c_i, c_y) \subseteq \Phi^{t-1}$, we obtain $\Phi^t_* = \Phi^{t-1} \setminus A(c_i, c_y)$, and hence $\Delta^t_* \phi = -d(c_i, c_y)$.

From Lemma 3, Lemma 4 and Lemma 5 together with $\Delta^t \phi \leq \Delta^t_* \phi$ and $OPT^t_{REC} = 1$, we immediately obtain the following bound.

Corollary 2. *For every step t, it holds that $OFF^t_{REC} + \Delta^t \phi \leq OPT^t_{REC}$.*

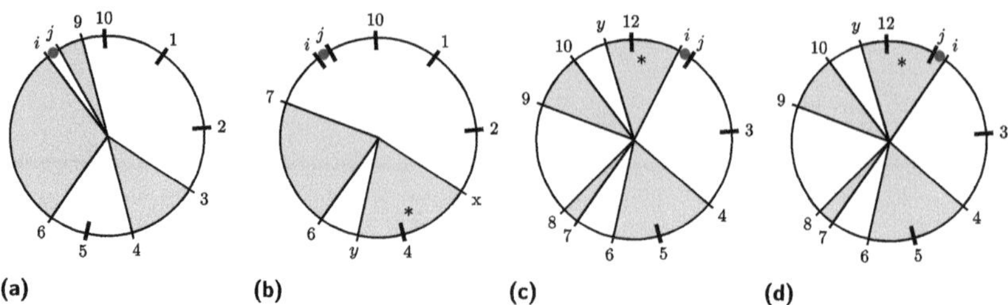

Fig. 5. Φ right before OPT deletes two adjacent cut-edges. Notation as in Fig. 3.

3.5   Approximation Ratio of OFF

Recall that before processing the first request, OFF performs the global rebalancing procedure described in Lemma 1. This guarantees that OFF satisfies the cut-edge invariants and remains $(1 + 1/k)$-balanced (and therefore also α-balanced, since $\alpha = 3/2 + 1/k$). The rebalancing procedure is invoked whenever OFF ceased to be α-balanced after applying the changes induced by OPT recolorings. Consequently, $OFF \in \mathcal{A}_\alpha^k$, and it remains to bound its total cost and compare it with that of OPT.

We begin with the following auxiliary lemma.

Lemma 6. *Whenever OPT is 1-balanced,* $\text{LESS}(\text{CUT}(OFF)) + \phi \geq n/2$.

Proof. Let z_{RR}, z_{RB}, z_{BR} and z_{BB} denote the number of nodes colored red by both OPT and OFF, red by OPT and blue by OFF, blue by OPT and red by OFF, and blue by both OPT and OFF, respectively. By the definitions of ϕ and $\text{LESS}(\text{CUT}(OFF))$, we obtain

$$
\begin{aligned}
\text{LESS}(\text{CUT}(OFF)) + \phi &= \min\{z_{\mathrm{RR}} + z_{\mathrm{BR}}, z_{\mathrm{BB}} + z_{\mathrm{RB}}\} \\
&\quad + \min\{z_{\mathrm{RB}} + z_{\mathrm{BR}}, z_{\mathrm{RR}} + z_{\mathrm{BB}}\}, \\
&\geq \min\{z_{\mathrm{RB}} + z_{\mathrm{RR}}, z_{\mathrm{BR}} + z_{\mathrm{BB}}\} \\
&= \min\{n/2, n/2\} = n/2,
\end{aligned}
$$

where the penultimate equality holds because OPT is 1-balanced.

In the following, we fix an input sequence σ and run both OPT and OFF on it. This induces a sequence of steps, and OFF performs global rebalancings between some of them. These rebalancings partition the sequence of steps into *phases*; the last phase may not necessarily end with a global rebalancing.

For any phase p, let $OFF_{\text{REC}}(p)$ denote the recoloring cost of OFF during p, and let $\Delta_p\phi$ denote the change in potential ϕ during the same phase, both measured excluding the rebalancing. The following lemma states that the amortized cost incurred by OFF in p is appropriately large, which later enables us to upper-bound the cost of the rebalancing procedure.

Lemma 7. *For any phase p, it holds that* $OFF_{\text{REC}}(p) + \Delta_p\phi \geq n/(2k)$.

Proof. Let $\mathcal{C}_b$ and $\mathcal{C}_e$ denote the sets of cut-edges of $O\!F\!F$ at the beginning and at the end of phase p, respectively; the latter is this set immediately before the global rebalancing. Then,

$$\text{LESS}(\mathcal{C}_e) < n - \alpha \cdot (n/2) = n/4 - n/(2k), \quad \text{(as rebalancing was triggered)}$$
$$\text{LESS}(\mathcal{C}_b) \geq n/2 - n/(2k). \quad\quad\quad\quad\quad\quad\quad\quad \text{(by Lemma 1)}$$

Next, we show that

$$O\!F\!F_{\text{REC}}(p) \geq \text{LESS}(\mathcal{C}_b) - \text{LESS}(\mathcal{C}_e). \tag{1}$$

To this end, assume without loss of generality that red is the less frequent color in $\mathcal{C}_e$. If red is also the less frequent color in $\mathcal{C}_b$, then (1) follows immediately. Otherwise, blue was less frequent in $\mathcal{C}_b$, and then there exist a moment within p when exactly $n/2$ nodes were colored red. Hence, $O\!F\!F_{\text{REC}}(p) \geq n/2 - \text{LESS}(\mathcal{C}_e) \geq \text{LESS}(\mathcal{C}_b) - \text{LESS}(\mathcal{C}_e)$.

We now derive a lower bound on $\Delta_p \phi$. The last step of each phase corresponds to the final recoloring performed by $O\!PT$ when serving some request. Consequently, $O\!PT$ is 1-balanced at that time. By Lemma 6, the potential value immediately before rebalancing is at least $n/2 - \text{LESS}(\mathcal{C}_e)$. Since the potential at the beginning of p is at most $n/2$, it follows that

$$\Delta_p \phi \geq -\text{LESS}(\mathcal{C}_e). \tag{2}$$

Combining (1) and (2) yields $O\!F\!F_{\text{REC}}(p) + \Delta_p \phi \geq \text{LESS}(\mathcal{C}_b) - 2 \cdot \text{LESS}(\mathcal{C}_e) \geq n/(2k)$.

We can finally prove Theorem 1.

Proof (of Theorem 1.). As established above, $O\!F\!F \in \mathcal{A}_\alpha^k$, so it remains to bound its total cost. Fix an input sequence σ, and let it consist of h phases $p_1, p_2, \ldots, p_h$.

For each phase p, let $O\!F\!F(\tilde{p})$ and $\Delta_{\tilde{p}} \phi$, be the cost of $O\!F\!F$ within p with rebalancing, and the change of potential within p including the rebalancing. Let $O\!PT(p)$ denote the cost of $O\!PT$ in phase p. The rebalancing performed at the end of p incurs a cost of at most n, and the corresponding change in potential is at most $n/2$. Hence, for each phase p,

$$
\begin{aligned}
O\!F\!F(\tilde{p}) &+ \Delta_{\tilde{p}} \phi \\
&\leq O\!F\!F_{\text{HIT}}(p) + O\!F\!F_{\text{REC}}(p) + \Delta_p \phi + (3/2) \cdot n \\
&\leq O\!F\!F_{\text{HIT}}(p) + (3k+1) \cdot (O\!F\!F_{\text{REC}}(p) + \Delta_p \phi) &&\text{(by Lemma 7)} \\
&\leq O\!F\!F_{\text{HIT}}(p) + (3k+1) \cdot O\!PT_{\text{REC}}(p) &&\text{(by Corollary 2)} \\
&\leq O\!PT_{\text{HIT}}(p) + (3k+1) \cdot O\!PT_{\text{REC}}(p) &&(\text{CUT}(O\!F\!F) \subseteq \text{CUT}(O\!PT)) \\
&\leq (3k+1) \cdot O\!PT(p).
\end{aligned}
$$

The initial rebalancing performed by $O\!F\!F$ at the beginning of σ incurs a cost of at most n, and the corresponding change in potential is at most $n/2$. Therefore,

$$\begin{aligned}
\textsc{Off}(\sigma) + \Delta_\sigma \phi &= (3/2) \cdot n + \sum_{i=1}^{h}(\textsc{Off}(\tilde{p}_i) + \Delta_{\tilde{p}_i}\phi) \\
&= (3/2) \cdot n + \sum_{i=1}^{h}(3k+1) \cdot \textsc{Opt}(p_i) \\
&= O(k) \cdot \textsc{Opt}(\sigma) + O(n).
\end{aligned}$$

Since the potential ϕ is initially 0 and always non-negative, we have $\Delta_\sigma \phi \geq 0$, and thus the theorem follows.

4   Online Algorithm

We first recall the definition of a metrical task system (MTS). An MTS is defined on a metric space $(\mathcal{S}, d)$, where $\mathcal{S}$ is a set of states and d specifies the distance between any two states. There is an initial state $x_0 \in S$.

The request sequence $\langle c_t : \mathcal{S} \to \mathbb{R}^+, t \geq 1 \rangle$ consists of cost functions c_t, and an algorithm has to produce a sequence of states $\langle x_t \in \mathcal{S}, t \geq 1 \rangle$. The total cost of such a solution is $\sum_t c_t(x_t) + d(x_{t-1}, x_t)$.

Proof (of Theorem 2.). We first argue that the online bisection problem on n nodes, restricted to algorithms from class $\mathcal{A}_\alpha^k$, forms a metrical task system. Each state in $\mathcal{S}$ is a set of cut-edges $\mathcal{C}$ such that $|\mathcal{C}| \leq 2k$ and $\mathcal{C}$ is α-balanced. Before serving the input sequence, every algorithm from class $\mathcal{A}_\alpha^k$ performs global rebalancing using the procedure from Lemma 1. This corresponds to selecting the initial state $x_0 \in \mathcal{S}$. The cost of this initial rebalancing can be neglected, as it is identical for all algorithms in $\mathcal{A}_\alpha^k$. The distance d between two states is defined as the minimum number of nodes that have to be recolored to change one state into the other. The value of $c_t(x) \in \{0, 1\}$ is the hit cost incurred if an algorithm state is x.

By the result of Bubeck et al. [12], there exists a randomized $O(\log^2 |\mathcal{S}|)$-competitive algorithm for every MTS. Let $\textsc{Onl}$ be their algorithm for the MTS instance described above. In this case, $|\mathcal{S}| = \sum_{i=1}^{k} \binom{n}{2i} \leq k \cdot \binom{n}{2k} \leq k \cdot n^{2k}$, and thus $\log^2 |\mathcal{S}| = O(k^2 \cdot \log^2 n)$. Clearly, $\textsc{Onl} \in \mathcal{A}_\alpha^k$, and for every (offline) algorithm $\textsc{Off} \in \mathcal{A}_\alpha^k$ and every input σ, it holds that $\mathbf{E}[\textsc{Onl}(\sigma)] \leq O(k^2 \cdot \log^2 n) \cdot \textsc{Off}(\sigma) + \beta$, where β is a parameter depending on $\mathcal{S}$, but independent of σ.

5   Conclusions

In this paper, we designed a randomized $O(\varepsilon^{-3} \cdot \log^2 n)$-competitive algorithm for the online bisection problem with ring demands, requiring clusters of size $3/4 + \varepsilon$. No super-constant lower bound is known for this variant; the current general randomized lower bound of $\Omega(\log n)$ does not appear to be adaptable to the ring demands. A natural direction for future work is to close the gap between upper and lower bounds and, perhaps more importantly, to reduce the required augmentation factor to $1 + \varepsilon$.

One approach that could bring progress toward the general case of online bisection is to study variants in which requests are restricted to a set Q different from the cycle. For instance, the case where Q is a tree seems to require substantially different techniques.

References

1. Andreev, K., Räcke, H.: Balanced graph partitioning. Theory Comput. Syst. **39**(6), 929–939 (2006). https://doi.org/10.1007/s00224-006-1350-7
2. Arora, S., Karger, D.R., Karpinski, M.: Polynomial time approximation schemes for dense instances of NP-hard problems. J. Comput. Syst. Sci. **58**(1), 193–210 (1999). https://doi.org/10.1006/jcss.1998.1605
3. Avin, C., Bienkowski, M., Loukas, A., Pacut, M., Schmid, S.: Dynamic balanced graph partitioning. SIAM J. Discret. Math. **34**(3), 1791–1812 (2020). https://doi.org/10.1137/17M1158513
4. Avin, C., Cohen, L., Parham, M., Schmid, S.: Competitive clustering of stochastic communication patterns on a ring. Computing **101**(9), 1369–1390 (2019). https://doi.org/10.1007/S00607-018-0666-X
5. Avin, C., Loukas, A., Pacut, M., Schmid, S.: Online balanced repartitioning. In: Proceedings of 30th International Symposium on Distributed Computing (DISC), pp. 243–256 (2016). https://doi.org/10.1007/978-3-662-53426-7_18
6. Azar, Y., Machluf, C., Patt-Shamir, B., Touitou, N.: Competitive vertex recoloring. Algorithmica **85**(7), 2001–2027 (2023). https://doi.org/10.1007/S00453-022-01076-X
7. Bienkowski, M., Böhm, M., Koutecký, M., Rothvoß, T., Sgall, J., Veselý, P.: Improved analysis of online balanced clustering. In: Proceedings of 19th Workshop on Approximation and Online Algorithms (WAOA), pp. 224–233 (2021). https://doi.org/10.1007/978-3-030-92702-8_14
8. Bienkowski, M., Even, G.: An improved approximation algorithm for dynamic minimum linear arrangement. In: Proceedings of 41st Symposium on Theoretical Aspects of Computer Science (STACS). LIPIcs, vol. 289, pp. 15:1–15:19. Schloss Dagstuhl – Leibniz-Zentrum für Informatik (2024). https://doi.org/10.4230/LIPICS.STACS.2024.15
9. Bienkowski, M., Schmid, S.: A subquadratic bound for online bisection. In: Proceedings of 41st Symposium on Theoretical Aspects of Computer Science (STACS), pp. 14:1–14:18. Schloss Dagstuhl – Leibniz-Zentrum für Informatik (2024). https://doi.org/10.4230/LIPICS.STACS.2024.14
10. Borodin, A., Linial, N., Saks, M.E.: An optimal on-line algorithm for metrical task system. J. ACM **39**(4), 745–763 (1992). https://doi.org/10.1145/146585.146588
11. Borodin, A., El-Yaniv, R.: Online Computation and Competitive Analysis. Cambridge University Press (1998)
12. Bubeck, S., Cohen, M.B., Lee, J.R., Lee, Y.T.: Metrical task systems on trees via mirror descent and unfair gluing. In: Proceedings of 30th ACM-SIAM Symposium on Discrete Algorithms (SODA), pp. 89–97. SIAM (2019). https://doi.org/10.1137/1.9781611975482.6
13. Even, G., Naor, J., Rao, S., Schieber, B.: Fast approximate graph partitioning algorithms. SIAM J. Comput. **28**(6), 2187–2214 (1999). https://doi.org/10.1137/S0097539796308217

14. Feige, U., Krauthgamer, R.: A polylogarithmic approximation of the minimum bisection. SIAM J. Comput. **31**(4), 1090–1118 (2002). https://doi.org/10.1137/S0097539701387660
15. Feige, U., Krauthgamer, R., Nissim, K.: Approximating the minimum bisection size. In: Proceedings of 32nd ACM Symposium on Theory of Computing (STOC), pp. 530–536 (2000). https://doi.org/10.1145/335305.335370
16. Forner, T., Räcke, H., Schmid, S.: Online balanced repartitioning of dynamic communication patterns in polynomial time. In: 2nd Symposium on Algorithmic Principles of Computer Systems (APOCS), pp. 40–54 (2021). https://doi.org/10.1137/1.9781611976489.4
17. Henzinger, M., Neumann, S., Räcke, H., Schmid, S.: Tight bounds for online graph partitioning. In: Proceedings of 32nd ACM-SIAM Symposium on Discrete Algorithms (SODA), pp. 2799–2818 (2021). https://doi.org/10.1137/1.9781611976465.166
18. Henzinger, M., Neumann, S., Schmid, S.: Efficient distributed workload (re-)embedding. In: Proc. SIGMETRICS/Performance Joint International Conference on Measurement and Modeling of Computer Systems, pp. 43–44 (2019). https://doi.org/10.1145/3309697.3331503
19. Krauthgamer, R., Feige, U.: A polylogarithmic approximation of the minimum bisection. SIAM Rev. **48**(1), 99–130 (2006). https://doi.org/10.1137/050640904
20. Krauthgamer, R., Naor, J., Schwartz, R.: Partitioning graphs into balanced components. In: Proceedings of 20th ACM-SIAM Symposium on Discrete Algorithms (SODA), pp. 942–949 (2009). https://doi.org/10.1137/1.9781611973068.102
21. Olver, N., Pruhs, K., Schewior, K., Sitters, R., Stougie, L.: The itinerant list update problem. In: Proceedings of 16th Workshop on Approximation and Online Algorithms (WAOA), pp. 310–326 (2018). https://doi.org/10.1007/978-3-030-04693-4_19
22. Pacut, M., Parham, M., Schmid, S.: Brief announcement: deterministic lower bound for dynamic balanced graph partitioning. In: Proceedings of 39th ACM Symposium on Principles of Distributed Computing (PODC), pp. 461–463 (2020). https://doi.org/10.1145/3382734.3405696
23. Pacut, M., Parham, M., Schmid, S.: Optimal online balanced graph partitioning. In: Proceedings of 40th IEEE International Conference on Computer Communications (INFOCOM), pp. 1–9 (2021). https://doi.org/10.1109/INFOCOM42981.2021.9488824
24. Patt-Shamir, B., Rosén, A., Umboh, S.W.: Colorful vertex recoloring of bipartite graphs. In: Proceedings of 42nd Symposium on Theoretical Aspects of Computer Science (STACS). LIPIcs, vol. 327, pp. 70:1–70:19. Schloss Dagstuhl – Leibniz-Zentrum für Informatik (2025). https://doi.org/10.4230/LIPICS.STACS.2025.70
25. Räcke, H.: Optimal hierarchical decompositions for congestion minimization in networks. In: Proceedings of 40th ACM Symposium on Theory of Computing (STOC), pp. 255–264 (2008). https://doi.org/10.1145/1374376.1374415
26. Räcke, H., Schmid, S., Zabrodin, R.: Approximate dynamic balanced graph partitioning. In: Proceedings of 34th ACM Symp. on Parallelism in Algorithms and Architectures (SPAA), pp. 401–409. ACM (2022). https://doi.org/10.1145/3490148.3538563
27. Räcke, H., Schmid, S., Zabrodin, R.: Polylog-competitive algorithms for dynamic balanced graph partitioning for ring demands. In: Proceedings of 35th ACM Symposium on Parallelism in Algorithms and Architectures (SPAA), pp. 403–413. ACM (2023). https://doi.org/10.1145/3558481.3591097

28. Räcke, H., Schmid, S., Zabrodin, R.: Tight bounds for online balanced partitioning in the generalized learning model. In: Proceedings of 37th ACM Symposium on Parallelism in Algorithms and Architectures (SPAA), pp. 240–254. ACM (2025). https://doi.org/10.1145/3694906.3743327
29. Rajaraman, R., Wasim, O.: Improved bounds for online balanced graph repartitioning. In: Proceedings of 30th European Symposium on Algorithms (ESA), pp. 83:1–83:15 (2022). https://doi.org/10.4230/LIPIcs.ESA.2022.83
30. Rajaraman, R., Wasim, O.: Competitive capacitated online recoloring. In: Proceedings of 32nd European Symposium on Algorithms (ESA). LIPIcs, vol. 308, pp. 95:1–95:17. Schloss Dagstuhl – Leibniz-Zentrum für Informatik (2024). https://doi.org/10.4230/LIPICS.ESA.2024.95
31. Saran, H., Vazirani, V.V.: Finding k cuts within twice the optimal. SIAM J. Comput. **24**(1), 101–108 (1995). https://doi.org/10.1137/S0097539792251730
32. Sergeev, A., Balso, M.D.: Horovod: fast and easy distributed deep learning in tensorflow (2018), unpublished
33. Simon, H.D., Teng, S.: How good is recursive bisection? SIAM J. Comput. **18**(5), 1436–1445 (1997). https://doi.org/10.1137/S1064827593255135
34. Sleator, D.D., Tarjan, R.E.: Amortized efficiency of list update and paging rules. Commun. ACM **28**(2), 202–208 (1985). https://doi.org/10.1145/2786.2793

On the Solvability of Byzantine-Tolerant Reliable Communication in Dynamic Networks

Silvia Bonomi[1] , Giovanni Farina[2(✉)] , and Sébastien Tixeuil[3,4]

[1] Sapienza University of Rome, Rome, Italy
[2] Department of Engineering, Niccolò Cusano University, Rome, Italy
giovanni.farina@unicusano.it
[3] Sorbonne Université, CNRS, LIP6, Paris, France
[4] Institut Universitaire de France, Paris, France

Abstract. A reliable communication primitive guarantees the delivery, integrity, and authorship of messages exchanged between correct processes of a distributed system. We investigate the necessary and sufficient conditions for reliable communication in dynamic networks, where the network topology evolves over time despite the presence of a limited number of Byzantine faulty processes that may behave arbitrarily (i.e., in the globally bounded Byzantine failure model). We identify classes of dynamic networks where such conditions are satisfied, and extend our analysis to message losses, local computation with unbounded finite delay, and authenticated messages.

Keywords: Reliable Communication · Byzantine fault-tolerance · Dynamic Network · Evolving Graph

1 Introduction

The reliable communication primitive is a fundamental building block for distributed systems. It guarantees the proper exchange of messages between correct processes, even if they are not directly connected by a communication link or if some participating processes behave maliciously (i.e., are Byzantine). In particular, the primitive ensures the *authorship, integrity,* and *delivery* of the information exchanged between correct processes. More precisely, it mandates that *(i)* all messages exchanged between correct processes are not modified during their propagation (integrity), *(ii)* messages eventually reach their destination (delivery), and *(iii)* the author of a message cannot be forged (authorship). Implementations of the reliable communication primitive have been studied in several settings [2,3,12,22,26,30,31]. In this paper, we consider the *globally bounded Byzantine failure model* (i.e., there is an upper bound f on the number of Byzantine faulty processes, and f is known to all correct processes), and a *dynamic*

This work is dedicated to Alexandre Maurer, whose work sparked this research journey.

© The Author(s), under exclusive license to Springer Nature Switzerland AG 2026
C. Georgiou (Ed.): SIROCCO 2026, LNCS 16488, pp. 112–130, 2026.
https://doi.org/10.1007/978-3-032-26465-7_7

communication network. To the best of our knowledge, the work of Maurer et al. [26] is the only one that analyzes the solvability of the primitive in such a setting. It characterizes the necessary and sufficient conditions for reliable communication from a specific source to a defined target at a given time. However, the verification of the conditions identified by Maurer et al. [26] is equivalent to solving a NP-complete problem [16,18].

In this work, we first extend such conditions to characterize when *all* correct processes can achieve reliable communication in a synchronous system *independently of the diffusion time.* We identify classes of dynamic networks that *(i)* satisfy the solvability conditions *(ii)* and where verifying that a network belongs to these classes is polynomial in the number of processes in the system. We then expand our analysis to include an asynchronous system with lossy links and find that the solvability conditions for synchronous systems also apply to asynchronous ones. Finally, we examine the case of authenticated messages.

2   Related Work

The reliable communication problem, which aims to implement a primitive to guarantee the delivery, integrity, and authorship of messages exchanged in a distributed system, has been the subject of extensive research in static networks under various assumptions. These include various types of faults, such as omissions, crashes, and arbitrary faults; alternative fault distributions, including deterministic and probabilistic models; and the impact of these faults on links [29], processes, or both. In a seminal work, Dolev [12] identified the necessary and sufficient condition for this problem in static networks with reliable and authenticated links, assuming an upper bound f on the number of Byzantine faulty processes. The condition states that the network must be $(2f + 1)$-connected to tolerate f such processes.

Subsequent work investigated more constrained process failure distributions. Koo [19] analyzed the reliable communication problem assuming only a fraction of nodes in a process's neighborhood can be compromised. Pelc and Peleg [31] generalized Koo's results by characterizing a failure model with an upper bound on faulty processes in each node's neighborhood and defining a corresponding solution. Pagourtzis et al. [28] further generalized these models by assuming non-homogeneous local bounds on the number of faulty processes in each node's neighborhood. They also showed this failure model can be extended by assuming specific sets of potentially faulty processes (the *general adversary model*), and that knowledge of the network topology increases the number of faulty processes that can be tolerated in the non-homogeneous, locally bounded setting.

Most solutions to the reliable communication problem rely on node-disjoint path redundancy, thus requiring highly connected networks. Consequently, several works have investigated weaker Byzantine-tolerant reliable communication primitives for use in loosely connected networks. These primitives may allow a small minority of correct processes to either deliver invalid messages or fail to deliver genuine ones [23–25].

Over the past two decades, the integration of computing and communication capabilities into a growing number of devices (*e.g.*, IoT networks) has spurred increased interest in the modeling and analysis of dynamic distributed systems. Most of the dynamic distributed system models proposed so far can be categorized as either *open* or *closed*. The former involves new processes continuously entering and leaving the system (a phenomenon often referred to as *churn*), while the latter assumes a fixed set of processes whose communication links may change over time. In the context of closed dynamic networks, Maurer et al. [26] identified the necessary and sufficient conditions for solving a single instance of the reliable communication problem in the presence of a subset of f Byzantine faulty processes. Bonomi et al. [2,5] identified the solvability conditions assuming the homogeneous locally bounded failure model of Pelc and Peleg [31]. Maurer [21] later extended the primitive to also withstand transient process failures.

Cryptography (specifically, digital signatures), by ensuring the authenticity and integrity of exchanged information, can be used to achieve Byzantine-tolerant reliable communication [10,14]. The main advantage of such cryptographic tools is that they enable reliable communication with simpler solutions and under weaker connectivity requirements. However, their correctness depends on the underlying cryptosystem and the assumption that the adversary has bounded computing power. A common assumption of Byzantine-tolerant reliable communication protocols is the use of authenticated point-to-point channels, which prevents a process from impersonating multiple others (a Sybil attack) [13]. The primary distinction between cryptographic (authenticated) and non-cryptographic (unauthenticated) protocols for reliable communication lies in how cryptographic primitives are used: non-cryptographic protocols can only use digital signatures between neighbors for authentication, while cryptographic protocols use them to allow message verification even between nodes that are not directly connected. Finally, it is worth noting that cryptography is not strictly required to implement an authenticated channel [32].

This work builds upon the seminal characterization of the reliable communication problem in closed dynamic networks by Maurer et al. [26], extending it in several directions by: *(i)* specifying the solvability conditions for any pair of processes at any time; *(ii)* identifying classes of dynamic networks where these conditions hold; and *(iii)* considering weaker or alternative models in which messages can be lost and local computation delays are unknown.

3   Graphs and Evolving Graphs

A static undirected *graph* is a pair $G = (V, E)$ of sets V and E such that $E \subseteq \binom{V}{2}$. The elements p_i of V are the *vertices* (or *nodes*) of the graph, whereas the elements of E are the (undirected) *edges* [11]. Two vertices p_s, p_t connected by an edge $\{p_s, p_t\} \in E$ are called *neighbors*. A sequence of distinct nodes $P = (p_1, p_2, \ldots, p_m)$ constitutes a *path* if every pair of consecutive nodes p_i and p_{i+1} in the sequence satisfies the condition that they are neighbors. Nodes p_1 and p_m in P are referred to as *endpoints*. Two or more paths are *disjoint* if they share no node except their endpoints. A graph is *connected* if there exists a path between every pair of nodes. A graph is k *-connected* if removing any subset $S \subset V$ of $k - 1$ nodes (and all the edges having at least one node in S) results in a connected subgraph. If a graph is k-connected, then there exists a set of k disjoint paths between all pairs of nodes [27]. The *node connectivity* of a graph is the minimum number of nodes that have to be removed from the graph to disconnect it [11].

An *evolving graph* (*a.k.a.* temporal graph) $\mathcal{G} = (G_0, G_1, \ldots, G_j, \ldots)$ [15] is a sequence of static undirected graphs, where each graph $G_j := (V, E_j \subseteq \binom{V}{2})$ denotes a *snapshot* of $\mathcal{G}$. All snapshots share the same set of vertices V, whereas the set of edges may change at every snapshot. An evolving graph is defined over a set of time instants $\mathcal{T} \subseteq \mathbb{N}$, potentially infinite, drawn from the natural numbers, called the *lifetime* of $\mathcal{G}$. Specifically, every snapshot $G_j \in \mathcal{G}$ is associated with time instant $j \in \mathcal{T}$, and vice-versa. We say that a particular edge e is *present* (or *appears*) at time j if $e \in E_j$ (*i.e.*, e is among the edges of snapshot G_j). The graph $\mathbb{G} = (V, E = \bigcup_{j \in \mathcal{T}} E_j)$ is the *underlying graph*. We refer to V and E as the *vertex set* and *edge set*, respectively, of the evolving graph.

Given a subset $T \subseteq \mathcal{T}$, a *temporal subgraph* $\mathcal{G}_T$ of $\mathcal{G}$ is the evolving graph that restricts the lifetime of $\mathcal{G}$ to the instants $j \in T$, namely, $\mathcal{G}_T$ contains only the snapshots G_j in $\mathcal{G}$ such that $j \in T$. Then, $\mathcal{G}_{[x,y]}$ is the temporal subgraph induced by the contiguous interval $[x, y]$ of $\mathcal{T}$, i.e., $\mathcal{G}_{[x,y]}$ limits the lifetime of $\mathcal{G}$ to the period $[x, y]$. Similarly, the temporal subgraph $\mathcal{G}_{[x,*]}$ restricts the lifetime of $\mathcal{G}$ to the time instants after x (x included). A *spatial subgraph* $\mathcal{G}[\bar{V}, \bar{E}]$ is the evolving graph resulting from $\mathcal{G}$ when considering the set $\bar{V} \subseteq V$ as vertex set, and $\bar{E} \subseteq (E \cap \binom{\bar{V}}{2})$ as edge set. We specify a spatial subgraph only by its vertex set $\bar{V}$, namely $\mathcal{G}[\bar{V}]$, if its edge set $\bar{E}$ consists of all the edges in the edge set that have both endpoints in $\bar{V}$, i.e. $\bar{E} = E \cap \binom{\bar{V}}{2}$. A *spatial temporal* subgraph $\mathcal{G}[\bar{V}]_T$ of $\mathcal{G}$ considers a subset T of the lifetime $\mathcal{T}$, a subset $\bar{V}$ of the vertices V as vertex set, and $\bar{E} = E \cap \binom{\bar{V}}{2}$ as edge set. Figure 1a shows a graphical example of an evolving graph spanning over three time instants, while Fig. 2 presents a spatial temporal subgraph of the former, removing node p_2 and snapshot G_2.

A *journey* is the analogue of a path in an evolving graph.

Definition 1. (Journey [26]).[1] *Given an evolving graph* $\mathcal{G} = (G_0, G_1, \ldots, G_j, \ldots)$, *where each* $G_j = (V, E_j)$, *and two of its nodes* $p_1, p_m \in V$, *a journey from* p_1 *to* p_m, *denoted with* $p_1 \rightsquigarrow p_m$, *is a pair* $J = (A, B)$ *of two sequences* A *and* B *such that:* A *is a sequence of distinct nodes* $(p_1, p_2, \ldots, p_m)$ *and* B *is a strictly increasing sequence of time instants* $(j_I, j_{II}, \ldots, j_{m-1})$, *with* $j_\iota \in \mathcal{T}$, *such that for all* $i \in \{1, \ldots, m - 1\}$, *it holds that* $\{p_i, p_{i+1}\} \in E_{j_\iota}$.

---

[1] Any definition or theorem followed by a reference has been defined or proven in that reference. All other definitions and theorems are novel to this work. This definition has been simplified due to the absence of the latency function in the model we adopted, and has been adapted to a discrete lifetime.

Definition 2. (Set $\Sigma(\mathcal{G}, p_s, p_t)$ of node sets between two vertices [26]). *Given an evolving graph $\mathcal{G}$ and two of its nodes $p_s, p_t \in V$, $\Sigma(p_s, p_t)$ refers to the set of node sets $\{\{p_1, \ldots, p_l\} | (p_s, p_1, \ldots, p_l, p_t)$ is a journey in $\mathcal{G}\}$.*

Definition 3. (Hitting set [17]). *Let $\Omega = \{S_1, S_2, \ldots, S_m\}$ be a family of subsets of a universe U, where $S_i \subseteq U$ for each $i \in \{1, \ldots, m\}$. A set $H \subseteq U$ is called a hitting set for Ω if it intersects every set in Ω, that is,*

$$\forall i \in \{1, \ldots, m\}, \quad H \cap S_i \neq \emptyset.$$

Definition 4. (Minimum Hitting Set [17] and MinCut [26]). *Let $\Omega = \{S_1, S_2, \ldots, S_m\}$ be a family of subsets of a universe U, where $S_i \subseteq U$ for each $i \in \{1, \ldots, m\}$. A set $H \subseteq U$ is called a minimum hitting set for Ω if:*

- *H is a hitting set for Ω, i.e., $H \cap S_i \neq \emptyset$ for all $i \in \{1, \ldots, m\}$, and*
- *H has the smallest possible cardinality among all hitting sets for Ω, i.e., for every hitting set $H' \subseteq U$, it holds that $|H| \leq |H'|$.*

We refer with $MinCut(\Omega)$ to the cardinality of a minimum hitting set for Ω.

Definition 5. (Dynamic minimum cut size k between two nodes and $p_s \leadsto_k p_t$ [26]). *Given an evolving graph $\mathcal{G}$, two of its nodes $p_s, p_t \in V$, the dynamic minimum cut size k from p_s to p_t is the smallest number of other nodes to remove from $\mathcal{G}$ so that no journey exists from p_s to p_t. Specifically,*

$$DynMinCut(\mathcal{G}, p_s, p_t) = MinCut(\Sigma(\mathcal{G}, p_s, p_t))$$

Note that if $\exists j \in \mathcal{T} : \{p_s, p_t\} \in E_j$, then $DynMinCut(\mathcal{G}, p_s, p_t) = \infty$.

We denote with $p_s \leadsto_k p_t$ a set of journeys in $\mathcal{G}$ from p_s to p_t having a dynamic minimum cut size at least k.

In the same way, various families of graph have been defined in graph theory (trees, planar graphs, grids, etc.), and several classes of evolving graphs have been characterized in the literature [8,9]. Specifically, a class of evolving graphs groups all graphs that satisfy a specific set of properties. We recall or define some relevant classes to our work in Sect. 5.1.

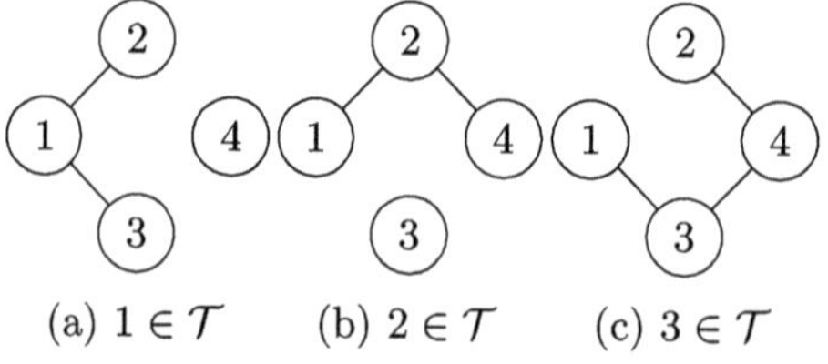

Fig. 1. An evolving graph example.

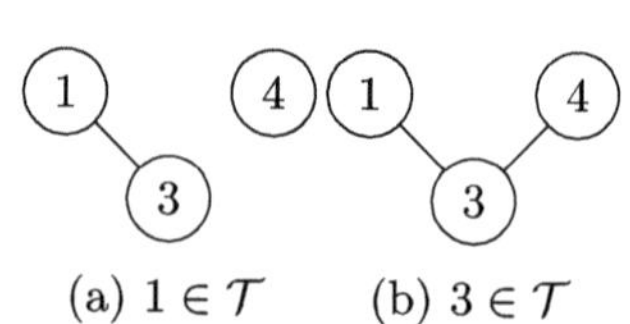

Fig. 2. A spatial temporal subgraph of the evolving graph in Fig. 1.

4 System Model and Problem Statement

We consider a distributed system composed of a fixed set of n processes $N = \{p_1, p_2 \ldots, p_n\}$, each one associated with a unique integer identifier. The evolution of the system is characterized by events occurring at specific times defined by a fictitious global clock spanning the natural numbers $\mathbb{N}$.

Processes can communicate with each other by exchanging *messages* over a *dynamic communication network* composed of *point-to-point links*. The dynamic communication network is modeled by an evolving graph $\mathcal{G} = (G_0, G_1, \ldots, G_j, \ldots)$. Each *snapshot* $G_j = (V,\ E_j)$ corresponds to the actual communication network at time j where $V = N$ represents the set of processes participating in the system and $E_j \subseteq N \times N$ is the actual set of *existing (present)* edges at time j (i.e., communication links available for the point-to-point communication). In the following, we will interchangeably use the terms *node* and *process*, and the terms *link* and *edge*. The evolving graph characterizes the communication network for the entire lifetime of the system. At each time j, processes can only communicate by using present links, i.e., they can send/receive messages to/from their neighbors in the snapshot G_j. We refer to *multicast* when a process sends a message through all of its available links, namely, to all of its current neighbors. Each message m is associated with a *source/author* and a *sender*: the source is the process *that generates* message m, the sender is the process *that relays* message m through a link. The source and sender of a message may coincide.

At each time instant j, every process executes the following concurrent steps: *compute*, *send*, and *receive*. Specifically, it carries out local computation and prepares (enqueues) messages to be sent to its neighbors, transmits these messages (if any), and receives messages from other processes (if any). Consequently, a message is able to traverse only one link during a single time instant j.

Processes execute a distributed protocol $\mathcal{P}$. Processes can be either *correct* or *Byzantine faulty*. A correct process executes the protocol $\mathcal{P}$, Byzantine faulty processes can behave arbitrarily instead. In particular, while running $\mathcal{P}$, faulty processes can send arbitrary messages or omit to send/receive all or part of them. We assume that at most f processes can be faulty (globally bounded Byzantine failure model).

To model the asynchrony and delays that may occur in the system, we consider two types of point-to-point communication primitives that characterize the behavior of the links (PL and FLL), and two alternative settings for the local computation delay of processes (SC and AC):

- *perfect link* (PL): it provides the *reliable delivery* property [7], namely that if a correct process p_s sends a message m to a correct process p_r at time j via the present link, then p_r receives m at the same time j;
- *fair-loss link* (FLL): it guarantees the *fair-loss* property [7], namely that if a correct process p_s infinitely often (at distinct times) sends a message m to a correct process p_r via the present link, then p_r receives m an infinite number of times;

- *synchronous computation* (SC): the local computation time (i.e., the time to perform the compute step) is negligible and is assumed to be equal to 0;
- *asynchronous computation* (AC): the local computation (i.e., the compute step) takes a finite and unknown amount of time.

For the sake of modeling, we assume that *(i)* link properties only hold when links are present, that *(ii)* links have *unbounded capacity* (namely, if a correct process p_s sends an arbitrary set M of messages to a correct process p_r at time j, then p_r receives all messages in M at the same time instant j (PL or FLL) or they are lost (FLL)), and *(iii)* that processes can instantly detect whether their links are available or not. The set of assumptions PL and SC characterizes a synchronous distributed system where processes and links are able to accommodate every message propagation enabled by the dynamic communication network $\mathcal{G}$, namely, every journey in $\mathcal{G}$ represents a feasible propagation pattern for a message between its endpoints (for an example, the journey $((p_s, p_r, p_t), (1, 2))$ models the possible propagation of a message exchanged at time 1 from p_s to p_r and then forwarded by p_r to p_t at time 2). It follows that a message generated by a process p_s at time j in a PL-SC system can potentially reach any process p_t such that there exists a journey from p_s to p_t in $\mathcal{G}_{[j,*]}$. The FLL assumption characterizes potentially asynchronous and lossy links in this setting, meaning that a process may attempt a finite but unknown number of times to send a message on a link that is infinitely often present before its first reception. The AC assumption characterizes the potential inability of processes to perform timely computation and generate messages to send for a finite amount of time. Note that the AC assumption does not prevent processes from receiving messages.

Finally, we consider two alternative settings that limit the capability of faulty processes:

- *authenticated links* (AL): the identity of the sender of a message m, i.e., the process sending m through a point-to-point link, cannot be forged;
- *authenticated messages* (AM): the identity of the author of a message m, namely, the process that generated a message m, cannot be forged.

Note that the AM assumption can guarantee the authenticity of the author of a message over multiple links, while the AL assumption can guarantee the authenticity of the author only if it matches the sender of the message, and that the authenticated message setting does not implicitly assume authenticated links.

In the rest of the paper, we will indicate the setting under consideration, in terms of links and local computation assumptions, by specifying a triple $\langle \alpha, \beta, \gamma \rangle$ where $\alpha \in \{PL, FLL\}$, $\beta \in \{SC, AC\}$ and $\gamma \in \{AL, AM\}$.

The Reliable Communication Problem

We aim at analyzing the *reliable communication problem*, whose goal is the definition of a communication primitive that allows correct processes, not directly connected by a link, to exchange *contents* guaranteeing their authorship, integrity, and delivery.

Let us denote as *source* or *author* the process p_s that generates a content and as *target* p_t the peer to which such content is addressed. A Reliable Communication (RC) primitive is accessible by every process in the system and exposes two operations: RC.send(p_t, c) and RC.deliver(p_s, c). The send operation is invoked by the source to disseminate a content, and the deliver operation notifies a process about the delivery of a content.

A protocol $\mathcal{P}$ implements a reliable communication primitive if it satisfies the following properties:

- *safety*: if p_t is a *correct* process and delivers a content c from p_s, then p_s previously sent c;
- *liveness*: if p_s is a *correct* process and sends a content c to a correct process p_t, then p_t eventually delivers c from p_s.

For the sake of notation, we denote by *content* the payload exchanged by a reliable communication primitive, and by *message* the unit of information exchanged by a distributed protocol over a point-to-point link.

We say that an *instance* of the reliable communication problem *starts at time* j (or simply *at time* j) if at time j the RC.send operation is executed, and that it *terminates at time* j if the target process p_t executes the RC.deliver(p_s, c) operation for the first time at time j.

5   Solvability Conditions

We characterize the solvability of the reliable communication problem in several settings. We start by recalling the result of Maurer et al. [26] who established the necessary and sufficient conditions for a *one-to-one* (i.e., from a defined source to a fixed target) reliable communication starting at time j, in a setting where the links are perfect and authenticated and the computation is syn chronous. We then extend their conditions to any starting time and any pair of processes. Afterwards, we look for further classes of evolving graphs where the learned conditions are verified. Interestingly, the stricter enabling class we identify for the PL and SC setting remains minimal also for the weakest setting we consider, namely asynchronous computation and fair-loss links; another class instead, allows to upper bound the latency of any reliable communication instance when synchronous computation and perfect links are assumed. Finally, we extend all of our results to the settings where messages are authenticated, and we provide an analysis on the computational complexity of asserting class membership for the dynamic network classes we identified. All the results that follow, cited or provided, are based on the existence of a specific set of journeys in the communication network that support the propagation of a content in the considered settings. Note that past theorems and definitions may be rephrased to fit our notations.

Due to space limitations, some of the intermediate results and proofs are reported in the technical report version of this paper [6].

5.1   Classes of Evolving Graphs

In this paper, we consider various classes of evolving graphs. While Definitions 6–11 were previously considered in the literature [9], Definitions 12-17 are newly defined to address the presence of Byzantine processes.

Definition 6. (Class $\mathcal{J}_{(s,t)}$ - Temporal Reachability). *The class $\mathcal{J}_{(s,t)}$ is the set of all evolving graphs $\mathcal{G}$ where there exists a journey from node p_s to node p_t.*

Definition 7. (Class $\mathcal{TC}$ - Temporal Connectivity). *The class $\mathcal{TC}$ is the set of all evolving graphs $\mathcal{G}$ where $\forall p_s, p_t \in V$, there exists $(p_s \rightsquigarrow p_t) \in \mathcal{G}$ (the class of evolving graphs where a journey exists between every pair of nodes).*

Definition 8. (Class $\mathcal{J}^{\mathcal{R}}_{(s,t)}$ - Recurrent Reachability). *The class $\mathcal{J}^{\mathcal{R}}_{(s,t)}$ is the set of all evolving graphs $\mathcal{G}$ where $\forall j \in \mathcal{T}$, $\mathcal{G}_{[j,*]} \in \mathcal{J}_{(s,t)}$.*

Definition 9. (Class $\mathcal{TC}^{\mathcal{R}}$ - Recurrent temporal connectivity). *The class $\mathcal{TC}^{\mathcal{R}}$ is the set of all evolving graphs $\mathcal{G}$ with infinite lifetime where $\forall j \in \mathcal{T}$, $\mathcal{G}_{[j,*]} \in \mathcal{TC}$ (the class where, for every time instant $j \in \mathcal{T}$, the temporal subgraph $\mathcal{G}_{[j,*]}$ is temporally connected).*

Definition 10. (Class C^* - Always-connected snapshots, or 1-interval connectivity). *The class C^* is the set of all evolving graphs $\mathcal{G}$ where $\forall G_j \in \mathcal{G}$, G_j is connected (the class where every snapshot is a connected graph).*

Definition 11. (Class $\mathcal{E}^{\mathcal{R}}$ - Recurrent Edges). *The class $\mathcal{E}^{\mathcal{R}}$ is the set of all evolving graphs $\mathcal{G}$ with infinite lifetime where $\forall e \in E$, $\forall j \in \mathcal{T}$, $\exists l > j, e \in E_l$ (the class where every edge is present infinitely often).*

Definition 12. (Class $\mathcal{J}_{(s,t,k)}$ - k-journeys from p_s to p_t). *The class $\mathcal{J}_{(a,b,k)}$ is the set of all evolving graphs $\mathcal{G}$ where $\exists (p_s \rightsquigarrow_k p_t) \in \mathcal{G}$ (the class where there exists a set of journeys with a dynamic minimum cut of size at least k from node p_s to node p_t).*

Definition 13. (Class $\mathcal{J}^{\mathcal{R}}_{(s,t,k)}$ - Recurrent k-journeys from p_s to p_t). *The class $\mathcal{J}^{\mathcal{R}}_{(s,t,k)}$ is the set of all evolving graphs $\mathcal{G}$ with infinite lifetime where $\forall j \in \mathcal{T}$, $\mathcal{G}_{[j,*]} \in \mathcal{J}_{(s,t,k)}$ (the class where the temporal subgraph $\mathcal{G}_{[j,*]}$ is in $\mathcal{J}_{(s,t,k)}$ for every time $j \in \mathcal{T}$).*

Definition 14. (Class $\mathcal{TC}_k$ - Temporal k-Connectivity). *The class $\mathcal{TC}_k$ is the set of all evolving graphs $\mathcal{G}$ where $\forall p_s, p_t \in V$, $\exists (p_s \rightsquigarrow_k p_t) \in \mathcal{G}$ (the class where there exists a set of journeys having a dynamic minimum cut of size at least k between every pair of nodes).*

Definition 15. (Class $\mathcal{TC}^{\mathcal{R}}_k$ - Recurrent k-Temporal-Connectivity). *The class $\mathcal{TC}^{\mathcal{R}}_k$ is the set of all evolving graphs $\mathcal{G}$ with infinite lifetime where $\forall j \in \mathcal{T}$, $\mathcal{G}_{[j,*]} \in \mathcal{TC}_k$ - the class where the temporal subgraph $\mathcal{G}_{[j,*]}$ is in $\mathcal{TC}_k$ for every time $j \in \mathcal{T}$.*

Definition 16. (Class $\mathcal{C}_k^*$ - 1-interval k-connectivity). *The class $\mathcal{C}_k^*$ is the set of all evolving graphs $\mathcal{G}$ where $\forall G_j \in \mathcal{G}$, G_j is a k-connected graph (the class where the node connectivity of every snapshot is at least k).*

Definition 17. (Class $\mathcal{E}_k^{\mathcal{R}}$ (Recurrent Edges k-connected)). *The class $\mathcal{E}_k^{\mathcal{R}}$ is the set of all evolving graphs $\mathcal{G}$ with infinite lifetime where, given $\mathbb{G} = (V, E)$ as underlying graph of $\mathcal{G}$, $\mathbb{G}$ is a k-connected graph and $\forall e \in E$, $\forall j \in \mathcal{T}$, $\exists l > j, e \in E_l$ (the class where the underlying graph is k-connected and every edge is present infinitely often).*

5.2 Authenticated Links

Maurer et al. [26] characterized the strict condition to solve a single one-to-one instance of the reliable communication problem in the *perfect authenticated links* and *synchronous computation* setting. In other words, they identified the message propagation pattern that the processes and the communication network must support (i.e., the "minimum" set of journeys that a content must traverse) in order to solve a single instance of the reliable communication problem under the considered settings. We recall their contribution in [6].

Theorem 1. (One-to-one RC at time j in $\langle PL, SC, AL \rangle$ [26]). *The reliable communication problem can be solved, starting at time j, from a defined source p_s to a fixed target p_t, in the perfect authenticated links and synchronous computation setting, if and only if $\mathcal{G}_{[j,*]} \in \mathcal{J}_{(s,t,2f+1)}$.*

From this seminal result [26], we can derive the class $\mathcal{J}_{(s,t,k)}$ as the one that characterizes the communication networks where one-to-one reliable communication in $\langle PL, SC, AL \rangle$ can be solved at least once.

We generalize the result by Maurer et al. [26] to any pair of processes and any time j.

Theorem 2. (RC at time j in $\langle PL, SC, AL \rangle$). *The reliable communication problem can be solved <u>at time</u> j, in the perfect authenticated links and synchronous computation setting, if and only if the dynamic subgraph $\mathcal{G}_{[j,*]} \in \mathcal{TC}_k$ and $k > 2f$.*

Proof. The claim follows from an extension of Theorem 1, by considering any pair of processes as the source and target of a reliable communication instance, and by the construction of class $\mathcal{TC}_k$ (Definition 14). Definition 12 identifies the class of evolving graphs where the strict condition for one-to-one reliable communication at time j holds (Theorem 1). Given any four nodes $p_s, p_t, p_u, p_v \in V$, $\mathcal{G}_{[j,*]} \in \mathcal{J}_{(s,t,2f+1)}$ does not imply $\mathcal{G}_{[j,*]} \in \mathcal{J}_{(u,v,2f+1)}$; therefore, the condition must thus be verified for every pair of nodes. Definition 14 extends Definition 12 by considering any pair of processes; the claim thus follows given the strictness of Theorem 1. $\square$

The $\mathcal{TC}_k^{\mathcal{R}}$ class identifies the communication networks where the reliable communication problem is solvable in $\langle PL, SC, AL \rangle$ at any time $j \in \mathcal{T}$.

Theorem 3 (RC in $\langle PL, SC, AL \rangle$). *The reliable communication problem can be solved starting <u>at any time</u> j, in the perfect authenticated links and synchronous computation setting, if and only if $\mathcal{G} \in \mathcal{TC}_k^{\mathcal{R}}$ and $k > 2f$.*

Proof. The claim follows from an extension of Theorem 2, by considering any starting time for a reliable communication instance, and by the construction of class $\mathcal{TC}_k^{\mathcal{R}}$ (Definition 15).

Definition 14 identifies the class of evolving graphs where the strict condition for reliable communication at time j holds (Theorem 2). Given $x, y \in \mathcal{T}$, where $y > x$, $\mathcal{G}_{[y,*]} \in \mathcal{TC}_k$ implies $\mathcal{G}_{[x,*]} \in \mathcal{TC}_k$, but the opposite relation does not hold; thus, the condition needs to be extended to any time $j \in \mathcal{T}$. Definition 15 extends Definition 14 by considering any time $j \in \mathcal{T}$; the claim thus follows given the strictness of Theorem 2.

We identify further dynamic network sub-classes of $\mathcal{TC}_k^{\mathcal{R}}$, thus providing additional classes where the primitive is feasible. We defined a sub-class of $\mathcal{E}^{\mathcal{R}}$ that relates to the $\mathcal{TC}_k^{\mathcal{R}}$ class and extends the result reported in the Theorem 3.

Theorem 4. *Let $\mathcal{G}$ be an evolving graph with infinite lifetime. If there exists a spatial subgraph $\mathcal{G}' := \mathcal{G}[V, \bar{E}]$ of class $\mathcal{E}_k^{\mathcal{R}}$ then $\mathcal{G}$ is in $\mathcal{TC}_k^{\mathcal{R}}$.*

Proof. Consider a k-connected graph $\mathbb{G}' = (V, \bar{E})$ where p_a and p_b are two of its nodes. It is known [11] that it is possible to identify a set of paths $p_a \to_k p_b$ between p_a, p_b in $\mathbb{G}'$ such that its minimum cut is at least k (namely, there exists a set of paths $p_a \to_k p_b$ between p_a, p_b in $\mathbb{G}'$ such that it is not possible to identify a subset $S \subset V \setminus \{p_a, p_b\}$ of size $k - 1$ in which each path in $p_a \to_k p_b$ shares at least one node with S). If $\mathbb{G}'$ is the underlying graph of an evolving graph $\mathcal{G}'$ of class $\mathcal{E}^{\mathcal{R}}$ (thus $\mathcal{G}' \in \mathcal{E}_k^{\mathcal{R}}$) , then there always exists a set of journeys $p_a \rightsquigarrow_k p_b$ traversing the paths $p_a \to_k p_b$, because every edge re-appears infinitely often. It follows that $\mathcal{G}' \in \mathcal{TC}_k^{\mathcal{R}}$ and the claim follows for any temporal graph $\mathcal{G}$ having as underlying graph $\mathbb{G} = (V, E \supseteq \bar{E})$.

Corollary 1 (RC in $\langle PL, NC, AL \rangle$ - recurrent edges). *The reliable communication problem can be solved starting at any time j, in the perfect authenticated links and synchronous computation setting, if there exists a spatial subgraph $\mathcal{G}' := \mathcal{G}[V, \bar{E}]$ in $\mathcal{G}$ such that $\mathcal{G}' \in \mathcal{E}_k^{\mathcal{R}}$ and $k > 2f$.*

Proof. It follows from Theorems 3 and 4. Theorem 3 characterizes class $\mathcal{TC}_k^{\mathcal{R}}$ as the one where reliable communication is solvable at any time when $k > 2f$; Theorem 4 identifies $\mathcal{E}_k^{\mathcal{R}}$ class as a subclass of $\mathcal{TC}_k^{\mathcal{R}}$.

Relations between recurrent reachability/connectivity and recurrent edges classes exist in both directions, as shown in the following.

Theorem 5. *If an evolving graph $\mathcal{G}$ is in $\mathcal{J}_{(s,t)}^{\mathcal{R}}$ then there exists a spatial subgraph $\mathcal{G}' := \mathcal{G}[\bar{V}, \bar{E}]$ of class $\mathcal{E}^{\mathcal{R}}$ having a path between p_s and p_t in its underlying graph $\bar{\mathbb{G}} = (\bar{V}, \bar{E})$.*

Proof. The $\mathcal{J}^{\mathcal{R}}_{(s,t)}$ class guarantees the existence of a journey from node p_s to node p_t in all temporal subgraphs $\mathcal{G}_{[j,*]}$ of $\mathcal{G}$.

Let $J_1 = (A_1, B_1)$ be a journey $(p_s \rightsquigarrow p_t) \in \mathcal{G}$, and let x_1 and y_1 be respectively the lowest and highest time instant associated to an edge in J_1, namely the first the and last elements of B_1. Let $J_2 = (A_2, B_2)$ be a journey $(p_s \rightsquigarrow p_t) \in \mathcal{G}_{[y_1+1,*]}$, and let x_2 and y_2 be respectively the lowest and highest time instant associated to an edge in J_2. The power set of a set R is the set of all subsets of R. The power set of a set that has a finite number of elements has a finite number of elements as well. It follows that, continuing the reasoning above, and thus identifying edge set $A_1, A_2, \ldots$ there is at least one edge set A_j that occurs infinitely often, and the claim follows.

Corollary 2. *If an evolving graph $\mathcal{G}$ is in $\mathcal{J}^{\mathcal{R}}_{(s,t,k)}$ then there exists a spatial subgraph $\mathcal{G}':=\mathcal{G}[\bar{V}, \bar{E}]$ of class $\mathcal{E}^{\mathcal{R}}$ having a set of k disjoint paths between p_s and p_t in its underlying graph $\bar{\mathbb{G}} = (\bar{V}, \bar{E})$.*

Proof. The claim follows for the same argument provided in Theorem 5.

The $\mathcal{J}^{\mathcal{R}}_{(s,t,k)}$ class guarantees the existence of a set of journeys from p_s to p_t, having a dynamic minimum cut of size at least k, for all temporal subgraphs $\mathcal{G}_{[j,*]}$ of $\mathcal{G}$, namely $\forall j \in \mathcal{T}, \exists (p_a \rightsquigarrow_k p_b) \in \mathcal{G}_{[j,*]}$.

Let P_1 be a set of journeys $(p_a \rightsquigarrow_k p_b) \in \mathcal{G}$, let x_1 and y_1 be respectively the lowest and highest time instant associated to an edge of a journey in P_1, and let $E_1 \subseteq E$ be the set of edges in P_1. Let P_2 be a set of journeys $(p_a \rightsquigarrow_k p_b) \in \mathcal{G}_{[y_1+1,*]}$, let x_2 and y_2 be respectively the lowest and highest time instant associated to an edge of a journey in P_2, and let $E_2 \subseteq E$ be the set of edges in P_2. The power set of a set that has a finite number of elements has a finite number of elements as well. It follows that, continuing the reasoning above, and thus identifying edge set $E_1, E_2, \ldots$, there is at least one edge set E_j that occurs infinitely often, and the claim follows.

Corollary 3. *Let $\mathcal{G}$ be an evolving graph with infinite lifetime. If $\mathcal{G}$ is in $\mathcal{TC}^{\mathcal{R}}_k$ then there exists a spatial subgraph $\mathcal{G}':=\mathcal{G}[V, \bar{E}]$ of class $\mathcal{E}^{\mathcal{R}}_k$*

Proof. The claim follows for the same argument provided in Corollary 2, considering any pair of nodes p_s, p_t.

We prove that the classes $\mathcal{C}^*_k$ and $\mathcal{TC}^{\mathcal{R}}_k$ are also related. Specifically, $\mathcal{C}^*_k$ is a sub-class of $\mathcal{TC}^{\mathcal{R}}_k$ if $\mathcal{G}$ has infinite lifetime, and we accordingly extend previous solvability results on the reliable communication problem.

Theorem 6. *Given an evolving graph $\mathcal{G}$ with infinite lifetime, if $\mathcal{G} \in \mathcal{C}^*_k$ then $\mathcal{G}_{[j,j+n-k]} \in \mathcal{TC}_k$ for any $j \in \mathcal{T}$, and thus $\mathcal{G} \in \mathcal{TC}^{\mathcal{R}}_k$.*

Proof. Consider an evolving graph $\mathcal{G} \in \mathcal{C}^*_k$ with V as vertex set, $|V| = n$, and a pair of its nodes $p_s, p_t \in V$.

Let $\Pi_{(s,t)}$ be the set of all the journeys from p_s to p_t in the temporal subgraph $\mathcal{G}_{[j,j+n-k]}$. Note that every temporal subgraph $\mathcal{G}_{\bar{T}}$ of an evolving graph $\mathcal{G}$ in $\mathcal{CK}^*_k$ is by definition also in $\mathcal{CK}^*_k$.

Let S be a subset of $k - 1$ nodes of V not containing p_s and p_t, namely $S \subset V \setminus \{p_s, p_t\}$, $|S| = k - 1$, and let $\mathcal{G}'$ be the spatial temporal subgraph of $\mathcal{G}$ such that $\mathcal{G}' := \mathcal{G}[V \setminus S]_{[j,j+n-k]}$. The evolving graph $\mathcal{G}'$ is 1-interval connected by construction because at least k nodes must be removed from $\mathcal{G}$ to disconnect any of its snapshots.

Let $\Pi[V \setminus S]_{(s,t)}$ be the set of all the journeys from p_s to p_t in $\mathcal{G}'$. It has been proven in [20] that $n' - 1$ instants, where n' is the number of nodes in an evolving graph, are sufficient to traverse a journey between any two nodes in a 1-interval connected graph (class $\mathcal{C}^*$); the evolving graph $\mathcal{G}'$ is composed of $n - (k - 1)$ nodes, thus a journey from p_s to p_t can always be traversed in at most $n - (k - 1) - 1 = n - k$ instants, and thus $\Pi[V \setminus S]_{(s,t)} \neq \emptyset$.

It follows that there exists a set of journeys with a dynamic minimum cut size at least equal to k in $\mathcal{G}_{[j,j+n-k]}$ from p_s to p_t because there exists at least one journey in $\Pi_{(s,t)}$ from p_s to p_t when removing any subset $S \subset V \setminus \{p_s, p_t\}$ of $k - 1$ nodes.

Given that, for any $j \in \mathcal{T}$, $\mathcal{G}_{[j,j+n-k]} \in \mathcal{TC}_k$, it follows that $\mathcal{G} \in \mathcal{TC}_k^{\mathcal{R}}$ by Definition 15.

Corollary 4 (RC in $\langle PL, SC, AL \rangle$ - 1-interval). *The reliable communication problem can be solved starting at any time j, in the perfect authenticated links and negligible computation setting, if $\mathcal{G} \in \mathcal{C}_k^*$ and $k > 2f$. Furthermore, it can be solved in $n - k$ time.*

Proof. It follows from Theorems 2 and 6. Theorem 2 characterizes class $\mathcal{TC}_k$ as the one where reliable communication is solvable when $k > 2f$; Theorem 6 identifies $\mathcal{C}_k^*$ class as a subclass of $\mathcal{TC}_k^{\mathcal{R}}$ where all of its temporal subgraphs with lifetime $n - k$ are in $\mathcal{TC}_k$. The upper bound on the latency follows from the fact that $\forall j \in \mathcal{T}, \mathcal{G}_{[j,j+n-k]} \in \mathcal{TC}_k$, thus $p_s \leadsto_k p_t$ are traversable in $n - k$ times for whatever pair of p_s and p_t.

For the sake of completeness, we state a relation that exists between evolving graphs classes $\mathcal{C}_k^*$ and $\mathcal{E}_k^{\mathcal{R}}$.

Theorem 7. *Let $\mathcal{G}$ be an evolving graph with infinite lifetime. If $\mathcal{G} \in \mathcal{C}_k^*$ (1-interval k-connectivity) then there exists a spatial subgraph $\mathcal{G}[V, E^{\mathcal{R}}]$ of class $\mathcal{E}_k^{\mathcal{R}}$ (recurrent edges k-connected).*

Proof. If an evolving graph $\mathcal{G}$ is 1-interval k-connected and has an infinite lifetime, then a subset of its edges $E^{\mathcal{R}} \subseteq E$ must be present within an infinite number of snapshots. Indeed, the number of nodes in $\mathcal{G}$ is finite and equals to n, and the number of possible edges is finite as well (at most n^2). It follows that some edges in E must re-appear infinitely often. We prove that if $\mathcal{G}$ is 1-interval k-connected then the set of edges $E^{\mathcal{R}}$ that re-appears infinitely often forms a k-connected graph $\mathbb{G}' = (V, E^{\mathcal{R}})$.

Let us partition the edges of E in $\mathcal{G}$ in two sets: $E^{\mathcal{R}}$ containing all the edges that re-appear infinitely often and $\tilde{E}$ that are present a finite number of times in $\mathcal{G}$. Let t_z be the time when the last appearance of an edge in $\tilde{E}$ occurs in $\mathcal{G}$.

It follows that starting at time t_{z+1} all edges in $\mathcal{G}$ must appear infinitely often. The 1-interval k-connectivity property of $\mathcal{G}$ requires that all the edges $E^{\mathcal{R}}$ must form a k-connected graph, and the claim follows.

Finally, we study the solvability conditions of the reliable communication problem while relaxing the assumptions of perfect links and synchronous computation.

Theorem 8 (One-to-one RC in $\langle FLL/AC, AL \rangle$). *Given a setting where either links are fair-loss, or local computation is asynchronous, or both, the one-to-one reliable communication problem can be solved starting at any time j if and only if $\mathcal{G} \in \mathcal{J}^{\mathcal{R}}_{(s,t,k)}$ and $k > 2f$.*

Proof. Provided in [6].

Theorem 9 (RC in $\langle FLL/AC, AL \rangle$). *Given a setting where either links are fair-loss, or local computation is asynchronous, or both, the any-to-any reliable communication problem can be solved starting at any time j if and only if $\mathcal{G} \in \mathcal{TC}^{\mathcal{R}}_k$ (Recurrent k-Temporal-Connectivity) and $k > 2f$.*

Proof. The claim follow by extending arguments provided in Theorem 8 to any pair of nodes. Given any four nodes $p_s, p_t, p_u, p_v \in V$, $\mathcal{G} \in \mathcal{J}^{\mathcal{R}}_{(s,t,k)}$ does not imply $\mathcal{J}^{\mathcal{R}}_{(u,v,k)}$; therefore, the condition must thus be verified for every pair of nodes. Definition 14 extends Definition 12 by considering any pair of processes; the claim thus follows given the strictness of Theorem 8.

Different from the $\langle PL, SC, AL \rangle$ setting, the start time of the RC instance in the $\langle FLL/AC, AL \rangle$ case is irrelevant for the solvability conditions of the examined problems. Further details are reported in Corollaries 8 and 9 in [6].

All the additional results identified for the defined sub-classes of $\mathcal{TC}^{\mathcal{R}}_k$ extend in the setting where either links are fair-loss, or local computation is asynchronous, or both.

Corollary 5 (RC in $\langle FLL/AC, AL \rangle$). *Given a setting where either links are fair-loss, or local computation is asynchronous, or both, the reliable communication problem can be solved starting at any time j if $\mathcal{G} \in \mathcal{E}^{\mathcal{R}}_k$ (recurrent edges k-connected) and $k > 2f$.*

Proof. It follows combining the results from Theorems 4 and 9.

Corollary 6 (RC in $\langle FLL/AC, AL \rangle$). *Given a setting where either links are fair-loss, or local computation is asynchronous, or both, the reliable communication problem can be solved starting at any time j, if $\mathcal{G} \in \mathcal{C}^*_k$ (1-interval k-connectivity) and $k > 2f$.*

Proof. It follows combining results from Theorems 6 and 9.

5.3   Authenticated Messages

Theorem 1 by Maurer et al. [26] identifies the base condition enabling one-to-one reliable communication from a defined source p_s and a specific target p_t starting at time j, that is, the existence of a set of journeys $p_s \leadsto_k p_t$ in $\mathcal{G}_{[j,*]}$ with $k > 2f$. More specifically, there must exist a set of journeys $p_s \leadsto_{2f+1} p_t$ in $\mathcal{G}_{[j,*]}$ that cannot be cut by any set of $2f$ nodes [26]. Maurer et al. [26] additionally studied the one-to-one at time j specification in the perfect links, synchronous computation and *authenticated message* setting. We recall its solution in [6] and the identified solvability condition in the following.

Theorem 10 (One-to-one RC at time t_j in $\langle PL, SC, AM \rangle$ [26]). *The one-to-one reliable communication problem can be solved starting at time j from a process p_s to a process p_t, in the perfect link, synchronous computation, and authenticated messages setting, if and only if it exists a set of journeys $p_s \leadsto_k p_t$ in $\mathcal{G}_{[t_i,*]}$ and $k > f$.*

All extension results are collected in the following Corollary.

Corollary 7 (RC in $\langle *, *, AM \rangle$). *All the results available on the reliable communication problem for the authenticated link setting (AL), specifically Theorems 2, 3, 8, 9, and 11, and Corollaries 1, 4, 5, 6, 8 and 9, extend to the authenticated message setting (AM) while requiring $k > f$ (instead of $2f$). More in detail, the solvability conditions to the reliable communication problem in the authenticated message settings are the ones reported in Table 1.*

Proof. The Corollary follows from the same argument given for the results presented in Subsect. 5.2. Theorem 10 provides the network conditions for solving the one-to-one problem at a given time. The extension follows by identifying classes of evolving graphs for which such conditions are verified, considering every pair of processes and infinitely often occurrences of the conditions. The results differ on the parameter k, which must be greater than f. Note that the Maurer et al. solution reported in Algorithm 1 [6] needs to be modified as reported in Algorithm 2 [6] to extend to fair-loss links and/or asynchronous computation settings.

5.4   On the Complexity of Verifying Class Membership

The evolution of the communication network of a distributed system can be *assumed*, in the sense that in certain real deployments it is reasonable to consider a particular model for the dynamic communication network. For example, it could be reasonable to assume that a swarm of mobile robots, moving inside a limited area, are repeatedly able to establish temporary communication links, and the resulting dynamic communication network provides recurrent temporal connectivity (class $\mathcal{TC}^{\mathcal{R}}$). Alternatively, the *complete characterization* of the evolution of a communication network, such as an evolving graph detailing the sets of available links over time, can be *known in advance*. For example, considering the same example of a swarm of mobile robots, if the schedule of the exact movements of all the robots are known in advance, it is possible to deduce exactly when every pair of robot is able to establish a communication link. In the latter setting, it is worth to notice that if a characterization of the communication network is provided as an evolving graph, the verification of class membership can be impractical to perform. More in detail, it has been proven [16,18,33] that it is NP-complete to decide whether the dynamic minimum cut size from a node p_s to p_t in an evolving graph is equal to a certain value k. It follows that the solvability conditions presented in Theorems 1, 2, 3, 9, and 11, and Corollaries 8, and 9, are NP-complete to verify on any temporal subgraph of the evolving graph. On the other hand, conditions defined on the recurrent edges k-connected ($\mathcal{E}_k^{\mathcal{R}}$) and 1-interval k-connectivity ($\mathcal{C}_k^*$) classes can be verified with a polynomial algorithm on any temporal subgraph of an evolving graph, motivating the analysis of such subclasses of $\mathcal{TC}_k^{\mathcal{R}}$, particularly in light of the result presented in Corollary 3.

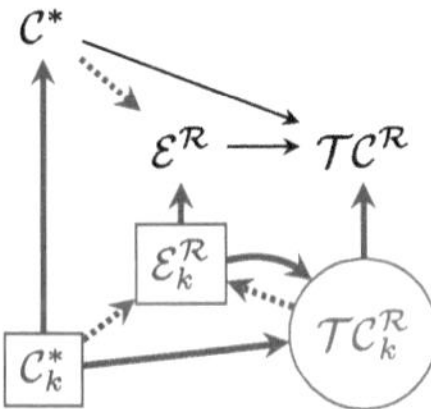

Fig. 3. Relations between classes of evolving graphs. The classes and relations presented in this work are depicted in square bold blue, dashed edges represent the inclusion relation of a spatial subgraph. In the red circle is the minimal class of evolving graphs where the any-to-any reliable communication problem is solvable at any time under all the settings considered. (Color figure online)

Table 1. Strict Solvability Conditions

	Solvability Conditions
$\langle AL, PL, SC \rangle$	1-to-1 at j : $\mathcal{J}_{(a,b,k)} \wedge k > 2f$ [26] 1-to-1 at any j : $\mathcal{J}_{(a,b,k)}^{\mathcal{R}} \wedge k > 2f$ *-to-* at j : $\mathcal{TC}_k \wedge k > 2f$ *-to-* at any j : $\mathcal{TC}_k^{\mathcal{R}} \wedge k > 2f$
$\langle AL, FLL, * \rangle \langle AL, *, AC \rangle$	1-to-1 at (or at any) j : $\mathcal{J}_{(a,b,k)}^{\mathcal{R}} \wedge k > 2f$ *-to-* at (or at any) j : $\mathcal{TC}_k^{\mathcal{R}} \wedge k > 2f$
$\langle AM, PL, SC \rangle$	1-to-1 at j : $\mathcal{J}_{(a,b,k)} \wedge k > f$ [26] 1-to-1 at any j : $\mathcal{J}_{(a,b,k)}^{\mathcal{R}} \wedge k > f$ *-to-* at j : $\mathcal{TC}_k \wedge k > f$ *-to-* at any j : $\mathcal{TC}_k^{\mathcal{R}} \wedge k > f$
$\langle AM, FLL, * \rangle \langle AM, *, AC \rangle$	1-to-1 at (or at any) j : $\mathcal{J}_{(a,b,k)}^{\mathcal{R}} \wedge k > f$ *-to-* at (or at any) j : $\mathcal{TC}_k^{\mathcal{R}} \wedge k > f$

6 Conclusion

In this work, starting from the seminal contribution of Maurer et al. [26], we characterized the conditions that allow reliable communication between all processes at any time, and identified classes of dynamic networks that satisfy them. All the relations we identified between the classes of evolving graphs are summarized in Fig. 3. In particular, class $\mathcal{TC}_k^{\mathcal{R}}$ is the smallest class of evolving graph for which the problem is solvable under all the settings we considered. Classes $\mathcal{E}_k^{\mathcal{R}}$ and $\mathcal{CK}_k^{*}$ are subclasses of $\mathcal{TC}_k^{\mathcal{R}}$ that can be verified in polynomial time on any temporal subgraph of an evolving graph. All the identified results are outlined in Table 1.

Several interesting lines of future research include: compare our deterministic classes of dynamic networks with those induced by probabilistic models, and identify (with high probability) equivalence conditions between the two models; analyze real datasets of dynamic networks (vehicles, drones, etc.), verifying whether identified conditions are satisfied; extend the study to open dynamic networks (where infinitely many processes may join and leave), or to the more demanding reliable broadcast problem [1,4] (where the sender also can be Byzantine).

Acknowledgments. This work was partially supported by ANR project SAPPORO 2019-CE25-0005.

Disclosure of Interests. The authors have no competing interests to declare that are relevant to the content of this article.

References

1. Bonomi, S., Decouchant, J., Farina, G., Rahli, V., Tixeuil, S.: Practical byzantine reliable broadcast on partially connected networks. In: 41st IEEE International Conference on Distributed Computing Systems, ICDCS 2021, Washington DC, USA, July 7–10, 2021. pp. 506–516. IEEE (2021). https://doi.org/10.1109/ICDCS51616.2021.00055
2. Bonomi, S., Farina, G., Tixeuil, S.: Reliable Broadcast in Dynamic Networks with Locally Bounded Byzantine Failures. In: Izumi, T., Kuznetsov, P. (eds.) SSS 2018. LNCS, vol. 11201, pp. 170–185. Springer, Cham (2018). https://doi.org/10.1007/978-3-030-03232-6_12
3. Bonomi, S., Farina, G., Tixeuil, S.: Multi-hop byzantine reliable broadcast with honest dealer made practical. J. Braz. Comput. Soc. **25**(1), 9:1–9:23 (2019). https://doi.org/10.1186/s13173-019-0090-x
4. Bonomi, S., Farina, G., Tixeuil, S.: Reliable broadcast despite mobile byzantine faults. In: Bessani, A., Défago, X., Nakamura, J., Wada, K., Yamauchi, Y. (eds.) 27th International Conference on Principles of Distributed Systems, OPODIS 2023, December 6–8, 2023, Tokyo, Japan. LIPIcs, vol. 286, pp. 18:1–18:23. Schloss Dagstuhl - Leibniz-Zentrum für Informatik (2023). https://doi.org/10.4230/LIPICS.OPODIS.2023.18

5. Bonomi, S., Farina, G., Tixeuil, S.: Reliable communication in dynamic networks with locally bounded byzantine faults. J. Parallel Distrib. Comput. **193**, 104952 (2024). https://doi.org/10.1016/j.jpdc.2024.104952
6. Bonomi, S., Farina, G., Tixeuil, S.: On the solvability of byzantine-tolerant reliable communication in dynamic networks (2025). https://arxiv.org/abs/2503.22452
7. Cachin, C., Guerraoui, R., Rodrigues, L.E.T.: Introduction to Reliable and Secure Distributed Programming (2. ed.). Springer, Cham (2011). https://doi.org/10.1007/978-3-642-15260-3
8. Casteigts, A.: A Journey through Dynamic Networks (with Excursions) (2018). https://tel.archives-ouvertes.fr/tel-01883384
9. Casteigts, A., Flocchini, P., Quattrociocchi, W., Santoro, N.: Time-varying graphs and dynamic networks. Int. J. Parallel Emerg. Distrib. Syst. **27**(5), 387–408 (2012). https://doi.org/10.1080/17445760.2012.668546
10. Castro, M., Liskov, B.: Practical byzantine fault tolerance. In: Seltzer, M.I., Leach, P.J. (eds.) Proceedings of the Third USENIX Symposium on Operating Systems Design and Implementation (OSDI), New Orleans, Louisiana, USA, February 22–25, 1999, pp. 173–186. USENIX Association (1999). https://dl.acm.org/citation.cfm?id=296824
11. Diestel, R.: Graph Theory. Springer Berlin Heidelberg (2017). https://doi.org/10.1007/978-3-662-53622-3
12. Dolev, D.: Unanimity in an unknown and unreliable environment. In: 22nd Annual Symposium on Foundations of Computer Science, Nashville, Tennessee, USA, 28–30 October 1981, pp. 159–168. IEEE Computer Society (1981). https://doi.org/10.1109/SFCS.1981.53
13. Douceur, J.R.: The sybil attack. In: Peer-to-Peer Systems, First International Workshop, IPTPS 2002, Cambridge, MA, USA, March 7–8, 2002, Revised Papers, pp. 251–260 (2002). https://doi.org/10.1007/3-540-45748-8_24
14. Drabkin, V., Friedman, R., Segal, M.: Efficient byzantine broadcast in wireless ad-hoc networks. In: 2005 International Conference on Dependable Systems and Networks (DSN 2005), 28 June–1 July 2005, Yokohama, Japan, Proceedings, pp. 160–169. IEEE Computer Society (2005). https://doi.org/10.1109/DSN.2005.42
15. Ferreira, A.: Building a reference combinatorial model for manets. IEEE Netw. **18**(5), 24–29 (2004). https://doi.org/10.1109/MNET.2004.1337732
16. Fluschnik, T., Molter, H., Niedermeier, R., Renken, M., Zschoche, P.: Temporal graph classes: a view through temporal separators. Theor. Comput. Sci. **806**, 197–218 (2020). https://doi.org/10.1016/j.tcs.2019.03.031
17. Garey, M.R., Johnson, D.S.: Computers and Intractability: A Guide to the Theory of NP-Completeness. Freeman, W. H (1979)
18. Kempe, D., Kleinberg, J.M., Kumar, A.: Connectivity and inference problems for temporal networks. J. Comput. Syst. Sci. **64**(4), 820–842 (2002). https://doi.org/10.1006/jcss.2002.1829
19. Koo, C.: Broadcast in radio networks tolerating byzantine adversarial behavior. In: Chaudhuri, S., Kutten, S. (eds.) Proceedings of the Twenty-Third Annual ACM Symposium on Principles of Distributed Computing, PODC 2004, St. John's, Newfoundland, Canada, July 25–28, 2004, pp. 275–282. ACM (2004). https://doi.org/10.1145/1011767.1011807,
20. Kuhn, F., Lynch, N.A., Oshman, R.: Distributed computation in dynamic networks. In: Schulman, L.J. (ed.) Proceedings of the 42nd ACM Symposium on Theory of Computing, STOC 2010, Cambridge, Massachusetts, USA, 5–8 June 2010, pp. 513–522. ACM (2010). https://doi.org/10.1145/1806689.1806760

21. Maurer, A.: Self-stabilizing byzantine-resilient communication in dynamic networks. In: Bramas, Q., Oshman, R., Romano, P. (eds.) 24th International Conference on Principles of Distributed Systems, OPODIS 2020, December 14–16, 2020, Strasbourg, France (Virtual Conference). LIPIcs, vol. 184, pp. 27:1–27:11. Schloss Dagstuhl - Leibniz-Zentrum für Informatik (2020). https://doi.org/10.4230/LIPIcs.OPODIS.2020.27
22. Maurer, A., Tixeuil, S.: On Byzantine Broadcast in Loosely Connected Networks. In: Aguilera, M.K. (ed.) DISC 2012. LNCS, vol. 7611, pp. 253–266. Springer, Heidelberg (2012). https://doi.org/10.1007/978-3-642-33651-5_18
23. Maurer, A., Tixeuil, S.: Byzantine broadcast with fixed disjoint paths. J. Parallel Distrib. Comput. **74**(11), 3153–3160 (2014). https://doi.org/10.1016/J.JPDC.2014.07.010
24. Maurer, A., Tixeuil, S.: Containing byzantine failures with control zones. IEEE Trans. Parallel Distrib. Syst. **26**(2), 362–370 (2015). https://doi.org/10.1109/TPDS.2014.2308190
25. Maurer, A., Tixeuil, S.: Tolerating random byzantine failures in an unbounded network. Parallel Process. Lett. **26**(1), 1650003:1–1650003:12 (2016). https://doi.org/10.1142/S0129626416500031
26. Maurer, A., Tixeuil, S., Défago, X.: Communicating reliably in multihop dynamic networks despite byzantine failures. In: 34th IEEE Symposium on Reliable Distributed Systems, SRDS 2015, Montreal, QC, Canada, September 28–October 1, 2015, pp. 238–245. IEEE Computer Society (2015). https://doi.org/10.1109/SRDS.2015.10
27. Menger, K.: Zur allgemeinen kurventheorie. Fundamenta Mathematicae **10**(1), 96–115 (1927). http://eudml.org/doc/211191
28. Pagourtzis, A., Panagiotakos, G., Sakavalas, D.: Reliable broadcast with respect to topology knowledge. Distrib. Comput. **30**(2), 87–102 (2017). https://doi.org/10.1007/s00446-016-0279-6
29. Pelc, A.: Reliable communication in networks with byzantine link failures. Networks **22**(5), 441–459 (1992). https://doi.org/10.1002/net.3230220503
30. Pelc, A.: Fault-tolerant broadcasting and gossiping in communication networks. Networks **28**(3), 143–156 (1996)
31. Pelc, A., Peleg, D.: Broadcasting with locally bounded byzantine faults. Inf. Process. Lett. **93**(3), 109–115 (2005). https://doi.org/10.1016/j.ipl.2004.10.007
32. Zeng, K., Govindan, K., Mohapatra, P.: Non-cryptographic authentication and identification in wireless networks. IEEE Wireless Commun. **17**(5), 56–62 (2010). https://doi.org/10.1109/MWC.2010.5601959
33. Zschoche, P., Fluschnik, T., Molter, H., Niedermeier, R.: The complexity of finding small separators in temporal graphs. J. Comput. Syst. Sci. **107**, 72–92 (2020). https://doi.org/10.1016/J.JCSS.2019.07.006

A Lightweight Approach for State Machine Replication

Christian Cachin[1] , Jinfeng Dou[2]([✉]) , Christian Scheideler[2] ,
and Philipp Schneider[3]

[1] University of Bern, Bern, Switzerland
christian.cachin@unibe.ch
[2] Paderborn University, Paderborn, Germany
jfdou@mail.upb.de, scheideler@upb.de
[3] CISPA Helmholtz Center for Information Security, Saarbrücken, Germany
philipp.schneider@cispa.de

Abstract. We present a lightweight solution for state machine replication with commitment certificates. Specifically, we adapt and analyze a median rule for the stabilizing consensus problem [16] to operate in a client-server setting where arbitrary servers may be blocked adaptively based on past system information. We further extend our protocol by compressing information about committed commands, thus keeping the protocol lightweight, while still enabling clients to easily prove that their commands have indeed been committed. Our approach guarantees liveness as long as at most a constant fraction of servers are blocked, ensures safety under any number of blocked servers, and supports fast recovery even after all servers are blocked. In addition to offering near-optimal asymptotic performance in several respects, our method is fully decentralized, unlike other near-optimal solutions that rely on leaders. In particular, our solution is robust against adversaries that target key servers (which captures insider-based denial-of-service attacks), whereas leader-based approaches fail under such a blocking model.

Keywords: Analysis of Consensus Dynamics · Distributed
Algorithms · State Machine Replication

1 Introduction

In the *state machine replication* (SMR) problem [29], a set of servers is required to replicate a state machine in a consistent way by agreeing on an order in which commands from clients are to be committed on it. Formally, a *state machine* $(\mathcal{S}, \mathcal{C})$ consists of a *state space* $\mathcal{S}$ and a collection of *commands* $\mathcal{C}$ acting on that state space. Each server maintains a copy of the state machine (simply called a *shared state* in the following). The clients may send their commands to any of the servers. The goal is to satisfy the following conditions:

Philipp Schneider was partially supported by a grant from Avalanche, Inc. to the University of Bern.

C. Georgiou (Ed.): SIROCCO 2026, LNCS 16488, pp. 131–150, 2026.
https://doi.org/10.1007/978-3-032-26465-7_8

- **Safety**: At any point in time, for any pair of correct servers, the sequence of committed commands on one server is a prefix of the sequence on the other.
- **Liveness**: Every command that was submitted to a correct server is eventually committed on all correct servers.

Safety and liveness imply that if every server executes the commands in the order in which they were committed by that server, the sequence of transitions on the shared state will be the same for each correct server, and any transition at one correct server will eventually be performed by all other correct servers. SMR captures the core consistency problem that any blockchain system faces: obtaining consensus on a total order of transactions. In this sense, blockchain protocols can be viewed as specific implementations of SMR in which the replicated object is a transaction log.

An important SMR application is a system that manages financial transactions, which requires maintaining both the shared state (account balances) and a record of transactions (as proof for their commitment). In cryptocurrencies, transactions are typically recorded on a large ledger that is replicated over many machines, for example, Bitcoin's ledger exceeds 720 GB which is maintained by thousands of full nodes [22]. A much more space-efficient alternative for servers maintains only the shared state and shifts the burden of maintaining a proof that a transaction took place to the originating clients, who are naturally incentivized to do so, to be able to prove successful commitment of their transactions to third parties.

We present a scalable and robust solution to the SMR problem that provides safety and liveness under a blocking adversary and minimizes the amount of information that must be maintained by the servers by offloading the responsibility of certifying the commitment of commands to the clients. Specifically, we require clients to certify commitment of their commands to other clients, *without* using long-term cryptographic signatures, where servers may act only as verifiers that retain a small amount of metadata but not the complete history of committed commands. This poses several intertwined challenges, especially under failures. We adopt a *blocking-failure* model under an adaptive adversary that has full information with a one-round delay. Adaptive blocking failures subsume both crash-stop and crashrecovery behavior since such an adversary may permanently or temporarily block servers. The core difficulty is that the adversary can potentially isolate groups of servers from each other by alternate blockings, making it hard to maintain safety.

Unlike many contemporary solutions for fault-tolerant SMR, which use leaders that can be easily suppressed by such an adaptive adversary, our protocol is leaderless and, to our knowledge, the first to realize SMR via the median-rule consensus dynamics [16]. We prove safety and liveness properties of our protocol in scenarios with increasing difficulty, for which we provide a formal framework by defining a sequence of core problems that iteratively build on each other. This work focuses on the *theoretical* foundations of SMR under a blocking adversary based on the median rule by providing an analysis of the consensus dynamics in the style of [8,16] and using these insights to obtain a light-weight protocol that is robust to blocking failures.

1.1 Model

Client-Server Model. We distinguish between *clients* and *servers*: clients issue commands, while servers maintain a copy of the state machine. We assume a fixed set of servers $\{1,\ldots,n\}$. The set of clients may change arbitrarily over time. We focus on minimizing communication overhead, latency, and storage, and therefore, any local computations are assumed to be negligible (which is indeed the case in our solution).

Network Model. Communication between clients and servers is done by point-to-point message passing. While clients can be addressed directly, for servers we assume the weaker gossip communication model (see, e.g., [21]) where servers can exchange a point-to-point message with anyone but *cannot* choose whom to contact. Messages are exchanged using either a *push* operation, which sends a message to a random server, or a *pull* operation, which asks a random server to reply to the sender, where every server has the same probability to be chosen as the target of the operation. Gossip-based protocols are highly practical due to their inherent load balancing, rapid convergence, simplicity, and robustness under stress or disruption. For example, they play a key role in Avalanche consensus [2,28] and anonymous networks like Tor. Because the gossip model is used for the servers, neither servers nor clients need to know the server identifiers or the exact number n; having some polynomial estimate of n is sufficient for our protocols to work.

Synchrony Assumptions. In *synchronous message passing*, communication takes place in discrete time steps called *rounds*, and any push or pull operation initiated at the beginning of some round is completed before the next round starts. By contrast, *asynchronous message passing* provides no timing guarantees: messages may get arbitrarily delayed. In this work, we assume synchronous message passing for server-to-server communication and asynchronous message passing for interactions between clients and servers.

Failure Model. We assume that the clients cannot impersonate other clients but may otherwise behave in a Byzantine manner. Servers are subject to blocking failures that are adversarially triggered but otherwise correctly follow the given protocol. The blocking adversary can isolate any server at any point in time, preventing it from sending or receiving messages in a given round. A server does not know whether it is isolated or not, and in case of a failed push or pull request, no information is given on who of the two involved parties caused the failure. This covers real-world phenomena such as denial-of-service attacks or network failures. It also captures aspects of network asynchrony or unreliable links, in the sense that blocked parts of the network experience delays or message loss. Because blocked servers are effectively cut out of the protocol, this model also subsumes the crash-recovery model, with the adversary controlling the timing of crashes and subsequent recovery. We consider a *late* adversary that adapts its blocking decisions based on previously observed system states (e.g. [1,27]) which allows us to rely on randomness to achieve network-wide outcomes that are outside the adversary's control. Lateness is a natural assumption, as information about the servers first has to be aggregated and evaluated by an adversary in order to target its attack.

Definition 1 (α-late, β-blocking adversary). *Let $\alpha \in \mathbb{N}_0$ and $0 \le \beta \le 1$ be fixed parameters.*

- *In round r, the α-late adversary only knows the local states (including random choices) of the servers up to the beginning of round $r - \alpha$, i.e., it cannot condition its current decisions on events happening after this point.*
- *In each round, the β-blocking adversary can block up to a β-fraction of servers. For simplicity, we assume that a server will either be completely blocked or completely unblocked during a round. A blocked server cannot send or receive any messages in that round.*

We consider a 1-late adversary: in round t it knows the entire system state only up to the beginning of round $t - 1$. This one-round opacity is crucial for fast commitment, because with $\Theta(n)$ adaptive crash failures under a *full*-information adversary, any synchronous randomized consensus protocol needs $\tilde{\Theta}(\sqrt{n})$ rounds [7]. Further, we assume that the adversary cannot observe which client requests have arrived or will arrive from the beginning of round $t - \alpha$ on. This assumption is necessary: if the late adaptive adversary would know (or even schedule) client server communication, it could simply block the servers scheduled to receive client requests and thereby prevent any client-server progress.

The model we consider is incomparable to, and *not* weaker than the classic Byzantine model, where the set of failing nodes is assumed to be static. In particular, Byzantine fault-tolerant protocols typically assume a fixed, sufficiently large majority that never fails, whereas here, any server may fail at any time. Leader-based consensus protocols cannot maintain liveness in this model as any leader selected in a given round may immediately be blocked in subsequent rounds.

Probabilistic Concepts. We use the standard concept of *with high probability* (w.h.p.) where the total probability of algorithm failure is upper bounded by $1/n^c$ for *any* constant $c > 0$. This ensures that the likelihood that our algorithm does not satisfy safety and liveness vanishes for sufficiently large n. We further discuss how to deal with the unlikely event of a single failure in Sect. 6.

1.2   Overview

Our goal is a robust protocol for state-machine replication (SMR) that is lightweight in terms of memory usage, allows signature-free certification of commitment of commands, and is highly scalable in terms of communication overhead and latency. Specific objectives are:

- **Small latency** from receiving a client-issued command by some server to the commitment of the command on all non-blocked servers.
- **Small communication overhead** defined as the additional amount of information the server has to send and receive per command compared to receiving that command once.
- **Small memory requirement per server**, where a server only has to store the shared state, the non-committed commands and a small amount of additional information.
- **Small memory requirement per client**, where a client only has to store small certificates for each of its own committed commands.
- **Liveness** against a 1-late adversary blocking a constant fraction of servers ($\Theta(1)$-blocking).
- **Safety** even against a 1-late adversary potentially blocking all servers (1-blocking).
- **Fast recovery** after any period of time with a 1-late 1-blocking adversary.

Our solution also avoids reliance on cryptographic signatures, which is motivated by the fact that signatures cause computational overhead, might expire, keys can get stolen, or even be broken at some point (if certain cryptographic assumptions turn out to be false). Hence, small commitment certificates cannot be simple signed statements by the server. Our solution only assumes a publicly known collision-resistant hash function, i.e., a function h for which it is computationally hard to find $x \neq y$ with $h(x) = h(y)$.

In the following, we formally describe the problems that we are tackling towards a solution satisfying the criteria above. We develop this solution step-by-step in a sense that a solution of a simpler problem is used for the solution to the next, more complex problem. We start with a simple distributed algorithm for the *stabilizing consensus problem*, which adapts the classic consensus problem to capture blocked servers. We call servers *useful* if they are currently non-blocked and store a value.[1]

Definition 2 (Stabilizing Consensus Problem). *Every server holds an arbitrary initial value. A protocol solves the stabilizing consensus problem if it satisfies:*

- **Agreement***: There exists a round after which all useful servers hold the same value.*
- **Availability***: In each round, at least a constant fraction of servers is useful.*
- **Validity***: If a server stores some value x at the end of a round, then some server must have stored x at the beginning of that round.*

Note that a protocol ensuring agreement should eliminate values from blocked servers to prevent the survival of outdated ones. Our agreement requirement for *useful* servers is analogous to Byzantine agreement (BA), where only *correct*

---

[1] The subsequent definitions are framed for the synchronous model that we consider in this work, but can be rephrased more generally.

servers must agree. The key difference is that the set of useful servers changes over time, due to the adaptive adversary and the randomness of gossip. A main challenge, therefore, is to ensure that a constant fraction of servers remains useful (available) at all times despite this shifting membership. We address this problem in Sect. 2 (details in Sect. 2 of the full version [11]) by combining a simple median rule in [16] with undecided-state dynamics (see, e.g., [3]). In this median rule, each server in each round requests the value from a random, constant-size subset of other servers, adopts the median value if enough values are received, and otherwise deletes its value, thereby becoming useless (i.e., not useful).

We then adapt this algorithm to solve the *stabilizing SMR problem* in Sect. 3 (details in Sect. 3 of the full version [11]), whose goal is to reach agreement on an ordered sequence of client-issued commands called *log*, even under an adversary that may block servers. Here, we say a command is *injected* as soon as it is first received from the client by a non-blocked server and assume that every command is unique (so that a client command does not appear twice in a log by mistake). Analogously to the single value case, we call non-blocked servers with a non-empty log *useful*.

Definition 3 (Stabilizing SMR Problem). *Each server starts with a log containing a seed command (so all servers are initially useful). A protocol solves the problem if it satisfies:*

- **Agreement***: For every injected command x, there exists a round after which all useful servers contain x at the same position in their logs.*
- **Availability***: In each round, at least a constant fraction of servers is useful.*
- **Validity***: If a server has some command x in its log at the end of a round, then it was either injected by a client or some server had x in its log at the beginning of that round.*

We show in Sect. 3 that the median rule can be adapted to work in the context of SMR by using the following idea: In each round, each server requests the logs from a random, constant-size subset of other servers. If enough logs are received, it adopts the median log (according to lexicographic order), appending all previously seen commands that are not contained in the median log to the end, and otherwise becomes useless (deletes its log). The *latency* of an algorithm that solves this problem is the number of rounds from the injection until the agreement property is satisfied.

Our solution in Sect. 3 can already be employed to implement state machine replication with small latency under a blocking adversary. However, this has the obvious drawback that entire logs (that can grow arbitrarily large) must be memorized and exchanged. Therefore, as next step in our iteration, we devise locally checkable rules for servers to determine when commands can be safely *committed* in Sect. 4 (details in Sect. 4 and Sect. 5 of the full version [11]). Committed commands can be executed on the local state (by order of time of commitment) and subsequently forgotten, with the guarantee that any other non-blocked server will commit the same commands in the same order. We encapsulate this in the "commitment problem", which mirrors the standard SMR problem to our setting:

Definition 4 (Commitment Problem). *A protocol solves the problem if it satisfies:*

- **Strong Safety**: *Any two useful servers have the same sequence of committed commands.*
- **Availability**: *In each round, at least a constant fraction of servers is useful.*
- **Liveness**: *Every injected command is eventually committed by all useful servers.*

When satisfying the criteria above, useful servers can execute commands on the shared state whenever they consider them to be committed and forget about them afterwards. This way, useful servers only need to maintain a shared state and a log of those commands that are not yet committed, leading to a significant reduction in the size of the messages as well as the storage needed by the servers. Servers that have been useless for a long period of time (e.g., due to frequent adversary blockings), will eventually be updated with the shared state by useful servers when they are able to successfully contact them again.

The clear drawback of deleting committed commands is that it erases the history of commands (e.g., transactions in a blockchain). This is the next problem we address: preserving the history without the servers needing to store it. Our solution, given in Sect. 4 (details in Sect. 5 of the full version [11]), is to offload the main burden of storing committed commands to the clients that issued them together with a small certificate that allows clients to prove to any third party that their command is indeed part of the committed history, whereas the servers only store a small amount of metadata to verify certificates. Note that our approach makes the client completely responsible for storing its issued commands and the associated certificate. However, loss of this data by one client never affects certificates of others.

Finally, we address in Sect. 5 (details in Sect. 6 of the full version [11]) the problem of recovering from any number of blocked servers over any period of time. A central challenge that arises from such an adversary is that the number of useful servers might be driven to zero. In our previous approach, we rely on responses from useful servers in order to transition previously useless servers to useful again, which fails in this setting. Worse still, an adversary may keep the number of useful servers at a small but changing minority, which poses the risk of disagreement on the sequence of committed commands. To address this, we make use of two additional protocols on top of our solution for the Commitment Problem: One that maintains the most recent shared state and non-committed commands (checkpoint protocol) and one that decides whether a reset to a prior checkpoint is required (reset protocol). For the first one, the servers take checkpoints of the shared state and disseminate these to agree on a most recent one. For the second one, the servers use a consensus mechanism to decide whether to reset the system or not. Formally, our protocol solves the following problem.

Definition 5 (Recovery Problem). *A protocol solves the recovery problem if it satisfies:*

- **Monotonicity***: Under any blocking adversary, for every server i and all $t < t'$, the committed sequence at time t is a prefix of the committed sequence at time t'.*
- **Recovery***: Once the blocking adversary is below its intended threshold, eventually strong safety, availability and liveness of Definition 4 hold again.*

Monotonicity ensures that no server starts an "alternate" commitment sequence; a situation akin to double spending in blockchains. Recovery guarantees that if any server has committed a command, it will eventually appear in every useful server's committed sequence once the adversary reverts to a bounded attack.

Our Contributions. Technically, we combine the median rule of [16] with undecided-state dynamics (e.g., [3]) and extend it to SMR with lightweight servers. To our knowledge, this is the first use of median-rule dynamics for SMR and the first analysis under a late blocking adversary. Prior work largely targets Byzantine faults and has either higher overheads or is leader-based and thus cannot ensure liveness against our adaptive blocking adversary.

Our main result is a protocol that meets all performance criteria listed at the beginning of Sect. 1.2. Concretely, it achieves logarithmic (in n) communication per client command and logarithmic latency. Further, server space is logarithmic in the length of the committed history plus logarithmic space per client. Clients only store logarithmic information for each command they issue. Our protocol guarantees liveness against any 1-late, 1/10-blocking adversary and strong safety (Definition 4) against any 1-late adversary, with no bound on the number of blocked servers. Finally, it provides logarithmic-time *recovery* from any number of blocked servers under a 1-late adversary (Definition 5). Our protocol compares favorably with other gossip-based blockchain protocols, in particular Avalanche, which achieves the same performance but can only provide liveness against $O(\sqrt{n})$ blocking failures (whereas we tolerate $\Omega(n)$) and does not consider the ramifications of keeping servers lightweight.

Further, we show that servers do not need to store the full command history, as is common in blockchains. Instead, commitment certificates are offloaded to the issuing clients. Servers keep only the shared state and the pool of uncommitted commands. Clients need certificate updates only when they submit a new command, and can remain offline otherwise. Our approach has additional benefits to privacy: after a command is committed, only the client will retain command-specific information. Technically, the recovery protocol is the most delicate component. Our techniques require new insights into the median rule under blockings and two tightly coupled subprotocols, enabling rapid (logarithmic-time) recovery after arbitrary blocking attacks. Due to space constraints, the remainder of the article takes the form of an extended abstract. Detailed algorithmic information and in-depth proofs are given in the full version [11].

1.3   Related Work

Leader and DAG Based Consensus Protocols. Most practical Byzantine fault-tolerant (BFT) consensus protocols follow either a leader-based or a DAG-based approach. Examples of leader-based protocols are PBFT [12], HotStuff [34], Autobahn [19], and ProBFT [6], and examples of DAG-based protocols are DAG-Rider [24], Narwhal [15], Bullshark [30], and Shoal++ [4]. Most of the BFT protocols can tolerate large-scale Byzantine behavior in the network. However, with the advent of trusted execution environments (TEEs), such strong fault tolerance might not be strictly necessary: adversarial peers can block a trusted device or obstruct message delivery, but cannot tamper with its internal execution. This has led to efficient consensus protocols based on trusted components [13,25,33], even before the blockchain era.

All of the works above assume that the set of participants under adversary control is static. Although we consider only attacks that block participants, the blocking can change *adaptively* from round to round. This rules out leader-based approaches since such an adversary can simply block a leader once it has been elected with a denial-of-service (DoS) attack. Heavily concentrating communication on a single participant also leads to imbalances in communication load and raises fairness concerns. Although rotating the leader over time can address fairness, our protocol avoids leaders altogether by being fully decentralized. In addition, while many state-of-the-art protocols rely on batching, coding, or threshold signatures to achieve near-optimal message complexity, our approach achieves near-optimal performance *without* such mechanisms.

The primary advantage of DAG-based protocols is that they can guarantee liveness under full asynchrony, whereas our protocol offers liveness under partial synchrony, once enough participants are synchronous. That said, this advantage comes with a caveat that is inherent to any protocol for the fully asynchronous model, namely that consensus can make very slow progress (even when randomized). In particular, a classical lower bound shows that for any integer k, an f-resilient algorithm over n processes fails to terminate within $k(n-f)$ steps with probability at least $1/c^k$ (for some constant c) [5]. Thus, asynchrony must persist for a long time before one can benefit from *any* protocol that offers liveness under asynchrony, whereas our protocol recovers quickly once a period of arbitrary asynchrony ends.

Gossip Based Consensus Protocols. In contrast to leader-based or DAG-based protocols, our approach relies on the gossip communication model. Gossip-based protocols have been studied extensively for various tasks, including information dissemination [23], aggregation [21], network coding [20], and consensus [16]. See [8] for a survey on gossip-based protocols. Due to their fast convergence and resilience under stress and disruptions, they have also been employed in various blockchain solutions, such as Bitcoin [14] and Tendermint [10], for network maintenance and information dissemination. Most closely aligned with our work are anti-entropy protocols [9,26,32], including the Snow consensus protocol used in Avalanche [28]. While many of these protocols have been analyzed under message loss and some under Byzantine behavior (e.g., [2,28]), their efficiency and robustness are often evaluated primarily through simulations. In contrast, we provide a rigorous analysis, building on works such as [16,27]. For the gossip model, it is known that under $\Theta(n)$ adaptive crash failures by a full-information adversary, any synchronous randomized consensus protocol needs $\tilde{\Theta}(\sqrt{n})$ rounds [7]. We bypass this lower bound by withholding new information from the adversary for one round, which allows the servers to update their state in an unpredictable way. Similar to related approaches like YOSO [17], this makes it hard for the adversary to start targeted blocking attacks.

Certification of Client Commands. Our approach to generate client certificates is based on a Merkle hash forest, which builds on the Merkle Mountain Range technique used in Ethereum and other blockchains [31]. While methods to store a compressed representation of the Merkle hash forest on servers have been used before, the novel challenge we address is ensuring that clients only need to receive the necessary hashing information once, at the moment the commitment of a command is acknowledged by a server, yet are still able to prove to any useful server, at any later time, that their command was committed, even though the servers just store a compressed version of the Merkle hash forest.

2   Consensus with a Median Rule

We start with an analysis of our proposed mechanism for stabilizing consensus that combines the median rule in [16] with undecided-state dynamics (e.g., [3]). The specific algorithm of the (k, l)-median rule can be found in Algorithm 1. Roughly, each server requests values from k random peers, and if it receives at least ℓ it adopts the median value as its own, else it adopts $\perp$ (corresponding to the undecided state). Since blocked servers will never receive any replies, their value will be equal to $\perp$ at the end of the round. The validity property (Definition 2) is trivially satisfied by the (k, ℓ)-median rule. Thus, it remains to show agreement and availability. Throughout the paper, we will focus on the specific case that $k = 6$ and $\ell = 3$ since that turns out to be the most suitable choice of parameters for our goals.

Availability. We call a server *useful* in round t if it stores a value at the beginning of t and is non-blocked during round t, and otherwise it is called *useless*. By definition, availability only holds as long as a constant fraction of servers is useful. We will show three results that provide important insights into availability when using the $(6, 3)$-median rule. The proofs are relatively technical and are given in full detail in Sect. 2.1 of the full version [11]. Here, we give an intuitive understanding of the claims and the way we use them later on.

The first result shows at which point a so-called *spiral-of-death* occurs, which describes the event where the number of useful servers (almost inevitably) goes to 0. In Algorithm 1 a server becomes useless if it does not obtain enough responses from others. However, this means that there is a threshold for the number of

---

Algorithm 1. The (k, l)-median rule

Preconditions: Let $k, \ell > 1$ with $k \geq \ell$ and ℓ odd. Assume that initially each server i stores an arbitrary value $x_i \in K$, where K is a discrete space with a total order.

Each server i does the following each round:

- send k value requests to servers chosen uniformly and independently at random
- if $x_i \neq \perp$ then for any value request received from some server j, send x_i back to j
- if at least ℓ replies are received, choose a subset of ℓ of these replies uniformly at random and set x_i to the median of the values sent by these replies
- if less than ℓ replies are received, set $x_i := \perp$

---

useful servers under which it is very unlikely for servers to sample enough useful others, so the servers are trapped in a negative feedback loop where ever fewer useful servers cause even more to become useless. Below the given threshold, the number of useful servers decays with double exponential speed in the number of rounds (i.e., is completed after $O(\log \log n)$ rounds) even if no server is actually blocked.

Lemma 1. *If the fraction of useful servers is at most $\frac{1}{3} - \varepsilon$ for any constant $\varepsilon > 0$ then even if no server is blocked, within $O(\log \log n)$ rounds no server is useful anymore, w.h.p.*

On the positive side, there is a minimum fraction for the number of useful servers, where that fraction stays stable, even if the adversary blocks a certain fraction of servers. This will define our "operating range" where our system guarantees liveness. Note that the specific thresholds of useful servers (3/4) and adversary ratio (1/10) are subject to our choice of parameters $(6, 3)$ in the median rule. In the interest of keeping the (already extensive) analysis manageable, we settle on this set of parameters, as this turns out to have suitable properties for our purposes.

Lemma 2. *If the initial fraction of useful servers is at least $1/2$ then for any 1-late $1/10$-blocking adversary, the fraction of useful servers monotonically converges to at least $3/4$ in just $O(\log n)$ rounds, w.h.p., and once it is at least $3/4$, it will be at least $3/4$, w.h.p., for any number of rounds that is polynomial in n.*

Another result we want to highlight shows that the $(6, 3)$-median rule preserves agreement under network partitions because for any isolated group of at most $7n/10$ servers, their values will all be $\perp$ within $O(\log n)$ rounds, w.h.p. This will be very useful later, when we show how to recover from arbitrary blocking attacks. Specifically, we exploit that the adversary can only choose between a perpetual death spiral (if it keeps blocking a fixed set of $3n/10$ servers thus essentially halting commitment of commands entirely) or allowing committed commands to be spread among the useful servers, thus ensuring their survival.

Lemma 3. *If at least a $\frac{3}{10}$-fraction of servers is permanently blocked, then irrespective of the number of useful servers, within $O(\log n)$ rounds no server is useful anymore, w.h.p.*

Agreement. We show that, perhaps interestingly, applying the $(6,3)$-median rule to the set of *all servers* can be reduced to applying the $(3,3)$-median rule only to the set of *useful servers*, which allows us to disregard useless severs and brings simplifications for the subsequent analysis of the agreement property. Thus, it suffices to focus on the subsets of useful servers and to prove the following statement inspired by the analysis of the median rule in [16]. More details and a generalization to a wider class of "(k,ℓ)-rules" can be found in Sect. 2.2 of the full version [11].

Theorem 1. *For any sequence $(U_1, U_2, U_3, \dots)$ of sets of useful servers satisfying $n/4 \leq |U_t| \leq n$ for all t, the $(3,3)$-median rule applied by U_{t+1} on U_t for all $t \geq 1$ achieves agreement in $O(\log n)$ rounds, w.h.p.*

Combining Lemma 1 (if the fraction of useful servers drops below $1/3$, it will rapidly spiral to 0) with Theorem 1 (if $n/4$ servers are continuously useful we reach agreement quickly), we obtain agreement in the general setting. Note that a blocking bound on the adversary is not even needed since the $(6,3)$-median rule trivially achieves agreement on $\perp$ if the fraction of useful servers ever drops below $1/3$.

Corollary 1. *For any 1-late adversary, the $(6,3)$-median rule achieves agreement in $O(\log n)$ rounds, w.h.p.*

When combining this corollary with Lemma 2 ($3n/4$ servers are useful under a limited adversary), we obtain the main result of this section.

Theorem 2. *If the adversary is 1-late and at least $n/4$ servers are useful in each round, the $(6,3)$-median rule solves the stabilizing consensus problem (Definition 2) in $O(\log n)$ rounds, w.h.p. Furthermore, given a 1-late $1/10$-blocking adversary, at least $3/4$ of the servers are useful w.h.p., for any number of rounds that is polynomial in n.*

3   SMR with an Extended Median Rule

Next, we extend our consensus protocol to a solution of the stabilizing SMR problem under a blocking adversary (Definition 3). We call a command *injected* once it is first received from the client by a non-blocked server. Here, clients are expected to send the same command multiple times to a random server to improve the chance of a successful injection (as a command sent to a blocked server is lost). We assume here that every client command is unique (a mechanism to resolve ambiguities is introduced in the next section.) The details of the extended (k,ℓ)-median rule can be found in Algorithm 2.

Algorithm 2. The extended (k, ℓ)-median rule

Preconditions: Each server i maintains a log $L_i \in K^*$, where K^* contains all finite sequences of commands from a totally ordered set K without repetitions. We use lexicographic order to impose a total order on these logs. Initially, $L_i = (x_0)$ for all i, where x_0 is a seed command. In every round, any set of client commands $x \in K$ can be injected at any subset of servers.

Each server i does the following each round:

- for every command x received from a client that is not yet contained in L_i, server i sends $\sigma \log n$ *append requests* to servers chosen uniformly and independently at random, for a sufficiently large constant $\sigma \geq 1$
- server i sends k *log requests* to servers chosen uniformly and independently at random
- if $L_i \neq \perp$ then for any *log request* received by server i from a server j, i sends L_i back to j
- if server i receives at least ℓ replies
  - server i chooses a subset M of size ℓ from the received logs uniformly at random
  - server i sets $L_i := L_i' \circ \bar{L}$, where L_i' is the median of M and $\bar{L}$ contains (in any order) all values in logs in M or in *append requests* received in that round that are *not* in L_i'
- if server i receives less than ℓ logs, it sets $L_i := \perp$

The first step amplifies the presence of any newly injected command x, giving it a high probability to reach all servers in subsequent rounds. Afterwards, the servers request logs from each other and select the median log from the responses, appending any missing commands. This process ensures that, over time, the servers converge on an ordering of commands that have circulated long enough. Similarly to the previous section, we call a server *useful* in round t if it stores a non-empty log at the beginning of t and is non-blocked during round t. We establish the following theorem, the proof in Sect. 3 of the full version [11].

Theorem 3. *If the adversary is 1-late and at least $n/4$ servers are useful in each round, the extended $(6, 3)$-median rule solves the stabilizing SMR problem (Definition 3) in $O(\log n)$ rounds, w.h.p. Furthermore, given a 1-late $1/10$-blocking adversary, at least $3/4$ of the servers are useful for polynomially many rounds, w.h.p.*

4   Compact SMR

This section summarizes, first, the compact state-machine replication (SMR) protocol (the details in Sect. 4 of the full version [11]) and, second, the command certification mechanism (the details in Sect. 5 of the full version [11]). The goal is to keep the history *compact*, that is, committed prefixes of logs should be executed on the shared state and then be pruned, while preserving the guarantees of our stabilizing SMR protocol (see Definition 3). To prune server logs, we build on the extended (k, ℓ)-median rule and attach an age to each command. We define a commit threshold $T \geq \tau \log n$, based on the time of $\tau \log n$ rounds (Theorem 3) until a command attains (w.h.p.) the same position in every non-empty log after injection. Each server keeps any command in its local log for at most T rounds. When a command reaches age T, it can be executed on the shared state and removed. This reduces the server logs to the commands injected within $O(T)$ rounds.

Two challenges necessitate changes to the design once this compactness rule is added. First, we need to take into account client behavior that might break some of the assumptions that we made in the previous section. In particular, clients may inject commands multiple times in order to improve their chances of reaching an unblocked server (i.e., we have to handle copies with different time stamps) and Byzantine clients may even inject conflicting commands. This was not an issue if the entire history is kept on each server, as such conflicts can be resolved locally in a consistent fashion, but need to be dealt with once we make the protocol compact. Second, clients need to be able to prove to third parties that their commands were committed.

We expect (non-Byzantine) clients to keep submitting their current command x to a random server until a server confirms that x has been committed, before submitting the next. Algorithm 5 in [11] handles the problem of multiple submissions as well as Byzantine deviations from this client protocol. To enforce exactly-once execution even under Byzantine client behavior, clients must attach to every command their identifier and a per-client sequence number that increments by exactly 1 from the previous command. Each server maintains, per client c, the largest committed sequence number $sn(c)$ and *accepts* a newly injected command x only if $sn(x) = sn(c) + 1$ and no command from c with that number is in its log. Upon acceptance, the server gossips x to $\sigma \log n$ random peers (as in the extended median rule), together with the current round number to track age. The command then goes through the process of broadcasting and eventual commitment (age $\geq T$) whereas age disagreements are reconciled via the median rule. After committing x, the server updates $sn(c) \leftarrow sn(x)$. If a client submits different commands with sequence number $sn(c)+1$, these can only be accepted if their injection times are at most T_B rounds apart, where $T_B = O(\log n)$ denotes the broadcast time of a command (w.h.p.). When choosing $T > 2T_B$, all servers will learn about these conflicting commands before committing them, so that all can be replaced by $\perp$ (the void command). When a client submits a command x with $sn(x) = sn(c)$ (or $x' \neq x$ with $sn(x') = sn(c)$ if the client acts Byzantine), the server informs the client that a command under that sequence number has already been committed (acting as commitment confirmation for x).

To allow checks of commitment proofs from the clients, the useful servers maintain root hashes of the Merkle hash forest whose leaves correspond to the log of committed commands and logarithmically many hashes per client (see Sect. 5 of [11]). Upon receiving x by a client for some command that was already committed, the server returns a certificate of x consisting of sibling hashes of the path from the leaf corresponding to x to the respective forest root. At any later time, the client can present its certificate to any useful server, which verifies it by comparing the computed root hash with its current (root or client) hashes.

5   Recovery

We now introduce a *recovery protocol* to provide resilience against an adversary capable of blocking an arbitrary number of servers for an unlimited duration (i.e., the recovery problem; see Definition 5). We call any period with less than $n/4$ useful servers a *surge*. Any period where at least $n/4$ servers are useful is considered *benign*. While the network will deteriorate into a death spiral, i.e., all servers become useless, somewhat above $n/4$ servers (see Lemma 1), we can still guarantee proper functioning of our prior protocols as long as $n/4$ servers are useful. However, our previous protocols are clearly not designed to handle a situation where all servers become useless, as they will lose all information on non-committed commands.

Therefore, we require servers to maintain persistent information on their states and logs, while at the same time keeping the protocol *compact*, i.e., allowing servers to eventually commit commands to their shared state and subsequently delete them. The primary challenge is that during a surge the adversary could allow some servers to progress and commit commands while preventing others from learning these. If the adversary then reverses this situation and permits the previously blocked servers to progress, those servers might commit a different set of commands, in violation of Definition 5. Our goal in this section is to ensure that the sequence of committed commands does not fork even under a surge and quickly return to a valid solution for the commitment problem (Definition 4), once the adversary becomes benign again.

Theorem 4. *The recovery protocol (Algorithm 3) solves the recovery problem (Def. 5) and returns to a solution for the commitment problem (Def. 4) $O(\log n)$ rounds after a surge.*

We begin with a brief overview of the recovery protocol, followed by pseudocode (Algorithm 3). In the recovery protocol, time is divided into periods of T rounds, referred to as *T-windows*. Whenever a T-window ends and the protocol behaves as expected, servers commit commands and create a new *checkpoint* that reflects the current state of servers. A checkpoint C_i of server i is a triple (S, P, W), where S is the current state of the state machine, P is a sequence of sufficiently old (but not yet committed) commands, and W is the T-window index when the checkpoint was taken. The parameters S and P represent a valid state of server i at some point, while W provides a priority ordering (where newer checkpoints take precedence). We also maintain a reset variable $R_i \in$ {reset, no-reset, $\perp$} for each server i, indicating whether i intends to revert to a previous checkpoint. If $R_i =$ no-reset, server i expects normal operation and a benign adversary. If $R_i = \perp$, server i believes a surge is currently in progress. If $R_i =$ reset, server i considers the surge over and that a rollback to a prior checkpoint is needed.

The complete recovery protocol can be viewed as two separate protocols: the *reset protocol* and the *checkpoint protocol* that run alongside the extended median rule, and incorporates the functionality of the compact median rule with certificates. The *reset protocol* is governed by each server's reset state, R_i. *At the end* of each T-window, if server i has an empty log L_i (from the extended median protocol), it concludes that it was blocked and sets $R_i = $ reset. Otherwise, $R_i = $ no-reset. *During* a T-window, in every round, each server i queries the reset states R_j of k randomly chosen servers. If at least ℓ responses are received and any of them is no-reset, the server sets $R_i = $ no-reset; if all responses are reset, it sets $R_i = $ reset. If fewer than ℓ responses are received, R_i becomes $\perp$, and a server in the $\perp$ state does not answer queries about its own state R_i. This design ensures that if the adversary surges during a T-window, the system falls into a "death spiral" where all servers eventually switch to $R_i = \perp$. Otherwise, the servers converge on either reset or no-reset. Finally, if a server ends a T-window with $R_i = $ reset, it rolls back to a previously agreed-upon checkpoint.

The *checkpoint protocol* revolves around the triple C_i. Servers exchange checkpoints by issuing k random queries, analogous to how they exchange logs L_i or states R_i. The key distinction is that checkpoints are prioritized by age, given by the third parameter W. If the newest received checkpoint (S', P', W') has a higher number W' than its own checkpoint, it immediately adopts it and updates its state $S_i := S'$ and its log $L_i := P'$, since the server is outdated. This procedure spreads the newest checkpoints (those with the largest W) within one T-window, assuming $T = O(\log n)$ is sufficiently large.

For conciseness, we assume in this section that the functionality of the compact median protocol with certificates is subsumed in the state machine, in particular, the required data structure centered around client sequence numbers (Sect. 4) and the Merkle hash forests (Sect. 5 in [11]). The techniques presented in Sects. 4 and 5 of the full version [11] can be adapted to the recovery protocol. Consequently, we assume here that client commands are unique.

The main technical challenge is to prove that the way these protocols interact ensures safety and recovery with a surging adversary. We outline qualitatively why Algorithm 3 never violates monotonicity and regains strong safety, availability, and liveness within $O(\log n)$ rounds once the blocking adversary is again benign, i.e., 1/10-bounded. This sketch takes a simplistic view, geared towards a high-level understanding. The detailed proof in Sect. 6 of the full version [11].

Proof (Proof Sketch of Theorem 4).

Monotonicity: This property is easiest to see by following the life cycle of a single command x in the *checkpoint protocol*. Let W be the next T-window after x is injected. We call W *good* if a sufficient number of servers is useful for most of the T-Window W, i.e., it allows a solution of the stabilizing SMR problem (Definition 3), that is, successful gossip of values and stabilization of commands within logs. If W is good, then a critical mass of servers hold x at the same log position and each of those servers copy x into their pre-committed pool P at the end of W (reaching the age threshold of T). If the next window $W + 1$ is

---

Algorithm 3. Recovery Protocol

Preconditions:

- S_i, L_i: **current** state and log of server i (initially start state s_0 and seed command x_0)
- $R_i \in \{\mathbf{reset}, \mathbf{no\text{-}reset}, \bot\}$: server i's willingness to roll back (initially $\mathbf{no\text{-}reset}$)
- $C_i = (S, P, W)$: parameters we intend to rescue in case of a surge:
  - S: last observed shared state (initially the start state s_0)
  - P: sequence of "pre-committed" commands (initially $\bot$)
  - W: number of T-window (initially 0)

Each round during a T-window each server i does: *(on top of extended median rule)*

- Send k requests to random servers *(same as in the extended median protocol)*
- If a request was received from server j and $R_i \neq \bot$, then
  - send C_i and R_i to server j
- If at least ℓ replies were received, then
  - If $\mathbf{no\text{-}reset}$ was received in one reply, $R_i := \mathbf{no\text{-}reset}$, else $R_i := \mathbf{reset}$
  - let $C' = (S', P', W')$ be the received checkpoint with largest W' *(break ties arbitrarily)*
  - If $W' > W$
    - set $S_i := S'$, $L_i := P'$ *(bring server up to date)*
    - set $C_i := C'$ *(adopt newer checkpoint)*
- If less than ℓ replies were received, set $R_i := \bot$

Between T-windows do:

- If $R_i = \mathbf{reset}$, then set $S_i := S$, $L_i := P$, where $C_i = (S, P, W)$ *(rollback)*
- If $L_i \neq \bot$, then
  - for current checkpoint $C_i = (S, P, W)$, commit all commands in P on S_i and remove the prefix P from L_i *(if L_i would become empty, append a dummy command x_d).*
  - make new checkpoint $C_i := (S_i, P_i, W')$, where S_i is the current state, P_i is the longest prefix of L_i of commands with age $\geq T$ and W' is the next T-window number
  - set $R_i := \mathbf{no\text{-}reset}$
- If $L_i = \bot$, then $R_i := \mathbf{reset}$

---

also good, the checkpoint protocol forces all useful servers to adopt the freshest checkpoint. So every command in P, including x, is *committed* (in the same order by each server that does so) by the end of $W + 1$. Overall, x is committed after $T = O(\log n)$ rounds.

If the adversary launches a surge, it has only two options: either let the command propagate so it enters the checkpoint variable P of a critical mass of up-to-date servers, or trigger a death spiral early in the window. If the death spiral starts before enough servers pre-commit x, every server becomes useless and clears its log; x may then vanish entirely, requiring the client to reinject it. Crucially, if *any* server ever commits x, then x must already have been pre-committed at the end of some good T-window W. Because pre-commitment requires an age of T rounds, x lived through the full duration of W and was therefore allowed to spread through logs and appears in the up-to-date checkpoint of a critical mass of servers which can no longer be "washed out" by the adversary. From that point forward the adversary again has only two choices. It may keep triggering death spirals every window, preventing those servers from propagating their checkpoints. But this prohibits that any other server commits commands or creates newer checkpoints! If the adversary stops causing spirals, then a most up-to-date checkpoint containing x will spread and every server will eventually commit x. In both cases no server commits a command that would reorder or exclude x, so monotonicity is preserved.

Recovery: We have to consider how the checkpoint protocol interacts with the *reset protocol*, which governs the reset variables R_i and the rollback mechanism. During normal operation where an adversary behaves benign, we have (1) only good T-windows and (2) a critical mass of useful servers start with the priority state $R_i = \texttt{no-reset}$ on which all useful servers will eventually agree by the priority rule. Because $\texttt{no-reset}$ disables rollbacks, command commitment proceeds normally, and safety, availability, and liveness are maintained (see Algorithm 3).

It remains to argue that we return to such a normal mode of operation after a period where all T-windows experience early death-spirals, causing all servers to end in the undecided states ($\bot$) in the checkpoint and reset protocols. This means that no server will trigger a rollback nor commit new commands which preserves monotonicity, as argued above. Assume that W is the first good T-window after this period. Because every server is useless ($L_i = \bot$) when W begins, each sets $R_i = \texttt{reset}$ (see Algorithm 3). Specifically, no server adopts the higher-priority value $\texttt{no-reset}$, so the priority rule (see Definition 3.5 in [11]) forces all useful servers to adopt $R_i = \texttt{reset}$ by the end of W. Therefore, at the end of W, all servers will roll back to the checkpoint they stored before the period of death spirals, which allows them to continue normal operation.

6   Conclusion

We introduced a lightweight solution for state machine replication under an adversary capable of blocking any number of servers. As shown in [16], the median rule can tolerate $O(\sqrt{n})$ adversarial servers, suggesting that our approach can be extended to handle not just blocked but also $O(\sqrt{n})$ malicious servers. Furthermore, we anticipate that it can accommodate server churn by allowing the adversary to have a β-fraction of blocked, joining or leaving servers in each round, thus removing the requirement of a static server set.

Our $1/10$ bound for blocked servers to ensure liveness is not fundamental. By tuning parameters k, ℓ, the protocol tolerates any 1-late $(1 - \varepsilon)$-blocking adversary for constant $\varepsilon > 0$. However, our choice of parameters provides some measure of partition tolerance. With our chosen parameters, safety even holds under *any* partition as all but at most one component will "spiral to death" (see Lemma 3). This provides a trade-off in the sense of the CAP theorem between safety, liveness, and partition tolerance [18].

Moreover, we believe our protocols can be extended so that commitment errors are not persistent. First of all, we ensure that commitment errors are very unlikely and, therefore, rare in the first place. Second, the proof of Theorem 3 implies that the extended median rule achieves agreement on the position of a command x within $O(\log n)$ rounds, w.h.p., *irrespective* of how the logs look like initially, i.e., commitment errors only have limited effects on other commands. Third, our recovery protocol only takes another checkpoint of a shared state every $T = \Theta(\log n)$ rounds so that there is sufficient time to arrive at a consensus checkpoint that resolves disagreement on the shared state caused by a commitment error, by making use of the median rule. This pushes the probability of a *persistent* error to a point where it can be truly ignored.

References

1. Ahmadi, M., Ghodselahi, A., Kuhn, F., Molla, A.R.: The cost of global broadcast in dynamic radio networks. In: Proceedings of of OPODIS 2015 (2015)
2. Amores-Sesar, I., Cachin, C., Schneider, P.: An analysis of avalanche consensus. In: Proceedings of SIROCCO 2024 (2024)
3. Angluin, D., Aspnes, J., Eisenstat, D.: A simple population protocol for fast robust approximate majority. Distrib. Comput. **21**(2), 87–102 (2008)
4. Arun, B., Li, Z., Suri-Payer, F., Das, S., Spiegelman, A.: Shoal++: High throughput dag bft can be fast! ArXiv (2024)
5. Attiya, H., Censor-Hillel, K.: Lower bounds for randomized consensus under a weak adversary. SIAM J. Comput. **39**(8), 3885–3904 (2010)
6. Avelas, D., Heydari, H., Alchieri, E., Distler, T., Bessani, A.: Probabilistic byzantine fault tolerance. In: Proceedings of ACM PODC 2024 (2024)
7. Bar-Joseph, Z., Ben-Or, M.: A tight lower bound for randomized synchronous consensus. In: Proceedings of ACM PODC 1998 (1998)
8. Becchetti, L., Clementi, A., Natale, E.: Consensus dynamics: an overview. SIGACT News **51**(1), 58–104 (2020)
9. Birman, K.P., Hayden, M., Özkasap, Ö., Xiao, Z., Budiu, M., Minsky, Y.: Bimodal multicast. ACM Trans. Comput. Syst. **17**(2), 41–88 (1999)
10. Buchman, E., Kwon, J., Milosevic, Z.: The latest gossip on BFT consensus. CoRR, abs/1807.04938 (2018)
11. Cachin, C., Dou, J., Scheideler, C., Schneider, P.: A lightweight approach for state machine replication. CoRR, abs/2509.17771 (2025)
12. Castro, M., Liskov, B.: Practical byzantine fault tolerance. In: Proceedings of OSDI 1999 (1999)
13. Chun, B.-G., Maniatis, P., Shenker, S., Kubiatowicz, J.: Attested append-only memory: making adversaries stick to their word. In: Proceedings of SOSP 2007 (2007)
14. Cruciani, A., Pasquale, F.: Dynamic graph models inspired by the bitcoin network-formation process. In: Proceedings of ICDCN 2023 (2023)
15. Danezis, G., Kokoris-Kogias, L., Sonnino, A., Spiegelman, A.: Narwhal and tusk: a dag-based mempool and efficient BFT consensus. In: Proceedings of EuroSys '22 (2022)

16. Doerr, B., Goldberg, L.A., Minder, L., Sauerwald, T., Scheideler, C.: Stabilizing consensus with the power of two choices. In: Proceedings of ACM SPAA 2011 (2011)
17. Gentry, C., et al: YOSO: you only speak once - secure MPC with stateless ephemeral roles. In: Proceedings of CRYPTO 2021, pp. 64–93 (2021). https://doi.org/10.1007/978-3-030-84245-1_3
18. Gilbert, S., Lynch, N.A.: Brewer's conjecture and the feasibility of consistent, available, partition-tolerant web services. SIGACT News **33**(2), 51–59 (2002)
19. Giridharan, N., Suri-Payer, F., Abraham, I., Alvisi, L.: and Natacha Crooks. Seamless high speed BFT. In: Proceedings of SOSP, Autobahn (2024)
20. Haeupler, B.: Analyzing network coding gossip made easy. In: Proceedings of STOC 2011 (2011)
21. Haeupler, B., Mohapatra, J., Su, H.-H.: Optimal gossip algorithms for exact and approximate quantile computations. In: Proceedings of ACM PODC 2018 (2018)
22. Bitcoin Blockchain Size (I:BBS) (2025). https://ycharts.com/indicators/bitcoin_blockchain_size
23. Karp, R.M., Schindelhauer, C., Shenker, S., Vöcking, B.: Randomized rumor spreading. In: Proceedings of FOCS 2000 (2000)
24. Keidar, I., Kokoris-Kogias, E., Naor, O., Spiegelman, A.: All you need is DAG. In: Proceedings of ACM PODC 2021 (2021)
25. Levin, D., Douceur, J.R., Lorch, J.R., Moscibroda, T.: Small trusted hardware for large distributed systems. In: Proceedings of NSDI, Trinc (2009)
26. Petersen, K., Spreitzer, M., Terry, D.B., Theimer, M., Demers, A.J.: Flexible update propagation for weakly consistent replication. In: Proceedings of ACM SOSP 1997 (1997)
27. Robinson, P., Scheideler, C., Setzer, A.: Breaking the $\omega(\sqrt{\log n})$ barrier: Fast consensus under a late adversary. In: Proceedings of ACM SPAA 2018 (2018)
28. Team Rocket, Yin, M., Sekniqi, K., van Renesse, R., Sirer, E.G.: Scalable and probabilistic leaderless BFT consensus through metastability. CoRR, abs/1906.08936 (2019)
29. Schneider, F.B.: Implementing fault-tolerant services using the state machine approach: a tutorial. ACM Comput. Surv. **22**(4), 299–319 (1990)
30. Spiegelman, A., Giridharan, N., Sonnino, A., Kokoris-Kogias, L.: Bullshark: DAG BFT protocols made practical. In: Proceedings of ACM CCS 2022, pp. 2705–2718 (2022)
31. Peter Todd. Merkle mountain ranges (2012). https://github.com/opentimestamps/opentimestamps-server/blob/master/doc/merkle-mountain-range.md
32. van Renesse, R., Dumitriu, D., Gough, V., Thomas, C.: Efficient reconciliation and flow control for anti-entropy protocols. In: Proceedings of LADIS 2008, pp. 6:1–6:7 (2008)
33. Veronese, G.S., Correia, M., Bessani, A.N., Lung, L.C., Veríssimo, P.: Efficient byzantine fault-tolerance. IEEE Trans. Comput. **62**(1), 16–30 (2013)
34. Yin, M., Malkhi, D., Reiter, M.K., Golan-Gueta, G., Abraham, I.: Hotstuff: BFT consensus with linearity and responsiveness. Proc. of ACM PODC **2019**, 347–356 (2019)

Silent Self-stabilising Leader Election in Programmable Matter Systems with Holes

Jérémie Chalopin[1], Shantanu Das[1], and Maria Kokkou[2]

[1] Aix Marseille Univ, CNRS, LIS, Marseille, France
{jeremie.chalopin,shantanu.das}@lis-lab.fr
[2] Paderborn University, Paderborn, Germany
maria.kokkou@uni-paderborn.de

Abstract. Leader election is a fundamental problem in distributed computing, particularly within programmable matter systems, where coordination among simple computational entities is crucial for solving complex tasks. In these systems, particles (i.e., constant-memory computational entities) operate in a regular triangular grid as described in the geometric Amoebot model. While leader election has been extensively studied in non self-stabilising settings, self-stabilising solutions remain more limited. In this work, we study the problem of self-stabilising leader election in connected (but not necessarily *simply* connected) configurations. We present the first self-stabilising algorithm for connected programmable matter systems that guarantees the election of a unique leader under an unfair scheduler, for oblivious particles (i.e., particles with no persistent memory) that share a common sense of direction. Our approach leverages particle movement, a capability not previously exploited in the self-stabilising context. We show that movement in conjunction with particles sharing a sense of orientation and operating in a grid can overcome classical impossibility results for constant-memory systems established by Dolev, Gouda and Schneider (1999).

Keywords: Leader Election · Programmable Matter · Self-Stabilisation · Silent · Deterministic · Unique Leader · Agreement on Directions · Holes · Oblivious

1 Introduction

Programmable Matter involves large collections of simple computational entities, called particles, that can change their physical properties (e.g., shape) in a programmable way and need to collaboratively accomplish a given task in a geometric environment. In this work, we assume the geometric environment to be a regular triangular grid. One of the central objectives of these systems

---

M. Kokkou—Most of this work was done while the author was affiliated with Aix-Marseille University.

C. Georgiou (Ed.): SIROCCO 2026, LNCS 16488, pp. 151–171, 2026.
https://doi.org/10.1007/978-3-032-26465-7_9

is to be able to form any desired configuration from an arbitrary initial configuration in an efficient way with respect to time, energy and computational power. Leader election can be used as an intermediate step to designing robust algorithms for more complex problems, such as the one mentioned before, by electing a particle that can coordinate the system and break symmetries. Leader election introduced in [26] is a classical problem in distributed computing, often addressed under the assumption that each node has a unique identifier. In the case of unique identifiers, it is easy to see that if nodes can exchange information, the node with the smallest or the greatest identifier can be elected. In our work, as particles have constant memory, we cannot assume unique identifiers. Leader election in anonymous systems (i.e., networks where nodes do not have unique identifiers) is impossible to solve without additional assumptions due to symmetries [2]. To overcome this constraint, one solution is to employ randomisation [24] or to characterise networks where the problem can be solved [32]. In this paper, we use a different combination of assumptions, namely common sense of direction and movement capabilities, to elect a unique leader.

Even though the large scale of programmable matter systems increases the likelihood of faults occurring and makes fault tolerance even more critical, fault-tolerant approaches to problems remain limited. In particular, self-stabilisation which is a broad way to model diverse faults such as memory corruption, particle crashes and failures in communication resulting in an arbitrarily initialised configuration, has been largely overlooked in previous work. An algorithm is self-stabilising if, from any arbitrary initial configuration, every execution of the algorithm reaches a valid configuration (whose precise definition depends on the problem) in finite time and all subsequent configurations are valid. To the best of our knowledge, [7] gives the only self-stabilising algorithm for programmable matter. The problem considered therein is leader election in simply connected systems, under a Gouda fair scheduler [23]. A Gouda fair scheduler imposes that for every configuration that appears infinitely often during an execution of an algorithm, every possible successor configuration must also appear infinitely often and is the strongest kind of fairness per [15]. A particle configuration $\mathcal{P}$ occupying a subset of nodes of an infinite regular triangular grid G_Δ is said to be *simply connected* if it is connected and $G_\Delta \backslash \mathcal{P}$ is also connected. In connected systems, we call connected components of $G_\Delta \backslash \mathcal{P}$ that are surrounded by particles, *holes*. The aim of this paper is to give a self-stabilising approach for the leader election problem in programmable matter systems that are connected but not necessarily simply connected, complementing the results of [7] for simply connected systems without holes. Our method can directly be combined with any *stationary* (i.e., when particles do not have movement capabilities) self-stabilising algorithm that requires a unique leader. As we consider oblivious particles without states or persistent memory, our algorithm does not have an explicit leader state but elects a leader based on local conditions that we formally define in Sect. 3. Informally, we show that eventually there exists exactly one particle that is locally lowermost and rightmost, which implies that this particle is globally lowermost and rightmost. We define this particle to be the leader. Our algorithm can be trivially modified to include a marked leader (see Observation 2).

We study self-stabilising leader election in connected programmable matter systems embedded in a regular triangular grid, where each node is incident to six edges labelled from 0 to 5. When the particles are stationary, this problem is significantly more difficult for arbitrary connected configurations compared to the simply connected setting presented in [7]. For example, suppose that the particles do not agree on orientation and the system is not simply connected. Then it is possible to construct a cyclic configuration where all particles have the same local information (e.g., Fig. 1). In this setting, the results of [14] determine that silent (i.e., all particles eventually stop performing any actions, such as updating their internal variables) self-stabilising leader election cannot be solved with constant memory. In this work, the algorithm being silent implies that particles eventually stop moving. To overcome the impossibility result of [14] we assume that particles agree on all directions. We consider the problem within the geometric Amoebot model and present a solution that uses movement, leading to a less general version of self-stabilising leader election in connected configurations. As proved in [12], moving cannot maintain connectivity in a self-stabilising context for programmable matter, without additional assumptions. This is due to the fact that particles may all start in an expanded state (i.e., occupying two neighbouring nodes) and immediately be instructed to contract (i.e., occupy one node), disconnecting the system with no way of reconnecting, while the system is not in a valid state. Therefore, we need to assume that particles can *sense* their surroundings in a way that the information on whether neighbouring nodes are occupied by other particles or empty cannot be corrupted.

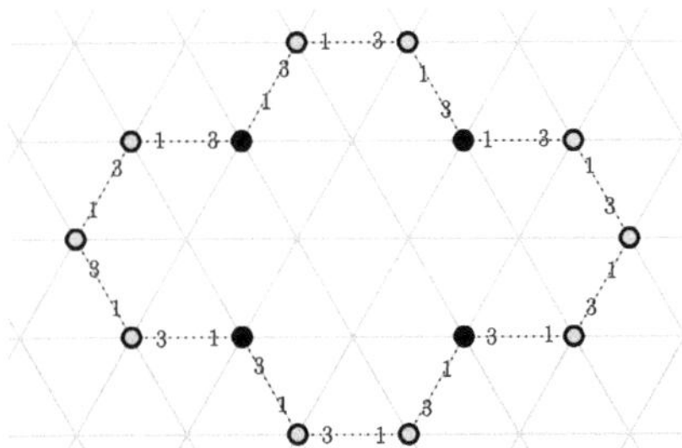

Fig. 1. A particle configuration where all particles share identical local information. Blue and black particles have opposite chiralities (i.e., senses of rotational orientation). Numbers denote (consecutive) edge labels from 0 to 5. (Color figure online)

1.1   Related Work

Programmable matter was introduced in [30] and has since been widely studied both within a theoretical context and a practical one (e.g., [28,29]). In this work we focus on its theoretical aspect, for which multiple models have been defined. One of the most popular active models (i.e., when the computational entities are also the building blocks of the system) is the *Amoebot model* [9,11] that has also been the basis for SILBOT [8] and the Reconfigurable Circuits extension [19]. Multiple other models exist such as [1,18,22,31]. We focus on leader election results within Amoebot which is the model used in this work.

Table 1. Deterministic Leader Election in triangular grids. "Simply Connected" denotes particle systems without *holes*. "Chirality" is a common sense of rotational orientation. "Movement" is the ability of particles to move to neighbouring nodes. A "Sequential (Seq.) Scheduler" activates one particle at a time. An "Asynchronous (Asynch.) Scheduler" activates particles independently. A "Fair" scheduler eventually activates all activable particles. An "Unfair" scheduler activates a number of activable particles. Under a "Gouda Fair" scheduler, every successor of a recurring configuration is recurring. *Agreement on the directions along one axis. †Agreement on all directions, which implies chirality.

Paper	Leaders	Simply Connected	Chirality	Movement	Scheduler	Self-Stabilising
[16]	6	X	✓	X	Seq. Fair	X
[13]	3	✓	X	X	Asynch. Fair	X
[4]	6	X	✓	X	Asynch. Fair	X
[20]	1	✓	✓	X	Seq. Fair	X
[17]	1	X	X	✓	Seq. Fair	X
[16]	1	X	✓	✓	Seq. Fair	X
[5]	1	✓	X	X	Seq. Fair	X
[6]	1	X	X*	X	Asynch. Fair	X
[7]	1	✓	X	X	Seq. Gouda Fair	✓
This Work	1	X	✓†	✓	Seq. Unfair	✓

Leader election is a very well studied problem within Amoebot, with results under various assumptions. It has been studied both in the three-dimensional setting (e.g., [5,21]) and in two dimensions. In the 2D case, both randomised (e.g., [12]) and deterministic algorithms have been proposed. In the deterministic approach particles are often assumed to agree on rotational orientation (known as particles having common *chirality*) like for example in [4,16,20]. In [6] the authors assume agreement on one axis of the triangular grid and show that this assumption is not comparable to agreement on chirality. Earlier work on leader election, as for example [16,17,20], assumes a sequential scheduler (i.e., one particle is active at any time). However, the problem has also been studied under an asynchronous scheduler in [4,6,13]. In terms of fairness, all previous leader election algorithms assume a fair scheduler (i.e., a scheduler that eventually activates every particle that can be activated). However, although this is not stated explicitly, we believe that most algorithms, especially [6,16,20], also work under an unfair scheduler (i.e., at any time at least one particle that can be activated is chosen but some particles may be perpetually ignored as long as another activable particle exists in the system). Most results in the literature consider stationary particles, with the exception of [16,17] which use the movement capabilities of programmable matter. Finally, [13,20] consider simply connected particle configurations whereas [4,6,16,17] allow for the particle system to contain holes. The results for the two-dimensional deterministic case in the Amoebot model are also summarised in Table 1.

In the same model, [7] studied self-stabilising leader election in the context of programmable matter for the first time, demonstrating that geometry can be leveraged to overcome the impossibility results established for general graphs in [14]. In particular, [7] gives a deterministic self-stabilising leader election algorithm for particles with constant memory when the particle system is simply connected and particles are activated by a Gouda fair scheduler. To the best of our knowledge, [7] is the only paper studying self-stabilisation in the context of programmable matter. Some earlier work also discusses self-stabilisation in programmable matter but in slightly different settings. In [12], the authors discuss the possibility of making their randomised leader election algorithm self-stabilising by combining it with techniques from [3,25]. However, in that case, it is assumed that particles have $O(\log^* n)$ memory, where n is the number of particles in the system, bypassing the constant memory constraint of programmable matter systems. More recently, [10] introduced a deterministic self-stabilising algorithm for constructing a spanning forest for particles with constant memory. However, in that case it is assumed that at least one non-faulty special particle always remains in the system, making the design of self-stabilising leader election algorithms particularly important. Hence the field of self-stabilisation within programmable matter systems remains largely unexplored as highlighted in [9].

Within the SILBOT model, Navarra and Piselli [27] introduced the idea of moving particles with a lower neighbour downwards until the particle system forms a single line. While their algorithm also yields a unique lowermost rightmost particle, it is not self-stabilising. Their approach assumes that every particle is initially contracted, movement is done via expansions and contractions and particles are allowed to become disconnected during execution. In a self-stabilising setting, every particle state allowed by the algorithm is a potential state of a particle in the initial configuration. Hence, in the self-stabilising context, the algorithm of [27] would allow particles to be initially expanded and for the system to initially be disconnected. If all particles in the system are initially expanded, instructing them to contract may cause disconnection. Moreover, if the system is initially disconnected, the particles have no way of knowing or reconnecting. Therefore, although we adopt the idea of moving particles with a lower neighbour down, directly using the algorithm of [27] is not possible. We address the aforementioned challenges by introducing atomic moves that consist of at most one contraction and at most one expansion, as well as a set of conditions that preserve connectivity at every step. Finally, [27] relies on additional assumptions such as two hop visibility, which we do not assume.

1.2 Our Contributions

We present a silent, self-stabilising leader election algorithm that deterministically ensures that in any arbitrarily initialised connected system, there eventually exists a unique locally lowermost rightmost particle, which is defined to be the leader. Being silent is in general a desirable property of self-stabilising algorithms as it implies smaller communication bandwidth [14]. In the context of our work, where particles do not communicate with each other, our algorithm being silent implies that particles eventually stop moving. This property allows our algorithm to be combined with other stationary self-stabilising algorithms. In order to overcome the additional difficulties introduced in a connected system instead of a simply connected one, we use atomic moves consisting of at most one contraction and at most one expansion. Algorithm 1 is the first self-stabilising algorithm that works in a connected configuration (instead of a simply connected configuration like [7]). Furthermore, this is the first self-stabilising algorithm for programmable matter that works under an unfair scheduler. In order to achieve this, we assume that particles agree on all directions of the grid and are activated sequentially. The latter assumption means that only one particle is active at a time, which is a standard assumption in programmable matter systems. We additionally assume that particles are oblivious, making our algorithm the first self-stabilising leader election algorithm for programmable matter where particles do not need persistent memory. Our algorithm (Sect. 3) only depends on an active particle detecting which nodes in its neighbourhood are occupied by other particles, but particles cannot exchange any additional information. In particular, particles cannot exchange messages or read the state of neighbouring particles like in previous work within programmable matter.

2 Model and Preliminaries

Let G_Δ be an infinite regular triangular grid. We assume the particle system $\mathcal{P}$ occupies a connected subset of nodes in G_Δ. Each computational entity in $\mathcal{P}$ is called a *particle*. We assume that each particle is *oblivious* (i.e., has no memory), has no communication capabilities and can be either *contracted* occupying one node or *expanded* occupying two neighbouring nodes. Notice that the state of the particle is thus only defined by whether it is expanded or contracted. Each node can be occupied by at most one particle at any time. We call the two endpoints of an expanded particle the *head* and *tail* of the particle. A contracted particle p is incident to six ports, each corresponding to one of the six neighbouring nodes of p in G_Δ, which are arranged consecutively in cyclic order around p. An expanded particle is incident to eight ports, each corresponding to one of the eight nodes around it in G_Δ. We define the neighbourhood of each endpoint of an expanded particle to be the same as the neighbourhood of a contracted particle, that is, to be the six nodes reachable by ports. We consider the neighbourhood of an expanded particle to be the union of the neighbourhood of the two endpoints of the particle. This means that we consider the tail (resp. head) of an expanded particle to be part of the neighbourhood of the head (resp. tail) of the particle. We write *occupied neighbourhood* of a particle p or $N(p)$ to denote the nodes that are neighbouring to p and are occupied by particles. We use the notation $N[p] = N(p) \cup \{p\}$ to refer to the occupied neighbourhood of p and the node(s) occupied by p. We call a particle in the occupied neighbourhood of p a *neighbour* of p. Finally, we assume that a particle p knows whether two adjacent nodes in $N(p)$ are occupied by one expanded particle or by two different particles. Notice that if p is adjacent to only one endpoint of an expanded particle it does not know whether the neighbouring particle is expanded or contracted. We discuss the importance of this assumption in Sect. 3.

Within the Amoebot model, particles move using two main operations: *expansion* to a neighbouring node and *contraction* to the node occupied by the head of the particle. An expansion is only possible for a contracted particle and a contraction is only possible for an expanded particle. Contrary to Amoebot, here we assume that particles have two *contract* operations: *contract to head* and *contract to tail*. The new *contract to tail* operation does not alter the model significantly as it is equivalent to an expanded particle contracting to head, expanding in the opposite direction and contracting to head a second time.

We say that a particle for which some condition is enabled is *activable*. We call an activable particle that is chosen by the scheduler *activated*. When a particle is activated, it detects which of its neighbouring nodes are occupied, whether any of those nodes are occupied by an expanded particle and, based on this information, it performs at most one contraction and at most one expansion, in this order. Operations performed during a single activation of the particle are called a *move* and a move is assumed to be atomic. That is, when a particle is activated it performs all operations that are part of the move before becoming inactive and while a particle is active no other particle becomes activated. Notice that since a move consists of at most one contraction and at most one expansion, at least one of the nodes the particle occupied before its activation remains occupied by the same particle after its activation. Atomic moves are particularly important in this context, as they guarantee that the system remains connected after every *move*. Without this assumption, the impossibility result of [12] forbids movement within the self-stabilising context.

We assume that all particles have a common sense of orientation (i.e., all particles agree on all directions), as shown in Fig. 2. We define a *step* of the execution to be the time needed for a particle to become activated, execute a given algorithm once and become deactivated. We assume that particles are activated by a *sequential unfair* scheduler. A sequential scheduler refers to the synchronicity of the system and guarantees that only one particle is active at any step and is a usual assumption within programmable matter systems (e.g., [16,17,20]). An unfair scheduler concerns the fairness of activations and represents the weakest fairness condition per [15]: at each step, some activable particle is activated. In

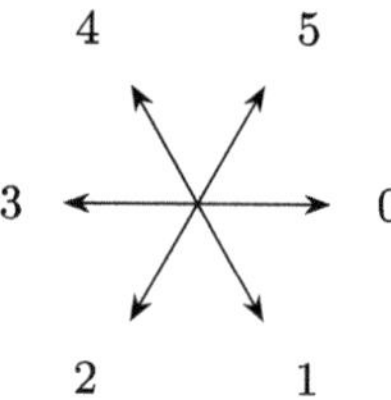

Fig. 2. Directions of particles

contrast to a fair scheduler, it does not require that every activable particle is eventually activated, and thus it is possible that any number of activable particles are perpetually ignored as long as at least one other activable particle exists in the system.

The pseudocode is composed of a set of states which in turn are composed of a set of conditions and actions. Each line of the algorithm is of the form $c_i : a_1, \ldots, a_m$ where c_i is the i-th condition and each $a_j \in \{a_1, \ldots, a_m\}$ is an action. Every time a particle is activated, it evaluates the conditions in its current state in order and if a condition is satisfied the particle performs the corresponding actions and finishes the round without evaluating the remaining conditions.

3   Silent Self-stabilising Leader Election with Movement

The algorithm we give follows the core idea presented in [27]. That is, the goal is to move particles that have a lower neighbour downwards if an empty lower node exists. However, in this work we also assume that any number of particles may initially be expanded and particles do not have 2–hop visibility. Since the labels of *head* and *tail* are usually part of the memory and we consider oblivious particles, every time an expanded particle is activated it assigns its head to be the end occupying the lower node if one exists, otherwise it assigns the head to be the end occupying the rightmost node. This, although not part of the Amoebot model, is not too restrictive as any particle for which the above orientation is not true could contract and expand in the opposite direction to achieve the described positioning.

Informally, the algorithm is the following. A contracted particle that has exactly one lower neighbour (i.e., direction 1 or 2 of Fig. 2) expands downwards without disconnecting its occupied neighbourhood. Any contracted particle that has either zero or two occupied lower neighbouring nodes and that has an upper neighbour to the right (i.e., in direction 5 of Fig. 2), expands to the right (i.e., direction 0). An expanded particle contracts to its head as long as it does not disconnect its neighbours. If an expanded particle with at least one lower neighbour cannot contract without disconnecting its occupied neighbourhood, it tries to improve its position. This is done by remaining expanded and either moving one of its endpoints to a lower position that does not disconnect its neighbours or by moving the tail to a node that allows a different particle to move without disconnecting the system. An example of the former case is shown in Fig. 3. A central step in proving the correctness of our algorithm (i.e., Lemma 2) is showing that:

> When executing this algorithm there eventually exists exactly one particle that has no lower neighbours and no neighbour to the right (i.e., in directions 0, 1, 2 and 5). This particle is defined to be the leader.

We now describe how a particle moves without disconnecting its neighbourhood. Let p be an expanded particle and let h and t be the head and tail of p respectively. Call v the lower common neighbouring node of h and t. If p is expanded diagonally, call w the higher common neighbour of h, t. If for every particle in $N(t)$ there exists a path to h that only passes through occupied nodes in $N(p)\backslash\{t\}$, p contracts to h without disconnecting its neighbourhood. Otherwise, if v is empty and for every particle in $N(t)$ there exists a path to v that only passes through v and occupied nodes in $N[h]\backslash\{t\}$, p contracts to head and expands to v so that p occupies v and the original node of h. An example of this case is shown in the first three subfigures of Fig. 3. If p is expanded horizontally, v is empty and for every particle in $N(h)$ there exists a path to v that only passes through v and occupied nodes in $N[t]\backslash\{h\}$, p contracts to tail and expands to v so that p occupies v and the original node of t. An example of this case is shown in the fourth subfigure of Fig. 3. When no such v that preserves connectivity exists, if p is expanded diagonally and t is the lower common neighbour of a horizontally expanded particle, p contracts to head and expands to w so that p occupies w and the original node of h.

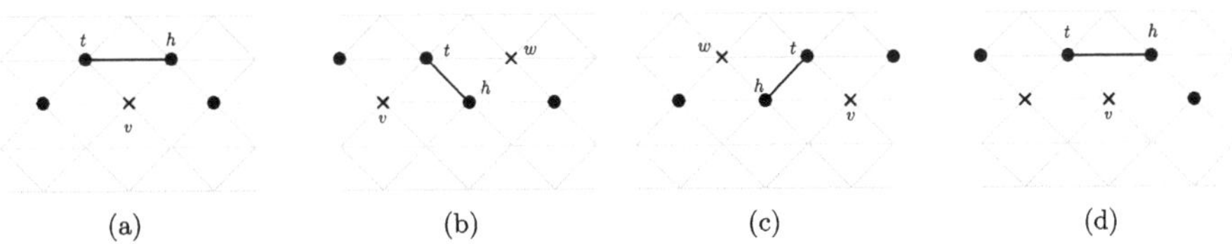

(a)   (b)   (c)   (d)

Fig. 3. An expanded particle (symbolised by two circles connected with a line) that cannot contract without disconnecting its neighbours (depicted as black circles). The tail is denoted by t and the head by h. Nodes marked by x are assumed to be empty.

Pseudocode

We use the following conditions in state **Expanded**:

E1 Contracting to head does not disconnect neighbours. For example, the blue expanded particle in Fig. 4a.

E2 There exists a lower empty common neighbour, v, such that $N(p)\backslash\{t\} \cup \{v\}$ is connected. For example, the black square expanded particle in Fig. 4a.

E3 The particle p is horizontally expanded and there exists a lower empty node, u, that is neighbouring to the tail such that $N(p)\backslash\{h\} \cup \{u\}$ is connected. For example, the white circle expanded particle in Fig. 4a.

E4 The tail is the lower common neighbour of an expanded particle and the higher common neighbour of the head and tail, w, is empty. For example, the white square expanded particle in Fig. 4a and the pink expanded particle in Fig. 4b.

We use the following conditions in state `Contracted`:

C1 Out of the two lower neighbours one is occupied and one is empty. For example, the blue contracted particle in Fig. 4a.

C2 Both lower neighbours are empty or both lower neighbours are occupied, there exists an occupied neighbour in direction 5 and the right neighbouring node (i.e., in direction 0) is empty. For example, the grey contracted particle in Fig. 4a.

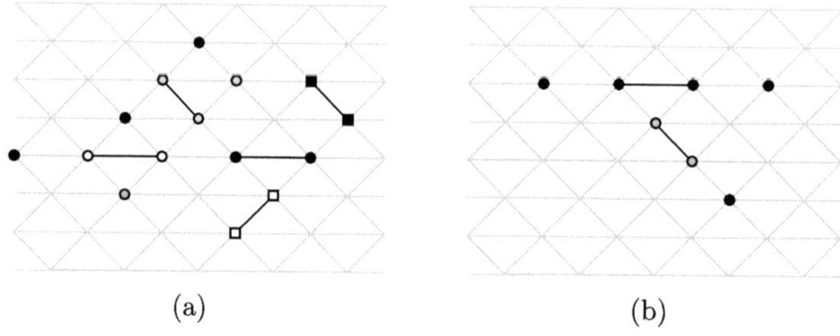

(a)   (b)

Fig. 4. (a) An example configuration containing particles that satisfy all conditions. The blue expanded particle satisfies E1, the black square expanded particle satisfies E2, the white circle expanded particle satisfies E3, the white square expanded particle satisfies E4, the blue circle contracted particle satisfies C1 and the grey contracted particle satisfies C2. (b) A configuration where the only satisfied condition is E4 (for the pink expanded particle). (Color figure online)

In the pseudocode, we write h to denote the node occupied by the head of an expanded particle and t to denote the node occupied by the tail of an expanded particle. Nodes v, u, w are those defined in the conditions E2, E3 and E4 respectively. The comments in the pseudocode are the nodes occupied by the particle after its activation.

The ability of a particle to distinguish whether two of its neighbouring nodes are occupied by a single expanded particle or by two distinct particles is essential for the evaluation of E4, which in turn allows progress in configurations such as the one depicted in Fig. 4b. If a particle satisfying E4 were to move without

---

Algorithm 1: Silent and Self–Stabilising Leader Election

<u>In state **Expanded**:</u>

1.1   mark the lowest endpoint (or rightmost endpoint if both endpoints are in the same row) as head and the remaining endpoint as tail

1.2   E1: contract to head, **Contracted**;   // occupies h

1.3   E2: contract to head, expand to v, **Expanded**;   // occupies h, v

1.4   E3: contract to tail, expand to u, **Expanded**;   // occupies t, u

1.5   E4: contract to head, expand to w, **Expanded**;   // occupies h, w

<u>In state **Contracted**:</u>

1.6   C1: expand to empty lower neighbour, **Expanded**;

1.7   C2: expand to empty right neighbour, **Expanded**;

---

this distinction, an unfair scheduler could repeatedly activate only that particle, causing it to oscillate between two nodes indefinitely and preventing any progress.

Observe that if a particle satisfies E1, E4 or C2 no endpoint of the particle occupies a lower node after its activation. By definition, an expanded particle can only move one of its endpoints to a lower node through E2 or E3 if the expanded particle has a lower neighbour and a contracted particle only expands to a lower node if it has a lower neighbour by definition of C1. Therefore:

Observation 1. *A contracted particle p that occupies some node v can only occupy a node lower than v after a move if p has a lower neighbour when it is activated.*

4   Proof of Correctness

We show that the particle system remains connected and that there is an activable particle in every step or there is a unique particle that does not have a neighbour in directions 0, 1, 2 and 5. We call a configuration with no activable particle a *final* configuration. By slight abuse of notation we refer to a node occupied by a particle p as p. Throughout this section we use h and t to denote the head and tail of an expanded particle. When the particle we refer to is not clear from the context, we write p_h, p_t instead of h, t for the head and tail of a particle p. We call the node at direction i of h (resp. of t) h_i (resp. t_i), regardless of whether it is empty or occupied.

We will show that every final configuration has the following property.

Proposition 1. *Every particle in a final configuration is in one of the following cases:*

1. Contracted and has either zero or two lower neighbours.

2. Horizontally expanded, contracting disconnects its neighbours and has no lower neighbours.

We first establish the following lemma.

Lemma 1. *Consider a particle p in a final configuration C s.t. for any p' above p or p' at the same height but on the left of p, Proposition 1 holds. Then Proposition 1 holds for p.*

Proof. It is easy to see that any contracted particle with one empty and one occupied lower neighbouring node is activable due to C1. Hence we immediately get that if p is contracted in a final configuration C it has either zero or two lower neighbours. We now show that if p has a lower neighbour in C, p is contracted. We split the proof into two cases based on whether p is expanded horizontally or diagonally and we show that either p is expanded horizontally with no lower neighbours in C or we get a contradiction to C being final.

Case 1. Particle p is expanded horizontally.

If the occupied neighbourhood of p is connected, p is activable due to E1 and C is not final. So let us assume that $N(p)$ is not connected and consider cases based on $N(p)$.

Case 1.1. Neighbour t_3 is empty.

Observe that in this case t_4 must be empty since by assumption the lemma holds for t_4 (i.e., a particle at t_4 cannot have only one lower neighbour regardless of whether it is occupied by an expanded or a contracted particle). The only remaining neighbour of t that is not a neighbour of h is t_2. We consider two cases based on whether t_2 is occupied. This is shown in Fig. 5. Let us begin by assuming t_2 is empty. Then p is activable by E1 as all occupied neighbours of t are also neighbours of h. So let us assume that t_2 is occupied. Then if t_1 is empty, p is activable by E2. The resulting configuration is connected as all neighbours of h are still neighbouring to p and t_2 is neighbouring to t_1 that is now occupied by p. So let us assume that t_1 is occupied. Then since t_2 is neighbouring to t_1, all neighbours of p are connected to h and p is activable by E1.

(a) t_2 empty   (b) t_2 occupied

Fig. 5. Black circles represent particles. Two black circles connected with a line represent an expanded particle. White circles can be empty or occupied by particles. Nodes marked by **x** are assumed to be empty.

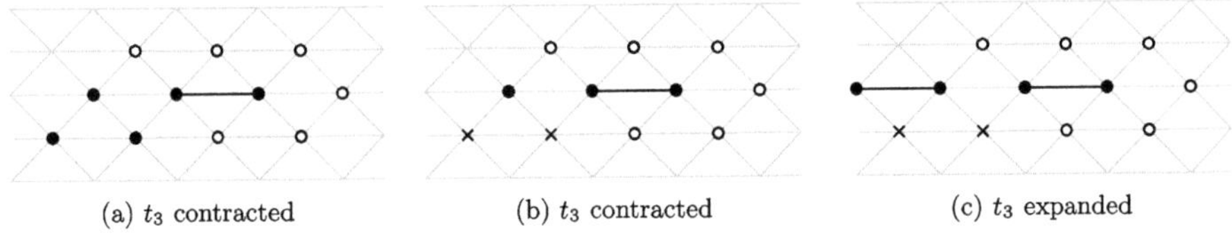

(a) t_3 contracted   (b) t_3 contracted   (c) t_3 expanded

Fig. 6. Black circles represent particles. Two black circles connected with a line represent an expanded particle. White circles can be empty or occupied by particles. Nodes marked by x are assumed to be empty.

Case 1.2. Neighbour t_3 is occupied.

Let us first assume that t_2 is occupied (i.e., Fig. 6a). If t_1 is occupied, p is activable due to E1. The resulting configuration is connected due to the neighbourhood of t being connected and h neighbouring to t_1 which is also neighbouring to the occupied neighbour of t, t_2. If t_1 is empty, p is activable due to E2. This is a valid configuration as h is still occupied by p so neighbours of h remain connected, the neighbourhood of t is connected and t_1 that is now occupied by p is neighbouring to the occupied neighbour of t, t_2.

Let us now assume that t_3 does not have lower neighbours, or equivalently that t_2 is not occupied since the lemma holds for t_3. Notice that since p cannot know whether t_3 is contracted or expanded even though two cases are possible for t_3 as shown in Figs. 6b and c the analysis for both is common. If $h_2 = t_1$ is occupied and h_1 is empty, we consider two cases based on whether the particle occupying h_2, q, is contracted or expanded. If q is contracted, q is activable from C1 if it has a unique lower neighbour or from C2 due to h, otherwise. As a contracted particle expanding cannot disconnect the system the resulting configuration is connected. If q is expanded, it must be expanded diagonally and q is activable from E4. Since both t_2 and h_1 are empty in this case q moving does not disconnect its neighbourhood as the only neighbour of q_t that is not a neighbour of q_h is p which is still a neighbour of q in the new configuration. Let us now assume that h_1 is occupied and h_2 is empty. Then, if h_5 is occupied by the lemma statement h_0 must also be occupied. Therefore, for every neighbour of h that is not a neighbour of t there is a path to h_1 that only passes through occupied nodes in $N(h)$. In this case, p is either activable by E3 and in the resulting configuration occupies t and h_2 or by E1. In the former case, as all neighbours of t are still neighbouring to t, the neighbours of h are connected and h_2 is neighbouring to the occupied neighbour of h, h_1 the resulting configuration is connected. The latter case is possible if t_4 and $t_5 = h_4$ are also occupied and the resulting configuration is connected since t_3, t_4, t_5 are connected and t_5 is neighbouring to h. Suppose now that h_1 and h_2 are both occupied. Then p is activable either by E3 and in the resulting configuration occupies t and t_2 or by E1. In the former case, if h_5 is occupied, h_0 must also be occupied by the lemma statement. Since h_0 is neighbouring to h_1, for every neighbour of h that is not a neighbour of t there is a path to $t_1 = h_2$ and this path only passes through occupied nodes in $N(h)$. Since t is neighbouring to t_1 and is additionally connected to all its neighbours, the resulting configuration is connected. The latter case is possible if $t_5 = h_4$ and t_4 are both occupied and the resulting configuration is connected since t_3, t_4, t_5 are connected and t_5 is neighbouring to h. Finally, if both h_2 and h_1 are empty Proposition 1 holds.

Therefore, if p is expanded horizontally, Proposition 1 holds.

Case 2. Particle p is expanded diagonally.

We consider the case of p being expanded towards direction 1 (i.e., $h_4 = t$ and $h = t_1$) and the other case is symmetric. If the occupied neighbourhood of p is connected without t, p is activable due to E1. So we assume that the occupied neighbourhood of p is not connected without t. The only neighbours of t that are not neighbours of h are t_3, t_4 and t_5. By assumption, if t_4 is occupied, t_3 must be occupied and if t_5 is occupied, t_0 must be occupied. Hence we do not need to consider t_4 separately to t_3 or t_5 separately to t_0. Furthermore, t_0 is neighbouring to h so if t_5 is occupied it is always connected to the neighbourhood of h. Therefore, the only neighbours of p that we need to consider are t_2, t_3. If t_3 is not occupied or if t_3 is occupied and t_2 is occupied, p is immediately activable by E1. The resulting configuration is valid as in either case if t_2 is occupied, it is a neighbour of h. So let us suppose that t_3 is occupied and t_2 is not occupied. Then p is activable by E2. The resulting configuration is connected as the neighbours of t are connected and t now occupies t_2 that is neighbouring to the occupied node t_3.

From Case 1 and Case 2 if p is expanded, either it has no lower neighbour as is the second case of Proposition 1 or C is not final which is a contradiction. $\square$

We can now prove Proposition 1.

Proof of Proposition 1. Suppose now that Proposition 1 does not hold for all particles. Let q be the topmost leftmost particle among the particles for which Proposition 1 does not hold. Then for all particles above q and in the same height but on the left of q the property holds. From Lemma 1, Proposition 1 then also holds for q, which is a contradiction. Hence, the proposition holds. $\square$

We now show that the final configuration has a unique leader.

Lemma 2. *A final configuration contains exactly one leader, that is, a particle that does not have any neighbours in directions 0,1,2 and 5.*

Proof. Suppose a final configuration does not have a leader. Consider the lowest row of particles and take the rightmost particle in this row, p. By definition, p does not have neighbours in directions 0,1 and 2. Hence, p must have a neighbour in direction 5, p_5. From Proposition 1, p_5 must have a second lower neighbour, but by assumption p_0 (i.e., the neighbour of p in direction 0) is empty. So this scenario is not possible and p is a leader in the final configuration.

Let us now suppose that there exist at least two leaders in the final configuration. Call the leader that is not globally lowermost rightmost p'. Then there exists a shortest path from p' to p that minimises the number of particles in the highest row of the path. We denote that path $p' \rightsquigarrow p$. Take q to be the first particle on that path that has a lower neighbour. From Proposition 1, since q has a lower neighbour, it must be contracted and have a second lower neighbour. Notice that q is either at the same row as p' or higher.

Let us first assume that q is in the same row as p'. Then the predecessor of q on $p' \rightsquigarrow q$ cannot be the neighbour of q in direction 0 or in direction 3 since both of those nodes share a lower common node with q, and q would not be the first particle in $p' \rightsquigarrow p$ that has a lower neighbour. Furthermore, the predecessor of q on $p' \rightsquigarrow p$ cannot be in direction 5 or 4 of q as q is a lower neighbour of those nodes and q would not be the first particle on $p' \rightsquigarrow p$ to have a lower neighbour. Hence the predecessor of q on the path must be one of the neighbours of q in direction 1 or 2. However, both of those neighbours are lower than p' and as a result q would not be the first particle in the path to have a lower neighbour. Therefore, this case is not possible.

Let us now suppose that q is at some row that is higher than p'. Since p is a globally lowermost rightmost node $p' \rightsquigarrow p$ must eventually move down again. Take q' to be the first particle of $p' \rightsquigarrow p$ that is at the highest row of the path. The predecessor of q' on the path cannot be one of the neighbours of q' in directions 0,3,4 or 5 otherwise q' would not be the first particle to be in the highest row of the path. Therefore, the predecessor of q' is one of the neighbours of q' in directions 1 or 2. Notice that from Proposition 1 since one of the lower neighbours of q' is occupied, both neighbours in directions 1 and 2 must be occupied. Let us now consider the successor of q' in $p' \rightsquigarrow p$. Since q' is at the highest row of the path, its successor on the path cannot be in direction 4 or 5. Without loss of generality, let us assume that the predecessor of q' on the path is in direction 1 and the case for the predecessor being in direction 2 is symmetric. If the successor of q' is in direction $j \in \{0, 2\}$, $p' \rightsquigarrow q'_1, q'_j \rightsquigarrow p$ is a shorter path than $p' \rightsquigarrow q'_1, q', q'_j \rightsquigarrow p$. This contradicts $p' \rightsquigarrow p$ being a shortest path and as a result this case is not possible. Finally, suppose the successor is in direction 3. Then since q'_2 is occupied, $p' \rightsquigarrow q'_1, q'_2, q'_3 \rightsquigarrow p$ is a path with fewer particles in the highest row that does not include q', a contradiction. Therefore, this case is not possible either.

Consequently, a final configuration has exactly one leader. $\square$

Finally, we show that a final configuration is reached from any starting configuration and for any order of activations. We call the lowest row that contains a particle the *horizontal boundary* of the system. We define the *vertical position* of a particle to be the head's distance to the horizontal boundary. For a contracted particle, the vertical position is the distance of the particle to the horizontal boundary. Consider all north-west to south-east diagonals of the grid (e.g., diagonals marked by a dotted line in Fig. 7a). Call *diagonal boundary* the rightmost such diagonal that contains a particle (e.g., the diagonal marked in Figs. 7a and b). Observe that this particle is not necessarily a globally rightmost particle in the system. The *horizontal position* of a particle is the horizontal distance of the particle to the diagonal boundary (e.g., Fig. 7b). For a contracted particle the

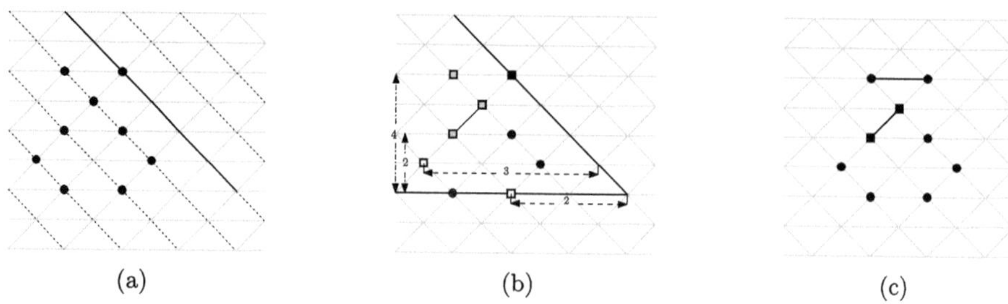

Fig. 7. (a) Dotted lines represent all north-west to south-east diagonals on the grid and the black line represents the diagonal boundary. (b) The diagonal and horizontal boundary are marked by black lines, the particle represented as a black square is the particle that defines the diagonal boundary, an example of the distance to the diagonal boundary is shown for the two particles marked as white squares and an example of the distance to the horizontal boundary is shown for the particles marked as blue squares. (c) An example of a blocking particle marked by square endpoints. (Color figure online)

horizontal distance is the distance of the particle to the diagonal boundary and for an expanded particle the horizontal distance is the distance of the head to the diagonal boundary. Finally we write *blocking particle* to denote a diagonally expanded particle whose tail is neighbouring to both the head and tail of an expanded particle (e.g., Fig. 7c).

We define *progress* to be a decrease on one of the following criteria, evaluated in order. Once a criterion is satisfied, the remaining criteria are not evaluated.

P1 The sum of the vertical positions of the particles.
P2 The sum of the horizontal positions of the particles.
P3 The number of diagonally expanded particles.
P4 The number of blocking particles.
P5 The number of horizontally expanded particles.

The convergence argument below relies on invariants guaranteed by the movement rules defined in Algorithm 1. In particular, particles only move to a lower row if a lower neighbour exists, do not cause the configuration to become disconnected and never move in directions 4 or 5.

Lemma 3. *Starting from any arbitrary initial configuration any sequential unfair execution of Algorithm 1 eventually reaches a final configuration.*

Proof. We prove this lemma by first showing that if an activable particle moves there is progress. We consider all cases of activable particles.

- A particle that satisfies C1: If a particle expands diagonally, by construction of the algorithm the particle expands to a lower node and as a result P1 is decreased.
- A particle that satisfies C2: In this case a contracted particle expands towards direction 0, decreasing the horizontal distance of the particle to the

diagonal boundary, that is, decreasing P2. Furthermore, C2 only applies to contracted particles moving to an empty neighbour in the same row hence P1 does not change.

- A particle that satisfies E1: There are two possibilities for this case: a diagonally expanded particle contracts to a lower node or a horizontally expanded particle contracts to the right. In the former case P3 is reduced. Additionally, since the vertical and horizontal positions of a particle are only determined by the position of the head, which in this case does not move, P1 and P2 do not change. In the latter case, P4 or P5 is reduced, depending on the configuration. Criteria P1, P3 are affected by particles being or becoming diagonally expanded and as a result do not change. Criterion P2 is not reduced as a particle satisfying E1 contracts to the node occupied by its head and as a result does not change its distance to the diagonal boundary.

- A particle that satisfies E2 or E3: Once again, this condition can either be satisfied by a horizontally expanded or a diagonally expanded particle. If the particle is diagonally expanded it must satisfy E2. In this case, the particle becomes horizontally expanded thus reducing P3. Notice that the position of the head does not change hence P1 and P2 do not change. If the particle is expanded horizontally, the particle becomes diagonally expanded to a lower node decreasing P1.

- A particle that satisfies E4: In this case a diagonally expanded particle moves but remains diagonally expanded. The action corresponding to E4 reduces P4. Furthermore, since the position of the head does not change, P1 and P2 do not change and since the particle remains diagonally expanded, P3 does not change.

Therefore as long as there is an activable particle in the system, progress is ensured. We also need to show that eventually there do not exist activable particles in the system. We prove this by showing that no particle moves lower than the horizontal boundary and no particle moves to the right of the diagonal boundary. From Observation 1, a particle only moves to a lower row if it has a lower neighbour. Hence particles in the lowest row of the system never move downwards. By construction of the algorithm particles move to distance at most one during an activation so particles that are not on the diagonal boundary cannot cross it in one activation. So let us suppose that there exists a particle p that is the first particle that can cross the diagonal boundary during an execution of Algorithm 1. From the structure of the grid, p cannot cross the diagonal boundary when expanding or contracting to a lower neighbour. The only way p can cross the diagonal boundary is by moving to direction 5 or 0. In Algorithm 1, particles never move to direction 5. Furthermore, in Algorithm 1, a particle only moves to direction 0 only if it has a neighbour in direction 5 through condition C2. However, a neighbour in direction 5 is beyond the diagonal boundary. As we have assumed that p is the first particle that crosses the diagonal boundary, this is a contradiction.

Since the positions that the particle system can occupy are bounded below and to the right and particles never move in any other direction, eventually no particle is activable.   □

From Proposition 1 and Lemmas 2 and 3 we get:

Theorem 1. *Algorithm 1 eventually reaches a final configuration that contains exactly one particle without neighbours in directions 0,1,2 and 5, in a silent and self-stabilising manner.*

Observation 2. *Algorithm 1 can be trivially transformed to an algorithm where the leader is explicitly marked.*

One way to perform this transformation is by adding a single bit of memory to each particle that can be set to 0 to denote that a particle cannot be a leader based on local conditions and set to 1 otherwise. The correctness of our algorithm implies that eventually only one particle has its variable set to 1.

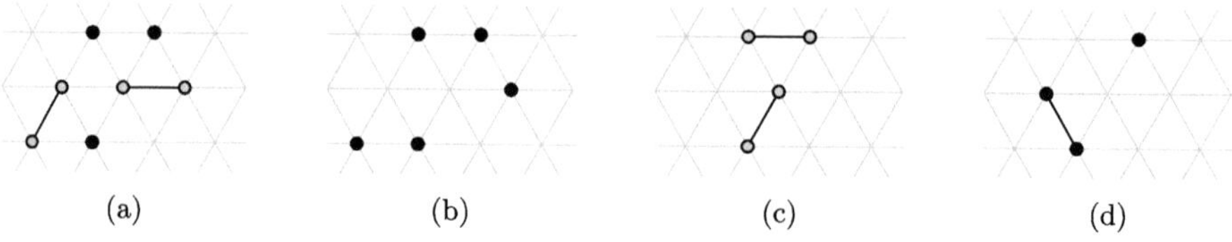

(a)   (b)   (c)   (d)

Fig. 8. Two examples of neighbouring particles activated simultaneously disconnecting the system. Suppose the blue expanded particles of Figure (a) (resp. Figure (c)) are simultaneously activated. Then E1 is satisfied for both particles (resp. E1 and E4 are satisfied for each expanded particle) and the resulting configuration becomes disconnected as shown in Figure (b) (resp. Figure (d)). (Color figure online)

5   Conclusion

We presented the first self-stabilising result in programmable matter for the case of an unfair scheduler and for the case of systems containing holes. As we now know that even in a self-stabilising setting, using the movement capabilities of particles can lead to solving problems that appear very challenging in the stationary setting, a natural direction for future work is studying what other problems would benefit from particle movement in a self-stabilising context. Another interesting direction would be to study self-stabilising leader election in connected systems under weaker assumptions. For example, one could consider substituting the agreement on all directions with a common sense of rotational orientation (i.e., chirality). A starting point could be to attempt to compact the system (i.e., "fill in" the holes). However, this setting presents additional challenges as the particles cannot locally recognise the inside and the outside of the configuration. Hence, oblivious particles may not be able to use such a method. In the non self-stabilising context there exist methods to calculate this information (e.g., [16,17]) with constant memory but it is not clear whether a self-stabilising counterpart for these methods can be designed. A different example is considering a synchronous or asynchronous scheduler instead of a sequential one. Although Algorithm 1 works if the activated particles are not neighbouring, it is easy to see that this is not the case for neighbouring activable particles (e.g., Fig. 8).

The most interesting open question is whether it is possible to design a stationary self-stabilising leader election algorithm using constant memory for arbitrary connected configurations. We conjecture that the design of such an algorithm is impossible, even if particles agree on all directions of the grid.

Acknowledgments. JC was partially funded by ANR project MIMETIQUE "Mineurs métriques" (ANR-25-CE48-4089-01). MK was supported by the DFG Project SCHE 1592/10-1.

Disclosure of Interests. The authors have no competing interests to declare that are relevant to the content of this article.

References

1. Almethen, A., Michail, O., Potapov, I.: Pushing lines helps: efficient universal centralised transformations for programmable matter. Theoret. Comput. Sci. **830**, 43–59 (2020). https://doi.org/10.1016/J.TCS.2020.04.026
2. Angluin, D.: Local and global properties in networks of processors (extended abstract). In: Proceedings of the 12th Annual ACM Symposium on Theory of Computing STOC, pp. 82–93. ACM (1980). https://doi.org/10.1145/800141.804655
3. Awerbuch, B., Ostrovsky, R.: Memory-efficient and self-stabilizing network reset. In: PODC 1994, pp. 254–263. ACM (1994). https://doi.org/10.1145/197917.198104
4. Bazzi, R.A., Briones, J.L.: Stationary and deterministic leader election in self-organizing particle systems. In: Ghaffari, M., Nesterenko, M., Tixeuil, S., Tucci, S., Yamauchi, Y. (eds.) SSS 2019. LNCS, vol. 11914, pp. 22–37. Springer, Cham (2019). https://doi.org/10.1007/978-3-030-34992-9_3
5. Briones, J.L., Chhabra, T., Daymude, J.J., Richa, A.W.: Invited paper: asynchronous deterministic leader election in three-dimensional programmable matter. In: ICDCN 2023, pp. 38–47. ACM (2023). https://doi.org/10.1145/3571306.3571389
6. Chalopin, J., Das, S., Kokkou, M.: Deterministic leader election for stationary programmable matter with common direction. In: International Colloquium on Structural Information and Communication Complexity, pp. 174–191. Springer, Heidelberg (2024). https://doi.org/10.1007/978-3-031-60603-8_10
7. Chalopin, J., Das, S., Kokkou, M.: Deterministic self-stabilising leader election for programmable matter with constant memory. In: 38th International Symposium on Distributed Computing (DISC). LIPIcs, vol. 319, pp. 13:1–13:17. Schloss Dagstuhl - Leibniz-Zentrum für Informatik (2024). https://doi.org/10.4230/LIPICS.DISC.2024.13

8. D'Angelo, G., D'Emidio, M., Das, S., Navarra, A., Prencipe, G.: Asynchronous silent programmable matter achieves leader election and compaction. IEEE Access **8**, 207619–207634 (2020). https://doi.org/10.1109/ACCESS.2020.3038174

9. Daymude, J.J., Richa, A.W., Scheideler, C.: The canonical amoebot model: algorithms and concurrency control. Distrib. Comput. **36**(2), 159–192 (2023). https://doi.org/10.1007/s00446-023-00443-3

10. Daymude, J.J., Richa, A.W., Weber, J.W.: Bio-inspired energy distribution for programmable matter. In: ICDCN 2021, pp. 86–95. ACM (2021). https://doi.org/10.1145/3427796.3427835

11. Derakhshandeh, Z., Dolev, S., Gmyr, R., Richa, A.W., Scheideler, C., Strothmann, T.: Brief announcement: Amoebot - a new model for programmable matter. In: 26th ACM Symposium on Parallelism in Algorithms and Architectures, SPAA, pp. 220–222. ACM (2014). https://doi.org/10.1145/2612669.2612712

12. Derakhshandeh, Z., Gmyr, R., Strothmann, T., Bazzi, R., Richa, A.W., Scheideler, C.: Leader election and shape formation with self-organizing programmable matter. In: Phillips, A., Yin, P. (eds.) DNA 2015. LNCS, vol. 9211, pp. 117–132. Springer, Cham (2015). https://doi.org/10.1007/978-3-319-21999-8_8

13. Di Luna, G.A., Flocchini, P., Santoro, N., Viglietta, G., Yamauchi, Y.: Shape formation by programmable particles. Distrib. Comput. **33**(1), 69–101 (2020). https://doi.org/10.1007/S00446-019-00350-6

14. Dolev, S., Gouda, M.G., Schneider, M.: Memory requirements for silent stabilization. Acta Informatica **36**(6), 447–462 (1999). https://doi.org/10.1007/s002360050180

15. Dubois, S., Tixeuil, S.: A taxonomy of daemons in self-stabilization. arXiv preprint (2011). https://doi.org/10.48550/arXiv.1110.0334

16. Dufoulon, F., Kutten, S., Moses Jr., W.K.: Efficient deterministic leader election for programmable matter. In: PODC 2021, pp. 103–113. ACM (2021). https://doi.org/10.1145/3465084.3467900

17. Emek, Y., Kutten, S., Lavi, R., Moses Jr., W.K.: Deterministic leader election in programmable matter. In: ICALP 2019. LIPIcs, vol. 132, pp. 140:1–140:14. Schloss Dagstuhl - Leibniz-Zentrum für Informatik (2019). https://doi.org/10.4230/LIPIcs.ICALP.2019.140

18. Fekete, S.P., Gmyr, R., Hugo, S., Keldenich, P., Scheffer, C., Schmidt, A.: CADbots: algorithmic aspects of manipulating programmable matter with finite automata. Algorithmica **83**(1), 387–412 (2020). https://doi.org/10.1007/s00453-020-00761-z

19. Feldmann, M., Padalkin, A., Scheideler, C., Dolev, S.: Accelerating Amoebots via reconfigurable circuits. arXiv preprint (2021). https://arxiv.org/abs/2105.05071

20. Gastineau, N., Abdou, W., Mbarek, N., Togni, O.: Distributed leader election and computation of local identifiers for programmable matter. In: Gilbert, S., Hughes, D., Krishnamachari, B. (eds.) ALGOSENSORS 2018. LNCS, vol. 11410, pp. 159–179. Springer, Cham (2019). https://doi.org/10.1007/978-3-030-14094-6_11

21. Gastineau, N., Abdou, W., Mbarek, N., Togni, O.: Leader election and local identifiers for three-dimensional programmable matter. Concurr. Comput. Pract. Exp. **34**(7) (2022). https://doi.org/10.1002/cpe.6067

22. Gmyr, R., Kostitsyna, I., Kuhn, F., Scheideler, C., Strothmann, T.: Forming tile shapes with a single robot. In: 33rd European Workshop on Computational Geometry (EuroCG 2017) (2017). https://doi.org/10.1007/S11047-019-09774-2

23. Gouda, M.G.: The theory of weak stabilization. In: Datta, A.K., Herman, T. (eds.) WSS 2001. LNCS, vol. 2194, pp. 114–123. Springer, Heidelberg (2001). https://doi.org/10.1007/3-540-45438-1_8

24. Itai, A., Rodeh, M.: Symmetry breaking in distributed networks. Inf. Comput. **88**(1), 60–87 (1990). https://doi.org/10.1016/0890-5401(90)90004-2
25. Itkis, G., Levin, L.: Fast and lean self-stabilizing asynchronous protocols. In: FOCS 1994, pp. 226–239. IEEE Computer Society (1994). https://doi.org/10.1109/SFCS.1994.365691
26. Le Lann, G.: Distributed systems - towards a formal approach. In: IFIP 1977, pp. 155–160. North-Holland (1977). https://inria.hal.science/hal-03504338
27. Navarra, A., Piselli, F.: Asynchronous silent programmable matter: line formation. In: International Symposium on Stabilizing, Safety, and Security of Distributed Systems, pp. 598–612. Springer, Heidelberg (2023). https://doi.org/10.1007/978-3-031-44274-2_44
28. Piranda, B., Bourgeois, J.: Geometrical study of a quasi-spherical module for building programmable matter. In: Groß, R., et al. (eds.) Distributed Autonomous Robotic Systems. SPAR, vol. 6, pp. 387–400. Springer, Cham (2018). https://doi.org/10.1007/978-3-319-73008-0_27
29. Piranda, B., Bourgeois, J.: Datom: A deformable modular robot for building self-reconfigurable programmable matter. In: Matsuno, F., Azuma, S., Yamamoto, M. (eds.) DARS 2021. SPAR, vol. 22, pp. 70–81. Springer, Cham (2022). https://doi.org/10.1007/978-3-030-92790-5_6
30. Toffoli, T., Margolus, N.: Programmable matter: concepts and realization. Int. J. High Speed Comput. **5**(2), 155–170 (1993). https://doi.org/10.1016/0167-2789(91)90296-L
31. Woods, D., Chen, H.-L., Goodfriend, S., Dabby, N., Winfree, E., Yin, P.: Active self-assembly of algorithmic shapes and patterns in polylogarithmic time. In: Proceedings of the 4th conference on Innovations in Theoretical Computer Science, pp. 353–354 (2013). https://doi.org/10.1145/2422436.2422476
32. Yamashita, M., Kameda, T.: Computing on anonymous networks: part I-characterizing the solvable cases. IEEE Trans. Parallel Distrib. Syst. **7**(1), 69–89 (1996). https://doi.org/10.1109/71.481599

Leveraging Structural Knowledge for Solving Election in Anonymous Networks with Shared Randomness

Jérémie Chalopin$^{(\boxtimes)}$ and Emmanuel Godard$^{(\boxtimes)}$

CNRS & Université Aix-Marseille, LIS, Marseille, France
{jeremie.chalopin,emmanuel.godard}@lis-lab.fr

Abstract. We study the classical Election problem in anonymous networks, where solutions can rely on the use of random bits, which may be either shared or unshared among nodes. We provide a complete characterization of the conditions under which a randomized Election algorithm exists, for arbitrary structural knowledge. Our analysis considers both Las Vegas and Monte Carlo randomized algorithms, under the assumptions of shared and unshared randomness. In our setting, random sources are considered shared if the output bits are identical across specific subsets of nodes. The algorithms and impossibility proofs are extensions of those of Chalopin et al. (2012) for the deterministic setting. Our results are a complete generalization of those from Fraigniaud et al. (2024). Moreover, as applications, we consider many specific knowledge: no knowledge, a bound on the size, a bound on the number of nodes sharing a source, the size, or the full topology of the network. For each of them, we show how the general characterizations apply, showing they actually correspond to classes of structural knowledge. We also describe also how randomized Election algorithms from the literature fits in this landscape. We therefore provide a comprehensive picture illustrating how knowledge influences the computability of the Election problem in arbitrary anonymous graphs with shared randomness.

Keywords: Leader Election · randomized algorithms · structural knowledge

1 Introduction

The Leader Election, or Election, problem is one of the paradigms of the theory of distributed computing. A distributed algorithm solves the Election problem if in the final configuration exactly one process is marked as ELECTED and all other processes are labeled NON-ELECTED. Election algorithms constitute a building block for many other distributed algorithms: the elected vertex acts as coordinator, initiator, and more generally performs some special role (cf. [23, p. 262]). The election problem was first studied by LeLann [14] who gives a solution in rings where each process has a unique name. Solutions to this problem

C. Georgiou (Ed.): SIROCCO 2026, LNCS 16488, pp. 172–192, 2026.
https://doi.org/10.1007/978-3-032-26465-7_10

are studied under two classical assumptions (see [21, Chapter 3] for details): each process is identified by a unique name (or identifier): its identity; processes have initially the same state (anonymous networks). If processes have initially unique identifiers, it is always possible to solve this problem, e.g., by electing the process with the smallest identifier. Nevertheless, if we consider *anonymous/homonymous* networks where processes do not have unique identifiers, it is not always possible to solve the election problem. Angluin [1] has introduced the classical proof techniques used for showing the impossibility of an Election algorithm even knowing the full topology of the network. This technique is based on graph coverings, which is a notion known from algebraic topology [15]. Finally, several characterizations of graphs for which there exists an Election algorithm have been obtained [3,5,17,25].

It is known that randomized algorithms can solve the Election problem in situation where Angluin-like results prohibit a deterministic solution. An early example of such result is [16]. It is often said that randomness helps to perform "symmetry breaking" for Election but it is a misconception to say this is always sufficient to have a solution. In this paper, we present new impossibility results that are still valid for randomized algorithms without enough structural knowledge. We present two general characterizations of solvability of Election by a Las Vegas or a Monte Carlo algorithm given any arbitrary knowledge, in the general case of shared and unshared random sources. Our contribution is to specify the exact limit of computability. The paper explains how randomness helps, or not, to leverage any structural knowledge about the underlying network in order to actually break symmetry, and solve the Election problem. We also discuss how our impossibility results match known randomized Election algorithms.

Computing With Knowledge. We encode a given arbitrary knowledge as an arbitrary family of graphs $\mathcal{F}$, which is the set of graphs with the given value of knowledge (e.g. the same given size). Solving with this knowledge amounts to find an Election algorithm that is correct on any graph from $\mathcal{F}$. From the general characterizations, we consider, in the Application section, these following structural knowledge that are classically considered. We denote $\mathcal{G}$ the set of all graphs. We consider

- *no knowledge* that is $\mathcal{F} = \mathcal{G}$;
- *bound* S on the size, $\mathcal{F} = \{\mathbf{G} \in \mathcal{G}, |\mathbf{G}| \leq S\}$;
- *strict* $2-$ *approximation* T on the size of the network, $\mathcal{F} = \{\mathbf{G} \in \mathcal{G}, \frac{1}{2}T < |\mathbf{G}| \leq T\}$;
- *the size* S of the network, $\mathcal{F} = \{\mathbf{G} \in \mathcal{G}, |\mathbf{G}| = S\}$;
- *the topology* $\mathbf{G}$ of the network, $\mathcal{F} = \{\mathbf{G}\}$.

We will see in Sect. 5.1 that this is actually representative of all the possible computability cases.

It is known from Angluin and later results, that so-called "symmetric", or more accurately "non-minimal" as described later, graphs do not admit a deterministic algorithm, even knowing the exact topology of the network $\mathbf{G}$ (in this case $\mathcal{F} = \{\mathbf{G}\}$). Here we prove that, given enough structural knowledge, it is possible to elect with a Monte Carlo randomized algorithm in any anonymous network. In some sense (that will be made formal later), for randomized algorithms with unshared sources, all networks are *minimal*. This situation is different from the deterministic case where some anonymous networks do not admit any Election algorithm, even knowing the entire topology of the graph. We therefore provide a comprehensive picture illustrating how randomness influences the computability of the Election problem in arbitrary anonymous graphs. In the general case, when a bound on the size is known, there is only a Monte Carlo algorithm. When random sources are symmetry-breaking, e.g. when there is at least one unshared source, there is a Las Vegas Election algorithm when the size of the network is known. When the network is already symmetry-breaking (covering-minimal) without random sources, then the computability power of deterministic algorithms is the same as randomized algorithms for any structural knowledge. Those results demonstrate that randomness, distributed computability-wise, can help leverage knowledge to have a randomized Election algorithm when there is no existing deterministic Election algorithm knowing the topology. Finally, it is also shown that without enough information on the network, it could be still impossible to Elect even with a randomized algorithm, if we require the termination to be explicit. In some sense, randoms bits, even shared, do provide symmetry-breaking, however they are not enough to achieve termination detection. Complementary knowledge is needed to leverage randomization.

Proof Techniques and Contributions. A general characterization about leveraging knowledge to solve Election in the deterministic setting has been done in [5]. The main tool is the notion of quasi-coverings. This notion captures the phenomenon which appears in the family formed by "all trees and a triangle" and quoted by Angluin: *"the existence of a large enough area of one graph that looks like another graph"* [1, p. 87, l. 13–17]. Here we consider networks where nodes have access to (possibly shared) i.i.d. random sources. In this work, to represent the symmetry relevant to randomized algorithms with shared sources, we consider graphs where nodes are labeled by the source of randomness it has access to. So in the shared randomness setting, two nodes that share the same source have the same label. The labeling is denoted by b, and the set of nodes having the same label is called a $B-$ class. However, it is not directly possible to use the results of [5] considering $B-$ labeled graph since, in general, a node has no (direct) access to its label b.

Besides showing that the proof methods from [5] can be extended (with some technical care) to the new setting of shared sources, the main interest of this study are the applications for standard knowledge, as shown in Sect. 5.1:

- there exists just 3 classes of knowledge (exact size/topology, some bounds, no knowledge) and we have, through Theorems 2.1 and 2.2, a precise hierarchy of computability
- known classical randomized Election Algorithms fit nicely into this hierarchy, and our work explains how and why. See also the detailed discussion in Sect. 5.

– up to our knowledge, the knowledge considered at Sect. 5.2 is the first to consider networks of unbounded diameter for which randomized election is still solvable. This seems surprising given the results from the literature.

Related Works. Leader Election is a long standing problem in distributed computing. Angluin introduced graph coverings to capture all the symmetries in anonymous and homonymous distributed systems. The notion of symmetry relevant for the message passing model is captured by *symmetric coverings* of graphs, see Sect. 3.2. This work has been extended by many researchers and several characterizations of graphs and deterministic models for which there exists an election algorithm have been obtained [3,5,17,25].

Shared sources of randomness can be used to improve the complexity of algorithms as recently shown in [2]. Here, for computability, sharing the same source for all nodes could actually have an adverse effect. Regarding both time and message complexity aspects relative to knowledge, the most recent advances for randomized Election are given in [13].

The closest previous work using arbitrary knowledge is [5] in the deterministic setting, and it is [9] in the general setting of shared randomness. Relatively to [5], the novelty is an extension of the deterministic quasi-covering characterization to the randomized setting. In [9], the notion of shared sources of randomness is introduced (under the terminology "biased"). Comparing to [9], we consider the same randomness setting, but for more general graph topologies than cliques. It is possible to derive here the characterizations given in [9], since a clique is $B-$ covering minimal if and only if the gcd of the size of its $B-$ classes is 1. We underline that our results show the impact of structural knowledge in the context of randomized algorithms. In some sense, in cliques, the knowledge of the size, hence the topology of the network, can be locally derived from the degree. There is no difference between no knowledge or full knowledge in this family of graphs.

Note also that we do not consider Election with implicit termination (i.e. eventually stabilizing to only one ELECTED node). Considering knowledge, this setting is solved in [19], it is possible to have Election with implicit termination without any knowledge with a Monte Carlo algorithm.

2   The Model and Main Technical Results

Our model is the usual asynchronous message passing model [5,24,25]. A network is represented by a simple connected graph $G = (V(G), E(G))$ where vertices correspond to processes and edges to direct communication links. The initial state of each process is represented by a label $\lambda(v)$ associated to the corresponding vertex $v \in V(G)$; we denote by $\mathbf{G} = (G, \lambda)$ such a labeled graph. When $\lambda(v) \neq \lambda(u)$ for two different nodes u and v, we can consider that $\lambda(v)$ is the *identity* of the node v. When $\lambda(u) = \lambda(v)$ for all nodes u, v, then the network is said to be *anonymous*. In the general case, the network is said to be *homonymous*.

We assume that each process can distinguish the different edges that are incident to it, i.e., for each $u \in V(G)$ there exists a bijection δ_u between the neighbors of u in G and $[1, \deg_G(u)]$. We denote by δ the set of functions $\{\delta_u \mid u \in V(G)\}$. The numbers associated by each vertex to its neighbors are called *port-numbers*, δ is called a *port-numbering* of G. Each process v has access at each step to a source of random bits $b(v)$. We denote by $b(u, t)$ the t−th bit drawn by u at source $b(u)$. In the case of a shared source between u and v, the nodes get always the same output as the other, i.e. $b(u, t) = b(v, t)$ for all t. We also denote b the label corresponding to the random source that is attached to a given vertex. We denote by $(\mathbf{G}, \delta, b)$ the labeled graph $\mathbf{G}$ with the port-numbering δ and sources b.

Each process v in the network represents an entity that is capable of performing computation steps, drawing random bits from its (maybe shared) source, sending messages via some port and receiving any message via some port as was sent by the corresponding neighbors. We consider asynchronous systems, i.e., each computation step may take an unpredictable (but finite) amount of time. We consider only reliable systems: no fault can occur on processes or communication links. We also assume the channels are FIFO, i.e., for each channel, the messages are delivered in the order they have been sent. This delivery depends on a scheduling that is chosen by the adversary.

A deterministic algorithm solves the Election problem on the family $\mathcal{F}$ if, for any execution starting from a graph in $\mathcal{F}$, a final configuration is reached where exactly one node is in state ELECTED and all the other nodes are in state NON-ELECTED. We assume that the states ELECTED and NON-ELECTED are terminal, i.e., once a node enters in this state, it will not leave this state afterwards. A randomized algorithm is an algorithm that can use the random sources b at any step. We consider a random source to be uniform over time, that is the probability to draw a 1 or a 0 is the same (and non-zero) at any given invocation; and that the sources are independent and identically distributed. Given a randomized algorithm and a fixed schedule, the local state of a node u at time s is a random variable $state(u, s)$, that may depend on the previous state and on the incoming messages. The probability of an execution is associated to the random variable of the global state. It is therefore the probability of the associated set of random draws at the shared sources, since the schedule is fixed. The following definitions are standard. A *Las Vegas algorithm* is an algorithm that terminates with probability $0 < p \leq 1$, and whose final configuration is correct (i.e., there is exactly one node in the ELECTED state, and all other nodes are in the NON-ELECTED state). A *Monte Carlo algorithm* is an algorithm that always terminates, and whose final configuration is correct with probability $0 < p \leq 1$. A randomized algorithm solves a problem against an asynchronous *non-adaptive scheduler* if it is correct for any fixed schedule. When the adversary can choose the nodes that are scheduled at the next step knowing not only all local states but also the random bits that were drawn, we say that the adversary is adaptive. Here, the impossibility proofs are given in the non-adaptive setting, whereas the correctness of the algorithms are shown for the adaptive setting.

2.1   Main Results

A symmetric covering is a graph homomorphism such that there is a local bijection at each node, see Sect. 3.2 for the formal definition. From now on, we assume all coverings to be surjective and when applied to labeled graphs, each label is preserved. A quasi-covering is intuitively a partial graph homomorphism that behaves like a covering on a subpart of the graph, see Definition 4.1 for a formal definition. These notions are extended to the $B-$ labeled version of graphs $(\mathbf{G}, b)$. In order to clearly distinguish from coverings on the underlying graph, we will denote the extension $B-$ coverings and $B-$ quasi-coverings. A graph is said to be minimal if any covering is actually an isomorphism. A graph G with a $B-$ labeling b is $B-$ minimal if (G, b) is minimal. When there is no pair of nodes sharing a source, all nodes have a different label and (G, b) is $B-$ minimal. This is also the case when there is at least one unshared source (that is used by only one node).

We consider any recursive family of graphs $\mathcal{F}$ (encoded as symmetric $B-$ labeled digraphs, see later for the details), that is, there is an algorithm that decides whether a given graph belongs to $\mathcal{F}$. This is a natural assumption to get actual algorithm parameterized by $\mathcal{F}$, consequently, the Election algorithms we give are the most general election algorithm possible. It is summarized by the following theorems that consider both shared and unshared sources through the $B-$ labeling.

Theorem 2.1. *Let $\mathcal{F}$ be a recursive family of connected symmetric $B-$ labeled digraphs. There exists a Las Vegas Election algorithm for $\mathcal{F}$ if and only if every labeled digraphs of $\mathcal{F}$ is $B-$ minimal, and there exists a recursive function $\tau :$ $\mathcal{F} \to \mathbb{N}$ such that for every labeled symmetric digraph $(\mathbf{D}, b)$ of $\mathcal{F}$, there is no quasi-covering of $\mathbf{D}$ of radius greater than $\tau(\mathbf{D})$ in $\mathcal{F}$, except $\mathbf{D}$ itself.*

Going for Monte Carlo algorithms enables some incorrect runs so it is possible to consider also non $B-$ minimal graphs, and it is needed to consider only proper quasi-coverings, that is quasi-coverings that are not actually coverings.

Theorem 2.2. *Let $\mathcal{F}$ be a recursive family of connected symmetric $B-$ labeled digraphs. There exists a Monte Carlo Election algorithm for $\mathcal{F}$ if and only if there exists a recursive function $\tau : \mathcal{F} \to \mathbb{N}$ such that for every labeled symmetric digraph $\mathbf{D}$ of $\mathcal{F}$, there is no proper quasi-covering of $\mathbf{D}$ of radius greater than $\tau(\mathbf{D})$ in $\mathcal{F}$, except $\mathbf{D}$ itself.*

3   Symmetric Coverings and the Election Problem for a Labeled Graph

3.1   Preliminaries

In the following, we will consider directed graphs (digraphs) with multiple arcs and self-loops. A *digraph* $D = (V(D), A(D), s_D, t_D)$ is defined by a set $V(D)$ of vertices, a set $A(D)$ of arcs and by two maps s_D and t_D that assign to each arc two elements of $V(D)$: a source and a target (in general, the subscripts will be omitted). If a is an arc, the arc a is said to be going out of $s(a)$ and coming into $t(a)$; we also say that $s(a)$ and $t(a)$ are incident to a. Let a be an arc, if $s(a) = u$ and $t(a) = v$ then v is an out-neighbor of u and u is an in-neighbor of v. A *symmetric* digraph D is a digraph endowed with a symmetry, that is, an involution $Sym : A(D) \to A(D)$ such that for every $a \in A(D), s(a) = t(Sym(a))$. In a symmetric digraph D, the degree of a vertex v is $\deg_D(v) = |\{a \mid s(a) = v\}| = |\{a \mid t(a) = v\}|$ and we denote by $N_D(v)$ the set of neighbors of v which is equal to the set of out-neighbors of v and to the set of in-neighbors of v.

Given two vertices $u, v \in V(D)$, a *path* π of length p from u to v in D is a sequence of arcs $a_1, a_2, \ldots a_p$ such that $s(a_1) = u, \forall i \in [1, p-1], t(a_i) = s(a_{i+1})$ and $t(a_p) = v$. If for each $i \in [1, p-1]$, $a_{i+1} \neq Sym(a_i)$, π is *non-stuttering*. A digraph D is *strongly connected* if for all vertices $u, v \in V(D)$, there exists a path from u to v in D. In a symmetric digraph D, the *distance* between two vertices u and v, denoted $\text{dist}_D(u, v)$ is the length of the shortest path from u to v in D. In a symmetric digraph $\mathbf{D}$, we denote by $\mathbf{B_D}(v_0, r)$, the labeled ball of center $v_0 \in V(D)$ and of radius r that contains all vertices at distance at most r of v_0 and all arcs whose source or target is at distance at most $r - 1$ of v_0.

A *homomorphism* γ between the digraph D and the digraph D' is a mapping $\gamma : V(D) \cup A(D) \to V(D') \cup A(D')$ such that for each arc $a \in A(D)$, $\gamma(s(a)) = s(\gamma(a))$ and $\gamma(t(a)) = t(\gamma(a))$. A homomorphism $\gamma : D \to D'$ is an *isomorphism* if γ is bijective, in this case, we note $D \simeq D'$. Throughout the paper we will consider digraphs where the vertices and the arcs are labeled with labels from a label set $L \times B$ where L is a recursive set (representing any additional information like pseudonyms) and B denotes the set of random sources. Given a set of labels L, a digraph D labeled over L will be denoted by (D, λ), where $\lambda : V(D) \cup A(D) \to L$ is the labeling function. A mapping $\gamma : V(D) \cup A(D) \to V(D') \cup A(D')$ is a homomorphism from (D, λ) to (D', λ') if γ is a digraph homomorphism from D to D' which preserves the labeling, i.e., such that $\lambda'(\gamma(x)) = \lambda(x)$ for every $x \in V(D) \cup A(D)$. Labeled digraphs will be designated by bold letters like $\mathbf{D}, \mathbf{D'}, \ldots$

With the set of labels $L = \mathbb{N} \times \mathbb{N}$, we denote by $\mathcal{D}_{L \times B}$ the set of all symmetric digraphs $\mathbf{D} = (D, \lambda)$ where for each $a \in A(D)$, there exist $p, q \in \mathbb{N}$ such that $\lambda(a) = (p, q)$ and $\lambda(Sym(a)) = (q, p)$ and for each $v \in V(D)$, $\lambda(v) \in L$ and $\{p \mid \exists a, \lambda(a) = (p, q)$ and $s(a) = v\} = [1, \deg_D(v)]$. In other words, $\mathcal{D}_{L \times B}$ is the set of digraphs that locally look like some digraphs obtained from a simple labeled graph $\mathbf{G}$ with port-numbering labels from $\mathbb{N}$.

To get from graphs to symmetric digraph, we follow the presentation of [5]. Let (G, λ) be a labeled graph with the port-numbering δ. We will denote by $(\text{Dir}(\mathbf{G}), \delta)$ the symmetric labeled digraph $(\text{Dir}(G), (\lambda, \delta))$ constructed in the following way. The vertices of $\text{Dir}(G)$ are the vertices of G and they have the same labels in $\mathbf{G}$ and in $\text{Dir}(\mathbf{G})$. Each edge $\{u, v\}$ of G is replaced in $(\text{Dir}(\mathbf{G}), \delta)$ by two arcs $a_{(u,v)}, a_{(v,u)} \in A(\text{Dir}(G))$ such that $s(a_{(u,v)}) = t(a_{(v,u)}) = u$, $t(a_{(u,v)}) = s(a_{(v,u)}) = v$, $\delta(a_{(u,v)}) = (\delta_u(v), \delta_v(u))$ and $\delta(a_{(v,u)}) = (\delta_v(u), \delta_u(v))$. Note that this digraph does not contain multiple arcs or loops. The object we use for our study is $(\mathrm{Dir}(G), (\lambda, \delta, b))$ and results are stated in full generality for symmetric labeled digraphs.

In the course of an execution, a node is said to be *activable* if its has pending operation or pending incoming messages. A scheduler is a family of iterated choices of a non-empty subset of activable nodes at each step. A distributed algorithm is probabilistic when nodes have local access (as formalized above) to a bounded number of *random bits* at each step. For simplicity, we assume here there is access to exactly one random bit at each invocation. We consider both the asynchronous setting (at each step, an adversary chooses a subset of activable nodes) and the synchronous setting (at each step, all node are activated and their messages are delivered).

3.2 Symmetric Coverings

This section presents a first tool: symmetric coverings, then it recalls the characterization of labeled graphs which admit a Las Vegas Election for some knowledge and it presents the Election algorithm and its main properties. The algorithm here is an adaptation of [5], additional proofs are in the full version [7]. The fundamental notion of symmetric coverings are presented in [4].

A labeled digraph $\mathbf{D}$ is a *covering* of a labeled digraph $\mathbf{D}'$ via φ if φ is a homomorphism from $\mathbf{D}$ to $\mathbf{D}'$ such that each arc $a' \in A(D')$ and for each vertex $v \in \varphi^{-1}(t(a'))$ (resp. $v \in \varphi^{-1}(s(a'))$, there exists a unique arc $a \in A(D)$ such that $t(a) = v$ (resp. $s(a) = v$) and $\varphi(a) = a'$. A symmetric labeled digraph $\mathbf{D}$ is a *symmetric covering* of a symmetric labeled digraph $\mathbf{D}'$ via φ if $\mathbf{D}$ is a covering of $\mathbf{D}'$ via φ and if for each arc $a \in A(D)$, $\varphi(Sym(a)) = Sym(\varphi(a))$. The homomorphism φ is a *symmetric covering projection* from $\mathbf{D}$ to $\mathbf{D}'$. A symmetric labeled digraph $\mathbf{D}$ is *symmetric-covering minimal*, or minimal, if there does not exist any symmetric labeled digraph $\mathbf{D}'$ not isomorphic to $\mathbf{D}$ such that $\mathbf{D}$ is a symmetric covering of $\mathbf{D}'$. To distinguish with $B-$ labeled digraphs, we will say that a digraph $(\mathbf{D}, b)$ is $B-$ *symmetric covering minimal*, or $B-$ minimal, when $(\mathbf{D}, b)$ is minimal. Note that when the sources are unshared, each $B-$ label occurs only once, therefore, all networks endowed with at least one unshared source are $B-$ minimal. We use the following notation, given a set of sources S (or equivalently a set of $B-$ labels) and $t \in \mathbb{N}$, we denote by X_S the random variable corresponding to draws from each sources of S.

The following lemma shows the importance of symmetric coverings when we deal with anonymous networks. This is the counterpart of the lifting lemma that Angluin gives for coverings of simple graphs [1] and the proof can be found in [3,6]. Here we adapt it to random sources: it is possible to take the execution steps of the lower graph and carry them over (aka lifting) to the corresponding nodes, via the covering; in such a way that the randomized execution still produces on the upper graph $\mathbf{D}$ a symmetric covering of $\mathbf{D}'$ with the same probability.

Lemma 3.1 (Probabilistic Lifting Lemma). *Let $\mathbf{D}$ and $\mathbf{D}'$ be two $B-$ labeled symmetric digraphs of $\mathcal{D}_{L \times B}$. If $\mathbf{D}$ is a symmetric covering of $\mathbf{D}'$ via*

φ, then any execution of an algorithm $\mathcal{A}$ on $\mathbf{D}'$ with probability $p > 0$ can be lifted up to an execution on $\mathbf{D}$ with probability p, such that at the end of the execution, for any $v \in V(D)$, v is in the same state as $\varphi(v)$.

Proof. We prove it for one step of execution on $\mathbf{D}'$, that executes with probability $p > 0$ on a set of nodes V'. For each v such that $\varphi(v) = v'$ with $v' \in V'$, we can apply the same execution step because of the local bijection. From the $B-$ symmetric covering, all those v share the same random source as v', so the new global state of $\mathbf{D}$ has probability $Pr(X_{S'} = x')$, where S' is the set of sources corresponding to V' and x' the bits obtained at this one step execution. This is exactly probability p.

3.3 Election in a $B-$ Labeled Graph and Symmetric Coverings

First, we give a characterization of networks where Election can be solved in the asynchronous message passing system. This statement means that for the moment, we consider we know the topology of the graph. The *number of sheets* q of a covering is the number of preimages of any node (being a covering, all nodes have the same number of preimages when the covering is surjective).

Theorem 3.2. *Given a $B-$ labeled graph $\mathbf{G} = (G, \lambda, b)$ with a port-numbering δ, there exists a Las Vegas Election algorithm for $(\mathbf{G}, \delta)$ if and only if $(Dir(G), (\lambda, b, \delta))$ is symmetric covering minimal.*

Proof (Necessary part). The necessary part of this theorem is a direct consequence of Lemma 3.1. Assume we have a Las Vegas Election algorithm for $\mathbf{G}$, consider $\mathbf{G}' \neq \mathbf{G}$ such that $\mathbf{G}$ a covering $\mathbf{G}'$. Even though the Election algorithm is "meant" for $\mathbf{G}$, it is possible to consider a synchronous execution of this algorithm on $\mathbf{G}'$. Every step can be lifted to the synchronous execution on $\mathbf{G}$, so it will terminate with some positive probability. Consider now the graphs with final labeling: it is consistent with a symmetric covering and, since $\mathbf{G}' \neq \mathbf{G}$, the number of sheets is greater than 2, there will be more than one *elected* node on $\mathbf{G}$. A contradiction.

3.4 A Las Vegas Election Algorithm Knowing the Size

The sufficient part needs the following naming algorithm (it will also be used later). The aim of a naming algorithm is to get to a final configuration where all nodes have unique identities. Again this is an essential prerequisite to many other distributed algorithms that work correctly only under the assumption that all nodes can be unambiguously identified. The enumeration problem is a variant of the naming problem. The aim of a distributed enumeration algorithm is to attribute to each network vertex a unique integer in such a way that this yields a bijection between the set $V(G)$ of vertices and $\{1, 2, \ldots, |V(G)|\}$.

In Algorithm 1, we describe a randomized enumeration algorithm knowing the size; by this way we obtain an election algorithm by considering that the vertex having the number $|V(G)|$ is elected (vertices know $|V(G)|$). This algorithm is an extension of [5] which is inspired from the one presented in [6], which was an adaptation of the enumeration algorithm given by Mazurkiewicz in [17].

Informal Description. We first give a general description of our algorithm $\mathcal{M}$, when executed on a connected labeled simple graph $\mathbf{G}$ with port-numbering δ and random sources b.

During the execution of the algorithm, each vertex v attempts to get its own unique identity which is a number between 1 and $|V(G)|$. At each step of the algorithm, it invokes the random source b in order to produce incrementally a binary sequence $\bar{b}(v)$. This sequence will eventually be different with the one of other nodes that do not share the same random source. Once a vertex v has chosen a number $n(v)$, it sends it to each neighbor u with the initial label, the port-number $\delta_v(u)$ and the sequence $\bar{b}$. When a vertex u receives a message from one neighbor v, it stores the number $n(v)$ with the port-numbers $\delta_u(v)$ and $\delta_v(u)$. From all information it has gathered from its neighbors, each vertex can construct its *local view* (which is the set of numbers of its neighbors associated with the corresponding port-numbers). Then, a vertex broadcasts its number, its label, its $\bar{b}$ sequence and its mailbox (which contains a set of *local views*). If a vertex u discovers the existence of another vertex v with the same tentative number then it should decide if it changes its own. To this end it compares its local view with the local view of v. If the label of u together with the random bits sequence $\bar{b}(u)$ or the local view of u is strictly weaker, then u picks another number—its new temporary identity—and broadcasts it again with its local view and new $\bar{b}$ sequence. To end of the computation, the node waits until it sees the number $|V(G)|$ in its mailbox. At this moment if the digraph $(Dir(G), (\lambda, \delta))$ is $B-$ symmetric covering minimal, then every vertex will have a unique number from $\{1, 2, \ldots, |V(G)|\}$: the algorithm is an Enumeration algorithm.

Labels. We consider a network $(\mathbf{G}, \delta)$ where $\mathbf{G} = (G, \lambda)$ is a simple labeled graph and where δ is a port-numbering of $\mathbf{G}$. The function $\lambda : V(G) \to L$ is the initial labeling. Note that the $B-$ label, that is the random source, is not known by the node.

We assume there exists a total order $<_L$ on L. We extend the order $<_L$ to $L \cup \{\perp\}$ (assuming that $\perp \notin L$) as follows: for all $\ell \in L$, $\perp < \ell$.

We say that $\bar{b} <_B \bar{b'}$ if $\bar{b}$ is before $\bar{b'}$ in the alphabetic order on binary strings.

During the execution, the label of each v is a tuple $(\lambda(v), \bar{b}, n(v), N(v), M(v))$ where:

- $\lambda(v) \in L$ is the initial label of v.
- $n(v) \in \mathbb{N}$ is the current *number* of v computed by the algorithm; initially $n(v) = 0$.
- $\bar{b}(v)$ is a finite sequence of $\{0, 1\}$.
- $N(v) \in \mathcal{P}_{\mathrm{fin}}(\mathbb{N} \times L \times \{0, 1\}^* \times \mathbb{N}^2)$, where $\mathcal{P}_{\mathrm{fin}}(-)$ denotes the set of finite subsets, is the *local view* of v. At the end of the execution, if $(m, \ell, \bar{b}, p, q) \in N(v)$, then v has a neighbor u whose number is m, whose label is ℓ, whose random sequence has prefix $\bar{b}$ and the arc from u to v is labeled (p, q). Initially $N(v) = \{(0, \perp, \varepsilon, 0, q) \mid q \in [1, \deg_G(v)]\}$.
- $M(v)$ is a set, it is the *mailbox* of v; initially $M(v) = \emptyset$. An element of $M(v)$ has the following form: $(m, \ell, \bar{b}, N)$ where $m \in \mathbb{N}$, $\ell \in L$, $\bar{b}$ in $\{0, 1\}^*$ and N is

a local view. It contains all information received by v during the execution of the algorithm. If $(m, \ell, \overline{b}, N) \in M(v)$, it means that at some previous step of the execution, there was a vertex u such that $n(u) = m$, $\lambda(u) = \ell$, $\overline{b}(u) = \overline{b}$ and $N(u) = N$.

Messages. Nodes exchange messages of the form $< (n, \ell, \overline{b}, M), p >$. If a vertex u sends a message $< (n, \ell, \overline{b}, M), p >$ to one of its neighbor v, then the message contains the following information: n is the current number $n(u)$ of u, ℓ is the label $\lambda(u)$ of u, $\overline{b}$ is the sequence of random bits, M is the mailbox of u, and $p = \delta_u(v)$.

An Order on Local Views. The interesting properties of the algorithm rely on a total order on local views, which has to be adapted from [5] to take into account the sequences of random bits. The idea is to complement the λ label with the sequence of random bits, and when comparing such extended labels, to use the alphabetic order, this way a previous sequence coming from the same node is always ordered before the current sequence.

Given two distinct sets $N_1, N_2 \in \mathcal{P}_{\mathrm{fin}}(\mathbb{N} \times L \times \{0,1\}^* \times \mathbb{N}^2)$, we define $N_1 \prec N_2$ if the maximum of the symmetric difference $N_1 \bigtriangleup N_2 = (N_1 \setminus N_2) \cup (N_2 \setminus N_1)$ for the lexicographic order belongs to N_2. One also says that $(\ell, \overline{b}, N) \prec (\ell', \overline{b'}, N')$ if either $\ell <_L \ell'$, or $\ell = \ell'$ and $\overline{b} <_B \overline{b'}$; or $\ell = \ell'$ and $\overline{b} = \overline{b'}$ and $N \prec N'$. We denote by $\preceq$ the reflexive closure of $\prec$. When doing comparison between mailboxes (equality or set-inclusion), this is done without considering the bits sequences, and we keep the same $=$ or $\leq$ operators to have lighter notations.

Consider the mailbox $M = M(v)$ of a vertex v during the execution of Algorithm $\mathcal{M}$ on a graph $(\mathbf{G}, \overline{b}, \delta)$. We say that an element $(n, \ell, \overline{b}, N) \in M$ is *maximal* in M if there does not exist $(n, \ell', \overline{b'}, N') \in M$ such that $(\ell, \overline{b}, N) \prec (\ell', \overline{b'}, N')$. We denote by $S(M)$ the set of maximal elements of M. From Proposition 3.3, after each step of Algorithm $\mathcal{M}$, $(n(v), \lambda(v), \overline{b}, N(v))$ is maximal in $M(v)$. The set $S(M)$ is said *coherent* if it is non-empty and if for all $(n_1, \ell_1, \overline{b_1}, N_1) \in S(M)$, for all $(n_2, \ell_2, \overline{b_2}, p, q) \in N_1, p \neq 0, n_2 \neq 0$ and $\ell_2 \neq \perp$ and for $(n_2, \ell'_2, \overline{b'}, N'_2) \in S(M)$ (there is only one by maximality), we have $\ell_2 = \ell'_2$, $\overline{b'}$ is a prefix of $\overline{b_2}$, and $(n_1, \ell_1, \overline{b_1}, q', p') \in N'_2$.

Action **I** can be executed by a node on wake-up only if it has not received any message. It chooses the number 1, updates its mailbox and informs its neighbors.

Action **R** describes the instructions the vertex v_0 has to follow when it receives a message $< (n_1, \ell_1, \overline{b_1}, M_1), p_1 >$ from a neighbor via port q_1. First, it memorizes and it updates its mailbox by adding M_1 to it. Then it modifies its number if it is equal to 0 or if there exists $(n(v_0), \ell', \overline{b'}, N') \in M(v_0)$ such that $(\lambda(v_0), \overline{b}(v_0), N(v_0)) \prec (\ell', \overline{b'}, N')$. The new number is the next available number. Then, it updates its local view by removing elements which corresponds to the port q_1 (if they exist) and by adding $(n_1, \ell_1, \overline{b_1}, p_1, q_1)$ to $N(v_0)$. Then, it adds its new state to its mailbox. Finally, if its mailbox has been modified

---

Algorithm 1: Algorithm $\mathcal{M}$, with $n = |V(G)|$.

$\mathbf{I}$: $\{n(v_0) = 0$ and no message has arrived at $v_0\}$
begin
    $n(v_0) := 1$;
    $\overline{b}(v_0) := \overline{b}(v_0)rbit()$;
    $M(v_0) := \{(n(v_0), \lambda(v_0), \overline{b}(v_0), \emptyset)\}$;
    for $i := 1$ **to** $\deg(v_0)$ **do**
        send $< (n(v_0), \lambda(v_0), \overline{b}(v_0), M(v_0)), i >$ through i ;

$\mathbf{R}$: $\{$A message $< (n_1, \ell_1, \overline{b_1}, M_1), p_1 >$ has arrived at v_0 through port $q_1\}$
begin
    $M_{old} := M(v_0)$;
    $M(v_0) := M(v_0) \cup M_1$;
    if $n(v_0) = 0$ *or*
      $\exists(n(v_0), \ell', \overline{b'}, N') \in M(v_0)$ *such that* $(\lambda(v_0), \overline{b}(v_0), N(v_0)) \prec (\ell', \overline{b'}, N')$
    then
        $n(v_0) := 1 + \max\{n' \mid \exists(n', \ell', \overline{b'}, N') \in M(v_0)\}$;
    $N(v_0) := N(v_0) \setminus \{(n', \ell', \overline{b'}, p', q_1) \mid \exists(n', \ell', \overline{b'}, p', q_1) \in$
    $N(v_0)\} \cup \{(n_1, \ell_1, \overline{b_1}, p_1, q_1)\}$;
    $M(v_0) := M(v_0) \cup \{(n(v_0), \lambda(v_0), \overline{b}(v_0), N(v_0))\}$;
    if $M(v_0) \neq M_{old}$ **then**
        for $i := 1$ **to** $\deg(v_0)$ **do**
            send $< (n(v_0), \lambda(v_0), \overline{b}(v_0), M(v_0)), i >$ through port i ;

$\mathbf{C}$: $\{M(v_0)$ is coherent and there is no $(n, \ell, \overline{b}, N) \in M(v_0)\}$
begin
    $\overline{b}(v_0) := \overline{b}(v_0)rbit()$;
    for $i := 1$ **to** $\deg(v_0)$ **do**
        send $< (n(v_0), \lambda(v_0), \overline{b}(v_0), M(v_0)), i >$ through port i ;

---

by the execution of all these instructions, it sends its number and its mailbox to all its neighbors. If the mailbox of v_0 is not modified by the execution of the action $\mathbf{R}$, it means that the information v_0 has about its neighbor (i.e., its number) was correct, that all the elements of M_1 already belong to $M(v_0)$, and that for each $(n(v_0), \ell, \overline{b}(v_0), N) \in M(v_0)$, $(\ell, \overline{b}, N) \preceq (\lambda(v_0), \overline{b}(v_0), N(v_0))$. This algorithm halts when $n(v_0) = |V(G)|$, and v_0 is elected; or when $|V(G)|$ appears in $M(v_0)$ and v_0 is non-elected.

Action $\mathbf{C}$ is extending the random bits sequence in order to help break symmetries between nodes not sharing the same random source. It is required that $M(v)$ is coherent to apply it so that this does not block progress for the $\mathbf{R}$ rule.

3.5   Some Properties of Algorithm $\mathcal{M}$

We consider an execution ρ of $\mathcal{M}$ on $(\mathbf{G}, b, \delta)$ and for each vertex $v \in V(G)$, we denote by $(\lambda(v), n_i(v), \bar{b}_i(v), N_i(v), M_i(v))$ the state of v after the ith computation step of ρ on v. If the vertex v executes an action from the step i to the step $i+1$, it is said active at step $i+1$. The following proposition summarizes properties that are satisfied during an execution ρ on $(\mathbf{G}, b, \delta)$.

Proposition 3.3. *Consider a vertex v and a step i. Then, $n_i(v) \leq n_{i+1}(v)$, $\bar{b}_i(v) \leq_B \bar{b}_{i+1}(v)$, $N_i(v) \preceq N_{i+1}(v)$, and $M_i(v) \subseteq M_{i+1}(v)$. For each $(m, \ell, \bar{b}, N) \in M_i(v)$ and each $m' \in [1, m]$, $\exists (m', \ell', \bar{b}', N') \in M_i(v), \exists v' \in V(G)$ such that $n_i(v') = m'$.*

Proof. We suppose that some internal event is executed at step $i+1$ by some vertex $v \in V(G)$. The property is obviously true for any vertex $w \in V(G) \setminus \{v\}$ and it is easy to see that $M_i(v) \subseteq M_{i+1}(v)$.

If $n_i(v) \neq n_{i+1}(v)$, then $n_{i+1}(v) = 1 + \max\{n' \mid (n', \ell', \bar{b}, \mathcal{N}') \in M_i(v)\}$ and either $n_i(v) = 0 < n_{i+1}(v)$ or $(n_i(v), \lambda(v), N_i(v)) \in M_i(v)$ and therefore $n_i(v) < n_{i+1}(v)$.

The random bits sequence is extended by its suffix, so $\bar{b}_i(v) \leq_B \bar{b}_{i+1}(v)$.

If $N_i(v) \neq N_{i+1}(v)$, then v has received a message $< (n', \cdots, M'), p >$ through port q and $N_{i+1}(v) = N_i(v) \setminus \{(n'_{old}, p, q)\} \cup \{(n', p, q)\}$ for some (previous) number n'_{old}. Let v' be the neighbor of v such that $\delta_v(v') = q$; we know that $\delta_{v'}(v) = p$.

If $(n'_{old}, p, q) \notin N_i(v)$, then $\max N_{i+1}(v) \triangle N_i(v) = (n', p, q) \in N_{i+1}(v)$ and then $N_i(v) \prec N_{+1}(v)$.

If $(n'_{old}, p, q) \in N_i(v)$, then $n'_{old} \neq n'$. Let $j < i+1$ be the computation step where v' has sent the message $< (n', \cdots, M'), p >$. We know that $n'_{old} \leq n' = n_j(v')$ and consequently, $\max N_{i+1}(v) \triangle N_i(v) = (n', p, q) \in N_{i+1}(v)$ and $N_i(v) \prec N_{+1}(v)$. Note that the previous inequality is obtained independently from the b label, by definition of $\prec$.

For the second part of the proposition: We first note that $(m, \ell, \beta, \mathcal{N})$ is added to $\bigcup_{v \in V(G)} M_i(v)$ at some step i only if there exists a vertex $v' \in V(G)$ such that $n_i(v') = m$, $\lambda(v') = \ell$, $\bar{b}(v') = \beta$ and $N_i(v') = \mathcal{N}$.

Given a vertex $v \in V(G)$, a step i and an element $(m, \ell, \beta, \mathcal{N}) \in M_i(v)$, let $m' \leq M$ and $U = \{(u, j) \in V(G) \times \mathbb{N} \mid j \leq i, n_j(u) = m'\}$ and $U' = \{(u, j) \in U \mid \forall (u', j') \in U, (\lambda(u'), N_{j'}(u')) \prec (\lambda(u), N_j(u))$ or $(\lambda(u'), N_{j'}(u')) = (\lambda(u), N_j(u))$ and $j' \leq j\}$. Since $(m, \ell, \beta, \mathcal{N}) \in M_i(v)$, U and U' are both non-empty and it is easy to see that there exists i_0 such that for each $(u, j) \in U'$, $j = i_0$.

If $i_0 < i$, let $(u, i_0) \in U'$; we know that $n_{i_0+1}(u) \neq n_{i_0}(u)$, but this is impossible, since by maximality of $(\lambda(u), \bar{b}(u), N_{i_0}(u))$, u cannot have modified its number. Consequently, $i_0 = i$ and there exists $v' \in V(G)$ such that $n_i(v') = m'$. This ends the proof.

From [6], we know that once $n(v)$, $N(v)$ and $M(v)$ have reached their final values for all v, then $S(M(v))$ is coherent for any v. This is also the case when adding $\bar{b}$, thus, if $S(M(v))$ is not coherent, we know that $M(v)$ will be modified.

If the set $S(M)$ is coherent, one can construct a labeled symmetric digraph $\mathbf{D}_M = (D_M, \lambda_M)$ as follows. The set of vertices $V(D_M)$ is the set $\{n \mid \exists(n, \ell, N) \in S(M)\}$. For any $(n, \ell, N) \in S(M)$ and any $(n', \ell', p, q) \in N$, there exists an arc $a_{n,n',p,q} \in A(D_M)$ such that $t(a) = n, s(a) = n'$, $\lambda_M(a) = (p, q)$. Since $S(M)$ is coherent, we can define Sym by $Sym(a_{n,n',p,q}) = a_{n',n,q,p}$.

One can show that Algorithm $\mathcal{M}$ terminates with probability 1. Consider two nodes with different sources, since the sources are independent, with probability 1, the finite sequences of random bits will eventually be different. So by rule $\mathbf{R}$, they will have different numbers.

When $\mathcal{M}$ terminates, the final labeling verifies the following properties: the digraph $(Dir(G), (\lambda, \delta))$ is a symmetric covering of $\mathbf{D}_M$ (see Proposition 4.1 in [6]). Thus if $(Dir(G), (\lambda, \bar{b}, \delta))$ is symmetric covering minimal then $\mathbf{D}_M$ is isomorphic to $(Dir(G), (\lambda, \delta))$ and therefore the set of numbers is exactly $[1, |V(G)|]$: each vertex has a unique number. Moreover, termination detection of the algorithm is possible. Indeed, once a vertex gets the identity number $|V(G)|$ (which is known by each vertex), from Proposition 3.3, it knows that all the vertices have different identity numbers that will not change any more and it can conclude that the computation is over. In this case, one can also solve the election problem, since this vertex can take the label *elected* and broadcasts the information that a vertex has been elected. Finally, we obtain Theorem 3.2 presented above.

4   Quasi-coverings and The Election Problem for a Family of Labeled Graphs

4.1   Quasi-coverings

In the previous section, we assumed the exact size of the network is known, here we consider general structural knowledge. This section presents the second tool we use: quasi-coverings. This tool provides necessary conditions for the randomized Election in a family of labeled graphs for both unshared and shared random sources.

Quasi-coverings have been introduced to study the termination detection problem [18]. The idea behind quasi-coverings is to enable the simulation of local computations on a given graph in a restricted area of a larger graph, such that a replay technique can be used to prove impossibility results by contradiction. The restricted area where we can perform the simulation will shrink while the number of simulated steps increases, so the replay technique cannot be used when a bound is known. In [10], the definition of quasi-coverings have been slightly modified to express more easily this property as a Quasi-Lifting Lemma. The next definition is an adaptation of this tool to labeled digraphs and is illustrated in Fig. 1.

Definition 4.1. *Given two symmetric labeled digraphs $\mathbf{D}_0, \mathbf{D}_1$, an integer r, a vertex $v_1 \in V(D_1)$ and a homomorphism γ from $\mathbf{B}_{\mathbf{D}_1}(v_1, r)$ to $\mathbf{D}_0$, the digraph $\mathbf{D}_1$ is a* quasi-covering *of $\mathbf{D}_0$ of center v_1 and of radius r via γ if there exists a symmetric labeled digraph $\mathbf{D}_2$ that is a symmetric covering of $\mathbf{D}_0$ via a homomorphism φ and if there exist $v_2 \in V(D_2)$ and an isomorphism ψ from $\mathbf{B}_{D_1}(v_1, r)$ to $\mathbf{B}_{D_2}(v_2, r)$ such that for any $x \in V(B_{D_1}(v_1, r)) \cup A(B_{D_1}(v_1, r))$, $\gamma(x) = \varphi(\psi(x))$.*

We define the number of sheets q *to be the minimal cardinality of the sets of preimages by γ: $q = \min_{v \in V(D_0)} |\{w \in \gamma^{-1}(v) | B_{D_1}(w, 1) \subset B_{D_1}(v_1, r)\}|$. We say that a quasi-covering is* proper *if $B_{D_1}(v_1, r-1)$ is not D_1. Any non-proper quasi-covering is a covering.*

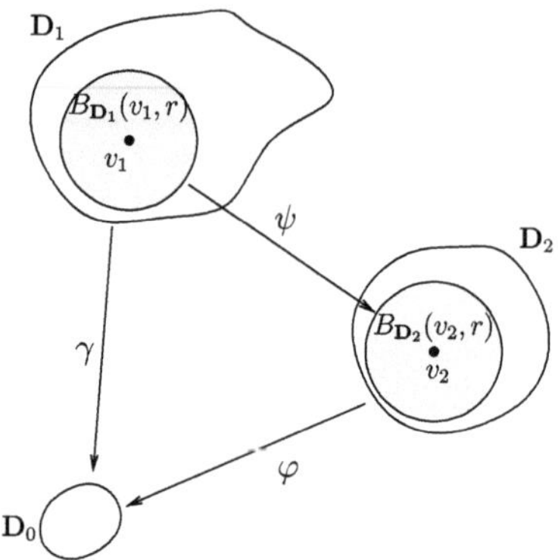

Fig. 1. Quasi-coverings diagram. The ball $B_{D_1}(v_1, r)$ captures *"the existence of large enough area of one graph"* ($\mathbf{D}_1$) *"that looks locally like another graph"* ($\mathbf{D}_0$).

Lemma 4.2. *Let $\mathbf{D}_1$ be a proper quasi-covering of $\mathbf{D}_0$ of center v_1 and radius r via γ. Then, for any $q \in \mathbb{N}$, if $r \geq q|V(D_0)|$ then γ has at least q sheets.*

Proof. Denote $\mathbf{D}_2$ the associated covering via φ. The quasi-covering being proper, we have that $|B_{\mathbf{D}_1}(v_1, r)| \geq r \geq q|V(\mathbf{D}_0)|$, hence $|V(\mathbf{D}_2)| \geq q|V(\mathbf{D}_0)|$. We can deduce that $\mathbf{D}_2$ has at least q sheets. Now, consider a spanning tree T of $\mathbf{D}_0$ rooted on $\gamma(v_1)$. Note T_1 the lifting via φ of T rooted on $v_2 = \psi(v_1)$. By a theorem of Reidemeister [20], there are $q-1$ disjoint lifted spanning trees $T_2, \ldots, T_q$ on $\mathbf{D}_2$ such that the subgraph induced by $T_1 \cup \cdots \cup T_q$ is connected. As T has a diameter at most $|V(\mathbf{D}_0)| - 1$, we have that $T_1 \cup \cdots \cup T_q \subset B_{\mathbf{D}_2}(v_2, q|V(\mathbf{D}_0)|)$. That means that every vertex of $\mathbf{D}_0$ has at least q preimages in $B_{\mathbf{D}_2}(v_2, r)$, hence in $B_{\mathbf{D}_1}(v_1, r)$.

We precise the shrinking of the radius after k rounds of a synchronous execution.

Lemma 4.3 (Quasi-Lifting Lemma). *Let* $\mathbf{D}_1$ *be a symmetric labeled digraph that is a quasi-covering of* $\mathbf{D}_0$ *of center* v_1 *and of radius* r *via* γ. *Let* $k < r$ *be a non negative integer. For any algorithm* $\mathcal{A}$, *any source labeling* b_0 *and* b_1 *such that* $(\mathbf{D}_1, b_1)$ *be a symmetric labeled digraph that is a quasi-covering of* $(\mathbf{D}_0, b_0)$ *of center* v_1 *and of radius* r *via* γ. *Let* $\mathbf{D}'_0$ *be the digraph obtained after* k *rounds of a random synchronous execution of* $\mathcal{A}$ *on* $(\mathbf{D}_0, b_0)$ *with probability* $p > 0$. *Then there exists* $\mathbf{D}'_1$ *obtained after a random synchronous execution of* $\mathcal{A}$ *on* $(\mathbf{D}_1, b_1)$ *with probability* p *that is a quasi-covering of* $\mathbf{D}'_0$ *of center* v_1 *and of radius* $r - k$.

Proof. Consider an algorithm $\mathcal{A}$ and a digraph $\mathbf{D}_1 = (D_1, \lambda_1, b_1)$ that is a quasi-covering of $\mathbf{D}_0 = (D_0, \lambda_0, b_0)$ of center v_1 and of radius r via γ. There exists a symmetric labeled digraph $\mathbf{D}_2 = (D_2, \lambda_2, b_2)$ that is a symmetric covering of $\mathbf{D}_0$ via a homomorphism φ and a vertex $v_2 \in V(D_2)$ such that $(B_{D_1}(v, r), \lambda_1, b_1)$ is isomorphic to $(B_{D_2}(v, r), \lambda_2, b_2)$ via an isomorphism ψ and for any $v \in B(v_1, r)$, $\gamma(v) = \varphi(\psi(v))$.

Let $\mathbf{D}'_0 = (D_0, \lambda'_0)$ (resp. $\mathbf{D}'_1 = (D_1, \lambda'_1), \mathbf{D}'_2 = (D_2, \lambda'_2)$) be the labeled digraph where for each v, $\lambda'_0(v)$ (resp. $\lambda'_1(v)$, $\lambda'_2(v)$) is the state of v in D_0 (resp. D_1, D_2) after a computation step of $\mathcal{A}$ on $\mathbf{D}_0$ with probability $p > 0$. To prove the lemma, it is sufficient to show that we can have a similar step on $\mathbf{D}_1, \mathbf{D}_2$ with probability also p while $\mathbf{D}'_1$ is a quasi-covering of $\mathbf{D}'_0$ of center v_1 and of radius $r - 1$ via γ. From Lemma 3.1, we know that we can obtain, with probability p, $\mathbf{D}'_2$ that is a covering of $\mathbf{D}'_0$. Moreover, for each $v \in V(B_{\mathbf{D}_1}(v_1, r - 1))$, $\lambda'_1(v) = \lambda'_2(\varphi(v))$ since $(B_{\mathbf{D}_1}(v, 1), \lambda_1, b_1)$ is isomorphic to $(B_{\mathbf{D}_2}(\varphi(v), 1), \lambda_2, b_2)$. Consequently, $(B_{\mathbf{D}_1}(v, r - 1), \lambda'_1, b_1)$ is isomorphic to $(B_{\mathbf{D}_2}(v, r - 1), \lambda'_2, b_2)$ via ψ, so $\mathbf{D}'_1$ is a quasi-covering of $\mathbf{D}'_0$ of center v_1 and of radius $r - 1$ via γ.

The probability of such a configuration is $Pr(X_{S_1} = x^1)$ where S_1 is the set of sources in $B_{\mathbf{D}_1}(v_1, r - 1)$ and x^1 the bits drawn on these sources. By composition $\phi \circ \psi$, the set of sources in $\mathbf{D}_0$ is also S_1. Hence this probability is equal to p.

The following is the counterpart of the lifting lemma for quasi-coverings.

Corollary 4.4 (Randomized Quasi-Lifting corollary). *Let* $\mathbf{D}_1$ *be a quasi-covering of* $\mathbf{D}_0$ *of center* v_1 *and of radius* r *via* γ. *For any algorithm* $\mathcal{A}$, *after* r *rounds of a random synchronous execution of an algorithm* $\mathcal{A}$ *on* $\mathbf{D}_1$ *with probability* $p > 0$, *then* v_1 *is in the same state as* $\gamma(v_1)$ *after* r *rounds of the synchronous execution of* $\mathcal{A}$ *on* $\mathbf{D}_0$ *with probability* p.

4.2 Las Vegas and Monte Carlo Election in a Family of Labeled Graphs

Using the Randomized quasi-lifting lemma, we give two necessary conditions for Las Vegas and Monte Carlo Election algorithms.

Proposition 4.5 (LV Necessary condition). *Let* $\mathcal{F}$ *be a recursive family of connected* $b-$ *labeled digraphs that are symmetric covering minimal, such that there is a Las Vegas Election algorithm for this family. Then there exists a computable function* $\tau : \mathcal{I} \to \mathbb{N}$ *such that for all labeled digraph* $\mathbf{D}$ *of* $\mathcal{F}$, *there is no quasi-covering of* $\mathbf{D}$, *distinct of* $\mathbf{D}$, *of radius greater than* $\tau(\mathbf{D})$ *in* $\mathcal{F}$.

Proof. Let $\mathcal{A}$ denote an election algorithm on $\mathcal{F}$. Consider a labeled digraph $\mathbf{D} \in \mathcal{F}$, Since this is a Las Vegas algorithm, there exists some terminating synchronous execution of $\mathcal{A}$, that is correct on $\mathbf{D} \in \mathcal{F}$. Denote T the number of rounds of this (finite) random synchronous successful execution on $\mathbf{D}$. We have a corresponding sequence $\mathcal{C} = (\mathbf{C}_0 = \mathbf{D}, \mathbf{C}_1, ..., \mathbf{C}_T)$ where $\mathbf{C}_i$ is the labeled graph obtained after the ith round. No step of $\mathcal{A}$ can be applied on any vertex of $\mathbf{C}_T$, (at the end of the round t no message is sent by any vertex). This execution is associated with some probability $p > 0$. Define $\tau(\mathbf{D}) = 2|V(\mathbf{D})| + T$. Then τ has the desired property.

By contradiction, let $\mathbf{D}' \in \mathcal{F}$ be a quasi-covering of $\mathbf{D}$ of radius $\tau(\mathbf{D})$, distinct of $\mathbf{D}$. By iteration of Lemma 4.3, we get with some non null probability $\mathbf{D}''$ such that $\mathbf{D}''$ is a quasi-covering of $\mathbf{C}_T$ of radius $\tau(D) - T = 2|V(D)|$. The labeled digraph $\mathbf{D}$ being symmetric covering minimal and distinct of $\mathbf{D}'$, this final quasi-covering $\mathbf{D}''$ of $\mathbf{C}_n$ is proper. Hence, since by construction the label *elected* appears exactly once in $\mathbf{C}_T$., we have that by Lemma 4.2, the label *elected* appears at least twice in $\mathbf{D}''$. A contradiction.

Now we consider Monte Carlo algorithms. Since they can fail for some executions, the previous technique does not apply. The radius condition will be necessary only for proper quasi-coverings.

Proposition 4.6 (MC Necessary condition). *Let $\mathcal{F}$ be a recursive family of connected $b-$ labeled digraphs such that there is a Monte Carlo Election algorithm for this family. Then there exists a computable function $\tau : \mathcal{I} \to \mathbb{N}$ such that for all labeled digraph $\mathbf{D}$ of $\mathcal{F}$, there is no proper quasi-covering of $\mathbf{D}$ of radius greater than $\tau(\mathbf{D})$ in $\mathcal{F}$.*

Proof. Let $\mathcal{A}$ denote a Monte Carlo election algorithm on $\mathcal{F}$ with correctness $\varepsilon > 0$. We consider the synchronous schedule of algorithm $\mathcal{A}$ on $\mathbf{D}$, Since $\mathcal{A}$ is a Monte Carlo Election algorithm, there exists a set of random bits sequences b_u, $u \in V(\mathbf{D})$, and a time $T \in \mathbb{N}$ at which the algorithm ends correctly. We denote $p > 0$ the probability of the set of sequences $b_u(1), \cdots, b_u(T)$, $u \in V(\mathbf{D})$.

Assume there is a proper quasi-covering $\mathbf{K}_1$ of $\mathbf{D}$ of radius $T + 2V(\mathbf{D})$. By iteration of Lemma 4.3, we can lift the execution. We denote b_1 the sequence of bits quasi-lifted to $\mathbf{K}_1$ from $\mathbf{D}$ on the T rounds. This sequence has some probability $p_1 > 0$. Assume now there is a proper quasi-covering $\mathbf{K}$ of $\mathbf{D}$ of radius $R = N(T + 2V(\mathbf{D})$, where N is such that $(1 - p_1)^N < \frac{1}{2}\varepsilon$. This proper quasi-covering can be decomposed in N disjoint regions that define a quasi-covering of radius $T + 2V(\mathbf{D})$. For a given quasi-covering, the probability of lifting from $\mathbf{D}$ and b to $\mathbf{K}_1$ and b_1 is at least p_1. When such a lifting occurs, we have that the *elected* label appears twice on $\mathbf{K}_1$. Hence, the probability that there is an incorrect output in one of the N disjoint regions is at least $1 - \frac{1}{2}\varepsilon$, a contradiction with the level of correctness for $\mathcal{A}$. So there are no proper quasi-covering of D of radius R and setting $\tau(\mathbf{D})$ as R concludes the proof.

The sufficient parts needed to prove Theorem 2.1 and 2.2 are presented in the full version [7] since they are extensions of the algorithms from [5].

5   Applications

5.1   Representative Cases of Structural Knowledge

We present a summary of the consequences of the two characterizations and discuss relation with works from the literature.

Knowledge	$B-$**Minimal Graphs**		
	None	**Sharing Bound/Bound**	**2-Approx/Size/Topology**
Deterministic	✗	✗	✗ ([1] for rings)
Las Vegas	✗	✗ ([12] for rings)	✓ ([12] for rings)
Monte Carlo	✗ ([12] for rings)	✓ ([22] for rings)	✓ ([8] with vhp)

Fig. 2. Summary of our Election computability results for $B-$ minimal graphs and various knowledge, with previously known results.

We consider unshared, shared randomness, and also bounded sharing randomness (in Sect. 5.2). There are three cases: the general case, the $B-$ minimal graphs, and the minimal graphs. Note that $(\mathbf{G}, b)$ being $B-$ minimal does not imply that $\mathbf{G}$ is minimal, but the converse is true. A $B-$ minimal graph could be an anonymous graph with at least one unshared source of randomness, a covering-minimal graph or a non covering-minimal graph where the shared sources do not align with the symmetry from the covering structure. Comparing to [9], we remark that $B-$ minimality extends the condition given in [9] for cliques. E.g., consider rings, if the gcd of the size of the B classes is exactly one then the ring is $B-$ minimal.

When a graph is not $B-$ minimal, then it does not admit a Las Vegas Election algorithm even knowing the topology (including the random sources). When it is $B-$ minimal, then it admits a Las Vegas Election algorithm provided we have enough knowledge. In particular, a consequence of Theorem 2.1, is that $B-$ minimal graphs admits a Las Vegas Election algorithm knowing the size. Knowing a bound on the size does provide a (uniform) τ function for limiting proper quasi-covering but not quasi-covering, because coverings are quasi-coverings of any radius. So for having Las Vegas Election, enough knowledge to rule out coverings within the same knowledge is necessary. This is the case of the strict 2-approximation knowledge, since any strict covering is at least twice as large. Therefore, while knowing the topology is the strongest possible knowledge, it is actually not necessary, nor to actually know the size.

What about Monte Carlo Election algorithm in the general case? From Theorem 2.2, we get that it is not possible to have an Election algorithm when nothing is known (because this enables quasi-coverings of arbitrary large radius). However, knowing a bound on the size does provide a way for limiting proper quasi-covering, but it is also the case for other bounds, like the sharing bound in Sect. 5.2 that enables a non-uniform τ function and is therefore a more generic example. Finally, when considering minimal graphs, it appears the characterizations are equivalent:

Theorem 5.1. *Let $\mathcal{F}$ be a family of covering-minimal graphs, then it is possible to solve Election with a deterministic algorithm on $\mathcal{F}$ if and only if it is possible to solve Election with a Las Vegas algorithm on $\mathcal{F}$ if and only if it is possible to solve Election with a Monte Carlo algorithm on $\mathcal{F}$.*

We also discuss previous works, that were only on anonymous rings. This shows how our general results are extending all the known cases. These results are summarized in Fig. 2.

- [1] the seminal work of Angluin is the first proof of the impossibility of election in anonymous algorithms. It was done in the local model which is a stronger model than asynchronous message passing.
- [11,12]: Itai and Rodeh gave an impossibility proof for Las Vegas algorithms on anonymous rings knowing a bound. In his textbook [24, Th. 9.12], Tel also presents this proof for rings. Itai and Rodeh gave a probabilistic Election algorithm when the size of the graph is known. Some precise complexity bounds are also given.
- [22]: Schieber and Snir present a Monte Carlo algorithm knowing a bound on the size.
- [8]: Codenotti *et al.* present an Election algorithm that is correct with v.h.p[1] with 1 random bit, knowing the size of the network. This result can be easily extended to knowing only a bound using more random bits.

When the topology is known, probabilistic algorithms are better solutions than deterministic algorithms. Because it not possible to lift executions forever, knowing the exact size or topology means it is possible to wait for Mazurkiewicz' algorithm to terminate. That there is no enumeration yet can be easily checked from the knowledge.

5.2   Bounded Sharing of Sources of Randomness

We consider now the family $\mathcal{B}_K$ of graphs where for every graph, the shared sources are known (that is there is bijection between the label and the sources) and where the number of nodes sharing a source with another node is bounded by some number $K \in \mathbb{N}$. We have a Monte Carlo Election algorithm, this is actually a corollary of Lemma 4.2. Since there exists $B-$ coverings in $\mathcal{B}_K$, there is no Las Vegas algorithm for this knowledge. We underline that the nodes need to know the class of their random sources. Otherwise, since networks in $\mathcal{B}_K$ have unbounded size, there would be unbounded proper quasi-coverings, so it is impossible to solve Election in the unlabeled version of $\mathcal{B}_K$.

Proposition 5.2. *Let $K \geq 1$, there is a Monte Carlo Election algorithm for $\mathcal{B}_K$.*

Proof. Lemma 4.2 implies that there is no proper quasi-covering of radius $(K + 1)|V(D)|$ for $\mathbf{D} \in \mathcal{B}_K$. So $\mathcal{B}_K$ satisfies the condition for Theorem 2.2 with $\tau(\mathbf{D}) = (K + 1)|V(D)|$. Therefore Monte Carlo Election is possible in $\mathcal{B}_K$ for any K.

---

[1] very high probability.

References

1. Angluin, D.: Local and global properties in networks of processors. In: Proceedings of the 12th Symposium on Theory of Computing, pp. 82–93 (1980)
2. Balliu, A.: Local advice and local decompression. CoRR abs/2405.04519 (2024)
3. Boldi, P.: Symmetry breaking in anonymous networks: characterizations. In: Proceedings of the 4th Israeli Symposium on Theory of Computing and Systems, pp. 16–26. IEEE Press (1996)
4. Boldi, P., Vigna, S.: Fibrations of graphs. Discrete Math. **243**, 21–66 (2002)
5. Chalopin, J., Godard, E., Métivier, Y.: Election in partially anonymous networks with arbitrary knowledge in message passing systems. Distrib. Comput. **25**(4), 297–311 (2012)
6. Chalopin, J., Métivier, Y.: An efficient message passing election algorithm based on Mazurkiewicz's algorithm. Fundam. Inform. **80**(1–3), 221–246 (2007)
7. Chalopin, J., Godard, E.: Leveraging structural knowledge for solving election in anonymous networks with shared randomness. CoRR abs/2603.05118 (2026)
8. Codenotti, B., Gemmell, P., Pudlak, P., Simon, J.: On the amount of randomness needed in distributed computations. In: OPODIS, pp. 237–248. Hermes (1997)
9. Fraigniaud, P., Gelles, R., Lotker, Z.: The topology of randomized symmetry-breaking distributed computing. J. Appl. Comput. Topol. **8**(4), 909–940 (2024)
10. Godard, E., Métivier, Y.: A characterization of families of graphs in which election is possible. In: Nielsen, M., Engberg, U. (eds.) FoSSaCS 2002. LNCS, vol. 2303, pp. 159–171. Springer, Heidelberg (2002). https://doi.org/10.1007/3-540-45931-6_12
11. Itai, A., Rodeh, M.: Symmetry breaking in distributed networks. In: IEEE 54th Annual Symposium on Foundations of Computer Science, pp. 150–158. IEEE Computer Society (1981)
12. Itai, A., Rodeh, M.: Symmetry breaking in distributed networks. Inf. Comput. **88**(1), 60–87 (1990)
13. Kowalski, D.R., Mosteiro, M.A.: Time and communication complexity of leader election in anonymous networks. In: ICDCS, pp. 449–460. IEEE (2021)
14. LeLann, G.: Distributed systems: towards a formal approach. In: Gilchrist, B. (ed.) Information Processing 1977, pp. 155–160. North-Holland (1977)
15. Massey, W.S.: A Basic Course in Algebraic Topology. Graduate Texts in Mathematics. Springer-Verlag (1991)
16. Matias, Y., Afek, Y.: Simple and efficient election algorithms for anonymous networks. In: Bermond, J.-C., Raynal, M. (eds.) WDAG 1989. LNCS, vol. 392, pp. 183–194. Springer, Heidelberg (1989). https://doi.org/10.1007/3-540-51687-542
17. Mazurkiewicz, A.: Distributed enumeration. Inf. Proc. Lett. **61**, 233–239 (1997)
18. Métivier, Y., Muscholl, A., Wacrenier, P.-A.: About the local detection of termination of local computations in graphs. In: Krizanc, D., Widmayer, P. (eds.) SIROCCO 97, Proceedings in Informatics, pp. 188–200. Carleton Scientific (1997)
19. Métivier, Y., Robson, J.M., Zemmari, A.: Analysis of fully distributed splitting and naming probabilistic procedures and applications. Theor. Comput. Sci. **584**, 115–130 (2015)
20. Reidemeister, K.: Einführung in die Kombinatorische Topologie. Vieweg, Brunswick (1932)
21. Santoro, N.: Design and Analysis of Distributed Algorithm. Wiley (2007)
22. Schieber, B., Snir, M.: Calling names on nameless networks. Inf. Comput. **113**(1), 80–101 (1994)

23. Tanenbaum, A., van Steen, M.: Distributed Systems - Principles and Paradigms. Prentice Hall (2002)
24. Tel, G.: Introduction to Distributed Algorithms. Cambridge University Press (2000)
25. Yamashita, M., Kameda, T.: Computing on anonymous networks: part i - characterizing the solvable cases. IEEE Trans. Parallel Distrib. Syst. 7(1), 69–89 (1996)

Maintaining a Bounded Degree Expander in Dynamic Peer-to-Peer Networks

Antonio Cruciani[(✉)](ID)

Aalto University, Espoo, Finland
`antonio.cruciani@aalto.fi`

Abstract. We study the problem of maintaining robust and sparse overlay networks in fully distributed settings where nodes continuously join and leave the system. This scenario closely models real-world unstructured peer-to-peer networks, where maintaining a well-connected yet low-degree communication graph is crucial. We generalize a recent protocol by Becchetti et al. [SODA 2020], which relies on a simple randomized connection strategy to build an expander topology with high probability, to a dynamic network setting with churn. In this work, the network dynamism is governed by an oblivious adversary that controls which nodes join and leave the system in each round. The adversary has full knowledge of the system and unbounded computational power, but cannot see the random choices made by the protocol. Our analysis builds on the framework of Augustine et al. [FOCS 2015], and shows that our distributed algorithm maintains a constant-degree expander graph with high probability, despite a continuous adversarial churn with a rate of up to $\mathcal{O}(n/\log^k n)$ per round, where n is the stable network size and $k \geq 1$ is an integer. The protocol and proof techniques are not new, but together they resolve a specific open problem raised in prior work. The result is a simple, fully distributed, and churn-resilient protocol with provable guarantees that align with observed empirical behavior.

Keywords: P2P Networks · Expander Graph · Dynamic Graph

1 Introduction

In this work, we study a simple *dynamics* that builds and maintains a sparse and well-connected graph despite *adversarial churn* at each round.

As a motivating example, consider peer-to-peer (P2P) networks that underpin major blockchain systems such as Bitcoin and Ethereum, providing decentralized communication and resilience against single points of failure. These overlays are governed by strict privacy rules restricting leaks of sensitive information about peers. Compliance with such privacy rules makes it difficult to employ distributed protocols that explicitly use standard message-passing techniques. For example, in the P2P Bitcoin network, it is not possible to use random walks to "uniformly spread" node IDs (in this case IP addresses) and provide peers with a

C. Georgiou (Ed.): SIROCCO 2026, LNCS 16488, pp. 193–213, 2026.
https://doi.org/10.1007/978-3-032-26465-7_11

fresh set of uniformly random IDs from which to sample new neighbors. Indeed, after an initial bootstrap phase in which nodes rely on DNS seeds for node discovery, nodes running the Bitcoin Core implementation turn to a decentralized policy to rebuild their neighborhood when their degree drops below a configured threshold. Each node has a minimum and a maximum number of neighbors that it must maintain (respectively 8 and 125, in the default configuration), and it locally stores a large list of IP addresses of active nodes. Every time the number of current neighbors drops below the configured minimum value, it tries to form new connections to nodes sampled from its list. Such a list is periodically shared with its neighbors and updated with lists received from them. In the long run, each node samples its neighbors from a list that represents a sufficiently random subset of the network. This sampling-based mechanism, despite being decentralized and oblivious to the global structure of the network, enables the construction of a sparse and robust overlay that induces good expansion properties.

In particular, Becchetti et al. [11] formalized and analyzed a dynamic random graph model inspired by the Bitcoin protocol, showing that the resulting network converges rapidly to a constant-degree expander with high probability. Formally, in [11], the authors proposed a simple and lightweight distributed protocol that extracts an n-vertex sparse expander subgraph H from any n-vertex dense expander graph G. The algorithm seeks to maintain a network in which each node has its degree bounded between two constants d and Δ, with $d < \Delta$. Initially, each node has no neighbors in the expanding subgraph H. At each round, each node that has degree below d selects random neighbors to establish d incident edges in H and sends an edge-creation request to each of these sampled neighbors. Subsequently, upon receiving requests, each node accepts or rejects them based on a threshold rule. More precisely, it accepts all incoming requests from the current round unless doing so would result in more than Δ total requests. If the limit is exceeded, it rejects all requests received in that round. Each node in the network keeps sending requests until its degree is in the range $[d, \Delta]$. In [11] the authors showed that if the protocol is run on a dense expander graph G, then the completion time is $\mathcal{O}(\log n)$ and the computed sparse subgraph H is a good expander graph with high probability. The setting considered in [11] is static: the underlying graph does not change, leaving as an open problem the study of the process in when the graph changes over time.

In [13,14], a generalized RAES protocol is presented and empirically evaluated in a dynamic setting where nodes join and leave the network according to a stochastic churn process (more on this model in Sect. 3). Their studies revealed that, in practice, the RAES protocol succeeds in maintaining a well-connected core with good empirical expansion properties. Here, by *core* we mean a large subset of nodes such that if we consider the induced subgraph by that set of vertices we have a bounded-degree expander.

In this paper, we formally address the open question posed by Becchetti et al. [11] by adapting their RAES protocol to a model with adversarial churn. Our solution builds directly on the analytical framework developed by Augustine et al. [8], and shows that a RAES-style protocol can maintain expansion with high probability even under continuous adversarial churn. This work serves as a theoretical closure to earlier experimental studies of RAES variants under churn [14]. Our analysis formally confirms the empirical behavior observed in simulations. The result is a modest but rigorous endpoint to a research line focused on the resilience of randomized overlay networks.

2 Related Works

There has been significant prior work on designing peer-to-peer (P2P) protocols that maintain desirable graph properties such as connectivity, low diameter, and good expansion, while also supporting fundamental distributed tasks including search and storage, broadcast, agreement, and the maintenance of distributed data structures. A central challenge is to build and maintain a sparse network of peers that remains connected and robust under continuous faults and churn.

From a theoretical perspective, two models have been introduced to capture the dynamics of such networks in which nodes can continuously join and leave.

The Dynamic Network with Churn (DNC) model formalizes adversarial churn in which an oblivious adversary can add and remove nodes over time. For a comprehensive overview of this model and its algorithmic challenges, we refer to the survey [7]. Within this model, several fundamental problems have been studied, including storage and search [6], information spreading [5], leader election [3], and distributed data structure maintenance [4]. Of particular relevance, Augustine et al. [8] presented the first distributed protocol that can maintain an expander graph under continuous adversarial churn of up to $\mathcal{O}(n/\log^k n)$ nodes per round for $k > 0$. While the protocol achieves strong guarantees (ensuring that a large expander subgraph persists with high probability) it is also technically intricate, relying on a delicate combination of randomization and structural maintenance.

A complementary line of work considers stochastic churn models (see, for example, [16]), where node turnover is governed by random processes rather than an adversary. Recently, Becchetti et al. [12] introduced the streaming node-churn process, where each node has a deterministic lifetime of t rounds before leaving and being replaced by a newcomer that attaches to existing nodes via uniform random sampling. This yields a sequence of random graphs with continuous turnover, and the authors showed that such graphs preserve expansion and support efficient flooding protocols. More recently, Angileri et al. [2] studied a streaming churn process where node departures occur continuously and newcomers again connect at random. In contrast to the fixed-lifetime model of Becchetti et al., this variant captures a more stochastic form of churn, in which nodes may leave at arbitrary rounds, making it closer to real-world dynamics. They established threshold conditions under which both expansion and rumor spreading remain efficient despite persistent churn. Similarly, Angileri et al. [2] considered a simple distributed protocol to build and maintain the dynamic graph [11] (we will discuss this protocol in detail in Sect. 3). Our work considers the same simple distributed protocol but in a different dynamic environment, in which an adversary can add and remove up to $\mathcal{O}(n/\log^k n)$ nodes at each round where $k \geq 1$ is a constant.

3 Preliminaries

A *dynamic graph*[1] $\mathcal{G}$ is a family of *simple* graphs $\mathcal{G} = \{G_t = (V_t, E_t) : t \in \mathbb{N}\}$. We call G_t the *snapshot* of the dynamic graph at time t. For any two set of vertices $S, T \subseteq V_t$, $E(S, T)$ denotes the set of edges crossing the cut (S, T), that is $E(S, T) = \{(u, v) \in E_t : u \in S, v \in T\}$. For a graph $G_t = (V_t, E_t)$, its edge expansion is

$$\alpha(G_t) = \min_{\substack{S \subseteq V_t \\ 0 < |S| \leq |V_t|/2}} \frac{|E(S, V_t \setminus S)|}{|S|}.$$

We call G_t an α-(edge)-expander if $\alpha(G_t) \geq \alpha$ for a constant $\alpha > 0$. Intuitively, $\alpha(G_t)$ measures how many edges leave a set S per vertex in S in the sparsest cut: if $\alpha(G_t)$ is a constant, then every S with $|S| \leq |V_t|/2$ has $\Omega(|S|)$ edges to $V_t \setminus S$, ruling out bottlenecks and ensuring strong connectivity. In particular, in bounded-degree graphs, constant edge expansion is a standard notion of being "expander-like".

The Dynamic Network with Churn Model. We consider a synchronous dynamic network controlled by an *oblivious* adversary. The adversary fixes in advance the entire churn sequence. The network size is stable: $|V_t| = n$ for all t. Each node has a unique identifier from a universe of size $\mathrm{Poly}(n)$. For the first $B = \Theta(\log n)$ rounds no churn occurs, i.e., $V_1 = \cdots = V_B$. During these rounds, the protocol starts from an empty overlay with n nodes and runs a specific distributed protocol to construct an initial bounded-degree expander overlay. This assumption is standard in the *Dynamic Network with Churn (DNC)* model (see, e.g., [8,9]), and prevents the adversary from isolating new nodes completely.

Intuitively, *churn* captures how many nodes leave and join the system from one round to the next: an adversary may delete up to m nodes and insert up to m new nodes per round (so the network size stays n), but the identities and incident edges of churned nodes can change arbitrarily. Formally, in each round t, it removes a set $C_{\mathrm{out}} \subseteq V_{t-1}$ and inserts a set C_{in} with $|C_{\mathrm{out}}| = |C_{\mathrm{in}}| \leq m$, where $m \in \mathcal{O}(n/\log^k n)$ for a fixed constant $k > 0$, and the network size is stable: $V_t = (V_{t-1} \setminus C_{\mathrm{out}}) \cup C_{\mathrm{in}}$ with $|V_t| = n$. When a node $u \in C_{\mathrm{in}}$ joins, before it can use the sampling primitive the adversary may initialize overlay edges incident to u, subject to the degree bound Δ; in particular, the adversary may choose the initial neighbors of u so that u starts with degree in $[d, \Delta]$. In addition, we require the adversary to ensure that each new node must be connected to at least one node already present in the network at time t, i.e. a node in $V_{t-1} \setminus C_{\mathrm{out}}$. Whenever a node $u \in V_t$ needs to create new overlay edges, it can sample a node ID uniformly at random from V_t.

Our goal is to design a simple distributed protocol that maintains a graph process $\mathcal{G} = \{G_t = (V_t, E_t) : t \geq 1\}$, such that for every $t \geq B$, the snapshot G_t has, with high probability, edge expansion bounded below a constant $\alpha > 0$

---

[1] In this paper we will use dynamic-graph and dynamic-network interchangeably.

while respecting degree constraints $d \leq d(u) \leq \Delta$ for all $u \in V_t$, where $d(u)$ is the degree of node $u \in V_t$ and d and Δ are fixed constants with $d < \Delta$. Throughout, we assume that at every round t, nodes can sample vertices uniformly at random from V_t.

Remark. Although the assumption that a node can pick its neighbors uniformly at random among all nodes of the network is unrealistic in many scenarios, the edge-creation process in our model is reminiscent of the way some unstructured peer-to-peer networks such as the Bitcoin Network maintain a "random" topology. This assumption matches the random-oracle style models in prior work (e.g., [11,12,14]), and can later be replaced by almost-uniform random walk sampling as in [8,9].

The RAES Protocol. Intuitively, *RAES (Request a link, then Accept if Enough Space)* [11] is a local "rewiring" process: nodes that fall below the minimum degree proactively contact random peers to create new edges, while nodes that receive too many requests selectively accept/drop edges to keep degrees bounded. This constant-degree random rewiring is what preserves expansion over time. Formally, RAES is a random graph model defined by three parameters $n \in \mathbb{N}, d \in \{1, \ldots, n-1\}, c > 1$, in which each one of n nodes has degree at least d and at most $cd = \Delta$. The random graph is generated according to the discrete random process described in Algorithm 1. The process terminates when all nodes have degree in $[d, \Delta]$.

Algorithm 1: Overview of a RAES-style protocol.

---

1 Let $G = (V, \{\emptyset\})$.
2 **foreach** $t \geq 0$ **do**
3   **Phase 1 (reconnection):** Each node u with degree $d(u) < d$ picks $d - d(u)$ new neighbors uniformly at random and sends them a connection request.
4   **Phase 2 (degree adjustment):** Each node u with degree $d(u) > \Delta$ selects $d(u) - \Delta$ neighbors uniformly at random and drops the connections to them.
5 **end**

The RAES model can be seen as a simplified version of the network-formation process implemented in Bitcoin-core [1,15]. The protocol converges in $\mathcal{O}(\log n)$ rounds to an expander graph with high probability [11]. However, this is not guaranteed to happen when nodes continuously join and leave the network. Recently, Angileri et al. [2] analyzed RAES in the streaming churn model and proved that it still maintains good expansion properties. Our results differ in that we show RAES remains resilient even against an adversary capable of applying churn of up to $\mathcal{O}(n/\log^k n)$ nodes per round.

4   Our Contribution

We address the problem of defining a variation of the RAES protocol that can build and maintain a dynamic expander graph despite an adversarial churn of $\mathcal{O}(n/\log^k n)$ at each round. Our construction relies on periodic randomized neighbor refreshing and pruning of high-degree nodes, and remains lightweight in terms of memory and messaging overhead. Our solution tackles the major open problem in [11] by building directly on the framework developed by Augustine et al. [8]. More precisely, our results can be summarized as follows:

- **The D-RAES Protocol.** We introduce D-RAES, a dynamic extension of RAES that incorporates a simple periodic randomized *edge-refreshing* step.
- **Necessity of edge refreshing.** We show that without the refreshing phase, an adversary can gradually erode the expansion of the network while keeping all degrees within $[d, \Delta]$ (Theorem 1). This shows that randomized refreshing of links is not only natural, but also *necessary* for preserving a well-connected P2P network.
- **Expander maintenance under churn.** Using the Υ-process framework of Augustine et al. [8], we show that D-RAES maintains an $(n - o(n))$-sized expander core with constant degree and constant expansion, despite continuous adversarial churn of up to $\mathcal{O}(n/\log^k n)$ nodes per round (Theorem 2).
- **Validation of prior empirical findings.** More broadly, our results (similarly to what showed in [2]) confirm the empirical findings in [13,14] and show that a RAES-like approach can maintain a constant-degree expander graph despite adversarial churn.

In what follows, we provide an overview of the main results.

The D-RAES Protocol. We now introduce D-RAES, a dynamic extension of the RAES protocol that is resilient to a continuous adversarial churn of up to $\mathcal{O}(n/\log^k n)$ nodes per round. The execution of the protocol is divided into two main phases: a bootstrap phase and a maintenance phase. During the bootstrap phase, the goal is to construct a bounded-degree expander graph. In the maintenance phase, the protocol continually repairs and adapts the network in response to churn events. The bootstrap phase begins with a graph of n nodes and no edges. We run the RAES protocol (Algorithm 1) for $B = \mathcal{O}(\log n)$ rounds. As shown in [11], this results in an expander graph whp. (see Theorem 2.1 in [11]). After this phase, the adversary is allowed to churn nodes, and each node executes a maintenance cycle composed of three phases (Algorithm 2).

The high-level idea of the protocol is that each node seeks to maintain a bounded-degree graph by keeping its degree between two parameters d and Δ, where $d < \Delta$. This simple procedure mimics the behavior of the Bitcoin network-formation process [1]. We require nodes that are not churned out by the adversary to refresh their neighbor lists with probability $1/\log^k n$. This prevents an oblivious adversary from incrementally building structures that gradually degrade,

---

Algorithm 2: Overview of the D-RAES protocol.

---

1 Let G be the graph obtained after the Bootstrap Phase.

2 **foreach** $t > B$ **do**

3   **Phase 1 (refresh neighbors):** With probability $1/\log^k n$, each node u with degree $d(u) \in [d, \Delta]$ drops all its neighbors.

4   **Phase 2 (reconnection):** Each node u with degree $d(u) < d$ picks $d - d(u)$ new neighbors uniformly at random.

5   **Phase 3 (degree adjustment):** Each node u with degree $d(u) > \Delta$ selects $d(u) - \Delta$ neighbors uniformly at random and drops the connections to them.

6 **end**

---

and ultimately destroy, expansion. Thus, on average, nodes refresh their neighborhoods every polylog(n) rounds. Indeed, the authors in [13, 14] experimentally showed that refreshing long-lasting edges may help the process recover after churn. The protocol reconnects when a node's number of neighbors falls below d: it infers that it is no longer well-connected and tries to sample new random neighbors from the network. In addition, the protocol preserves bounded degrees by "pruning" neighbors of nodes that exceed Δ.

As mentioned above, our goal is to keep the network close to a random constant-degree graph at every round, w.h.p. Throughout, we fix the degree parameters d and Δ as constants with $d < \Delta$. Beyond reconnections triggered by lost edges, in every round each node independently deletes all its edges and reconnects with probability $\Theta(1/\log^k n)$. This refreshing step continuously creates new "random enough" edges in the network, which is useful for showing expansion properties in each round. Moreover, without such a phase in the protocol (or an analogous step), it is impossible to maintain a constant-degree expander graph under adversarial churn.

Theorem 1. *Assume that after the bootstrap phase, the graph G_t is a constant-degree expander in which every node has degree in $[d, \Delta]$, where d and Δ are suitable constants with $3 \leq d < \Delta$ and $\Delta \geq 2d$. Suppose that the maintenance protocol does not include an edge-refreshing phase. Then there is an adversarial strategy with a churn budget of $m = \Theta(n/\log^k n)$ that (1) maintains a constant-degree graph in which each node has degree in $[d, \Delta]$ and (2) makes the graph no longer an expander.*

Proof. We define a multi-round adversarial strategy that constructs a set S of size $s = \Theta(n/\log^k n)$ whose edge expansion becomes $o(1)$ if the maintenance protocol has no edge-refreshing phase.

Let $c = \Delta - d$. Since $\Delta \geq 2d$ and $d \geq 3$, we have $3 \leq d \leq c$. We build S in $\tau = \Theta(\log s)$ rounds by inserting disjoint layers $S_1, S_2, \ldots, S_\tau$ with $|S_1| = d$, and $|S_j| = c|S_{j-1}| = dc^{j-1}$ for $j \geq 2$. Let $S^{(j)} = \bigcup_{i=1}^{j} S_i$ and $\sigma_j = |S^{(j)}|$. Then $\sigma_j = \sum_{i=1}^{j} dc^{i-1} \leq d \cdot \frac{c^j}{c-1}$, and $\sigma_\tau = \Theta(dc^\tau) = \Theta(s) = \Theta(n/\log^k n)$. In each round j we churn in exactly $|S_j|$ nodes and churn out exactly $|S_j|$ nodes, so the per-round churn is at most $|S_\tau| = dc^{\tau-1} = \Theta(s) = \Theta(n/\log^k n)$. Fix in advance a disjoint set $R_0 \subseteq R = V \setminus S$ of size $|R_0| = d + \sum_{j=1}^{\tau} |S_j| = d + \sigma_\tau$, and an arbitrary partition $R_0 = R_0^{(0)} \sqcup R_0^{(1)} \sqcup \cdots \sqcup R_0^{(\tau)}$ with $|R_0^{(0)}| = d$ and $|R_0^{(j)}| = |S_j|$ for $1 \leq j \leq \tau$. The adversary will churn out $R_0^{(j)}$ in round j (and churn in S_j), independently of the algorithm's random choices. In round 1 the adversary churns in S_1 and churns out $R_0^{(1)}$. To satisfy the model requirement, the adversary connects each $u \in S_1$ to a distinct node in $R_0^{(0)}$ (one edge per u), and wires the remaining $d - 1$ incident edges of each u inside S_1 so that every node in S_1 has degree exactly d.

For each round $j = 2, 3, \ldots, \tau$, the adversary churns in S_j and churns out $R_0^{(j)}$. It then assigns exactly c children in S_j to each parent $u \in S_{j-1}$. For every new node $v \in S_j$, the adversary creates exactly one edge from v to its parent in S_{j-1}, and wires the remaining $d - 1$ incident edges of v inside S_j so that every $v \in S_j$ has degree exactly d. Consequently, each parent $u \in S_{j-1}$ gains exactly c additional incident edges, so its degree becomes $d + c = \Delta$ after round j and it never takes further children. Thus, throughout the construction every node in $S^{(j)}$ has degree in $[d, \Delta]$ and never drops below d, hence nodes in $S^{(j)}$ never invoke the reconnection phase.

When $R_0^{(j)}$ is churned out in round j, at most $\Delta|S_j|$ edges are deleted, so at most $\Delta|S_j|$ surviving nodes in R may lose at least one neighbor. Each such node can create at most Δ reconnection requests, hence the total number of reconnection requests in round j is at most $\Delta^2|S_j|$. Each request samples its other endpoint uniformly from V, and therefore hits the current set $S^{(j)}$ with probability σ_j/n. Let Y_j be the number of reconnection edges created in round j whose endpoint lies in $S^{(j)}$. Conditioned on the (deterministic) upper bound $\Delta^2|S_j|$ on the number of requests, Y_j is stochastically dominated by a binomial random variable with parameters $\Delta^2|S_j|$ and σ_j/n, and thus

$$\mathbf{E}[Y_j] \leq \Delta^2|S_j| \cdot \frac{\sigma_j}{n} \leq \Delta^2(dc^{j-1}) \cdot \frac{dc^j}{(c-1)n} = \mathcal{O}\left(\frac{c^{2j}}{n}\right).$$

Let $Y = \sum_{j=1}^{\tau} Y_j$. Summing the geometric series gives $\mathbf{E}[Y] = \mathcal{O}\left(\frac{c^{2\tau}}{n}\right)$.

Since $\sigma_\tau = \Theta(dc^\tau) = \Theta(s)$, we have $c^{2\tau} = \Theta(s^2)$ and hence $\mathbf{E}[Y] = \mathcal{O}\left(\frac{s^2}{n}\right) = \mathcal{O}\left(\frac{n}{\log^{2k} n}\right)$. Moreover, Y is dominated by a sum of independent Bernoulli trials, so a standard Chernoff bound implies $Y = \mathcal{O}\left(\frac{n}{\log^{2k} n}\right)$ w.h.p.

The only *forced* edges crossing the cut $(S^{(\tau)}, R)$ are the d initial edges from S_1 to $R_0^{(0)}$; all other crossing edges arise from accidental reconnections counted in Y plus a ΔY additional factor that takes care of additional reconnections. Therefore, w.h.p.,

$$|E(S^{(\tau)}, R)| \leq d + Y + \Delta Y = \mathcal{O}(1) + \mathcal{O}\left(\frac{n}{\log^{2k} n}\right)$$

Recalling $|S^{(\tau)}| = \sigma_\tau = \Theta(n/\log^k n)$, we obtain

$$\frac{|E(S^{(\tau)}, R)|}{|S^{(\tau)}|} \leq \mathcal{O}\left(\frac{\log^k n}{n}\right) + \mathcal{O}\left(\frac{1}{\log^k n}\right) = o(1)$$

w.h.p. $\square$

In particular, the above theorem applies to any maintenance protocol whose actions are limited to (i) adding edges only for nodes with degree below d and (ii) deleting edges only for nodes with degree above Δ (i.e., Algorithm 2 without Phase 1), and hence it is not specific to RAES.

The graph produced after each iteration of Algorithm 2 (lines 2–6), is the result of the interaction between two entities: the oblivious adversary and Algorithm 2. To analyze the distributed protocol behavior under churn, we use the same approach of Augustine et al. [8] and we define a family of processes whose behavior is: (1) the adversary's move; (2) the actions by the nodes; and, (3) the random bits available to the process itself. As in [8], we refer to a member of this family of processes as the Υ-process.

Overview of the Process. We present a high-level description of the process and intuitions behind its analysis and we refer to Sect. 5 for a complete description and analysis of the process. The main idea is that the process captures both, the distributed protocol's and the adversary's actions by first applying the adversarial churn to the graph and then steps (1–3) in Algorithm 2 at each round. We have that the Υ-process starts from a bounded degree expander graph that was created during the bootstrap phase. At each iteration it generates a new graph $G_t = (V_t, E_t)$, given the graph at $t-1$. The process ensures that nodes with a degree less than d and a life-span greater than $\Omega(\log n)$ will gain at least once a degree between d and Δ in $\mathcal{O}(\log n)$ rounds. Moreover, to argue that at each round we have a large expander subgraph we have to take into account that: (1) the (adversarial) churn is $\mathcal{O}(n/\log^k n)$, (2) the number of nodes that choose to refresh their neighborhood is $\mathcal{O}(n/\log^k n)$ whp., and (3) the number of "unlucky" nodes that after the reconnection phase had degree exactly d and that after the degree adjustment phase lost some neighbors (due to some highly connected node with degree greater than Δ dropping a random subset of their neighbors) is $\mathcal{O}(n/\log^k n)$ whp. By iteratively using the results by Bagchi et al. in [10], the fact that nodes sample from a uniform distribution over V_t and that no node can have degree less than d for $\Omega(\log n)$ consecutive rounds whp. we can argue that at the end of each iteration t, the Υ-process produces a graph G_t that contains a large core with good expansion properties. This result implies that the D-RAES protocol maintains a graph with a $(n - o(n))$-sized constant expander subgraph in which all the nodes have degree between d and Δ. Our main result can be summarized as follows.

Theorem 2 (Main Theorem). *Let d and Δ be two suitable constants such that $d < \Delta$. Despite an adversarial churn rate of $\mathcal{O}(n/\log^k n)$ for any $k \geq 1$, the D-RAES protocol maintains a dynamic graph $\mathcal{G} = \{G_t = (V_t, E_t)\}_{t \geq 1}$ such that, with high probability, for at least n^c rounds (for any arbitrarily large constant $c \geq 1$), each snapshot G_t contains a connected subgraph C_t on $n - o(n)$ nodes that satisfies: (1) each node in C_t has degree in $[d, \Delta]$; and, (2) C_t has edge expansion of at least α, for some constant $\alpha > 0$.*

5   The Υ-Process for Simple Expander Maintenance

Algorithm 3: Overview of the Υ-process

---

1 Let $G_1 - (V_1, E_1)$ be a graph obtained after the bootstrap phase of length $\Theta(\log n)$, such that: (1) G_1 is a bounded-degree expander with edge expansion $\alpha > 0$; (2) Every node $u \in V_1$ has degree in the range $d \leq d(u) \leq \Delta$.

2 **for** $t = 2, 3, 4, \ldots$ **do**

    // Churn

3   A set $C_{\text{out}} \subseteq V_{t-1}$ of at most $O(n/\log^k n)$ nodes is removed.

4   A set C_{in} of the same size is added.

5   Define $V_t = (V_{t-1} \setminus C_{\text{out}}) \cup C_{\text{in}}$.

6   Let $F_t = \{(u, v) \in F_{t-1} \mid u, v \in V_t\}$.

    // Edge Refresh Phase

7   **foreach** $v \in V_t \setminus C_{in}$ **do**

8   Node v independently drops all of its incident edges with probability $1/\log^k n$.

9   **end**

    // Connection Phase

10   **while** $\exists v \in V_t$ with $d(v) < d$ **do**

11   Sample a node u uniformly at random from $V_t \setminus N(v)$, and add the edge (v, u) to E_t.

12   **end**

    // Degree-Adjusting Phase

13   **while** $\exists v \in V_t$ with $d(v) > \Delta$ **do**

14   Sample a node u uniformly at random from $N(v)$, and remove the edge (v, u) from E_t.

15   **end**

    // Finalize graph

16   Set $G_t = (V_t, E_t)$.

17 **end**

As stated above, the main idea behind the Υ-process is that it captures the actions of both the distributed protocol and the adversary. The Υ-process starts from a bounded-degree expander graph created during a bootstrap phase of $\Theta(\log n)$ rounds. At each iteration of the for-loop (lines 2–17), it generates a new graph $G_t = (V_t, E_t)$ from G_{t-1}.

Our goal is to show that (i) the sequence $(G_t)_{t\geq 1}$ consists of expander graphs and (ii) the execution of the maintenance protocol (right after the bootstrap phase) can be viewed as a Υ-process. To this end, for all $t \geq 1$, the graph output by the Υ-process at round t corresponds to G_{t+B}, the graph output by the D-RAES protocol in round $t + B$. Moreover, in each G_t, all nodes have degree at most Δ, and a subgraph of G_t contains nodes with degree in $[d, \Delta]$.

The main invariant maintained by the protocol is the degree of each node. If a node's degree falls below the threshold d (due to churn), the protocol creates new incident edges until its degree is at least d. If a node's degree exceeds Δ, it drops some neighbors so that its degree falls back into the allowed range $[d, \Delta]$. As mentioned before, the protocol aims to keep the graph close to a random bounded-degree graph in every round w.h.p. Thus, in addition to reconnections caused by churn, in every round each node drops all its neighbors and reconnects with probability $\Theta(1/\log^k n)$. This refreshing step periodically injects new random edges into the graph.

Let $\hat{V} \subseteq V_t$ be the set of nodes that have degree less than d, such that $C_{\mathrm{in}} \subseteq \hat{V}$, $|\hat{V}| = \mathcal{O}(n/\log^{k-1} n)$, and $\hat{V}$ contains only nodes that in the past $\Theta(\log n)$ rounds were not part of any such set $\hat{V}$. Lemma 3 shows that the Υ-process guarantees that no node remains trapped in $\hat{V}$ for more than $\Omega(\log n)$ contiguous rounds. Consequently, each node attains a degree between d and Δ within $\mathcal{O}(\log n)$ rounds. Moreover, lines 10–15 guarantee that the process creates new edges by picking their endpoints uniformly at random from the current vertex set. This ensures that the graph remains "sufficiently random." To show that the graphs generated by the Υ-process contain a large core with good expansion, we use two facts: (1) adversarially removing $\mathcal{O}(n/\log^k n)$ nodes from an expander graph leaves a large expander subgraph; and (2) the number of nodes with degree less than d after the reconnection phase (lines 10–15) is bounded by $\mathcal{O}(n/\log^k n)$ w.h.p.

5.1   Analysis of the Υ-Process

We start our analysis by showing that a graph built and maintained by a Υ-process is an expander graph. It suffices to show that a graph in which each node has between d and Δ edges, generated by sampling endpoints uniformly at random from the vertex set, has edge expansion at least some constant $\alpha' > 0$. This can be seen as an alternative proof of Theorem 2.2 in [11], showing that a random graph with degrees in $[d, \Delta]$ enjoys good expansion properties.

Theorem 3. *Let $G = (V, E)$ be a random graph on n vertices formed by the following random process. Each node $u \in V$ creates d neighbors choosing them from V with probability $1/n$, and each node u that has degree $d(u)$ greater than Δ drops $d(u) - \Delta$ neighbors uniformly at random. (Hence, each node has degree at most Δ.) Then, with high probability, G has expansion at least α', where $\alpha' > 0$ is a suitable constant.*

Proof. The proof of this theorem follows the same steps of the proof of expansion in [8]. Let S be a subset of size s. We upper-bound the probability that too

204   A. Cruciani

many edges incident at S have their end within S itself. We first need to show that $|E(S,\overline{S})| \geq \alpha'|S|$. Since nodes in S have degree at least d, we have that $d|S| = |E(S,\overline{S})| + |E(S,S)|$. Where $|E(S,S)|$ is the set of edges in S that have both endpoints in S. Thus we require $d|S| - |E(S,S)| \geq \alpha'|S|$, and we need to upper bound $\mathbf{Pr}(|E(S,S)| \geq (d-\alpha')|S|)$. To this end, let $\gamma = d - \alpha'$, and let $e_1,\ldots,e_{sd}$ be the edges leaving S. We know that each endpoint of edges e at node v has uniform probability to be any node of the set V, which consists of n nodes in the graph. Define X_i to be the random variable that is 1 if the i-th edge e_i of S starting in $u_i \in S$ has its other endpoint inside S.

The upper bound for the probability that an edge falls back into S is s/n. Since the probability that e endpoints to a specific node in S is at most $1/n$, we can sum up over all elements of S to bound the probability that e points to a node in S by s/n. Now, conditioning on the event that $X_1 = 1,\ldots,X_{t-1} = 1$, decreases the number of available connection points for e inside S. Thus, we have

$$\mathbf{Pr}\left(X_t = 1 \;\Big|\; \bigcap_{i=1}^{t-1}\{X_i = 1\} \right) \leq \frac{s}{n}$$

for any $2 \leq t \leq sd$. By the chain rule of conditional probability, we obtain

$$\mathbf{Pr}\left(\bigcap_{i=1}^{t}\{X_i = 1\} \right) = \mathbf{Pr}\left(X_t = 1 \;\Big|\; \bigcap_{i=1}^{t-1}\{X_i = 1\} \right) \cdot \mathbf{Pr}\left(\bigcap_{i=1}^{t-1}\{X_i = 1\} \right) =$$

$$\mathbf{Pr}(X_1 = 1) \prod_{i=2}^{t} \mathbf{Pr}\left(X_i = 1 \;\Big|\; \prod_{j=1}^{i-1} X_j = 1 \right) \leq \left(\frac{s}{n}\right)^{t}$$

Now we bound the probability that at least $s\gamma$ of the sd indicators are 1. If $\sum_{i=1}^{sd} X_i \geq s\gamma$, then there exists a subset $I \subseteq \{1,\ldots,sd\}$ with $|I| = s\gamma$ such that $X_i = 1$ for all $i \in I$. There are $\binom{sd}{s\gamma}$ choices for I, and for each fixed I, by the bound above (and since conditioning can only decrease availability), $\mathbf{Pr}\left(\bigcap_{i \in I}\{X_i = 1\} \right) \leq \left(\frac{s}{n}\right)^{s\gamma}$. Therefore, by a union bound, $\mathbf{Pr}\left(\sum_{i=1}^{sd} X_i \geq s\gamma \right) \leq \binom{sd}{s\gamma}\left(\frac{s}{n}\right)^{s\gamma}$. Finally, taking a union bound over all $\binom{n}{s}$ choices of S yields

$$\mathbf{Pr}\left(\exists S : |S| = s \wedge |E(S,S)| \geq s\gamma \right) \leq \binom{n}{s}\binom{sd}{s\gamma}\left(\frac{s}{n}\right)^{s\gamma}.$$

We upper bound the above inequality as follows: for sets of size $s \in o(n)$ we have

$$\binom{n}{s}\binom{sd}{s\gamma}\left(\frac{s}{n}\right)^{s\gamma} \leq \left(\frac{en}{s}\right)^{s}\left(\frac{esd}{s\gamma}\right)^{s\gamma}\left(\frac{1}{n}\right)^{s\gamma} = \left(\frac{e}{s}\right)^{s} s^{s\gamma}\left(\frac{ed}{\gamma}\right)^{s\gamma} n^{s(1-\gamma)} =$$

$$e^{s} s^{s(\gamma-1)} n^{s(1-\gamma)}\left(\frac{ed}{\gamma}\right)^{s\gamma} = 2^{\beta' s} 2^{s(\gamma-1)\log s} 2^{s(1-\gamma)\log n} 2^{\beta\gamma s} =$$

$$2^{s(\beta' + \beta\gamma + (\gamma-1)\log s + (1-\gamma)\log n)}$$

Where $\beta = \log(d \cdot e/\gamma)$ and $\beta' = \log_2 e$. To show that this inequality holds, we notice that the term $(1 - \gamma) \log n$ in the exponent dominates and yields an upper bound of $2^{-\ell_s \log n} = 1/n^{\ell_s}$ for sufficiently large d.

In the second case, the size $s = h \cdot n$ where $h \leq 1/2$, we can approximate the binomial coefficient $\binom{n}{k}$ with $2^{nH(k/n)}$ where $H(x) = -x \log_2(x) - (1-x) \log_2(1-x)$ is the binary entropy function of x and we can upper bound the inequality as

$$\binom{n}{s} \binom{sd}{s\gamma} \left(\frac{s}{n}\right)^{s\gamma} \leq$$
$$2^{n(-h \log(h) - (1-h) \log(1-h) - hd(\gamma/d) \log(\gamma/d) + (1-\gamma/d) \log(1-\gamma/d)) + \log(\beta)\gamma h}$$

Where in this case $\beta = s/n$.

The quantity

$$(-h \log(h) - (1 - h) \log(1 - h) - hd(\gamma/d) \log(\gamma/d) + (1 - \gamma/d) \log(1 - \gamma/d))$$

will be negative for all values of $h \leq 1/2$ for sufficiently large constant values of h. Thus,

$$\mathbf{Pr}(\exists S\,,\, |S| = s \wedge |E(S,S)| \geq (d - \alpha')hn) \leq 2^{-n}$$

this is much smaller than $1/n^{\ell}$ for any constant value of ℓ. Thus, over all s we can choose $\max_s \ell_s$ and set the constant degree d appropriately so that $\ell_s \geq 4$. Thus over all $\Theta(n)$ set sizes $s \in [1, n/2]$, with probability at least $(1 - 1/n^3)$ the graph G has and edge expansion α'. $\qquad\square$

In order to show that after every churn the resulting graph contains an expanding *core*, we make use of the following adaptation of Theorem 2.1 in [10] proposed by Augustine et al. in [8].

Lemma 1 (Adaptation of Theorem 2.1 in [10]). *Let G be a n-node graph with expansion α and constant degree d and suppose that all nodes in a set F are removed from G, where $|F| = o(n)$. Then, for any positive constant $c < 1$, there exists a subgraph H of G such that (1) H has expansion $c \cdot \alpha$ and (2)* $|H| \geq n - |F| \left(1 + \frac{1}{\alpha(1-c)}\right).$

The above lemma implies that any n-node bounded-degree expander graph with constant edge expansion α will, after a churn of $\mathcal{O}(n/\log^k n)$ nodes, contain a large subset of nodes H that induces an expander subgraph.

At each round t, every node independently erases its neighbor list with probability $1/\log^k n$ and selects d new neighbors uniformly at random from V_t. This random edge refresh step does not affect the expansion of the well-connected core of the graph. In particular, Lemma 1 ensures that with high probability, there will be a good expanding subset of nodes even after the edge refresh step. Indeed, on average, this step causes $n/\log^k n$ nodes to drop their whole neighborhood and initiate new connections, thereby introducing $d \cdot n/\log^k n$ new edges into the network. While this process contributes to re-randomizing the edge set and counteracts the adversarial action, it can also induce some side effects. For instance, nodes whose degree exceeds Δ will prune their connections to restore their local bounded-degree structure, which might inadvertently remove edges within the expanding core. Additionally, some nodes in H may have degree exactly d, and if they lose neighbors during this process, their degree may fall below d, causing them to lose their local bounded-degree property.

Therefore, it is crucial to show that the number of nodes whose degree drops below d due to the degree adjustment phase (Phase 3 in Algorithm 2 and lines 13–15 in Algorithm 3) remains small. We argue that this effect is negligible w.h.p. and does not significantly impact the expansion properties of the core subgraph H.

Lemma 2. *Let $G_t = (V_t, E_t)$ be the graph at round t of the D-RAES protocol, where each node has degree in $[d, \Delta]$ and $d < \Delta$ are fixed constants. Then, with high probability:*

1. *The number of nodes whose degree falls below d after the pruning phase (due to being dropped by a neighbor while having degree exactly d) is at most $\mathcal{O}(n/\log^k n)$.*
2. *The resulting graph contains a core of size $n - o(n)$ that maintains edge expansion $\alpha' > 0$ with high probability.*

Proof. We split the analysis into three steps: first, we upper-bound the number of nodes with degree greater than Δ, subsequently, we show that the number of nodes that have degree less than d after the degree-adjustment phase of Algorithm 3 is upper-bounded by $\mathcal{O}(n/\log^k n)$. Finally, we show that there exists a big "core" that preserves a good edge expansion.

Step 1: Bounding the Number of High-Degree Nodes. Let $R_t \subseteq V_t$ be the set of nodes that refresh their neighbors in round t, each independently and with probability $1/\log^k n$. Then, $\mathbf{E}[|R_t|] = \frac{n}{\log^k n}$. Using the Chernoff bound $\mathbf{Pr}(X > (1+\delta)\mu) \leq \exp\left(-\frac{\delta^2 \mu}{3}\right)$ where $\mu = \mathbf{E}[|R_t|]$ and $\delta = 1$ we have that $\mathbf{Pr}\left(|R_t| > \frac{2n}{\log^k n}\right) \leq \exp\left(-\frac{n}{3\log^k n}\right)$ thus for sufficiently large values of n and $k \geq 2$ with probability at least $1 - 1/n^c$ for $c \geq 2$ we have $|R_t| \leq 2n/\log^k n$.

Each node in R_t initiates d connection requests to nodes chosen uniformly at random. So the total number of new connection requests is $T \leq 2dn/\log^k n$. For any node $v \in V_t$, let Y_v denote the number of new connection requests v receives. Then $Y_v \sim \mathrm{Bin}(T, 1/n)$ and $\mathbf{E}[Y_v] = \frac{T}{n} \leq \frac{2d}{\log^k n} = o(1)$. Since d is constant. Thus we have that only a $\mathcal{O}(1/\log^k n)$ fraction of nodes can exceed Δ. This is not a problem, since Phase 3 of the protocol "prunes" these high-degree nodes. Similarly, using a balls into bins argument we can bound the maximum number of connection requests a node receives and (eventually) might prune in the degree reduction phase. The following claim will be useful for the next step of the proof.

Claim 1. Let $T \leq C n / \log^k n$ for some constant $C \geq 1$ be the total number of new connection requests in the round, thrown u.a.r. over V_t. For $v \in V_t$, let $Y_v \sim \text{Bin}(T, 1/n)$ be the number of requests that target v, and let $Y_{\max} = \max_v Y_v$. Then, for $L_n = \frac{(k+3)\log n}{\log \log n}$, we have $\mathbf{Pr}\left(Y_{\max} \geq L_n\right) \leq n^{-3}$ for all n large enough. Consequently, during the degree adjusting phase each node u can drop up to $r_u = d(u) - \Delta \leq d + Y_u \leq d + L_n$ with probability at least $1 - n^{-3}$.

Proof (Proof of Claim 5.1.). For each v, with $\mu = \mathbf{E}[Y_v] = T/n \leq 2d / \log^k n$ and any $L \geq 1$, a standard Chernoff bound gives $\mathbf{Pr}\left(Y_v \geq L\right) \leq \left(\frac{e\mu}{L}\right)^L$. Thus by union bound,

$$\mathbf{Pr}\left(Y_{\max} \geq L\right) \leq n \cdot \left(\tfrac{e\mu}{L}\right)^L = \exp\left(\log n + L(1 + \log \mu - \log L) \right).$$

With $L = L_n$ we have

$$\mathbf{Pr}\left(Y_{\max} \geq L_n\right) \leq \exp\left(\log n - (k+1)(k+3)\log n + o(\log n) \right)$$

$$= \exp\left(-((k+1)(k+3) - 1)\log n + o(\log n) \right) \leq n^{-3}.$$

for large enough n (since for $k \geq 1$, $(k+1)(k+3) - 1 \geq 7$). Finally, we observe that at the start of the round every node has degree at most Δ, then after the churn and the edge refresh phase we have that nodes in the graph can send at most d new link requests and that can receive Y_u new request from other nodes. So, the degree of each node u is bounded by $d(u) \leq \Delta + d + Y_u$ and the number of neighbors it has to drop in the degree reduction step is

$$r_u = d(u) - \Delta \leq d + Y_u \leq d + L_n$$

whp for each node u. $\qquad\square$

Step 2: Bounding Nodes Dropped Below Degree d. Let $F = \{u \in V_t : d(u) > \Delta\}$ the set of overfull vertices after the reconnection phase and $m = \sum_{u \in F} r_u$ where $r_u = d(u) - \Delta$. To upper bound m, for a node u consider the number of connection requests initiated and received after the churn event, let them be S_u and Y_u respectively. Clearly $S_u \leq d$ and $Y_u \leq T$ therefore (from Step 1) $m \leq 2T = \mathcal{O}(\frac{n}{\log^k n})$. Next, for each $u \in F$, let π_u be an independent uniform random permutation of $N(u)$, and let the pruning phase drop the first r_u elements of π_u. Fix any $U \subseteq V_t$ such that each node in U has degree exactly d before the degree adjustment phase and define

$$X = \sum_{u \in F} \sum_{j=1}^{r_u} \mathbf{1}\{\pi_u(j) \in U\}.$$

X counts the number of edges dropped by nodes in F that share one endpoint in U. Let D be the number of *distinct* vertices in U that are "hit" by the pruning step, then it holds $D \leq X$.

We condition on the event $\mathcal{E} = \{Y_{\max} \leq L_n\}$ from Claim 1, which holds with probability $\mathbf{Pr}(\mathcal{E}) \geq 1 - n^{-3}$ for all large n. On $\mathcal{E}$ we have $r_u \leq d + L_n$ for all u; hence

$$\sum_{u \in F} r_u^2 \leq (\max_{u \in F} r_u) \sum_{u \in F} r_u \leq (d + L_n) \sum_{u \in F} r_u = (d + L_n) m. \qquad (1)$$

Observe that changing a π_u for some $u \in F$ affects X by at most r_u. Thus we can say that X is r_u–Lipschitz per node. Fix all the random choices made up to the degree-adjusting phase, let us call them A. Conditioned on these choices, the randomness left is in the independent permutations. To this end, we consider $\mu = \mathbf{E}[X \mid A]$ and apply McDiarmid's inequality for any $\lambda > 0$,

$$\mathbf{Pr}\left(|X - \mu| \geq \lambda\right) \leq \mathbf{Pr}\left(|X - \mu| \geq \lambda \wedge \mathcal{E}\right) + \mathbf{Pr}\left(\neg \mathcal{E}\right)$$

$$\leq 2 \exp\left(-\frac{2\lambda^2}{\sum_{u \in F} r_u^2}\right) + n^{-3} \leq 2 \exp\left(-\frac{2\lambda^2}{(d + L_n)m}\right) + n^{-3}.$$

Where the last step uses (1). Furthermore, $X \leq \sum_{u \in F} r_u = m$, and given Step 1 we have that $X = \mathcal{O}(n/\log^k n)$ whp. Now, the probability that a drop event hits a node in U is $|U|/n$. Moreover, conditioning on neighborhoods,

$$\mu = \sum_{u \in F} r_u \cdot \frac{|N(u) \cap U|}{d(u)} \leq m = \mathcal{O}\left(\frac{n}{\log^k n}\right).$$

Let us assume to have a large mean, $\mu \geq 4\sqrt{(d + L_n)\,m\log n}$. Set $\lambda = \mu/2$. Then,

$$\mathbf{Pr}\left(|X - \mu| \geq \frac{1}{2}\mu \wedge \mathcal{E}\right) \leq 2 \exp\left(-\frac{2\mu^2}{4(d + L_n)m}\right) \leq 2 \exp\left(-2\log n\right) = 2n^{-2}$$

Thus, with probability at least $1 - 2n^{-2} - \mathbf{Pr}(\neg\mathcal{E}) \geq 1 - 3n^{-2}$, $\frac{1}{2}\mu \leq X \leq \frac{3}{2}\mu \leq \frac{3}{2}m$. Next, assume to have a small mean $\mu < 4\sqrt{(d + L_n)\,m\log n}$. Set $\lambda = \sqrt{(d + L_n)\,m\log n}$, we have

$$\mathbf{Pr}\left(|X - \mu| \geq \lambda \wedge \mathcal{E}\right) \leq 2 \exp\left(-\frac{8(d + L_n)m\log n}{4(d + L_n)m}\right) = 2 \exp\left(-2\log n\right) = 2n^{-2}$$

Since $\mathbf{Pr}(\neg\mathcal{E}) \leq n^{-3}$, it follows that $\mathbf{Pr}(|X - \mu| \geq \lambda) \leq 2n^{-2} + n^{-3} \leq 3n^{-2}$. Therefore, with probability at least $1 - 3n^{-2}$ we have

$$X \leq \mu + \lambda \leq m + \sqrt{(d + L_n)\,m\log n} = \mathcal{O}\left(\frac{n}{\log^k n}\right).$$

Step 3: Expansion is Preserved. Let $S \subseteq V_t$ be the set of nodes affected in this round, those that dropped below d. We showed $|S| = \mathcal{O}(n/\log^k n)$. By invoking Lemma 1, we can say that removing or modifying a sublinear set of nodes or edges in a bounded-degree expander preserves edge expansion $\alpha' > 0$ with high probability. $\square$

The above lemma, shows that the degree adjustment step in the D-RAES protocol does not jeopardize the expansion of the graph. Despite the randomized pruning and churn, the number of nodes whose degree drops below the minimum threshold remains sublinear with high probability, ensuring that the expander core remains robust and well-connected over time.

We are now ready to put everything together and show that if the D-RAES along with the adversary's behavior has been an Υ-process until some round $t - 1$, then it will continue to be an Υ-process in the current round whp.

Lemma 3. *Suppose the D-RAES protocol has been a Υ-process until round $t-1$. Then, with high probability, it will continue to be an Υ-process in round t and the graph G_t that it creates at time t will also contain a large $n - o(n)$-sized expander subgraph with expansion at least α.*

Proof. The graph after the bootstrap phase is an expander. The Υ-process also starts with the graph being an expander graph (line 1 of Algorithm 3). We now show that the graph generated henceforth by the protocol will be an Υ-process. Moreover, in lines (3–6) the behavior of the Υ-process matches the behavior of the adversary. In line 7, the Υ-process refreshes the edges of randomly chosen vertices, that corresponds to Phase 2 in the expander maintenance protocol. After refreshing a random subset of nodes, the new edges are chosen uniformly at random from the vertex set. Precisely, recall that in the maintenance protocol, when a node has fewer than d neighbors, it tries to connect until it succeeds (or is churned out). Thus, it seeks neighbors until some round and then gets an edge uniformly at random. The Υ-process delineates the two decisions, namely (i) when to add an edge and (ii) how to add an edge.

The edges are added to the graph in line 9 of the Υ-process definition. Each edge is selected uniformly at random from the set of nodes. Moreover, in lines (11–13) all the nodes that gained more than Δ neighbor proceed with deleting some of their connections as in Phase 4 of the maintenance protocol.

As a final step we must ensure that nodes with degree less than d are able to gain (at least once) the minimum allowed degree d in reasonable time. To this end, denote X_i be the set of nodes that have less than d edges in round i. Now we must show that the nodes in (say) $X_{i-\tau}$ have all obtained degree d at least once by round i.

By the protocol, if a node has degree less than d, it performs at most d random sampling attempts in each round to reconnect to new neighbors.

Assume conservatively that u performs d independent uniform samples from $V \setminus \{u\}$ in each of the τ rounds from $i - \tau$ to i. Let $p \in (0, 1)$ be a lower bound on the success probability of a single sampling trial (i.e., the probability that the sampled node is connectable, not churned, and not already adjacent to u). This is justified if at least a $1 - \varepsilon$ fraction of the nodes are connectable in each round, for some constant $\varepsilon < 1$.

Over τ rounds, node u performs $T = d \cdot \tau = \Theta(\log n)$ independent trials, each with success probability at least p. We pessimistically assume that u performs

T independent random connection attempts over the τ rounds. In reality, u may perform fewer trials (e.g., if it reaches degree d earlier), so this assumption yields a conservative lower bound on the probability that u succeeds in restoring its degree. Let X be the total number of successful connections made by u during this period. Then $X \sim \text{Bin}(T, p)$, and $\mu := \mathbf{E}[X] = pT = \Theta(\log n)$.

We want to bound the probability that $X < d$, i.e., that u fails to reach degree d. Since $d \ll \mu$, we can define $\delta := 1 - \frac{d}{\mu} \in (0, 1)$, and apply the Chernoff bound:

$$\mathbf{Pr}(X < d) = \mathbf{Pr}(X < (1 - \delta)\mu) \leq \exp\left(-\frac{\delta^2 \mu}{2}\right) = \exp\left(-\frac{(1 - d/\mu)^2 \mu}{2}\right)$$

We want $\exp\left(-\frac{(1-d/\mu)^2 \mu}{2}\right) \leq \frac{1}{n^c}$. To this end, assume that $\mu = c_1 \log n$, then

$$\delta^2 \mu = \left(1 + \frac{d^2}{c_1^2 \log^2 n} - \frac{2d}{c_1 \log n}\right) c_1 \log n = c_1 \log n - 2d + \frac{d^2}{c_1 \log n} =$$

$$c_1 \log n - 2d + \mathcal{O}\left(\frac{1}{\log n}\right)$$

Therefore, $\frac{\delta^2 \mu}{2} = \frac{c_1}{2} \log n - d + \mathcal{O}\left(\frac{1}{\log n}\right)$. Putting all together,

$$\mathbf{Pr}(X < d) \leq \exp\left(-\frac{c_1}{2} \log n - d + \mathcal{O}\left(\frac{1}{\log n}\right)\right) =$$

$$n^{-c_1/2} \cdot e^d \cdot (1 + o(1)) = \mathcal{O}\left(\frac{1}{n^c}\right)$$

for $c = \frac{c_1}{2} - \varepsilon > 0$, where $\varepsilon = o(1)$. Therefore, the probability that u fails to reach degree d during the interval $[i - \tau, i]$ is inverse polynomial in n. Applying a union bound over all nodes in $X_{i-\tau}$ (of size at most n), we get:

$$\mathbf{Pr}(\exists u \in X_{i-\tau} \text{ s.t. } u \text{ does not reach degree } d) \leq n \cdot \frac{1}{n^c} = \frac{1}{n^{c-1}}.$$

Hence, with high probability, all nodes in $X_{i-\tau}$ reach degree at least d in some round between $i - \tau$ and i. $\qquad\square$

We showed that D-RAES maintains the structural guarantees of the Υ-process during rounds whp. As a result, the protocol ensures that a large expander subgraph persists over time, despite continuous adversarial churn. This establishes D-RAES as a robust and self-healing protocol for dynamic networks, capable of maintaining strong connectivity and expansion properties over time.

Moreover, we observe that our results hold even when nodes are not sampling from a *perfect* uniform distribution. Indeed, it suffices that each node samples from an *almost-uniform distribution*, where the probability of selecting any given peer is within a constant factor of $1/n$. Formally, in any round t, whenever a node samples a new neighbor, the endpoint is drawn from a distribution $\mathcal{D}_t$ over

V_t satisfying the following. There exists a set $S_t \subseteq V_t$ with $|S_t| \geq \beta n$ for a fixed constant $\beta \in (0,1]$ and a constant $c_1 > 0$ such that for all $v \in S_t$,

$$\mathcal{D}_t(v) \geq \frac{c_1}{n}.$$

and There exist constants $\varepsilon \in (0,1)$ and $\eta \in (0,1)$ such that for every $S \subseteq V_t$ with $|S| \leq \varepsilon |V_t|$,

$$\sum_{v \in S} \mathcal{D}_t(v) \leq (1+\eta)\frac{|S|}{n}.$$

Corollary 1. *All results established under uniform sampling continue to hold if each node $v \in V_t$ samples neighbors according to the distribution $\mathcal{D}_t(v)$ defined above.*

Proof (Theorem 3 under almost-uniform distribution.). In the proof of Theorem 3, every time we used $\mathbf{Pr}(\text{endpoint} \in S) \leq \frac{|S|}{n}$ for $|S| \leq \varepsilon n$, we instead invoke the small-set upper bound,

$$\mathbf{Pr}_{v \sim \mathcal{D}_t}(v \in S) = \sum_{v \in S} \mathcal{D}_t(v) \leq (1+\eta)\frac{|S|}{|V_t|}.$$

Thus all expectations and Chernoff exponents are scaled by a factor of at most $(1+\eta)$, and the theorem holds with constants adjusted accordingly. $\square$

Proof (Lemma 2 under almost-uniform distribution.). For a fixed node $u \in V_t$ and a single request, take $S = \{u\}$ to get $p_u = \mathbf{Pr}(v = u) = \mathcal{D}_t(u) \leq \frac{1+\eta}{n}$. With m requests in the round, $Y_u \preceq \text{Bin}(m, p_u)$ and $\mathbf{E}[Y_u] \leq (1+\eta)m/n$. By Chernoff, $\mathbf{Pr}(Y_u \geq (1+\delta)\mathbf{E}[Y_u] + c\log n) \leq n^{-c'}$ for suitable constants $c, c' > 0$. A union bound over $u \in V_t$ yields

$$Y_{\max} = \max_{u \in V_t} Y_u = \mathcal{O}\!\left(\frac{m}{n} + \log n\right) \quad \text{w.h.p.}$$

Exactly as in the uniform case, each node can lose at most $d + Y_u$ edges in the round, so at most $\mathcal{O}(n/\log^k n)$ nodes fall below degree d, and pruning them preserves a linear-size core with constant edge expansion (constants changed by $(1+\eta)$ only). $\square$

6   Conclusion

We presented a fully distributed and lightweight protocol for maintaining a constant-degree expander graph despite a continuous adversarial churn of up to $\mathcal{O}(n/\log^k n)$ nodes per round where $k > 0$. Despite this strong adversary, our protocol ensures that the resulting overlay graph remains an expander with high probability over time. Moreover, this work demonstrates that robustness and good connectivity can be achieved under far weaker assumptions, without relying on global knowledge or heavy coordination among nodes. Our analysis suggests that if nodes in the network periodically refresh their neighborhoods, the Bitcoin network-creation protocol can maintain an expander graph with good edge expansion under heavy adversarial churn using only local dynamics (i.e., without global knowledge of the network structure). Finally, our result closes an open problem in [11] where the authors suggested studying their protocol under churn.

Acknowledgments. This work was supported in part by the Research Council of Finland, Grant 363558.

References

1. Bitcoin core P2P network. https://en.wikipedia.org/wiki/Bitcoin_Core
2. Angileri, F., Clementi, A., Natale, E., Salvi, M., Ziccardi, I.: Threshold-driven streaming graph: expansion and rumor spreading (2025). https://arxiv.org/abs/2507.23533
3. Augustine, J., Avin, C., Liaee, M., Pandurangan, G., Rajaraman, R.: Information spreading in dynamic networks under oblivious adversaries. In: Gavoille, C., Ilcinkas, D. (eds.) DISC 2016. LNCS, vol. 9888, pp. 399–413. Springer, Heidelberg (2016). https://doi.org/10.1007/978-3-662-53426-7_29
4. Augustine, J., Cruciani, A., Gillani, I.A.: Maintaining distributed data structures in dynamic peer-to-peer networks (2024). https://doi.org/10.48550/ARXIV.2409.10235
5. Augustine, J., Kulkarni, T., Sivasubramaniam, S.: Leader election in sparse dynamic networks with churn. Internet Math (2016)
6. Augustine, J., Molla, A.R., Morsy, E., Pandurangan, G., Robinson, P., Upfal, E.: Storage and search in dynamic peer-to-peer networks. In: 25th ACM Symposium on Parallelism in Algorithms and Architectures, SPAA '13, Montreal, QC, Canada - 23–25 July 2013. ACM (2013)
7. Augustine, J., Pandurangan, G., Robinson, P.: Distributed algorithmic foundations of dynamic networks. SIGACT News (2016)
8. Augustine, J., Pandurangan, G., Robinson, P., Roche, S.T., Upfal, E.: Enabling robust and efficient distributed computation in dynamic peer-to-peer networks. In: IEEE 56th Annual Symposium on Foundations of Computer Science, FOCS 2015, Berkeley, CA, USA, 17–20 October, 2015. IEEE Computer Society (2015)
9. Augustine, J., Pandurangan, G., Robinson, P., Upfal, E.: Towards robust and efficient computation in dynamic peer-to-peer networks. In: Proceedings of the Twenty-Third Annual ACM-SIAM Symposium on Discrete Algorithms, SODA 2012, Kyoto, Japan, 17–19 January 2012. SIAM (2012)
10. Bagchi, A., Bhargava, A., Chaudhary, A., Eppstein, D., Scheideler, C.: The Effect of Faults on Network Expansion. Theory Comput, Syst (2006)
11. Becchetti, L., Clementi, A., Natale, E., Pasquale, F., Trevisan, L.: Finding a bounded-degree expander inside a dense one. In: Proceedings of the 2020 ACM-SIAM Symposium on Discrete Algorithms, SODA 2020, Salt Lake City, UT, USA, 5–8 January 2020. SIAM (2020)
12. Becchetti, L., Clementi, A., Pasquale, F., Trevisan, L., Ziccardi, I.: Expansion and Flooding in Dynamic Random Networks with Node Churn. Random Struct, Algorithms (2023)

13. Cruciani, A., Pasquale, F.: Brief announcement: dynamic graph models for the bitcoin P2P network: simulation analysis for expansion and flooding time. In: Stabilization, Safety, and Security of Distributed Systems - 24th International Symposium, SSS 2022, Clermont-Ferrand, France, 15–17 November 2022, Proceedings. Lecture Notes in Computer Science, Springer (2022)
14. Cruciani, A., Pasquale, F.: Dynamic graph models inspired by the bitcoin network-formation process. In: 24th International Conference on Distributed Computing and Networking, ICDCN 2023, Kharagpur, India, 4–7 January 2023. ACM (2023)
15. Nakamoto, S.: Bitcoin: A peer-to-peer electronic cash system (2009). http://www.bitcoin.org/bitcoin.pdf
16. Pandurangan, G., Raghavan, P., Upfal, E.: Building low-diameter P2P networks. In: 42nd Annual Symposium on Foundations of Computer Science, FOCS 2001, Las Vegas, Nevada, USA, 14–17 October 2001. IEEE Computer Society (2001)

Fast Distributed Sampling of Colorings
of Trees with Few Colors

Varsha Dani$^{(\boxtimes)}$ and Asya Vitko

Rochester Institute of Technology, Rochester, USA
{varsha.dani,av8258}@rit.edu

Abstract. The problem of generating a uniformly, or almost uniformly, random proper q-coloring of a given graph in polynomial time is an interesting and challenging sampling problem that has been widely studied in the sequential setting. Recently there has been interest in distributed algorithms for the problem, where the goal is to get parallel speedup, so that the running time is polylogarithmic in n. Existing approaches converge in logarithmic time but with a small increase in the number of colors required, which, for most of the sequential results, is already more than the maximum degree of the graph. We study the problem of distributed sampling of q-colorings in the special case where the graph is a tree. Regardless of the maximum degree of the tree, which may be as large as $\Omega(n)$, we allow the number of available colors, q, to be as small as three. We present a distributed CONGEST algorithm that produces an almost uniform proper q-coloring of the tree. Additionally, if the tree is rooted, a modification of our algorithm produces a uniformly random proper q-coloring. Both algorithms succeed with probability 1, and have a running time that is $O(\log^2 n)$ with high probability.

Keywords: Distributed Algorithm · Graph colorings · Sampling

1 Introduction

The problem of sampling (almost) uniformly random colorings of a given graph on n nodes was first studied in the statistical physics literature, and has a long and distinguished history (see, for example, the monograph by Chen et al. [3, Section 12.2] for a survey of some recent results). It has long been conjectured that, when the number of colors exceeds the maximum degree by at least 2, almost-uniformly random colorings can be sampled in $O(n \log n)$ time, using a very simple Markov chain known as the Glauber dynamics. Although significant progress has been made in special cases, such as when there are more colors, or the graph has additional properties, much remains unknown.

Much more recently, in the last couple of decades, there has been significant progress on distributed algorithms for this problem. See, for example, [6–10]. Here, the hope, which still remains elusive, is that a full parallel speedup by a factor $\Theta(n)$ is possible for this problem. This is known to be true when the number of colors is large enough, in which case the overall running time becomes poly-logarithmic in n.

C. Georgiou (Ed.): SIROCCO 2026, LNCS 16488, pp. 214–233, 2026.
https://doi.org/10.1007/978-3-032-26465-7_12

In the present work, we consider the case of distributed sampling of colorings when the graph is a tree. This seems like a modest goal, since trees are a very nice class of graphs. In the sequential setting, it is trivial to sample a uniformly random coloring of any tree in linear time.[1] The behavior of Markov chains for coloring trees has been studied in detail; see, for example, [14,18].

Our main contribution is polylog(n)-time distributed algorithms for approximately and exactly sampling a coloring of a tree even when the number of colors is as small as 3. This is stated more precisely in the following two theorems.

Theorem 1. *Let T be a tree on n vertices, let $q \geq 3$, and let π be the uniform distribution over proper q-colorings of T. There is a CONGEST algorithm that, given $\varepsilon > 0$, outputs a q-coloring whose distribution μ satisfies*

$$d_{\mathrm{TV}}(\mu, \pi) \leq \varepsilon.$$

The running time is $O(\log(n)\log(n/\varepsilon))$, both in expectation and with probability at least $1 - 1/n^2$.

If we assume that the communication network of n processors is a **rooted** tree, in which each node knows which neighbor is its parent, we obtain an exact sampler. We prove

Theorem 2. *Let T be a rooted tree on n vertices and let $q \geq 3$. There is a CONGEST algorithm that, given a constant $\alpha \geq 1$, outputs a uniformly random proper q-coloring of T. The running time of the algorithm is $O(\log^2(n))$, both in expectation and with probability at least $1 - n^{-\alpha}$.*

The main idea behind our algorithm is to decompose the input tree into long paths and small diameter components and deal with those separately. This approach is inspired by the rake-and-compress algorithm due to Reif and Tate [21] for solving problems on trees efficiently in parallel. Bonamy et al. [1] recently adapted this algorithm to solve a distributed recoloring problem.

A crucial difference between our algorithm and Reif and Tate's rake-and-compress algorithm is that we only remove paths of degree 2 vertices (i.e. compress) if they are sufficiently long. This is necessary because the colors of vertices in a random coloring are inherently correlated. To achieve efficiency in approximate sampling we need multiple vertices to color in parallel, but if they are too close to each other, correlations between colors are strong and the parallelism skews the distribution by a lot. Correlations between colors of vertices decay with graph distance between them, so vertices can be "forgiven" for choosing colors independently in parallel if they are far apart, and this threshold is what controls how long a path needs to be in order to be removed in the compress step.

---

[1] Note, however, that this trivial algorithm seems like it cannot be parallelized to run in sub-diameter time.

1.1 Related Work

One algorithmic solution is the Markov chain Monte Carlo method that is a randomized algorithm used to generate samples approximately from the target distribution. Glauber dynamics is one possible Markov chain for sampling proper q-colorings of graphs. It is known to have a connected state space whenever the number of colors is at least $\Delta + 2$, and it is an open problem to show that this many colors suffice for Glauber dynamics to have $O(n \log n)$ mixing time. Jerrum [17], and independently Salas and Sokal [22] showed that Glauber dynamics has $O(n \log n)$ mixing time when the number of colors is more than twice the maximum degree Δ of a graph. In subsequent work, considerable effort has gone into lowering the number of colors.

In particular, Vigoda [23] analyzed an alternative Markov chain called flip dynamics and showed that it has polynomial mixing time when the number of colors is at least $\frac{11}{6}\Delta$. The $O(n^2)$ mixing time of Glauber dynamics then follows from this result by comparison to the flip dynamics. Further improvements on the range of colors have been achieved under various restrictions on the input graph. For example, if the graph is assumed to have large girth $\Omega(\log \Delta)$, where Δ is maximum degree, and furthermore, $\Delta = \Omega(\log n)$, Dyer and Frieze [5] prove $O(n \log n)$ mixing time of Glauber dynamics when $k > \alpha\Delta$ where $\alpha \approx 1.763....$ Further improvements on girth and degree requirements were given in Hayes [15], Hayes and Vigoda [16], Frieze and Vera [11], Dyer et al. [5]. We refer the reader to the survey by Frieze and Vigoda [12] for details on the special cases considered in the literature. Very recently Carlson and Vigoda [2] improved the upper bound on the number of colors q for general graphs down to $q > 1.809\Delta$.

Moving on, an alternative algorithmic approach to sampling is based on decay of correlations. A deterministic algorithm for sampling colorings of graphs approximately uniformly at random has been given in Gamarnik and Katz [13]. The assumption on the input graph is that it is triangle-free and the number of colors is at least $\alpha\Delta$, where α is an arbitrary constant larger than $\alpha^{**} = 2.8432....$

Recently, there has been interest in sampling graph colorings in the distributed setting. Feng, Sun, Yin [8], Fischer and Ghaffari [10], Feng, Hayes, Yin [6] analyze distributed Markov chains and show $O(\log n/\varepsilon)$ mixing time when the number of colors is at least $(2+\delta)\Delta$, where $\delta > 0$ and $\varepsilon > 0$ is an error parameter. These works achieve an optimal speed-up of Glauber dynamics and pay by a slight increase in the number of colors required. Feng and Yin [9] gave a distributed algorithm based on strong spatial mixing, in the LOCAL model. We note that these algorithms could sample q-coloring on trees in $O(\log(n/\varepsilon)$ time for large numbers of colors – note that the maximum degree of a tree may be linear in n. The appeal of our approach is that it works for $q \geq 3$, regardless of the maximum degree of the graph. The problem of sampling colorings has been studied in the special case where the input graph is a tree. In the single processor setting, the primary motivation has been to gain insight into how Glauber dynamics works. A series of works including Goldberg et al. [14], Lucier and Molloy [18], etc. Establishes polynomial mixing time of Glauber dynamics on a complete d-ary tree for all $d \geq 2$ and the number of colors q at least 3.

2   Notation and Preliminaries

We use standard graph terminology and notation throughout. In particular, a **tree** $T = (V, E)$ of size n is an acyclic connected graph with n vertices. We call $v \in V$ a **high degree vertex** in a tree, if $\deg(v) > 2$. A tree with no high degree vertices is a path. We denote the maximum degree of a graph by Δ. P_k will denote a path of length k, i.e. with $k + 1$ vertices and k edges.

A **rooted tree** is a tree with a designated vertex r, called the **root**, such that all the edges of the tree are oriented towards r. If a rooted tree is the communication graph of a network of processors, then we assume that each vertex knows which of its neighbors is its parent in the tree and which ones are its children. Not that the directionality of the edges is only a structural information and that communication can still occur in either direction. In a rooted tree, every vertex except the root has **outdegree** 1 (and the root has outdegree 0), and every vertex except the leaves have **indegree** at least 1.

A **distance-b power graph** G^b of a graph G is a graph constructed by adding edges between vertices at distance at most b in G.

An **independent set** in a graph G is a set $S \subset V$ such that no two vertices S are adjacent in G. A **maximal independent set (MIS)** in G is an independent set that is maximal *i.e.* adding any other vertex to the MIS would violate the independence property.

For $q \in \mathbb{N}$ and a graph $G = (V, E)$, a **proper q-coloring** of G is a mapping $f : V \to [q]$ such that for any $x, y \in V$, if $(x, y) \in E$, then $f(x) \neq f(y)$.

2.1   Sampling

Let Ω be a finite set of elements. A probability distribution on Ω is a function $\mu : \Omega \to [0, 1]$ such that $\sum_{x \in \Omega} \mu(x) = 1$. Sampling from μ means choosing an element from Ω, so that each x is chosen with probability $\mu(x)$. The uniform distribution π is the one in which all elements have equal probability $1/|\Omega|$.

When the set Ω is explicitly enumerated, sampling from it is easy. However, one is often interested in sampling from a set that is not explicitly written down, but instead expressed succinctly as a set of structures with some property. For example, given a graph, Ω might be the set of all its spanning trees, or the set of all maximal independent sets, or the set of all proper q-colorings. In all of these, the size of Ω can be exponential in the size of the graph. The goal is to generate a sample from the distribution in polynomial time in n, the size of the graph (i.e. the problem representation) rather than the size of Ω itself. The problem of sampling from the uniform distribution from such a set Ω is intimately connected with the problem of counting the number of elements in Ω, and in many cases is known to be #P-complete. Thus *exact* sampling is often intractable, and is replaced by a weaker goal of *approximate* sampling, *i.e.* generating a sample from a distribution that is in some sense "close" to the target one. Typically, closeness between distributions is measured in terms of the *total variation distance*.

Definition 1. *The **total variation distance** between two probability distributions μ, ν on a space Ω is given by*

$$d_{TV}(\mu, \nu) = \frac{1}{2} \sum_{x \in \Omega} |\mu(x) - \nu(x)|.$$

Definition 2. *Let π be a distribution on Ω. An **exact sampler** is an algorithm that generates an element of Ω according to the distribution π. An **approximate sampler** is an algorithm that, given an error parameter $\varepsilon > 0$, generates an element of Ω according to some distribution μ such that $d_{TV}(\mu, \pi) \leq \varepsilon$.*

2.2   Distributed Algorithms

Distributed algorithms aim to solve problems in a setting where both the computational power as well as the input to the problem are *distributed* among several machines that can communicate with (some of) each other over a communication network. Typically, the communication network is itself the input graph, although other models have also been studied. Each vertex of the communication graph G has a processor that is capable of performing computations, as well as communicating with its neighbors in the graph. It is sometimes assumed that the processors have unique IDs. However we do not require this assumption, *i.e.* we work in a network of anonymous processors. Each processor is aware of n, the size of the network, as well as its own neighbors in the graph, but may not know anything else about the topology of the graph. To model the reality that sending messages over networks is much slower than performing CPU operations, in the idealized setting, it is generally assumed that local computation is free, and one is interested in the amount of communication required to solve a problem.

In the LOCAL model of distributed computation, an algorithm proceeds in synchronous rounds. In each round, each processor (i) optionally sends a message to each of its neighbors, (ii) receives the messages (if any) sent by its neighbors, and (iii) performs some local computation based on its input, its state and the messages received. The output of the algorithm may itself be distributed, in that each processor only computes a small piece of it, and different processors may remain communicative for different numbers of rounds. The running time of the algorithm is the number of rounds of communication required for all the vertices to compute (their piece of) the output and terminate. In the LOCAL model, there is no limit on the size of the messages that can be sent. We work in the more restricted CONGEST model, where each processor is only allowed to send $O(\log n)$ bits per neighbor per round.

3   Approximate and Exact Samplers

In this section we describe our approximate and exact samplers. Both use the same approach of decomposing the tree into a hierarchical collection of so-called "long" paths (to be defined later) and small diameter components. The approximate and exact samplers color "long" paths using two different methods tailored for the corresponding task. The method to color small diameter components is the same in both samplers. It is helpful to start by considering the two extreme cases, (i) where the input tree has small (*i.e.*, $O(\log n)$) diameter and (ii) where the input tree is a path, meaning that its diameter is maximum.

If the tree has diameter $O(\log n)$, then the process of repeatedly stripping leaves off (after having identified themselves to their "parent") results in either a single vertex or two vertices connected by an edge remaining after $O(\log n)$ rounds. At this point, the remaining vertex becomes the root (if two vertices remain they collectively select one of them to be the root) and the rest of the tree is oriented towards it via the parent pointers. (When the tree is already rooted this process follows the existing pointers and ends up at the root). Then the root chooses a uniformly random color, and in the subsequent $O(\log n)$ rounds a vertex whose parent chose a color the previous round chooses a uniformly random color different from its parent's color. The resulting coloring is proper and uniformly random.

The situation is different on a path, since the above process would take linear time to run. In the next sections we discuss how to sample colorings on a path in polylogarithmic time, first approximately, then exactly. This serves as a warm up, but will ultimately be a subroutine in our algorithms for trees.

3.1   Coloring a Path Almost Uniformly at Random

If a path is to be colored in $\text{polylog}(n)$ rounds, there must be at least one round in which many nodes must select colors simultaneously. Consider the set of nodes that selects their colors in such a round. Since they have no knowledge of each other's choices, these nodes must act independently, each choosing out of q choices. If they do not get recolored, in the final coloring the marginal distributions of the colors chosen by these nodes are independent. However, this is not true of the marginal distributions of the colors of a set of (> 1) vertices in a uniform coloring. Here, once the color of any vertex is fixed, the color of every other vertex is correlated with the color of the initially colored vertex. What saves us is that these correlations decay the further we go from the initial vertex. So, if we go far enough, the marginal distribution is close to uniform, and although sampling the color from a uniform distribution will introduce some error into the sample, hopefully this error can be kept small.

How far do we need to go for the correlations to have sufficiently decayed? An easy inductive calculation shows that the correlation between the colors of vertices on the path decays exponentially with the distance between them, which means that if we pick vertices that are logarithmically far apart, already their colors are almost independent in a uniformly random coloring, and so, by choosing them independently we are not skewing the distribution too much (although of course this statement needs to be made quantitatively more precise). But now, note that if u and v are distance $d = \Theta(\log n)$ apart and have been colored, then there are at most $(q-1)^{d-1} = \text{poly}(n)$ ways to properly color the vertices in between them (the exact number depends on whether or not u and v chose the same color), so these can be enumerated locally and a uniformly random one of them can be selected and described in $O(\log n)$ bits, and quickly conveyed to all the intermediate vertices. Moreover, the coloring of the path from u to v thus obtained is fairly close to uniform. Specifically, a straightforward calculation shows

Lemma 1. *Let u, v be the endpoints of a path P_d of length $d > 1$. Let π the uniform distribution on q-colorings of P_d and μ be the distribution obtained by by coloring u, v independently and uniformly at random from q choices, and coloring $P_d \setminus \{u, v\}$ uniformly at random among all the colorings compatible with u and v's colors. Then*

$$d_{TV}(\mu, \pi) = \frac{1}{q(q-1)^{d-1}}.$$

This suggests an algorithm for quickly distributedly coloring the whole path with an almost uniform q-coloring. Let $\varepsilon > 0$ be the desired error parameter for the approximately uniform coloring of the path. Let

$$b := \left\lceil \frac{\log n - \log q + \log(1/\varepsilon)}{\log(q-1)} \right\rceil + 1$$

Suppose we were able to select "fencepost" vertices that are distance b apart on the path. Then we could color the fencepost vertices independently and fill in the segments between them by selecting a random coloring compatible with the endpoints. This would result in each segment being colored almost uniformly up to an error of

$$\frac{1}{q(q-1)^{b-1}} = \frac{1}{q(q-1)^{\lceil(\log n - \log q + \log(1/\varepsilon))/\log(q-1)\rceil}} \leq \frac{q\varepsilon}{qn} = \frac{\varepsilon}{n}.$$

Assuming that the errors in the individual segments add up nicely (and we will show this later, in Lemma 6 which is a general lemma about colorings on trees), this would then give a coloring that was within total variation distance ε of uniform. But there is still a gap: how can a distributed algorithm executing on a path P on n vertices *quickly* find fencepost vertices that are exactly distance b apart? The answer is that sadly, it cannot. However, what it *can* do quickly is find fencepost vertices that are between distance b and $2b$ apart. That is, we choose the fencepost vertices to be a $(b, 2b)$-ruling set. There are sophisticated algorithms for finding ruling sets in general graphs (see [19,20]). However, in our case, since the underlying graph is a path, and the distance parameters are b and $2b$, this can be accomplished by simulating Luby's algorithm for finding maximal independent sets on P^b, the distance-b power graph of P. Since Luby's algorithm runs in $O(\log n)$ with high probability, such a simulation is trivial in the LOCAL model in $O(b \log n) = O(\log^2 n)$ time. In the CONGEST model, it is not possible to share all the messages that Luby's algorithm generates, in a single step, since each node has $2b$ virtual neighbors, but only two neighbors in the actual communication network which is the path P. Thus a naive simulation of Luby's algorithm would need to spread these messages out in time, for a total running time of $O(b^2 \log n) = O(\log^3 n)$. However, the insight is that in fact the messages can be aggregated, because when looking for a local maximum of some function in one's neighborhood, one only needs to forward the maximum value one has seen to one's neighbors, not the vector of all received values. This is a standard trick, and we omit the details. Thus, Luby's algorithm can be simulated in $O(\log^2 n)$ expected time in CONGEST as well.

We note here that if we assumed that the nodes had unique identifiers, then we could use the techniques of Cole and Vishkin [4] to select the fenceposts in $O(b \log^* n) = O(\log n \log^* n)$ time. Even without existing unique identifiers, we could generate random unique identifiers by the Birthday paradox (although then the algorithm would have a small chance of failing.) This might be worth doing, if the graph were known to be a path. However, our main motivation is to use the path algorithm as a subroutine for our algorithm on trees. Since our overall algorithm for trees is going to have an $O(\log^2 n)$ running time anyway, the fencepost selection is not the bottleneck, and we may as well run the Luby simulation, which, although slower, definitely succeeds and allows us to assume an anonymous network.

Once the fenceposts have been found, they can choose colors independently. Then the segments in between can be uniformly colored conditioned on the endpoints in $O(b) = O(\log n)$ time, by everyone locally enumerating all the compatible colorings in a canonical way, and a designated vertex, say one of the endpoints of the segment, selecting one of them at random and telling everyone in the segment which one was selected. Then each vertex colors itself based on knowing how far it is from the endpoints and consulting its local list of colorings. There are more sophisticated methods of accomplishing this that do not rely on there being only polynomially many compatible colorings, but this is good enough for our purposes.

The fact that the segments can have length between b and $2b$ only improves the error bound, so modulo proving that the individual pieces can be stitched together (Lemma 6) this shows that an almost uniform q-coloring of the path can be sampled in $O(\log^2 n)$ time (or $O(\log n \log^* n)$ time if the processors had unique IDs).

3.2   Coloring a Path Exactly Uniformly at Random

We now describe how to modify the above approximate sampling algorithm to get an exactly uniform sample. For simplicity, we will assume that the path is directed, *i.e.* one of its endpoints is the root, and all the edges are oriented towards it. This assumption is not necessary for the path but it makes describing the algorithm simpler, and moreover, it is the version we will use when we extend the algorithm to rooted trees.

As in the approximate sampler, we select fenceposts at distances between b and $2b$ apart. We want these fencepost vertices to be able to select their colors simultaneously and independently, but the problem is that when they have done that, they have already sampled from the wrong marginal distribution, albeit very slightly (because of the decay of correlations). In order to fix this error, we want to put in a correction so that most of the time, each such vertex sticks with its independent choice of color, but some of the time, just often enough to compensate for the error, it does something different, that involves waiting to hear what the previous fencepost vertex has done.

To make this more precise we make the following observations. Let P be a segment with ℓ vertices, and endpoints u, v. Then there are $q(q-1)^{(\ell-1)}$ ways to color this segment. Let us organize these colorings into a $q \times q$ array of buckets where rows and columns represent the color choices of u and v respectively, and a (proper) coloring of the segment is placed in bucket (i, j) if it is compatible with u choosing color i and v choosing color j. Now observe that by symmetry of colors, all off-diagonal buckets (where u and v chose different colors) contain the same number of colorings, and all diagonal buckets (where u and v chose the same color) contain the same number of colorings. Moreover,

- for odd ℓ, diagonal buckets have one more coloring than off-diagonal ones,
- for even ℓ, off-diagonal buckets have one more coloring than diagonal ones.

In fact this happens because a 2-coloring of the segment has same-colored endpoints when ℓ is odd and differently colored endpoints when ℓ is even.

If we remove one 2-coloring from each diagonal bucket when ℓ is odd and one 2-coloring from each off-diagonal bucket when ℓ is even, then there are an equal number of colorings compatible with any possible coloring of endpoints. We will use *Rest* to denote the set of all colorings remaining in the buckets. As a result, the endpoints of the segment can now choose colors independently, uniformly at random and then choose a coloring for the segment in between uniformly at random from the bucket determined by their color choices. The overall coloring of the segment will be exactly uniformly random over the colorings in *Rest*. Most of the time the segment will color itself this way. Indeed, this happens with probability proportional to the size of *Rest*.

To account for the 2-colorings that we removed from the table, we put them into another set that we call *Excess*, and some of the time (*i.e.* with probability proportional to the size of *Excess*,) the segment will color itself by selecting a 2-coloring uniformly from *Excess*.

To actually implement this distributedly on a *directed* path, we will make each fencepost responsible for deciding whether the segment above it will color itself from *Excess* or *Rest*. The probability of *Excess* is given by $\frac{q}{q(q-1)^{\ell-1}}$ (for odd ℓ) and $\frac{q^2-q}{q(q-1)^{\ell-1}}$ (for even ℓ) and the probability of *Rest* is given by $1 - \Pr[\textit{Excess}]$.

Now, the root can choose a random color and each fencepost that selected *Rest* for the segment above it can choose a color independently and uniformly at random, and convey that choice upstream to the fencepost above it. The fenceposts that chose *Excess* will just convey this fact to the fencepost above them and wait to receive a color. When fencepost u knows its own color (either by choosing it itself, or by receiving it from its upstream neighbor) and has received either (*Rest*, color-choice) or (*Excess*, $-$) from its downstream fencepost, it selects a coloring for the segment below it, and sends it to the segment.

If *Rest* was chosen, it selects this coloring uniformly from the appropriate bucket in *Rest*, to be compatible with the color choices of both endpoints. If *Excess* was chosen, then if the segment below has an odd number of vertices (including both fenceposts), u distributes the unique 2-coloring from *Excess* compatible with its color choice to the segment, and if the segment has an even number of vertices then it distributes a uniformly random one of the $q - 1$ 2-colorings from *Excess* that are compatible with its choice.

Effectively, this means every segment gets colored from the correct distribution, although the time taken to achieve this depends on the length of the longest maximal sequence of consecutive segments that chose to color from *Excess*.

We still need to show that having each segment colored from the uniform distribution in such a way that they agree at the endpoints, is enough to give the uniform distribution on the whole path. But this follows by repeatedly applying Lemma 6 with the error parameters set to zero.

We have not yet said how to pick the threshold distance between the fenceposts. In the previous section, when we were talking about approximate sampling, we set the threshold b controlling the distance between fenceposts in order to ensure that the error arising from any given segment was at most ε/n. Here, we do not want any error, and are using the trick of separating out the *Excess* set to ensure that. However, we also do not want too many segments to pick *Excess* since many consecutive segments picking *Excess* will cause the running time to increase. (In particular, if all the segments pick *Excess*, the algorithm will color the vertices sequentially.) So we pick b to make the probability of a segment choosing *Excess* small.

Let $\alpha > 1$ be constant, and let $b = (\alpha + 1) \cdot \log_{q-1} n + 1$. The fenceposts will be selected to be between b and $2b$ distance apart.

Lemma 2. *Let S be a set of $\frac{n}{b}$ segments of length at least b each.*

$$\Pr[\text{no segment chose Excess}] \geq 1 - \frac{1}{n^\alpha}$$

We will use this to show that with probability at least $1 - \frac{1}{n^\alpha}$, the algorithm runs to completion in time $O(\log^2 n)$.

Finally, we remark that although it was convenient to have the path be directed so that a predetermined endpoint of a segment could make decisions for that segment, this is not necessary. With a little more work, we can have the two endpoints of a segment decide things (like picking *Excess* vs. *Rest*) collectively. Moreover, they can also find maximal consecutive sequences of segments that chose *Excess* in time linear in the length of the segment. Since it hardly ever happens that any segment chose *Excess*, this does not affect the high probability running time.

3.3   Sampling Colorings on Trees

We now show how to extend these ideas to sampling colorings on trees in $O(\log^2 n)$ time. For general trees we will show how to approximately sample

---

Algorithm 1

1: **procedure** COL-SAMPLER(s)   ▷ s is either APPROX or EXACT
2:   ▷ When $s = EXACT$, T must be rooted.
3:     **for** $3 \ln n$ rounds **do**   ▷ Rake-and-Compress style decomposition
4:         run IDENTIFY-LONG-PATH(s)
5:         **if** in a long path **then** inform your neighbors. and proceed to line 14
6:         **if** not in a long path **then**
7:             update your list of children by removing those who are in a long path,
                and update your degree accordingly
8:         **for** b rounds **do**   ▷ Recursively strip leaves
9:             **if** a leaf **then**
10:                **if** unrooted tree **then** mark your unique neighbor as your parent
11:                Inform your parent of being a leaf
12:                Decrease your degree by the number of leaves that contacted you.
13:     ▷ Decomposition complete. Vertices not in long paths start coloring, in the
        reverse order of being marked. Vertices in long paths may have started already.
14:     **if** in a long path **then**
15:         run SELECT-FENCEPOSTS
16:         **if** $s = APPROX$ **then** run COLOR-LONG-PATH
17:         **else** run COLOR-LONG-PATH-EXACT
18:     **if** your degree is 0 and not in a long path **then**
19:         choose a color uniformly at random
20:         send your color to all your neighbors
21:     **else if** received your parent's color c **then**
22:         choose a uniformly random color from $[q] \setminus \{c\}$
23:         send this color to all your neighbors

---

a q-coloring to within total variation distance ε from uniform. If the tree is rooted, then we can also sample exactly from the uniform distribution.

The first step is to decompose the tree using a Rake-and-compress style algorithm, where we alternate between rake steps (stripping leaves) and compress steps (removing paths). The difference is that in the compress steps we remove a path only if its length is at least b where $b = \Theta(\log n)$ is a specified parameter set according to the discussions in Sects. 3.1 and 3.2. In the exact sampling setting, we additionally require that the path is oriented, $i.e.$ all its edges point in the same direction.

Definition 3. *A **long path** in a given tree T is a connected induced subgraph of T with at least b vertices, each with degree at most 2 in T. Thus the induced subgraph is a path of length at least b. A **long oriented path** in a given rooted tree T is a connected induced subgraph of T with at least b vertices such that each vertex has at most one child in T. Thus the induced subgraph is an oriented path of length at least b.*

Since we have to discover paths of length b, each compress step is going to take $\Theta(b)$ rounds. To balance this out, in the rake step, we do b rounds of leaf stripping. As we will see later, $O(\log n)$ iterations of raking and compressing are sufficient to empty out the tree.

Algorithm 2. IDENTIFY-LONG-PATH

1: **procedure** IDENTIFY-LONG-PATH(s)   ▷ s is either APPROX or EXACT
2:     **if** s is APPROX **then**
3:         Only vertices of degree 1 or 2 participate in this protocol.
4:     **else if** s is EXACT **then**
5:         Only vertices of indegree 0 or 1 participate in this protocol.
6:         ▷ This means that the algorithm is running on an induced subgraph which is disjoint union of paths and singleton vertices. If the tree is rooted, the paths are oriented. Vertices will gather the degrees of the vertices in their radius-b neighborhood in this induced subgraph.
7:     $msg \leftarrow$ your degree
8:     Send msg to your neighbor(s).
9:     Receive messages from your neighbor(s)
10:     **for** $b - 1$ rounds **do**
11:         **if** a message is received from a neighbor **then**
12:             forward it to your other neighbor (if any).
13:         Use received messages to infer geometry of your radius-b neighborhood.
14:     **if** your radius-b neighborhood is a path of length at least b **then**
15:         Mark yourself as in the long (oriented) path.

This results in a hierarchical decomposition of the tree into rooted components and long paths, where the hierarchy is based on the rake/compress phase in which the component is discovered. The components then color themselves in the reverse order of discovery phase. In the rooted components, individual vertices color themselves in breadth-first order from the root, with each vertex choosing a random color different from its parent's color, in the round after its parent. The "long" paths are colored using the methods of approximate and exact coloring described earlier for paths. Note that for exact sampling, we assumed that a long path is oriented one way because it can be colored efficiently from the conditional uniform distribution if conditioning is on a color of only one vertex (orientation is always towards the root).

The pseudocode for the full algorithm is given in Algorithm 1. The subroutine SELECT-FENCEPOSTS runs the simulation of Luby's MIS algorithm on the distance-b power graph of the long path that is running it. Due to space limitations we omit the pseudocode in this version.

4   Correctness

It is fairly easy to see that Algorithm 2 enables nodes to identify themselves as belonging to a long path: the algorithm runs on the subgraph induced by nodes of degree 1 and 2, (or indegree 0 and 1 if the tree is rooted) and is therefore operating on a disjoint union of paths and singletons. Within this subgraph, a node's radius-b neighborhood is a path, and it is easy to identify whether or not its length is at least b. Finding the fenceposts follows standard algorithms.

The alternation between identifying long paths and b rounds of stripping leaves is done $3 \ln n$ times. We need to show that this process empties out the

---

Algorithm 3. COLOR-LONG-PATH

1: **procedure** COLOR-LONG-PATH
2:     **if** you are a fencepost **then**
3:         **if** you have a parent **then**
4:             Choose a random color different from your parent's color.
5:         **else** Choose a random color.
6:         Send your color to everyone in the segment(s) adjacent to you
7:             ▷ *Msg not forwarded beyond the next fencepost. Takes $\leq 2b$ rounds.*
8:         Send your color to all your other neighbors.
9:     **else**
10:         Within the first $2b$ rounds,
11:             **when** you receive the color of one of the fenceposts from your neighbor,
12:                 Store and forward to the other neighbor.   ▷ *this will happen twice*
13:                 Also record your distance from the fencepost
14:     ▷ *Now everyone in segment knows colors of endpts and their distance from each.*
15:     The segment elects a leader from among the two fenceposts
16:     **if** leader **then**
17:         $Q \leftarrow$ uniformly random coloring of segment conditioned on fencepost colors.
18:         Send the lexicographic index of Q to everyone in the segment.
19:     **if** not a fencepost **then**
20:         Receive lexicographic index of Q.
21:         Color yourself according to Q based on your distance from the leader.

---

tree. To show this we need several lemmas relating the number of leaves in a tree and the existence of long paths.

Lemma 3. *Let T be a rooted tree of size n such that all vertices are either leaves, the root, or have indegree at least 2. Let ℓ be the number of leaves (without the root if it has indegree 1) and $k = n - \ell$ be the number of non-leaf vertices (including the root if it has indegree 1). Then $\ell \geq \frac{n}{2}$. If T is unrooted of size n such that all vertices have degree either 1 or at least 3, and ℓ is the number of leaves, the same lower bound on the number of leaves is true.*

Proof. The sum of the degrees in T is $2(n-1)$. Thus

$$2(n-1) \geq \ell + \deg(\text{root}) + \sum_{i=1}^{k-1} \deg(v_i) \geq \ell + \deg(\text{root}) + 3k - 3.$$

Rearranging terms gives $2\ell \geq n + \deg(\text{root}) - 3 + 2 \geq n$. $\square$

Lemma 4. *Let T be a (rooted) tree of size n. If there are no long (oriented) paths in T, then the number of leaves is at least $\frac{n}{2b}$.*

Proof. Vertices of degree 2 in T (or in-degree 1 if it is a rooted tree) can be viewed as "beads" on the edges of a "skeleton" tree T' with the same number of leaves, ℓ and satisfying the hypotheses of Lemma 3. It follows that T' has at most $2\ell - 1$ edges. If there are no long (oriented) paths in $T4$, that implies there are at most $b - 1$ beads per edge of T'. Thus $n \leq 2\ell + (2\ell - 1)(b - 1) \leq 2\ell b$, and the result follows. $\square$

Algorithm 4

1: **procedure** COLOR-LONG-PATH-EXACT
2: **if** top fencepost in your long path (i.e. root, or parent is outside path) **then**
3:   **if** root **then** Choose uniformly random color
4:   **else** After parent chooses color, choose a uniformly random different color.
5: **else if** fencepost with a parent in your long path **then**
6:   $\ell \leftarrow$ length of the segment above you (including fenceposts.)
7:   $p \leftarrow \frac{1}{(q-1)^{\ell-1}}$ (odd ℓ) or $\frac{1}{(q-1)^{\ell-2}}$ (even ℓ)
8:   Choose $Excess$ with probability p;
9:   **if** $Excess$ **then** $msg \leftarrow (Excess, -)$
10:   **else** Choose a uniformly random color c $\triangleright$ *(with probability $1-p$)*
11:    $msg \leftarrow (Rest, c)$
12:   Send msg up to the other endpoint of the segment (above you.)
13:   $\triangleright$ *Now all the segments are marked $Excess$ or $Rest$, all fenceposts with Rest-segment below them know the color of the other endpoint. All fenceposts except those with Excess-segment above them have chosen their own color.*
14: All fenceposts with a segment below them do the following:
15: **When** you know your own color $\triangleright$ *if $Excess$ in segment above, then wait*
16: **if** segment below marked $Rest$ **then**
17:   Choose a random coloring from $Rest$ bucket compatible with your color and the color of the other endpoint.
18: **else**
19:   Choose random 2-coloring compatible with your color from $Excess$ bucket.
20: Distribute index of chosen coloring to the segment below you.
21: Once colored, send your color to children (if any) that are not in your long path

Lemma 5. *Let T be a given input tree (either rooted or not). After $3 \ln n$ iterations of line 2 of Algorithm 1, all vertices in T have identified either as being in a long path or as a leaf with a pointer to the parent.*

Proof. Assume that the input tree T is rooted. We show that in each round of recursion, the size of the input tree graph decreases by a constant factor. Since in the worst case, the initial call to IDENTIFY-LONG-PATH does not identify any long paths, we may w.l.o.g. Assume that each round of recursion starts with b rounds of leaf stripping and is followed by one call to IDENTIFY-LONG-PATH.

When a long path is identified in the graph, we can think of it as being removed from the graph and a graph entering a recursive call may be a forest of unrooted (approximate sampling) or rooted (exact sampling) trees.

Let N_1 be the number of vertices in the largest tree in the beginning of a recursive call. Let N_2 be the number of vertices after b rounds of leaf stripping and let L be the number of leaves in the largest tree at that point. Let N_3 be the number of vertices after the call to IDENTIFY-LONG-PATH in the largest tree.

We analyze two cases:

1. $L < \frac{N_2}{2b}$. In this case by Lemma 4 there must be at least one (oriented) long path with b or more degree 2 vertices and $N_3 \leq N_2 - b$. Note that since there

is at least one oriented long path after b rounds of leaf stripping, it must be true that it was not there before b rounds of leaf stripping. This means that b rounds of leaf stripping in the first iteration decreased N_1 by a factor of $\frac{N_1}{2b}$ and then by at least $L(b-1)$ (since each leaf that is left after $b-1$ rounds of leaf stripping must have had at least $b-1$ vertices attached to it before):

$$N_2 \leq N_1 - \frac{N_1}{2b} - L(b-1)$$
$$= N_1\left(1 - \frac{1}{2b}\right) - \frac{N_2}{2b}(b-1)$$
$$= 1.5N_2 \leq N_1\left(1 - \frac{1}{2b}\right)$$
$$= N_2 \leq \frac{2}{3}\left(1 - \frac{1}{2b}\right)N_1$$

Now we get:

$$N_3 \leq \frac{2}{3}N_1\left(1 - \frac{1}{2b}\right) - b$$

2. $L \geq \frac{N_2}{2b}$. In this case by Lemma 4 there are no (oriented) long paths with b or more degree 2 vertices and $N_3 = N_2$. We can give the following range on N_1 in terms of L and N_2. Each leaf must have had a diameter b component attached that was removed by b rounds of leaf stripping. So, N_1 is at least $Lb + N_2$. Furthermore, it is possible that each vertex that is not a leaf had a diameter b component attached to it. To maximize the number of vertices in a tree with diameter b, assume a complete binary tree with $2^b - 1$ vertices. Hence, N_1 is at most $N_2 \cdot 2^b$. We will assume that $N_1 = N_2 + Lb$ since this is when N_1 has decreased the least by b rounds of leaf stripping. Then using our assumption that $N_1 = N_2 + Lb$:

$$N_1 \geq N_2 + \frac{N_2}{2b} \cdot b = 1.5N_2$$
$$N_2 = N_3 \leq \frac{2}{3}N_1$$

We showed that after a recursive call the largest tree in the forest entering the recursive call decreases by at least $\frac{1}{3}$, i.e., the whole input graph decreases by at least $\frac{1}{3}$ with each round of recursion. Now we calculate the recursion depth starting with n vertices:

$$n\left(1 - \frac{1}{3}\right)^k \leq \frac{n}{e^{k/3}}.$$

Let $k = 3\ln n$. After $O(\log n)$ rounds, we reach the base case. $\qquad\square$

All that remains is to show that the resulting colorings have the correct distribution. We begin by observing how sampling errors accumulate, when different pieces of the tree are colored separately and then stitched together.

Let T be a tree, and (v, w) be an edge in T. The $T = T_1 \cup T_2$ where T_1 and T_2 are trees, $v \in T_1$, $w \in T_2$ and (v, w) is a cut between T_1 and T_2. Let π be the uniform distribution on colorings of T, π_1 be the uniform distribution on colorings of T_1 and π_2^c be the uniform distribution on colorings of T_2 that are compatible with the color at v being c (so that the color at w is not c).

Suppose that μ_1 is a distribution on colorings of T_1 that is within ε_1 of uniform, i.e. $d_{TV}(\mu_1, \pi_1) \leq \varepsilon_1$. Also, for each $c \in [q]$, let μ_2^c be a distribution on colorings of T_2 that are compatible with the color at v being c such that $d_{TV}(\mu_2^c, \pi_2^c) \leq \varepsilon_2$. Now consider the following process to color the whole tree T:

- First sample a coloring of T_1 from μ_1. Let c be the color assigned to v.
- Now sample a coloring of T_2 from μ_2^c.
- The resultant coloring is a proper coloring of T.

Let μ be the distribution of the coloring of T generated by this process, and let $\varepsilon = \varepsilon_1 + \varepsilon_2$. The next lemma shows that μ is within ε of uniform.

Lemma 6. *Let μ, π and ε be as defined above. Then $d_{TV}(\mu, \pi) < \varepsilon$.*

Proof. Fix a coloring f of T. Then $\mu(f)$ is the probability that process describes above generates f. Let f_1 be the coloring of T_1 obtained by restricting f to the vertices in T_1 and f_2 be the coloring of T_2 obtained by restricting f to the vertices in T_2. Note that since we started out with a proper coloring of T, f_2 is automatically a coloring of T_2 that is compatible with the color at v. Then by definition of the process $\mu(f) = \mu_1(f_1)\mu_2^{f(v)}(f_2)$. Also it is easy to see that $\pi(f) = \pi_1(f_1)\pi_2^{f(v)}(f_2)$ Taking the absolute difference and applying the triangle inequality we have

$$|\mu(f) - \pi(f)| = |\mu_1(f_1)\mu_2^{f(v)}(f_2) - \pi_1(f_1)\pi_2^{f(v)}(f_2)|$$
$$\leq |\mu_1(f_1) - \pi_1(f_1)| \cdot \mu_2^{f(v)}(f_2) + \pi_1(f_1) \cdot |\mu_2^{f(v)}(f_2) - \pi_2^{f(v)}(f_2)|$$

Thus

$$2d_{TV}(\mu, \pi) = \sum_{f=(f_1,f_2)\in\Omega} |\mu(f) - \pi(f)| = \sum_{f_1}\sum_{f_2} |\mu(f) - \pi(f)|$$
$$\leq \sum_{f_1}\sum_{f_2} |\mu_1(f_1) - \pi_1(f_1)|\mu_2^{f(v)}(f_2) + \pi_1(f_1)|\mu_2^{f(v)}(f_2) - \pi_2^{f(v)}(f_2)|$$
$$= \sum_{f_1} |\mu_1(f_1) - \pi_1(f_1)| + \sum_{f_2} |\mu_2^{f(v)}(f_2) - \pi_2^{f(v)}(f_2)|$$
$$\leq 2d_{TV}(\mu_1, \pi_1) + 2d_{TV}(\mu_2^{f(v)}, \pi_2^{f(v)}) \leq 2\varepsilon_1 + 2\varepsilon_2 = 2\varepsilon$$

Here we have used the fact that $\sum_{f_2} \mu_2^{f(v)}(f_2) = 1$ and $\sum_{f_1} \pi_1(f_1) = 1$ because $\mu_2^{f(v)}$ and π_1 are probability distributions. Dividing by 2 gives the result. $\qquad\square$

With this machinery, we can inductively prove that when the algorithm iteratively subdivides the graph via the modified Rake-and-Compress process and then puts it back together, the errors in the colorings that are being stitched back together remain under control.

Approximate Sampler. To see that the coloring produced by Algorithm 1 with $s = APPROX$ is almost uniformly random, note that any vertex that is not in a long path chooses its color uniformly at random conditioned on the choice of its parent. Thus, each component that is a logarithmic size tree colors itself sequentially and therefore exactly from the correct distribution, with the first vertex to be colored choosing its color to be compatible with its parent, if any. Each component that is a segment in long path colors itself according to the uniform distribution conditioned on the colors of its two bounding fenceposts. By the discussion in Sect. 3.1 the resulting distribution of the coloring of the segment is at most ε/n away from uniform. By Lemma 6, these pieces can be stitched together, and the overall error is at most the sum of the individual errors on the pieces. Since there are n vertices, there are fewer than n pieces to be stitched together, and thus the overall error is at most ε. Thus we have sketched a proof of the following

Theorem 3. *Let T be a tree on n vertices, $q \geq 3$, and $\varepsilon > 0$. Then Algorithm 1 with $s = APPROX$ generates a proper q-coloring of T within total variation distance ε of uniform distribution.*

Exact Sampler. To see that Algorithm 1 with $s = EXACT$ produces a uniformly random coloring, note that any vertex that is not in a long oriented path chooses its color uniformly at random conditional on the choice of its parent unless it is the root that chooses a color uniformly at random independently of any other vertex. As discussed in Sect. 3.2, the distribution produced by COLOR-LONG-PATH-EXACT is uniform on colorings of the long path. So we only need to show that the pieces can be stitched together. But again, this follows inductively from Lemma 6, noting this time that since the error in each piece is zero, this is also true for the whole tree, and we get

Theorem 4. *Let T be a rooted tree on n vertices and $q \geq 3$. Then Algorithm 1 with $s = EXACT$ generates a uniformly random proper q-coloring of T.*

We defer rigorous proofs of Theorems 3 and 4 to the full version of the paper.

5   Running Time

For both the approximate and exact samplers, we note that the running time of the subroutines identifying long paths is easily seen to be $O(b)$. Also, SELECT-FENCEPOSTS (a simulation of Luby's algorithm on the distance-b power graph of a path) runs in time $O(b \log n)$ in expectation and with high probability.

For the approximate sampler on trees, the only remaining piece is to note that the subroutine COLOR-LONG-PATH runs in time $O(b)$. Together with the correctness (Theorem 3), this proves Theorem 1.

For the exact sampler on rooted trees, it is more tricky to estimate the running time of COLOR-LONG-PATH-EXACT. Here, by Lemma 2, with probability at least $1 - n^{-\alpha}$, all the segments of long paths choose *Rest*, and be colored in time $O(b)$. It follows that the overall running time of the algorithm is at most $O(b \log n) = O(\log^2 n)$ with high probability. In order to show that the expected running time is also $O(\log^2 n)$, we need to show that even when some segments choose *Excess*, the running time does not blow up too much. However, if there are segments that chose *Excess*, then the vertices in a maximal sequence of consecutive segments that chose *Excess* must color sequentially. The maximum number of vertices needing to color sequentially is n, so the worst case time to color them is at most $O(n)$. Noting that the bad event happens with probability at most n^{α}, where $\alpha > 1$, we see that the expected running time of exact sampler is also $O(\log^2 n)$. This, together with the correctness (Theorem 4) completes the proof of Theorem 2.

6   Concluding Remarks and Open Questions

We have shown that it is possible to sample nearly uniform colorings of trees in $O(\log^2 n)$ time with high probability. Our approach is based on identifying long paths, over which correlations have decayed sufficiently to allow endpoints to color independently uniformly at random. The coloring for the interior of the path can then be sampled from the correct distribution conditioned on the colors of the endpoints. The running time of $O(\log^2 n)$ seems forced for this approach, due to graphs like the beaded binary tree with $b - 1$ beads per edge, which has diameter $O(\log^2 n)$, and no long paths enabling simultaneous independent coloring of their endpoints. See Fig. 1. This naturally leads to the question of whether a faster sampling algorithm is possible using some other approach. For example, is it possible to decompose the tree into low-diameter clusters that are not paths, whose boundaries could be independently colored from a distribution close to the correct marginal? If such clusters contained high-degree vertices, would it still be possible to color their interiors with few colors?

When we have a rooted tree, we can use the same approach to sample exactly a uniform coloring. The assumption that the tree is rooted is crucial (even though it was not necessary when it was actually a path.) The reason for this is that in the unlikely event that all segments of a long path chose *Excess*, that path must color itself sequentially, and one of the endpoints must be willing to accept a color chosen for it by the other. But if both endpoints have a parent in the decomposition that needs to be colored before them, then in this bad event, the algorithm fails to produce a valid coloring. This might not seem like such a terrible thing, since it happens with vanishingly small probability, but actually, it destroys the entire algorithm! This is because Bayes' Theorem tells us that if the algorithm has a small chance to fail, this actually affects the distribution of the coloring it produces in the good event. In other words, a sampler that produces an exact sample with high probability is not an exact sampler at all! Naturally, this leads us to ask about the complexity of exactly sampling proper colorings of an unrooted tree. Can it be done in time that is asymptotically smaller than the diameter of the tree, or is there a lower bound?

Finally, are there other graph classes to which this techniques may be applied?

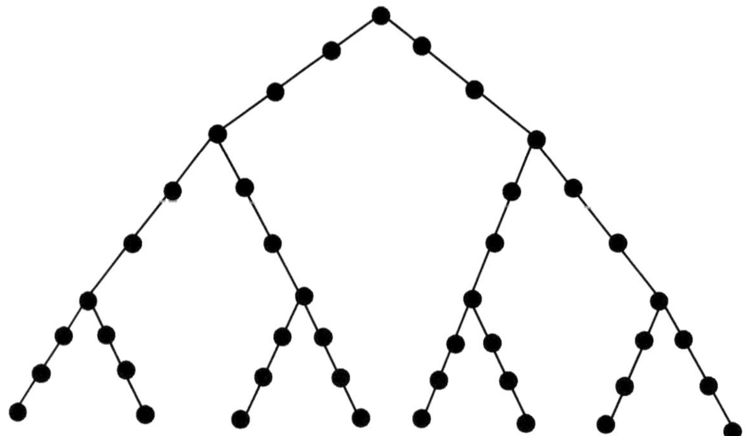

Fig. 1. A beaded binary tree, with $b - 1$ beads per edge ($b = 3$ in this example). This has diameter $\Theta(\log^2 n)$ but no long paths that can be removed.

Acknowledgements. We thank Ivona Bezáková, Tom Hayes, and the anonymous reviewers for many helpful comments.

References

1. Bonamy, M., Ouvrard, P., Rabie, M., Suomela, J., Uitto, J.: Distributed recoloring. In: 32nd International Symposium on Distributed Computing, pp. 1 (2018)
2. Carlson, C., Vigoda, E.: Flip dynamics for sampling colorings: improving ($11/6—\varepsilon$) using a simple metric. In: Proceedings of the 2025 Annual ACM-SIAM Symposium on Discrete Algorithms (SODA), pp. 2194–2212. SIAM (2025)
3. Chen, Z., Stefankovic, D., Vigoda, E.: Spectral independence and local-to-global techniques for optimal mixing of Markov chains (2025)
4. Cole, R., Vishkin, U.: Deterministic coin tossing with applications to optimal parallel list ranking. Inf. Control **70**(1), 32–53 (1986)
5. Dyer, M., Frieze, A.: Randomly coloring graphs with lower bounds on girth and maximum degree. Random Struct. Algorithms **23**(2), 167–179 (2003)
6. Feng, W., Hayes, T.P., Yin, Y.: Distributed symmetry breaking in sampling (optimal distributed randomly coloring with fewer colors). arXiv preprint arXiv:1802.06953 (2018)

7. Feng, W., Hayes, T.P., Yin, Y.: Distributed metropolis sampler with optimal parallelism. In: Proceedings of the 2021 ACM-SIAM Symposium on Discrete Algorithms (SODA), pp. 2121–2140. SIAM (2021)
8. Feng, W., Sun, Y., Yin, Y.: What can be sampled locally? In: Proceedings of the ACM Symposium on Principles of Distributed Computing, pp. 121–130 (2017)
9. Feng, W., Yin, Y.: On local distributed sampling and counting. In: Proceedings of the 2018 ACM Symposium on Principles of Distributed Computing, pp. 189–198 (2018)
10. Fischer, M., Ghaffari, M.: A simple parallel and distributed sampling technique: local Glauber dynamics. In: 32nd International Symposium on Distributed Computing (2018)
11. Frieze, A., Vera, J.: On randomly colouring locally sparse graphs. Discrete Math. Theoretical Comput. Sci. **8** (2006)
12. Frieze, A., Vigoda, E.: A survey on the use of Markov chains to randomly sample colourings. Oxford Lecture Series Math. Appl. **34**, 53 (2007)
13. Gamarnik, D., Katz, D.: Correlation decay and deterministic FPTAS for counting colorings of a graph. J. Discrete Algorithms **12**, 29–47 (2012)
14. Goldberg, L.A., Jerrum, M., Karpinski, M.: The mixing time of Glauber dynamics for coloring regular trees. Random Struct. Algorithms, **36**(4), 464–476 (2010)
15. Hayes, T.P.: Randomly coloring graphs of girth at least five. In: Proceedings of the Thirty-fifth Annual ACM Symposium on Theory of Computing, pp. 269–278 (2003)
16. Hayes, T.P., Vigoda, E.: Coupling with the stationary distribution and improved sampling for colorings and independent sets. Ann. Appl. Probability**16**(3), 1297–1318 (2006)
17. Jerrum, M.: A very simple algorithm for estimating the number of k-colorings of a low-degree graph. Random Struct. Algorithms **7**(2), 157–165 (1995)
18. Lucier, B., Molloy, M.: The Glauber dynamics for colorings of bounded degree trees. SIAM J. Discret. Math. **25**(2), 827–853 (2011)
19. Maus, Y., Peltonen, S., Uitto, J.: Distributed symmetry breaking on power graphs via sparsification. In: Proceedings of the 2023 ACM Symposium on Principles of Distributed Computing, pp. 157–167 (2023)
20. Pai, S., Pandurangan, G., Pemmaraju, S.V., Riaz, T., Robinson, P.: Symmetry breaking in the congest model: time-and message-efficient algorithms for ruling sets. In: 31st International Symposium on Distributed Computing (DISC 2017), volume 91, page 38. Schloss Dagstuhl–Leibniz-Zentrum fuer Informatik (2017)
21. Reif, J.H., Tate, S.R.: Dynamic parallel tree contraction. In: Proceedings of the Sixth Annual ACM Symposium on Parallel Algorithms and Architectures, pp. 114–121 (1994)
22. Salas, J., Sokal, A.D.: Absence of phase transition for antiferromagnetic Potts models via the Dobrushin uniqueness theorem. J. Stat. Phy. **86**(3), 551–579 (1997)
23. Vigoda, E.: Improved bounds for sampling colorings. J. Math. Phys. **41**(3), 1555–1569 (2000)

Distributed Sparsest Cut via Eigenvalue Estimation

Yannic Maus[ID] and Tijn de Vos[(✉)][ID]

Institute of Algorithms and Theory, TU Graz, Graz, Austria
{yannic.maus,tijn.devos}@tugraz.at

Abstract. We give new, improved bounds for approximating the sparsest cut value or in other words the conductance ϕ of a graph in the CONGEST model. As our main result, we present an algorithm running in $O(\log^2 n/\phi)$ rounds in which every vertex outputs a value $\tilde\phi$ satisfying $\phi \leq \tilde\phi \leq \sqrt{2.01\phi}$. In most regimes, our algorithm improves significantly over the previously fastest algorithm for the problem [Chen, Meierhans, Probst Gutenberg, Saranurak; SODA 25]. Additionally, our result generalizes to k-way conductance.

We obtain these results, by approximating the eigenvalues of the normalized Laplacian matrix $L := I - \mathrm{Deg}^{-1/2} A \, \mathrm{Deg}^{-1/2}$, where, A is the adjacency matrix and Deg is the diagonal matrix with the weighted degrees on the diagonal. We show our algorithms are near-optimal by proving a lower bound for computing the smallest non-trivial eigenvalue of L, even in the stronger LOCAL model.

The previous state of the art sparsest cut algorithm is in the technical realm of expander decompositions. Our algorithms, on the other hand, are relatively simple and easy to implement. At the core, they rely on the well-known *power method*, which comes down to repeatedly multiplying the Laplacian with a vector. This operation can be performed in a single round in the CONGEST model.

All our algorithms apply to weighted, undirected graphs. Our lower bounds apply even in unweighted graphs.

Full version: https://arxiv.org/abs/2508.19898.

Keywords: CONGEST · Sparsest Cut · Laplacian · Eigenvalues · Spectral Graph Theory

1 Introduction

A graph cut is a partition of the vertices into two disjoint subsets, where the size of the cut is the total number of edges crossing between them, and the sparsity of the cut measures how small this cut is relative to total edge weight of the

The author ordering was randomized using https://www.aeaweb.org/journals/policies/random-author-order/ generator. Citations of this work should list the authors separated by ⓡ instead of commas.

smaller side, i.e., in comparison to the sum of its vertex degrees. Graph cuts are a central object in theoretical computer science and algorithm design and have been extensively studied in various settings and models of computation, both explicitly studied, e.g., in [6,24,30,46,50,65,68], and as central subroutines, e.g., in [23,64,72].

Cuts are especially important in communication networks because they represent the capacity for information to flow between different parts of the system. A sparse cut—where only a few edges connect two large subsets—can become a bottleneck, severely limiting bandwidth or throughput. A central question for guaranteeing the performance of network algorithms is to determine the minimum sparsity of cuts in a given communication network. For example the runtime of the famous PUSH-PULL protocol depends on the sparsest cut value [41]. More generally, graphs without sparse cuts support fast mixing of random walks [69], and enable efficient routing due to their strong connectivity [39,40]. This motivates the use of expander decompositions, which partition a graph into *high-conductance* clusters (i.e., no sparse internal cuts), and sparse inter-cluster connections. Such decompositions are powerful algorithmic tools: thanks to efficient routing, many algorithms run significantly faster on high-conductance subgraphs, allowing problems to be solved locally within clusters before handling the sparse inter-cluster parts. This strategy has been used in many applications, see, e.g., [18–20,28,31]. The distributed expander decompositions [19–21,23] are all constructed by repeatedly computing sparsest cuts.

In this work, we present simple, time and bandwidth efficient distributed algorithms to approximate the sparsest cut value. Our randomized algorithms run in the classic CONGEST model of distributed computing where a communication network is abstracted as an n-vertex graph with vertices being computing entities and edges serving as bandwidth-limited communication links. Communication happens in synchronous rounds, in each of which each vertex can send a $O(\log n)$-bit message to each of its neighbors and the complexity measure is the number of communication rounds until the vertices have computed their outputs, e.g., until they have output an approximate value of the sparsest cut.

Formally, the *sparsity* of a set (or cut) $S \subseteq V$ in a graph $G = (V, E)$ is defined as as

$$\phi(S) := \frac{w(E(S, V \setminus S))}{\min\{\mathrm{Vol}(S), \mathrm{Vol}(V \setminus S)\}} \, ,$$

where $w(T) := \sum_{e \in T} w(e)$ for any edge set T and the volume $\mathrm{Vol}(S)$ of a set of vertices S is the sum of the weighted degrees of the vertices in the set: $\sum_{v \in S} \sum_{uv \in E} w(uv)$. The value $\phi(S)$ is also known as the *conductance* of the set S. The *sparsest cut* $\phi(G) \in [0, 1]$ of a graph G is the minimum sparsity of a subset $S \subseteq V$. This is also known as the *conductance* of the graph.

The relative notion $\phi(G)$ can be viewed as a normalized quantification of cut size. In contrast to computing minimum cuts, which quantify the absolute size of a cut, determining the sparsest cut or the conductance is not only NP-complete [59] but also APX-hard under the unique games conjecture [22]. Consequently, although no polynomial-time algorithm can approximate the optimum arbitrarily well (unless $P = NP$), a variety of approximation algorithms with provable—albeit weaker—guarantees have been developed across different computational models. Next, we present our results and compare them with the state of the art in the field. As the sparsest cut and the conductance have been extensively studied we provide further background and related work in Sect. 4.

2   Our Contribution on Sparsest Cut Approximation

Our first result is an efficient CONGEST algorithm to approximate the sparsest cut.

Theorem 1. *There is a randomized* CONGEST *algorithm that, given an undirected weighted n-node graph with sparsest cut ϕ, w.h.p. gives an approximation of the sparsest cut in $O(\log^2 n/\phi)$ rounds. In particular, every vertex outputs $\tilde{\phi}$ such that $\phi \leq \tilde{\phi} \leq \sqrt{2.01\phi}$.*

In general, there are two approaches for developing approximation algorithms for the sparsest cut, the *flow approach*, that we detail in Sect. 4, and the *spectral approach*, which we use to prove Theorem 1. On a high-level, one computes the spectrum (or parts of it) of the graph, i.e., its eigenvalues, and then uses Cheeger's Inequality[1] to derive an approximation of $\phi(G)$ from the eigenvalues. Due to the limitations imposed by Cheeger's Inequality, the best possible approximation achievable through spectral methods is $\sqrt{2\phi}$. Our technical result is slightly stronger than Theorem 1. In fact, we can attain this theoretical bound – up to an arbitrarily small additive error – in $O(\log^2 n/\varepsilon^2 + \log n/\varepsilon^4)$ rounds. See the proof of Theorem 1 for the details.

For unweighted graphs, we compare our result against the previously best algorithm by Chen, Meierhans, Probst Gutenberg, and Saranurak that provides a $O(\phi \log^2 n)$-approximation of ϕ [23][2] Our approximation is more precise than [23] when $\phi = \Omega(1/\log^4 n)$, and is faster in all cases: [23] takes $O(\text{poly}\log n/\phi^4)$ rounds. Upon inspection of their $\text{poly}\log n$, they have a total round complexity of at least $O(\log^{20} n)$ in the regime where their approximation is more precise.

Prior to [23], Das Sarma, Molla, and Pandurangan [67] gave a different algorithm to approximate the sparsest cut, which also works for weighted graphs. They computed an $O(\sqrt{\phi}\text{poly}\log n)$-approximation in $O(\frac{1}{b}(n+\frac{1}{\phi})\log^2 n)$ rounds if the graph has a sparse cut of *balance b*, i.e., both sides S of the cut satisfy $\text{Vol}(S) \geq 2b|E|$. Building on the methods of [67], Kuhn and Molla improved the approximation ratio to $O(\sqrt{\phi \log n})$ and the runtime to $O(D + \frac{\log^2 n}{b\phi})$ [50]. For balanced cuts $b = \Omega(1)$, we improve their approximation ratio by a factor $\sqrt{\log n}$,

---

[1] Cheeger's Inequality [1,2,71] relates the second-smallest eigenvalue λ_2 of the normalized Laplacian to the graph's conductance ϕ, showing that $\frac{1}{2}\lambda_2 \leq \phi \leq \sqrt{2\lambda_2}$. See Theorem 7 for the formal statement.

[2] They do not state this result explicitly, but they implement the cut-matching game from [64] (see Appendix A) in the distributed setting. As stated in [64], this cut-matching game gives such an approximation.

while matching their running time. For unbalanced cuts, also their algorithm can take as much as $\Omega(n^2)$ time, so we do not only improve the approximation ratio, but also the running time exponentially.

We note that [23,50,67] do not only provide an approximate cut value, but also give a corresponding cut.

k-Way Sparsest Cut. There exists a natural generalization of the sparsest cut to *multi-cuts* [51]: the *k-way sparsest cut* or *k-way conductance* ϕ_k is defined follows:

$$\phi_k := \min_{V_1,V_2,\ldots,V_k \subset V} \max_{i=1,\ldots,k} \frac{|E(V_i, V \setminus V_i)|}{\mathrm{Vol}(V_i)},$$

where the minimum is taken over disjoint, non-empty V_i. Note that $\phi_2 = \phi$. The k-way conductance captures how well-connected a graph is across multiple parts; it can describe multi-partition bottlenecks, which standard conductance may miss. This is in particular relevant for real-world networks that usually consists of multiple clusters.

We prove the following theorem for approximating the k-way sparsest cut.

Theorem 2. *There is a randomized* CONGEST *algorithm that, given a constant $k \geq 2$ and undirected weighted graph with k-way sparsest cut ϕ_k, w.h.p. gives an approximation of the k-way sparsest cut in $O(\log^2 n\,\mathrm{poly}(\phi_k^{-1}))$ rounds. In particular, every vertex outputs $\tilde{\phi}_k$ such that $\phi_k \leq \tilde{\phi}_k \leq O(\sqrt{\phi_k})$.*

To the best of our knowledge, we are the first to study the k-way conductance in the distributed setting.

Lower Bounds on Approximating Sparse Cuts. Generally, it is known that approximating the sparsest cut takes $\Omega(D)$ rounds. In particular, Das Sarma, Molla, and Pandurangan [67] show a $\tilde{\Omega}(D + \sqrt{n})$ CONGEST lower bound for any multiplicative approximation in weighted graphs. They reduce the spanning connected subgraph problem to a sparsest cut instance with edge weights that are either 0 or 1. This means that the lower bound shows that it is hard to decide whether $\phi = 0$ holds or not. For ϕ bounded away from zero, there is no such lower bound. Our upper bound of $O(\log^2 n/\phi)$ rounds, Theorem 1, indeed takes D rounds, since $D = O(\log n/\phi)$. However, for $\phi = \omega(1/\sqrt{n})$, the upper bound does not have a $\sqrt{n}$-term.

We prove a $\Omega(D)$ lower bound that holds even for unweighted graphs and in the LOCAL model. LOCAL is identical to CONGEST, except that there is no bound on the message size. Even for a class of fixed diameter, any algorithm needs $\Omega(D)$ time for a $O(n)$-approximation.

Theorem 3. *Let $D \leq n/2$ be a parameter and consider the class of graphs with diameter D. An algorithm that with probability $> \frac{1}{2}$ satisfies that every vertex v of a graph G outputs a value $\tilde{\phi}_v \geq \phi(G)$, for sparsest cut $\phi(G)$, and at least one vertex has $\phi_v \leq \Theta(n \cdot \phi)$ needs $\Omega(D)$ rounds in LOCAL.*

Note that the $\Omega(D)$ lower bound in Theorem 3 holds even in the case where only a single vertex needs to witness the cut.

The above proof is about discerning graphs with sparsity $1/n$ and $1/n^2$. If *every vertex* needs to output a correct estimation, a diameter lower bound exists for larger values of ϕ.

Theorem 4. *Let $0 < \varepsilon < 1$ be a constant and let $\phi > 1/n^{1-\varepsilon}$. An algorithm that with probability $> \frac{1}{2}$ satisfies that every vertex v outputs a value $\tilde{\phi}_v$ such that $\phi \le \tilde{\phi} \le O(n^{1+\varepsilon} \cdot \phi)$, where ϕ is the sparsest cut value of the graph needs at least $\Omega(D)$ rounds in the* LOCAL *model.*

Our CONGEST upper bound for approximating the sparsest cut w.h.p. is $O(\log^2 n/\phi)$ – only a factor $\log n$ away from optimal, since the graphs from the above observation have sparsest cut ϕ and diameter $\Theta(\log n/\phi)$ [25]. We note that with constant probability, we match the lower bound, see Sect. 5.

3   Our Contributions on Spectrum Approximation

Our core technical contributions are efficient CONGEST algorithms to compute the approximate (partial) spectrum of a graph. In essence, Theorems 1 and 2 then follow as direct consequences via Cheeger's Inequality. Nevertheless, we chose to present these theorems first, as they are more accessible to a broader audience and can be compared with prior work.

Eigenvalues of the Normalized Laplacian. The normalized Laplacian of a graph is the matrix defined as $L := I - \mathrm{Deg}^{-1/2} A \, \mathrm{Deg}^{-1/2}$, where A is the adjacency matrix and Deg is the (weighted) degree matrix. See our full version for more details. Its spectrum captures many central properties of the graph, e.g., various types of its connectedness like k-way conductance [51] and small set expansion [5], or how close it is to being bipartite [9,55]. We provide the following theorem to compute an approximation of that spectrum.

Theorem 5 (Eigenvalue estimation). *Let $\varepsilon > 0$ be a parameter and $k \in \mathbb{N}$ be a constant. There are randomized* CONGEST *algorithms that, given an undirected, weighted graph $G = (V, E)$, with high probability approximate the eigenvalues $\lambda_1 \le \lambda_2 \le \ldots \le \lambda_n$ of the graph's normalized Laplacian as follows:*

1. $\lambda_1, \ldots, \lambda_k$: an additive ε-approximations in $O(\log^2 n \cdot \mathrm{poly}(\varepsilon^{-1}))$ rounds,
2. λ_2: an additive ε-approximation in
$$O\left(\frac{\log^2 n}{\varepsilon} + \frac{\log n}{\varepsilon} \cdot \left\lceil \frac{\lambda_2}{\varepsilon} \right\rceil \right) = O\left(\frac{\log^2 n}{\varepsilon} + \frac{\log n}{\varepsilon^2}\right) \text{ rounds,}$$
3. λ_n: a multiplicative $(1 \pm \varepsilon)$-approximation in $O\left(D + \frac{\log^2 n}{\varepsilon}\right)$ rounds.

Eigenvalue λ_2 is the eigenvalue approximating the sparsest cut via Cheeger's Inequality. It could either be approximated via the second algorithm, or slightly slower via the first.

For the smaller eigenvalues, Theorem 5 states additive approximations avoiding the diameter dependence, e.g., when ε is an arbitrarily small constant Theorem 5 approximates λ_2 in $O(\log^2 n)$ rounds even though the diameter may be up to linear in n.

As ε can be arbitrary in Theorem 5, we can obtain multiplicative approximations by setting $\varepsilon = \varepsilon' \lambda_2$ for any $\varepsilon' > 0$. However, this does not circumvent the diameter lower bound of Theorem 6 presented below. By Theorem 7 and the fact that if G has k-way sparsest cut ϕ_k then it has diameter $D = O(k \log n / \phi_k)$ (see our full version), $D = O(\log n / \lambda_2)$ holds for any graph, so the diameter term is then always asymptotically smaller than the overall runtime of the algorithm.

The main prior work for distributed eigenvalue approximation is by Kempe and McSherry [48]. They provide a distributed algorithm that, for constant k, approximates the k-largest/smallest eigenvalues in $O(\tau_{\mathrm{mix}} \log^2 n)$ rounds. We note that the mixing time can be as large as $n^{\Omega(1)}$. This happens when λ_2 is really small (in which case our algorithms are also slow), but also when the graph is (close to) bipartite. In the latter case, our algorithms can be exponentially faster. Furthermore, an important caveat here is that Kempe and McSherry do not obtain their result in the CONGEST model: they do not discuss the bandwidth constraint. They do specify that they only need $\mathrm{poly}(k)$ messaged per edge per round. However, they do not take the *size* of these messages into account. In our work, this is a non-trivial contribution, as intermediate values may grow fast. We think similar techniques might be able to work for their approach as well, but this requires non-trivial adjustments and additional analysis.

Later, Becchetti et al. [12] gave an algorithm for finding *balanced* cuts, where our algorithm works for *all* cuts. We provide more details on this algorithm in Sect. 5.

An alternative approach to distributed eigenvalue computation is via computing a spectral sparsifier, i.e., a sparse subgraph H with $\tilde{O}(n/\varepsilon^2)$ edges that approximately preserve the graph's spectrum. Next, the sparsifier H can be gathered at one vertex of the graph that can locally compute the eigenvalues of H and hence obtain approximations of all eigenvalues of G. Computing H is actually relatively fast and only requires $\mathrm{poly}(\log n, \varepsilon^{-1})$ rounds [49]. Collecting H at a single vertex is the expensive part, requiring $\tilde{O}(n/\varepsilon^2)$ rounds. This is exponentially slower than Theorem 5, though this more general method immediately computes the full spectrum while we focus on single eigenvalues.

We note that all our upper bounds even hold in the more restricted Broadcast CONGEST model in which a vertex needs to send the same message to all of its neighbors in each round. All our algorithms become a $\log n$-factor faster if we only ask for constant probability as typical in property testing, see the discussion in Sect. 5.

Lower Bound. All of our multiplicative upper bounds take diameter time. This means that at the end of the algorithm, every vertex can easily output the same eigenvalue or sparsest cut estimate. One may ask whether one can obtain faster algorithms if the output is more local. Perhaps every vertex outputs the sparsest cut it sees in some neighborhood, and there is a guarantee that at least one vertex will see an approximately sparsest cut. In Theorem 3, we showed that this is not true for sparsest cut approximation. We also show that approximating λ_2 at even one node requires $\Omega(D)$ rounds.

Theorem 6. *Any algorithm that with probability $> \frac{1}{2}$ ensures that all vertices output a value $\tilde{\lambda}_2 \geq \lambda_2$, and at least one vertex additionally satisfies $\tilde{\lambda}_2 \leq 2\lambda_2$ requires $\Omega(D)$ rounds.*

An $\Omega(D)$ lower bound could also follow from our sparsest cut lower bounds via Cheeger's Inequality, but such an approach incurs an inherent quadratic loss due to the approximation gap in Cheeger's.

Decision Problem and Connections to Property Testing. For the lower bounds in Theorem 3 (and similarly for Theorem 6), the vertices that do not output a correct value, still need to output a value $\tilde{\phi} \geq \phi$. If we do not do this, then a trivial algorithm where every vertex outputs a random number between 0 and 1 will be correct most of the time. In other words, we aim to solve the decision problem: "is there a cut sparser than ϕ?" If all vertices say "no", the answer is no. If at least one vertex answers "yes", the answer is yes. As we are only solving the approximate version of the question this is closely related to the concept of *property testing* in CONGEST, introduced in [17] and extensively studied since then, e.g., [32,52]. "Conductance property testing" has been explicitly studied by [8,33] and Theorem 1 improves significantly on their results. We detail the relation to property testing and their results in Sect. 4.

Also the eigenvalues of the adjacency matrix and the non-normalized Laplacian describe many graph properties. Among other properties, they relate to the size of independent sets (Hoffman's bound) [44], the chromatic number [74], the average density of cuts [44], the toughness of the graph [54], Hamiltonicity [34], the matching number [43], and the existence of a perfect matching [16].

Approximating the Entire Spectrum. Via similar methods, one can compute a multiplicative approximation of the entire spectrum. However, the output will not reveal how many eigenvalues there are of a certain approximation, i.e., it gives the spectrum *without multiplicity*. The running time of such an algorithm is $n^{o(1)}(\sqrt{n}+D)/\varepsilon^2$ rounds, see our full version for details. Note that in particular this gives a multiplicative approximation of the smallest non-zero eigenvalue λ_2. In case λ_2 is small – roughly $\lambda_2 = o(1/\sqrt{n})$ – this is faster than Theorem 5.

4   Related Work

Sparsest Cut. As mentioned there are two approaches to solving the sparsest cut problem. The *spectral approach* used in this paper and the *flow approach*. The spectral approach encompasses techniques like Cheeger's Inequality, spectral sparsifiers (discussed above), and also random walks. For instance, the results of [8,29,33,50] rely on random walks, which are considered spectral in nature since their convergence analysis depends on spectral properties. This approach is inherently limited by Cheeger's Inequality, capping the approximation factor at $\sqrt{2\phi}$, the guarantee we match in this work.

The flow approach, based on the *cut-matching game*, computes a number of flows that will either guarantee expansion or find a sparse cut. Theoretically, this can give a $(\phi\,\text{poly}\log n)$-approximation. In the sequential setting, the state-of-the-art is a $O(\phi\sqrt{\log n})$-approximation by Arora, Rao, and Vazirani [6]. In the distributed setting, the state-of-the-art is the aforementioned $O(\phi\log^2 n)$-approximation [23]. Before this recent result, the flow based gave worse approximations: [19,20] gave a $\tilde{\phi} \leq O(\phi^{1/3}\log^{5/3} n)$-approximation in $O(D \cdot \text{poly}\log n, \phi^{-1})$ rounds, for $\phi = O(1/\log^5 n)$. Additionally, Chang and Saranurak [21] gave a deterministic version of that result with additional subpolynomial factor in the round complexity.

Property Testing. In our paper, we are essentially solving the decision problem: "does G have sparsest cut at least ϕ?" In property testing, the goal is to solve a relaxed variant of the corresponding decision problem: if the input network satisfies a property, then, with constant probability, all the vertices accept but if the input network is ε-far[3] from satisfying the property, then at least one vertex rejects. Testing for sparsest cuts has explicitly been targeted in this setting by [8,33]. For a fixed ϕ, [8], improving on [33], solves this question as follows. All vertices output "yes", with probability at least $2/3$ if the sparsest cut is at least ϕ, and at least one vertex outputs "no", with probability at least $2/3$ if G is ε-far from having sparsest cut above $\phi^2/2880$. Similar to our result, the ϕ^2 term stems from Cheeger's Inequality. Our results improve upon this in several ways. For achieving a constant probability, we only need $O(\log n/\phi)$ rounds, as compared to $O(\frac{\log n}{\varepsilon \cdot \phi^2})$ rounds in their algorithm. Most notably, we do not solve the property testing version, and do not require that the instance is ε-far from having a sparse cut above $O(\phi^2)$. Thus, in some sense we are solving their version with $\varepsilon = 1/n^2$. Additionally, our results extend to weighted graphs and the constant in our approximation factor is significantly better. Lastly, we also approximately compute the sparsest cut value instead of only solving the decision problem.

Cut Sparsifiers. We have already discussed how to use spectral sparsifiers to approximate the spectrum in $\tilde{O}(n/\varepsilon^2)$ rounds [49]. They can also directly be used for approximating sparsest cuts without going through Cheeger's Inequality: $(1 \pm \varepsilon)$-approximate spectral sparsifiers are $(1 \pm \varepsilon)$-cut sparsifiers. This means that in $\tilde{O}(n/\varepsilon^2)$ rounds, we can collect a subgraph H in one vertex, in which *all* cuts are at most a factor $(1 \pm \varepsilon)$ away from the cut in G. In particular, we can find a $(1 \pm \varepsilon)$-approximation of the sparsest cut, and more generally a $(1 \pm \varepsilon)$-approximation of the k-way sparsest cut in $\tilde{O}(n/\varepsilon^2)$ rounds.

Laplacian Paradigm. The *Laplacian paradigm* is an umbrella term for algorithmic techniques relying on the Laplacian and its properties. This line of research was initiated by Spielman and Teng [72], who showed that linear equations in the Laplacian matrix of a graph can be solved in near-linear time. Algorithms within the Laplacian paradigm combine numerical techniques – from the matrix

---

[3] This refers to εm changes to the graph. For a precise definition, see, e.g., [8].

point of view – with combinatorial techniques – from the graph point of view. Nowadays, it encompasses techniques like solving Laplacian systems, spectral sparsifiers, electrical flow, effective resistance, expander decompositions, continuous optimization, interior-point methods, gradient descent, and preconditioning. This has had many applications, including but not limited to flow problems [7,27,47,56,57,60–62,70], bipartite matching [15], and (parallel) shortest paths [4,53].

Also in the distributed world, this has booked many successes, e.g., [3,13,35–38,73]. With this paper, we hope to contribute to a better understanding of the Laplacian matrix and its applications in a distributed setting.

Comparison to the Min-Cut Problem. In the minimum cut (min-cut) problem, the goal is to find a cut S of minimum value $|E(S, V \setminus S)|$. Although the problem statement seems similar to the sparsest cut problem, it has a very different computational complexity. As said, in the sequential setting, it is NP-hard to approximate the sparsest cut (under the unique games conjecture) [22,59]. On the other hand, there are linear time algorithms for computing the exact min-cut [46].

In the distributed setting, we show that the $\Omega(\sqrt{n} + D)$ lower bound does not apply for approximating the sparsest cut problem. The min-cut problem however has a complexity of $\tilde{\Theta}(\sqrt{n} + D)$ [30,66], where the lower bound holds even for a $\mathrm{poly}(n)$-approximation.

5 Technical Overview

As mentioned, Theorems 1 and 2 follow as direct consequences from our eigenvalue estimation results via Cheeger's Inequality. Here, we focus on our core technical contribution: efficient CONGEST algorithms to compute the approximate (partial) spectrum of a graph. The main ingredient of our algorithms is the well-known *power method* for approximating the largest eigenvalue of a matrix.

The Power Method Algorithm. Let M be any matrix. The power method, also known as *power iteration* or *Von Mises iteration*, starts with a random vector and converges to the eigenvector corresponding to the largest eigenvalue of M. It is a standard technique in numerical linear algebra, see, e.g., [42]. The procedure is as follows.

Power Method

1: **Input:** Matrix $M \in \mathbb{R}^{n \times n}$, number of iterations k.
2: **Initialize:** A random vector $x_0 \in \mathbb{R}^n$.
3: **for** $i = 1$ to k **do**
4:     $x_i \leftarrow M x_{i-1}$.
5: **Output:**
   – Approximate dominant eigenvalue: $\lambda \approx \frac{x_k^T M x_k}{x_k^T x_k}$;
   – Approximate dominant eigenvector: x_k.

With constant probability over the randomness of the start vector x_0, the power method outputs a vector x_k whose *Rayleigh coefficient* $\frac{x_k^T M x_k}{x_k^T x_k}$ is close to the *largest* eigenvalue of the matrix M. The main intuition why this happens is as follows: Any vector can be written as a combination of the matrix' eigenvectors and when you apply the matrix multiple times, the contribution from the eigenvector with the largest eigenvalue (in magnitude) dominates. So, over time, the method "filters out" all directions except the one corresponding to the largest eigenvalue. This works only if the random start vector x_0 has a nonzero component in the dominant eigenvector's direction; beyond the choice of this initial vector, the process is fully deterministic.

In this paper, we only need the power method for *positive semi-definite (PSD)* matrices, which are symmetric matrices with non-negative eigenvalues. Then all eigenvalues are nonnegative and we can assume the eigenvectors to be orthonormal. The power method also converges slightly faster on PSD matrices – by a factor 2 to be precise.

Lemma 1 (Power Method). *Let M be a positive semi-definite matrix with eigenvalues $0 \leq \mu_1 \leq \cdots \leq \mu_n$. Let $x_0 \sim \{-1, 1\}^n$ be a uniformly random vector and $x_k = M^k x_0$. For $\varepsilon \geq 16/n$ and $k \geq \Theta(\log n/\varepsilon)$, it holds with constant probability that*

$$(1 - \varepsilon)\mu_n \leq \frac{x_k^T M x_k}{x_k^T x_k} \leq \mu_n.$$

The power method is suitable for distributed applications, since matrix vector multiplication is easy in the CONGEST model: this can be done in $O(1)$ rounds where each vertex of the communication network holds an entry of the vector, and each vertex knows the entries of the matrix in its row and column. Important is that the only non-zero entries in a row or column correspond to a neighboring vertex. This is exactly the case when the matrix is closely related to the adjacency matrix – such as the Laplacian.

Only the final step, of computing the Rayleigh coefficient of x_k takes $O(D)$ time. We note that the power method is a widely used routine. Also decentralized implementations have been known for a long time, e.g., [14, 63] or for the special case of PageRank [68]. However, to the best of our knowledge, the procedure and its extensions have not been studied in the context of the CONGEST model.

One difficulty with implementing the power method in the CONGEST model as is, is that values grow exponentially with k and hence after a few iterations and they cannot be send to neighbors using $O(\log n)$ bits per message. Fortunately, the method is extremely robust. It still converges quickly after truncating each value after the $O(\log n)$ most significant bits; if one additionally remembers the order of magnitude of the values one can approximately compute the Rayleigh coefficient at the end of the algorithm – see our full version for a formal statement. More involved methods, like the Lanczos method (see, e.g., [42]) might be able to return similar results. However, the Lanczos method is inherently unstable. It is unclear whether this can be adapted to work (efficiently) in the CONGEST model.

Averaging Dynamics. In community detection, average dynamics is a well-known concept. The idea is that each node updates its value to the average of its neighbors. If G is connected and not bipartite, this always converges. The update step is comparable is the same in spirit as a step in the power method, but not entirely equal. In particular, Becchetti et al. [12] use average dynamics in the distributed setting. In case of a sufficiently small balanced cut, and some additional technical assumptions, they can provide an approximate sparsest cut. Since the approximation factor depends on the technical assumptions, we will not state their exact guarantees here. With a similar approach, Beccheretti et al. [11] can find a sparse cut efficiently if both of the parts do not contain sparse cuts. Moreover, the average dynamics has been studied as a tool for community dynamics in related models that do not directly compare to the CONGEST model, e.g., the asynchronous, opportunistic communication model [10] and the asynchronous gossip model [58].

The Graph Laplacian Matrix. We denote $\mathbb{1}$ for the vector with 1 in each entry and $\sqrt{\deg} = \mathrm{Deg}^{1/2}\,\mathbb{1}$ for the vector with $(\sqrt{\deg})_v = \sqrt{\deg(v)}$ on index (equals vertex) v.

Recall that the normalized Laplacian $L := I - \mathrm{Deg}^{-1/2}\,A\,\mathrm{Deg}^{-1/2}$ has smallest eigenvalue $\lambda_1 = 0$. This can be seen since $\sqrt{\deg}$ is an eigenvector of L eigenvalue 0:

$$L\sqrt{\deg} = (I - \mathrm{Deg}^{-1/2}\,A\,\mathrm{Deg}^{-1/2})\sqrt{\deg} = \sqrt{\deg} - \mathrm{Deg}^{-1/2}\,A\mathbb{1},$$

Note that $A\mathbb{1}$ counts the number of 1 s in each row[4], so this exactly sums up to the degree: $L\sqrt{\deg} = \sqrt{\deg} - \mathrm{Deg}^{-1/2}\,\deg = 0$. Hence, the smallest interesting eigenvalue to study is λ_2.

Approximating λ_2. To approximate the smallest non-zero eigenvalue of the Laplacian L, we consider the matrix $M := 2I - L$, which has eigenvalues $0 \leq \mu_1 \leq \cdots \leq \mu_n$, satisfying $\mu_i = 2 - \lambda_{n-i+1}$. In particular, this means that $\mu_n = 2$ and $\mu_{n-1} = \lambda_2$. In order to compute λ_2, one would like to subtract the components in the direction $v_n = \sqrt{\deg}$, the eigenvector corresponding to the largest eigenvalue μ_n. As a result, the prior largest eigenvalue is shifted to 0, and the power method converges to the second largest eigenvalue instead.

As per the discussion above, we know the largest eigenvector $v_n = \sqrt{\deg}$ exactly. We can also subtract the components in this direction exactly. However, a significant facet here is the bit complexity. As we discussed before, small errors incurred from rounding are not an issue when we are approximating the *largest* eigenvalue. However, due to rounding when we are approximation the second-largest eigenvalue, our vector will not remain perpendicular to v_n. Hence, given enough iterations, the process will always converge to the largest eigenvalue. Naively, we can combat this by projecting the current vector x on the subspace orthogonal to v_n in every step, or in other words, by removing components in

---

[4] In weighted graphs, this is the sum of the weights in each row. Since the degrees are also weighted degrees, the proof remains the same.

direction v_n. This requires computing the inner product between v_n and x. The latter is no problem in the centralized setting, but computing this inner product requires $\Omega(D)$ rounds in CONGEST. Hence we want to limit how often we do this. We show that the error blows up at a rate that means that we only need to project periodically, in total at most $\lceil \frac{\lambda_2}{\varepsilon} \rceil$ times. In order to perform this efficiently, we show that all interesting cases actually have a diameter small enough to repeatedly perform these projections without increasing the runtime too much.

Approximating $\lambda_1, \ldots, \lambda_k$. We compute the eigenvalue approximations sequentially. For approximating λ_i, we use the same general approach as for λ_2. Instead of projecting on the subspace orthogonal the largest eigenvalue, we project on the subspace orthogonal to the largest $i-1$ eigenvalues, and remove the resulting parts from consideration. The key challenge is that we do not know the corresponding eigenvectors exactly but they are only approximately known from our prior steps. We show that the power method still converges despite these inaccuracies in the eigenvectors that we project on. This is one of the most technical parts of this paper and appears in our full version.

Probabilistic Guarantees. The power method as stated in Lemma 1 is correct with constant probability. This means that we can for example can also obtain our sparsest cut result, Theorem 1, in $O(\log n/\phi)$ rounds but with *constant* probability. To boost the probability, we run $O(\log n)$ independent instances of the power method and return the maximum. Since we are looking for the largest eigenvalue, and we know that we cannot overshoot (see the proof in our full version), this gives the required approximation with high probability.

Lower Bound Constructions. We construct graphs by combining well-understood components—such as cliques, paths, and star graphs—where the sparsest cut is easy to determine. Using these building blocks, we define two graph families with significantly different sparsest cut values, yet with locally identical neighborhoods around certain vertices. As a result, these vertices cannot distinguish between the two families and thus cannot accurately approximate the sparsest cut without global information. This implies that approximating the sparsest cut requires $\Omega(D)$ rounds in our constructions.

It is challenging to use a similar approach to obtain a lower bound for eigenvalue approximation, as determining the eigenvalues of any graph is highly nontrivial. The eigenvalues of few specific graphs have been computed, like paths, cycles, and cliques, but determining them remains hard in general. This stems partly from the fact that gluing together graphs can have big effects on the eigenvalues. Cauchy's interlacing eigenvalue theorem [45] gives some bounds, but this is unfortunately of no help. Another approach is to use the fact that we know the sparsest cut, together with Cheeger's Inequality. Rephrased Cheeger's Inequality gives $\phi^2/2 \leq \lambda_2 \leq 2\phi$. So it gives a linear upper bound on the eigenvalue given the sparsest cut, but it has a square in the lower bound. At the end of the day, this means that only using Cheeger's would result in a lower bound of the form $\Omega(\sqrt{D})$. For our $\Omega(D)$ lower bound, we need a better upper bound on the eigenvalues of the graphs used in the lower bound construction. We exploit that eigenvalues can also be bounded by specific vectors. The simplest such statement is that the largest eigenvalue of a matrix M equals $\max_{x \in \mathbb{R}^n} \frac{x^T M x}{x^T x}$. Hence any x can provide a lower bound for the largest eigenvalue. We use a similar statement for the second smallest eigenvalue and construct an appropriate vector x to prove a tighter upper bound on the eigenvalues of our constructed graphs. In total, we are able to provide upper and lower bounds that characterize the eigenvalues of the graphs used in our lower bound construction up to a constant factor.

Sparsest Cuts and Cheeger's Inequality. Finally, let us explain how the eigenvalue results enable us to derive an approximation of the sparsest cut.

Let us obtain some intuition why eigenvalue λ_2 relates to the connectedness of the graph. In the extreme case that $\lambda_2 = 0$ holds the graph is disconnected: On each connected component, the degree vector is still an eigenvector with eigenvalue 0. Hence a vector that has $\sqrt{\deg}$ on one connected component, and all 0s on the other connected component is also an eigenvector – and linearly independent of $\sqrt{\deg}$. The reverse direction, i.e., that the graph is connected if $\lambda_2 \neq 0$ holds, is also true but its proof is slightly more involved, so we omit it in this overview, see e.g. [26].

Cheeger's Inequality [1,2,71] gives a more precise statement about the connectedness of the graph and the second smallest eigenvalue: it relates λ_2 to the sparsest cut ϕ.

Theorem 7 (Cheeger's Inequality). *Let $G = (V, E)$ be an undirected, weighted graph, then*

$$\frac{\lambda_2}{2} \leq \phi \leq \sqrt{2\lambda_2} \ .$$

The fact that $\lambda_2 = 0$ holds if and only if the graph is disconnected is a corollary of Theorem 7.

Since Cheeger's Inequality states that the value of λ_2 approximates ϕ, we can find an approximation $\tilde{\lambda}_2$ for λ_2 with Theorem 5 and use it to output an approximation $\tilde{\phi} = \sqrt{2\tilde{\lambda}_2}$ of the sparsest cut, establishing Theorem 1.

For larger values of k, similar statements hold. First, we remark that $\lambda_k = 0$ if and only if the graph consists of at least k connected components. One direction of this statement is again easy to see: as before, on each connected component the $\sqrt{\deg}$ vector is an eigenvector with eigenvalue 0. In total, this gives k independent eigenvalues with eigenvector 0 – in other words, $\lambda_k = 0$.

Similar as for $k = 2$, this generalizes by relating λ_k to ϕ_k: Lee, Gharan, and Trevisan showed the following theorem which we then use to establish Theorem 2 via Theorem 5.

Theorem 8 (Higher-Order Cheeger's Inequality, [51]). *Let $G = (V, E)$ be an undirected, weighted graph, then $\frac{\lambda_k}{2} \leq \phi_k \leq O(k^2)\sqrt{\lambda_k}$.*

Acknowledgement. We would like to thank Leo Wennmann, for the many hours of discussion on this topic. We would like Joachim Orthaber and Malte Baumecker, for thinking along. We would like to thank Faith Ellen, Sebastian Brandt, Alexandre Nolin, and Eva Rotenberg, for the initial discussions that were the inspiration for this research. We would like to thank Schloss Dagstuhl, since the research was initiated during the Dagstuhl seminar *Graph Algorithms: Distributed Meets Dynamic.*

This is a low-co2 research paper: https://tcs4f.org/low-co2-v1. This research was developed, written, submitted and presented without the use of air travel.

This research was funded in whole or in part by the Austrian Science Fund (FWF) https://doi.org/10.55776/P36280 and https://doi.org/10.55776/I6915. For open access purposes, the author has applied a CC BY public copyright license to any author-accepted manuscript version arising from this submission.

The authors have no competing interests to declare that are relevant to the content of this article.

References

1. Alon, N.: Eigenvalues and expanders. Comb. **6**(2), 83–96 (1986). https://doi.org/10.1007/BF02579166
2. Alon, N., Milman, V.D.: λ_1, isoperimetric inequalities for graphs, and superconcentrators. J. Comb. Theory B **38**(1), 73–88 (1985). https://doi.org/10.1016/0095-8956(85)90092-9
3. Anagnostides, I., Lenzen, C., Haeupler, B., Zuzic, G., Gouleakis, T.: Almost universally optimal distributed Laplacian solvers via low-congestion shortcuts. In: Proceedings of the 36th International Symposium on Distributed Computing, DISC 2022. LIPIcs, vol. 246, pp. 6:1–6:20. Schloss Dagstuhl - Leibniz-Zentrum für Informatik (2022). Announced at PODC 2022
4. Andoni, A., Stein, C., Zhong, P.: Parallel approximate undirected shortest paths via low hop emulators. In: Proceedings of the 52nd Annual ACM SIGACT Symposium on Theory of Computing, STOC 2020, pp. 322–335. ACM (2020)
5. Arora, S., Barak, B., Steurer, D.: Subexponential algorithms for unique games and related problems. J. ACM **62**(5), 42:1–42:25 (2015). https://doi.org/10.1145/2775105. Announced at FOCS '10
6. Arora, S., Rao, S., Vazirani, U.V.: Expander flows, geometric embeddings and graph partitioning. J. ACM **56**(2), 5:1–5:37 (2009). https://doi.org/10.1145/1502793.1502794. Announced at STOC'04
7. Axiotis, K., Mądry, A., Vladu, A.: Circulation control for faster minimum cost flow in unit-capacity graphs. In: Proceedings of the 61st IEEE Annual Symposium on Foundations of Computer Science, FOCS 2020, pp. 93–104. IEEE (2020)
8. Batu, T., Trehan, A., Trehan, C.: All you need are random walks: fast and simple distributed conductance testing. In: International Colloquium on Structural Information and Communication Complexity, pp. 64–82. Springer (2024)
9. Bauer, F., Jost, J.: Bipartite and neighborhood graphs and the spectrum of the normalized graph Laplacian. Commun. Anal. Geom. **21** (10 2009). https://doi.org/10.4310/CAG.2013.v21.n4.a2
10. Becchetti, L., et al.: Average whenever you meet: opportunistic protocols for community detection. In: Azar, Y., Bast, H., Herman, G. (eds.) 26th Annual European Symposium on Algorithms, ESA 2018, 20–22 August 2018, Helsinki, Finland. LIPIcs, vol. 112, pp. 7:1–7:13. Schloss Dagstuhl - Leibniz-Zentrum für Informatik (2018). https://doi.org/10.4230/LIPICS.ESA.2018.7

11. Becchetti, L., Clementi, A., Natale, E., Pasquale, F., Raghavendra, P., Trevisan, L.: Friend or foe? Population protocols can perform community detection. CoRR abs/1703.05045 (2017). http://arxiv.org/abs/1703.05045
12. Becchetti, L., Clementi, A.E.F., Natale, E., Pasquale, F., Trevisan, L.: Find your place: simple distributed algorithms for community detection. SIAM J. Comput. **49**(4), 821–864 (2020). https://doi.org/10.1137/19M1243026. Announced at SODA'17
13. Becker, R., Forster, S., Karrenbauer, A., Lenzen, C.: Near-optimal approximate shortest paths and transshipment in distributed and streaming models. SIAM J. Comput. **50**(3), 815–856 (2021). Announced at DISC 2017
14. Bertsekas, D., Tsitsiklis, J.: Parallel and Distributed Computation: Numerical Methods. Athena Scientific (2015)
15. van den Brand, J., et al.: Bipartite matching in nearly-linear time on moderately dense graphs. In: Proceedings of the 61st IEEE Annual Symposium on Foundations of Computer Science, FOCS 2020, pp. 919–930. IEEE (2020)
16. Brouwer, A.E., Haemers, W.H.: Eigenvalues and perfect matchings. Linear Algebra Appl. **395**, 155–162 (2005)
17. Censor-Hillel, K., Fischer, E., Schwartzman, G., Vasudev, Y.: Fast distributed algorithms for testing graph properties. Distributed Comput. **32**(1), 41–57 (2019). https://doi.org/10.1007/S00446-018-0324-8. Announced at DISC '16
18. Censor-Hillel, K., Gall, F.L., Leitersdorf, D.: On distributed listing of cliques. In: Emek, Y., Cachin, C. (eds.) PODC '20: ACM Symposium on Principles of Distributed Computing, Virtual Event, Italy, 3–7 August 2020, pp. 474–482. ACM (2020). https://doi.org/10.1145/3382734.3405742
19. Chang, Y., Pettie, S., Zhang, H.: Distributed triangle detection via expander decomposition. In: Chan, T.M. (ed.) Proceedings of the Thirtieth Annual ACM-SIAM Symposium on Discrete Algorithms, SODA 2019, San Diego, California, USA, 6–9 January 2019, pp. 821–840. SIAM (2019). https://doi.org/10.1137/1.9781611975482.51
20. Chang, Y., Saranurak, T.: Improved distributed expander decomposition and nearly optimal triangle enumeration. In: Robinson, P., Ellen, F. (eds.) Proceedings of the 2019 ACM Symposium on Principles of Distributed Computing, PODC 2019, Toronto, ON, Canada, 29 July–2 August 2019, pp. 66–73. ACM (2019). https://doi.org/10.1145/3293611.3331618
21. Chang, Y., Saranurak, T.: Deterministic distributed expander decomposition and routing with applications in distributed derandomization. In: Irani, S. (ed.) 61st IEEE Annual Symposium on Foundations of Computer Science, FOCS 2020, Durham, NC, USA, 16–19 November 2020, pp. 377–388. IEEE (2020). https://doi.org/10.1109/FOCS46700.2020.00043
22. Chawla, S., Krauthgamer, R., Kumar, R., Rabani, Y., Sivakumar, D.: On the hardness of approximating multicut and sparsest-cut. Comput. Complex. **15**(2), 94–114 (2006). https://doi.org/10.1007/S00037-006-0210-9. Announced at CCC'05
23. Chen, D., Meierhans, S., Gutenberg, M.P., Saranurak, T.: Parallel and distributed expander decomposition: simple, fast, and near-optimal. In: Azar, Y., Panigrahi, D. (eds.) Proceedings of the 2025 Annual ACM-SIAM Symposium on Discrete Algorithms, SODA 2025, New Orleans, LA, USA, 12–15 January 2025, pp. 1705–1719. SIAM (2025). https://doi.org/10.1137/1.9781611978322.53
24. Chen, L., Kyng, R., Gutenberg, M.P., Sachdeva, S.: A simple framework for finding balanced sparse cuts via APSP. In: Kavitha, T., Mehlhorn, K. (eds.) 2023 Symposium on Simplicity in Algorithms, SOSA 2023, Florence, Italy, 23–25 January 2023, pp. 42–55. SIAM (2023). https://doi.org/10.1137/1.9781611977585.CH5

25. Chierichetti, F., Giakkoupis, G., Lattanzi, S., Panconesi, A.: Rumor spreading and conductance. J. ACM **65**(4), 17:1–17:21 (2018). https://doi.org/10.1145/3173043
26. Chung, F.R.: Spectral graph theory, vol. 92. American Mathematical Soc. (1997)
27. Cohen, M.B., Mądry, A., Sankowski, P., Vladu, A.: Negative-weight shortest paths and unit capacity minimum cost flow in $\tilde{o}(m^{10/7} \log w)$ time (extended abstract). In: Proceedings of the Twenty-Eighth Annual ACM-SIAM Symposium on Discrete Algorithms, SODA 2017, pp. 752–771. SIAM (2017)
28. Daga, M., Henzinger, M., Nanongkai, D., Saranurak, T.: Distributed edge connectivity in sublinear time. In: Charikar, M., Cohen, E. (eds.) Proceedings of the 51st Annual ACM SIGACT Symposium on Theory of Computing, STOC 2019, Phoenix, AZ, USA, 23–26 June 2019, pp. 343–354. ACM (2019). https://doi.org/10.1145/3313276.3316346
29. Das, K., Sun, S.: Extremal graph on normalized Laplacian spectral radius and energy. Electron. J. Linear Algebra **29**, 237–253 (2015)
30. Dory, M., Efron, Y., Mukhopadhyay, S., Nanongkai, D.: Distributed weighted mincut in nearly-optimal time. In: Khuller, S., Williams, V.V. (eds.) STOC 2021: 53rd Annual ACM SIGACT Symposium on Theory of Computing, Virtual Event, Italy, 21-25 June 2021, pp. 1144–1153. ACM (2021). https://doi.org/10.1145/3406325.3451020
31. Eden, T., Fiat, N., Fischer, O., Kuhn, F., Oshman, R.: Sublinear-time distributed algorithms for detecting small cliques and even cycles. Distributed Comput. **35**(3), 207–234 (2022). https://doi.org/10.1007/S00446-021-00409-3. Announced at DISC '19
32. Even, G., et al.: Three notes on distributed property testing. In: Richa, A.W. (ed.) 31st International Symposium on Distributed Computing, DISC 2017, 16–20 October 2017, Vienna, Austria. LIPIcs, vol. 91, pp. 15:1–15:30. Schloss Dagstuhl - Leibniz-Zentrum für Informatik (2017). https://doi.org/10.4230/LIPICS.DISC.2017.15
33. Fichtenberger, H., Vasudev, Y.: A two-sided error distributed property tester for conductance. In: 43rd International Symposium on Mathematical Foundations of Computer Science (MFCS 2018), pp. 19–1. Schloss Dagstuhl–Leibniz-Zentrum für Informatik (2018)
34. Fiedler, M., Nikiforov, V.: Spectral radius and hamiltonicity of graphs. Linear Algebra Appl. **432**(9), 2170–2173 (2010)
35. Forster, S., Goranci, G., Liu, Y.P., Peng, R., Sun, X., Ye, M.: Minor sparsifiers and the distributed Laplacian paradigm. In: Proceedings of the 62nd IEEE Annual Symposium on Foundations of Computer Science, FOCS 2021, pp. 989–999. IEEE (2021)
36. Forster, S., de Vos, T.: The Laplacian paradigm in the broadcast congested clique. In: Proceedings of the ACM Symposium on Principles of Distributed Computing, PODC 2022, pp. 335–344. ACM (2022)
37. Forster, S., de Vos, T.: Brief announcement: the Laplacian paradigm in deterministic congested clique. In: Oshman, R., Nolin, A., Halldórsson, M.M., Balliu, A. (eds.) Proceedings of the 2023 ACM Symposium on Principles of Distributed Computing, PODC 2023, Orlando, FL, USA, 19–23 June 2023, pp. 75–78. ACM (2023). https://doi.org/10.1145/3583668.3594577
38. Ghaffari, M., Karrenbauer, A., Kuhn, F., Lenzen, C., Patt-Shamir, B.: Near-optimal distributed maximum flow. SIAM J. Comput. **47**(6), 2078–2117 (2018). Announced at PODC 2015

39. Ghaffari, M., Kuhn, F., Su, H.: Distributed MST and routing in almost mixing time. In: Schiller, E.M., Schwarzmann, A.A. (eds.) Proceedings of the ACM Symposium on Principles of Distributed Computing, PODC 2017, Washington, DC, USA, 25–27 July 2017, pp. 131–140. ACM (2017). https://doi.org/10.1145/3087801.3087827

40. Ghaffari, M., Li, J.: New distributed algorithms in almost mixing time via transformations from parallel algorithms. In: Schmid, U., Widder, J. (eds.) 32nd International Symposium on Distributed Computing, DISC 2018, New Orleans, LA, USA, 15–19 October 2018. LIPIcs, vol. 121, pp. 31:1–31:16. Schloss Dagstuhl - Leibniz-Zentrum für Informatik (2018). https://doi.org/10.4230/LIPICS.DISC.2018.31

41. Giakkoupis, G.: Tight bounds for rumor spreading in graphs of a given conductance. In: Schwentick, T., Dürr, C. (eds.) 28th International Symposium on Theoretical Aspects of Computer Science, STACS 2011, 10–12 March 2011, Dortmund, Germany. LIPIcs, vol. 9, pp. 57–68. Schloss Dagstuhl - Leibniz-Zentrum für Informatik (2011). https://doi.org/10.4230/LIPICS.STACS.2011.57

42. Golub, G.H., Van Loan, C.F.: Matrix Computations. JHU Press (2013)

43. Gu, X., Liu, M.: A tight lower bound on the matching number of graphs via Laplacian eigenvalues. Eur. J. Comb. **101**, 103468 (2022). https://doi.org/10.1016/J.EJC.2021.103468

44. Haemers, W.H.: Interlacing eigenvalues and graphs. Linear Algebra Appl. **226**, 593–616 (1995)

45. Hwang, S.G.: Cauchy's interlace theorem for eigenvalues of Hermitian matrices. Am. Math. Mon. **111**(2), 157–159 (2004)

46. Karger, D.R.: Minimum cuts in near-linear time. J. ACM **47**(1), 46–76 (2000). https://doi.org/10.1145/331605.331608. Announced at STOC '96

47. Kelner, J.A., Lee, Y.T., Orecchia, L., Sidford, A.: An almost-linear-time algorithm for approximate max flow in undirected graphs, and its multicommodity generalizations. In: Proceedings of the Twenty-Fifth Annual ACM-SIAM Symposium on Discrete Algorithms, SODA 2014, pp. 217–226. SIAM (2014)

48. Kempe, D., McSherry, F.: A decentralized algorithm for spectral analysis. J. Comput. Syst. Sci. **74**(1), 70–83 (2008). https://doi.org/10.1016/J.JCSS.2007.04.014. Announced at STOC'04

49. Koutis, I., Xu, S.C.: Simple parallel and distributed algorithms for spectral graph sparsification. ACM Trans. Parallel Comput. **3**(2), 14:1–14:14 (2016). https://doi.org/10.1145/2948062

50. Kuhn, F., Molla, A.R.: Distributed sparse cut approximation. In: Anceaume, E., Cachin, C., Potop-Butucaru, M.G. (eds.) 19th International Conference on Principles of Distributed Systems, OPODIS 2015, 14–17 December 2015, Rennes, France. LIPIcs, vol. 46, pp. 10:1–10:14. Schloss Dagstuhl - Leibniz-Zentrum für Informatik (2015). https://doi.org/10.4230/LIPICS.OPODIS.2015.10

51. Lee, J.R., Gharan, S.O., Trevisan, L.: Multi-way spectral partitioning and higher-order Cheeger inequalities. In: Karloff, H.J., Pitassi, T. (eds.) Proceedings of the 44th Symposium on Theory of Computing Conference, STOC 2012, New York, NY, USA, 19–22 May 2012, pp. 1117–1130. ACM (2012). https://doi.org/10.1145/2213977.2214078

52. Levi, R., Medina, M., Ron, D.: Property testing of planarity in the congest model. In: Proceedings of the 2018 ACM Symposium on Principles of Distributed Computing, pp. 347–356 (2018)

53. Li, J.: Faster parallel algorithm for approximate shortest path. In: Proceedings of the 52nd Annual ACM SIGACT Symposium on Theory of Computing, STOC 2020. pp. 308–321. ACM (2020)

54. Liu, B., Chen, S.: Algebraic conditions for t-tough graphs. Czechoslov. Math. J. **60**(4), 1079–1089 (2010)
55. Liu, S.: Multi-way dual Cheeger constants and spectral bounds of graphs. Adv. Math. **268**, 306–338 (2015)
56. Liu, Y.P., Sidford, A.: Faster divergence maximization for faster maximum flow. CoRR abs/2003.08929 (2020). https://arxiv.org/abs/2003.08929
57. Liu, Y.P., Sidford, A.: Faster energy maximization for faster maximum flow. In: Proceedings of the 52nd Annual ACM SIGACT Symposium on Theory of Computing, STOC 2020, pp. 803–814. ACM (2020)
58. Mallmann-Trenn, F., Musco, C., Musco, C.: Eigenvector computation and community detection in asynchronous gossip models. In: Chatzigiannakis, I., Kaklamanis, C., Marx, D., Sannella, D. (eds.) 45th International Colloquium on Automata, Languages, and Programming, ICALP 2018, 9–13 July 2018, Prague, Czech Republic. LIPIcs, vol. 107, pp. 159:1–159:14. Schloss Dagstuhl - Leibniz-Zentrum für Informatik (2018). https://doi.org/10.4230/LIPICS.ICALP.2018.159
59. Matula, D.W., Shahrokhi, F.: Sparsest cuts and bottlenecks in graphs. Discret. Appl. Math. **27**(1-2), 113–123 (1990). https://doi.org/10.1016/0166-218X(90)90133-W
60. Mądry, A.: Navigating central path with electrical flows: from flows to matchings, and back. In: Proceedings of the 54th Annual IEEE Symposium on Foundations of Computer Science, FOCS 2013, pp. 253–262. IEEE Computer Society (2013)
61. Mądry, A.: Computing maximum flow with augmenting electrical flows. In: Proceedings of the IEEE 57th Annual Symposium on Foundations of Computer Science, FOCS 2016, pp. 593–602. IEEE Computer Society (2016)
62. Peng, R.: Approximate undirected maximum flows in $O(m\mathrm{polylog}(n))$ time. In: Proceedings of the Twenty-Seventh Annual ACM-SIAM Symposium on Discrete Algorithms, SODA 2016, pp. 1862–1867. SIAM (2016)
63. Penna, F., Stańczak, S.: Decentralized eigenvalue algorithms for distributed signal detection in wireless networks. IEEE Trans. Signal Process. **63**(2), 427–440 (2014)
64. Saranurak, T., Wang, D.: Expander decomposition and pruning: faster, stronger, and simpler. In: SODA, pp. 2616–2635. SIAM (2019)
65. Sarma, A.D., Gollapudi, S., Panigrahy, R.: Sparse cut projections in graph streams. In: Fiat, A., Sanders, P. (eds.) Algorithms - ESA 2009, 17th Annual European Symposium, Copenhagen, Denmark, 7–9 September 2009, Proceedings. LNCS, vol. 5757, pp. 480–491. Springer (2009). https://doi.org/10.1007/978-3-642-04128-0_43
66. Sarma, A.D., et al.: Distributed verification and hardness of distributed approximation. SIAM J. Comput. **41**(5), 1235–1265 (2012). https://doi.org/10.1137/11085178X. Announced at STOC '11
67. Sarma, A.D., Molla, A.R., Pandurangan, G.: Distributed computation of sparse cuts via random walks. In: Das, S.K., et al. (eds.) Proceedings of the 2015 International Conference on Distributed Computing and Networking, ICDCN 2015, Goa, India, 4–7 January 2015, pp. 6:1–6:10. ACM (2015). https://doi.org/10.1145/2684464.2684474
68. Sarma, A.D., Molla, A.R., Pandurangan, G., Upfal, E.: Fast distributed PageRank computation. Theor. Comput. Sci. **561**, 113–121 (2015). https://doi.org/10.1016/J.TCS.2014.04.003. Announced at ICDCN'13
69. Sarma, A.D., Nanongkai, D., Pandurangan, G., Tetali, P.: Distributed random walks. J. ACM **60**(1), 2:1–2:31 (2013). https://doi.org/10.1145/2432622.2432624

70. Sherman, J.: Nearly maximum flows in nearly linear time. In: Proceedings of the 54th Annual IEEE Symposium on Foundations of Computer Science, FOCS 2013, pp. 263–269. IEEE Computer Society (2013)
71. Sinclair, A., Jerrum, M.: Approximate counting, uniform generation and rapidly mixing Markov chains. Inf. Comput. **82**(1), 93–133 (1989). https://doi.org/10.1016/0890-5401(89)90067-9
72. Spielman, D.A., Teng, S.: Nearly-linear time algorithms for graph partitioning, graph sparsification, and solving linear systems. In: Proceedings of the 36th Annual ACM Symposium on Theory of Computing (STOC 2004), pp. 81–90. ACM (2004)
73. de Vos, T.: Minimum cost flow in the CONGEST model. In: Rajsbaum, S., Balliu, A., Daymude, J.J., Olivetti, D. (eds.) Structural Information and Communication Complexity - 30th International Colloquium, SIROCCO 2023, Alcalá de Henares, Spain, 6–9 June 2023, Proceedings. LNCS, vol. 13892, pp. 406–426. Springer (2023). https://doi.org/10.1007/978-3-031-32733-9_18. Announced at PODC'23
74. Wilf, H.S.: The eigenvalues of a graph and its chromatic number. J. Lond. Math. Soc. **1**(1), 330–332 (1967)

Cow Path by Finite Agent: Time vs Pebbles

Stefan Dobrev[1] , Rastislav Královič[2]([envelope]) , Richard Královič[3] ,
Dana Pardubská[2] , and Peter Rossmanith[4]

[1] Slovak Academy of Sciences, Bratislava, Slovakia
stefan.dobrev@savba.sk
[2] Comenius University, Bratislava, Slovakia
{kralovic,pardubska}@dcs.fmph.uniba.sk
[3] ETH Zürich, Zürich, Switzerland
[4] RWTH Aachen University, Aachen, Germany
rossmani@cs.rwth-aachen.de

Abstract. We consider the classical cow-path/treasure-hunt problem
on a discrete infinite line, being solved by a deterministic finite state
agent with s states and k pebbles.

We show asymptotically optimal solutions for small values of k, as
well as an efficient algorithm for general k. For non-constant number
of pebbles we show that $O(\log \log n)$ pebbles are sufficient to find the
treasure located at distance n within $O(n \log n)$ steps. Having more pebbles does not help, as we show a lower bound $\Omega(n \log n)$ steps even with
unlimited number of pebbles. Randomization can break this bound, as
we show that a randomized agent can solve the problem with expected
$O(n \log \log n)$ steps using $O(\log \log n)$ pebbles.

Along the way, we introduce two subproblems that might be of independent interest, and use the solutions to those as building blocks for
our solutions to the treasure-hunt problem.

In fact, the core of the paper is a result on how to efficiently travel
with a counter implemented by pebbles, so that the amortized cost of
the travel is significantly smaller than the traveled distance times the
counter size, despite always having the counter nearby for incrementing
in each travel step.

Keywords: Finite agents · Cow path problem · Treasure hunt ·
Pebbles · Discrete line

1 Introduction

A cow stands on the bank of a river, staring at the greener pastures on the other
side. Somewhere there, at an unknown distance, in an unknown direction, is a
bridge leading to the tastier future. If only the cow knew how to get there!

Stefan Dobrev has been supported by grant VEGA 2/0117/25. Dana Pardubská has
been supported by grant VEGA 1/0140/25.

C. Georgiou (Ed.): SIROCCO 2026, LNCS 16488, pp. 253–271, 2026.
https://doi.org/10.1007/978-3-032-26465-7_14

This (ok, ok, we omitted a few details: it is a smart cow, and wants to minimize the worst case competitive ratio between the traveled distance and the actual distance to the bridge) is the classical *online cow path problem*, which, together with its numerous variants and extensions, has been thoroughly investigated for decades.

Similarly, in the area of graph and distributed algorithms, (cooperative) graph and area exploration are areas that have seen intense and longstanding research interest, with a vast accumulated body of knowledge, for numerous models and their variants. In particular, graph exploration and the closely related *treasure hunt* problem have been investigated from the point of view of *What are the weakest agents that can still do it?*. As such, there is considerable research into the capabilities of finite state agents (FSAs). As those are typically too weak to achieve anything interesting in the non-constant size input graphs, they need to be provided with a supplemental power, often in the form of a finite set of undistinguishible pebbles that can be placed in (and picked-up from) the explored environment.

In contemplating on how to employ FSA with pebbles to efficiently explore complex 2D areas, we have discovered that the natural 1D subproblem (efficiently exploring a discrete infinite line, i.e. the cow-path problem, or, as we prefer to call it, TREASUREHUNT) has not been solved. This is rather peculiar, as the solution for the whole 2D grid is simple and asymptotically optimal [17].

1.1 Related Work

Search games have been studied for more that half a century. Earliest works about *linear search* such as [3,5,22,26] introduce a setting where a point on a line is chosen according to some probability distribution and a *seeker* chooses a trajectory. The goal is to find a trajectory with minimal length from start to the *hider*. The original problem has been formulated also as a two-player zero-sum game [4], in the online algorithms setting [27], and generalized to other domains [22]. Randomized solutions have been analyzed in [2]. There is a significant number of results on various other aspects of the problem, see e.g. [1,23],

We are, however, interested in version with discrete space, which leads into the area of *graph exploration* problems. In this context, the cow path problem where the underlying metric space is a graph is known under the name *treasure hunt*. The relation between exploration and treasure hunt is obvious: if we are interested in the adversarial scenario in the treasure hunt, the algorithm must explore the whole graph before the treasure is found. The literature about graph exploration is vast. Taking some liberties, one can say that the entire graph theory originated from a graph exploration problem [18]. The problems where there is a local entity with limited access to the graph have been first studied in relation to specific heuristics for concrete problems [31], and also gave rise to a large body of literature. For our purposes, the relevant context is graph exploration using mobile agents. There are various flavors of the model, but essentially, there is a (or potentially several) computational entity (a.k.a. agent or robot) that is located in a vertex, can see the local neighborhood (usually labels of outgoing edges, sometimes label of the current vertex or labels of neighboring vertices) and can move from one vertex to a neighboring vertex (for a survey of models and results see e.g. [20]).

In [6] it has been shown, in the context of directed graphs, that a finite automaton cannot explore/construct a map of all graphs without using some mechanism to mark vertices. If a bound on the size of the graph is known, it is shown that one pebble is enough. If the graph is completely unknown, $\Omega(\log \log n)$ pebbles are needed. Memory requirements for the agent have been considered in [21] where the agent was to perform perpetual exploration of all edges of the graph. It was shown that $\Omega(D \log d)$ memory bits are needed in order to explore all regular graphs with diameter D and degree d. Exploration of several special graph classes has also been considered, e.g. in [13] it is proven that trees can be explored with $O(\log \log \log n)$ bits of memory.

Relevant to our investigation is the result from [14] that states that $\Theta(\log \log n)$ distinguishable pebbles are needed for an agent with sublogarithmic memory to explore all graphs. The paper also provided an algorithm that used $O(\log \log n)$ memory bits. The result was improved in [15] to achieve constant memory, and the algorithm worked in time polynomial in the size of the graph. It was also shown that $\Omega(\log \log n)$ pebbles are needed even if the pebbles are replaced by finite automata that can move. A previous result [8] states that if the graph is a maze (subgraph of infinite grid equipped with compass sense of direction), it can be explored with two pebbles.

Most of the exploration results concern finite graphs, but there are also results about infinite structures, e.g., [11] considers randomized treasure hunt protocols in infinite grids with many agents with the aim to achieve finite mean hitting time in every vertex. [30] studies exploration of infinite trees with a 1-state (a.k.a. memoryless) agent with pebbles.

The majority of the works about exploration/treasure hunt analyze the worst case over a class of graphs, but there are also many papers dealing with the competitive ratio, e.g. [16, 19, 29].

A closely related concept originated from the formal computational models, where automata/Turing machines that can place pebbles on the tape have been considered, e.g. [10]. More recently, the expressive power (i.e., which classes of graphs can be recognized) of weighted pebble walking graph automata has been considered in [9]. In [28] it has been proven that in weighted graph walking automata with labeled vertices, drop-once pebbles can be avoided at the expense of more states.

Various other versions of the model have been investigated, e.g., in [7, 24] a version of treasure hunt is studied, in which the pebbles are placed in advance by an oracle that knows the location of the treasure and wants to help the agent in finding it. [12] is concerned with collision-free exploration by two agents in the same model of pebbles placed by oracle.

Finally, there is a line of research, e.g. [25] where the agent is a finite automaton with no pebbles, but the edge labels are set by oracle.

1.2   Our Results

We introduce two problems that might be of independent interest:

- *The DISTANCEBB (s, k) problem:* What is the maximal distance an s-state agent with k pebbles can reach before terminating?
- *The TRAVELCOUNTER (k) problem:* How to efficiently keep track of the traveled distance (i.e., how to maintain a counter that counts the distance traveled so far)? Here, the cost is the time needed by the agent to travel to a distance n while maintaining the counter.

We show that the answers to the DISTANCEBB problem are s, $2s$, and $2^{\Theta\left(\sqrt{s \log s}\right)}$ for $k = 0, 1, 2$, respectively. For $k = 3$, there is no computable upper bound on the distance, as the agent can simulate a Turing machine.

For TRAVELCOUNTER, we show a simple solution with cost $O\left(kn^{\frac{k-1}{k-2}}\right)$ and a general solution for larger k of cost $O\left(10^r n^{1+\frac{1}{4^r}}\right)$, where $r = \lfloor k/5 \rfloor$. Hence, $k = O(\log \log n)$ pebbles are sufficient to reduce the cost to $O(n \log n)$.

We use these results to build solutions to the TREASUREHUNT problem and establish a trade-off between the number of pebbles and the required time: For $k \leq 1$ the problem is unsolvable. For $k = 2, 3$ we present algorithms based on the optimal solution to DISTANCEBB. We also prove that for $k = 2$ our algorithm is asymptotically optimal. For $k \geq 4$ we use the solutions of TRAVELCOUNTER to construct algorithms for TREASUREHUNT: for $4 \leq k \leq 10$ pebbles, the cost of our algorithm is $O\left(n^{\frac{1}{k-2}}\right)$, and for $k \geq 11$ the cost is $O\left(10^r n^{\frac{1}{4^r}}\right)$ where $r = \lfloor k/5 \rfloor$. Hence, with $O(\log \log n)$ pebbles, the TREASUREHUNT can be solved in $O(n \log n)$ steps.

On the other hand, we show that $\Omega(n \log n)$ steps are needed to solve TREASUREHUNT even with unlimited number of pebbles. This can be improved if the agent is allowed to use randomization: even with one pebble, the randomized agent can solve the TREASUREHUNT in expected finite time. With $O(\log \log n)$ pebbles, the randomized agent can beat the deterministic lower bound, and solve the problem in expected time $O(n \log \log n)$.

Due to space constraints, proofs marked as ✂, and some algorithms are omitted and will appear in the journal version of this paper.

2   Model and Preliminaries

2.1   Model

A deterministic finite-state agent moves on a discrete infinite line, and can mark nodes of the line by placing undistinguishable pebbles. The agent starts with k pebbles in its bag, and can place a pebble on the current node (if its bag is not empty), or pick up a pebble from the current node (if there is one). The agent does not know the number of pebbles currently in its bag, it only can sense whether the bag is empty or not.

In particular, the line (also referred to as *tape*) consists of *places* (also *nodes* or *cells*) $\{c_i \mid c_i \in \mathbb{Z}_2\}_{i\in\mathbb{Z}}$. If $c_i = 1$ we say that place i contains a pebble. At the beginning $c_i = 0$ for all i. The agent has states Σ, where $|\Sigma| = s$. After t steps, the agent is located on a position $p_t \in Z$, initially $p_0 = 0$. In each step, the transition function $\delta : \Sigma \times \mathbb{Z}_2 \times \mathbb{Z}_2 \to \Sigma \times \mathbb{Z}_2 \times \{-1, 1\}$ is applied, i.e., the agent considers its state, the state of the current cell (whether there is a pebble or not), and a flag telling whether there are some pebbles left in its bag. Based on this information it changes its state, updates the state of the current cell (by placing or removing a pebble), and updates its position[1]. If a termination is needed by the algorithm, we add a special `terminate` action as a possible outcome of a transition. Also, the agent must not place a pebble if its bag is empty, i.e., it must always hold $\sum_{i\in\mathbb{Z}} c_i \leq k$.

Note that in this model, there is no need for multiplicity detection; furthermore, the transition function is truly finite and does not depend on k. As there is a single agent, the time is discrete, corresponding to applications of the agent's transition function.

2.2   The Problem

We consider the classical cow-path problem (a.k.a. treasure hunt/search in linear space): At an unknown location on the line, there is a treasure to be found. The cost measure is the total distance traveled by the agent until the treasure is found. We are interested in the competitive ratio of the cost vs the distance n of the treasure from the agent's initial location.

2.3   Preliminaries

For the description of our algorithms it is often convenient to distinguish several types of pebbles that would play different roles. The pebbles themselves are identical, but we can implement a constant number of *flavors* using the following technique: The discrete line is divided into blocks of size f, where f is an appropriately chosen constant. One cell of the higher-level algorithm (i.e., solving the cow-path problem) is implemented by one block of f cells. The offset within a block corresponds to a *flavor*; the agent can assign flavors to pebbles by selecting the drop location within the block. Analogously, the agent knows the flavors of the pebbles it finds in this block, based on their offsets.

Obviously, this technique incurs an $O(f)$ cost per logical place (and hence $O(f)$ penalty for the competitive ratio), however, in this paper we are interested in asymptotics. Observe that we can have multiple pebbles in the same (logical) place (i.e. block), as long as they have different flavors. Note that the pebble's flavor persists only while it is dropped, once it is picked-up, if the agent wants to maintain its flavor, it has to remember it in its state.

---

[1] There is never a need for the agent to stay at the same place, so the number of steps is always the total distance traveled.

Another simplification used by our algorithms is the ability of the agent to check whether its bag contains less than some small constant number x of pebbles, which is used in the construction of the recursive counter. This can be implemented, using $O(x)$ states and steps, by (up to x times) dropping a pebble and walking right, using a flavor dedicated for this task only. The subsequent cleanup also costs only $O(x)$ states and $O(x)$ steps.

In our constructions, we shall often use two pebbles located at a distance d from each other (i.e., the number of empty cells between them is $d - 1$) to store a value d. Changing the stored value by some constant c is easy: the agent just picks the rightmost pebble, and moves it c steps to the right or left; $O(c)$ states are sufficient for this. However, we shall also need multiplication by a rational (constant) number $r = \frac{p}{q}$, i.e., the rightmost pebble must be moved so that the new distance between the pebbles is $\lfloor dr \rfloor$. This can be achieved with one additional pebble by an agent moving the pebbles at various speeds.

Lemma 1 ($\succ\!\!\prec$). *Consider initial position with two pebbles with mutual distance d, and the agent located on the left pebble. Let $r = p/q$ for some co-prime p, q. The task of moving the right pebble so that the distance between the pebbles is $d' = \lfloor rd \rfloor$ can be achieved using one extra pebble, $O(p + q)$ states and $O((pd)^2)$ time.*

The previous lemma was formulated in a setting where no other pebbles were involved. When using in further constructions, this will usually not be the case, since there will be other pebbles around. However, we can reserve one flavor specifically for the multiplication algorithm, and use it every time a distance must be multiplied. This way we can make sure there is no interference from other parts of the algorithm.

In order not to obscure the conceptual ideas by tedious technicalities, we avoid overly optimizing the construction; our choices are guided by the aim to keep the presentation simple, while still achieving the desired asymptotic complexity bounds.

3   Know Where You Are: Traveling with a Counter

Our aim is to formally capture the notion of an agent knowing how much it has traveled, and being able to efficiently use this knowledge. An agent marking the origin using a single pebble, and then just moving on, in fact encodes the distance traveled (it is the distance between the pebble and the agent). However, this encoding is very brittle: since every move of the agent changes the stored distance, it is not possible to e.g. copy the value to another counter, or to shift the entire encoding to a new position; indeed, the only reasonable usage is to return back to the starting position.

Perhaps a better problem would be: *Given an input value (encoded in unary by two pebbles at distance n), copy/move this input value to another location (e.g. identified by another pebble).* This is actually a very useful sub-problem, but we would like to abstract it a bit more, to prevent the agent using the input pebbles for solving it. Hence, our formulation:

The TRAVELCOUNTER **problem:** *On an infinite line, to the right of the agent's origin, there is a read-once marker (i.e. it disappears once the agent finds it) saying* half-way to the treasure. *When the agent encounters this marker, at a distance n from the origin, it has to reach the node at distance n to the right of the marker and terminate. The cost is the total distance traveled by the agent, as a function of n.*

The basic idea for solving TRAVELCOUNTER is that the agent uses its pebbles to implement a counter that it carries along (i.e., it periodically shifts the entire counter so that it is always close at hand) and increments it as it travels rightward. Upon finding the midway marker, the agent switches to decrementing the counter and terminates when the counter reaches 0.

Our next aim is to implement this idea: we want to maintain a counter that supports increment and decrement, and the entire counter can be efficiently shifted to the right. Instead of having a counter of arbitrary length, we shall implement a fixed-length counter. A counter c is initialized to a distance d given by some configuration of pebbles, and using k pebbles can store values up to $e(c; d, k)^2$. When an attempt is made to increment the counter beyond $e(c; d, k)$, an overflow is detected (we say the counter *expires*). Note that we have, at this point, deliberately not defined the size of the counter. It depends on the actual counter implementation, and is not necessarily the distance between the left-most and right-most pebbles of the counter.

This fixed-length approach allows us to solve the TRAVELCOUNTER by iterative doubling: initialize a counter of size d, and travel right while incrementing it. If the halfway marker was found, continue traveling while decrementing the counter. If the counter expired, move the counter back to the starting position, double the distance d, and try again. Since doubling d increases $e(d, k)$ more than twice, the whole process can be amortized by the cost of the final iteration.

Moreover, this design will be convenient also later as a subroutine to TREASUREHUNT. The idea there is to use a counter with a distance d that counts to some value $e(d, k)$ while traveling in one direction, and when the counter expires, double the maximal value of the counter and switch direction. Note that in order to achieve the asymptotically optimal competitive ratio, the value does not need to be doubled precisely; we will be able to increase d to d' in a way that $e(d', k)$ is good enough for our purposes.

3.1   Simple Counter

We first show a simple implementation SIMPLECOUNTER (d, k), that will nevertheless be useful as a building block for more efficient counters. Here we assume

---

[2] We shall later use several counters, so it is convenient that notation $e(c; d, k)$ states explicitly which counter we are referring to. If part of the information is clear from the context, we shall use $e(d, k)$, or $e(c)$.

$k \geq 3$, with two pebbles at distance d from each other used as an input, and the agent starting atop the left pebble. Implementing the counter means showing how to perform the following operations: a) initializing it, b) incrementing it, c) shifting the counter right, and d) recognizing when the counter has expired.

We will use three pebble flavours: *leftmost, inner* and *rightmost*, with the input (border) pebbles specifying the counter size d being the *leftmost* and *rightmost* ones. The border pebbles will keep their distance, while the inner pebbles will encode the value of the counter.

Let $\Gamma(d, k)$ denote all k-pebble configurations with the border pebbles at distance d from each other. For a configuration $\gamma \in \Gamma(d, k)$, let χ_γ be the binary string of length $d - 1$ with 0's representing the placement of inner pebbles of γ and 1's representing empty places. We will write $\gamma \prec \gamma'$ if $\chi_\gamma \prec \chi_{\gamma'}$. From the construction of SIMPLECOUNTER it follows that one increment of SIMPLE-COUNTER applied to a configuration γ results in a configuration γ' that is the successor of γ (Fig. 1).

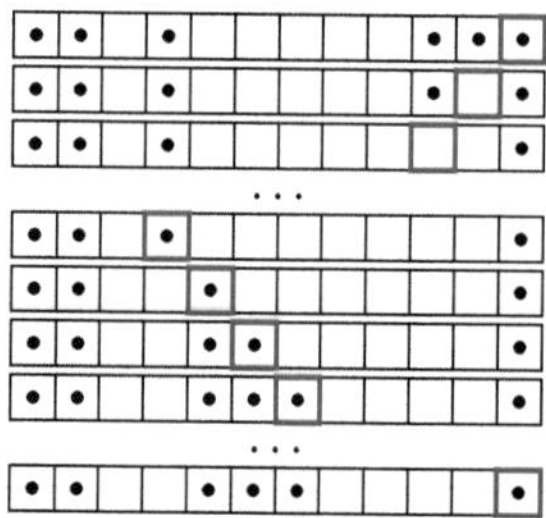

Fig. 1. Incrementing simple counter with $d = 11$, $k = 6$. Agent's position in blue.

Since the counter's starting configuration is the smallest one, and the counter does not expire before reaching the largest configuration, we have the following:

Lemma 2. *SIMPLECOUNTER counts to* $\binom{d-1}{k-2}$, *and the cost of each operation is* $O(d)$.

Corollary 1 (✂).   *Using k pebbles, the* TRAVELCOUNTER *problem can be solved with cost* $O(kn^{(k-1)/(k-2)})$.

3.2   Two Level Counter

The problem with SIMPLECOUNTER is that the cost of updating and shifting it is $O(d)$. While this seems inevitable, due to the need to shift the counter in each step, we can actually do better.

The basic idea is to divide the counter into two parts: a large prefix counter c_p of size $d_p = d$, which is moved rarely, and a much smaller suffix counter c_s that counts up to d', which should be roughly the size of d, and is moved in every step (see Fig. 2). When the suffix counter expires, the prefix counter is incremented and shifted d' to the right, the suffix counter is reinitialized, and the whole process repeats until the prefix counter expires. Since the prefix counter is incremented and shifted only once in d' steps, the heavy cost of updating and moving it is amortized among those d' steps. The goal is to make the amortized per-step cost of counting proportional not to the size of the large prefix counter, but to the size of the small suffix counter.

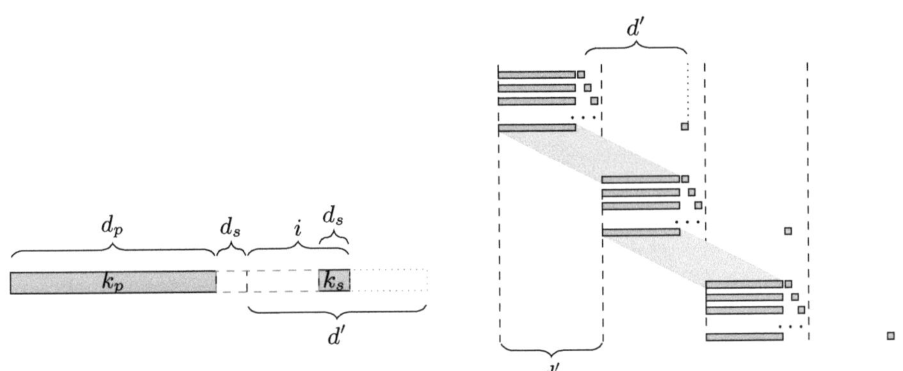

Fig. 2. Left: the structure of TwoLevelCounter, with the suffix counter having value i. Right: advancing the TwoLevelCounter across expirations of the suffix counter.

As TwoLevelCounter is just a stepping stone to the more efficient Rec-Counter, we skip optimizing it and instead employ a simple, fixed-split approach. The size of the prefix counter $d_p = d$ is given as an input. The suffix counter uses 6 pebbles, while the prefix counter uses the remaining $k - 6$ pebbles[3]. The size d_s of the suffix counter needs to be computed by the algorithm. We require that a) $d' = e(c_s; d_s, 6) \in d + o(d)$ (so that amortization works), and b) computing d_s should be simple and efficient.

In TwoLevelCounter, c_p and c_s are implemented using SimpleCounter, however a few details need to be adapted. First, initializing TwoLevel-Counter means initializing c_p, computing d_s and initializing c_s as well (both initializations using SimpleInit). Second, when c_s expires, c_p needs to be incremented and efficiently moved d' positions to the right. This is crucial, as using the same approach as with SimpleCounter to shift c_p d' times would cost $O(d'd_p)$, i.e. no real saving w.r.t. just using SimpleCounter. Instead, when c_s expires, the whole c_s is dragged to the left until c_p is encountered. Then c_p is incremented, and c_s is used to move c_p, one pebble after another, by d' places to the right, incurring a cost of only $O(d'd_s k_p)$.

Lemma 3 ($\times$). *The* TwoLevelCounter *counts up to* $(d + o(d))\binom{d-1}{k-8}$, *and the amortized cost of each operation is* $O(kd_s) = O(kd^{1/4})$.

3.3 Recursive Counter

Now we apply the idea of the two-level counter recursively: While we have enough pebbles and the counter size is not a small constant, use 5 pebbles for a prefix counter (starting with size d at the topmost level), compute the appropriate size of suffix counter and proceed recursively in the suffix (see procedure RECINIT).

This results in a chain of simple counters $c_r, c_{r-1} \ldots, c_0$, where for $i > 0$, each c_i has size d_i and uses 5 pebbles. Note that c_i, together with all counters c_j with $j < i$, implements a recursive counter c_i^* that counts to e_i^*.

A critical problem with the concept of a recursive counter is that the recursive call stack cannot fit in the agent's state. Hence, the agent's environment must provide sufficient information to guide the agent's execution. To that effect, we heavily employ pebble flavors.

Each pebble has a *role*, i.e. *leftmost, inner, rightmost*, used by the algorithm to recognize the boundaries of the simple counters. Similarly, the simple counters themselves (i.e. the pebbles of the counter) have a *role*: *top-level, mid-level* or *bottom-level*. These roles allow the algorithm to seamlessly operate on counters, and move between them and within the boundaries of the overall recursive counter.

The initialization procedure has size d_r as input, and sets up the counters left-to right: starting with a distance d_i as input, it creates a simple counter c_i with size d_i and 5 pebbles, sets the new value $d_{i-1} = \lfloor \sqrt[4]{6d_i} \rfloor$ on the right, and continues to create counter c_{i-1}. The procedure stops when it either runs out of pebbles (i.e., has less than 10 pebbles left), or the distance is less than 10. In the latter case it sets the final counter c_0 to $k_0 = 6$ and $d_0 = \lfloor \sqrt[4]{24} \rfloor$. This choice of parameters guarantees two important properties: the smaller counter c_{i-1}^* counts approximately to the size of the previous counter c_i, i.e., $e_{i-1}^* \approx 6d_i$. Moreover, the sizes of the counters decrease so that $d_{r-i} \in \Theta(d^{1/4^i})$.

When counter c_i^* expires, the counter c_{i+1} (i.e. its 5 pebbles) should be shifted right by e_i^* and subsequently incremented. To do this efficiently, similarly to TWOLEVELCOUNTER, the idea is to shift the pebbles of c_{i+1} one by one, using c_i^* recursively to count to e_i^*.

To that end, we employ two more per-counter variables: a three-way *phase* (*forward, returning,* and *crossing*) and a two-way *direction* (*rightward, leftward*). Note that all our algorithms/code are presented assuming the counter's direction is *rightward*. If the counter's direction is *leftward*, just flip all references to left/right and *leftmost/rightmost*.

In the *forward* phase, c_i explores rightwards, as well as brings a pebble of c_{i+1} (if c_i is not top-level). In the *returning* phase, c_i returns for the next pebble of c_{i+1}, while in the *crossing* phase it crosses from the *leftmost*, just brought-in, pebble of c_{i+1} to the *rightmost* pebble of c_{i+1}, so that after shifting c_{i+1}, c_i^* is correctly placed just right of it.

There are several problems that need resolving to make this work: primarily due to finite state of the agent not allowing to have per recursion level (stack) variables.

Algorithm 1. High level algorithm for c_i^*

1: count rightward in state *normal* until expiration $\qquad\qquad$ ▷ counting to e_i^*
2: **for** all 5 pebbles of c_{i+1} **do** $\qquad\qquad$ ▷ shift c_{i+1} distance e_i^* rightward
3: $\qquad$ travel leftward in state *returning* until a pebble p is found
4: $\qquad$ pick-up p and travel rightward in state *forward* until expiration $\qquad$ ▷ e_i^*
5: $\qquad$ drop p
6: **end for**
7: travel rightward in state *crossing* until c_{i+1} is crossed $\qquad\qquad$ ▷ distance d_i

---

− The agent cannot just walk leftward, it needs to bring the counter c_i^* with itself, as it will need it in the next *forward* phase. Going light and recomputing d_i from d_{i+1} is too costly (and impossible when bringing next pebbles of c_{i+1}). Even bringing just d_i naively is too costly[4]. Hence, the recursive travel leftward is used to bring c_i^* to pebble of c_{i+1} that needs shifting. Also note that we might need to travel more than e_i^*, as also the inter-pebble distance between pebbles of c_{i+1} needs to be crossed. Therefore, upon expiration, a *returning* counter just reinitializes and continues its travel, without affecting c_{i+1}.

− The agent cannot pick p and carry it to its destination, without losing its flavor. We resolve this by not carrying p, but dragging it behind the *leftmost* pebble of c_i. Note that we might as well do this already in the first forward travel of c_i^*; going light, only to return later for the first pebble of c_{i+1} is wasteful. Furthermore, c_{i+1} itself might have been dragging a pebble of c_{i+2} and so on. In effect, the *leftmost* pebble of c_i might have a multi-level *tail* of higher level *leftmost* pebbles dragging each other, with only the end of the tail not being a *leftmost* pebble. Note that the dragging of the tail itself is not done by recursive returns for the pebbles in the tail, but at the lowest level by DRAGGINGSHIFT.

− At the moment c_i^* has shifted the last pebble of c_{i+1} (recognized by being *leftmost*), the whole c_{i+1} (including its tail) is in the correct shifted location. However, c_i^* itself is not at a correct place to the right of c_{i+1}, it is just to the right of the *leftmost* pebble of c_{i+1}. Hence c_i^* must cross c_{i+1}. As the distance is d_{i+1}, naive crossing is again too costly and this has to be done recursively as well, in the *crossing* phase.

− There is another problem: c_i^* has to cross the pebbles it dragged-in, causing potential conflicts with two (or even more, due to recursion) pebbles of the same flavor having to occupy the same place. In fact, this might happen not only during to final crossing, but also before: c_i^* has some size, if the dragged-in pebbles were originally closer than that size, there would be overlap between c_i^* and the previously dragged-in pebble. We resolve this problem as follows: First, we assign a tag *ignore* to dragged-in pebbles when logically dropping them; the algorithm ignores these pebbles, unless explicitly stated. When a *forward* counter c_i^* expires, while dragging the righmost pebble of c_{i+1} and it is time to shift the

---

[4] $O(d_i d_{i+1})$, one can do slightly better by bringing just a counter c_{i-1} with the count to d_i frozen in it, so it can reconstruct it; the cost would be $O(d_{i-1}d_{i+1})$, which is still too much.

rest of c_{i+1}, the agent checks whether there is an *ignore* pebble in the way. If no, the recursive shifting can be safely employed. However, if there is an *ignore* pebble, a safe, but costly NAIVESHIFT is employed, which shifts the whole c_{i+1} (and its tail) at a cost of d_{i+1}^2. The idea is that this happens sufficiently rarely to not be of concern. Furthermore, this prevents recursively piling *ignore* pebbles of different counters in an overlapping manner, which would have caused problems for the *crossing* phase. Finally, when an *ignore* pebble exits the rear end of a *crossing* counter c_i, its *ignore* tag is removed. If it was a *rightmost* pebble, this marks the end of the crossing phase, c_i^* is reinitialised right next to c_{i+1}, its phase is changed to *forward* and the agent is moved to the rightmost pebble of c_{i+1} (see DRAGGINGSHIFT and NEWPHASE). The whole counting continues in the main loop by incrementing c_{i+1}, as the agent is now in c_{i+1}.

The main procedure (see Algorithm 2) is initially called with the agent atop the left pebble of the input specifying the size d of the top-level counter.

Algorithm 2. Algorithm RECCOUNTER(d, k)

1: call RECINIT(d, k) ▷ also sets direction flag of each c_i to *right*
2: **while** true **do**   ▷ the agent is at the *rightmost* pebble of the current counter
3:     let c_i be the counter the agent is in   ▷ c_i needs shifting
4:     **if** c_i is the bottom-level counter **then**
5:         **if** there is a pebble to the right **then**   ▷ this ignores *ignore* pebbles
6:             call NEWPHASE (*forward*, {compactR, flip})
7:         **else**
8:             call DRAGGINGSHIFT () ▷ shift c_0 and its tail right, might exit *crossing* phase
9:         **end if**
10:     **end if**
11:     **if** SIMPLEINC () returned *expired* **then**
12:         **if** c_i is top-level **then**
13:             **return** *expired*   ▷ the final end
14:         **else if** c_i is a *returning* counter **then**
15:             call REINIT (c_i^*) ▷ continue traveling, not affecting c_{i+1}
16:         **else**   ▷ c_i is *forward*, a *crossing* counter would detect end before expiration
17:             let p be the dragged-in pebble   ▷ p is a pebble of c_{i+1}
18:             **if** p is *leftmost* **then**
19:                 call NEWPHASE (*crossing*, {keep})   ▷ c_{i+1} shifted, now cross it
20:             **else if** p is *rightmost* and UNSAFEFORRECURSION () **then**
21:                 call NAIVESHIFT ()   ▷ unsafe to shift c_{i+1} recursively, do it naively
22:             **else**
23:                 mark p as *ignore*
24:                 call NEWPHASE (*returning*, {flip, skip}) ▷ recursively bring next pebble
25:             **end if**
26:         **end if**
27:     **end if**
28: **end while**

The subroutine DRAGGINGSHIFT is called whenever a counter c_i, together with its dragged tail, needs shifting one position right (i.e. for c_0 in the main loop, or as a subroutine in NAIVESHIFT). It starts atop the *rightmost* pebble of c_i, and returns either OK, with the agent at the same place, or *crossComplete*, with the agent atop the *rightmost* pebble of freshly shifted c_{i+1}, and reinitialized c_i^* to the right of it. The subroutine NAIVESHIFT is called when c_i^* has expired and it is the time to shift c_{i+1}, however, there are *ignore* pebbles in the way, preventing shifting c_{i+1} recursively. NAIVESHIFT shifts c_{i+1} and its tail rightward to c_i by repeatedly using DRAGGINGSHIFT. The subroutine NEWPHASE (phase, options) is used for preparing c_i^* for the start of the next phase. This is a generic subroutine used in several situations, the options argument allows it to prepare c_i^* according to what is needed. It also adjusts c_i of the main loop: If the *keep* option is provided, $i \leftarrow i+1$, otherwise $i \leftarrow 0$. Let *lifetime* denote one full counting cycle of c_i^*, from initialization to expiration. Note that during its lifetime, c_i travels in only one direction (its subcounters might not).

Lemma 4 (✄). *The* crossing *counter c_i correctly identifies the* rightmost *pebble of shifted c_{i+1}, and clears all* ignore *pebbles created by shifting c_{i+1}.*

Theorem 1. RECCOUNTER *correctly counts.*

Proof (Proof outline).
   First, observe that this is in fact an algorithm for a finite state machine. There are no loop variables or per-level information remembered by the agent, only pebble flavors are used everywhere. The proof itself is by induction on i, that c_i^* correctly counts. The base step follows from the correctness of SIMPLE-COUNTER (or counting in state), the induction step follows by careful analysis of the construction. The non-recursive subroutines are all relatively straightforward exercises that can be made to work, the important and tedious part is verifying that the logical boundaries they work with indeed correspond to the ones implied from the pebble flavors. The crucial step is showing that the recursion works properly as well, in particular that there are no interference problems between recursion calls at different levels. This boils down to showing that *ignore* pebbles do not cause problems by having overlapping ranges. Lemma 4 is crucial to that effect.

Lemma 5 (✄). *The total cost of* NAIVESHIFT *charged to an* ignore *pebble p of counter c_{i+1} (during one stretch of time it had* ignore *flag) is $O(d_{i+1}^2)$.*

   Let t_i^* denote the total cost of c_i^* counting to e_i^* (excluding the computation of d_i, but including everything else) and let $x_i^* = \frac{t_i^*}{e_i^*}$ be the overhead (amortized cost per counting step) of c_i^*.

Lemma 6. $x^i \in O(10^i d_0)$

Proof. By induction on i that the statement holds for c_i^*. The base step follows from Lemma 2, and trivially if the lowest-level counting is done in agent's states.

The computation and initialisation of d_j for $j < i$ costs $O(d_i^{3/2})$ is done once, at the very beginning, and is overwhelmed by $e_i^* \in O(d_i^4)$. The cost of counting to e_{i+1}^* is divided into segments of e_i^* steps, divided by the moments of incrementing and shifting c_{i+1}. The cost of each segment can be divided into

- t_i^* for the first counting to e_i^* by c_i^* in the *forward* phase between two increments of c_{i+1}
- $O(d_i)$ for UNSAFEFORRECURSION
- the cost of shifting each remaining pebble of c_{i+1}
  - $O(d_i^2)$ for preparing (compacting, flipping, reinitializing) c_i^* for *returning* travel
  - $t_i^* + g_j x_i^*$ for traveling left until finding the next pebble of c_{i+1}, where g_j is the distance between the consecutive pebbles of c_{i+1} in their position before shifting
  - $O(d_i^2)$ for preparing c_i^* for *forward* travel
  - at most t_i^* for c_i^*'s travel in *crossing* phase
  - $O(d_i^2)$ for NAIVESHIFT charged to c_i
- $O(e_i^*)$ cost for dragging pebbles of c_{i+1}, incurred by DRAGGINGSHIFT

Note that $\sum_j g_j = d_{i+1} \le e_i^*$ and therefore $\sum_j g_j x_i^* \le t_i^*$. Hence, the overall cost incurred in one segment is $t_i^* + 4(2t_i^* + O(d_i^2)) + \sum_j g_j x_i = 10t_i^* + O(d_i^2)$, and the overhead is therefore $(10t_i^* + O(d_i^2))/e_i^* = 10x_i^* + o(1)$, using $t_i^* = e_i^* x_i^*$ and $e_i^* \in O(d_i^4)$. Applying the induction hypothesis $x_i^* = O(10^i d_0)$ completes the proof.

Note that each level of recursion reduces k by 5 and $\log d$ by a factor of 4, hence if $5k > \log_4 \log d$, the recursion stops due to $d_0 \le 10$.

Theorem 2. *If $5k < \log_4 \log n$ then the amortized cost of exploring one step rightward using RECCOUNTER is $O(10^r n^{\frac{1}{4^r}})$ where $r = \lfloor k/5 \rfloor$, otherwise the amortized cost is $O(\log n)$.*

4   Treasure Hunt

Now let us proceed to the main treasure hunt problem. Recall that a configuration is given by the position of the agent, its state, and the content of the tape. Since the cells are symmetric, the behavior of the agent is invariant w.r.t. a shift of the tape. Hence, if a configuration repeats shifted by some distance in some direction, the agent starts cycling in that direction. Call two configurations *equivalent*, if they are shifted instances of each other.

First, let us consider the Max Distance Busy Beaver problem, which is of independent interest: *The DISTANCEBB (s, k) problem:* What is the maximal distance an s-state agent with k pebbles can reach before terminating?

Theorem 3 (✂). *The values of DISTANCEBB (s, k) satisfy the following:*

- *DISTANCEBB $(s, 0) = s$,*

- $\textsc{DistanceBB}\,(s,1) = 2s$,
- $\textsc{DistanceBB}\,(s,2) = 2^{\Theta(\sqrt{s\log s})}$,
- *There is no computable upper bound on* $\textsc{DistanceBB}\,(s,k)$ *for* $k \geq 3$.

Proof (Proof idea:). The algorithm with two pebbles uses them to delimit a distance n. Then it uses its states to check whether n is divisible by the first k primes where $k \approx \sqrt{s}$. If yes, it terminates, otherwise increases n. Hence, the overall time corresponds to the primorial $p_k\# = \prod_{i=1}^{k} p_k = e^{(1+o(1))k\log k}$. The corresponding upper bound is obtained by observing the behavior of the agent when both pebbles are placed at a distance n: there are at most $O(s^3)$ non-equivalent configurations with $n \leq s$. For $n > s$ (called *sparse configuration*), however, the agent must eventually travel from one endpoint to the other, and during this travel its states must change in a cycle. By counting the lcm of all possible cycles, we conclude that there are only finitely many classes of sparse configurations, such that if two configurations from the same class are entered, the agent starts cycling. Counting the number of such configurations gives the desired bound.

In order to see that there is no computable upper bound for $k \geq 3$ pebbles, it is sufficient to realize that an agent with three pebbles can simulate a two-counter machine, which is Turing complete.

It is not hard to observe that one pebble is not enough to find the treasure:

Theorem 4 ($\ltimes$). *It is impossible to find the treasure with less than 2 pebbles.*

With two pebbles, the agent can use them to delimit the explored distance, and expand the boundaries in an alternating pattern. This takes $O(n^2 s)$ steps, and it is essentially the best what can be done:

Theorem 5. *With $k = 2$ pebbles, $\Theta(n^2/s)$ time steps are needed and sufficient to solve the* $\textsc{TreasureHunt}$ *problem.*

Proof. Upper bound: The idea is that the explored area is delimited by pebbles, and expansion is alternating on both sides. In particular, the agent has one state in which it travels to the left until a pebble is encountered, and another state for traveling to the right. The remaining $s - 2$ states are divided into two groups: one group is used to move the left pebble $(s-2)/2$ steps to the left (after which a right traversal state is entered), and the other set of $(s-2)/2$ states is used to move the right pebble to the right. Overall, the traveled distances in alternating directions are of lengths $\sum_{0<1\leq 4n/(s-2)} i(s-2)/2 = O(n^2/s)$.

Lower bound: In order to eventually reach every point on the line, the agent must periodically switch between the expansion of the left and right border of the explored interval. Denote by E the explored interval, and $P \subseteq E$ the (possibly empty) interval currently delimited by the pebbles. Call a configuration *tight* if $|P| \leq s$ (in particular, any configuration with less than two pebbles placed is tight). If two equivalent tight configurations appear, the agent starts drifting into one direction, never exploring the other part. Hence, at most $O(s^3)$ tight configurations may appear overall, meaning that after some finite number of steps, no tight configuration appears. Suppose now that the agent is about to expand the right border of E (in a configuration where $|P| > s$). Since fetching the left pebble would create a tight configuration, the agent can use only the right pebble. It means that the right pebble of P must be located near the right border of E, and the agent may move it by at most s steps. After spending some $O(s)$ steps, the agent must start traveling to the left, and the bound follows.

With three pebbles we can use the same idea of expanding the explored region, only this time the third pebble can be used to perform the DISTANCEBB protocol, and make the expansion faster.

Theorem 6 (✂). *Let* $f(s) = $ DISTANCEBB $(2, (s-2)/2) = 2^{\Theta(\sqrt{s \log s})}$. *With* $k = 3$ *pebbles,* $\frac{n^2}{f(s)} + O(n)$ *time steps are sufficient to solve the* TREASUREHUNT *problem.*

Once we have at least 4 pebbles, we can efficiently use TRAVELCOUNTER to count, so we can use the classic distance-doubling technique. Whenever the TRAVELCOUNTER expires, change the travel direction and properly adjust counter size d, so that now it counts to approximately double the previous distance. Repeat the process until the treasure is found. The approximation ratio is then driven by the overhead (amortized cost per new exploration step) of using TRAVELCOUNTER. Which counter, and hence how to adjust the counter size d, depends on k: For $k \leq 10$, SIMPLECOUNTER is used, counting to $\binom{d-1}{k-2} \in O(d^{k-2})$, and d is multiplied by a close rational approximation of $\sqrt[k-2]{2}$. On the other hand, for $k \geq 11$, RECCOUNTER is used, counting to $O(d^4)$, and d is multiplied by a close rational approximation of $\sqrt[4]{2}$. Applying Lemma 2 and Theorem 2 yields

Theorem 7. *The* TREASUREHUNT *problem can be solved using* 1 *agent and* k *pebbles with an approximation ratio of*

- $O(n^{\frac{1}{k-2}})$ *with* $4 \leq k \leq 10$ *pebbles*
- $O(10^r n^{\frac{1}{4r}})$ *with* $k \geq 11$ *pebbles, where* $r = \lfloor k/5 \rfloor$

The previous theorem implies that with $O(\log \log n)$ pebbles, it is possible to solve the TREASUREHUNT problem in $O(n \log n)$ steps. Next, we show that it cannot be solved faster, even with unlimited number of pebbles. Note that if the agent has an unlimited number of pebbles (i.e., the pebble bag is always full), the setting is just a standard Turing machine with two-way unbounded tape. The input is given as a single "one" at a distance n in either direction from the starting point. The task is to move the head to that position. Using a *crossing-sequence* argument, we are able to prove the following:

Theorem 8 (✂). *With unlimited number of pebbles, the agent needs* $\Omega(n \log n)$ *steps to solve the* TREASUREHUNT *problem.*

The previous theorem concerns the scenario where the agent has from the beginning a bag with unlimited supply of pebbles. However, if the agent could request new pebbles during the computation, it would give him an additional counter that would help to overcome the lower bound. In particular, consider the following scenario with *on-demand pebbles*: the agent starts with an empty pebble bag, and empty tape. It can move on the tape, place, and collect pebbles as usual, only in this setting if the bag is empty, the agent may request a new pebble (that then immediately appears in the bag). Then the agent can effectively use its pebble bag as a counter:

Theorem 9 (✂). *In the scenario with on-demand pebbles, the* TREASURE-HUNT *problem can be solved in $O(n)$ steps.*

Next, we consider randomization where the agent can in each step flip a fair coin, and we are interested in the expected time to find the treasure. If the agent has no pebbles, and performs a simple (possibly biased) random walk, there is always a place with infinite hitting time. However, even with a single pebble, the agent now can find the treasure in expected finite time: use the pebble to mark the origin, and perform a simple random walk, but always slightly biased towards the origin.

Theorem 10 (✂). *For any $\delta > 1$, a randomized agent with one pebble can find the treasure in expected time $O(\delta^n)$.*

When there are more than constant number of pebbles, a randomized agent can use random choices to drag a more succinct counter.

Theorem 11 (✂). *A randomized agent using $O(\log \log n)$ pebbles can find the treasure in expected time $O(n \log \log n)$.*

Proof (Proof outline) The overall idea is straightforward: the agent marks the origin with a dedicated pebble (using a unique flavor), and proceeds in a series of *phases*. Each phase starts from the origin, and consist of two *incursions*: one to the right and one to the left. The expected length of the incursions increases exponentially, until eventually some incursion hits the treasure.

The main building block in implementing the incursions is a *flavored counter*. The counter uses pebbles of three unique flavors: *bitter*, *sweet*, and *spicy*, to store binary representations of two values. A *threshold T* is stored in a continuous sequence of places. On each place, a bitter or a sweet pebble is placed, representing zeroes and ones with the most significant bit on the left (assuming the right incursion). Overlaid over the threshold, a *counter $C \leq T$* is stored on the same sequence of places, such that the presence of a spicy pebble on a given place means a set bit. Note that with this representation, a counter of length d can represent numbers $0, \ldots, 2^d - 1$. Incrementing/decrementing (with a simultaneous check for overflow/underflow) of T or C can be performed in $O(d)$ (amortized $O(1)$) time. Moreover, in $O(d)$ time the whole counter can be shifted by one place, and also the value C can be *reset* (i.e., let $C \leftarrow T$) in $O(d)$ time.

The agent always drags with it a flavored counter whose threshold T is the number of the current phase (starting from 1). The aim of one incursion in phase T is to move $\approx 2^T$ steps in the given direction. Each incursion consists of a number of *rounds*. A round starts with the counter $C = T$, and repeatedly flips a coin. If there are T consecutive outcomes 1, the whole incursion is finished, and the agent moves (still carrying the counter) back to the origin. If a coin flip in a given round produces 0, the round is aborted, the agent moves one step further (shifting the counter), resets C, and starts another round.

The incursion with threshold T can be viewed as a process of repeatedly flipping a coin until T consecutive ones appear for the first time. It can be shown that the expected cost of phase T (provided that phase T actually happens) is $O(2^T \log T)$. Using this fact, we can show that the expected overall cost, i.e., sum of costs of all phases, is $O(n \log \log n)$.

References

1. Alpern, S., Gal, S.: The Theory of Search Games and Rendezvous. International Series in Operations Research & Management Science. Springer, US (2006)
2. Baezayates, R.A., Culberson, J.C., Rawlins, G.J.: Searching in the plane. Inform. Comput. **106**(2), 234–252 (1993)
3. Beck, A.: On the linear search problem. Israel J. Math. **2**(4), 221–228 (1964)
4. Beck, A., Newmann, D.J.: Yet more on the linear search problem. Israel J. Math. **8**(4), 419–429 (1970)
5. Bellman, R.: Problem 63–9, an optimal search. SIAM Rev. **5**(3), 274–274 (1963)
6. Bender, M.A., Fernández, A., Ron, D., Sahai, A., Vadhan, S.: The power of a pebble: exploring and mapping directed graphs. Inf. Comput. **176**(1), 1–21 (2002)
7. Bhattacharya, A., Gorain, B., Mandal, P.S.: Treasure hunt in graph using pebbles. In: Devismes, S., Petit, F., Altisen, K., Di Luna, G.A., Anta, A.F., eds., Stabilization, Safety, and Security of Distributed Systems - 24th International Symposium, SSS 2022, Clermont-Ferrand, France, November 15-17, 2022, Proceedings, volume 13751 of LNCS, pp. 99–113. Springer (2022)
8. Blum, M., Kozen, D.: On the power of the compass (or, why mazes are easier to search than graphs). In: 19th Annual Symposium on Foundations of Computer Science, Ann Arbor, Michigan, USA, 16-18 October 1978, pp. 132–142. IEEE Computer Society (1978)
9. Bollig, B., Gastin, P., Monmege, B., Zeitoun, M.: Logical characterization of weighted pebble walking automata. In: Henzinger, T.A., Miller, D., eds., Joint Meeting of the Twenty-Third EACSL Annual Conference on Computer Science Logic (CSL) and the Twenty-Ninth Annual ACM/IEEE Symposium on Logic in Computer Science (LICS), CSL-LICS '14, Vienna, Austria, July 14–18, 2014, pp. 19:1–19:10. ACM, (2014)
10. Chang, J.H., Ibarra, O.H., Palis, M.A., Ravikumar, B.: On pebble automata. Theor. Comput. Sci. **44**, 111–121, (1986)
11. Cohen, L., Emek, Y., Louidor, O., Uitto, J.: Exploring an infinite space with finite memory scouts. In: Klein, P.N., ed., Proceedings of the Twenty-Eighth Annual ACM-SIAM Symposium on Discrete Algorithms, SODA 2017, Barcelona, Spain, Hotel Porta Fira, January 16-19, pp. 207–224. SIAM (2017)

12. Das, S.K., Dhar, A.K., Gorain, B., Mahawar, M.: Collision-free exploration by mobile agents using pebbles. In: Korman, A., Chakraborty, S., Peri, S., Boldrini, C., Robinson, P., eds., Proceedings of the 26th International Conference on Distributed Computing and Networking, ICDCN 2025, Hyderabad, India, January 4–7, 2025, pp. 161–170. ACM (2025)
13. Diks, K., Fraigniaud, P., Kranakis, E., Pelc, A.: Tree exploration with little memory. J. Algorithms **51**(1), 38–63 (2004)
14. Disser, Y., Hackfeld, J., Klimm, M.: Undirected graph exploration with $\theta(\log \log n)$ pebbles. In: Krauthgamer, R., ed., Proceedings of the Twenty-Seventh Annual ACM-SIAM Symposium on Discrete Algorithms, SODA 2016, Arlington, VA, USA, January 10-12, 2016, pp. 25–39. SIAM (2016)
15. Disser, Y., Hackfeld, J., Klimm, M.: Tight bounds for undirected graph exploration with pebbles and multiple agents. J. ACM, **66**(6), 40:1–40:41 (2019)
16. Dynia, M., Łopuszański, J., Schindelhauer, C.: Why robots need maps. In: Prencipe, G., Zaks, S. (eds.) SIROCCO 2007. LNCS, vol. 4474, pp. 41–50. Springer, Heidelberg (2007). https://doi.org/10.1007/978-3-540-72951-8_5
17. Emek, Y., Langner, T., Stolz, D., Uitto, J., Wattenhofer, R.: How many ants does it take to find the food? Theor. Comput. Sci. 608:255–267 (2015). Structural Information and Communication Complexity
18. Euler, L.: Solutio problematis ad geometriam situs pertinentis. Commentarii Academiae Scientiarum Imperialis Petropolitanae **8** 128–140 (1736)
19. Fleischer, R., Trippen, G.: Exploring an unknown graph efficiently. In: Brodal, G.S., Leonardi, S. (eds.) ESA 2005. LNCS, vol. 3669, pp. 11–22. Springer, Heidelberg (2005). https://doi.org/10.1007/11561071_4
20. Flocchini, P., Prencipe, G., Santoro, N.: Distributed computing by mobile entities, Current Research in Moving and Computing, vol. 11340 LNCS. Springer (2019)
21. Fraigniaud, P., Ilcinkas, D., Peer, G., Pelc, A., Peleg, D.: Graph exploration by a finite automaton. Theor. Comput. Sci. **345**(2–3), 331–344 (2005)
22. Gal, S.: A general search game. Israel J. Math. **12**(1), 32–45 (1972)
23. Gal, S.: Search Games. Mathematics in science and engineering : a series of monographs and textbooks. Academic Press (1980)
24. Gorain, B., Mondal, K., Nayak, H., Pandit, S.: Pebble guided optimal treasure hunt in anonymous graphs. Theor. Comput. Sci. **922**, 61–80 (2022)
25. Gąsieniec, L., Klasing, R., Martin, R., Navarra, A., Zhang, X.: Fast periodic graph exploration with constant memory. J. Comput. Syst. Sci. **74**(5), 808–822 (2008)
26. Isaacs, R.: Differential Games: A Mathematical Theory with Applications to Warfare and Pursuit. Control and Optimization. Dover books on mathematics, Wiley (1965)
27. Kao, M.-Y., Reif, J.H., Tate, S.R.: Searching in an unknown environment: An optimal randomized algorithm for the cow-path problem. Inf. Comput. **131**(1), 63–79 (1996)
28. Martynova, O., Okhotin, A.: A time to cast away stones. In: Nagy, B., ed., Implementation and Application of Automata - 27th International Conference, CIAA 2023, Famagusta, North Cyprus, September 19-22, 2023, Proceedings, vol. 14151 of LNCS, pp. 242–253. Springer (2023)
29. Papadimitriou, C.H., Yannakakis, M.: Shortest paths without a map. Theor. Comput. Sci. **84**(1), 127–150 (1991)
30. Pattanayak, D., Pelc, A.: Graph exploration by a deterministic memoryless automaton with pebbles. Discret. Appl. Math. **356**, 149–160 (2024)
31. Rosenkrantz, D.J., Stearns, R.E., Lewis II, P.M.: An analysis of several heuristics for the traveling salesman problem. SIAM J. Comput. **6**(3), 563–581 (1977)

Multiparty Equality in the Local Broadcast Model

Louis Esperet[1]($\boxtimes$) and Jean-Florent Raymond[2]

[1] CNRS, Université Grenoble Alpes, G-SCOP, Grenoble, France
`louis.esperet@grenoble-inp.fr`
[2] CNRS, ENS de Lyon, Université Claude Bernard Lyon 1, LIP, UMR 5668,
Lyon, France
`jean-florent.raymond@cnrs.fr`

Abstract. In this paper we consider the *multiparty equality problem* in graphs, where every vertex of a graph G is given an input, and the goal of the vertices is to decide whether all inputs are equal. We study this problem in the *local broadcast model*, where a message sent by a vertex is received by all its neighbors and the total cost of a protocol is the sum of the lengths of the messages sent by the vertices. This setting was studied by Khan and Vaidya, who gave in 2021 a protocol achieving a 4-approximation in the general case.

We study this multiparty communication problem through the lens of network topology. We design a new protocol for 2-connected graphs, whose efficiency relies on the notion of total vertex cover in graph theory. This protocol outperforms the aforementioned 4-approximation in a number of cases. To demonstrate its applicability, we apply it to obtain optimal or asymptotically optimal protocols for several natural network topologies such as cycles, hypercubes, and grids. On the way we also provide new bounds of independent interest on the size of total vertex covers in regular graphs.

Keywords: Distributed equality testing · packing and covering boundaries of cuts · total vertex cover

1 Introduction

We consider the *multiparty equality problem* in graphs, where every vertex of a graph G is given a k-bit input, and the goal of the vertices is to decide whether all inputs are the same. Each vertex can communicate with its neighbors in the graph, and the cost of the protocol is the total number of bits transmitted during the communication phase. After this phase, each vertex either accepts or rejects the instance; if every vertex was assigned the same input, then all vertices must accept the instance, and if two of the inputs differ then at least one vertex must reject the instance. The *complexity* of the multiparty equality problem is the minimum cost of a protocol solving the problem. Note that we only consider protocols that are deterministic and *static* [AES17, KV21, LV11], in

C. Georgiou (Ed.): SIROCCO 2026, LNCS 16488, pp. 272–291, 2026.
https://doi.org/10.1007/978-3-032-26465-7_15

the sense that the set of vertices sending messages and the size of their messages is independent of their input strings (they only depend on G and k). One the other hand, the content of the messages is allowed to depend on the input strings. See [AES17] for a discussion on non-static protocols.

In the classical *point-to-point* communication model, each vertex communicates with its neighbors on different channels (one channel per vertex), so that sending the same message of ℓ bits to d neighbors costs $d\ell$ bits of communication. A natural lower bound on the complexity of the multiparty equality problem in this model can be obtained by observing that at least k bits need to be sent through every cut of the graph in every protocol. As a consequence, as proved in [CR15, AES17], the complexity is at least k times the minimum fractional transversal of cuts in the graph (or by duality, the maximum fractional packing of cuts), see Sect. 2.2 for more details. Alon, Efremenko and Sudakov [AES17] showed that this linear programming lower bound can be attained asymptotically for a number of graph classes, including Hamiltonian graphs, and moreover they gave a protocol of cost within a factor $4/3$ of the optimal for every graph. To the best of our knowledge, it is unknown whether computing the optimal cost of a protocol can be done in polynomial time.

Much less is known in the *local broadcast* communication model, which is the main focus of this paper. In this model, each message sent by a vertex v is transmitted to *all* the neighbors of v, and the number of bits of this message is counted only once in the complexity of the protocol. The *total cost* of a protocol Π on G, denoted $\mathsf{cost}_\Pi(G, k)$, is the sum of the number of bits broadcast by each vertex. The *total complexity* (minimum cost of a protocol solving the problem) of the multiparty equality problem in the local broadcast communication model on G with k bit inputs is denoted by $\mathsf{OPT}(G, k)$. We will be mostly interested in the *per-bit complexity* $\mathsf{OPT}(G) = \lim_{k\to\infty} \frac{1}{k} \mathsf{OPT}(G, k)$, whose existence directly follows from Fekete's subadditive lemma [Wik26]. Similarly, we define the *per-bit cost* of a protocol Π as $\mathsf{cost}_\Pi(G) = \lim_{k\to\infty} \frac{1}{k}\mathsf{cost}_\Pi(G, k)$ (this limit does not exist for all protocols, but it does in all the protocols we consider in the paper). As in the point-to-point communication model, a simple linear programming lower bound on the complexity of the problem can be obtained by noting that for every cut, the sum of the number of bits broadcast by the vertices incident to the cut has to be at least k. This implies that a natural lower bound on $\mathsf{OPT}(G)$ is the maximum fractional packing (or minimum fractional transversal) of boundaries in the graph G, where a *boundary* is the set of vertices incident to the edges of a given cut in the graph.

In the definition of a protocol for equality above, we have required that when two inputs differ, this is detected by at least one vertex. We note that when focusing on the per-bit complexity $\mathsf{OPT}(G)$ or the per-bit cost of a protocol, it would be equivalent to ask the stronger requirement that at then end of the protocol, all vertices know whether they have the same input or not. This is because if two inputs differ, then some vertex will detect it, and this vertex can then communicate this information to all vertices along a spanning tree, costing a number of bits that depends only on G, not on the length k of the input. The contribution of this additional constant cost in the per-bit complexity vanishes as $k \to \infty$.

The complexity of multiparty equality in the local broadcast model was studied by Khan and Vaidya [KV21]. They first studied so-called *simple protocols*, where each vertex either broadcasts its entire input, or remains inactive. Each vertex then checks that the inputs received from its neighbors match its own input, and accepts the instance if and only if this is the case. They related such protocols to the notion of a weakly connected dominating set. A *weakly connected dominating set* S in a graph G, is a subset of the vertices of G such that the set of edges incident to S induces a spanning and connected subgraph of G. The minimum size of a weakly connected dominating set in G is denoted by $\mathsf{wds}(G)$.

Khan and Vaidya proved the following characterization of simple protocols [KV21].

Theorem 1 ([KV21]). *A simple protocol solves the multiparty equality problem if and only if the set $S \subseteq V$ of vertices chosen to transmit their entire input is a weakly connected dominating set of G. In particular, $\mathsf{OPT}(G) \leq \mathsf{wds}(G)$.*

Let us denote by Π_0 the simple protocol of Theorem 1, of per-bit cost $\mathsf{cost}_{\Pi_0}(G) = \mathsf{wds}(G)$. The authors of [KV21] use the result above to provide examples where the multiplicative gap between the minimum cost of a simple protocol and OPT is of order $\Omega(\log n)$ (here and in the remainder of the paper, n stands for the number of vertices of the graph under consideration). Khan and Vaidya then studied general (non-simple) protocols, and designed a protocol Π_1 which is within factor 4 of the optimal.

Theorem 2 ([KV21]). *For any graph G and integer k, there is a protocol Π_1 for multiparty equality in the local broadcast model whose total cost is at most $4k$ times the maximum fractional packing of boundaries, and in particular at most $4\,\mathsf{OPT}(G,k)$.*

We note that it appears to be unknown whether $\mathsf{OPT}(G)$ and $\mathsf{OPT}(G,k)$ can be computed in polynomial time.

Our Results

In this paper, we study the multiparty equality problem in the local broadcast model through the lens of network topology (or equivalently, graph classes).

We first provide a couple of interesting applications of Theorem 1: an optimal protocol for trees, and an asymptotically optimal protocol for hypercubes.

We then design a new protocol in 2-connected graphs, which outperforms Theorem 2 on a number of natural graph classes. Our protocol uses ideas introduced by Alon, Efremenko and Sudakov [AES17] in the point-to-point model, relying on classical constructions in extremal combinatorics. Recall that a *vertex cover* in a graph G is a subset of vertices intersecting every edge of G, and a *total dominating set* in G is a subset X of vertices such that every vertex in G has a neighbor in X. The efficiency of our protocol depends on the minimum size of a *total vertex cover* in the graph G, denoted by $\mathsf{tvc}(G)$, where a total vertex cover is a subset of vertices which is both a vertex cover and a total dominating set. We prove the following result.

Theorem 3. *For any 2-connected graph G, there is a protocol Π_2 for multiparty equality in the local broadcast model whose per-bit cost is at most $\frac{1}{2}\mathsf{tvc}(G)$, and in particular $\mathsf{OPT}(G) \leq \frac{1}{2}\mathsf{tvc}(G)$.*

We emphasize that only the vertices of a total vertex cover send messages in the protocol Π_2, as opposed to the protocol of [AES17] whose correctness relies on the fact that every vertex communicates.

Theorem 3 motivates the study of total vertex covers in graphs, for which we obtain new results which might be of independent interest. Our first application concerns the class of cycles. The linear programming lower bound on $\mathsf{OPT}(C_n)$ is of order $n/3$ (assigning weight $\frac{1}{3}$ to each vertex). On the other hand, as $\mathsf{wds}(C_n) = \lfloor n/2 \rfloor$, the simple protocol of Theorem 1 has per-bit cost $\lfloor n/2 \rfloor$, and it can be checked that the protocol of Theorem 2 has per-bit cost $\frac{2}{3}n - \frac{2}{3}$ or $\frac{2}{3}n - \frac{1}{3}$, depending on the parity of n. As an immediate application of Theorem 3, we obtain an almost optimal protocol for cycles.

Corollary 1. *For any integer $n \geq 3$, $\frac{n}{3} \leq \mathsf{OPT}(C_n) \leq \frac{n+1}{3}$, and for every integer $n \equiv 0 \pmod 3$, $\mathsf{OPT}(C_n) = \frac{n}{3}$.*

We then consider hypercubes, a well-studied graph topology. It is known that d-dimensional hypercubes Q_d have weakly connected dominating sets of size matching asymptotically the linear programming lower bound $\frac{2^d}{d+1}$ [Gri21], and therefore the protocol Π_0 of Theorem 1 is asymptotically best possible in this class. However the bounds on the size of weakly connected dominating sets depend on non-trivial results on the density of primes (even in the most simple case $d = 2^\ell - 1$). We give a simple and self-contained proof of an upper bound on $\mathsf{tvc}(Q_d)$ in this case, which directly implies that Π_2 is asymptotically optimal for these graphs as well.

Corollary 2. *Let $\ell \geq 2$ be an integer and let $d = 2^\ell - 1$. Then the protocol Π_2 for equality in the hypercube Q_d has per-bit cost at most*

$$\frac{2^d}{d+1} + \frac{2^{d/2}}{d+1} = \mathsf{OPT}(Q_d) + O\left(\sqrt{\mathsf{OPT}(Q_d)}\right).$$

We next consider the classical n by n square grid, which is denoted by G_n. The linear programming lower bound on $\mathsf{OPT}(G_n)$ is of order $n^2/5$ (assigning weight $\frac{1}{5}$ to each vertex), but a simple counting argument shows that $\mathsf{wds}(G_n) \geq n^2/4$, and thus simple protocols cannot be optimal. The protocol of Theorem 2 has many possible outcomes in a grid, depending on the order in which the vertices are chosen, and therefore it is not clear if it can be optimal for some well-chosen ordering. We have found some natural orderings for which the protocol of Theorem 2 has per-bit cost $\frac{2}{5}n^2$, that is twice the linear programming lower bound. On the other hand, as a direct application of Theorem 3, we obtain an asymptotically optimal protocol for grids.

Corollary 3. $\mathsf{OPT}(G_n) = (\frac{1}{5} + o(1))n^2$.

We then study d-regular graphs for $d \geq 3$. An interesting property of these classes is that although the classes are very large (containing roughly $2^{(d/2-1)n\log n}$ non-isomorphic n-vertex graphs), the linear programming lower bound in this case can be expressed easily as $\frac{n}{d+1}$, which allows to compare explicitly the quality of protocols on a large class of graphs by simply bounding the cost of protocols on the entire class (instead of comparing the cost of the protocol and the linear programming lower bound on every single graph in the class).

It was proved in [CG17] that every cubic graph on n vertices has a total vertex cover on at most $3n/4$ vertices. We extend this result to every degree by proving that for $d \geq 3$, every d-regular graph on n vertices has a total vertex cover on at most $\frac{d}{d+1} \cdot n$ vertices. This is optimal for every d, since any total vertex cover of the complete graph K_{d+1} (which is d-regular) contains at least d vertices. It was proved in [CG17] that there are two more extremal connected graphs in the case $d = 3$, and all the other connected cubic graphs have a total vertex cover with less than $3n/4$ vertices. Our result below implies that for $d \geq 5$, complete graphs are the only extremal examples.

Theorem 4. *For every $d \geq 3$, every d-regular graph on n vertices has a total vertex cover on at most $\frac{d}{d+1} \cdot n$ vertices. For $d \geq 5$, every connected d-regular graph on n vertices distinct from K_{d+1} has a total vertex cover on at most $\frac{d-\epsilon}{d+1} \cdot n$ vertices, with $\epsilon = \frac{1}{2d+1}$.*

Combining Theorem 4 and Theorem 3 for the upper bound, and using the linear programming lower bound of $\frac{n}{d+1}$ alluded to above, we immediately obtain the following.

Corollary 4. *For any $d \geq 3$ and any 2-connected d-regular graph G, the protocol Π_2 of Theorem 3 has per-bit cost at most $\frac{d}{2d+2} \cdot n = \frac{d}{2} \cdot \mathsf{OPT}(G)$. If moreover, $d \geq 5$ and $G \neq K_{d+1}$, then Π_2 has per-bit cost at most $\frac{d-\epsilon}{2} \cdot \mathsf{OPT}(G)$, for some $\epsilon > 0$ depending only on d.*

Corollary 4 improves on the 4-approximation of Theorem 2 for any degree $d \leq 8$.

Organization of the Paper

In Sect. 2 we introduce the necessary notation, the linear programming lower bounds and two useful lemmas. Section 3 is devoted to the study of simple protocols. In Sect. 4 we introduce a new protocol for 2-connected graphs based on total vertex covers and provide several applications. Directions for future research are given in Sect. 5.

2 Preliminaries

2.1 Notation

In this paper, log denotes the binary logarithm. Let G be a graph. For two disjoint sets $S, S' \subseteq V(G)$, we denote by $E(S, S')$ the set of edges of G with the one endpoint in S and the other one in S', and the *cut* defined by S is $E(S, \bar{S})$, where $\bar{S} = V(G) \setminus S$. The *boundary* $B(S)$ of the cut defined by S consists of all vertices incident to $E(S, \bar{S})$. Observe that for every $v \in V(G)$, the trivial boundary $B(\{v\})$ is precisely the closed neighborhood $N[v]$ of v in G (that is, v together with its set of neighbors in G).

In the remainder we only consider connected graphs (otherwise the problem we consider has no solution, as vertices in different components cannot communicate to verify that their inputs are equal). A graph G is *2-connected* if it has at least 3 vertices and G remains connected after the removal of any vertex.

2.2 A Linear Programming Lower Bound

Consider the following covering linear program for boundaries.

Program $\mathsf{Cov}_{\mathrm{bnd}}(G)$

variables: $x(v)$ for every $v \in V(G)$

function to minimize: $\displaystyle\sum_{v \in V(G)} x(v)$

subject to the constraints: $\begin{cases} \forall S \subsetneq V(G) \text{ s.t. } S \neq \emptyset, \displaystyle\sum_{v \in B(S)} x(v) \geq 1 \\ \forall v \in V(G), \ x(v) \geq 0. \end{cases}$

Optimal value: $\tau^*_{\mathrm{bnd}}(G)$

The dual packing linear program is the following.

Program $\mathsf{Pack}_{\mathrm{bnd}}(G)$

variables: $y(S)$ for every non-empty $S \subsetneq V(G)$

maximize: $\displaystyle\sum_{S \subsetneq V(G), \ S \neq \emptyset} y(S)$

subject to: $\begin{cases} \forall v \in V(G), \displaystyle\sum_{S, \ v \in B(S)} y(S) \leq 1 \\ \forall S \subsetneq V(G) \text{ s.t. } S \neq \emptyset, \ y(S) \geq 0 \end{cases}$

Optimal value: $\nu^*_{\mathrm{bnd}}(G)$

Note that by linear programming duality, $\tau^*_{\mathrm{bnd}}(G) = \nu^*_{\mathrm{bnd}}(G)$ for any graph G. It will be also useful to consider the simple variants of the two linear programs above, $\mathsf{Cov}_{\mathrm{balls}}(G)$ and $\mathsf{Pack}_{\mathrm{balls}}(G)$, where instead of considering all boundaries

$B(S)$, we only consider the trivial boundaries (of the form $B(\{v\})$, for some v). Let $\tau^*_{\text{balls}}(G) = \nu^*_{\text{balls}}(G)$ be the associated optimal values.

Observing that for any non-empty cut $E(S, \bar{S})$, at least k bits in total have to be broadcast by the vertices incident to the cut, the following was proved in [KV21].

Theorem 5 ([KV21]). *For any graph G and integer k, $\mathsf{OPT}(G, k) \geq \tau^*_{\text{bnd}}(G) \cdot k$, and in particular $\mathsf{OPT}(G) \geq \tau^*_{\text{bnd}}(G) \geq \tau^*_{\text{balls}}(G)$.*

We also consider the integer parameters $\tau_{\text{bnd}}(G)$, $\nu_{\text{bnd}}(G)$, $\tau_{\text{balls}}(G)$, $\nu_{\text{balls}}(G)$, which are defined similarly as their fractional counterparts, but optimizing over the integers instead of the real (or rational) numbers. For instance, as $B(\{v\}) = N[v]$ for every vertex v, $\tau_{\text{balls}}(G)$ is equal to the minimum size of a set S, such that $V(G) = \bigcup_{v \in S} N[v]$, or equivalently $\tau_{\text{balls}}(G)$ is the *domination number* of G, the minimum size of a dominating set in G. Therefore, $\tau^*_{\text{balls}}(G)$ can be considered as the fractional domination number of G. The following simple result will be useful in the remainder of the paper.

Lemma 1. *If G is an n-vertex graph with maximum degree Δ, then $\tau^*_{\text{bnd}}(G) \geq \tau^*_{\text{balls}}(G) \geq \frac{n}{\Delta+1}$. Moreover, if G is Δ-regular, then $\tau^*_{\text{balls}}(G) = \frac{n}{\Delta+1}$.*

Proof. Setting $y(S) = \frac{1}{\Delta+1}$ for every vertex boundary S of the form $S = B(\{v\}) = N[v]$ for some $v \in V(G)$, we obtain a feasible solution to the program $\mathsf{Pack}_{\text{balls}}(G)$, and thus $\tau^*_{\text{balls}}(G) = \nu^*_{\text{balls}}(G) \geq \frac{n}{\Delta+1}$. When G is Δ-regular, setting $x(v) = \frac{1}{\Delta+1}$ for every vertex $v \in V(G)$, we obtain a feasible solution to the program $\mathsf{Cov}_{\text{balls}}(G)$. It follows that $\tau^*_{\text{balls}}(G) \leq \frac{n}{\Delta+1}$, and thus $\tau^*_{\text{balls}}(G) = \frac{n}{\Delta+1}$, as desired. $\qquad\square$

We note that we will only use the first part of the statement, in combination with Theorem 5.

Finally, we will use the following well-known fact about 2-connected graphs.

Lemma 2. *Every 2-connected graph G on n vertices has a 2-connected spanning subgraph H on at most $2n - 3 \leq 2n$ edges.*

Proof. Every 2-connected graph G has an ear-decomposition such that every ear is open (the two endpoints of the ear are distinct), see [Whi32]. Include in H all the ears from the ear-decomposition, except those consisting of a single edge. Note that we start with a cycle (of length at least 3), and every time we add k new vertices to H, we add $k + 1 \leq 2k$ edges to H. Thus H has at most $2(n - 3) + 3 = 2n - 3$ edges. $\qquad\square$

3   Simple Protocols

We recall that in *simple protocols* for equality, each vertex either broadcasts its entire input, or does not send any bit of communication. As stated in Theorem 1, the set S of vertices broadcasting their input in such a protocol is a *weakly connected dominating set*, which implies that $\mathsf{OPT}(G) \leq \mathsf{wds}(G)$ for any graph G. In this section, we explore a number of interesting consequences of this result.

Let $\mathsf{vc}(G)$ denote the minimum size of a *vertex cover* of a graph G (a set of vertices intersecting every edge of G). Note that $\mathsf{wds}(G) \leq \mathsf{vc}(G)$. We obtain the following simple result.

Theorem 6. *For any tree T, the simple protocol in which every vertex of a vertex cover broadcasts its input is optimal among all protocols. In particular* $\mathsf{OPT}(T) = \mathsf{vc}(T)$.

Proof. Let T be a tree. Since the minimal cuts of T are single edges, $\tau^*_{\mathrm{bnd}}(T)$ coincides with the optimal solution of the linear relaxation of vertex cover in T. But since T is bipartite, it follows from Kőnig's theorem that this optimal solution is equal to $\mathsf{vc}(T)$. As there is a protocol for equality with per-bit cost $\mathsf{wds}(G) \leq \mathsf{vc}(T)$, the per-bit complexity of equality in trees is precisely the vertex cover number. $\qquad\square$

As observed in the previous section, $\tau_{\mathrm{balls}}(G)$ is the domination number of G, and this can be used to connect $\tau_{\mathrm{balls}}(G)$ and $\mathsf{wds}(G)$ as follows.

Lemma 3. *For any connected graph G,* $\tau_{\mathrm{balls}}(G) \leq \mathsf{wds}(G) \leq 2\,\tau_{\mathrm{balls}}(G) - 1$.

Proof. Since a weakly dominating set is a dominating set, we have $\tau_{\mathrm{balls}}(G) \leq \mathsf{wds}(G)$, so it remains to prove $\mathsf{wds}(G) \leq 2\,\tau_{\mathrm{balls}}(G)$. Consider a dominating set D of size $\tau_{\mathrm{balls}}(G)$ in G. We assume that G has more than one vertex otherwise the statement is trivially true. Let H be the subgraph of G induced by all edges that are incident to a vertex of D. Since D is a dominating set, H is a spanning subgraph of G of minimum degree at least 1, and with at most $\tau_{\mathrm{balls}}(G)$ connected components. Let E' be a set of edges of $E(G) \setminus E(H)$ of minimum size such that the subgraph of G induced by the edges of $E(H) \cup E'$ is connected. As H has at most $\tau_{\mathrm{balls}}(G)$ connected components, $|E'| \leq \tau_{\mathrm{balls}}(G) - 1$. Let D' be a subset of vertices of G obtained by doing the following for each edge $e \in E'$: select an endpoint of e arbitrarily and add it to D'. Then $D \cup D'$ has size at most $2\,\tau_{\mathrm{balls}}(G) - 1$ and it can be checked that $D \cup D'$ is a weakly dominating set of G, as desired. $\qquad\square$

Recall that $\tau^*_{\mathrm{balls}}(G) \leq \mathsf{OPT}(G)$. In particular, for any graph G for which $\tau_{\mathrm{balls}}(G)$ is very close to $\tau^*_{\mathrm{balls}}(G)$, combining Theorem 1 with Lemma 3 immediately provides a good approximation of the optimal broadcast protocol.

Corollary 5. *For every graph G, there is a simple protocol for equality with per-bit cost at most* $2 \cdot \dfrac{\tau_{\mathrm{balls}}(G)}{\tau^*_{\mathrm{balls}}(G)} \cdot \mathsf{OPT}(G)$.

For instance, the d-dimensional hypercube Q_d with $d = 2^k - 1$, for some integer k, satisfies $\tau^*_{\mathrm{balls}}(Q_d) = \tau_{\mathrm{balls}}(Q_d) = \frac{2^d}{d+1}$, and thus Corollary 5 implies that the broadcast protocol based on weakly dominating sets is within a multiplicative factor 2 of the optimal protocol for these graphs.

Note that for hypercubes, we can use the stronger results obtained by Griggs in [Gri21], showing that Q_d has a connected dominating set of size $(1+o(1))\frac{2^d}{d+1}$ as $d \to \infty$, and in particular $\mathsf{wds}(Q_d) = (1+o(1))\frac{2^d}{d+1}$. Theorem 1 then gives an asymptotically optimal (simple) protocol for equality in hypercubes. Alternatively, we describe in the next section a protocol Π_2 which has per-bit cost $\frac{2^d}{d+1} + 2^{d/2}$ on the hypercube Q_d, see Sect. 4.2 for details.

4   Total Vertex Covers and a New Protocol

4.1   The New Protocol

Recall that a *total vertex cover* in a graph G is a vertex subset that is both a total dominating set and a vertex cover. The minimum size of such a set is denoted by $\mathsf{tvc}(G)$. See Figs. 2 and 3 for illustrations of total vertex covers in grids. In this section we prove Theorem 3, restated below as Theorem 7.

Theorem 7. *Let G be a 2-connected graph G and k be an integer. Then there is a protocol Π_2 for equality in G of total cost $\mathsf{cost}_{\Pi_2}(G, k) \leq (k/2 + o(k)) \cdot \mathsf{tvc}(G)$, and thus $\mathsf{OPT}(G) \leq \mathsf{cost}_{\Pi_2}(G) \leq \frac{1}{2}\mathsf{tvc}(G)$.*

We emphasize that in our protocol, only the vertices of a total vertex cover of G send a message; all the other vertices remain silent.

Note that it might be the case that a 2-connected graph G contains a 2-connected spanning subgraph H with $\mathsf{tvc}(H) < \mathsf{tvc}(G)$, in which case it is natural to run the equality protocol in H rather than in G. We therefore obtain the following immediate corollary of Theorem 7, which will be used extensively in our applications.

Corollary 6. *For any 2-connected spanning subgraph H of G, there is a protocol for equality in the local broadcast model in G whose per-bit cost is at most $\frac{1}{2}\mathsf{tvc}(H)$, and in particular $\mathsf{OPT}(G) \leq \frac{1}{2}\mathsf{tvc}(H)$.*

Remark 1. In terms of transversals, a total vertex cover is an (integral) transversal of open neighborhoods (total dominating set) and of edges (vertex cover). As we are dealing with graphs with no isolated vertices, a total vertex cover always exists, for instance every vertex cover of such a graph G is dominating and can be made total by adding a neighbor of each of its elements, so $\mathsf{tvc}(G) \leq 2\mathsf{vc}(G)$.

Our protocol Π_2 of Theorem 7 relies on a technical lemma (Lemma 4 below) from [AES17] and used there in the different setting of point-to-point communication. Before we can formally state this result, we need to introduce some terminology. Let H be a graph with n vertices $v_1, \ldots, v_n$. Let F be a graph with its vertices partitioned into n classes $U_1, \ldots, U_n$. A subgraph of F isomorphic to H is called a *special copy* of H if for every $i \in \{1, \ldots, k\}$ the vertex corresponding to v_i in the copy belongs to U_i. We say that F is a *faithful host* for H if the two following conditions are met:

1. The edges of F can be partitioned into edge-disjoint special copies of H; and
2. F contains no other special copy of H than the aforementioned $|E(F)|/|E(H)|$ copies defining its edge set.

See Fig. 1 for an illustration (the three special copies of the triangle in the faithful host are depicted with different colors and width).

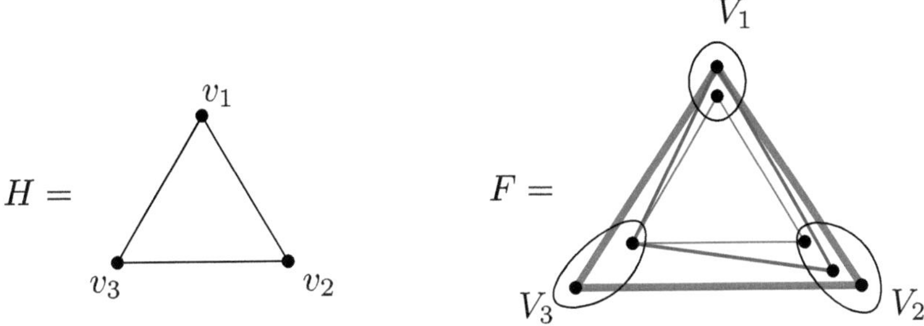

Fig. 1. A faithful host of the triangle.

Lemma 4 ([AES17, Lemma 3.3]). *Let H be a 2-connected n-vertex graph and let m be a positive integer. Then there is a faithful host for H with classes of vertices $U_1, \ldots, U_n$, each of size nm, containing a least $m^2/e^{10\sqrt{\log m \log n}}$ special copies of H.*

We are now ready to prove the main result of this section.

Proof of Theorem 3. Let n denote the number of vertices of G, that we call $v_1, \ldots, v_n$, and let m be the minimum integer such that $\frac{m^2}{e^{10\sqrt{\log m \log n}}} \geq 2^k$. By Lemma 4 there is a faithful host F for G with classes of vertices $U_1, \ldots, U_n$, each of size nm, containing a least 2^k special copies of G. For every $i \in \{1, \ldots, n\}$, let us name $u_i^1, \ldots, u_i^{nm}$ the vertices of U_i. We associate to each k-bit word w a special copy G_w of G in F in an injective way (i.e. if $w \neq w'$ then $G_w \neq G_{w'}$). Since there are at least 2^k special copies, this is always possible.

For a fixed assignment $\lambda \colon V(G) \to \{0,1\}^k$ of k-bit inputs to the vertices of G, let us define the *identity* of a vertex v_i of G as the integer $1 \leq j \leq nm$ such that the vertex of the special copy $G_{\lambda(v_i)}$ corresponding to v_i is u_i^j. In other words, $V(G_{\lambda(v_i)}) \cap U_i = \{u_i^j\}$. Such an integer always exists by the definition of a special copy. Notice that the identity of a vertex v_i depends on its input $\lambda(v_i)$.

For every edge $v_i v_j \in E(G)$, we say that the identity a_i of v_i is *consistent* with the identity a_j of v_j if:

1. there is an edge in F between $u_i^{a_i}$ and $u_j^{a_j}$; and
2. this edge belongs to the special copy $G_{\lambda(v_j)}$.

Observe that due to the second item, this relation is not symmetric. However, given a_i, the vertex v_j can check whether a_i is consistent with a_j.

We now fix an optimal total vertex cover S of G, and we are ready to describe the protocol Π_2. Given an assignment λ of k-bit inputs to the vertices of G, the protocol is the following:

Protocol Π_2

Communication: Each vertex v of S broadcasts its identity to its neighbors and the other vertices remain silent. *Decision:* A vertex v of G accepts the instance if and only if all identities received from its neighbors are consistent with its own identity.

This completes the description of the protocol Π_2. Recall that we chose F and the function $w \mapsto G_w$ depending only on G, and in particular they do not depend on the assignment of inputs λ. So using them and their own inputs, the vertices can indeed compute their own identity and check consistency with those possibly sent by their neighbors.

Let us now show that the protocol is correct. Suppose first that λ assigns the same word w to every vertex of G. Then for every edge vv' of G, the identity of v is trivially consistent with that of v', since these are defined with respect to the same special copy G_w of G. Hence in this case every vertex accepts the instance.

Conversely, suppose that every vertex accepts the instance. For every $i \in \{1, \ldots, n\}$, let a_i be the identity of v_i. Recall that S is a vertex cover, so for every edge $v_i v_j$ of G, at least one of the two endpoints lies in S, say $v_i \in S$. It follows that v_i sends its identity a_i to v_j. As v_j accepts the instance, $u_i^{a_i} u_j^{a_j}$ is an edge in F. Hence F has a subgraph G' on vertex set $\{u_i^{a_i}\}_{i \in \{1, \ldots, n\}}$ that is isomorphic to G and where for every $i \in \{1, \ldots, n\}$ the vertex corresponding to v_i lies in the vertex subset U_i. The subgraph G' of F is a thus a special copy of G in F, and by the definition of a faithful host G' is one of the special copies that partition the edges of F, say $G' = G_w$ for some k-bit word w. Since S is a total vertex cover, every vertex v_j of G has a neighbor $v_i \in S$. By the second item in the definition of consistency, the edge $v_i^{a_i} v_j^{a_j}$ of F belongs to the special copy $G_{\lambda(v_j)}$. As noted above this edge also belongs to $G' = G_w$ so by definition of faithful hosts, $\lambda(v_j) = w$. This shows that all vertices of G have the same input, as desired.

It remains to bound the cost of the protocol. Recall that only the vertices in S broadcast their identity. Also, recall that the identity of a vertex is an integer of $\{1, \ldots, nm\}$, and that n (the number of vertices of G) is a constant while

$k \to \infty$. By the choice of m we have

$$2\log(m-1) \le k + 10\log(e)\sqrt{\log(m-1)\log n}$$

$$\log m = \frac{k}{2} + O(\sqrt{\log m \log n})$$

$$= \frac{k}{2} + O(\sqrt{k \log n})$$

The total cost of the protocol is thus at most

$$|S| \cdot \log mn = |S| \cdot \left(\frac{k}{2} + O\left(\sqrt{k \log n}\right) + \log n\right)$$

$$= \mathsf{tvc}(G) \cdot \left(\frac{k}{2} + o(k)\right).$$

It follows that the per-bit cost of the protocol is at most $\frac{1}{2}\mathsf{tvc}(G)$, which completes the proof. $\qquad\square$

4.2 Applications

Complete Bipartite Graphs $K_{2,t}$. We start by giving a simple example of a family of graphs where the protocol Π_2 of Theorem 7 outperforms the protocols Π_0 of Theorem 1 and Π_1 of Theorem 2. The complete bipartite graph $K_{2,t}$ has a total vertex cover that consists of three vertices: the two vertices of degree t and one vertex of degree 2. According to Theorem 7, we thus have $\mathsf{cost}_{\Pi_2}(K_{2,t}) \le 3/2$. This is tight as we also have $\mathsf{OPT}(K_{2,t}) \ge 3/2$ thanks to the lower bound $\mathsf{OPT}(K_{2,t}) \ge \tau^*_{\mathrm{bnd}}(K_{2,t})$ (Theorem 5). On the other hand, we can observe (see [KV21]) that on $K_{2,t}$ the cost of the protocols Π_0 and Π_1 is always at least 2.

Cycles. We immediately deduce from Theorem 7 an almost optimal protocol for equality in cycles.

Corollary 7. *On input C_n, the protocol Π_2 of Theorem 7 has per-bit cost at most $\frac{n+1}{3} \le \mathsf{OPT}(C_n) + \frac{1}{3}$. Moreover, if $n \equiv 0 \pmod 3$, Π_2 has per-bit cost $\frac{n}{3} = \mathsf{OPT}(C_n)$.*

Proof. In a cycle C_n we can construct a total vertex cover by selecting all vertices except those whose index is 0 modulo 3. So $\mathsf{tvc}(C_n) \le \frac{2}{3}(n+1)$ and the protocol of Theorem 7 has per-bit cost at most $(n+1)/3$ (and at most $n/3$ if $n \equiv 0 \pmod 3$).

On the other hand, by Lemma 1, $\tau^*_{\mathrm{balls}}(C_n) = n/3$. Overall we get:

$$\frac{n}{3} = \tau^*_{\mathrm{balls}}(C_n) \le \tau^*_{\mathrm{bnd}}(C_n) \le \frac{1}{k}\mathsf{OPT}(C_n, k) \le \mathsf{cost}_{\Pi_2}(C_n) \le \frac{n+1}{3},$$

as desired. $\qquad\square$

Hypercubes. In Sect. 3, we observed that there is a simple protocol for equality in the d-dimensional hypercube Q_d of per-bit cost $(1 + o(1))\frac{2^d}{d+1}$, asymptotically matching the fractional lower bound $\frac{2^d}{d+1}$. The efficiency of this protocol was based on a recent result of Griggs on connected dominating sets in hypercubes [Gri21]. We note that this result itself is based on classical results on q-ary codes and crucially relies on the density of primes, even for simple cases such as $d = 2^\ell - 1$ (for some integer ℓ) where the domination number of Q_d is well understood. It turns out that Corollary 6 can be used to give an alternative protocol for equality in the hypercube Q_d, $d = 2^\ell - 1$, of cost at most $\frac{1}{d+1}(2^d + 2^{d/2})$, which only relies on basic arguments (once we assume Lemma 4, which is based on a non-trivial construction of dense sets of integers without long arithmetic progression [Beh46]).

Theorem 8. *Let $\ell \geq 2$ be an integer and let $d = 2^\ell - 1$. Then the hypercube Q_d has a spanning 2-connected subgraph H with* $\mathsf{tvc}(H) \leq 2 \cdot (2^{d-\ell} + 2^{d/2-\ell})$.

Proof. We start by recalling a number of classical properties of Hamming codes. Let $d = 2^\ell - 1$ and let H be an ℓ by d binary matrix whose column vectors $h_1, \ldots, h_d$ are all the non-zero vectors in $\mathrm{GF}(2)^\ell$. We assume for convenience that $h_1 = \mathbf{1}$ (the all 1 vector). Let C_0 be the subgroup of $\mathrm{GF}(2)^d$ consisting of all vectors y such that $Hy = 0$. For every $1 \leq i \leq d$, we set $C_i = C_0 + e_i$, where e_i denotes the vector of $\mathrm{GF}(2)^d$ whose entries are all 0 except at coordinate i (the vectors e_i, $1 \leq i \leq d$, form the standard basis of $\mathrm{GF}(2)^d$ if viewed as a vector space, and a generating set if viewed as an additive group). We view the sets C_i both as subsets of the vertex set $V(Q_d)$ and as cosets of the subgroup C_0 of $\mathrm{GF}(2)^d$. In particular the sets C_i, $0 \leq i \leq d$, partition $V(Q_d)$ and all have cardinality $\frac{2^d}{d+1}$. The crucial property of this construction is that for any $x \in C_i$ and any $j \neq i$, x has exactly one neighbor y in C_j: $y = x + e_s$, where s is the index of the column $h_i + h_j$ in H. Note that the translation vector e_s only depends on i and j, so there is indeed a perfect matching between C_i and C_j in Q_d.

We now consider $S = C_0 \cup C_1$ (which we view both as a subset of vertices of Q_d and as a subgroup of $\mathrm{GF}(2)^d$). Let G_S be the subgraph of Q_d induced by all edges having at least one endpoint in S. Note that G_S is a spanning subgraph of Q_d: all vertices of S have degree d in S, and all vertices not in S have degree 2 (being adjacent to exactly one vertex of C_0 and one vertex of C_1, by the paragraph above). Moreover all the vertices of S are in the same orbit under the action of the automorphism group of G_S, so no vertex of S is a cut-vertex in G_S (otherwise all of them would be cut-vertices), and thus all connected components of G_S are 2-connected.

Claim. G_S has at most $2^{d/2-\ell}$ connected components.

Proof of Claim. Let X be a connected component of G_S and let $B = X \cap C_0$. For any $b \in B$, the vertices of B at distance 3 from b in G_S are of the form $b + e_1 + e_i + e_{\sigma(i)}$, where $2 \leq i \leq d$ and $\sigma(i)$ is the index of the column $h_1 + h_i =$

$1 + h_i$ in H. Write $v_i = e_1 + e_i + e_{\sigma(i)}$ for any $2 \leq i \leq d$. The observation above implies that B is equal to $b + V$, where V denotes the subgroup generated by the vectors v_i, $2 \leq i \leq d$. Note that $v_i = v_{\sigma(i)}$ for any $2 \leq i \leq d$, but if we define V' as a subset of V containing exactly only one of v_i and $v_{\sigma(i)}$ for any $2 \leq i \leq d$, the vectors of V' are linearly independent (each one has Hamming weight 3, and their supports are pairwise disjoint apart from the first coordinate which is common to the support of all vectors of V'). It follows that V has dimension at least $|V'| = \frac{d+1}{2}$, and thus $|B| \geq 2^{(d+1)/2}$. Note that $|X| = (d+1)|B|$, since each vertex of $X \setminus B$ has exactly one neighbor in B, and thus $|X| \geq (d+1)2^{(d+1)/2} = 2^{(d+1)/2+\ell}$. It follows that G_S has at most

$$\frac{2^d}{2^{(d+1)/2+\ell}} = 2^{d-(d+1)/2-\ell} \leq 2^{d/2-\ell}$$

components, which concludes the proof of the claim. ∎

Consider the graph R obtained from Q_d by contracting each component of G_S into a single vertex. As Q_d is connected, R is also connected, so it contains a spanning tree $\tilde{T}$. Each edge $\tilde{e} \in E(\tilde{T})$ corresponds to at least one edge e in Q_d between two connected components of G_S, say X_i and X_j. We observe that whenever there is such an edge e, there is actually at least one other edge e' between X_i and X_j which is not incident to e. To see this, write $e = xy$, and assume $x \in C_s$ and $y \in C_t$ (note that $s, t \geq 2$, since otherwise e would lie in G_S). Observe that by definition of G_S, we have $x' = x + e_s + e_t \in X_i$ and $y' = y + e_t + e_s \in X_j$. As x and y are adjacent in Q_d and $x - y = x' - y'$, x' and y' are also adjacent, so we can set $e' = x'y'$.

For each edge $\tilde{e} \in E(\tilde{T})$, we consider the two edges e and e' in Q_d defined above and add to S one endpoint from each edge. Let S' be the resulting vertex set, with $|S'| \leq |S| + 2 \cdot 2^{d/2-\ell}$. Note that the subgraph $G_{S'}$ of Q_d consisting of all edges incident to S' is spanning and 2-connected (recall that each connected component of G_S is 2-connected), and

$$\mathsf{tvc}(G_{S'}) \leq |S'| \leq 2 \cdot \frac{2^d}{d+1} + 2 \cdot 2^{d/2-\ell} = 2 \cdot \left(2^{d-\ell} + 2^{d/2-\ell}\right),$$

so the theorem follows by taking $H = G_{S'}$. □

By Corollary 6 we obtain the following as an immediate consequence.

Corollary 8. *Let $\ell \geq 2$ be an integer and let $d = 2^\ell - 1$. Then the protocol Π_2 for equality in the hypercube Q_d has per-bit cost at most*

$$\frac{2^d}{d+1} + \frac{2^{d/2}}{d+1} = \mathsf{OPT}(Q_d) + O\left(\sqrt{\mathsf{OPT}(Q_d)}\right).$$

Grids. We also obtain an asymptotically optimal protocol for equality in grids.

Corollary 9. *In the $n \times n$ square grid G_n, the protocol Π_2 of Theorem 7 has per-bit cost at most $\frac{1}{5} n^2 + 2n = (1 + o(1))\mathsf{OPT}(G_n)$.*

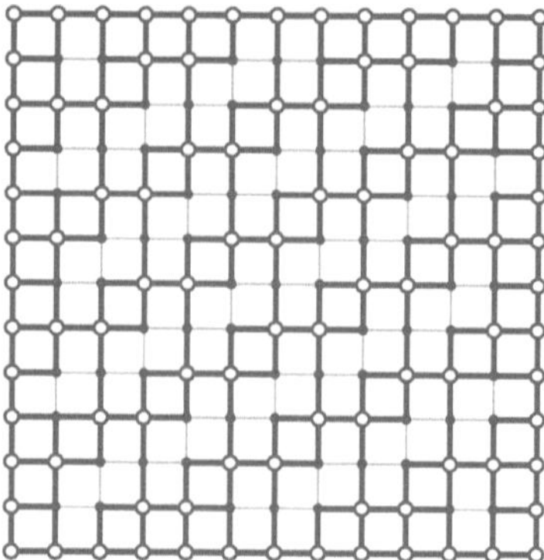

Fig. 2. The vertex set S (depicted as white circles) and the spanning 2-connected subgraph G_S of the square grid, in red. (Color figure online)

Proof. In the $n \times n$ square grid $G = G_n$, consider the set S of vertices $(i, j) \in [n]^2$ which either lie on the outerface, or are such that $i \in \{3j - 2, 3j - 1\}$ (mod 5) (in words, in row j of the grid, we add to S all vertices located in columns whose index is $3j - 2$ or $3j - 1$ modulo 5). Let G_S be the subgraph of G induced by the edges incident to S (see Fig. 2 for an illustration). Observe that G_S is a spanning subgraph of G and is 2-connected. By definition of G_S, it has a S as a total vertex cover so $\mathsf{tvc}(G_S) \leq |S| \leq \frac{2}{5} n^2 + 4n$. By Corollary 6, the protocol Π_2 has per-bit cost at most $\frac{1}{2} |S| \leq \frac{1}{5} n^2 + 2n$. By Lemma 1 we have $\mathsf{OPT}(G) \geq \frac{1}{5} n^2$, and the result follows. □

Similarly, we obtain asymptotically optimal protocols for equality in triangular grids and grids with all diagonals.

Corollary 10. *In the $n \times n$ triangular grid T_n, the protocol Π_2 of Theorem 7 has per-bit cost at most $\frac{1}{7} n^2 + 2n = (1 + o(1)) \mathsf{OPT}(T_n)$. In the $n \times n$ grid $P_n \boxtimes P_n$ with all diagonals (i.e., the strong product of two paths P_n), the protocol Π_2 of Theorem 7 has per-bit cost at most $\frac{1}{9} n^2 + 2n = (1 + o(1)) \mathsf{OPT}(P_n \boxtimes P_n)$.*

Proof. The proof is identical to that of Corollary 9. We only need to find total vertex covers in some spanning 2-connected subgraph of the triangular grid (with $\frac{2}{7} n^2 + 4n$ vertices), and of the grid with all diagonals (with $\frac{2}{9} n^2 + 4n$ vertices). Such sets are depicted in Fig. 3. □

We note that the lower order term in all these results can easily by improved by a factor of 2 (we have chosen not to do so for the sake of simplicity). It is not immediately clear how to reduce the lower order term to a constant.

Regular Graphs. The following was proved in [CG17], under a different terminology.

Theorem 9 ([CG17]). *Every cubic graph on n vertices has a total vertex cover on at most $3n/4$ vertices.*

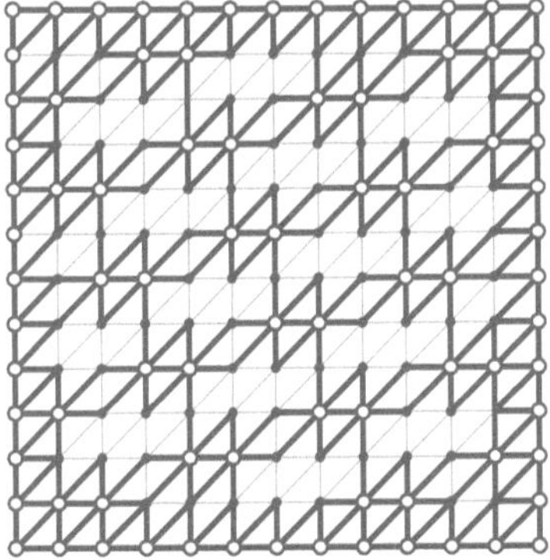

Fig. 3. Total vertex covers (in white) of 2-connected spanning subgraphs (in red) of the triangular grid (left) and the grid with all diagonal (right). (Color figure online)

Combining Theorem 9 and Theorem 7 for the upper bound and using Lemma 1 for the lower bound, we directly obtain the following $\frac{3}{2}$-approximation for equality in cubic 2-edge-connected graphs.

Corollary 11. *For any n-vertex 2-edge-connected cubic graph G, the protocol Π_2 of Theorem 7 has per-bit cost at most $3n/8 \leq \frac{3}{2}\,\mathsf{OPT}(G)$.*

Remark 2. We can obtain a more efficient protocol for random cubic graphs as they are almost surely Hamiltonian [RW94], using the fact that n-cycles have a total vertex cover of size $(2/3 + o(1))n$. This approach gives a protocol of per-bit cost $(1/3 + o(1))\,n \leq (\frac{4}{3} + o(1))\,\mathsf{OPT}(G)$ for random cubic graphs, improving on Corollary 11 for almost all cubic graphs.

Cubic graphs of large girth share many properties with random cubic graphs (techniques solving problems in one class often work to solve problems in the other). We prove the following counterpart of the result above for cubic graphs of large girth (we can actually use the same proof to give another proof of the $(1/3 + o(1))\,n$ result for random cubic graphs without using the Hamiltonicity of random cubic graphs, but we omit the details).

Theorem 10. *For any $\epsilon > 0$, there is an integer g such that the following holds. If G is an n-vertex cubic graph which is 2-edge-connected and has girth at least g, then G has a 2-connected spanning subgraph G' with $\mathsf{tvc}(G') \leq (\frac{2}{3} + 2\epsilon)n$, and thus the protocol Π_2 of Theorem 7 has per-bit cost $(\frac{1}{3} + \epsilon)n \leq (\frac{4}{3} + \epsilon)\,\mathsf{OPT}(G)$.*

Proof. Let M be a perfect matching and let $C_1, \ldots, C_\ell$ be the disjoint cycles in the subgraph of G induced by the edges of $E(G) \setminus M$ (each cycle has length at least g, by definition). In each cycle C_i, there is a total vertex cover S_i of size $\lceil 2|C_i|/3 \rceil \leq (2/3 + \epsilon)|C_i|$, for sufficiently large g. Let H be the multigraph on ℓ vertices obtained from G by contracting each cycle C_i into a single vertex v_i. This graph is 2-connected, and by Lemma 2, it has a 2-connected spanning subgraph H' with at most $2\ell - 2 \leq 2\ell$ edges. Let G' be the subgraph of G consisting of the union of the cycles C_i and the edges of H'. This graph G' is a 2-connected spanning subgraph of G. For each edge of H', add one of its endpoints in a new set S_0. Then $\bigcup_{i=0}^{\ell} S_i$ is a total vertex cover of G' of size at most $(2/3 + \epsilon)n + 2\ell \leq (2/3 + \epsilon)n + 2n/g \leq (2/3 + 2\epsilon)n$ for sufficiently large g. By Corollary 6, we obtain $\mathsf{cost}(G) \leq \frac{1}{2}\,\mathsf{tvc}(G') \leq (1/3 + \epsilon)n$, as desired. $\square$

By extending the proof of Theorem 9 we can prove that for $d \geq 3$, every d-regular graph on n vertices has a total vertex cover on at most $\frac{d}{d+1} \cdot n$ vertices. This is optimal for every d, since any total vertex cover of the complete graph K_{d+1} (which is d-regular) contains at least d vertices. It was proved in [CG17] that there are two more extremal connected graphs in the case $d = 3$, and all the other connected cubic graphs have a total vertex cover with less than $3n/4$ vertices. The result below implies that for $d \geq 5$, complete graphs are the only extremal examples.

Theorem 11. *For every $d \geq 3$, every d-regular graph G on n vertices has a total vertex cover on at most $\frac{d}{d+1} \cdot n$ vertices. For $d \geq 5$, every connected d-regular graph G on n vertices distinct from K_{d+1} has a total vertex cover on at most $\frac{d-\epsilon}{d+1} \cdot n$ vertices, with $\epsilon = \frac{1}{2d+1}$.*

Proof. Let S be a total vertex cover with the minimum number of vertices and let $T = V(G) \setminus S$. For every $i \in \{0, \ldots, d-1\}$, let S_i denote the subset of those vertices of S that have exactly i neighbors in T. Because S is a total vertex cover and G is d-regular, there is no vertex in S with d neighbors in T, hence $S = S_0 \cup \cdots \cup S_{d-1}$. Also, since S is a vertex cover, there are no edges between vertices in T.

The edges between S and T can be counted in two different ways, which yields the following equality:

$$\sum_{i=0}^{d-1} i|S_i| = d|T|. \tag{1}$$

As a consequence, we have:

$$|S| = d|T| + |S_0| - \sum_{i=1}^{d-1}(i-1)|S_i|. \tag{2}$$

Note that each vertex $u \in S_0$ has at least one neighbor in S_{d-1}, since otherwise we could remove u from S and still have a total vertex cover, which would contradict the minimality of S. On the other hand, each vertex of S_{d-1} has at most one neighbor in S_0, so it follows that $|S_0| \leq |S_{d-1}|$. By (2), it follows that

$$|S| \leq d|T| - \sum_{i=1}^{d-2}(i-1)|S_i| - (d-3)|S_{d-1}| \tag{3}$$

If $|T| \geq \frac{n}{d+1}$, then $|S| = n - |T| \leq \frac{d}{d+1} \cdot n$. Otherwise $|T| \leq \frac{n}{d+1}$, and (3) implies that $|S| \leq \frac{d}{d+1} \cdot n$, which proves the first part of the statement.

We now assume for the remainder of the proof that $d \geq 5$, $G \neq K_{d+1}$, and that G is connected. If $|T| \geq (\frac{1+\epsilon}{d+1}) \cdot n$, then $|S| \leq \frac{d-\epsilon}{d+1} \cdot n$, as desired. So we can assume that $|T| \leq (\frac{1+\epsilon}{d+1}) \cdot n$.

Claim. For every $u \in T$, $N(u) \cap S_1$ induces a clique in G and u has a neighbor in $S_2 \cup \cdots \cup S_{d-1}$.

Proof of Claim. To show the first part of the statement, suppose towards a contradiction that u has two neighbors $v, w \in S_1$ that are not adjacent. Since $v, w \in S_1$, all the neighbors of v and w distinct from u are in S. Then observe that $S \setminus \{vw\} \cup \{u\}$ is a total vertex cover, a contradiction to the minimality of S. If u has no neighbor in $S_2 \cup \cdots \cup S_{d-1}$, recall that it can neither have neighbors in T nor in S_0, hence $N(u) \subseteq S_1$. By the first part of the statement, $G[\{u\} \cup N(u)]$ is a clique. As G is d-regular and connected, $V(G) = \{u\} \cup N(u)$ and thus $G = K_{d+1}$, a contradiction. ∎

We now count the number of edges between T and $S_2 \cup \cdots \cup S_{d-1}$. On the one hand, the claim above shows that this number is at least $|T|$. On the other hand, it is at most $\sum_{i=2}^{d-1} i|S_i|$. We thus obtain $|T| \leq \sum_{i=2}^{d-1} i|S_i|$ and thus

$$\frac{|T|}{2} \leq \sum_{i=2}^{d-1} \frac{i}{2} \cdot |S_i| \leq \sum_{i=2}^{d-2} (i-1)|S_i| + (d-3)|S_{d-1}|,$$

where we have used that $d \geq 5$. By (3), it follows that we have

$$|S| \leq d|T| - |T|/2 = (d - \tfrac{1}{2})|T| \leq (d - \tfrac{1}{2})(\tfrac{1+\epsilon}{d+1}) \cdot n = \tfrac{d-\epsilon}{d+1} \cdot n$$

for $\epsilon = \frac{1}{2d+1}$, as desired. □

Theorem 11 can be combined with Theorem 7 to prove the following.

Corollary 12. *For any $d \geq 3$ and any 2-connected d-regular graph G, the protocol Π_2 of Theorem 7 has per-bit cost at most $\frac{d}{2d+2} \cdot n = \frac{d}{2} \cdot \mathsf{OPT}(G)$. If moreover, $d \geq 5$ and $G \neq K_{d+1}$, then the protocol Π_2 has per-bit cost at most $\frac{d-\epsilon}{2} \cdot \mathsf{OPT}(G)$, for some $\epsilon > 0$ depending only on d.*

Observe that complete graphs K_{d+1} have a very efficient protocol of per-bit cost 1, where a single vertex broadcasts its whole input. In combination with the corollary above, this outperforms the 4-approximation given by Theorem 2 whenever $d \leq 8$.

5   Conclusion

5.1   Monotone Total Vertex Cover

Given a 2-connected graph G, let $\mathsf{tvc}^{\downarrow}(G)$ be the minimum of $\mathsf{tvc}(H)$ for all 2-connected spanning subgraphs H of G. Equivalently, $\mathsf{tvc}^{\downarrow}(G)$ is the minimum cardinality of a subset S of vertices of G such that the subgraph G_S of G consisting of all edges incident to S is spanning and 2-connected. Notice the similarity with the definition of $\mathsf{wds}(G)$, which is the minimum cardinality of a subset S of vertices of G such that the subgraph G_S of G consisting of all edges incident to S is spanning and connected. A simple rephrasing of Corollary 6 is that there is protocol for equality in the local broadcast model in any 2-connected graph G with per-bit cost at most $\frac{1}{2}\mathsf{tvc}^{\downarrow}(G)$. Consequently, when $\frac{1}{2}\mathsf{tvc}^{\downarrow}(G)$ is close to $\tau^*_{\mathrm{bnd}}(G)$ we obtain almost-optimal protocols for equality in G. This is the case for any graph that contains $K_{2,t}$ as a spanning subgraph (Sect. 4.2), for hypercubes (Theorem 8), and for grids (Corollary 9). It was also used implicitly in Remark 2 that any n-vertex Hamiltonian graph G satisfies $\mathsf{tvc}^{\downarrow}(G) \le \frac{2}{3}(n+1)$, and in Theorem 10 to obtain an efficient protocol for cubic graphs of large girth.

We believe that independently of its connections with multiparty equality, this common variant of total vertex covers and weakly connected dominating sets is worth further investigation. The parameter $\mathsf{tvc}^{\downarrow}$ is in some sense much better behaved than tvc: adding edges to G does not increase $\mathsf{tvc}^{\downarrow}(G)$, while this might increase $\mathsf{tvc}(G)$.

5.2   Open Problems

A natural problem is whether the fractional lower bound $\tau^*_{\mathrm{bnd}}(G)$ can always be attained by $\mathsf{OPT}(G)$. We have not been able to find a graph for which the two parameters provably differ. A natural class to consider for potential counterexamples is the class of 2-edge-connected cubic graphs, which has a clean expression for τ^*_{bnd}. For this class we have only been able to find protocols of per-bit cost $3n/8$, while the fractional lower bound is $n/4$. Note that if we have $\mathsf{OPT}(G) = \tau^*_{\mathrm{bnd}}(G)$ for every graph G, then $\mathsf{OPT}(G)$ can indeed be computed in polynomial time.

Another interesting problem is to bound the per-bit complexity of equality as a function of the number of vertices, regardless of any fractional lower bound. This question makes sense for the class of all graphs, but also for specific graph classes studied in structural and algorithmic graph theory, such as planar graphs or graphs of bounded treewidth.

We have seen that for various types of grids we could obtain asymptotically optimal protocols for equality, using total vertex covers in some 2-connected subgraphs, of size at most twice the fractional lower bound. The three types of grids we have considered can all be seen as Cayley graphs of $\mathbb{Z}^2$, with different generating sets. As the three constructions are very similar, a natural question is whether our constructions can be generalized to any Cayley graph of $\mathbb{Z}^2$.

It remains an open question whether the upper bound of $4\,\mathsf{OPT}(G)$ on the cost of the protocol Π_1 in Theorem 2 can be improved.

Finally, in this paper we have only considered protocols that are deterministic and static. It is an interesting problem to understand whether significantly better bounds can be obtained for protocols that are randomized and/or non-static.

Acknowledgements. We thank Moritz Mühlenthaler and Alantha Newman for helpful discussions at the early stages of the project, and Zoltán Szigeti for pointing out references [Gri21] and [Whi32] to us. We also thank ChatGPT for the suggested approaches for bounding the number of components of G_S in the proof of Theorem 8.

References

[AES17] Alon, N., Efremenko, K., Sudakov, B.: Testing equality in communication graphs. IEEE Trans. Inf. Theory **63**(11), 7569–7574 (2017)

[Beh46] Behrend, F.A.: On sets of integers which contain no three terms in arithmetical progression. Proc. Natl. Acad. Sci. **32**(12), 331–332 (1946)

[CG17] Chen, X., Gao, T.: A note on α-total domination in cubic graphs. Discret. Appl. Math. **217**, 718–721 (2017)

[CR15] Chattopadhyay, A., Rudra, A.: The range of topological effects on communication. In: Halldórsson, M.M., Iwama, K., Kobayashi, N., Speckmann, B. (eds.) ICALP 2015. LNCS, vol. 9135, pp. 540–551. Springer, Heidelberg (2015). https://doi.org/10.1007/978-3-662-47666-6_43

[Gri21] Griggs, J.R.: Spanning trees and domination in hypercubes. Integers, vol. 21A, Paper A13, p. 11 (2021)

[KV21] Khan, M.S., Vaidya, N.H.: Testing equality under the local broadcast model. In: Jurdziński, T., Schmid, S. (eds.) SIROCCO 2021. LNCS, vol. 12810, pp. 262–276. Springer, Cham (2021). https://doi.org/10.1007/978-3-030-79527-6_15

[LV11] Liang, G., Vaidya, N.: Multiparty equality function computation in networks with point-to-point links. In: Kosowski, A., Yamashita, M. (eds.) SIROCCO 2011. LNCS, vol. 6796, pp. 258–269. Springer, Heidelberg (2011). https://doi.org/10.1007/978-3-642-22212-2_23

[RW94] Robinson, R.W., Wormald, N.C.: Almost all regular graphs are Hamiltonian. Random Struct. Algorithms **5**(2), 363–374 (1994)

[Whi32] Whitney, H.: Non-separable and planar graphs. Trans. Am. Math. Soc. **34**, 339–362 (1932)

[Wik26] Wikipedia contributors. Fekete's lemma (2026). Accessed 23 Feb 2026

Universal Dancing by Luminous Robots Under Sequential Schedulers

Caterina Feletti[1,2](✉) [ID], Paola Flocchini[2] [ID], Debasish Pattanayak[3] [ID],
Giuseppe Prencipe[4] [ID], and Nicola Santoro[1] [ID]

[1] School of Computer Science, Carleton University, Ottawa, Canada
`caterinafeletti@cunet.carleton.ca`, `santoro@scs.carleton.ca`
[2] School of Electrical Engineering and Computer Science, University of Ottawa,
Ottawa, Canada
`paola.flocchini@uottawa.ca`
[3] Department of Computer Science and Engineering, Indian Institute of Technology
Indore, Indore, India
`debasish@iiti.ac.in`
[4] Dipartimento di Informatica, Università di Pisa, Pisa, Italy
`giuseppe.prencipe@unipi.it`

Abstract. The `Dancing` problem requires a swarm of n autonomous mobile robots to form a sequence of patterns, i.e., perform a *choreography*. Existing work has proven that some crucial restrictions on choreographies and initial configurations (e.g., on repetitions of patterns, periodicity, symmetries, contractions/expansions) must hold so that the `Dancing` problem can be solved under certain robot models. Here, we prove that these necessary constraints can be dropped by considering the $\mathcal{LUMI}$ model (i.e., where robots are endowed with a light whose color can be chosen from a constant-size palette) under the quite unexplored *sequential scheduler*. We formalize the class of `Universal Dancing` problems which require a swarm of n robots starting from any initial configuration to perform a (periodic or finite) sequence of arbitrary patterns, only provided that each pattern consists of n vertices (including multiplicities). However, we prove that, to be solvable under $\mathcal{LUMI}$, the length of the feasible choreographies is bounded by the compositions of n into the number of colors available to the robots. We provide an algorithm solving `Universal Dancing` by exploiting the peculiar capability of sequential robots to implement a distributed counter. Even assuming non-rigid movements, our algorithm ensures spatial homogeneity of the performed choreography.

Keywords: Luminous Robots · Sequence of Patterns · Pattern Formation · Sequential Scheduler

1   Introduction

The *Look-Compute-Move* (LCM) is a theoretical model used to describe distributed systems of mobile robots, a.k.a. swarms [29]. Generally, a swarm is

C. Georgiou (Ed.): SIROCCO 2026, LNCS 16488, pp. 292–312, 2026.
https://doi.org/10.1007/978-3-032-26465-7_16

modeled as a set of punctiform robots that can move on the Euclidean plane. The robots are idle by default and are repeatedly activated by a scheduler. As soon as activated, a robot performs an LCM cycle: it takes the snapshot of the system (*Look*), it executes a deterministic algorithm calculating a position (*Compute*), and eventually it moves straight towards the computed position. By repeating the LCM cycle infinitely, the robots solve a given problem: typically, robots are required to arrange in the environment to satisfy some conditions (e.g., Scattering [18,36]) or according to some patterns (e.g., Pattern Formation [2,7,9,19,27,28,41,43,45], Gathering [1,5,10,24,37,39,40]). To design robust algorithms, the literature considers limited robots: they are *anonymous* and *indistinguishable* (no internal/external ids), *autonomous* (no central control), and *homogeneous* (they execute the same algorithm). Mostly, robots are assumed to be partially or totally disoriented: there might not be agreement between their local coordinate systems, on the unit of distance, or on chirality (i.e., clockwise orientation of the plane). Robots' movements may be *rigid* or *non-rigid* depending on the impossibility or possibility to be stopped by an adversary, respectively.

In the early literature, starting from the pioneering work of [42], robots are assumed to be *oblivious* and *silent*, i.e., with neither a persistent memory nor communication means. This minimal LCM sub-model, called $\mathcal{OBLOT}$, has been widely studied to both explore its power and delimit its limitations regarding computability. Unsurprisingly, not all problems can be solved without memory or communication. The more recent sub-model $\mathcal{LUMI}$ has been introduced by Das et al. [14] to overcome such limitations: here, robots are assumed to be *luminous*, i.e., endowed with a persistent *light*, whose value, called *color*, can be updated at each LCM cycle choosing from a $O(1)$-size palette of colors. Being visible to all robots in the swarm, the robot's light serves as an internal persistent memory and an external communication means.

Beyond the presence/absence of lights, the setting under which robots are activated and synchronized can affect their computational power. In the general *asynchronous* setting (ASYNCH), the robots are activated without any assumptions on the duration of an LCM cycle (except that it is finite), nor on the synchronization among them. In the *semi-synchronous* setting (SSYNCH), time is divided into atomic discrete *rounds*; at each round, an arbitrary non-empty subset of the robots is activated and they execute their LCM cycle in perfect synchrony. In the special case *fully synchronous* (FSYNCH), all the robots are activated simultaneously at every round. Note that, under SSYNCH (and thus ASYNCH), robots do not know the activation schedule, which is determined by an adversarial but *fair* scheduler that activates each robot infinitely often.

The literature has long focused on these three synchronization settings, studying the computational power of the model X^S, where $X \in \{\mathcal{OBLOT}, \mathcal{LUMI}\}$ defines memory/communication and $S \in \{\text{FSYNCH}, \text{SSYNCH}, \text{ASYNCH}\}$ [3,14,23,30]. Until recently, the *sequential* setting (SEQ), which activates only one robot at a round, remained nearly unexplored. Recent works have addressed this setting and its sub-settings [22] (e.g., the famous *round-robin*), mainly considering fault-prone swarms [11,16,17], and Pattern Formation and Gathering problems [25,32,33].

1.1 Pattern Formation

Pattern Formation is the problem requiring robots, within finite time, to rearrange themselves so that their positions in the plane form a given geometric figure (the *pattern*), up to rotation, reflection, translation, or scaling, and then stop moving. Which patterns are formable depends on many factors, first and foremost on the model X^S. For a given model X^S, the main focus has been on determining which patterns are formable from a given initial configuration, and, more importantly, which patterns are formable from every initial configuration (a.k.a. Arbitrary Pattern Formation) [2,7,9,19,27,28,41,43,45].

Clearly, to form a pattern, there must be at least as many robots as there are points in the pattern; we shall call this the *trivial assumption* and assume it to hold. Most of the algorithmic research has however relied on a variety of non-trivial assumptions, such as: restricting the type of allowed initial configurations (e.g., the robots occupy distinct initial locations); imposing restrictions on the number of robots or the size of the pattern (e.g., the size of the swarm is a prime number, or it is equal to the number of points in the pattern[1]); requiring specific symmetry relationship between the initial configuration and the pattern; the robots have some agreement on coordinate systems or on chirality; the movements of the robots are rigid; one of the robots is visibly different from all the others (i.e., there is a *leader*), etc. (see, e.g., [7–9,26,28,42,44]).

The most general problem in this class, Universal Pattern Formation (UPF), requires the robots to form *any* arbitrary pattern given in input, starting from *any* arbitrary initial configuration, regardless of the number of robots, and of the number of points in the pattern, under just the trivial assumption. As for the power of the robots, the only requirement is strong multiplicity detection (i.e., robots can detect the exact number of robots occupying the same location), which is required by the nature of the problem. This problem is generally unsolvable in $\mathcal{OBLOT}$ under FSYNCH (and, thus, SSYNCH) even with a leader, full agreement on the coordinate systems, and rigid movements. However, it has recently been shown that, except for point formation, Universal Pattern Formation is solvable in $\mathcal{OBLOT}$ under SEQ without any additional assumption [25]. This implies that UPF, including point formation, is solvable under $\mathcal{LUMI}^{\text{SEQ}}$. This result brings to light the strong computational power that robots have under the sequential schedulers in regards to pattern formation problems.

1.2 Sequence of Patterns: Dancing

Pattern Formation can be a primitive task to be repeatedly achieved in a more complex task. Examples include Flocking, requiring the robots to construct a pattern and then maintaining it while moving [4,34], and Dancing, as nicely

---

[1] Multiple robots may lie on the same point of the pattern.

named in [12], requiring the swarm to form a given ordered sequence of patterns (or *choreography*) [13,15], which is the subject of our investigation.

Interestingly, in [15], it was shown that an $\mathcal{OBLOT}^{\text{SSYNCH}}$ swarm can *dance*. However, the possibility to "perform a choreography" $\mathcal{S}$ is subject to several constraints: on the patterns (i.e., they must have the same number of points and degree of symmetry[2] and must be all distinct); on the number of robots (i.e., it must be equal to the number of points of the patterns); on the initial configuration (i.e., the robots must start from distinct locations and their positions must have the same symmetricity as the patterns); and on the structure of the choreography (i.e., the sequence must be periodic). Under these inevitable constraints, an algorithm was presented that allows $\mathcal{OBLOT}$ robots to perform a choreography employing a peculiar technique, based on the related distances of selected robots, to collectively memorize the index of the next pattern to be formed [15]; this algorithm assumes chirality agreement and rigid movements.

The impact of $\mathcal{LUMI}$'s memory/communication means on the feasibility of `Dancing` was studied next [13]. It was shown that, assuming $\mathcal{LUMI}$ and global chirality, the feasible sequences are subject to fewer constraints, even considering `ASYNCH` and non-rigid movements; more precisely, a swarm can perform a periodic choreography containing pattern repetitions and contractions/expansions, starting from any configuration with robots at distinct locations, subject to weaker symmetry conditions on the patterns and initial configuration.

The results of [13,15] have highlighted a key fact in the passage from `Pattern Formation` to `Dancing`. Let $\mathcal{P}(X^S)$ be the set of patterns formable under X^S: given a set $P \subseteq \mathcal{P}(X^S)$, it does not mean that any periodic sequence of patterns chosen from P is a feasible choreography under X^S. In other words, *a sequence of feasible patterns is not necessarily a feasible sequence.*

1.3   Contribution: Universal Dancing

As mentioned, `Universal Pattern Formation` is solvable in $\mathcal{LUMI}^{\text{SEQ}}$ without any additional assumption [25]; that is, luminous-sequential robots can form any pattern. In this paper, we show that *a sequence of arbitrary patterns is performable* in $\mathcal{LUMI}^{\text{SEQ}}$, independently of any property (e.g., symmetry, size, shape, etc.) of the patterns or of the initial configuration, whether the sequence is periodic or not. In other words, the sequential scheduler enables a swarm of $\mathcal{LUMI}$ robots to solve what we shall call the `Universal Dancing` problem.

Our proof is constructive: we develop an algorithm, establish its correctness, and analyze its properties. The main ingredient of our solution is the implementation of a distributed colored counter, which allows them to keep track of the current pattern being formed in the choreography: this new technique exploits the sequential nature of the scheduler to implement Gray code through robots'

---

[2] Conditions on the symmetry of the patterns and of the initial configuration derive from the fact that symmetric robots can be activated simultaneously under `SSYNCH` (and, thus, `ASYNCH`) and they may perform a symmetric movement, thus never "breaking" the original symmetry.

lights. The formation of each individual pattern is based on a novel technique that makes the robots match with their respective target points, exploiting properties of Dyck words on the Boolean alphabet. Our solution tolerates non-rigid movements. Yet, despite non-rigidity, our solution guarantees an interesting spatial property which provides homogeneity and stability to the choreography performance: the smallest circles enclosing the patterns of the choreography (except for patterns with only two or three points) formed by the swarm are concentric.

Note that, unlike previous solutions [13,15], our algorithm does not assume chirality agreement among the robots, and it allows a swarm to perform choreographies of finite length (in addition to the periodic ones). However, we prove that, to be performable under $\mathcal{LUMI}$, the length/period of the choreographies is bounded by the compositions of n into the number of colors available to the robots. Note also that our solution adopts a novel pattern formation procedure, which differs from that in [25] for two main reasons. First, it allows the formation of patterns where the number of robots assigned to each point is fixed and must be respected. Second, each pattern is formed in $O(1)$ time[3] w.r.t. the swarm cardinality n, rather than in $O(n)$ time as in [25].

2   Preliminaries

2.1   Model

We consider a swarm of n mobile computational entities, a.k.a. robots, $\mathcal{R} = \{r_1, \ldots, r_n\}$, acting in the Euclidean plane $\mathbb{R}^2$. Robots are assumed to be autonomous (i.e., without any central control), anonymous and indistinguishable (i.e., devoid of internal and external ids), homogeneous (i.e., they execute the same algorithm), and punctiform. Each robot r has its own local coordinate system Ξ_r. We assume that robots are *disoriented*, thus their local coordinate systems may be totally different (no global agreement on axes, unit distance, origin, chirality); moreover, the local coordinate system may change from one robot's activation to the next one. For simplicity, we assume each Ξ_r is egocentric, i.e., it defines its origin in the current position of r. We consider the $\mathcal{LUMI}$ model (i.e., *luminous*), where each robot r is embedded with a persistent light lig_r whose color can be chosen from a constant-size palette $\mathcal{L}$. We assume that $\mathcal{L}$ always contains the default color off, which all robot lights are initialized to. Moreover, r is provided with a sensing system that allows it to perceive the positions (according to its current Ξ_r) and colors of all the robots in the swarm. By default, a robot is idle. A scheduler is responsible for the robots' activation times. Once activated, a robot r performs a *Look-Compute-Move* cycle.

- *Look:* r obtains a snapshot σ of the positions according to Ξ_r occupied by all the robots, and the corresponding lights' colors.
- *Compute:* r executes the algorithm, say $\mathbb{A}$, giving it σ in input, and computes a destination as a point and a new color for its light lig_r. Formally, it computes $\mathbb{A}(\sigma) = (p', c)$, with $p' \in \mathbb{R}^2$ and $c \in \mathcal{L}$. Then, r updates the color of lig_r to c.

---

[3] Measured in *epochs*, as explained later.

– *Move:* r moves to the computed destination p' traveling along a straight
  trajectory.

We assume *non-rigid* movements: each robot may be stopped by an adversary
before reaching its destination, but always after having traveled at least a distance δ, where $\delta > 0$ is arbitrarily small. The guaranteed minimum distance δ is
a fixed constant, but unknown to the robots.

We consider the sequential class of schedulers, abbreviated as SEQ. Time is
logically divided into discrete and atomic rounds. Within each round, exactly
one robot is activated and completes one LCM cycle. Formally, a SEQ scheduler
$\mathfrak{S}$ defined for a swarm $\mathcal{R}$ is a function $\mathfrak{S} : \mathbb{N} \to \mathcal{R}$ which defines for any instant
time $t \in \mathbb{N}$ the activated robot. When needed, we can replace the function-like
notation of $\mathfrak{S}$ and define it through the *activation sequence* $\mathfrak{S}(0)\mathfrak{S}(1)\dots$. We
assume that the scheduler satisfies the *fairness* condition, i.e., for any $r \in \mathcal{R}$
and any $t \in \mathbb{N}$, there is a time $t' > t$ such that $\mathfrak{S}(t') = r$. Time is measured
in *epochs*: the first epoch starts with the first activation of $\mathcal{R}$; each epoch ends
as soon as all robots have been activated; the next epoch starts with the next
activation.

2.2   (Sequences of) Patterns

Patterns and Vertices. Let us consider an absolute[4] coordinate system $\hat{\Xi}$ on
the Euclidean plane $\mathbb{R}^2$; unless otherwise specified, we consider the positions of
the points of the plane according to $\hat{\Xi}$. We indicate with $d(\cdot,\cdot)$ the Euclidean
distance between two points.

A *pattern* $\Pi = \{\!\{v_1,\dots,v_n\}\!\}$ is a multiset[5] of positions $v_i \in \mathbb{R}^2$, called *vertices*. We denote with $shape(\Pi)$ the set of the unique positions in Π. A pattern
Π can belong to one of the four classes: $\Pi \in$ Point if $shape(\Pi)$ is a singleton;
$\Pi \in$ TwoPoints if $|shape(\Pi)| = 2$; $\Pi \in$ ThreePoints if $|shape(\Pi)| = 3$; otherwise, $\Pi \in$ NPoints. NLine is the special subclass of NPoints where the positions
of Π are aligned. We denote with $\mathscr{P}(\Pi)$ the set of patterns similar to Π, i.e.,
all the patterns obtained from Π by any composition of non-degenerate similarity transformations: uniform scaling with a non-zero scale factor, translation,
rotation, and reflection. Formally, $\Pi' \in \mathscr{P}(\Pi)$ if there exists a non-degenerate
similarity transformation $\tau : \Pi \to \Pi'$.

A   pattern   can   be   also   defined   by
the set notation $\Pi = \{(v_1,\#_1),\dots,(v_m,\#_m)\}$, where $\#_i \in \mathbb{N}_{>0}$ indicates the
multiplicity of the relative vertex and where $\sum_{j=1}^{m} \#_j = n$. We refer to $(v_i,\#_i)$
as a *multivertex* of Π.

Configurations and SEC. Let $\mathcal{R} = \{r_1,\dots,r_n\}$ be a swarm of robots. A *configuration* of $\mathcal{R}$ at time t is the multiset $C(t) = \{\!\{(p_1,c_1),\dots,(p_n,c_n)\}\!\}$ containing,
for each $r_i \in \mathcal{R}$, its position $p_i \in \mathbb{R}^2$ and its color c_i at time t. In the *initial*

---

[4] Unknown by the robots.
[5] We will use the notations $\{\!\{\}\!\}$ and $\{\}$ to indicate a multiset and a set, respectively.

configuration $C(0)$, all the colors are set to off; no other assumptions are made. We will omit the time t when no ambiguity arises. Given a configuration C, we denote with $C_{|\mathbb{R}^2}$ the multiset containing only the positions in C. We say that a multivertex $(v_i, \#_i)$ is *saturated* if exactly $\#_i$ robots lie on v_i in C; on the contrary, we say that it is *unsaturated* (*oversaturated*, resp.) if it is covered by fewer than (more than, resp.) $\#_i$ robots. We say that $\mathcal{R}$ forms a pattern Π at time t if $C_{|\mathbb{R}^2} \in \mathscr{P}(\Pi)$.

Given a pattern Π, we indicate with $SEC(\Pi)$ the *smallest enclosing circle* of Π and with $\omega(\Pi)$ the center of $SEC(\Pi)$. We remind that the SEC of a set of points is unique, and at least three (or two antipodal) points of the set lie on its perimeter. With a slight abuse of notation, given a configuration C, we indicate with $SEC(C)$ and $\omega(C)$ the smallest circle enclosing the points in $C_{|\mathbb{R}^2}$ and its center, respectively.

Choreographies. We define a *choreography* as $\mathcal{S} = (\Pi_0, \ldots, \Pi_{q-1})^x$ where each Π_i is a pattern and $x \in \{1, \infty\}$. It must be $\Pi_{i+1} \notin \mathscr{P}(\Pi_i)$; if $\mathcal{S}$ is *periodic* (i.e., if $x = \infty$), then it must also hold that $\Pi_0 \notin \mathscr{P}(\Pi_{q-1})$. If $\mathcal{S}$ is periodic, we assume that the sequence $\Pi_0, \ldots, \Pi_{q-1}$ cannot be written as $(\Pi_0, \ldots, \Pi_{h-1})^{\frac{q}{h}}$ for any $h < q$. We say that q is the *length* (*period*, resp.) of $\mathcal{S}$ if $x = 1$ ($x = \infty$, resp.).

We say that $\mathcal{R}$ *performs* $\mathcal{S}$ if, for any $j = 1, \ldots, x$, there exists a series of increasing finite times $\{t_{i+(j-1)q}\}_{i=0,\ldots,q-1, j=1,\ldots,x}$ such that the swarm forms Π_i at time $t_{i+(j-1)q}$. If $x = 1$, then the swarm must remain still after t_{q-1}. Indeed, a choreography $\mathcal{S}$ must satisfy the *trivial assumption* which states that each pattern of $\mathcal{S}$ must have n vertices to be performed by a n-swarm $\mathcal{R}$.

2.3   The Dancing Problems

Given a swarm $\mathcal{R}$, the general Dancing problem requires $\mathcal{R}$ to perform any *feasible* choreography. A choreography is feasible if it satisfies some necessary conditions so that a swarm of n robots can perform it; indeed, the trivial assumption is one of them. Moreover, some constraints may be satisfied by the initial configuration of $\mathcal{R}$ so that it can perform a feasible choreography. Formally, we can define a Dancing problem for a swarm $\mathcal{R}$ of n robots as the tuple $\mathfrak{D} = \langle \Sigma(n), \mathcal{I}(n), \phi \rangle$, where $\Sigma(n)$ is a set of patterns with n vertices, $\mathcal{I}(n)$ is a set of initial configurations for a swarm of n robots, and ϕ is a predicate on choreographies (e.g., limiting their length, pattern repetitions, etc.). Thus, $\mathcal{S} = (\Pi_0, \ldots, \Pi_{q-1})^x$ is a *feasible* choreography for $\mathfrak{D}$ if $\Pi_i \in \Sigma(n)$ for any $i \in [0, q-1]$ and $\mathcal{S}$ satisfies ϕ. Note that, for $\mathfrak{D}$ to be well defined, each $\Pi \in \Sigma(n)$ must appear in at least one feasible choreography; namely, ϕ cannot exclude a pattern of $\Sigma(n)$ from all the feasible choreographies. An algorithm $\mathbb{A}$ solves $\mathfrak{D}$ if, for any swarm $\mathcal{R}$ starting from a configuration in $\mathcal{I}(n)$, it makes $\mathcal{R}$ perform any feasible choreography for $\mathfrak{D}$.

A Dancing problem $\langle \Sigma(n), \mathcal{I}(n), \phi \rangle$ is said to be Universal if $\Sigma(n) = (\mathbb{R}^2)^n$ (i.e., any pattern with n vertices), $\mathcal{I}(n) = (\mathbb{R}^2 \times \{\text{off}\})^n$ is the set of all possible initial configurations where robots are off-colored, and ϕ can only bound the length/period of the choreographies. As we will see, this paper solves Universal

`Dancing` under a specific bound ϕ. We here prove that if we drop such a bound, i.e., if ϕ is a tautology $\top$, then the problem is unsolved under our model. Formally:

Theorem 1. *The* $\langle(\mathbb{R}^2)^n, (\mathbb{R}^2 \times \{\mathsf{off}\})^n, \top\rangle$ *problem cannot be solved in* $\mathcal{LUMI}^{SEQ}$ *even if robots have rigid movements and share a global coordinate system.*

Proof. By contradiction, let $\mathbb{A}$ be an algorithm for $\langle(\mathbb{R}^2)^n, (\mathbb{R}^2 \times \{\mathsf{off}\})^n, \top\rangle$ under $\mathcal{LUMI}^{SEQ}$ with $k > 1$ colors. Let $\mathcal{R}$ be a swarm of n robots, and let $z = \binom{n+k-1}{k-1}$ be the number of color-compositions of $\mathcal{R}$. Let $\mathcal{S} = (\mathsf{P}_1, \Pi_1, \ldots, \mathsf{P}_z, \Pi_z, \mathsf{P}_{z+1}, \Pi_{z+1})$ be a feasible choreography, such that $\mathsf{P}_i \in \mathtt{Point}$ for any $i \in [1, z+1]$ and $\Pi_i \neq \Pi_j$ for any $i \neq j \in [1, z+1]$. Namely, $\mathcal{R}$ is asked to perform a choreography that requires the swarm to gather into a point before forming each pattern of the series $\Pi_1, \ldots \Pi_{z+1}$. By the definition of choreography, we know that $\Pi_i \notin \mathtt{Point}$. Consider an execution of $\mathbb{A}$ under a *round-robin* scheduler $\mathfrak{S}$ (i.e., a `SEQ` scheduler where each epoch lasts n rounds and robots are always activated in the same order). Let t_b be the first time when the swarm forms a point P_b where robots have the same color-composition as while forming a previous point P_a, with $a < b$. Note that t_b exists since the maximum number of k-colorings for a swarm of n robots is z. Let t_a be the time when P_a is formed under $\mathfrak{S}$. W.l.o.g., assume the same colors in P_a are assigned to the same robots in P_b.

Consider the `SEQ` scheduler $\mathfrak{S}' = \mathfrak{S}(0) \ldots \mathfrak{S}(t_a) \left(\mathfrak{S}(t_{a+1}) \ldots \mathfrak{S}(t_b)\right)^{\infty}$ such that it equals $\mathfrak{S}$ until t_b and then activates the same sequence of robots as starting from t_{a+1}. It is easy to prove that $\mathfrak{S}'$ guarantees the fairness condition too: in fact, all the robots are activated at least once during the time $[t_{a+1}, t_b]$ in $\mathfrak{S}$. This is true since, in that time, the swarm passes from a `Point` pattern (i.e., P_a), to a non-point pattern (i.e., Π_a), and lastly it gathers again into a point (i.e., P_b): to perform this sequence of patterns, at least one epoch is needed.

So, if we consider the swarm under $\mathfrak{S}'$, then, after time t_b, the robots will perform the same actions as in the interval $[t_{a+1}, t_b]$ in a loop, since they will take the same snapshots as in that time frame. This results in the swarm never terminating. Contradiction achieved. $\qquad\square$

3   Techniques

Our algorithm uses a palette $\mathcal{L} = \{\ell_1, \ldots, \ell_{k-3}, \mathsf{L}_1, \mathsf{L}_2, \mathsf{L}_3\}$ of $k \geq 4$ colors which allows a n-size swarm $\mathcal{R}$ to perform any feasible choreography $\mathcal{S} = (\Pi_0, \ldots, \Pi_{q-1})^x$ with $x \in \{1, \infty\}$ that satisfies $q \leq \binom{n+k-7}{k-4}$. The colors L_1, L_2, and L_3 are destined for three robots called *leaders*. All the other $n-3$ robots, called *non-leaders*, will assume colors in $\{\ell_1, \ldots, \ell_{k-3}\}$. Using those colors, the non-leaders implement a counter which, thanks to Gray Code (Sect. 3.1), encodes the index i of the pattern $\Pi_i \in \mathcal{S}$ to be formed. Then, the leaders must set the univocal position of the *actual pattern* $\Pi \in \mathscr{P}(\Pi_i)$ on whose vertices robots must arrange themselves. To this aim, robots need to agree on a global ranking of the multivertices of Π_i (Sect. 3.2) which allows them to elect some vertices. Exploiting this ranking, the leaders choose some vertices of Π and arrange themselves on a triangle, called *chiral angle* (Sect. 3.3), that provides a global orientation to $\mathcal{R}$ and the position of Π. Once Π is fixed, the non-leaders must move to their designated pattern points, for which we employ a Dyck word–based matching (Sect. 3.4).

We now describe in detail the main concepts and techniques adopted by our algorithm, which combine both the power of $\mathcal{LUMI}^{\mathrm{SEQ}}$ and some concepts adapted from other fields.

3.1   Colored Counter and Composition Gray Codes

One of the main benefits of the sequential schedulers is the possibility of implementing a *distributed counter* through the robots' lights, by exploiting the Gray code. The size of the counter (i.e., the maximum value that can be counted) increases with the number of robots and colors. In Sect. 4, we will explain how our algorithm uses this technique to keep track of the ongoing pattern that is being formed, and to reset the counter in case of periodic choreographies. Thus, the counter size defines a tight bound on the length (if finite) /period (if periodic) q of the choreographies performable by a swarm of n robots with k colors according to our algorithm.

The $n-3$ non-leader robots will use their lights, colored using all the colors in $\{\ell_1, \ldots, \ell_{k-3}\}$. We assume that such colors are totally ordered: w.l.o.g., let $\ell_1 < \cdots < \ell_{k-3}$, and we assume that $\ell_1 = \mathsf{off}$, i.e., the color each robot is initialized. We implement a counter whose value iterates over the range of integers $[0, z-1]$, where $z = \binom{n+k-7}{k-4}$ corresponds to the number of weak compositions of $n-3$ into $k-3$ parts[6]. For the sake of simplicity, in the remainder of this section, we will use n and k instead of $n-3$ and $k-3$, respectively, thus illustrating the counter technique for a general set of n robots using $k \geq 2$ colors $\{\ell_1, \ldots, \ell_k\}$.

Given a configuration C, we define the *composition vector* (or simply, *counter*) as the tuple $X = (x_1, x_2, \ldots, x_k)$, where x_i denotes the number of robots in C with color ℓ_i. Let $\mathfrak{X}(n, k)$ be the set of all $z = \binom{n+k-1}{k-1}$ composition vectors made with n robots and k colors. If there exists a univocal method to order the elements in $\mathfrak{X}(n, k)$ so that $X_0 < \cdots < X_{z-1}$, then the robots can encode the composition vector X_a with the integer a, which will be the current value of the swarm counter. Another desirable property of this order is that any two consequent vectors $X_a = (x_1, \ldots, x_k)$ and $X_{a+1} = (x'_1, \ldots, x'_k)$ (with $a < z - 1$) differ at exactly two indexes: i.e., there exist $i \neq j \in \{1, \ldots, k\}$ such that $x_i = x'_i - 1$ while $x_j = x'_j + 1$. This means that if the swarm forms a composition vector X_a and wants to increment the counter by 1, it is sufficient for a ℓ_i-colored robot to turn its light into ℓ_j, thus updating the composition vector into X_{a+1}.

---

[6] A weak composition of n into k parts is an ordered representation of n as the sum of k non-negative integers.

To implement the order of $\mathfrak{X}(n,k)$ that fits our purposes, we use *Gray code* for compositions as described by Klingsberg [38]. In that work, the authors present a fast algorithm to generate the Gray codes[7] to represent the compositions of n into k parts. In particular, the algorithm produces the ordered list $\mathrm{L}(n,k) = \langle X_0, \ldots, X_{z-1} \rangle$ of all the Gray codes of all the $z = \binom{n+k-1}{k-1}$ compositions. We illustrate the recursive method to generate the list of gray codes $\mathrm{L}(j,k)$ for any values $j \geq 0$ and $k \geq 2$. The reverse of the list is denoted by $-\mathrm{L}(j,k)$. For the base case, $k = 2$, we have $\mathrm{L}(j,2) = \langle X_0, \ldots, X_j \rangle$ where $X_a = (j-a, a)$. For an arbitrary $k > 2$, the gray code can be obtained by recursion as follows,

$$\mathrm{L}(j, k+1) = \oplus_{l=0}^{j}(-1)^l[\mathrm{L}(j-l, k) \otimes \{l\}]$$

where $\oplus$ is the concatenation operator, and $\otimes$ is the Cartesian product of the sets. From the results of Klingsberg [38], we know that this Gray code construction follows the same property: it begins with the composition vector $X_0 = (n, 0, \ldots, 0)$ and ends with $X_{z-1} = (0, \ldots, 0, n)$.

3.2　Multivertices Ranking

We now describe how robots obtain an unambiguous rank of the multivertices of a pattern $\Pi = \{(v_1, \#_1), \ldots, (v_m, \#_m)\} \in \mathtt{NPoints}$ to be formed with n vertices (and m multivertices). To lighten the notation, we often indicate a multivertex $(v_i, \#_i)$ as only v_i. Let Ω be the $SEC(\Pi)$ whose center is O. Suppose, w.l.o.g., that the positions of the multivertices in Π are given considering a coordinate system whose origin and unit distance are $O = (0,0)$ and $radius(\Omega) = 1$, respectively. Let Π_O denote Π without the multivertex lying in O, if it exists, and let $m' = |shape(\Pi_O)| \in \{m, m-1\}$. For any multivertex v_i, we define:

1. $\Psi(v_i)$ as the radial projection of v_i on Ω, if $v_i \in \Pi_O$ (i.e., the intersection between the radius where v_i lies and Ω). Let $\{\psi_1, \ldots, \psi_{m''}\}$ be the set of all the radial projections, where $m'' \leq m'$, assuming w.l.o.g. that $[\psi_1, \ldots, \psi_{m''}]$ is the cyclic order[8] according to the clockwise orientation of Ξ.
2. $\theta_i = \angle \psi_j O \psi_{j+1}$ and $\hat{\theta}_i = \angle \psi_j O \psi_{j-1}$ where $\psi_j = \Psi(v_i)$. If v_i lies on O, we set $\theta_i = \hat{\theta}_i = 0$.
3. $\mu(v_i) = (\rho(v_i), \theta_i, \#_i)$ and $\hat{\mu}(v_i) = (\rho(v_i), \hat{\theta}_i, \#_i)$ where $\rho(v_i) = 1 - d(v_i, O)$.

The multivertices of Π belong to concentric circles of Ω. Then, it is possible to unambiguously define two cyclic orders on Π_O, using the radial projections and the distances from O: one clockwise according to Ξ, and the other counterclockwise. Let $\mathcal{A} = [v_{a_1}, \ldots, v_{a_{m'}}]$ be the clockwise one, and let $\mathcal{B} = [v_{b_1}, \ldots, v_{b_{m'}}]$ be the counterclockwise[9]. Starting from each $v_{a_i} \in \mathcal{A}$ we

---

[7] Gray code (patented in 1953 by Frank Gray [31]) is a binary encoding method with the additional property that the representations of two consecutive integers differ by only one bit.

[8] We here consider indexes in the circular range $[1, \cdots, m'']$.

[9] $a_1, \ldots, a_{m'}$ and $b_1, \ldots, b_{m'}$ represent two permutations of the m' indexes of the multivertices of Π_O.

define the string $CW(v_{a_i}) = \mu(v_{a_i})\mu(v_{a_{i+1}})\dots\mu(v_{a_{i-1}})$ (clockwise); from each $v_{b_i} \in \mathcal{B}$ we define the string $CCW(v_{b_i}) = \hat{\mu}(v_{b_i})\hat{\mu}(v_{b_{i+1}})\dots\hat{\mu}(v_{b_{i-1}})$ (counter-clockwise). Let $\gamma(v_i) = \min\{CW(v_i), CCW(v_i)\}$, where the total order $\leq$ of the strings is given by considering the three numerical orders (distances, angles, and multiplicities) in the triples[10]. If v_i lies on O, we set $\gamma(v_i) = (\rho(v_i), \theta_i, \#_i)$ which is $(1, 0, \#_i)$ by definition. Formally, given two triples $(\rho, \theta, \#)$ and $(\rho', \theta', \#')$ from the domain $[0,1] \times [0, 2\pi) \times [1, n]$, we define the following relation:

$$(\rho, \theta, \#) \leq (\rho', \theta', \#') \iff \begin{cases} \rho < \rho' & \text{or} \\ \rho = \rho' \wedge \theta < \theta' & \text{or} \\ \rho = \rho' \wedge \theta = \theta' \wedge \# \leq \#' \end{cases}$$

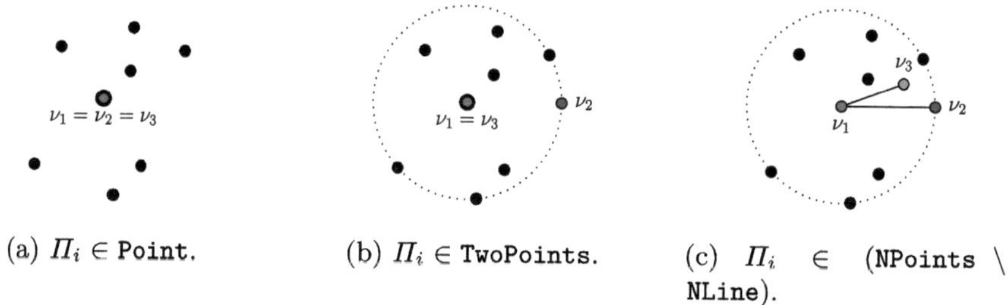

(a) $\Pi_i \in$ Point.   (b) $\Pi_i \in$ TwoPoints.   (c) $\Pi_i \in$ (NPoints \ NLine).

Fig. 1. Chiral angles and supporting circles in some different scenarios.

So, the multivertices of Π can be partitioned in equivalence classes $[v_1]_{\equiv}, \dots, [v_s]_{\equiv}$ so that $1 \leq s \leq m$ and $v_j \in [v_i]_{\equiv}$ iff $\gamma(v_j) = \gamma(v_i)$. Indeed, it is possible to define a total strict order (*ranking*) among the classes $[v_{\iota_1}]_{\equiv} < \dots < [v_{\iota_s}]_{\equiv}$ which is obtained[11] by considering the corresponding strings $\gamma(v_{\iota_j})$ for any $1 \leq j \leq s$. Note that, according to the definition of $\leq$, the multivertices in $[v_{\iota_1}]_{\equiv}$ lie on Ω (in fact, they have the minimal value of $\rho(\cdot)$). Moreover, if a multivertex lies on $\omega(\Pi)$, then $[v_{\iota_s}]_{\equiv}$ is a singleton containing only such a multivertex.

Let $\Pi' \in \mathscr{P}(\Pi)$ be a similar pattern to Π, and let $\tau : \Pi \to \Pi'$ be the related similarity transformation. It is obvious that, if $\Pi/_{\equiv} = \{[v_1], \dots, [v_s]\}$, then $\Pi'/_{\equiv} = \{[\tau(v_1)], \dots, [\tau(v_s)]\}$. Moreover, the ranking in Π is preserved in Π', i.e., $[\tau(v_{\iota_1})]_{\equiv} < \dots < [\tau(v_{\iota_s})]_{\equiv}$.

3.3   Chiral Angle

Let C be a configuration from which the swarm must start the formation of a pattern $\Pi_i \in \mathcal{S}$. Being totally disoriented, the robots need to univocally establish

---

[10] Indeed, any $v_i \in \Pi_O$ corresponds to some $v_{a_j} \in \mathcal{A}$ and some $v_{b_h} \in \mathcal{B}$.
[11] $(\iota_1, \dots, \iota_s)$ represents a permutation of $\{1, \dots, s\}$.

the position, orientation, and scale of the *actual pattern* $\Pi \in \mathscr{P}(\Pi_i)$ they have to arrange on. Thus, before forming Π_i, our algorithm includes a preliminary phase where the leaders L_1, L_2, and L_3, place themselves on three points ν_1, ν_2, ν_3 respectively. The formed triangle $\triangle\nu_1\nu_2\nu_3$ (possibly degenerate) is called *chiral angle*, and provides the swarm a partial (if the triangle is degenerate) or total (if the triangle is not degenerate) global coordinate system of the plane. Notably, ν_1 represents its origin; if $\nu_1 \neq \nu_2$, then ν_2 represents the coordinate $(0,1)$ (thus fixing the unit distance and the x-axis); if ν_3 is not aligned with ν_1 and ν_2, then ν_3 represents a y-positive coordinate (thus fixing the y-axis, and thus the clockwise orientation of the plane).

Once L_1 and L_2 have fixed ν_1 and ν_2 for Π_i, all the robots can construct the circle Ω_i whose center is ν_1 and whose radius is $d(\nu_1, \nu_2)$. We call Ω_i as the *supporting circle* of Π_i. If $\Pi_i \in (\texttt{Point} \cup \texttt{NPoints})$, then the swarm must form Π so that $\Omega_i = SEC(\Pi)$ (trivially, it means that if $\Pi_i \in \texttt{Point}$, then Ω_i will be a degenerate circle). Otherwise, if $\Pi_i \in (\texttt{TwoPoints} \cup \texttt{ThreePoints})$, then the swarm must form Π so that $\overline{\nu_1\nu_2}$ is the (longest) edge of Π. Note that, in all the cases, all the vertices of Π are contained within Ω_i.

Note that our strategy for constructing the supporting circles is to guarantee a spatial homogeneity in the $\mathcal{S}$ performance: notably, all the supporting circles are concentric. In fact, regardless of Π_i, ν_1 is static at the same point of the plane, which corresponds to $\omega(C)$ if $C_{|\mathbb{R}^2} \in \texttt{NPoints}$, otherwise ν_1 corresponds to the position of L_1, denoted by $pos(\mathsf{L}_1)$ (thus, L_1 does not move since it already lies on ν_1). Moreover, given any subsequence $\Pi_a, \ldots, \Pi_b$ of $\mathcal{S}$, if $\Pi_i \notin \texttt{Point}$ for any $i \in [a, b]$, then $\Omega_a, \ldots, \Omega_b$ are equal. We now explain how to compute ν_2 and ν_3 for the different cases, and the actual pattern $\Pi \in \mathscr{P}(\Pi_i)$ to be formed.

If $\Pi_i \in \texttt{Point}$, the chiral angle (and thus Ω_i) degenerates on the same point $\nu_1 = \nu_2 = \nu_3$, which is the vertex at which the swarm will gather (see Fig. 1a). Formally, $\Pi = \{(\nu_1, n)\}$.

If $\Pi_i \in \texttt{TwoPoints}$, then $\nu_3 = \nu_1$, while ν_2 is a different point: the swarm will arrange itself on these two vertices with the respective multiplicities. The point ν_2 is computed in this way: if L_2 does not lie on ν_1, then its position becomes the new ν_2 for Π_i (see Fig. 1b); otherwise, the position $(0,1)$ according to the local coordinate system of L_2 becomes the new ν_2. Formally, if $\Pi_i = \{(v_1, \#_1), (v_2, \#_2)\}$ with $\#_1 \geq \#_2$, then $\Pi = \{(\nu_1, \#_1), (\nu_2, \#_2)\}$.

If $\Pi_i \in \texttt{ThreePoints}$, then ν_1, ν_2, ν_3 are three distinct points forming the target triangle on which the swarm must arrange. Point ν_2 is computed as before, and it fixes the longest edge $\overline{\nu_1\nu_2}$ of the target pattern Π. Once L_1 and L_2 have fixed ν_1 and ν_2, then L_3 chooses the position[12] of ν_3, so that $\triangle\nu_1\nu_2\nu_3 \in \mathscr{P}(\Pi_i)$ and $d(\nu_1, \nu_2) \geq d(\nu_1, \nu_3) \geq d(\nu_2, \nu_3)$. Formally, if $\Pi_i = \{(v_1, \#_1), (v_2, \#_2), (v_3, \#_3)\}$ with $d(v_1, v_2) \geq d(v_1, v_3) \geq d(v_2, v_3)$, with $\#_1 \geq \#_2$, and with $\#_1 \geq \#_3$ if $d(v_1, v_3) = d(v_1, v_2)$, then $\Pi = \{(\nu_1, \#_1), (\nu_2, \#_2), (\nu_3, \#_3)\}$.

If $\Pi_i \in \texttt{NPoints}$, then ν_1, ν_2, ν_3 are three distinct points forming a triangle with $d(\nu_1, \nu_2) \geq d(\nu_1, \nu_3)$. Even in this case, ν_2 is computed as for the $\texttt{TwoPoints}$ case. The swarm must form Π so that $SEC(\Pi) = \Omega_i$ (which is defined by ν_1

---

[12] Different positions of ν_3 can be found in order to form the target triangle.

and ν_2), so that ν_2 corresponds to one vertex of Π. The precise position of Π within Ω_i will be given by L_3 once set on ν_3. Let us describe how L_3 computes ν_3. Assume that the ranking of the multivertices of Π_i is $[v_{\iota_1}]_\equiv < \cdots < [v_{\iota_s}]_\equiv$. Then ν_2 will be one multivertex of Π corresponding to one multivertex of Π_i in $[v_{\iota_1}]$. As seen in Sect. 3.2, we know that the vertices in the minimal class $[v_{\iota_1}]$ lie on $SEC(\Pi_i)$. So, L_3 chooses one vertex in $[v_{\iota_1}]$, say w.l.o.g. v_{ι_1}, and then it computes a similarity transformation τ such that $\tau(v_{\iota_1}) = \nu_2$. If $\Pi_i \in \mathtt{NLine}$, then L_3 chooses the multivertex closest to ν_2 but not lying on ν_1, and moves there. Otherwise, L_3 chooses the multivertex closest to ν_2 but not collinear with ν_1 and ν_2: if multiple multivertices are eligible, then L_3 chooses one belonging to the lowest class in the ranking (see Fig. 1c). This strategy allows all robots to unambiguously reconstruct $\tau(\Pi_i) = \Pi$.

3.4   Robot-Vertex Matching with Dyck Words

Our algorithm adopts a technique to match each robot with its target vertex by exploiting the Dyck words on the Boolean alphabet. Dyck words are well-parenthesized strings over an alphabet of brackets [6,35]; in our case, 0 is the opening bracket, while 1 is the closing one.

Given a Boolean string x, $|x|$ denotes its length, and $|x|_0$ ($|x|_1$, resp.) denotes the number of 0s (1s, resp.) contained in x. The empty string (i.e., without symbols) is denoted by ϵ. For any $i \in [0, |x|]$, we indicate with $\delta_x(i) = |y|_0 - |y|_1$ where y is a prefix of x of length i. A Boolean string x is *balanced* if $|x|_0 = |x|_1$. Given a balanced string x, we say that x is *minimal* if it cannot be non-trivially factorized into multiple balanced strings. E.g., 110100 is minimal, while 010011 is not minimal since it can be factorized into 01 and 0011.

We consider the Dyck language $\mathcal{L}_{\mathsf{Dyck}} = \{x \in \{0,1\}^* \mid |x|_0 = |x|_1 \wedge (\delta_x(i) \geq 0\ \forall i \in [0, |x|])\}$. In other terms, x is a Dyck word if it is balanced and any prefix of x must not have more 1s than 0s. Equivalently, $x \in \mathcal{L}_{\mathsf{Dyck}}$ if *(i)* $x = \epsilon$, or *(ii)* $x = 0y1z$ for some $y, z \in \mathcal{L}_{\mathsf{Dyck}}$ where the 0 and 1 that envelops y are a pair of *matched brackets*. If $x = x_1 \cdots x_m$ is a Dyck word, then $x_b = 1$ is matched with $x_a = 0$ where $a = \max\{1 \leq i < b \mid x_i = 0 \wedge \delta_x(i) - 1 = \delta_x(b)\}$.

4   Algorithm

We present an algorithm for $\mathtt{Universal\ Dancing}$ for a swarm $\mathcal{R}$ of $n \geq 3$ robots that satisfies the assumptions in Sect. 2. Using $k \geq 4$ colors, it enables $\mathcal{R}$ to perform any feasible choreography $\mathcal{S} = (\Pi_0, \ldots, \Pi_{q-1})^x$ with $x \in \{1, \infty\}$ and $q \leq \binom{n+k-7}{k-4}$. The following theorem summarizes our main contribution; the correctness and complexity proofs can be found in the full version [21].

Theorem 2. *The $\mathtt{Universal\ Dancing}$ problem $\mathfrak{D}_U = ((\mathbb{R}^2)^n, (\mathbb{R}^2 \times \{\mathtt{off}\})^n, \phi)$ where ϕ only requires that any choreography has length/period $q \leq \binom{n+k-7}{k-4}$ for $k \geq 4$, can be solved under $\mathcal{LUMI}^{SEQ}$ by a swarm of n robots with k colors, even assuming non-rigid movements.*

The core of our algorithm consists of three phases, namely PHASE 1, PHASE 2, and PHASE 3, which are repeated cyclically until $\mathcal{S}$ ends. For each $\Pi_i \in \mathcal{S}$, PHASE 1 aims at setting the chiral angle; PHASE 2 aims at making robots form Π_i; PHASE 3 aims at updating the counter value. If the $\mathcal{S}$ is periodic, then the algorithm execution never ends. Before entering the loop of the three phases, we need an initial phase PHASE 0 to set up the three leader robots.

4.1   PHASE 0 - Election of leaders

This phase starts from the initial configuration C (where all the robots are off-colored) and terminates when the three leaders have elected themselves by setting the dedicated colors. No robot moves during PHASE 0. If $C_{|\mathbb{R}^2} \notin$ ThreePoints, the first activated off robot lying on $SEC(C)$ sets its color to L_2. Otherwise, an off robot lying on one of the longest edges of the triangle sets to L_2. Let us see which off robot becomes L_1: if $C_{|\mathbb{R}^2} \in$ Point, the next activated off robot sets its color to L_1. If $C_{|\mathbb{R}^2} \in$ (TwoPoints $\cup$ ThreePoints), the off robot lying on the other endpoint of the (longest) edge of $C_{|\mathbb{R}^2}$ sets to L_1, so that $pos(\mathsf{L}_1) \neq pos(\mathsf{L}_2)$. Otherwise, the off robot closest to $\omega(C)$ on a distinct position from $pos(\mathsf{L}_2)$ becomes L_1. Note that, in this phase, L_2 always lies on $SEC(C)$, while $pos(\mathsf{L}_1) = pos(\mathsf{L}_2)$ iff $C_{|\mathbb{R}^2} \in$ Point.

Lastly, the next activated off robot turns its color to L_3, thus completing the three leaders' setting. When no ambiguity arises, we denote with L_1, L_2, and L_3 both the colors and the related leader robots. All the other $n-3$ non-leaders are off, thus the counter value is 0: now the loop can start with the formation of Π_0 (i.e., the first pattern of the choreography).

4.2   PHASE 1 - Chiral Angle Setup

Let C be the current configuration. Let the current counter vector be $X_i = (x_1, \ldots, x_{k-3})$, where x_j represents the number of robots of color $\ell_j \in \mathcal{L} \setminus \{\mathsf{L}_1, \mathsf{L}_2, \mathsf{L}_3\}$, for $j \in [1, k-3]$. This means that i is the counter's value and that Π_i is the ongoing pattern to be formed in the choreography. PHASE 1 starts when Π_i is not formed by the swarm and the three leaders are not located on the chiral angle related to C and Π_i. In this phase, the three leaders L_1, L_2, L_3 compute the chiral angle $\triangle \nu_1 \nu_2 \nu_3$ as explained in Sect. 3.3, and sequentially reach the relative vertices. Specifically, L_1 moves to $\omega(C)$ if $C_{|\mathbb{R}^2} \in$ NPoints, otherwise it stays still since it is already on ν_1. Then, L_2 calculates the position of ν_2 for Π_i, and moves to ν_2. Note that, if $C_{|\mathbb{R}^2} \notin$ Point, $\nu_2 = pos(\mathsf{L}_2)$; otherwise, all the robots lies in $(0,0)$ (since all have an egocentric coordinate system) and L_2 is required to move in a distinct position, conventionally to $(0,1)$ (thus, the request is satisfied even if L_2 is stopped before reaching its point $(0,1)$). Lastly, L_3 calculates and moves to ν_3, completing the chiral angle $\triangle \nu_1 \nu_2 \nu_3$ for Π_i. No other robot moves in this phase.

4.3 PHASE 2 - Pattern Formation

This phase starts when the leaders have formed the chiral angle for Π_i and ends as soon as the swarm forms the pattern $\Pi \in \mathscr{P}(\Pi_i)$ which is unequivocally defined by the chiral angle. Let r be an activated non-leader robot. Thanks to the counter's value of the swarm, r detects the pattern Π_i to be formed. If Π_i is not formed and the triangle $\triangle L_1 L_2 L_3$ constitutes a valid chiral angle for Π_i, then r knows it is in PHASE 2. Thus, r detects the actual pattern Π on whose vertices robots must arrange themselves. Let us distinguish the two cases:

Case $\Pi \notin$ NPoints. If $\Pi \in$ Point (thus, $\nu_1 = \nu_2 = \nu_3$), then r reaches the gathering point where the leaders lie. If $\Pi \in (\text{TwoPoints} \cup \text{ThreePoints})$, then if r lies on a (un)saturated multivertex of Π, it stays still. Otherwise, it reaches the closest unsaturated multivertex of Π. The leaders do not move, since they already lie on their target vertices.

Case $\Pi \in$ NPoints. Let C be the current configuration, where L_1, L_2, and L_3 form a non-degenerate chiral angle. Let Ω be the supporting circle for Π, centered in L_1 and such that L_2 belongs to its boundary. We remind that, in this case, L_2 and L_3 already lie on their target vertices of Π by construction, thus they will not move during PHASE 2. In this phase, all non-leaders reach their target vertices of Π, and subsequently, L_1 possibly moves to the last missing vertex left free. Note that L_1 already lies on its target vertex (and thus it will not move in this phase) only if ν_1 is a vertex of Π. If $\nu_1 \notin \Pi$, then, robots must properly agree on the target (multi)vertex to be left free for L_1: notably, they select the closest multivertex to L_1 (in case of equidistance, the choice is made following the orientation given by the chiral angle).

Let D be the *main diameter*, i.e., the diameter of Ω starting from L_2. Given a vertex v of Π, we indicate with $v_\perp$ its projection on D. We call the segment $\overline{vv_\perp}$ the *line projection* of v. Let $\Pi_\perp = \{v_\perp \mid v \in \Pi\}$. This case is handled in four sub-phases: *(i)* all non-leaders move to D perpendicularly, *(ii)* they shift along D to arrange on the vertices of $\Pi_\perp$ (except for the three vertices which are intended for the leaders), *(iii)* they move perpendicularly w.r.t. D to reach the corresponding target vertices of Π, and *(iv)* L_1 reaches the last missing vertex of Π. Note that this strategy (i.e., projecting Π on D and making robots arrange on $\Pi_\perp$ before reaching Π) guarantees no waiting times for robots and a constant bound on the maximum distance traveled by each robot: in this way, the number of epochs remains $O(1)$ w.r.t. n, even under non-rigid movements. We explain the four sub-phases in detail:

Migration Towards D. All the $m = n - 3$ non-leader robots reach D moving along a perpendicular trajectory.

Arrangement on D. Once all the m non-leaders have reached D, they compute $\Pi_\perp$ and remove from it the projections of the three vertices intended for the leaders. In this sub-phase, the non-leaders move along D to reach the projection in $\Pi_\perp$ of their target vertex. They use the following matching algorithm to detect their target projection. Let r be an activated non-leader on D. It computes the Boolean string $w \in \{0,1\}^{\leq 2m}$ that represents the ordered arrangement of non-leaders and projections along D, starting from the closest to L_2 (see Fig. 2). In particular, each 1 represents a non-leader that does not lie on a projection, while each 0 represents a projection not covered by a non-leader. Multiplicities (multivertices, resp.) on D are treated by unrolling and representing them through factors of adjacent 1 s (0 s, resp.). Then, w can be factorized uniquely into minimal-length factors, such that each one is either a Dyck word or a reverse of a Dyck word. Let $x = x_1, \ldots, x_h$ be such a factor of w; w.l.o.g., assume x is a Dyck word. So, if $x_i = 1$ corresponds to r, then r must reach the projection represented by the corresponding opening 0 in x, say $v_\perp$.

Note that during the movement towards $v_\perp$, r may be stopped on a (previously) uncovered projection, say $v'_\perp$. Then, at the next round, the corresponding 1 and 0 related to r and $v'_\perp$ are removed from w, and the matching algorithm can restart from the new arrangement string. It may also happen that, during its trajectory towards $v_\perp$, r is stopped on a non-vertex point[13]. In this case, the new arrangement string and thus the new matching can change. However, the new matching always ensures that the new intended projection for r is in the same direction as $v_\perp$ (thus, r does not have to retrace its trajectory backwards).

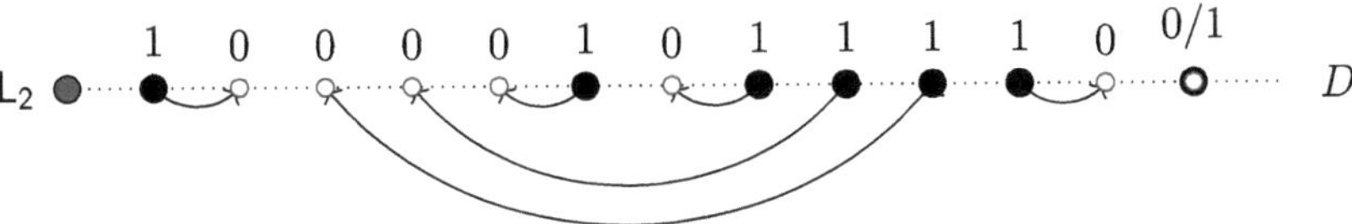

Fig. 2. Here, $w = 100001011110$ is factorized in $x = 10$, $y = 00010111$, and $z = 10$. x^R, y, and z^R are Dyck words. The rightmost robot and the projection where it lies are not included in w.

Back to the Vertices. This sub-phase starts once all the non-leader robots have arranged themselves on the vertex projections on D, and ends when all non-leader robots have reached the corresponding vertices traveling perpendicularly to D.

Let us explain the invariant that each robot r can evaluate to understand that this sub-phase is in progress. Thanks to the counter (kept by the non-leaders) and the chiral-angle (kept by the leaders), r detects Π_i (the pattern of the choreography), the supporting circle Ω_i, and the actual pattern Π to be formed (so that $\Omega_i = SEC(\Pi)$). If Π is formed, then PHASE 2 is terminated. Otherwise, for each vertex v of Π not intended for a leader, r checks that a distinct non-leader robot lies on $\overline{vv_\perp}$. Assume r is a non-leader robot lying on D, which has positively checked the invariant for this sub-phase. Then it unambiguously chooses

---

[13] Note that this case also comprehends the case when r stops on a multivertex (over)saturated.

the closest uncovered vertex[14] whose projection corresponds to its current position on D, and for which there does not yet exist a robot moving towards it. Note that multiple vertices (belonging to both the semi-circles cut by D) can have the same projections; in this case, r unambiguously elects the target vertex by considering the clockwise orientation of the plane. After the vertex choice, r starts traveling perpendicularly to D towards the computed vertex.

Robot r may be stopped before reaching its vertex. If r is a non-leader robot not lying on D, then it evaluates the sub-phase invariant. Let h be the segment perpendicular to D which starts from D, contains r, and ends at Ω_i. Let $v_1, \ldots, v_s$ be the list of vertices along h so that $d(v_i, D) \geq d(v_{i+1}, D)$. Then r moves to v_j where $j \in [1, s]$ is the greatest index such that v_j is not covered and r lies on the segment $[v_j, v_{j_\perp})$.

L_1 *Towards its Vertex.* Once all the m robots have reached their target vertices, the last missing vertex, say w, must be covered by L_1. Let C be the current configuration: remind that L_1 lies on $\omega(C)$. By construction, w has been selected for L_1 among the closest to $\omega(C)$. If $\omega(C) = w$, then L_1 does not move since it already covers the last vertex. Otherwise, L_1 moves to w. Assume L_1 is stopped before reaching w, and let C' be the resulting configuration. Thus, any activated non-leader robot sees that L_1 does not lie on $\omega(C')$ and that the swarm does not form Π: thus, it does nothing. Once reactivated, L_1 recomputes and reaches w.

4.4   PHASE 3 - Counter Update

Let C be the current configuration and i be the counter value, which points to the pattern Π_i of the choreography $\mathcal{S} = (\Pi_0, \ldots, \Pi_{q-1})^x$. This phase starts when $C_{|\mathbb{R}^2} = \Pi$, where $\Pi \in \mathscr{P}(\Pi_i)$ is the pattern defined by the chiral angle (detectable even after the movement of L_1). Let the current counter vector be $X_i = (x_1, \ldots, x_{k-3})$, where x_j represents the number of robots of color $\ell_j \in \mathcal{L} \setminus \{\mathsf{L}_1, \mathsf{L}_2, \mathsf{L}_3\}$, for $j \in [1, k-3]$. We distinguish three actions:

- **Termination.** If $i = q - 1$ and $x = 1$, the choreography is terminated. Thus, the swarm does not update the counter, and it freezes in Π_{q-1}.
- **Increment.** If $i < q - 1$, then the swarm must increment the counter from i to $i + 1$. Let X_{i+1} be the next vector for counter $i + 1$. From the Gray code construction, there are exactly two differences between X_i and X_{i+1} corresponding to one decrement value and one increment value. Let a and b be the two indices that change between X_i and X_{i+1}. There must be x_a robots with color ℓ_a. When a robot with color ℓ_a gets activated and realizes that pattern Π_i is formed, it changes its color to ℓ_b. Now the counter vector corresponds to $i+1$, and all robots realize that the pattern Π_{i+1} is not formed. PHASE 1 now restarts the chiral angle setting with L_1, L_2, and L_3.
- **Resetting.** If $i = q - 1$ and $x = \infty$, then the swarm must reset the counter to the initial value X_0, where all the non-leader robots are off-colored. However, since a swarm passing from X_{q-1} to X_0 under **SEQ** creates other counter

---

[14] Indeed, it can belong to an unsaturated multivertex.

vectors and may create unambiguous configurations, the swarm must mark the reset through an unequivocal configuration. Specifically, we make the leader L_3 set its color to L_2; in this way, the presence of two L_2 robots signals non-leader robots that they have to reset the counter. Once all non-leader robots have turned into off, one of the two L_2 robots must turn into L_3. If it is possible to establish which of the two L_2 robots was the former L_3 (e.g., if one L_2 does not lie on $SEC(C)$), then leaders maintain their former roles.

5   Conclusions

In this paper, we have studied the computational power of $\mathcal{LUMI}$ robots under sequential schedulers, concerning their ability to perform sequences of patterns (a.k.a. choreographies). We have proved that their peculiar capability of implementing a distributed counter mechanism allows them to solve the Universal Dancing problem, which requires a swarm to perform (periodic or finite) sequences of any type of pattern, starting from any initial configuration. We have proved that the number of robots and available colors define a bound on the length/period of the feasible choreographies. We have presented an algorithm that solves Universal Dancing for completely disoriented robots and ensures spatially homogeneous choreography, even with non-rigid movements.

Two possible future research lines can follow this paper: the first can define other classes of Dancing problems, and investigate under which assumptions they are solved. Secondly, further work may deeply investigate the distinctive power of robots under sequential schedulers.

Acknowledgement. This work was partly supported by NSERC through the Discovery Grant program. This research was done while Caterina Feletti was visiting Profs. Flocchini and Santoro while she was a Ph.D. student (Università degli Studi di Milano). A brief announcement of this work appears in [20].

References

1. Bramas, Q., Tixeuil, S.: Wait-free gathering without chirality. In: 22nd International Coloqium of Structural Information and Communication Complexity (SIROCCO), pp. 313–327 (2015)
2. Bramas, Q., Tixeuil, S.: Probabilistic asynchronous arbitrary pattern formation (Short Paper). In: 18th International Symposium on Stabilization, Safety, and Security of Distributed Systems (SSS), pp. 88–93 (2016)
3. Buchin, K., Flocchini, P., Kostitsyna, I., Peters, T., Santoro, N., Wada, K.: Autonomous mobile robots: refining the computational landscape. In: 23rd IPDPS Workshop on Advances in Parallel and Distributed Computational Models (APDCM), pp. 88–93 (2021)

4. Canepa, D., Dèfago, X., Izumi, T., Potop-Butucaru, M.: Flocking with oblivious robots. In: 18th International Symposium on Stabilization, Safety, and Security of Distributed Systems (SSS), pp. 94–108 (2016)
5. Chaudhuri, S.G., Mukhopadhyaya, K.: Leader election and gathering for asynchronous fat robots without common chirality. J. Discrete Algorithms **33**, 171–192 (2015)
6. Chomsky, N., Schützenberger, M.P.: The algebraic theory of context-free languages. In: Computer Programming and Formal Systems. Studies in Logic and the Foundations of Mathematics, vol. 35, pp. 118–161. Elsevier (1963)
7. Cicerone, S., Di Stefano, G., Navarra, A.: Asynchronous arbitrary pattern formation: the effects of a rigorous approach. Distrib. Comput. **32**(2), 91–132 (2019)
8. Cicerone, S., Di Stefano, G., Navarra, A.: Embedded pattern formation by asynchronous robots without chirality. Distrib. Comput. **32**(4), 291–315 (2019)
9. Cicerone, S., Stefano, G.D., Navarra, A.: Solving the pattern formation by mobile robots with chirality. IEEE Access **9**, 88177–88204 (2021)
10. Cieliebak, M., Flocchini, P., Prencipe, G., Santoro, N.: Distributed computing by mobile robots: gathering. SIAM J. Comput. **41**(4), 829–879 (2012)
11. Clemente, S., Feletti, C.: Fault detection and identification by autonomous mobile robots. In: 4th Symposium on Algorithmic Foundations of Dynamic Networks (SAND), pp. 10:1—-10:20 (2025)
12. Das, S., Flocchini, P., Prencipe, G., Santoro, N.: Synchronized dancing of oblivious chameleons. In: 7th International Conference on Fun with Algorithms (FUN), vol. 8496, pp. 113–124. Springer (2014)
13. Das, S., Flocchini, P., Prencipe, G., Santoro, N.: Forming sequences of patterns with luminous robots. IEEE Access **8**, 90577–90597 (2020)
14. Das, S., Flocchini, P., Prencipe, G., Santoro, N., Yamashita, M.: Autonomous mobile robots with lights. Theoret. Comput. Sci. **609**, 171–184 (2016)
15. Das, S., Flocchini, P., Santoro, N., Yamashita, M.: Forming sequences of geometric patterns with oblivious mobile robots. Distrib. Comput. **28**(2), 131–145 (2015)
16. Défago, X., Gradinariu, M., Messika, S., Raipin-Parvédy, P.: Fault-tolerant and self-stabilizing mobile robots gathering. In: Dolev, S. (ed.) DISC 2006. LNCS, vol. 4167, pp. 46–60. Springer, Heidelberg (2006). https://doi.org/10.1007/11864219_4
17. Défago, X., Potop-Butucaru, M., Tixeuil, S.: Fault-tolerant mobile robots. Chapter 10 of [29], pp. 234–251 (2019)
18. Dieudonné, Y., Petit, F.: Scatter of robots. Parallel Process. Lett. **18**(1), 75–184 (2009)
19. Dieudonné, Y., Petit, F., Villain, V.: Leader election problem versus pattern formation problem. In: 24th International Symposium on Distributed Computing (DISC), pp. 267–281 (2010)
20. Feletti, C., Flocchini, P., Pattanayak, D., Prencipe, G., Santoro, N.: Brief announcement: universal dancing by luminous robots under sequential schedulers. In: 39th International Symposium on Distributed Computing (DISC), vol. 356, pp. 56:1–56:7 (2025)
21. Feletti, C., Flocchini, P., Pattanayak, D., Prencipe, G., Santoro, N.: Universal dancing by luminous robots under sequential schedulers. arXiv abs/2508.15484 (2025)
22. Feletti, C., Flocchini, P., Santoro, N.: On the computational power of mobile robots under sequential schedulers. In: 27th International Symposium on Stabilization, Safety, and Security of Distributed Systems (SSS). Springer (2025)

23. Feletti, C., Mambretti, L., Mereghetti, C., Palano, B.: Computational power of autonomous robots: transparency vs. opaqueness. Theor. Comput. Sci. **1036**, 115153 (2025)
24. Flocchini, P.: Gathering. Chapter 4 of [29], pp. 63–82 (2019)
25. Flocchini, P., Navarra, A., Pattanayak, D., Piselli, F., Santoro, N.: Oblivious robots under sequential schedulers: universal pattern formation. In: 32nd International Colloquium on Structural Information and Communication Complexity (SIROCCO), vol. 15671, pp. 297–314. Springer (2025)
26. Flocchini, P., Prencipe, G., Santoro, N., Viglietta, G.: Distributed computing by mobile robots: uniform circle formation. Distrib. Comput. **30**(6), 413–457 (2017)
27. Flocchini, P., Prencipe, G., Santoro, N., Widmayer, P.: Hard tasks for weak robots: the role of common knowledge in pattern formation by autonomous mobile robots. In: 10th International Symposium on Algorithms and Computation (ISAAC), pp. 93–102 (1999)
28. Flocchini, P., Prencipe, G., Santoro, N., Widmayer, P.: Arbitrary pattern formation by asynchronous, anonymous, oblivious robots. Theoret. Comput. Sci. **407**(1), 412–447 (2008)
29. Flocchini, P., Prencipe, G., Santoro, N.: Distributed Computing by Mobile Entities. Springer (2019)
30. Flocchini, P., Santoro, N., Sudo, Y., Wada, K.: On asynchrony, memory, and communication: separations and landscapes. In: 27th International Conference on Principles of Distributed Systems (OPODIS), pp. 28:1–28:23 (2023)
31. Frank, G.: Pulse code communication, US Patent 2,632,058 (1953)
32. Frei, F., Wada, K.: Brief announcement: distinct gathering under round robin. In: 38th International Symposium on Distributed Computing (DISC), vol. 319, pp. 48:1–48:8 (2024)
33. Frei, F., Wada, K.: Brief announcement: the virtue of self-consistency. In: 39th International Symposium on Distributed Computing (DISC), vol. 356, pp. 57:1–57:7 (2025)
34. Gervasi, V., Prencipe, G.: Coordination without communication: the case of the flocking problem. Discret. Appl. Math. **144**(3), 324–344 (2004)
35. Ginsburg, S.: The Mathematical Theory of Context Free Languages. McGraw-Hill Book Company (1966)
36. Izumi, T., Kaino, D., Potop-Butucaru, M.G., Tixeuil, S.: On time complexity for connectivity-preserving scattering of mobile robots. Theoret. Comput. Sci. **738**, 42–52 (2018)
37. Kamei, S., Lamani, A., Ooshita, F., Tixeuil, S.: Asynchronous mobile robot gathering from symmetric configurations without global multiplicity detection. In: 18th International Colloquium on Structural Information and Communication Complexity (SIROCCO), pp. 150–161 (2011)
38. Klingsberg, P.: A Gray code for compositions. J. Algorithms **3**(1), 41–44 (1982). https://doi.org/10.1016/0196-6774(82)90006-2
39. Pattanayak, D., Augustine, J., Mandal, P.S.: Randomized gathering of asynchronous mobile robots. Theoret. Comput. Sci. **858**, 64–80 (2021)
40. Pattanayak, D., Mondal, K., H., R., Mandal, P.S.: Gathering of mobile robots with weak multiplicity detection in presence of crash-faults. J. Parallel Distrib. Comput. **123**, 145–155 (2019)
41. Prencipe, G.: Pattern formation. In: Chapter 3 of [29], LNCS, vol. 11340, pp. 37–62. Springer (2019)
42. Suzuki, I., Yamashita, M.: Distributed anonymous mobile robots: formation of geometric patterns. SIAM J. Comput. **28**(4), 1347–1363 (1999)

43. Vaidyanathan, R., Sharma, G., Trahan, J.: On fast pattern formation by autonomous robots. Inf. Comput. **285**, 104699 (2022)
44. Yamashita, M., Suzuki, I.: Characterizing geometric patterns formable by oblivious anonymous mobile robots. Theoret. Comput. Sci. **411**(26–28), 2433–2453 (2010)
45. Yamauchi, Y., Yamashita, M.: Randomized pattern formation algorithm for asynchronous oblivious mobile robots. In: 28th International Symposium on Distributed Computing (DISC), pp. 137–151 (2014)

Polynomial Time Local Decision Revisited

Laurent Feuilloley[1] , Soumyadeep Paul[2(✉)] , and Ami Paz[3]

[1] CNRS, INSA Lyon, UCBL, LIRIS, UMR5205, 69622 Villeurbanne, France
`laurent.feuilloley@cnrs.fr`
[2] Tata Institute of Fundamental Research, Mumbai, India
`soumyadeep.paul@tifr.res.in`
[3] LISN—CNRS & Paris-Saclay University, Bures-sur-Yvette, France
`ami.paz@lisn.fr`

Abstract. We consider three classification systems for distributed decision tasks: With unbounded computation and certificates, defined by Balliu, D'Angelo, Fraigniaud, and Olivetti [JCSS'18], and with (two flavors of) polynomially bounded local computation and certificates, defined in recent works by Aldema Tshuva and Oshman [OPODIS'23], and by Reiter [PODC'24]. The latter two differ in the way they evaluate the polynomial bounds: the former considers polynomials with respect to the size of the graph, while the latter refers to being polynomial in the size of each node's local neighborhood.

We start by revisiting decision without certificates. For this scenario, we show that the latter two definitions coincide: roughly, a node cannot know the graph size, and thus can only use a running time dependent on its neighborhood.

We then consider decision with certificates. With existential certificates (Σ_1-type classes), a larger running time defines strictly larger classes of languages: when it grows from being polynomial in each node's view, through polynomial in the graph's size, and to unbounded, the derived classes strictly contain each other. With universal certificates (Π_1-type classes), on the other hand, we prove a surprising incomparability result: having running time bounded by the graph size sometimes allows us to decide languages undecidable even with unbounded certificates.

We complement these results with other containment and separation results, which together portray a surprisingly complex lattice of strict containment relations between the classes at the base of the three classification systems.

Keywords: Distributed decision · Distributed certification · Distributed complexity theory

1 Introduction

Decision tasks constitute the core of computational complexity theory, and their role in theoretical computer science is crucial. In his 2010 talk [6], Fraigniaud

C. Georgiou (Ed.): SIROCCO 2026, LNCS 16488, pp. 313–330, 2026.
https://doi.org/10.1007/978-3-032-26465-7_17

suggested distributed decision tasks as a base for a complexity theory for distributed computing. Following this, Fraigniaud, Korman, and Peleg [7] started the systematic study of distributed decision tasks, a project that continues until today. They defined several classes of graph languages, where the basic one is LD, consisting of all languages that can be decided by the following procedure. The input is a labeled graph, representing a communication network; the nodes of the graph communicate for a constant time, and then a Turing machine at each node performs a time-unbounded local computation and decides if to accept or reject. An input graph is accepted if all the Turing machines at its nodes accept. A simple example is the language of properly k-colored graphs: each node is labeled by a color in $\{1, \ldots, k\}$, and in the decision algorithm accepts if its color is different from those of its neighbors. It is easy to see that if the graph is properly k-colored then all nodes accept, while otherwise at least two of them reject.

The same work also defines the class NLD, where each node is equipped with a *certificate* of unbounded size, and a configuration is in the language if there exists a certificate assignment that makes all the nodes accept. This latter notion is very similar to the notion of *proof labeling schemes*, introduced by Korman, Kutten, and Peleg [8] a few years beforehand, and coincides with it for many languages. An example of a certification scheme (valid both for NLD and as a Proof Labeling Scheme) is for k-colorability, the claim that the (initially unlabeled) graph has a proper k-coloring. To certify this, each node gets a color in $\{1, \ldots, k\}$ as a certificate, and accepts iff its certificate is different from those of its neighbors.

Later on, Balliu, D'Angelo, Fraigniaud, and Olivetti [2] introduced a hierarchy for distributed decision inspired by the polynomial hierarchy in classic complexity theory. This hierarchy captured the classes already known and allowed to define new classes of distributed decision tasks. They studied the relation between these new classes, and in particular they showed that their hierarchy collapses to the second level: Π_2^{local} contains all decidable distributed languages.

An interesting artifact of their definition is that any language that is stable under the so-called lift operation can be certified using $O(n^2)$-bit certificates. This is a very large class of language, and contains, e.g., the language of all non-3-colorable graphs. To certify such a property, each node is simply given a map of all the graph, and verifies locally that it is consistent with its view and that the given graph has the property (e.g., is not 3-colorable). This is allowed since the local computation at each node is unbounded and not accounted for, as is common in distributed graph algorithms.

Recently, Aldema Tshuva and Oshman [1] considered the case where local computation is bounded, limited to polynomial in the size of the graph. Shortly after, Reiter [9] suggested a similar model, but where the local computation is polynomial in the view of the node, that is, in the size of the neighborhood rather than the full graph. Both these works defined hierarchies that resemble the centralized polynomial hierarchy, and studied relations between the classes in these hierarchies. Aldema Tshuva and Oshman showed that their hierarchy

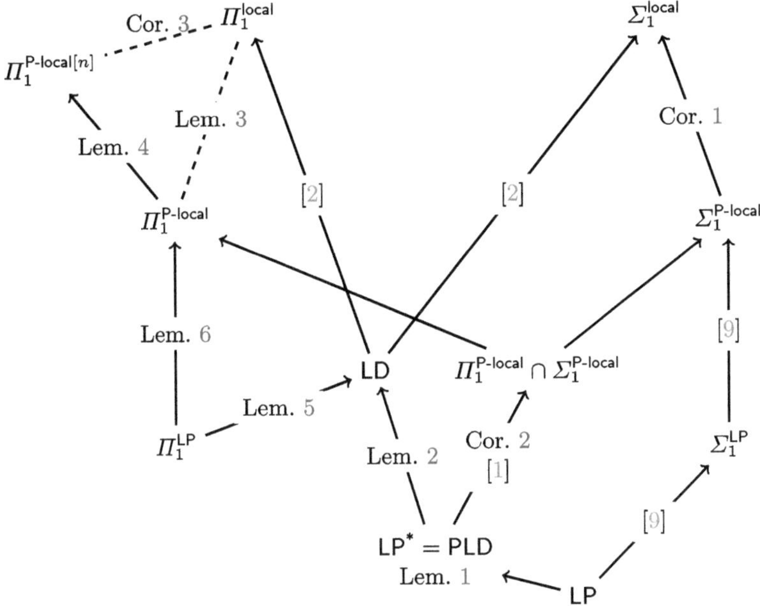

Fig. 1. We consider the classes with universal quantifiers (Π_1-type, left), deterministic computation (center) and existential quantifiers (Σ_1-type, right). Solid arrows represent strict containment except for $\text{LP} \subseteq \text{LP}^*$ where the strictness remains open. The dotted line refers to the fact that the classes are incomparable. Only the known relations that are relevant to the paper are represented on the figure.

coincides with the centralized hierarchy (restricted to graphs) starting from the second level. Reiter proved that his hierarchy coincides with the centralized one for graphs of a single node. A common theme of these works is that they essentially resolve the relations from level 2 of the hierarchies and above, while leaving intriguing open questions regarding the relations in the lower levels of the hierarchies, and between them.

1.1 Our Results

The central goal of our work is to understand the relations between the distributed complexity classes defined in the aforementioned works. While much of this comparison has been carried out for the higher levels of the hierarchy by Aldema Tshuva and Oshman [1] and Reiter [9], several gaps remain in the lower hierarchy levels. Our main results are depicted in Fig. 1.

Intuitively, one would expect the following relation between classes of decision tasks, both regarding computation time and certificate sizes.

$$\begin{array}{ccccc} \text{polynomial in} & \subsetneq & \text{polynomial in} & \subsetneq & \text{unbounded} \\ \text{local view} & & \text{graph size} & & \end{array}$$

Surprisingly, this turns out not to always be the case. While this is true for the existential quantifier (classes of type Σ_1 defined with "$\exists$ certificate c"), this is not the case without certificates, or with the universal quantifier (class of type Π_1 defined with "$\forall$ certificate c").

We restrict our attention to constant verification radius, do not consider randomization, and focus on ID-oblivious certification, that is, the certificate assignment is independent of the IDs.

Without Certificates: Equality of LP* and PLD. The first, and perhaps most fundamental comparison we present is between certificate-free classes: the class LP*, which is closely related to the class LP defined by Reiter [9], and the class PLD defined by Aldema Tshuva and Oshman [1]. In both LP and LP*, a node must decide by performing computation in time polynomial in the size of its local view, whereas in PLD, decisions must be taken in time polynomial in the graph size. The subtle difference between LP and LP* is that an LP* algorithm only needs to be correct for globally unique IDs, while an LP algorithm must be correct for any locally unique ID assignment. Therefore, an LP algorithm is also an LP* algorithm, i.e., LP $\subseteq$ LP*. All these three classes are contained in LD, where the local computation is unbounded.

The containment LP* $\subseteq$ PLD is almost trivial, and one is tempted to speculate that proving LP* $\subsetneq$ PLD is just as simple. After all, in a low-degree graph LP* allows much less local computation time than PLD. However, in Sect. 3, we prove this speculation to be wrong.

$$\mathsf{LP} \subseteq \mathsf{LP}^* = \mathsf{PLD} \subsetneq \mathsf{LD}$$

Roughly speaking, we show that a PLD algorithm cannot fully utilize its supposed global polynomial-time bound, since it lacks knowledge of the total graph size.

Continuing this section, we show that this simple idea is instrumental in proving separations between distributed decision classes. One result asserts that PLD $\subsetneq$ P $\cap$ LD, which also implies PLD $\subsetneq$ LD. That is, polynomial time local decision is strictly weaker than centralized polynomial-time decision (P) and local decision with unbounded local time (LD). This was proved in [1] using a carefully crafted language called ITER-BOUND, and applying a computability argument; here, we give a much simpler proof, based on the fact that the local polynomial time cannot be fully utilized.

Existential Certificates. In the case of existential certificates, the classes $\Sigma_1^{\mathsf{LP}}(\mathsf{NLP})$, $\Sigma_1^{\mathsf{P\text{-}local}}(\mathsf{NPLD})$ and $\Sigma_1^{\mathsf{local}}(\mathsf{NLD})$ behave "as expected".

$$\Sigma_1^{\mathsf{LP}}(\mathsf{NLP}) \subsetneq \Sigma_1^{\mathsf{P\text{-}local}}(\mathsf{NPLD}) \subsetneq \Sigma_1^{\mathsf{local}}(\mathsf{NLD})$$

The containments in both cases follow easily from the definitions since an existential certificate from a stricter space is still an existential certificate when we are allowed larger certificates. Note that this simple argument does not work when we consider the corresponding Π classes below: in the case of Π classes we need to ensure that the algorithm accepts for all certificates in a larger set of possible certificates. Intuitively speaking, for Σ we can "use the same certificate", while for Π we "need to accept on more certificates".

The inequality $\mathsf{NLP} \neq \mathsf{NPLD}$ was proved in [9] using the language `NOT-ALL-SELECTED`, which is the language of graphs where the nodes are given labels 0 or 1 and at least one of the nodes is given the label 0. The inequality $\mathsf{NPLD} \neq \mathsf{NLD}$ is a simple consequence of Corollary 1 we prove at the end of Sect. 2. There, we define the language $\mathsf{node}_{\mathsf{LSP}}$ which is in LP but not in the the centralized polynomial hierarchy PH, while NPLD is clearly a subset of PH.

Universal Certificates: Certificate-Bounded Separations. Up until here, we showed that for local computation, time that is polynomial in the graph size is not more powerful than having it polynomial only in the local view. For existential certificates, we showed that certificates with size polynomial in the graph size are slightly more powerful, and lies between certificates with size bounded by the local view size, and unbounded certificates. In Sect. 4 we move to consider universal certificates.

In Sect. 4.1 we present a result of the opposite flavor: In some cases, bounding the certificates by the graph size lets us solve problems which would not be solvable with unbounded certificates. Concretely, $\Pi_1^{\mathsf{P\text{-}local}} \not\subseteq \Pi_1^{\mathsf{local}}$. To prove this separation, we use the language `AGTG` of n-node paths with each node i labeled x_i, such that $x_i > n$ for all i. There is a simple $\Pi_1^{\mathsf{P\text{-}local}}$ algorithm for it, when bounding the certificate sizes by the polynomial $Q(n) = n$: node i checks that x_i is larger than the size of its certificate. As another application of the `AGTG` language, we prove that $\mathsf{PLD} \subsetneq \Pi_1^{\mathsf{P\text{-}local}} \cap \mathsf{NPLD}$. This was claimed in [1], and here we provide a simple, locality-based proof of it.

To prove the aforementioned separation, we use the fact that the nodes can deduce information on the value of n. In their work [1], Aldema Tshuva and Oshman defined the class $\Pi_1^{\mathsf{P\text{-}local}[n]}$, which is the same as the class $\Pi_1^{\mathsf{P\text{-}local}}$, but with the nodes knowing n. Since `AGTG` used to separate $\Pi_1^{\mathsf{P\text{-}local}}$ and Π_1^{local} is using information on n learned by the nodes in a $\Pi_1^{\mathsf{P\text{-}local}}$ algorithm, one may suspect that the nodes can learn n, yielding $\Pi_1^{\mathsf{P\text{-}local}[n]} = \Pi_1^{\mathsf{P\text{-}local}}$. In Sect. 4.2 we disprove this suspicion, and show $\Pi_1^{\mathsf{P\text{-}local}} \subsetneq \Pi_1^{\mathsf{P\text{-}local}[n]}$. This, on the other hand, begs the question whether knowing n makes the class $\Pi_1^{\text{P-local}[n]}$ as strong as Π_1^{local}, which we also answer in the negative: we show that $\Pi_1^{\text{P-local}[n]}$ and Π_1^{local} are incomparable.

In Sect. 4.3 we consider the "weaker" class Π_1^{LP}, where the certificate sizes are bounded by the local view size. We complement the aforementioned inequality $\Pi_1^{\text{P-local}} \not\subseteq \Pi_1^{\text{local}}$ by showing that Π_1^{LP} is strictly contained in both classes. The containment claims were claimed by Reiter [9] without a proof, while the separation was left open in his work. For both cases, we complement Reiter's containment claims with formal proofs, and prove the corresponding separation results.

$$\Pi_1^{\text{LP}} \subsetneq \Pi_1^{\text{P-local}} \not\subseteq \Pi_1^{\text{local}}$$

$$\Pi_1^{\text{LP}} \subsetneq \Pi_1^{\text{local}}$$

In fact, in order to prove $\Pi_1^{\text{LP}} \subsetneq \Pi_1^{\text{local}}$, we prove a more refined result: $\Pi_1^{\text{LP}} \subsetneq \text{LD}$. To this end, we show that a Π_1^{LP} algorithm can be simulated by an LD algorithm of double the locality radius. It is unclear whether a simulation with the same locality is possible. A similar argument is used to simulate a Π_1^{LP} algorithm by a $\Pi_1^{\text{P-local}}$ algorithm.

2   Model and Definitions

Let us define the model formally. We follow closely the definitions and notations of [1].

2.1   General Definitions

We consider simple graphs on n nodes. In some cases the nodes will have input labels, for example a color for each node. A *graph configuration* (G, x) is a graph G, equipped with an assignment of inputs, $x : V \to S$ (where S is some input set). We use $N_G^t(v)$ to denote the distance-t neighborhood of v, and $\#N_G^t(v)$ the number of nodes in it. We also use $|N_{G,x,id}^t(v)|$ for the number of bits in v's distance-t neighborhood, where we take into account the IDs and certificates given to the nodes (see definitions below).

Identifiers. The distributed certification literature contains several models for identifiers. Unless stated otherwise, we use the classic version where every node is given a unique integer encoded on $O(\log n)$ bits. For most classes, that is LD and PLD, and the ones with superscripts local and P-local, the certificates should not depend on the identifiers, in the sense that the identifiers are chosen adversarially after the certificates are chosen. See [3,4] for discussions of other models, and [5] for another convention.

The identifiers in the LP class and the ones with LP superscript behave differently. As computation time in these classes depends only on the local view, the identifier's uniqueness need not be universal: when considering a t-local algorithm, the identifiers in every distance-t ball around a node must be distinct, but not in the whole graph.

Languages, Neighborhoods, Local Decision Algorithms. In local decision, it is common to use the vocabulary from language theory, and we define a *distributed language* as a set of graph configurations. In the following, we might simply refer to a *language*. Note that the identifiers do not appear in the definition of a distributed language. An example of a language is the set of all the graphs for which the inputs encode a proper coloring.

Let $N^t_{G,x,id}(v)$ denote the t-neighborhood of v in the identified configuration (G, x, id), including the identifiers and the inputs of the nodes in the t-neighborhood. Let $N^t_{G,x}(v)$ be the same but without the identifiers.

Next, we formally define local distributed algorithms. In a distributed algorithm, each node observes the neighborhood around itself and then decides whether to accept or reject.

Definition 1 (Local decision algorithms). *A t-local decision algorithm A is a computable mapping from identified neighborhoods of size t to Boolean output values,* accept *or* reject. *When t is constant, we refer to such an algorithm as an* LD *-algorithm.*

If $A(N^t_{G,x,id}(v))$ accepts at all nodes $v \in V(G)$, then we say that A accepts (G, x, id). We say that A decides the distributed language L if for every graph configuration (G, x) and for every identifier assignment id, $(G, x) \in L \Leftrightarrow A(G, x, id) =$ accept. Given a t-local decision algorithm, we refer to t as the algorithm's locality radius.

Deterministic Classes. We first define the deterministic class without local computational constraints.

Definition 2 (The class LD). *A distributed language L is in the class* LD *if it can be decided by a t-local decision algorithm A for some constant t.*

Definition 3 (The class PLD). *A distributed language L is in the class* PLD *if there exist a polynomial P such that for all $n > 0$, L can be decided on any n-node graph by an LD-algorithm running in $P(n)$ time.*

Definition 4 (The class LP). *A distributed language L is in the class* LP *if there exist a constant t and a polynomial P such that L can be decided by an* LD*-algorithm with locality t running in $P(|N^t_{G,x,id}(v)|)$ time on each node v of a graph G, where the IDs are t-locally unique.*

Definition 5 (The class LP^*). *A distributed language L is in the class LP^* if there exist a constant t and a polynomial P such that L can be decided by an* LD*-algorithm with locality t running in $P(|N^t_{G,x,id}(v)|)$ time on each node v of a graph G, but the IDs are globally unique.*

With these definitions, we have $\mathsf{LP} \subseteq \mathsf{LP}^*$.

Existential Quantifier: Σ_1-Type Classes

Definition 6 (The class NLD $= \Sigma_1^{\text{local}}$). *A distributed language L is in the class* $\mathsf{NLD} = \Sigma_1^{\text{local}}$ *if there exists an* LD*-algorithm $\mathbf{A}$ such that for every configuration (G,x):*

$$(G,x) \in L \Rightarrow \exists c, \forall id, (\mathbf{A} \text{ accepts } (G,(x,c),id)),$$

$$(G,x) \notin L \Rightarrow \forall c, \forall id, (\mathbf{A} \text{ rejects } (G,(x,c),id)).$$

Note that the order of quantifier encodes what we discussed earlier: the identifiers are chosen adversarially after the certificates.

Definition 7 (The class NPLD $= \Sigma_1^{\text{P-local}}$). *A distributed language L is in the class* $\mathsf{NPLD} = \Sigma_1^{\text{P-local}}$ *if there exist an* LD*-algorithm $\mathbf{A}$ and polynomials P and Q such that for every n-node configuration (G,x):*

$$(G,x) \in L \Rightarrow \exists c, \forall id, (\mathbf{A} \text{ accepts } (G,(x,c),id)),$$

$$(G,x) \notin L \Rightarrow \forall c, \forall id, (\mathbf{A} \text{ rejects } (G,(x,c),id)),$$

where in addition, $\mathbf{A}$ must run in $P(n)$ time at each node, and c must satisfy $|c(v)| \leq Q(n)$ for every node v.

Note that the polynomials P and Q are chosen before the graph configuration, which is crucial in our proof of Lemma 3. Also note that the nodes generally do not know n, and therefore cannot evaluate $P(n)$, yet the algorithm $\mathbf{A}$ must be designed so that it runs in $P(n)$ time.

Definition 8 (The class NLP $= \Sigma_1^{\text{LP}}$). *A distributed language L is in the class* $\mathsf{NLP} = \Sigma_1^{\text{LP}}$ *if there exist $t \in \mathbb{N}$, a t-round* LD*-algorithm and polynomials P and Q such that for every n-node configuration (G,x) and every t-locally unique ID assignment:*

$$(G,x) \in L \Rightarrow \exists c \leq Q, (\mathbf{A} \text{ accepts } (G,(x,c),id)),$$

$$(G,x) \notin L \Rightarrow \forall c \leq Q, (\mathbf{A} \text{ rejects } (G,(x,c),id)),$$

where in addition, $\mathbf{A}$ must run in $P(|N^t_{G,x,id}(v)|)$ time at each node v, and $\forall c \leq Q$ stands for $|c(v)| \leq Q(|N^t_{G,x,id}(v)|)$ for each $v \in V$.

Universal Quantifier: Π_1-Type Classes

Definition 9 (The class Π_1^{local}). *A distributed language L is in the class Π_1^{local} if there exists an* LD-*algorithm $\boldsymbol{A}$ such that for every configuration (G, x):*

$$(G, x) \in L \Rightarrow \forall c, \forall id, (\boldsymbol{A} \text{ accepts } (G, (x, c), id)),$$

$$(G, x) \notin L \Rightarrow \exists c, \forall id, (\boldsymbol{A} \text{ rejects } (G, (x, c), id)).$$

Definition 10 (The class $\Pi_1^{\text{P-local}}$). *A distributed language L is in the class $\Pi_1^{\text{P-local}}$ if there exists an* LD-*algorithm $\boldsymbol{A}$ and polynomials P and Q such that for every n-node configuration (G, x):*

$$(G, x) \in L \Rightarrow \forall c \leq Q, \forall id, (\boldsymbol{A} \text{ accepts } (G, (x, c), id)),$$

$$(G, x) \notin L \Rightarrow \exists c \leq Q, \forall id, (\boldsymbol{A} \text{ rejects } (G, (x, c), id)),$$

where in addition, $\boldsymbol{A}$ must run in $P(n)$ time at each node, and $\forall c \leq Q$ is a shorthand for $\forall c \in \{c : V \to \{0, 1\}^* \mid \forall v \in V, |c(v)| \leq Q(n)\}$.

Definition 11 (The class Π_1^{LP}). *A distributed language L is in the class Π_1^{LP} if there exists $t \in \mathbb{N}$, a t-round* LD-*algorithm $\boldsymbol{A}$ and polynomials P and Q such that for every n-node configuration (G, x) and every t-locally unique ID assignment:*

$$(G, x) \in L \Rightarrow \forall c \leq Q, (\boldsymbol{A} \text{ accepts } (G, (x, c), id)),$$

$$(G, x) \notin L \Rightarrow \exists c \leq Q, (\boldsymbol{A} \text{ rejects } (G, (x, c), id)),$$

where in addition, $\boldsymbol{A}$ must run in $P(|N_{G,x,id}^t(v)|)$ time at each node v, and $\forall c \leq Q$ stands for $\forall c \in \{c : V \to \{0, 1\}^* \mid \forall v \in V, |c(v)| \leq Q(|N_{G,x,id}^t(v)|)\}$.

Note that there are two ways to define a bound on the certificate size after a universal quantifier: either we enumerate all the certificates *of the given size*, or all the certificates *up to a given size*. This is an important distinction since the first setting leaks more information about the size of the graph. We use the second definition.

In our definitions, we separately write the conditions for $(G, x) \in$ L and $(G, x) \notin$ L instead of using a single if-and-only-is statement, since we want the algorithm to either accept for all ID assignment, or to reject for all of them (see also [2, Sec. 1.1]).

2.2 A Simple Observation

Note that a consequence of the definitions is that $\Pi_1^{\text{LP}}, \Sigma_1^{\text{LP}} \in$ PH and $\Pi_1^{\text{P-local}}, \Sigma_1^{\text{P-local}} \in$ PH (remember that PH stands for the polynomial hierarchy in centralized complexity theory). Now, we consider a language $\mathsf{L}_{\text{SP}} \in$ EXPSPACE $\setminus$ PSPACE, which exists by the space hierarchy theorem. We construct a language $\mathtt{node}_{\mathsf{L}_{\text{SP}}}$ using L_{SP} as follows.

$$\mathtt{node}_{\mathsf{L}_{\text{SP}}} = \{(G, x) \mid G \text{ contains a single node labeled } x, \text{ and } x \in \mathsf{L}_{\text{SP}}\}$$

It is easily seen that $\mathsf{node}_{\mathsf{L_{SP}}} \in \mathsf{LD}$ since a single node is allowed to use unbounded resources for its local computation. On the other hand, $\mathsf{node}_{\mathsf{L_{SP}}} \notin \mathsf{PH}$, since such an algorithm could be simulated by a centralized machine to compute $\mathsf{L_{SP}}$ in polynomial space (remember that $\mathsf{PH} \subseteq \mathsf{PSPACE}$). This yields the following corollary.

Corollary 1.

$$\mathsf{node}_{L_{SP}} \in \mathsf{LD} \setminus \left(\Pi_1^{\mathsf{LP}} \cup \Sigma_1^{\mathsf{LP}} \cup \Pi_1^{\mathsf{P\text{-}local}} \cup \Sigma_1^{\mathsf{P\text{-}local}} \right).$$

We notice that the corollary also holds if the nodes know n, since a centralized machine simulating the local algorithm knows the size of the graph.

3   Polynomial in the Graph vs. in the Local View

It can be easily seen that $\mathsf{LP}^* \subseteq \mathsf{PLD}$. A node in an LP^* algorithm, by definition, is only allowed to use time polynomial in the size of its neighborhood. A node in a PLD algorithm, on the other hand, is permitted to use time polynomial in the size of the graph. The following result shows that these two notions overlap exactly. A PLD algorithm cannot see the whole graph and therefore cannot exploit the time permitted by its definition.

Lemma 1. $LP^* = \mathsf{PLD}$.

Proof. It is easy to see that $\mathsf{LP}^* \subseteq \mathsf{PLD}$: The size of a node's neighborhood is at most n, and the local input and ID of each node is polynomial in n. Therefore, the running time of an LP^* algorithm at a node is also polynomial in n, and the same algorithm is a PLD algorithm.

To show $\mathsf{PLD} \subseteq \mathsf{LP}^*$ we consider a PLD algorithm $\mathbf{A}$ of radius r on a graph G. Intuitively, we want to claim that the algorithm does not know the graph's size, and thus can only use time polynomial in its view. The formalization, however, is a bit trickier.

Let P be the polynomial bounding the running time of $\mathbf{A}$ as a function of the number n of nodes. Assume w.l.o.g. that P is non-decreasing for all $n \geq 0$; if this is not the case, P can be replaced by a bigger polynomial as follows. Let $P(n) = a_k n^k + \ldots + a_1 n + a_0$, with $a_k \neq 0$. Clearly, $a_k > 0$, as otherwise the algorithm's running time would have to be negative for a large enough n. Let c be the largest local maxima of P on any $n \geq 0$, which must exist since P is not monotone. Then $\bar{P}(n) = a_k n^k + c$ is monotone on the desired range, and satisfies $P(n) \leq \bar{P}(n)$ for all $n \geq 0$, hence also bounds the local running time of $\mathbf{A}$. Thus, we can henceforth assume P is monotonously increasing on $n \geq 0$.

We pick an arbitrary node $u \in V(G)$, and that the local computation time of $\mathbf{A}$ in u is polynomial in the size of u's r-neighborhood and input, hence $\mathbf{A}$ is also a legitimate LP^* algorithm with the same polynomial P bounding its running time (but this time, as a function of the view size and not of n). Let λ_r be the total size of the labels in u's r-neighborhood, including IDs. If the r-neighborhood of u contains all of G then $\mathbf{A}$'s running time is bounded by $P(n)$, while an LP* algorithm is allowed to run for time $P(n + \lambda_r)$. As P is monotone, we are done.

Otherwise, recall that $\#N^r[u]$ denotes the number of nodes in u's r-neighborhood. If $\#N^r[u] + \lambda_r \geq n$ then $\mathbf{A}$'s running time is still under $P(\#N^r[u] + \lambda_r)$, and we are done as before.

Assume this is not the case. Let v be a node in the $(r+1)$-neighborhood of u but not in its r-neighborhood. Consider the graph G' which is the same as G on the r neighborhood of u and on v, and extended by a path of label-less nodes from v, so that the total number of nodes is $n' = \#N^r[u] + \lambda_r$. Now, the view of u in both G and G' is the same, and therefore the running time of $\mathbf{A}$ on both graphs must be identical, and bounded by $P(\#N^r[u] + \lambda_r) = P(n')$. Thus, $\mathbf{A}$ is an LP* algorithm, as claimed. $\qquad\square$

Using Lemma 1, we can give a simpler proof of the fact that $\mathsf{PLD} \subsetneq \mathsf{P} \cap \mathsf{LD}$. This was proved in [1] using more involved, ad hoc arguments.

Lemma 2. $\mathsf{PLD} \subsetneq \mathsf{P} \cap \mathsf{LD}$.

By Lemma 1, it suffices to prove that $\mathsf{LP}^* \subsetneq \mathsf{P} \cap \mathsf{LD}$, which we do in the following two claims.

Claim. $\mathsf{LP}^* \subseteq \mathsf{P} \cap \mathsf{LD}$.

Proof. Every LP* algorithm can be simulated by a centralized machine in poly n time. Additionally, every LP* algorithm is also an LD algorithm. $\qquad\square$

Claim. $\mathsf{LP}^* \neq \mathsf{P} \cap \mathsf{LD}$.

Proof. To show the separation, we consider a language $\mathsf{L} \in \mathsf{EXP} \setminus \mathsf{P}$, which exists by the time hierarchy theorem. Using L, we define

$$\mathtt{path_L} = \{G \mid G \text{ is an } n\text{-node path with labels } (n, n), \ldots, (n, 2), (n, 1, \varphi)$$
$$\text{where } \varphi \text{ is a word of size at most } \log n \text{ in } \mathsf{L}\}.$$

We assume, for the sake of contradiction, that there exists an LP* algorithm $\mathbf{A}$ of locality radius r for $\mathtt{path_L}$.

We consider the following centralized algorithm for determining if a word φ satisfies $\varphi \in \mathsf{L}$. We consider all n large enough such that $\log n > 2r$ and such that ψ, ψ' used later in the proof are of size at most $\log n$ each.

- Consider the path graph G' with labels $(n, \log n), (n, \log n - 1), \cdots, (n, 1, \varphi)$
- Simulate $\mathbf{A}$ on G'
- Accept if and only if all the node labeled $(n, r), (n, r-1), \cdots, (n, 1, \varphi)$ accept. We call these nodes $u_r, u_{r-1}, \cdots, u_1$.

To show the correctness of our algorithm we notice that, in the case where $\mathbf{A}$ accepts G , all nodes in G accept and therefore $u_r, \cdots, u_1$ must also accept in our algorithm in G' since their local views are the same.

324   L. Feuilloley et al.

Now we consider the case that $\mathbf{A}$ rejects G. We can assume that there exists two words ψ, ψ' such that $\psi \in \mathsf{L}$ and $\psi' \notin \mathsf{L}$: both $\varnothing$ and the set $\{0,1\}^*$ are in P, while $\mathsf{L} \notin \mathsf{P}$, so L is neither of them.

Consider the two paths with labels

$$G_1 : (n, n), \ldots, (n, r), \ldots, (n, 1, \psi)$$

$$G_2 : (n, n), \ldots, (n, r), \ldots, (n, 1, \psi').$$

The local view of all nodes (n, i) with $i > r$ is the same in both instances, but G_1 should be accepted and while G_2 should be rejected. Therefore, all of these nodes must accept (in both cases), and the only rejecting nodes can be the ones with $i \leq r$. Therefore, our algorithm sees a rejecting node in one of $u_r, \cdots, u_1$.

Since $\mathbf{A}$ is an LP^* algorithm, it runs in each node in time polynomial with respect to the size of its neighborhood, which is of size $O(\log n)$. Therefore, our algorithm simulates $2r$ many executions of $\mathbf{A}$, each taking $\mathrm{poly}(\log n)$ time, for a total of $\mathrm{poly}(\log n)$ time. Hence, our centralized algorithm L' is a poly-time verifier for L: it runs in $\mathrm{poly}(\log n)$ time on inputs of size $\log n$. But we assumed $\mathsf{L} \in \mathsf{EXP} \setminus \mathsf{P}$, a contradiction. Therefore, such a PLD algorithm $\mathbf{A}$ cannot exist. $\square$

4 Universal Certificates and the Graph Size

In this section we discuss universal certificates. We show that giving certificates of length polynomial in the size of the graph end up "leaking" information to the nodes. We then show that this only gives a lower bound on n, knowing n exactly makes the model even more powerful. Unlike using certificates that are polynomial in n, we show that using certificates polynomial in the view of each node behaves "as expected", i.e., is strictly weaker than having unbounded certificates. We conclude with a few implications of the aforementioned results, at the form of extremely simple proofs of several separation results.

4.1 Bounded Certificates Leak Information

One might guess that having a bound on the size of certificates limits the power of the model, and this is indeed true in many cases. The next result, however, shows the opposite may also happen: the size limit might enable to solve problems which couldn't be solved with unbounded certificates. It is easy to see that $\mathsf{node}_{\mathsf{LSP}} \in \varPi_1^{\mathsf{local}} \setminus \varPi_1^{\mathsf{P\text{-}local}}$. The next result shows that $\varPi_1^{\mathsf{P\text{-}local}}$ and $\varPi_1^{\mathsf{local}}$ are incomparable.

Lemma 3. $\varPi_1^{\mathsf{P\text{-}local}} \not\subset \varPi_1^{\mathsf{local}}$.

We consider the language $\mathtt{AGTG}$ (All Greater Than size of Graph) of n-node path with labels

$$x_1, \cdots, x_n$$

such that for all i, $x_i > n$. We show that this language is in $\varPi_1^{\mathsf{P\text{-}local}}$ but not in $\varPi_1^{\mathsf{local}}$.

Claim. $\text{AGTG} \in \Pi_1^{\text{P-local}}$.

Proof. Recall that a language is in $\Pi_1^{\text{P-local}}$ if there exists a polynomial Q and an algorithm that uses certificates up to size $Q(n)$ on an n-node graph. To prove $\text{AGTG} \in \Pi_1^{\text{P-local}}$, we use $Q(n) = n$ as the polynomial bounding the certificates, and the following local decision algorithm.

For a node $u \in V$, let $c(u)$ denote the certificate it receives, and $|c(u)|$ its length. Node u accepts if $x_u > |c(u)|$, and rejects otherwise. If $x_u > n$ then $x_u > |c(u)|$ for all the certificates, and u always accepts; if $x_u > n$ for all nodes u, then they all accept. Conversely, if $x_v \leq n$ for some node v then this node will reject, e.g., for a certificate with $|c(v)| = n$. □

Claim. $\text{AGTG} \notin \Pi_1^{\text{local}}$.

Proof. Assume for contradiction that there is an algorithm $\mathbf{A}$ for AGTG, with locality r. Consider three path graphs with input labels as follows, where we take n large enough so that $n > 2r$.

- $G_1 \in \text{AGTG}$ is an n-node graph with labels

$$n + 1, n + 2, \ldots, n + 2$$

- $G_2 \in \text{AGTG}$ is an $(n + 1)$-node graph with labels

$$n + 2, n + 2, \ldots, n + 2, n + 2$$

- $G_3 \notin \text{AGTG}$ is an $(n + 1)$-node graph with labels

$$n + 1, n + 2, \ldots, n + 2, n + 2$$

In all these graphs, the IDs start by 1 on the left and grow consecutively.

Note that $G_1, G_2 \in \text{AGTG}$, so in both graphs, any assignment of certificates to the nodes make all of them accept. Consider an assignment of certificates to G_3. The nodes $1, \ldots, r+1$ have the same view as in the same assignment to G_1, and thus they all accept. The other nodes of G_3, $r + 2, \ldots, n + 1$ have the same view as in the same assignment to G_2, so they all accept as well. Hence, all nodes must accept under all certificate assignments; however, $G_3 \notin \text{AGTG}$, rendering $\mathbf{A}$ wrong. □

While $\text{AGTG} \in \Pi_1^{\text{P-local}}$ was a surprising result that required some work, It can be easily seen that $\text{AGTG} \in \Sigma_1^{\text{P-local}}$ (i.e., NPLD).

Claim. $\text{AGTG} \in \text{NPLD}$.

Proof. The ith node is given the certificate $(1^i, 1^n)$. The nodes can then check that the certificates are increasing consistently and consecutively among their neighbors. A node with only one neighbor then checks that its certificate is $(1, 1^n)$ and its neighbor's certificate is $(11, 1^n)$, or its certificate is $(1^n, 1^n)$ and its neighbors certificate is $(1^{n-1}, 1^n)$. After verifying this, all nodes have the correct value of n and can make sure that their inputs are greater than n. □

With this claim in hand, the language ALTG can also be used to give a very simple proof of the separation $\mathsf{PLD} \subsetneq \Pi_1^{\mathsf{P\text{-}local}} \cap \mathsf{NPLD}$, which was also claimed in [1].

Corollary 2. $\mathsf{PLD} \subsetneq \Pi_1^{\mathsf{P\text{-}local}} \cap \mathsf{NPLD}$.

Proof. The containment is immediate from the definitions. We already know from Lemma 3 that $\mathsf{ALTG} \in \Pi_1^{\mathsf{P\text{-}local}} \setminus \Pi_1^{\mathsf{local}}$ and we know that $\mathsf{PLD} \subseteq \mathsf{LD} \subseteq \Pi_1^{\mathsf{local}}$. As $\mathsf{ALTG} \in \mathsf{NPLD}$, the claim follows.   □

In Appendix A we give another proof of the aforementioned result. While our proof above uses locality, the proof in appendix is based on ideas from [2] and is reliant on computational constraints.

4.2 Knowing n Exactly

Recall that $\Pi_1^{\mathsf{P\text{-}local}[n]}$ is defined similarly to $\Pi_1^{\mathsf{P\text{-}local}}$, but giving each node the value of n as additional information. We can easily see that $\Pi_1^{\mathsf{P\text{-}local}} \subseteq \Pi_1^{\mathsf{P\text{-}local}[n]}$: given a $\Pi_1^{\mathsf{P\text{-}local}}$ algorithm **A**, we can also consider **A** as a $\Pi_1^{\mathsf{P\text{-}local}[n]}$ algorithm that ignores n. The previous result implies that polynomial certificates leak some information about n, so one may suspect that $\Pi_1^{\mathsf{P\text{-}local}} = \Pi_1^{\mathsf{P\text{-}local}[n]}$. The following lemma proves this suspicion to be wrong.

Lemma 4. $\Pi_1^{\mathsf{P\text{-}local}} \subsetneq \Pi_1^{\mathsf{P\text{-}local}[n]}$.

We consider the language ALTG (All Lesser Than size of Graph) of n-node paths with labels

$$x_n, x_{n-1}, \ldots, x_1$$

such that for all i, $x_i < n$. We show that this language is in $\Pi_1^{\mathsf{P\text{-}local}[n]}$ but not in $\Pi_1^{\mathsf{P\text{-}local}}$.

Claim. $\mathsf{ALTG} \in \Pi_1^{\mathsf{P\text{-}local}[n]}$.

Proof. Each node can check the condition directly since it knows the size of the graph.   □

Claim. $\mathsf{ALTG} \notin \Pi_1^{\mathsf{P\text{-}local}}$.

Proof. Assume there exists a $\Pi_1^{\mathsf{P\text{-}local}}$ algorithm **A** for ALTG with locality radius r. Let $Q(n)$ be the bound on certificate sizes as a function of n.

Take n large enough so that $n > 2r$ and $Q(n+1) \geq Q(n)$, and consider the following instances

  - $G_1 \in \mathsf{ALTG}$ is an $(n+1)$-node graph labeled

$$n, \quad n-1, \ldots, n-1, n-1;$$

- $G_2 \in \mathtt{ALTG}$ is an n-node graph labeled

$$n-1, n-1, \ldots, n-1;$$

- $G_3 \notin \mathtt{ALTG}$ is an n-node graph labeled

$$n, \quad n-1, \ldots, n-1.$$

We assume the IDs of the nodes start with 1 on the left and increase consecutively. G_1 and G_2 are clearly accepting instances, so in both, all nodes accept under all certificate assignments.

Now, the view of the $r+1$ left-most vertices is the same in both G_1 and G_3, so they must behave the same in both graphs. Similarly, the views of the nodes from $r+1$ to n is the same in both G_2 and G_3, so they must behave the same in those graphs. Therefore, for any certificate assignment, each node of G_3 must behave as a node of G_1 or of G_2 under the same certificate assignment (and this assignment can occur in G_1 since $Q(n+1) \geq Q(n)$), and accept. However, $G_3 \notin \mathtt{ALTG}$, a contradiction. $\qquad\square$

We now show, as corollary of this lemma and Lemma 3, that $\Pi_1^{\mathsf{P\text{-}local}[n]}$ and Π_1^{local} are incomparable.

Corollary 3. $\Pi_1^{\mathsf{P\text{-}local}[n]}$ *and* Π_1^{local} *are incomparable.*

Proof. We notice that $\mathtt{node}_{\mathsf{LsP}} \in \Pi_1^{\mathsf{local}} \setminus \Pi_1^{\mathsf{P\text{-}local}[n]}$ from Corollary 1, implying $\Pi_1^{\mathsf{local}} \not\subset \Pi_1^{\mathsf{P\text{-}local}[n]}$. On the other hand, if $\Pi_1^{\mathsf{P\text{-}local}[n]} \subseteq \Pi_1^{\mathsf{local}}$ then with Lemma 4 above, we get $\Pi_1^{\mathsf{P\text{-}local}} \subseteq \Pi_1^{\mathsf{local}}$. But we have proved this to be false in Lemma 3, so $\Pi_1^{\mathsf{P\text{-}local}[n]}$ and Π_1^{local} are incomparable. $\qquad\square$

4.3 Certificates Polynomial in the View

In Lemma 3 we show that $\Pi_1^{\mathsf{P\text{-}local}}$ is not contained in Π_1^{local}. We now examine the relation of Π_1^{LP} to both these classes. The idea for the inclusions $\Pi_1^{\mathsf{LP}} \subseteq \Pi_1^{\mathsf{local}}$ and $\Pi_1^{\mathsf{LP}} \subseteq \Pi_1^{\mathsf{P\text{-}local}}$ was outlined in [9]. We prove the inclusions here for completeness and also additionally show that the inclusions are strict.

We start by proving $\Pi_1^{\mathsf{LP}} \subsetneq \Pi_1^{\mathsf{local}}$. In fact, we prove something stronger: $\Pi_1^{\mathsf{LP}} \subsetneq \mathtt{LD}$.

Lemma 5. $\Pi_1^{\mathsf{LP}} \subsetneq \mathtt{LD} \subseteq \Pi_1^{\mathsf{local}}$.

Proof. We start by proving $\Pi_1^{\mathsf{LP}} \subseteq \mathtt{LD}$. Consider a Π_1^{LP} algorithm $\mathbf{A}$ with locality radius r and where the bound on the certificates is $Q(x)$ as a function of the size of the view of each node. We construct an $\mathtt{LD}$ algorithm $\mathbf{A}'$ of locality radius $2r$ as follows.

Each node $v \in V(G)$ checks its $2r$-neighborhood $N^{2r}(v)$. For each node u in its r-neighborhood, v can compute the size of u's distance-r neighborhood, $|N^r(u)|$. Then, v simulates $\mathbf{A}$ on all assignments of certificates to itself and its distance-r neighborhood, where node $u \in N^r(v)$ can get certificates of size at most $Q(|N^r(u)|)$. Node v accepts if and only if the simulation of $\mathbf{A}$ accepts on all these certificate.

Our new algorithm is clearly in LD, since there are only finitely many possible certificate. To show the correctness of this algorithm, we notice that if $\mathbf{A}$ is executed on an accepting instance, then every node must accept, and do so for all possible assignments of certificates in its neighborhood; hence, every node will accept in $\mathbf{A}'$ as well. On the other hand, in case of a rejecting instance, there exists a node v and an assignment of certificates to its neighborhood, such that v rejects in $\mathbf{A}$, and consequently, in $\mathbf{A}'$ as well.

To show that the inclusion is strict, we consider $\mathtt{node}_{\mathsf{L}_{\mathsf{SP}}}$. It is easily seen that $\mathtt{node}_{\mathsf{L}_{\mathsf{SP}}} \in \mathsf{LD}$ since a single node is allowed to use unbounded resources for its local computation. On the other hand, $\mathtt{node}_{\mathsf{L}} \notin \Pi_1^{\mathsf{LP}}$. $\qquad\square$

Next, we show similar results (containment and strictness) for $\Pi_1^{\mathsf{P\text{-}local}}$.

Lemma 6. $\Pi_1^{\mathsf{LP}} \subsetneq \Pi_1^{\mathsf{P\text{-}local}}$.

Proof. Given a Π_1^{LP} algorithm $\mathbf{A}$ with locality radius r and the bound on the certificates being $Q(x)$ as a function of the size of the view of each node. Similar to Lemma 1, we assume that Q' is a non-decreasing polynomial such that $Q'(x) \geq Q(x)$ for all $x \geq 0$. We construct a $\Pi_1^{\mathsf{P\text{-}local}}$ algorithm $\mathbf{A}'$ of radius $2r$ and certificates are bounded by $R(x) = Q'(x^2 h(x))$ where $h(x)$ is a polynomial upper bound on the size of labels.

Each node $v \in V(G)$ aggregates its $2r$-neighborhood $N^{2r}(v)$. For each node u in its r-neighborhood, v can compute the size of u's distance-r view, denoted $|N^r_{G,x,id}(u)|$.

Node v first examines the certificate sizes: if for some $u \in N^r(v)$ (including v itself), $|c(u)| > Q(|N^r_{G,x,id}(u)|)$ then v accepts. Otherwise v runs $\mathbf{A}$ on its r-neighborhood and outputs accordingly.

Clearly, $\mathbf{A}'$ is a legitimate $\Pi_1^{\mathsf{P\text{-}local}}$ algorithm. To show the correctness of $\mathbf{A}'$, we notice that if $\mathbf{A}$ is executed in an accepting instance then all nodes must accept. For $\mathbf{A}'$ on the same instance and $v \in V(G)$, either one of the certificates in its r-neighborhood was too large (in which case it accepts) or $\mathbf{A}$ is simulated and $\mathbf{A}'$ also accepts. On the other hand, for a rejecting instance, there must be a node v and an assignment of certificates to its neighborhood such that v rejects when simulating $\mathbf{A}$. We have taken Q' to be non-decreasing $Q'(x) \geq Q(x)$ for all $x \geq 0$ and $n^2 h(n) \geq |N^r_{G,x,id}(u)|$ for all u. Therefore while simulating $\mathbf{A}$ all the certificates with size $|c(u)| \leq Q(|N^r_{G,x,id}(u)|)$ will be considered. Therefore, the rejecting certificates must also be accounted for when running $\mathbf{A}'$ and therefore must result in rejection. Unlike Lemma 1, we couldn't directly assume Q is a non-decreasing function since $\mathbf{A}$ is an arbitrary algorithm and we can only ensure it behaves as expected if certificates are bounded by Q.

For the separation, recall that in the proof of Lemma 3 we have shown a language $\mathtt{AGTG}$ satisfying $\mathtt{AGTG} \in \Pi_1^{\mathsf{P\text{-}local}}$ but $\mathtt{AGTG} \notin \Pi_1^{\mathsf{local}}$. Lemma 5 asserts that $\Pi_1^{\mathsf{LP}} \subseteq \Pi_1^{\mathsf{local}}$, and hence $\mathtt{AGTG} \notin \Pi_1^{\mathsf{LP}}$. The claim follows. $\qquad\square$

Acknowledgments. Ami Paz was supported by Supported by ANR project DIDYA (ANR-25-CE48-0897).

Disclosure of Interests. The authors have no competing interests to declare that are relevant to the content of this article.

A   An Alternative Proof of Claim 2

Recall that Claim 2 asserts that $\mathsf{PLD} \subsetneq \Pi_1^{\mathsf{P\text{-}local}} \cap \mathsf{NPLD}$. We give another proof of this claim. The containment is immediate, so we only have to show separation, which we do next, using the language $\mathtt{ITER}$ defined in [2].

Claim. $\mathtt{ITER} \in (\mathsf{NPLD} \cap \Pi_1^{\mathsf{P\text{-}local}}) \setminus \mathsf{LD}$.

Proof. We follow the footsteps of in [2], who defined a language $\mathtt{ITER}$ to separate Π_1 from LD. The language it composed of labeled paths of the following structure. One node p is the *pivot* node, and is labeled by a Turing machine M and two inputs a and b to it. Each other node u is labeled with the machine M, with its distance $d(u,p)$ from the pivot p, and with the configuration of M after $d(u,p)$ steps: when starting from a if it is on the left of p (denoted $\mathrm{config}(M,a,d(u,p)))$, and when starting from b when it is on its right (denoted $\mathrm{config}(M,b,d(u,p)))$. Here, the sides are arbitrary, and need only be consistent among the different nodes. Finally, the endpoints of the path must both contain halting configurations, and at least one of these configurations must also be accepting.

We define a new language $\mathtt{ITER}^-$ which is the same as $\mathtt{ITER}$ but with the condition that both states at the endpoints only need to be halting. To show that $\mathtt{ITER}^- \in \Pi_1^{\mathsf{P\text{-}local}}$, we present the following algorithm. Each node first checks if all the nodes got the same machine and if the distances they received is consistent with each other. The pivot checks if one of its neighbors got a and the other got b as the input to M. The nodes then check if the Turing machine configurations are consecutive according to their distance from the pivot. The nodes with degree 1 check if their configuration is halting. A node rejects if any of these checks fails.

To check $\mathtt{ITER}$, we use a similar algorithm, with certificate lengths bounded by the identity polynomial $Q(n) = n$. Each node first checks if $(G,x) \in \mathtt{ITER}^-$, and each node but the pivot decides according to this check. If the pivot would have rejected in the check for $\mathtt{ITER}^-$, it rejects for $\mathtt{ITER}$ as well. Otherwise, the pivot interprets the length of the certificate as a non-negative integer $k \le n$, where n is the number of nodes. The pivot rejects if both $\mathrm{config}(M,b,k)$ and $\mathrm{config}(M,a,k)$ are rejecting configurations, and accepts otherwise.

For correctness, first note that the check for $\mathtt{ITER}^-$ ensures the syntactic correctness, and that both endpoints of the path have halting configurations. If both are rejecting, then the machine halts and rejects on both a and b in less than n steps (for each), as the path length is n. In this case, when the pivot gets a certificate of some length $k \le n$, it will see that both $\mathrm{config}(M,b,k)$ and config(M, a, k) are rejecting, and will reject. Finally, we notice that the algorithm runs in polynomial local time (polynomial in n). Therefore, ITER $\in \Pi_1^{\text{P-local}}$.

Proving ITER $\in$ NPLD directly is not hard. However, we take a different path, utilizing known results regarding relationships between classes of tasks. First, we notice that it is easy to check in a centralized manner that a labeled graph is in ITER$^-$, by checking the syntax of the labels and simulating M on a and b. Additionally, it is trivial to check that the states at both endpoints are halting and that at least one of them is accepting. All this can be done deterministically in time polynomial in the length of the path and the encoding of the machine and states, and therefore ITER $\in$ P $\subseteq$ NP. We have shown ITER $\in \Pi_1^{\text{P-local}}$ and we know that $\Pi_1^{\text{P-local}} \subseteq$ NLD, so ITER $\in$ NLD. We also know that and NPLD $=$ NLD $\cap$ NP, and therefore we conclude ITER $\in$ NPLD.

Finally, it was proved in [2, Proposition 7] that ITER $\notin$ LD, and this holds in our case as well. $\qquad\square$

References

1. Aldema Tshuva, E., Oshman, R.: On polynomial time local decision. In: OPODIS. LIPIcs, vol. 286, pp. 27:1–27:17. Schloss Dagstuhl - Leibniz-Zentrum für Informatik (2023)
2. Balliu, A., D'Angelo, G., Fraigniaud, P., Olivetti, D.: What can be verified locally? J. Comput. Syst. Sci. **97**, 106–120 (2018)
3. Feuilloley, L.: Introduction to local certification. Discret. Math. Theor. Comput. Sci. **23**(3) (2021). https://doi.org/10.46298/DMTCS.6280
4. Feuilloley, L., Fraigniaud, P.: Survey of distributed decision. Bull. EATCS **119** (2016). http://eatcs.org/beatcs/index.php/beatcs/article/view/411
5. Feuilloley, L., Fraigniaud, P., Hirvonen, J.: A hierarchy of local decision. Theor. Comput. Sci. **856**, 51–67 (2021)
6. Fraigniaud, P.: Distributed computational complexities: are you Volvo-addicted or NASCAR-obsessed? In: PODC, pp. 171–172. ACM (2010)
7. Fraigniaud, P., Korman, A., Peleg, D.: Towards a complexity theory for local distributed computing. J. ACM **60**(5), 35:1–35:26 (2013)
8. Korman, A., Kutten, S., Peleg, D.: Proof labeling schemes. Distrib. Comput. **22**(4), 215–233 (2010)
9. Reiter, F.: A LOCAL view of the polynomial hierarchy. In: PODC, pp. 347–357 (2024). https://doi.org/10.1145/3662158.3662774

Proving There Is a Leader Without Naming It

Laurent Feuilloley[2], Josef Erik Sedláček[1](✉), and Martin Slávik[1]

[1] Faculty of Information Technology, CTU in Prague, Prague, Czech Republic
{sedlajo5,slavim17}@fit.cvut.cz
[2] CNRS, INSA Lyon, UCBL, LIRIS, UMR5205, 69622 Villeurbanne, France

Abstract. Local certification is a mechanism for certifying to the nodes of a network that a certain property holds. In this framework, nodes are assigned labels, called certificates, which are supposed to prove that the property holds. The nodes then communicate with their neighbors to verify the correctness of these certificates.

Certifying that there is a unique leader in a network is one of classical problems in this setting. It is well-known that this can be done using certificates that encode node identifiers and distances in the graph. These require $O(\log n)$ and $O(\log D)$ bits respectively, where n is the number of nodes and D is the diameter. A matching lower bound is known in cycle graphs (where n and D are equal up to multiplicative constants).

A recent line of work has shown that network structure greatly influences local certification. For example, certifying that a network does not contain triangles takes $\Theta(n)$ bits in general graphs, but only $O(\log n)$ bits in graphs of bounded treewidth. This observation raises the question: Is it possible to achieve sublogarithmic leader certification in graph classes that do not contain cycle graphs? And since in that case we cannot write identifiers in a certificate, do we actually need identifiers at all in such topologies? We prove the following results.

- For graphs with constant diameter, which is the most natural way to rule out cycle graphs in this context, $\Omega(\log n)$-bit certificates are still required.
- For anonymous chordal graphs and anonymous grids, a leader can be certified using $O(\log D)$ bits. In particular, in chordal graphs with small enough diameter, we get a sublogarithmic certification. These two graph classes enforce in two different ways the fact that, unlike cycle graphs, the network has no large "hole".
- In graphs with logarithmic minimum degree, we obtain an $O(\log \log n)$ leader certification. Here, identifiers are actually used, but they are not stored verbatim in the certificates. This indicates that sparsity also plays a role in the fact that cycle graphs are hard instances.

We also discuss the types of properties to which these results apply beyond leader election, as well as the impact of the identifier range.

Keywords: local certification · locally checkable proofs · proof-labeling schemes · graph structure · leader election

C. Georgiou (Ed.): SIROCCO 2026, LNCS 16488, pp. 331–350, 2026.
https://doi.org/10.1007/978-3-032-26465-7_18

1   Introduction

Local Certification and Certification Size. Local certification is a model of distributed computing, where the nodes of a network have to verify a property, with the help of an oracle. More precisely, each node of the network is first given a *certificate* by a *prover*, then it communicates with its neighbors, and finally outputs a binary decision, *accept* or *reject* [8]. Such a scheme is correct for verifying a given property if the following holds: for any network configuration, there exists an assignment of certificates such that all nodes accept, if and only if the configuration satisfies the property. One can consider properties of the graph itself, such as having an odd number of nodes, or properties of an input labeling, for example *having a unique leader* consists of having exactly one node with input label 1 (selected) and all other nodes with input label 0 (non-selected).

The main measure of quality of a local certification is the size of the certificates used, which one wants to minimize. The certificates are simply bit strings used as labels, hence this size is measured in bits. Another aspect is the communication radius of the nodes. In the original model, *proof-labeling schemes* [21], the radius is 1, which means that every node just sends and receives one message from each (direct) neighbor. A more general model, *locally checkable proof* model [19], allows for any constant radius.

Example: Certifying a Leader. Let us describe the classic way to certify that there exists a *unique leader* in a graph. This will serve as an example for the notions given above and will also be the key problem in this paper.

On a correct instance, the prover does the following:

1. It writes the identifier of the selected node into the certificate of all nodes.
2. It chooses a spanning tree rooted at the selected node.
3. It writes into the certificate of every node the identifier of its parent in the tree, as well as its distance to the root (in the tree). (If the node is the root, it has no parent.)

Every node can check the local consistency of this labeling by communicating with its neighbors. More precisely, after reading the certificates of its neighbors and its own, it can check the following:

1. The claimed identifier of the root is the same for itself and its neighbors.
2. If the node has label 1 (selected), then its identifier is the one appearing in the certificate, it has not been given a parent identifier, and its distance is 0.
3. Otherwise, it has label 0 and a parent identifier that corresponds to a neighbor (parent) whose distance is one less than its own.

It is clear that in correct instances the prover's strategy described above makes all nodes accept. Now, intuitively, if the instance is not correct, then either there are several leaders, which is detected using the leader identifiers in the certificates, or there is no leader and this is detected when checking the spanning tree, which cannot point to a selected node.

On graphs with n nodes and diameter D, this certification uses $O(\log n + \log D)$ bits. Indeed, the standard hypothesis is that identifiers are encoded on $O(\log n)$ bits and the distances can be encoded on $O(\log D)$ bits. If we do not insist on making the diameter appear explicitly in the complexity this boils down to $O(\log n)$, since $D \leq n$.

Having a leader is actually one of the many problems for which the optimal certification size is $\Theta(\log n)$, and it is an essential primitive for all these problems. Let us mention that the classic terminology in distributed computing is *leader election*, but since there is no election involved here, we will refer to this problem as *(having a) unique leader*.

How Does the Topology Impact the Hardness of Certification? In the domain of local certification, there are important recent efforts to understand how the topology of the graph influences the hardness of certification. In other words, if we assume that the graph belongs to some structurally constrained graph class, does it make certifying some property easier? And if so, what properties?

In that direction, we have seen a lot of progress on the upper bound side, in particular in the *compact certification* regimes, that is, the certifications of (at most) logarithmic size. These take the form of meta-theorems inspired by the meta-theorem in algorithmic graph theory [23,25]. More precisely, they are theorems of the following form: In graph class X, certifying a property of type Y can be done with $O(\log n)$ bits, where X is typically defined by a bounded parameter (*e.g.* treewidth), and Y is a logic capturing many classic properties (first order logic or monadic second order logic) [6,9,17,18].

The impact of such structural restrictions can sometimes be spectacular. For example, certifying that a graph has no triangles requires a polynomial number of bits in general graphs, but one of these meta-theorems ([6]) automatically implies that logarithmic certificates are enough in bounded treewidth graphs. This line of work has had impact beyond local certification, when the ideas have been transferred to the CONGEST model, see [13–15].

There is nothing similar for lower bounds. That is, the lower bounds are proved in a few very specific graphs, and if one wants to understand the hardness of verifying a property in a graph class that does not contain these special graphs, then there is simply no lower bound available. To our knowledge, there are three lower bound techniques for proving $\Omega(\log n)$ lower bounds. The best known lower bound is by Göös and Suomela [19] (generalizing a proof of [20]) but it is only proved for cycles. The paper [11] also has a logarithmic lower bound that applies to different problems, but it is also only for cycles. Finally, some bounds are obtained by reduction to 2-party communication complexity (see *e.g.* [3]), but again the structure of the lower bound instances is very rigid, in the sense that it must encode a fixed partition into two well-structured parts.

This situation indicates that we might get new meta-theorems in the $o(\log n)$ regime for interesting properties, if only we can rule out cycles and structures coming from communication complexity reductions. In particular, the neighborhood diversity parameter [24] is promising since when it is bounded, the diameter is also bounded, which rules out the first obstacle, and also the structure of the graph must be very simple, which rules out the second.

The Göös-Suomela Lower Bound. In this paper, we will in particular focus on the Göös-Suomela lower bound, and try to understand to what extent it can be generalized and what its inherent limitations are.[1]

In order to have a more informed discussion on the power and limitations of the Göös-Suomela lower bound, let us sketch the technique. Consider the task of verifying that there is a unique leader and assume that there exists a local certification with $o(\log n)$ bits for it. We consider a family of *yes*-instances, which are cycle graphs with exactly one leader, with specific identifier assignments.[2] From these, we can create a family of new instances by cutting several of these cycles and plugging them into a larger cycle. These are *no*-instances because they have several leaders, but a counting argument shows that at least one of these must be accepted. This is a contradiction with the correctness of the certification scheme, and establishes the $\Omega(\log n)$ bound.

In the original paper [19], the lower-bound technique is described as a general framework and applied to a few concrete problems. Intuitively, the lower bound applies to properties where it is required that *some pattern appears at most once* in the graph. Having a unique leader is such a property, since we want at most one leader. Actually, for this paper it is relevant to see unique leader as the conjunction of two problems: At-Most-One-Selected (AMOS) [16] and At-Least-One-Selected (ALOS) [11]. In this paper, for all results AMOS and unique leader are equivalent, and we use AMOS, which better captures the intuition of the lower bound.

In Which Topologies Does the Göös-Suomela Technique Apply? In the proof of the Göös-Suomela lower bound, the structure of the lower bound instances is very rigid, since they are cycle graphs only. It is a strength, in the sense that it shows that even in a very restricted setting the lower bound holds, but it is also a weakness. Indeed, the proof does not apply to settings where we restrict ourselves to a graph class that does not contain infinitely many cycle graphs. In particular, unlike other lower bounds, it is not sufficient to have a cycle in the graph to apply the result. The main question of this paper is the following:

Question 1. What are the graph structural constraints that allow a $\Omega(\log n)$ lower bound, and what are the ones that allow a $o(\log n)$ upper bound?

Since identifiers are encoded on $\Theta(\log n)$ bits, this question is tightly connected to a second question.

---

[1] Throughout the paper, we will use *Göös-Suomela lower bound* to refer to the $\Omega(\log n)$ lower bound in [19], but it should be noted that the same paper has several important lower bounds in the quadratic regime too.

[2] Throughout the paper, we will use the words *cycle graph* to insist on the fact that the full graph considered is a cycle.

Question 2. What are the graph structural constraints that allow certification in anonymous graphs?

In order to answer these questions, we will inspect the natural features of cycle graphs one after the other. A first aspect is that cycles are obviously not acyclic. The complexity of leader election in trees is known to be constant: it is sufficient to give every node its distance modulo three from the leader. The reason why this works is that it basically gives an orientation to each edge, and having a unique sink is easy to check locally in trees. Note that in comparison with the classic scheme, in trees, not only can one avoid identifiers in the certificates, but also compress the distance to only three different labels.

Let us now explore other structural aspects of cycle graphs in more detail.

The Role of the Diameter. Another important aspect of cycles is their linear diameter, which is especially relevant for our problem since the diameter appears naturally in the bounds. A natural question is whether the logarithmic lower bound still holds in low-diameter graphs. Our first result is to prove that it does.

Theorem 1. *Certifying AMOS in a graph with bounded diameter D requires certificates of size $\Omega(\log n)$.*

This theorem undermines the hopes of establishing a sublogarithmic metatheorem based on neighborhood diversity (or similar parameters) that we mentioned before (and, indeed, it is not hard to see that Theorem 1 extends to bounded neighborhood diversity).

The proof of this theorem revisits the proof of [19], with two essential modifications. Although this is the case in the original proof, one does not need the *yes*-instances to be connections of long paths: we can replace them by paths of constant length with an arbitrary dense and large part added at one end. Second, one can combine four of these small parts, hence keeping the diameter under control, when the original proof was just considering arbitrary combinations.

At an intuitive level, what is needed for the proof to work is to have some "hole" in the graph, and that around this hole there are at least two places that are "thin". See Fig. 1. However, good and general definitions of what a hole is and what it means for a region to be thin remain elusive. In the following, we prove that one can go below $\Omega(\log n)$ ruling out holes, for a specific definition, or ruling out sparse graphs. But we also show that these definitions do not capture all the relevant cases.

The Role of the "Hole". A possible definition for a hole is a large enough induced cycle, that is, a set of nodes such that the edge set restricted to this set of nodes forms a cycle. Graphs with no induced cycles of some length are well-studied in graph theory. The most classic such class (besides trees) is the class of *chordal graphs*, which are the graphs that have no induced cycles of length larger than 3. These are basically the graphs that can be organized as trees of cliques, and they are a good example of a class for which there is no hole in the intuitive sense. See Fig. 1 for an example.

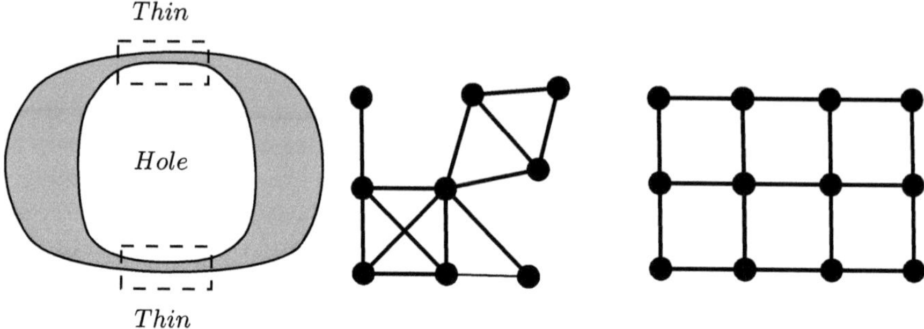

Fig. 1. Left picture: illustration of the type of graphs for which the Göös-Suomela proof works, with a hole and two thin parts (the graph is the gray part). Middle picture: a chordal graph. Right picture: a 2-by-3 grid.

For chordal graphs, we show that there exists a local certification that only depends on the diameter, hence, being sublogarithmic if the diameter is small enough. And in the spirit of Question 2, we prove that we can do so in anonymous graphs.

Theorem 2. *In anonymous graphs, there exists a 2-local proof-labeling scheme* $(f, \mathcal{A})$ *of size* $O(\log D)$ *that accepts a chordal graph* G *if and only if* $G \in \mathcal{P}$, *that is, if* G *has at most one selected vertex.*

The certificates we use are very simple: they are only the distances to the selected node. The challenging part is to design the verification made at the nodes, and to prove correctness. For this the key part is to understand and use what the neighborhood of a node looks like in chordal graphs, which is also why we need radius-2, so that nodes can see these connections.

In the context of the paper, the take-away of this theorem is that defining holes as forbidden induced subgraphs leads to "hole-free" graphs of small diameter breaking the lower bound, and that identifiers are not needed. But there are other cases where we can avoid identifiers, with a less conservative definition of a hole. An example is grid graphs (see Fig. 1), where there are large induced cycles: consider, for example, the nodes at the border of the grid. They form an induced cycle of linear length. In these graphs we have a local certification, even in the anonymous setting.

Theorem 3. *In anonymous graphs, there exists a 1-local proof-labeling scheme of size* $O(\log D)$ *that accepts a labeled grid graph of diameter at most* D *if and only if at most one vertex is selected.*

Note that here we only need radius 1, proving that the 2 of the previous result is not required to work in structured anonymous graphs. Also note that the logarithm of the diameter of the grid is of order $\Theta(\log n)$ so we do not break the lower bound in that case.

As mentioned earlier, the right definition of a hole eludes our understanding. Let us formulate this as an open problem (leaving aside the dense case that we discuss later).

Open problem 1. *In which (sparse) graphs does AMOS require $\Omega(\log n)$ bits? Is there a good notion of "hole", such that ruling out this structure captures the cases where we can go below $\Theta(\log n)$?*

An intuitive definition for a hole would be that it is a cycle in a graph, that would act as an obstacle in a road network: the paths that connect two diametrically opposite nodes of the cycle can be partitioned in two groups, those that "go north of the obstacle" and those that "go south of the obstacle". To our surprise, we were unable to find such a notion in the literature. Note that in grids and chordal graphs, there is no such hole, while the construction of Göös-Suomela does have such a structure.

Paper [5] independently considered similar questions. More precisely, the authors consider a setting where the certificates are constant-size labels on the edges of the graph, and they want to verify that the graph has a unique leader or a correct spanning tree. They prove that they can achieve this in chordal graphs and in so-called K_4-free dismantlable graphs. In a very recent paper by the same group [4], the authors improve our Theorem 2 and 3 to a larger class of graphs, the meshed graphs, and improve the certificate size, making great progress on Open problem 1. They also certify the structure of these graphs.

The Impact of Sparsity/Density. Let us now discuss one more aspect of the cycle topology that makes Göös-Suomela proof work: the cycles are sparse graphs. In particular, the places where we cut and plug different instances are "thin", in the sense that there are not too many nodes close to these cuts. If this were not the case, the amount of information available in the certificates around the cut would not be negligible compared to the number of instances considered, and the counting argument would not work.

Hence the question: What happens if the graph is dense everywhere? Is the sparsity requirement an artifact of the proof, or does density help? We show that density does help.

Theorem 4. *In graphs where every node has degree $\alpha \log^2 n$, for a large enough constant α, AMOS can be certified with $O(\log \log n)$ bits with verification radius 2.*

Interestingly, in the case of that theorem, even though the identifiers cannot be encoded in the certificates due to the lack of space, we do use them. The trick is that when we need to provide an identifier to a node, we can cut this identifier into many smaller pieces, and distribute the pieces to the neighbors of the node. The node can then collect these pieces from its neighbors' certificates.

The Role of the Identifier Range. Our focus has been mostly to understand the scope of the Göös-Suomela technique in terms of topology. Another aspect of the technique to be questioned is the identifier range. Indeed, the construction of the instances leading to a contradiction requires the identifier range to be quadratic. Again, the question is: is this necessary, or is it an artifact of the proof? If the identifier range is of the form $[1, n + c]$ where c is a constant, then the following theorem proves that once again the lower bound can be broken.

Theorem 5. *Let G be a graph with bounded diameter D. If there exists a vertex whose identifier is of constant size relative to the size of G, then AMOS can be verified with certificates of size $O(\log D)$.*

What are the Relevant Properties Beyond AMOS and Unique Leader? We have mentioned before that meta-theorems usually have two restrictions: one on the topology of the graph and one on the set of problems considered. Our focus is on the former, but the second is also interesting. We have focused on AMOS and unique leader for simplicity, but our questions are relevant for any property in the logarithmic regime.

For example, Göös and Suomela consider two other problems: verifying that a set of pointers forms a spanning tree and verifying that the graph has an odd number of nodes. It is not hard to argue that spanning tree reduces to AMOS, using the notion of local reduction recently introduced in [7], but it is unclear whether this could be achieved for the odd number of nodes. This prompts the following question.[3]

Open problem 2. *Can we characterize the properties that have $\Theta(\log n)$ complexity, at least on cycles? Is there a property that is complete for local reduction?*

In this direction, let us note that a recent paper proved that in anonymous cycles without input labels, there is a gap in the complexity between $\Theta(1)$ and $\Theta(\log n)$, in the sense that no property can have optimal certificate size strictly in between these regimes [2]. This means that in that restricted setting, the logarithmic regime forms a complexity class that is well-separated from the lower complexities.

2   Model, Definitions and Notation

All graphs in this paper are undirected, connected, simple graphs, with inputs labels on the nodes, denoted by $G = (V, E, L)$ where $L \colon V \to \{0, 1\}^*$ encodes the labeling. We denote by n the number of vertices and by D the diameter of the graph. Unless specified otherwise, the vertices are assigned *unique identifiers* encoded on $O(\log n)$ bits. We use the word *anonymous* when there is no identifiers. Neighbors of a vertex v are denoted as $N_G(v)$, and if G is clear from the context, $N(v)$ is used. Distance between two vertices u, v is denoted as $d_G(u, v)$,

---

[3] Some variant of this question appears in [8] as Open Problem 11.

and the subscript is omitted if G is clear from the context. We denote the set of vertices within distance r from v as $V[v, r]$, also called the r-local neighborhood of v.

A *graph property* is formally a set of graphs that is closed under isomorphism, that is, its membership does not depend on the choice of identifiers. Note that it may depend on the labels of the graph. A *certificate assignment* P for G is a function $P \colon V(G) \to \{0,1\}^*$ that associates with each vertex a *certificate*. We say that P has size s if $|P(v)| \le s(n)$ for every v. A *verifier* is a function that takes as an input a graph G, its certificate assignment P and $v \in V(G)$ and outputs either 0 or 1.

The induced subgraph $G[V[v, r]]$ is denoted as $G[v, r]$ and the restriction of P to $V[v, r]$ is denoted as $P[v, r]$, that is $P[v, r] \colon V[v, r] \to \{0,1\}^*$. A verifier $\mathcal{A}$ is *r-local* if $\mathcal{A}(G, P, v) = \mathcal{A}(G[v, r], P[v, r], v)$ for all G, P, and v.

An r-local *proof labeling scheme* certifying a property of labeled graphs $\mathcal{P}$ is a pair $(f, \mathcal{A})$, where $\mathcal{A}$ is an r-local verifier and f, called the *prover*, assigns to each $G \in \mathcal{P}$ a certificate assignment P such that the following properties hold.

- *Completeness*: If $G \in \mathcal{P}$, then $\mathcal{A}(G[v, r], P[v, r], v) = 1$ for all v, where $P = f(G)$.
- *Soundness*: If $G \notin \mathcal{P}$, then for every certificate assignment P', there is v such that
$$\mathcal{A}(G[v, r], P'[v, r], v) \ = \ 0.$$

We say that $(f, \mathcal{A})$ has size $s : \mathbb{N} \to \mathbb{N}$ if $|f(G)(v)| \le s(|V(G)|)$ for all $G \in \mathcal{P}$ and all $v \in V(G)$.

A *chordal graph* is a graph with no induced cycles of length 4 or more.

The $k \times q$ square grid graph is the cartesian product of a path on k vertices and a path on q vertices. A *grid graph* is one of these graphs with arbitrary k and q.

3   Logarithmic Lower Bound in Constant Diameter Graphs

In this section we prove the following theorem:

Theorem 1. *Certifying AMOS in a graph with bounded diameter D requires certificates of size $\Omega(\log n)$.*

The basic idea of the proof is similar to that introduced by Göös and Suomela in their proof of the $\Omega(\log n)$ lower bound on certificate size for spanning trees and leader election [19] (Theorem 5.1). They considered graph properties on cycles. The problem is that cycles have large diameter relative to the number of vertices. The only change is that we will take a clique with a path extending from one of its vertices and ending in another one or a *connection* of such graphs. This way we can make the yes-instance any size necessary, without increasing the diameter.

We will connect two graphs, which will result in no-instance. By *connection* we mean taking two graphs, removing the edge in the middle of the path in each graph, and adding two edges to connect the corresponding endpoints of the two paths.

Then, we will assume that there is a proof labeling scheme $(f, \mathcal{A})$ of size $o(\log(n))$. Finally, we will take the graph created by connecting yes-instances, retaining the identifiers and certificates of the original graphs. This way, the verifier will have to accept the combined graph even though it will be a no-instance.

In the context of the AMOS problem, consider several graphs, each with one selected vertex. By connecting two graphs, we obtain a graph with two selected vertices. The verifier will also have to accept this connected graph.

Proof. Consider a family of graphs $\mathcal{F}$, which includes graphs that have diameter at most d and consist of a cycle, where any vertex v can be replaced with a clique K, such that the two edges incident to v are connected to any two vertices of K. It is possible to have a constant number of bits of auxiliary information on vertices, such as labels or colors. Fix a radius r and a diameter d. We assume that d is much larger than r but at least $5r$. Let $\mathcal{P} \subseteq \mathcal{F}$ be a graph property such that every graph $G \in \mathcal{P}$ has diameter at most $d/2$ and one selected vertex. Assume there is an r-local proof labeling scheme $(f, \mathcal{A})$ of size $o(log(n))$.

We show that there are always yes-instances that can be connected to form an instance that inherits the certificates from the yes-instances. The verifier will accept each yes-instance, and therefore it will also accept the connected instance.

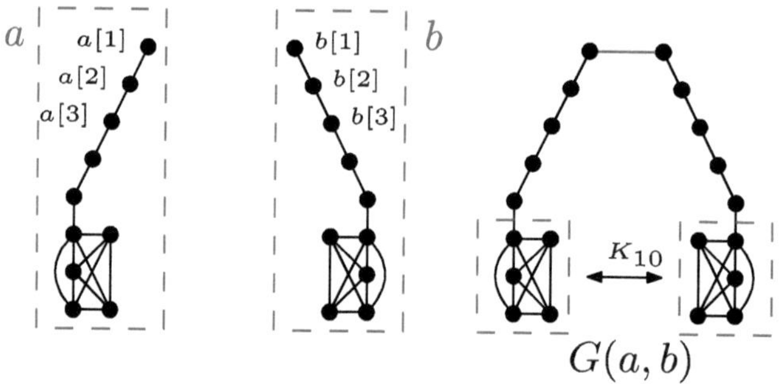

Fig. 2. An example of a graph $G(a, b)$ consisting of a and b.

Similarly to the proof in [19], we split $n = n_A + n_B$, where $n_A = \lfloor n/2 \rfloor$ and $n_B = \lceil n/2 \rceil$. Fix a partition of the set of identifiers $\{1, ..., n^2\}$ into $2n$ subsets $a_1, ..., a_n, b_1, ..., b_n$ so that each $a \in A := \{a_1, ..., a_n\}$ is of size n_A, and each $b \in B := \{b_1, ..., b_n\}$ is of size n_B. Let $a[i]$ (resp., $b[i]$) denote the i-th identifier in a (resp., b) in the natural order.

We define a family of yes-instances $G(a, b)$ indexed by pairs $(a, b) \in A \times B$. The graph $G(a, b)$ consists of:

- a path $a[1], a[2], \ldots, a[2r + 1], \ldots, a[k]$,

- a path $b[1], b[2], \ldots, b[2r+1], \ldots, b[\ell]$,
- a clique consisting of the vertices $a[k+1], \ldots, a[n_A]$ and $b[\ell+1], \ldots, b[n_B]$,
- and the edges $\{a[1], b[1]\}, \{a[k], a[k+1]\}, \{b[\ell], b[\ell+1]\}$.

For an example, see Fig. 2.

Recall that we assume that $\mathcal{P}$ requires only an $o(\log(n))$-bits certificate to be verified. Let $c(a, b)$ denote a color of $G(a, b)$, consisting of all the labels and certificates within distance $2r+1$ of the vertices $a[1]$ and $b[1]$. Formally $c(a, b)$ is defined as follows:

$$c(a,b) = \begin{pmatrix} f(G(a,b))(a[2r+1]), \ L(G(a,b))(a[2r+1]), \ \ldots, \ f(G(a,b))(a[1]), \\ L(G(a,b))(a[1]), \ f(G(a,b))(b[1]), \ L(G(a,b))(b[1]), \ \ldots, \\ f(G(a,b))(b[2r+1]), \ L(G(a,b))(b[2r+1]) \end{pmatrix}$$

It holds that the number of bits of $c(a, b)$ is $o(r \log(n))$.

Let $K_{n,n} = (A \cup B, E)$ be a complete bipartite graph with $E = \{\{a, b\} : a \in A, b \in B\}$. We define an edge coloring of $K_{n,n}$ as follows: the color of the edge $\{a, b\} \in E$ is $c(a, b)$. For sufficiently large n, the number of bits in $c(a, b)$ is smaller than $\log(n)/3$. Therefore, the number of distinct colors in $K_{n,n}$ is smaller than $\sqrt[3]{n}$. Hence there is a subset of edges $H \subseteq E$ such that $|H| > |E|/\sqrt[3]{n} = n^{5/3}$ and all edges of H have the same color. In the original proof, the authors apply the result due to Bondy and Simonovits [1] to show that in H there is a $2k$-cycle where all the edges have the same color. We only need a weaker result, namely *Kővári–Sós–Turán theorem* [22], from which it follows that for a sufficiently large n, the subgraph $(A \cup B, H)$ necessarily contains a 4-cycle. Let the vertices of this cycle be a_i, b_i, a_j, b_j in this order, where $a_i, a_j \in A$ and $b_i, b_j \in B$. As all edges of the cycle have the same color, we have $c(a_i, b_i) = c(a_j, b_j) = c(a_i, b_j) = c(a_j, b_i)$.

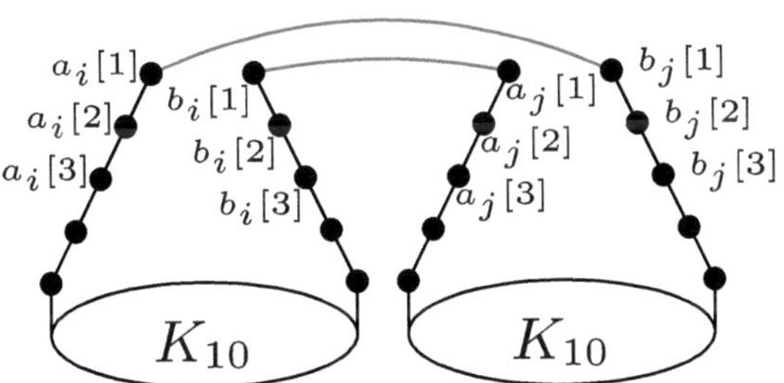

Fig. 3. An example of a graph created by connecting two yes-instances $G(a_i, b_i)$ and $G(a_j, b_j)$.

Now we connect the instances $G(a_i, b_i)$ and $G(a_j, b_j)$ and construct a no-instance. See Fig. 3 for an example.

That is, we take the vertex-disjoint graphs $G(a_i, b_i)$ and $G(a_j, b_j)$, remove the edges $\{a_i[1], b_i[1]\}$ and $\{a_j[1], b_j[1]\}$, and add $\{b_i[1], a_j[1]\}$ and $\{b_j[1], a_i[1]\}$. For each vertex v, we keep the auxiliary information $L(v)$ and the certificates $P(v)$ from the graphs $G(a_i, b_i)$ and $G(a_j, b_j)$. Note that since we connect instances with diameter at most $d/2$, the diameter of the resulting instance is at most d and thus it still belongs to $\mathcal{F}$.

It remains to argue that the computation of $\mathcal{A}$ on the connected instance G, with the labels L and the certificate assignment P, is accepting. To see this, pick a vertex v. Then there exists i such that $v \in V(G(a_i, b_i))$. If v is far from $a_i[1]$ and $b_i[1]$, then the local neighborhood of v looks identical in G and $G(a_i, b_i)$. Because $G(a_i, b_i)$ is a yes-instance, $\mathcal{A}(v)$ accepts. If v is close to $b_i[1]$, then the local neighborhood of v looks identical in G and $G(a_j, b_i)$, which is another yes-instance. Similarly, if v is near $a_i[1]$, then its local neighborhood looks identical in G and $G(a_i, b_j)$, which is also a yes-instance. In all cases, $\mathcal{A}(v)$ accepts. Thus, the connected graph is accepted by all vertices. If $G \notin \mathcal{P}$, we have a contradiction. We can therefore conclude that the graph property $\mathcal{P}$ does not admit proof labeling scheme of size $o(\log n)$.

For the AMOS problem, place one selected vertex in each yes-instance. When these yes-instances are combined, the resulting graph contains more than one selected vertex. Thus, the graph with more than one selected vertex is accepted. $\qquad\square$

Observation 6. *Certifying AMOS in bipartite graphs, and thus also in perfect graphs, with bounded diameter, requires certificates of size $\Omega(\log n)$.*

Proof. We can achieve the same result for bipartite graphs by subdividing each edge once, that is, by inserting a vertex into each edge. Since all bipartite graphs are perfect, the lower bound also applies to perfect graphs. $\qquad\square$

Observation 7. *Certifying AMOS in graphs with bounded neighborhood diversity requires certificates of size $\Omega(\log n)$.*

Proof. Our yes-instances also have small neighborhood diversity, since each vertex on the path can form its own set, and the clique forms a single set. Therefore, the lower bound $\Omega(\log n)$ also holds for the smaller class of graphs with bounded neighborhood diversity. $\qquad\square$

4   Log-Diameter Certification in Anonymous Chordal Graphs

Let $\mathcal{F}$ be the family of all labeled chordal graphs with diameter at most D, and let $\mathcal{P} \subseteq \mathcal{F}$ denote the set of graphs satisfying the AMOS property, meaning that each $G \in \mathcal{P}$ contains at most one selected vertex. In this section we will prove the following theorem:

Theorem 2. *In anonymous graphs, there exists a 2-local proof-labeling scheme $(f, \mathcal{A})$ of size $O(\log D)$ that accepts a chordal graph G if and only if $G \in \mathcal{P}$, that is, if G has at most one selected vertex.*

Let us first describe the scheme, namely the prover strategy on yes-instances and the verification at the vertices.

Let G be a yes-instance and $P = f(G)$ be the certificate assignment for G. Let s be the selected vertex. If no vertex is selected, then s is chosen arbitrarily. The certificate of s is $P(s) = 0$.

For any other $v \in V$, the certificate assignment is $P(v) = d(v, s)$.

Verification on a vertex v consists of the following steps:

- If v is selected and $P(v) \neq 0$, the verifier $\mathcal{A}(v)$ rejects.
- If $P(v) = 0$ and there exists $y \in N(v)$ such that $P(y) \neq 1$, the verifier $\mathcal{A}(v)$ rejects.
- If $P(v) > 0$, then:

  R1: If for all $u \in N(v)$ we have $P(u) \geq P(v)$, or if there exists $u \in N(v)$ such that $|P(u) - P(v)| > 1$, the verifier $\mathcal{A}(v)$ rejects.

  R2: If there exist vertices $u_1, u_2 \in N(v)$ such that $P(u_1) = P(u_2) = P(v) - 1$ and there is no edge $\{u_1, u_2\}$ then the verifier $\mathcal{A}(v)$ rejects.

  R3: If there exists a vertex $u \in N(v)$ with $P(u) = P(v) - 1$ and a vertex $y \in N(v)$ with $P(y) = P(v)$, then for each such y, if
  (a) $u \notin N(y)$, and
  (b) there exists $z \in N(y)$ such that $P(z) = P(v) - 1$ and $z \notin N(v)$
  the verifier $\mathcal{A}(v)$ rejects.

- Otherwise, the verifier $\mathcal{A}(v)$ accepts.

If the condition in R2 is not satisfied, the input graph is either not chordal, as there exists a cycle $v, u_1, \ldots, u_2$ of length greater than 3, or there are two vertices s_1, s_2. See Fig. 4 for a visualization of this case.

For the case of R3, see Fig. 5.

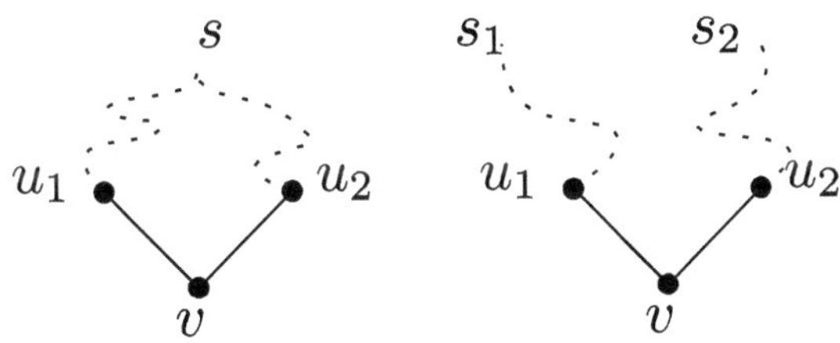

Fig. 4. Visualization of a case that R2 prevents.

Proof (Proof of Theorem 2). First, we show that if a graph is accepted, it must contain at most one selected vertex.

Proof of $\Rightarrow$:

We can assume that there is a vertex s with $P(s) = 0$. If not, by R1 the verifier would reject the vertex with the smallest certificate, as it would have no neighbor with a smaller certificate.

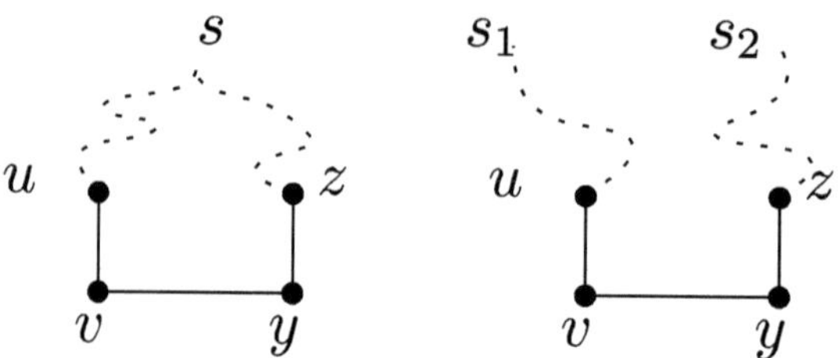

Fig. 5. Visualization of a case that R3 prevents. Note that even if there would be an edge between u and z the cycle would still be too long.

The proof proceeds by induction on the distance from the vertex s. We assume that for any vertex v with $d(v, s) < k$, we have $P(v) = d(v, s)$.

Base case: Every vertex $u \in G[s, r]$ can verify that its certificate matches its actual distance from s.

Induction step: We show that, under the induction hypothesis, for any vertex v with $d(v, s) = k$, either $P(v) = d(v, s)$ or the verifier rejects at some vertex. Consider a vertex v with $d(v, s) = k$ and any neighbor $u \in N(v)$ with $d(u, s) = k - 1$.

Let $w \in N(u)$ be the neighbor of u such that $d(w, s) = k - 2$.

- If $P(v) < k - 2$ or $P(v) > k$, the verifier $\mathcal{A}(v)$ rejects according to R1.
- If $P(v) = k - 2$, recall that vertex u sees its neighbor w with $P(w) = k - 2$. However, there cannot be an edge $\{v, u\}$; if such an edge existed, it would imply that $d(v, s) \leq k - 1$, which is not the case. Therefore, the verifier $\mathcal{A}(u)$ rejects according to R2.
- Now suppose that $P(v) = k - 1$. Vertex v must have a neighbor y with $P(y) = k - 2$; otherwise, the verifier $\mathcal{A}(v)$ would reject according to R1. However, y cannot have $d(y, s) = k - 2$, as that would imply $d(v, s) \neq k$. This means that $P(y) \neq d(y, s)$ and y is attempting to *deceive* the verifier. Since $y \in N(v)$ and $d(v, s) = k$, there are only three possible values for $d(y, s)$:
  1. If $d(y, s) = k - 1$, we reach a contradiction with the induction hypothesis, which states that the certificates are correct for all vertices at distance less than k from s.
  2. If $d(y, s) = k$, then y cannot be adjacent to any vertex at distance $k - 2$, as that would imply $d(y, s) \leq k - 1$. In particular, y cannot be adjacent to w. Now, if there is an edge between u and y, the verifier $\mathcal{A}(u)$ rejects according to R2, because $P(w) = P(y) = k - 2$, $w, y \in N(u)$, but $\{w, y\} \notin E$. If there is no edge $\{u, y\}$, then both $\mathcal{A}(u)$ and $\mathcal{A}(v)$ reject due to R3, reason being that the vertex v cannot be adjacent to w and y is not adjacent to u.
  3. If $d(y, s) = k + 1$, then u cannot be adjacent to y, as that would imply $d(y, s) \leq k$. Without the edge $\{u, y\}$, the verifier $\mathcal{A}(v)$ rejects according to R2.

All possibilities for the distance of such a *deceiving* vertex y have been exhausted, each leading to a contradiction. Therefore, no such vertex y exists, and consequently no such vertex v exists either.

- The only remaining option is that $P(v) = k = d(v, s)$, which is the correct certificate.

For the converse implication, we show that any yes-instance is always accepted.
Proof of $\Leftarrow$:

If there is exactly one selected vertex s, then for every vertex v, the certificate is $P(v) = d(v, s)$, and it holds that $P(s) = 0$. If there is no selected vertex in G, then any vertex can serve as s, and the certificate $P(s) = 0$ is assigned accordingly.

R1 is always satisfied, since the certificate corresponds to the distance from s.

R2 is satisfied because, if two vertices x, y with $d(x, s) = d(y, s)$ have a common neighbor v with $d(v, s) = d(x, s) + 1$, there must be an edge $\{x, y\}$. If such an edge does not exist, then the vertices x, v, y would form part of a cycle of length at least 4, since there exist paths from both x and y to s, which contradicts the assumption that the graph is chordal.

R3 is satisfied for a reason similar to that of R2. Consider two vertices v, y with $d(v, s) = d(y, s)$, and two other vertices $u \in N(v)$ and $z \in N(y)$, such that $d(u, s) = d(z, s) = d(v, s) + 1$.

If neither of the edges $\{v, z\}$ or $\{y, u\}$ exists, then the vertices u, v, y, z would form part of a cycle of length at least 4, similarly to the case of R2. Hence, the graph would not be chordal.

Therefore, all rules are satisfied, and the graph is accepted.

Since only the distances are stored, the certificates have size $O(\log(D))$. The verifier only checks vertices up to distance 2, thus it is 2-local.

We have thus shown that the 2-local proof-labeling scheme $(f, \mathcal{A})$ of size $O(\log(D))$ accepts a chordal graph if and only if it contains at most one selected vertex. $\qquad\square$

5   Log-Diameter Certification in Anonymous Grid Graphs

Let $\mathcal{F}$ be the family of all labeled grid graphs with diameter at most D, and let $\mathcal{P} \subseteq \mathcal{F}$ denote the set of graphs satisfying the AMOS property, meaning that each $G \in \mathcal{P}$ contains at most one selected vertex.

In this section, we prove the following:

Theorem 3. *In anonymous graphs, there exists a 1-local proof-labeling scheme of size $O(\log D)$ that accepts a labeled grid graph of diameter at most D if and only if at most one vertex is selected.*

Again, let us first describe the prover strategy on yes-instances and then the verification at the vertices.

Let s be the selected vertex and $P(s) = 0$ the certificate of s. If no vertex is selected, an arbitrary vertex is chosen as s. For any other vertex v, the certificate is $P(v) = d(v, s)$.

Verification on vertex v:

1. If v is selected and $P(v) \neq 0$, then $\mathcal{A}(v)$ rejects.
2. If $P(v) = 0$ and there is a vertex $y \in N(v)$ such that $P(y) \neq 1$, then $\mathcal{A}(v)$ rejects.
3. If for any v there are two or more vertices $w \in G[v, r]$ such that $P(w) = 0$, then $\mathcal{A}(v)$ rejects.
4. If for any v the certificate $P(v) = k$ and there is a vertex $y \in N(v)$ such that $P(y) \notin \{k - 1, k + 1\}$, then $\mathcal{A}(v)$ rejects.
5. If for any v the certificate $P(v) = k > 0$ and there is no $y \in N(v)$ such that $P(y) = k - 1$, then $\mathcal{A}(v)$ rejects.
6. If for any v there are more than two vertices $y \in N(v)$ such that $P(y) = k - 1$, then $\mathcal{A}(v)$ rejects.
7. Otherwise, $\mathcal{A}(v)$ accepts.

Proof. The proof of the left-to-right implication proceeds by induction on the distance from vertex s. In the case there are several vertices w with $P(w) = 0$, one of them is selected as s.

We can assume that there is such a vertex s with $P(s) = 0$, otherwise, on the vertex w with the smallest $P(w)$, the verifier $\mathcal{A}(w)$ would reject according to the condition 5, as there would be no vertex in $N(w)$ with a smaller certificate.

We assume that for any vertex v with $d(v, s) < k$, we have $P(v) = d(v, s)$.

Base case: If s is a selected vertex, the certificate $P(s) = 0$; otherwise, $\mathcal{A}(s)$ would reject according to condition 1, and every $v \in N(s)$ has $P(v) = 1$ according to condition 2.

If there are multiple vertices w with $P(w) = 0$ in the local neighborhood of a vertex, the verifier rejects at that vertex.

Induction step: We show that under the induction hypothesis for a vertex v with $d(v, s) = k$ either $P(v) = d(v, s) = k$ or there is a vertex y such that $\mathcal{A}(y)$ rejects.

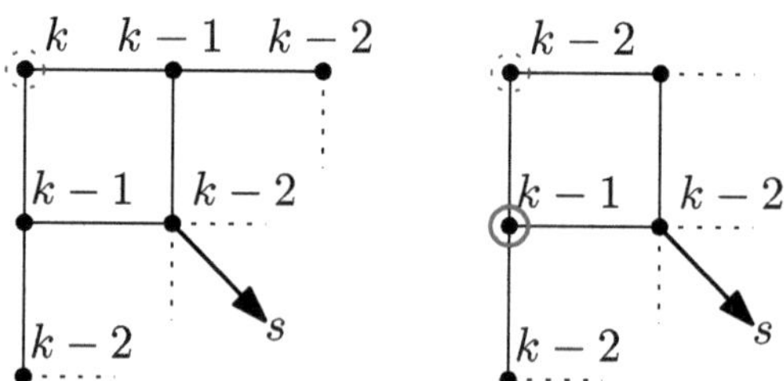

Fig. 6. Visualization of the case, where v has both coordinates different from s. The vertex in the dotted circle is v. The vertex in the red circle is the vertex, where the verifier rejects. (Color figure online)

There are two cases, which will be solved separately:

1. Assume that vertex v has both coordinates different from those of s. In this case v has two neighbors $y_1, y_2 \in N(v)$ such that $P(y_1) = P(y_2) = k-1$. The certificate $P(v)$ can be equal to k, in which case it is the correct distance, or $P(v) = k-2$. In all other cases, the vertices y_1, y_2 would reject due to condition 4.

   Now assume that $P(v) = k-2$. Since v differs in both coordinates, at least one of y_1 or y_2 must also differ in both coordinates. If not, they would be neighboring to s and they would reject due to condition 3 as $k-1 = 0$. Without loss of generality, let y_1 be the vertex that differs in both coordinates.

   The vertex y_1 has to have two neighbors at distance $k-2$ from s equal to $k-2$ and v would be a third neighbor with $P(v) = k-2$ and thus $\mathcal{A}(y_1)$ would reject due to condition 6.

   See Fig. 6 for a visualization of this case.

   Thus the only option is that $P(v) = k = d(v, s)$, which is the correct certificate.

2. Now assume that vertex v differs from s in only one coordinate in the grid. Let $y \in N(v)$ be the vertex with $d(y, s) = P(y) = k-1$.

   The certificate $P(v)$ can, again, be either k or $k-2$, otherwise $\mathcal{A}(y)$ would reject. If $P(v) = k$ the certificate is correct, so let us assume that $P(v) = k-2$ and vertex v is trying to deceive the verifier.

   Let v_N, v_E, v_S, v_W denote the neighbors of y, and let $v = v_N$ and $P(v_S) = k-2$.

   Let us emphasize that the vertices v_S, v_E, v_W must have a correct certificate $P(v_i) = d(v_i, s)$ for $i \in \{S, E, W\}$. For the vertex v_S, this holds by the induction hypothesis since $d(s, v_S) < k$, and v_E, v_W can have the certificate equal to either $k-2$ or k. However, if $P(v_E) = k-2$ or $P(v_W) = k-2$, there would be 3 neighbors of y with certificate $k-2$ and thus $\mathcal{A}(y)$ would reject. The only possibility is that v_S, v_E, v_W have the correct certificate.

   The vertices v and v_E have a common neighbor v_C. As $P(v) = k-2$ and $P(v_E) = k$, the only possible certificate is $P(v_C) = k-1$. But then v_E has three neighbors whose certificates are equal to $k-1$ and $\mathcal{A}(v_E)$ rejects.

   See Fig. 7 for a visualization of this case.

   Thus we showed that the only possibility is $P(v) = k$ which is the correct certificate.

And thus we have shown that if our proof labeling scheme accepts, the AMOS property holds.

Now we show that any yes-instance is always accepted. Assume that there is one selected vertex s and that for every v the certificate $P(v) = d(v, s)$. If there is no selected vertex, an arbitrary vertex is chosen instead.

Because $P(v) = d(v, s)$, the conditions in points 1, 2, and 4 cannot be true. Since there is at most one selected vertex, the condition in point 3 will also never be true. The condition in point 5 is also never true, because the certificate is a distance from a specific vertex. If there is a vertex with distance k, there needs to be a neighbor with distance $k-1$. Lastly, the condition in point 6 cannot be true, since in a grid it is not possible for three different neighbors to be closer to a given vertex.

We have thus shown both implications, and the theorem is proved.   □

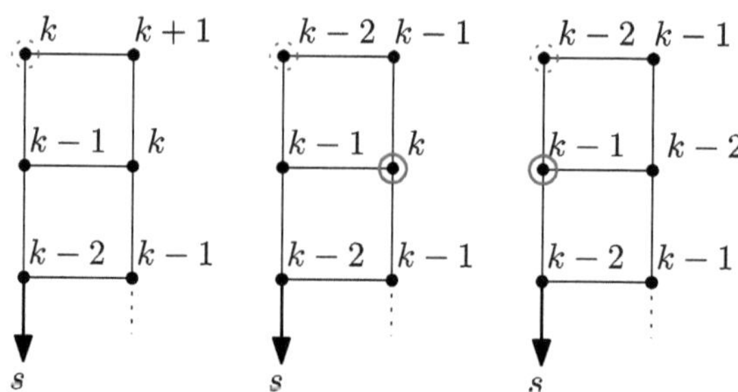

Fig. 7. Visualisation of the case, where v has one coordinate different from s. The vertex in the dotted circle is v. The vertex in the red circle is the vertex, where the verifier rejects. (Color figure online)

6   Sublogarithmic Upper Bounds in Everywhere-Dense Graphs

Up to this point, we have explored two aspects of the topology of the lower bound: the diameter and the presence of a hole. We now turn our attention to the density of the graph. For the Göös-Suomela technique to work, it is essential to be able to cut yes-instances into pieces and combine these pieces without too many vertices noticing the difference. If this cannot be done, then the counting argument fails. We prove that if the graph is dense everywhere, in the crude sense that the degree is relatively high for all vertices, then the lower bound cannot work, since we have a sublogarithmic upper bound.

Theorem 4. *In graphs where every node has degree* $\alpha \log^2 n$, *for a large enough constant* α, *AMOS can be certified with* $O(\log \log n)$ *bits with verification radius 2.*

Due to space limitations, we present only a sketch of the proof. The complete proof is given in the full version of the paper [12]. We now briefly outline the technique. For AMOS, we would like to give the identifier of the selected vertex (if it exists) to all vertices, but this would require $\Theta(\log n)$ bits. The idea is to cut this identifier into small pieces and distribute them among the vertices. Then a vertex uses one round of communication to gather all the pieces and recover the leader identifier, and one round to check that it has been given the same as its neighbors, and that if it is selected then this is its own identifier. Arguing that there exists a good distribution of small enough pieces can be done via the probabilistic method, in a similar way to [6,10].

7 Sublogarithmic Upper Bound with Small Identifiers

In this section, we prove the following theorem.

Theorem 5. *Let G be a graph with bounded diameter D. If there exists a vertex whose identifier is of constant size relative to the size of G, then AMOS can be verified with certificates of size $O(\log D)$.*

The idea of the proof is to choose the vertex with the smallest identifier as the root of a spanning tree, and then accumulate the number of selected vertices from the leaves towards the root.

For the complete proof, see [12].

Corollary 8. *If the identifiers are in $[1 + k, n + h]$ for some constant integers h and k, with $k \leq h$, then AMOS on a graph with a bounded diameter D can be done with certificates of size $O(\log D)$.*

The corollary follows directly from the theorem.

Acknowledgments. This work was supported by the Grant Agency of the Czech Technical University in Prague, grant No. SGS23/205/OHK3/3T/18, and by the ANR grant PREDICTIONS - ANR-23-CE48-0010. The authors thank Dušan Knop and Jan Matyáš Křišťan for discussions.

References

1. Bondy, J.A., Simonovits, M.: Cycles of even length in graphs. J. Comb. Theory Ser. B **16**(2), 97–105 (1974)
2. Bousquet, N., Feuilloley, L., Zeitoun, S.: Complexity landscape for local certification. In: Kowalski, D.R. (ed.) 39th International Symposium on Distributed Computing, DISC 2025, LIPIcs, vol. 356, pp. 18:1–18:21 (2025)
3. Censor-Hillel, K., Paz, A., Perry, M.: Approximate proof-labeling schemes. Theor. Comput. Sci. **811**, 112–124 (2020)
4. Chalopin, J., Chepoi, V., Kokkou, M.: Distance-based certification for leader election in meshed graphs and local recognition of their subclasses. CoRR, abs/2602.12894 (2026)
5. Chalopin, J., Kokkou, M.: Constant-size certificates for leader election in chordal graphs and related classes. CoRR, abs/2511.19208 (2025)
6. Cook, L., Kim, E.J., Masařík, T.: A tight meta-theorem for LOCAL certification of MSO2 properties within bounded treewidth graphs. In: Proceedings of the ACM Symposium on Principles of Distributed Computing, PODC 2025, pp. 110–120. ACM (2025)
7. Esperet, L., Zeitoun, S.: Reductions in local certification. In: Graph-Theoretic Concepts in Computer Science - 51st International Workshop, WG 2025 (2025). https://doi.org/10.1007/978-3-032-11835-6_14
8. Feuilloley, L.: Introduction to local certification. Discret. Math. Theor. Comput. Sci. **23**(3) (2021)
9. Feuilloley, L., Bousquet, N., Pierron, T.: What can be certified compactly? Compact local certification of MSO properties in tree-like graphs. In: PODC 2022: ACM Symposium on Principles of Distributed Computing, pp. 131–140. ACM (2022)

10. Feuilloley, L., Fraigniaud, P., Hirvonen, J., Paz, A., Perry, M.: Redundancy in distributed proofs. Distrib. Comput. **34**(2), 113–132 (2021)
11. Feuilloley, L., Hirvonen, J.: Local verification of global proofs. In: 32nd International Symposium on Distributed Computing, DISC 2018, vol. 121, pp. 25:1–25:17. Schloss Dagstuhl - Leibniz-Zentrum für Informatik (2018)
12. Feuilloley, L., Sedláček, J.E., Slávik, M.: Proving there is a leader without naming it. arXiv preprint arXiv:2511.15491 (2025)
13. Fomin, F.V., Fraigniaud, P., Golovach, P.A., Montealegre, P., Rapaport, I., Todinca, I.: Distributed model checking in graphs classes of bounded expansion. CoRR, abs/2411.14825 (2024)
14. Fomin, F.V., Fraigniaud, P., Golovach, P.A., Montealegre, P., Rapaport, I., Todinca, I.: Brief announcement: deciding FO formulas efficiently in congested networks. In: Proceedings of the ACM Symposium on Principles of Distributed Computing, PODC, vol. 2025, pp. 310–313 (2025)
15. Fomin, F.V., Fraigniaud, P., Montealegre, P: Distributed model checking on graphs of bounded TreeDepth. In: 38th International Symposium on Distributed Computing, DISC 2024, LIPIcs, vol. 319, pp. 25:1–25:20 (2024). https://doi.org/10.1007/s00453-025-01349-1
16. Fraigniaud, P., Korman, A., Peleg, D.: Towards a complexity theory for local distributed computing. J. ACM **60**(5), 35:1–35:26 (2013)
17. Fraigniaud, P., Mazoit, F., Montealegre, P., Rapaport, I., Todinca, I.: Distributed certification for classes of dense graphs. In: 37th International Symposium on Distributed Computing, DISC 2023, LIPIcs, vol. 281, pp. 20:1–20:17 (2023)
18. Fraigniaud, P., Montealegre, P., Rapaport, I., Todinca, I.: A meta-theorem for distributed certification. Algorithmica **86**(2), 585–612 (2024)
19. Göös, M., Suomela, J.: Locally checkable proofs in distributed computing. Theory Comput. **12**(1), 1–33 (2016)
20. Korman, A., Kutten, S.: Distributed verification of minimum spanning trees. Distrib. Comput. **20**(4), 253–266 (2007)
21. Korman, A., Kutten, S., Peleg, D.: Proof labeling schemes. Distrib. Comput. **22**(4), 215–233 (2010)
22. Kővári, P., T Sós, V., Turán, P.: On a problem of K. Zarankiewicz. In: Colloquium Mathematicum, vol. 3, pp. 50–57. Polska Akademia Nauk. Instytut Matematyczny PAN (1954)
23. Kreutzer, S.: Algorithmic meta-theorems. In: Esparza, J., Michaux, C., Steinhorn, C. (eds.) Finite and Algorithmic Model Theory, London Mathematical Society Lecture Note Series, vol. 379, pp. 177–270. Cambridge University Press (2011)
24. Lampis, M.: Algorithmic meta-theorems for restrictions of treewidth. Algorithmica **64**(1), 19–37 (2012)
25. Siebertz, S., Vigny, A.: Advances in algorithmic meta theorems (invited paper). In: 44th IARCS Annual Conference on Foundations of Software Technology and Theoretical Computer Science, FSTTCS 2024, LIPIcs, vol. 323, pp. 2:1–2:29 (2024)

Fast Distributed Computation of Compact Routing Schemes

Jinfeng Dou[1], Thorsten Götte[2](✉), Henning Hillebrandt[1],
Christian Scheideler[1], and Julian Werthmann[1]

[1] Paderborn University, Paderborn, Germany
`{jfdou,hhilleb,scheidel,jwerth}@mail.upb.de`
[2] University of Hamburg, Hamburg, Germany
`thorsten.goette@uni-hamburg.de`

Abstract. We consider the problem of computing compact routing tables for weighted, undirected graphs. Our main contribution is a unified distributed framework for constructing compact routing schemes for graphs that admit a small collection of short paths that nearly separate the graph. The framework is fully distributed and relies only on two generic primitives: single-source approximate distance computation and minor-aggregation. Both are efficiently implementable in CONGEST and the novel HYBRID model. In particular, they require $\tilde{O}(\mathrm{HD})$ rounds in the CONGEST model where HD is the graph's hop-diameter and $\tilde{O}(1)$ rounds in HYBRID.

Specifically, we apply our framework to four different important graph families. In all four cases, we assume that the graphs are weighted, undirected and have polynomially bounded edge weights.

1. Our first algorithm is designed for the HYBRID model and constructs a routing scheme for general graphs. With high probability, and for any $k > 4$, the scheme achieves stretch k^2 while using labels and tables of size $\tilde{O}(n^{1/k})$ and running in $\tilde{O}(n^{4/k})$ rounds.
2. The second algorithm handles universally $\tilde{O}(1)$-path separable graphs. A universally k-separable graph can recursively be separated into subgraphs with a constant fraction of the original size by removing k shortest path—independent of the weight function on the edges. For $\epsilon \leq 1$, we obtain a stretch of $1 + \epsilon$ with labels and tables of size of $\tilde{O}(\epsilon^{-2})$ in $\tilde{O}(\epsilon^{-4})$ rounds in HYBRID and $\tilde{O}(\epsilon^{-4} \cdot \mathrm{HD})$ rounds in CONGEST.
3. The third algorithm is devised for planar graphs. For any $\epsilon \leq 1$, we obtain a stretch of $1 + \epsilon$ with label and table size of $O(\epsilon^{-1} \log^7 n)$ in $\tilde{O}(\epsilon^{-3})$ rounds in HYBRID and $\tilde{O}(\epsilon^{-3} \cdot \mathrm{HD})$ rounds in CONGEST.
4. The final algorithm is for Unit Disk Graphs (UDGs) in the HYBRID model. For any $\epsilon \leq \frac{1}{2}$, we obtain a stretch of $1 + \epsilon$ with label and table size of $\tilde{O}(\epsilon^{-4})$ in $\tilde{O}(\epsilon^{-5})$ rounds in HYBRID.

Keywords: Compact Routing · Planar Graphs · Unit Disk Graph · HYBRID model

C. Georgiou (Ed.): SIROCCO 2026, LNCS 16488, pp. 351–370, 2026.
https://doi.org/10.1007/978-3-032-26465-7_19

1   Introduction

Routing schemes are distributed algorithms that determine how data packets are forwarded through a network. Designing efficient routing schemes is a fundamental task in distributed computing, since the quality of the routing infrastructure directly affects the performance and reliability of higher-level protocols. As a result, the distributed construction of efficient routing schemes has been studied extensively in both theory and practice (e.g., [7, 12, 27]).

A routing scheme assigns to each node v a routing table $\mathcal{R}_v$ and to each destination t a short label $\mathcal{L}_t$. The label is attached to messages intended for t and provides intermediate nodes with just enough information to determine the next hop. Formally, when a node v receives a message carrying the label $\mathcal{L}_t$, it consults $\mathcal{R}_v$ to select a neighbor $w \in N(v)$. Repeating this local forwarding rule from a source s produces a routing path to t.

A straightforward approach is to let every node store the complete network topology and compute routes locally. This would clearly yield shortest paths and would not even require labels. However, the resulting routing tables are far too large for practical use and prohibitively expensive to construct in distributed models. Indeed, without labels all routing schemes more or less degenerate to this case: There are constant-degree networks in which some nodes must receive $\Omega(n)$ messages to compute a label-free routing scheme [27]. This motivates the study of *compact routing schemes*, where routing tables and labels are required to be strictly sublinear in the number of nodes n. The performance of a routing scheme is quantified by its *stretch*, the ratio between the length $d_{P_{st}}(s,t)$ of the route computed for a pair (s,t) and the true shortest-path distance $d_G(s,t)$. A scheme has stretch α if $d_{P_{st}}(s,t) \leq \alpha \cdot d_G(s,t)$ for all $s,t \in V$. The central objective is therefore to design routing schemes that simultaneously achieve low stretch, small tables, and short labels, while remaining feasible to compute efficiently in the distributed setting.

We consider the construction of routing schemes in CONGEST and the novel HYBRID model [2]. In both models, there exist graphs that require $\Omega(n^c)$ rounds to compute a routing scheme for some $c \in \Theta(1)$ (cf. [26, 27]). We therefore ask whether constant-stretch compact routing schemes can be constructed efficiently for non-trivial graph classes beyond these worst-cases. In particular, we seek schemes that can be built in $\tilde{O}(\mathrm{HD})$ rounds in the CONGEST model (where HD is the graph's hop-diameter) and $\tilde{O}(1)$ rounds in the HYBRID model. We answer this question in the affirmative and present a general framework for constructing such routing schemes. The framework is based on a very weak form of vertex separators that can be computed efficiently in a distributed manner. We apply our framework to several graph classes, including planar graphs, unit disk graphs, and universally k-path separable graphs. The latter class includes K_r-free graphs and graphs of bounded tree-width. We obtain schemes with stretch $1 + \epsilon$ and tables of size $\tilde{O}(\mathrm{poly}(\epsilon^{-1}))$. Note that our focus is on theoretical feasibility rather than optimizing the dependency on ϵ^{-1} or logarithmic factors.

In the remainder of this section, we present the necessary preliminaries and give an overview of our results. In Sect. 2, we describe our framework for constructing routing schemes in a model-agnostic fashion. Then, in Sect. 3, we apply the framework to construct our routing schemes. Due to space constraints, many proofs and additional material are deferred to [11].

1.1 Preliminaries and Notations

We assume familiarity with basic notions from graph theory and algorithmic geometry. In this work, we only consider *weighted, undirected* graphs $G = (V, E, \ell)$ where $\ell : E \to \mathbb{R}_{\geq 0}$ assigns a *length/weight* to each edge. We assume that all edge weights are polynomial in n so they can be encoded in $O(\log n)$ bits. For completeness, we include the largest weight W in the relevant lemmas. Throughout this work, we denote the distance between a node $v \in V$ and a set $S \subseteq V$ as $d(v, S)$. This distance is defined as the (weighted) length of the shortest path between v and the node $w \in S$ closest to v. We use $d_H(v, S)$ if the distance is with respect to a subgraph $H \subseteq G$. Further, for a subgraph $H \subseteq G$, a subset $S \subseteq H$, and a distance δ, we define $B_H(S, \delta) = \{v \in V \mid d_H(v, S) \leq \delta\}$ to be the *ball* that contains all nodes within distance δ of any node of S in H. For $H = G$ we omit the subscript. $\tilde{O}(\cdot)$ hides polylogarithmic factors. Finally, we say that an event occurs with high probability (w.h.p.) if it occurs with probability at least $1 - n^{-c}$ for a constant $c \geq 1$.

1.2 Models of Computation

We consider algorithms that can be implemented in multiple models of distributed computation. Our primary setting is the classical CONGEST model [33], where the network is represented by a static graph $G = (V, E)$, i.e., the communication graph is equal to the input graph. Each node has a unique identifier of $O(\log n)$ bits taken from the interval $[1, \ldots, n^c]$ for a constant $c \in \Theta(1)$. The computation proceeds in synchronous rounds: in each round, nodes first receive all messages sent to them in the previous round, perform arbitrary local computation, and may then send a distinct $O(\log n)$-bit message to each of their neighbors in G. We also make use of the recently introduced HYBRID model (cf. [2]). Just as in CONGEST, time is synchronous, and nodes may send $O(\log n)$-bit messages to all of their neighbors in a graph G (this is called the *local* mode). In addition, each node can contact up to $O(\log n)$ arbitrary nodes per round, provided that no node receives more than $O(\log n)$ such messages (this is called the *global* mode). If a node receives more than $O(\log n)$ messages, an arbitrary subset is dropped. Whereas the CONGEST model captures traditional wired networks, the HYBRID model is motivated by systems such as sensor networks in which devices combine short-range communication with occasional long-range or cellular transmissions.

1.3 Related Work

In the CONGEST model, there is a plethora of results for constructing routing schemes in general graphs [12, 13, 27–29]. In particular, Elkin and Neiman [13] give a solution with stretch $O(k)$, routing tables of size $\tilde{O}(n^{1/k})$, routing labels of size $\tilde{O}(k)$ that can be computed in $\widetilde{O}(\text{HD} + n^{1/2+1/k}) \cdot n^{o(1)}$ rounds, which is close to optimal in all parameters. For more restricted graphs, Izumi, Kitamura, Naruse, and Schwartzman [22] introduce a fully polynomial-time distributed tree decomposition algorithm. It yields a decomposition of width $O(\tau^2 \log n)$ in $\tilde{O}(\tau^2 \text{HD} + \tau^3)$ rounds, where τ is the graph's treewidth. Additionally, they present a novel concept of a stateful walk constraint, which naturally defines a set of feasible walks in the input graph based on their local properties. Further, for planar graphs, Li and Parter [30] present an exact routing scheme that can be computed in $\tilde{O}(\text{HD}^2)$ time with labels and tables of size $\tilde{O}(\text{HD})$.

In the HYBRID model, Kuhn and Schneider [26] proved that it takes $\tilde{O}(n^{1/3})$ rounds to compute exact routing schemes with labels of size $O(n^{2/3})$ on unweighted graphs in the HYBRID model and provide an algorithm that matches this. They also give polynomial time lower bounds of $\Omega(n^{1/f(k)})$ for routing schemes with stretch k on weighted graphs. Here, $f(k)$ is a polynomial function in k. They also provide algorithms with near-matching upper bounds for this setting. However, for both their lower and upper bounds, they assume unlimited communication along the local edges. Further, there are many works that considered routing on UDGs with up to h so-called radio holes ([7,15,24]). Most recently, Coy et al. [7] presented a scheme with stretch 36 and tables of size $O(h^2 \log n)$. The scheme can be computed in $O(h^2 + \log n)$ steps.

1.4 Our Contributions

We develop a framework for constructing compact routing schemes in both the CONGEST and the HYBRID model. The key insight is that whenever a graph class admits an efficiently computable (weak) form of a separator, the computation of the routing scheme reduces to building a few approximate shortest path trees. We apply this framework to four important graph families: general graphs, universally k-path separable graphs, planar graphs, and unit disk graphs (UDGs). Theorem statements for each class are given below.

We begin with a general result for the HYBRID model:

Theorem 1 (Arbitrary Undirected Graphs). *Let $G = (V, E, \ell)$ be a weighted graph with poly-bounded positive edge weights. Then, w.h.p., for any $k > 4$, a routing scheme of stretch $O(k^2)$ with labels and tables of size $O(n^{1/k} \log^2 n)$ can be constructed in $\tilde{O}(n^{4/k})$ rounds in the HYBRID model.*

Our construction nearly matches the lower bound of [26], which states that routing schemes with stretch k require $O(n^{1/f(k)})$ rounds in a different variant of the HYBRID model. They assume that an unlimited number of bits can be sent per local edge, whereas in our setting, only $O(\log n)$ bits can be sent per edge per round. Further, note that, for general graphs, the best we can hope for is a stretch of $2k - 1$ with routing tables of size $\tilde{O}(n^{1/k})$ due to Erdös' girth conjecture [36] and we are not too far away from that. On the negative side, the runtime is sublinear only for $k > 4$, which leaves plenty of room for improvement in this regime.

A natural next step is to consider graph classes that possess stronger separator structure. One such class is the family of *universally k-path separable graphs*, introduced by Abraham and Gavoille [1]. Informally, these are graphs that, under any assignment of positive edge weights, admit a separator obtained by recursively deleting at most k shortest paths. Surprisingly, this property captures many important topological families, including planar graphs, bounded-treewidth graphs, and, more generally, all graphs excluding a fixed clique minor K_r [1,8]. A formal definition is given in Definition 5 in Sect. 3.

Theorem 2 (Universally k-Path Separable Graphs). *Let $G = (V, E, \ell)$ be a weighted, universally $\tilde{O}(1)$-path separable graph with poly-bounded positive edge weights. Then, w.h.p., for any $\epsilon \leq 1$, a routing scheme of stretch $1 + \epsilon$ with labels and tables of size $\tilde{O}(\epsilon^{-2})$ can be computed in $\tilde{O}(\epsilon^{-4})$ rounds in HYBRID and in $\tilde{O}(\epsilon^{-4} \cdot \mathrm{HD})$ rounds in CONGEST.*

Our guarantees are comparable to the sequential scheme of Abraham and Gavoille [1], though with additional polylogarithmic factors and a (much) larger dependence on ϵ^{-1}. On the flip side, our approach avoids the expensive $n^{O(r)}$-time embedding used in [1] for K_r-minor-free graphs and yields efficient fully distributed constructions. To the best of our knowledge, this is the first distributed construction with stretch $1 + \epsilon$ for this vast and essential class.

If we have a slightly better understanding of the graph class, we can compute even better separators and obtain smaller tables and labels. For planar graphs, it holds:

Theorem 3 (Planar Graphs). *Let $G = (V, E, \ell)$ be a weighted planar graph with poly-bounded positive edge weights. Then, w.h.p., for any $\epsilon \leq 1$, a routing scheme of stretch $1 + \epsilon$ and size $O(\epsilon^{-1} \log^7 n)$ can be computed in $\tilde{O}(\epsilon^{-3})$ rounds in HYBRID and $\tilde{O}(\epsilon^{-3} \cdot \mathrm{HD})$ rounds in CONGEST.*

Here, we save a factor of ϵ^{-1} in the table/label size compared to Theorem 2. Compared to the exact routing scheme of Li and Parter [30] that takes $\tilde{O}(\mathrm{HD}^2)$ time in CONGEST, w.h.p, and creates tables of size $\tilde{O}(\mathrm{HD})$, we have two benefits: Our routing achieves smaller tables and significantly faster distributed construction for graphs with large hop diameter. On the flip side, we only achieve a $(1 + \epsilon)$-stretch instead of exact shortest paths.

Theorem 4 (Unit Disk Graphs). *Let $G = (V, E, \ell)$ be a unit disk graph. Then, w.h.p., for any $\epsilon \leq 1/2$, a routing scheme of stretch $1 + \epsilon$ and size $\tilde{O}(\epsilon^{-4})$ can be computed in $\tilde{O}(\epsilon^{-5})$ rounds in HYBRID.*

For UDGs, *all* previous distributed routing constructions either depended polynomially on n or required assumptions on the number of radio holes [6,7,21]. Our algorithm is the first to achieve a polylogarithmic dependence on n together with a $(1 + \epsilon)$-stretch for arbitrary $\epsilon \in (0, \frac{1}{2}]$. Despite the high dependencies on ϵ^{-1} and $\log n$, this proves that (in principle) it is possible to efficiently compute routing schemes for UDGs in a distributed manner *completely independent* of the number of radio holes.

1.5 Algorithmic Tools

Rather than relying on model-specific tricks, our algorithms reduce to $\tilde{O}(1)$ invocations of a $(1 + \epsilon)$-approximate shortest-path routine combined with simple aggregations on suitable subsets of the graph. In this section, we will clarify what these operations do and how efficiently they can be implemented in CONGEST and HYBRID.

First, we formalize the class of approximate SETSSP algorithms. For our algorithms, we must be able to compute the shortest paths to a subset of nodes and to virtual nodes that may not be part of the original input graphs. We define this problem as follows: Let $G := (V, E)$ be a weighted graph and let $G' := (V', E', \ell)$ with $V' := V \cup \{s_1, s_2, \dots\}$ be the graph that results from adding $\tilde{O}(1)$ virtual nodes to G. Each virtual node can have an edge of polynomially bounded weight to every virtual and non-virtual node in G'. Finally, let $S \subseteq V'$ be an arbitrary subset of virtual and non-virtual nodes. Then, an algorithm that solves $(1 + \epsilon)$-approximate set-source shortest paths with virtual nodes computes the following: Each node $v \in V' \backslash S$ learns a predecessor $p_v \in N(v)$ on a path of length at most $(1 + \epsilon)d(v, S)$ to some node in S and marks the edge $\{v, p_v\}$. Together, all the marked edges imply an approximate shortest path tree T^1 rooted in set S. Further, each node $v \in V'$ learns its distance $d_T(v, S) \leq (1 + \epsilon)d(v, S)$ to S in tree T, i.e., its exact distance to S in T and its $(1 + \epsilon)$-approximate distance to S in G'. Note that, if we can compute SETSSP on a graph G in τ time, we can also compute it on any set of disjoint subgraphs of G in τ time. To be precise, let $C_1, \dots, C_N$ with $C_i = (V_i, E_i)$ be a set of disjoint subgraphs of G and let $S_1, \dots, S_N$ with $S_i \subseteq V_i$ be subsets of nodes from each C_i. Suppose, we want to compute a SETSSP from each S_i in C_i. Then, we simply assign a prohibitively high length to each edge between two subgraphs $C_i \neq C_j$, which causes no (approximate) shortest path to ever contain an edge between C_i and C_j. Our second building block are so-called *minor aggregations*, which were first introduced in [16,17]. Consider a network $G = (V, E)$ and a (possibly adversarial) partition of vertices into disjoint subsets $V_1, V_2, \dots, V_N \subseteq V$, each of which induces a *connected* subgraph $G[V_i]$. We will call these subsets *minors*. Further, let each node $v \in V$ have private input x_v of length $\tilde{O}(1)$, i.e., a value that can be sent along an edge in $\tilde{O}(1)$ rounds. Finally, we are given an aggregation function $\bigotimes$ like SUM, MIN, AVG, ... A *minor aggregation* computes these functions in all minors $G[V_i]$. Note that the diameter of these minors might be (much) larger than the diameter of G.

Having established these two operations, the natural question is how long do they take to implement in CONGEST and HYBRID? For the CONGEST model, the answer is straightforward:

Lemma 1 (Complexity in CONGEST). *Let $G = (V, E, \ell)$ be a graph that excludes a fixed minor K_r, then SETSSP can be computed in $\tilde{O}(r\epsilon^{-2}\text{HD})$ rounds and minor aggregation in $\tilde{O}(r\text{HD})$ rounds of CONGEST.*

---

[1] Technically, for a set S with $|S| \geq 2$, the algorithm produces a forest with the individual trees rooted in the nodes S. However, we slightly abuse notation and refer to it as a tree.

The bound for SETSSP was shown in [34] and the bound for MINAGG was shown in [18]. For the HYBRID model, the situation is a bit more difficult. Instead of relying on algorithms made for HYBRID, we use the following generic result that lets us efficiently simulate a wide class of CRCW PRAM algorithms in the HYBRID model with small overhead.

Proposition 1. *Let I be the input to a CRCW PRAM algorithm $\mathcal{A}$ with work W and depth D. Suppose each node stores at most a items of I. Then, $\mathcal{A}$ can be simulated in the HYBRID model in $\tilde{O}(a + \frac{W}{n} + D)$ rounds, w.h.p. Further, any node stores at most $\tilde{O}(|O|/n)$ items of the output, w.h.p., where $|O|$ denotes the size of the output.*

We elaborate on the simulation and prove the proposition in the full version. That being said, Rozhoň (r) al. [34] showed that SETSSP can be solved with work $\tilde{O}(\epsilon^{-2}m)$ and depth $\tilde{O}(1)$ on a graph with m edges. Further, they showed that minor aggregation can be solved with linear work in $\tilde{O}(1)$ depth in the PRAM. We want to simulate the respective algorithms in HYBRID. Note that the input to these problems is the graph G itself and each node in G initially stores all its neighbors (which could be up to n). However, it is known that on a sparse graph with arboricity α, we can locally assign each edge to either of its endpoints, such that each node gets assigned at most $O(\alpha)$ edges using a Nash-Williams Decomposition. The assignment can be computed in $O(\log n)$ rounds of CONGEST [3]. Further, a graph with arboricity α has at most $O(\alpha \cdot n)$ edges. Therefore, we get the following result.

Lemma 2 (Complexity in HYBRID). *Let $G = (V, E, \ell)$ be a graph of arboricity α. Then, w.h.p., SETSSP can be computed in $\tilde{O}(\alpha\epsilon^{-2})$ rounds and minor aggregation in $\tilde{O}(\alpha)$ rounds of HYBRID.*

2 A Distributed Framework for Compact Routing Schemes Using Separators

In this section, we describe a framework for the construction of compact routing schemes that uses approximate SETSSP computations, minor aggregations, and an oracle that constructs a special type of separator that we introduce hereafter. Generally, a *weak $\mathcal{D}$-separator* S ensures that in the graph $G \setminus S$, all nodes have at most a constant fraction of nodes in distance $\mathcal{D}$. In particular, in contrast to a *classical* separator, $G \setminus S$ might still be connected. In this work, we use the following special type of weak separators introduced in [10], namely

Definition 1 (Weak κ-Path $(\mathcal{D}, \epsilon)$-Separator). *Let $G := (V, E, \ell)$ be a weighted graph, $\mathcal{D} > 1$ be an arbitrary distance parameter, and $\epsilon > 0$ be an approximation parameter. Then, we call the set $S := \bigcup_{i=1}^{\kappa} \mathcal{P}_i$ with $\mathcal{P}_i := \{P_i, B_i\}$ a weak κ-path separator, if it holds:*

1. Each P_i is path of length at most $4\mathcal{D}$.
2. Each $B_i \subseteq B_G(P_i, \epsilon\mathcal{D})$ is a set of nodes surrounding path P_i.

3. For all $v \in V \setminus S$ it holds $|B_{G \setminus S}(v, \mathcal{D})| \leq (7/8) \cdot n$ (or $V \setminus S$ is empty).

Note that this definition is generic enough to include, for example, separators of k shortest paths (where each set B_i only contains the path itself) and *traditional* vertex separators (where each path is a single node). In the following, we assume that we have access to an oracle constructing these separators:

Definition 2 (Separator Oracle $\mathcal{O}_\kappa^{\mathcal{D},\epsilon}$). *Let $G = (V, E, \ell)$ be a weighted graph and let $\mathcal{C}_1, \ldots, \mathcal{C}_N$ be a series of N disjoint connected subgraphs of G. Further, let $\mathcal{D} \geq 1$ and $\epsilon \leq 1$ be parameters. Then, an application of the oracle $\mathcal{O}_\kappa^{\mathcal{D},\epsilon}$ computes a κ-path weak $(\mathcal{D}, \epsilon)$-separator in every $\mathcal{C}_1, \ldots, \mathcal{C}_N$.*

Given this definition, the main result of this section is the following:

Theorem 5. *Consider a weighted graph $G := (V, E, \ell)$ with maximum edge weight W. Suppose that we have black-box access to an oracle $\mathcal{O}_\kappa^{\mathcal{D},\epsilon}$ for G. Then, a compact routing scheme with stretch $(1 + \epsilon)$ and labels/tables of size $O(\kappa \cdot \epsilon^{-1} \cdot \log^7(nW))$ can be computed with $O(\log^3 nW)$ applications of $\mathcal{O}_\kappa^{\mathcal{D}',\epsilon'}$ with $\epsilon' \in \Omega(\epsilon/\log^2 n)$ and $\mathcal{D}' \in O(Wn)$. Further, the algorithm requires $\tilde{O}(\kappa \cdot \epsilon^{-1} \log W)$ minor aggregations and $\tilde{O}(\kappa \cdot \epsilon^{-1} \log W)$ $(1 + \epsilon'')$-approximate SETSSP computations where $\epsilon'' \in \Omega(\epsilon/\log^3 n)$.*

On a high level, our framework works as follows: Just as in previous works (cf. [1,12,13,22,30,35]), the construction is divided into two phases, a so-called *covering phase* and a *computation phase*. In the *covering phase*, we compute a series of subforests of $G := (V, E, \ell)$ that approximate the distances between all pairs of nodes. By *approximate*, we mean that the distance between two nodes in a tree, i.e., the shortest path in the tree, is *close* to their actual shortest path in G. In the subsequent *computation phase*, we compute the actual labels and tables for the routing scheme based on these forests. Formally, we define the forests constructed in the covering phase as follows:

Definition 3 (Tree Cover). *Consider a weighted graph $G := (V, E, \ell)$ and parameter $\epsilon > 0$. A $(1 + \epsilon)$-approximate tree cover with overlap $t \geq 1$ for G is a series of t subforests $\mathfrak{T} := \{\mathcal{F}_1, \ldots, \mathcal{F}_t\}$ with $\mathcal{F}_i \subseteq G$, s.t., for each pair $v, w \in V$, there is a forest $\mathcal{F}_i \in \mathfrak{T}$ with a tree $T \in \mathcal{F}_i$ with root r where $\tilde{d}_T(v, w) := d_T(v, r) + d_T(r, w) \leq (1 + \epsilon) \cdot d_G(v, w)$.*

Note that each node $v \in V$ is in at most t trees, as it can be in at most one tree per forest. In the computation phase, we then construct an *exact* compact routing scheme for each individual tree in $\mathfrak{T}$ and combine its labels and tables to obtain the routing scheme for G. If we want to route a message from s and t in G, we simply pick the tree with the least distance between s and t and route the message according to this tree's routing scheme. Crucially, the size of the resulting labels and tables depends on the number of trees a node is contained in. Further, the stretch only depends on how well the trees approximate the actual distances since the routing in the tree does not add additional distortion.

The remainder of this section is structured as follows: In Sect. 2.1 we show how to construct a $(1 + \epsilon)$-approximate tree cover with low overlap $\tilde{O}(\epsilon^{-1} \cdot \kappa \cdot \log W)$

using approximate SETSSP computations, minor aggregations, and the oracle (Proposition 2). Then, in Sect. 2.2 we sketch how we obtain the routing scheme from a tree cover using only $\tilde{O}(\epsilon^{-1} \cdot \kappa \cdot \log W)$ minor aggregations (Proposition 3). Together, the two proposition then imply Theorem 5.

2.1   Covering Phase: Tree Covers From Weak Separators

In this section, we show the following technical result:

Proposition 2. *Consider a weighted graph $G := (V, E, \ell)$ with maximum edge weight W. Suppose that we have black-box access to an oracle $O_\kappa^{\mathcal{D},\epsilon}$ for G. Then, a $(1 + \epsilon)$-approximate tree cover with overlap $O(\kappa \cdot \epsilon^{-1} \cdot \log^4(nW))$ can be computed with $O(\log^3(nW))$ applications of $O_\kappa^{\mathcal{D}',\epsilon'}$ with $\epsilon' \in \Omega(\epsilon/\log^2 n)$ and $\mathcal{D}' \in O(\mathcal{D} \cdot \log^2 n)$. The algorithm requires $\tilde{O}(\kappa \cdot \epsilon^{-1} \log W)$ minor aggregations and $\tilde{O}(\kappa \cdot \epsilon^{-1} \log W)$ $(1 + \epsilon'')$-approximate SETSSP computations where $\epsilon'' \in \Omega(\epsilon/\log^3 n)$.*

On a high level, our algorithm is a distributed and parallel implementation of Thorup's algorithm for tree covers [35] that was also used by Abraham and Gavoille for k-path separable graphs [1]. However, our weak κ-path $(\mathcal{D}, \epsilon)$-separator differs from the (classical) k-path separator used in these algorithms. Not only does it contain more paths and additional nodes, but the paths are only approximate shortest paths, and when removed, they do not necessarily create disjoint connected subsets. For these reasons, simply replacing the separators does not work. Our construction is based on so-called $(\epsilon, \mathcal{D})$-additive tree covers, which are defined as follows.

Definition 4 ($((\epsilon, \mathcal{D})$-additive Tree Cover)). *Let $\mathcal{D}, \epsilon \geq 0$ be parameters. An $(\epsilon, \mathcal{D})$-additive tree cover with overlap $t \geq 1$ for a graph G is a series of rooted trees $\mathcal{T}(\epsilon, \mathcal{D}) := (T_1, T_2, \dots)$, s.t. it holds:*

1. *Each node $v \in V$ is in at most t trees.*
2. *For each pair $v, w \in V$ with $d(v, w) < 2\mathcal{D}$, there is a tree $T \in \mathcal{T}$ with $d_T(v, w) \leq (1 + \epsilon) \cdot d_G(v, w) + \epsilon\mathcal{D}$.*

In the following, we will show that we can compute a polylogarithmic-size $(\epsilon, \mathcal{D})$-additive tree cover for any distance $\mathcal{D}$ and error parameter ϵ. We show the following lemma:

Lemma 3. *Consider a weighted graph $G := (V, E, \ell)$. Suppose that we have black-box access to an oracle $O_\kappa^{\mathcal{D},\epsilon}$ for G. Then, an $(\epsilon, \mathcal{D})$-additive tree cover with overlap $O(\kappa \cdot \epsilon^{-1} \cdot \log^4 n)$ can be computed with $O(\log^2 n)$ applications of $O_\kappa^{\mathcal{D}',\epsilon'}$ with $\epsilon' \in \Omega(\epsilon/\log^2 n)$ and $\mathcal{D}' \in O(\mathcal{D} \cdot \log^2 n)$. The algorithm requires $\tilde{O}(\kappa \cdot \epsilon^{-1})$ minor aggregations and $\tilde{O}(\kappa \cdot \epsilon^{-1})$ $(1 + \epsilon'')$-approximate SETSSP computations where $\epsilon'' \in \Omega(\epsilon/\log^3 n)$.*

Given an algorithm that computes these covers for all possible values of $\mathcal{D}$, there is a straightforward algorithm to create a proper tree cover. The high-level idea behind the construction is to consider the distance scales $\mathcal{D}_i := 2^i$ for

$i \in [1, \lceil \log(nW) \rceil]$ separately. For each of these scales, we compute a separate tree cover that approximates the distance between all pairs of nodes in the distance at most $2\mathcal{D}_i$. The resulting collection of these $O(\log(nW))$ tree covers $\mathfrak{T} := \{\mathcal{T}(\epsilon, 1), \ldots, \mathcal{T}(\epsilon, nW)\}$ is the desired *tree cover*. It is easy to see that for each pair of nodes, such a $\mathfrak{T}$ contains a tree that approximates the distance between them. Thus, together with Lemma 3, this approach produces a tree cover with overlap $O(\epsilon^{-1}\kappa \log^5(nW))$ and proves Proposition 2. For the details, we refer to the full version.

In the remainder of this section, we present the algorithm behind Lemma 3. In addition to the weak path separators, we will also need a generic clustering algorithm to resize the graphs, namely:

Theorem 6 (Pseudo-Padded Decomposition(cf. [9, 10])). *Let $\mathcal{D} > 0$ be a distance parameter, ϵ be an error parameter, and $G := (V, E, \ell)$ be a (possibly weighted) undirected graph. Then, for $\epsilon \in o(1/\log n)$ there is an algorithm that computes a series of connected clusters $\mathcal{K} = K_1, \ldots, K_N$ with strong diameter $4(1 + \epsilon)\mathcal{D}$ where for all nodes $v \in V$ and all $\epsilon \leq \gamma \leq \frac{1}{32}$, it holds $\mathbf{Pr}[B(v, \gamma\mathcal{D}) \subset K(v)] \geq e^{-\Theta((\gamma+\epsilon)\log n)} - O(1/n^c)$. Here, $K(v)$ denotes the cluster that contains v. The algorithm can be implemented with one $(1 + \epsilon)$-approximate SetSSP computation and $\tilde{O}(1)$ minor aggregations.*

Now, we can start with the construction: Recall that the tree cover is parameterized with a distance bound $\mathcal{D} \in [1, nW]$ and a parameter $\epsilon > 0$ that trades the number of trees with the multiplicative and additive distortion. For our algorithm, we need some *helper variables* that are based on these parameters. Note that the values for the variables are chosen with hindsight such that they can be used more easily in the analysis. We do not claim that our specific choices are optimal; they are chosen for convenience. They can likely be optimized within constant and probably even logarithmic factors. First, we define the *relaxed* distance parameter $\mathcal{D}' := 6400 \cdot \mathcal{D} \cdot \log^2(n)$ and the error parameter $\epsilon_{pd} := \frac{1}{16000 \log^2(n)}$. These will be input parameters for our pseudo-padded decomposition algorithm promised by Theorem 6 (This choice will ensure that a path of length $\mathcal{D}$ is not cut by the padded decomposition algorithm with probability $1 - O\left(\frac{1}{\log n}\right)$, so we can apply it $O(\log n)$ times). Further, we need the following three parameters: $\epsilon_p = \epsilon/12$, $\epsilon_t = \epsilon/12$, and $\epsilon_s = \frac{\epsilon_p}{6400 \log^2(n)}$. All these parameters will be used in different subroutines.

We can now describe the main loop of the algorithm. On a high level, our algorithm is a classical recursive divide-and-conquer algorithm that creates tree covers for subgraphs of decreasing size. For the *divide* step, we use a padded decomposition to create subgraphs of diameter $\mathcal{D}' \in O(\mathcal{D}\log^2 n)$. The *conquer* step works in five synchronized phases that compute and remove a weak $(\mathcal{D}', \epsilon_s)$-separator, which ensures that the size of each subgraph shrinks by a constant factor each step. In the following, we call a node, which was not yet part of a separator, an *uncharted* node. A single recursive *conquer* step works as follows:

(Step 1) Create Partitions: Let $C_1, C_2, \ldots$ be the connected subgraphs of uncharted nodes of arbitrary diameter (where initially, it holds $C_1 := G$). Compute a pseudo-padded decomposition with diameter $\mathcal{D}'$ and error parameter ϵ_{pd} in each subgraph using the algorithm from Theorem 6. The resulting partitions are connected subgraphs $P_1, P_2, \ldots$ with diameter at most $\mathcal{D}'$.

(Step 2) Create Weak Separators in All Partitions: In each partition P_i, we compute a separator using $\mathcal{O}_\kappa^{\mathcal{D}', \epsilon_s}$. As the distance parameter for the separator, we choose $\mathcal{D}'$, and for the approximation parameter, we pick ϵ_s. This results in a weak κ-path $(\mathcal{D}', \epsilon_s)$-separator that consists of κ paths of length at most $4\mathcal{D}'$ and nodes in distance at most $\epsilon_s \mathcal{D}' = \epsilon_p \mathcal{D} = O(\epsilon \mathcal{D})$ to these paths.

(Step 3) Create Portals on Separators: On each separator path $\mathcal{P}_{i_j}$ computed in the previous step, mark a set of nodes, s.t., each $v \in \mathcal{P}_{i_j}$ has a marked node $p \in \mathcal{P}_{i_j}$ in distance at most $\epsilon_p \cdot \mathcal{D}$. We refer to the marked nodes as portals. As the length of each path is $4\mathcal{D}' \in O(\mathcal{D} \cdot \log^2 n)$, there are at most $O(\epsilon_p^{-1} \cdot \log^2 n)$ portals. This sums up to $O(\kappa \cdot \epsilon_p^{-1} \cdot \log^2 n)$ portals for all paths.

(Step 4) Grow Trees from Portals: Compute the actual trees of the tree cover by performing a $(1 + \epsilon_t)$-approximate SETSSP from each portal within their respective partition. Given our bound on the portals, there are $O(\kappa \cdot \epsilon_p^{-1} \cdot \log^2 n)$ approximate SETSSP computations.

(Step 5) Prepare Next Recursion: Every node on the separator removes itself and its incident edges from the graph. These nodes will not partake in future iterations. All remaining uncharted nodes compute their respective connected component for the next recursion.

As we removed weak $\mathcal{D}'$-separators in each connected subgraph, each node has at most $(7/8) \cdot n$ other nodes in distance $\mathcal{D}'$ in the resulting partitions. We repeat this process until all uncharted subgraphs are empty. As the size of the uncharted components shrinks by a factor of $7/8$ in each step, the process can be stopped after $8 \log n$ recursions. The detailed proof is provided in the full version.

2.2   Computing Phase: Compact Routing Schemes Using Tree Covers

Given a valid tree cover, we can show the following technical result:

Proposition 3. *Let $G := (V, E, \ell)$ be weighted graphs with edge weights bounded by W. Suppose that we have a $(1 + \epsilon)$-approximate tree cover $\mathfrak{T} := \{\mathcal{F}_1, \ldots, \mathcal{F}_t\}$*

of G with overlap t. Then, we can compute a routing scheme with stretch $(1+\epsilon)$ and routing labels and tables of size $O\left(t \cdot \log^2 n\right)$ in $\tilde{O}(t)$ minor aggregations.

On a high level, our construction mirrors the approach of Elkin and Neiman [14], which in turn was influenced by the seminal paper of Thorup and Zwick [36]. For this, each node in a (rooted) tree needs to learn its DFS labels, i.e., the first and last visit of a DFS started at the root. Further, it needs to count the number of its descendants in the tree and share this number with its parent. The parent declares the child with most descendants to be its *heavy child*. Given this information, the label of a node v then consists of its entry and exit label and all the identifiers of all non-heavy children from the root to v. The DFS labels allow us to route *upward* in the tree until we find the subtree that contains the target, and the identifier of the non-heavy children allow us to route *down* to the target. The former works by checking if the target's entry label is between the current node's entry and exit labels. The latter works by moving to the current node's heavy child by default unless one of its non-heavy children's identifiers is in the target label. As there can be at most $O(\log n)$ non-heavy children with identifiers of size $O(\log n)$ and DFS labels require $O(\log n)$ bits, the label size for a single tree is $O(\log^2 n)$. Summing up all labels for all trees yields the desired result. We will use some techniques developed by Ghaffari and Zuzic for computations in trees [19] to compute the schemes. More precisely, we use them to show that all of the operations sketched above can be implemented with $\tilde{O}(1)$ minor aggregations for each forest of the tree cover. Due to space constraints, the full description and analysis are deferred to the full version.

3   Our Routing Schemes

Given the framework introduced in the previous section, we explain how to build our routing schemes for various graph classes and prove Theorems 1, 2, 3, and 4.

3.1   Undirected Graphs (Proof of Theorem 1)

Given the machinery introduced in the previous section, the problem of constructing a compact routing scheme can be reduced to finding a tree cover. For general graphs with polynomially bounded edge weights, tree covers can be constructed by repeatedly constructing pseudo-padded decompositions from Theorem 6. Using it as a black box, we show the following general lemma:

Lemma 4. *Let $G = (V, E, \ell)$ be a graph with poly-bounded edge weights. For $k > 4$ we can construct a $O(k^2)$-approximate tree cover with overlap $O\left(n^{1/k} \log n\right)$ within $\tilde{O}\left(n^{4/k}\right)$ time in HYBRID, w.h.p.*

The algorithm works in two steps. First, we create a sparse k-spanner of G of arboricity $O(n^{1/k})$ using the $O(k)$-round CONGEST algorithm of [4]. This allows for efficient SetSSP computations. Then, we construct $O(n^{1/k})$ pseudo-padded decompositions, such that, w.h.p., for any two nodes in distance kD, there is a cluster in these partitions that contains both. The spanning trees of the clusters then form a tree cover. Using this tree cover in the construction from Proposition 3, we obtain the routing scheme in $\tilde{O}(n^{4/k})$ additional minor aggregations in HYBRID, w.h.p. This results in a runtime of $\tilde{O}(n^{4/k})$, w.h.p. This proves Theorem 1.

3.2   Universally k-Path Separable Graphs (Proof of Theorem 2)

We now consider the vast class of universally k-path separable graphs. Diot and Gavoille [8] formalize this graph class as follows:

Definition 5 (Universally k-Path Separable Graphs [1,8]). *A weighted graph $G := (V, E, \ell)$ with n vertices is k-path separable, if there exists a subset of vertices S, called a k-path separator, such that:*

1. $S := \mathcal{P}_0 \cup \mathcal{P}_1 \cup \mathcal{P}_2 \cup \ldots$, *where each* $\mathcal{P}_i := \{P_{i_1}, P_{i_2}, \ldots\}$ *is a set of shortest paths in* $G \setminus \bigcup_{j<i} \mathcal{P}_j$.
2. *The total number of paths in S is at most k, i.e.,* $\sum_{\mathcal{P}_i \in S} |\mathcal{P}_i| \leq k$.
3. *Each connected component in $G \setminus S$ contains at most $\frac{n}{2}$ nodes.*
4. *Either $G \setminus S$ is empty or k-path separable.*

If G is k-path separable for any weight function, we call G universally k-path separable.

We want to apply our separator construction framework from Theorem 5 to prove the theorem. This framework requires an oracle $\mathcal{O}_\kappa^{\mathcal{D},\epsilon}$ that lets us efficiently compute separators for any partition of G. To show that such an oracle exists, we exploit the following technical result from [10]:

Theorem 7 (Thm. 14 in [10]). *Consider a weighted k-path separable graph $G := (V, E, \ell)$ of weighted diameter $\leq \mathcal{D}$. For $\epsilon \geq 0$, there is an algorithm constructing a weak $O(\epsilon^{-1} \cdot k \cdot \log n)$-path $(\mathcal{D}, \epsilon)$-separator, w.h.p. It uses $\tilde{O}(\epsilon^{-1} \cdot k \cdot \log n)$ minor aggregations and $O(\epsilon^{-1} \cdot k \cdot \log n)$ 2-approximate SETSSP computations.*

Recall that every subgraph of a k-path separable graph is also k-path separable, so the algorithm can compute a separator on any partitioning $\mathcal{C}_1, \ldots, \mathcal{C}_N$. Thus, there is an oracle $\mathcal{O}_\kappa^{\mathcal{D},\epsilon}$ with $\kappa \in O(\epsilon^{-1} \cdot k \cdot \log n)$. Plugging this into Theorem 5 gives us a $(1+\epsilon)$-approximate routing scheme with tables/labels of size $O(k \cdot \epsilon^{-2} \cdot \log^8 n)$. The required number of minor aggregations and SETSSP computations to construct the separator is $\tilde{O}(k \cdot \epsilon^{-1})$. Finally, recall that $(1 + \epsilon)$-approximate SETSSP computations and minor aggregations, w.h.p., require $\tilde{O}\left(k\epsilon^{-2}\right)$ time in HYBRID and $\tilde{O}\left(k \cdot \epsilon^{-2} \cdot \text{HD}\right)$ time in CONGEST as the graphs exclude K_{2k} [8]. This yields the time complexities from Theorem 2.

3.3 Planar Graphs (Proof of Theorem 3)

Recall that planar graphs are graphs that can be drawn onto plane without two edges crossing. The construction for planar graphs follows our same basic scheme as before. However, we use a different oracle to construct the separators. In contrast to our previous weak separator construction, this is a *classical* vertex separator whose removal leaves connected components of a constant fraction of the original size. Notably, for the construction of these separators, we will *not* (only) use the minor aggregation framework and instead present bespoke algorithms for CONGEST and HYBRID that use additional techniques. That being said, we show the following technical result.

Theorem 8. *Consider a weighted planar graph $G := (V, E, \ell)$ and a collection of N node-disjoint subgraphs $\mathcal{C}_1, \ldots, \mathcal{C}_N \subset G$ with $C_i = (V_i, E_i)$. Then, there is an algorithm that constructs 4-path separators $S_1, \ldots, S_N$ of $4\,(1 + \epsilon)$ approximate shortest paths in all $\mathcal{C}_1, \ldots, \mathcal{C}_N$. Each connected component in $C_i \setminus S_i$ consists of at most $(3/4) \cdot |V_i|$ nodes. The algorithm can, w.h.p., be implemented in $\tilde{O}(\epsilon^{-2} \cdot \mathrm{HD})$ time in* CONGEST *and $\tilde{O}(\epsilon^{-2})$ time in* HYBRID.

Using this theorem, we can construct a 4-path separator in both HYBRID and CONGEST in arbitrary decompositions of a planar graph G. The algorithm is based on [30] but optimized for the use in disjoint subgraphs which required some extensions. We defer the full description and the proof to the full version. Alternatively, the deterministic separator construction by Jauregui, Montealegre, and Rapaport [23] (developed in parallel with our work) can also be used. Asymptotically, their algorithm has the same runtime as ours. Thus, using either separator algorithm as an oracle $\mathcal{O}_\kappa^{\mathcal{D},\epsilon}$ in the construction gives us labels and tables of size $O(\epsilon^{-1} \log^5(nW))$. Recall that the construction of the separators takes $\tilde{O}(1)$ time in HYBRID and $\tilde{O}(\mathrm{HD})$ time in CONGEST. The remaining operations are $O(\epsilon^{-1})$ approximate SETSSP computations and minor aggregations. Thus, the total complexity is $\tilde{O}(\epsilon^{-3})$ in HYBRID and $\tilde{O}(\epsilon^{-3} \cdot \mathrm{HD})$ in CONGEST, w.h.p. This proves Theorem 3.

3.4 Unit Disk Graphs (Proof of Theorem 4)

Finally, we consider unit disk graph (UDGs). Recall that a UDG is a graph $G = (V, E)$ for which there exists a mapping of vertices to points in the Euclidean plane $\mathbb{R}^2$ such that two vertices are adjacent if and only if the Euclidean distance between their points is at most 1. For our algorithm, we assume that initially all nodes $v \in V$ know their coordinates $(x_v, y_v) \in \mathbb{R}^2$ in the plane. To apply our framework, we must show how to compute suitable $(\mathcal{D}, \epsilon)$-separators and approximate shortest paths in the HYBRID model.

We begin by computing the separators. The construction splits into two diameter regimes. When the weighted diameter of a component $\mathcal{C}_i$ is *smaller* than ϵ^{-1}, a simple geometric construction suffices.

Lemma 5. *Let $\mathcal{C}$ be a connected subgraph of a UDG G of weighted diameter $\mathcal{D}$. Then we can construct a weak $O((\mathcal{D}/\epsilon)^2)$-path $(\mathcal{D}, \epsilon)$-separator for $\mathcal{C}$ in $O(\log n)$ rounds in the CONGEST model (using only edges of $\mathcal{C}$).*

Proof. For the separator, we first compute an MIS $\mathcal{N}_i \subseteq V_i$ in the subgraph $\mathcal{C}_i^{(\epsilon)}$ induced by all edges of length at most ϵ. As $\mathcal{C}_i^{(\epsilon)}$ is a proper subgraph of $\mathcal{C}_i$, we can run any CONGEST algorithm on $\mathcal{C}_i^{(\epsilon)}$. Thus, an MIS can be computed in $O(\log n)$ CONGEST rounds (e.g., using Luby's algorithm [32]). We will see that $S = \cup_{v \in \mathcal{N}_i}(v, B(v, \epsilon))$ is a weak $O((\mathcal{D}/\epsilon)^2)$-path $(\mathcal{D}, \epsilon)$-separator. To this end, we first argue why it is a separator. Note that every $u \in V_i$ is contained in (at least) one ball $B(v, \epsilon)$ with $v \in \mathcal{N}_i$. Otherwise, it could be added to $\mathcal{N}_i$. This is a contradiction as $\mathcal{N}_i$ is maximal. Thus, the balls $(B(v, \epsilon))_{v \in \mathcal{N}_i}$ contain all nodes in V_i. This proves that $C_i \setminus S_i$ is empty, and therefore S_i is a separator for C_i. Second, we must argue that $\mathcal{N}_i$ contains $O(\epsilon^{-2})$ nodes. Consider the disk $\mathfrak{D}_v$ of diameter ϵ around $v \in \mathcal{N}_i$. Note that two disks $\mathfrak{D}_v, \mathfrak{D}_w$ with $v, w \in \mathcal{N}_i$ are disjoint as otherwise the distance between v and w would be ϵ. The disk $\mathfrak{D}_i$, which covers C_i, has an area of at most $\pi \mathcal{D}_i^2$ and each disk $\mathfrak{D}_v$ around each $v \in \mathcal{N}_i$ covers an area of $\pi \epsilon^2$. Thus, $\mathfrak{D}_i$ can be covered by $O((\mathcal{D}_i/\epsilon)^2)$ such balls/disks. Thus, the nodes $\mathcal{N}_i$ and their ϵ-balls form a weak $O((\mathcal{D}/\epsilon)^2)$-path $(\mathcal{D}, \epsilon)$-separator as claimed.

When the diameter of a component $\mathcal{C}_i$ becomes *larger* than ϵ^{-1}, the separators created by the geometric approach from Lemma 5 would become too large. In this regime, we instead build separators via Delaunay triangulations of the point set and extend them to separators for the UDG. The algorithm consists of the following four steps:

> ***(Step 1) Delaunay Triangulation.*** Compute the Delaunay triangulation $DT(V_i)$ of the point set V_i by simulating the PRAM algorithm of Blelloch, Gu, Shun, and Sun [5].
>
> ***(Step 2) Approximate Shortest-Path Tree.*** Compute an approximate shortest-path tree T_i of $DT(V_i)$ rooted at an arbitrary node $s \in V_i$ using the PRAM algorithm of Rozhoň ⓡ al. [34].
>
> ***(Step 3) Separator in $DT(V_i)$.*** Compute a separator S_i^{DT} of $DT(V_i)$ by simulating the PRAM algorithm of Kao, Teng, and Toyama [25]. The algorithm outputs a separator composed of two tree paths $P_1 = (s, \ldots, v)$ and $P_2 = (s, \ldots, w)$ in T_i together with an edge $\{v, w\}$.
>
> ***(Step 4) Expansion to UDG Separator.*** Let $S_i^{UDG} := B(S_i^{DT}, 1)$, i.e., all nodes within distance 1 of the Delaunay separator.

Given this algorithm, we can show the following:

Lemma 6. *Consider a UDG $G := (V, E, \ell)$ and a collection of N node-disjoint subgraphs $\mathcal{C}_1, \ldots, \mathcal{C}_N \subset G$ with $\mathcal{C}_i = (V_i, E_i)$. Then, for each $\epsilon > 0$ and $\mathcal{D} \geq \epsilon^{-1}$, we can compute a weak $(\mathcal{D}, \epsilon)$-separator in each $\mathcal{C}_i$ in $\tilde{O}(1)$ time in HYBRID.*

Proof. We must show that S_i^{UDG} is a 2-path weak $(\mathcal{D}, \epsilon)$-separator for the UDG $\mathcal{C}_i$. We begin with structure. The Delaunay graph is a 2.5-spanner of the UDG [31], so each tree path P_1 and P_2 has length at most $(1 + \epsilon) \cdot 2.5\mathcal{D} \leq 4\mathcal{D}$ for sufficiently small ϵ. Moreover, for $\mathcal{D} \geq \epsilon^{-1}$ we have $B(P_1 \cup P_2, 1) \subseteq B(P_1 \cup P_2, \epsilon\mathcal{D})$, so the radius condition is satisfied.

Next, we argue why S_i^{UDG} is a separator. The cycle separator S_i^{DT} forms a Jordan curve in the plane that separates V_i into an interior and an exterior region, each containing at most $(2/3)|V_i|$ vertices. Hence any UDG edge $\{x, y\} \in E_i$ connecting a vertex inside the curve to one outside must geometrically cross at least one Delaunay edge in S_i^{DT}. To argue that S_i^{UDG} blocks all such crossings, we use the notion of *cross-dominating* edges coined by Harb, Huang, and Zheng [20]. An edge $\{v, w\}$ (interpreted as a line from v to w) is cross-dominating if every UDG edge $\{x, y\}$ crossing $\{v, w\}$ has an endpoint in distance at most 1 from either v or w; equivalently, $\{x, v\}$, $\{x, w\}$, $\{y, v\}$, or $\{y, w\}$ is an edge of the UDG. First, we show that all UDG edges are cross-dominating: if $\{x, y\}$ crosses $\{v, w\}$, then one endpoint, say x, is within distance $1/2$ of the crossing point, and the crossing point is within distance $1/2$ of either v or w, so by the triangle inequality x is adjacent to v or w. Moreover, Harb, Huang, and Zheng [20, Lemma 12] showed that all edges in the Delaunay triangulation of a UDG (including the edges that are not part of the UDG) are cross-dominating as well. Consequently, any UDG edge crossing the Delaunay separator S_i^{DT} has an endpoint within distance 1 of a vertex $v \in S_i^{DT}$. By construction, $S_i^{UDG} = B(S_i^{DT}, 1)$ contains *all* such vertices, i.e., every node that is close to some Delaunay edge in the separator is indeed included. Hence every path of $\mathcal{C}_i$ that uses an edge crossing the separator must contain a vertex of S_i^{UDG}, proving that S_i^{UDG} is indeed a separator.

For the runtime, we first consider the PRAM algorithm of Blelloch, Gu, Shun, and Sun that has $\tilde{O}(n)$ work and $\tilde{O}(1)$ depth. Since the input consists of the node's coordinates, each node holds exactly one input item. Thus, Step 1 can be simulated in $\tilde{O}(1)$ HYBRID rounds. The resulting Delaunay graph has at most $6|V_i|$ edges (because it is planar), so after Step 1 each node holds $O(\log n)$ edges w.h.p. As this graph is the input to the algorithms in Steps 2 and 3 (and therefore already evenly distributed), they can be simulated in $\tilde{O}(\epsilon^{-2})$ time and $\tilde{O}(1)$ time respectively. Finally, Step 4 requires only one round as the nodes we add are adjacent, which proves the runtime.

Thus, we obtain a $O(\epsilon^{-4})$-path separator in either case.

We conclude with the SETSSP computations on G. As stated before, we can efficiently compute SETSSP on graphs of low arboricity. Unfortunately, a UDG may have arboricity n when all nodes lie within distance 1 of each other. Instead, we first construct a sparse $1 + \epsilon$ spanner and compute the shortest paths on this spanner.

Lemma 7. *Let $G = (V, E)$ be a UDG. Then, we can construct a $(1 + \epsilon)$-spanner $G_\epsilon = (V, E_\epsilon)$ of arboricity $O(\epsilon^{-2})$ in $O(\log n)$ CONGEST rounds.*

Proof. Consider the graph $G^{(\epsilon)}$ that only contains edges of length at most ϵ. Then, compute an MIS $\mathcal{N}_\epsilon$ in $G^{(\epsilon)}$ using, e.g., Luby's algorithm, in $O(\log n)$ rounds. Next, build a *cluster* for each net node. Each node $v \in V \setminus \mathcal{N}_\epsilon$ then joins the cluster of its closest node in $\mathcal{N}_\epsilon$. To construct the spanner, each node $v \in V$ only keeps the edge to its cluster head and drops all other edges to nodes in the same cluster and among all edges connecting to nodes in other clusters, keeps only the shortest edge to each distinct cluster.

We must show that G_ϵ has arboricity $O(\epsilon^{-2})$, is connected, and has a stretch of $(1+\epsilon)$. Each node in G_ϵ keeps $O(\epsilon^{-2})$ edges, since it keeps at most one edge to each cluster. There can be at most $O(\epsilon^{-2})$ cluster heads within distance 1 as all cluster heads are at a distance of at least ϵ from each other. Thus, we can create an orientation where each node has $O(\epsilon^{-2})$ outgoing edges. This is equivalent to having an arboricity of $O(\epsilon^{-2})$. For each edge $\{v, w\} \in E$ that is not included in the spanner, the corresponding path in G_ϵ can be realized as follows: If v and w are in the same cluster, we simply go via the cluster head which causes a path length of 2ϵ as both nodes are in distance at most ϵ to the cluster head. If v and w are in different clusters, we can go from v to the closest node w' in w's cluster. Per construction, it holds $d(v, w') \leq d(v, w)$. Then, we go from w' to the cluster head and finally to w. Again, this detour has a length of at most 2ϵ. This shows that G_ϵ is connected, and that each path of length k with h hops in G corresponds to a path of length at most $k + 2\epsilon h$ in G_ϵ. In a UDG, for every shortest path of length k there is a path of length k with at most $h \leq 4k$ hops. This follows from the fact that any two consecutive edges of length less than $1/2$ can be shortcut. By the pigeonhole principle, there can be at most $2k$ edges of length $1/2$ in a path of length k. Thus, if each edge of length $\leq \frac{1}{2}$ is followed by an edge of length $> 1/2$, this gives $4k$ hops in total. Thus, it follows that the total stretch of G_ϵ is at most $(1 + 8\epsilon)$. Setting $\epsilon' = \epsilon/8$ gives the desired stretch of $(1 + \epsilon')$, proving the lemma.

On G_ϵ we can then simulate the algorithm of Rozhoň ⓡ al. in $\tilde{O}(\epsilon^{-4})$ rounds and, for an appropriate choice of ϵ, obtain approximate shortest paths on G. This proves Theorem 4.

4   Conclusion

We presented a distributed framework for constructing compact routing schemes that yields efficient distributed constructions for several important graph classes. Our results demonstrate that compact routing schemes with near-optimal stretch can, in principle, be computed efficiently in both the CONGEST and the HYBRID model for a wide range of graph families. However, the primary goal of this work is to establish theoretical feasibility rather than practical efficiency. In particular, the current constructions exhibit large dependencies on $\log n$ and on the approximation parameter ϵ^{-1} in both the label sizes and the running times. Reducing these dependencies—ideally to near-linear or polylogarithmic factors in ϵ^{-1} with significantly smaller logarithmic overhead—remains an important direction for future work and is necessary for these techniques to become practically relevant.

References

1. Abraham, I., Gavoille, C.: Object location using path separators. In: Ruppert, E., Malkhi, D. (eds.) Proceedings of the Twenty-Fifth Annual ACM Symposium on Principles of Distributed Computing, PODC 2006, Denver, CO, USA, 23–26 July 2006. pp. 188–197. ACM (2006). https://doi.org/10.1145/1146381.1146411
2. Augustine, J., Hinnenthal, K., Kuhn, F., Scheideler, C., Schneider, P.: Shortest paths in a hybrid network model. In: Proceedings of the 2020 ACM-SIAM Symposium on Discrete Algorithms, SODA 2020, Salt Lake City, UT, USA, 5–8 January 2020. pp. 1280–1299. SIAM (2020). https://doi.org/10.1137/1.9781611975994.78
3. Barenboim, L., Elkin, M.: Sublogarithmic distributed MIS algorithm for sparse graphs using Nash-Williams decomposition. Distrib. Comput. **22**(5–6), 363–379 (2010). https://doi.org/10.1007/s00446-009-0088-2
4. Baswana, S., Sen, S.: Simple algorithms for spanners in weighted graphs. In: Encyclopedia of Algorithms, pp. 1981–1986. Springer, New York (2016). https://doi.org/10.1007/978-1-4939-2864-4_10
5. Blelloch, G.E., Gu, Y., Shun, J., Sun, Y.: Parallelism in randomized incremental algorithms. J. ACM **67**(5), 27:1–27:27 (2020). https://doi.org/10.1145/3402819
6. Castenow, J., Kolb, C., Scheideler, C.: A bounding box overlay for competitive routing in hybrid communication networks. In: Mukherjee, N., Pemmaraju, S.V. (eds.) 21st International Conference on Distributed Computing and Networking, ICDCN 2020, Kolkata, India, 4–7 January 2020, pp. 14:1–14:10. ACM (2020). https://doi.org/10.1145/3369740.3369777
7. Coy, S., Czumaj, A., Scheideler, C., Schneider, P., Werthmann, J.: Routing schemes for hybrid communication networks. In: Rajsbaum, S., Balliu, A., Daymude, J.J., Olivetti, D. (eds.) Structural Information and Communication Complexity - 30th International Colloquium, SIROCCO 2023, Proceedings. LNCS, Alcalá de Henares, Spain, 6–9 June 2023, vol. 13892, pp. 317–338. Springer, Heidelberg (2023). https://doi.org/10.1007/978-3-031-32733-9_14
8. Diot, E., Gavoille, C.: Path separability of graphs. In: Lee, D.-T., Chen, D.Z., Ying, S. (eds.) FAW 2010. LNCS, vol. 6213, pp. 262–273. Springer, Heidelberg (2010). https://doi.org/10.1007/978-3-642-14553-7_25
9. Dou, J., Götte, T., Hillebrandt, H., Scheideler, C., Werthmann, J.: Brief announcement: Distributed construction of near-optimal compact routing schemes for planar graphs. In: Proceedings of the 2023 ACM Symposium on Principles of Distributed Computing, PODC 2023, Orlando, FL, USA, 19–23 June 2023, pp. 67–70. ACM (2023). https://doi.org/10.1145/3583668.3594561
10. Dou, J., Götte, T., Hillebrandt, H., Scheideler, C., Werthmann, J.: Distributed and parallel low-diameter decompositions for arbitrary and restricted graphs. In: 16th Innovations in Theoretical Computer Science Conference, ITCS 2025. LIPIcs, 7–10 January 2025, Columbia University, New York, NY, USA, vol. 325, pp. 45:1–45:26. Schloss Dagstuhl - Leibniz-Zentrum für Informatik (2025). https://doi.org/10.4230/LIPICS.ITCS.2025.45
11. Dou, J., Götte, T., Hillebrandt, H., Scheideler, C., Werthmann, J.: Distributed construction of near-optimal compact routing schemes for planar graphs (2023). https://arxiv.org/abs/2305.02854

12. Elkin, M., Neiman, O.: On efficient distributed construction of near optimal routing schemes: extended abstract. In: Giakkoupis, G. (ed.) Proceedings of the 2016 ACM Symposium on Principles of Distributed Computing, PODC 2016, Chicago, IL, USA, 25–28 July 2016, pp. 235–244. ACM (2016). https://doi.org/10.1145/2933057.2933098

13. Elkin, M., Neiman, O.: Near-optimal distributed routing with low memory. In: Proceedings of the 2018 ACM Symposium on Principles of Distributed Computing, PODC '18, pp. 207–216, Association for Computing Machinery, New York, NY, USA (2018). https://doi.org/10.1145/3212734.3212761

14. Elkin, M., Neiman, O.: Efficient algorithms for constructing very sparse spanners and emulators. ACM Trans. Algorithms **15**(1), 4:1–4:29 (2019). https://doi.org/10.1145/3274651

15. Feldmann, M., Hinnenthal, K., Scheideler, C.: Fast hybrid network algorithms for shortest paths in sparse graphs. In: Proceedings of the 24th International Conference on Principles of Distributed Systems (OPODIS), pp. 31:1–31:16 (2020)

16. Ghaffari, M., Haeupler, B.: Distributed algorithms for planar networks I: planar embedding. In: Giakkoupis, G. (ed.) Proceedings of the 2016 ACM Symposium on Principles of Distributed Computing, PODC 2016, Chicago, IL, USA, 25–28 July 2016, pp. 29–38. ACM (2016). https://doi.org/10.1145/2933057.2933109

17. Ghaffari, M., Haeupler, B.: Distributed algorithms for planar networks II: low-congestion shortcuts, MST, and Min-Cut. In: Krauthgamer, R. (ed.) Proceedings of the Twenty-Seventh Annual ACM-SIAM Symposium on Discrete Algorithms, SODA 2016, Arlington, VA, USA, 10–12 January 2016, pp. 202–219. SIAM (2016). https://doi.org/10.1137/1.9781611974331.ch16

18. Ghaffari, M., Haeupler, B., Zuzic, G.: Hop-constrained oblivious routing. In: Proceedings of the 53rd Annual ACM SIGACT Symposium on Theory of Computing, Virtual Italy, June 2021, pp. 1208–1220. ACM (2021). https://doi.org/10.1145/3406325.3451098

19. Ghaffari, M., Zuzic, G.: Universally-optimal distributed exact Min-Cut. In: Proceedings of the 2022 ACM Symposium on Principles of Distributed Computing, Salerno Italy, July 2022, pp. 281–291. ACM (2022). https://doi.org/10.1145/3519270.3538429

20. Harb, E., Huang, Z., Zheng, D.W.: Shortest path separators in unit disk graphs. In: Chan, T., Fischer, J., Iacono, J., Herman, G. (eds.) 32nd Annual European Symposium on Algorithms (ESA 2024). Leibniz International Proceedings in Informatics (LIPIcs), vol. 308, pp. 66:1–66:14. Schloss Dagstuhl – Leibniz-Zentrum für Informatik, Dagstuhl, Germany (2024). https://doi.org/10.4230/LIPIcs.ESA.2024.66

21. Hillebrandt, H.: Verteiltes Berechnen kompakter Routingtabellen in Unit Disk Graphen. Bachelor's thesis, Paderborn University (2022)

22. Izumi, T., Kitamura, N., Naruse, T., Schwartzman, G.: Fully polynomial-time distributed computation in low-treewidth graphs. In: Agrawal, K., Lee, I.A. (eds.) SPAA '22: 34th ACM Symposium on Parallelism in Algorithms and Architectures, Philadelphia, PA, USA, 11–14 July 2022, pp. 11–22. ACM (2022). https://doi.org/10.1145/3490148.3538590

23. Jauregui, B., Montealegre, P., Rapaport, I.: Deterministic distributed DFS via cycle separators in planar graphs. In: Balliu, A., Kuhn, F. (eds.) Proceedings of the ACM Symposium on Principles of Distributed Computing, PODC 2025, Hotel Las Brisas Huatulco, Huatulco, Mexico, 16–20 June 2025, pp. 268–277. ACM (2025). https://doi.org/10.1145/3732772.3733558

24. Jung, D., Kolb, C., Scheideler, C., Sundermeier, J.: Competitive routing in hybrid communication networks. In: Algorithms for Sensor Systems - 14th International Symposium on Algorithms and Experiments for Wireless Sensor Networks, ALGO-SENSORS 2018, Revised Selected Papers, Helsinki, Finland, 23–24 August 2018, pp. 15–31 (2018)
25. Kao, M.Y., Teng, S.H., Toyama, K.: Improved parallel depth-first search in undirected planar graphs. In: Goos, G., Hartmanis, J., Dehne, F., Sack, J.R., Santoro, N., Whitesides, S. (eds.) Algorithms and Data Structures. LNCS, vol. 709, pp. 409–420. Springer, Heidelberg (1993). https://doi.org/10.1007/3-540-57155-8_266
26. Kuhn, F., Schneider, P.: Routing schemes and distance oracles in the hybrid model. In: Scheideler, C. (ed.) 36th International Symposium on Distributed Computing, DISC 2022. Leibniz International Proceedings in Informatics (LIPIcs), vol. 246, pp. 28:1–28:22. Schloss Dagstuhl – Leibniz-Zentrum für Informatik, Dagstuhl, Germany (2022). https://doi.org/10.4230/LIPIcs.DISC.2022.28
27. Lenzen, C., Patt-Shamir, B.: Fast routing table construction using small messages: extended abstract. In: Symposium on Theory of Computing Conference, STOC'13, Palo Alto, CA, USA, 1–4 June 2013, pp. 381–390 (2013). https://doi.org/10.1145/2488608.2488656
28. Lenzen, C., Patt-Shamir, B.: Fast partial distance estimation and applications. In: Georgiou, C., Spirakis, P.G. (eds.) Proceedings of the 2015 ACM Symposium on Principles of Distributed Computing, PODC 2015, Donostia-San Sebastián, Spain, 21–23 July 2015, pp. 153–162. ACM (2015). https://doi.org/10.1145/2767386.2767398
29. Lenzen, C., Patt-Shamir, B., Peleg, D.: Distributed distance computation and routing with small messages. Distrib. Comput. **32**(2), 133–157 (2018). https://doi.org/10.1007/s00446-018-0326-6
30. Li, J., Parter, M.: Planar diameter via metric compression. In: Charikar, M., Cohen, E. (eds.) Proceedings of the 51st Annual ACM SIGACT Symposium on Theory of Computing, STOC 2019, Phoenix, AZ, USA, 23–26 June 2019, pp. 152–163. ACM (2019). https://doi.org/10.1145/3313276.3316358
31. Li, X.Y., Calinescu, G., Wan, P.J., Wang, Y.: Localized Delaunay triangulation with application in ad hoc wireless networks. IEEE Trans. Parallel Distrib. Syst. **14**(10), 1035–1047 (2003). https://doi.org/10.1109/TPDS.2003.1239871
32. Luby, M.: A simple parallel algorithm for the maximal independent set problem. SIAM J. Comput. **15**(4), 1036–1053 (1986). https://doi.org/10.1137/0215074
33. Peleg, D.: Distributed Computing: A Locality-Sensitive Approach. Society for Industrial and Applied Mathematics, USA (2000)
34. Rozhon, V., Grunau, C., Haeupler, B., Zuzic, G., Li, J.: Undirected $(1+\epsilon)$-shortest paths via minor-aggregates: near-optimal deterministic parallel and distributed algorithms. In: Leonardi, S., Gupta, A. (eds.) STOC '22: 54th Annual ACM SIGACT Symposium on Theory of Computing, Rome, Italy, 20–24 June 2022, pp. 478–487. ACM (2022). https://doi.org/10.1145/3519935.3520074
35. Thorup, M.: Compact oracles for reachability and approximate distances in planar digraphs. J. ACM **51**(6), 993–1024 (2004). https://doi.org/10.1145/1039488.1039493
36. Thorup, M., Zwick, U.: Compact routing schemes. In: Rosenberg, A.L. (ed.) Proceedings of the Thirteenth Annual ACM Symposium on Parallel Algorithms and Architectures, SPAA 2001, Heraklion, Crete Island, Greece, 4–6 July 2001, pp. 1–10. ACM (2001). https://doi.org/10.1145/378580.378581

Online Exploration of Grid Graphs
with Multiple Searchers

Yuya Higashikawa[(✉)][iD], Shuichi Miyazaki[(✉)][iD], and Daiki Okayama[(✉)][iD]

Graduate School of Information Science, University of Hyogo, Kobe, Japan
`{higashikawa,shuichi}@sis.u-hyogo.ac.jp`, `okymd4aiki@gmail.com`

Abstract. In this paper, we study the problem of exploring an unknown grid graph by multiple searchers. All searchers start from a single vertex, and each vertex in the graph must be visited by at least one searcher. The objective is to minimize the time required until every vertex has been visited and all searchers have returned to the starting vertex. We assume that the searchers can communicate with each other by reading and writing information at any vertex they visit. In prior work, Ortolf and Schindelhauer proposed an online exploration algorithm for an $n \times n$ grid graph with disjoint rectangular obstacles. They showed that its competitive ratio is $\mathcal{O}(\log^2 n)$. We propose an online algorithm for arbitrary grid graphs that achieves a competitive ratio of $\Theta(k/\log k + \min(c, k))$, where k is the number of searchers and c is the number of hole corners in the grid graph. Our result improves on that of Ortolf and Schindelhauer when c and k are relatively small compared to the graph size. In particular, when c is a constant, our algorithm achieves a constant competitive ratio that is independent of the graph size.

Keywords: Online algorithms · Graph exploration · Competitive ratio

1 Introduction

We study the online graph exploration problem with multiple searchers. This problem models real-world urgent situations, such as rapid life-saving activities during the collapse of buildings due to a massive earthquake.

The *online graph exploration problem* is formally defined as follows. Consider an unknown graph $G = (V, E)$, where k searchers are initially located at a starting vertex $s \in V$. In each discrete time step, every searcher may either move to an adjacent vertex or remain at its current position. Initially, the searchers know only the adjacency information of the starting vertex s (i.e., the incident edges and the neighboring vertices). When a searcher visits a vertex v for the first time, all edges incident to v and the identities of its adjacent vertices become known to the searchers (hence the term *online*). The objective is to minimize the total number of time steps required until every vertex has been visited by at least one searcher and all searchers have returned to s. We assume that each searcher has unlimited memory and computational power and can communicate with others locally by reading and writing data at visited vertices.

C. Georgiou (Ed.): SIROCCO 2026, LNCS 16488, pp. 371–390, 2026.
https://doi.org/10.1007/978-3-032-26465-7_20

Let $\mathcal{G}$ denote a family of graphs, and assume that the searchers know that the unknown graph is a member of this family. Let ALG be an online exploration algorithm for $G \in \mathcal{G}$ with k searchers. Let $cost_{\mathsf{ALG}}(G, k)$ be the time when exploration is completed and all searchers return to s. Also, let OPT be an optimal offline exploration algorithm for $G \in \mathcal{G}$ with k searchers, and let $cost_{\mathsf{OPT}}(G, k)$ be defined similarly. Then, the competitive ratio for ALG is defined as follows:

$$\sup_{G \in \mathcal{G}} \frac{cost_{\mathsf{ALG}}(G, k)}{cost_{\mathsf{OPT}}(G, k)}.$$

In this paper, we focus on grid graphs, a natural and practically relevant setting: real-world exploration regions can be modeled as grid graphs by virtually constructing a grid based on the searcher's visibility distance, treating each cell as a vertex, and defining edges between adjacent cells (see Fig. 1).

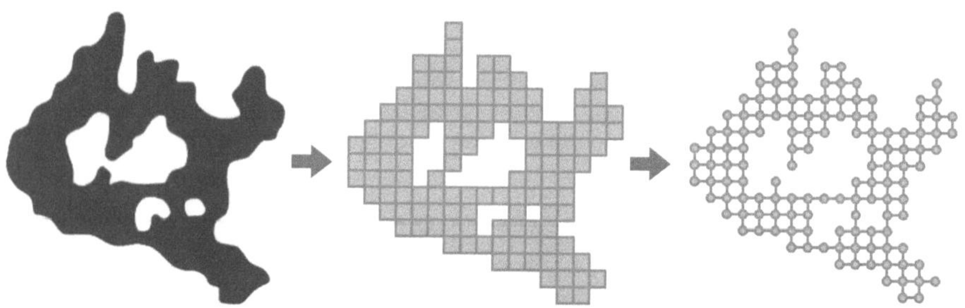

Fig. 1. Modeling an unknown region as a grid graph

To the best of our knowledge, the only prior work on online exploration of grid graphs with multiple searchers is by Ortolf and Schindelhauer [27]. For $n \times n$ grid graphs with multiple rectangular holes, Ortolf and Schindelhauer [27] presented an algorithm with a competitive ratio of $\mathcal{O}(\log^2 n)$. They also established lower bounds of $\Omega(\log k / \log \log k)$ and $\Omega(\sqrt{\log k} / \log \log k)$ for deterministic and randomized algorithms using k searchers, respectively.

Our Results. We construct an online algorithm that achieves a competitive ratio of $\Theta(k / \log k + \min(c, k))$, where c denotes the number of hole corners in the grid graph. Our result improves on the previous result of Ortolf and Schindelhauer [27] when the number of hole corners c is relatively small. We also establish a lower bound of $\Omega(k / \log k)$ for a restricted class of algorithms, which we call *tree-greedy* algorithms.

Related Work. The online graph exploration problem has been extensively studied. Rosenkrantz et al. [29] analyzed several heuristics for the traveling salesman problem (TSP). Although their results were obtained in the offline setting, Kalyanasundaram and Pruhs [22] observed that the Nearest Neighbor algorithm

(NN) extends naturally to the online setting, achieving a competitive ratio of $\Theta(\log n)$ on weighted graphs with n vertices.

The same authors initiated the study of the online exploration problem and proposed the ShortCut algorithm for planar graphs with a competitive ratio of 16. Megow et al. [25] generalized this result to graphs of genus at most g, showing that a variant of ShortCut, called Blocking, achieves a competitive ratio of $16(1+2g)$. They also showed that Blocking cannot have a constant competitive ratio on general graphs. Recently, Baligács et al. [2] improved the upper bound to $16(1+2g/3)$. On the negative side, Birx et al. [3] proved that no online algorithm for weighted graphs can achieve a competitive ratio better than $10/3 - \varepsilon$, even on planar graphs. For directed graphs, Foerster and Wattenhofer [16] proved a lower bound of $n-1$ on n-vertex graphs and presented a matching upper bound.

Several graph classes have been studied in detail. For cycles, Miyazaki et al. [26] gave an algorithm with a competitive ratio of $(1 + \sqrt{3})/2$ and showed that it is optimal. For tadpole graphs, Brandt et al. [5] showed that NN achieves a ratio 2 and proved that this is optimal. For unicyclic graphs, Kobayashi and Li [23] obtained a ratio of $5/2$. Fritsch [18] proved that Blocking achieves $5/2+\sqrt{2}$ on cactus graphs. For unweighted graphs, DFS is 2-competitive and optimal [26]. Megow et al. [25] analyzed graphs with c-distinct edge weights and obtained a $2c$-competitive algorithm.

For grid graphs, Icking et al. [20] proved a lower bound of $2 - \varepsilon$ and observed that DFS is 2-competitive. For grid graphs without holes, Icking et al. [20] presented a $(4/3)$-competitive algorithm and showed a lower bound of $7/6 - \varepsilon$. Kolenderska et al. [24] later improved the upper bound to $5/4$ and established a lower bound of $20/17 - \varepsilon$. More recently, Brock et al. [7] obtained a new lower bound of $13/11 - \varepsilon$. We also note that the offline version of the exploration problem is $\mathcal{NP}$-hard even on grid graphs, as the Hamiltonian Cycle problem remains $\mathcal{NP}$-complete in this setting [21].

The multiple-searcher setting increases the complexity further, and several works have focused on specific graph classes. Higashikawa et al. [19] developed a 1.5-competitive algorithm for cycles, which matches their lower bound. For trees, Fraigniaud et al. [17] proposed an $\mathcal{O}(k/\log k)$-competitive algorithm, and Higashikawa et al. [19] refined it into the BEER algorithm with a competitive ratio of $k/\log k + o(1)$. Dynia et al. [12,14] showed a lower bound of $\Omega(\log k/\log \log k)$ for any deterministic algorithm, and Higashikawa et al. [19] additionally proved an $\Omega(k/\log k)$ lower bound for any greedy algorithm. After nearly two decades of a barrier imposed by greedy approaches, Cosson and Massoulié [8] achieved a breakthrough by presenting an $\mathcal{O}(\sqrt{k})$-competitive algorithm under the unlimited communication model.

Other special cases and variants have also been investigated. Ortolf and Schindelhauer [28] proposed an algorithm for trees achieving a competitive ratio of $\mathcal{O}(k^{o(1)})$ when $k = 2^{\omega(\sqrt{\log D \log \log D})}$ and $n = 2^{\mathcal{O}(2^{\log D})}$, where D is the height of the tree and n is the number of vertices. Dynia et al. [13] introduced the parameter *density* for trees and proposed an algorithm with a competitive ratio of $\mathcal{O}(D^{1-p})$, where p denotes the density of the input tree. Additionally, Brass et al. [6] gave an algorithm for exploring trees with running time $2n/k + \mathcal{O}((k + D)^{k-1})$. Disser et al. [12] clarified the range of the number of searchers required to achieve a constant competitive ratio for tree exploration. van den Akker et al. [1] analyzed tadpole graphs and obtained competitive ratios between 3/2 and 5/2 depending on the number of searchers. Dereniowski et al. [11] showed that any unweighted graph can be explored in $O(D)$ time using $Dn^{1+o(1)}$ searchers, where D is the maximum distance from the starting vertex to any vertex.

Further variations include minimizing the maximum distance traveled by any searcher [1,14], battery-constrained exploration [10], asynchronous settings [8,9], advice complexity [4], and learning-augmented online algorithms [15].

2   Preliminaries

We define G^∞ as an infinite graph whose vertex set consists of all points with integer coordinates in the plane, and two vertices are adjacent if and only if their Euclidean distance is one [21]. A *grid graph* is defined as a finite connected subgraph of G^∞ induced by a subset of its vertices [21]. Since every grid graph is planar, we use the terminology of planar graphs without further notice. A *hole* is defined as a bounded face of a grid graph whose area is at least two. By definition, every hole is an orthogonal polygon, and each vertex of such a polygon coincides with a vertex of the grid graph. A vertex of the grid graph corresponding to a convex corner of a hole is called a *hole corner*, whereas a vertex corresponding to a convex corner of the outer face is called an *outer corner*. These two types of vertices are collectively referred to as *corner vertices* (see Fig. 2). The *coordinate* of a vertex is the integer coordinate $(x, y) \in \mathbb{Z}^2$ in the orthogonal coordinate system of G^∞ to which the vertex belongs. Hereafter, we may denote the coordinate of a vertex $v \in V$ by $v = (v_x, v_y)$ whenever there is no risk of confusion.

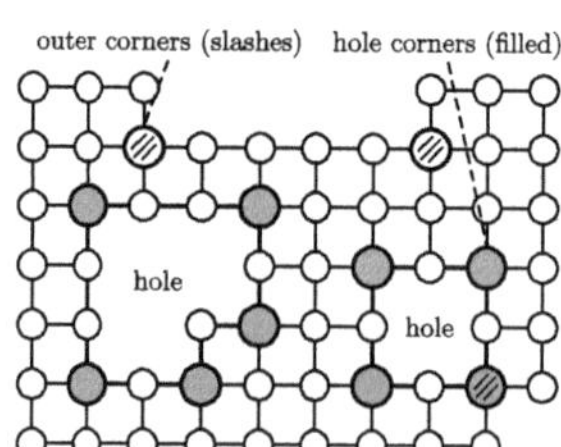

Fig. 2. Corner vertices

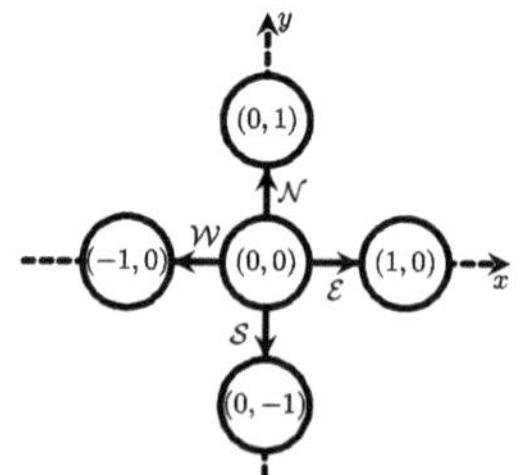

Fig. 3. Directions

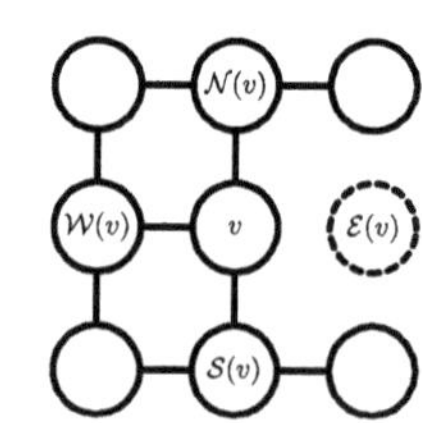

Fig. 4. Adjacent vertices

As will be described in Sect. 3, our exploration algorithm implicitly embeds a directed tree into a grid graph. To represent the direction of each edge, we introduce four symbols, $\mathcal{N}, \mathcal{E}, \mathcal{S}, \mathcal{W}$, corresponding to the four cardinal directions. Each directed edge in a directed tree can be uniquely associated with one of these directions according to the difference of the coordinates of its endpoints. As shown in Fig. 3, we say that the direction of a directed edge (u, v) is $\mathcal{N}$ if $v_x - u_x = 0$ and $v_y - u_y = 1$, $\mathcal{E}$ if $v_x - u_x = 1$ and $v_y - u_y = 0$, $\mathcal{S}$ if $v_x - u_x = 0$ and $v_y - u_y = -1$, and $\mathcal{W}$ if $v_x - u_x = -1$ and $v_y - u_y = 0$. We refer to a directed edge as an $\mathcal{N}$ edge, $\mathcal{E}$ edge, $\mathcal{S}$ edge, or $\mathcal{W}$ edge according to its direction. For convenience, we define $\mathcal{N}(v) = (v_x, v_y + 1)$, $\mathcal{E}(v) = (v_x + 1, v_y)$, $\mathcal{S}(v) = (v_x, v_y - 1)$, and $\mathcal{W}(v) = (v_x - 1, v_y)$. Figure 4 shows these adjacent vertices around v. Note that, for $\delta \in \{\mathcal{N}, \mathcal{E}, \mathcal{S}, \mathcal{W}\}$, $\delta(v)$ may not belong to the vertex set V of the grid graph. Furthermore, for some integer $m > 0$, we define $\delta^m(v)$ as the vertex obtained by applying δ m times to v.

A *directed path* is a sequence of directed edges $P = (e_1, e_2, \ldots, e_{|P|})$ such that each directed edge $e_i = (v_{i-1}, v_i)$ determines a corresponding sequence of vertices $(v_0, v_1, \ldots, v_{|P|})$. We call the set of vertices $v_1, v_2, \ldots, v_{|P|-1}$ the *internal vertices* of P. The *length* of P is the number of edges contained in it and is denoted by $|P|$. For $0 \le i < j \le |P|$, we denote by $P[i, j]$ the *subpath* of P from v_i to v_j, that is, $P[i, j] = ((v_i, v_{i+1}), \ldots, (v_{j-1}, v_j))$. Given our definition of edge directions, a *bend* of a path P is an internal vertex v_i such that the directions of the two consecutive edges e_i and e_{i+1} are different.

For a graph $G = (V, E)$, the *distance* between two vertices $u, v \in V$ is the length of a shortest path between them and is denoted by $d_G(u, v)$. Let s be the starting vertex of the exploration. We define

$$D(G) = \max_{v \in V} d_G(s, v),$$

that is, $D(G)$ is the maximum distance from s to any vertex of G.

3   An Online Exploration Algorithm for Grid Graphs

Our algorithm WRAP (Wall-Reactive Algorithm for Path-branching) consists of two parts. When a searcher first visits an unknown vertex, all edges incident to that vertex are revealed. The first part of our algorithm determines which of the newly revealed edges should be used by the searchers. The second part decides how the searchers traverse the remaining traversable edges. We carefully design the first part of the algorithm so that the set of selected edges forms a tree. With this design, we can adapt an online tree exploration algorithm to grid graphs. We use BEER (Branch Evenly, Explore, Return), the sophisticated online tree exploration algorithm by Higashikawa et al. [19], as the second part of our algorithm. BEER is a slight modification of the algorithm proposed by Fraigniaud et al. [17]. Both algorithms are depth-first-search-type algorithms for multiple searchers. At any time during the algorithm, the number of searchers in each unfinished subtree is kept approximately balanced. Once there are no unvisited vertices or searchers in a subtree, the searchers immediately return to the parent vertex.

This section focuses on explaining WRAP. To provide an intuitive understanding of the algorithm, we start by giving a static definition of the tree embedded by WRAP into a grid graph without holes in Sect. 3.1. In the remaining part of the subsection, we describe how searchers can embed the same tree into grid graphs without holes using only their local knowledge. We then apply the algorithm to grid graphs that may contain holes. Section 3.2 introduces several issues that occur in such cases and exceptional rules to avoid them. The analysis of the competitive ratio will be given in Sect. 4.

3.1   How to Embed Trees Into Grid Graphs Without Holes

Before describing the algorithm, we first give a constructive definition of the tree embedded into a given graph. We begin with subgraph $T_0 = (\{s\}, \emptyset)$ where s is the starting vertex. For $i = 1, 2, \ldots$, we repeat the following procedure until $V(T_i)$ becomes identical to $V(G)$.

1. Initialize T_{2i-1} as T_{2i-2}. For each vertex $v \in V(T_{2i-1})$, if $\mathcal{E}(v)$ is contained in $V(G)$ but not in $V(T_{2i-1})$, add $\mathcal{E}(v)$ and $(v, \mathcal{E}(v))$ to $V(T_{2i-1})$ and $E(T_{2i-1})$, respectively. We do the same for $\mathcal{W}(v)$. Repeat this process iteratively also for the newly added vertices, until no further vertices can be added to T_{2i-1}.
2. Initialize T_{2i} as T_{2i-1}. For each vertex $v \in V(T_{2i})$, if $\mathcal{N}(v)$ is contained in $V(G)$ but not in $V(T_{2i})$, add $\mathcal{N}(v)$ and $(v, \mathcal{N}(v))$ to $V(T_{2i})$ and $E(T_{2i})$, respectively. We do the same for $\mathcal{S}(v)$. Repeat this process iteratively also for the newly added vertices, until no further vertices can be added to T_{2i}.

Fig. 5 shows an example of tree construction.

Next, we describe how searchers can embed the tree defined above in an online fashion. Initially, the searchers are located at the starting vertex s and at most 4 edges incident to s are revealed. For $\delta \in \{\mathcal{N}, \mathcal{E}, \mathcal{S}, \mathcal{W}\}$, if $\delta(s)$ is contained in $V(G)$, then WRAP embeds the edge $(s, \delta(s))$ into the tree. As mentioned earlier, the traversal of the searchers is governed by the BEER algorithm. It remains to specify which edges are discarded from the grid graph when a searcher first visits a vertex v. Suppose that a searcher traverses an edge (u, v), visiting vertex v for the first time. Let δ denote the direction of (u, v). If $\delta(v)$ is contained in $V(G)$, WRAP embeds the edge $(v, \delta(v))$ into the tree. Let δ' denote either of the other two directions orthogonal to δ (e.g., when δ is $\mathcal{N}$, δ' is either $\mathcal{E}$ or $\mathcal{W}$). If $\delta'(v)$ is contained in $V(G)$, the edge $(v, \delta'(v))$ is also embedded into the tree if either of the following conditions is satisfied:

- $\delta'(u)$ is not contained in $V(G)$.
- (u, v) is neither $(s, \mathcal{N}(s))$ nor $(s, \mathcal{S}(s))$, u is not a bend of the directed path from s to v in the embedded tree, and there exists an edge $(u, \delta'(u))$ in the embedded tree.

The following observation can be established straightforwardly. However, its proof is omitted here, as it is a special case of Lemma 3, which will be presented later.

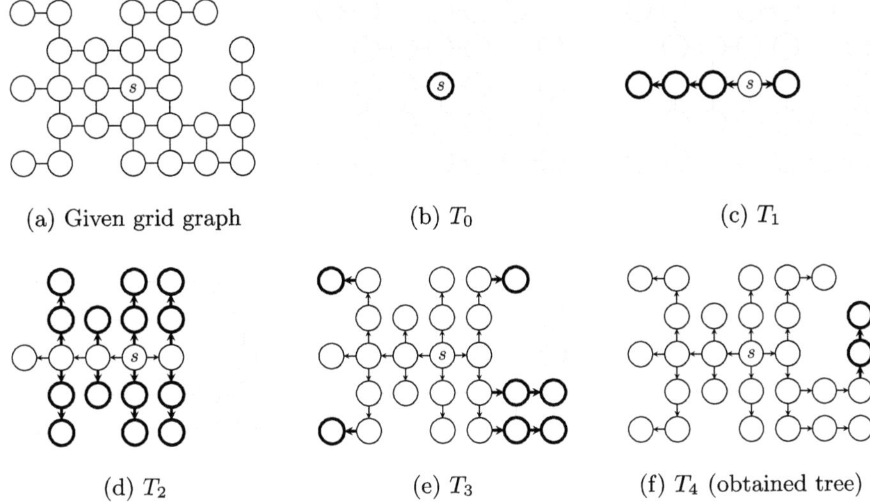

(a) Given grid graph   (b) T_0 (c) T_1

(d) T_2 (e) T_3 (f) T_4 (obtained tree)

Fig. 5. Compositional definition of the tree embedded into a grid graph without holes. Newly added vertices and edges are highlighted by bold lines.

Remark 1. Let G be a grid graph without holes. Then the tree defined above is a shortest-path tree of G rooted at s.

3.2   Exceptional Rules for Grid Graphs with Holes

We generalize the above algorithm to general grid graphs, which may contain holes. Two issues immediately arise. First, two or more edges would share the same head, creating cycles in the embedded structure. Second, Remark 1 may no longer hold, since holes may force detours around them.

The latter issue is addressed in Sect. 4.1, where we analyze the competitive ratio. In this subsection, we focus on the former one. We assume that a group of searchers traverses an edge (u, v) for the first time and visits vertex v, although this group may not be the first one to visit v. We then consider two cases: (i) v is already visited by other searchers traversing another edge before the current group arrives at v, and (ii) multiple groups arrive at v simultaneously traversing different edges. In case (i), we regard the head of the edge (u, v) as a distinct leaf vertex v' of the tree, different from the original vertex v. In case (ii), when unvisited neighbors of v still exist within the searchers' local knowledge, exactly one of the groups that intended to explore those neighbors continues the exploration. The remaining groups treat v as a distinct leaf vertex v' as in case (i). These exceptional rules ensure that the embedded structure can still be regarded as a tree. The number of vertices in the embedded tree is at most $4|V|$ because each vertex in the grid graph has at most four adjacent vertices. Note that two groups of searchers never cross in the middle of an edge (i.e., in one step, one group traverses (u, v) and another group traverses (v, u)), since it cannot happen that two groups of searchers simultaneously lie on both u and v. This is because all the searchers are initially at the same vertex s and always keep moving, while grid graphs are bipartite.

We denote by $T_{\mathsf{WRAP}}(G)$ the tree embedded into a grid graph G by WRAP. As the last part of this subsection, we introduce several definitions to analyze the competitive ratio of WRAP. A *U-shaped path* in $T_{\mathsf{WRAP}}(G)$ is defined as a directed path that contains exactly two bends and three distinct directions. Let $P = ((v_0, v_1), (v_1, v_2), \ldots, (v_{|P|-1}, v_{|P|}))$ be a U-shaped path and let v_i, v_j $(i < j)$ be the bends of P. Further assume that the three directions $\delta_1, \delta_2, \delta_3$ on P appear in this order from v_0 to $v_{|P|}$. A vertex v_k is defined as a *U-shaped vertex* of P if it is the minimum-index vertex such that for every vertex v_l with $k \leq l \leq j$, there exists an edge $(v_l, \delta_3(v_l))$ in $T_{\mathsf{WRAP}}(G)$ (see Fig. 6). Note that $i + 1 < k$ is required because the existence of edge $(v_{i+1}, \delta_3(v_{i+1}))$ violates the embedding rule. An important property derived from this definition is that $\delta_3(v_{k-1})$ does not belong to $V(G)$; in other words, the face bounded by v_{k-1}, v_k, and $\delta_3(v_k)$ corresponds to either a hole or the outer face.

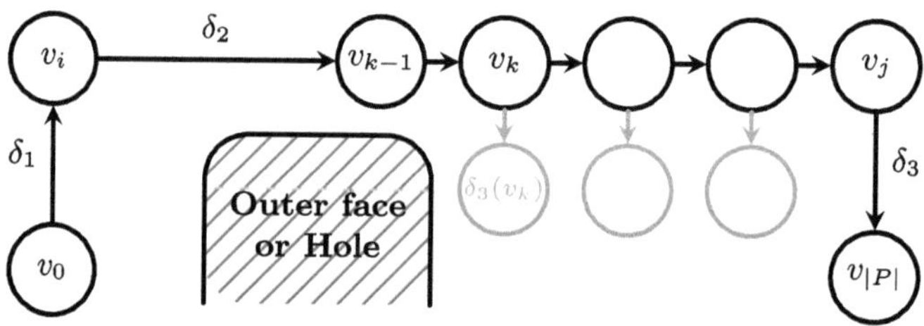

Fig. 6. U-shaped path and U-shaped vertex v_k. Gray vertices and edges are contained in $T_{\mathsf{WRAP}}(G)$, not in P. (Color figure online)

We call v_k a *hole U-shaped vertex* if a hole is incident to all of v_{k-1}, v_k, and $\delta_3(v_k)$. Otherwise, we call v_k an *outer-boundary U-shaped vertex*. Note that only the corner vertices can be U-shaped vertices. Although U-shaped vertices, hole U-shaped vertices, and outer-boundary U-shaped vertices are defined on a U-shaped path, we extend them to any directed path P in $T_{\mathsf{WRAP}}(G)$ by applying them to each U-shaped subpath of P.

4 Competitive Analysis of WRAP

The main theorem of this paper is as follows.

Theorem 1. *The competitive ratio of the* WRAP *algorithm for grid graphs with at most c hole corners is $\Theta(k/\log k + \min(c, k))$, where k is the number of searchers.*

In the following subsections, we analyze the upper bound and the lower bound on the competitive ratio of the WRAP algorithm separately.

4.1   Upper Bound

The goal of this subsection is to prove the following lemma.

Lemma 1. *The competitive ratio of the* WRAP *algorithm for grid graphs with at most c hole corners is* $\mathcal{O}(k/\log k + \min(c, k))$, *where k is the number of searchers.*

We first derive a lower bound for $cost_{\mathsf{OPT}}(G, k)$. Ortolf and Schindelhauer [27] proved a similar bound for $n \times n$ square grid graphs with disjoint rectangular holes.

Lemma 2. *The cost of the optimal offline algorithm exploring a grid graph $G = (V, E)$ is at least $cost_{\mathsf{OPT}}(G, k) \geq \max\{2D(G), |V|/k\}$, where k is the number of searchers.*

Proof. In any algorithm, at least one searcher has to go to the farthest vertex in G and return to s, which takes at least $2D(G)$ steps. Also, to visit all vertices, at least one searcher has to visit $|V|/k$ vertices, so the cost is also at least $|V|/k$. This leads to $cost_{\mathsf{OPT}}(G, k) \geq \max\{2D(G), |V|/k\}$.

Next, we prove an upper bound for $cost_{\mathsf{WRAP}}(G, k)$. Since $cost_{\mathsf{WRAP}}(G, k)$ coincides with the cost of BEER exploring $T_{\mathsf{WRAP}}(G)$, we only need to focus on the properties of $T_{\mathsf{WRAP}}(G)$. According to Higashikawa et al. [19], the cost of BEER depends on the depth of the tree $T_{\mathsf{WRAP}}(G)$. The cost also depends on the total edge lengths in the tree (in our case, we focus on the number of vertices because all edges have unit length) and the number of searchers k. As we mentioned in the previous section, the number of vertices in the tree is at most $4|V|$. Therefore, we only need to bound the depth of the tree $T_{\mathsf{WRAP}}(G)$ by some factor of $D(G)$ because the term $D(G)$ appears in the lower bound for $cost_{\mathsf{OPT}}(G, k)$, shown in Lemma 2.

We use U-shaped vertices to bound the depth of $T_{\mathsf{WRAP}}(G)$ and prove the following lemma.

Lemma 3. *Let P be a directed path in $T_{\mathsf{WRAP}}(G)$ from u to v for some $u, v \in T_{\mathsf{WRAP}}(G)$ which does not contain any hole U-shaped vertices as its internal vertices. Then $|P| = d_G(u, v)$.*

The proof of this lemma follows from the following two lemmas. Note that the path P may contain some outer-boundary U-shaped vertices as its internal vertices. Lemma 5 states that such vertices are unavoidable for any shortest u-v path in G (see Fig. 7). Hence we can decompose P at these vertices, and apply Lemma 4 to each subpath to conclude that $|P| = d_G(u, v)$.

Lemma 4. *Let P be a directed path in $T_{\mathsf{WRAP}}(G)$ from u to v for some $u, v \in T_{\mathsf{WRAP}}(G)$ which does not contain any U-shaped vertices as its internal vertices. Then $|P| = d_G(u, v)$.*

Lemma 5. *Let P be a directed path in $T_{\mathsf{WRAP}}(G)$ from u to v for some $u, v \in T_{\mathsf{WRAP}}(G)$ which does not contain any hole U-shaped vertices as its internal vertices. Then any shortest path from u to v in G must pass through all outer-boundary U-shaped vertices in P.*

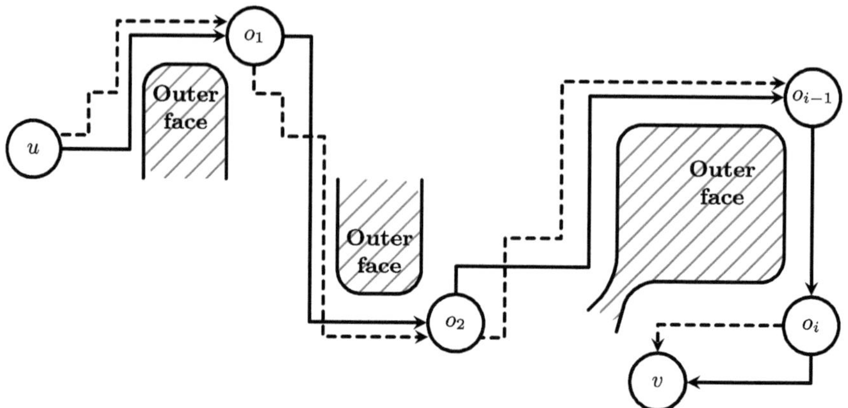

Fig. 7. Path P from u to v in $T_{\mathsf{WRAP}}(G)$ (solid) and an example shortest u-v path in G (dashed). The vertices $o_1, o_2, \ldots, o_i$ are outer-boundary U-shaped vertices on P.

Proof of Lemma 4. We easily see that P does not contain any U-shaped subpath. To complete the proof, it suffices to show that P uses at most two directions if P does not contain any U-shaped subpath. We actually prove its contrapositive, that is, P contains some U-shaped subpath if it uses at least three directions.

Let $P = ((u_0 = u, u_1), (u_1, u_2), \ldots, (u_{|P|-1}, u_{|P|} = v))$. Suppose that P consists of edges in at least three directions, and let $\delta_1, \delta_2, \delta_3$ be the directions of the edges in the order they appear along P from u to v. Let i be the minimum index such that the direction of edge (u_i, u_{i+1}) is δ_3. Then, the direction of the edge (u_{i-1}, u_i) is either δ_1 or δ_2, and suppose it is δ_2 without loss of generality. Let j be the maximum index such that $j < i$ and the direction of (u_{j-1}, u_j) is δ_1. This leads to the existence of a U-shaped subpath in P. Thus, if P does not contain any U-shaped subpath, it must use at most two directions. This proves the contrapositive and thus the lemma.

Proof of Lemma 5. We prove this lemma by mathematical induction on the number of outer-boundary U-shaped vertices contained in P as its internal vertices. In both the base case and the inductive step, we assume that there exists a shortest u-v path P' in G that does not pass through at least one outer-boundary U-shaped vertex in P. We then show that its length is strictly greater than $|P|$, which contradicts the minimality of $|P'|$.

Base case: Suppose that P contains exactly one outer-boundary U-shaped vertex o as its internal vertex. We show that any shortest path from u to v in G must pass through o. Without loss of generality, assume that P is composed of the edges of direction $\mathcal{N}, \mathcal{E}, \mathcal{S}$, and these directions appear in this order along P from u to v (see Fig. 8). Now suppose there exists a shortest path P' in G between u and v that does not pass through o. Because P' passes through some vertex t above o (i.e., $t = \mathcal{N}^m(o)$ for some $m > 0$), P' needs more $\mathcal{N}$ edges than P to reach t from u and more $\mathcal{S}$ edges than P to reach v from t. Note that any u-v

path in G must have at least $(v_x - u_x)$ $\mathcal{E}$ edges, and the number of $\mathcal{E}$ edges in P coincides with this lower bound. We thus conclude that $|P'| > |P|$ holds, which contradicts the minimality of $|P'|$.

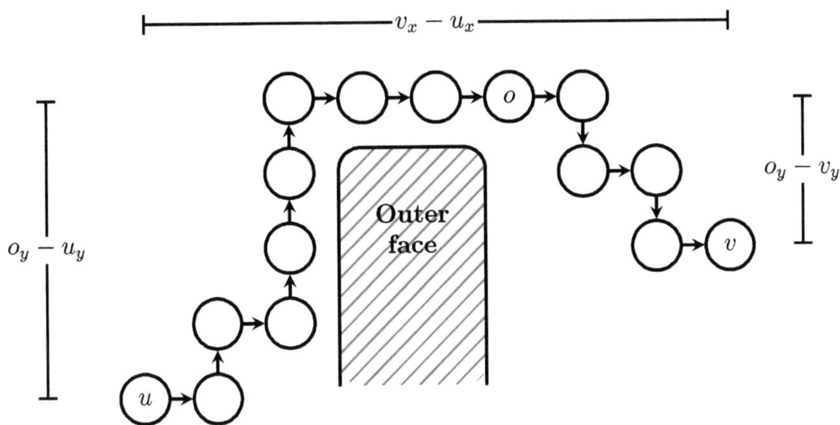

Fig. 8. A path P in the base case

Inductive Hypothesis: Suppose that P contains i outer-boundary U-shaped vertices as its internal vertices. We assume that any shortest path from u to v in G must pass through all of them.

Inductive Step: Suppose that P contains $i+1$ outer-boundary U-shaped vertices as its internal vertices, and denote them by $o_1, o_2, \ldots, o_{i+1}$ in the order they appear along P from u to v. We now show that any shortest path from u to v in G must pass through all of them. We assume that there exists a shortest path P' from u to v in G that does not pass through at least one outer-boundary U-shaped vertex in P. In fact, we may further assume that P' does not pass through all of them. If P' passes through some outer-boundary U-shaped vertex o_j in P, then we can decompose P into two subpaths: one from u to o_j and the other from o_j to v. Since each subpath contains at most i outer-boundary U-shaped vertices as its internal vertices, the inductive hypothesis implies that any shortest path from u to o_j, as well as from o_j to v, in G must pass through all the outer-boundary U-shaped vertices in the corresponding subpath of P. Hence, it suffices to consider the case where P' does not share any of $o_1, o_2, \ldots, o_{i+1}$.

Next, we consider the positional relation between adjacent outer-boundary U-shaped vertices o_j and o_{j+1} in P for each $1 \leq j \leq i$. Without loss of generality, we assume that o_j is the head of some $\mathcal{E}$ edge in P. Then, o_{j+1} is either the tail of some $\mathcal{N}$ edge or the tail of some $\mathcal{W}$ edge in $T_{\mathsf{WRAP}}(G)$ (see Fig. 9).

In the former case, any u-v path in G necessarily intersects the subpath of P from o_j to o_{j+1} because o_j and o_{j+1} face the outer face. As mentioned above,

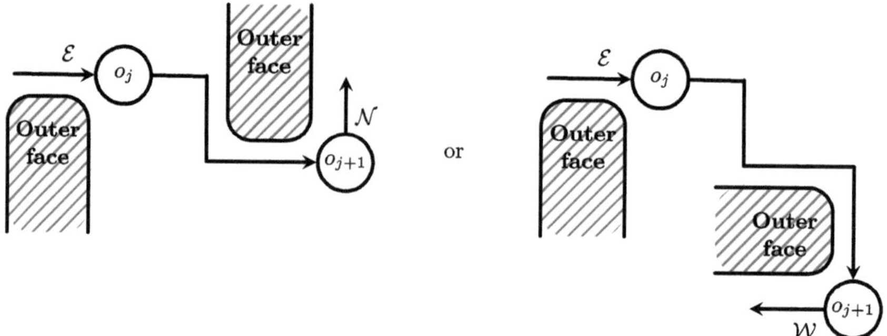

Fig. 9. Positional relation between o_j and o_{j+1} in P

P' does not share any vertex with this subpath, so we only need to consider the latter case. In the latter case, P' must pass through some vertex t_j above o_j (i.e., $t_j = \mathcal{N}^m(o_j)$ for some $m > 0$) and some vertex t_{j+1} to the right of o_{j+1} (i.e., $t_{j+1} = \mathcal{E}^n(o_{j+1})$ for some $n > 0$). Similarly, P' must pass through some vertices $t_1, t_2, \ldots, t_{i+1}$ such that t_j lies on the inner side of o_j (i.e., on the side opposite to the outer face) for each $1 \le j \le i+1$ (see Fig. 10).

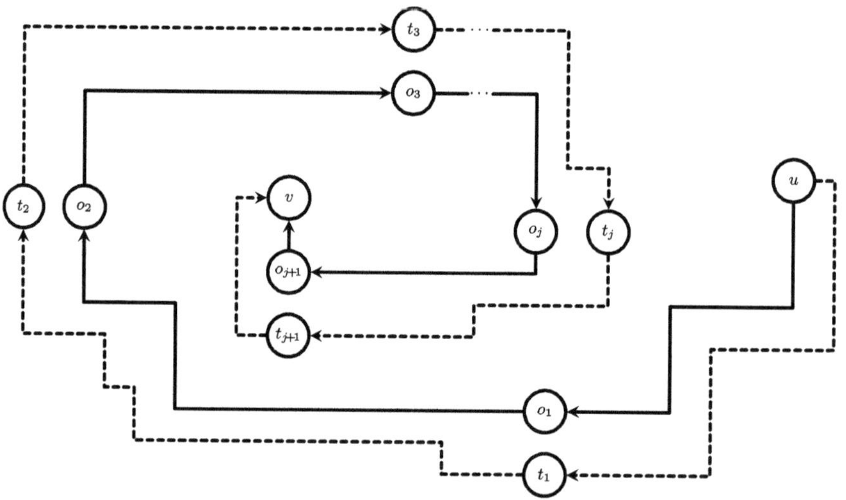

Fig. 10. Paths P (solid) and P' (dashed) in the inductive step

By construction, the subpath of P' from u to t_1, each subpath from t_j to t_{j+1} for $1 \le j \le i$, and the subpath from t_{i+1} to v are all strictly longer than the corresponding subpaths in P (from u to o_1, from o_j to o_{j+1}, and from o_{i+1} to v, respectively). Summing over all these subpaths, we conclude that $|P'| > |P|$. Therefore, any shortest path from u to v must pass through all outer-boundary

U-shaped vertices $o_1, \ldots, o_{i+1}$. This completes the proof of the inductive step and thus the lemma.

Lemma 6. *The depth of the tree embedded by* WRAP *into a grid graph* $G = (V, E)$ *with at most* c *hole corners is at most* $D(T_{\mathsf{WRAP}}(G)) \leq (2c + 1)D(G)$.

Proof. Let t be a vertex farthest from the starting vertex s in $T_{\mathsf{WRAP}}(G)$, and P be a directed path in $T_{\mathsf{WRAP}}(G)$ from s to t. We assume that P contains c' hole U-shaped vertices $u_1, u_2, \ldots, u_{c'}$. Note that $c' \leq c$ holds because a hole U-shaped vertex must be a hole corner. By Lemma 3, we have

$$|P| = |P[s, u_1]| + \sum_{i=1}^{c'-1} |P[u_i, u_{i+1}]| + |P[u_{c'}, t]|$$

$$= d_G(s, u_1) + \sum_{i=1}^{c'-1} d_G(u_i, u_{i+1}) + d_G(u_{c'}, t) \quad \text{by Lemma 3}$$

$$\leq d_G(s, u_1) + \sum_{i=1}^{c'-1} \big(d_G(u_i, s) + d_G(s, u_{i+1})\big)$$

$$+ \big(d_G(u_{c'}, s) + d_G(s, t)\big) \qquad\qquad \text{by the triangle inequality}$$

$$\leq (2c' + 1)D(G) \qquad\qquad\qquad\qquad \text{by } d_G(s, v) \leq D(G) \quad \forall v \in V$$

$$\leq (2c + 1)D(G),$$

which completes the proof.

We now obtain the upper bound for the competitive ratio of the WRAP algorithm.

Lemma 7. *The cost of the* WRAP *algorithm for exploring a grid graph* $G = (V, E)$ *with at most* c *hole corners is at most*

$$cost_{\mathsf{WRAP}}(G, k) \leq \frac{2((4|V| - 1) + \min(2(c + 1)D(G), 4|V|)\lfloor \log k \rfloor)}{1 + \lfloor \log k \rfloor},$$

where k *is the number of searchers.*

Proof. Let us begin by recalling the analysis of the BEER algorithm by Higashikawa et al. [19]. According to their study, the cost of the BEER algorithm for exploring a tree T is at most $2(|V| - 1 + D(T)\lfloor \log k \rfloor)/(1 + \lfloor \log k \rfloor)$ with k searchers. Recall that the number of vertices in the tree $T_{\mathsf{WRAP}}(G)$ is at most $4|V|$, and its depth is at most $(2c + 1)D(G)$ by Lemma 6. The depth of a tree is at most the number of its vertices, so we have $D(T_{\mathsf{WRAP}}(G)) \leq \min((2c+1)D(G), 4|V|)$. Substituting these into the above inequality, we obtain the lemma.

Finally, we conclude this subsection by showing the competitive ratio of the WRAP algorithm, combining Lemmas 2 and 7.

$$\frac{cost_{\mathsf{WRAP}}(G,k)}{cost_{\mathsf{OPT}}(G,k)} \leq \min \left\{ \frac{2((4\,|V|-1)+\min(2(c+1)D(G),4\,|V|)\lfloor \log k\rfloor)}{(2D(G))(1+\lfloor \log k\rfloor)}, \frac{2((4\,|V|-1)+\min(2(c+1)D(G),4\,|V|)\lfloor \log k\rfloor)}{(|V|/k)(1+\lfloor \log k\rfloor)} \right\}$$

$$\leq 8 \cdot \min\left\{\frac{1}{D(G)},\frac{k}{|V|}\right\} \cdot \frac{|V|+\min((c+1)D(G),|V|)\lfloor \log k\rfloor}{1+\lfloor \log k\rfloor},$$

which is in $\mathcal{O}(k/\log k + \min(c,k))$ because $|V| \cdot \min(1/D(G),k/|V|) \leq k$ and $\min((c+1)D(G),|V|) \cdot \min(1/D(G),k/|V|) \leq \min(c+1,k)$ hold.

4.2   Lower Bound

In this subsection, we prove the following lemma.

Lemma 8. *The competitive ratio of the* **WRAP** *algorithm for grid graphs with at most c hole corners is at least $\Omega(k/\log k + \min(c,k))$, where k is the number of searchers.*

The proof combines two lower bounds: $\Omega(k/\log k)$ and $\Omega(\min(c,k))$. We establish them separately in Lemmas 9 and 10, respectively. The first of our lower bounds strongly relies on the result of Higashikawa et al. [19]. The primary difference between our setting and theirs is that we consider embeddable trees in grid graphs with unit edge lengths, whereas they consider general trees with arbitrary edge lengths.

Lemma 9. *For any $\delta > 0$, the competitive ratio of the* **WRAP** *algorithm for grid graphs is at least $\lceil k/(1+\lfloor \log k\rfloor)\rceil - \delta$, where k is the number of searchers.*

Proof. An adversary provides a grid graph $G = (V,E)$ as input (see Fig. 11). We call a vertex of degree three a *T-junction*. The graph contains k T-junctions, which are connected by a path of length $2k-1$ where T-junctions and degree-2 vertices alternate, starting from s: $s \to$ 1st T-junction $\to$ degree-2 vertex $\to$ 2nd T-junction $\to \cdots \to$ degree-2 vertex $\to$ kth T-junction. We refer to this path as the *spine*. The spine is monotone in the sense that it proceeds only downward or rightward: it first departs s downward, and at each T-junction it either continues straight (downward or rightward) or switches to the other direction (rightward or downward). Each T-junction has an attached straight path of length d, called a *rib*. Each rib extends orthogonally to the next edge of the spine after its T-junction; that is, if the spine proceeds downward after the T-junction, the rib extends rightward, and if it proceeds rightward, the rib extends downward.

Next, we describe how the adversary determines the directions of the spine and the ribs at each T-junction. For each T-junction from the first to the $(k-1)$st,

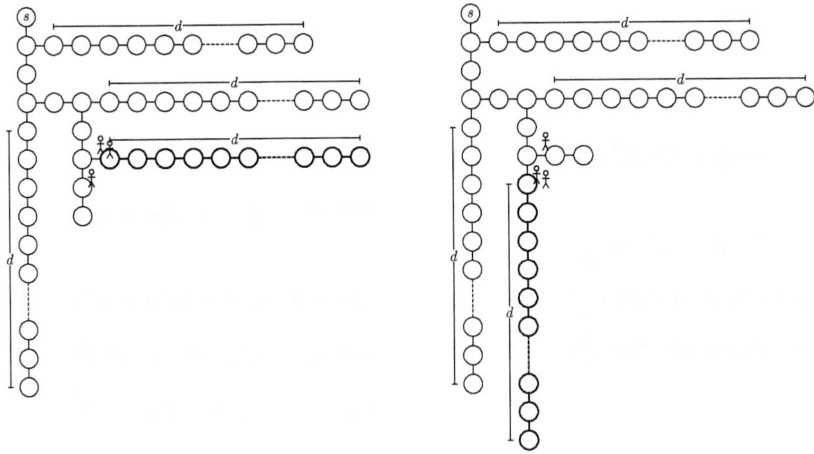

Fig. 11. Grid graphs constructed by an adversary. Directions of the spine and the ribs are determined at each T-junction based on the behavior of WRAP.

at the moment when the T-junction is first reached, the adversary presents two incident edges–one downward and one rightward. If k' searchers have reached the T-junction, then the WRAP algorithm commits to sending $\lceil k'/2 \rceil$ searchers along one of these edges and $\lfloor k'/2 \rfloor$ along the other. The adversary then designates the side that receives $\lceil k'/2 \rceil$ searchers as the rib, and sets the other side to be the next edge of the spine. For the kth T-junction, the orientation of the attached rib is arbitrary; for convenience, we assume that it extends to the right.

Eventually, at some T-junction, all remaining searchers will be exploring some ribs. When these searchers finish exploring their respective ribs and return to the T-junction, the structure of the grid graph ensures that all searchers meet again at that T-junction. After the rendezvous, they start exploration from the same T-junction in the same manner.

Suppose that all searchers meet at a T-junction $n-1$ times, for some integer $n \geq 1$. For each integer p with $1 \leq p \leq n-1$, let t_p denote the time step when all searchers gather at the T-junction for the p-th time. We also define $t_0(= 0)$ and t_n as the time steps when all searchers are at the starting vertex s. The exploration occurring between t_{p-1} and t_p is referred to as *stage* p $(1 \leq p \leq n)$. Note that at time t_{n-1}, all searchers meet at a T-junction, and therefore at least one unexplored rib remains in stage n.

Since at least one rib is explored in each stage, we have $t_p - t_{p-1} \geq 2d$ for every p $(1 \leq p \leq n)$. Thus, $cost_{\mathsf{WRAP}}(G, k) = t_n = \sum_{p=1}^{n}(t_p - t_{p-1}) \geq 2nd$. Because at most $1 + \lfloor \log k \rfloor$ ribs are explored in each stage, the integer n must satisfy $n(1 + \lfloor \log k \rfloor) \geq k$. Moreover, the optimal offline exploration time clearly satisfies $cost_{\mathsf{OPT}}(G, k) \leq 2d + 2(2k - 1)$. Therefore, we have

$$
\frac{cost_{\mathsf{WRAP}}(G, k)}{cost_{\mathsf{OPT}}(G, k)} \geq \frac{2nd}{2d + 2(2k - 1)}
$$
$$
= n\left(1 - \frac{2k - 1}{d + (2k - 1)}\right)
$$
$$
\geq \left\lceil \frac{k}{1 + \lfloor \log k \rfloor} \right\rceil \left(1 - \frac{2k - 1}{d + (2k - 1)}\right).
$$

Assuming $d \gg k$, this completes the proof.

Lemma 10. *The competitive ratio of the* WRAP *algorithm for grid graphs with at most c hole corners is at least $\Omega(\min(c, k))$, where k is the number of searchers.*

Proof. Consider the grid graph G shown in Fig. 12(a), which consists of a starting vertex, two subgrids called the *rectangular part* and the *brickwork part*, and a single vertex u connecting these two parts. The rectangular part consists of $(k+1) \times (\lfloor \log k \rfloor + 1)$ vertices, and the brickwork part consists of $(c/2+1) \times k - c/2$ vertices.

First, we describe the structure of the brickwork part, which contains h holes. The brickwork part is obtained by removing $c/2$ vertices from a rectangular grid of $(c/2 + 1) \times k$ vertices, called G'. Consider the horizontal rows of G' in the upward order. If h is even, we remove the leftmost and the second rightmost vertices at $(4i-2)$th horizontal row of G' for $i = 1, 2, \ldots, h/2$ and the rightmost and the second leftmost vertices at $(4i)$th horizontal row of G' for $i = 1, 2, \ldots, h/2$. If h is odd, we apply the same removal at $(4i - 2)$th horizontal row of G' for $i = 1, 2, \ldots, (h+1)/2$, and at $(4i)$th horizontal row of G' for $i = 1, 2, \ldots, (h-1)/2$. Then the resulting graph is the brickwork part. At the bottom of G, s, the lowest row of the rectangular part, u, and the lowest row of the brickwork part are aligned horizontally in this order from left to right.

We apply WRAP to the graph G. The time step when vertex u is reached is $\lfloor \log k \rfloor + 2$ if WRAP has always made at least half of the searchers go rightward at each vertex on the path from s to u.

At time step $\lfloor \log k \rfloor + 4$, the searcher that has been moving straight so far reaches the first branch of the brickwork part. We assume that WRAP lets this searcher proceed straight (rightward). Furthermore, we assume that WRAP lets the searcher move rightward at each of the following $k - 4$ branching points. Afterward, the searcher detours around the hole, and then we suppose that it continues straight toward the rectangular part again. At this point, the remaining $k - 1$ searchers that have been exploring the rectangular part may begin to explore the brickwork part. However, they only follow the already embedded tree constructed by the single searcher. Because the single searcher would possibly continue to detour around the holes in the same fashion, the exploration cannot be parallelized at all. Consequently, WRAP can embed a tree $T_{\mathsf{WRAP}}(G)$ of depth at least $ck/4 + c/4 + k + \lfloor \log k \rfloor + 2$. Since any searcher has to return to the starting vertex using edges of $T_{\mathsf{WRAP}}(G)$ after the exploration, the cost of WRAP is at least $2D(T_{\mathsf{WRAP}}(G)) = ck/2 + c/2 + 2k + 2\lfloor \log k \rfloor + 4$ (see Fig. 12(b)).

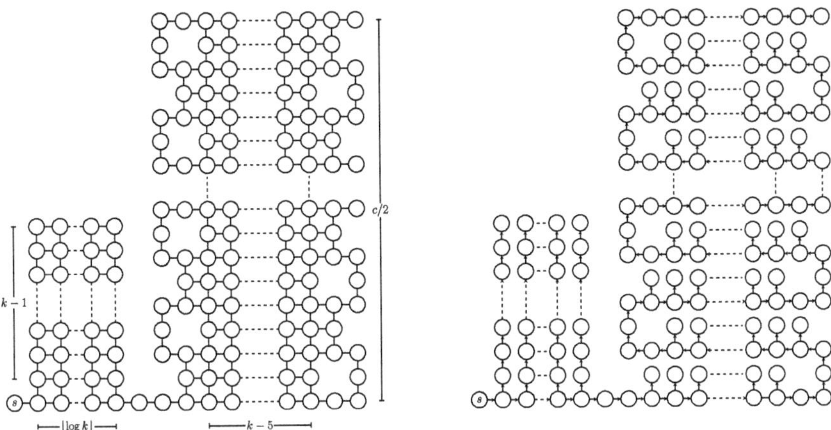

(a) The grid graph G given by an adversary

(b) The tree embedded by WRAP into the grid graph G

Fig. 12. The grid graph G and the tree embedded by WRAP into G. The numbers in the figure indicate the lengths of the corresponding paths.

For the optimal offline algorithm, we consider the following exploration strategy. In the first phase, the searchers move to the bottom vertices of each column in the brickwork part while passing through the rectangular part. Namely, for each searcher i ($1 \le i \le k$), it first explores the i-th row of the rectangular part, and then moves to the bottom vertex of the i-th column of the brickwork part. Obviously, searcher 1 travels the longest distance, which is $2k + \lfloor \log k \rfloor + 3$. In the second phase, each searcher explores its assigned column upward and continues the exploration by detouring obstacles whenever encountered. Even for the searcher that travels the longest distance, the total distance is at most $3c/4 + 1$. After that, all searchers return to the starting vertex in at most $c/2 + k + \lfloor \log k \rfloor + 2$ steps. Therefore, the total exploration time is at most $5c/4 + 3k + 2\lfloor \log k \rfloor + 6$. We use this as an upper bound on the cost of the optimal offline algorithm. Therefore, the competitive ratio of the WRAP algorithm for the grid graph G is at least

$$\frac{cost_{\mathsf{WRAP}}(G, k)}{cost_{\mathsf{OPT}}(G, k)} \ge \frac{ck/2 + c/2 + 2k + 2\lfloor \log k \rfloor + 4}{5c/4 + 3k + 2\lfloor \log k \rfloor + 6}$$

$$\ge \frac{ck/2}{41/4 \cdot \max(c, k)}$$

$$\in \Omega(\min(c, k)).$$

5 Discussion

In this paper, we proposed an algorithm for the online exploration of grid graphs with multiple searchers that achieves a competitive ratio of $\Theta(k/\log k +$

$\min(c, k))$, where c denotes the number of hole corners in the grid graph. There is still a gap between our upper bound and the lower bound $\Omega(\log k / \log \log k)$ for general deterministic algorithms by Ortolf and Schindelhauer [27]. We begin this section by establishing a lower bound on the competitive ratio for a restricted class of algorithms called *tree-greedy* algorithms. This class extends the *greedy* algorithms [19] defined for trees to general graphs as follows.

Definition 1 (tree-greedy algorithm). *An online exploration algorithm for general graphs is called tree-greedy if, when the input graph is a rooted tree, it always assigns searchers to unexplored subtrees, and each searcher returns to the root after completely exploring the assigned subtree.*

We can generalize Lemma 9 to *tree-greedy* algorithms as follows. The proof closely follows that of Lemma 9 and is therefore omitted.

Theorem 2. *For any $\delta > 0$, there is no tree-greedy online graph exploration algorithm for grid graphs with k searchers that has a competitive ratio less than $\lceil k/(1 + \lfloor \log k \rfloor) \rceil - \delta$.*

In the last part of this section, we briefly mention some possible directions for future work. The first direction is to study how changes in the communication model among searchers would affect WRAP and its analysis. We recall the efficient collective tree exploration algorithm of Cosson and Massoulié [8] under the unlimited communication model.

Lemma 11 (Cosson and Massoulié [8]). *There exists a collective tree exploration algorithm ALG for a tree $T = (V, E)$ with cost*

$$cost_{ALG}(T, k) \leq \frac{2\,|V|}{\sqrt{k}} + \mathcal{O}\left(\sqrt{k} \cdot D(T)\right),$$

where k is the number of searchers.

If we use this algorithm as a subroutine instead of BEER in WRAP, the same analysis as in Sect. 4.1 shows that the competitive ratio of the modified WRAP is

$$\frac{cost_{WRAP}(G, k)}{cost_{OPT}(G, k)} \leq \frac{2V|/\sqrt{k} + \mathcal{O}\left(\sqrt{k} \cdot \min((c + 1)D(G), |V|)\right)}{\max(2D(G), |V|/k)}$$

$$\leq \sqrt{k} \cdot \frac{2V|/k + \mathcal{O}\left(\min(c + 1, k) \cdot \max(2D(G), |V|/k)\right)}{\max(2D(G), |V|/k)}$$

$$\in \mathcal{O}(\sqrt{k} \cdot \min(c + 1, k)).$$

When c is a constant, this modification achieves a competitive ratio of $\mathcal{O}(\sqrt{k})$, which is better than the original WRAP's $\mathcal{O}(k / \log k)$.

The second direction is to extend our results to more general graph classes beyond grid graphs. Our algorithm and analysis rely heavily on the geometric properties of grid graphs, not only in the analysis of WRAP but also in the behavior of the algorithm itself (e.g., the coordinate system and the directional structure of edges). Even for planar graphs with unit-length edges, adapting WRAP and its analysis is far from straightforward.

Acknowledgments. This work was supported by JST Moonshot R&D Program Japan Grant Number JPMJMS2238.

Disclosure of Interests. The authors have no competing interests to declare that are relevant to the content of this article.

References

1. van den Akker, E., Buchin, K., Foerster, K.T.: Multi-agent online graph exploration on cycles and tadpole graphs. In: International Colloquium on Structural Information and Communication Complexity, pp. 513–519. Springer (2024). https://doi.org/10.1007/978-3-031-60603-8_31
2. Baligács, J., Disser, Y., Heinrich, I., Schweitzer, P.: Exploration of graphs with excluded minors. J. Comput. Syst. Sci., 103725 (2025)
3. Birx, A., Disser, Y., Hopp, A.V., Karousatou, C.: An improved lower bound for competitive graph exploration. Theoret. Comput. Sci. **868**, 65–86 (2021)
4. Böckenhauer, H.J., Fuchs, J., Unger, W.: Exploring sparse graphs with advice. Inf. Comput. **289**, 104950 (2022)
5. Brandt, S., Foerster, K.T., Maurer, J., Wattenhofer, R.: Online graph exploration on a restricted graph class: optimal solutions for tadpole graphs. Theoret. Comput. Sci. **839**, 176–185 (2020)
6. Brass, P., Cabrera-Mora, F., Gasparri, A., Xiao, J.: Multirobot tree and graph exploration. IEEE Trans. Rob. **27**(4), 707–717 (2011)
7. Brock, M., Brückmann, M., Langetepe, E., Wude, R.: Simple grid polygon online exploration revisited. arXiv preprint arXiv:2407.17208 (2024)
8. Cosson, R., Massoulié, L.: Collective tree exploration via potential function method. In: Proceedings of the Innovations in Theoretical Computer Science, pp. 1–22 (2024)
9. Cosson, R., Massoulié, L.: Asynchronous collective tree exploration: a distributed algorithm, and a new lower bound. arXiv preprint arXiv:2507.15658 (2025)
10. Davoodi, M., Delfaraz, E., Ghobadi, S., Masoori, M.: Multi-robot exploration on grids with a bounded time. Sci. Iranica **28**(Special issue on collective behavior of nonlinear dynamical networks), 1515–1528 (2021)
11. Dereniowski, D., Disser, Y., Kosowski, A., Pająk, D., Uznański, P.: Fast collaborative graph exploration. Inf. Comput. **243**, 37–49 (2015)
12. Disser, Y., Mousset, F., Noever, A., Škorić, N., Steger, A.: A general lower bound for collaborative tree exploration. Theoret. Comput. Sci. **811**, 70–78 (2020)
13. Dynia, M., Kutyłowski, J., der Heide, F.M., Schindelhauer, C.: Smart robot teams exploring sparse trees. In: International Symposium on Mathematical Foundations of Computer Science, pp. 327–338. Springer (2006). https://doi.org/10.1007/11821069_29
14. Dynia, M., Łopuszański, J., Schindelhauer, C.: Why robots need maps. In: International Colloquium on Structural Information and Communication Complexity, pp. 41–50. Springer (2007). https://doi.org/10.1007/978-3-540-72951-8_5

15. Eberle, F., Lindermayr, A., Megow, N., Nölke, L., Schlöter, J.: Robustification of online graph exploration methods. In: Proceedings of the AAAI Conference on Artificial Intelligence, vol. 36, pp. 9732–9740 (2022)
16. Foerster, K.T., Wattenhofer, R.: Lower and upper competitive bounds for online directed graph exploration. Theoret. Comput. Sci. **655**, 15–29 (2016)
17. Fraigniaud, P., Gasieniec, L., Kowalski, D.R., Pelc, A.: Collective tree exploration. Netw. Int. J. **48**(3), 166–177 (2006)
18. Fritsch, R.: Online graph exploration on trees, unicyclic graphs and cactus graphs. Inf. Process. Lett. **168**, 106096 (2021)
19. Higashikawa, Y., Katoh, N., Langerman, S., Tanigawa, S.: Online graph exploration algorithms for cycles and trees by multiple searchers. J. Comb. Optim. **28**(2), 480–495 (2014)
20. Icking, C., Kamphans, T., Klein, R., Langetepe, E.: Exploring simple grid polygons. In: International Computing and Combinatorics Conference, pp. 524–533. Springer (2005). https://doi.org/10.1007/11533719_53
21. Itai, A., Papadimitriou, C.H., Szwarcfiter, J.L.: Hamilton paths in grid graphs. SIAM J. Comput. **11**(4), 676–686 (1982)
22. Kalyanasundaram, B., Pruhs, K.R.: Constructing competitive tours from local information. Theoret. Comput. Sci. **130**(1), 125–138 (1994)
23. Kobayashi, K.M., Li, Y.: An improved upper bound for the online graph exploration problem on unicyclic graphs. J. Comb. Optim. **48**(1), 4 (2024)
24. Kolenderska, A., Kosowski, A., Małafiejski, M., Żyliński, P.: An improved strategy for exploring a grid polygon. In: International Colloquium on Structural Information and Communication Complexity, pp. 222–236. Springer (2009). https://doi.org/10.1007/978-3-642-11476-2_18
25. Megow, N., Mehlhorn, K., Schweitzer, P.: Online graph exploration: new results on old and new algorithms. Theoret. Comput. Sci. **463**, 62–72 (2012)
26. Miyazaki, S., Morimoto, N., Okabe, Y.: The online graph exploration problem on restricted graphs. IEICE Trans. Inf. Syst. **92**(9), 1620–1627 (2009)
27. Ortolf, C., Schindelhauer, C.: Online multi-robot exploration of grid graphs with rectangular obstacles. In: Proceedings of the Twenty-Fourth Annual ACM Symposium on Parallelism in Algorithms and Architectures, pp. 27–36 (2012)
28. Ortolf, C., Schindelhauer, C.: A recursive approach to multi-robot exploration of trees. In: International Colloquium on Structural Information and Communication Complexity, pp. 343–354. Springer (2014). https://doi.org/10.1007/978-3-319-09620-9_26
29. Rosenkrantz, D.J., Stearns, R.E., Lewis, P.M., II.: An analysis of several heuristics for the traveling salesman problem. SIAM J. Comput. **6**(3), 563–581 (1977)

Towards Optimal Distributed Delta Coloring

Manuel Jakob$^{(\boxtimes)}$ and Yannic Maus

TU Graz, Rechbauerstraße 12, 8010 Graz, Austria
`{m.jakob,yannic.maus}@tugraz.at`

Abstract. In contrast to the $(\Delta + 1)$-vertex coloring problem, the Δ-vertex coloring problem cannot be solved with a simple sequential greedy algorithm. As a result it has become one of the prototypical problems for understanding the complexity of non-greedy distributed graph problems on constant-degree graphs. The major open problem is whether the problem can be solved deterministically in logarithmic time, which would match the lower bound [Chang et al., FOCS'16]. Despite recent progress in the design of efficient Δ-coloring algorithms, we lack an asymptotically optimal algorithm.

In this work we present a $O(\log n)$-round deterministic Δ-coloring algorithm for locally dense constant-degree graphs, matching the lower bound for the problem on general graphs. For general Δ the algorithms' complexity is $\min\{\widetilde{O}(\log^{5/3} n), O(\Delta + \log n)\}$. Almost all recent distributed and sublinear graph coloring algorithms (also for coloring with more than Δ colors) decompose the graph into sparse and dense parts. Our algorithm works for the case that this decomposition has no sparse vertices. Ironically, in recent (randomized) Δ-coloring algorithms, dealing with sparse parts was relatively easy and these dense parts arguably posed the major hurdle. We present a solution that addresses the dense parts and may have the potential for extension to sparse parts.

Our approach is fundamentally different from prior deterministic algorithms and hence hopefully contributes towards designing an optimal algorithm for the general case, and potentially also for other non-greedy problems. Additionally, we leverage our result to also obtain a randomized $\min\{\widetilde{O}(\log^{5/3} \log n), O(\Delta + \log \log n)\}$-round algorithm for Δ-coloring locally dense graphs that also matches the lower bound for the problem on general constant-degree graphs [Brandt et al.; STOC'16].

Keywords: distributed algorithms · LOCAL model · Vertex Coloring

This research was funded in whole or in part by the Austrian Science Fund (FWF) https://doi.org/10.55776/P36280, https://doi.org/10.55776/I6915. For open access purposes, the author has applied a CC BY public copyright license to any author-accepted manuscript version arising from this submission.

1   Introduction

In the 1940ies Brooks showed that any connected graph with maximum degree Δ admits a proper vertex coloring with Δ colors, unless it is a clique on $\Delta + 1$ vertices or an odd cycle [8]. Recently, this problem has received ample attention in various sublinear models of computation, e.g., in streaming [2], massively parallel computing [12], or most prominently in distributed message passing models [3,6,9,17,18,23,30,33]. We continue with introducing the standard distributed message passing model and our results. Thereafter we explain why the Δ-coloring problem, our results and techniques are of particular interest.

The LOCAL *Model of Distributed Computing* [27]. A communication network is modeled as an n-node graph, where vertices represent computing entities and edges serve as communication channels. Communication occurs in synchronous rounds, with each node sending unbounded messages to neighbors. Nodes have unlimited computation time, and an algorithm's round complexity is the number of rounds until every node outputs its part in a globally consistent solution, e.g., its color. Recent graph coloring algorithms in distributed and other models rely on decomposing the graph into sparse and dense vertices, which are largely treated separately. A vertex is sparse if it has many non-edges in its neighborhood, and dense otherwise. A graph is locally dense if it contains no sparse vertices. Greedy problems are well-suited for parallelization, yielding highly efficient algorithms. On constant-degree graphs, these problems can be solved in $\Theta(\log^* n)$ rounds [27,31,32]. The Δ-coloring problem is fundamentally different and for a long time people asked for such an algorithm despite almost finding a logarithmic-time algorithm. While coloring with a single color less is probably of no importance to any application, the problem is of an entirely different nature. If we process many nodes in parallel and greedily color large parts of the graph, we are likely to run into situations where extending the coloring to a valid Δ-coloring is impossible. Thus, even on constant-degree graphs, the Δ-coloring problem has a $\Omega(\log n)$ lower bound for deterministic round complexity and an $\Omega(\log \log n)$ lower bound for randomized round complexity [6,9]. Understanding, whether these lower bounds are tight (at least on constant-degree graphs) has become one of the major open problem of the field, see, e.g., [3]:

Is there a logarithmic-time deterministic distributed algorithm for the Δ-coloring problem?

In this paper, we make partial progress towards answering this question affirmatively. Recent graph coloring algorithms in distributed and other models rely on decomposing the graph into sparse and dense vertices, which are largely treated separately. A vertex is *sparse* if it has many non-edges in its neighborhood, and *dense* otherwise. A graph is locally dense if it contains no sparse vertices. See the discussion in Sects. 1.1 and 1.2 for more details on locally dense graphs and Sect. 2 for its formal definition.

Theorem 1. *There is a deterministic* $\min\{\widetilde{O}(\log^{5/3} n), O(\Delta + \log n)\}$*-round*[1] LOCAL *algorithm for* Δ*-coloring locally dense graphs that do not contain a* $\Delta+1$ *clique.*

On constant-degree graphs the complexity of our algorithm matches the lower bound for the problem on general graphs [9]. On general locally dense graphs it improves the complexity from $O(\log^4 n)$ to $\widetilde{O}(\log^{5/3} n)$, which is more than a quadratic improvement [5]. In general, it is well-known that the randomized complexity and the deterministic complexity of local distributed graph problems are extremely interconnected and that this is even necessary [9].

We also leverage our deterministic algorithm by using it in a shattering framework and obtain the following randomized result.

Theorem 2. *There is a randomized algorithm with runtime* $\min\{\widetilde{O}(\log^{5/3} \log n), O(\Delta + \log \log n)\}$ *that w.h.p.* Δ*-colors locally dense graphs.*

1.1 Background and Motivation

In this section we provide further background on the Δ-coloring problem and answer the question why designing an optimal algorithms is a significant and worthwhile goal.

Fundamental Difference Between an Optimal and Almost-Optimal Algorithm. Recently, Bourreau, Brandt, and Nolin made notable progress on developing an optimal algorithm for Δ-coloring. They designed an algorithm that runs in $O(\log n \cdot \log^* n)$ rounds on constant-degree graphs [5]. While this is a significant result, it does not provide a resolution to the open problem whether there exists a deterministic Δ-coloring algorithm that runs in logarithmic time. Moreover, the authors argue that their approach cannot be further improved within the constraints of their algorithmic framework. Hence, despite seemingly almost closing the question, they still explicitly pose the following open question [5]: *What is the (randomized and deterministic) complexity of* Δ*-coloring on constant-degree graphs?* In general, there is a fundamental difference between an optimal and an almost-optimal algorithm. Also, the authors of [5] provide further reasons why removing the additional $\log^* n$ factor is of such significance.

According to a result of Chang, Kopelowitz, and Pettie [10], every so-called locally checkable labeling problem (LCLs) is either solvable in $O(f(\Delta) \cdot \log^* n)$ rounds deterministically or has a $\Omega(\log n)$ lower bound. In a nutshell, LCLs are problems on constant-degree graphs for which a $O(1)$-round LOCAL algorithm can verify a solution. Examples are many graph coloring problems or the maximal independent set problem. The all important question within this classification is whether the $\Omega(\log n)$ lower bound is tight.

In this work we make partial progress in showing that the Δ-coloring problem can be solved in $O(\log n)$ rounds, at least on locally dense constant-degree graphs. Extending our approach to all constant-degree graphs and proving that

---

[1] $\widetilde{O}(f(n))$ hides factors that are poly-logarithmic in $f(n)$.

the complexity of Δ-coloring depends only logarithmically on n and therefore proving the tightness of its lower bound would represent a breakthrough. To the best of our knowledge there are only very few problems where the $\Omega(\log n)$ lower bound for constant degrees is tight, namely sinkless orientation [20] and its siblings [19], hypergraph sinkless orientation [7], and $(3/2\Delta)$-edge coloring [7].

A New Approach for Solving Δ-Coloring. As mentioned, Bourreau, Brandt, and Nolin argued that is is unlikely to further improve their approach [5]. From a very high-level point of view their algorithm uses some form of symmetry-breaking on a virtual graph built by so-called degree choosable components (DCC). As DCCs can have diameter $\Theta(\log n)$, and symmetry-breaking generally requires at least $\Omega(\log^* n)$ time, the $O(\log n \log^* n)$ runtime seems to be the limit of this approach. This was already observed earlier by Balliu, Brandt, Kuhn, and Olivetti in [3] where they explicitly ask for a Δ-coloring algorithm not relying on this technique; see Sect. 1.2 for more details. Our algorithm for the non-greedy Δ-coloring problem is genuinely different: We split the graph into clusters, and then use logarithmic time to provide *slack* to each cluster. e form of having a distinct slack triad for each clique.

As a result, solving the clusters is a greedy problem and greedy problems are well understood with a large existing toolbox ready for solving them. Hopefully this novel approach can be also used as a building block for designing optimal algorithms further non-greedy problems in the field. In other words, our algorithm can also be seen as an $O(\log n)$-round reduction of the Δ-coloring problem to various greedy problems like maximal matching, *degree* $+ 1$-list coloring, and the ruling set problem. It is interesting to explore under which settings such reductions are possible. To our knowledge, prior to this work, the only known reductions targeting a non-greedy problem reduce to LLL, another inherently non-greedy problem.

Locally Dense Graphs Have Been the Most Challenging Part in Most Prior Works. Most recent distributed graph coloring algorithms (but also in models as streaming, massively parallel computation, etc.) rely on decomposing the input graph into a set of sparse vertices and the set of dense vertices, e.g., $[1, 2, 11, 15, 21\text{--}23, 25]$. Sparse vertices are relatively easy to deal with in randomized Δ-coloring algorithms. It is well-known and widely used, see e.g., [13] and all of the aforementioned papers, that the simplest one-round coloring algorithm— in this algorithm each node picks a random candidate color and permanently adopts the color if no neighbors tries the same color—is likely to produce permanent slack for sparse vertices. A node receives *permanent slack* if two of its neighbors are colored with the same color, as it loses only one color of its palette of available colors but two competitors for these colors. Hence, coloring a node with permanent slack brings us back to the greedy regime, i.e., we obtain a problem whose flavor is similar to the one of $(\Delta + 1)$-coloring. This slack generation for sparse graphs has been leveraged for Δ-coloring in $[2, 15, 23]$, but also to obtain very efficient $(\Delta + 1)$-coloring algorithms in various papers before. In contrast, dense parts of the graph are much more challenging to deal with as dependencies are larger and it is much more difficult to produce slack. With Theorems 1 and 2, the search for an optimal Δ-coloring algorithm has narrowed to sparse graphs.

Concurrent Work. In concurrent work, Bourreau, Brandt, and Nolin made notable progress toward developing an optimal algorithm for Δ-coloring. They obtained an algorithm that runs in optimal $O(\log n)$ rounds for graphs with constant maximum degree Δ [4]. Their work (different from [5]) uses similar building blocks as our approach, i.e., a form of slack-triads and a reduction to the hypergraph sinkless orientation problem, see Sect. 1.2 for details. The benefit of their work is that it works for general graphs unless our work that only applies to locally dense graphs. The benefit of our work is that it can be extended to work with *easier* subroutines. In fact, using the building blocks of our work, Jakob, Maus, and Schager have designed an $O(\log n)$-round reduction of the $(2\Delta - 2)$-edge coloring problem to the *probably much easier* $2\Delta - 1$-edge coloring problem [26] that works for general graphs. The $2\Delta - 2$-edge coloring problem is the same as the Δ-coloring problem for line graphs, and line graphs are very similar to locally dense graphs. Such a result cannot be obtained with [4] as on general graphs it inherently relies on the computation of a so-called maximal independent set whose best upper bound currently is superlogarithmic [16]. We hope that the approach presented in our work can serve as a blueprint for further improvements for other non-greedy problems.

1.2   Technical Overview and Related Work

Prior Deterministic Algorithms. The Δ-coloring problem is easy in areas of the graph where there is a node with degree $< \Delta$. We can stall coloring that node, providing temporary slack to its neighbors as the number of competitors for colors reduces due to the stalled neighbor. By iterating this stalling procedure, we obtain multiple layers around the original node, where each layer consists of vertices at the same distance from the origin. Coloring is then performed layer by layer, starting from the outermost layer and progressing inward to the node with degree $< \Delta$. Prior deterministic algorithms leverage this idea and use the concept of so-called degree choosable components (DCC) [14,18,33,35]. The crucial structural theorem forming the base for prior results claims that any node is contained in a DCC of at most logarithmic diameter. On the positive side a DCC of logarithmic diameter can be solved by brute-force in logaritmic time in the **LOCAL** model, regardless of how we have colored other vertices. The main issue is that DCCs for different vertices are neighboring and may even overlap. Thus, they cannot be dealt with simultaneously. Hence, some form of symmetry-breaking between the DCCs is required. As symmetry-breaking usually requires at least $\Omega(\log^* n)$ time, and DCCs have a logarithmic diameter, this approach can probably, even in the best case, only lead to algorithms with runtime $O(\log n \cdot \log^* n)$. Due to this observation Balliu, Brandt, Kuhn, and Olivetti even explicitly asked for a genuinely different approach to attack the Δ-coloring problem [3].

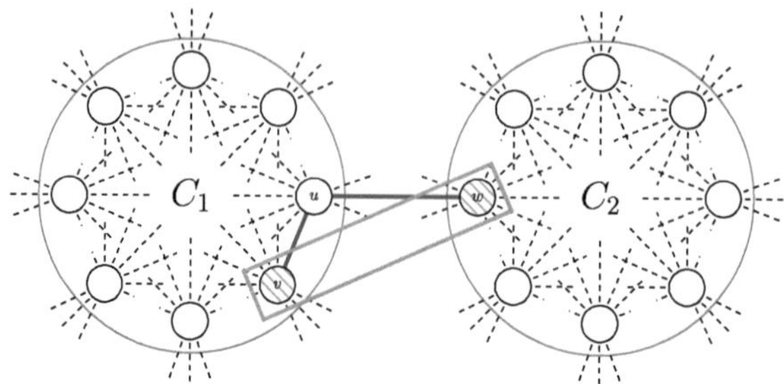

Fig. 1. For each hard clique, such as C_1 and C_2, we identify slack triads—for example, (u, v, w) in C_1. The slack pair vertices, v and w, are then same-colored (see Fig. 2), providing slack to vertex u.

Our Approach. Our approach is inspired by the recent development in randomized algorithms for the problem, namely [15,23]. In both of these the focus is on locally producing permanent slack as explained for the case of sparse nodes in the previous section. **Slack Triads (Fig. 1).** To achieve this, we aim to find many so-called slack triads[2]. A slack triad is a triple of nodes u, v, and w such that v and w are both neighbors of u, but v and w are non-adjacent. In that case, we can same-color v and w providing slack to u. We call u the *slack vertex* and v and w the *slack pair* vertices. Using a similar layering approach as for nodes with degree $< \Delta$, we can color all nodes reaching u via a short (optimally constant-hop) path of uncolored vertices. The main obstacle is that slack triads should be

i) non-overlapping, ii) easily be same-colorable, and iii) be locally everywhere in the graph.

The first property is important as the slack at u is useless if u appeared in some other slack triad where u is actually colored. Also, if v and w appear as slack pair vertices in other slack triads we may end up having to same-color large subsets of vertices. In order to satisfy condition *ii)* we ensure that the conflict graph of same-coloring the respective vertices of all slack triads has maximum degree $\Delta - 1$. Note that this is non-trivial as potentially both slack pair vertices could have up to $\Delta - 1$ neighboring conflicting slack triads, resulting in a maximum degree of $2\Delta - 2 \gg \Delta - 1$. See Fig. 2 for an illustrations of the virtual conflict graph formed by slack triads. Property iii) is clearly needed to color all vertices of the graph.

Finding Slack Triads in Extremely Locally Dense Graphs. The details of our algorithm for finding a set of slack triads satisfying properties i)–iii) are involved. For illustration purposes let us focus on some locally really dense part of the graph that only consists of adjacent cliques of size Δ. Fix one such clique C.

---

[2] A similar yet slightly different concept first appeared in a prior randomized algorithm under the name of a T-node [18].

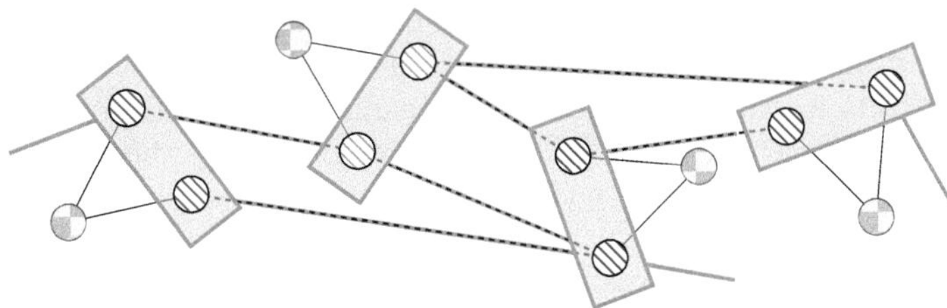

Fig. 2. For coloring the hard cliques in the graph, we identify slack pair vertices (orange boxes), which provide the slack vertices (checkboard) with one unit of slack. To color the slack pair vertices, we construct a virtual graph where each slack pair (orange box) is treated as a single vertex. Edges between these vertices (orange) exist if there is an underlying edge in the original graph (black). (Color figure online)

As there are no $\Delta + 1$ cliques in the graph each vertex u of C has one external neighbor $v_u \notin C$. For this exposition also assume that each node in C has a distinct external neighbor. The high level idea is to find two edges (u_1, v_{u_1}) and (u_2, v_{u_2}) leaving the clique that are not claimed by the clique on the other side. If we find these edges, nodes u_1 and v_{u_1} and u_2 form a slack triad, as u_1 is adjacent to v_{u_1} and u_2, and v_{u_1} and u_2 are non-adjacent.

The *sinkless Orientation Problem* has distributed complexity $\Theta(\log n)$ and asks to orient the edges of a graph such that every node with degree at least 3 has one outgoing edge. By splitting each vertex into two virtual vertices, one can also ensure that every node with degree 6 has at least two outgoing edges. If we now split each clique into two virtual *vertices* and orient the intra-clique edges, we can achieve that each clique has found two edges (its outgoing edges) that are not claimed by the clique at the other end and we can form a slack triad with slack pair vertices v_{u_1} and u_2. This construction satisfies property $i)$ and $iii)$. But we may entirely violate property $ii)$ as all the other edges incident to the respective cliques of v and w may be *claimed* by other cliques and hence it may be that the entire cliques of v_{u_1} and u_2 are used in other slack triads. In order to ensure property $ii)$ we thus use another logarithmic-time algorithm to sparsify the set of participating intra-cluster edges. This completes the high level procedure of finding slack triads in the case where the graph locally only consists of Δ cliques.

Finding Slack Triads in Locally Dense Graphs. When the graph is less dense, each clique can have up to $\Omega(\Delta)$ outgoing edges. If we would mimic the same approach, it may be that one vertex has multiple outgoing and multiple incoming edges. In that case it is unclear whether it should take part in the slack triad of its own clique or the slack triad of a neighboring clique. The first idea is to compute a maximal matching of intra-cluster edges and restrict the previous algorithm to the edges in the matching. The benefit is that every node has only one incident intra-cluster edge and the same reasoning as before works fine. The challenge is that a maximal matching is a greedy-type problem and hence it does not satisfy the locally everywhereness of property iii), that is, we may have parts in the graph that have no matching edge. Now, if we would simply proceed we may run into a situation where vertices cannot be colored in the sequel, not even existentially. Hence, in our full solution, we re-balance the matching to also achieve property *iii*). To that end we develop a proposal algorithm in which cliques propose to grab intra-cluster edges. We manage proposals such that each intra-cluster edge only receives few proposals, but each clique sends many of them. Hence, on average each clique can grab some edges. We indeed ensure that *every* clique grabs sufficiently many edges by reducing this re-balancing problem to the hyperedge grabbing problem of [7]. This overview omits several technical details and in our full algorithm we also deal with parts of the graph that do not form proper cliques.

Why Does Our Approach Not (Yet) Extend to Sparse Graphs? In principle the approach of finding slack triads seems to be a promising candidate to extend to sparse graphs, and the same is true for the general scheme all of our subroutines. Instead of applying it to cliques, one may apply it to constant-radius subgraphs that contain enough outgoing edges (to send a large number of proposals). The main point where our technique does not extend is that we are unable to glue two edges grabbed by such a part together to form a slack triad. While we still think that our general approach is fruitful, a full solution should probably be less focused on edges but rather on higher order objects such as hyperedges. Ironically, as already mentioned earlier, for large Δ sparse parts are extremely simple for randomized algorithms as slack is produced everywhere with high probability with a one round color trial procedure. The algorithm of Bourreau, Brandt, and Nolin in [4] finds a way to select suitable slack triads even in the sparse parts of a graph. Their method avoids gluing of edges to form slack triads but directly places slack-triad candidates in sparse parts of the graph. Then, they use the hypergraph sinkless orientation problem to select slack triads such that all parts of the graph have a short suitable paths to the slack vertex of a slack triad.

Outline. In Sect. 2, we introduce locally dense graphs. In Sect. 3, we present our deterministic Δ-coloring algorithm along with all essential proofs. Appendix A complementary subroutines. Full proofs and supplementary results regarding the role of Δ-coloring in the complexity of local graph problems are available in the full version of the paper (https://arxiv.org/abs/2504.03080).

2   Preliminaries: ACD, Locally Dense Graphs, and Hyperedge Grabbing

Notation. Given a graph $G = (V, E)$ and a vertex $v \in V$, let $N(v)$ denote the set of v's neighbors. A clique or an almost clique C is a subgraph of G with additional properties specified below. Let $V(C)$ represent the set of vertices contained in C. Sometimes, we also simply write $v \in C$ to depict a vertex in a given clique C.

Given a set of cliques $\mathcal{C}$, we define $V(\mathcal{C}) = \bigcup_{C \in \mathcal{C}} V(C)$ as the union of the vertex sets of all cliques in $\mathcal{C}$. Furthermore, let $\deg(C) = |\{\{u,v\} \in E \mid u \in C, v \notin C\}|$ denote the degree of a clique C, defined as the number of outgoing edges of the clique. Throughout let $\Delta = \max_{v \in V} |N(v)|$ be the maximum degree of the input graph G. For an integer k let $[k]$ denote the set $\{0, \dots, k-1\}$. Let v be a node with available color palette $P(v)$ in a subgraph $\tilde{G} \subseteq G$. The *slack* of v in $\tilde{G}$ is $|P(v)| - d$, where d is the number of uncolored neighbors of v in $\tilde{G}$. A vertex has *slack* if its slack is positive.

We next explain the necessary basics of the almost clique decomposition that we require for our theorem. In the following $0 < \eta, \varepsilon < 1$ are sufficiently small constants. Two adjacent nodes u and v are *friends*, if $|N(v) \cap N(u)| \geq (1-\eta)\Delta$. A vertex is *$\eta$-dense* if it has at least $(1-\eta)\Delta$ friend neighbors, otherwise it is *η-sparse*.

Claim ([1]). Any η-sparse vertex has at most $(1 - \eta^2)\binom{\Delta}{2}$ edges in the subgraph induced by its neighborhood.

Based on these definitions, any graph can be decomposed into sparse and dense vertices, which are further partitioned into *almost cliques (ACs)*. Different coloring algorithms provide slightly varying guarantees for these ACs. In the basic version of the decomposition, each connected component of the graph induced by dense vertices and friend edges forms an AC [1,24]. This decomposition can be computed in $O(1)$ rounds in the LOCAL model, the ACs have diameter two, and each AC is of size $(1 \pm O(\eta))\Delta$ [1,24]. We use the following almost clique-decomposition (ACD) that can be obtained via a deterministic $O(1)$-round postprocessing of the basic ACD [15,23]:

Lemma 1 (ACD computation [2,15,23,24]). *Let $\varepsilon = 1/63$. For any graph $G = (V, E)$, there is a partition (almost-clique decomposition (ACD) of V into sets V_{sparse} and $C_1, C_2, \dots, C_t$ such that each node in V_{sparse} is $\varepsilon/108$-sparse and for every $i \in [t]$,*

(i) $(1 - \varepsilon/4)\Delta \leq |C_i| \leq (1 + \varepsilon)\Delta$,
(ii) Each $v \in C_i$ has at least $(1 - \varepsilon)\Delta$ neighbors in C_i: $|N(v) \cap C_i| \geq (1 - \varepsilon)\Delta$,
(iii) Each node $u \notin C_i$ has at most $(1 - \varepsilon/2)\Delta$ neighbors in C_i: $|N(u) \cap C_i| \leq (1 - \varepsilon/2)\Delta$.

Further, there is a deterministic $O(1)$-round LOCAL algorithm to compute a valid ACD.

Observation 1. *Any vertex v of an AC C has at most $\varepsilon\Delta$ neighbors outside of C.*

Definition 1 (Locally dense graph). *We call a graph* locally dense *if the ACD computation executed with that $\varepsilon = 1/63$ does not contain any nodes that are classified as sparse.*

While Δ-coloring algorithms (Theorems 1 and 2) work for any Δ, for $\Delta < 63$ any locally dense graph can only consists of isolated cliques due to the choice of ε. We believe that the parameter ε can be made larger classifying more graphs as locally dense at the cost of complicating the algorithm.

Hyperedge Grabbing (HEG). In a hypergraph, the *minimum degree δ* is the smallest number of hyperedges incident to any vertex, while the *(maximum) rank r* is the largest number of vertices contained in any hyperedge. Given a hypergraph with rank r and minimum degree δ, the *hyperedge grabbing problem (HEG)* asks each vertex to grab one of its incident hyperedges such that no hyperedge is grabbed by more than one vertex. The problem is equivalent to the hypergraph sinkless orientation problem from [7] and can be solved in logarithmic time with their algorithm if the hypergraph's rank is sufficiently smaller than the minimum degree.

Lemma 2 ([7]). *There is a deterministic $O(\log_{\frac{\delta}{r}} n)$-round algorithm for computing an HEG in any n-node multihypergraph with minimum degree δ and maximum rank $r < \delta$.*

3   Deterministic Δ-Coloring Locally Dense Graphs

The goal of this section is to prove Theorem 1.

Theorem 1. *There is a deterministic $\min\{\widetilde{O}(\log^{5/3} n), O(\Delta + \log n)\}$-round[3] LOCAL algorithm for Δ-coloring locally dense graphs that do not contain a $\Delta+1$ clique.*

The definitions of the terms in the high-level overview in Algorithm 1, i.e., hard cliques, easy cliques, and loopholes, follow in Sect. 3.1. The bulk of the paper will be coloring the vertices in hard cliques in Sect. 3.2 to 3.7. The last step of coloring easy cliques and loopholes is detailed on in Sect. 3.9. The short proof of Theorem 1 combining all previous lemmas appears in Sect. 3.10.

Algorithm 1. Δ-coloring locally dense graphs (high-level overview)

1: Compute an ACD (for $\varepsilon = 1/63$) and form the ordered partition of the nodes.
2: Color vertices in hard almost cliques
3: Color vertices in easy almost cliques and loopholes

3.1   Definitions: Loopholes and Hard/Easy Almost-Cliques

Any node in a graph with degree less than Δ can be greedily (in a centralized setting) colored with one of the Δ colors, regardless of how its neighbors have been colored. Thus, it forms in some sense a loophole for the Δ-coloring problem. Another loophole is given by a non-clique four cycle [14,18,35]. A non-clique four cycle in a graph G consists of four vertices v_0, v_1, v_2, v_3 that form a four cycle, i.e., $\{v_i, v_{i+1 \bmod 4}\} \in E(G)$ for $i = 0, 1, 2, 3$ and $G[\{v_0, v_1, v_2, v_3\}]$ does not form a clique. In fact, it is known that any non-clique even length cycle is a loophole. We summarize these loopholes in the following definition.

---

[3] $\widetilde{O}(f(n))$ hides factors that are poly-logarithmic in $f(n)$.

Definition 2 (Loophole). *Consider a clique C in a graph G. A loophole is a subgraph which has one of the following shapes:*

1. *A vertex in C with a degree less than Δ, or*
2. *A non-clique cycle of even length*

A loophole vertex *is a vertex contained in some loophole.*

These loopholes are also known as *degree choosable components*, or as *deg*-list colorable graphs. A graph G is *deg-list colorable* if, for any list assignment where each vertex $v \in V(G)$ is assigned a list of at least $\deg(v)$ colors, there exists a proper coloring of G from the lists.

Lemma 3 ([14,18,35]). *Non-clique cycles of even length are deg-list colorable.*

Lemma 3 is useful, as we can compute any Δ-coloring of $V \setminus L$ to a coloring of V if $G[L]$ is a loophole. In contrast to prior work based on such loopholes, we only consider loopholes of constant size which is crucial for obtaining a flat logarithmic runtime, see Sect. 1.2.

Due to Lemma 3, it will be easier to color almost cliques that intersect a loophole. The bulk of our algorithm deals with the remaining hard cliques, as defined next.

Definition 3 (Easy/Hard ACs). *An almost clique is called hard if it does not contain any vertex belonging to a loophole of at most 6 vertices; otherwise, it is called easy.*

Let $\mathcal{C}_{hard}$ be the set of all hard cliques in G. Further, we refer $\mathcal{V}_{hard} = \bigcup_{C' \in \mathcal{C}_{hard}} V(C')$ as the set of vertices that are in a hard clique and $\mathcal{E}_{hard}$ as the edges between vertices in $\mathcal{V}_{hard}$ whose endpoints lie in different cliques. We often omit the 'almost' for *hard almost cliques*.

Lemma 4. *The following hold for each hard clique C:*

1. *C forms a clique,*
2. *Each vertex $v \in C$ has $e_C = \Delta - |C| + 1$ neighbors outside of C ,*
3. *There is no vertex $w \notin C$ with two neighbors in C .*

Lemma 4 is a direct consequence of the definition of hard cliques. For example if Part 3 would not hold, one could identify a loophole in the clique.

3.2   Coloring Hard Cliques: High Level Overview (Algorithm 2)

High Level Overview (Pseudocode in Algorithm 2). Hard cliques, introduced in Definition 3, are cliques that do not intersect any loophole and therefore lack access to an existing slack source. To address this we identify a collection of so-called non-overlapping *slack triads*, see Definition 4 below. A slack triad for a hard clique C consists of a vertex $u \in C$ and two non-adjacent neighbors $v \in C$ and $w \notin C$ of u. Once identified these nodes, we aim at same-coloring the *slack pair* v and w (Step 8, Sect. 3.6), providing slack to the uncolored node

u, effectively providing a toehold to the whole clique such that all nodes can be colored efficiently, see Step 9 and Sect. 3.7. A key challenge is to ensure that we can even effectively same-color the slack pairs. Consider the virtual graph consisting of one vertex for each such slack pair and an edge between two 'slack pair vertices' if there is an edge between any of their corresponding vertices in the underlying graph G. Same-coloring the vertices in each slack pair corresponds to Δ-coloring this virtual graph. Poorly chosen pairs can yield virtual degrees up to $2\Delta - 2$, making this extremely difficult. The bulk of this section (Step 1 to Step 7 dealt with in Sects. 3.3 to 3.5) aims to identify these slack triads. See Sect. 1.2 for intuition on these steps. Phase 1 is presented in Sect. 3.3 and contains the initial maximal matching computation as well as the explained proposal algorithm to modify the matching such that conditions i)–iii) from Sect. 1.2 are satisfied. The latter is the most involved part of our algorithm.

Let $\mathcal{C}$ ($\mathcal{C}_{hard}$) denote the set of all almost cliques (hard cliques). Define the subgraph

$$G' := G\left[\{C \in \mathcal{C}_{hard} \mid \forall v \in V(C), N(v) \cap \mathcal{V}_{hard} \neq \emptyset\}\right]$$

that consists of all hard almost cliques in $\mathcal{C}_{hard}$ where each vertex of the clique has at least one neighbor in a hard clique. We begin with a high level overview on the algorithm. Thereafter we detail on each step and its properties in a separate section.

Algorithm 2. Coloring vertices in hard cliques (high level overview)

Phase 1: Balanced Matching (Section 3.3)
  1: Compute Maximal Matching F_1 in G'
  2: Compute a HEG on the hypergraph
  3: Rearrange edges in F_1 to vertex that grabbed the edge to obtain matching $F2$
  4: Orient edges in F_2 to the vertex that grabbed the edge.
Phase 2: Sparsifying the matching (Section 3.4)
  5: Apply the Degree Splitting to reduce incoming and outgoing edges per clique.
  6: Discard all outgoing edges per clique except two
Phase 3: Slack Triad Forming (Section 3.5)
  7: Define a slack triad from the two vertices with an outgoing edge per clique
Phase 4: Coloring (Sections 3.6 and 3.7)
  8: Compute a coloring of the slack pairs in the graph induced by them.
  9: Color remaining hard vertices with $O(1)$ rounds of $deg + 1$-list coloring instances

---

3.3   Phase 1: Balanced Matching

The first step of the coloring is to determine a matching in the graph $(\mathcal{V}_{hard}, \mathcal{E}_{hard})$ that considers only edges of $E(G)$ whose endpoints lie in different hard cliques. The main part of this stage is to rearrange and orient the matching F_1 such that each participating clique ends up with at least 28 incident outgoing edges. Let $\mathcal{C}_{HEG} \subseteq \mathcal{C}_{hard}$ be the set of all hard cliques for which each vertex is adjacent to at least one vertex in another hard clique. Define the following multihypergraph H to apply Lemma 2 on it.

$$H = (V_H, E_H) \ .$$

The vertex set V_H. The vertex set V_H consists of 28 virtual vertices for each hard clique $C \in \mathcal{C}_{HEG}$ that are obtained by partitioning C into sets $Q_C^1, \ldots, Q_C^{28}$.

Intuition For the Proposal Algorithm. Each virtual sub clique sends out one request for each of its vertices to grab a close-by edge of F_1; different vertices of the sub clique send requests to different edges, as otherwise loopholes would exist. Then, the hypergraph H has one hyperedge for each edge of F_1 consisting of the sub cliques requesting to grab that edge. In a solution to the HEG problem on H sub clique exclusively grabs one edge of F_1. In a second step this relation is used to modify the matching F_1 and to orient the resulting edges such that each sub clique obtains one outgoing edge. This totals in 28 outgoing edges for each hard clique in $\mathcal{C}_{HEG}$. **The edge set E_H.** Formally, describing the edge set of H is more involved, in particular, as we require several technical definitions to later formally define the matching F_2 stemming from a solution to HEG on H. Let $N_{out}(v)$ be the neighbors of v that are not in the same clique. To this end, define $f : V(\mathcal{C}_{HEG}) \to V(F_1)$:

$$f(v) = \begin{cases} v & \text{if } v \text{ has incident edge in } F_1 \\ u & \text{otherwise, where } u \text{ is the vertex with min. ID in } N_{out}(v) \cap V_{hard} \end{cases}$$

The function $f(v)$ is well-defined because every vertex v belongs to one of the participating cliques. This ensures that v either has an incident edge in F_1 or a neighbor in $N_{out}(v) \cap V_{hard}$. Note that if $f(v) = u$ with $u \neq v$, then u has an incident edge in F_1 as F_1 is a maximal matching between hard vertices and both v and u are hard vertices. Let $\phi(v)$ be the unique edge of F_1 incident to $f(v)$. For a vertex $v \in V(\mathcal{C}_{HEG})$ let $Q_i(v) \in V_H$ denote the sub clique that contains v. The hypergraph H has one hyperedge $f_e = \{Q_i(v) \mid v \in V, \phi(v) = e\}$ for each edge $e \in F_1$ and f_e contains exactly those sub cliques that request to grab edge e.

The following lemma shows that all vertices of a sub clique request to grab distinct sets of edges. It is proven by contradiction: If two vertices of a sub clique would request to grab the same edge, one can construct a loophole intersecting their hard clique.

Lemma 5. *For each $C \in \mathcal{C}_{HEG}, i \in [28]$ we have $|f(V(Q_C^i))| = |\phi(V(Q_C^i))| = |Q_C^i|$.*

Let $r_H = \max_{e \in F_1} |f_e|$ be the rank of the hypergraph H and let $\delta_H = \min_{Q \in V_H} |\{f \in E_H \mid Q \in f\}|$ be the minimum degree of H. In order to apply Lemma 2 for computing an HEG of H, we show that the rank r_H is smaller than the minimum degree δ_H.

(a) The red edges indicate a partial maximal matching on a section of a graph that result after Step 1. The proposals of the vertices u and v are indicated by the blue arrows.

(b) The green oriented edges show the partial matching after the HEG procedure in Step 2.

Fig. 3. This example illustrates the intuition behind the HEG procedure in Algorithm 2, applied to three cliques with their respective partitions. It demonstrates the process of edge flipping triggered by the HEG. Initially, vertices request to grab an edge, as indicated by the blue arrows based on the function f. This request can either target an adjacent matching edge (e.g., vertex v) or a matching edge adjacent to a neighbor (e.g., vertex u). As the algorithm progresses, the vertices (u, v, w) form the slack triad for the bottom clique assuming u becomes the slack vertex.

Lemma 6. $\delta_H > 1.1 r_H$ *holds.*

Intuitively, Lemma 6 states that each subclique sends out more requests to grab edges than any edge in the initial maximal matching receives. As a result, on average, each subclique can claim at least one edge exclusively. Furthermore, Lemma 2 guarantees that such an assignment can be computed efficiently in $O(\log_{r_H/\delta_H} n) = O(\log n)$ rounds.

Computing F_2 From a Solution to HEG on H. Given the matching F_1 obtained in Step 1 of Algorithm 2, along with the result of the subsequent HEG instance, we now demonstrate the method for constructing a matching F_2 together with an orientation of its edges ensuring that each clique is incident to at least 28 outgoing edges from F_2.

We obtain the set F_2 by starting with the empty set and by adding edges to F_2 via performing the following process for each edge $e \in F_1$ and corresponding hyperedge $f_e \in E_H$. Let $\phi''(f_e) \in V_H \cup \{\bot\}$ be the sub clique that grabbed the hyperedge f_e based on the result of the HEG on H obtained via Lemma 2. If $\phi''(f_e) \neq \bot$ let $v_e = \phi'(f_e) \in V(\mathcal{C}_{HEG})$ be the unique vertex of the sub clique that sent a request to edge e. For each edge $e \in F_1$ we add the edge $\{v_e, f(v_e)\}$ to F_2 and orient it to $f(v_e)$. See Fig. 3 for an illustration of this process. The next lemma states the properties of the resulting matching F_2.

Lemma 7 (Balanced Matching). *F_2 is a matching whose edges are directed and for each hard clique C at least one of the following holds:*

- *Type I: C has at least 28 outgoing edges in F_2, or*
- *Type II: C has an adjacent easy AC.*

3.4 Phase 2: Sparsifying the Core Matching

This sparsification step aims to limit the number of incident edges for each hard clique, which is essential for coloring slack pairs in Step 8; see Sect. 3.6. We split each hard clique C into two subsets using a more structured approach than in the previous step. Let $Q_C^+ \subseteq C$ denote the set of vertices that have an outgoing edge in F_2. The remaining vertices, $Q_C^- = C \setminus Q_C^+$, consist of those incident to an incoming edge in F_2 or are not incident to an edge in F_2 at all. Let $\mathcal{Q}^+ = \{Q_C^+ \mid C \in \mathcal{C}_{hard}\}$ and $\mathcal{Q}^- = \{Q_C^- \mid C \in \mathcal{C}_{hard}\}$ be the sets of all such sub cliques. Construct a virtual graph G_Q with vertex set $\mathcal{Q}^+ \cup \mathcal{Q}^-$. Two vertices in G_Q are connected by an edge if there exists an edge in F_2 with endpoints in their corresponding sub-cliques. We apply the degree-splitting algorithm from Lemma 14 to G_Q to limit the number of edges incident to each hard clique, retaining 2 outgoing edges and imposing an upper bound on incoming edges. The outcome is summarized in the following lemma:

Lemma 8 (Low-Degree Balanced Matching). *Given the graph G_H and the Matching F_2 with the properties from Lemma 7, the second phase of Algorithm 2 computes a oriented matching $F_3 \subseteq F_2$ with the following property: each hard clique C has less than $\frac{1}{2}(\Delta - 2\varepsilon\Delta - 1)$ incoming edges in F_3 and additionally one of the following holds:*

- *Type I^+: C is adjacent to exactly 2 outgoing edges in F_3, or*
- *Type II: C has an adjacent easy clique.*

3.5 Phase 3: Forming Slack Triads

We use the matching F_3 to define a slack triad for each hard clique, thereby providing it with a source for permanent slack. Also see Fig. 1.

Definition 4 (Slack Triad). *An ordered triple of vertices (u, v, w) is a slack triad if $v, w \in N(u)$ and v and w are non-adjacent. In this case we call u the slack vertex of the slack triad and v, w form the slack pair. We also refer v and w as slack pair vertices.*

Given the matching F_3, for each hard clique C, we select an arbitrary tail of one of its outgoing edges, denoted as e_1 in F_3, and set it as the slack node for the corresponding slack triad of C. The slack triad is then completed by including the head of e_1 and the tail of the other outgoing edge of C in F_3 as the slack pair vertices. Note that the slack pair vertices are indeed non-adjacent as required since otherwise there would be another vertex in C that would define a loophole with the vertices of the slack triad.

Lemma 9 (Forming slack triads). *Given the Matching F_3 with the properties of Lemma 8, in $O(1)$ rounds one can compute a collection $\mathcal{S}$ of slack triads with the following properties:*

- *i) Each clique of Type I^+ from Lemma 8 contains a slack node of a slack triad of $\mathcal{S}$.*
- *ii) The slack triads in $\mathcal{S}$ are vertex disjoint.*
- *iii) Each clique contains at most $\frac{1}{2}(\Delta - 2\varepsilon\Delta - 1) + 1$ slack pair vertices.*

3.6   Phase 4A: Coloring Slack Pairs

We start the coloring process with the slack pairs of the slack triads $\mathcal{S}$. Since there is no edge between the two slack pair vertices one can assign both the same color providing the slack node one unit of slack without violating the coloring. Nevertheless, vertices of the slack triads can be adjacent and consequently we need to coordinate color choices between the different slack pairs. Define the virtual graph $G_V = (V_V, E_V)$ capturing the conflict relation between slack pairs, where V_V contains one vertex for each slack pair in $\mathcal{S}$ and there exists an edge in E_V between two slack pairs if there is an edge in the original graph between any of the slack pairs' vertices. See Fig. 2 for an illustration. Lemma 10 proves that this virtual graph instance can indeed be colored via a MaxDegree + 1-coloring procedure, when using color space $[\Delta]$.

Lemma 10. *The maximum degree of G_V is at most $\Delta - 2$.*

3.7   Phase 4B: Coloring Remaining Hard Vertices

Lemma 11. (Coloring). *In Step 9 all remaining vertices in hard cliques can be colored with a two deg + 1-list coloring instances.*

3.8   Runtime of Algorithm 2

Let $T_{MM}(n, \Delta)$ denote the round complexity for computing a maximal matching, T_{SP} for computing the degree splitting, and let $T_{deg+1}(n, \Delta)$ represent the round complexity to compute a $deg + 1$-list coloring in a graph with n vertices and maximum degree Δ. Additionally, let $T_{HEG}(n)$ be the round complexity of computing a hyperedge grabbing solution in a hypergraph with n vertices and minimum degree at least by a 1.05 factor larger than the maximum rank.

Lemma 12. *The round complexity of Algorithm 2 is upper bounded by*

$$O(T_{MM}(n, \Delta) + T_{SP}(n) + T_{deg+1}(n, \Delta) + T_{HEG}(n)).$$

This round complexity is upper bounded by $\min\{O(\Delta + \log n), \widetilde{O}(\log^{5/3} n)\}.$

3.9   Coloring Easy Cliques and Loopholes (Algorithm 1, Line 3)

Loophole Coloring. In this section, we describe Step 3, which handles the coloring of vertices in easy almost-cliques and the remaining vertices in loopholes.

Algorithm 3. Coloring of loopholes and easy cliques

1: Each loophole vertex votes for one of its loopholes; $\mathcal{L}$ contains all loopholes with a vote
2: Construct virtual graph $G_{\mathcal{L}}$ of $\mathcal{L}$
3: Compute a 6-ruling set $\mathcal{L}_{rs}$ in $G_{\mathcal{L}}$
4: Run BFS with depth 25 from $\mathcal{L}_{rs}$ to layer remaining vertices by depth.
5: **for** $i = 25 \ldots 1$ **do**
6:    Perform $(\deg +1)$-list coloring for vertices in layer i
7: **end for**
8: Color the vertices in $\mathcal{L}_{rs}$ by bruteforce in $O(1)$ rounds

---

Let $T_{6-rs}(n, \Delta)$ be the complexity to compute a 6-ruling set.

Lemma 13. *Algorithm 3 computes a Δ-coloring in $T_{6-rs} + O(T_{deg+1})$ rounds.*

3.10   Proof of Theorem 1

The validity of the coloring follows from Lemma 11 and Lemma 13. Lemma 11 shows that a valid Δ-coloring can be computed for all vertices in hard cliques, while Lemma 13 ensures that the Δ-coloring can be completed for the remaining vertices in easy cliques and loopholes. For the runtime we get the following: In Step 1, computing the ACD has a round complexity of $O(1)$ by Lemma 1. By Lemma 12, the step of Algorithm 1 that colors vertices in hard cliques requires at most $\min\{O(\Delta + \log n), \widetilde{O}(\log^{5/3} n)\}$ rounds. The last two steps of coloring vertices in easy cliques and last the vertices in loopholes, detailed in Algorithm 3, can be done in $O(\Delta) + \min\{O(\Delta + \log n), \widetilde{O}(\log^{5/3} n)\}$ rounds due to Lemma 13. Computing the 6-ruling set requires $O(\Delta'^{\frac{2}{r+2}}) = O(\Delta^{\frac{8}{r+2}}) = O(\Delta)$ rounds. Combining these results, we conclude that the total round complexity is in $\min\{O(\Delta + \log n), \widetilde{O}(\log^{5/3} n)\}$.

A   Complementary Subroutines

A.1   Degree Splitting

Lemma 14 (Degree splitting[19]). *For every $\varepsilon > 0$, there are deterministic $O\left(\varepsilon^{-1} \cdot \log \varepsilon^{-1} \cdot \left(\log \log \varepsilon^{-1}\right)^{1.71} \cdot \log n\right)$-round distributed algorithms for computing directed and undirected degree splittings with the following properties:*

1. *For directed degree splitting, the discrepancy at each node v of degree $d(v)$ is at most $\varepsilon \cdot d(v) + 1$ if $d(v)$ is odd and at most $\varepsilon \cdot d(v) + 2$ if $d(v)$ is even.*
2. *For undirected degree splitting, the discrepancy at each node v of degree $d(v)$ is at most $\varepsilon \cdot d(v) + 4$.*

Corollary 1. *For $i \in \mathbb{N}_{>0}$ and given $\varepsilon > 0$, there exists a deterministic $O(\log n)$ round algorithm to split the edges of a graph into $k = 2^i$ parts such that the following holds for any of the k parts:*

For each node v the number of edges contained in the part and incident to v lies in the interval

$$[deg(v)/2^i - \varepsilon d(v) - a, deg(v)/2^i + \varepsilon d(v) + a] , \tag{1}$$

where $a = 2 \sum_{j=0}^{i-1}(1/2 + \varepsilon/4)^j$.

A.2 List Coloring

Lemma 15 (List coloring [29]). *There is a deterministic distributed algorithm to $(deg+1)$-list-color any graph with maximum degree Δ in $O(\sqrt{\Delta \log \Delta}) + O(\log^* n)$ rounds.*

A.3 Ruling Sets

Lemma 16 (Ruling Sets [28,34]). *For any constant integer $r \geq 2$, there is a deterministic LOCAL algorithm that computes $(2,r)$-ruling in $O(\Delta^{\frac{2}{r+2}}) + \log^* n$ rounds on any graph with maximum degree Δ.*

References

1. Assadi, S., Chen, Y., Khanna, S.: Sublinear algorithms for $(\Delta+1)$ vertex coloring. In: Proceedings of the SIAM-ACM Symposium on Discrete Algorithms (SODA), pp. 767–786 (2019). https://doi.org/10.1137/1.9781611975482.48, full version at arXiv:1807.08886
2. Assadi, S., Kumar, P., Mittal, P.: Brooks' theorem in graph streams: a single-pass semi-streaming algorithm for Δ-coloring. In: Proceedings of the 54th Annual ACM SIGACT Symposium on Theory of Computing, pp. 234–247 (2022)
3. Balliu, A., Brandt, S., Kuhn, F., Olivetti, D.: Distributed Δ-coloring plays hide-and-seek. In: Proceedings of the 54th ACM Symposium on Theory of Computing (STOC) (2022)
4. Bourreau, Y., Brandt, S., Nolin, A.: Faster distributed Δ-coloring via a reduction to MIS. CoRR abs/2508.01762 (2025). https://doi.org/10.48550/ARXIV.2508.01762, to appear in SODA 2026
5. Bourreau, Y., Brandt, S., Nolin, A.: Faster distributed Δ-coloring via ruling subgraphs. In: Proceedings of the 57th Annual ACM Symposium on Theory of Computing (STOC 2025). ACM (2025). https://doi.org/10.1145/3717823.3718320
6. Brandt, S., et al.: A lower bound for the distributed Lovász local lemma. In: Proceedings of the ACM Symposium on Theory of Computing (STOC) (2016)
7. Brandt, S., Maus, Y., Narayanan, A., Schager, F., Uitto, J.: On the locality of hall's theorem. In: Azar, Y., Panigrahi, D. (eds.) Proceedings of the 2025 Annual ACM-SIAM Symposium on Discrete Algorithms, SODA 2025, New Orleans, LA, USA, January 12-15, 2025, pp. 4198–4226. SIAM (2025). https://doi.org/10.1137/1.9781611978322.143
8. Brooks, R.L.: On colouring the nodes of a network. Math. Proc. Cambridge Philos. Soc. **37**(2), 194–197 (1941). https://doi.org/10.1017/S030500410002168X

9. Chang, Y., Kopelowitz, T., Pettie, S.: An Exponential Separation between Randomized and Deterministic Complexity in the LOCAL Model. In: Proceedings of the IEEE Symposium on Foundations of Computer Science (FOCS), pp. 615–624 (2016)

10. Chang, Y.J., Kopelowitz, T., Pettie, S.: An exponential separation between randomized and deterministic complexity in the LOCAL model. In: Proceedings of the 57th IEEE Symposium on Foundations of Computer Science (FOCS 2016), pp. 615–624. IEEE Computer Society (2016). https://doi.org/10.1109/FOCS.2016.72

11. Chang, Y.J., Li, W., Pettie, S.: Distributed $(\Delta + 1)$-coloring via ultrafast graph shattering. SIAM J. Comput. **49**(3), 497–539 (2020)

12. Coy, S., Czumaj, A., Davies, P., Mishra, G.: Parallel derandomization for coloring (2024). note: https://arxiv.org/abs/2302.04378v1 contains the Delta-coloring algorithm

13. Elkin, M., Pettie, S., Su, H.: $(2\Delta - 1)$-edge-coloring is much easier than maximal matching in the distributed setting. In: Proceedings of the Twenty-Sixth Annual ACM-SIAM Symposium on Discrete Algorithms, SODA 2015, San Diego, CA, USA, January 4-6, 2015, pp. 355–370 (2015). https://doi.org/10.1137/1.9781611973730.26

14. Erdős, P., Rubin, A., Taylor, H.: Choosability in graphs. In: Proceedings of the West Coast Conference on Combinatorics, Graph Theory and Computing, vol. 26, pp. 125–157. Congressus Numerantium (1979)

15. Fischer, M., Halldórsson, M.M., Maus, Y.: Fast distributed Brooks' theorem. In: Proceedings of the SIAM-ACM Symposium on Discrete Algorithms (SODA), pp. 2567–2588 (2023). https://doi.org/10.1137/1.9781611977554.ch98

16. Ghaffari, M., Grunau, C.: Near-optimal deterministic network decomposition and ruling set, and improved MIS. In: 65th IEEE Annual Symposium on Foundations of Computer Science, FOCS 2024, Chicago, IL, USA, October 27-30, 2024, pp. 2148–2179. IEEE (2024). https://doi.org/10.1109/FOCS61266.2024.00007

17. Ghaffari, M., Hirvonen, J., Kuhn, F., Maus, Y.: Improved distributed delta-coloring. In: Proceedings of the 2018 ACM Symposium on Principles of Distributed Computing, PODC 2018, Egham, United Kingdom, July 23-27, 2018, pp. 427–436 (2018). https://dl.acm.org/citation.cfm?id=3212764

18. Ghaffari, M., Hirvonen, J., Kuhn, F., Maus, Y.: Improved distributed Δ-coloring. In: Proceedings of the 37th ACM Symposium on Principles of Distributed Computing (PODC 2018), pp. 427–436. ACM (2018). https://doi.org/10.1145/3212734.3212764

19. Ghaffari, M., Hirvonen, J., Kuhn, F., Maus, Y., Suomela, J., Uitto, J.: Improved distributed degree splitting and edge coloring. In: Proceedings of the International Symposium on Distributed Computing (DISC), pp. 19:1–19:15 (2017)

20. Ghaffari, M., Su, H.: Distributed degree splitting, edge coloring, and orientations. In: Proceedings of the SIAM-ACM Symposium on Discrete Algorithms (SODA), pp. 2505–2523 (2017)

21. Halldórsson, M.M., Kuhn, F., Maus, Y., Tonoyan, T.: Efficient randomized distributed coloring in CONGEST. In: Proceedings of the ACM Symposium on Theory of Computing (STOC), pp. 1180–1193 (2021). full version at CoRR abs/2105.04700

22. Halldórsson, M.M., Kuhn, F., Nolin, A., Tonoyan, T.: Near-optimal distributed degree+1 coloring. In: Leonardi, S., Gupta, A. (eds.) STOC 2022: 54th Annual ACM SIGACT Symposium on Theory of Computing, Rome, Italy, June 20 - 24, 2022, pp. 450–463. ACM (2022). https://doi.org/10.1145/3519935.3520023

23. Halldórsson, M.M., Maus, Y.: Distributed delta-coloring under bandwidth limitations. In: Alistarh, D. (ed.) 38th International Symposium on Distributed Computing, DISC 2024, October 28 to November 1, 2024, Madrid, Spain. LIPIcs, vol. 319, pp. 31:1–31:22. Schloss Dagstuhl - Leibniz-Zentrum für Informatik (2024). https://doi.org/10.4230/LIPICS.DISC.2024.31
24. Harris, D.G., Schneider, J., Su, H.H.: Distributed $(\Delta+1)$-coloring in sublogarithmic rounds. J. ACM **65**, 19:1–19:21 (2018)
25. Harris, S.G., Schneider, J., Su, H.H.: Distributed $(\Delta + 1)$-coloring in sublogarithmic rounds. In: Proceedings of the 48th Symposium on the Theory of Computing (STOC) (2016)
26. Jakob, M., Maus, Y., Schager, F.: Towards optimal distributed edge coloring with fewer colors. In: Kowalski, D.R. (ed.) 39th International Symposium on Distributed Computing, DISC 2025, October 27-31, 2025, Berlin, Germany. LIPIcs, vol. 356, pp. 37:1–37:26. Schloss Dagstuhl - Leibniz-Zentrum für Informatik (2025). https://doi.org/10.4230/LIPICS.DISC.2025.37
27. Linial, N.: Locality in distributed graph algorithms. SIAM J. Comput. **21**(1), 193–201 (1992)
28. Maus, Y.: Distributed graph coloring made easy. In: Agrawal, K., Azar, Y. (eds.) SPAA 2021: 33rd ACM Symposium on Parallelism in Algorithms and Architectures, Virtual Event, USA, 6-8 July, 2021, pp. 362–372. ACM (2021). https://doi.org/10.1145/3409964.3461804
29. Maus, Y., Tonoyan, T.: Local conflict coloring revisited: Linial for lists. In: Attiya, H. (ed.) 34th International Symposium on Distributed Computing, DISC 2020, October 12-16, 2020, Virtual Conference. LIPIcs, vol. 179, pp. 16:1-16:18. Schloss Dagstuhl - Leibniz-Zentrum für Informatik (2020). https://doi.org/10.4230/LIPIcs.DISC.2020.16
30. Maus, Y., Uitto, J.: Efficient CONGEST algorithms for the Lovász local lemma. In: Gilbert, S. (ed.) Proceedings of the International Symposium on Distributed Computing (DISC). LIPIcs, vol. 209, pp. 31:1–31:19. Schloss Dagstuhl - Leibniz-Zentrum für Informatik (2021)
31. Naor, M.: A lower bound on probabilistic algorithms for distributive ring coloring. SIAM J. Discr. Math. **4**(3), 409–412 (1991)
32. Panconesi, A., Rizzi, R.: Some simple distributed algorithms for sparse networks. Distrib. Comput. **14**(2), 97–100 (2001)
33. Panconesi, A., Srinivasan, A.: The local nature of Δ-coloring and its algorithmic applications. Combinatorica **15**(2), 255–280 (1995). https://doi.org/10.1007/BF01200759
34. Schneider, J., Elkin, M., Wattenhofer, R.: Symmetry breaking depending on the chromatic number or the neighborhood growth. Theor. Comput. Sci. **509**, 40–50 (2013). https://doi.org/10.1016/j.tcs.2012.09.004
35. Vizing, V.: Vextex coloring with given colors. Metody Diskretn. Anal., 29:3–10 (1976)

Extending the Writing Distance: the $\mathrm{R}(d_r)\mathrm{W}(d_w)$ Communication Model for Self-stabilizing Distributed Algorithms

Hirotsugu Kakugawa[1(✉)], Sayaka Kamei[2], Masahiro Shibata[3], and Fukuhito Ooshita[4]

[1] Ryukoku University, Otsu, Shiga, Japan
kakugawa@rins.ryukoku.ac.jp
[2] Hiroshima University, Higashi Hiroshima, Hiroshima, Japan
s10kamei@hiroshima-u.ac.jp
[3] Kyushu Institute of Technology, Iizuka, Fukuoka, Japan
shibata@csn.kyutech.ac.jp
[4] University of Hyogo, Kobe, Hyogo, Japan
f-oosita@gsis.u-hyogo.ac.jp

Abstract. Self-stabilization is a versatile methodology for designing fault-tolerant distributed algorithms for transient faults. Many self-stabilizing distributed algorithms adopt the state-reading model (or locally shared memory model), in which each process can read the local variables of its direct neighbor processes, in addition to its own local variables. In this paper, we propose a new model, named the $\mathrm{R}(d_r)\mathrm{W}(d_w)$ model. In this model, each process can read the local variables of processes within a distance of d_r (≥ 1) and write the local variables of processes within a distance of d_w (≥ 0). We present several self-stabilizing distributed algorithms in the proposed model. Furthermore, we present a transformer that directly simulates the $\mathrm{R}(1)\mathrm{W}(1)$ model in the synchronous message passing model.

Keywords: distributed algorithm · self-stabilization · communication model · the $\mathrm{R}(1)\mathrm{W}(1)$ model

1 Introduction

Self-stabilization is a versatile methodology for designing fault-tolerant distributed algorithms for transient faults [1,4,5]. A transient fault is defined as the corruption of data, such as message corruption, message loss, memory corruption and rebooting. Self-stabilizing systems automatically recover from any kind and any finite number of transient faults. It is considered a self-organizing system because it does not require globally synchronized initialization or resetting, and it automatically converges to a legitimate configuration after faults occur. However, arbitrary initial configurations and asynchronous executions make designing and verifying self-stabilizing distributed algorithms difficult.

C. Georgiou (Ed.): SIROCCO 2026, LNCS 16488, pp. 411–429, 2026.
https://doi.org/10.1007/978-3-032-26465-7_22

1.1 Background

Many self-stabilizing distributed algorithms adopt a communication model called the *state-reading model* (also known as the *locally shared memory model*). Dijkstra adopted this model in his paper on self-stabilization [4], and it has since become widely accepted in the research community. In the state-reading model, each process has some *local variables*, and each process can read the local variables of its neighbors without any delay. Furthermore, Dijkstra also assumes the *composite atomicity model* (also known as the *atomic-state model*) for atomicity of the process execution. According to this model, each process performs the following three substeps atomically in a single step: (1) reads its own and neighbors' local variables, (2) performs computations locally based on these values, and (3) writes the results to its own local variables.

In general, the asynchronous execution and the locality of information exchange make designing self-stabilizing distributed algorithms difficult. The asynchronous execution of processes is modeled by a *daemon*. The *central daemon* is a process scheduler that selects one process at each step. The *distributed daemon* selects any nonempty set of processes at each step. A daemon is *unfair* if it is allowed not to select a specific process as long as possible. The locality of information exchange is modeled by the state-reading model. Each process can only communicate with its direct neighbors by reading their local variables. This paper focuses on the locality of information exchange.

1.2 Related Works

The first work to extend the reading distance is the distance-two model proposed by Gairing et al. [6]. In this model, each process can read the local variables of processes within a distance of two in a single step. They also propose two transformers from the distance-two model to the ordinary state-reading model under the central or distributed daemons. The overhead factor on the time complexity (the convergence time from arbitrary initial configurations) is m (resp., $O(n^2 m)$) in the case of the central (resp., distributed) daemon, where n is the number of processes and m is the number of communication links. Goddard et al. [7] propose the *distance-k model*. This model extends the reading distance further, and each process can read local variables of process within a distance of k in a single step. They also propose a transformer to the ordinary state-reading model under the central daemon, and the overhead factor of time and space complexities are $n^{O(\log k)}$. Turau [19] proposes the *expression model* which is a variation of the distance-two model. In this model, each process exports an expression on its local variables and those of its neighbors. An expression is considered as an aggregation of local variable values. By reading a value of an expression of a neighbor, a process can indirectly access local variables at a distance of two. He proposed two transformers from the expression model to the ordinary state-reading model under the central or distributed daemons, and the overhead factor of time complexity is both $O(m)$.

Self-stabilizing distributed algorithms designed in the ordinary state-reading model do not run in real distributed computing environments. For example, they must be converted into the message passing model. Transformations from the (distance-one) state-reading model to the asynchronous message passing model are proposed in [8,9,14]. A basic technique in common to these works is that each process has a *cache* of its neighbor's local variables, and each process reads the cache to simulate reading its neighbor's local variables. Cohen et al. [3] propose transformers from the (distance-one) state-reading model to the link-register model with read/write atomicity. Here, a link register is an abstraction of a unidirectional communication channel. A sender process writes a value to the register, which is then read by a receiver process. Their transformers adopt (distance-one) local mutual exclusion to simulate the composite atomicity.

We refer to the self-stabilizing algorithms related to this paper. A 1-MIS (Maximal Independent Set) algorithm in the distance-3 model under the unfair central daemon is proposed in [10], with a time complexity of $O(n)$. Here, 1-MIS is a locally improved MIS with a set size. A 1-MIS is maximal iff any superset of it is not independent. A maximal matching algorithm in the ordinary state-reading model under the unfair distributed daemon is proposed in [13], with a time complexity of $O(m)$. A maximal k-dependent set algorithm, where $k > 0$, in the expression model under the unfair central daemon is proposed in [19], with a time complexity of $O(n)$. Here, a k-dependent set is a (sub)set of processes such that each process in the set has at most k neighbor processes in the set.

1.3   Contribution of This Paper

Works on the generalization of the reading distance can be found in [6,7,19]. However, to the authors' knowledge, no studies have been conducted on generalizing the writing distance. In this paper, we propose a new model, named the R(d_r)W(d_w) model, that extends the writing distance. Each process in the R(d_r)W(d_w) model is allowed to read local variables of processes within a distance of d_r (≥ 1) and allowed to write local variables of processes within a distance of d_w (≥ 0) in a single step.

The distance-two (resp., distance-k) model is equivalent to R(2)W(0) (resp., R(k)W(0)). The distance-two and distance-k models generalize the reading distance, while the proposed R(d_r)W(d_w) model generalizes both reading and writing distances.

The R(d_r)W(d_w) model provides a coarser grain of atomicity compared to the existing distance-k model. In the existing distance-k model, handshaking sequences, involving several steps between two or more processes, are designed in self-stabilizing distributed algorithms. Recovery actions must be designed for initial configurations involving illegitimate intermediate handshaking steps. In contrast, such handshaking sequences are unnecessary in the R(d_r)W(d_w) model because they are completed in a single step, and recovery actions are not required. Therefore, the proposed R(d_r)W(d_w) model helps designers in developing simpler algorithms with easier proofs of correctness, and such algorithms are transformed automatically into a realistic distributed computing model. A drawback of the proposed model is the model transformer. Because the atomic action becomes coarser when d_r and d_w become increase, the efficiency of transforming from the proposed $R(d_r)W(d_w)$ model to a real distributed system is important.

We present several self-stabilizing algorithms to demonstrate the model's benefits in the design and verification of algorithms. Specifically, the 1-MIS algorithm presented in this paper under the $R(2)W(1)$ model is simple.

Finally, we present a simple transformation from the $R(1)W(1)$ model to the synchronous message passing model. In the synchronous message passing model, the initial system state may include arbitrary messages that are already present in the communication channels. Despite this possibility, correctness is established due to the synchrony assumptions regarding message arrival within one synchronous round. Existing transformation schemes take two steps, for example, from the distance-k model to the message passing model via the ordinary state-reading model. Our transformation scheme, on the other hand, takes a single step, i.e., from the $R(1)W(1)$ model directly to the message passing model.

In general, when an algorithm in the $R(d_r)W(d_w)$ model is transformed, the performance of the transformed version is not better than the algorithm in the ordinary $R(1)W(0)$ model because the designers of algorithms optimize it extensively. However, if we design an efficient transformer, transformed version will be competitive.

1.4 Organization of This Paper

In Sect. 2, we explain the computational model and terminology used in this paper, and we present the $R(d_r)W(d_w)$ model. In Sect. 3, we present a 1-MIS algorithm SS1MIS in the $R(2)W(1)$ model, a maximal matching algorithm SSMM in the $R(1)W(1)$ model, and a maximal k-dependent set algorithm SSMKDEP in the $R(1)W(1)$ model. In Sect. 4, we present a transformer TrR1W1 that simulates the $R(1)W(1)$ model in the synchronous message passing model. In Sect. 5, we conclude this paper. Proof of correctness of SS1MIS is presented in Appendix. Due to space limitations, proofs of correctness of other algorithms are omitted, however, proofs of correctness of SSMM and SSMKDEP are found in [11].

2 Preliminary

A distributed system is represented by a graph $G = (V, E)$, where V is the set of processes and $E \subseteq V \times V$ is the set of bidirectional communication links between processes. The number of processes is denoted by n $(= |V|)$. The processes are denoted by $P_0, P_1, ..., P_{n-1}$. The set of neighbor processes of P_i is denoted by N_i $(= \{P_j \in V \mid (P_i, P_j) \in E\})$. The set of processes at a distance of d from P_i is denoted by $N_i^{(d)}$. Note that $N_i = N_i^{(1)}$ holds. The set of processes within distance d or less from P_i is denoted by $N_i^{(\leq d)}$. For example, $N_i^{(\leq 2)} = N_i^{(1)} \cup N_i^{(2)}$. Note that P_i is not included in $N_i^{(\leq d)}$. The degree (the number of neighbors) of

P_i is denoted by $\deg_i$ ($= |N_i|$), and the maximum degree is denoted by Δ ($= \max_{P_i \in V}\{\deg_i\}$).

2.1   The R(d_r)W(d_w) Model

We propose a new computational model, named the R(d_r)W(d_w) model. Informally speaking, in this model, each process P_i (1) reads the local variables of P_i and the processes in $N_i^{(\leq d_r)}$, (2) performs computations locally based on these values, and (3) writes the results to the local variables of P_i and processes in $N_i^{(\leq d_w)}$, in a single step. According to our model, the ordinary state-reading model adopted in [4] is denoted by R(1)W(0). The distance-k model proposed in [7] is denoted by R(k)W(0).

2.2   Self-stabilization in the R(d_r)W(d_w) Model

A self-stabilizing distributed algorithm is a type of fault-tolerant distributed algorithm designed for transient faults. Let q_i be the local state of process $P_i \in V$. The *local state* of a process is the tuple of its local variable values. A *configuration* of a distributed system, denoted by $(q_0, ..., q_i, ..., q_{n-1})$, is a tuple of the local states of $P_0, ..., P_i, ..., P_{n-1}$. By Γ, we denote the set of all configurations. The correct system states of a distributed system are specified by a set of *legitimate* configurations, denoted by Λ ($\subseteq \Gamma$).

A self-stabilizing distributed algorithm is described as a set of rules in the form of a *guarded command*, which is written as $G \longrightarrow C$. Here, G is a *guard* which is a Boolean expression on the local variables of P_i and processes in $N_i^{(\leq d_r)}$, and C is a *command* which is a series of statements to update the local variables of P_i and processes in $N_i^{(\leq d_w)}$. We say that a process is *enabled* iff it has a guard that evaluates to true. Otherwise, the process is *disabled*. From the local variables of processes within the read distance d_r, P_i computes, in a command, the new values of the local variables of processes within the write distance d_w. For the execution model of processes, we assume *the composite model*: an atomic step of a process consists of the three substeps. First, the guards are evaluated based on the local variables. Second, the new values of the local variables are computed according to the command whose corresponding guard evaluates to true. Finally, the new values are written to the local variables.

A daemon is a process scheduler that selects process(es) to execute from the enabled processes. In this paper, we assume the unfair central daemon. The *central daemon* selects exactly one process at each step. It is *unfair* if it is adversarial, i.e., it is possible that it will avoid selecting a specific process unless that process is the only enabled process.   In the R(d_r)W(d_w) model, where $d_w > 1$, we do not consider the distributed daemon which selects one or more process(es) at each step because two or more processes write to the same local variable at the same time.

The central daemon selects an enabled process whose guard evaluates to true. Let γ be any configuration, and γ' be the configuration that follows γ.

Algorithm 1: SS1MIS in the R(2)W(1) model for 1-MIS

Local variable

    $x_i \in \{0,1\}$ $//\ x = 1$ iff P_i is in the independent set

  def Rule 1: $//$ Independence

      $x_i = 1 \wedge \exists P_j \in N_i : x_j = 1 \longrightarrow$

        $x_i := 0$

  def Rule 2: $//$ Maximality

      $x_i = 0 \wedge \forall P_j \in N_i : x_j = 0 \longrightarrow$

        $x_i := 1$

  def Rule 3: $//$ 1-MIS

      $x_i = 1 \wedge \forall P_j \in N_i : x_j = 0$

      $\wedge\ \exists P_k, P_\ell \in N_i : P_k \notin N_\ell \wedge (\forall P_z \in N_k \cup N_\ell \backslash \{P_i\} : x_z = 0) \longrightarrow$

        $x_i := 0;\ x_k := 1;\ x_\ell := 1$

This binary relation is denoted by $\gamma \to \gamma'$. We assume that any execution is *maximal*, meaning that the execution continues until there are no more enabled processes.

A distributed system is *self-stabilizing* with respect to Λ iff the following two conditions are satisfied:

1. *Closure*: For any legitimate configuration $\gamma \in \Lambda$, if there exists an enabled process in γ, then any configuration γ' that follows γ is also legitimate.
2. *Convergence*: For any (possibly illegitimate) starting configuration $\gamma \in \Gamma$, the distributed system eventually reaches a legitimate configuration $\gamma' \in \Lambda$.

3   Self-stabilizing Algorithms in the Proposed Model

In this section, we present some self-stabilizing algorithms in the R(2)W(1) and R(1)W(1) models to demonstrate the proposed model.

3.1   1-MIS in the R(2)W(1) Model

In this subsection, we present a self-stabilizing distributed 1-MIS algorithm SS1MIS in the R(2)W(1) model under the unfair central daemon. The proposed algorithm is presented in Algorithm 1. Computing a 1-MIS can be considered selecting as many local servers as possible in a greedy manner, ensuring that no two servers are adjacent to each other. Intuitively speaking, a 1-MIS is an MIS (maximal independent set) where one cannot remove a node and replace it with two neighbors. That is, it is an improved MIS in terms of set size by greedily repeating the local replacements. This problem is interesting because 1-MIS is computed with local information within a distance of two or more, while MIS is computed with local information within a distance of one.

The set $S \subseteq V$ is an *independent set (IS)* of a graph $G = (V, E)$ iff $\forall P_i, P_j \in S : (P_i, P_j) \notin E$. An independent set S of a graph G is a *maximal independent set (MIS)* iff any superset of S is not an independent set of G. A maximal independent set $S \subseteq V$ is a *1-MIS* of a graph G iff, for any three distinct processes $P_i, P_k, P_\ell \in V$ such that $P_i \in S$ and $P_k, P_\ell \notin S$, $S \backslash \{P_i\} \cup \{P_k, P_\ell\}$ is not an independent set.

For each process P_i, $x_i = 1$ iff it is a member of an IS. Let γ be any configuration of SS1MIS, and let $S(\gamma) = \{P_i \in V \mid x_i = 1 \text{ in } \gamma\}$. A configuration γ of SS1MIS is legitimate iff $S(\gamma)$ is a 1-MIS. By Λ, we denote the set of legitimate configurations. There are three rules in SS1MIS:

- Rule 1: If P_i is in S but S is not an IS, then P_i leaves S to make S independent.
- Rule 2: If P_i is not in S but S is not a MIS, then P_i joins S to make S a MIS.
- Rule 3: If P_i is in S and there exist two neighbors, say P_k and P_ℓ, such that P_k and P_ℓ are not in S and P_i is the only neighbor in S for P_k and P_ℓ, then to make S a 1-MIS, P_i leaves S and invites P_k and P_ℓ to join S. The condition $P_k \notin N_\ell$ in the guard guarantees that P_k and P_ℓ are not neighbors each other, and in a resulting configuration, the independence condition is satisfied at P_k and P_ℓ.

In Rule 3, P_i reads local variables of processes within a distance of two, and it finds two neighbors P_k and P_ℓ that can safely be invited to S. Then, P_i invites P_k and P_ℓ to S by writing their local variables. These actions are simply performed in a single step.

Lemma 1. (Closure) *For any configuration $\gamma \in \Gamma$, no process is enabled in γ iff $\gamma \in \Lambda$.*

Outline of the proof of the convergence: For each configuration $\gamma \in \Gamma$, let $C(\gamma) = |\{P_i \in V \mid \exists P_j \in N_i : x_i = x_j = 1\}|$, $I(\gamma) = |\{P_i \in V \mid x_i = 1 \wedge \forall P_j \in N_i : x_j = 0\}|$, and $S(\gamma) = \{P_i \in V \mid x_i = 1 \text{ in } \gamma\}$. Intuitively speaking, $C(\gamma)$ is the number of processes such that the guard of Rule 1 is true, $I(\gamma)$ is the number of processes such that $x = 1$ and the guard of Rule 1 is false, and $S(\gamma)$ is an independent set iff $C(\gamma) = 0$.

Executing Rule 1 decreases the value of C by at least one, but never decreases the value of I. Executing Rule 2 never changes the value of C, but increases the value of I by one. Executing Rule 3 never changes the value of C, but increases the value of I by at least one. Because $0 \leq C(\gamma) \leq n$ and $0 \leq I(\gamma) \leq n$ hold, at most $2n$ steps are enough to converge for any initial configuration.

Lemma 2. (Convergence) *Starting from any configuration $\gamma_0 \in \Gamma$, any execution reaches a legitimate configuration $\gamma \in \Lambda$ within $2n$ steps.*

Theorem 1. *SS1MIS is self-stabilizing with respect to Λ under the unfair central daemon in the R(2)W(1) model, and its time complexity is $O(n)$.*

A 1-MIS algorithm in the R(3)W(0) model is proposed in [10], and algorithms in the ordinary R(1)W(0) model are proposed in [15, 16, 18]. Unfortunately, design and proof of correctness of these algorithms are long and complex.

In contrast, **SS1MIS** presented in this paper is quite simple due to the R(2)W(1) model.

Let us observe the complexity of the design of a self-stabilizing 1-MIS algorithm in the R(3)W(0) model in [10]. The difficulty lies in flipping states of three processes P_i, P_k, P_ℓ such that $x_i = 1, x_k = x_\ell = 0$. The algorithm SS1MIS in the R(2)W(1) model in this paper, flipping the states of three processes is done in a single step. On the other hand, in the algorithm in the R(3)W(0) model in [10], flipping the states of three processes is divided into several steps of the following sequence: (1) P_i raises a flag to start flipping, (2) P_k flips its state, (3) P_ℓ flips its state, and (4) P_i lowers a flag and flip its state. The ability of reading distance three is used to check whether no flag is raised within distance three and no two processes executes the flipping sequence. However, in a self-stabilizing setting, two or more processes within distance three may raise a flag in the initial configuration, and a cancellation procedure for the flipping sequence must be designed in the algorithm. Such a cancellation procedure is necessary in the R(k)W(0) model for any $k \geq 3$, i.e., enlarging the read distance does not simplify the complexity of algorithm design.

3.2   Maximal Matching in the R(1)W(1) Model

In this subsection, we propose a self-stabilizing distributed maximal matching algorithm SSMM in the R(1)W(1) model under the unfair central daemon. The proposed algorithm is presented in Algorithm 2. Computing a maximal matching can be considered selecting as many communication links as possible in a greedy manner such that the two end processes of a selected link can communicate with each other simultaneously without interference from other processes.

A *matching* M of a graph $G = (V, E)$ is a subset of links E such that, no two links share a common end process. A matching M is *maximal* iff $M \cup \{(P_i, P_j)\}$ is not a matching for each link $(P_i, P_j) \in E \backslash M$.

For each process P_i, the local variable q_i points to a matching process. We say that P_i *points* to $P_j \in N_i$ iff $q_i = P_j$. A link $(P_i, P_j) \in E$ is a *matching* iff $P_j = q_i$ and $P_i = q_j$ hold. We say that $P_j \in N_i$ is a *matching neighbor* of P_i iff (P_i, P_j) is a matching. If P_j is a matching neighbor of P_i, we say that the pair of processes is a *matching pair*. We say that P_i is *free* iff $q_i = \perp$ holds. We say that q_i of P_i is *incorrect* iff $q_i \in N_i$ and $q_j \neq P_i$ hold, where $P_j = q_i$. Let γ be any configuration of SSMM, and let $M(\gamma) = \{(P_i, P_j) \mid q_i = P_j \in N_i \wedge q_j = P_i \in N_j \text{ in } \gamma\}$. A configuration γ of SSMM is legitimate iff $M(\gamma)$ is a maximal matching of G. Let Λ be the set of legitimate configurations.

The basic idea of SSMM is to force P_j to form a matching pair with P_i when P_j is free. According to Rules 1, 2, 3 and 4, P_i forms a matching pair with a neighbor if such one exists, and the matching pair remains forever. Thus, these rules increase the number of matching pairs. If $q_i \in N_i$ holds and each neighbor $P_j \in N_i$ is not free, then q_i is incorrect. In this case, P_i executes Rule 5 and gives up forming a matching because P_i does not know whether q_j is incorrect or not for each neighbor $P_j \in N_i$. Then the incorrect q_i becomes free. This rule decreases the number of processes with an incorrect q. If there is a neighbor

---

Algorithm 2: SSMM in the R(1)W(1) model for maximal matching

Local variable

   $q_i \in N_i \cup \{\bot\}$ // the matching neighbor of P_i

  def Rule 1: // Free P_i accepts P_j, and make a matching

      $q_i = \bot \wedge \exists P_j \in N_i : q_j = P_i \longrightarrow$

         $q_i := P_j$

  def Rule 2: // Force P_i and P_j to make a matching

      $q_i = \bot \wedge \exists P_j \in N_i : q_j = \bot \longrightarrow$

         $q_i := P_j; q_j := P_i$

  def Rule 3: // Force P_j to make a matching with P_i

      $q_i \in N_i \wedge q_j = \bot$, where $P_j = q_i \longrightarrow$

         $q_j := P_i$

  def Rule 4: // P_i switches to P_k to make a matching

      $q_i \in N_i \wedge (q_j \notin \{P_i, \bot\}$, where $P_j = q_i) \wedge \exists P_k \in N_i : q_k \in \{P_i, \bot\} \longrightarrow$

         $q_i := P_k; q_k := P_i$

  def Rule 5: // P_i gives up

      $q_i \in N_i \wedge (q_j \notin \{P_i, \bot\}$, where $P_j = q_i) \wedge \forall P_k \in N_i : q_k \notin \{P_i, \bot\} \longrightarrow$

         $q_i := \bot$

$P_j \in N_i$ such that q_j is incorrect, then the guard of Rule 4 at P_j becomes true. If P_j executes Rule 4, then P_j and P_i become a matching pair (if P_j selects P_i in Rule 4).

Lemma 3. (Closure) *For any configuration $\gamma \in \Gamma$, no process is enabled in γ iff $\gamma \in \Lambda$.*

Outline of the proof of the convergence: Let $A(\gamma) = |M(\gamma)|$ and $B(\gamma) = |\{P_i \in V \mid q_i \in N_i \wedge q_j \notin \{P_i, \bot\}$, where $P_j = q_i\}|$. Intuitively speaking, A represents the number of matching pairs, and B represents the number of processes P_i such that the value of q_i is incorrect. For any configuration γ, $0 \leq A(\gamma) \leq \lfloor n/2 \rfloor$ and $0 \leq B(\gamma) \leq n$ hold. Executing Rules 1,2,3 or 4 increases the value of A by one, however, executing Rule 5 does not. Executing Rules 4 or 5 decreases the value of B by one, however, executing Rules 1, 2 or 3 does not. For any execution of a rule, $A(\gamma) = A(\gamma')$ and $B(\gamma) = B(\gamma')$ do not occur at the same time. Because $0 \leq A(\gamma) \leq \lfloor n/2 \rfloor$ and $0 \leq B(\gamma) \leq n$ hold, at most $3n/2$ steps are enough to converge for any initial configuration.

Lemma 4. *For any two configurations γ, γ' such that $\gamma \rightarrow \gamma'$, $A(\gamma) \leq A(\gamma')$ and $B(\gamma) \geq B(\gamma')$ hold. Furthermore, $A(\gamma) < A(\gamma')$ or $B(\gamma) > B(\gamma')$ holds.*

Lemma 5. (Convergence) *Starting from any configuration $\gamma_0 \in \Gamma$, any execution reaches a legitimate configuration $\gamma \in \Lambda$ within $3n/2$ steps.*

Theorem 2. *SSMM is self-stabilizing with respect to Λ under the unfair central daemon in the R(1)W(1) model, and its time complexity is $O(n)$.*

In [13], a self-stabilizing distributed algorithm under the unfair distributed daemon is proposed, and its time complexity is $O(m)$. Compared to the algorithm in [13], the description and the proof of correctness of SSMM is simple.

3.3 Maximal k-Dependent Set in the R(1)W(1) Model

In this subsection, we propose a self-stabilizing distributed maximal k-dependent set algorithm SSMKDEP in the R(1)W(1) model under the unfair central daemon. The proposed algorithm is presented in Algorithm 3. Computing a maximal k-dependent set can be considered selecting as many local servers as possible in a greedy manner such that each server is adjacent to at most k other servers.

For each integer $k \geq 0$, a k-*dependent set* S of a graph $G = (V, E)$ is a subset of processes $S \subseteq V$ such that, for each process $P_i \in S$, $|N_i \cap S| \leq k$ holds. A k-dependent set S is *maximal* iff any superset of S is not a k-dependent set. The definition is a generalization of a maximal independent set (MIS), i.e., the definitions of a maximal 0-dependent set and a maximal independent set are equivalent. Intuitively speaking, a k-dependent set S is a relaxed independent set such that, for each process in S, at most k of its neighbors are permitted to be in S. Let $S_i = N_i \cap S$. According to the definition, a set of processes $S \subseteq V$ is a maximal k-dependent set iff the following local conditions hold for each $P_i \in V$.

- k-Dependency: $P_i \in S \Rightarrow |S_i| \leq k$.
- Maximality: $P_i \in V \backslash S \Rightarrow |S_i| > k \vee \exists P_j \in N_i \cap S : |S_j| = k$.

Each process P_i has two local variables: x_i, which represents whether P_i is a member of S or not, and c_i, which counts the number of neighbor processes in S. When P_i joins or leaves S, P_i increments or decrements, resp., c_j by one for each neighbor P_j. P_i verifies the value of c_i by counting the number of neighbors P_j such that $x_j = 1$. If the value of c_i is incorrect, P_i fixes the value of c_i by executing Rule 1. If the value of c_i becomes correct, it remains so thereafter. Then, each process P_k in two hops from P_i knows the value of $|S_j|$, where P_j is the process between P_k and P_i.

Let Γ be the set of all configurations of SSMKDEP, and let Λ be the set of legitimate configurations. A configuration γ is legitimate iff the following three conditions are satisfied for each $P_i \in V$ in γ.

- Correctness of the count: $c_i = Count_i()$, where $Count_i()$ is the number of neighbors with $x = 1$. (See Algorithm 3.) If this condition does not hold, P_i executes Rule 1.
- k-Dependency: $x_i = 1 \Rightarrow c_i \leq k$. If this condition does not hold, P_i executes Rule 2.
- Maximality: $x_i = 0 \Rightarrow c_i > k \vee \exists P_j \in N_i : x_j = 1 \wedge c_j = k$. If this condition does not hold, P_i executes Rule 3 to increase the number of processes with $x = 1$ to make the k-dependent set maximal. Because $x_j = 0$ or $c_j < k$ holds for each neighbor P_j, an execution of Rule 3 at P_i never violates the k-dependency condition.

Algorithm 3:   SSMKDEP in the R(1)W(1) model for maximal k-dependent set

---

Local variable
    $x_i \in \{1, 0\}$ // whether a member of the set or not
    $c_i \in \{0, 1, ..., |N_i|\}$ // #neighbors s.t. $x_j = 1$
Macro
    $Count_i() \equiv |\{P_j \in N_i \mid x_j = 1\}|$

def Rule 1: // Fix the counter
    $c_i \neq Count_i() \longrightarrow$
        $c_i := Count_i()$

def Rule 2: // k-Dependency
    $x_i = 1 \wedge c_i = Count_i() \wedge c_i > k \longrightarrow$
        $x_i := 0$
        for each $P_j \in N_i$ s.t. $c_j > 0$:
            $c_j := c_j - 1$

def Rule 3: // Maximality
    $x_i = 0 \wedge c_i = Count_i() \wedge c_i \leq k \wedge (\forall P_j \in N_i : x_j = 0 \vee c_j < k) \longrightarrow$
        $x_i := 1$
        for each $P_j \in N_i$ s.t. $c_j < |N_j|$:
            $c_j := c_j + 1$

Lemma 6. (Closure) *For any configuration $\gamma \in \Gamma$, no process is enabled in γ iff $\gamma \in \Lambda$.*

Note that, in the initial configuration, the values of c_i for each P_i may or may not be correct. So, when P_i reads c_j of a neighbor $P_j \in N_i$, the value c_j may or may not be correct.

Outline of the proof of the convergence: For each P_i, if the values of c_i is incorrect, P_i is enabled by Rule 1. If P_i executes Rule 1, then the value of c_i becomes correct, and it is remains so. Therefore, P_i executes Rule 1 at most once. When P_i executes Rule 3, $x_i = 0$ and $c_i \leq k$ holds, and we have $x_i = 1$ and $c_i \leq k$ after P_i executes Rule 3. Then, for any execution of P_i and its neighbors, the condition $c_i \leq k$ is maintained as long as $x_i = 1$ holds. Therefore, P_i executes Rule 3 at most once. By the condition of $c_i > k$ in the guard of Rule 2, P_i never executes Rule 2 three times because, if it does, it must execute Rule 3 twice, which never occurs. Therefore, P_i executes Rule 2 at most twice. Therefore, each process executes a rule at most 4 times, and hence at most $4n$ steps are enough to converge from any initial configuration.

Lemma 7. *For each process $P_i \in V$, if $c_i = Count_i()$ holds, it remains so thereafter.*

Lemma 8. *For each process $P_i \in V$, the number of executions of Rule 1 is at most one. If P_i executes Rule 1, it is the first execution of P_i.*

Lemma 9. *For each process $P_i \in V$, the number of executions of Rule 3 is at most one.*

Lemma 10. *For each process $P_i \in V$, the number of executions of Rule 2 is at most two.*

Lemma 11. (Convergence) *Starting from any configuration $\gamma_0 \in \Gamma$, any execution reaches a legitimate configuration $\gamma \in \Lambda$ within $4n$ steps.*

Theorem 3. *SSMKDEP is self-stabilizing under the unfair central daemon in the R(1)W(1) model, and its time complexity is $O(n)$.*

A maximal k-dependent set algorithm, where $k > 0$, in the expression model under the unfair central daemon is proposed in [19], with a time complexity of $O(n)$. In the expression model, each process (indirectly) reads the local variables within two hops. It is transformed by the transformer proposed in [19] to the composite atomicity model under the unfair distributed daemon. Then, it must be transformed to the message passing model by another transformer. In contrast to this, each process in our SSMKDEP reads and writes the local variables of its one-hop neighbors. Furthermore, the transformer proposed in this paper directly transforms SSMKDEP to the message passing model.

4   A Transformer to the Message Passing Model

In this section, we propose a transformer TrR1W1 for self-stabilizing algorithms in the R(1)W(1) model to the synchronous message passing model with a local broadcast primitive.

4.1   A Transformer

The transformer is presented in Algorithm 4. It uses a voting mechanism based on process identifiers for distance-two mutual exclusion to avoid conflicts of writes to the same local variables. We use the following terms: a *target algorithm* (e.g., SSMM) is an algorithm in the R(1)W(1) model that is to be simulated, and a *transformed algorithm* is an algorithm in the synchronous message passing model that is transformed by TrR1W1. We assume a network $G = (V, E)$ of processes $V = \{\mathcal{P}_0, \mathcal{P}_1, ...\mathcal{P}_{n-1}\}$ in the synchronous message passing model. Each process $\mathcal{P}_i$ simulates P_i of the target algorithm. We assume that each process has a unique identifier.

We assume the synchronous message passing model with reliable communication. Process execution is synchronized in *round*. In each round, each process synchronously sends a message by the **bcast** primitive, receives all messages from neighbors, and updates its local variables by local computation. The primitive sends a message to direct neighbor processes. The proposed transformer is described as a series of *phases*, and we assume that each phase is a synchronized round. Phase synchronization can be achieved by using a GPS receiver at

---

Algorithm 4: TrR1W1 for each process $\mathcal{P}_i \in V$

Local variable

x_i // The state of the target algorithm

$C_i[\mathcal{P}_j]$ // Cache of x_j for each $\mathcal{P}_j \in N_i^{(1)}$

g_i // Whether there is a guard which evaluates to true

w_i // A winner process identifier

M_i // A set of messages

while true:

  Phase 1:   // Cache refresh & evaluation of guards

    bcast $\langle 1, x_i \rangle$

    receive; $M_i :=$ messages received

    Update C_i according to M_i

    $g_i :=$ (**true** iff there is a true guard)

  Phase 2: // Voting

    if g_i:

      bcast $\langle 2, \mathcal{P}_i \rangle$

    receive; $M_i :=$ messages received

    $w_i := \bot$

    if $M_i \neq \emptyset$:   // Select the winner at $\mathcal{P}_i$

      $w_i :=$ (the smallest process identifier in M_i)

      if g_i:

        $w_i := \min\{w_i, \mathcal{P}_i\}$

  Phase 3:   // The winner executes a command

    if $w_i \neq \bot$:

      bcast $\langle 3, w_i \rangle$

    receive; $M_i :=$ messages received

    if $g_i \wedge (\mathcal{P}_i$ *is the winner at each neighbor*):

      Execute a command and update x_i and C_i

  Phase 4:   // Value propagation to one-hop neighbors

    if (A command is executed in Phase 3):

      bcast $\langle 4, x_i, C_i \rangle$

    receive; $M_i :=$ messages received

    Update C_i and x_i according to M_i

  Phase 5:   // Value propagation to two-hop neighbors

    if (x_i is updated in Phase 4):

      bcast $\langle 5, x_i \rangle$

    receive; $M_i :=$ messages received

    Update C_i according to M_i

---

each process (e.g., [12,17]) or by building a BFS tree with the process having the smallest identifier as the root (e.g., [2]). In this case, each process would synchronize with the phase number of the root process.

In the problem setting of self-stabilization, the communication channels may include arbitrary messages in the initial configuration. Despite this possibility, the correctness of the transformation is established due to the synchrony assumptions regarding message arrival within one synchronous round. Specifically, the transformer sends a message tagged with a phase number, and no more than one message is sent per sender per phase. Therefore, the receiver filters multiple messages from the same sender and messages tagged with an incorrect phase number.

First, let us explain the main idea of the transformer. A process $\mathcal{P}_i$ with a guard evaluates to true (i.e., $\mathcal{P}_i$ is enabled), enters the critical section, executes the command corresponding to the guard evaluates to true, broadcasts new values of local variables of $\mathcal{P}_i$ and its neighbors, and exits the critical section. Entry to the critical section is controlled so that no two processes within distance two are not in their critical sections at the same time. In other words, the execution of a guarded command is controlled by the local mutual exclusion within a distance of two. This local mutual exclusion ensures that the executions of the target processes are serializable and that an equivalent execution exists under the central daemon. The priority for entering the critical section is defined by process identifier, and, therefore, any fairness is not guaranteed. Consequently, if the target algorithm in the R(1)W(1) model is correct under the unfair central daemon, the transformed version is also correct.

Next, we explain the local variables of each process $\mathcal{P}_i$. In general, each process P_i of the target algorithm has one or more local variables. For the sake of simplicity, however, it is assumed that each process P_i has a single local variable x_i. The local variables of the transformed algorithm of $\mathcal{P}_i$ include x_i and some housekeeping variables. The primary housekeeping variable is a cache. Each $\mathcal{P}_i$ has a *cache* $C_i[\mathcal{P}_j]$ of x_j for each $\mathcal{P}_j \in N_i$. Instead of reading x_j of neighbor $\mathcal{P}_j$, $\mathcal{P}_i$ reads the cache $C_i[\mathcal{P}_j]$. If $\mathcal{P}_i$ updates the value of x_i, then $\mathcal{P}_i$ broadcasts the new value of x_i to its neighbors, and neighbors update their caches. If P_i updates the value of x_j of some neighbor, it updates the cache for $\mathcal{P}_j$, and $\mathcal{P}_i$ broadcasts the new value of x_j to neighbors. If $\mathcal{P}_j$ finds that x_j is updated by $\mathcal{P}_i$, $\mathcal{P}_j$ broadcasts the new value of x_j to neighbors. Subsequently, each neighbor $\mathcal{P}_k$ of $\mathcal{P}_j$ updates its cache. To simulate the target algorithm in the message passing model, it is important to ensure the correctness of cache contents. In this paper, we refer to this correctness as *cache coherency*.

Definition 1. *We say that cache is* coherent *iff, for each $\mathcal{P}_i \in V$, $C_i[\mathcal{P}_j] = x_j$ holds for each $\mathcal{P}_j \in N_i$ and for each local variable x_j of $\mathcal{P}_j$.*

The target algorithm in the R(1)W(1) model is simulated in five phases. The transformer consists of series of five synchronized phases, and the execution of these fives phases is referred to as a *cycle*. The central daemon is simulated using the distance-two local mutual exclusion. This ensures that no two processes within two hops execute their guarded commands simultaneously.

- Phase 1: Each process $\mathcal{P}_i$ (locally) broadcasts the value of x_i, and each neighbor that receives it updates its cache. Then, $\mathcal{P}_i$ computes in g_i whether some guards of the target algorithm are true or not.
- Phase 2: If one or more guards of the target algorithm are true, then $\mathcal{P}_i$ broadcasts its process identifier. This is the request message for the distance-two local mutual exclusion. Subsequently, $\mathcal{P}_i$ receives messages from its neighbors. It selects in w_i the smallest process identifier among the requesting processes in neighbors (and $\mathcal{P}_i$ if it is requesting too). We say that w_i is the *winner* at $\mathcal{P}_i$.
- Phase 3: $\mathcal{P}_i$ broadcasts the winner w_i. Thereafter, if $\mathcal{P}_i$ has a guard that evaluates to true and its process identifier is the locally smallest among the requesting neighbors, then $\mathcal{P}_i$ executes the command of the target algorithm. If two or more guards evaluate to true, one of the corresponding commands is executed. If none of the guards evaluate to true at this phase, no command is executed. Since P_i is the winner at $P_j \in N_i$, a neighbor P_k of P_j cannot be the winner at P_j at the same time. Hence, the distance-two mutual exclusion is achieved.
- Phase 4: If $\mathcal{P}_i$ executed the command in the previous phase, then it broadcasts the values to neighbors. Then, $\mathcal{P}_i$ receives a message that includes new values, and updates its cache accordingly.
- Phase 5: If the local variables of $\mathcal{P}_i$ are updated in the previous phase, then it broadcasts the values to neighbors. Then, $\mathcal{P}_i$ receives a message including new values, and updates its cache accordingly. Note that this phase can be omitted because an equivalent action is implicitly taken in the Phase 1 in the next cycle. However, we left it to present the actions explicitly when writes to the neighbor local variables occur.

4.2   Proof of Correctness

To verify a self-stabilizing algorithm in message passing communication, we must consider spurious (garbage) messages in communication channels in initial configurations. Because we assume the synchronous message passing model, each spurious messages arrive at its destination process within a phase. In the proposed algorithm, such spurious messages are discarded by the following way, but these actions are not explicitly described in the Algorithm 4. Each message is tagged with phase number, however, if a process executing in Phase f receives a message tagged with a different phase number $f'(\neq f)$, then such a message is discarded. In each phase, a process sends a message at most once by the **bcast** primitive, however, if a process receives two or more messages from the same process in a phase, then such messages are discarded. A process may receive a spurious message not discarded by above method. In such a case, a process handles such a message as if it is a correct one, and no spurious messages left in communication channels. Despite this general possibility, we can assume that there are no spurious messages in the Phase 1 of the first cycle. Under synchronous rounds with reliable message delivery, this is possible by adopting the last message from each neighbor in the corresponding communication channel because each process definitely sends a message in Phase 1 of each cycle. Therefore, without loss of generality, we assume that there are no spurious messages and that the cache contents may or may not be correct in an initial configuration of an execution of the transformer.

Lemma 12. *The cache becomes coherent after each process executes Phase 1.*

Outline of the proof of the correctness: If there is one or more processes with a true guard, the process with the smallest identifier enters the critical section because it has the highest priority. Hence, in each cycle, at least one process executes a guarded command of the target algorithm. If the target algorithm converges in at most T steps, the transformed algorithm converges in at most $O(T)$ cycles ($O(T)$ rounds). Entry to a critical section is mutually exclusive for processes within a distance of two. Therefore, no two processes can update the same local variables and corresponding cache at the same time. Thus, if the cache is coherent, it remains so. Consequently, for any execution of processes under the transformer, there is an equivalent execution of the target algorithm under the central daemon.

Lemma 13. *No two processes $\mathcal{P}_i \in V$ and $\mathcal{P}_j \in N_i^{(\leq 2)}$ execute a guarded command at the same time.*

Lemma 14. *If the cache becomes coherent, it remains so thereafter.*

Lemma 15. *For each cycle $t \geq 2$, if there exists an enabled process, then at least one process executes a command.*

Lemma 16. *Any execution by TrR1W1 simulates the execution of the target algorithm in the R(1)W(1) under the unfair central daemon.*

Theorem 4. *Let A be a self-stabilizing algorithm in the R(1)W(1) model that stabilizes in T_A steps in the worst case under the unfair central daemon, and let S_A be the space complexity of A per process. Let A' be the transformed version of A by TrR1W1. Then, A' is a self-stabilizing algorithm in the synchronous message passing model that stabilizes in $O(T_A)$ rounds, and its space complexity is $O(\Delta(\Delta S_A + \log n))$ per process.*

Let us explain the space complexity. In A', each process has a cache for each neighbor's local variables, and the total size of these caches is $O(\Delta S_A)$ per process. In addition, each process has a message buffer to receive messages from neighbors. The message size sent in Phase 1 (resp., Phases 2, 3, 4 and 5) is $O(S_A)$ (resp., $O(\log n)$, $O(\log n)$, $O(\Delta S_A)$ and $O(\log n)$). Specifically, in Phase 4, a message sent by $\mathcal{P}_i$ in Phase 4 contains the entire cache C_i, whose size is $O(\Delta S_A)$. As each process receives messages from neighbors in each phase, the size of the message buffer is $O(\Delta(\Delta S_A + \log n))$ per process. In total, the space complexity of A' is $O(\Delta(\Delta S_A + \log n))$.

5   Conclusion

In this paper, we proposed a new communication model, the $R(d_r)W(d_w)$ model, which generalizes the writing distance. The 1-MIS algorithm presented in this paper is quite simple due to the $R(2)W(1)$ model, while the 1-MIS algorithm in the $R(3)W(0)$ model proposed in [10] is complex. Our transformation scheme consists of a single step: from the $R(1)W(1)$ model directly to the message passing model.

Self-stabilizing distributed algorithms in the literature for 1-MIS, maximal matching, and maximal k-dependent set problems, for example, are highly optimized by the their designers. However, transformed versions of the proposed algorithms in the $R(2)W(1)$ and $R(1)W(1)$ models by the proposed transformer are, in general, not better than the algorithms in the literature. This paper contributes by showing that the $R(d_r)W(d_w)$ model greatly simplifies the design of algorithms. If transformers from the $R(d_r)W(d_w)$ model to realistic computational models are developed, the performance of the transformed algorithms becomes competitive. An important future task is to develop transformers for the $R(1)W(1)$ and $R(d_r)W(d_w)$ models that highly optimize the transformation.

An interesting research question about the $R(d_r)W(d_w)$ model is: What are the minimum values for d_r and d_w that result in a convergence time of self-stabilizing distributed algorithms in $O(n)$?

Acknowledgement. This work was partially supported by JSPS KAKENHI Grant Numbers JP20KK0232, JP23K11059, JP23K28037, JP25K14995, and JP25K03101.

A   Proof of Correctness of **SS1MIS**

We show the proof of correctness of the proposed algorithm SS1MIS in the $R(2)W(1)$ model. In the proof for SS1MIS, we use the following definition: $S(\gamma) = \{P_i \in V \mid x_i = 1 \text{ in } \gamma\}$. Remember that Rule 1 is the independence rule, Rule 2 is the maximality rule, and Rule 3 is the rule for flipping three processes for 1-MIS.

Lemma 1. (Closure) *For any configuration $\gamma \in \Gamma$, no process is enabled in γ iff $\gamma \in \Lambda$.*

Proof. ($\Rightarrow$) Let γ be any configuration such that no process is enabled in γ. The set $S(\gamma)$ is an IS by Rule 1, and it is an MIS by Rule 2. By Rule 3, there exists no three distinct processes $P_i, P_k, P_\ell \in V$ such that $x_i = 1$ and $x_k = x_\ell = 0$ and $S(\gamma)\backslash\{P_i\} \cup \{P_k, P_\ell\}$ is an IS. Hence the set $S(\gamma)$ is a 1-MIS.

($\Leftarrow$) Let γ be any legitimate configuration. Because $S(\gamma)$ is a 1-MIS, each $P_i \in V$ is not enabled by Rule 1, 2 and 3. $\qquad\square$

Lemma 2. (Convergence) *Starting from any configuration $\gamma_0 \in \Gamma$, any execution reaches a legitimate configuration $\gamma \in \Lambda$ within $2n$ steps.*

Proof. Let $C(\gamma)$ be the number of processes such that the guard of Rule 1 is true in γ, i.e., $C(\gamma) = |\{P_i \in V \mid \exists P_j \in N_i : x_i = x_j = 1\}|$. We have $0 \leq C(\gamma) \leq n$. $C(\gamma)$ counts the number of conflicting processes. Here, we say that a process P_i is conflicting iff $x_i = 1$ and there exists a neighbor P_j such that $x_j = 1$. $S(\gamma)$ is not an independent set iff there exists a conflicting process in γ. Any execution of Rule 1 decreases the number of conflicting processes.

Let $I(\gamma)$ be the number of processes such that $x = 1$ and the guard of Rule 1 is false in γ, i.e., $I(\gamma) = |\{P_i \in V \mid x_i = 1 \wedge \forall P_j \in N_i : x_j = 0\}|$. We have $0 \leq I(\gamma) \leq n$. $I(\gamma)$ counts the number of independent processes. Here, we say that a process P_i is independent iff $x_i = 1$ and $x_j = 0$ for each neighbor P_j.

Let γ' is any configuration that follows γ. Let us compare the sizes of S and I in γ and γ'.

If some process executes Rule 2 in γ, then the number of independent processes increases by one but no new conflicting process appears. Hence we have $I(\gamma) < I(\gamma')$ and $C(\gamma) = C(\gamma')$.

By the R(2)W(1) model, in a single step, P_i can verifies that it is the only process with $x = 1$ for neighbors P_k and P_ℓ, and P_i can modify the values x_i, x_k and x_ℓ. If some process executes Rule 3 in γ, then the number of independent processes increases by one. No new conflicting process appears because P_i is the only neighbor of P_k and P_ℓ such that $x = 1$ and the condition $P_k \notin N_\ell$ holds. Hence we have $I(\gamma) < I(\gamma')$ and $C(\gamma) = C(\gamma')$.

If some process executes Rule 1 in γ, then the number of conflicting processes decreases at least by one, and the number of independent processes never decreases. Hence we have $C(\gamma) > C(\gamma')$ and $I(\gamma) \leq I(\gamma')$.

For any execution of a rule, C decreases at lease by one or I increases by one. Because $0 \leq C(\gamma), I(\gamma) \leq n$ holds, the total number of executions of rules is bounded by $2n$. Therefore, for any initial configuration γ_0, any execution starting from γ_0 reaches a configuration in which no process is enabled within $2n$ steps. By Lemma 1, it is a legitimate configuration. $\square$

Theorem 1. *SS1MIS is self-stabilizing with respect to Λ under the unfair central daemon in the R(2)W(1) model, and its time complexity is $O(n)$.*

Proof. The closure property is shown in Lemma 1, and the convergence property and the convergence time are shown in Lemma 2. $\square$

References

1. Altisen, K., Devismes, S., Dubois, S., Petit, F.: Introduction to distributed self-stabilizing algorithms. Morgan & Claypool (2019)
2. Arora, A., Gouda, M.G.: Distributed reset. IEEE Trans. Comput. **43**(9), 1026–1038 (1994)
3. Cohen, J., Manoussakis, G., Pilard, L.: From state to link-register model: a transformer for self-stabilizing distributed algorithms. In: 2023 25th International Symposium on Symbolic and Numeric Algorithms for Scientific Computing (SYNASC), pp. 114–121 (2023)

4. Dijkstra, E.W.: Self-stabilizing systems in spite of distributed control. Commun. ACM **17**(11), 643–644 (1974)
5. Dolev, S.: Self-stabilization. The MIT Press (2000)
6. Gairing, M., Goddard, W., Hedetniemi, S.T., Kristiansen, P., McRae, A.A.: Distance-two information in self-stabilizing algorithms. Parallel Process. Lett. **14**(03n04), 387–398 (2004)
7. Goddard, W., Hedetniemi, S.T., Jacobs, D.P., Trevisan, V.: Distance-k knowledge in self-stabilizing algorithms. Theoret. Comput. Sci. **399**(1), 118–127 (2008)
8. Herman, T.: Models of Self-Stabilization and Sensor Networks. In: Das, S.R., Das, S.K. (eds.) IWDC 2003. LNCS, vol. 2918, pp. 205–214. Springer, Heidelberg (2003). https://doi.org/10.1007/978-3-540-24604-6_20
9. Huang, S.T., Wuu, L.C., Tsai, M.S.: Distributed execution model for self-stabilizing systems. In: Proceedings of the 14th International Conference on Distributed Computing Systems (ICDCS), pp. 432–439 (1994)
10. Kakugawa, H., Kamei, S., Shibata, M., Ooshita, F.: A self-stabilizing distributed algorithm for the 1-mis problem under the distance-3 model. Concurrency Comput. Pract. Experience **36**(26), e8281 (2024)
11. Kakugawa, H., Kamei, S., Shibata, M., Ooshita, F.: The R(1)W(1) communication model for self-stabilizing distributed algorithms (2025). https://arxiv.org/abs/2510.04644
12. Kim, R., Nagayama, T., Jo, H., Jr, B.S.: Preliminary study of low-cost GPS receivers for time synchronization of wireless sensors. In: Sensors and Smart Structures Technologies for Civil, Mechanical, and Aerospace Systems, vol. 8345, pp. 352–360. SPIE (2012)
13. Manne, F., Mjelde, M., Pilard, L., Tixeuil, S.: A new self-stabilizing maximal matching algorithm. Theoret. Comput. Sci. **410**(14), 1336–1345 (2009)
14. Mizuno, M., Kakugawa, H.: A timestamp based transformation of self-stabilizing programs for distributed computing environments. In: Babaoğlu, Ö., Marzullo, K. (eds.) WDAG 1996. LNCS, vol. 1151, pp. 304–321. Springer, Heidelberg (1996). https://doi.org/10.1007/3-540-61769-8_20
15. Namba, E.: A hierachical self-stabilizing 1-MIS algorihtm. Master's thesis, Osaka University (2017). (in Japanese)
16. Shi, Z., Goddard, W., Hedetniemi, S.T.: An anonymous self-stabilizing algorithm for 1-maximal independent set in trees. Inf. Process. Lett. **91**, 77–83 (2004)
17. Sterzbach, B.: GPS-based clock synchronization in a mobile, distributed real-time system. Real-Time Syst. **12**(1), 63–75 (1997)
18. Tanaka, H., Sudo, Y., Kakugawa, H., Masuzawa, T., Datta, A.K.: A self-stabilizing 1-maximal independent set algorithm. J. Inf. Process. **29**, 247–255 (2021)
19. Turau, V.: Efficient transformation of distance-2 self-stabilizing algorithms. J. Parallel Distrib. Comput. **72**(4), 603–612 (2012)

Indirect Coflow Scheduling

Alexander Lindermayr[1]([✉])[iD], Kirk Pruhs[2][iD], Andréa W. Richa[3][iD],
and Tegan Wilson[4][iD]

[1] Institut für Mathematik, Technische Universität Berlin, Berlin, Germany
`alexander.lindermayr@tu-berlin.de`
[2] Computer Science Department, University of Pittsburgh, Pittsburgh, USA
`kirk@cs.pitt.edu`
[3] School of Computing and Augmented Intelligence, Arizona State University,
Tempe, USA
`aricha@asu.edu`
[4] Khoury College of Computer Sciences, Northeastern University, Boston, MA, USA
`te.wilson@northeastern.edu`

Abstract. We consider routing in reconfigurable networks, which is also known as coflow scheduling in the literature. The algorithmic literature generally (perhaps implicitly) assumes that the amount of data to be transferred is large. Thus the standard way to model a collection of requested data transfers is by an integer demand matrix D, where the entry in row i and column j of D is an integer representing the amount of information that the application wants to send from machine/node i to machine/node j. A feasible coflow schedule is then a sequence of matchings, which represent the sequence of data transfers that covers D. In this work, we investigate coflow scheduling when the size of some of the requested data transfers may be small relative to the amount of data that can be transferred in one round. In particular, we investigate algorithms that employ fractional matchings and/or that employ indirect routing, and compare the relative utility of these options. We design algorithms that perform much better for small demands than the algorithms in the literature that were designed for large data transfers.

Keywords: coflow scheduling · reconfigurable networks · indirect routing · online · approximation · completion time · makespan

1 Introduction

We consider routing in reconfigurable networks, also known as *coflow scheduling*, whose topologies dynamically adapt to the structure of the communication traffic [5,12]. There is currently no consensus in the community on what the best reconfigurable network design is, and the community lacks models and metrics to rigorously study and compare different designs [5]. Our high level goal in this work is to fill some of this gap.

C. Georgiou (Ed.): SIROCCO 2026, LNCS 16488, pp. 430–449, 2026.
https://doi.org/10.1007/978-3-032-26465-7_23

1.1   Background and Motivation

In coflow scheduling, there is a layer, which we will call the coflow layer, that sits underneath the application layer, and above the network layer, in the network protocol stack. The application passes the coflow protocol a collection of requests for data transfers that the application wants to execute. The task of the coflow layer is to sensibly schedule/manage when these requests for data transfers are passed to the networking layer. Most notably the coflow layer should not overwhelm the network with more requests than the network can simultaneously support.

The algorithmic literature in this area generally models this informal goal by the formal constraint that at all times the pairs of nodes communicating form a matching M, which in this context is a set $M = \{(s_1, t_1), (s_2, t_2), \ldots, (s_n, t_n)\}$ of source-destination pairs of nodes with distinct sources and distinct sinks (so $i \neq j$ implies $s_i \neq s_j$ and $t_i \neq t_j$). A coflow schedule is then a sequence of matchings $M_1, \ldots, M_T$, where matching M_t is passed to the networking layer at time t, and during the time interval $[t, t+1]$ the network layer transmits a unit of data from s_i to t_i for each $(s_i, t_i) \in M_t$.

The input passed to the coflow layer is assumed to consist of an integer demand matrix D, where D_{ij}, the entry in row i and column j of D, is an integer representing the amount of information that the application wants to send from machine/node i to machine/node j (see, e.g., [2, 11, 13–15, 23, 25, 35, 37]). Then the objective is to optimize some standard quality-of-service metric, like minimizing *makespan*, which is the time when the last unit of data is transmitted, or minimizing the *average completion (or delay) time*, which is the average time that it takes a unit of data to reach its destination. Some of the coflow scheduling literature also considers generalizations of this basic setting, see Sect. 1.3.

Originally, the proposal of a coflow layer was to handle large numbers of data transfer requests, whose sizes were also large [12], and so this has been the, perhaps implicit, assumption in most of the algorithmic literature. This is reflected in the modeling assumption that the demands D_{ij} are integer. Our goal in this work was to examine coflow scheduling when the amount of data transfer requests may be small, as one could conceive in certain data-parallel applications. We model this by allowing the demands D_{ij} to be arbitrary nonnegative rational numbers; in particular demands may be less than 1.

To understand the additional issues that arise if some of the requested data transfers are small, consider the demand matrix D where each entry $D_{ij} = \frac{1}{2n^{3/2}}$, where n is the number of nodes used by the application. Then these data transfers can be supported by routing up to a unit of data from node i to node j at the time t where $t = (j - i) \mod n$. This results in a makespan of $n - 1$ (and average completion time of $(n-1)/2$), and it might seem that obtaining sublinear makespan is impossible, as D cannot be expressed as a linear combination of less than $n - 1$ matchings.

However, a makespan of $O(\sqrt{n})$ can be achieved if the coflow scheduler can indirectly route data, as it is commonly assumed in the reconfigurable networks literature [1, 3, 6, 18, 33, 40]. As an example of indirect routing, a unit of data with

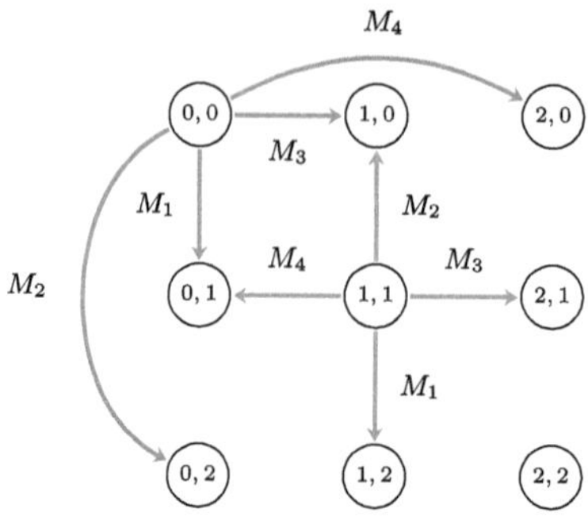

Fig. 1. The data transmissions for nodes $(0, 0)$ and $(1, 1)$ for the 3×3 grid formed from $n = 9$ nodes. The matchings M_1 and M_2 belong to Phase 1, and the matchings M_3 and M_4 belong to Phase 2.

source s_i and destination t_i could be routed using two matchings M_1 and M_2: M_1 could send the data from source node s_i to an intermediate node k, and M_2 could route this data from node k to destination node t_i. One can achieve a makespan of $O(\sqrt{n})$ (for the instance where each $D_{ij} = \frac{1}{2n^{3/2}}$) in the following way. The n nodes are conceptually assigned to nodes in an $\sqrt{n} \times \sqrt{n}$ square grid G. Then the data transfers are divided into two phases, and each phase is divided into $\sqrt{n} - 1$ subphases. In subphase k of Phase 1, the node in row i and column j of G routes to the node in row $[(i + k) \mod \sqrt{n}]$ and column j all of its data whose final destination is in row $[(i + k) \mod \sqrt{n}]$. Thus after the first phase, the current location of each unit of data is in the same row as its final destination. Then subphase k of Phase 2, the node in row i and column j of G routes to the node in row i and column $[(j + k) \mod \sqrt{n}]$ all of its data whose final destination is that node. See Fig. 1 for an illustration of this algorithm when $n = 9$.

Here we consider eight variations of coflow scheduling with rational demand matrices, where "eight" comes from there being two options to each of the following three characteristics:

Direct vs. Indirect Routing. We consider both allowing and disallowing indirect transfers.

Makespan vs. Average Completion Time Objective. We consider both of the two most commonly considered quality-of-service objectives, makespan and average completion time (which are essentially the infinity norm and one norm of the delays for the data units).

Fractional vs. Integral Routing. One conceptual "solution" for coflow scheduling of small data transfers is to allow the network layer to route a fractional matching in each unit of time. In this context, a fractional matching is given by a collection $\{(s_1, t_1, p_1), (s_2, t_2, p_2), \ldots, (s_n, t_n, p_n)\}$ of triples (s_i, t_i, p_i) indicating that p_i fractional units of data are routed from s_i to t_i, such that for all nodes v, $\sum_{i:s_i=v} p_i \leq 1$ and $\sum_{i:t_i=v} p_i \leq 1$. Note that a fractional matching transfers the same amount of data per unit time as an integer matching, so it does not violate the unit throughput constraints at the network layer and thus it would be feasible in several networking scenarios. In contrast, such a relaxation is probably not feasible in settings where the network is optical and the matching is being implemented by the rotation of mirrors [5,31,33]. Thus we consider both allowing fractional matchings and restricting matchings to be integral.

For each of these eight variations, the goal is to find the best approximation ratio that is achievable by a polynomial-time algorithm. Table 1 summarizes the best-known approximation ratios for all the variations of coflow scheduling.

Table 1. Overview of known approximation guarantees. We have provided references to some of the results, as appropriate; for the others, the corresponding approximation bounds follow directly from well-known standard approximation techniques.

	fractional matching		integral matching	
	direct	indirect	direct	indirect
makespan	1 [38]	1 [38]	1	$O(\log n)$
average completion	1	$O(\log n)$	$\sqrt{2}$ [17]	$O(\log n)$

For direct integral routing for the makespan objective, optimal schedules can be computed using an optimal algorithm for edge coloring a bipartite graph [38]. For fractional routing with the makespan objective, the optimal makespan is the same for both direct and indirect routing because the fractional edge coloring number for a bipartite graph is the same as the maximum coloring number of the two underlying bipartite graphs [38]. Finally it is straightforward to model fractional direct routing to optimize average completion time with a polynomial-size linear program. An $O(\log n)$-approximation is achievable for the rest of the variants by modeling the problem as a linear program, where the edges in each time step are over-capacitated by $O(\log n)$ [19]. It can be established that this over-capacitation is sufficient via the probabilistic method. For direct integral routing for average completion time, rounding the demands up to the next integer essentially does not change the problem. Thus, can use the $\sqrt{2}$-approximation for integer demands to obtain a $\sqrt{2}$-approximation for fractional demands.

In this paper, we focus on the variants where a $O(1)$-approximation does not (to the best of our knowledge) follow directly from known results, which all involve indirect routing.

1.2 Summary of Our Results

We present two main results, stated in Theorems 1 and 2. Theorem 1 presents the *first $O(1)$-approximation algorithm for indirect fractional routing for the average completion time* objective:

Theorem 1. *There is a polynomial-time algorithm* ALG *for indirect routing with fractional matchings that outputs, for any valid instance, a schedule whose average completion time is at most 16 times the optimal average completion time. The algorithm only uses direct routing schedules, so the approximation bound is valid for both the direct and indirect routing settings with fractional matchings.*

The algorithm ALG is the natural greedy algorithm that routes an arbitrary maximal matching at each unit of time. Perhaps the limited utility of indirectness in the context of fractional routing for the objective of average completion time is somewhat surprising. Although recall that a similar situation arises for the makespan objective, where indirect routing is of no benefit.

Our algorithm introduces a novel dual fitting framework. As is usually the case in approximation algorithms, the critical step is to find the "right" lower bounds to the optimum to compare against. To that end, we introduce two relaxations of the problem. In the *Sender Bound Problem*, there are only capacity constraints on the amount of data a sender can send in a unit of time, but there are no constraints on the amount of data a receiver can receive in a unit of time. Similarly, in the *Receiver Bound Problem*, there are only capacity constraints on the amount of data a receiver can receive in a unit of time, but there are no constraints on the amount of data a sender can send in a unit of time. We consider the natural linear programming formulations PS and PR for the sender and receiver bound problems, and their respective duals DS and DR. We then use dual feasible solutions for DS and DR as our lower bounds. We are not aware of a similar "double" dual fitting analysis in the literature.

Our second main result appears in Theorem 2, with a full characterization of the *worst-case makespan and average completion time* for *indirect integral routing*, with respect to two parameters n and B. In the future, we plan to leverage the bounds in Theorem 2 towards determining whether a $O(1)$-approximation for indirect integral routing is possible.

Theorem 2. *Let D be a rational demand matrix where the maximum row or column sum is at most B. There is a polynomial-time algorithm* ALG *that uses indirect integral routing, and guarantees makespan and average completion time*

$$\begin{cases} O(\log n) & \text{if } B \leq 2 \text{ ,} \\ O(\frac{B \log n}{\log B}) & \text{if } 2 \leq B \leq n \text{ , and} \\ O(B) & \text{if } n \leq B \text{ .} \end{cases}$$

Further if each entry of D is $\frac{B}{n}$ then the optimal schedule has makespan and average completion time $\Omega(\max\{\log n, \frac{B \log n}{\log B}, B\})$. Thus, algorithm ALG *is worst-case optimal with respect to both objectives.*

Theorem 2 confirms the intuition that the worst-case input should be when the demand is evenly spread out. As $\lceil B \rceil$ is a clear lower bound on the optimal makespan (and optimal average completion time), we also derive the following corollary to the theorem:

Corollary 1. *Algorithm* ALG *from Theorem 2 attains an $O(\log n)$-approximation ratio for both makespan and average completion times, for all B.*

In some sense, the challenge of obtaining an $O(1)$-approximation appears to be to identify instances that admit schedules with less than worst-case objective value.

If $B \leq 2$, we can use Valiant's hypercube design [41] to achieve $O(\log n)$ makespan by using routing paths with $O(\log n)$ intermediate nodes. In a nutshell, this approach tries to maximize the usage of intermediate nodes, because there is very little demand to route. Accordingly, the $\Omega(\log n)$ makespan lower bound relies purely on topological properties, and does not take demands into account. Alternatively, if $B \geq n$, we can use a single round-robin design and route flow directly from sources to destinations in maximum matchings to achieve $O(B)$ makespan—there is no need for intermediate nodes because there are no small demands that can be "combined." The $\Omega(B)$ lower bound relies purely on the maximum demand requested per source or destination node, without taking the network topology into account.

The challenge in the $2 \leq B \leq n$ regime is thus to interpolate between these two extreme cases. For the upper bound, we use a generalization of the hypercube design, which uses $dn^{1/d}$ distinct matchings, for some dimension parameter d. Each matching must be repeated with a multiplicity m that depends on B, n, and d, and increases as d increases, resulting in $mdn^{1/d}$ total makespan. Setting d appropriately results in the desired makespan bound $O(B \log n / \log B)$. To prove the matching lower bound, we carefully partition routings into two categories. If a source can route to a large fraction of destinations using "short" paths with few intermediate nodes (even if only a small fraction of demand is routed there), we show a lower bound purely on network topology properties. Otherwise, if the routing uses "long" paths with many intermediate nodes for a large fraction of the total demand, we can prove a large makespan via a topology-independent averaging argument. This results in the desired lower bound $\Omega(B \log n / \log B)$ for an appropriate threshold of "short" versus "long" paths.

1.3 Related Work

Coflow scheduling was popularized by Chowdhury and Stoica [12], and followed by heuristics for online and offline settings [13,14]. A recent overview of reconfigurable networking can be found in [5].

There is some literature on direct integral routings to optimize weighted completion time. Marx [32] showed that this problem is APX-hard. The natural greedy algorithm is a 2-approximation [8,9]. Gandhi and Mestre [17] give an improved $\sqrt{2}$-approximation, and Halldórsson, Kim, and Sviridenko [21] show a 1.83-approximation for a more general setting. Other works in this area consider non-preemptive variants, where large demands must be scheduled consecutively in time [16,20,29]. The fractional preemptive variants of these problems are also captured by the general polytope scheduling problem, as any feasible instantaneous allocation belongs to the matching polytope [22,24].

There is also some literature on the situation where there are several different applications, each with their own demand matrix, and the objective is to minimize the sum of the makespans over the different applications. This literature considers direct integral routing for the average completion time objective. The problem is APX-hard [32], and an even stronger hardness-of-approximation result ruling out any factor better than 2 follows from a reduction to the concurrent open shop problem [36], which is hard under the Unique Games Conjecture [7]. The first constant-factor approximation was shown by Qiu, Stein, and Zhong [35], and after several improvements [2,28,39], the current best approximation ratio is 3.415 [37]. The special case where each coflow corresponds to the set of incident edges of a vertex is called *data migration* and also has been studied extensively [16,17,26,29,34]. Other notable results are online algorithms [10,15,27,30], a matroid generalization [23], and generalization for general graphs [11,25]. In particular some elements of our dual fitting analysis derive from the dual fitting analysis in [15].

The second main area of related work is in Oblivious Reconfigurable Networks (ORNs). The theoretical problem was formalized recently [4], modeling the constraints of various proposed data center architectures using fast circuit switch technology [1,3,18,33,40]. The ORN model allows for multi-hop indirect routing, its key connection to our work. However, it also focuses on the streaming setting, where traffic demands arrive over time and must be continuously fulfilled. Additionally, they focus on obliviousness, and frame their results as a guarantee on the minimum amount of traffic which can be fulfilled, rather than as a guaranteed approximation ratio. One contribution of the ORN area is a generalized hypercube-style design with a tunable hop parameter [3,4,44]. Our work in Sect. 4 uses similar ideas, but applied to a different use case. Randomized oblivious connection schedules with some adaptive routing have also been considered in theory [43], focusing on the same tradeoff guarantees as in the oblivious literature. It is still unknown what can be done with a fully adaptive design.

2   Notation and Formal Definitions

We follow broadly the definitions and notations used in [4]. Our setting is a network with a collection $N = \{0, \ldots, n-1\}$ of n nodes. The input is an $n \times n$ demand matrix D with nonnegative rational entries, where D_{ij} specifies the amount of data that needs to be transferred from node i to node j.

We define a particular flow network derived from the demand matrix D that allows us to characterize feasible solutions for the problems we consider. The graph (or network) G has vertex set $N \times \{0, \ldots, T\}$, for some $T \in \mathbb{N}$. The edge set of G is partitioned into edges E_{phys} that we will label as *physical*, and edges E_{virt} that we will label as *virtual*. The physical edges are of the form $(i,t) \to (j,t+1)$ for all $i \neq j \in N$ and $t \in \{0, \ldots, T-1\}$. The virtual edges are of the form $(i,t) \to (i,t+1)$ for all $i \in N$ and $t \in \{0, \ldots, T-1\}$. For all $i, j \in N$ and $t \in \{1, \ldots, T\}$, let $\mathcal{P}(i,j,t)$ be the set of all directed paths from vertex $(i,0)$

to vertex (j, t) in G. We define $\mathcal{P} := \cup_{i,j \in N, t \geq 1} \mathcal{P}(i, j, t)$. An *indirect fractional routing* is a flow $f : \mathcal{P} \to \mathbb{R}_{\geq 0}$. We say that the routing (or flow) f is *feasible* for demands D if it satisfies the following constraints:

Capacity Constraints: each vertex has a total outgoing flow over physical edges of at most 1, that is, for each $t \in \{0, \ldots, T-1\}$ and $i \in N$,

$$\sum_{j \in N \setminus \{i\}} \sum_{P \in \mathcal{P}} f(P) \cdot \mathbf{1}[((i, t), (j, t+1)) \in P] \leq 1 \, ,$$

and each vertex has a total incoming flow over physical edges of at most 1, that is, for each $t \in \{0, \ldots, T-1\}$ and $j \in N$,

$$\sum_{i \in N \setminus \{j\}} \sum_{P \in \mathcal{P}} f(P) \cdot \mathbf{1}[((i, t), (j, t+1)) \in P] \leq 1 \, .$$

Demand Satisfaction: for each $i, j \in N$, $\sum_{t=1}^{T} \sum_{P \in \mathcal{P}(i,j,t)} f(P) \geq D_{ij}$.

If a routing f routes α units of flow along a path P from $(i, 0)$ to (j, t) that contains a physical edge $(a, s) \to (b, s+1)$, then α units of data with source i and destination j are transmitted from node a to node b at time s.

A routing f is an *integral* routing if every vertex in G has at most one incoming physical edge with positive flow, and at most one outgoing physical edge with positive flow; hence, for all $t \in \{1, \ldots, T\}$, the physical edges between vertex sets $\{(i, t)\}_{i \in N}$ and $\{(j, t+1)\}_{j \in N}$ with positive flow form a matching in G. A routing f is a *direct* routing if it sends positive flow only over paths that contain at most one physical edge. A direct fractional routing and a direct integral routing can thus be viewed as a sequence of fractional or integral matchings $M_0, \ldots, M_{T-1}$ in the complete bipartite graph between two copies of the node set N that covers D, respectively. Note that with our definitions, direct routings are a subset of indirect routings, and integral routings are a subset of fractional routings.

We say that a feasible routing f for the network G has a *makespan* of T, if the last unit of data was delivered at time T. The *completion time* t for a unit of data with source i and destination j is the smallest t such that this data arrives at a node of the form (j, t). Thus, the total completion time of a schedule is then

$$\sum_{t=1}^{T} \sum_{i, j \in N} \sum_{P \in \mathcal{P}(i,j,t)} t \cdot f(P) \, .$$

3 Fractional Matching, Indirect Routing, and Average Completion Time

In this section we prove Theorem 1. For clarity of explanation, we prove the theorem for the total sum of completion times, which is equivalent to the average completion time (up to a factor of $1/\sum_{i,j} D_{ij}$). We start with a description of the polynomial-time algorithm ALG that gives us Theorem 1.

Algorithm **ALG***:* At each time t, the fractional matching M_t is an arbitrary maximal fractional matching of the residual demand matrix $D(t)$, where for all $i, j \in N$,

$$D_{ij}(t) := D_{ij} - \sum_{t'=0}^{t-1} (M_{t'})_{ij}$$

where $(M_{t'})_{ij}$ denotes the amount of data on edge (i, j) in $M_{t'}$.

The most important step in obtaining approximation ratio results is to find "good" lower bounds to the optimal objective value, which we will denote by OPT. Here we consider the following two lower bounds, each of which are derived by relaxing the constraints in two different (but symmetric) ways.

Sender Bound Problem: For each fractional matching $M = \{(s_i, r_i, p_i)\}$ and for all nodes v, we require that $\sum_{i:s_i=v} p_i \leq \frac{1}{4}$. However, $\sum_{i:r_i=v} p_i$ can be unbounded.

Receiver Bound Problem: For each fractional matching $M = \{(s_i, r_i, p_i)\}$ and for all nodes v, we require that $\sum_{i:r_i=v} p_i \leq \frac{1}{4}$. However, $\sum_{i:s_i=v} p_i$ can be unbounded.

In the sender bound problem there is no bound on the rate that data can be transferred into a node, and in the receiver bound problem there is no bound on the rate that data can be transferred out of a node. Instead of limiting the amount of flow that can be transferred into or out of a node to one, as it may seem natural, we limit it to $\frac{1}{4}$. This setting arises due to technical reasons and makes our dual fitting arguments more convenient. Note that

$$\text{OPT}^S \leq 4 \cdot \text{OPT} \quad \text{and} \quad \text{OPT}^R \leq 4 \cdot \text{OPT} \tag{1}$$

where OPT^S and OPT^R are optimal solutions to the sender bound and receiver bound problems, respectively. This is because replicating each matching in OPT four times results in a solution that is feasible for both the sender bound problem and the receiver bound problem, and increases the objective value by at most a factor of 4.

We now give a linear programming formulation (PS) for the sender bound problem, and a linear programming formulation (PR) for the receiver bound problem. For convenience we are going to rescale time so that every demand D_{ij} is an integer. Such a rescaling does not affect the approximation ratio. In each formulation, the intended meaning of the variable x_{ijt} is the amount of data with source node i destination node j that is transmitted at time t.

$$\text{(PS) min} \sum_{i \in N} \sum_{j \in N} \sum_{t=0}^{T} t \cdot x_{ijt}$$

$$\text{s.t.} \sum_{t=0}^{T} x_{ijt} \geq D_{ij} \qquad \forall i, j \in N$$

$$\sum_{j \in N} x_{ijt} \leq \frac{1}{4} \qquad \forall i \in N,\ 0 \leq t \leq T$$

$$x_{ijt} \geq 0 \qquad \forall i, j \in N, 0 \leq t \leq T$$

$$\text{(PR) min} \sum_{i \in N} \sum_{j \in N} \sum_{t=0}^{T} t \cdot x_{ijt}$$

$$\text{s.t.} \sum_{t=0}^{T} x_{ijt} \geq D_{ij} \qquad \forall i, j \in N$$

$$\sum_{i \in N} x_{ijt} \leq \frac{1}{4} \qquad \forall j \in N,\ 0 \leq t \leq T$$

$$x_{ijt} \geq 0 \qquad \forall i, j \in N, 0 \leq t \leq T$$

We now give the dual linear program (DS) of the primal linear program (PS), and the dual linear program (DR) of the primal linear program (PR). In these dual programs the α variables are associated with the first set of constraints in the primal, and the β variables are associated with the second set of constraints.

$$\text{(DS) max} \sum_{i,j \in N} D_{ij} \cdot \alpha_{ij}^{S} - \sum_{i \in N} \sum_{t=0}^{T} \beta_{it}^{S}$$

$$\text{s.t.}\ \alpha_{ij}^{S} - t \leq 4 \cdot \beta_{it}^{S} \qquad \forall i, j \in N,\ 0 \leq t \leq T$$

$$\alpha_{ij}^{S}, \beta_{it}^{S} \geq 0 \qquad \forall i, j \in N,\ 0 \leq t \leq T$$

$$\text{(DR) max} \sum_{i,j \in N} D_{ij} \cdot \alpha_{ij}^{R} - \sum_{j \in N} \sum_{t=0}^{T} \beta_{jt}^{R}$$

$$\text{s.t.}\ \alpha_{ij}^{R} - t \leq 4 \cdot \beta_{jt}^{R} \qquad \forall i, j \in N,\ 0 \leq t \leq T$$

$$\alpha_{ij}^{R}, \beta_{jt}^{R} \geq 0 \qquad \forall i, j \in N,\ 0 \leq t \leq T$$

We now define dual feasible solutions for (DS) and (DR) related to the execution of the algorithm ALG. Recall that $D_{ij}(t)$ denotes the amount of data with source i and destination j that ALG has not transmitted by time t. Let $D_i^S(t) = \sum_j D_{ij}(t)$ be the amount of data with source i that ALG has not transmitted by time t, and let $D_j^R(t) = \sum_i D_{ij}(t)$ be the amount of data with destination j that ALG has not transmitted by time t. Finally let D_i^S denote $D_i^S(0)$ and $D_j^R = D_j^R(0)$.

Now, we can define dual solutions for (DS) and (DR).

- For all $i, j \in N$, we set $\alpha_{ij}^S = D_i^S(0)$ and $\alpha_{ij}^R = D_j^R(0)$.
- For all $i, j \in N$, we set $\beta_{it}^S = \frac{1}{4}D_i^S(t)$ and $\beta_{jt}^R = \frac{1}{4}D_j^R(t)$.

Let $\mathrm{DS}(\alpha^S, \beta^S)$ and $\mathrm{DR}(\alpha^R, \beta^R)$ be the respective objective values of (DS) and (DR) for these solutions. For convenience, we use ALG below to denote both the algorithm and the value it outputs for the objective function. We first show in Lemma 1 that the sum of these dual objectives upper bounds ALG/2. Then in Lemma 2 we show that the respective dual solutions are feasible.

Lemma 1. $\mathrm{DS}(\alpha^S, \beta^S) + \mathrm{DR}(\alpha^R, \beta^R) \geq \frac{1}{2}\mathrm{ALG}$.

Proof. Recall that

$$\mathrm{DS}(\alpha^S, \beta^S) + \mathrm{DR}(\alpha^R, \beta^R)$$

$$= \sum_{i,j \in N} D_{ij}\alpha_{ij}^S - \sum_{i \in N}\sum_{t=0}^{T} \beta_{it}^S + \sum_{i,j \in N} D_{ij}\alpha_{ij}^R - \sum_{j \in N}\sum_{t=0}^{T} \beta_{jt}^R .$$

We first analyze $\mathrm{DS}(\alpha^S, \beta^S)$. Consider a particular sender receiver pair (i, j). Let T_{ij} denote the collection of times t when ALG sends a positive amount of data from i to j. If ALG does not send data from i to j at time t it must be the case that either ALG is sending unit of data out of sender i or into receiver j. Since there are at most $D_i^S + D_j^R - 2D_{ij}$ such times, and sending all data from i to j takes at most D_{ij} (fractional) time, for every $t \in T_{ij}$ it is the case that

$$t \leq D_i^S + D_j^R - D_{ij} .$$

Thus the completion time of any unit of data with source i and destination j is at most $D_i^S + D_j^R - D_{ij}$. This gives

$$\mathrm{ALG} \leq \sum_{i,j \in N} D_{ij} \cdot (D_i^S + D_j^R - D_{ij})$$

$$\leq \sum_{i,j \in N} D_{ij} \cdot (D_i^S + D_j^R)$$

$$= \sum_{i,j \in N} \left(D_{ij}\alpha_{ij}^S + D_{ij}\alpha_{ij}^R\right) .$$

The equality follows by definition of the α variables. Now note that

$$\frac{1}{2}\mathrm{ALG} = \frac{1}{4}\sum_{t=0}^{T}\left(\sum_{i \in N} D_i^S(t) + \sum_{j \in N} D_j^R(t)\right) = \sum_{t=0}^{T}\sum_{i \in N} \beta_{it}^S + \sum_{t=0}^{T}\sum_{j \in N} \beta_{jt}^R$$

The first equality follows because $\sum_i D_i^S(t) + \sum_j D_j^R(t)$ is equal to twice the total data at time t that ALG has not yet transmitted. The second equality follows from the definition of β variables. Combining these two bounds on ALG, we conclude

$$\mathrm{DS}(\alpha^S, \beta^S) + \mathrm{DR}(\alpha^R, \beta^R)$$

$$= \sum_{i,j \in N} D_{ij} \alpha_{ij}^S - \sum_{i \in N} \sum_{t=0}^T \beta_{it}^S + \sum_{i,j \in N} D_{ij} \alpha_{ij}^R - \sum_{j \in N} \sum_{t=0}^T \beta_{jt}^R$$

$$\geq \mathrm{ALG} - \frac{1}{2}\mathrm{ALG} = \frac{1}{2}\mathrm{ALG} \ .$$

This completes the proof of the lemma. $\qquad\square$

Lemma 2. *The dual solution (α^S, β^S) is feasible for the linear program* (DS) *and the dual solution (α^R, β^R) is feasible for the linear program* (DR).

Proof. First consider the linear program (DS). Since at any time at most one unit can be sent from i, we have $4\beta_{it}^S = D_i^S(t) \geq D_i^S - t = \alpha_{ij}^S - t$, which verifies that the dual constraints of (DS) hold. The argumentation for the linear program (DR) is symmetric. $\qquad\square$

We now conclude the proof of Theorem 1:

Proof of (Theorem 1). We now conclude by noting

$$4 \cdot \mathrm{OPT} + 4 \cdot \mathrm{OPT} \geq \mathrm{OPT}^R + \mathrm{OPT}^S$$

$$\geq \mathrm{DS}(\alpha^S, \beta^S) + \mathrm{DR}(\alpha^R, \beta^R) \geq \frac{1}{2} \cdot \mathrm{ALG} \ .$$

The first inequality follows from the observation in Line (1). The second inequality follows from weak duality and the dual feasibility (from Lemma 2). Finally, the last inequality follows from Lemma 1. Thus we can conclude that the approximation ratio of ALG is at most 16. $\qquad\square$

4   Integral Matching and Indirect Routing

In this section, we present the proof of Theorem 2. We first consider the special case where every entry of the demand matrix is B/n, and show worst-case upper and lower bounds on makespan and average completion time. At the end of this section, we will then show that we can lift these results to the general setting while only losing small constants.

We distinguish three main cases, $B > n$, $B < 2$, and $2 \leq B \leq n$, which we handle in the following. All of the proposed algorithms below run in polynomial time.

Lemma 3. *If all demands are equal to B/n and $B > n$, then there exists an indirect integral routing scheme with makespan and average completion time at most $O(B)$. Moreover, every indirect integral routing scheme has makespan and average completion time at least $\Omega(B)$.*

Proof. We use a *single round-robin* design, which is in fact a direct routing scheme. However, we will see that it achieves a best-possible makespan in the worst-case (up to a constant) even among indirect routing schemes.

The connection schedule consists of n distinct matchings, equal to the set of all cyclic permutations of n, with each matching repeated $\lceil \frac{B}{n} \rceil$ times. With this connection schedule, every possible source-destination pair is directly connected with multiplicity $\lceil \frac{B}{n} \rceil$. The routing protocol chooses to always route flow on direct connections. This gives us total makespan equal to the total number of matchings, $\lceil \frac{B}{n} \rceil n \leq 2B$.

To prove the lower bound, note that every indirect routing scheme must be able to route all demands out of every source, and into every destination. In particular, the maximum row or column sum of the demand matrix is a lower bound on the makespan, and the maximum row or column sum is exactly B when all demands are equal to B/n. Moreover, the median completion time of demands transmitted by any sender is at least $B/2$, and therefore, the average completion time of all demands is $\Omega(B)$. $\qquad\square$

Lemma 4. *If all demands are equal to B/n and $B < 2$, then there exists an indirect integral routing scheme with makespan and average completion time at most $O(\log n)$. Moreover, every indirect integral routing scheme has makespan and average completion time at least $\Omega(\log n)$.*

Proof. We use a variant of Valiant's hypercube design [42]. Assume w.l.o.g. that n is a power of 2, and represent each node $u \in \{1, \ldots, n\}$ in binary. That is, $u = (u_1, \ldots, u_{\log_2(n)})$ where $u_i \in \{0, 1\}$ for all i. The connection schedule $\mathcal{M}$ will consist of exactly $\log_2(n)$ matchings. For each $i \in \{1, \ldots, \log_2(n)\}$, the ith matching connects nodes which match in all but the ith coordinate. That is,

$$M_i(u_1, \ldots, u_{\log_2(n)}) = (u_1, \ldots, u_{i-1}, u_i \oplus 1, u_{i+1}, \ldots, u_{\log_2(n)}).$$

The routing protocol routes flow on the shortest path from source to destination. That is, to route from u to v, a single physical edge is taken for every index for which u and v do not match. This strategy obtains makespan $\log_2(n)$. All that is left is to show that this routing protocol does not overload the physical edges from our matchings.

Consider a node's binary representation. On average each node u will agree with other nodes v on half of their binary indices. Therefore every node pair u, v is connected by a routing path with an average of $\log_2(n)/2$ physical edges. Because demands are uniform, all flow in the network travels along $\log_2(n)/2$ physical edges on average. Additionally, this also implies that the total flow Bn will be evenly load-balanced across all $n \log_2(n)$ physical edges of the network, leading to exactly

$$\frac{\log_2(n)}{2} \cdot \frac{Bn}{n \log_2(n)} \leq 1$$

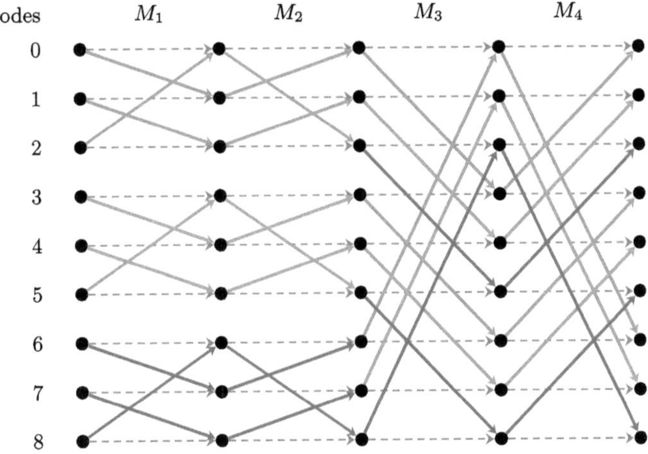

Fig. 2. The time-expanded integral routing scheme of a hypercube with dimension $d = 2$ and $n = 9$.

flow traversing each physical edge, using $B \leq 2$. Thus, the flow is feasible on $\mathcal{M}$.

To prove the lower bound, note that in order to route uniform demands B/n for any $B > 0$, there must be some routing path between every source-destination pair u, v. This is only possible when the number of distinct paths which leave any fixed node u is at least n. Given some makespan bound L, the number of distinct paths leaving a fixed node u using exactly $1 \leq d \leq L$ physical edges is equal to $\binom{L}{d}$. Thus, the number of distinct paths leaving u using at most L physical edges is exactly $\sum_{d=1}^{L} \binom{L}{d} = 2^L - 1$. Therefore, it must be the case that $n \leq 2^L$, or equivalently, $L \geq \log_2(n)$. Using the same argument on source u for reaching $n/2$ destinations, we can see the median completion time of demands sent from u is at least $\log_2(n)/2$, hence the average completion time of all demands is $\Omega(\log n)$. $\qquad\square$

For the case $2 \leq B \leq n$, we split our results into two lemmas. We start with the upper bounds.

Lemma 5. *If all demands are equal to B/n and $2 \leq B \leq n$, then there exists an indirect integral routing scheme with makespan and average completion time at most $O(B \log n / \log B)$.*

Proof. Let $d = \lceil \log_2 n / \log_2 B \rceil$ and assume w.l.o.g. that $n^{1/d}$ is an integer. Represent nodes $u \in \{0, \ldots, n-1\}$ as d-tuples $u = (u_1, \ldots, u_d)$, where each $u_i \in \{0, \ldots, n^{1/d} - 1\}$. For our connection schedule, we use a single period of the Elementary Basis connection schedule (Sect. 4.1 of [4]), illustrated in Fig. 2 for dimension parameter $d = 2$ and explained in detail below. We will use multiplicity of matchings $\lceil B/n^{1/d} \rceil$. For each index $i \in \{1, \ldots, d\}$ and each scale factor $s \in \{1, \ldots, n^{1/d} - 1\}$, we define the matching $M_{t=(i,s)}$ which connects nodes u

to nodes v which match u in all but the ith coordinates, and which differ from u in the ith coordinate by exactly $+s(\mathrm{mod}\ n^{1/d})$. That is,

$$M_{t=(i,s)}(u) = (u_1, \ldots, u_{i-1}, u_i + s(\mathrm{mod}\ n^{1/d}), u_{i+1}, \ldots, u_d).$$

Our connection schedule repeats each matching M_t exactly $\lceil B/n^{1/d} \rceil$ times. Hence, the length of the schedule is equal to $T = d \cdot (n^{1/d} - 1) \cdot \lceil B/n^{1/d} \rceil$.

To route between an arbitrary node pair u to v, greedily route flow across any physical edge which connects to a node with decreased Hamming distance to v (i.e. it matches v in the modified ith coordinate). This process will use at most d physical edges to route between each pair u, v.

We next show that no edge is overloaded. Since there are $n^{1/d}$ choices for each of the d entries of node's tuples, on average each node u agrees with another node v on $d/n^{1/d}$ entries. Therefore, every node pair u, v is connected by a routing path using an average of $d - d/n^{1/d}$ physical edges. Because uniform traffic is being routed, flow will be evenly balanced across all physical edges. Since a total of Bn flow is routed over Tn physical edges, the load on each edge is

$$\left(d - \frac{d}{n^{1/d}} \right) \cdot \frac{Bn}{Tn} = \left(d - \frac{d}{n^{1/d}} \right) \cdot \frac{B}{d \cdot (n^{1/d} - 1) \cdot \left\lceil \frac{B}{n^{1/d}} \right\rceil}$$

$$= \frac{B}{n^{1/d} \cdot \left\lceil \frac{B}{n^{1/d}} \right\rceil} \le 1 \ .$$

Finally, we can bound the makespan as follows:

$$T = \left\lceil \frac{B}{n^{1/d}} \right\rceil \cdot dn^{1/d}$$

$$\le dn^{1/d} + dB$$

$$= \left\lceil \frac{\log_2 n}{\log_2 B} \right\rceil \cdot \left(n^{1/\left\lceil \frac{\log_2 n}{\log_2 B} \right\rceil} + B \right)$$

$$\le \left(\frac{\log_2 n}{\log_2 B} + 1 \right) \cdot \left(n^{\frac{\log_2(B)}{\log_2(n)}} + B \right)$$

$$= \left(\frac{\log_2 n}{\log_2 B} + 1 \right) \cdot 2B \in \mathcal{O}\left(\frac{B \log_2(n)}{\log_2(B)} \right).$$

This completes the proof of the lemma. $\qquad\qquad\qquad\qquad\qquad\qquad\square$

Lemma 6. *If all demands are equal to B/n and $2 \le B \le n$, then every indirect integral routing scheme has makespan and average completion time at least $\Omega(B \log n / \log B)$.*

Proof. Fix any integral routing scheme f and let T be its makespan. For any node pair u, v, let $S_{u,v}$ denote the minimum number of physical edges used to route demands from u to v, and let h be the median of $S_{u,v}$ over all node pairs u, v. Let $d = \frac{1}{3} \log_2 n / \log_2 B$. We distinguish whether $h \ge d$ or $h < d$.

Case 1: $h \geq d$. Because we assumed f obtained makespan T, there are exactly nT total physical edges that may be used to route flow. Additionally, there are Bn total units of flow that need to be routed across the entire network. In particular, each node pair u, v with $S_{u,v} \geq h$ requires at least h physical edges per unit flow. Thus, there is a total of $\frac{1}{2}Bn$ demand that needs at least h physical edges per unit flow. Thus, the average amount of flow per physical edge is at least $\frac{Bnh}{2nT} \geq \frac{Bd}{2T}$. Since each physical edge has unit capacity and we assumed that f was feasible, it must be that $T \geq Bd/2 \in \Omega(B \log_2(n)/\log_2(B))$.

Case 2: $h < d$. By the definition of h, for half of the node pairs f routes some flow using at most h physical edges. Thus, there must exist a sender u^* that can route flow to at least $n/2$ receivers using at most h physical edges each. Therefore, there must exist at least $n/2$ distinct paths from u^* that reach those receivers within makespan T using at most h physical edges. We next compute how many such paths exist. There are $\binom{T}{i}$ distinct paths using exactly i physical edges that obtain makespan T. Thus, there are $\sum_{i=1}^{h} \binom{T}{i}$ distinct paths with at most h physical edges within makespan T. Thus, it must be that $n/2 \leq \sum_{i=1}^{h} \binom{T}{i}$.

In the following, we derive a lower bound on T from this inequality. We first note that the proof of Lemma 4 shows that for any $B > 0$, it holds that $T \geq \log_2 n$, and thus, $T \geq \log_2 n / \log_2 B = 3d$ since we assume that $B \geq 2$. We can now observe that

$$\sum_{i=1}^{h} \binom{T}{i} \leq 2 \binom{T}{h} \leq 2 \frac{T^h}{h!} \ ,$$

where the first inequality holds using $h \leq d \leq T/3$, and the second inequality is a well-known approximation of the binomial coefficient. Rearranging $n/2 \leq 2T^h/h!$ gives us

$$T \geq \left(h! \cdot \frac{n}{4} \right)^{1/h} = n^{1/h} \cdot (h!)^{1/h} \cdot \left(\frac{1}{4} \right)^{1/h} .$$

Using Stirling's approximation $h! \geq \sqrt{2\pi h} \cdot (\frac{h}{e})^h$, we can derive

$$T \geq \frac{h}{e} n^{1/h} \cdot \left(\frac{\sqrt{2\pi h}}{4} \right)^{1/h} \geq \frac{h}{e} n^{1/h} \ ,$$

because $(\sqrt{2\pi h}/4)^{1/h}$ converges to 1 from above as $h \to \infty$.

The derivative of $h \cdot n^{1/h}$ is equal to $n^{1/h}(h - \ln n)/h$, which is negative for all $2 \leq h < \ln n$. Hence, the function $h \cdot n^{1/h}$ is strictly decreasing on this interval. Since $\ln n > \frac{1}{2} \log_2 n \geq \frac{1}{2} \log_2 n / \log_2 B \geq d$, we can conclude that $h \cdot n^{1/h} \geq d \cdot n^{1/d}$ for all $2 \leq h \leq d$. Thus, f has makespan at least $T \geq h \cdot n^{1/h}/e \in \Omega(B \log_2(n)/\log_2(B))$. This completes the proof of Case 2.

Note that by our choice of h, our lower bounds on the makespan also apply to the median completion time, hence also give the same lower bound on the average completion time up to constants. This completes the proof of the lemma.

$\square$

This completes our results for the uniform demand setting. To lift our results to the general setting, we use the following well-known reduction.

Lemma 7. *Given a connection schedule $\mathcal{M} = M_0, \ldots, M_{T-1}$ and routing protocol f_{unif} over $\mathcal{M}$ that is feasible for uniform demands B/n and obtains makespan T, then for any demand matrix D with row and column sums no more than B, we can build a routing f_D over the connection schedule $\mathcal{M} \circ \mathcal{M}$ that obtains makespan $2T$.*

Proof. This is a natural application of Valiant Load Balancing [42], which is described at a high level below. To route r demand between any node pair u, v, first traffic is routed from u to all intermediate nodes i in the network in equal shares r/n, using f_{unif}. Then, traffic is routed from intermediate nodes to its destination using f_{unif}. This allows us to treat routing any demand D with row and column sums no more than B as if it is two copies of uniform demand, requesting B/n demand between node pairs. $\qquad\square$

5 Conclusion

In this paper, we focus on two of the variants of coflow scheduling with rational demand matrices, for which $O(1)$-approximations were not previously known: We first present a 16-approximation algorithm for minimizing the average completion time under indirect fractional matching routings. Secondly, we address both the makespan and the average completion time objectives under indirect integral routing, and provide a full characterization of the worst-case runtimes under both objectives for this regime. While this falls short of providing $O(1)$-approximations for indirect integral routing, our proposed algorithm provides $O(\log n)$-approximations for the two objectives, in addition to being worst-case optimal; we also believe that the worst-case analysis will be helpful in determining whether a $O(1)$-approximation for indirect integral routing is possible. If it is, then we will have shown, together with the results in this paper, that constant-approximation algorithms exist for all possible coflow scheduling variants in Table 1.

Acknowledgments. This research was conducted while the authors were participants in the Simons Institute program on Algorithmic Foundations for Emerging Computing Technologies. AL and TW were Research Fellows at the Simons Institute for the Theory of Computing when this research was conducted. KP was supported by National Science Foundation grant CCF-2209654. AR was supported in part by research grants NSF-CCF-2312537 and 2106917, and U.S. ARO MURI W911NF-19-1-0233.

References

1. Addanki, V., Avin, C., Schmid, S.: Mars: near-optimal throughput with shallow buffers in reconfigurable datacenter networks. Proc. ACM Meas. Anal. Comput. Syst. **7**(1), 2:1–2:43 (2023). https://doi.org/10.1145/3579312

2. Ahmadi, S., Khuller, S., Purohit, M., Yang, S.: On scheduling CoFlows. Algorithmica **82**(12), 3604–3629 (2020). https://doi.org/10.1007/s00453-020-00741-3

3. Amir, D., Saran, N., Wilson, T., Kleinberg, R., Shrivastav, V., Weatherspoon, H.: Shale: a practical, scalable oblivious reconfigurable network. In: SIGCOMM, pp. 449–464. ACM (2024). https://doi.org/10.1145/3651890.3672248

4. Amir, D., Wilson, T., Shrivastav, V., Weatherspoon, H., Kleinberg, R., Agarwal, R.: Optimal oblivious reconfigurable networks. In: STOC, pp. 1339–1352. ACM (2022). https://doi.org/10.1145/3519935.3520020

5. Avin, C., Schmid, S.: Revolutionizing datacenter networks via reconfigurable topologies. Commun. ACM **68**(6), 44–53 (2025). https://doi.org/10.1145/3708980

6. Ballani, H., et al.: Sirius: a flat datacenter network with nanosecond optical switching. In: SIGCOMM, pp. 782–797. ACM (2020). https://doi.org/10.1145/3387514.3406221

7. Bansal, N., Khot, S.: Optimal long code test with one free bit. In: FOCS, pp. 453–462. IEEE Computer Society (2009). https://doi.org/10.1109/FOCS.2009.23

8. Bar-Noy, A., Bellare, M., Halldórsson, M.M., Shachnai, H., Tamir, T.: On chromatic sums and distributed resource allocation. Inf. Comput. **140**(2), 183–202 (1998). https://doi.org/10.1006/inco.1997.2677

9. Bar-Noy, A., Halldórsson, M.M., Kortsarz, G., Salman, R., Shachnai, H.: Sum multicoloring of graphs. J. Algorithms **37**(2), 422–450 (2000). https://doi.org/10.1006/jagm.2000.1106

10. Bhimaraju, A., Nayak, D., Vaze, R.: Non-clairvoyant scheduling of CoFlows. In: WiOpt, pp. 81–88. IEEE (2020). https://dl.ifip.org/db/conf/wiopt/wiopt2020/32.pdf

11. Chowdhury, M., Khuller, S., Purohit, M., Yang, S., You, J.: Near optimal CoFlow scheduling in networks. In: SPAA, pp. 123–134. ACM (2019). https://doi.org/10.1145/3323165.3323179

12. Chowdhury, M., Stoica, I.: CoFlow: a networking abstraction for cluster applications. In: HotNets, pp. 31–36. ACM (2012). https://doi.org/10.1145/2390231.2390237

13. Chowdhury, M., Stoica, I.: Efficient CoFlow scheduling without prior knowledge. In: SIGCOMM, pp. 393–406. ACM (2015). https://doi.org/10.1145/2785956.2787480

14. Chowdhury, M., Zhong, Y., Stoica, I.: Efficient CoFlow scheduling with VARYS. In: SIGCOMM. pp. 443–454. ACM (2014). https://doi.org/10.1145/2619239.2626315

15. Dinitz, M., Moseley, B.: Scheduling for weighted flow and completion times in reconfigurable networks. In: INFOCOM, pp. 1043–1052. IEEE (2020). https://doi.org/10.1109/INFOCOM41043.2020.9155537

16. Gandhi, R., Halldórsson, M.M., Kortsarz, G., Shachnai, H.: Improved bounds for scheduling conflicting jobs with minsum criteria. ACM Trans. Algorithms **4**(1), 11:1–11:20 (2008). https://doi.org/10.1145/1328911.1328922

17. Gandhi, R., Mestre, J.: Combinatorial algorithms for data migration to minimize average completion time. Algorithmica **54**(1), 54–71 (2009). https://doi.org/10.1007/s00453-007-9118-2

18. Ghorbani, S., Yang, Z., Godfrey, P.B., Ganjali, Y., Firoozshahian, A.: DRILL: micro load balancing for low-latency data center networks. In: SIGCOMM, pp. 225–238. ACM (2017). https://doi.org/10.1145/3098822.3098839

19. Gonnet, G.H.: Expected length of the longest probe sequence in hash code searching. J. ACM **28**(2), 289–304 (1981)

20. Halldórsson, M.M., Kortsarz, G., Shachnai, H.: Minimizing average completion of dedicated tasks and interval graphs. In: Goemans, M., Jansen, K., Rolim, J.D.P., Trevisan, L. (eds.) APPROX/RANDOM -2001. LNCS, vol. 2129, pp. 114–126. Springer, Heidelberg (2001). https://doi.org/10.1007/3-540-44666-4_15

21. Halldórsson, M.M., Kortsarz, G., Sviridenko, M.: Sum edge coloring of multigraphs via configuration LP. ACM Trans. Algorithms **7**(2), 22:1–22:21 (2011). https://doi.org/10.1145/1921659.1921668

22. Im, S., Kulkarni, J., Munagala, K.: Competitive algorithms from competitive equilibria: Non-clairvoyant scheduling under polyhedral constraints. J. ACM **65**(1), 3:1–3:33 (2018). https://doi.org/10.1145/3136754

23. Im, S., Moseley, B., Pruhs, K., Purohit, M.: Matroid CoFlow scheduling. In: ICALP. LIPIcs, vol. 132, pp. 145:1–145:14. Schloss Dagstuhl - Leibniz-Zentrum für Informatik (2019). https://doi.org/10.4230/LIPIcs.ICALP.2019.145

24. Jäger, S., Lindermayr, A., Megow, N.: The power of proportional fairness for non-clairvoyant scheduling under polyhedral constraints. In: SODA, pp. 3901–3930. SIAM (2025). https://doi.org/10.1137/1.9781611978322.132

25. Jahanjou, H., Kantor, E., Rajaraman, R.: Asymptotically optimal approximation algorithms for CoFlow scheduling. In: SPAA, pp. 45–54. ACM (2017). https://doi.org/10.1145/3087556.3087567

26. Khuller, S., Kim, Y.A., Wan, Y.J.: Algorithms for data migration with cloning. SIAM J. Comput. **33**(2), 448–461 (2004). https://doi.org/10.1137/S009753970342585X

27. Khuller, S., Li, J., Sturmfels, P., Sun, K., Venkat, P.: Select and permute: an improved online framework for scheduling to minimize weighted completion time. Theor. Comput. Sci. **795**, 420–431 (2019). https://doi.org/10.1016/j.tcs.2019.07.026

28. Khuller, S., Purohit, M.: Brief announcement: improved approximation algorithms for scheduling co-flows. In: SPAA, pp. 239–240. ACM (2016). https://doi.org/10.1145/2935764.2935809

29. Kim, Y.A.: Data migration to minimize the total completion time. J. Algorithms **55**(1), 42–57 (2005). https://doi.org/10.1016/j.jalgor.2004.07.009

30. Lindermayr, A., Liu, Z., Megow, N.: Polytope scheduling with groups: unified models and optimal guarantees. In: IPCO. Springer (2026), to appear

31. Liu, H., et al.: Lightwave fabrics: at-scale optical circuit switching for datacenter and machine learning systems. In: Proceedings of the ACM SIGCOMM 2023 Conference, pp. 499–515. ACM SIGCOMM 2023, Association for Computing Machinery, New York, NY, USA (2023). https://doi.org/10.1145/3603269.3604836

32. Marx, D.: Complexity results for minimum sum edge coloring. Discret. Appl. Math. **157**(5), 1034–1045 (2009). https://doi.org/10.1016/j.dam.2008.04.002

33. Mellette, W.M., Forencich, A., Athapathu, R., Snoeren, A.C., Papen, G., Porter, G.: Realizing RotorNet: toward practical microsecond scale optical networking. In: SIGCOMM, pp. 392–414. ACM (2024). https://doi.org/10.1145/3651890.3672273

34. Mestre, J.: Adaptive local ratio. SIAM J. Comput. **39**(7), 3038–3057 (2010). https://doi.org/10.1137/080731712

35. Qiu, Z., Stein, C., Zhong, Y.: Minimizing the total weighted completion time of CoFlows in datacenter networks. In: SPAA, pp. 294–303. ACM (2015). https://doi.org/10.1145/2755573.2755592

36. Queyranne, M., Sviridenko, M.: A (2+epsilon)-approximation algorithm for the generalized preemptive open shop problem with minsum objective. J. Algorithms **45**(2), 202–212 (2002). https://doi.org/10.1016/S0196-6774(02)00251-1

37. Rohwedder, L., Schnaars, L.: 3.415-approximation for CoFlow scheduling via iterated rounding. In: ICALP. LIPIcs, vol. 334, pp. 128:1–128:19. Schloss Dagstuhl - Leibniz-Zentrum für Informatik (2025), https://doi.org/10.4230/LIPIcs.ICALP.2025.128
38. Schrijver, A., et al.: Combinatorial Optimization: Polyhedra and Efficiency, vol. 24. Springer (2003). https://link.springer.com/book/9783540443896
39. Shafiee, M., Ghaderi, J.: Brief announcement: a new improved bound for CoFlow scheduling. In: SPAA, pp. 91–93. ACM (2017). https://doi.org/10.1145/3087556.3087598
40. Shrivastav, V., et al.: Shoal: a network architecture for disaggregated racks. In: NSDI, pp. 255–270. USENIX Association (2019). https://www.usenix.org/conference/nsdi19/presentation/shrivastav
41. Valiant, L.G.: A scheme for fast parallel communication. SIAM J. Comput. $11(2)$, 350–361 (1982). https://doi.org/10.1137/0211027
42. Valiant, L.G., Brebner, G.J.: Universal schemes for parallel communication. In: STOC, pp. 263–277. ACM (1981). https://doi.org/10.1145/800076.802479
43. Wilson, T., Amir, D., Saran, N., Kleinberg, R., Shrivastav, V., Weatherspoon, H.: Breaking the VLB barrier for oblivious reconfigurable networks. In: STOC, pp. 1865–1876. ACM (2024). https://doi.org/10.1145/3618260.3649608
44. Wilson, T., Amir, D., Shrivastav, V., Weatherspoon, H., Kleinberg, R.: Extending optimal oblivious reconfigurable networks to all N. In: APOCS, pp. 1–16. SIAM (2023). https://doi.org/10.1137/1.9781611977578.ch1

Byzantine Approximate Agreement Cross-chain Task

Maurice Herlihy[1], Bo Pan[2]([✉]), Maria Potop-Butucaru[2],
and Liuba Shrira[3]

[1] Brown University Computer Science Dept, Providence, RI 02912, USA
[2] Sorbonne Université, CNRS, LIP6, 75005 Paris, France
{bo.pan,maria.potop-butucaru}@lip6.fr
[3] Brandeis University Computer Science Dept, Waltham, MA 02454, USA

Abstract. We introduce the *Byzantine Approximate Agreement Cross-chain Task* in the *smart contract model*, a recently proposed framework for capturing computation in blockchain-based systems. In this model, a set of m parties, of which up to a minority may be Byzantine, interact via n trusted smart contracts deployed on multiple independent ledgers (blockchains).

We present two protocols that solve the Byzantine Approximate Agreement Cross-chain Task and prove their correctness. Both protocols are optimal with respect to Byzantine resilience - tolerating a minority of Byzantine parties - and time complexity, completing in two rounds in synchronous executions. We further analyze their bit complexity within the smart contract model. The first protocol requires $\mathcal{O}(k)$ bits of local memory per party, where k denotes the number of bits needed to encode the proposed values, and achieves a total message bit complexity of $\mathcal{O}(n \cdot m \cdot k)$. The second protocol reduces the local memory usage at each party to $\mathcal{O}(1)$ bits, at the cost of increasing the total message bit complexity to $\mathcal{O}(n^2 \cdot m \cdot k)$.

Keywords: Cross-chain tasks · Blockchains oracles · Approximate Agreement · Byzantine fault-tolerance

1 Introduction

Approximate Byzantine Agreement introduced by Dolev et al. in [6] addresses the challenge of reaching agreement on real values in the presence of Byzantine faults. The problem has been introduced as a relaxation of exact consensus, where processes converge to values within some ϵ of each other, and within the range of correct inputs.

In [6] the authors assume a model in which processes can send messages containing arbitrary real values, and can store arbitrary real values. Each process starts with an arbitrary real value. Informally stated, approximate agreement must satisfy the following two conditions:

- *Agreement.* All non-faulty processes eventually halt with output values that are within ϵ of each other (with $\epsilon > 0$ as small as desired);
- *Validity.* The value output by each non-faulty process must be within the range of the initial values of the non-faulty processes.

If the non-faulty processes start with the same initial value, the final values are required to be the same as the common initial value.

Variants of this problem have been proposed recently in [8] and [10]. In [10] the authors propose *median approximate agreement* with a validity condition, *median validity*, which requires that correct processes should output the median of the correct processes' input values. In [8], the authors propose an approximation for the k-th smallest value under an *interval validity* condition.

The study of Approximate Agreement problem was motivated by a broad range of applications (e.g. large scale sensor and robot networks, continuous cyber-physical systems, federated learning etc) where exact consensus is sometimes impossible and its approximate version is good enough.

Blockchain oracles are one of these applications. Oracles are systems that connect blockchains with the outside world by providing decentralized applications with the external information needed for smart contract execution. In decentralized price oracles (e.g [4]), oracle nodes fetch price data from different off-chain sources (exchanges, APIs). Because of timing, network delays, and different sources, honest nodes will have different price observations, though usually close to each other. These values are not identical, therefore the exact consensus is not realistic.

Nodes iteratively share their price estimates with others. Each node updates its estimate based on the set of values received, often taking a median or weighted average within the range of honest values (convex hull). After a number of rounds, all honest nodes hold values that are very close to each other — within a small tolerance. The final agreed value is then published to be used by *decentralized finance* applications.

At the core of the distributed oracle price problem is the *approximated agreement* and not exact consensus. In [7] the authors were the first to make the connection between the *price oracle* problem and the classical *Approximate Byzantine Agreement* problem [6]. Additionally, they proposed an implementation of price oracles in asynchronous Byzantine settings using an Approximate Byzantine Agreement primitive.

Interestingly, in order to formalize the blockchain oracle technology as an approximate agreement problem (e.g. [3,5,7]) one should first formalize the approximate agreement problem itself in a model that captures the specificity of computations with smart contracts. In [2] the authors introduced *the smart contract model*, the first framework that captures the specificities of the computation in blockchain technologies supporting smart contracts. In this model, a collection of m potentially Byzantine parties interact through n trusted smart contracts residing on multiple, independent ledgers (blockchains). Tasks to be solved are formulated using elementary game-theoretic notions, taking into account the utility to each party of each possible outcome.

Our Contribution. This paper defines the *Byzantine Approximate Agreement Cross-chain Task* in *the smart contract model* introduced in [2]. Furthermore, we design and prove correct two protocols to solve *Byzantine Approximate Agreement Cross-chain Task* in the smart contract model. The first protocol assumes that both parties and smart contracts perform local computation while in the second protocol the computation is performed only by smart contracts. Our protocols are optimal in terms of both Byzantine resilience (tolerating a minority of Byzantine participants) and time complexity (two rounds in synchronous settings).

Moreover, we investigate the bit complexity of our protocols. The first protocol uses $\mathcal{O}(k)$ bits at each party (k represent the number of bits necessary to encode the proposed values). The total bit complexity of messages exchanges is $\mathcal{O}(n \cdot m \cdot k)$. The second protocol uses only $\mathcal{O}(1)$ bits on the parties side while the total bit complexity of messages exchanged is $\mathcal{O}(n^2 \cdot m \cdot k)$.

2   The Smart Contract Model

This section reviews the *smart contract model* [2]). The smart contract model draws inspiration from classical distributed computing models, but it diverges in several fundamental ways. In traditional models, a task is defined by its inputs and outputs: each process selects an input and, after communicating with others via messages or shared memory, produces an output consistent with the task specification.

Smart contracts abstract the underlying blockchain to provide a trusted, deterministic mechanism for coordinating autonomous parties. Smart contracts are deterministic state machines that change state in response to authenticated messages from parties, and their code and state are publicly observable and replicated across multiple repositories, ensuring trustworthiness.

To execute a task, parties agree on a *protocol*: a prescribed sequence of steps. *Compliant* parties follow this protocol, whereas *deviating* parties may act arbitrarily. Because no party can assume compliance from others, protocols must guarantee both *safety*—no compliant party is worse off than at the start—and *liveness*—if all parties comply, everyone benefits. Tasks are formulated using elementary game-theoretic notions, expressed in terms of each party's utility for possible outcomes. Parties provide inputs but deviations can alter it. Unlike in classical models, the outputs of the task are determined by the contracts themselves, which are the only trusted authorities controlling.

A *cross-chain system* $CCS = (\mathcal{P}, \mathcal{C})$ is composed of a finite set of *parties* $\mathcal{P} = \{P_1, \ldots, P_m\}$, $m \geq 2$ and a finite set of *smart contracts* $\mathcal{C} = \{C_1, \ldots, C_n\}$, $n \geq 2$. Parties and smart contracts are both modeled as *interface automata* [1].

Given a cross-chain system CCS $= (\mathcal{P}, \mathcal{C})$ where $\mathcal{P}$ is a set of m parties and $\mathcal{C}$ a set of n smart contracts a *cross-chain task* is a tuple $(\mathcal{I}_P, \mathcal{I}_C, \mathcal{O}_C, U)$, where:

- $\mathcal{I}_P$ is a set of m-element *input party vectors*, representing each party's input to the task,

- $\mathcal{I}_C$ is a set of n-element *input contract state vectors*, representing each contract's state before executing the task,
- $\mathcal{O}_C$ is a set of n-element *output contract state vectors*, representing each contract's state after executing the task, and
- $U : \mathcal{I}_P \times \mathcal{I}_C \times \mathcal{O}_C \to \mathbb{R}^m$ is a *utility function* that characterizes how each party values each possible transition.

The utility for an individual party P is written $U(I_P, I_C, O_C)[P]$, and the utility for a coalition $\mathcal{Q} \subset \mathcal{P}$ is defined to be

$$U(I_P, I_C, O_C)[\mathcal{Q}] := \sum_{Q \in \mathcal{Q}} U(I_P, I_C, O_C)[Q].$$

The utility function captures the notion of "better off" and "worse off" for parties. A *transition* is a triple $(I_P, I_C, O_C) \in \mathcal{I}_P \times \mathcal{I}_C \times \mathcal{O}_C$. Party P considers transition (I_P, I_C, O_C) *acceptable* if $U(I_P, I_C, O_C)[P] \geq 0$, and *preferred* if $U(I_P, I_C, O_C)[P] > 0$. A transition is *acceptable* if it is acceptable to all parties, and *preferred* if it is preferred by all parties.

Note that a task's set of output contract states must encompass all reachable output contract states, even those produced when parties deviate maliciously or irrationally from the protocol. Because parties are autonomous (and possibly Byzantine), a task definition is not expressed in terms of parties' states, only in terms of the input values they provide to the task.

For a task to be *feasible* (capable of solution), it must satisfy certain additional feasibility conditions. Because deviating parties can always obstruct progress, the null transition must always be acceptable. For any input vectors $I_P \in \mathcal{I}_P$ and $I_C \in \mathcal{I}_C$,

$$\mathcal{I}_C \subset \mathcal{O}_C \text{ and } (I_P, I_C, I_C) \text{ is an acceptable transition.} \tag{1}$$

Each task must be solvable in principle: for all input vectors $I_P \in \mathcal{I}_P, I_C \in \mathcal{I}_C$, there must exist a preferred transition:

$$\exists O_C \in \mathcal{O}_C \text{ such that } (I_P, I_C, O_C) \text{ is a preferred transition.} \tag{2}$$

A task will have no solution if a *deviating* party Q can trick a *compliant* party P into negative utility simply by lying about Q's input. For any two input party vectors I_P, I_P', and for every party P,

$$\text{if } I_P[P] = I_P'[P] \text{ and } U(I_P, I_C, O_C)[P] \geq 0, \text{ then } U(I_P', I_C, O_C)[P] \geq 0. \tag{3}$$

A hidden input might shift a compliant party's utility from one non-negative quantity to another, but never from non-negative to negative.

To execute a task, parties agree on a sequence of contract calls called a *cross-chain protocol*. As noted, *compliant* parties follow the agreed-upon protocol, while *deviating* parties need not.

When describing a protocol execution, we indicate which parties are compliant by a *compliance set* $\mathcal{Q} \subset \mathcal{P}$, where $P \in \mathcal{Q}$ means P is compliant.

Given a cross-chain system $CCS = (\mathcal{P}, \mathcal{C})$ where $\mathcal{P}$ is a set of m parties and $\mathcal{C}$ is a set of n smart contracts, a cross-chain protocol is a tuple $(\mathcal{I}_P, \mathcal{I}_C, \mathcal{O}_C, \Xi)$, where

- $\mathcal{I}_P$ is a set of m-element *input party vectors*,
- $\mathcal{I}_C$ is a set of n-element *input contract state vectors*,
- $\mathcal{O}_C$ is a set of n-element *output contract state vectors*,
- $\Xi : \mathcal{I}_P \times \mathcal{I}_C \times 2^{\mathcal{P}} \to 2^{\mathcal{O}_C}$, the *execution function*, is a map that carries a input party vector, an input contract state vector, and a compliance set to a set of output contract state vectors representing possible outcomes.

The protocol itself is the automaton obtained by the composition of automata modeling parties in $\mathcal{P}$ and interface automata modeling smart contracts in $\mathcal{C}$.

The execution of a cross-chain protocol is an execution fragment starting in a state $(I_P, I_C) \in \mathcal{I}_P \times \mathcal{I}_C$ and terminating in a state in $\Xi(I_P, I_C, \mathcal{Q})$ where $\mathcal{Q} \subseteq \mathcal{P}$ indicates which parties were compliant during the protocol execution.

A cross-chain protocol for a cross-chain task is *correct* if each execution of the protocol satisfies the following properties:

- *Coalition Nash Equilibrium:* Informally, we want to ensure that no rational party has an incentive to deviate: no coalition of parties can increase its utility by deviating from the protocol while the remaining parties comply. More precisely, for all coalitions $\mathcal{Q} \subset \mathcal{P}$, input vectors $I_P \in \mathcal{I}_P, I_C \in \mathcal{I}_c$, conforming executions $O_C \in \Xi(I_P, I_C, \mathcal{P})$, and $\mathcal{Q}$-deviating executions $O_C' \in \Xi(I_P, I_C, \mathcal{P} \backslash \mathcal{Q})$, conforming is the better strategy for $\mathcal{Q}$

$$U(I_P, I_C, O_C)[\mathcal{Q}] \geq U(I_P, I_C, O_C')[\mathcal{Q}]. \tag{4}$$

- *Liveness:* If all parties are compliant then the protocol's transitions are preferred:

$$(\forall O_C \in \Xi(I_P, I_C, \mathcal{P})) \, (\forall P \in \mathcal{P}) \, U(I_P, I_C, O_C)[P] > 0 \tag{5}$$

- *Safety:* No compliant party ends up worse off:

$$(\forall O_C \in \Xi(I_P, I_C, \mathcal{Q})) \, (\forall Q \in \mathcal{Q}) \, U(I_P, I_C, O_C)[Q] \geq 0. \tag{6}$$

In a cross-chain system $CCS = (\mathcal{P}, \mathcal{C})$, parties in $\mathcal{P}$ communicate with contracts in $\mathcal{C}$ via messages. Compliant parties do not communicate directly with other parties, and contracts do not communicate directly with contracts. Communication channels are *authenticated*: a message's sender cannot be forged, and *reliable*: a channel does not create, lose, or duplicate messages.

We consider executions proceed in synchronous rounds, each round is composed of four *synchronized* phases: *send phase, contract-local phase, read phase* and *party-local phase*. A detailed explanation of each one of these phases follows.

1. In the *send phase*, each party optionally sends a message to one or more contracts.
2. In the *contract-local phase*, each contract receives the messages in an arbitrary order and undergoes state changes in response.
3. In the *read phase* each party reads the new contract state.
4. In the *party-local phase*, each party optionally executes a local computation and prepares a new message.

3   Approximate Agreement Cross-Chain Task

In the following we specify the ϵ-*Approximate Agreement Cross-chain Task* in the in the smart contract model Section 2.

The system is composed of a finite set of *parties* $\mathcal{P} = \{P_1, \ldots, P_m\}$, $m \geq 2$, a finite set of *smart contracts* $\mathcal{C} = \{C_1, \ldots, C_n\}$, $n \geq 2$. Each party P_i has an initial value $v_i \in \mathcal{D}$. Informally, the ϵ-*Approximate Agreement Cross-chain Task* ensures that all the smart contracts have to output (deliver) values that are within ϵ of each other, and the output values must be within the range of the initial values of non-faulty parties.

Using the formalism introduced in Section 2, the ϵ-*Approximate Agreement Cross-chain Task* is defined as follows:

- the input party vectors $\mathcal{I}_P = \mathcal{D}^m$,
- the input contract state vectors $\mathcal{I}_C = (\bot, \ldots, \bot)$,
- the output contract state vectors $\mathcal{O}_C = \{o = (o_1, \ldots, o_n), o \in [min(\mathcal{D}), max(\mathcal{D})]^n\}$
- The utility profile is

$$U(I_P, I_C, O_C)[P_i] = \begin{cases} 1 & \text{if } O_C = (o_1, \ldots, o_n) \in [min(I_P), max(I_P)]^n, \forall j, k, |o_j - o_k| \leq \epsilon \\ 0 & \text{if } O_C = (o_1, \ldots, o_n) \notin [min(I_P), max(I_P)]^n, \forall j, k, |o_j - o_k| \leq \epsilon \\ -1 & \text{otherwise.} \end{cases}$$

$$(7)$$

The parties thus get positive utility if the values delivered lie within the range of the inputs, and within ϵ of each other. They have zero utility if the values lie within ϵ but outside the range, and negative utility if some values are more than ϵ apart, where $\epsilon \geq 0$ is a negligible constant.

A protocol implementing the ϵ-*Approximate Agreement Cross-chain Task* has execution function $\Xi : \mathcal{I}_P \times \mathcal{I}_C \times 2^{\mathcal{P}} \to 2^{\mathcal{O}_C}$, $\Xi(I_P, I_C, Map) = \{o = (o_1, \ldots o_n) \in \mathcal{O}_C, \forall o_i \in [min(I_P), max(I_P)] \text{ and } \forall j, k, |o_j - o_k| \leq \epsilon\}$.

In this paper we consider a system with m parties $P_1, \ldots, P_m$ with at most t Byzantine parties and n contracts $C_1, \ldots, C_n$. Each party P_i has an initial value $v_i \in \mathcal{D}$.

Given that a Byzantine party can have multiple initial values, to be sent to different contracts, $\mathcal{I}_P$ is defined as follows to properly capture the Byzantine task:

$$\mathcal{I}_P = \mathcal{S}^m, \text{ where } \mathcal{S} = \{P \subset \mathcal{D} : 1 \leq \mathrm{Card}(P) \leq n\}.$$

$\mathcal{I}_P$ is thus a Cartesian product space of non-empty finite subsets of $\mathcal{D}$ with size limited to n. For an input $I_P \in \mathcal{I}_P$, we write $I_P = (S_1, S_2, \ldots, S_m)$ where $S_j \in \mathcal{S}$. S_j represents the finite set of party P_j's initial values, ready to be sent to the contracts. Note that a compliant party P_j always has only one initial value, meaning that the corresponding component S_j is a singleton. $min(I_P)$ and $max(I_P)$ consider all the values that appear in these subsets (i.e., in $S_1 \cup S_2 \cup \cdots \cup S_m$).

A protocol implementing the *Byzantine ϵ-Approximate Agreement Cross-chain Task* has execution function $\Xi : \mathcal{I}_P \times \mathcal{I}_C \times 2^{\mathcal{P}} \to 2^{\mathcal{O}_C}$, which must satisfy one of the following additional property:

- *Strong Validity:* Every contract output must fall within the range of the compliant inputs, and within ϵ of each other:
  $\Xi(I_P, I_C, Map) = \{o = (o_1, \ldots o_n) \in \mathcal{O}_C, \forall o_i \in [min(V_c), max(V_c)]$ and $\forall j, k, |o_j - o_k| \leq \epsilon\}$, where $V_c = \{I_P[i], Map[i] = 1\}$
  Here, V_c represents the set of input values of the compliant parties. We call the interval $[min(V_c), max(V_c)]$ the *compliant range*.
- *Weak Validity (Convergence):* Every contract output are within ϵ of each other, but may fall out of the range of the inputs:
  $\Xi(I_P, I_C, Map) = \{o = (o_1, \ldots o_n) \in \mathcal{O}_C, \forall j, k, |o_j - o_k| \leq \epsilon\}$.

In the following we compute the upper bound on the number of Byzantine parties in order to solve the Byzantine ϵ-Approximate Agreement Cross-chain Task with strong validity in the smart contract model. We consider a system with m parties $P_1, \ldots, P_m$ with at most t Byzantine parties and n contracts $C_1, \ldots, C_n$. Each party P_i has an initial value $v_i \in \mathcal{D}$.

Theorem 1. *In the smart contract model, if $m \leq 2t$, no cross-chain protocol can solve the Byzantine ϵ-Approximate Agreement task, i.e., satisfying Coalition Nash Equilibrium, Liveness, Safety (defined in Section 2), and Strong Validity (define in Section 3), with respect to the utility function (in Section 3).*

Proof. Assume for contradiction that such a cross-chain protocol exists for $m \leq 2t$. There are t Byzantine parties and $m - t$ compliant parties.

Let x_1 and x_2 be two different values in $\mathcal{D}$. Let us consider two executions E_1 and E_2:

- Both executions begin with the same initial contract state I_C.
- In E_1: The set of compliant parties $\mathcal{Q}^{E_1}$ is $\{P_1, \ldots, P_{m-t}\}$, and their initial value is x_1. The t Byzantine parties $\{P_{m-t+1}, \ldots, P_m\}$ have the initial value x_2.
- In E_2: The set of compliant parties $\mathcal{Q}^{E_2}$ is $\{P_{t+1}, \ldots, P_m\}$ with initial value x_2. We recall that $m - t \leq t$. Parties $P_1, \ldots, P_{m-t}$ are Byzantine with initial value x_1, and $P_{m-t+1}, \ldots, P_t$ (if $m \leq 2t - 1$) are Byzantine with initial value x_2.

We notice that E_1 and E_2 have indeed the same input party vector: $I_P^{E_1} = I_P^{E_2} = (x_1, \ldots, x_1, x_2, \ldots, x_2)$, $m - t$ instances of x_1 followed by t instances of x_2. In each round, the Byzantine parties can arrange the set of messages that each contract receives identically in both executions.

In E_1, for any compliant P_i, by *Safety* we have $U(I_P, I_C, O_C)[P_i] \geq 0$. Furthermore, by *Validity*, all outputs of the contracts are in the compliant range, so $U(I_P, I_C, O_C)[P_i] = 1$. As all the compliant parties have input value x_1, the compliant range is $\{x_1\}$, hence *Validity* is satisfied if and only if all contract outputs are x_1, i.e.

$$\Xi(I_P^{E_1}, I_C, \mathcal{Q}^{E_1}) = \{(x_1, \ldots, x_1)\}$$

By construction of E_2, the Byzantine parties can replicate in E_2 the same messages as in E_1. From the perspective of the contracts, executions E_1 and E_2

are indistinguishable, so the output contract state vector $(x_1, \ldots, x_1)$ which is feasible in E_1 is also feasible in E_2, i.e.

$$(x_1, \ldots, x_1) \in \Xi(I_P^{E_2}, I_C, \mathcal{Q}^{E_2})$$

However, in E_2, all the compliant parties have initial value x_2, hence the compliant range is $\{x_2\}$. Since $x_1 \notin \{x_2\}$, *Validity* is not satisfied in E_2, therefore contradiction.

Note that the adversarial strategy used in this proof does not require equivocation: in each round, each Byzantine party fixes a value to broadcast to every contract. Therefore, the impossibility does not depend on sending different messages to different contracts.

Corollary 1. *The impossibility of Theorem 1 still holds even if messages are signed and non-equivocation is enforced (i.e., in each round a party must send the same message to all contracts).*

We further establish a lower bound on the communication rounds, demonstrating that the Byzantine ϵ-Approximate Agreement task in the smart contract model cannot be solved in a single round. This impossibility holds for both Strong and Weak Validity.

Theorem 2. *At least two rounds of communication are necessary to solve the Byzantine ϵ-Approximate Agreement task with both Strong and Weak Validity in the smart contract model, even in the presence of only one Byzantine party.*

Proof. We aim to prove that, after one round of communication, the outputs of the contracts can either differ by more than ϵ or are not within the compliant range, thereby demonstrating that the task is not solved after one round. Indeed, since a Byzantine party can send different values to different contracts, each contract may observe a different set of inputs, and then the outputs may differ, regardless of the function used by the contracts to attempt agreement.

We show this by contradiction. Suppose that the Byzantine ϵ-Approximate Agreement task can be solved after one single round.

Consider 2 contracts C_1 and C_2, and 3 parties P_1, P_2 and P_3.

Let $x_1 < x_2 < x_3 < x_4$ be four values in $\mathcal{D}$ such that $x_3 - x_2 > \epsilon$.

First, let us construct an execution E_1: P_1 is Byzantine, P_2 and P_3 are compliant. The Byzantine party P_1 sends x_2 to C_1, and x_3 to C_2. Compliant P_2 sends x_1 to both C_1 and C_2, and compliant P_3 sends x_4 to both C_1 and C_2.

For C_1, the input party vector is (x_2, x_1, x_4), and the output of C_1, denoted by o_1, lies in the compliant range $[x_1, x_4]$. For C_2, the input party vector is (x_3, x_1, x_4), and the output of C_2, denoted by o_2, lies in the compliant range $[x_1, x_4]$ (Fig 1).

If $|o_1 - o_2| > \epsilon$, this means after the first round, agreement is not achieved, since the utility function would evaluate to -1. Hence, at least two rounds are necessary.

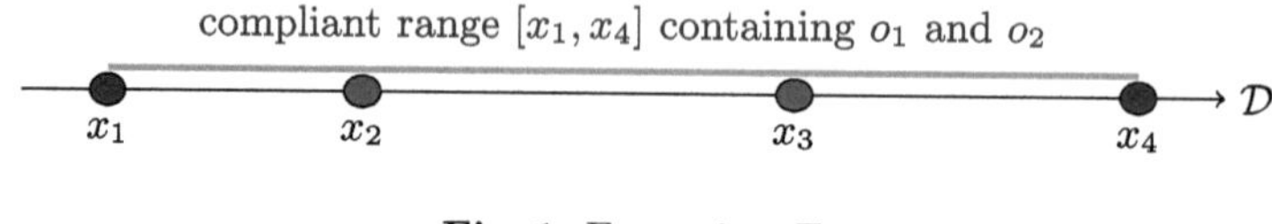

Fig. 1. Execution E_1.

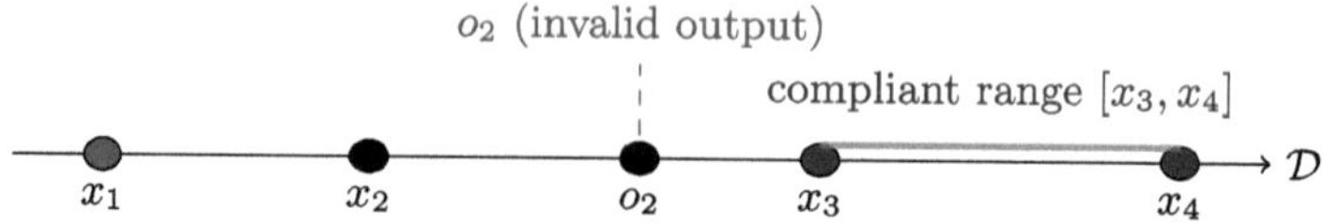

Fig. 2. Case 1, Execution E_2: $o_2 < x_3$.

If $|o_1 - o_2| \le \epsilon$, at least one of the following two cases holds: (1) $o_2 < x_3$ (Fig. 2), (2) $o_1 > x_2$. (Otherwise $o_2 \ge x_3$ and $o_1 \le x_2$ yield $o_2 - o_1 \ge x_3 - x_2 > \epsilon$.).

Case 1. If $o_2 < x_3$, now consider another execution E_2, where P_1 is compliant and sends x_3 to both contracts, P_2 is Byzantine and sends x_1 to both contracts, P_3 is compliant and sends x_4 to both contracts. For C_2, E_1 and E_2 are indistinguishable after only one round of communication, as the input vectors are the same (x_3, x_1, x_4). Therefore, the output o_2 from E_1 is also feasible in E_2. However, in E_2, the compliant range is $[x_3, x_4]$. Since $o_2 < x_3$, this yields a contradiction to *Validity*.

Case 2. If $o_1 > x_2$, similarly consider E_2 where P_1 is compliant and sends x_2 to both contracts, P_2 is compliant and sends x_1 to both contracts, P_3 is Byzantine and sends x_4 to both contracts. The input vector is (x_2, x_1, x_4). By the same reasoning as the previous case, the output o_1 from E_1 is feasible in E_2, but since $o_1 > x_2$ while the compliant range is $[x_1, x_2]$, this also violates *Validity*.

The proof above shows a case of 3 parties with 1 Byzantine, and it can be easily extended to $m > 3$ parties with 1 Byzantine, for example, by having all the additional compliant parties replicate the actions of P_3 as defined in the construction.

This two-round lower bound also holds for the task with Weak Validity. To prove this, we first establish a lemma concerning any potential one-round solution.

Lemma 1. *If the Byzantine ϵ-Approximate Agreement task with Weak Validity is solvable in one single round, then all contract outputs must lie within the range spanned by the initial inputs, including those from Byzantine parties.*

Proof. From a contract's perspective, in a single-round protocol, it is unable to distinguish between an execution E_1 with Byzantine input values and an all-compliant execution E_2, if the contract receives the identical input vector in both scenarios.

By *Liveness*, the contract's output in the all-compliant execution E_2 must be in the range of the inputs so that the utility function returns strictly positive. Since the contract cannot distinguish E_1 from E_2 (as its input vector is the same), its feasible range in E_1 must be identical to its feasible range in E_2. Therefore, any valid contract output in E_1 must also be in this range.

Building upon this lemma, we can now formally state and prove the impossibility of one round for the Weak Validity case.

Theorem 3. *At least two rounds of communication are necessary to solve the Byzantine ϵ-Approximate Agreement task with Weak Validity in the smart contract model, even in the presence of only one Byzantine party.*

Proof. We prove by contradiction. Suppose that the task with Weak Validity can be solved after one single round.

Consider 2 contracts C_1 and C_2, and 3 parties P_1, P_2 and P_3, where at most one party can be Byzantine. Let o_i^E denote the output of contract C_i in execution E.

Let $x_1 < x_2 < x_3 < x_4 < x_5 < x_6$ be six values in $\mathcal{D}$ such that $x_{i+1} - x_i > \epsilon$ for $i = 1..5$ and $x_4 - x_3 > 3\epsilon$. We construct a chain of three executions, E_1, E_2, E_3, linking them by indistinguishable contract views.

- Construct E_1 as follows: P_1 is Byzantine, sends x_1 to C_1 and x_4 to C_2. P_2 is compliant and sends x_2 to both contracts. P_3 is compliant and sends x_3 to both contracts.
  C_1 receives (x_1, x_2, x_3), by Lemma 1, $o_1 \in [x_1, x_3]$. C_2 receives (x_4, x_2, x_3), so $o_2 \in [x_2, x_4]$. By *Weak Validity*, $o_1 - o_2 < \epsilon$. Combining all these bounds, we have:
$$\begin{cases} o_1^{E_1} \in [x_2 - \epsilon, x_3] \\ o_2^{E_1} \in [x_2, x_3 + \epsilon] \\ |o_1^{E_1} - o_2^{E_1}| \leq \epsilon \end{cases}$$

- Construct E_2: P_2 is Byzantine, sends x_2 to C_2 and x_5 to C_1. P_1 is compliant and sends x_4 to both contracts. P_3 is compliant and sends x_3 to both contracts.
  For C_1, by Lemma 1, $o_1 \in [x_3, x_5]$. For C_2, it receives the same input as in E_1, so it is unable to distinguish E_2 from E_1. Therefore, its feasible range of outputs must be the same in both executions, meaning that any valid output $o_2^{E_2}$ must lie in the range $[x_2, x_3 + \epsilon]$. With $o_1 - o_2 < \epsilon$, we have:
$$\begin{cases} o_1^{E_2} \in [x_3, x_3 + 2\epsilon] \\ o_2^{E_2} \in [x_3 - \epsilon, x_3 + \epsilon] \\ |o_1^{E_2} - o_2^{E_2}| \leq \epsilon \end{cases}$$

- Construct E_3: P_3 is Byzantine, sends x_3 to C_1 and x_6 to C_2. P_1 is compliant and sends x_4 to both contracts. P_2 is compliant and sends x_5 to both contracts.
  For C_1, it is unable to distinguish E_3 from E_2, so any valid $o_2^{E_3}$ should lie in the range $[x_3 - \epsilon, x_3 + 2\epsilon]$. While For C_2, it has the input (x_4, x_5, x_6), so $o_1^{E_3} \in [x_4, x_6]$. But as we took $x_4 - x_3 > 3\epsilon$, $o_1^{E_3} - o_2^{E_3} \geq x_4 - (x_3 + 2\epsilon) > \epsilon$. This shows that *Weak Validity* is violated.

Thus, our initial assumption that the task is solvable in one round must be false. The proof illustrates a case of 3 parties with 1 Byzantine. It can be extended to $m > 3$ parties with 1 Byzantine, by constructing m executions with the same core pattern.

4 Approximate Byzantine Agreement Cross-chain Protocols

In this section, we focus on the task with Strong Validity. We propose two protocols that solve this task in two variants of the model: in the first variant parties are allowed to execute local computations, while in the second variant parties do not execute local computations (they only facilitate the communication between smart contracts).

Dolev et al. [6] introduced the idea of achieving agreement by discarding the extreme values and then aggregating the remaining inputs with an averaging rule. Stolz and Wattenhover [10] considered Byzantine agreement with median validity, as another rule. Melnyk and Wattenhofer [8] later generalized this to an approximation for the k-th smallest value under interval validity.

Inspired by these observations, we introduce two abstract functions f and g to capture the essence of the averaging steps in our protocol. The role of f is to aggregate the values received by each contract after discarding the t smallest and t largest ones, while g is used to combine the outputs of all contracts. We do not commit to one particular function, but instead require only the range-preserving property.

Formally, with the assumption of $m \geq 2t + 1$, we define two functions f and g.

$$f : \mathcal{D}^{m-2t} \to [min(\mathcal{D}), max(\mathcal{D})]$$

The function f takes as input a sequence of $m - 2t$ values, and outputs a single value such that

$$f(x_1, \ldots, x_{m-2t}) \in [min(x_1, \ldots, x_{m-2t}), max(x_1, \ldots, x_{m-2t})]$$

$$g : [min(\mathcal{D}), max(\mathcal{D})]^n \to [min(\mathcal{D}), max(\mathcal{D})]$$

The function g takes as input a sequence of n values, and outputs a single value such that

$$g(x_1, \ldots, x_n) \in [min(x_1, \ldots, x_n), max(x_1, \ldots, x_n)]$$

Both f and g can be any form of average function, in a very general sense. Typical example is the arithmetic mean. Other examples include: the median [10], the k-th smallest [8], the weighted mean, the p-norm means, the min, the max, trimmed and step-k means [6], etc. All functions satisfying the key requirement that the output lies within the minimum and maximum of the inputs. This abstraction is unifying generalization of these previous approaches.

In our protocols written using the formalism of [9], only this range-preserving property is required.

4.1 Byzantine Approximate Agreement Cross-chain Protocol with party computation

---

Algorithm 1. Byzantine Approximate Agreement Cross-chain Protocol

---

```
 1: procedure PARTYPROTOCOL(v_i)                          ▷ Executed by each party P_i
 2:     begin synchronous round 1
 3:         send phase: send v_i to all contracts {C_1, ..., C_n}
 4:         read phase: O ← {o_1, ..., o_n}    ▷ Read outputs from all contracts updated
       after contract-local phase
 5:         party-local phase: v_i ← g(o_1, ..., o_n)
 6:     end synchronous round 1
 7:     begin synchronous round 2
 8:         send phase: Send updated v_i to all contracts {C_1, ..., C_n}
 9:         read phase: O ← {o_1, ..., o_n}    ▷ Read outputs from all contracts updated
       after contract-local phase
10:     end synchronous round 2
11: end procedure

12: procedure CONTRACTPROTOCOL                            ▷ Executed by each contract C_j
13:     for r = 1 to 2 do
14:         begin synchronous round r                     ▷ contract-local phase
15:             V[1..m] ← [∞, ..., ∞]
16:             for each value v_i received during round r from P_i do
17:                 V[i] ← v_i
18:             end for           ▷ If no value is received from P_i, V[i] remains ∞
19:             V ← sort(V)
20:             if r = 1 then                              ▷ Round 1
21:                 o_j ← f(V[t+1], ..., V[m-t])
22:             else                                       ▷ Round 2
23:                 o_j ← V[t+1]        ▷ Subarray V[t+1 ... m-t] is consistent
24:             end if
25:             Set o_j as available for parties to read
26:         end synchronous round r
27:     end for
28: end procedure
```

In the following we present a first protocol where parties are allowed to execute local computations. The protocol runs in two synchronous rounds. We recall that executions proceed in synchronous rounds, each round composed of four phases: *send phase*, *contract-local phase*, *read phase* and optional *party-local phase*.

– Synchronous round 1
   1. *send phase*: Each party P_i sends its initial value v_i to all contracts.
   2. *contract-local phase*: Each contract C_j processes the inputs received in send phase:

   (a) For each party P_i from which no value was received, C_j assigns a default value ∞.

   (b) C_j collects all values (received or default) into an array $V[1..m]$ and sorts them in non-decreasing order.

   (c) C_j computes its output $o_j = f(V[t+1], \ldots, V[m-t])$. By discarding the t smallest and t largest values, the impact of both missing values (∞) and malicious outliers is mitigated.

  3. *read phase*: Each party reads the outputs o_j from all contracts C_j.

  4. *party-local phase*: Each party P_i computes its new $v_i = g(o_1, \ldots, o_n)$.

– Synchronous round 2

  1. *send phase*: Each party P_i sends its updated v_i to all contracts.

  2. *contract-local phase*: Each contract C_j processes the inputs received in send phase:

   (a) For each party P_i from which no value was received, C_j assigns ∞.

   (b) C_j sorts all m values in array $V[1..m]$.

   (c) The subarray $V[t+1..m-t]$ is guaranteed to consist of the same value v_c (proof below). The contract updates its output $o_j = v_c$.

  3. *read phase*: Each party reads the outputs o_j from all contracts C_j.

Lemma 2. *If $m \geq 2t+1$, at the end of Round 1, the output o_j of each contract C_j lies within the compliant range.*

Proof. During the *contract-local phase*, each contract C_j processes the inputs as specified in *ContractProtocol*. According to Lines 15–18, C_j maintains an array V of size m, where each entry is either a value received from party P_i or a default value ∞ if the input is missing. Among these m values, at most t values are Byzantine (either sent by Byzantine parties or assigned as ∞ due to absence).

As shown in Line 19, C_j sorts all values in non-decreasing order. Let $V[1 \ldots m]$ be the sorted array.

Let k ($k \leq t$) be the number of values in V that are strictly smaller than $\min(comp)$. Note that since ∞ is the largest possible value, it will always be positioned at the end of the sorted array and thus k only accounts for Byzantine outliers.

Then, we have $V[k+1] \geq \min(comp)$. Since $k \leq t$, it follows that $V[t+1] \geq V[k+1]$, and thus $V[t+1] \geq \min(comp)$.

Similarly, let k' be the number of values strictly larger than $\max(comp)$. These values include both Byzantine outliers and missing inputs (∞). Since the total number of such values is at most t, we have $V[m-t] \leq \max(comp)$.

Therefore, the trimmed subarray $V[t+1 \ldots m-t]$ (in Line 21) contains only values within the compliant range $[\min(comp), \max(comp)]$. Consequently, the output $o_j = f(V[t+1], \ldots, V[m-t])$ also lies within this range, assuming f is a function within the bounds of its inputs.

Lemma 3 (Validity). *If $m \geq 2t+1$, at the end of Round 2, all outputs o_j are equal and lie within the compliant range.*

Proof. In the read phase of Round 1, each compliant party P_i reads the outputs $O = \{o_1, \ldots, o_n\}$ from all contracts (Line 4). According to Lemma 2, each o_j already lies within the compliant range. Since the functions $g(\cdot)$ and the set O are identical for all compliant parties, they all compute the same updated value $v_i = g(o_1, \ldots, o_n)$ (Line 5). Let v_c denote this common value, which is also within the compliant range.

In Round 2, each party P_i sends v_c to all contracts (Line 8). Each contract C_j then processes these inputs (Lines 15–18). Among the m entries in array V, at least $m - t$ entries are from compliant parties that successfully submitted v_c. The remaining at most t entries consist of either Byzantine values or default values ∞ assigned due to missing inputs (Line 15).

After sorting V in non-decreasing order (Line 19), we consider the distribution of these values. There are at most t "non-compliant" values (Byzantine or ∞).

- If a non-compliant value is smaller than v_c, it can occupy at most the first t positions ($V[1 \ldots t]$).
- If a non-compliant value is larger than v_c (including all ∞ values), it can occupy at most the last t positions ($V[m - t + 1 \ldots m]$).

Since $m \geq 2t + 1$, the number of v_c entries ($m - t$) is strictly greater than the number of potentially smaller outliers (t). Thus, the $(t + 1)$-th element must be v_c. More generally, the entire subarray $V[t + 1 \ldots m - t]$ is guaranteed to consist of the identical value v_c.

Consequently, as specified in Line 23, each contract updates its output to $o_j = V[t + 1] = v_c$. This ensures that all contracts compute the exact same output, which remains within the compliant range.

Lemma 4 (Liveness). *If all parties are compliant, then the protocol's transitions are preferred:*

$$(\forall O_C \in \Xi(I_P, I_C, \mathcal{P})) \, (\forall P \in \mathcal{P}) \, U(I_P, I_C, O_C)[P] > 0$$

Proof. Following Lemma 3, if all parties are compliant, at the end of the protocol, for any O_C, all outputs o_j are equal and lie within the compliant range, hence within the input range. By the definition of utility function (Equation 7), we have

$$(\forall P \in \mathcal{P}) \, U(I_P, I_C, O_C)[P] = 1 > 0.$$

Lemma 5 (Safety). *If $m \geq 2t + 1$, no compliant party ends up worse off:*

$$(\forall O_C \in \Xi(I_P, I_C, \mathcal{Q})) \, (\forall Q \in \mathcal{Q}) \, U(I_P, I_C, O_C)[Q] \geq 0$$

where $\mathcal{Q} \subset \mathcal{P}$ is a compliance set.

Proof. Following Lemma 3, if $m \geq 2t + 1$, then at the end of the protocol, all outputs o_j are equal and lie within the compliant range. So we have

$$(\forall Q \in \mathcal{Q}) \, U(I_P, I_C, O_C)[Q] = 1.$$

Lemma 6 (Coalition Nash Equilibrium). *If $m \geq 2t + 1$, no coalition of parties can increase its utility by deviating from the protocol while the remaining parties comply. More precisely, for all coalitions $\mathcal{Q} \subset \mathcal{P}$, input vectors $I_P \in \mathcal{I}_P, I_C \in \mathcal{I}_c$, conforming executions $O_C \in \Xi(I_P, I_C, \mathcal{P})$, and $\mathcal{Q}$-deviating executions $O'_C \in \Xi(I_P, I_C, \mathcal{P} \setminus \mathcal{Q})$, conforming is the better strategy for $\mathcal{Q}$*

$$U(I_P, I_C, O_C)[\mathcal{Q}] \geq U(I_P, I_C, O'_C)[\mathcal{Q}].$$

Proof. For any coalition $\mathcal{Q}$, under a conforming execution, as shown in the previous lemma, every compliant party obtains utility 1, so

$$(\forall Q \in \mathcal{Q}) \quad U(I_P, I_C, O_C)[Q] = 1.$$

For any deviating execution yielding O'_C, by the definition of the utility function we have

$$(\forall Q \in \mathcal{Q}) \quad U(I_P, I_C, O'_C)[Q] \leq 1.$$

Summing over all members Q of $\mathcal{Q}$, we have

$$U(I_P, I_C, O'_C)[\mathcal{Q}] \leq U(I_P, I_C, O_C)[\mathcal{Q}].$$

Summing up these lemmas, we have:

Theorem 4. *If $m \geq 2t + 1$, the two-round protocol described above is a correct cross-chain protocol for the Byzantine ϵ-Approximate Agreement task, i.e., it satisfies* Coalition Nash Equilibrium, Liveness, Safety, *and* Validity.

4.2   Byzantine Approximate Agreement Cross-chain Protocol without party computation

In the following we present a second protocol in a version of the model where parties are not allowed to execute local computations however parties are still allowed to communicate with smart contracts. The protocol runs in two synchronous rounds:

- Round 1
    1. *send phase*: Each party P_i sends its initial value v_i to all contracts.
    2. *contract-local phase*: Each contract C_j processes the inputs received in send phase:
        (a) For each party P_i from which no value was received, C_j assigns a default value ∞.
        (b) C_j collects all values (received or default) into an array $V[1..m]$ and sorts them in non-decreasing order.
        (c) C_j computes its output $o_j = f(V[t + 1], \ldots, V[m - t])$.
    3. *read phase*: Each party P_i reads the outputs o_j from all contracts C_j and stores them in a local array $Out_i[1..n]$.
    4. *party-local phase*: No computation is performed.
- Round 2

Algorithm 2. Byzantine Approximate Agreement Cross-chain Protocol (without party computation)

1: **procedure** PARTYPROTOCOL(v_i)   ▷ Executed by each party P_i
2:     **begin synchronous round 1**
3:         *send phase*: send v_i to all contracts $\{C_1, \ldots, C_n\}$
4:         *read phase*: $Out_i \leftarrow \{o_1, \ldots, o_n\}$ ▷ Read and store outputs from all contracts
5:         *party-local phase*: No local computation allowed
6:     **end synchronous round 1**
7:     **begin synchronous round 2**
8:         *send phase*: send $Out_i[1..n]$ to all contracts $\{C_1, \ldots, C_n\}$
9:         *read phase*: $O \leftarrow \{o_1, \ldots, o_n\}$ ▷ Read final outputs from contracts
10:     **end synchronous round 2**
11: **end procedure**

12: **procedure** CONTRACTPROTOCOL   ▷ Executed by each contract C_j
13:     **for** $r = 1$ **to** 2 **do**
14:         **begin synchronous round** r ▷ *contract-local phase*
15:             $V[1..m] \leftarrow [\infty, \ldots, \infty]$
16:             **if** $r = 1$ **then**   ▷ Round 1: Processing received values
17:                 **for** each value v_i received during round 1 from P_i **do**
18:                     $V[i] \leftarrow v_i$
19:                 **end for**
20:                 $V \leftarrow \text{sort}(V)$
21:                 $o_j \leftarrow f(V[t+1], \ldots, V[m-t])$
22:             **else**   ▷ Round 2: Processing received arrays
23:                 **for** each array Out_i received during round 2 from P_i **do**
24:                     $V[i] \leftarrow g(Out_i[1], \ldots, Out_i[n])$ ▷ g is executed by the contract
25:                 **end for**
26:                 $V \leftarrow \text{sort}(V)$
27:                 $o_j \leftarrow V[t+1]$ ▷ Subarray $V[t+1 \ldots m-t]$ is consistent
28:             **end if**
29:             Set o_j as available for parties to read
30:         **end synchronous round** r
31:     **end for**
32: **end procedure**

---

1. *send phase*: Each party P_i sends its stored array $Out_i[1..n]$ to all contracts.
2. *contract-local phase*: Each contract C_j processes the received arrays:
   (a) For each party P_i from which no array was received, C_j assigns a default value ∞.
   (b) For each array Out_i successfully received from party P_i, C_j computes $V[i] = g(Out_i[1], \ldots, Out_i[n])$.
   (c) Upon each received Out, computes $g(Out[1], \ldots, Out[n])$. Stores the values in array $V[1..m]$.
   (d) C_j sorts the resulting array $V[1..m]$ in non-decreasing order.

(e) The subarray $V[t+1\ldots m-t]$ is guaranteed to consist of the same value v_c (proof below). The contract updates its output $o_j = v_c$.

3. *read phase*: Each party reads the final outputs o_j from the contracts.

Lemma 7. *If $m \geq 2t+1$, at the end of Round 1, the output o_j of each contract C_j lies within the compliant range.*

Proof. Note that the message exchange and the contract-local computation f in Round 1 are identical to those described in Algorithm 1. Therefore, the proof follows directly from the same logic as Lemma 2.

Lemma 8 (Validity). *If $m \geq 2t+1$, at the end of Round 2, all outputs o_i are equal and lie within the compliant range.*

Proof. During the *read phase* of Round 1 (Line 4), every compliant party P_i reads the same set of contract outputs $O = \{o_1, \ldots, o_n\}$. By Lemma 7, each $o_j \in O$ already lies within the compliant range. Consequently, all compliant parties store an identical array $Out_i = O$ and send this same array to all contracts during the *send phase* of Round 2 (Line 8).

In the *contract-local phase* of Round 2, each contract C_j processes these inputs (Lines 23–25). For each array Out_i received from a compliant party, the contract computes $V[i] = g(Out_i[1], \ldots, Out_i[n])$. Since g is a deterministic function and the input arrays from compliant parties are identical and consist of values in the compliant range, the computed results $V[i]$ are all equal to a single value v_c, which also lies within the compliant range.

The array V of size m is composed of:

- At least $m - t$ entries equal to v_c (resulting from arrays sent by compliant parties).
- At most t entries that are either non-compliant values (computed from Byzantine arrays) or default values ∞ (assigned in Line 15 for missing inputs).

As shown in Line 26, C_j sorts the array V. Given that $m \geq 2t+1$, the number of v_c entries $m - t > t$. Therefore, even if all t Byzantine or missing values are smaller (or larger) than v_c, they will be restricted to the prefix $V[1\ldots t]$ (or the suffix $V[m - t + 1 \ldots m]$). This guarantees that the subarray $V[t+1\ldots m-t]$ consists entirely of the value v_c. Thus, according to Line 27, each contract sets its output $o_j = V[t+1] = v_c$. This ensures that all contract outputs are identical and remain within the compliant range.

Lemma 9 (Liveness). *If all parties are compliant, then the protocol's transitions are preferred:*

$$(\forall O_C \in \Xi(I_P, I_C, \mathcal{P})) \ (\forall P \in \mathcal{P}) \ U(I_P, I_C, O_C)[P] > 0$$

Proof. Following Lemma 8, if all parties are compliant, at the end of the protocol, for any O_C, all outputs o_j are equal and lie within the compliant range. By the definition of utility function (Equation 7), we have

$$(\forall P \in \mathcal{P}) \ U(I_P, I_C, O_C)[P] = 1 > 0.$$

Lemma 10 (Safety). *If $m \geq 2t + 1$, no compliant party ends up worse off:*

$$(\forall O_C \in \Xi(I_P, I_C, \mathcal{Q}))\ (\forall Q \in \mathcal{Q})\ U(I_P, I_C, O_C)[Q] \geq 0$$

where $\mathcal{Q} \subset \mathcal{P}$ is a compliance set.

Proof. Following Lemma 8, if $m \geq 2t + 1$, then at the end of the protocol, all outputs o_j are equal and lie within the compliant range. So we have

$$(\forall Q \in \mathcal{Q})\ U(I_P, I_C, O_C)[Q] = 1.$$

Lemma 11 (Coalition Nash Equilibrium). *If $m \geq 2t + 1$, no coalition of parties can increase its utility by deviating from the protocol while the remaining parties comply. More precisely, for all coalitions $\mathcal{Q} \subset \mathcal{P}$, input vectors $I_P \in \mathcal{I}_P, I_C \in \mathcal{I}_c$, conforming executions $O_C \in \Xi(I_P, I_C, \mathcal{P})$, and $\mathcal{Q}$-deviating executions $O'_C \in \Xi(I_P, I_C, \mathcal{P} \setminus \mathcal{Q})$, conforming is the better strategy for $\mathcal{Q}$*

$$U(I_P, I_C, O_C)[\mathcal{Q}] \geq U(I_P, I_C, O'_C)[\mathcal{Q}].$$

Proof. For any coalition $\mathcal{Q}$, under a conforming execution, as shown in the previous lemma, every compliant party obtains utility 1, so

$$(\forall Q \in \mathcal{Q})\quad U(I_P, I_C, O_C)[Q] = 1.$$

For any deviating execution yielding O'_C, by the definition of the utility function we have

$$(\forall Q \in \mathcal{Q})\quad U(I_P, I_C, O'_C)[Q] \leq 1.$$

Summing over all members Q of $\mathcal{Q}$, we have

$$U(I_P, I_C, O'_C)[\mathcal{Q}] \leq U(I_P, I_C, O_C)[\mathcal{Q}].$$

Summing up these lemmas, we have:

Theorem 5. *If $m \geq 2t+1$, the two-round protocol without party computation, is a correct cross-chain protocol for the Byzantine ϵ-Approximate Agreement task, i.e., it satisfies* Coalition Nash Equilibrium, Liveness, Safety, *and* Validity.

4.3 Bit Complexity Analysis

We assume values are encoded on k bit-length. For both contracts and parties, we analyze the *bit complexity* of the two protocols (with and without parties computation).

- Computation Memory Complexity (in bits): the *extra* memory required for local computation, *excluding* the primary buffers used to store received data.
- Message Space Complexity (in bits): the total number of bits all entities send and receive.

For computation memory, assume computations (sorting, f, g) are space-efficient:

- Sorting: Performed in-place (e.g., Heapsort) directly on the receive buffer (V or Out). This requires only $\mathcal{O}(k)$ additional space for a temporary swap.
- Functions f and g: Use simple calculations. This requires only $\mathcal{O}(k)$ additional space for temporary variables.

Protocol 1: With Party Computation.

- Contract: Sorts V in-place on its buffer and computes f. Computation memory: $\mathcal{O}(k)$.
- Party: Sorts received values in-place on its buffer and Computes g. Computation memory: $\mathcal{O}(k)$.
- Message bit Complexity: $\mathcal{O}(n \cdot m \cdot k)$. (Communicates k-bit values on each channel between n contracts and m parties and terminates after 2 rounds).

Protocol 2: Without Party Computation.

- Contract: All sorting and f function computations can be done in-place on buffer. Computation memory: $\mathcal{O}(k)$.
- Party: Performs no local computation. Computation memory: $\mathcal{O}(1)$.
- Message bit Complexity: Dominated by the communication of Out arrays, each of size $\mathcal{O}(n \cdot k)$. The total message complexity is $\mathcal{O}(n^2 \cdot m \cdot k)$.

5 Conclusion

This paper builds on top of *the smart contract model* introduced in [2]. We define the *Byzantine Approximate Agreement Cross-chain Task* and propose optimal protocols that implement this task. Our protocols tolerate a minority of Byzantine participants and need only two rounds in synchronous settings. Moreover, we investigate the bit complexity of our protocols in the smart contract model. The first protocol uses $\mathcal{O}(k)$ bits at each party (k represent the number of bits necessary to encode the proposed values). The total bit complexity of messages exchanges is $\mathcal{O}(n \cdot m \cdot k)$. The second protocol uses only $\mathcal{O}(1)$ bits on the parties side while the total bit complexity of messages exchanged is $\mathcal{O}(n^2 \cdot m \cdot k)$. An interesting open question is the extension of the *the smart contract model* to the asynchronous settings and the study of the *Byzantine Approximate Agreement Cross-chain Task* in the asynchronous settings. Another interesting line of research is the comparison of the smart contract model with respect to the classical models in distributed computing (e.g. shared memory, client-server where servers are correct etc).

References

1. de Alfaro, L., Henzinger, T.A.: Interface automata. In: Tjoa, A.M., Gruhn, V. (eds.) Proceedings of the 8th European Software Engineering Conference held jointly with 9th ACM SIGSOFT International Symposium on Foundations of Software Engineering 2001, Vienna, Austria, September 10-14, 2001, pp. 109–120. ACM (2001). https://doi.org/10.1145/503209.503226
2. Amoussou-Guenou, Y., Herlihy, M., Jayanti, S., Potop-Butucaru, M., Rajsbaum, S.: The smart contract model. CoRR abs/2502.05280 (2025). https://doi.org/10.48550/ARXIV.2502.05280

3. Bandarupalli, A., Bhat, A., Bagchi, S., Kate, A., Liu-Zhang, C., Reiter, M.K.: Delphi: efficient asynchronous approximate agreement for distributed oracles. In: 54th Annual IEEE/IFIP International Conference on Dependable Systems and Networks, DSN 2024, Brisbane, Australia, June 24-27, 2024, pp. 456–469. IEEE (2024). https://doi.org/10.1109/DSN58291.2024.00051
4. Breidenbach, L., Cachin, C., Coventry, A., Juels, A., Miller, A.: ChainLink off-chain reporting protocol (2021). https://blogchain.link/off-chain-reporting-live-on-mainnet
5. Chakka, P., Joshi, S., Kate, A., Tobkin, J., Yang, D.: Oracle agreement: from an honest super majority to simple majority. In: 43rd IEEE International Conference on Distributed Computing Systems, ICDCS 2023, Hong Kong, July 18-21, 2023, pp. 714–725. IEEE (2023). https://doi.org/10.1109/ICDCS57875.2023.00025
6. Dolev, D., Lynch, N.A., Pinter, S.S., Stark, E.W., Weihl, W.E.: Reaching approximate agreement in the presence of faults. J. ACM **33**(3), 499–516 (1986). https://doi.org/10.1145/5925.5931
7. Lys, L., Potop-Butucaru, M.: Distributed blockchain price oracle. In: Koulali, M., Mezini, M. (eds.) Networked Systems - 10th International Conference, NETYS 2022, Virtual Event, May 17-19, 2022, Proceedings. LNCS, vol. 13464, pp. 37–51. Springer (2022). https://doi.org/10.1007/978-3-031-17436-0_4
8. Melnyk, D., Wattenhofer, R.: Byzantine agreement with interval validity. In: 37th IEEE Symposium on Reliable Distributed Systems, SRDS 2018, Salvador, Brazil, October 2-5, 2018, pp. 251–260. IEEE Computer Society (2018). https://doi.org/10.1109/SRDS.2018.00036
9. Raynal, M.: Fault-Tolerant Message-Passing Distributed Systems - An Algorithmic Approach. Springer (2018). https://doi.org/10.1007/978-3-319-94141-7
10. Stolz, D., Wattenhofer, R.: Byzantine agreement with median validity. In: Anceaume, E., Cachin, C., Potop-Butucaru, M.G. (eds.) 19th International Conference on Principles of Distributed Systems, OPODIS 2015, December 14-17, 2015, Rennes, France. LIPIcs, vol. 46, pp. 22:1–22:14. Schloss Dagstuhl - Leibniz-Zentrum für Informatik (2015). https://doi.org/10.4230/LIPICS.OPODIS.2015.22

Asynchronous Fault-Tolerant Mutual Visibility

Subhajit Pramanick[1], Saswata Jana[2], and Partha Sarathi Mandal[2]($\boxtimes$)

[1] Institute of Computer Science, University of Wrocław, 50-383 Wrocław, Poland
[2] Indian Institute of Technology Guwahati, Guwahati 781039, India
`psm@iitg.ac.in`

Abstract. The mutual visibility problem needs a set of N autonomous mobile robots to reach a configuration on the 2D plane where every pair of robots can see each other, i.e., no robot lies on the line segment connecting any two others. We study the *fault-tolerant mutual visibility problem* under the barebones luminous model (each robot has a light that can flash a color from a finite prefixed color set), where the objective is to reach a configuration in which every pair of non-faulty robots are mutually visible, despite the presence of at most $f(< N)$ robots prone to mobility failures. Mobility fault is a fault model in the existing literature that makes a robot immobile. However, the faulty robot executes the algorithms and its light remains functional. Unlike existing studies that assume coordinate agreement or partial synchrony, we consider the asynchronous ($\mathcal{ASYNC}$) setting and disoriented robots (do not share a coordinate system or orientation), with both N and f unknown.

We propose a deterministic $O(N)$-time algorithm in terms of epochs that utilises $O(1)$ colors and ensures collision-free movements, where epoch is the smallest time interval in which every robot completes at least one full LCM cycle. In addition, our algorithm solves a useful subproblem of detecting the global innermost layer under asynchronous setting only with the help of local view of the robots. The layer structure of any robot configuration represented as a sequence of disjoint convex polygons, that offers a way to organize progress even without shared coordinate system.

Keywords: Mobile robots · Mutual Visibility · Fault tolerance · Asynchronous Scheduler · Luminous robots

1 Introduction

Motivation and Background. The mutual visibility problem is a fundamental coordination task in swarm robotics that has received considerable attention in

Subhajit Pramanick is supported by the Polish National Science Centre project no. 2020/39/B/ST6/03288.

Saswata Jana is supported by the Prime Minister's Research Fellowship (PMRF) scheme of the Govt. of India (PMRF-ID: 1902165).

the past decade. In the usual 2D plane, two robots are said to be mutually visible if no third robot lies on the line segment joining them. Starting from an arbitrary initial deployment of N robots placed at distinct locations, the goal is to reach a configuration where every pair of robots is mutually visible. This problem is significant both intrinsically and as a building block for other classical tasks such as gathering, pattern formation, and leader election.

Introduced by Di Luna et al. [7], the problem is studied under the weak robot model [5], where robots are point-shaped, autonomous, anonymous, homogeneous, and disoriented, operating in *Look–Compute–Move* (LCM) cycles. Traditionally, the activation of the robots are controlled by one of three standard adversarial schedulers: fully-synchronous ($\mathcal{FSYNC}$), semi-synchronous ($\mathcal{SSYNC}$) and asynchronous ($\mathcal{ASYNC}$). Building upon this base model, most of the existing literature [4,9,11,15,16] studies the problem under the *luminous* ($\mathcal{LUMI}$) robot model, where each robot is augmented with an externally visible persistent light, which can determine a color from a prefixed color set, enabling a weak form of communication. Such a model is not only considered for the mutual visibility problem, but in other popular swarm robotic problems like gathering and pattern formation [6,10,13]. Under this model, the problem has been examined under various additional assumptions, such as knowledge of N, agreement on both coordinate axes, or on a single axis.

In this paper, we focus on the *fault-tolerant* variant of the mutual visibility problem under the barebones $\mathcal{LUMI}$ model, without relying on any additional assumptions. A fault model, known as the *mobility fault*, is already well-established in this context, where the mobility of a faulty robot is disrupted permanently. However, the functioning of the light remains intact. The best-known non–fault-tolerant result is by Sharma et al. [14], who proposed an $O(1)$-time mutual visibility algorithm for disoriented $\mathcal{ASYNC}$ robots. However, the fault-tolerant variants studied so far rely on stronger assumptions. Aljohani and Sharma [1] solved the problem under $\mathcal{SSYNC}$, assuming the robots share a global coordinate system and that at most one robot may be faulty. Poudel et al. [8] extended the problem to the $\mathcal{ASYNC}$ setting and proposed an $O(N)$ algorithm, allowing multiple faulty robots but assuming agreement on one coordinate axis. Under the $\mathcal{ASYNC}$ setting, Pramanick et al. [11] introduced a new variant of the fault-tolerant mutual visibility problem (under the same mobility fault model), termed mutual visibility with angular inaccuracy, assuming the same one-axis agreement. Recently, in [12], Pramanick et al. dealt fault-tolerance with disoriented robots but with the assumption of $\mathcal{FSYNC}$ scheduler. Despite that, they proposed an $O(N^2)$ algorithm.

Although established in the literature, it is straightforward to observe that with three collinear disoriented robots, if the middle one becomes faulty, breaking the collinearity is impossible: the adversary can mirror the local coordinate systems of the two non-faulty robots, forcing symmetric movements. A similar argument extends to a configuration where a faulty robot is placed at the center of a regular polygon formed by the remaining $N-1$ (possibly non-faulty) robots [12]. These impossibility arguments and the difficulty in this problem stem from the lack of a common coordinate system among the robots. Let us call them *impossible configurations.*

In this paper, apart from the above configurations leading to impossibilities, we are investigating the following problem.

Problem Definition. Given N disoriented, opaque luminous robots placed at distinct positions on the plane, of which up to $f(< N)$ may incur mobility faults at arbitrary times (both N and f unknown), the goal is to reach a configuration where (i) no three non-faulty robots are collinear, and (ii) no faulty robot lies between any two non-faulty robots.

Contribution. Any fault-tolerant algorithm for mutual visibility is primarily judged in terms of three metrics: (i) assumption of the scheduler (ii) time complexity, and (iii) number of colors. In this paper, we consider a barebones model for fault-tolerant mutual visibility and solve the problem by presenting an $O(N)$ algorithm under $\mathcal{ASYNC}$ to tolerate $f < N$ faulty robots. Our algorithm operates with $O(1)$ colors and specifically requires 35 distinct colors. Another metric, widely addressed in mutual visibility literature, is collision avoidance, where a collision refers to two robots occupying the same point at the same time. Our algorithm ensures collision-free movements for the robots.

Additionally, our technique has two byproducts. (1) As no robot moves outside the convex hull formed by their initial positions during the entire execution, our technique preserves a *spatial boundary*, defined as the convex hull of the initial configuration. This property aligns with a recent emerging line of research on space-contained formulation of distributed coordination problems, where the goal is to achieve the desired configuration while keeping robot movements within specified geometric limits. (2) As a given configuration of the robots can be globally divided into *disjoint convex layers* of robots (formally defined in Sect. 3), our technique can distinguish a particular global layer by coloring all the robots on it with a designated color, even if the robots are incapable of seeing the global configuration (and thus the layers). This can be a useful subproblem in distributed robotics (e.g. in sequence of pattern formation), which we highlight more in Sect. 3.1.

Challenges and Techniques. Note that the adversary controls the activation schedule, the initial configuration, and the orientation of each robot's local coordinate system. For disoriented robots, if all are allowed to move simultaneously, an adversary can always enforce collinearity among any three robots, even when all are non-faulty. So, serializing the robots (with some geometric constraints) becomes an intuitive strategy to overcome such problems. When robots share one coordinate axis, serialization becomes simpler. For instance, if all agree on the y-axis direction, the algorithm can proceed from the northernmost to the southernmost robots along virtual horizontal lines (used in [8,11]). With disoriented robots, serialization becomes significantly more difficult. Obstructed visibility further complicates the problem, particularly when both N and f are unknown. Robots may remain unaware about large portion of the configuration due to obstructions. Identifying faulty robots remains challenging, even with the aid of lights. $\mathcal{ASYNC}$ settings become another major challenge as the robots are susceptible to outdated view (as a moving robot can be seen), which potentially directs the robots to act on erroneous computations.

We use the concept of *disjoint convex layers* (see Fig. 1 and it is formally defined later in Sect. 3) to systematically decide the order of robot movements. At a broad level, the outermost convex layer is composed of robots positioned along the boundary of the convex hull of the entire configuration. The remaining robots form successive inner layers by recursively computing convex hulls after excluding those already on the outer layers. This process yields a hierarchy of non-overlapping convex layers. It is important to note that these globally defined layers may not coincide with the ones perceived locally by individual robots. Under $\mathcal{ASYNC}$, the initial layers might not be preserved, as some robots of a layer may start moving while others remain inactive.

The concept of layers raises two interesting questions: *Q1. Can we detect a specific global layer (e.g. the innermost one in the initial configuration) under $\mathcal{ASYNC}$?* By detection, we mean that the robots on that layer must color themselves with a designated color. *Q2. Can we color all the disjoint layers using distinct colors under $\mathcal{ASYNC}$, assuming there are sufficiently many colors?* The answer of Q2 is out of our context. However, we affirmatively answer Q1 in Sect. 3.1 by treating it as a subproblem and use it in our algorithm. Once the innermost layer of the initial configuration is detected, we move the non-faulty robots on the outermost layer to distinct positions on the innermost layer. We tackle two cases: (A) the innermost layer is non-linear, and (B) it is linear. In Case (A), to ensure correctness under $\mathcal{ASYNC}$, each robot that attempts to move inward undergoes a carefully orchestrated sequence of color transitions (Subroutine FAULT-DETECTION-NONLINEAR) that allows it to determine whether it has actually reached the innermost layer or has become faulty en route. Once all the non-faulty robots are positioned on the innermost layer, they are further repositioned within it to distinct locations forming the vertices of a convex polygon entirely contained inside the layer. In Case (B), we rely on a query-feedback mechanism (using colors) to detect the center of linear layer and eventually consider an ellipse (whose major axis lies on that layer) on each of the half planes delimited by the line containing the linear innermost layer. Later, we coordinate in such a way that all the robots lying on a half plane agree on a single ellipse, which is challenging specially under $\mathcal{ASYNC}$.

2   Model and Preliminaries

Robot Model. We consider N autonomous, anonymous and homogeneous point robots deployed on distinct points on the Euclidean plane. Each robot is endowed with an externally visible light that emit ψ (a constant) number of colors (one at a time), enabling coordination through observed colors. The robots are *disoriented* which means that they share no global orientation or coordinate system. With a slight abuse of notation, we use r to denote both the robot and its position on the plane. Each robot r is equipped with its own local coordinate system centered at its current location, so two robots may perceive the same point differently. We assume *obstructed visibility* (*opaque* robots), wherein two robots can see each other if and only if no other robot lies on the line segment joining them. This prevents robots from knowing N. Up to $f < N$, f not known, robots may experience *mobility faults*, becoming permanently immobile while their lights remain functional. Faults may occur at any time.

Configuration and View of the Robots. At any time $t \geq 0$, the configuration is $\{(r_1^t, r_1^t.color), (r_2^t, r_2^t.color), \ldots, (r_N^t, r_N^t.color)\}$, where each tuple consists of the position of a robot r_i^t and the color of its light $r_i^t.color$ at time t. We denote the convex hull of all robots at time t by $\mathcal{CH}^t$. For a robot r, we denote the convex hull of all the visible robots by $\mathcal{CH}_r^t$. When the context is clear, we omit the time superscripts from the notations.

Activation Cycles. A robot is either active or inactive. When active, it executes *Look-Compute-Move* (LCM) cycles, as follows. *Look:* it captures the position and the light color of every visible robot, including its own. *Compute:* It runs the algorithm and computes a destination point and possibly a new light color. *Move:* Finally, updating the color, it moves straight to its destination or stays put. The robots loose all their memory except the current color of the light whenever they finish an LCM cycle.

Activation Scheduler. We consider an adversarial $\mathcal{ASYNC}$ scheduler, the weakest among all standard schedulers. In $\mathcal{ASYNC}$, robots may be activated at arbitrary times with no global clock or synchrony, and each LCM phase may experience unpredictable delays. A robot may remain inactive for an arbitrarily long time, but fairness ensures that every robot is activated infinitely often. For comparison, in $\mathcal{FSYNC}$, all robots execute their LCM cycles synchronously in global rounds, while in $\mathcal{SSYNC}$, any non-empty subset of robots performs its cycles synchronously in each round. Time in $\mathcal{ASYNC}$ is measured in *epochs*, the smallest interval during which every robot completes at least one full LCM cycle.

3 $\mathcal{ASYNC}$ Algorithm for Fault-Tolerant Mutual Visibility

In this section, we describe our algorithm in the $\mathcal{ASYNC}$ setting. We present the algorithm using a combination of intuitive explanations and pseudocode for selected subroutines. While the overall strategy is explained in descriptive terms (with sufficient technicalities), we include pseudocode for certain components whose behavior would otherwise require lengthy and repetitive rule-based specifications.

Algorithms for swarm robotic problems often require robots to "wait" or "maintain the status quo." This simply means that when a robot observes that a required geometric or configurational condition is not satisfied in its current snapshot, it performs no action, namely, it neither changes its current color nor its position. Since all robots execute the same algorithm, it suffices to present the algorithm from the perspective of a robot r. Initially, all robots start with color OFF.

Algorithmic Preliminaries and Notations. Let us first define some useful terminologies.

▶ For a line L, we use $\mathcal{H}_L^1$ and $\mathcal{H}_L^2$ (resp. $\overline{\mathcal{H}}_L^1$ and $\overline{\mathcal{H}}_L^2$) to denote the two open (resp. closed) half-planes delimited by L.

▶ **Global Convex Layers:** The boundary of the (global) convex hull $\mathcal{CH}$ of all robots present on the plane, denoted by $\mathcal{L}^1$, is the *outer-most* layer of robots. For $j \geq 2$, the *j-th layer* $\mathcal{L}^j$ is the boundary of the convex hull of all robots excluding the ones on $\mathcal{L}^1 \cup \mathcal{L}^2 \cup \cdots \cup \mathcal{L}^{j-1}$. $\mathcal{L}^k$ represents the *inner-most layer* such that $\mathcal{L}^{k+1}$ does not exist (see Fig. 1).

▶ **Corner, Boundary and Interior Robots:** A robot r is called a *corner robot* if there exist two distinct lines, L_r^1 and L_r^2, such that r lies at their point of intersection, and all other robots visible to r are located in the region $\overline{\mathcal{H}}_{L_r^1}^i \cap \overline{\mathcal{H}}_{L_r^2}^j$ for some $i, j \in \{1, 2\}$. Otherwise, if there is a line L_r passing through r such that all robots visible to r lie entirely within one of the two closed half-planes $\overline{\mathcal{H}}_{L_r}^1$ or $\overline{\mathcal{H}}_{L_r}^2$, the robot r is called a *boundary robot*. Else, r is classified as an *interior robot*.

▶ For a robot r, $\mathcal{CH}_r^{\mathtt{COL}^*}$ denotes the convex hull of robots visible to r excluding those with color COL, while $\mathcal{CH}_r^{\mathtt{COL}}$ denotes the convex hull of visible robots colored COL.

▶ The line segment (resp. infinite line) joining r and r' is denoted by $\overline{rr'}$ (resp. $\overleftrightarrow{rr'}$). $dist(r, L)$ denotes the shortest distance between r and line L.

3.1   A Subproblem: Determining Innermost Layer in $\mathcal{ASYNC}$

A solution to this subproblem benefits both our algorithm and real-world applications. For instance, during the 2020 Olympic opening ceremony, coordinated drone formations, resembling the "dancing problem" in swarm robotics [2,3], demonstrated the need for such layered coordination. In practice, robots are opaque, and assigning distinct colors to layers can aid various tasks. Here, we address Q1 by identifying the global innermost layer $\mathcal{L}^k$ (generalization is possible to answer Q2): robots on $\mathcal{L}^k$ adopt color INNERMOST, while others switch to OUTER. This is achieved using only six colors. A robot with color OFF changes its color to OUTER, if it finds itself on the boundary of $\mathcal{CH}_r$; and to INNER otherwise. After that the action of robot is as follows (also refer to Fig. 1).

▶ $r.color = $ OUTER : The robot r maintains the status quo, if it observes any robot with a color from {OFF, INNER, NEXT, NOT-NEXT}, thereby allowing

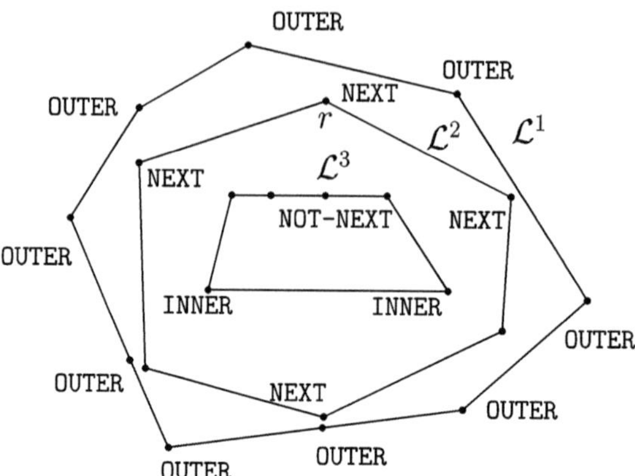

Fig. 1. The disjoint convex layers with $k = 3$. In the detection process of global innermost layer, when the robots lying on $\mathcal{L}^i$ color themselves with OUTER, the robots on the immediate subsequent layer $\mathcal{L}^{i+1}$ switches to NEXT and all other robots to NOT-NEXT.

robots to complete the detection of the actual innermost layer. If no such robot is there, it proceeds to the algorithm in Sect. 3.2. Moreover if r finds all the robots are with color OUTER or INNERMOST and lying on the convex hull $\mathcal{CH}_r$, it switches to INNERMOST, and directly executes the subroutine MOVEMENT-FROM-INNERMOST-LAYER.

▶ *r.color* = INNER: If a robot colored OFF is visible to r, it waits. Once none remain, r disregards all visible OUTER-colored robots and computes the convex hull $\mathcal{CH}_r^{\text{OUTER}^*}$ of the rest. If r finds itself as a corner or boundary robot on this hull, it changes its color to NEXT from INNER, otherwise to NOT-NEXT. The color NEXT indicates that the robot r currently lies on a layer of robots, outside of which all robots have already turned their color to OUTER, signifying that they are not part of the actual innermost layer.

▶ *r.color* = NEXT : Upon observing an INNER-colored robot, r maintains the status quo. When no INNER-colored but a NOT-NEXT-colored robot is present, indicating that r does not belong to the innermost layer, it switches to OUTER. When neither is visible, r switches to INNERMOST.

▶ *r.color* = NOT-NEXT : If r observes a robot r' with color NEXT, it maintains its current color until r' receives the signal that r' cannot be a part of the innermost layer and switches to OUTER. Otherwise, r updates to INNER from NOT-NEXT. As a result, some interior robots may alternate between INNER and NOT-NEXT colors multiple times during this process.

An INNERMOST-colored robot waits until no NEXT-colored robots are visible. These INNERMOST-colored robots form the global innermost layer, after which the goal is to move the OUTER-colored corner robots on the outermost layer to points on this layer.

3.2   Algorithm for Mutual Visibility

Under $\mathcal{ASYNC}$, corner robots on the outermost layer $\mathcal{L}^1$ may lack full visibility of the configuration and might be activated before the innermost layer $\mathcal{L}^k$ is correctly identified, causing premature movements. Even after $\mathcal{L}^k$ is distinctly colored, visibility may remain limited (i.e., obstructed).

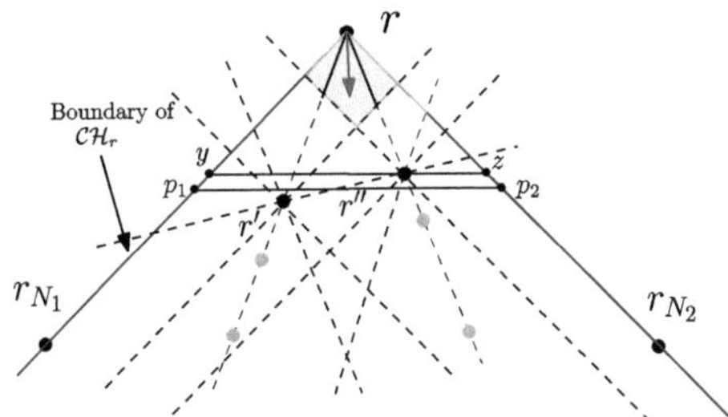

Fig. 2. The highlighted area is the visible area for the corner robot r

To mitigate this, we use the notion of a *visible area*, introduced by Sharma *et al.* [15], which is based on a Euclidean geometric property. For completeness of this paper, we recall a brief description of the visible area for a corner robot r (also see Fig. 2).

Let r_{N_1} and r_{N_2} be the counterclockwise and clockwise neighbors of r on $\mathcal{CH}_r$, and let p_1 and p_2 be the midpoints of $\overline{r r_{N_1}}$ and $\overline{r r_{N_2}}$, respectively. The visible area of r is initially defined as the triangle $\Delta r p_1 p_2$. If this triangle contains other robots, it is shrunk by a line parallel to $\overline{p_1 p_2}$ passing through the nearest such robot. The resulting region is further refined by intersecting it with half-planes induced by lines passing through visible robots and parallel to lines $\overleftrightarrow{r r''}$, for all r'' visible to r, thereby eliminating positions that could cause collinearity or obstruct visibility. Finally, boundary points of the resulting region and points collinear with any visible robot other than r_{N_1} and r_{N_2} are excluded.

In this paper, we denote this region by $\textsc{VisibleArea}(r, \mathcal{CH}_r)$. Moving within this region retains the corner status while gaining visibility of all stationary robots. So, we have the following lemma from [15].

Lemma 1. *If the robot r moves to any point strictly inside the region* $\textsc{VisibleArea}(r, \mathcal{CH}_r)$ *and no other robot is moving simultaneously with r, then r remains a corner of the convex hull $\mathcal{CH}_r$ and all other stationary robots become visible to r.*

During relocation of non-faulty robots from layers $\mathcal{L}^1, \ldots, \mathcal{L}^{k-1}$ to $\mathcal{L}^k$, robots already on $\mathcal{L}^k$ (colored `INNERMOST`) remain stationary with a specific color until all non-faulty robots arrive. This ensures that $\mathcal{L}^k$ serves as a stable geometric reference throughout the relocation process[1]. Thus, a robot from its visible area can verify if the detection of $\mathcal{L}^k$ is over or not. We divide the description into two major cases depending on whether the innermost layer $\mathcal{L}^k$ is non-linear (Case A) or linear (Case B).

Case A: Algorithm for Non-linear Innermost Layer. The objective is to move all corner robots on the current outermost layer to distinct points on $\mathcal{L}^k$ (after detection) without collisions, where the movements of corner robots convert the adjacent boundary robots into new corners.

If r observes any robot with a color from the set {OFF, NEXT, NOT-NEXT, INNER}, it maintains the status quo, as this indicates that the innermost layer is not yet determined. Otherwise, r determines the convex hull $\mathcal{CH}_r^{\text{FAULT}^*}$ of all visible robots excluding those colored FAULT. Evidently, $\mathcal{CH}_r = \mathcal{CH}_r^{\text{FAULT}^*}$ when no robot is with the color FAULT. If r finds a MOVE1-colored robot, it takes no action in the current LCM cycle. When no such robot is present, r first determines whether it is a corner, boundary or an interior robot on the convex hull $\mathcal{CH}_r^{\text{FAULT}^*}$. If it is a corner robot with color OUTER, r moves to a point within VISIBLEAREA$(r, \mathcal{CH}_r^{\text{FAULT}^*})$ after changing its color to CORNER. In all other situations (boundary or interior), it maintains its color and position.

When $r.color =$ CORNER, r checks for a MOVE1-colored robot. The presence of such a robot, due to $\mathcal{ASYNC}$, may obstruct r's visibility of the innermost layer. If present, r stays put, but reverts its color to OUTER. Otherwise, it calculates the center of gravity (CG) c_g of the convex hull of all currently visible INNERMOST-colored robots and determines its target point t_r on $\mathcal{L}^k$ by following FIND-TARGET$(r, \mathcal{L}^k, c_g)$. When the point of intersection of $\mathcal{L}^k$ and $\overline{rc_g}$ is unoccupied, t_r is that point. Else, t_r is an unoccupied point on $\mathcal{L}^k$ very close to the above point of intersection (see Algorithm 1). After changing its color to MOVE1, r moves to the point t_r. After activation with MOVE1, it switches to MOVE1-END without any further movement.

In this movement towards the innermost layer, r might encounter mobility fault. If it has failed to reach the innermost layer, we want it to detect and accordingly change its color to FAULT by checking some geometric constraints. Let $S =$ {MOVE1-END, CONF, N-CONF, INTERIM, INNERMOST, BOUNDARY-IM} denote the set of colors used by the subroutine FAULT-DETECTION-NONLINEAR to determine whether or not a movement of the robot r was successfully executed.

▶ *Subroutine* FAULT-DETECTION-NONLINEAR: This subroutine for r begins only after all visible OUTER-colored robots have switched to some color in S, indicating that each such robot has completed its movement toward the innermost layer, either successfully or unsuccessfully in case of a fault. Let $\mathcal{CH}_r^S$ denote the convex hull of all visible robots with colors in S. Since a successful movement of a corner robot r from an outer layer to $\mathcal{L}^k$ turns it to a boundary robot there, r can no longer remain a corner on $\mathcal{CH}_r^S$. If

---

[1] This relocation process is not needed when there is only one layer in the initial configuration. The single layer case can be handled by the later part of the algorithm.

Algorithm 1: Subroutine $\textsc{Find-Target}(r, \mathcal{C}, p)$

---

1 $p_r \leftarrow$ the point of intersection of $\mathcal{C}$ and the line segment $\overline{rp}$ // $\mathcal{C}$ is the layer
   where r is supposed to reach

2 if p_r *is not occupied by any robot* **then**

3 $t_r \leftarrow p_r$

4 else

5   Find all r' such that
     $dist(r', \overleftrightarrow{rp}) = \min\{dist(r'', \overleftrightarrow{rp}) \mid r''$ is visible to r and does not lie on $\overleftrightarrow{rp}\}$

6 $p_{r'} \leftarrow$ the point of intersection of $\mathcal{C}$ and $\overline{r'p}$

7 $t_r \leftarrow$ a point on the arc joining the points p_r and $p_{r'}$ along $\mathcal{C}$ such that
     $dist(p_r, t_r) = \frac{1}{3}dist(p_r, p_{r'})$

8 return t_r

---

r still finds itself a corner on $\mathcal{CH}_r^S$, it switches directly to FAULT. When a faulty corner robot sets its current color to FAULT, its neighbouring boundary non-faulty robots (and eventually interior ones, if exist) become the new corners of $\mathcal{CH}_r^S$. To make r distinguish between the two scenarios depicted in Fig. 3, an intricate signaling sequence through color transitions is used (formally given in Algorithm 2). In Fig. 3 (left), r is lying on the boundary of $\mathcal{CH}_r^S$, but in reality, it has failed to reach a point on the innermost layer. In another configuration depicted in Fig. 3 (right), r has successfully reached the innermost layer. In both of the figures, the convex hull $\mathcal{CH}_r^S$ is marked (in blue dotted lines) to indicate that it is not possible for r to differentiate the two scenarios without further computations. We in Algorithm 2 make r involved in a signaling process using a constant number of colors with its neighbours in $\mathcal{CH}_r^S$ to solve this problem.

Being a boundary robot on $\mathcal{CH}_r^S$, r's action depends on the current color of it and its neighbouring robots on $\mathcal{CH}_r^S$. If r is adjacent to a INNERMOST-colored robot, it first updates its color to CONF to signal the other neighbour r_{N_2}. Robot r_{N_2} upon seeing r_1 with CONF and the other neighbour still with MOVE1-END, changes to N-CONF. After that, r takes the color INTERIM, and then r_{N_2} adapts CONF to signal its other neighbour. This process continues until a robot finds both of its neighbours with a color in {CONF, N-CONF, INTERIM, INNERMOST}. When such a situation occurs, a robot switches to BOUNDARY-IM, which gets propagated towards the INNERMOST-colored robots later on.

Proceeding from the stage where all non-faulty robots lie on the innermost layer, a robot r executes $\textsc{Movement-From-Innermost-Layer}$ when all visible robots are colored BOUNDARY-IM, INNERMOST, or FAULT.

▶ *Subroutine* $\textsc{Movement-From-Innermost-Layer}$: The aim is to move the corner robots of the innermost layer within their visible areas so that their neighbouring boundary robots become new corners of the convex hull. An INNERMOST-colored robot r turns CORNER-IM (resp. BOUNDARY-IM) if it

---

Algorithm 2: Subroutine FAULT-DETECTION-NONLINEAR

---

1   $S \leftarrow \{$MOVE1-END, CONF, N-CONF, INTERIM, INNERMOST, BOUNDARY-IM$\}$

2   $r_{N_1}, r_{N_2} \leftarrow$ The neighbours of r on the convex hull $\mathcal{CH}_r^S$

3   **if** *r is a corner robot on the convex hull $\mathcal{CH}_r^S$* **then**

4   r changes its color to FAULT

5   **else if** *r is boundary robot on $\mathcal{CH}_r^S$* **then**

6   **if** *r.color $\in \{$MOVE1-END, N-CONF$\}$ & both r_{N_1}.color, r_{N_2}.color $\in \{$INNERMOST, CONF, N-CONF, INTERIM$\}$* **then**

7   r changes its color to BOUNDARY-IM

8   **else if** *r.color $\in \{$MOVE1-END, CONF, N-CONF, INTERIM$\}$ & one neighbour r_{N_1} is with r_{N_1}.color = BOUNDARY-IM* **then**

9   r changes its color to BOUNDARY-IM

10   **else if** *r.color = CONF with r_{N_1}.color = $\{$INNERMOST, INTERIM$\}$ & r_{N_2}.color $\in \{$CONF, N-CONF$\}$* **then**

11   r changes its color to BOUNDARY-IM

12   **else if** *r.color = MOVE1-END & r_{N_1}.color $\in \{$INNERMOST, INTERIM$\}$ & r_{N_2}.color = MOVE1-END* **then**

13   r changes its color to CONF

14   **else if** *r.color = MOVE1-END & r_{N_1}.color = CONF & r_{N_2}.color = MOVE1-END* **then**

15   r changes its color to N-CONF

16   **else if** *r.color = CONF & r_{N_1}.color = N-CONF* **then**

17   r.color $\leftarrow$ INTERIM

18   **else if** *r.color = N-CONF & r_{N_1}.color = INTERIM & r_{N_2}.color = MOVE1-END* **then**

19   r changes its color to CONF

20   **else**

21   r maintains the status quo

---

is a corner (resp. boundary) robot on $\mathcal{CH}_r^{\text{FAULT}^*}$ and waits until all robots on $\mathcal{CH}_r^{\text{FAULT}^*}$ are similarly recolored. Then, a robot with the color CORNER-IM waits for its neighbouring BOUNDARY-IM-colored robots to switch to MY-TURN, and moves within VISIBLE-AREA$(r, \mathcal{CH}_r^{\text{FAULT}^*})$ with a color MOVE-IN (which later switches to MOVE-FIN), making neighbours (now with MY-TURN) new corners. Seeing this, MY-TURN robots turn to CORNER-IM or BOUNDARY-IM, depending on whether they become a corner or boundary of $\mathcal{CH}_r^{\text{FAULT}^*}$. If these neighbours adopt BOUNDARY-IM, it indicates that the movement of the former robot is unsuccessful due to fault and hence it changes its color to FAULT. This is formally described in Algorithm 3.

This subroutine makes every non-faulty robots a corner of a convex hull and hence mutual visibility of those robots is achieved.

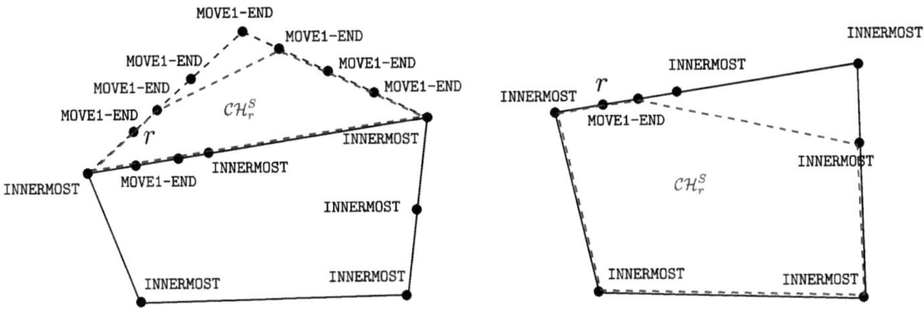

Fig. 3. (left) r failed to reach the innermost layer (right) r has reached to the innermost layer

Case B: Algorithm for Linear Innermost Layer. When the innermost layer consists of one non-faulty robot, we can simply move it to a point on the layer $\mathcal{L}^{k-1}$, as such a robot can detect the layer $\mathcal{L}^{k-1}$ easily sitting at $\mathcal{L}^k$. In this process, we reset the color of the robots on the outer layers to OFF and restart the layer detection procedure once again.

When there are more than one robots on $\mathcal{L}^k$, we modify the algorithm presented in Sect. 3.1 as follows. When a robot r with color NEXT observes that the convex hull $\mathcal{CH}_r^{\text{NEXT}}$ formed by the NEXT-colored robots is a line (i.e., it sees at most two such robots), it switches to LINEAR instead of INNERMOST. We refer to the linear innermost layer by $\mathbb{L}$ henceforth. In this case, our target is to bring the non-faulty robots lying on each of the half-planes $\overrightarrow{\mathcal{H}_{\mathbb{L}}^1}$ and $\overrightarrow{\mathcal{H}_{\mathbb{L}}^2}$ to distinct points on an ellipse whose major axis coincides with $\mathbb{L}$. There might be two half-ellipses on two half-planes. Since they share the same major axis, joining two half-ellipses still gives a convex curve.

Now, the major challenge is determining two central robots (who will be colored CENTER in this process, and will later act as the major axis) on $\mathbb{L}$ under $\mathcal{ASYNC}$. A inward signal propagation from the two terminal robots on $\mathbb{L}$ does not work under $\mathcal{ASYNC}$. So, we take the help of the robots (now colored OUTER) lying on layer $\mathcal{L}^{k-1}$, as such robots lying on the open half-plane $\mathcal{H}_{\mathbb{L}}^i$ (for $i = 1, 2$) can see all robots on $\mathbb{L}$. We first find at most two *marker* robots on each half-plane from the layer $\mathcal{L}^{k-1}$ and color them accordingly. We use the following subroutine.

▶ *Subroutine* FINDING-MARKERS: To find such a robot, an OUTER-colored robot r checks if two robots having the color LINEAR are visible or not. If not, it maintains the status quo. Otherwise, it computes a line L_r passing through its own position and parallel to $\overline{r_1 r_2}$, where r_1 and r_2 are two visible LINEAR-colored robots. Then, if it observes any robot lying strictly between the two lines L_r and $\overleftrightarrow{r_1 r_2}$, it is not eligible to become a marker. If instead, no such robot is seen, r calculates the midpoint m_r of $\mathbb{L}$ and considers the line $L_{m_r}^\perp$ through m_r perpendicular to $\overleftrightarrow{r_1 r_2}$. Let p_r be the point of intersection of L_r and $L_{m_r}^\perp$. If p_r is occupied by r itself or p_r is visible but unoccupied, it switches

---

Algorithm 3: MOVEMENT-FROM-INNERMOST-LAYER

---

1 **if** $r.color =$ INNERMOST **then**

2   **if** r *is a corner robot on* $\mathcal{CH}_r^{FAULT^*}$ **then**

3   r changes its color to CORNER-IM

4   **else**

5   r changes its color to BOUNDARY-IM

6 **else if** $r.color =$ CORNER-IM & *both* $r_{N_1}.color,$ $r_{N_2}.color \in$ {CORNER-IM, FINISH} **then**

7   r changes its color to FINISH

8 **else if** $r.color =$ BOUNDARY-IM & *one neighbour with color* CORNER-IM **then**

9   r changes its color to MY-TURN

10 **else if** $r.color =$ CORNER-IM & $r_{N_1}.color =$ MY-TURN, & $r_{N_2}.color \in$ {MY-TURN, CORNER-IM, FINISH} **then**

11   r computes VISIBLE-AREA$(r, \mathcal{CH}_r^{FAULT^*})$

12   r changes its color to MOVE-IN and moves to a point within it

13 **else if** $r.color =$ MOVE-IN **then**

14   r changes its color to MOVE-FIN

15 **else if** $r.color =$ MY-TURN & *one neighbour with color MOVE-FIN* **then**

16   **if** r *is a corner robot on* $\mathcal{CH}_r^{FAULT^*}$ **then**

17   r changes its color to CORNER-IM

18   **else**

19   r changes its color to BOUNDARY-IM

20 **else if** $r.color =$ MOVE-FIN **then**

21   **if** $r_{N_1}.color =$ *BOUNDARY-IM* **then**

22   r changes its color to FAULT

23   **else if** $r_{N_1}.color, r_{N_2}.color \in$ {CORNER-IM, FINISH} **then**

24   r changes its color to FINISH

25   **else**

26   r waits without any changes

27 **else**

28   r maintains the status quo

---

to MARKER. After this process, each open half-plane $\mathcal{H}_{\mathbb{L}}^i$ contains at least one MARKER-colored robots. Now the LINEAR-colored robots start updating their color in a query-feedback fashion using a sequence of color transitions with marker robots.

▶ *Subroutine* CENTER-DETECTION: We refer to a LINEAR-colored robot terminal on $\mathbb{L}$, if it sees exactly one other robot with color LINEAR. Such a robot waits until the required number of marker robots are detected. Once done, a terminal robot r on $\mathbb{L}$ changes its color to CENTER?, indicating a query to the marker robots on whether it is a center or not. Upon seeing a CENTER?-colored robot, a marker r_m waits until it finds two CENTER?-colored robot. When two such robots are visible, and there is at most one LINEAR-colored robots lying between these two robots, r_m changes its color to YES and to NO otherwise. For the robots $r_1, r_2, \ldots, r_s$ (in order) lying on $\mathbb{L}$, we color the two robots $r_{s/2}$ and $r_{s/2+1}$ with CENTER when s is even. When s is odd, we color the robots $r_{\lfloor s/2 \rfloor}$ and $r_{\lfloor s/2 \rfloor+2}$ with CENTER, and the robot $r_{\lfloor s/2 \rfloor+1}$ is eventually moved to a point on the ellipse. After observing all MARKER robots change their respective colors either to YES or NO, a CENTER?-colored robot r updates to N-CENTER, when it finds NO on them, and CENTER otherwise. Once both the CENTER?-colored robots switch to N-CENTER or CENTER, r_m reverts its color to MARKER. This process continues until exactly two robots are colored CENTER.

After the above process, we now have two CENTER-colored robots r_c and r_c' and at least one r_m with MARKER in each $\overline{\mathcal{H}}_{\mathbb{L}}^i$.

▶ *Movement of the Marker Robots*: We now start moving the marker robots on an ellipse $\mathbb{E}(r_c, r_c', b)$, where the major axis is $\overline{r_c r_c'}$ and the lengths of the minor axis is $2b$. We consider the (perpendicular) distance between the marker robot r_m and $\mathbb{L}$ as b. Note that the values of b may differ for the two half-planes $\mathcal{H}_{\mathbb{L}}^1$ and $\mathcal{H}_{\mathbb{L}}^2$. In this process, r_m moves to the point of intersection of the ellipse and the line segment $\overline{r_m cen}$ after changing the color to MOVE-M, where cen is the midpoint of $\overline{r_c r_c'}$. If r_m is unable to see two CENTER-colored robots due to the movement of another marker robot, it changes its color to OUTER. Upon activation with MOVE-M, r_m needs to detect whether or not its movement has created a valid ellipse for other robots to move on. It does so by calculating an ellipse $\mathbb{E}'(r_c, r_c', r_m)$ that passes through r_m with the major axis being $\overline{r_c r_c'}$. If $\mathbb{E}'(r_c, r_c', r_m)$ intersects any line $L_{r'}$, it updates its color to F-MARKER, and to G-MARKER otherwise, where r' lies on half-plane $\mathcal{H}_{L_{r_m}}^i$ that does not contain r_c. We now discuss movement strategy for the robots from outer layers toward the ellipse.

▶ *Movement From an Outer Layer to an Ellipse*: A corner robot on the outermost layer must see the CENTER-colored and marker robots to use them as references for computing its target point on the ellipse. As earlier, such a robot r moves within $\textsc{VisibleArea}(r, \mathcal{CH}_r^{\text{FAULT}^*})$ after switching to CORNER. After this movement, it waits till robots with a color in {LINEAR, MARKER, MOVE-M} are present. Once the waiting ends, if r observes two CENTER-colored robots r_c and r_c' and a robot with color G-MARKER or F-MARKER lying on the half-plane $\mathcal{H}_L^i$ for $L = \overleftrightarrow{r_c r_c'}$ in which r itself lies, it calculates the ellipse depending on the color of the marker robots, as follows. If r finds a G-MARKER robot r_m on $\mathcal{H}_L^i$, it chooses the ellipse $\mathcal{E} = \mathbb{E}'(r_c, r_c', r_m)$ that passes through r_m and has the major axis as $\overline{r_c r_c'}$. In case of r seeing a F-MARKER robot r_m (w.l.o.g. this is the nearest F-MARKER robot to $\overleftrightarrow{r_c r_c'}$, when two such markers are present) on $\mathcal{H}_L^i$, it selects the ellipse $\mathcal{E} = \mathbb{E}(r_c, r_c', b)$ (b is defined as above). After this computation, it finds t_r by following $\textsc{Find-Target}(r, \mathcal{E}, cen)$ and moves to it after changing its color to MOVE2. In all other situations, r updates its color to FAULT. Upon activation with MOVE2, a robot changes its color to

MOVE2-END without any further movement. Moreover, a CORNER-colored robot reverts to OUTER seeing any MOVE2-colored robot, as such a robot may block its view under $\mathcal{ASYNC}$ to see center or marker robots.

Now we want the non-faulty robots with the color MOVE2-END to determine whether they have successfully reached the desired ellipse or not using the following subroutine.

▶   ***Subroutine*** FAULT-DETECTION-LINEAR: After activation with color MOVE2-END, if r observes a robot with a color in {OUTER, CORNER, MOVE2}, it maintains the status quo. Once none are visible, it checks if it can see two CENTER-colored robots r_c and r'_c. If not, it updates its color to FAULT. If yes, let r_m be a G-MARKER robot visible to r. If the two ellipses $\mathbb{E}'(r_c, r'_c, r)$ and $\mathbb{E}'(r_c, r'_c, r_m)$ coincide, r has reached the target ellipse and turns FINISH. If the two ellipses are not the same, it must have become faulty and changes its color to FAULT. It is also possible that r_c and r'_c are visible to r, but the G-MARKER-colored r_m is not. In such a situation, let, for $L_r \parallel \overleftrightarrow{r_c r'_c}$ passing through r, $\mathcal{H}^i_{L_r}$ be the half-plane that does not contain r_c or r'_c. We now need a redefined the notion of *terminal robot*, where r is terminal on L_r if it has at most one MOVE2-END-colored neighbour on L_r. When all visible robots on $\mathcal{H}^i_{L_r}$ turn their color to FAULT and r is terminal on L_r (as otherwise, r waits), it starts computing the ellipses that passes through r_c, r'_c and every visible MOVE2-END-colored robot. r sets its color to FAULT, if either there cannot be such an ellipse through r, or among all such ellipses, the minor axis of its own is not the minimum ones. Even if r lies on the one with the smallest minor axis, it cannot confirm if r is non-faulty or not, since there could be some non-faulty robots (not visible to r due to $\mathcal{ASYNC}$) coming to create a new ellipse (with smaller minor axis). Hence it requires further computations to determine that. r now calculates p_r, the point of intersection of L_r and the line perpendicular to $\overleftrightarrow{r_c r'_c}$ passing through the midpoint of $\overline{r_c r'_c}$. r changes its color to READY if any one of the conditions hold: (1) r has no neighbour on L_r (2) r has only one neighbour r_{N_1} on L_r with $dist(r, p_r) \leq dist(r_{N_1}, p_r)$ (3) r has two neighbours r_{N_1} and r_{N_2} on L_r with $r_{N_2}.color =$ FAULT, $r_{N_1}.color \in$ {MOVE2-END, READY}, and $dist(r, p_r) \leq dist(r_{N_1}, p_r)$. Once all the robots that lie on the region bounded by $\mathbb{L}$ and L_r switch their color to FINISH or FAULT-F, it will then decide its final color. When a FAULT-colored robot r observes that all the robots lies on the region bounded by by $\mathbb{L}$ and L_r are with color FINISH or FAULT-F, it switches to FAULT-F. While, a FINISH-colored robot, with the same condition, computes all the ellipses that pass through r_c, r'_c and all the visible READY or FINISH-colored robots on $\mathcal{H}^i_{\mathbb{L}}$ that contains itself. If r has the minimum minor axis among all such ellipses, it updates its color to FINISH; otherwise to FAULT-F.

▶   ***Movement of a Marker Robot:*** When a marker robot r_m finds no robot with a color from the set {OUTER, CORNER, MOVE2, MOVE2-END}, it turns its color to FINISH (resp. FAULT-F) if $r_m.color =$ G-MARKER (resp. F-MARKER).

Algorithm 4: MOVEMENT-FROM-$\mathbb{L}$-TO-ELLIPSE

---

1 **if** $r.color = \textit{N-CENTER}$ **then**

2 $\quad$ $L_r \leftarrow$ The line passing through r and another robot with the color CENTER or N-CENTER

3 $\quad$ **if** r *finds exactly one other robot on L_r with color CENTER or N-CENTER and all robot lying on $\mathcal{H}^i_{L_r}$ are colored either with FAULT-F or FINISH* **then**

4 $\quad\quad$ $t_r \leftarrow$ The point with $\overline{rt_r} \perp L_r$ and $dist(r, t_r) = \frac{1}{2}\min\{dist(r', L_r) \mid r' \text{ is visible to } r\}$

5 $\quad\quad$ r moves to t_r with the color MOVE3

6 $\quad$ **else if** r *finds no CENTER-colored robot* **then**

7 $\quad\quad$ $t_r \leftarrow$ A point that is not on $\overleftrightarrow{r'r''}$ for any two visible robots r' and r''

8 $\quad\quad$ r moves to t_r with color FINISH

9 **else if** $r.color = \textit{MOVE3}$ **then**

10 $\quad$ **if** *two CENTER-colored robots are not visible* **then**

11 $\quad\quad$ r changes its color to FAULT-F

12 $\quad$ **else**

13 $\quad\quad$ $r_c, r'_c \leftarrow$ The two CENTER-colored robot and $\mathbb{L} \leftarrow \overleftrightarrow{r_c r'_c}$

14 $\quad\quad$ **if** *at least one FINISH-colored robot r' is visible on the half-plane $\mathcal{H}^i_{\mathbb{L}}$ where r itself is situated* **then**

15 $\quad\quad\quad$ $\mathcal{E} \leftarrow$ The ellipse passing through r' with major axis as $\overline{r_c r'_c}$

16 $\quad\quad$ **else**

17 $\quad\quad\quad$ $b \leftarrow \frac{1}{2}\min\{dist(r'', \mathbb{L}) \mid r'' \text{ is on } \mathcal{H}^i_{\mathbb{L}} \text{ and } r''.color = \text{FAULT-F}\}$

18 $\quad\quad\quad$ $\mathcal{E} \leftarrow$ the ellipse with the major axis as $\overline{r_c r'_c}$, and the minor axis length as $2b$

19 $\quad\quad$ $t_r \leftarrow$ FIND-TARGET$(r, \mathcal{E}, cen)$

20 $\quad\quad$ r moves to t_r with the color MOVE4

21 **else if** $r.color = \textit{MOVE4}$ **then**

22 $\quad$ r computes the ellipse $\mathcal{E}$, described in Line 13 and 18

23 $\quad$ **if** r *has reached on a point on $\mathcal{E}$* **then**

24 $\quad\quad$ r changes its color to FINISH

25 $\quad$ **else**

26 $\quad\quad$ r changes its color to FAULT-F

27 **else if** $r.color = \textit{CENTER}$ **then**

28 $\quad$ $L_r \leftarrow$ The line passing through r and another robot with the color CENTER or N-CENTER

29 $\quad$ **if** r *sees exactly one other robot with color CENTER or N-CENTER* **then**

30 $\quad\quad$ r changes its color to FINISH

31 **else**

32 $\quad$ r maintains the status quo

▶ ***Movement of Robots from*** $\mathbb{L}$**:** Now the non-faulty robots placed on the ellipses on two sides of $\mathbb{L}$ achieved mutual visibility. Only the robots, currently on $\mathbb{L}$ (that are now colored with N-CENTER or CENTER) are yet to be positioned on an ellipse. As this step is simple, we present only the highlevel idea of this part and move the formal steps to Algorithm 4. We start from the terminal ones and move such a robot r perpendicularly against $\mathbb{L}$. This movement should enable r to see the two CENTER-colored robots r_c and r'_c. If not, r must be faulty and color itself with FAULT-F. Otherwise, r moves to the ellipse passing through r_c, r'_c and some FINISH-colored robots (if exists) on the half plane $\mathcal{H}^i_{\mathbb{L}}$ where r itself is situated. In case absence of FINISH-colored robots, r computes the ellipse with minor axis as the distance between the nearest FAULT-colored robot and $\mathbb{L}$. After the sequential movement of the N-CENTER robots, the CENTER-colored robots eventually changes its color to FINISH.

Let us recall the impossible configuration (the initial configurations that lead us to unsolvability of the mutual visibility problem under the mobility fault) mentioned in Sect. 1. The above algorithm solves mutual visibility apart from those impossibility configurations. In particular, if the innermost layer is linear and there are odd number of robots present on that layer such that the central robot is equidistant from both of its neighbouring robots on that layer, our algorithm cannot solve mutual visibility for a faulty central robot. So we state the following theorem.

Theorem 1. *Apart from the impossibility configurations, our algorithm achieves mutual visibility of $N - f$ non-faulty robots without collisions in $O(N)$ epochs under $\mathcal{ASYNC}$ using $O(1)$ colors, where $f(< N)$ robots may experience mobility faults.*

4   Conclusion

We presented an $\mathcal{ASYNC}$ $O(N)$ algorithm for the fault-tolerant mutual visibility problem under a minimal model with disoriented robots and a constant number of colors. An important direction for future work is to establish tight lower bounds on the time and color complexities of the fault-tolerant mutual visibility problem. Another interesting extension is to study the problem in the fat robot model, where robots are represented as unit disks rather than points. Although the mutual visibility problem has been studied in this model under the assumption of one-axis agreement among the robots, removing this assumption and dealing with fully disoriented fat robots remains a challenging and open direction. We also believe that fault-tolerant mutual visibility can be studied on grid graphs embedded in the Euclidean plane. In such settings, it is possible to establish impossibility results, particularly when all grid points within the bounding rectangle (of the positions of the robots) are occupied by robots. However, for other initial configurations, achieving mutual visibility would require the development of new techniques.

References

1. Aljohani, A., Sharma, G.: Complete visibility for mobile agents with lights tolerating a faulty agent. In: 2017 IEEE International Parallel and Distributed Processing Symposium Workshops (IPDPSW), pp. 834–843 (2017). https://doi.org/10.1109/IPDPSW.2017.145
2. Das, S., Flocchini, P., Prencipe, G., Santoro, N.: Synchronized dancing of oblivious chameleons. In: Ferro, A., Luccio, F., Widmayer, P. (eds.) Fun with Algorithms, pp. 113–124. Springer, Cham (2014). https://doi.org/10.1007/978-3-319-07890-8_10
3. Das, S., Flocchini, P., Prencipe, G., Santoro, N.: Forming sequences of patterns with luminous robots. IEEE Access **8**, 90577–90597 (2020). https://doi.org/10.1109/ACCESS.2020.2994052
4. Di Luna, G., Flocchini, P., Gan Chaudhuri, S., Poloni, F., Santoro, N., Viglietta, G.: Mutual visibility by luminous robots without collisions. Inf. Comput. **254**(P3), 392–418 (2017). https://doi.org/10.1016/j.ic.2016.09.005
5. Flocchini, P., Prencipe, G., Santoro, N., Widmayer, P.: Hard tasks for weak robots: the role of common knowledge in pattern formation by autonomous mobile robots. In: ISAAC 1999. LNCS, vol. 1741, pp. 93–102. Springer, Heidelberg (1999). https://doi.org/10.1007/3-540-46632-0_10
6. Flocchini, P., Prencipe, G., Santoro, N., et al.: Distributed computing by mobile entities. Curr. Res. Moving Comput. **11340**(1) (2019). https://doi.org/10.1007/978-3-030-11072-7
7. Luna, G.A.D., Flocchini, P., Poloni, F., Santoro, N., Viglietta, G.: The mutual visibility problem for oblivious robots. In: Proceedings of the 26th Canadian Conference on Computational Geometry, CCCG 2014, Halifax, Nova Scotia, Canada, 2014. Carleton University, Ottawa, Canada (2014). http://www.cccg.ca/proceedings/2014/papers/paper51.pdf
8. Poudel, P., Aljohani, A., Sharma, G.: Fault-tolerant complete visibility for asynchronous robots with lights under one-axis agreement. Theoret. Comput. Sci. **850**, 116–134 (2021). https://doi.org/10.1016/j.tcs.2020.10.033
9. Poudel, P., Sharma, G., Aljohani, A.: Sublinear-time mutual visibility for fat oblivious robots. In: Proceedings of the 20th International Conference on Distributed Computing and Networking, ICDCN 2019, pp. 238–247. Association for Computing Machinery, New York, NY, USA (2019). https://doi.org/10.1145/3288599.3288602
10. Pramanick, S., Jana, S., Bhattacharya, A., Mandal, P.S.: Distributed uniform partitioning of a region using opaque async luminous mobile robots. In: Proceedings of the 25th International Conference on Distributed Computing and Networking, pp. 55–64 (2024). https://doi.org/10.1145/3631461.3631555
11. Pramanick, S., Jana, S., Bhattacharya, A., Mandal, P.S.: Mutual visibility of luminous robots despite angular inaccuracy. Theor. Comput. Sci. **1011**, 114723 (2024). https://doi.org/10.1016/j.tcs.2024.114723. https://www.sciencedirect.com/science/article/pii/S0304397524003402
12. Pramanick, S., Jana, S., Mandal, P.S.: Fault-tolerant mutual visibility without any axis agreement in presence of mobility failure. Theoret. Comput. Sci. **1025**, 114970 (2025). https://doi.org/10.1016/j.tcs.2024.114970
13. Pramanick, S., Jana, S., Mandal, P.S., Sharma, G.: Asynchronous gathering of opaque robots with mobility faults. arXiv preprint arXiv:2509.10711 (2025). https://doi.org/10.48550/ARXIV.2509.10711
14. Sharma, G., Vaidyanathan, R., Trahan, J.L.: Constant-time complete visibility for robots with lights: the asynchronous case. Algorithms **14**(2) (2021). https://doi.org/10.3390/a14020056

15. Sharma, G., Vaidyanathan, R., Trahan, J.L., Busch, C., Rai, S.: Complete visibility for robots with lights in $O(1)$ time. In: Bonakdarpour, B., Petit, F. (eds.) SSS 2016. LNCS, vol. 10083, pp. 327–345. Springer, Cham (2016). https://doi.org/10.1007/978-3-319-49259-9_26
16. Vaidyanathan, R., Busch, C., Trahan, J.L., Sharma, G., Rai, S.: Logarithmic-time complete visibility for robots with lights. In: 2015 IEEE International Parallel and Distributed Processing Symposium, IPDPS 2015, pp. 375–384 (2015). https://doi.org/10.1109/IPDPS.2015.52

Distributed MIS Algorithms for Rational Agents Using Games

Nithin Salevemula[(✉)] and Shreyas Pai

Indian Institute of Technology Madras, Chennai, India
`nithinprakash9999@gmail.com`, `shreyas@cse.iitm.ac.in`

Abstract. We study the problem of computing a Maximal Independent Set (MIS) in distributed networks, where each node is a rational agent that receives a payoff depending on whether it is included in the MIS. In classical distributed computing, it is typically assumed that nodes follow the prescribed algorithm faithfully. However, this assumption fails when nodes are rational agents whose utilities depend on the algorithm's output. In such cases, nodes may deviate from the algorithm if it increases their expected payoff.

Classical solutions for MIS assume that nodes generate random bits honestly or rely on unique identifiers to break symmetry. However, in rational settings, nodes may manipulate randomness to gain a strategic advantage, and relying solely on unique identifiers can result in unfairness, where some nodes have zero probability of joining the MIS and thus no incentive to participate. To address these challenges, we propose two algorithms that work under a utility model, where agents are incentivized to compute locally correct solutions while also exhibiting preferences among these solutions. In these algorithms, randomness is generated through interactions between neighboring nodes, which can be viewed as simple games, where no single node can unilaterally change the outcome. This approach allows us to break symmetry while being compatible with rational behavior.

For both algorithms, we show that regardless of the execution history that has occurred, no agent can improve its expected utility by deviating from that stage, provided no other agents deviate. This is a much stronger guarantee compared to Trembling Hand Perfect Equilibrium, which is typically used in such scenarios. Both algorithms guarantee that when all the nodes follow the algorithm, every node has a positive probability of joining the MIS, and that the final output is a correct Maximal Independent Set. Finally, for both algorithms, we can guarantee termination in $O(\log n)$ rounds with high probability under mild additional assumptions, where n is the number of nodes in the network.

1 Introduction

In many classical distributed computing settings, some fraction of the nodes is assumed to be byzantine while the rest are obedient. An obedient node follows the prescribed algorithm without deviation, whereas byzantine nodes are assumed to be controlled by an adversary that is actively trying to ensure that the algorithm's goals are not achieved. Such a setup is valid as long as the obedient nodes follow the prescribed algorithm perfectly and the fraction of byzantine nodes is not too high. However, in many real-world scenarios, the situation is a bit more nuanced: nodes in the network often have their own incentives, which makes algorithm design challenging even without the presence of a byzantine adversary. In this work, we take a "middle path" of assuming that each node in the network is a selfish agent with its own utility function that it wants to maximize. If we allow for arbitrary utility functions, the behavior of the rational nodes will be similar to that of a byzantine node[1]. Therefore, we restrict our attention to utility functions where nodes are incentivized to compute a correct solution, but may still have a preference over which correct solution they want to compute. See Sect. 2 for a full description of our model.

Consider the Maximal Independent Set (MIS) problem as a working example. Although all nodes are primarily interested in ensuring that the MIS is computed correctly, they also prefer to be included in the set. As a result, a node may deviate from the prescribed algorithm if doing so increases its chance of joining the MIS. This behavior is referred to as *rationality* in the game-theoretic literature, where agents (nodes) act to maximize their individual utility. Deviations due to individual rationality can harm both the correctness and termination guarantees of classical MIS algorithms. Therefore, we need to design new algorithms that are resilient to rational behavior. Such algorithms guarantee that nodes, acting in their own self-interest, still prefer to follow the algorithm rather than deviate.

Challenges for Computing MIS with Rational Agents. Classical distributed algorithms for computing a Maximal Independent Set (MIS), such as Luby's algorithm [14] and the algorithm by Métivier et al. [16], are not suitable in rational settings where nodes may deviate in order to maximize their own utility. As an illustrative example, let us examine both these algorithms under the utility model where nodes are incentivized to be included in the MIS.

In Luby's algorithm [14], each node i proposes to join the MIS with probability $1/2d(i)$, where $d(i)$ is the degree of the node i. A node successfully joins the MIS if none of its neighbors propose in the same round. However, this approach fails in a rational setting: since the decision to propose is determined by internal randomness, a rational node can always falsely claim that it has proposed to join the MIS with probability $1/2d(i)$, but it got lucky in every round. If all nodes act this way, no node ever joins the MIS, and the algorithm never terminates. In the algorithm of Métivier et al. [16], each node generates a rank uniformly at random from the interval $[0, 1]$. A node joins the MIS if its rank is lower than all of its neighbors' ranks. Again, this algorithm will not work if nodes prefer joining the MIS: a rational node can simply report a rank of 0 in every round, ensuring it always appears eligible to join. If all nodes behave similarly, no node is eliminated, no progress is made, and the algorithm stalls indefinitely.

---

[1] Albeit in this case, all the byzantine nodes may not be controlled by a single adversary.

Given the above discussion, one may argue that we should then just focus on deterministic MIS algorithms, as there has been impressive progress on this front [9]. However, deterministic algorithms have the following problem: a node may realize that it can never join the MIS by following the algorithm, even though none of its neighbors have currently joined the MIS. In such a situation, it will have no incentive to participate further in the algorithm. As a simple example, consider a deterministic algorithm where, in each round, a node joins the MIS if its ID is smaller than those of all its neighbors. If a node i has a neighbor j with the globally minimum ID, i knows it can never join the MIS even though j has not yet joined the MIS. Therefore, i has no incentive to participate in the algorithm. In fact, any deterministic algorithm would face the same problem when nodes are rational agents aiming to maximize their own utility. This problem even holds for algorithms that have a randomized part followed by a deterministic part.

These examples demonstrate that classical MIS algorithms do not translate directly to settings with rational agents. Therefore, new algorithms must be designed that are resilient to deviations that arise from rational behavior and guarantee participation from every node.

Our Contributions. We use the classical framework of *extensive-form games* to analyze the MIS problem in distributed networks with rational agents. Each node in the network is modeled as a rational player, motivated by the incentive to be included in the MIS. We define a *strategy algorithm* that specifies, for each node, the action it should take in every round until termination, as a function of its state—including those that may arise due to deviations from the prescribed algorithm, either by itself or by other nodes. We then propose two such strategy algorithms in which nodes have no unilateral[2] incentive to deviate at any state, even at states that occur as a result of earlier deviations. We refer to this property as a *belief-independent sequential equilibrium*, which provides a stronger guarantee than Nash equilibrium, sequential equilibrium, or trembling-hand perfect equilibrium in games of imperfect information.

Furthermore, when all agents follow the strategy algorithm, the nodes joining the independent set form a valid MIS, and every node has a non-zero probability of being included in the MIS. The following is a brief description of our proposed strategy algorithms.

- The first algorithm (Sect. 3): In each iteration, every active node plays a simple two-player game of rock-paper-scissors with each of its neighbors in order to decide who gets to join the MIS. Only a node that wins all its games against its neighbors in an iteration gets to join the MIS. This rule allows us to ensure that no agent can benefit from unilaterally deviating from the algorithm at any point. Moreover, when all nodes follow the algorithm, we can guarantee termination in $O(\log n)$ rounds with high probability, assuming the maximum degree of the network graph is constant, where n is the number of nodes in the network.

---

[2] That is, we assume that collusions cannot be formed.

– The second algorithm (Sect. 4) uses lightweight cryptographic assumptions to generate randomness in a way that prevents manipulation. Each agent computes its priority for the current round by combining its own random value with a signed random value received from one of its neighbors. Since the randomness is jointly determined, no agent can unilaterally bias the outcome. These priorities are then used to simulate one round of the algorithm of Métivier et al. [16]. Repeating this process, the algorithm guarantees termination in $O(\log n)$ rounds with high probability.

2 The LOCAL Model with Rational Agents

We work in the LOCAL model, a classic synchronous message-passing model of distributed computing [13]. The network is abstracted as $G = (V, E)$, an undirected graph, where V is the set of nodes (agents) and $E \subseteq V \times V$ is the set of edges. As usual we denote $n = |V|$ and $m = |E|$. Each node represents a selfish agent that acts to maximize its own utility, and each edge $(i, j) \in E$ indicates that agents i and j can communicate directly. We assume no prior communication occurs between the agents before the algorithm begins. Each agent is expected to irrevocably output one of three values: 1, declaring itself as a member of the MIS; 0, declaring itself to not belong to the MIS; or $\perp$, indicating an abort. The output of a node, once computed, is visible to all the neighbors of that node.

The utility of each node depends only on its own output and those of its neighbors. As discussed earlier, if we allow for arbitrary utilities, the behavior of the rational nodes will be similar to that of Byzantine nodes, which will lead to trivial impossibilities. Therefore, we consider a particular family of utility functions in which nodes are incentivized to compute a locally correct solution. Additionally, each node i gets utility value $v_i > 0$ if it outputs 1 and all its neighbors output 0. More precisely, the utility function for a node i can be defined as a function on its own output and its neighbors' output. Let $\text{out}(i) \in \{1, 0, \perp\}$ denote the output of node i and let $\text{out}(N(i))$ denote the list of outputs of all its neighbors. Then, the utility function u_i for node i is defined in Eq. 1. Here we slightly abuse notation by interpreting $\text{out}(N(i))$ as a set in the case analysis. The conditions are evaluated in order; once a condition is satisfied, the subsequent conditions are not considered, even though they may be applicable.

$$u_i\big(\text{out}(i), \text{out}(N(i))\big) = \begin{cases} 0, & \text{if } \text{out}(i) = \perp \text{ or } \perp \in \text{out}(N(i)) \quad \text{(locally aborted)}, \\ 0, & \text{if } \text{out}(i) = 0 \text{ and } 1 \in \text{out}(N(i)) \quad \text{(locally valid, } i \text{ not in MIS)}, \\ v_i, & \text{if } \text{out}(i) = 1 \text{ and } 1, \perp \notin \text{out}(N(i)) \quad \text{(locally valid, } i \text{ in MIS)}, \\ -\infty, & \text{otherwise} \quad \text{(locally invalid solution)}. \end{cases}$$

(1)

Given the above model and assumptions, our goal is to design a distributed algorithm in which nodes, despite being able to deviate, find it optimal to follow the algorithm. However, if a deviation does occur, we cannot simply ignore the deviating node; the algorithm must still prescribe how it should optimally behave from that point onward. In other words, the algorithm should tell each node what to do in every situation it could possibly face, even those that would occur only if some of them deviated earlier. This is precisely analogous to the notion of a *strategy* in game theory. To capture this requirement, we introduce the notion of a *strategy algorithm*. Intuitively, it specifies how a node should act in every possible situation it may encounter, including those that arise due to deviations by itself or its neighbors. To define this formally, we first define the notion of a *state*, and then use it to precisely characterize what constitutes a strategy algorithm.

Definition 1 (State). *The* state *of a node i at the beginning of round t consists of all messages sent and received by i in rounds $t' < t$, the values of its local variables (including any private randomness), and any observable outputs of its neighbors from earlier rounds.*

Definition 2 (Strategy Algorithm). *A strategy algorithm in the LOCAL model with rational nodes is a special type of algorithm, which specifies, for each node i, the action it should take in every round until termination as a function of its state, including states that may arise due to deviations from the prescribed algorithm by itself or by other nodes.*

Remark 1. Providing a strategy algorithm to the nodes specifies, for every round, the exact internal computation and external action prescribed for each possible state. However, each node remains free to deviate from the suggested behavior. We classify deviations into three types: (i) deviations in internal deterministic computations, (ii) deviations in internal randomized computations (e.g., replacing prescribed randomness with deterministic choices), and (iii) deviations in external actions (such as sending incorrect messages, omitting required messages, outputting values at unintended times, or outputting values different from those prescribed by the algorithm). We assume that a node cannot deviate in its internal deterministic computations. This assumption is without loss of generality: any deviation in internal deterministic computation affects the execution only when it causes unintended external behavior. Hence, for any such deviation, it suffices to consider an equivalent execution in which the node performs the deterministic computation correctly but deviates directly in the corresponding external action.

Intuition for our Utility Function and Modeling Choices. Our aim in this paper is to study rational behavior in the LOCAL model. A basic feature in many LOCAL model algorithms is that the nodes perform computation for a certain number of rounds and finally produce a correct output upon termination. When the nodes are rational agents, we want them to terminate at some point; therefore, it is essential that once a node commits to an output, it cannot be changed. Moreover, our utility function is well-defined only once a node and its neighbors have computed their outputs, and allowing nodes to change their outputs makes it difficult to calculate their utility. We can still design algorithms where nodes are allowed to change their output by having nodes compute a temporary output that can be changed. But before termination, the nodes have to irrevocably commit to this output, and the utility is calculated based on the committed outputs of all nodes.

Next, we motivate our choice of utility function. If all nodes are in a locally valid solution, we have computed a (globally) correct MIS, and since we are interested in computing a correct MIS solution, we require that all nodes prefer a locally valid solution over a locally invalid solution. In fact, we do not want the nodes to try to join the MIS at a risk of being in a locally invalid solution with some probability. Hence, we assign a utility of $-\infty$ to nodes in a locally invalid solution. Moreover, MIS has the property that if a node is in a locally invalid solution, it can always change its own output to be in a locally valid solution. Since an output change is not allowed, this means that a node in a locally invalid solution has committed too early to its output, and such behavior must be appropriately penalized.

If we have the same utility for all locally valid solutions, we are in the standard LOCAL model, as the rational nodes will faithfully follow any algorithm that computes a correct MIS. Therefore, to make the model interesting, we need to assign different utility values to different locally valid solutions. There are indeed many choices here, but for the purposes of this paper, we study one family of utility functions where nodes always prefer locally valid solutions where they belong to the MIS. The other choices in this space are also interesting, especially the case where nodes prefer locally valid solutions where they are not in the MIS. Designing rationality-resilient algorithms for these alternative families of utility functions is left as an open problem.

We now address why we introduce the third output symbol, $\perp$. If we define the utility function with only two output labels 0 and 1, we may encounter the following scenario: if a node outputs 1 by deviating from the protocol to get higher utility, then the best response for all its neighbors is to output 0, since otherwise they obtain $-\infty$ utility. Therefore, the node that outputs 1 is getting away with its deviation simply because its neighbors can do nothing but support its action. To address this problem, we need a way for nodes to retaliate when their neighbors deviate from the algorithm and irrevocably output 1. We do this by introducing a new output symbol $\perp$ which can be interpreted as a credible threat. Now, if a node i deviates by outputting 1, its neighbors can output $\perp$ instead of 0 at no extra penalty to themselves, which makes the deviation of i not profitable. It is important to note that the output $\perp$ is only used as a credible threat to ensure nodes do not deviate from the algorithm. In a correct execution of the algorithm with no deviations, no node will ever actually output $\perp$. So a node outputting $\perp$ can be considered as a failure of the algorithm execution.

We also assume that the output of each node is visible to all of its neighbors. This assumption is necessary because, in our model, the utilities of nodes are based on their own output and the outputs of their neighbors. If outputs of neighbors are not directly observable, a node would have to rely solely on what its neighbors report as their output, which introduces the possibility of misreporting. In such a case, a trivial but undesirable outcome could arise where all nodes output 1 while falsely reporting to have output 0 to their neighbors, resulting in a configuration that is not a valid MIS, as every node is part of the MIS in reality. Hence, visibility of the neighbor's output is required to ensure that utilities are well-defined and correspond to actual local configurations.

2.1 MIS with Rational Nodes as Extensive-Form Game

As discussed in Sect. 2, we consider a model in which nodes are *rational* and interact with one another to change their states. Each node's utility depends on the final state of the network, making the overall system naturally analogous to a strategic game among the nodes. Since these notions are well formalized in the game-theoretic framework, we model our setting as an *extensive-form game.*

In an r-round LOCAL model algorithm, a node has no information about the graph outside its r-hop neighborhood. This means the corresponding extensive form game must be one with *imperfect information.* Since each node retains complete memory of all its past actions and observations, the game satisfies the property of *perfect recall.* Finally, because we assume synchronous communication rounds in which all nodes act simultaneously, the game can be viewed as an *extensive-form game with imperfect information, perfect recall, and simultaneous moves.* Formally, an extensive-form game is defined as a tuple consisting of several components (see [8] for a complete description). In our context, we do not require the full generality of this definition; it suffices to specify only the elements necessary to model our distributed setting. Accordingly, we work with a simplified version of the tuple and its associated definitions.

Definition 3 (Distributed MIS Problem with Rational Agents as an Extensive Form Game with Imperfect Information, Perfect Recall and Simultaneous Moves). [3] *Given a graph $G = (V, E)$, where V is the set of nodes (agents) and $E \subseteq V \times V$ is the set of edges and each edge $(i, j) \in E$ indicates that agents i and j can communicate directly. The MIS problem over G can be modeled as an extensive game, denoted by $\mathcal{G}$. Formally, we define $\mathcal{G}$ as a tuple $\mathcal{G} = \langle V, H, P, \{\mathcal{I}_i\}_{i \in V}, \{A_i\}_{i \in V}, \{\succsim_i\}_{i \in V} \rangle$ whose components are described below.*

- *V: the set of players, corresponding to the nodes of the graph.*
- *H: the set of all possible prefix-closed histories of messages exchanged between neighboring nodes and their outputs, subject to the following constraints: each node produces an output at most once, and once a node outputs, it becomes inactive—i.e., it can no longer send or receive messages.*
- *A history $h \in H$ is called terminal if it is infinite, or if all nodes output a value from $\{0, 1, \bot\}$. Denote by Z the set of all terminal histories.*

---

[3] This is an instance of an extensive form game, refer [8, Chapter 12] for the exact definitions of extensive form game with imperfect information, perfect recall and simultaneous moves.

- $P : H \setminus Z \to 2^V \setminus \{\emptyset\}$: *assigns to each nonterminal history h the set of players who move simultaneously at that history. $P(h)$ is the set of nodes that have not yet produced an output at history h*
- *Since any player $i \in V$ observes only the messages it has sent and received, together with the outputs of its neighbors, so every history $h \in H$ has a local projection onto the information accessible to i. Formally, we define the projection function $\mathrm{proj}_i : H \to H_{i,,}$ where H_i denotes the set of all possible local histories of player i. For any global history $h \in H$, the projection $\mathrm{proj}_i(h)$ is the subsequence of events in h that involve i—namely, all messages sent or received by i, together with the outputs of its neighbors observed by i. Two global histories $h, h' \in H$ are said to be* indistinguishable *to i if they induce the same local history, that is, $h \sim_i h' \iff \mathrm{proj}_i(h) = \mathrm{proj}_i(h')$. This indistinguishability relation $\sim_i$ partitions the set $\{h \in H \mid i \in P(h)\}$ of global histories where i is active into equivalence classes. We denote this partition by $\mathcal{I}_i$, where each element $I_i \in \mathcal{I}_i$ corresponds to the set of all global histories that induce the same local history to i. Each such class I_i is therefore an information set of player i, since player i cannot distinguish between any two global histories in the same class and therefore must choose the same action at all of them. Let $I_i(h_i)$ denote the set of all global histories that project local history h_i on i.*
- *At any information set $I_i \in \mathcal{I}_i$. The set of possible actions for player i, denoted $A_i(I_i)$, consists of any combination of: (1) perform internal computation, (2) send arbitrarily long messages to any subset of undecided neighbors, and (3) output a value in $\{0, 1, \bot\}$.*
- *For each player $i \in V$, a preference relation $\succsim_i$ is defined over terminal histories Z, representable by a local utility function $u_i : Z \to \mathbb{R}$. For an infinite history $h \in Z$, the utility of all nodes is defined to be 0. For a finite terminal history, the utility is given by the function in Eq. 1.*

Given the definition of the game, we can define pure, mixed, and behavioral strategies as follows:

Definition 4 (Pure, Mixed and Behavioral Strategies [18, Definitions 203.1, 212.1]). *A* pure strategy *of player $i \in V$ of an extensive-form game $\mathcal{G}$ is a function that assigns an action in $A_i(I_i)$ to each information set $I_i \in \mathcal{I}_i$. A* mixed strategy *of player i is a probability measure over the set of i's pure strategies. Whereas a* behavioral strategy *of player i is a collection $(\beta_i(I_i))_{I_i \in \mathcal{I}_i}$ of independent probability measures, where $\beta_i(I_i)$ is a probability measure over $A(I_i)$.*

Remark 2. Under this formulation, a strategy algorithm can be viewed as a *behavioral strategy*, since it specifies, for each node, the action (or distribution over actions) it should take at every possible state it may encounter, which corresponds to the local history in the extensive form game $\mathcal{G}$ defined above.

Next, we define various equilibrium notions for extensive-form games before introducing the equilibrium guarantee that can be obtained.

Definition 5 (Nash equilibrium [18, Chapter 11.5]). *A Nash equilibrium in mixed strategies of an extensive game is a profile $\sigma^* = (\sigma_i^*)_{i \in N}$ of mixed strategies with the property that for every player $i \in N$ we have $O(\sigma_{-i}^*, \sigma_i^*) \succeq_i O(\sigma_{-i}^*, \sigma_i)$ for every mixed strategy σ_i of player i, where $O(\sigma)$ denotes the expected outcome (or distribution over terminal histories) induced by the strategy profile σ and σ_{-i}^* denotes the equilibrium strategy profile of all players except i.*

Definition 6 (Sequential Equilibrium[18, Definition 222.1]). *A sequential equilibrium of an extensive-form game $\mathcal{G}$ is an assessment (β, μ), where $\beta = (\beta_i)_{i \in N}$ is a profile of behavioral strategies (which assign, for each information set $I_i \in \mathcal{I}_i$, a probability distribution over the available actions at I_i) and μ is a belief system, that is, a function that assigns to every player i and every information set $I_i \in \mathcal{I}_i$ a probability measure over the set of histories contained in I_i, conditional on I_i being reached. The assessment (β, μ) is a sequential equilibrium if it satisfies the following conditions:*

1. ***Sequential Rationality:*** *An assessment (β, μ) is said to be sequentially rational if, for every player $i \in V$ and every information set $I_i \in \mathcal{I}_i$, the strategy β_i prescribes actions that maximize i's expected utility at I_i, given the belief system μ and the strategies β_{-i} of the other players. Formally, let $O(\beta, \mu \mid I_i)$ denote the distribution over terminal histories induced by (β, μ) conditional on I_i being reached. Then (β, μ) is sequentially rational if $O(\beta, \mu \mid I_i) \succeq_i O((\beta_{-i}, \beta_i'), \mu \mid I_i)$ for every behavioral strategy β_i' of player i.*
2. ***Consistency:*** *An assessment (β, μ) is said to be consistent if there exists a sequence of assessments $\{(\beta^n, \mu^n)\}_{n=1}^{\infty}$ that converges to (β, μ) in Euclidean space, where each strategy profile β^n is completely mixed and each belief system μ^n is derived from β^n using Bayes' rule.*

Another equilibrium notion that is considered is called *Trembling Hand Perfect Equilibrium*, which is a refinement of sequential equilibrium with a particular assessment. It ensures that each player's strategy remains optimal, even if players occasionally make unintended moves with a very small probability, thereby ensuring that strategies are robust to such "trembles" in decision-making. While both sequential and trembling hand perfect equilibria provide a guarantee only with respect to a particular belief system (that is, a strategy is optimal given that belief system), Our strategy algorithms give behavioral strategies that admit a stronger guarantee: they are Sequentially Rational for *any* belief system. Hence, unlike sequential equilibrium, we do not define behavioral strategies relative to a belief system, But only over information sets. We formalize this stronger notion as a Belief-Independent Sequential Equilibrium.

Definition 7 (Belief-Independent Sequential Equilibrium). *A behavioral strategy profile $\beta^* = (\beta_i^*)_{i \in N}$ of an extensive-form game $\mathcal{G}$ is an Belief-Independent Sequential Equilibrium if, for every player i and every information set $I_i \in \mathcal{I}_i$, the behavioral strategy β_i^* is sequentially rational, regardless of player i's belief over the histories in I_i. Formally, for every player $i \in V$, every information set $I_i \in \mathcal{I}_i$, any belief system μ of player i, $O(\beta^*, \mu \mid I_i) \succeq_i O((\beta_{-i}^*, \beta_i'), \mu \mid$*

I_i) *for every behavioral strategy β_i' of player i. where β^*_{-i} denotes the equilibrium strategies of all players other than i in the profile β^*.*

Now we are ready to define the desirable properties of a strategy algorithm.

Definition 8 (Rationality Resilient Strategy Algorithm). *A* Strategy Algorithm *is said to be* rationality resilient*(with respect to the above MIS problem) if it satisfies the following properties*

1. *__Belief-Independent Sequential Equilibrium:__ The behavioral strategy corresponding to the strategy algorithm should induce Belief-Independent Sequential Equilibrium 7.*
2. *__Termination:__ If all nodes follow the algorithm, it must terminate after a finite number of rounds with high probability.*
3. *__Correctness:__ If all nodes follow the algorithm and terminate, the set of nodes that output 1 forms a valid Maximal Independent Set (MIS), and all remaining nodes output 0.*
4. *__Positive Inclusion Probability:__ If all nodes follow the algorithm, then each node must have a non-zero probability of eventually outputting 1 in every round where none of its neighbors has output 1. This ensures that no node prematurely drops out of participation based on the belief that it has no future chance of joining the MIS.*

2.2   Related Work

The study of incentive-compatible distributed algorithms has led to the field of *Distributed Algorithmic Mechanism Design (DAMD)* [6], which extends the classical *Algorithmic Mechanism Design (AMD)* framework to distributed settings where there is no trusted central authority. While AMD focuses on designing truthful mechanisms in centralized settings, DAMD addresses the challenge of ensuring that rational agents follow prescribed strategies when the computation is decentralized.

Nisan [17] gave a distributed mechanism for computing a truthful maximum independent set in chain networks. Later, Hirvonen and Ranjbaran [12] proposed a distributed mechanism for all local optimization problems, including Maximal Independent Set, that guarantees a Δ-approximation. However, both approaches require monetary transfers (payments) to third parties to enforce truthfulness – something we explicitly aim to avoid in our work. Moving beyond the third-party setting, other widely studied notions include *self-stabilization* [21] [22] and *fairness* [7] [2]. The work by Amoussou-Gueno et al. [3] analyzes the dynamics between rational and Byzantine players in blockchain consensus protocols, highlighting their implications for security and efficiency in decentralized systems.

Rationality has also been extensively studied in the context of the *Secret Sharing* problem. Halpern et al. [11] introduced the notion of rational secret sharing, showing that classical schemes fail when agents act in a selfish manner, and proposed randomized protocols that restore incentive compatibility. Subsequent works [1,10,15] explored alternative utility models and provided further constructions under these variations. Although the problem domain is different, these works share with ours the high-level goal of designing distributed algorithms that are resilient to rational deviations.

Solving *Locally Checkable Labeling (LCL) problems* with rational nodes was formalized as extensive-form games by Collet et al. [4]. They show that for all LCL problems solvable by greedy sequential algorithms – such as MIS, $(\Delta + 1)$-coloring, and maximal matching – there exist distributed algorithms that are robust to selfish behavior and form trembling hand perfect equilibria. While we adopt an equivalent extensive-form game framework, our model differs in several key respects. First, in their setting, actions are restricted to choosing labels, whereas in our model, nodes may also send arbitrary messages to their neighbors. Second, their formulation allows labels to be revised in later stages, while in our setting, label choices, once made, cannot be changed. Finally, in their model, the game always terminates in a valid LCL solution, whereas in our framework, the outcome may correspond to an invalid solution. In our work, we study the MIS problem under a specific family of utility functions and present a strategy that is sequentially rational irrespective of beliefs, which is a much stronger guarantee than trembling hand perfect equilibrium.

Fineman et al. [7] define fairness in the context of computing maximal independent sets as balanced inclusion probabilities across nodes. However, they do not allow nodes to have rational behavior, and hence their algorithm is not robust to strategic deviations. In contrast, Abraham et al. [2] study fair leader election for specific topologies such as chains and cliques. Their model assumes that agents strictly prefer the existence of some leader over no leader, which is conceptually similar to our assumption that agents prefer to be included in the MIS. Importantly, their protocols are also resistant to collusion. Our algorithms adopt a similar idea of generating randomness from inputs provided by multiple agents with conflicting preferences over the outcome.

3   A Strategy Algorithm for MIS with Rational Nodes

We now describe our first strategy algorithm, which employs a simple and symmetric tie-breaking mechanism: each node plays a Rock-Paper-Scissors (RPS) game with each of its neighbors, and only the nodes that win with all their neighbors are allowed to join the MIS. We note that the RPS game between two nodes i and j must be well defined even if one or both players choose not to play the game. If both nodes send valid moves to each other, then the outcome is determined by the standard RPS rules: rock breaks scissors, scissors cut paper, paper covers rock. If exactly one of the two nodes sends an invalid move or sends no move at all, then the other player wins. If both nodes fail to send valid moves, the result is a tie. We capture all these cases formally in the following definition.

Definition 9 (RPS Outcome Function). *Let* $rps_{i,j} : \{r, p, s, \phi\}^2 \rightarrow \{i, j, tie\}$ *be a function which determines the winner between two nodes i and j that are playing an RPS game with each other. Here r, p, and s correspond to* rock, paper, *and* scissors, *respectively, and ϕ denotes an invalid or missing move (i.e., any* *input not in $\{r, p, s\}$). When node i plays move s_i and node j plays move s_j, the function is defined as follows:*

$$
rps_{i,j}(s_i, s_j) = \begin{cases} i, & \text{if } (s_i, s_j) \in \{(r,s), (p,r), (s,p), (r,\phi), (p,\phi), (s,\phi)\} \\ j, & \text{if } (s_i, s_j) \in \{(s,r), (r,p), (p,s), (\phi,r), (\phi,p), (\phi,s)\} \\ tie, & \text{if } s_i = s_j \end{cases}
$$

RPS Algorithm Overview. The algorithm proceeds in *iterations*, and each iteration consists of *three rounds*. Initially, all nodes are in an **undecided** state. Once a node outputs a value in $\{0, 1, \perp\}$, it becomes **decided** and takes no further action. Each node maintains a **BeenCheated** flag, initialized to **false**, and in every iteration, the strategy algorithm proceeds through the following rounds:

- **Round 1 (Play RPS):** Each node i selects a move from $\{r, p, s\}$ uniformly at random for each of its undecided neighbors and sends it. The RPS games with different neighbors are treated independently, allowing the node to play distinct moves against each of its neighbors.
- **Round 2 (Join MIS if possible):** Each node i checks whether any neighbors has already output 1 or $\perp$. If such neighbors exist, they are considered to have deviated from the algorithm, since they were not supposed to do so under the prescribed algorithm. In that case, i ignores the rest of the algorithm and outputs $\perp$ in every subsequent round where it remains **undecided**. Otherwise, if no neighbor has output 1 or $\perp$, then if i wins against all its **undecided** neighbors according to Definition 9, it outputs 1 and joins the MIS. In addition, if i did not receive a move from an **undecided** neighbor in the previous round, it sets its **BeenCheated** flag to **true**.
- **Round 3 (Respond to neighbor outputs):** Each node i checks whether any neighbor j has output $\perp$. If such a node exists, i outputs $\perp$ in every subsequent round in which it remains **Undecided**.
  If any neighbor j has output 1 in previous round, then:
  - If i lost to all such neighbors then node i outputs 0 in every subsequent round while it remains undecided, unless **BeenCheated** is **true**, in which case it outputs $\perp$ in every subsequent round while it remains undecided.
  - Otherwise, if there exists a neighbor k that lost to i but still output 1 then i outputs $\perp$ in every subsequent round while it remains undecided.
  Node i outputs 1 if it has no undecided neighbors; otherwise, it proceeds to the next iteration.

3.1   Rationality Resilient RPS Algorithm

The distributed strategy algorithm described above is formalized in Algorithm 1. This is followed by an analysis showing that this strategy algorithm is rationality resilient, encapsulated in Theorem 1.

Algorithm 1: RPS based MIS Strategy algorithm for node i

---

1 **Initialization**
2   UndecidedNeighbors $\leftarrow N(i)$;
3   BeenCheated $\leftarrow$ false;

4 **if** $N(i) = \emptyset$ **then**
5   From this point onward, disregard the rest of the algorithm and Output 1 in every round where node i is still UNDECIDED;

6 **while** i *is* UNDECIDED **do**
    /* Round 1: Play RPS with Undecided Neighbors   */
7   **foreach** $j \in$ UndecidedNeighbors **do**
8   Choose strategy $s_i(j) \in \{r, p, s\}$ uniformly at random and send to j;
    /* Round 2: Join MIS if possible   */
9   **foreach** $j \in$ UndecidedNeighbors **do**
10   **if** j *has output* 1 *or* $\perp$ **then**
11   From this point onward, disregard the rest of the algorithm and Output $\perp$ in every round where node i is still UNDECIDED;
12   **else if** j *has output* 0 **then**
13   Remove j from UndecidedNeighbors;

14   **foreach** $j \in$ UndecidedNeighbors **do**
15   **if** *message* $s_j(i)$ *is* ϕ **then**
16   BeenCheated $\leftarrow$ true;
17   Compute $rps_{i,j}(s_i(j), s_j(i))$ as defined in Definition 9;
18   **if** $rps_{i,j}(s_i(j), s_j(i)) = i$ *for all* $j \in$ *UndecidedNeighbors* **then**
19   Output 1 (join MIS);
    /* Round 3: Observe Undecided Neighbors' Outputs   */
20   **if** *there exits a node in* UndecidedNeighbors *has output* $\perp$ **then**
21   From this point onward, disregard the rest of the algorithm and output $\perp$
22   **else if** *there exits a node in* UndecidedNeighbors *has output* 1 **then**
23   **if** *there exists a neighbor* j *with output* 1 *and* $rps_{i,j}(s_i(j), s_j(i)) \neq j$ **then**
24   BeenCheated $\leftarrow$ true;
25   From this point onward, disregard the rest of the algorithm and output $\perp$ if BeenCheated is **true**, and output 0 otherwise, in every round where node i is still UNDECIDED;

26   **else**
27   Remove all $j \in$ UndecidedNeighbors who output 0;
28   **if** UndecidedNeighbors *is empty* **then**
29   From this point onward, disregard the rest of the algorithm and Output 1 in every round where node i is still UNDECIDED;

Theorem 1. *Algorithm 1 is a Rationality Resilient Algorithm as defined in Definition 8.*

We prove Theorem 1 in four parts (Theorems 2, 3, 4, and 5). Theorem 2 requires intermediate results, which we establish through Lemmas 1 and 2.

Lemma 1. *Let the game be at an arbitrary history h with $i \in P(h)$, where $h \in I_i \in \mathcal{I}_i$. Suppose that one of i's UndecidedNeighbors (say, j) has its BeenCheated flag set to **true**. Then, regardless of the history h and of i's strategy from h onward, if all the other nodes follow Algorithm 1 from h onward, the utility of node i will be at most 0.*

Proof. According to Algorithm 1, node j outputs 0 only in Round 3 of an iteration, and even then, only if its BeenCheated flag is false. Since the BeenCheated flag, once set to true, is never reset to false, a node with BeenCheated = true will never output 0. Therefore, node j will only output 1 or $\perp$. In either case, the utility of all its neighbors, including i, is at most 0.

Lemma 2. *Let the game be at an arbitrary history h with $i \in P(h)$, where $h \in I_i \in \mathcal{I}_i$, and let h_i be the local history of node i. Then, provided that i and all other undecided nodes follow Algorithm 1 from this point onward, the expected utility of node i is at least 0.*

Proof. A node i receives a utility less than zero (i.e., $-\infty$) only in two cases:

1. i outputs 0, and none of its neighbors output 1, or
2. i outputs 1, and at least one of its neighbors also outputs 1.

Case 1 is not possible under the Algorithm 1: a node is instructed to output 0 only in Round 3 of an iteration, and only after observing at least one neighbor output 1. Hence, after any local history where the node i is undecided in Round 3 outputs 0, it must be the case that a neighbor has already output 1. Therefore, the first case cannot occur.

Case 2 is also prevented by Algorithm 1: a node outputs 1 only in Round 2 or Round 3 of an iteration.

- In Round 2, node i outputs 1 only if no neighbor has yet output 1 or $\perp$, and i has won the RPS game against all its undecided neighbors. Since all neighbors also follow the algorithm, any neighbor that loses to i in the RPS game will not output 1. Thus, no neighbor of i can simultaneously output 1.
- In Round 3, node i outputs 1 only if all of its neighbors have already output 0. Hence, it is impossible for a neighbor to output 1 in this case.

Therefore, Case 2 cannot occur. Combined with the fact that Case 1 is also impossible, we conclude that by following Algorithm 1, node i's utility is never less than 0.

Theorem 2. *The strategy corresponding to Algorithm 1 constitutes a Belief-Independent Sequential Equilibrium.*

Proof. Consider an arbitrary history h with $i \in P(h)$. Let h_i denote the local history of node i, which implies $h \in I_i(h_i) \in \mathcal{I}_i$. We show that the continuation strategy prescribed for i by Algorithm 1 from information set $I_i(h_i)$ is sequentially rational irrespective of the i's belief over $I_i(h_i)$, i.e., it gives the maximum expected payoff when all other nodes also follow Algorithm 1 from h. It follows that the strategy constitutes a sequential equilibrium for any belief system of i. and it follows that the strategy constitutes a Belief-Independent Sequential Equilibrium. As we mentioned in Sect. 2, we do not consider internal deviations except for randomness generation. We distinguish deviations as:

- *Undetectable deviations:* for example, choosing RPS moves with nonuniform probabilities. Since every sequence of moves is still possible under the prescribed uniform strategy (albeit with small probability), neighbors can never rule out a deviation with certainty, even after many observations. Similarly, voluntarily outputting 0 or $\perp$ earlier than prescribed may also be indistinguishable, since it could be a valid response to another neighbor having output 1, which remaining neighbors may not observe.
- *Detectable deviations:* e.g., failing to send a required/valid message, sending inconsistent messages, or outputting 1 when not eligible. Such deviations are caught by at least one neighbor, upon which the neighbor sets its `BeenCheated` flag to 1.

Case Analysis.

Case A: At h, i has a decided neighbor with output 1 or $\perp$. Then the maximum attainable payoff for i is 0. By Lemma 2, following the algorithm yields a payoff of at least 0. Hence, no profitable deviation exists, so the prescribed action is a best response.

Case B: At h, i do not have a decided neighbor with output 1 or $\perp$ and there exists an undecided neighbor that i has cheated. If the remaining undecided neighbors follow the algorithm, Lemma 1 implies the most i can obtain is 0; following the algorithm also yields payoff 0. Thus, no profitable deviation exists.

Case C: At h, i does not have a decided neighbor with output 1 or $\perp$ and i has not cheated any undecided neighbor.

- *Detectable deviation by i:* Some neighbor detects it and sets `BeenCheated=`1. By Lemma 1, the best payoff i can then secure is 0. By Lemma 2, sticking to the algorithm yields a payoff of at least 0, so no profitable deviation exists.
- *Undetectable deviation by i:* (i) Changing the probabilities with which i plays rock, paper, scissors does not improve i's win probability against neighbors who pick each move uniformly at random. Therefore, i's chance of joining the MIS is unchanged, and so is the expected payoff. (ii) Voluntarily outputting 0 or $\perp$ can yield a payoff at most 0, whereas Lemma 2 guarantees that following the algorithm yields payoff at least 0. Hence, no strictly profitable deviation exists.

Therefore, we have shown that for every history h with $i \in P(h)$, the prescribed strategy for i based on $h_i = \mathrm{proj}_i(h)$ gives maximum expected utility possible from h when all other node are following the algorithm from h, which proves the theorem.

We have shown that Algorithm 1 constitutes an Belief-Independent Sequential Equilibrium, meaning that no node has a unilateral incentive to deviate. When all nodes follow the prescribed strategy and no deviations occur, the execution of Algorithm 1 is equivalent to running Algorithm 2. To complete the proof of Theorem 1, we therefore analyze a simplified version of the algorithm in which the deviation-handling logic is removed.

Algorithm 2: RPS based MIS strategy algorithm for node i without deviations

---

1 **Initialization**
2   Initialize node i as undecided;
3   UndecidedNeighbors $\leftarrow N(i)$;
4 **while** *true* **do**
      /* Round 1: Play RPS with Undecided Neighbors   */
5   **foreach** $j \in UndecidedNeighbors$ **do**
6   Choose strategy $s_i(j) \in \{r, p, s\}$ uniformly at random and send to j;
      /* Round 2: Join MIS if possible   */
7   **if** $rps_{i,j}(s_i(j), s_j(i)) = i$ *for all* $j \in UndecidedNeighbors$ **then**
8   Output 1 (join MIS and terminate);
      /* Round 3: Observe Undecided Neighbors' Outputs   */
9   **if** *any* $j \in UndecidedNeighbors$ *has output* 1 **then**
10   Output 0 and terminate;
11   Remove all $j \in UndecidedNeighbors$ who output 0;
12   **if** UndecidedNeighbors *is empty* **then**
13   Output 1 (join MIS and terminate);

Theorem 3 (Termination). *Algorithm 2 terminates in $O(3^{4\Delta} \log n)$ rounds with high probability on graphs with maximum degree Δ.*

Theorem 4 (Correctness). *When all nodes follow Algorithm 2, after termination, the set of nodes that output 1 forms a valid Maximal Independent Set (MIS) of the network graph, and all remaining nodes output 0.*

Theorem 5 (Positive Probability of MIS Inclusion). *Under Algorithm 2, each node has a non-zero probability of eventually outputting 1, i.e., joining the MIS, in every round where none of its neighbors has output 1*

Proofs of Theorems 3, 4, and 5 appear in the full version of this paper [20].

4   A Faster Strategy Algorithm Using Cryptography

The RPS-based algorithm described in the previous section is not very efficient on graphs with high-degree nodes. The exponential dependence on degree arises because each node plays independent RPS games with its neighbors and can only join the MIS if it wins *all* of them. To improve the round complexity, we require an algorithm where each node plays a single game with all of its neighbors, under the condition that if a node wins, none of its neighbors can win. The algorithm by Métivier et al. [16], can be viewed as such a game: each node generates a random rank, and a node "wins" if its rank is lower than that of all its neighbors, in which case it joins the MIS. However, as discussed in Sect. 1, this algorithm fails in rational settings because nodes can bias their rank selection to gain an advantage.

A natural attempt to get around this obstacle is to have each node's rank also depend on inputs from its neighbors. For instance, if rank of node i is computed using randomness from both i and an arbitrarily chosen neighbor j, then neither i nor j can fully influence the outcome: i prefers a low rank in order to join the MIS, while j prefers i to have a high rank in order to block it from joining the MIS. This idea of *two-party shared randomness* ensures that the ranks will be *truly random* and cannot be changed unilaterally by any single party. To make this verifiable, nodes must prove the correctness of their computed rank to others. This requires sharing the opponent's input, which must be authenticated by some means. We perform authentication using digital signatures, which requires standard cryptographic assumptions.

Additional Assumptions. As mentioned, our approach relies on cryptographic tools; we assume that each node i is equipped with a public–private key pair and can sign messages using an *unforgeable digital signature scheme* [5,19]. To verify digital signatures, all nodes are assumed to know the identifiers and public keys of every other node in the network. Further, nodes can only broadcast to their neighbors.[4]

4.1   Rationality Resilient Rank-Based Strategy Algorithm

The algorithm proceeds in *iterations*, where each iteration consists of *five rounds*. Initially, all nodes are in the **undecided** state. Once a node outputs a value in $\{0, 1, \perp\}$, it becomes **decided**, meaning that its output is visible to all neighbors and it takes no further action in subsequent rounds. Each node maintains a

---

[4] The algorithm can, in principle, be extended to support unicast communication. However, doing so introduces several corner cases that would require substantially more discussion. One such case arises when a node can avoid detection by selecting multiple opponents simultaneously. Although this strategy does not yield a higher expected payoff than choosing a single opponent, we must still account for it, since the algorithm is required to prescribe the best continuation strategy for every possible history.

`BeenCheated` flag, initialized to `false`, and in every iteration, the algorithm proceeds through the following rounds:

- **Round 1: Opponent Selection.** Each node i selects an arbitrary undecided neighbor as its *opponent*, denoted by opp(i), and broadcasts this choice to all neighbors.
- **Round 2 (Randomness Generation and Exchange).** Each node i generates a $c \log n$ length bit string $r_{i \to i} \in \{0,1\}^{c \log n}$ uniformly at random and broadcasts it to all neighbors, where $c > 0$ is a fixed constant. For each neighbor j who selected i as an opponent in Round 1, node i generates a separate $c \log n$ length bit string $r_{i \to j} \in \{0,1\}^{c \log n}$ uniformly at random, signs it along with the current iteration counter, and broadcasts each signed message.
- **Round 3: Share Randomness of Opponent** Each node i that broadcast opp(i) in Round 1 and received $r_{\mathrm{opp}(i) \to i}$ computes its rank as $R_i = r_{i \to i} \oplus r_{\mathrm{opp}(i) \to i}$, and then broadcasts the signed message it received from opp(i) to all its neighbors.
- **Round 4: Calculate Ranks of Neighbors.** Each node i, for each of its neighbors j, after receiving a valid signed $r_{\mathrm{opp}(j) \to j}$ in the previous round, computes the rank $R_j = r_{j \to j} \oplus r_{\mathrm{opp}(j) \to j}$. If any undecided neighbor j did not broadcast some message in the previous 3 rounds as expected, then i assumes j's rank to be $\{1\}^{c \log n}$ and sets its `BeenCheated` flag to `true`, since such nodes are considered to have deviated from the algorithm. Similarly, if i deviated in a manner that can be detected by some of its neighbors(this includes the case where i fails to broadcast $r_{\mathrm{opp}(i) \to i}$ because it did not receive it from opp(i)), then it sets its own rank to $\{1\}^{c \log n}$ in order to stay consistent with neighbors that detect i's deviation, and avoid a potential $-\infty$ payoff. Next, node i checks whether any neighbor has already output 1 or $\perp$ in the current iteration; if so, it outputs $\perp$ in every subsequent round in which it remains `Undecided`. . Otherwise, it compares its rank with all its undecided neighbors. If $R_i < R_j$ for all such neighbors j, then node i outputs 1, joining the MIS and terminates.
- **Round 5: Reacting to Neighbor Decisions.** Each node i checks whether any undecided neighbor j has output $\perp$. If such a node exists, i outputs $\perp$ in every subsequent round in which it remains `Undecided`.
  Else, if any neighbor j has output 1 in previous round, then:
  - If, for all such j with output 1, it holds that $R_j < R_i$, then node i outputs 0 in every subsequent round while it remains undecided, unless `BeenCheated` is `true`, in which case it outputs $\perp$ in every subsequent round while it remains undecided.
  - Otherwise, if there exists a node j with $R_j > R_i$ that still outputs 1, then i outputs $\perp$ in every subsequent round while it remains undecided.
  If there are no `Undecided` neighbors, i outputs 1. otherwise, i proceeds to next iteration.

The complete pseudocode of the distributed strategy algorithm, together with all supporting theorems and proofs establishing its rationality resilience, is presented in the full version of this paper [20].

5   Conclusion and Future Work

We proposed a model that incorporates rational behavior in distributed message passing algorithms. We considered a utility function, where nodes are incentivized to compute a correct solution and prefer to be included in the MIS. We designed two algorithms that are resilient to rational behavior: no node has an incentive to deviate from the prescribed algorithm. Additionally, assuming that no node deviates from the algorithm, we can guarantee correctness, termination, and positive probability of inclusion.

However, each algorithm has certain drawbacks. The rank-based strategy algorithm relies on cryptographic assumptions, which restricts agents to have bounded local computation, a non-standard assumption in the context of distributed algorithms. Moreover, this algorithm may use large messages. A node that becomes the opponent of k neighbors will send $O(k \log n)$-bit messages over each incident edge. On the other hand, the RPS-based strategy algorithm avoids cryptographic assumptions and, under honest execution of the strategy, requires only $O(1)$-bit messages and therefore works in CONGEST. But its round complexity has an exponential dependence on the maximum degree of the network.

While our algorithms are resilient to unilateral deviations, they do not prevent coordination or implicit collusion among multiple nodes. For example, once a node realizes that it cannot join the MIS (because one of its neighbors has already output 1), it may still have an incentive to continue participating in the algorithm in a way that strategically reduces the chances of its neighbors, thereby improving the inclusion probability of the nodes with which it is colluding. Additionally, the two algorithms presented are somewhat sensitive to the assumptions about the underlying model and utility structure. If the utilities are perturbed even slightly, our equilibrium guarantees may not hold. For instance, if the utility of a node in a locally valid solution where it belong to the MIS is negative, our algorithms no longer ensure equilibrium. An important direction for future work, therefore, is to design algorithms that remain robust under a broader class of utility functions, collusion, or to establish *impossibility results* that characterize the precise limitations of such robustness.

Acknowledgements. The authors are grateful to the A. Raghunathan Center for Theoretical CS for support. We also thank anonymous reviewers for their helpful comments.

References

1. Abraham, I., Dolev, D., Gonen, R., Halpern, J.Y.: Distributed computing meets game theory: robust mechanisms for rational secret sharing and multiparty computation. In: ACM PODC 2006, pp. 53–62. https://doi.org/10.1145/1146381.1146393
2. Abraham, I., Dolev, D., Halpern, J.Y.: Distributed protocols for leader election: a game-theoretic perspective. ACM Trans. Economics and Comput. **7**(1), 4:1–4:26 (2019). https://doi.org/10.1145/3303712

3. Amoussou-Guenou, Y., Biais, B., Potop-Butucaru, M., Tucci Piergiovanni, S.: Rational vs byzantine players in consensus-based blockchains. In: AAMAS '20, pp. 43–51. https://dl.acm.org/doi/10.5555/3398761.3398772

4. Collet, S., Fraigniaud, P., Penna, P.: Equilibria of games in networks for local tasks. In: OPODIS 2018, vol. 125, pp. 6:1–6:16. https://drops.dagstuhl.de/entities/document/10.4230/LIPIcs.OPODIS.2018.6

5. Diffie, W., Hellman, M.E.: New directions in cryptography. IEEE Trans. Inf. Theory 22(6), 644–654 (1976). https://doi.org/10.1109/TIT.1976.1055638

6. Feigenbaum, J., Shenker, S.: Distributed algorithmic mechanism design: recent results and future directions. In: DIAL-M 2002, pp. 1–13. https://doi.org/10.1145/570810.570812

7. Fineman, J.T., Newport, C.C., Sherr, M., Wang, T.: Fair maximal independent sets. In: IPDPS 2014, pp. 712–721. https://doi.org/10.1109/IPDPS.2014.79

8. Fudenberg, D., Tirole, J.: Game theory (3. pr.). MIT Press (1991)

9. Ghaffari, M., Grunau, C.: Near-optimal deterministic network decomposition and ruling set, and improved MIS . In: FOCS 2024, pp. 2148–2179. https://doi.ieeecomputersociety.org/10.1109/FOCS61266.2024.00007

10. Gong, T., Liu, Z.: Rational secret sharing with competition. IACR Cryptol. ePrint Arch., p. 242 (2025). https://eprint.iacr.org/2025/242

11. Halpern, J.Y., Teague, V.: Rational secret sharing and multiparty computation: Extended abstract. CoRR (2006). http://arxiv.org/abs/cs/0609035

12. Hirvonen, J., Ranjbaran, S.: Designing local distributed mechanisms. CoRR (2024). https://doi.org/10.48550/arXiv.2411.06788

13. Linial, N.: Distributive graph algorithms-global solutions from local data. In: SFCS, pp. 331–335 (1987). https://doi.org/10.1109/SFCS.1987.20

14. Luby, M.: A simple parallel algorithm for the maximal independent set problem. In: Proceedings of the 17th Annual ACM Symposium on Theory of Computing, pp. 1–10. ACM (1985). https://doi.org/10.1145/22145.22146

15. Maleka, S., Shareef, A., Rangan, C.P.: The deterministic protocol for rational secret sharing. In: IPDPS 2008, pp. 1–7. https://doi.org/10.1109/IPDPS.2008.4536558

16. Métivier, Y., Robson, J.M., Saheb-Djahromi, N., Zemmari, A.: An optimal bit complexity randomized distributed MIS algorithm. Distributed Comput. 23(5-6), 331–340 (2011). https://doi.org/10.1007/s00446-010-0121-5

17. Nisan, N.: Algorithms for selfish agents. In: Meinel, C., Tison, S. (eds.) STACS 1999. LNCS, vol. 1563, pp. 1–15. Springer, Heidelberg (1999). https://doi.org/10.1007/3-540-49116-3_1

18. Osborne, M.J., Rubinstein, A.: A Course in game theory. The MIT Press, Cambridge, MA (1994). https://sites.math.rutgers.edu/~zeilberg/EM20/OsborneRubinsteinMasterpiece.pdf

19. Rivest, R.L., Shamir, A., Adleman, L.M.: A method for obtaining digital signatures and public-key cryptosystems. Commun. ACM 21(2), 120–126 (1978). https://doi.org/10.1145/359340.359342

20. Salevemula, N., Pai, S.: Distributed MIS algorithms for rational agents using games. CoRR (2025). https://doi.org/10.48550/arXiv.2511.16533

21. Yen, L., Huang, J., Turau, V.: Designing self-stabilizing systems using game theory. ACM Trans. Auton. Adapt. Syst. 11(3), 18:1–18:27 (2016). https://doi.org/10.1145/2957760

22. Yen, L.-H., Sun, G.-H.: Game-theoretic approach to self-stabilizing minimal independent dominating sets. In: Xiang, Y., Sun, J., Fortino, G., Guerrieri, A., Jung, J.J. (eds.) IDCS 2018. LNCS, vol. 11226, pp. 173–184. Springer, Cham (2018). https://doi.org/10.1007/978-3-030-02738-4_15

Uniform Deployment of Myopic Luminous Robots in Rings

Masahiro Shibata[1]($\boxtimes$), Sayaka Kamei[2], Fukuhito Ooshita[3],
and Hirotsugu Kakugawa[4]

[1] Kyushu Institute of Technology, Iizuka, Fukuoka, Japan
`shibata@csn.kyutech.ac.jp`
[2] Hiroshima University, Higashi Hiroshima, Hiroshima, Japan
`s10kamei@hiroshima-u.ac.jp`
[3] University of Hyogo, Kobe, Hyogo, Japan
`f-oosita@gsis.u-hyogo.ac.jp`
[4] Ryukoku University, Otsu, Shiga, Japan
`kakugawa@rins.ryukoku.ac.jp`

Abstract. In this paper, we consider the uniform deployment problem of myopic luminous robots in rings, requiring them to spread uniformly in the ring. Robots are myopic if they have a common limited visibility range and robots are luminous if hey are equipped with a light device that can emit a color from a finite set. The past related research considered uniform deployment for myopic and oblivious robots. Here, robots are oblivious if they have no memory and cannot memorize the history of past actions. In this case, it is shown that quiescent uniform deployment, requiring that robots stop moving after they reached a uniformly deployed configuration but they are allowed to resume moving when observing some configuration changes, is impossible. In this paper, we consider the feasibility of the uniform deployment problem by introducing lights. Let n be the number of nodes and k be the number of robots. First, we show that, even if robots behave fully synchronously and have an infinite number of light colors, they cannot achieve uniform deployment when either of the followings holds: *(i)* they do not have a common sense of direction, *(ii)* the visibility range is less than $\lfloor n/k \rfloor$, or *(iii)* the problem requires explicit termination detection. Next, for robots that behave semi-synchronously and have a common sense of direction and visibility range at least $\lfloor n/k \rfloor$, we propose an algorithm to solve the quiescent uniform deployment problem, by allowing robots to be luminous and have a constant number of light colors. This is a striking difference compared to the past result for oblivious robots.

Keywords: mobile robots · uniform deployment · myopic · luminous

1 Introduction

Background. Autonomous mobile robots aim to achieve some tasks with limited capabilities [1]. Most studies assume that robots are identical (they execute

C. Georgiou (Ed.): SIROCCO 2026, LNCS 16488, pp. 509–526, 2026.
https://doi.org/10.1007/978-3-032-26465-7_27

the same algorithm and cannot be distinguished by their appearance) and oblivious (they cannot remember their past actions). In addition, it is assumed that robots cannot communicate with others explicitly. Instead, they communicate implicitly using their positions.

There are a lot of studies considering problem solvability for the above robots in continuous environments (*a.k.a.* Euclidean space) [1,2], or in discrete environments (*a.k.a.* graphs) [3–8]. While classical robots are assumed to be oblivious, *luminous* robots have been considered. They are equipped with a light device that can emit a single non-volatile color from a constant number of colors visible to itself and other robots. Since the light color is non-volatile, it can be used as a constant space memory. The notion of luminous robots was introduced by Das et al. [9] with the initial goal to circumvent impossibility results that hold for oblivious robots in the continuous space. D'Emidio et al. [10] consider the solvability of several problems for luminous robots in the graph environment.

As an example of robots' coordination, the *uniform deployment* problem has been studied as a fundamental problem. This problem requires robots to spread uniformly in the network. Uniform deployment is useful in practice: when robots achieve uniform deployment, they can maximize the coverage area and execute some task such as patrolling, environment monitoring, and intruder detection efficiently [11]. The uniform deployment problem for mobile robots has been considered in cycles (*i.e.*, the continuous model) [12], and rings [13] and grids (*i.e.*, the discrete model) [11,14 16]. Notice that, while robots in the continuous space can freely move to a designated point in one movement, *e.g.*, an extremely close point or a faraway point from the current point, robots in the discrete space can move only to a neighboring node in one movement. Hence, designing algorithms for the discrete space is more challenging. In [11,13,14], robots are assumed to be *myopic*, that is, they have some common limited visibility range ϕ, which is a strictly weaker assumption than that for classical robots with unlimited visibility. For myopic and luminous robots, in [15,16], uniform deployment in grids is considered and is shown that robots can achieve it faster [15] or better [16]. Other than rings and grids, Shibata and Tixeuil [17] considered uniform deployment for luminous robots in a special kind of trees called *perfect ℓ-ary trees*, where every intermediate node has ℓ children and all leaf nodes have the same depth.

Although uniform deployment has been considered in rings, grids, and (a kind of) trees, to the best of our knowledge, the problem for myopic and luminous robots in ring networks has not been considered.

Our Contribution. In this paper, we consider the uniform deployment problem of myopic, opaque, and luminous robots in rings. We say that robots are *opaque* if robot r_i cannot observe robot r_j even within the visibility range when another robot r_h exists between r_i and r_j. The most related research is by Elor and Bruckstein [13]. They considered *quiescent* uniform deployment for myopic and oblivious robots. Here, intuitively, in the quiescent uniform deployment, when robots recognize that they reach a uniformly deployed configuration, they need to stop moving thereafter but are allowed to resume moving when observing some configuration changes. Even with this requirement, they showed that the problem is impossible. In this paper, we consider the feasibility of the uniform deployment problem by introducing lights. Let n be the number of nodes and k be the number of robots. First, by applying the impossibility results in [13] for oblivious robots to luminous robots, we show that, even if robots behave fully synchronously and have an infinite number of light colors, they cannot achieve uniform deployment when either of the followings holds: *(i)* they do not have a common sense of direction, *(ii)* the visibility range is less than $\lfloor n/k \rfloor$, or *(iii)* the problem requires explicit termination detection. Notice that, when explicit termination detection is required, robots need to eventually declare the execution termination and never move thereafter. Hence, uniform deployment with explicit termination detection is more difficult than the quiescent one. Next, for robots that behave semi-synchronously and have a common sense of direction and visibility range at least $\lfloor n/k \rfloor$, we propose an algorithm to solve the quiescent uniform deployment problem, by allowing robots to be luminous and use 20 light colors. This is a striking difference compared to the past result for oblivious robots. Notice that, since robots are myopic, it is possible that some robot never detects the existence of other robots in an unbalanced initial configuration. Even in this case, by using constant number of light colors, robots can reach a balanced (uniformly deployed) configuration, which is an interesting point. Due to the page limit, we omit to describe several proofs of lemmas and theorems.

2   Preliminaries

System Models. The system comprises n nodes and k robots. The nodes $v_0, v_1, \ldots, v_{n-1}$ construct a bidirected ring in this order. For simplicity, we consider mathematical operations to indices of nodes as operations modulo n. The *distance* between nodes v_p and v_q is defined as $\min(p - q, q - p)$. We call the direction from v_i to v_{i+1} (resp., v_i to v_{i-1}) the *forward* direction (resp., *backward* direction). Neither nodes nor links have any labels, and consequently robots cannot distinguish nodes and links.

We consider a set of k robots with the following characteristics and capabilities. Robots are *identical*, that is, they execute the same algorithm. Robots are *luminous*, that is, each robot has a device that can emit a light color (or state) visible to itself and others, from a discrete set *Col*. We denote by κ ($= |Col|$) the number of available colors. Note that, when $\kappa = 1$, robots are equal to being oblivious. Robots do not have other persistent memory and cannot remember the history of past actions. Robots do not have global knowledge such as k or n. Robots have a *common sense of direction*, that is, they agree on the forward and backward directions in the ring (we briefly describe why such an assumption is necessary in the next section). Robots are *myopic*, that is, they have *limited visibility range* ϕ and can observe information (*e.g..*, existence of a robot and its color if any) at each node within distance ϕ. However, robots are *opaque*, that is, even if robots r_i and r_j are within distance ϕ, they cannot observe each other when another robot r_h exists between r_i and r_j. We say that robots r_i and r_j are *adjacent* if there is no robot between them. Robots cannot communicate with others

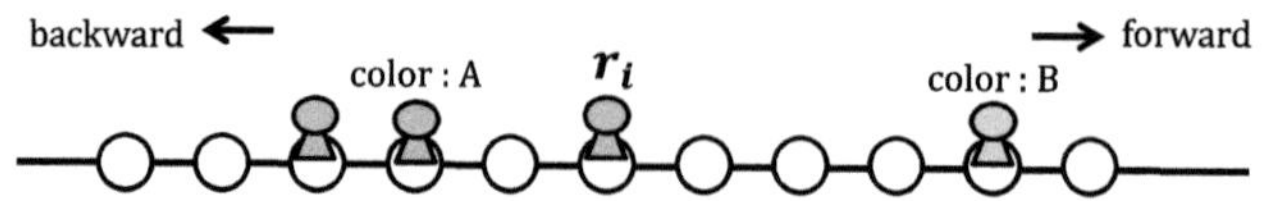

Fig. 1. Example of r_i's view.

explicitly, but they can communicate implicitly by observing positions and light colors of other robots (for collecting information), and by changing their light colors and moving (for sending information). Concretely, when collecting information, each robot r_i uses the $view_i$ information represented by the following 3-tuple: $view_i = ((bDis_i, bCol_i), col_i, (fDis_i, fCol_i))$, where $bDis_i$ (resp., $fDis_i$) is the distance to the backward (resp., forward) adjacent robot, $bCol_i$ (resp., $fCol_i$) is the light color emitted by the backward (resp., forward) adjacent robot, and col_i is the light color emitted by r_i itself. When the distance to the backward (resp., forward) adjacent robot is more than ϕ, $(bDis_i, bCol_i) = (\infty, \perp)$ (resp., $(fDis_i, fCol_i) = (\infty, \perp)$) holds. For example, in Fig. 1, $view_i = ((2, B), A, (4, A))$ (resp., $view_i = ((2, B), A, (\infty, \perp))$) holds when $\phi \geq 4$ (resp., when $\phi = 2, 3$). We assume that robots know the value of ϕ.

Each robot r_i executes the algorithm by repeating *Look-Compute-Move (LCM) cycles*. At the beginning of each cycle, r_i gets the view information mentioned above (Look phase). According to the observation, r_i computes the destination to move (possibly the current node, which implies r_i remains at the node) and changes its light color as necessary (Compute phase). If r_i decides to move, it moves to the node by the end of the cycle (Move phase). We introduce the notion of a *scheduler* that decides when each robot executes the phases. When the scheduler makes robot r execute some phases, we say the scheduler *activates* r. In this paper, we consider two types of synchronicity models: the FSYNC (fully synchronous) model and the SSYNC (semi-synchronous) model. In the *FSYNC model*, at each time step, all robots are activated and they execute an LCM cycle synchronously and concurrently. In the *SSYNC model*, at each time step, a scheduler activates a non-empty set of robots and the selected robots execute the cycle synchronously and concurrently. In this model, we assume that the scheduler is *fair*, that is, each robot is activated infinitely often. In the SSYNC model, we consider the scheduler as an adversary, that is, we assume that the scheduler is omniscient (it knows robot positions, algorithms, etc.), and tries to activate robots in such a way that they fail to execute the task.

A configuration C of the system is defined by the position and light color of all robots. In initial configuration C_0, all robots emit the same light color (or they are in the same state) and are placed at distinct nodes (but their placement is decided by the adversary). Throughout the algorithm execution, we assume that robots stay at some nodes (not on links). For an infinite sequence of configurations $E = C_0, C_1, \ldots, C_t, \ldots$ we say E is a fair execution from initial configuration C_0 if, for every instant t, C_{t+1} is obtained from C_t after a fair scheduler activates a non-empty subset of robots and they execute an LCM cycle. We say C_i is the i-th configuration of execution E.

Problem Definition. The *uniform deployment problem* requires robots to spread uniformly in the ring, that is, they should reach a configuration such that the distance between every adjacent robots is $\lfloor n/k \rfloor$ or $\lceil n/k \rceil$. In this paper, we consider two kinds of the uniform deployment problem: *explicitly terminating uniform deployment* and *quiescent uniform deployment*. In explicitly terminating uniform deployment, when robots recognize that they reach a uniformly deployed configuration, they emit a corresponding light color and declare the execution termination (*i.e.*, they never move thereafter). On the other hand, in quiescent uniform deployment, robots are allowed to resume moving when observing some configuration changes. We define the problems as follows.

Definition 1. *An algorithm solves the* explicitly terminating *uniform deployment problem iff every execution reaches a configuration such that, all robots emit a light color declaring the execution termination and never move thereafter. In the configuration, the distance between every adjacent robots is $\lfloor n/k \rfloor$ or $\lceil n/k \rceil$.*

Definition 2. *An algorithm solves the* quiescent *uniform deployment problem iff every execution reaches a configuration where the distance between every adjacent robots is $\lfloor n/k \rfloor$ or $\lceil n/k \rceil$ and no robot moves thereafter.*

3   Impossibility Results

In [13], it is shown that myopic oblivious robots cannot achieve uniform deployment if they do not have a common sense of direction or visibility range ϕ is less than $\lfloor n/k \rfloor$. These impossibilities also hold for luminous robots by similar proofs of those in [13]. The first impossibility is intuitively because, when robots do not have a common sense of direction, there exists a non-uniform initial configuration such that all robots get the same view information and the distance between adjacent robots do not change or oscillate during the execution.

Theorem 1. *When robots do not have a common sense of direction, there is no algorithm that achieves uniform deployment even for FSYNC robots with infinite visibility range and infinite number of light colors.*

The second impossibility is intuitively because there exists a non-uniform initial configuration from which robots never detect the existence of an adjacent robot (*i.e.*, the distance to an adjacent robot is ∞), and even if they continue to move in some direction or keep staying, the distance to adjacent robots are still ∞ (not one for uniform deployment).

Theorem 2. *When $\phi < \lfloor n/k \rfloor$, there is no algorithm that achieves uniform deployment even for FSYNC robots with a common sense of direction and infinite number of light colors.*

Next, we show that robots cannot achieve explicitly terminating uniform deployment. This impossibility holds intuitively because, when considering two executions E and E' such that (i) in E, k robots are already deployed uniformly in an n-node ring $\mathcal{R}$ with $n = dk$ for some positive integer d, and (ii) in E', k' robots are deployed in an n'-node ring $\mathcal{R}'$ with $n' = 3dk'$ so that almost all of the distances between adjacent robots are d, then several adjacent robots in E' execute in the exactly same way as that for a robot in E and they terminate the algorithm execution so that the distance between them is d, which violates the condition of uniform deployment in E'.

Theorem 3. *There is no algorithm that achieves explicitly terminating uniform deployment even for FSYNC robots with a common sense of direction, infinite visibility range, and infinite number of light colors.*

4   Proposed Algorithm

In this section, we propose an algorithm to solve the quiescent uniform deployment problem for SSYNC robots with visibility range at least $\lfloor n/k \rfloor$ and 20 light colors. By Theorem 2, this algorithm is visibility-optimal. At the beginning of the execution, all robots emit the same light color F (First). Robots first execute the phase named *base-electing phase* and then repeat the two phases named *interval-adjusting phase* and *merging phase*. In the base-electing phase, we elect some robot(s) as a *base*. After the election, robots are divided into groups each of whose most forward robot is a base. In the interval-adjusting phase, robots other than a base move and adjust distance intervals in their group, basically by increasing distances between adjacent robots one by one. When adjusting, a robot may observe a base robot in another group. In this case, after moving appropriately, robots enter the merging phase and two groups are merged into one group because the two groups may use different distance intervals and the configuration in that case is not a uniformly deployed one. In the following, we explain the details of each phase.

4.1   Base-Electing Phase

Each robot determines whether or not it becomes a base using distances between adjacent robots and light colors of the robots. Intuitively, we select robot r_i as a base when *(i)* the distance to its backward adjacent robot r^i_{back} is smaller than that to its forward adjacent robot and *(ii)* r^i_{back} recognizes that the distance to its backward adjacent robot is not smaller than that to its forward adjacent robot (*i.e..*, r_i). To this end, each robot r_i with light color F first compares the distance $bDis_i$ to the backward adjacent robot with the distance $fDis_i$ to the forward adjacent robot. When $bDis_i < \infty$ and $fDis_i = \infty$, r_i changes its light color to B (Base). When $bDis_i < fDis_i$ ($< \infty$) (resp., $bDis_i > fDis_i$), r_i changes its light color to C (Candidate) (resp., NB (Non-Base)). When $bDis_i = fDis_i < \infty$, r_i changes its light color to E (Equal), and when $bDis_i = fDis_i = \infty$, r_i changes

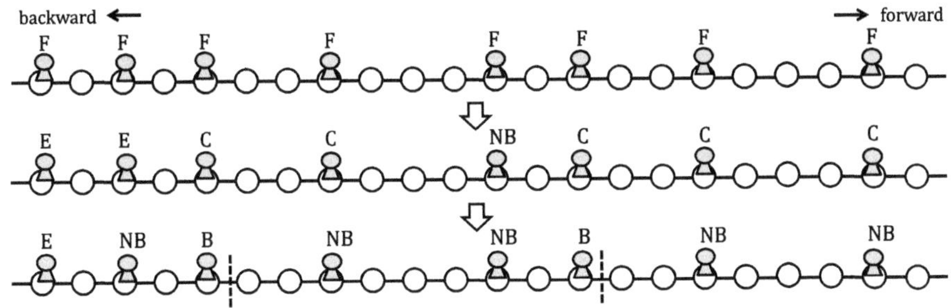

Fig. 2. Execution example of the base-electing phase (when $\phi \geq 4$).

its light color to NB and remains at the current node (it joins the forward group in the next section). Thereafter, a robot with light color B keeps its color (and enters the interval-adjusting phase). On the other hand, when its light color is C, if the color $bCol_i$ of its backward adjacent robot is NB or E and if the color $fCol_i$ of its forward adjacent robot is not B, r_i changes its light color to B. Otherwise, it changes its color to NB and enters the interval-adjusting phase. When its light color is E, if $bCol_i = E$ and $fCol_i = E$, r_i keeps the color E. Otherwise, r_i changes its color to NB. Notice that, when the initial configuration C_0 is an already uniformly deployed one, all robots emit the light color E and keep staying at their current node. This means that they already achieve quiescent uniform deployment. Hence, in the following, we assume that C_0 is not a uniformly deployed one. An example is given in Fig. 2. In this case, robots are divided into groups each of whose most forward robot emits the light color B (dashed lines in the figure). By this behavior, we can show in Lemma 1 that at least one robot changes its light color to B and the other robots emit the color NB unless C_0 is a uniformly deployed one.

The pseudocode of the base-electing phase is described in Algorithm 1. For the readability, we express robot r_i's action as (col_i, dir_i), where $col_i = \{Col, -\}$ represents the light color and $dir_i = \{\rightarrow, \leftarrow, -\}$ represents the moving direction for the current round. In col_i, "$-$" means that r_i keeps the current light color. In dir_i, "$\rightarrow$" (resp., "$\leftarrow$") means moving forward (resp., backward), and "$-$" means staying at the current node. Notice that, when r_i's light color is C or E, it is possible that the light color of its adjacent forward or backward robot is still F. In this case, to correctly judge its next behavior, r_i waits until the corresponding robot changes its light color (lines 8 to 14).

Concerning the base-electing phase, we have the following lemma.

Lemma 1. *After all robots terminate the base-electing phase, at least one robot emits the light color B and the other robots emit the light color NB unless C_0 is a uniformly deployed one.*

Algorithm 1: Base-electing phase

```
 1  // Behavior when its light color is F (First)
 2  if col_i = F then
 3      if (bDis_i < ∞) ∧ (fDis_i = ∞) then (B, −)
 4      else if bDis_i < fDis_i (< ∞) then (C, −)
 5      else if bDis_i > fDis_i then (NB, −)
 6      else if bDis_i = fDis_i < ∞ then (E, −)
 7      else if bDis_i = fDis_i = ∞ then (NB, −)
 8  // Behavior when its light color is C (Candidate)
 9  if col_i = C then
10      if (bCol_i = NB) ∨ (bCol_i = E) ∧ (fCol_i ≠ B) ∧ (fCol_i ≠ F) then (B, −)
11      else if (bCol_i ≠ F) ∧ (fCol_i ≠ F) then (NB, −)
12  // Behavior when its light color is E (Equal)
13  if col_i = E then
14      if (bCol_i = NB, B, or C) ∨ (fCol_i = NB, B, or C) then (NB, −)
```

4.2   Interval-Adjusting Phase

In this phase, each group adjusts distance intervals in the group. Concretely, robots in the group first move so that the distance between adjacent robots becomes 2 and then increase the distances one by one. To this end, like (a) to (b) of Fig. 3, each robot r_i with light color NB moves forward when $fDis_i \geq 3$. Notice that it is possible that r_i's backward adjacent robot becomes invisible if r_i moves forward when $bDis_i = \phi$. To avoid this, r_i waits until $bDis_i < \phi$ holds. When $fDis_i = 1$, r_i tries to move backward if the node is empty, to avoid a situation such that robots with light color NB stay at consecutive nodes and they cannot make the distance between them 2. When robot r_i with light color NB recognizes that the adjacent forward robot r_b emits the light color B, it stays at the node whose distance to r_b is 2 and emits the light color I2-A (Interval Increase A). Thereafter, like (b) to (c) of Fig. 3, similar to the above robot, a robot whose forward adjacent robot $r_{I2\text{-}A}$ emits the light color I2-A stays at a node with distance 2 to $r_{I2\text{-}A}$, emits the light color I2-A, and keeps staying at the current node. In a way that intermediate robots repeat such behaviors, the distance interval between robots in the group becomes 2. The most backward robot r_{back} in the group (*e.g.*, robot r_{back} with $bDis_{back} = \infty$) also stays at a node with distance 2 to the forward adjacent robot with light color $r_{I2\text{-}A}$. Thereafter, based on r_{back}, robots increase the distance interval in their group one by one as follows.

First, like (b) to (c) of Fig. 3, r_{back} emits the light color I2-B (Interval-Increase B), and moves to a backward neighboring node. When a robot r_i recognizes $bCol_i =$ I2-B, like (c) to (d) of Fig. 3, it also changes its light color to I2-B and moves to a backward neighboring node. Each intermediate robot r_i with $bCol_i =$ I2-B, $fCol_i =$ I2-A, and $bDis_i = fDis_i + 1$ repeats the above behaviors. On the other hand, like (d) to (e) of Fig. 3, the robot r_i with $fCol_i =$ B and $bDis_i = fDis_i + 1$ changes its light color I2-C and moves to a backward neighboring node. In this case, for this example, the distance between the robot with light color B and its backward robot is 3, and the other distances between robots in their group are 2. Thereafter, except for the most backward robot r_{back}, robot r_i with

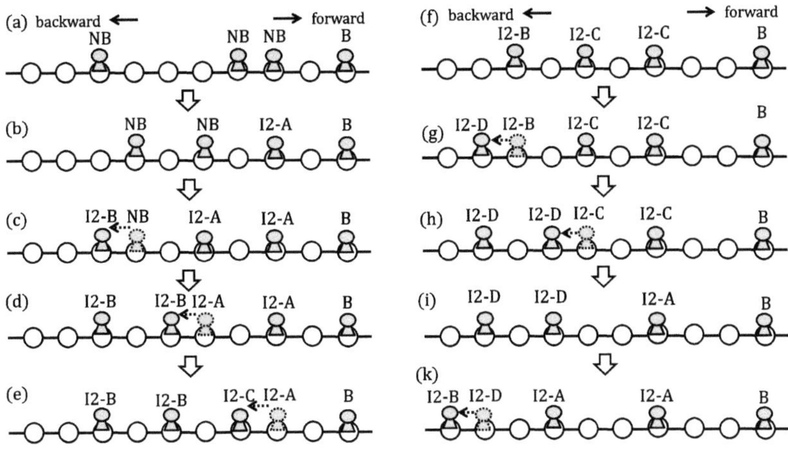

Fig. 3. Execution example of the interval-adjusting phase.

$fCol_i = $ I2-C changes its light color to I2-C, like (e) to (f) of Fig. 3. When r_{back} observes the color I2-C, like (f) to (g) of Fig. 3, it changes its light color to I2-D and moves to a backward neighboring node. Thereafter, each intermediate robot r_i with $bCol_i = $ I2-D, $fCol_i = $ I2-C, and $bDis_i = fDis_i + 1$ (resp., $bDis_i = fDis_i$) conveys its behavior by changing its light color to I2-D and moving to a backward neighboring node, like (g) to (h) of Fig. 3 (resp., remaining at the current node). When the robot r_i recognizes $bCol_i = $ I2-D, $fCol_i = $ B, and $bDis_i = fDis_i$ (resp., $bDis_i = fDis_i + 1$), it changes its light color to I2-A and remains at the current node, like (h) to (i) of Fig. 3 (resp., moves to a backward neighboring node). In this case, for this example, the distance between the robot r_b with light color B and its backward robot r_{back}^b is 3, the distance between r_{back}^b and its backward robot is 3, and the other distances between robots in their group is 2. Thereafter, like (i) to (k) of Fig. 3, each intermediate robot changes its light color to I2-A when it observes the color I2-A, and r_{back} changes its light color to I2-B and moves backward when it observes the color I2-A. Robots repeat the above behavior and increase their distance intervals one by one.

During the movement, eventually or from the beginning of this phase, the most backward robot r_{back} detects an existence of a robot r_a in the backward direction (*i.e.*, $bDis_{back} < \infty$). In this case, r_a is either *(i)* a robot that did not recognize the existence of adjacent robots in the base-electing phase (*i.e.*, $bDis_a = fDis_a = \infty$), or *(ii)* a base robot emitting the light color B. In case *(i)*, r_{back} (and the other robots in its group) first repeats the above behavior until $bDis_{back} = fDis_{back}$ or $bDis_{back} = fDis_{back} - 1$ holds, to smoothly perform the next behavior. Thereafter, r_{back} gives its role to r_a, that is, r_{back} becomes an intermediate robot and r_a becomes the most backward robot in the group. To this end, r_{back} changes its light color to what its forward adjacent robot emits (I2-A or I2-C). When r_a detects r_{back}'s color change to I2-A (resp., I2-C), it changes its light color to I2-B (resp., I2-D), becomes the most backward robot in the group, and the group continues to increase distance intervals. We briefly show in Lemma 2, after the behavior, $fDis_a$ is equal to the distance used in r_{back}'s group. In case *(ii)*, that is, when r_a emits the light color B, r_{back} (the other robots in the group) continues to perform the interval-adjusting phase until $bDis_{back} = fDis_{back}$ or $bDis_{back} = fDis_{back} + 1$ holds. Thereafter, r_{back} changes its light color to M (Merge) and enters the merging phase.

The pseudocode of the interval-adjusting phase is described in Algorithm 2. Notice that, in Algorithm 2, when r_i's light color is NB, it is possible that its backward adjacent robot is still executing the base-electing phase. In this case, r_i waits until the backward robot changes its light color in order to smoothly proceed executions (line 3). In addition, it is possible that, some robot r_i first recognizes $fCol_i = bCol_i = \infty$ in the base-electing phase, and then sets $col_i = NB$ in the former part of the interval-adjusting phase. In this case, r_i does not move until it detects the existence of a forward adjacent robot and the robot changes its light color to one telling r_i to move (or just change its light color), to smoothly perform the next behavior (lines 3, 6, and 7). Moreover, robots may observe light colors observed in the merging phase. To treat the colors, robots execute procedure *Adjust()*. The pseudocode of *Adjust()* is described in Algorithm 3. We describe how to use these colors in Sect. 4.3.

Concerning the interval-adjusting phase, we have the following lemma.

Lemma 2. *At least one robot changes its light color to M by the interval-adjusting phase unless C_0 is a uniformly deployed one.*

Proof. Let r_{back} be a most backward robot in a group and r_a (resp., r_{back+1}) be r_{back}'s backward (resp., forward) adjacent robot. In this case, There are two cases of the light color emitted by r_a: (A) the color NB and (B) the color B. We consider the cases in this order.

In case (A), by Algorithms 1 and 2, we can observe that (i) r_a and r_{back+1} do not move at the round when r_{back} moves, and (ii) r_{back} moves backward one by one, the value of $bDis_{back}$ decreases by one and the value of $fDis_{back}$ increases by one at each round when r_{back} moves. Thereafter, r_{back+1} moves (resp., does not move) backward when $bDis_{back+1} = fDis_{back+1} + 1$ (resp., $bDis_{back+1} = fDis_{back+1}$) holds (see Fig. 4(a) and (b), respectively). By these observations, when r_{back} moves backward and r_{back+1} finishes the behavior treating r_{back}'s movement, eventually $bDis_{back} = fDis_{back}$ or $bDis_{back} = fDis_{back} - 1$ holds. In the former case (Fig. 4(a)), all the distances in the group, including $bDis_{back}$ are the same. Hence, r_{back} gives its role to r_a and the group continues the behavior. In the latter case (Fig. 4(b)), when r_{back} gives its role to r_a, then r_a firstly moves backward and thereafter r_{back} finishes the behavior treating the movement by r_a, without moving. Hence, similarly to the former case, the new group can continue the behavior.

Next, we consider the case (B), that is, r_a emits the light color B. Notice that there exists at least one such robot by Lemma 1. In this case, r_{back} (an the other robots in the group) continues to move backward. Then, by considering the moving tactics described in the previous paragraph, eventually $bDis_{back} =$

Algorithm 2: Interval-adjusting phase

1 // Behavior when its light color is NB (Non-Base)
2 **if** $col_i = NB$ **then**
3   **if** $(3 \leq fDis_i < \infty) \wedge (fCol_i \neq$ I2-B or I2-D$) \wedge (bDis_i = \infty) \vee (bCol_i = B) \vee$ $((bCol_i = NB) \wedge (bDis_i < \phi))$ **then** $(-, \rightarrow)$
4   **else if** $(fDis_i = 1) \wedge (bDis_i \geq 2)$ **then** $(-, \leftarrow)$
5   **else if** $(fDis_i = 2) \wedge (fCol_i = B$ or I2-A$)$ **then** (I2-A, $-$)
6   **else if** $(fCol_i =$ I2-A$) \wedge (bDis_i = \infty) \vee (bCol_i = B)$ **then** (I2-B, $\leftarrow$)
7   **else if** $(fCol_i =$ I2-C$) \wedge (bDis_i = \infty) \vee (bCol_i = B)$ **then** (I2-D, $\leftarrow$)

8 // Behavior when its light color is I2-A (Interval-Increasing A)
9 **if** $col_i =$ I2-A **then**
10   **if** $bCol_i =$ I2-B **then**
11   **if** $(fCol_i =$ I2-A$) \wedge (bDis_i > fDis_i)$ **then** (I2-B, $\leftarrow$)
12   **else if** $(fCol_i =$ I2-A$) \wedge (bDis_i = fDis_i)$ **then** (I2-B, $-$)
13   **else if** $(fCol_i = B) \wedge (bDis_i > fDis_i)$ **then** (I2-C, $\leftarrow$)
14   **else if** $(fCol_i = B) \wedge (bDis_i = fDis_i)$ **then** (I2-C, $-$)
15      $Adjust()$

16 // Behavior when its light color is I2-B (Interval-Increasing B)
17 **if** $col_i =$ I2-B **then**
18   **if** $fCol_i =$ I2-C **then**
19   **if** $(bCol_i = B) \wedge (bDis_i = fDis_i$ or $fDis_i + 1)$ **then** (M, $-$)
20   **else if** $(bCol_i = NB) \wedge (bDis_i = fDis_i$ or $fDis_i - 1)$ **then** (I2-C, $-$)
21   **else if** $(bDis_i = \infty) \vee (bCol_i = NB) \vee (bCol_i = B)$ **then** (I2-D, $\leftarrow$)
22   **else** (I2-C, $-$)
23      $Adjust()$

24 // Behavior when its light color is I2-C (Interval-Increasing C)
25 **if** $col_i =$ I2-C **then**
26   **if** $bCol_i =$ I2-D **then**
27   **if** $(fCol_i =$ I2-C$) \wedge (bDis_i > fDis_i)$ **then** (I2-D, $\leftarrow$)
28   **else if** $(fCol_i =$ I2-C$) \wedge (bDis_i = fDis_i)$ **then** (I2-D, $-$)
29   **else if** $(fCol_i = B) \wedge (bDis_i > fDis_i)$ **then** (I2-A, $\leftarrow$)
30   **else if** $(fCol_i = B) \wedge (bDis_i = fDis_i)$ **then** (I2-A, $-$)
31      $Adjust()$

32 // Behavior when its light color is I2-D (Interval-Increasing D)
33 **if** $col_i =$ I2-D **then**
34   **if** $fCol_i =$ I2-A **then**
35   **if** $(bCol_i = B) \wedge (bDis_i = fDis_i$ or $fDis_i + 1)$ **then** (M, $-$)
36   **else if** $(bCol_i = NB) \wedge (bDis_i = fDis_i$ or $fDis_i - 1)$ **then** (I2-A, $-$)
37   **else if** $(bDis_i = \infty) \vee (bCol_i = NB) \vee (bCol_i = B)$ **then** (I2-B, $\leftarrow$)
38   **else** (I2-A, $-$)
39      $Adjust()$

Algorithm 3: Procedure $Adjust()$

1 **if** $(bCol_i = RI) \wedge (bDis_i = \phi)$ **then** $(-, \leftarrow)$
2 **if** $(fCol_i = RI) \wedge (fDis_i = \phi)$ **then** $(-, \rightarrow)$
3 **if** $(fCol_i = MF) \vee (bCol_i = MB)$ **then** (RI, $-$)
4 **if** $(fCol_i = ME$ or $RM)$ **then** (ME, $-$)
5 **if** $(bCol_i = Q) \vee (fCol_i = Q)$ **then** (Q, $-$)

$fDis_{back} + 3$ or $bDis_{back} = fDis_{back} + 2$ holds. When $bDis_{back} = fDis_{back} + 3$, after r_{back} moves backward and thereafter r_{back+1} moves backward (resp., does not move backward), $bDis_{back} = fDis_{back} + 2$ (resp., $bDis_{back} = fDis_{back} + 1$) holds. When $bDis_{back} = fDis_{back} + 2$, after r_{back} moves backward and thereafter r_{back+1} moves backward (resp., does not move backward), $bDis_{back} = fDis_{back} + 1$ (resp.,

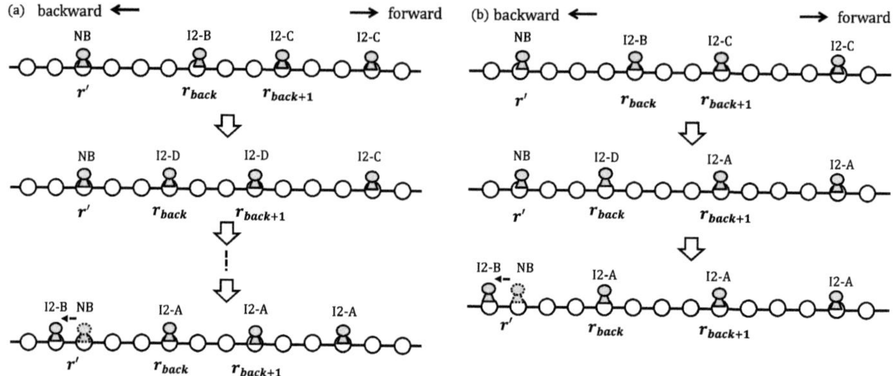

Fig. 4. Execution example that r_{back} detects the existence of r_a.

$bDis_{back} = fDis_{back}$) holds. In either case, by lines 19 and 35 of Algorithm 2, r_{back} changes its light color to M.

Therefore, the lemma holds. □

4.3 Merging Phase

In this section, several groups (if any) are merged into one group. In the previous interval-adjusting phase, each group increases their distance intervals until the most backward robot r_{back} in the group detects an existence of a robot r_a in the backward direction. When r_a emits the light color B and $bDis_{back} = fDis_{back}$ or $bDis_{back} = fDis_{back} + 1$ holds, r_{back} changes its light color to M and starts merging. Let G_b be the group to which r_{back} belongs and G_a be the group to which r_a belongs, and let d_a (resp., d_b) be the distance interval currently used in G_a (resp., G_b). That is, d_a is equal to $bDis_a$ and d_b is equal to $fDis_{back}$. In this case, since each group increases its distance interval independently, the values of d_a and d_b may be different. Then, G_a and G_b are merged so that the distance interval in the new group becomes $\min(d_a, d_b)$. Notice that adopting $\max(d_a, d_b)$ is not appropriate because $\max(d_a, d_b)$ may be already larger than the interval d_{true} which is the value when uniform deployment is achieved. We consider cases *(i)* $d_a > d_b + 1$, *(ii)* $d_a < d_b$, and *(iii)* $d_a = d_b$ or $d_a = d_b + 1$ in this order.

In case *(i)*, robots in G_a move forward to be merged. In this case, when r_a observes a robot with light color M in the forward direction, it compares the distances $bDis_a$ $(= d_a)$ and $fDis_a$ $(= d_b)$ to judge which distance interval is larger. Notice that, in the previous interval-adjusting phase, r_{back} continued to move backward to implicitly inform its distance interval d_b of r_a using $bDis_{back}$ $(= fDis_a)$. In case *(i)* $d_a > d_b + 1$, robot r_a changes its light color to MF (Move Forward), like Fig. 5(a). When the backward robot of r_a, say r_{a-1} (this robot emits light color I2-A, I2-B, I2-C, or I2-D in the interval-adjusting phase) observes the light color MF in the forward direction, it changes its light color to RI (Received Instruction). When r_a observes the color RI, it changes

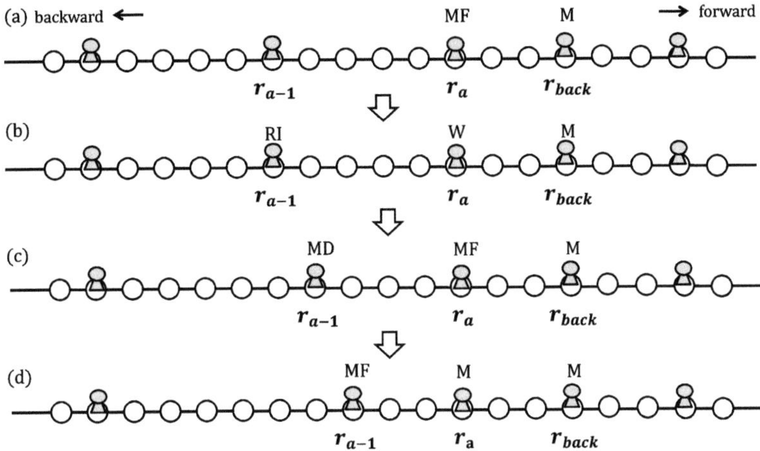

Fig. 5. Execution example of the merging phase.

its light color to W (Waiting), like Fig. 5(b). When r_{a-1} observes the color W, it moves close to r_a (i.e., moves forward), and changes its light color to MD (Movement Done). When r_a observes the light color MD and $bDis_a > fDis_a$ still holds, it changes its light color to MF (Fig. 5(c)). Robots r_a and r_{a-1} repeat the above behavior until $bDis_a = fDis_a$ holds. Thereafter, r_a changes its light color to M (Fig. 5(d)), and then r_{a-1} changes its light color to MF and instructs the backward robot of r_{a-1} about merging that r_a had executed just before. By repeating such behaviors, two groups are merged and the distance interval becomes d_b. At the end of merging, the most backward robot r_{back}^a in group G_a observes the light color M by its forward adjacent robot. In this case, r_{back}^a changes its light color to ME (Merge End), to notify the completion of merging. When each intermediate robot in the group, except for the second most forward robot $r_{sForward}$ (i.e.., the robot whose forward adjacent robot emits the light color B), observes the light color ME, it also changes its light color to ME and conveys the information. When $r_{sForward}$ observes the light color ME, it changes its light color to RM (Resume Moving). Thereafter, each intermediate robot in the group also changes its light color to RM and conveys the information. When r_{back}^a observes the light color RM, it changes its light color to I2-B, enters the interval-adjusting phase again, and the new group resumes increasing the distance interval.

In case *(ii)*, that is, when $d_a < d_b$, robots in G_b move backward to be merged. Basic behaviors are similar to the above case of *(i)*. First, when the robot r_a in group G_a recognizes $bDis_a (= d_a) < fDis_a (= d_b)$, it changes its light color to MB (Move Backward). When the forward adjacent robot of r_a (i.e.., r_{back}) observes the light color MB, r_{back} changes its light color to RI (the same color as that in the above paragraph). Thereafter, r_a changes its light color to W. In the remaining, robots in G_b continue to move backward until the distance interval of the group becomes d_a, in a similar way to the previous paragraph (several supplementary explanations are given later).

Finally, in case *(iii)*, that is, when $d_a = d_b$ or $d_a = d_b + 1$, robot r_a changes its light color to Q (Quiescent) and checks whether or not the current number of robot groups is exactly one. Concretely, when each intermediate robot observes the light color Q, it also changes its light color to Q, except for the case when it observes the light color B in the forward direction. Where there is no such robot observing the light color B, it means that the number of robot groups is already one, since the robot that previously emitted the light color B changed the light color to Q by detecting the above case *(iii)*. In this case, we can show in Lemma 3 that all robots emit the light color Q and the distance between each pair of two adjacent robots is $\lfloor n/k \rfloor$ or $\lceil n/k \rceil$. Otherwise, that is, when some robot r_i observes the light color B, it means that two groups G_a and G_b used the same distance intervals and they are now merged. In this case, since the current number of robot groups may be more than one, and since the current distance intervals may not be correct ones even if the current number of groups becomes one, r_i changes its light color to RM and robots in the group resume moving as described above. Robots repeat the interval-adjusting phase and the merging phase until the current number of the robot groups becomes one and the distance between each pair of adjacent robots becomes $\lfloor n/k \rfloor$ or $\lceil n/k \rceil$.

The pseudocode of the merging phase is described in Algorithm 4. Notice that, when robot r_i emits the light color RI and tries to move forward (resp., backward), it is possible that its backward (resp., forward) adjacent robot becomes invisible if the distance between them is ϕ. To avoid this, the adjacent robot moves close to r_i when it detects the fact (lines 1 and 2 in Algorithm 3). In addition, when robot r_i emitting the light color B recognizes that it needs to change its light color and move backward for merging, in order to memorize that it has emitted the color B, r_i uses light colors RIB (Receive Information Base) and MDB (Movement Done Base) corresponding to colors RI and MD, respectively. When r_i with light color MDB recognizes that its backward movement is completed by the light color M of the backward adjacent robot, it returns its light color to B. Other behaviors of the light colors of RIB and MDB are almost the same as those of RI and MD, respectively, and hence we omit the descriptions of the colors in the pseudocode for simplicity. Moreover, when some robot with some light color recognizes the color RM in the forward direction, it first changes its light color to ME in order to avoid a situation such that the most backward robot in the group also changes its light color to RM and the following behaviors do not proceed (line 4 in Algorithm 3 and line 46 in Algorithm 4). Furthermore, when some robot groups change their light colors to Q in order to merge but need to resume their behaviors thereafter, it is possible that, assuming that the distances used in the merged group are d' and $d' + 1$, the distance sequence of the group is like $(d' \ldots, d', d' + 1, \ldots, d' + 1, d, \ldots d, d' + 1, \ldots, d' + 1)$, that is, the distance $d' + 1$ appears consecutively at two points. In this case, robots may not be able to achieve uniform deployment for the following behaviors. To treat this, when each robot r_i with light color RM recognizes $bDis_i > fDis_i$, it moves

---

Algorithm 4: Merging phase

```
 1  // Behavior when its light color is B (Base)
 2  if col_i = B then
 3        if (fCol_i = M) ∧ (bDis_i > fDis_i + 1) then (MF, −)
 4        else if (fCol_i = M) ∧ (bDis_i < fDis_i) then (MB, −)
 5        else if (fCol_i = M) ∧ (bDis_i = fDis_i or fDis_i + 1) then (Q, −)
 6        else if (bCol_i = RI) ∧ (bDis_i = φ) then (−, ←)
 7        else if (bCol_i = MB) then (RIB, −)

 8  // Behavior when its light color is MF (Move Forward)
 9  if col_i = MF then
10        if bCol_i = RI then (W, −)

11  // Behavior when its light color is MB (Move Backward)
12  if col_i = MB then
13        if fCol_i = RI or RIB then (W, −)

14  // Behavior when its light color is RI (Receive Information)
15  if col_i = RI then
16        if (fCol_i = W) ∧ (bDis_i < φ) then (MD, →)
17        else if (bCol_i = W) ∧ (fDis_i < φ) then (MD, ←)

18  // Behavior when its light color is W (Waiting)
19  if col_i = W then
20        if (bCol_i = MD) ∧ (bDis_i > fDis_i) then (MF, −)
21        else if (bCol_i = MD) ∧ (bDis_i = fDis_i) then (M, −)
22        else if (fCol_i = MD) ∧ (fDis_i > bDis_i) then (MB, −)
23        else if (fCol_i = MD) ∧ (fDis_i = bDis_i) then (M, −)

24  // Behavior when its light color is MD (Movement Done)
25  if col_i = MD then
26        if (fCol_i = M) ∧ (bCol_i = I2-A, I2-B, I2-C, or I2-D) then (MF, −)
27        else if (fCol_i = M) ∧ (bCol_i ≠ I2-A, I2-B, I2-C, or I2-D) then (ME, −)
28        else if (bCol_i = M) ∧ (fCol_i = I2-A, I2-B, I2-C I2-D, or B) then (MB, −)
29        else if (fCol_i = MF) ∨ (bCol_i = MB) then (RI, −)

30  // Behavior when its light color is M (Merge)
31  if col_i = M then
32        if (bCol_i = MB) then (RI, −)
33        else if (bCol_i = ME) ∧ (fCol_i ≠ B) then (ME, −)
34        else if (bCol_i = ME) ∧ (fCol_i = B) then (RM, −)
35        else if (fCol_i = RM) then (ME, −)

36  // Behavior when its light color is ME (Merge Ending)
37  if col_i = ME then
38        if (fCol_i = RM) ∧ (bCol_i = ME or Q) then (RM, −)
39        else if (fCol_i = RM) ∧ (bCol_i ≠ I2-A, I2-B, I2-C, I2-D or M) then (I2-B, −)

40  // Behavior when its light color is RM (Resume Moving)
41  if col_i = RM then
42        if bDis_i > fDis_i then (−, ←)
43        else if bCol_i = I2-B then (I2-B, −)

44  // Behavior when its light color is Q (Quiescent)
45  if col_i = Q then
46        if (fCol_i = B or RM) then (ME, −)
```

---

backward even if its backward adjacent robot emits the color I2-B for resuming increasing distance interval (lines 42 and 43 in Algorithm 4).

Concerning the merging phase, we have the following lemma.

Lemma 3. *If C_0 is not a uniformly deployed one, all robots eventually change their light color to Q. When robots reach such a configuration, the distance between each pair of two adjacent robots is $\lfloor n/k \rfloor$ or $\lceil n/k \rceil$.*

Proof. When the number of current robot groups is more than one, by lines 38 and 46 of Algorithm 4, even when some robots change their light color to Q, they eventually change the light color to ME (and then RM) and resume merging. Hence, the number of robot groups decreases monotonically and eventually becomes one. In the following, we consider light color and the distances between adjacent robots in the case when the number of robot groups is 1.

First, we consider the case when $n \mod k = 0$. We assume that $n = dk$ holds for some positive integer d. Let r_b be a robot emitting a light color B and r_{back} be the most backward robot in the group (*i.e.*, a robot emitting a light color I2-B or I2-D). In this case, r_b and r_{back} are adjacent. We assume that robots $r_b, r_{back}, r_{back+1}, \ldots, r_{last-1}, r_{last}$ exist in this order and let D_{rbOut} (resp., D_{rbIn}) be the distance sequence from r_{back} to r_{back+1}, r_{back+1} to r_{back+2}, and $\ldots, r_{last-1}$ to r_{last} (resp., r_b to r_{back}, r_{back} to $r_{back+1}, \ldots, r_{last-1}$ to r_{last}, and r_{last} to r_b). In this case, by Algorithm 2, when the distance interval at some stage is d_i $(< d)$, D_{rbOut} changes as follows.

$$(d_i, d_i, \ldots, d_i, d_i)$$
$$\to (d_i + 1, d_i, \ldots, d_i) \to (d_i, d_i + 1, \ldots, d_i, d_i) \to \ldots \to (d_i, d_i, \ldots, d_i, d_i + 1)$$
$$\to (d_i + 1, d_i, \ldots, d_i, d_i + 1) \to \ldots \to (d_i, d_i, \ldots, d_i + 1, d_i + 1)$$
$$\to \ldots$$
$$\to (d_i, d_i + 1, \ldots, d_i + 1, d_i + 1)$$
$$\to (d_i + 1, d_i + 1, \ldots, d_i + 1, d_i + 1)$$

Hence, robots eventually reach a configuration that D_{rbIn} becomes $(d + 1, d - 1, d, d, \ldots, d)$. Thereafter, r_{back} eventually moves backward and the sequence becomes $(d, d, \ldots, d)$. Thus, r_b emits the light color Q and the other robots eventually emit the light color Q, satisfying the condition of the lemma.

Next, we consider the case of $n \mod k = 1$. We assume that $n = dk + 1$ holds for some integer d. In this case, by Algorithm 2, D_{rbIn} becomes $(d + 2, d - 1, d, d, \ldots, d)$. Thereafter, similarly to the above case, r_{back} moves backward and the distance sequence becomes $(d + 1, d, d, \ldots, d)$. Hence, r_{back} first changes its light color to Q and the other robots change their light colors to Q, satisfying the condition of the lemma.

Finally, we consider the case of $2 \leq n \mod k \leq k - 1$. We assume that $n = dk + q$ holds for some positive integers d and q $(2 \leq q \leq k - 1)$. In this case, by Algorithm 2, D_{rbIn} becomes $(d + q, d, d, \ldots, d)$. Thereafter, D_{rbIn} changes as follows:

$$(d + q, d, d, \ldots, d)$$
$$\to (d + q - 1, d + 1, d, d \ldots, d)$$
$$\to (d + q - 1, d, d + 1, d \ldots, d)$$
$$\to \ldots$$
$$\to (d + q - 1, d, d, d \ldots, d + 1)$$

Hence, by repeating the behavior, eventually the distance from r_b to r_{back} becomes $d + 2$ and the distance from r_{back} to r_{back+1} becomes d. Thereafter,

r_{back} moves backward and the distance from r_b to r_{back} becomes $d+1$. In addition, several robots among $r_{back+1}, r_{back+2}, \ldots$ move backward and eventually the distance from r_b to r_{back} becomes d. In this case, r_{back} first changes its light color to Q and the other robots changes their light colors to Q. Since each distance between adjacent robot is d or $d+1$, this placement satisfy the condition of uniform deployment.

Therefore, the lemma follows. $\qquad\qquad\square$

Concerning the proposed algorithm, we have the following theorem.

Theorem 4. *The proposed algorithm solves the quiescent uniform deployment problem for SSYNC robots with a common sense of direction, visibility range at least $\lfloor n/k \rfloor$, and 20 light colors.*

5   Conclusion

In this paper, we considered the uniform deployment problem for myopic luminous robots in rings. First, we showed that, even if robots are luminous, they cannot achieve uniform deployment when either of the followings holds: *(i)* they do not have a common sense of direction, *(ii)* visibility range is less than $\lfloor n/k \rfloor$, or *(iii)* the problem requires an explicit termination declaration. Next, we proposed an algorithm to achieve quiescent uniform deployment for SSYNC robots with a common sense of direction, visibility range at least $\lfloor n/k \rfloor$, and 20 light colors.

In future work, we plan to consider whether or not impossibility results hold even if we relax the ability of robots, *e.g.*, robots with distinct IDs of global knowledge such as n. Next, we plan to consider how smaller number of light colors robots can solve the problem when starting from specific initial configurations. Also, we plan to consider the solvability for ASYNC robots (there is no limit in each LCM phase and it can be executed at an arbitrary time).

Acknowledgments. This work was supported in part by JSPS KAKENHI No. JP20KK0232, JP23K11059, JP23K28037, JP25K14995, JP25K03101, and JP25K03078.

References

1. Suzuki, I., Yamashita, M.: Distributed anonymous mobile robots: formation of geometric patterns. SIAM J. Comput. **28**(4), 1347–1363 (1999)
2. Yamauchi, Y., Uehara, T., Kijima, S., Yamashita, M.: Plane formation by synchronous mobile robots in the three-dimensional Euclidean space. J. ACM (JACM) **64**(3), 1–43 (2017)
3. Cicerone, S., Di Stefano, G., Navarra, A.: Asynchronous robots on graphs: gathering. Distrib. Comput. Mob. Entities Curr. Res. Moving Comput. **11340**, 184–217 (2019)

4. D'Angelo, G., Navarra, A., Nisse, N.: Gathering and exclusive searching on rings under minimal assumptions. In: International Conference on Distributed Computing and Networking, pp. 149–164 (2014)
5. Flocchini, P., Ilcinkas, D., Pelc, A., Santoro, N.: Computing without communicating: ring exploration by asynchronous oblivious robots. Algorithmica **65**(3), 562–583 (2013)
6. Ooshita, F., Tixeuil, S.: Ring exploration with myopic luminous robots. Inf. Comput. **285**, 104702 (2022)
7. Devismes, S., Lamani, A., Petit, F., Raymond, P., Tixeuil, S.: Terminating exploration of a grid by an optimal number of asynchronous oblivious robots. Comput. J. **64**(1), 132–154 (2021)
8. Sangnier, A., Sznajder, N., Potop-Butucaru, M., Tixeuil, S.: Parameterized verification of algorithms for oblivious robots on a ring. Formal Methods Syst. Des. **56**(1), 55–89 (2020)
9. Das, S., Flocchini, P., Prencipe, G., Santoro, N., Yamashita, M.: Autonomous mobile robots with lights. Theoret. Comput. Sci. **609**, 171–184 (2016)
10. D'Emidio, M., Di Stefano, G., Frigioni, D., Navarra, A.: Characterizing the computational power of mobile robots on graphs and implications for the euclidean plane. Inf. Comput. **263**, 57–74 (2018)
11. Barriere, L., Flocchini, P., Mesa-Barrameda, E., Santoro, N.: Uniform scattering of autonomous mobile robots in a grid. Int. J. Found. Comput. Sci. **22**(03), 679–697 (2011)
12. Flocchini, P., Prencipe, G., Santoro, N.: Self-deployment of mobile sensors on a ring. Theoret. Comput. Sci. **402**(1), 67–80 (2008)
13. Elor, Y., Bruckstein, A.M.: Uniform multi-agent deployment on a ring. Theoret. Comput. Sci. **412**(8–10), 783–795 (2011)
14. Poudel, P., Sharma, G.: Fast uniform scattering on a grid for asynchronous oblivious robots. In: International Symposium on Stabilizing, Safety, and Security of Distributed Systems, pp. 211–228 (2020)
15. Poudel, P., Sharma, G.: Time-optimal uniform scattering in a grid. In: International Conference on Distributed Computing and Networking, pp. 228–237 (2019)
16. Kamei, S., Tixeuil, S.: An asynchronous maximum independent set algorithm by myopic luminous robots on grids. Comput. J. **67**(1), 57–77 (2024)
17. Shibata, M., Tixeuil, S.: Semi-uniform deployment of mobile robots in perfect ℓ-ary trees. Concurrency Comput.: Pract. Experience **35**(19), e7432 (2023)

A Formalization of Knowledge in Fault Tolerant Distributed Algorithms

Ron van der Meyden and Godfrey Wong

School of Computer Science and Engineering, UNSW Sydney, Sydney, Australia
r.vandermeyden@unsw.edu.au, godfrey.wong@student.unsw.edu.au

Abstract. Epistemic Logic has been shown to provide a useful abstract framework for reasoning about fault tolerant distributed algorithms. In particular, it provides a way to derive protocols that are optimal in the way that they use information. An example of this is results using notions of common knowledge to establish the optimality of consensus protocols, under a variety of failure models. Proofs in this area have, to date, been performed manually, and have consequently been error-prone. This paper addresses this weakness using formal methods. A formalization in the theorem prover Isabelle is developed of a general framework for epistemic reasoning about distributed algorithms, that can cover multiple failure models and concrete protocols. As an application of the framework, it is formally proved that for all patterns of information exchange among the agents, the implementation of a knowledge based program is optimal among protocols for simultaneous consensus that use that pattern of information exchange. Furthermore, the FloodSet protocol has been modelled in our framework and we verified knowledge properties about the protocol.

Keywords: Distributed algorithms · Epistemic logic · Reasoning about knowledge · Byzantine Agreement · Consensus · Fault tolerance · Isabelle · Higher order logic

1 Introduction

Epistemic logic provides a powerful formal framework for reasoning about knowledge in the analysis of fault tolerant distributed algorithms [12]. By characterizing the knowledge that an agent needs in order to take an action, it is possible to develop distributed algorithms that are optimal, in the sense of terminating as soon as any other algorithm that solves the same problem.

Examples of this approach include the work of Dwork and Moses [7], who studied the simultaneous consensus problem under crash failures and characterized the necessary and sufficient conditions for an agent to make a decision using a notion of "common knowledge". Using this characterization, they provide an algorithm that makes a decision as soon as any other algorithm that solves the problem. Other works have applied this approach to develop optimal protocols for other failure models and alternate specifications of consensus [1,5,13,18].

© The Author(s), under exclusive license to Springer Nature Switzerland AG 2026
C. Georgiou (Ed.): SIROCCO 2026, LNCS 16488, pp. 527–548, 2026.
https://doi.org/10.1007/978-3-032-26465-7_28

Frequently, these works have been based on "full-information exchange" protocols, in which in every round all the information an agent knows is transmitted and recorded into the state of each agent, leading to an exponential explosion in memory requirements. Often, we want to transmit and record less information than full information in distributed algorithms, to obtain a better message and space complexity. Motivated by this, Alpturer et al. [1] commenced the study of optimality of protocols with respect to more limited exchanges of information.

Proofs in this area can be complex, but have, to date, been performed manually and may contain errors. A notable example is in [13]. In that paper, a proof of optimality is erroneous, as was pointed out in [5]. This incident highlights a gap in the field. We need formal proofs that guarantee the correctness and optimality of distributed algorithms derived by reasoning about knowledge. By doing proofs inside a theorem prover, we can be more confident that our proofs are correct. This is the motivation for the present paper.

We develop a framework, in the Isabelle theorem prover, for reasoning about knowledge in distributed algorithms, enabling the formalization of proofs of optimality of protocols along the lines of the above-mentioned works. While there have been prior works on theorem proving for epistemic logic, they have concerned weaker notions of common knowledge than is required for the analysis of distributed algorithms, or have not had a focus on distributed computation. Our model uses interpreted systems, which can represent all possible behaviours of a distributed system, and allows us to reason about knowledge of a set of agents in which members of the set can change in different runs of an algorithm. To enable verification of the correctness and optimality of protocols, we use a model based on [1, 17] and verify some of their results in Isabelle. This model deals with protocols that may exchange less than full information with respect to a broad set of failure models. The main result (from [17]) that we prove formally states that implementations of a knowledge-based program yield protocols for Simultaneous Consensus that are an optimum, relative to a given information exchange protocol, in the sense of making decisions at the earliest possible time, amongst all protocols that use the same information exchange. As an example, we model the simple FloodSet [15] protocol and derive knowledge properties about it.

We begin by reviewing past literature and related work in Sect. 2. Then, in Sect. 3 we define an interpreted system and describe how we model an interpreted system in Isabelle. (Throughout the paper, we provide formal definitions in Isabelle with explanatory comments for the reader not already familiar this theorem prover.) Information exchange and action protocols are introduced in Sect. 4. Section 5 describes failure models. Generating an interpreted system from an information exchange protocol, action protocol, and a failure model is described in Sect. 6. We apply our model to the simultaneous consensus problem in Sect. 7. In Sect. 8, we define optimality and derive what knowledge conditions are necessary and sufficient for a simultaneous consensus protocol to be optimum. As our main application of the formal framework, we show that protocols that make their decision as soon as this knowledge condition arises are optimum among protocols using the same exchange of information. An example of modelling a concrete protocol using our framework is demonstrated in Sect. 9. Finally, we conclude this paper in Sect. 10 with a discussion of future work. Our presentation describes the theory and gives illustrative examples of its formalization in Isabelle, but omits many details of the latter for reasons of space[1].

2 Related Work

Epistemic logic has already been formalized in a wide variety of proof assistants. The work of From [10] has a formalization of epistemic logic in Isabelle, with proofs of soundness and completeness (based on [8]). The authors of [19] studied coalition logic, which is useful for reasoning about strategies, extended with common knowledge, and developed a proof of completeness. Their proof has been verified in the theorem prover Lean 4. In [3], the authors give a coinductive definition of common knowledge and prove it is equivalent to the relational definition of common knowledge. Their proofs were verified in the theorem provers Agda and Coq. Gammie [11] has a formalization of knowledge-based programs, which is an extension of standard programs that allow for testing of an agent's knowledge. The formalization of knowledge-based programs was done in Isabelle. So far, all formalizations of epistemic logic used operators for group knowledge with a rigid set of agents. Our work differs in that we allow for representing group knowledge among an indexical set of agents, which can change throughout a run depending on the time. This is necessary to capture reasoning about fault-tolerant consensus protocols. Another difference between our work and previous work is that previous work was based on Kripke structures for the logic of knowledge, while we use the richer setting of interpreted systems [8], which provides the expressive power that is needed for reasoning about both knowledge and time in distributed algorithms.

Consensus protocols have also been formalized [4,6,14,16]. In [6], the authors developed a framework and verified the correctness of six distinct consensus algorithms. A framework [14] was presented to verify the correctness of distributed algorithms that are described in pseudo code. There exists another framework [16] to verify the correctness of consensus algorithms. Included in the framework is an abstraction that classifies algorithms that share common ideas. Besides the correctness of consensus algorithms, the famous FLP impossibility result [9] has been verified in Isabelle [4]. Existing formalization of consensus algorithms only cover the correctness of algorithms or impossibility results and there has been no formalization that studies whether a consensus algorithm is deciding as soon as possible. Existing formalizations of consensus algorithms also do not use reasoning about knowledge.

3 Interpreted Systems

We begin by formalising *interpreted systems*, an abstract model of distributed systems, following [8], that provides semantics for reasoning about knowledge

---

[1] Isabelle source code is available at http://www.cse.unsw.edu.au/~meyden/research/kftda.html.

and time. We later refine this to a more concrete model of message passing systems with faulty agents.

Intuitively, an interpreted system represents all possible behaviours of a distributed system. Since we only model a synchronous message-passing system, it suffices to use natural numbers to represent the time.

type-synonym *time = nat*

A *run* is one possible behaviour of a system, and a point identifies a particular moment of time in a run. We model a run as a mapping from time to a world. In a concrete model, a world will represent the global state of a system at a moment of time, comprised of the state of an environment and a state of each of the agents in the system.

type-synonym *time = nat*

Here *'world* is a variable denoting a type of worlds, and the statement defines the type of runs over this type of worlds. The symbol $\Rightarrow$ is used to define the type of fuctions from the type on its left to the type on its right. A pair (r, m) comprised of a run r and a time m is a *point*. We use binary relations on points to represent points that are indistinguishable by an agent.

type-synonym *'world point = ('world run $\times$ time)*

Applications of epistemic logic to fault-tolerant protocols require reasoning about the shared knowledge of the set of non-faulty agents. This is an *indexical* set of agents whose members can vary between different points. An agent may not know whether it is a member of this set. We now show an example that illustrates why it is insufficient to reason about knowledge among a rigid set of agents. Consider two runs r and r' of the same protocol with three agents i, j, and k. During the first round, agent i crashes in run r and no failure occur in run r'. At time 1, the set of nonfailed agents in run r is $\{j, k\}$ and the set of nonfailed agents in run r' is $\{i, j, k\}$. During the second round, agent k fails in run r' and agent i continues to fail in run r. At time 2, the set of nonfailed agents in run r is $\{j\}$ and the set of nonfailed agents in run r' is $\{i, j\}$. This example is illustrated in Fig. 1.

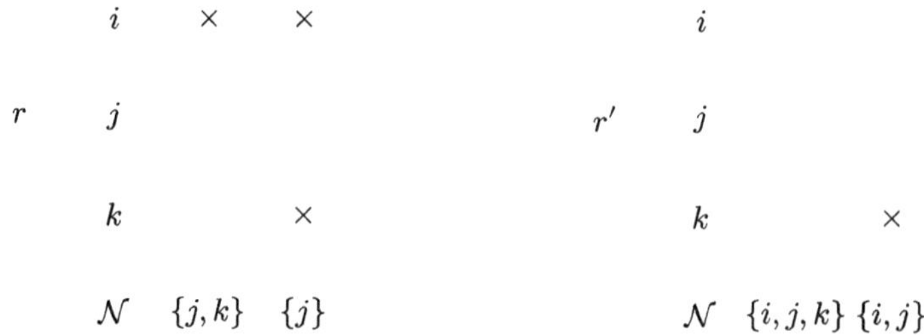

Fig. 1. Example showing the set $\mathcal{N}$ of nonfailed agents in two distinct runs

In our representation, an interpreted system $\mathcal{I}$ is a tuple ('**record**' in Isabelle) consisting of:

- *system*, a set $\mathcal{R}$ of runs,
- *relations*, giving a binary relation between points for each agent, representing points that the agent is unable to distinguish, given the information represented in its local state,
- a *valuation* function π mapping each point (r, m) of $\mathcal{I}$ to a function $\pi(r, m) :$ $Prop \to \{\textbf{True}, \textbf{False}\}$ that determines whether or not each atomic proposition from a set $Prop$ is true at the point,
- *index-set*, a function that outputs a set of agents given a point and the name of an "indexical set" (a set whose value depends on the point). (Our main application of this will be to represent the set of faulty agents, as illustrated above.)

Types $'agent, 'prop, 'world, 'index\text{-}name$ represent the sets agents, propositions $Prop$, worlds and names of indexical sets, respectively. In Isabele, 'τ set' represents the type of sets of elements of type τ, and 'τ rel' the type of binary relations over τ. Formally,

record $('agent, 'prop, 'world, 'index\text{-}name)$ $InterpretedSystem =$
  $system :: {}'world\ run\ set$
  $relations :: {}'agent \Rightarrow ('world\ point)\ rel$
  $valuation :: {}'world\ point \Rightarrow {}'prop \Rightarrow bool$
  $index\text{-}set :: {}'world\ point \Rightarrow {}'index\text{-}name \Rightarrow {}'agent\ set$

Interpreted systems provide the semantics for an *epistemic* logic of knowledge and time. In fault-tolerant distributed systems, agents have uncertainty about the global state of the system, and must reason based on the incomplete information encoded in their local states. Epistemic logic is suitable for the analysis of such systems because it allows us to express what agents know about their environment and each other.

We work with a modal logic that uses the atomic propositions along with the standard boolean operators $\neg, \vee, \wedge$. For an agent i and an *indexical* set $\mathcal{N}$ of agents (which may depend on the point at which we evaluate the formula) we also have unary epistemic operators $B_i^{\mathcal{N}}, EB_{\mathcal{N}}, CB_{\mathcal{N}}$ intuitively representing, respectively, agent i's individual belief, what all agents in the group $\mathcal{N}$ believe, and common belief amongst agents in the group $\mathcal{N}$.

The semantics of the logic in an interpreted system $\mathcal{I}$ with valuation function π is given by a binary relation $\models$, such that $(\mathcal{I}, r, m) \models \varphi$, for a point (r, m) of $\mathcal{I}$ and a formula φ, represents that φ is true at the point (r, m) of $\mathcal{I}$. The definition of this relation is given by an induction on the construction of the formula φ. For an atomic proposition p, we have $\mathcal{I}, (r, m) \models p$, if $\pi(r, m)(p) = \textbf{True}$. The semantics of the epistemic operators is given using a relation $\sim_i$ on points for each agent i. The points (r, m) and (r', m') are *indistinguishable* for agent i in interpreted system $\mathcal{I}$, written as $(r, m) \sim_{\mathcal{I}, i} (r', m')$, if both r and r' are in the set of runs and $((r, m), (r', m'))$ is in the relation of i. The intuition behind the definition of knowledge is that agent i knows φ if φ is true in all the points that agent i cannot distinguish from the current point. At this point we do not make any assumptions about the properties of the relation. (In the following Isabelle code defining the boolean function *related*, the parenthesized expression following "*bool*" defines syntactic sugar for this function matching our mathematical presentation. This syntactic sugar is used in the defining "where" clause.)

fun *related* :: *'world point* $\Rightarrow$ (*'agent, 'prop, 'world, 'index-name*) *InterpretedSystem* $\Rightarrow$ *'agent* $\Rightarrow$ *'world point* $\Rightarrow$ *bool* (- $\sim$-,- -)
  where
$(r,m) \sim_{I,i} (r',m') \longleftrightarrow ((r,m), (r',m')) \in$ *relations I i* $\wedge$ *r* $\in$ *system I* $\wedge$ *r'* $\in$ *system I*

To define the semantics of common knowledge relative to an indexical set S of agents, we use the notion of S-reachability. We say a point (r', m') is S-reachable from point (r, m) in k steps if there exist points $(r^0, m_0), \ldots, (r^k, m_k)$ such that $(r^0, m_0) = (r, m)$, $(r^k, m_k) = (r', m')$ and for all $0 \le j < k$, there exists agent i_j that is in both indexical sets $S(r^j, m_j)$ and $S(r^{j+1}, m_{j+1})$ such that $(r^j, m_j) \sim_{I,i_j} (r^{j+1}, m_{j+1})$. Furthermore, we say (r', m') is S-reachable from (r, m), and write $(r', m') \sim_{I,S} (r, m)$, if (r', m') is S-reachable from (r, m) in k steps for some $k > 0$. In Isabelle, we formalise the reachability relation as a transitive closure of the following relation. The *indexical-reachable1-rel* function gives the set of pairs of points that are S-reachable in one step for an indexical set S.

fun *indexical-reachable1-rel* :: (*'agent, 'prop, 'world, 'index-name*) *InterpretedSystem* $\Rightarrow$ *'index-name* $\Rightarrow$ (*'world point* $\times$ *'world point*) *set*
  where
indexical-reachable1-rel I S = { (w, w'). ($\exists$ $i \in$ *index-set I w S* $\cap$ *index-set I w' S*. $w \sim_{I,i} w'$) }

The *indexical-reachable-rel* function, which is defined as the transitive closure (*trancl*) of *indexical-reachable1-rel*, then gives a set binary relations that are S-reachable for an indexical set S.

fun *indexical-reachable-rel* :: (*'agent, 'prop, 'world, 'index-name*) *InterpretedSystem* $\Rightarrow$ *'index-name* $\Rightarrow$ (*'world point* $\times$ *'world point*) *set*
  where
indexical-reachable-rel I S = *trancl* (*indexical-reachable1-rel I S*)

In the more concrete setting to follow, we will use the indexical set name $S = \mathcal{N}$, representing the set of nonfaulty agents. Semantics of the modal operators is given as follows. For a formula φ and point (r, m) of an interpreted system $\mathcal{I}$, we say:

- agent i believes φ at (r, m), written as $\mathcal{I}, (r, m) \models B_i^{\mathcal{N}} \varphi$, if for all points (r', m') satisfying $(r, m) \sim_{I,i} (r', m')$, we have $\mathcal{I}, (r', m') \models i \in \mathcal{N} \Rightarrow \varphi$,
- everyone in $\mathcal{N}$ believes φ at (r, m), written as $\mathcal{I}, (r, m) \models EB_{\mathcal{N}} \varphi$, if $\mathcal{I}, (r', m') \models \varphi$ for every point (r', m') that is $\mathcal{N}$-reachable in 1 step from (r, m).

- φ is common belief among $\mathcal{N}$ at the point (r, m), written as $\mathcal{I}, (r, m) \models CB_{\mathcal{N}}\varphi$, if $\mathcal{I}, (r', m') \models \varphi$ for every point (r', m') that is $\mathcal{N}$-reachable from (r, m).

A formula φ is valid in interpreted system $\mathcal{I}$, written as $\mathcal{I} \models \varphi$, if for every point $(r, m) \in \mathcal{I}$, we have $\mathcal{I}, (r, m) \models \varphi$. We have verified in Isabelle that the semantics makes the following $S5_n$ axioms valid in all systems $\mathcal{I}$:

- Distribution axiom: $\models (CB_{\mathcal{N}}\varphi \wedge CB_{\mathcal{N}}(\varphi \Rightarrow \psi)) \Rightarrow CB_{\mathcal{N}}\psi$.
- Knowledge generalization rule: If $\mathcal{I} \models \varphi$ then $\mathcal{I} \models CB_{\mathcal{N}}\varphi$.
- Positive introspection axiom: $\models CB_{\mathcal{N}}\varphi \Rightarrow CB_{\mathcal{N}}CB_{\mathcal{N}}\varphi$.
- Negative introspection axiom: $\models \neg CB_{\mathcal{N}}\varphi \Rightarrow CB_{\mathcal{N}}\neg CB_{\mathcal{N}}\varphi$.

We now give some examples illustrating Isabelle proofs. The following two theorems were verified in Isabelle to test that our model of interpreted systems is correct. We have the following induction rule, which gives us a way of proving common knowledge.

Theorem 1 (Induction Rule). *If $\mathcal{I} \models \varphi \Rightarrow EB_{\mathcal{N}}(\varphi \wedge \psi)$ then $\mathcal{I} \models \varphi \Rightarrow CB_{\mathcal{N}}(\varphi \wedge \psi)$ for an indexical set $\mathcal{N}$ that is nonempty at every point.*

```
theorem Induction-Rule:
  assumes eq: I-rel-equiv I
  assumes E:  ∀ r' ∈ system I. ∀ m'. (I,(r',m') ⊨ φ ⟶ I,(r',m') ⊨ EB_S (Kand
φ ψ))
  assumes nonempty-S: ∀ r' ∈ system I. ∀ m'. index-set I (r',m') S ≠ empty
  shows ∀ r ∈ system I. ∀ m. (I,(r,m) ⊨ φ ⟶ I,(r,m) ⊨ CB_S (Kand φ ψ))

proof (safe)
  fix r m
  assume r: r ∈ system I
  assume phi: I,(r,m) ⊨ φ
  with E have I,(r,m) ⊨ CB_S (φ)
    apply auto
    by (erule trancl-induct) fastforce+
  with assms show I,(r,m) ⊨ CB_S (Kand φ ψ) by auto (metis (lifting) ext E
S5n-knowledge-EB index-reachableI index-reachable-in-system models.simps(4) r)
qed
```

We describe our proof in Isabelle as follows. First, we fixed a run $r \in system\ I$ and time m and then showed that $I, (r, m) \models CB_S\varphi$ by induction on the points that are S-reachable from (r, m) using trancl-induct, the induction rule for transitive closure. The fastforce proof method is then able to automatically solve the subgoals generated by the induction. We are able to conclude the proof by showing that $I, (r, m) \models CB_S(\varphi \wedge \psi)$ using sledgehammer, which generated a proof using the metis method. Sledgehammer was unable to generate the entire proof automatically so we had to specify that we wanted to do an induction. We also verified that $CB_S\varphi$ is a fixed point of $f(\psi) = EB_S(\varphi \wedge \psi)$.

Theorem 2 (Fixed-Point Theorem). *For a proposition φ and an indexical set $\mathcal{N}$ that is nonempty at every point, $\models CB_{\mathcal{N}}\varphi \Leftrightarrow EB_{\mathcal{N}}(\varphi \wedge CB_{\mathcal{N}}\varphi)$ is valid.*

theorem *Fixed-Point*:
  assumes *S5*: *I-rel-equiv I*
  assumes *nonempty-S*: $\forall$ *r$'$* $\in$ *system I.* $\forall$ *m$'$. index-set I (r$'$,m$'$) S* $\neq$ *empty*
  assumes *r*: *r* $\in$ *system I*
  shows $(I,(r,m) \models \mathbf{EB}_S\ (Kand\ \varphi\ (\mathbf{CB}_S\ \varphi))) \longrightarrow (I,(r,m) \models \mathbf{CB}_S\ \varphi)$

In order to prove this theorem in Isabelle, we split the goal into $I, (r, m) \models EB_{\mathcal{N}}(\varphi \wedge CB_{\mathcal{N}}\varphi) \Rightarrow CB_{\mathcal{N}}\varphi$ and $I, (r, m) \models CB_{\mathcal{N}}\varphi \Rightarrow EB_{\mathcal{N}}(\varphi \wedge CB_{\mathcal{N}}\varphi)$ and then solve each subgoal using the proof automation tool Sledgehammer.

4   Information Exchange and Action Protocols

To represent concrete distributed algorithms, and in particular, to reason about knowledge in practical algorithms that use limited exchanges of information, we follow an approach from [1]. We decompose distributed algorithms into two components $(P, \mathcal{E})$, comprised of an action protocol P and an information exchange protocol $\mathcal{E}$. An action protocol describes what actions an agent takes at each time, based on its local state. An information exchange protocol describes what information the agents record in their local states, and what messages an agent sends in a given local state.

We represent the states of the environment in which agents operate by a set L_e, defined more precisely below. Given a set of agents Agt, a local information exchange protocol $\mathcal{E}_i$ of agent $i \in Agt$ is a tuple $\langle L_i, I_i, A_i, M_i, \mu_i, \delta_i \rangle$ that consists of: a set of local states L_i, a set of initial states $I_i \subseteq L_i$, a set of allowed actions A_i for agent i, a set M_i of messages that are allowed to be sent by agent i, a message selection function $\mu_i : L_i \times A_i \to (Agt \to M_i \cup \{\bot\})$, and a transition function $\delta_i : L_i \times A_i \times \prod_{j \in Agt}(M_j \cup \{\bot\}) \to L_i$. Missing messages are represented by $\bot$.

The message selection function μ_i takes a local state and an action performed by an agent in a round to a tuple of messages that the agent sends in that round. The transition function δ_i updates the local state depending on the state of the environment, the action an agent performs in the round and the tuple of messages it receives in that round.

In Isabelle, we can represent the set L_i of local states, the set M_i of messages, and the set A_i of allowed actions, and using types $'state, 'msg, 'act$, respectively. For a type τ, the type 'τ option' represents $\tau \cup \{\bot\}$ ($\bot$ is represented as *None* in Isabelle). Hence, in the Isabelle representation of local information exchange protocols, we only include the set of initial states, the message selection function, and the transition function in an Isabelle record.

record (*'state, 'msg, 'act, 'agent*) *InfoExchange* =
  Initial :: *'state set*
  Transition :: *'state* $\Rightarrow$ *'act* $\Rightarrow$ (*'agent* $\Rightarrow$ *'msg option*) $\Rightarrow$ *'state*
  MsgSelect :: *'state* $\Rightarrow$ *'act* $\Rightarrow$ *'agent* $\Rightarrow$ *'msg option*

Formally, a joint information exchange protocol is a tuple $\langle \mathcal{E}_1, \ldots, \mathcal{E}_n \rangle$ containing a local information exchange protocol $\mathcal{E}_i$ for each agent i.

type-synonym $('agent, \,'state, \,'msg, \,'act)$ $JointInfo =$
$\quad 'agent \Rightarrow ('state, \,'msg, \,'act, \,'agent)$ $InfoExchange$

An action protocol describes what actions the agents perform at a given situation. A *local action protocol* $P_i : L_i \to A_i$ for agent i maps a local state of agent i to an action that i can perform. A joint *action protocol* P is a tuple $\langle P_1, \ldots, P_n \rangle$ of local action protocols for all agents. In Isabelle, we represent a joint action protocol using the following type.

type-synonym $('agent, \,'state, \,'act)$ $JointAction = \,'agent \Rightarrow \,'state \Rightarrow \,'act$

5   Failure Models

In distributed computing, failure models are used to describe assumptions about the ways that the system can fail, and protocols must be designed to achieve their goals even in the face of these failures. A description of a particular pattern of failures over time is called an *adversary*.

In our formalisation, we follow an abstract representation, from [17], for failure models in message passing systems, that captures three types of failures: blocking or corruption of messages at time or transmission, blocking or corruption of messages at a receiver, at time of reception, and corruption of the local state of an agent. (State perturbations have been included for generality of the framework, but our theorems about Simultaneous Consensus below assume that corruption of agent's local states does not occur.) An adversary is represented by a record consisting of a transmission adversary $tAdv$, that describes how, at each moment of time, and for each agent, a message sent by that agent to another agent is perturbed, a receiving adversary $rAdv$, that describes how, at each moment of time, and for each agent, a message that is ready to be received by that agent is perturbed, and a state perturbation adversary $sAdv$, that describes how, at each moment of time, the state of each agent is perturbed from the update that would otherwise be produced by it's state update function.

record $('agent, \,'msg, \,'state)$ $Adversary =$
$\quad tAdv :: nat \Rightarrow \,'agent \Rightarrow \,'agent \Rightarrow \,'msg\ option \Rightarrow \,'msg\ option$
$\quad rAdv :: nat \Rightarrow \,'agent \Rightarrow \,'agent \Rightarrow \,'msg\ option \Rightarrow \,'msg\ option$
$\quad sAdv :: nat \Rightarrow \,'agent \Rightarrow \,'state \Rightarrow \,'state$

Agents are assumed to run in the context of an external environment with states represented in Isabelle by a type $'env$. (This could be used to represent the external world on which agents act, or to keep a record of the actions that agents have performed.) A failure model describes the failures that could occur in a run of a protocol. It consists of a set of the initial states of the environment, an environment transition function, describing how environment states are updated as a function of the joint actions performed by the agents, and a set of possible adversaries.

record $(\mathit{'env}, \mathit{'agent}, \mathit{'act}, \mathit{'msg}, \mathit{'state})\ \mathit{Failure} =$
  $\mathit{eInitial} :: \mathit{'env\ set}$
  $\mathit{eTransition} :: \mathit{'env} \Rightarrow (\mathit{'agent} \Rightarrow \mathit{'act}) \Rightarrow \mathit{'env}$
  $\mathit{Adv} :: (\mathit{'agent}, \mathit{'msg}, \mathit{'state})\ \mathit{Adversary\ set}$

The set of nonfaulty agents is the set of agents such that $tAdv$ and $rAdv$ do not perturb any of the agents' messages and $sAdv$ does not perturb its state at any time.

fun $\mathit{nonFaulty} :: (\mathit{'agent}, \mathit{'msg}, \mathit{'state})\ \mathit{Adversary} \Rightarrow \mathit{'agent\ set}$
where
$\mathit{nonFaulty\ adv} = \{\ i.\ \forall\ m\ j\ msg\ s.\ (tAdv\ adv\ m\ i\ j\ msg = msg \wedge rAdv\ adv\ m\ j\ i\ msg$
$= msg \wedge sAdv\ adv\ i\ m\ s = s)\ \}$

6 Message Passing Systems

In distributed algorithms, agents communicate with each other by passing messages. In this section, we will explain how we model a message passing system.

A global state is a tuple comprised of the state of the external environment, an adversary, and a local state of each agent. We model this in Isabelle using a record that consists of an external environment state $EnvState$, an adversary $AdvState$, and a function $LocalState$ which represents the tuple of states in $\prod_{i \in Agt} L_i$.

record $(\mathit{'env}, \mathit{'agent}, \mathit{'msg}, \mathit{'state})\ \mathit{GlobalState} =$
  $\mathit{EnvState} :: \mathit{'env}$
  $\mathit{AdvState} :: (\mathit{'agent}, \mathit{'msg}, \mathit{'state})\ \mathit{Adversary}$
  $\mathit{LocalState} :: \mathit{'agent} \Rightarrow \mathit{'state}$

The following function $sent$ gives, in the context of an information exchange protocol E and agents running action protocol P, the message (or $\bot$) that is transmitted, at time m (i.e., in round $m + 1$), when the global state is s, from an agent i to an agent j, after perturbation by the transmission adversary.

fun $\mathit{sent} :: (\mathit{'agent}, \mathit{'state}, \mathit{'msg}, \mathit{'act})\ \mathit{JointInfo}$
  $\Rightarrow (\mathit{'agent}, \mathit{'state}, \mathit{'act})\ \mathit{JointAction}$
  $\Rightarrow (\mathit{'agent}, \mathit{'msg}, \mathit{'state})\ \mathit{Adversary}$
  $\Rightarrow (\mathit{'env}, \mathit{'agent}, \mathit{'msg}, \mathit{'state})\ \mathit{GlobalState}$
  $\Rightarrow \mathit{nat} \Rightarrow \mathit{'agent} \Rightarrow \mathit{'agent} \Rightarrow \mathit{'msg\ option}$
  where
$\mathit{sent\ E\ P\ adv\ s\ m\ i\ j} = tAdv\ adv\ m\ i\ j\ (MsgSelect\ (E\ i)\ (LocalState\ s\ i)\ (P\ i\ (LocalState$
$s\ i))\ j)$

Similarly, the following function $received$ gives the message (or $\bot$) that is received by agent j from agent i after perturbation by the receiving adversary.

fun $\mathit{received} :: (\mathit{'agent}, \mathit{'state}, \mathit{'msg}, \mathit{'act})\ \mathit{JointInfo}$
  $\Rightarrow (\mathit{'agent}, \mathit{'state}, \mathit{'act})\ \mathit{JointAction}$

$\Rightarrow$ (*'agent*, *'msg*, *'state*) *Adversary*
$\Rightarrow$ (*'env*, *'agent*, *'msg*, *'state*) *GlobalState*
$\Rightarrow$ *nat* $\Rightarrow$ *'agent* $\Rightarrow$ *'agent* $\Rightarrow$ *'msg option*
where
received E P adv s m j i = rAdv adv m i j (sent E P adv s m i j)

The adversary resolves all the nondeterminism that occurs during a run, as a consequence of failures. Consequently, a run is uniquely determined from the initial global state by the following induction. The adversary $r_a(m)$ in the global states $r(m)$ will be the same for all times m. For each round $k + 1$, the local state $r_i(k + 1)$ of agent i is determined as follows. First, each agent i uses the decision protocol P_i to select its action $a_i = P_i(r_i(k))$, and attempts to send the messages $\mu_i(r_i(k), a_i)$. Using the functions *sent* and *received*, the adversary $r_a(k)$ determines, for each agent i, an agent indexed vector v_i of messages (or $\perp$ in case of a message that was not sent or is not received). Agent i then attempts to update its local state to $\delta_i(r_i(k), a_i, v_i)$, but the state adversary *AdvState* may, in general, perturb this resulting state. The component *EnvState* in $r(k + 1)$ is determined from its value in $r(k)$ and the actions performed by the agents in the round. (The purpose of this component is primarily to record information about the history of actions performed.)

In Isabelle, a run of a protocol is modelled using the following function. (Lambda abstraction λ is used to represent tuples indexed over an agent i.)

fun *run* :: (*'agent*, *'state*, *'msg*, *'act*) *JointInfo*
  $\Rightarrow$ (*'agent*, *'state*, *'act*) *JointAction*
  $\Rightarrow$ (*'env*, *'agent*, *'act*, *'msg*, *'state*) *Failure*
  $\Rightarrow$ (*'env*, *'agent*, *'msg*, *'state*) *GlobalState*
  $\Rightarrow$ *nat*
  $\Rightarrow$ (*'env*, *'agent*, *'msg*, *'state*) *GlobalState*
where
run0: run Info P F State0 0 = State0 |
runSuc: run Info P F State0 (Suc m) =
  (*let rm = run Info P F State0 m;*
  actions = λ *i. P i (LocalState rm i)*
  in
  (|
    EnvState = eTransition F (EnvState rm) actions ,
    AdvState = AdvState rm,
    LocalState = (λ *i. sAdv (AdvState rm) i m (Transition (Info i) (LocalState rm i)*
  (*actions i*) (*received Info P (AdvState rm) (rm) m i*))) |))

Given an information exchange $\mathcal{E}$, decision protocol P, failure model $\mathcal{F}$, we construct an interpreted system $\mathcal{I}_{P,\mathcal{E},\mathcal{F}}$ as follows. The runs in the system of $\mathcal{I}_{P,\mathcal{E},\mathcal{F}}$ are generated by selecting an initial global state $r(0) = \langle s_e, s_1, \ldots, s_n \rangle$, where s_e encodes an external environment state and an adversary from the failure model and $s_i \in I_i$, for all $i \in Agt$, are initial local states of agents.

definition *System* :: (*'agent*, *'state*, *'msg*, *'act*) *JointInfo*

$\Rightarrow$ *('agent, 'state, 'act) JointAction*
$\Rightarrow$ *('env, 'agent, 'act, 'msg, 'state) Failure*
$\Rightarrow$ *('env, 'agent, 'msg, 'state) GlobalState run set*
where
System Info P Failure $\equiv$
  $\bigcup$ *e0 $\in$ eInitial Failure.*
  $\bigcup$ *l0 $\in$ { L. $\forall$ i. L i $\in$ Initial (Info i) }.*
  $\bigcup$ *adv0 $\in$ Adv Failure.*
  { run Info P Failure (| EnvState = e0, AdvState = adv0, LocalState = l0 |) }

In an interpreted system for a message passing system, we define two points (r, m) and (r', m') to be indistinguishable for agent i if the agent cannot distinguish them using its local state, that is, $(r, m) \sim_i (r', m')$ if $r_i(m) = r'_i(m')$. We have verified in Isabelle that this relation is an equivalence relation.

definition *MsgPassing-System :: ('agent, 'state, 'msg, 'act) JointInfo*
  $\Rightarrow$ *('agent, 'state, 'act) JointAction*
  $\Rightarrow$ *('env, 'agent, 'act, 'msg, 'state) Failure*
  $\Rightarrow$ *('env, 'agent, 'msg, 'state, 'prop) Interpretation*
  $\Rightarrow$ *(('env, 'agent, 'msg, 'state) GlobalState point $\Rightarrow$ 'index-name $\Rightarrow$ 'agent set)*
    $\Rightarrow$ *('agent, 'prop, ('env, 'agent, 'msg, 'state) GlobalState, 'index-name)*
InterpretedSystem
  where
MsgPassing-System Info P Failure Interpretation indexical-set $\equiv$ (|
  system = System Info P Failure,
  relations = λ i. { ((r,m), (r',m')). {r, r'} $\subseteq$ System Info P Failure $\wedge$ LocalState (r m) i = LocalState (r' m') i },
  valuation = Interpretation,
  index-set = indexical-set |)

7 Simultaneous Consensus

In this section we apply the general framework defined above to show an example of how to model a specific fault-tolerant distributed computing problem, known as the Simultaneous Byzantine Agreement (SBA) problem in the literature on reasoning about knowledge [7,8]. (In spite of the name, there is not an implication that the failure model is the Byzantine failure model.) The SBA problem is also called Simultaneous Consensus in other literature [2].

Furthermore, we explore what conditions are necessary to achieve protocols that provide *optimum* solutions to this problem. Specifically, we aim to find protocols that terminate at the earliest possible time in all runs.

In the Simultaneous Byzantine Agreement problem, agents from a set $Agt = \{1, \ldots, n\}$ communicate using a synchronous, round-based, message-passing network in order to decide on a value. Each agent starts with an initial value from the set $Values = \{\mathbf{True}, \mathbf{False}\}$. We assume that $t < n$ is the maximum number of faulty agents.

The action set for each agent i is $A_i = \{\text{decide}(v) \mid v \in \textit{Values}\} \cup \{\textbf{noop}\}$. In Isabelle, we model the action set using the option type, with **noop** represented by *None*.

type-synonym *SBA-value* = *bool*
type-synonym *SBA-action* = *SBA-value option*

We assume that the local state component of an agent always contains its initial value and the current time. In addition, an agent may store extra information, depending on the specific information exchange. We capture this information in Isabelle using a record *SBA-state*

record $('value, 'extra)$ *SBA-state* =
   init :: $'value$
   time :: *nat*
   extra :: $'extra$

The local state of an agent consists of its *SBA-state* as well as a component *decision-info* that is used to record information about actions (i.e., decisions made) that the agent has performed. (In the following, the operator $+$ is used to add a field to a record type.)

record $('value, 'extra, 'decision-info)$ *SBA-local* = $('value, 'extra)$ *SBA-state* $+$
   decision-info :: $'decision-info$

The specification of SBA can be stated as follows:

- **Unique Decision:** every agent decides at most once:
- **Simultaneous Agreement:** every nonfaulty agent decides on the same value simultaneously:
- **Validity:** if a nonfaulty agent decides on a value v, then there exists an agent such that its initial value is v.

(Our notion of Validity is stated in the form known as "Strong Validity" as opposed to Weak or Univalent Validity, which restrict the condition to runs in which all agents have the same initial value. However, for the case of $\textit{Values} = \{True, False\}$ the definitions coincide.) The system $\mathcal{I}_{E,P,F}$ generated by an information exchange protocol E, an action protocol P and a failure model F is defined to be an SBA-system if it satisfies all of the above conditions.

We remark that the above specification does not require termination, that is, that non-faulty agents eventually decide. In limited information exchange settings, this cannot be guaranteed, and we leave the proof of termination properties as separate, protocol-dependent matter. However, we note that optimal protocols, as defined below, will have the property of terminating whenever this is possible.

We say two runs r and r' *correspond* if they have the same initial states. This means the two runs have the same adversary and same initial states, but they could differ by being runs generated using different action protocols.

We define $n > 0$ to be the number of all agents, which corresponds with *total_agents* in Isabelle and $t < n$, which corresponds with *tolerance* in Isabelle.

consts
  total-agents :: *nat*
  tolerance :: *nat*

specification (*total-agents*) *n-gt-0* [*intro*]: *total-agents* > *0*

specification (*tolerance*) *t-lt-n* [*intro*]: *tolerance* < *total-agents*

We use the type *Agt*, which is natural numbers from 1 to n to represent the type for agents in the system.

typedef *Agt* = {*1 .. total-agents*}

In Isabelle, a locale is a sequence of parameters and assumptions. We work inside the following Isabelle locale for the remainder of this section to make our results more extensible. The *SBA-structure* is a record containing the information exchange, action protocol, failure model, interpretation function, and indexical set. We assume that the system is synchronous. To capture that at most t agents are faulty, we assume that the number of agents in the indexical set is at least $n - t$.

(′*env*, ′*prop*, ′*msg*, ′*extra*, ′*decision-info*) *SBA-structure* =
  Info :: (*Agt*, (*SBA-value*, ′*extra*, ′*decision-info*) *SBA-local*, ′*msg*, *SBA-action*) *JointInfo*
  ActionProtocol :: (*Agt*, (*SBA-value*, ′*extra*, ′*decision-info*) *SBA-local*, *SBA-action*) *JointAction*
  Failure :: (′*env*, *Agt*, *SBA-action*, ′*msg*, (*SBA-value*, ′*extra*, ′*decision-info*) *SBA-local*) *Failure*
  Interpretation :: (′*env*, *Agt*, ′*msg*, (*SBA-value*, ′*extra*, ′*decision-info*) *SBA-local*, ′*prop*) *Interpretation*
  indexical-set :: (′*env*, *Agt*, ′*msg*, (*SBA-value*, ′*extra*, ′*decision-info*) *SBA-local*) *GlobalState point* ⇒ *Agt set*

locale *SBA-locale* =
  fixes *S* :: (′*env*, ′*prop*, ′*msg*, ′*extra*, ′*decision-info*) *SBA-structure* (**structure**)
  assumes *card-N-ge-n-minus-t* [*intro*]: *card* (*indexical-set S* (*r,m*)) ≥ *total-agents* − *tolerance*
  and *synchronous*: ∀ *r* ∈ *System* (*Info S*) *P* (*Failure S*). ∀ *i*. *Time* (*r m*) *i* = *m*

In Isabelle, we define functions *Time*, *Deciding*, *Init* to get the time, action, and initial values from the local state of an agent respectively. We will construct an interpreted system for SBA and prove properties about it. We add the following three atomic propositions to our interpretation function:

- decides i v: agent i is deciding on value v.
- decide v: every agent in the indexical set is deciding on value v.
- ∃v: value v is an initial value of an agent in the current run.

fun *SBA-Interpretation* :: (*Agt*, (*SBA-value*, *'extra*, *'decision-info*) *SBA-local*, *SBA-action*) *JointAction* $\Rightarrow$ (*'env*, *Agt*, *'msg*, (*SBA-value*, *'extra*, *'decision-info*) *SBA-local*, *'prop SBA-prop*) *Interpretation* **where**
SBA-Interpretation P (*r,m*) (*exists v*) = ($\exists$ *i. Init r i = v*) |
SBA-Interpretation P (*r,m*) (*decides i v*) = (*Deciding P i* (*r m*) = *Some v*) |
SBA-Interpretation P (*r,m*) (*decide v*) = ($\forall$ *i* $\in$ *indexical-set S* (*r,m*). *Deciding P i* (*r m*) = *Some v*) |
SBA-Interpretation P (*r,m*) (*Prop ψ*) = *Interpretation S* (*r,m*) *ψ*

Using our framework in Isabelle, we verified the following theorem from [7] in the case of limited information exchange. This theorem shows that common belief of existence of a specific initial value among nonfaulty agents is a necessary condition to decide in the SBA problem.

Theorem 3. *Let $\mathcal{I}$ be an interpreted system for SBA. For all $r \in \mathcal{I}$, agent i and time m, we have $\mathcal{I}, (r, m) \models$ decides$i \; v \Rightarrow B_i^{\mathcal{N}} CB_{\mathcal{N}}(\exists v)$.*

theorem *SBA-CB*:
  assumes *SBA-protocol: SBA* (*Info S*) *P* (*Failure S*) (*indexical-set S*)
  shows *I-P P,(r,m)* $\models$ *Kprop* (*decides i v*) $\longrightarrow$ *I-P P,(r,m)* $\models$ $\mathbf{B}^{N}{}_{i}$ ($\mathbf{CB}_{N}$ (*Kprop* (*exists v*)))

To prove Theorem 3 in Isabelle, we first showed that $\mathcal{I} \models$ decide $v \Rightarrow \exists v$. Then, we proved that $\mathcal{I} \models$ decide $v \wedge \exists v \Rightarrow EB_{\mathcal{N}}(\text{decide } v \wedge \exists v)$ and then applied Induction Rule.

8   Optimality

In this section we focus on proving whether a SBA protocol is deciding as early as possible. We now define what it means for a SBA protocol to be optimum. Let P and P' be two decision protocols with identical information exchange $\mathcal{E}$, and let $\mathcal{F}$ be failure model. We write $P \leq_{\mathcal{E},\mathcal{F}} P'$ if for every run r of $\mathcal{I}_{P,\mathcal{E},F}$, and corresponding run r' of $\mathcal{I}_{P',\mathcal{E},\mathcal{F}}$, and for each agent i, if i decides at (r, m), then if agent i decides at (r', m') we have $m' \geq m$.

fun   *SBA-le*   ::   (*Agt*,   (*SBA-value*,   *'extra*,   *'decision-info*)   *SBA* *-local*, *'msg*, *SBA-action*) *JointInfo* $\Rightarrow$ (*'env*, *Agt*, *SBA-action*, *'msg*, (*SBA-value*, *'extra*, *'decision-info*) *SBA-local*) *Failure* $\Rightarrow$ (*Agt*, (*SBA-value*, *'extra*, *'decision-info*) *SBA-local*, *SBA-action*) *JointAction* $\Rightarrow$ (*Agt*, (*SBA-value*, *'extra*, *'decision-info*) *SBA-local*, *SBA-action*) *JointAction* $\Rightarrow$ *bool*
  where
SBA-le E F P P' = ($\forall$ *s i*. ((*run E P F s* $\in$ *System E P F* $\wedge$ *run E P' F s* $\in$ *System E P' F*) $\longrightarrow$ (*dtime E F P i s* $\leq$ *dtime E F P' i s*)))

Protocol P is an *optimum SBA protocol* with respect to information exchange $\mathcal{E}$ if it is an SBA protocol and for every SBA protocol P' that uses $\mathcal{E}$, we have $P \leq_{\mathcal{E},\mathcal{F}} P'$.

definition *Optimum* :: (*Agt*, (*SBA-value*, *'extra*, *'decision-info*) *SBA-local*, *'msg*, *SBA-action*) *JointInfo* $\Rightarrow$ (*'env*, *Agt*, *SBA-action*, *'msg*, (*SBA-value*, *'extra*, *'decision-info*) *SBA-local*) *Failure* $\Rightarrow$ (*Agt*, (*SBA-value*, *'extra*, *'decision-info*) *SBA-local*, *SBA-action*) *JointAction* $\Rightarrow$ ((*'env*, *'msg*, *'extra*, *'decision-info*) *SBA-global* *point* $\Rightarrow$ *Agt set*) $\Rightarrow$ *bool*
  where
Optimum E F P Nset $\equiv$ *SBA E P F Nset* $\wedge$ ($\forall$ *P'*. (*SBA E P' F Nset* $\longrightarrow$ *SBA-le E F P P'*))

Knowledge-based programs [8] are an extension of standard programs that allow for testing for knowledge of the agent running it. The following knowledge-based program optKBP is from [18], generalising earlier work of [7].

Algorithm 1. optKBP

---

  repeat noop
  until $B_i^{\mathcal{N}} CB_{\mathcal{N}} \exists v$ for some v
  if $B_i^{\mathcal{N}} CB_{\mathcal{N}} \exists$ **True then** decides i **True**
  else if $B_i^{\mathcal{N}} CB_{\mathcal{N}} \exists$ **False then** decides i **False**
  end if
  repeat noop
  until end

A concrete action protocol P *implements* optKBP with respect to an information exchange protocol $\mathcal{E}$ and a failure model $\mathcal{F}$ if at every point (r, m) of $\mathcal{I}_{P,\mathcal{E},\mathcal{F}}$, the action protocol P selects for agent i the same action as would be selected at that point by the program optKBP, with the truth value of the knowledge formulas $\phi = B_i^{\mathcal{N}} CB_{\mathcal{N}} \exists\ v$ determined by $\mathcal{I}_{P,\mathcal{E},\mathcal{F}}, (r, m) \models \phi$. In Isabelle, it is defined as follows.

definition *optKBP* :: (*Agt*, *'prop SBA-prop*, (*'env*, *Agt*, *'msg*, (*SBA-value*, *'extra*, *'decision-info*) *SBA-local*) *GlobalState*, *indexical-N*) *InterpretedSystem* $\Rightarrow$ (*Agt*, (*SBA-value*, *'extra*, *'decision-info*) *SBA-local*, *SBA-action*) *JointAction* $\Rightarrow$ *bool*
  where
optKBP I' P $\equiv$ $\forall$ *r* $\in$ *system I'*. $\forall$ *m i*. (*if* ($\exists$ *m'* < *m*. *Deciding P i* (*r m'*) $\neq$ *None*) *then Deciding P i* (*r m*) = *None else* (*if I',(r,m)* $\models$ *Kbelieves N i* (*Kcbelieves N* (*Kprop* (*exists True*))) *then Deciding P i* (*r m*) = *Some True else if I',(r,m)* $\models$ *Kbelieves N i* (*Kcbelieves N* (*Kprop* (*exists False*))) *then Deciding P i* (*r m*) = *Some False else Deciding P i* (*r m*) = *None*))

We define I_P to be a message passing system that is generated by the information exchange, failure model, interpretation function, and indexical set defined in the SBA_structure. Then, the interpreted system I is defined to be I_P with the same ActionProtocol from the *SBA_structure*.

definition *I-P* :: (*Agt*, (*SBA-value*, $'extra$, $'decision\text{-}info$) *SBA-local*, *SBA-action*)
JointAction $\Rightarrow$ (*Agt*, $'prop$ *SBA-prop*, ($'env$, *Agt*, $'msg$, (*SBA-value*, $'extra$,
$'decision\text{-}info$) *SBA-local*) *GlobalState*, *indexical-N*) *InterpretedSystem*
where
I-P P $\equiv$ *MsgPassing-System* (*Info S*) *P* (*Failure S*) (*SBA-Interpretation P*) (*N-set*)

definition *I* :: (*Agt*, $'prop$ *SBA-prop*, ($'env$, *Agt*, $'msg$, (*SBA-value*, $'extra$,
$'decision\text{-}info$) *SBA-local*) *GlobalState*, *indexical-N*) *InterpretedSystem*
where *I* $\equiv$ *I-P* (*ActionProtocol S*)

Furthermore, we define the function $nFaulty$ to return the set of agents that a nonfaulty at a given point.

fun *nFaulty* :: ($'env$, $'msg$, $'extra$, $'decision\text{-}info$) *SBA-global point* $\Rightarrow$ *Agt set*
where
nFaulty (r,m) = *nonFaulty* (*AdvState* (*r 0*))

Theorem 4. *Let P be an action protocol that implements optKBP with respect to information exchange $\mathcal{E}$ and failure model $\mathcal{F}$, and an indexical set $\mathcal{N}$ of nonfaulty agents. Then $\mathcal{I}_{P,\mathcal{E},\mathcal{F}}$ is an SBA-system, that is, satisfies the Simultaneous Consensus specification.*

We have verified that an implementation of optKBP satisfies the SBA specification when the indexical set $\mathcal{N}$ is the set of nonfaulty agents [17]. This shows that common belief of existence of a specific initial value among nonfaulty agents is a sufficient condition to decide in the SBA problem. Our proof in Isabelle follows the proof of the corresponding theorem in [17]. Simultaneous Agreement is proven by choosing the minimum time m such that there exists nonfaulty i that decides value v at time m. The definition of optKBP then shows that we have $B_i^{\mathcal{N}} CB_{\mathcal{N}} \exists v$. Then, we can show that $B_j^{\mathcal{N}} CB_{\mathcal{N}} \exists v$ for any nonfaulty j. We conclude the proof using the definition of optKBP and our choice of m.

theorem *SBA-optKBP*:
  assumes *N*: *indexical-set S* = *nFaulty*
  assumes *I′*: *I′* = *I-P P*
  assumes *opt*: *optKBP I′ P*
  shows *SBA* (*Info S*) *P* (*Failure S*) (*indexical-set S*)

We now set about showing that under certain side-conditions, an implementation of optKBP is in fact an *optimum* SBA protocol. To state these side-conditions, we need the following notions. Intuitively, an information exchange protocol *does not transmit information about actions* if it does not send what actions it has performed to other agents. This means the transition function and message selection function work independent of the action of the agent. Intuitively, this means that agents transmit information only about their initial values and failures that they have detected. It was shown in [17] that that these conditions are sufficient to ensure that an implementation of optKBP is optimum.

definition *ntransmit-action* :: (*Agt*, (*'value, 'extra, 'decision-info*) *SBA-local, 'msg, SBA-action*) *JointInfo* ⇒ *bool* **where**
ntransmit-action Info ≡ ∀ *i s1 s2 a1 a2 d1 d2 msg1 msg2. MsgSelect* (*Info i*) (*SBA-state.extend s1* (*SBA-local.fields d1*)) *a1* = *MsgSelect* (*Info i*) (*SBA-state.extend s1* (*SBA-local.fields d2*)) *a2*
∧ *SBA-state.truncate* (*Transition* (*Info i*) (*SBA-state.extend s1* (*SBA-local.fields d1*)) *a1 msg1*) = *SBA-state.truncate* (*Transition* (*Info i*) (*SBA-state.extend s1* (*SBA-local.fields d2*)) *a2 msg1*)
∧ *decision-info* (*Transition* (*Info i*) (*SBA-state.extend s1* (*SBA-local.fields d1*)) *a1 msg1*) = *decision-info* (*Transition* (*Info i*) (*SBA-state.extend s2* (*SBA-local.fields d1*)) *a1 msg2*)

We say a failure model *acts independently on message and action memory* if the *SBA-state* component of the local state is independent of the *decision-info* component and the *decision-info* component of the local state is independent of the *SBA-state* component after perturbation by the state perturbation adversary *sAdv*.

definition *independent-msg-act* :: (*'env, 'agent, 'act, 'msg,* (*SBA-value, 'extra, 'decision-info*) *SBA-local*) *Failure* ⇒ *bool* **where**
independent-msg-act F ≡ ∀ *adv* ∈ *Adv F.* ∀ *s s' i m d d'.* (*SBA-state.truncate* (*sAdv adv i m* (*SBA-state.extend s* (*SBA-local.fields d*))) = *SBA-state.truncate* (*sAdv adv i m* (*SBA-state.extend s* (*SBA-local.fields d'*))) ∧ *decision-info* (*sAdv adv i m* (*SBA-state.extend s* (*SBA-local.fields d*))) = *decision-info* (*sAdv adv i m* (*SBA-state.extend s'* (*SBA-local.fields d*))))

We say an information exchange *records decision information* if for every agent, the decision-info starts with *None* and becomes the value that the agent has decided upon after a decision has been made. The reason why sometimes we need to record decision information is that in some protocols we need to record the fact that the agent has decided to avoid a situation where an agent makes a decision multiple times, which will violate the Unique Decision rule. We will work inside the following locale, which is extended from *SBA-locale*, for the remainder of this section.

type-synonym *SBA-decision-info* = *SBA-action*
locale *SBA-record-decision-locale* = *SBA-locale S*
  for *S* :: (*'env, 'prop, 'msg, 'extra, SBA-decision-info*) *SBA-structure* (**structure**) +
  assumes *record-decision:* ∀ *r* ∈ *System* (*Info S*) (*ActionProtocol S*) (*Failure S*). ∀ *i.* (*decision-info* (*LocalState* (*r 0*) *i*) = *None* ∧ (∀ *m msg.* **let** *s* = *LocalState* (*r m*) *i*; *act* = *ActionProtocol S i s* **in** *decision-info* (*Transition* (*Info S i*) *s act msg*) = (**case** *act* **of** *None* ⇒ *decision-info s* | *-* ⇒ *act*)))

Our work in Isabelle has verified the following result from [17]. This theorem shows that, if the information exchange does not transmit information about actions and records decision information, an SBA action protocol that decides as soon as common belief of existence of a specific initial value is attained among nonfaulty agents is optimum. The theorem is inside the *SBA-record-decision-locale* locale. The implication of this result is that to check whether a concrete protocol is an optimum protocol for SBA, it suffices to check that agent i decides only at the first time $B_i^{\mathcal{N}} CB_{\mathcal{N}} \exists v$ is satisfied for some value v.

Theorem 5. *Let $\mathcal{E}$ be an information exchange protocol for SBA that does not transmit information about actions and records decision information. Let P be an implementation of optKBP with respect to information exchange $\mathcal{E}$, failure model $\mathcal{F}$ that acts independently on message and action memory, action protocol P, and the indexical set of nonfaulty agents. Then, P is an optimum SBA protocol with respect to $\mathcal{E}$ and $\mathcal{F}$.*

theorem *Optimality*:
  assumes N: *indexical-set* $S = nFaulty$
  assumes *sAdv-id*: $\forall\ adv \in Adv\ (Failure\ S).\ \forall\ i\ m.\ sAdv\ adv\ i\ m = id$
  assumes *ntransmit*: *ntransmit-action* (*Info S*)
  assumes *independent*: *independent-msg-act* (*Failure S*)
  assumes *opt*: *optKBP I* (*ActionProtocol S*)
  shows *Optimum* (*Info S*) (*Failure S*) (*ActionProtocol S*) (*indexical-set S*)

Our proof of Theorem 5 in Isabelle follows the proof (by contradiction) in [17]. The proof required roughly 500 lines of Isabelle code. A proof sketch was first encoded and then we tried to prove some statements automatically using Sledgehammer. In the case of Sledgehammer being unable to prove the statement, we would write a proof manually using a variety of tactics.

9 FloodSet

Theorem 5 gives general conditions that guarantee that a protocol is an optimum SBA protocol with respect to a given information exchange. In this section, we apply this result to an example of a simple information exchange, and prove in Isabelle that a variant of a well known textbook protocol is an optimum with respect to this information exchange. Specifically, we consider FloodSet [15], which is a simple protocol that solves simultaneous consensus under crash failures. Its simplicity serves as a good example to test our model in Isabelle.

The information exchange associated to FloodSet is given as follows. Each agent stores a set of possible decision values their local state. The type of messages sent by the agents is a set of SBA_value.

type-synonym *FloodSet-extra* $=$ *SBA-value set*
type-synonym *FloodSet-msg* $=$ *SBA-value set*

During every round, an agent sends the set of values in its local state to every agent. The following is the message selection function for FloodSet.

fun *FloodSet-Select* :: *FloodSet-local*
  $\Rightarrow$ *SBA-action*
  $\Rightarrow$ *'agent*
  $\Rightarrow$ *FloodSet-msg option*   **where**
FloodSet-Select local action i = Some (*extra local*)

The transition function adds the set of values received from other agents to the set of values in its local state by set union.

$FloodSet\text{-}Transition$ :: $FloodSet\text{-}local$ $\Rightarrow$ $SBA\text{-}action$ $\Rightarrow$ $('agent$ $\Rightarrow$ $FloodSet\text{-}msg$ $option)$ $\Rightarrow$ $FloodSet\text{-}local$ **where**
$FloodSet\text{-}Transition$ $local$ $action$ $vector$ $=$ $local($
  $time$:= Suc $(time\ local)$,
  $extra$:= $(extra\ local)$ $\cup$ $(\bigcup\ (Option.these\ (vector\ `\ UNIV)))$,
  $decision\text{-}info$:= if $action$ $\neq$ $None$ $then$ $action$ $else$ $decision\text{-}info$ $local$ $)$

The function $FloodSet\_init\_local$ returns a local state for a given initial value.

fun $FloodSet\text{-}init\text{-}local$ :: $SBA\text{-}value$ $\Rightarrow$ $FloodSet\text{-}local$ **where**
$FloodSet\text{-}init\text{-}local$ v $=$ $($ $init{=}v$, $time{=}0$, $extra{=}\{v\}$, $decision\text{-}info$ $=$ $None$ $)$

The following defines the FloodSet information exchange. The set of initial local states in this information exchange contains an initial state for each possible value v.

definition $FloodSet\text{-}Info$ :: $(FloodSet\text{-}local,$ $FloodSet\text{-}msg,$ $SBA\text{-}action,$ $'agent)$ $InfoExchange$
  where
$FloodSet\text{-}Info$ $\equiv$ $($
  $Initial$ $=$ $\bigcup$ $v.$ $\{$ $FloodSet\text{-}init\text{-}local$ v $\}$,
  $Transition$ $=$ $FloodSet\text{-}Transition$,
  $MsgSelect$ $=$ $FloodSet\text{-}Select$ $)$

There exists a pen and paper proof [2] that shows with respect to the FloodSet information exchange, the optimum protocol is the protocol that decides, in every run, on the minimum value in the agent's set, at time $\min\{t+1, n-1\}$. We will use it as our action protocol.

fun $FloodSet\text{-}Decision$ :: $FloodSet\text{-}local$ $\Rightarrow$ $SBA\text{-}action$ **where**
$FloodSet\text{-}Decision$ $local$ $=$ $(if$ $time$ $local$ $=$ min $(tolerance{+}1)$ $(total\text{-}agents{-}1)$ $then$
  $Some$ $(Min$ $(extra\ local))$ $else$ $None)$

Our model in Isabelle has successfully verified that in FloodSet, common belief is attained among nonfaulty agents when time $m \geq \min\{t+1, n-1\}$. The formal proof closely follows the pencil and paper one.

theorem $FloodSet\text{-}CB$:
  assumes r: $r \in system$ I
  assumes m: $m \geq min$ $(tolerance{+}1)$ $(total\text{-}agents{-}1)$
  obtains v **where** $I,(r,m) \models \mathbf{CB}_N$ $(Kprop$ $(exists\ v))$

10   Conclusion

We have formalized knowledge and belief in fault-tolerant distributed algorithms using Isabelle. Our work in Sect. 3 is the first formalization of epistemic logic adequate for consensus protocol applications, covering temporal as well as epistemic modalities, and using an indexical set of agents rather than a fixed set of agents. Using the framework we developed, we successfully verified that common belief of existence of intial value among nonfaulty agents is a necessary and sufficient condition to decide in the SBA (Simultaneous Consensus) problem. We also verified that, subject to some conditions on the information exchange, a consensus protocol that makes a unique decision as soon as common belief of an initial value is attained among nonfaulty agents, decides no later than any other consensus protocol using that information exchange. A simple concrete protocol FloodSet [15] has been modelled in Isabelle and we were able to verify theorems about knowledge properties of the protocol.

This work sets up a formal framework for verifying the correctness and optimality of simultaneous consensus protocols that have lower computational complexity, space complexity, and communication complexity than full-information protocols, with respect to a variety of failure models. In future work, we will apply the results of this paper to formally prove more optimality results such as in [1,2], by showing that a simultaneous consensus protocol implements optKBP.

Acknowledgments. This research is supported by an Australian Government Research Training Program (RTP) Scholarship held by Godfrey Wong.

Disclosure of Interests. The authors have no competing interests to declare that are relevant to the content of this article.

References

1. Alpturer, K., Halpern, J.Y., van der Meyden, R.: Optimal eventual byzantine agreement protocols with omission failures. In: Proceedings of 2023 ACM Symposium on Principles of Distributed Computing, pp. 244–252. PODC '23, Association for Computing Machinery, New York, NY, USA (2023). https://doi.org/10.1145/3583668.3594573
2. Alpturer, K., van der Meyden, R., Ruj, S., Wong, G.: Optimality of simultaneous consensus with limited information exchange. In: Proceedings of Twentieth Conference on Theoretical Aspects of Rationality and Knowledge (TARK 2025), pp. 175 – 189. Electronic Proceedings in Theoretical Computer Science, Düsseldorf, Germany (2025)
3. Baston, C., Capretta, V.: The coinductive formulation of common knowledge. In: Avigad, J., Mahboubi, A. (eds.) Interactive Theorem Proving, pp. 126–141. Springer International Publishing, Cham (2018)
4. Bisping, B., Brodmann, P.D., Jungnickel, T., Rickmann, C., Seidler, H., Stüber, A., Wilhelm-Weidner, A., Peters, K., Nestmann, U.: Mechanical verification of a constructive proof for FLP. In: Blanchette, J.C., Merz, S. (eds.) Interactive Theorem Proving, pp. 107–122. Springer International Publishing, Cham (2016)
5. Castañeda, A., Gonczarowski, Y.A., Moses, Y.: Unbeatable consensus. In: Kuhn, F. (ed.) Distributed Computing, pp. 91–106. Springer, Berlin Heidelberg, Berlin, Heidelberg (2014)

6. Debrat, H., Merz, S.: Verifying fault-tolerant distributed algorithms in the heard-of model. Archive of Formal Proofs (2012). https://isa-afp.org/entries/Heard_Of.html, Formal proof development

7. Dwork, C., Moses, Y.: Knowledge and common knowledge in a byzantine environment: crash failures. Inf. Comput. **88**(2), 156–186 (1990). https://doi.org/10.1016/0890-5401(90)90014-9

8. Fagin, R., Halpern, J., Moses, Y., Vardi, M.: Reasoning About Knowledge. The MIT Press (1995, paperback edition 2003)

9. Fischer, M.J., Lynch, N.A., Paterson, M.S.: Impossibility of distributed consensus with one faulty process. J. ACM **32**(2), 374–382 (1985). https://doi.org/10.1145/3149.214121

10. From, A.H.: Formalized soundness and completeness of epistemic logic. In: Silva, A., Wassermann, R., de Queiroz, R. (eds.) Logic, Language, Information, and Computation, pp. 1–15. Springer International Publishing, Cham (2021)

11. Gammie, P.: Verified synthesis of knowledge-based programs in finite synchronous environments. In: van Eekelen, M., Geuvers, H., Schmaltz, J., Wiedijk, F. (eds.) Interactive Theorem Proving, pp. 87–102. Springer, Berlin Heidelberg, Berlin, Heidelberg (2011)

12. Halpern, J.Y., Moses, Y.: Knowledge and common knowledge in a distributed environment. J. ACM **37**(3), 549–587 (1990). https://doi.org/10.1145/79147.79161

13. Halpern, J.Y., Moses, Y., Waarts, O.: A characterization of eventual byzantine agreement. SIAM J. Comput. **31**(3), 838–865 (2001). https://doi.org/10.1137/S0097539798340217

14. Küfner, P., Nestmann, U., Rickmann, C.: Formal verification of distributed algorithms - from pseudo code to checked proofs. In: IFIP TCS (2012). https://api.semanticscholar.org/CorpusID:15381678

15. Lynch, N.A.: Distributed Algorithms. Morgan Kaufmann Publishers Inc., San Francisco, CA, USA (1996)

16. Maric, O., Sprenger, C., Basin, D.: Consensus refined. In: 2015 45th Annual IEEE/IFIP International Conference on Dependable Systems and Networks, pp. 391–402 (2015). https://doi.org/10.1109/DSN.2015.38

17. Meyden, R.v.d.: Optimal simultaneous byzantine agreement, common knowledge and limited information exchange. CoRR **abs/2508.03418** (2025). https://doi.org/10.48550/ARXIV.2508.03418

18. Moses, Y., Tuttle, M.R.: Programming simultaneous actions using common knowledge. Algorithmica **3**, 121–169 (1988). https://doi.org/10.1007/BF01762112

19. Obendrauf, K., Baanen, A., Koopmann, P., Stebletsova, V.: Lean formalization of completeness proof for coalition logic with common knowledge. In: Bertot, Y., Kutsia, T., Norrish, M. (eds.) 15th International Conference on Interactive Theorem Proving (ITP 2024). Leibniz International Proceedings in Informatics (LIPIcs), vol. 309, pp. 28:1–28:18. Schloss Dagstuhl – Leibniz-Zentrum für Informatik, Dagstuhl, Germany (2024). https://doi.org/10.4230/LIPIcs.ITP.2024.28

Author Index

MIX
Papier aus verantwortungsvollen Quellen
Paper from responsible sources
FSC® C105338

If you have any concerns about our products,
you can contact us on
ProductSafety@springernature.com

In case Publisher is established outside the EU,
the EU authorized representative is:
Springer Nature Customer Service Center GmbH
Europaplatz 3, 69115 Heidelberg, Germany

Printed by Libri Plureos GmbH
in Hamburg, Germany